BRISTOL CITY
The Modern Era
– A Complete Record –

DESERT ISLAND FOOTBALL HISTORIES	ISBN
Aberdeen: A Centenary History 1903-2003	978-1-874287-57-5
Aberdeen: Champions of Scotland 1954-55	978-1-874287-65-0
Aberdeen: The European Era	978-1-905328-32-1
Bristol City: The Modern Era – A Complete Record	978-1-905328-27-7
Bristol City: The Early Years 1894-1915	978-1-874287-74-2
Bristol Rovers: The Bert Tann Era	978-1-905328-37-6
Cambridge United: The League Era – A Complete Record	978-1-905328-06-2
Cambridge United: 101 Golden Greats	978-1-874287-58-2
Carlisle United: A Season in the Sun 1974-75	978-1-905328-21-5
The Story of the Celtic 1888-1938	978-1-874287-15-5
Chelsea: Champions of England 1954-55	978-1-874287-94-0
Colchester United: Graham to Whitton – A Complete Record	978-1-905328-35-2
Colchester United: From Conference to Championship	978-1-905328-28-4
Coventry City at Highfield Road 1899-2005	978-1-905328-11-6
Coventry City: The Elite Era – A Complete Record	978-1-874287-83-4
Coventry City: An Illustrated History	978-1-874287-59-9
Derby County: Champions of England 1971-72, 1974-75	978-1-874287-98-8
Dundee: Champions of Scotland 1961-62	978-1-874287-86-5
Dundee United: Champions of Scotland 1982-83	978-1-874287-99-5
History of the Everton Football Club 1878-1928	978-1-874287-14-8
Halifax Town: From Ball to Lillis – A Complete Record	978-1-874287-26-1
Hereford United: The League Era – A Complete Record	978-1-874287-91-9
Hereford United: The Wilderness Years 1997-2006	978-1-905328-22-2
Huddersfield Town: Champions of England 1923-1926	978-1-874287-88-9
Ipswich Town: The Modern Era – A Complete Record	978-1-905328-24-6
Ipswich Town: Champions of England 1961-62	978-1-874287-63-6
The Old Farm: Ipswich Town v Norwich City	978-1-905328-12-3
Kilmarnock: Champions of Scotland 1964-65	978-1-874287-87-2
Leyton Orient: A Season in the Sun 1962-63	978-1-905328-05-5
Luton Town at Kenilworth Road: A Century of Memories	978-1-905328-10-9
Luton Town: The Modern Era – A Complete Record	978-1-874287-90-2
Luton Town: An Illustrated History	978-1-874287-79-7
Manchester United's Golden Age 1903-1914: Dick Duckworth	978-1-874287-92-6
The Matt Busby Chronicles: Manchester United 1946-69	978-1-874287-96-4
Motherwell: Champions of Scotland 1931-32	978-1-874287-73-5
Northampton Town: A Season in the Sun 1965-66	978-1-905328-01-7
Norwich City: The Modern Era – A Complete Record	978-1-874287-67-4
Peterborough United: The Modern Era – A Complete Record	978-1-874287-33-9
Peterborough United: Who's Who?	978-1-874287-48-3
Plymouth Argyle: The Modern Era – A Complete Record	978-1-874287-54-4
Plymouth Argyle: 101 Golden Greats	978-1-874287-64-3
Plymouth Argyle: Snakes & Ladders – Promotions and Relegations	978-1-905328-34-5
Portsmouth: The Modern Era	978-1-905328-08-7
Portsmouth: From Tindall to Ball – A Complete Record	978-1-874287-25-4
Portsmouth: Champions of England – 1948-49 & 1949-50	978-1-874287-50-6
The Story of the Rangers 1873-1923	978-1-874287-95-7
The Romance of the Wednesday 1867-1926	978-1-874287-17-9
Seventeen Miles from Paradise: Saints v Pompey	978-1-874287-89-6
The Southend United Chronicles 1906-2006	978-1-905328-18-5
Stoke City: The Modern Era – A Complete Record	978-1-874287-76-6
Stoke City: 101 Golden Greats	978-1-874287-55-1
Potters at War: Stoke City 1939-47	978-1-874287-78-0
Swansea City: Seasons in the Sun	978-1-905328-02-4
Third Lanark: Champions of Scotland 1903-04	978-1-905328-03-1
Tottenham Hotspur: Champions of England 1950-51, 1960-61	978-1-874287-93-3
West Bromwich Albion: Champions of England 1919-1920	978-1-905328-04-8
West Ham: From Greenwood to Redknapp	978-1-874287-19-3
West Ham: The Elite Era – A Complete Record	978-1-905328-33-8
Hammers Through the Looking Glass	978-1-905328-23-9
Wimbledon: From Southern League to Premiership	978-1-874287-09-4
Wimbledon: From Wembley to Selhurst	978-1-874287-20-9
Wimbledon: The Premiership Years	978-1-874287-40-7
Wrexham: The European Era – A Complete Record	978-1-874287-52-0
England's Quest for the World Cup – A Complete Record	978-1-905328-16-1
Scotland: The Quest for the World Cup – A Complete Record	978-1-897850-50-3
Ireland: The Quest for the World Cup – A Complete Record	978-1-897850-80-0
Blinded by the Lights: A History of Night Football in England	978-1-905328-13-0
Red Dragons in Europe – A Complete Record	978-1-874287-01-8
The Book of Football: A History to 1905-06	978-1-905328-00-4
Football's Twelve Apostles: The Making of the League 1886-1889	978-1-905328-09-3
Football's War & Peace: The Tumultuous Season of 1946-47	978-1-874287-70-4
Freestaters: Republic of Ireland 1921-39	978-1-905328-36-9

BRISTOL CITY

The Modern Era

— A Complete Record —

Series Editor: Clive Leatherdale
Series Consultant: Leigh Edwards

David Woods

DESERT ISLAND BOOKS LIMITED

Second Edition Published in 2007
First Edition Published in 2000

DESERT ISLAND BOOKS LIMITED
7 Clarence Road, Southend-on-Sea, Essex SS1 1AN
United Kingdom
www.desertislandbooks.com

British Library Cataloguing-in-Publication Data
A catalogue record for this book is available from the British Library

ISBN 978-1-905328-27-7

Printed in Great Britain
by
Biddles Ltd, King's Lynn

Photographs in this book are reproduced by kind permission of
The Bristol United Press, Kevin Brake, John Kelland, Joe Meredith.
All images between 1996-2002 are credited to Bristol City FC.
All images from 2002-03 are credited to Joe Meredith/Bristol City FC.

CONTENTS

AUTHOR'S NOTE

Grateful thanks are expressed to long-time City supporters Tom Hopegood and Tony Ticktum, as well as Jonathan Morgan, whose diligence in checking the seasonal summaries has been invaluable. Appreciation is also due to Brian Tabner for supplying the official home and away Football League attendances for the 1967-68 to 1998-99 period, and I am indebted to the many journalists who have unknowingly provided most of the raw material. Particularly, I acknowledge the help received during many years of research from Peter Godsiff, David Foot, the late George Baker, as well as Bill Pinnell (well-known to generations of Bristolians as ''The Traveller').

Given that I did not start keeping scrapbooks until the 1973-74 season, the kind gift of City cuttings covering the 1970 to 1979 period from Bristol Rovers fan Malcolm Norman is much appreciated. Others of differing allegiances to whom thanks are due include: Jim Brown (Coventry), Donal Cullen, Mike Davage (Norwich), Leigh Edwards (Bournemouth), Mike Jay (Bristol Rovers), Colin Jones (Swansea), Alan Lacock (Bristol Rovers), Johnny Meynell (Halifax), Ron Parrott (Hereford), Rev Nigel Sands (Crystal Palace), Ray Shoesmith (West Ham), Colin Timbrell (Gloucestershire FA Historian and Arsenal fan), Jeff Whitehead (Colchester), as well as the Ashton Gate Bard, Gareth Calway, and fellow City supporters Mervyn Baker, Kevin Brake, Phil Jones, Gerry Pearce, Matthew Stevens and Mike Swain.

Gratitude is also due to Andrew Crabtree, with whom I embarked with my first Bristol City book back in 1987, Lorna Parnell of the Football League, who has been of great help in supplying information and answering my queries, the staff at Bristol Central Library and the British Newspaper Library at Colindale, and Ed Furniss and Colin Sexstone of Bristol City FC for providing photographs.

DAVID WOODS
September 2007

Dedication

In memory of Clive Spratt, who died in March 2003. A much-valued friend and frequent companion on away trips.

INTRODUCTION

Bristol City would appear to be one of those clubs who are unable to stabilise. Throughout their history they have rarely managed more than five seasons at any one level. Many think of the present 'Championship' as being their natural home, but 1998-99's dire performances, and taking into account that ten of their 42 seasons at this level (albeit the old Division Two) took place before the Football League was extended, suggests that they will now be fighting above their weight.

This, of course, is not how it should be in so large a city as Bristol, which in the eighteenth century was second only to London. It certainly wasn't the intention of the founders of the club in 1894, when as Bristol South End they strove to be the cream of the top locals sides – Warmley, St George, Clifton Association, Eastville Rovers, and Bedminster.

South End turned professional on joining the First Division of the Southern League in 1897, whereupon they adopted their present name after appealing to the Football Association. Finishing runners-up three times, election to the Football League was secured for 1901-02, though not before 'survival of the fittest' had reduced Bristol's professional sides to the two we have today.

Warmley, St George, and Eastville Rovers also adopted professionalism in 1897, and Bedminster (founded as Southville in 1887) followed suit twelve months later. It just wasn't possible for Bristol to support the activities of five professional clubs and gradually they, along with the renowned Clifton Association Club, who gave up the battle in December 1897, started falling by the wayside.

In the east of the city bitter rivals Warmley and St George, both formed in 1882, died in 1899 after an earlier proposed amalgamation had been rejected, but south of the river better sense prevailed. The Bedminster board were the instigators of their amalgamation with Bristol City in the summer of 1900. Eastville Rovers, who became Bristol Rovers in 1899, doggedly soldiered on by themselves, very much in the same admirable way they still conduct their affairs.

City's early years in the Football League were their most successful. Finishing sixth in their first season, three successive fourth placings followed before promotion to the top flight was secured. In 1905-06 City only lost two League games on their way to amassing a record 66 points, as well as becoming the first club ever to win thirty League games in a season. Five years in the First Division then ensued, with the Championship being narrowly missed in 1906-07 and the FA Cup final reached in 1909. Relegation at the end of the 1910-11 campaign brought financial problems, and no sign of regaining lost status until finishing third in 1920-21. Since when, until the 1967-68 season which is the starting point of this book, it has been City's dismal lot to have operated at Third Division level for all but fourteen campaigns.

Not a record to boast about, given the club's undoubted potential, not to mention the high level of support that has been enjoyed over the years! Let us therefore read further to see what travails have taken place during the intervening period.

1

CONSOLIDATION 1967-1973

LEAGUE DIVISION 2	**1967-68**
Division 2	19th
League Cup	2nd Round
FA Cup	5th Round

The capture of England international Chris Crowe from Nottingham Forest had transformed City's 1966-67 campaign. Not only did their struggling side start winning, but they did so with a style and panache that thrilled the fans. The record signing of Hugh McIl-moyle from Wolverhampton Wanderers in early March appeared to be the icing on the cake: it was expected that a serious assault on reclaiming top-flight status after a 56-year gap would be made in 1967-68.

After a 1-0 home victory over Swindon in the first pre-season friendly on 3 August, a crowd of 7,719 were attracted to Ashton Gate four days later when the Supporters Club opened City's first shop. Unfortunately First Division visitors West Bromwich Albion proved much too strong as they strolled to a 4-1 success, but a 3-3 draw at Swindon the next evening kept hopes buoyant for the League campaign.

The atmosphere was electric at Ashton Gate for the opening fixture against Huddersfield Town, and all bode well after just two minutes when Crowe slid in the day's quickest goal. Unfortunately, this proved to be the calm before the storm: it was downhill all the way thereafter, with City losing 2-3 after Tony Ford had hit the post with a late penalty.

With only one win in the first eight League games, not to mention losing 0-5 at home to Everton in the League Cup, the axe fell on manager Fred Ford at an emergency board meeting. That was on the evening of 19 September, just three days after City's 2-4 home defeat by Blackpool. Unusually for a club in trouble, this sacking brought forth much protest, with letters streaming into the columns of the local *Green 'Un* and Gordon Parr leading a deputation of players to chairman Harry Dolman's house in Chew Magna to plead for Ford's reinstatement.

The decision stood, however, and whilst the search for a manager went on, club physiotherapist Les Bardsley took over for the third time as caretaker boss, with the assistance of chairman Dolman, and directors Norman Jones and Graham Whittock. Johnny Quigley was appointed captain in place of the dropped Gordon Low.

Torquay boss Frank O'Farrell was Dolman's first choice, but he turned his back, objecting to the unfair manner in which he considered his good friend Ford had been dismissed. Dolman then turned to Coventry City's assistant manager, Alan Dicks, who was interviewed by the board on 5 October and offered a three-year contract at £4,000 per annum, as well as a bonus of £1,000 should he succeed in preserving City's Second Division status.

A mediocre half-back with Millwall, Chelsea and Southend United, Dicks gained much valuable experience under Jimmy Hill at progressive-minded Coventry. At 33 years of age and having gained his full FA coaching badge in his early twenties, Dicks appeared to be the ideal man to lead City forward.

Commitments at Coventry, though, meant he was unable to take up full-time duties until 16 October, though he selected the side for the 1-1 home draw with Cardiff City two days earlier. His first signing was wing-half Ken Wimshurst from Southampton for a £12,000 fee, but his priority was a centre-forward, following Dolman's decision to transfer McIlmoyle to Carlisle United in exchange for £22,000 in late September.

Liverpool reserve Alf Arrowsmith was the initial target, but, on being rebuffed, Dicks turned to 23-year-old John Galley. Surprisingly, Rotherham boss Tommy Docherty agreed to let him go for £25,000, but on joining City in late November Galley's left ankle was in plaster.

Passed fit to make his debut on 16 December, Galley demonstrated that he was worth the wait, scoring all the goals in a 3-0 away win against Huddersfield. His haul of sixteen League goals that season proved to be a major factor in City's escape from the jaws of relegation. It was a close thing though, as many at Ashton Gate on the night of 29 March, when Rotherham took both points, were inclined to the opinion that relegation was inevitable.

Four wins from their last eight games hauled City back from the brink and, after beating Preston on 27 April to banish lingering fears of the drop, they put on a show the following week with a 4-2 win at Villa Park. It was there that keeper Barry Watling and former England and Bristol Boys skipper Geoff Merrick made their debuts.

Did You Know?

Stan Mortensen (ex-Blackpool & England) refereed when City beat Rovers at head-tennis to win the Fred Pontin Trophy at the Colston Hall in Dec 1968.

The FA Cup offered City respite from their relegation battle. Having negotiated replays to overcome Bristol Rovers and Middlesbrough, the fifth round was reached for the second successive year. Record receipts for both Ashton Gate and Eastville – £9,954 and £6,600 respectively – had been generated by the local derby clashes, whilst the fifth round game at Leeds yielded receipts of £15,250. This rough encounter, which City lost 0-2, boiled over in the second half when Gary Sprake, the Leeds keeper, was sent off for belting Chris Garland.

Among the back-room staff, former Rochdale boss Tony Collins was appointed chief scout in November, but the most significant newcomer was John Sillett, who took over coaching duties towards the end of the season. On the playing front, the departure of Quigley to Mansfield for £3,000 was viewed with alarm by most supporters, despite Dicks hoisting the club's record fee to £36,300 by bringing in Bobby Kellard from Portsmouth. Others who moved included Low to Stockport for £3,000, Lou Peters to Bournemouth for £5,000, whilst Ray Savino departed for King's Lynn in March.

Losses of £25,599 were announced for the season, despite the number of season ticket holders (at a cost of £10) rising from 1,442 to 2,017. This wasn't surprising, however, as the dross the fans were expected to watch drove average home gates down from 16,183 to 15,935. The deficit of £5,500 incurred by the hastily-arranged transfer of McIllmoyle added to the costs incurred in obtaining the services of Galley and Wimshurst. In the League Cup, receipts of £5,737 were realised from the Everton encounter, whilst in the League the largest return at Ashton Gate was for Birmingham City's visit on 30 December, when a crowd of 23,493 generated £4,818.

Match of the Season 1967-68

Charlton Athletic 1 Bristol City 2

Division 2, 20 April 1968

The emotions aroused by this game provoked a personal crisis for Alan Dicks, who had taken over from Fred Ford the previous October. With the season approaching its climax, City, with just four games left, were involved in a desperate fight to avoid relegation.

With Charlton just one place higher in the table, this clash was viewed as a game neither side could afford to lose.

It had been a struggle for Dicks to improve the club's fortunes, despite the shrewd signing of John Galley, who had started his City career with a hat-trick at Huddersfield. Wins proved hard to come by and many feared City were heading for a quick return to the lower reaches after just three seasons in Division Two.

'Do or die' at the Valley was, however, a worrying prospect for City. Charlton, unbeaten over the Easter period, were one of City's bogey sides and many fans had vivid memories of their overturning a 0-2 half-time FA Cup deficit at Ashton Gate in 1959-60 to win 3-2. Whilst Charlton were unchanged, City had Terry Bush taking over from flu victim Gordon Parr in the defensive wing-half position.

With Chris Crowe operating on the right wing, despite wearing the No 2 shirt, City made the better start in front of a near 12,000 crowd, and on a bumpy, hard pitch carried the game to their opponents. Keeper Charlie Wright did well to keep out Galley's 25-yarder, before City were rewarded with a well-taken goal after just eight minutes. Derrick hooked the ball into the middle from the left, and Galley's back-header set up Crowe, moving in from the right, to unleash a rocket into the far top corner.

Playing effectively in attack against a Charlton defence vulnerable to Galley and Garland's quick thrusts through the middle, City kept up the pressure to add another goal before half-time when a mis-hit ten-yard effort from the prolific Galley struck Paul Went and rolled into the net.

After the break, City were unfortunate not to increase their advantage when John Quigley's shot was cleared off the line by Peter Reeves. Charlton raised the tempo following the 65th-minute replacement of Matt Tees by substitute Stenson, and forced their way back into the game when Keith Peacock's corner from the left was headed low into the net by Harry Gregory. As City doggedly hung on, the tension was such that Dicks found he had temporarily lost the use of his legs.

On an afternoon of high drama City secured what was thought to be one of the most critical wins in their history, but as events turned out defeat did not mean relegation for the loser. Charlton rediscovered their form to attain fifteenth place at the season's end, while City finished in nineteenth spot to preserve their status and earn Dicks his £1,000 bonus.

LEAGUE DIVISION 2	**1968-69**
Division 2	16th
League Cup	3rd Round
FA Cup	3rd Round

After the struggles of the previous campaign, optimism among the fans wasn't high. Portents were grim, with many of the club's records being lost in July floods that saw Ashton Gate under water. However, the presence of record signing Kellard in City's line-up had 7,862 spectators turning up for the opening friendly against Southampton. The game was won 5-3, but as this was followed by a 1-3 defeat at Bournemouth and a 1-1 draw at Hereford, the jury was still out when City travelled to sun-drenched Craven Cottage for the League opener. A good performance against relegated Fulham, despite a 0-1 defeat, augured well, but with just one win from the opening twelve League games – coupled with the team earning a reputation for rough and negative play – pressure on the manager intensified. Shouts of 'Dicks must go' reverberated at home games as relegation became a serious threat. Matters came to a head in Alan Skirton's first match.

A £15,000 signing from Blackpool, Skirton had been a member of City's Youth team that had reached the semi-finals of the FA Youth Cup twelve years previously. He could do little, however, as Norwich's 1-0 win on 23 November provoked a mass demonstration demanding Dicks' head. Dolman responded by calling a crisis board meeting. The manager survived, despite having supervised just two wins from the first nineteen games and a lamentable total of thirteen goals. Dolman was concerned about the coverage of City's affairs in the local press. Having fallen out with Herbie Gillam, sports editor of the *Western Daily Press*, he accepted an invitation by Gordon Farnsworth, editor of the *Bristol Evening Post*, for a frank interview to be published in the *Green 'Un*. Unfortunately, the outcome demonstrated Dolman's paranoia over supporters having an outlet for their frustration. He complained that much of the criticism was destructive and also blamed the local press for raising false hopes of success among the fans.

Dicks decided on a bolder policy against Carlisle, but after City's attack-minded display at Brunton Park failed to reap its due reward, he reverted to type at Middlesbrough, where negative tactics brought a 1-4 defeat. The tide began to turn when both points were secured in a fortuitous 2-1 home success over Bury. With Galley regaining his form following an operation on an in-growing toenail, the following ten games – culminating in a 6-0 thrashing of Fulham – earned five wins and two draws.

Relegation fears were rekindled by a 1-2 defeat at Sheffield United, but only two defeats in the remaining nine games hoisted City up to sixteenth, eight points clear of the drop zone. The season ended at the Baseball Ground, where any optimism for the following season was shattered. City were annihilated 0-5 by champions Derby County.

A notable landmark had been achieved in the League Cup. City's 2-0 win over Newport, which ended a barren seven-year spell, was only their second success in the competition. Heady times followed with a 1-0 victory over Middlesbrough that earned another clash with First Division Leeds. The crowd of 16,359 did not have their enjoyment marred by a repeat of the previous season's ugly incidents but City proved to be no match for the defending League Cup holders.

The FA Cup took the Ashton Gate fans to Upton Park, where City faced a Hammers side which included all three of their England World Cup heroes. On a day that saw the opening of the East Stand, City gave Bobby Moore, Geoff Hurst and Martin Peters a far from easy time before losing 2-3.

Despite the number of season ticket holders increasing to 2,054, attendances continued to decline. City's operating loss of £20,252 was not so bad as the previous year, the opening of the Sunday Market in the officials' car park helping to stem the flow. Receipts of £4,426 were generated by City's largest home crowd of the season. The 20,632 who turned up for the Cardiff fixture on 28 September witnessed the first real flowering of the hooligan problem at Ashton Gate, with rival 'supporters' fighting in the Covered End.

Work on building Dolman's dream to replace the old Number Two stand – known affectionately as the Cowshed – that had been demolished in the summer of 1966, eventually started in January 1969, this at a projected cost of £180,000, which eventually rose to £235,000. At the time it was thought to be a gamble, but with the provision of a bowls area within the structure, which yielded an income of £12,000 per year, Dolman's wisdom in progressing with the project was soon vindicated. All sixteen club houses were sold, many at favourable prices, to the players and staff who occupied them. Mann the brewers lent £64,000 at an interest rate of 2.5 percent per annum over seven years, whilst the Football Association, the Supporters Club, 51 Club, and the directors themselves, who each pledged £3,000, all chipped in with loans. The Dolman Stand, as it was duly named, found itself ready for use for the start of the 1970-71 season, but as costs mounted Dicks was left with little money for new players. He was obliged to transfer Kellard to

Leicester for £49,000 in the summer of 1970 and Garland to Chelsea for £110,000 in September 1971.

Whilst the Supporters Club did not commence their Player of the Year awards until 1970-71, Kellard was City's undoubted star of 1968-69, his all-action play even winning over those fans who still bemoaned the loss of Quigley. It was fortunate then, that Dolman stymied Kellard's efforts to go back to Pompey by offering to buy his apparently unsaleable house on Hayling Island. Departures included Chris Crowe, whose idiosyncratic bouts of genius were never enough for Dicks; he negotiated his own transfer to Australian club Auburn of Sydney for a £3,000 fee.

In the Football Combination, City's reserves, after winning the Second Division Championship the previous season, finished in ninth place, whilst at youth-team level Sillett's work was beginning to bear fruit. The Colts occupied fourteenth spot (having been seventeenth in 1967-68) in the Western League, whilst the Youth team improved on last season's second round exit by reaching the third round of the FA Youth Cup. They beat Swindon 4-2, Plymouth 2-0, before losing 1-3 against Cardiff. Unfortunately, the Youths would be denied the splendid competition which since 1960-61 had been offered by the Wessex Youth League: it was allowed to die after City finished runners-up in 1967-68. During the competition's eight-season run, City's poorest campaign had been in 1963-64 when they finished fourth. Four times they won the Championship, doing the Cup and League double in 1965-66, and thrice finished as runners-up.

For the first team it was a poor season overall, best remembered for the fact that all City's forwards (Galley, Garland, Kellard, Sharpe and Skirton) scored in a 5-0 Gloucestershire Senior Professional Cup final triumph over Bristol Rovers in front of 14,735 fans at Eastville Stadium on 28 April.

The incorporation of the Football League Review into City's programme brought a threepence price increase to one shilling as the club carried on improving their publication, having radically changed its design in 1966-67. However, when Ashton Gate was used as a neutral venue in December (Exeter beat Nuneaton Borough 1-0 in a second replay of an FA Cup first round tie) a single-folded sheet of paper was produced for the 5,071 spectators who paid match receipts of £1,297.

This was the ninth occasion, and the last to date, in which Ashton Gate was used as a neutral venue in the FA Cup, though the ground – which was originally the home of Bedminster Cricket & Football Club – has also been used by other sports – rugby union, rugby league, American football, cricket, baseball, lacrosse.

Did You Know?

The Wurzels' song 'One for the Bristol City' was adopted as the official club song in September 1977.

Match of the Season 1968-69

Bristol City 6 Fulham 0

Division 2, 1 March 1969

Fulham's visit on a cold and windy St David's Day, brought to mind the fixture ten years previously when they had attracted 32,378 to Ashton Gate for a 1-1 top-of-the-table draw. At that time, Fulham – Johnny Haynes, Jimmy Hill, Roy Bentley, Jimmy Langley, Graham Leggatt *et al* – were headed for a second spell in the top flight. This time they were down at the foot of the Second Division, despite the recent £20,000 signing of Brian Dear from West Ham.

After Chris Garland had latched onto Bobby Kellard's pass to stroke the ball past Brian Williamson, City – who had only scored sixteen goals in fifteen previous League games – tore Fulham apart. George Cohen, a member of England's 1966 World Cup winning side, endured a torrid afternoon, in what was to be his final game. City scored four goals in the first half and two in the second.

Alan Skirton was much involved in the first-half action. He headed wide of an open net before his challenge for Galley's cross caused John Ryan to slice the ball between his own posts. Eleven minutes later he notched City's first successful penalty for almost two years after the Fulham keeper had grabbed Garland round the legs. It was then Skirton's cross from the left that Galley headed back for Gerry Sharpe to nod in at the far post.

After the break, Fulham offered little threat apart from a Haynes effort which Trevor Jacobs cleared off the line. Despite creating many chances it wasn't until five minutes from time that City added to the score, Garland following up to put Sharpe's blocked shot into the back of the net. Galley finished off the romp two minutes later, turning in Garland's centre as City notched up their biggest League victory since beating Notts County by the same score in December 1961.

The two vital points helped City's valiant war against the drop, but there was to be no escape for Fulham, who finished bottom, conceding over eighty goals, whilst only managing seven wins.

It would be 1970-71 before the two clubs met again, when Fulham, pressing for promotion from the Third Division, gave City two tough games in the quarter-finals of the Football League Cup.

LEAGUE DIVISION 2	**1969-70**
Division 2	14th
League Cup	2nd Round
FA Cup	3rd Round

In the summer of 1969 Dicks pulled off two brilliant buys from the North East, obtaining centre-half Dickie Rooks from Middlesbrough for £13,000 and full-back Brian Drysdale from Hartlepool for £10,000. Unbeaten in their four pre-season friendlies, City's League campaign started well when Galley headed in at the Open End for a 1-0 success over newly-promoted Watford. However, with Merrick having dislocated his elbow at Sheffield United in a 1-2 defeat, it was not long before the manager was under the cosh yet again. Ignoring the claims of the impressive Malcolm Clarke – signed from Cardiff – after he had played just two games, Dicks' outfit slumped, until perking up against bogey team Norwich City.

Despite his team winning 4-0, the Ashton Gate crowd's patience was sorely tested by Dicks' substitution of Jantzen Derrick by Danny Bartley. It took a 6-0 win over another bogey side – Charlton Athletic – three days later to change the mood. City embarked on a six-match unbeaten run which conversely ended against a Bolton side who viewed City as bit of a jinx.

With on-loan keeper Bob Wilson from Cardiff replacing the injured Mike Gibson, City went down in a 1-3 defeat at Bolton, but this proved to be but a brief interruption to a sparkling run of success. Four wins and three draws were secured from the following seven games before the Christmas break was spoilt by a 1-2 home defeat by Huddersfield. Two more losses ensued, including a 1-4 hammering at Norwich when Merrick made his long-awaited return. It was that sort of season. One defeat in eight games was the prelude to one win in the next eight. City plummeted down the table to finish fourteenth, having been at one stage as high as ninth.

Injuries took their toll, Merrick only playing one game after dislocating his elbow, whilst Galley was out of action with ankle trouble for long spells. Terry Bush, though, proved an admirable deputy with his wholehearted play and thunderbolt shooting. Gerry Sharpe was top scorer with eleven goals, but Garland caught the eye with his six, despite being embroiled in a wrangle over wages. Garland was called up for the England U-23 international squad against Wales at Ashton Gate in October. The crowd of 22,286 who saw England win 2-0 were disappointed that Garland was not picked (later that season he came on as substitute against Bulgaria).

In the League Cup – having disposed of Exeter – City were involved in a marathon second round tie with Leicester. They paid for missing their chances in the first two games and losing the toss for choice of venue for the second replay. Despite scoring first, they were undone by Andy Lochhead's hat-trick. In the FA Cup City were humiliated at Fourth Division Chester, where Billy Dearden's late goal punished them for trying to hold out for a replay.

Receipts of £5,874 were earned from the 24,905 spectators against Swindon, City's biggest home League crowd of the campaign. Season ticket sales dropped to 2,013, but with average home gates shooting up to 16,274 the club was able to declare its first profit since 1965-66 – a princely £3,856 being announced at the AGM held in the Indoor Bowls Club in the Dolman Stand.

The Youth side – containing Len Bond, Ray Cashley (an amateur full-back who impressed when taking over in goal from the injured Bond), Keith Fear, Billy Menmuir, Steve and Tom Ritchie – attracted much attention after disposing of Swindon, Cardiff, Plymouth and Bournemouth to reach the fifth round of the FA Youth Cup. A crowd of 10,178 (City's best FA Youth attendance since 18,181 turned up for the semi-final against Chelsea in April 1960) saw Leeds' youngsters beaten 2-1. Sadly, City lost 0-3 on aggregate in the semi-final against Tottenham.

The Colts finished fourteenth in the Western League, the same position as the previous year, while the Reserves, as well as reaching the final of the Somerset Professional Cup (losing 0-1 on aggregate against Bath City), made a strong bid for the Football Combination Championship before sliding back to fifth.

Though City retained their hold on the Gloucestershire Senior Professional Cup with a 2-1 home victory over Bristol Rovers, the curtain didn't come down on the season until almost two weeks later. Top Italian club Juventus came to Ashton Gate on 5 May, when goals from Gordon Parr and Skirton earned City a 2-1 win.

On the playing front, Tony Ford joined Bristol Rovers for £4,000 in December, and at the end of the season his long-time full-back partner Alec Briggs retired after thirteen years with the club. Popular Jack Connor, who had played over 400 games at the heart of City's defence, became player-coach. Manager Alan Dicks was rewarded for City's improved showing with a five-year contract at £5,000 per annum, after persuading the board to give Collins and Sillett new three-year agreements.

All in all, it was a much improved campaign after a poor start, with up-and-coming youngsters Gerry Gow, Ian Broomfield, Peter Spiring, Trevor Tainton having already played in the first team. Others, such as Ritchie, Rodgers, and the talented Fear, were hovering on the fringes, and the future prospects at Ashton Gate suddenly appeared much brighter.

Did You Know?

Walsall did not allow City to film the League Cup-tie at Fellows Park in 1981 because they were due to face City again in the League a few weeks later.

Match of the Season 1969-70

Bristol City 6 Charlton Athletic 0

Division 2, 23 September 1969

After two years at Ashton Gate, with no sign of improvement in City's fortunes, Alan Dicks was coming under heavy fire from the fans. Scoring only two goals, whilst losing five of their first seven League games of the season, City had slumped to 21st spot in the Second Division table.

Feelings were running high, so much so that the manager had endured severe abuse in the previous game against Norwich City, despite a 4-0 success bringing the poor run to an end. The Charlton game was seen as a huge test for both the manager and the team, and over 15,000 fans were in attendance as City responded with a performance which proved to be a turning point of their campaign.

Following Alan Skirton's early header from a corner, John Galley brought the crowd to their feet with a tremendous ten-yard volley – likely the most powerful ever seen at Ashton Gate – the ball nestling in the back stanchion of the Covered End goal. These two first-half strikes were only a prelude to what was to come.

Charlton's defence disintegrated after the break as Skirton led them a merry dance, not only adding to his goal haul, but also hitting the bar with a 20-yarder and forcing keeper Tony Burns into making three expert saves. Playing great football, City stacked up the goals. Two came from free-kicks, and two others were the product of defence-shattering bursts down the right, firstly by Bobby Kellard, then by Galley.

Whilst many fans remained critical of City's slow progress, fortunes improved as the season unfolded. Indeed, the Charlton game was part of a six-match unbeaten run. Dicks was slowly fashioning a side that was becoming more difficult to beat, ending the campaign in fourteenth place with 39 points, and actually scoring more goals than they conceded.

There is little doubt that the back-to-back home wins over Norwich and Charlton enabled the directors to keep faith with Dicks, and, whilst it would be a long time in coming, such faith was to be ultimately rewarded with promotion to the top flight.

LEAGUE DIVISION 2	**1970-71**
Division 2	19th
League Cup	Semi-Final
FA Cup	3rd Round

A season of contrasts, as City came close to reaching Wembley in the League Cup, whilst only just avoiding relegation. With the transfer of Kellard to Leicester to help pay for the Dolman Stand, and with Dicks having little money to spend on players, Gow kept his place for most of the season. He looked raw to start with, but by the end of the campaign his great determination had made him worthy of a regular place. Dicks did, however, part with £5,000 to Ipswich to bring Steve Stacey back to Ashton Gate after City had previously sold him to Wrexham for £2,000.

For the first time since 1963, when the FA lifted restrictions on the playing of pre-season friendlies, City went abroad for their early preparations. Two wins and a draw against Dutch sides Holstein Kiel (2-0), Go Ahead Deventer (1-1) and Veendam (2-1), followed by home wins over West Ham (1-0) and Go Ahead Deventer (2-0) had everyone fired up for the big kick-off against relegated Sunderland.

With the Dolman Stand, though still unfinished, in use for the opening match, Ashton Gate was treated to a thrilling encounter which City won by the odd goal in seven. A 1-1 draw at Charlton followed before City chalked up a long-awaited home success over Cardiff – Sharpe's late strike brought a 1-0 win to take City up to fourth place. Unfortunately, this proved to be as good as it was going to get. A 0-4 drubbing at Filbert Street precipitated a slump that saw City in relegation peril after losing 0-1 at Bolton. With just two wins from the following thirteen games, relegation appeared inevitable, until City's youngest forward line carved out a 3-2 home win over Millwall in late-February. Ten points from the following nine games saw City claim the dizzy heights of eighteenth, after beating Portsmouth 2-0 at home on 10 April.

It was the loan signings of half-backs Brian Hill from Coventry and Les Wilson from Wolves that saved City from the drop. The duo inspired a 3-0 win at Watford on their debuts and were part of the side that recovered from a 0-2 half-time deficit to defeat promotion-chasers Luton at Ashton Gate. Even so, City only mustered a meagre 31 points and Dicks was fortunate that relegated Blackburn (27 points) and Bolton (24) were so poor.

The FA Cup offered but a brief distraction as Southampton gained belated revenge for their 1909 defeat – when City marched on to reach the final – by overcoming Cashley's goalkeeping defiance to win 3-0 at the Dell in a twice-postponed third round tie. The real loss, though, came five days later when the brilliant Gerry Sharpe, only 24, broke his leg in a tackle with Middlesbrough's Eric McMordie in City's 0-2 defeat at Ashton Gate. After weeks in hospital, when infection raised fears of amputation, Sharpe embarked on a long period of recuperation. Sadly he was forced to retire following a gallant comeback bid in the Reserves the next season. He was rewarded with a Testimonial in December 1973 and deserved better than the 3,607 crowd who turned up to see a 0-1 defeat by Derby County.

With Dicks under fire again from his many critics, it was a wonder to many that he survived the season, but no doubt City's run in the League Cup helped. Certainly it improved his position enough to fiercely resist efforts at an Emergency Board Meeting in January to dismiss Collins as an economy measure. Dicks had his way and directors Lionel Smart and Graham Whittock resigned.

The League Cup run commenced with a goalless draw at Third Division Rotherham. City were fortunate not to be numbered among the victims on a night of shocks – Carlisle 2 Manchester City 1; Bristol Rovers 2 Newcastle 1; Lincoln 2 Sunderland 1; Sheffield United 1 Leeds 0. A 4-0 win in the replay flattered City, but a 1-0 success at First Division Blackpool gave no measure of their superiority. Revenge was then gained over Leicester for the previous season's defeat – Wimshurst's extra-time winner prevented the tie extending into another marathon – taking City into the quarter-finals, where they avoided First Division Tottenham, Coventry, Crystal Palace and Manchester United.

On being paired with Third Division pacemakers Fulham, many thought City would have an easy passage into the semi-finals, and whilst this is how it often looked in a 0-0 draw at rain-swept Craven Cottage, the replay was a different matter. City were outplayed, but Sharpe's penalty proved enough to clinch the tie in front of a 23,230 crowd.

With Spurs beating Coventry 4-1, Manchester United disposing of Crystal Palace 4-2 and Bristol Rovers losing a replay 0-1 against Aston Villa, all of City's possible opponents in the hat for the semi-final draw were clubs of distinguished cup pedigree. It did not therefore much matter that they were drawn to play the favourites, Tottenham Hotspur, though the task was made more difficult by being at home in the first leg. The game was postponed for a week because of a power workers dispute, but on the evening of 16 December, 30,201 fans paying record receipts of £13,931 saw Skirton put City ahead just after half-time. Unfortunately, Alan Gilzean headed in a brilliant equaliser for Spurs to leave everything to play for in the second leg.

Did You Know?

England played a World XI at cricket at Ashton Gate in September 1980. A year later rain restricted the crowd at a floodlight cricket match to 1,539.

A stern defensive battle at White Hart Lane kept Spurs at bay for ninety minutes, but City's defence cracked in extra-time. Martin Chivers and Jimmy Pearce broke down the barrier to end City's hopes of their first major cup final for almost 62 years. The defeat also brought to an end their best cup run since reaching the semi-finals of the FA Cup in 1920, when their injury-hit side lost 1-2 to Huddersfield Town at Stamford Bridge.

The Reserves were well in the running for the Football Combination Championship, heading the table for much of the season until a late slump brought a final placing of fourth, whilst in the Western League, the Colts dropped down to fifteenth. Following their heady efforts in reaching the semi-final in 1969-70, the Youths went out of the FA Youth Cup at the first time of asking – losing 0-3 at Bournemouth.

Having played 168 games and scored 46 goals, a diseased knee ended Bush's career at 28. He later became Assistant Secretary at Ashton Gate, before taking up a position with the Transport and General Workers Union. Derrick joined French First Division side Paris Saint-Germain on a free-transfer, whilst Dicks quickly signed John Emanuel from Welsh club Ferndale, after watching his superb performance as a trialist in City's drawn Gloucestershire Cup match at Eastville Stadium.

The £2,000 proceeds of Connor's Benefit against Wolves in March, which City lost 1-2 in front of 7,800 fans, were added to the monies raised from other events held throughout the year. Among these was an Old Players' Match between City and Rovers at Eastville, which attracted a 2,000 attendance. Goals from Ian Hamilton and Alfie Biggs gave Rovers a 2-0 win, avenging defeat in a similar fixture almost seven years earlier, when a crowd totalling 3,289 saw City win 6-3 at Eastville in 1964.

A total of 12,256 spectators were present at Eastville when Fear scored for City in the last unresolved Gloucestershire Cup final, before the introduction of the penalty shoot-out. A short trip to Spain then followed, where City, having lost 1-3 to Espanol, beat Calella 2-1. Garland was selected for the Football Association's five-week tour of Australia, whilst promising youngster Peter Spiring was loaned to American side Washington Darts for the summer.

Despite a new record number of 4,176 season ticket holders, finance remained a problem. With the burden of the Dolman Stand repayments creating losses of £500 per week, accountant Tony Sully, later to replace Bert Bush as Secretary, took on the duties of Financial Secretary. Any gains made by the League Cup run were offset by a drop of over two thousand in the home League average attendance, but Kellard's £49,000 transfer to Leicester City saved the day and a profit of £15,172 was announced at the AGM held on 10 December 1971.

Match of the Season 1970-71

Bristol City 1 Tottenham Hotspur 1

League Cup, semi-final, 1st leg, 16 December 1970

A season of giant-killing in the Football League Cup saw struggling Second Division Bristol City and promotion-chasing Aston Villa of the Third Division both reach the semi-finals. For City, Welsh Cup winners in 1933-34, it was their first major semi-final since 1919-20 when they lost 1-2 against Huddersfield Town at Stamford Bridge in the FA Cup.

After many years of failure in the League Cup, now in its eleventh year, City fans were surprised at their team's success, especially as they had to overcome bogey side Leicester along the way. Apart from the Filberts, City enjoyed the luck of the draw, only once facing a top-flight side, albeit struggling Blackpool, and playing Third Division Fulham in the quarter-finals. City's struggle in the League came as a blow to the fans, who had expected the club to build on the previous season's improvement. Naturally, the consequence of this was more criticism being heaped on Alan Dicks, so City's lucrative cup run did much to keep him in a job.

After a week's delay in playing the tie, due to a power workers dispute, cup fever was rampant at Ashton Gate. City faced a Spurs side packed with star names, and the crowd of 30,201 was slightly larger than the number who attended the second leg a week later. After a dour opening, City fans dreamed of a first trip to Wembley when Alan Skirton scored with a close-range shot just after the interval. However, Alan Gilzean's far-post header from a Martin Peters cross left everything to play for in the second leg.

Given little chance at White Hart Lane, City put up a sterling defensive performance to take the game into extra-time before succumbing to goals by Martin Chivers and Jimmy Pearce. Spurs went on to cup glory, beating Villa 3-1 in the final. For City, though, nothing changed; they struggled throughout the season in the League and eventually finished just above the relegation spot.

LEAGUE DIVISION 2	**1971-72**
Division 2	8th
League Cup	1st Round
FA Cup	3rd Round

After the disappointments of the previous campaign, Chairman Dolman demanded improvement in 1971-72. New signings included Gerry Sweeney from Morton for £22,000 and Dave Merrington, a free from Burnley. Things didn't look promising when Bristol Rovers beat City 3-1 at Ashton Gate on the newly-laid pitch in a joint benefit game for Bush and Ford. However, with homebred players such as Cashley, Merrick, Spiring, and Tainton establishing themselves, matters improved once the League campaign got underway. A 5-1 win at Hillsborough surprised all, but despite the transfer of Garland to Chelsea after just four games, City sustained the momentum – twice topping the table early on. Emanuel's dynamic runs from midfield were a revelation, and a massive following travelled to Swindon on 2 October.

They were rewarded by Spiring's second-half volley that kept City in a promotion spot. The following week a 2-1 home success over Watford gave City sixteen points from eleven games and lifted them to second. Unfortunately a 1-3 defeat in the next game in front of the Match of the Day cameras at Millwall, against opponents who often proved a good yardstick of City's progress, brought Ashton Alf (as City's supporters are known) back to reality. Despite paying Wolves £15,000 to sign 23-year-old Les Wilson permanently, heavy grounds and only one further win (5-3 over Orient) prior to the New Year not only squashed promotion hopes, but left City worrying about relegation yet again.

Galley's textbook header got 1972 off to a good start with a home victory over Birmingham, but it wasn't until 19 February when Charlton were beaten 2-0 at Ashton Gate that another two-point haul came City's way. During this period City had slumped from tenth to sixteenth, but a return of the firmer pitches and the recall of winger Danny Bartley heralded much improved form. Eight wins and three draws from the last thirteen games produced a final position of eighth, City's best showing since 1965-66.

In the League Cup, though, it was a case of 'after the Lord Mayor's show'. The previous year's epic deeds meant naught at Home Park, where Plymouth made City pay for failing to take advantage of their first-half chances. In the FA Cup it was a similar story, as early chances were squandered before City succumbed to Preston's late onslaught, when Dicks' gamble on Rooks' fitness backfired.

Did You Know?

When Sunday football began in Bristol in 1966, City supporters formed a team called Bristol Casuals, while Rovers fans called their team the Pirates.

City's on-field progress was reflected in the home attendances, which rose to an average of 15,225. The biggest was 23,525 who turned up for the visit of Cardiff City, whilst the lowest was against Charlton Athletic – just 10,207. Despite season ticket sales dropping to 3,912, the selling of Garland allowed a record profit of £64,637 to be declared at the AGM.

The Gloucestershire Cup final at Ashton Gate was drawn 1-1, but Bristol Rovers took the trophy by winning the penalty shoot-out 4-2. The next day City travelled to Ferndale to play the local side as part of the deal that had brought Emanuel to the club. Sweeney got on the scoresheet in a 5-1 win. At the end of the month City embarked on an ambitious four-match overseas tour, which brought victories over a Teheran Select XI (2-0), Persepolis (1-0), Appollo Limasol (1-0) and Famagusta (3-1) in the space of seven days.

This extended City's participation in 'friendlies' for the season to thirteen. In the pre-season, besides the Rovers match, other games resulted as follows – Newport Co (a) 2-1, Wolves (h) 0-1, Torquay (a) 0-1, Port Vale (a) 1-1. During the campaign a goalless draw was played out against West Brom at Ashton Gate on 30 November, with 4,884 in attendance to support a benefit match for Terry Bush. The remaining friendlies brought a 1-0 win at Southend, whilst a home clash with Morton in May drew just 1,700 spectators, who saw Gow's second-half penalty salvage a 1-1 draw.

With Cashley established in goal, Mike Gibson – arguably the best keeper City have ever had – was allowed to join Gillingham on a free transfer, having played 383 games in nine years. Gordon Parr, who had been with the club twice as long, sampled League of Ireland football with Waterford. Recurring knee trouble brought an end to the Ashton Gate career of Rooks, a centre-half who, despite supplanting the popular Connor in City's side, had won over the hearts of the fans with his sterling displays. Merrington, who had not played a senior game due to Achilles tendon trouble, retired along with Wimshurst.

They both joined City's backroom staff, which was reshuffled in the summer of 1972 following Collins' departure to become Chief Scout at Leeds United. Sillett became Chief Coach, Wimshurst was given charge of the reserves, while Merrington took over the youth team. In the previous season they had reached the fifth round of the FA Youth Cup by beating Bournemouth (h) 1-0, Plymouth

Argyle (a) 3-2, and Stoke City (h) 2-0 (after a 1-1 away draw), before losing 1-2 at Norwich. Tony Rance became Commercial Manager and later replaced Sully as Secretary.

The Colts did not operate in 1971-72, and their return for the following season, when they finished fifteenth in the Western League, proved to be their swan-song. The Reserves, who had won the Somerset Professional Cup in 1970-71 (beating Yeovil 4-3 on aggregate), retained the trophy by beating Taunton 6-1 at Wordsworth Drive and 3-1 at Ashton Gate three days later. In the Football Combination, a run of form from December until late January, with only one point dropped in seven matches, carried City into Championship contention, but with only four wins from their last fourteen games they had to settle for a final placing of eighth.

Match of the Season 1971-72

Sheffield Wednesday 1 Bristol City 5

Division 2, 21 August 1971

By 1971 the club's vigorous scouting network was beginning to bear fruit and the introduction of up-and-coming youngsters into the side, coupled with the signing of Gerry Sweeney from Morton, prompted this outstanding performance against Sheffield Wednesday early in the season.

The campaign had started brightly with Sweeney scoring on his debut in a 3-3 home draw with Millwall, but few fans could have anticipated what was to follow at Hillsborough a week later. The lack of goals since Dicks' arrival was forgotten as City, seizing the initiative from the start, ran riot to notch up their biggest away win for five years. They were three up by half-time, Galley sparking the action by finishing a four-man move with a shot into the top corner of Peter Grummitt's net. Two more strikes after the break put City five up before Mike Prendergast headed a late goal for the Owls.

This success gave City much confidence and they maintained a top-four placing throughout the autumn, before the goals dried up. City scored only two in eight League games during December and January, which brought a slump into the bottom half of the table. A late-season recovery secured a creditable finishing position of eighth to suggest that, after so many years of struggle, City had at last come to terms with Second Division football.

For the Owls, their course was set in the opposite direction. A second consecutive season of under-achievement for this famous club saw them finish in fourteenth place, an early warning of their demise that was to bring relegation in 1974-75.

LEAGUE DIVISION 2	**1972-73**
Division 2	5th
League Cup	2nd Round
FA Cup	4th Round

Despite the lack of any signings in the summer of 1972, Ashton Alf entertained promotion thoughts for the first time in a long while as City embarked on their round of pre-season friendlies. Two hefty wins over Port Vale and Leicester kept expectations high, and a large following travelled to a wet and windy Goldstone Ground for the League opener against newly promoted Brighton.

With Rodgers back at centre-half, after almost a year's absence with a serious knee-ligament injury, Bartley hooked home a volley for a deserved point; but City failed to win any of their first five matches. They even found themselves at the bottom after losing 1-2 at home to Sheffield Wednesday, at which point Sillett told City fans that their heroes were the best footballing side in the Second Division.

A 2-0 success at fellow strugglers Orient ended the drought, to set up a nine-match unbeaten run extending over six weeks. This culminated in a 2-0 win at Oxford, by which time City were in eighth place. Three successive defeats, including the heaviest loss of the season, a 1-5 drubbing at Fulham (when young full-back Steve Ritchie made his only League appearance), brought Ashton Alf back to earth. Failure to win at home until 25 November, when Sunderland were defeated 1-0, proved costly. Despite the record £70,000 signing from West Brom of Bobby Gould – who made a less than auspicious debut in a 0-1 home defeat by Burnley – patchy form up to the turn of the year saw City slipping down the table. Considering the time of year, it was appropriate that it should be at Millwall's Cold Blow Lane on 30 December that City slumped to thirteenth after losing 0-3.

It took the intervention of the FA Cup to raise spirits. Gould's last-gasp third round equaliser at Portsmouth prompted a brilliant display in the replay which was won 4-1. City fans then enjoyed the treat of a trip to First Division Wolves, where injury-hit City were perhaps unfortunate to lose an enthralling cup-tie.

Despite an amazing on-field bust up between Gould and Gow, which prompted the latter to be sensibly pulled off by Dicks, a 3-1 home win over Brighton put the season back on track. City's young side – reinforced by the signing of Donnie Gillies from Morton just before the transfer deadline (in exchange for Steve Ritchie and £30,000) – won eight and drew three of their last fourteen games. They climbed to fifth at the campaign's end, when their total of 63 goals was enough to gain entry to the following season's Watney Cup.

In round two of the League Cup, City put up a brave show at Upton Park before losing 1-2 against First Division West Ham. In the Gloucestershire Cup, City turned the tables on the Rovers with a 5-3 penalty shoot-out victory, following a 2-2 draw at Eastville.

Season ticket sales reached a new record with 4,282 sold at prices ranging between £10.50 and £13.50 to raise £42,139, but the home average attendance dropped dramatically to 12,892 – a reflection, perhaps, of the fact that it took City over three months to notch up their first home success. A loss of £20,912 was declared at the AGM. The fearless play of the rumbustious Gould earned him ten goals, whilst Galley – described by Dicks as the best signing he ever made – managed seven from his twenty games prior to joining Nottingham Forest for £30,000 in December.

The quicksilver Spiring, whose exciting bursts from midfield promised more than they achieved, also moved on. He signed for Liverpool in March, when Bill Shankly, who was always on the lookout for young players of potential, paid £55,000 for his services. At the end of the campaign long-serving full-back Trevor Jacobs joined Bristol Rovers on a free transfer, but Swansea City had to pay £12,000 to capture centre-half David Bruton.

Emanuel's sterling performances were recognised when he was called up for the Welsh squad for the end-of-season Home Internationals. By coming on as substitute during a 0-3 defeat by England at Wembley on 15 May and again during a 0-1 loss against Northern Ireland at Goodison Park four days later, he was able to upgrade his earlier amateur appearances for his country. Emanuel thereby became City's first full international since Dermot Curtis, who was in the Republic of Ireland side that lost 1-3 against Austria in Vienna in May 1958.

The youth policy, partly financed by insurance receipts (Sharpe £15,000, Rooks £5,000, and Merrington £3,500) was by now coming along nicely. The youth team, captained by 18-year-old Gary Collier, who made his League debut in a 3-1 win at Luton in March, reached the FA Youth Cup final for the only time.

Opening with a 0-0 draw at Southampton, City won the replay 2-0. An identical score, this time against Birmingham side Northfield Juniors, allowed City the opportunity to spot the talent of Clive Whitehead among the ranks of the opposition. A 1-0 win at Everton persuaded 6,781 to attend the home quarter-final with Arsenal, when goals from Collier and Price earned a place in the semi-finals for the third time and a controversial meeting with Sheffield United.

Did You Know?

The Young Robins Club was formed in 1967 for 11-18 year olds. Subscription was 2s 6d (12½ pence). Membership quickly topped 400, including 50 girls.

After Kevin Prue's two strikes earned a 2-2 draw at Bramhall Lane, the 7,906 fans at Ashton Gate for the second leg nine days later were bemused when United refused to play extra-time following a goalless ninety minutes. Thankfully, justice was done when Martyn Rogers' goal was enough to win the decider on Birmingham's neutral St Andrew's Ground. Unfortunately, City proved to be no match for Ipswich in the final. Having lost the first leg 0-3 at Portman Road, City never looked like pulling back the deficit in the second leg a week later.

Disappointment for the 6,032 crowd, maybe, but at least they enjoyed the consolation of Rogers' 90th-minute goal as City lost 1-4 on aggregate. A reward of sorts came later for the youngsters as they travelled to Holland in the close season and won the prestigious Blauw Wit tournament in Amsterdam. They also won the Bordeaux Etudiantes Youth Tournament and added to their successes in 1971 and 1972 by collecting the honours at the Tilberg Youth Tournament for the third time. By contrast, the Reserves had a poor season, relinquishing their hold on the Somerset Professional Cup after a 1-3 defeat at Bridgwater Town in the third round. They also finished seventeenth in the Football Combination.

Match of the Season 1972-73

Sunderland 2 Bristol City 2

Division 2, 31 March 1973

During a season which saw City continue their progress of the previous campaign, no greater test came than that at windy Roker Park. In-form Sunderland were seeking their fourth successive League victory, having recovered from a mid-season slump.

Fielding the same line-up that had achieved wins at Luton and at home to Aston Villa, City were confident of success at a venue that had often proved a happy hunting ground in the past – actually winning at Roker the week following Sunderland's record 9-1 thrashing of Newcastle at St James' Park in 1908-09.

City gave as good as they got early on, but when Geoff Merrick turned Dick Malone's cross into his own net on 35 minutes the spectre of City's record 1-6 FA Cup defeat at Roker Park in 1963-64 haunted the thoughts of the small band of Robins fans in the 33,255 crowd. Fortunately the interval was reached without the team conceding further goals, but Merrick left City a mountain to climb early in the second half when he attempted to head the ball back to his keeper. The alert Dave Watson nipped in to stretch out his foot and touch the ball over the head of the advancing Ray Cashley.

Now was the time for City's great team spirit to assert itself, and this is precisely what happened under the inspiring leadership of captain Merrick. Refusing to be cowed by his earlier errors, Merrick rallied his side with a headed goal in the 59th minute and continually drove his players forward in the search for the equaliser. With time running out it looked as though all the effort was to be in vain, but then midfield dynamo John Emanuel ensured City did not leave Roker without any reward. He seized on a half-clearance to send a great first-time left-footed shot rocketing into the net from 25 yards.

City's young side showed they had come of age and this fighting spirit was to be the basis of their promotion-winning side three years later. Four of City's final five games of the season were won, to take them up to fifth in the table, whilst Sunderland, with an identical record but inferior goal-average, were one place lower.

City and Sunderland would be promoted together, and their clash in this game highlighted the fact that both clubs were building squads with elevation to the top flight very much in mind.

2

ON THE RISE 1973-1979

LEAGUE DIVISION 2	**1973-74**
Division 2	16th
League Cup	3rd Round
FA Cup	6th Round

Whilst 1973-74, with a slide to sixteenth place, didn't appear to offer evidence of an upswing in City's fortunes, the signing of 21-year-old centre-forward Paul Cheesley from Norwich City for £30,000 – following Gould's £80,000 December move to West Ham and the free-transfer summer captures of Mike Brolly from Chelsea and Jimmy Mann from Leeds – meant all the pieces of the promotion jigsaw would come together.

A memorable FA Cup run that saw Leeds beaten 1-0 in a replay at Elland Road was the undoubted catalyst for the great events of the following two years, despite City losing to Liverpool by a solitary goal in the quarter-finals at Ashton Gate. Paradoxically, the start of City's long-term decline were sown this season – namely the seeds of the boardroom battles which eventually led to the formation of Bristol City (1982) plc.

We must not get ahead of events, however, as the feeling during the summer was one of anticipation of this being City's year. A 2-1 first round win at Peterborough in the Watney Cup on 11 August fuelled these hopes, which were not dampened by a 1-4 defeat against First Division Stoke in the semi-final at the Victoria Ground four days later.

After winning both their opening matches, slick Luton's 3-1 win at Ashton Gate brought Ashton Alf back to earth, but a 3-1 win over Hull saw City perched on top of the table. This game at windswept Ashton Gate is remembered for keeper Cashley's astonishing goal. With the wind behind them, the Tigers had the better of the first half and fully deserved the lead gained by Stuart Pearson's tap-in. After the break Tom Ritchie headed City level before Cashley made his mark with a clearance that sped through the air and bounced just outside the Hull penalty area before ballooning high into the net over keeper Jeff Wealands, who was caught ten yards off his line. The distance of the kick was originally hailed as being 98 yards, but measurement of the Ashton Gate pitch a few days later revised this downwards to 95 yards 2 feet – still a record for a League goal, beating Peter Shilton's effort against Southampton six years previously by two yards.

A 1-2 defeat at Hull saw City's players use up their unexpended energy with a late-night party in their hotel. Following complaints from the other residents Dicks slapped a £20 fine on every player, but Gould, who had not been involved, refused to pay and appealed to the Football Association. Within a few months Gould, a tremendous ambassador for the club who always took the trouble to talk to the fans, was transferred, with Dicks explaining that his star player had been unable to get on with his team-mates.

A week after the Hull affair, City recorded their first ever win over Scunthorpe, this in a replay of their second-round League Cup-tie. There followed two classic encounters with First Division Coventry, but Whitehead's goal was not enough at Highfield Road as the Sky Blues won 2-1.

The League campaign nosedived after this. Despite the arrivals of Cheesley and Ernie Hunt (the latter on a two-month loan from Coventry before City paid £7,000 for the 31-year-old's services) a 0-2 defeat on their New Year's Day debut against Orient heaped the pressure back on Dicks as City slumped to fourteenth. Dolman registered his concerns by leaving written instructions as he took off for his annual mid-winter holiday in the Barbados. The gist was that more money needed to be injected into the club, that Dicks ought not to be offered more than a one-year contract, and that if Dolman's views did not prevail he would consider that he had grounds for resigning.

It was in this uncertain atmosphere that Dicks prepared for the FA Cup, but in the home third-round tie with Hull at Ashton Gate keeper Bond was unable to emulate Cashley's goalscoring exploits as City could only scrape a 1-1 draw. A rare Tainton goal brought a hard-fought win in the replay at Boothferry Park. Before the next round, City played on a Sunday for the first time because of the national power crisis and the ban on the use of floodlights.

On a sunny afternoon at Burnden Park, Hunt's volley was insufficient to prevent Bolton winning 2-1, but in the wind and rain at soggy Hereford the following Saturday, Merrick's left-footed effort carried City through to the fifth round.

Few gave City much chance against Leeds, even with home advantage, but the First Division pacesetters were fortunate to escape with a 1-1 draw in front of a crowd of 37,141 paying record receipts of £28,111. Billy Bremner rifled a 25-yard shot into the top corner to give Leeds a first-half lead, but the visitors were rocking when Fear lobbed a 65th-minute equaliser. The incredible replay victory is covered in Match of the Season.

With Liverpool the quarter-final visitors, the fans flocked to the League match against Oxford, but the real attraction was the issue of vouchers for the cup-tie and, once these had been obtained, many of the 25,904 crowd did not hang around to watch City's 0-0 draw. Sadly, the FA Cup dream ended in front of 37,671 spectators, creating a new receipts record for Ashton Gate of £28,826. Shortly after half-time Rodgers, in for the injured Merrick, failed to deal with a Kevin Keegan cross and the ball, after hitting Drysdale, bounced obligingly into John Toshack's path.

Dolman had arrived back from the West Indies in time to see the famous win at Leeds, but was shocked to learn that the other directors accepted his resignation, as they were not prepared to accede to his demands. The rift was hushed up until after the Cup run. In due course it was announced that self-made millionaire Robert Hobbs was the new Chairman, while Dolman became the club's first president since Albert Denby in 1896 had followed Col Plant and John Durant in the role.

Cup glory brought honours for Gillies and Gow, both of whom were selected for Scotland's Under-23 squad against England at Newcastle. Gillies played the whole game, whilst Gow came on for the last half-hour in a 0-2 defeat.

In the League, it needed a hat-trick of wins in early April to keep relegation at bay. A close season tour to Greece did little to improve City's form, the best results being 1-1 draws against Olympiakos and Agrinion, following a 1-2 defeat by AEK Athens. Average home League attendance increased to 14,058, and with the income from the Cup revenue, a profit of £60,527 was announced at the AGM.

The Youths only reached the third round of the FA Youth Cup, but the growing reputation of City's youth policy earned a fixture with England Youth. A crowd of only 450 were present at Ashton Gate to see England (with Whitehead in their ranks) win 2-0.

Match of the Season 1973-74

Leeds United 0 Bristol City 1

FA Cup, 5th Round replay, 19 February 1974

A season that started brightly was only redeemed by City's best run in the FA Cup since they reached the semi-finals 54 years previously.

Did You Know?

City's 8 consecutive League wins in 1997-98 was well short of their record 14 League wins in 1906-07 – a record shared with Manchester U and Preston.

Prior to the Leeds epic, a fourteen-game sequence had brought City just two wins and nine goals between October and January, not to mention a 0-5 trouncing at Oxford on Boxing Day, which left Dicks fretting about his job.

Following the 1-1 draw at Ashton Gate, Leeds were overwhelming favourites for the replay. This game, which kicked-off at 2pm on account of the miners' strike affecting national power supplies, drew a huge crowd to Elland Road. Jim Evans, City's Promotions Manager, had booked the League Liner – a special Pullman carriage chartered by the Football League – for the Tuesday afternoon replay and sold enough tickets to fill it within an hour. Widespread absenteeism was reported in the Avon area as a mass exodus took place. Some of City's 8,000 travelling fans were locked out of Elland Road when the gates were closed half an hour before the kick-off, with 47,182 customers already inside the ground.

Leeds, brimming with ten internationals, played the free-flowing soccer for which they were renowned, but City kept them at bay with a mixture of luck and tenacity before, against the odds, taking a 73rd-minute lead. The Bristol hordes could hardly believe it as Gillies, having received a super pass from Fear, clipped the ball underneath Saturday's hero, keeper David Harvey. The remaining minutes were pure torture as Leeds strove to save the game, but City somehow kept their goal intact to achieve their greatest Cup success since beating Portsmouth 39 years previously. The result earned a mention on the front page of *The Times* and kept Alan Dicks in his job.

Leeds duly clinched the championship, but suffered their first League defeat of the season in their very next game. For City, their cup luck ran out at home to Liverpool in the quarter-finals, when John Toshack's shot was all that divided the sides at the end of a close game.

LEAGUE DIVISION 2	**1974-75**
Division 2	5th
League Cup	3rd Round
FA Cup	3rd Round

Dicks' brainchild 'All-In-the-Game' competition was staged at Ashton Gate on 28 July and filmed for transmission on ITV's World of Sport a month later. City came second with 250 points in this first pilot of a competition that was to run again in 1976 and 1977. Wolves were the winners with 315 points, whilst Derby (230) were third and Chelsea fourth (195).

The football started with a 5-0 home win over Dutch side Veendam, by which time Sillett – whose one-touch football coaching was such a feature of City's young side – had rowed with Dicks and left to take over as manager of Hereford. Wimshurst stepped up as Chief Coach, whilst Merrington – who had returned to Burnley – was succeeded by Don Mackay, a former Dundee United and Southend goalkeeper.

A goalless draw at Nottingham Forest was indicative of City's season to come: despite their neat, composed football, goals were at a premium. Dicks relied on Gow, Emanuel and Sweeney to provide the cutting thrust, but it wasn't until Mann's regular inclusion in the side from late October that the team started to click.

A slow start saw City as low as fifteenth after losing 0-2 at Oxford, but four straight wins hoisted them up to fourth after Emanuel's shot secured a 1-0 home win over Manchester United, who were suffering the indignity of a season in Division Two. Although City hovered among the promotion places throughout the campaign, and completed the double over the champions-to-be with a 1-0 victory at Old Trafford, the paucity of goals proved too big a handicap. With money in short supply, Dicks' interest in Wolves striker Hugh Curran was not followed up. City soldiered on, and on Good Friday a first-ever League win at Southampton put them in a promotion spot.

With a home game against fellow promotion chasers Norwich the following day, City fans travelling home from the Dell were intoxicated by thoughts of a long-cherished First Division place. Norwich, though, without a game the day before, looked the fresher side. Inspired by the play of Martin Peters, they deservedly won thanks to Colin Suggett's goal.

A 1-1 home draw against Bristol Rovers on Easter Tuesday, followed by wins over Notts County and Sheffield Wednesday, sustained City's interest, but a controversial defeat at Orient when the floodlights failed destroyed the dream. City were left to reflect on the Norwich defeat that effectively cost them promotion. Dicks made sure that in future years his side would never again have to play three games over the Easter period.

A final position of fifth was a great improvement and for the first time in many years City were an admired Second Division club. Surprisingly, the average home attendance barely increased, whilst the number of season tickets holders dropped from 4,269 to 3,863, no doubt put off by price increases for the best seats from £15.50 to £17. A loss of £68,456 was declared at the AGM.

In the League Cup, a 2-1 home victory over Cardiff was followed by an outstanding 4-1 win at Crystal Palace, which set up a home meeting with Liverpool in the third round. Given the fact of last season's FA Cup win for Liverpool over City, this opportunity for revenge over the First Division giants failed to generate much excitement. Only 25,753 out of 37,000 tickets were sold. Following a disappointing goalless draw City were put to the sword at Anfield where Liverpool achieved a 4-0 victory.

In the light of the previous year's exploits, the FA Cup was a big disappointment as City went out at the first time of asking – a 0-2 defeat at Sheffield United a poor reward for playing some good football. Failure was also City's fate in the County tourney. Bristol Rovers followed up the previous season's 2-0 win by retaining the trophy with a 2-1 extra-time success at Eastville in front of an 11,408 crowd. City collected a cup in early May when, having beaten Blackburn 2-0 and Stoke 1-0, the Pontins Five-a-Side Tournament at Southport was won by beating Sunderland 1-0 in the final.

A second benefit match for City's great servant Cliff Morgan – who captained the side in the 1930s – brought down the curtain at Ashton Gate when only 1,796 turned up to see Leicester win 4-2. For the players, though, there remained a trip to Norway. The highlight of a four-match tour was a 10-0 thrashing of Mo, following victories over Molde (2-0), Bodo-Glimt (1-0) and Mjolner (5-2).

In the Football Combination the Reserves emulated the seniors in making a strong bid for League honours, but at the end had to be satisfied with third place after losing their last three fixtures. Although it was a disappointing finish, it was still their highest position since finishing runners-up in 1954-55. Fortunately, they made no mistake in the Somerset Professional Cup, the last season before it was renamed the Somerset Premier Cup. In the final, Taunton Town were beaten 3-0 in the second leg at Wordsworth Drive, after City had beaten them 4-0 at Ashton Gate three days earlier. The Youths, though, could not follow suit in the FA Youth Cup, losing 0-1 at Ipswich in the third round after winning 3-2 at Plymouth.

Did You Know?

Mark Aizlewood is City's second most capped player. His 21 Welsh caps can't match the 26 England caps won by Billy Wedlock between 1907 and 1914.

Match of the Season 1974-75

Bristol City 0 Norwich City 1

Division 2, 29 March 1975

History shows that this was the season when Dicks convinced City fans that the team he was building could take the club into the highest echelons of the English game. Indeed, it was only defeat in this vital game on Easter Saturday that ultimately denied City promotion in 1974-75.

A first-ever League win at Southampton the previous day had put City in control of their own destiny and convinced the travelling horde of fans that the promotion prize was theirs. Unfortunately promotion rivals Norwich had the advantage of resting in a Bristol hotel while City were otherwise engaged on the South Coast, and whilst this did not have any apparent effect on the result, it was a situation that Dicks was at pains to ensure wasn't to happen at Easter time again.

City's team was built on the ethos of everyone working for each other, which in the absence of a prolific attack lent them defensive resilience. Despite the lack of goals, nine wins from a twelve-game run which culminated at Southampton suggested that City were coming through with a late dash to snatch the third promotion prize.

A bumper crowd of more than 22,000 were enticed to Ashton Gate on a fine sunny afternoon, but with Keith Fear returning after suspension in place of Tom Ritchie, the promotion dream faltered against impressive opponents who demonstrated class and composure under City's ceaseless, but often punchless, pressure. Guilty of over-elaboration, many City moves broke down through players being caught in possession. Colin Suggett, earlier denied when Geoff Merrick headed off the line, won the priceless points for Norwich as early as the seventeenth minute with a low right-footed volley after Ted MacDougall had hooked back Phil Boyer's cross.

Although City won three of their remaining six fixtures, this proved to be a vital win for Norwich that gave them the boost to secure promotion, a situation that would have been reversed if the result had gone the other way.

LEAGUE DIVISION 2	**1975-76**
Division 2	2nd (Promoted)
League Cup	2nd Round
FA Cup	3rd Round

Despite only being ninth favourites, at odds of 20-1 for promotion, belief was strong, both within the club and amongst the fans, that the prize could be won. It was, however, felt that a goalscorer was needed: Cheesley had only flattered to deceive in his infrequent appearances since joining from Norwich. As it turned out, it was the harnessing of Cheesley alongside the hard-working Ritchie that proved to be the final piece of the promotion jigsaw. Indeed, it was not long before Cheesley was being noted as a candidate for England honours. Merrick was in such outstanding form that Bristol City great John Atyeo was moved to comment that he was the best defender he had ever seen. The cultured Gary Collier at centre-half, together with the energetic Sweeney and the reliable Drysdale at full-back, as well as keeper Cashley enjoying his best ever season, all combined to ensure that City's defence could mop up the pressure and supply the platform for a return to the top flight.

After failing to qualify for the knock-out stages of the Anglo-Scottish Cup – when a defeat at Chelsea, a draw at Fulham and a home win over Norwich left City second in their group – a disputed, twice-taken penalty by Sweeney at Ashton Gate brought a winning, if shaky start to the League campaign. Sunderland were then sent packing as two goals from Mann and another from Brolly brought a 3-0 win, but successive 1-3 defeats at Hull and Southampton brought City down to earth. The smallest League derby attendance for years saw Cheesley get off the mark in a 1-1 draw at Ashton Gate, before the promotion march really got under way with wins over Blackburn and Oxford. It was in those matches that the Cheesley-Ritchie partnership began to spark, as they each scored twice to take City to the top of the table.

October brought a brilliant performance at Oldham, inspired by Whitehead's thirty-minute substitute appearance. He set up a headed goal for Cheesley and scored the fourth himself to earn City the plaudits from many rival managers as being the best side outside the First Division. Following a runaway 4-1 success at York, with Cheesley notching the only hat-trick of his career, City's nine-match unbeaten run came to an end when West Brom's player-boss Johnny Giles inspired his side's 2-0 win at Ashton Gate.

Three more scoreless games followed, before the BBC Match of the Day cameras recorded City's return to form in the reverse fixture against York, when Ritchie hit a hat-trick in another 4-1 win.

Did You Know?

Geoff Merrick conceded nine own-goals in seven seasons for Bristol City, out of a total of just 17 City own-goals in that period.

He scored twice the following week in a 2-1 success at Fulham and only a 0-1 defeat at Bolton disturbed City's progress up to the turn of the year.

In the FA Cup, few were particularly concerned over City's 1-2 exit as all efforts were now concentrated on the promotion prize. Against struggling Oxford at the Manor Ground the following week it might be thought that in a 1-1 draw City lost a point, but in effect this was a point gained because, following Cheesley's early headed goal, it was only Cashley's defiance between the sticks that averted a heavy defeat.

Dicks, recalling the previous season's Easter setback, persuaded Plymouth to bring forward their home fixture against City from Easter Saturday to 24 January, the date of the fourth round of the FA Cup. The game was poor and goalless, but the point earned was vital. By this time, though Collins had returned from Leeds as Assistant Manager, Hobbs dropped a bombshell by threatening to sell Merrick and Ritchie to Arsenal, who had bid £250,000 for the pair. Dicks, his sights fixed on promotion, insisted they stayed, but with the club facing an ultimatum from the bank the directors were sorely tempted. The argument raged for two weeks, but eventually the board announced that the pair would be staying. They appealed for supporters to purchase season tickets (£33 before 30 June, £40 thereafter) for the following year. The fans responded by purchasing over £66,000 worth in a few weeks and the financial showdown with the bank was averted.

Ritchie proved his worth by netting in a 1-1 home draw with Southampton and grabbing the winner at Orient to take City back to the top of the table. Having done so, it came as no surprise to City fans that their favourites lost the next fixture, though there was no fluke about Forest's 2-0 win at Ashton Gate. Two wins and a draw followed before a crucial encounter at West Brom. This fixture should have taken place on 28 February, but the Football League sanctioned a late postponement as nine City players, plus Dicks, had gone down with flu. Many City fans had already set off for the game and knew nothing of the postponement until they reached the ground.

The game was re-scheduled for 17 March. After Sweeney's drive earned a 1-0 win, few doubted that City were headed for the First Division. A 1-1 draw with promotion rivals Sunderland at Roker

Park cast aside many of the remaining doubts, with thoughts focusing instead on the Championship. Missed chances brought a 1-2 defeat at Blackpool and a further point was dropped in a 2-2 draw with Chelsea, which allowed Sunderland to take over pole position. After another point was lost at Eastville in a dire derby clash, City were left needing two points to clinch promotion, with two games remaining.

20 April 1976 will long be remembered by those City fans present at Ashton Gate. A rare Whitehead goal early in the game clinched a nervous victory over a Portsmouth side who belied their already relegated status by putting up a mighty struggle. Noisy were the celebrations that night as City clinched their long-awaited return to the top echelon of the English game.

With the Championship still up for grabs, City were deflated in their final game as Notts County won 2-1 at Ashton Gate. In the event, Sunderland's 2-0 home success over Portsmouth meant the Rokermen could not be overhauled, finishing three points clear. Fortunately, City found their form to beat Bristol Rovers 3-2 after extra-time in the Gloucestershire Cup final at Ashton Gate.

An open-topped bus tour of the city was followed by a civic reception at the Council House, whereupon the players went off to Spain to play a 1-1 draw with Orhuela Deportiva. For their achievement in winning promotion the players were awarded a bonus of £1,000, whilst the manager was rewarded with £5,000. The most-expensive season tickets had increased in cost to £23 and City's home League average attendances jumped to 16,204. This, coupled with no outgoings on transfer fees, meant that a relatively small deficit of £5,900 was announced at the AGM.

Match of the Season 1975-76

West Brom 0 Bristol City 1

Division 2, 17 March 1976

Although it would be fair to say that promotion is not won in a single game, there comes a defining moment in every campaign. Over the course of the season, City's twice-taken penalty in the opening fixture against Bolton comes to mind, but the match that the Robins' travelling fans were convinced clinched promotion was this rearranged epic battle at the Hawthorns on St Patrick's Day.

The first half of this thrilling encounter was played at a furious pace, with table-topping City more than holding their own against fellow promotion challengers. Just before half-time, Gerry Sweeney sent the massive contingent of City fans amongst the 26,000 crowd into raptures, finishing off a clever move by netting with a cross-shot from the right into the Birmingham End goal.

After the break it was a different story, as the Baggies seized control. Ray Cashley's goal was under almost constant siege as Albion did everything but score. Heroic defending and the intervention of the woodwork prevented an equaliser, though City missed the chance of putting the result beyond doubt when Paul Cheesley miskicked in front of an open net. It was just like the Leeds cup-tie again as the final minutes dragged agonisingly by, and the fans' relief was palpable when the final whistle blew.

Despite only winning two of their final eight games, City duly fulfilled the confidence of their fans by gaining promotion in their penultimate game, but they lost out on the Championship. West Brom bounced back from this defeat to put together a great winning run to clinch the third promotion spot. Only their inferior goal-average kept them below City.

LEAGUE DIVISION 1	**1976-77**
League Division 1	18th
League Cup	2nd Round
FA Cup	3rd Round

Dicks knew he had to strengthen his squad. He released Emanuel to Newport County and Brolly to Grimsby, and had funds available from the record number of 6,639 season tickets sold. Unfortunately, Burnley midfielder Doug Collins chose to join Plymouth on a free transfer, whilst a £55,000 bid for Mansfield striker Ray Clarke was rejected, as were overtures for Newcastle's John Tudor. It was therefore the promotion-winning side that quite properly participated in the pre-season Anglo-Scottish Cup. Despite home wins over West Brom and Notts County, a 2-4 defeat at Nottingham Forest was sufficient to deny them a place in the knock-out stages.

The fans were unconcerned though, their thoughts focused on City's League opener at sun-baked Highbury. City's shock win did scant justice to their superiority over an Arsenal side that included their record new-signing Malcolm Macdonald. Lauded by Brian Moore on ITV's The Big Match, City showed their win was no fluke as they went second in the table with a 4-1 home win over Sunderland, following a 1-1 draw with Stoke in their first home match. The Stoke game was marred by an injury that finished Cheesley's career. He fell awkwardly after contesting a high ball with keeper Peter Shilton and his right knee crumpled beneath him. He attempted a comeback in a 0-1 home defeat by Birmingham two months later, but eventually, following three operations and a lengthy stay at Farnham Park Rehabilitation Centre, near Slough, was obliged to hang up his boots.

Unbeaten in the first four League games, Dicks searched in vain for a striker as the goals dried up. A 1-2 defeat at Maine Road put a halt to City's promising start. Then, after a home draw against West Ham, City mustered just two goals in the next six games, losing them all. Len Bond, back at Ashton Gate after being loaned out and playing in America, ended Cashley's run of consecutive games when taking over in goal against Leicester. Bond pulled a groin muscle taking a goal-kick at Villa Park and never played for City again, joining Brentford in the summer. John Shaw was the next keeper to be drafted in, having waited two and a half years for his senior chance. His debut coincided with Cheesley's last game. Shaw seized his opportunity so firmly that he became a fixture in the side. By 1978-79 he was being tipped for Scottish international honours.

City tumbled dramatically down the table and had sunk to twentieth (out of 22) when Dicks made his first foray into the transfer market. It wasn't a forward he wanted, however, but one of England's greatest post-war defenders – 32-year-old Norman (bite your legs) Hunter. He signed a three-year contract after City paid Leeds £40,000 for his services. Known only by his reputation as a hard man, City supporters soon began to appreciate the other side of his character that had so endeared him to the Leeds fans over the course of thirteen years and 540 League appearances.

Instead of a ruthless clogger, City supporters learned that Hunter was an accomplished footballer. Possessed of a cultured left-foot, his passing and positional play were impeccable. Every time he surged forward it was like a one-man cavalry charge. Hunter, however, did not enjoy an auspicious City debut. It was at Derby, where he had been sent off after fighting with Francis Lee some years previously. He was given a rough ride by the home fans and received a first-half booking as City slipped to a 0-2 defeat.

Hunter's first home appearance coincided with Fear's return to the side. A sound display by Merrick – who had moved to left-back in place of Drysdale to accommodate the newcomer – helped City halt their losing run with a goalless draw. The following week saw Dicks splash out £50,000 to secure 29-year-old Liverpool midfielder Peter Cormack, who had been capped nine times by Scotland. Cormack's debut was at Tottenham and he was instrumental in the goal that brought City's later winner. His long diagonal pass set Merrick scurrying down the left to cross for Fear to net.

Things looked even brighter following a 3-1 home win over Norwich. And though City lost 1-2 at Anfield they extended Liverpool to the limit. Dicks then agreed a £100,000 fee to bring Chris Garland back from Leicester. A training ground bust-up that left Jeff Blockley with a broken jaw meant that Leicester boss Jimmy Bloomfield was anxious to offload the fair-haired striker who had made a name for himself as a First Division marksman since leaving City four years previously.

Garland's first match was at home to Leeds, when 31,400 spectators, City's biggest home crowd of the season, saw very little. After ten minutes fog enveloped the ground and though rumour suggested Garland had hit the bar with a header it was no surprise that the game was called off at half-time.

With Gow needing a cartilage operation and Ritchie unable to recapture his previous form, City had to wait until 22 January for their next win. After bowing out of the FA Cup 1-4 at Ipswich and then losing 1-2 at Old Trafford, City secured the double over Arsenal, helped by Cormack's two goals. Garland's first goal after his return earned a home point against Newcastle, but the crunch came at Sunderland, who had gone thirteen games without winning and

1,017 minutes of play without scoring a goal. Both sequences ended against City, the crucial goal dumping them back in trouble.

Dicks took the players to Torremolinos for a short break. Garland's goal accounted for Manchester City on their return, but only one win in the next nine games saw City entrenched at the bottom of the table. Cormack's penalty winner against Spurs heralded better things, and seven points from seven games, whilst not lifting City clear of the drop-line, kept them in with a chance of pulling clear with two matches left.

Garland's two goals beat champions Liverpool at Ashton Gate, whereupon City's fate was suddenly thrust into their own hands. With one match left, three days later, it didn't matter what the other clubs did; all City had to do was draw at Coventry. The record books show that was what happened, but behind the 2-2 scoreline was a story that no writer of fiction could ever dream up.

Match of the Season 1976-77

Coventry City 2 Bristol City 2

Division 1, 19 May 1977

Postponed on New Year's Day because of a frozen pitch, this game provided a climax to the season that no one present will ever forget. Having waited 65 years to regain First Division status, City looked to be making a quick return back to where they had come from.

Stoke and Tottenham were already down, but the third relegation spot rested between City, Sunderland and Coventry, each with 34 points. On this last fateful evening Sunderland were away at Everton. If Sunderland won, Coventry's inferior goal-difference (introduced to replace goal-average this season) meant they too would have to win to survive. Both games were due to kick off at the same time for this Thursday evening fixture, but this failed to take account of the sheer numbers of Bristolians converging on the ground. Many of the estimated 15,000 red-and-white bedecked West Country fans travelled up the M5 more in hope than expectation, almost resigned to relegation, but they reckoned without their team's fighting qualities – not to mention the consequences of the five-minute delay to the kick-off, brought about by the massive 36,000 crowd still trying to squeeze inside Highfield Road.

Coventry went in front after fifteen minutes through Tommy Hutchison, their Scottish International winger. When he doubled his tally shortly after the break it looked all up for the Robins. Fortunately, the players did not give up the ghost, and Gerry Gow revived hopes a few minutes later by scoring from twelve yards.

Did You Know?

When City beat St Albans 9-2 in the FA Cup in 1996, it was the first time City had been involved in an 11-goal match since beating Chichester 11-0 in 1960.

It was now all City, and with just eleven minutes left Donnie Gillies shot into the far corner of the Coventry net to level matters. A battle royal then ensued, but the Robins looked the more likely winners until the heart-pounding action came to an abrupt halt four minutes from time. The electronic scoreboard was flashing up the message that Sunderland had lost 0-2, the result of which was that both teams needed only to maintain the status-quo. The remaining minutes degenerated into farce, with the Robins retaining possession in their own half, the only danger being the prospect of a back-pass going astray. So passed the final minutes, until the bemused referee, Ron Challis, blew for time with both sets of fans deliriously happy.

Survival celebrations in Bristol were interrupted the following day when Hobbs, unbeknown to his colleagues, announced that potential directors could buy themselves vacancies on the board for £25,000 each. This bombshell stirred the other four directors into action and Hobbs was deposed as chairman on 23 May. Stephen Kew succeeded him with the backing of Norman Jones, Graham Griffiths and Bill Garland.

While Bristol City's tenure in the top flight would last only three more seasons, Coventry have lived a charmed life in its glorified ranks ever since.

LEAGUE DIVISION 1	**1977-78**
League Division 1	17th
League Cup	3rd Round
FA Cup	3rd Round

City's return to the First Division precipitated a change to the club badge. The design – a robin perched on a ball surmounted by the Clifton Suspension Bridge – was adopted in July 1976. Prior to 1972, the club badge had always been the Coat of Arms of the City and County of Bristol, though a robin had been worn on the players' shirts in 1949-50. However, with the increasing marketing of club products it was decided to hold a competition to design an official badge. Organised by the *Bristol Evening Post*, it attracted 300 entries and the winner was 57-year-old rugby fan Harry Winn. He received a prize of £50 for his simple design depicting a robin on a five-bar gate. This new crest appeared in the match programme but not on the players' shirts, which continued to bear the Bristol Coat of Arms right up until the end of the promotion campaign. It would not be until the 1994-95 season that the Suspension Bridge badge was supplanted and the Bristol Coat of Arms returned to grace City's shirts once more.

In the close season the big news focused on the boardroom battle. Hobbs had gathered around him a team of businessmen to fight for his reinstatement. Daily statements from one side and then the other enlivened the local newspapers for months. At the AGM, held in the packed Patrons Bar of the Dolman Stand, when a loss for the 1976-77 season of £113,039 was announced, the attempt by Hobbs and his followers to gain control was thwarted. Two new directors, Peter West and David Callow, were elected, and the following day solicitor Richard Castle joined them.

The power-struggle continued, however. In November the board called an extraordinary meeting, where it pledged to increase the share capital from £30,000 to £110,000. The resolution was carried at this stormy meeting by 306 votes, but there was a dispute over 500 shares. Had they gone against the motion, the outcome would effectively have unseated the board and restored majority-shareholder Hobbs to power. The matter was settled in an expensive High Court action the following summer. The result stood and Hobbs conceded defeat.

Following on from the tournaments staged in 1974 and 1976, the third and last 'All in the Game' soccer skills contest was held at Ashton Gate between 14-16 July. After beating St Mirren by 210 points to 145, City were knocked out in the semi-finals 130-110 by Manchester City. The final was won by Leicester 162-132.

In the pre-season qualifying for the Anglo-Scottish Cup, a 0-1 defeat at Birmingham did not deny City reaching the quarter-finals for the first time. Wins over Bristol Rovers and Plymouth carried them through. A 0-2 defeat in the first leg at Partick Thistle did not auger well for City's chances of making progress, but two goals from Mann and one from Whitehead in the return two weeks later set up a semi-final meeting with Hibernian. The first leg at Easter Road was a tempestuous affair, ending 1-1 despite Hunter (73rd-minute tackle on Ally McLeod) and Cormack (77th-minute head-butt on Des Bremner) being sent off. Shaw was City's hero, when saving McLeod's 84th-minute spot-kick, and Ritchie the villain, when his late miss prevented City pulling off a sensational win.

Hibs chairman Tom Hart described City as the 'Butchers of Bristol', and made clear that under no circumstances would his side play the second leg. He attempted to claim the tie, and then threatened to withdraw by paying a £2,000 fine, but City's demands for £12,000 compensation, coupled with the intervention of the Scottish and English League Secretaries, brought a change of heart. City won a thriller, 5-3, in front of 6,072 soaking fans at Ashton Gate.

It looked easy in the final when City won the first leg 2-1 in heavy rain at Love Street, Paisley (City: Mabbutt 20, Cormack 74; St Mirren: Abercrombie 87) in front of 7,800 spectators on 23 November, but St Mirren were a different proposition at Ashton Gate on 5 December. A 16,110 crowd were confident of City winning their first major trophy since lifting the Welsh Cup in 1934, but Bobby Reid gave the visitors a 68th-minute lead with an overhead kick from a narrow angle. City equalised two minutes later in their first concerted attack of the half when Kevin Mabbutt headed in Whitehead's inswinging corner. St Mirren kept pressing and Frank McGarvey headed what most considered to be a valid goal before colliding with keeper Shaw. Fortunately for City, referee Derek Nippard thought otherwise, and Saints' manager Alex Ferguson found himself in hot water after the game for his ill-tempered remarks to the official. The teams for the final were:

1st leg:

ST MIRREN: Hunter, Young, Beckett, Fitzpatrick, Reid, Dunlop (Hyslop 45), Copeland, Stark, McGarvey, Abercrombie, Munro.

BRISTOL CITY: Shaw, Sweeney, Gillies, Gow, Collier, Merrick, Tainton, Ritchie, Mabbutt, Cormack, Mann.

2nd leg:

BRISTOL CITY: Shaw, Gillies, Sweeney, Gow, Collier, Merrick, Tainton, Ritchie, Mabbutt, Mann, Whitehead.

ST MIRREN: Hunter, Beckett (Richardson 74), Young, Fitzpatrick, Reid, Copeland, McGarvey, Stark, Hyslop, Abercrombie, Munro.

Did You Know?

Against Oxford U in 1968, City sub Derrick did not wear No 12. He wore No 8, the same as the player he replaced, Garland. The referee did not notice.

In the League, City struggled early on with three defeats and two draws before recording their first win, 3-2 at home to West Ham. The next nine games brought only two more victories – Hunter's left boot flying off when he netted the decisive goal in a 3-2 home win over Leeds, and a 3-1 success against Derby. By then Dicks was desperately searching for a striker. Scarcity of goals was a headache, especially away from home where Gillies' effort in a 1-1 draw at Newcastle was City's first away strike of the season. Unable to sign Alan Gowling from Newcastle, Dicks turned his attention to 28-year-old Joe Royle from Manchester City. The England international centre-forward, who had been at Maine Road for three years since his transfer from Everton, was persuaded to come to Ashton Gate on loan. He made an immediate impact on his debut, scoring all City's goals in a 4-1 hammering of Middlesbrough.

After this there was no way the City fans were going to let Royle go, and an avalanche of letters to the press eventually persuaded the reluctant Royle to sign permanently. Of course, the goals were not to flow so easily again, the trend being set in Royle's first game after City had paid a £90,000 fee for his services.

His brilliant chip was disallowed at Derby, but the big centre-forward proved to be a great provider for others as City eventually came to terms with top flight soccer. Try as he might, Royle could not find the target. He went eleven matches without scoring, hitting the woodwork, having goals disallowed in consecutive games, and squandering a spot-kick against West Brom with a shot high into the crowd. A simple tap-in versus Norwich in February ended the drought as City embarked on a six-match unbeaten run.

The loss of Collier for the rest of the season after suffering knee damage in a 1-1 draw at Old Trafford allowed David Rodgers to make a triumphant return to the side; it was his goal that brought City their first ever win at West Ham. A harsh defeat by Everton wiped the smile off City's faces, and whilst just two wins from the final eleven games did not raise the spectre of relegation, it brought a disappointing finishing position of seventeenth.

A poor disciplinary record didn't help City's cause. Tainton, Sweeney and Gow had all been sent off during the spring. Having had almost 200 misconduct points, City were fined £800 by the FA.

Failure to cope with Third Division Wrexham in both the major cup competitions raised doubts as to City's overall ability. Whilst one defeat against such opposition could be explained away, to succumb twice suggested City were far from being a genuine top-flight side. The fans' small consolation was a thrilling 4-4 home draw with Wrexham in the third round of the FA Cup.

The close-season saw an end to physiotherapist Les Bardsley's 21-year association with the club. The popular ex-Bury player left to concentrate on his thriving private practice, whilst Bill Heather was appointed in his place. Bardsley was granted a testimonial in February 1978 against a Bobby Charlton XI.

Match of the Season 1977-78

Bristol City 4 Middlesbrough 1

Division 1, 26 November 1977

Every player hopes to make a good impression on his debut, and in this game Joe Royle's hopes were more than fulfilled. On loan from Manchester City, his four-goal haul made him an instant hit with the Ashton Gate fans, and many were the letters in the local press urging the reluctant player to make a permanent move.

City's poor return of just five goals from their previous six games had prompted manager Dicks to strengthen the attack, and Royle's first game attracted almost 21,000 fans for the visit of Middlesbrough. His four goals from just four chances demonstrated what City had been lacking since Paul Cheesley's career had been ended by injury during the preceding campaign.

Whilst Royle's goals – a header, followed by a right-footed shot and two with his left – were taken with the aplomb one would expect from a top-class international striker, it was his all-round ability that impressed the most as he added a new dimension to City's game.

After mulling over a permanent move for some weeks, Royle eventually decided to come to the West Country. Unfortunately, it was a case of 'after the Lord Mayor's Show' for quite a while as it was not until early February that Royle found the net again. Two games at the turn of the year illustrated his bad luck. On Boxing Day against West Brom he hit the crossbar and had a goal disallowed, and his fifth-minute effort against Nottingham Forest was struck off because Kevin Mabbutt had strayed offside.

Whilst Royle never recaptured the goalscoring exploits that had made him an instant idol, there is little doubt that – together with Norman Hunter – he supplied the class that enabled City not only to survive awhile in the top flight, but to be good enough to challenge for a European place in 1978-79.

LEAGUE DIVISION 1	**1978-79**
Division 1	13th
League Cup	2nd Round
FA Cup	4th Round

Whilst doubts over City's true abilities never entirely disappeared, on account of their failure yet again to overcome so-called inferior opposition in cup competitions – losing to Second Division Crystal Palace in both the League and FA Cup – they found themselves near the top of the table in the wage stakes. Other than Liverpool and Everton, City's were reputedly the highest paid players in the League, on a basic £300 per week, on a par with Aston Villa, Derby, Leeds, Manchester City and Nottingham Forest.

City returned to Scandinavia, where they had won six out of six games twelve months previously, for their pre-season action. This time they again managed a clean sweep, beating Vasteras SK, Edsbro IF, Enkopnings and IFK Eskilstuna, before returning to begin their defence of the Anglo-Scottish Cup. It could not have started better as Bristol Rovers were hammered 6-1 at Ashton Gate. Wins over Cardiff and Fulham enabled City to top their qualifying group. Unfortunately, in the quarter-finals St Mirren gained revenge for last season's defeat – winning 2-1 at Ashton Gate and drawing 2-2 at Love Street.

Opening their League campaign with a 2-1 win at newly promoted Bolton, City followed up with three points from their next two games. This raised hopes, until City lost 0-2 at bottom of the table Wolves. The points continued to accumulate on a fairly regular basis, however, and helped by Shaw keeping a clean-sheet at home to Coventry on Boxing Day, goals from Royle (three), Ritchie and Cormack produced City's best-ever win in the top division. What a change this made: instead of bracing themselves for another struggle against relegation, City fans saw their team firmly ensconced in the top half of the table and were talking about qualifying for Europe.

Climbing as high as fifth at one stage, City were still in with a shout of qualifying for the Fairs Cup as late as 10 April, when a 3-1 win over Chelsea left them a challenging seventh. City were disadvantaged in having fulfilled more fixtures than many of their rivals and added just three points from their final five games. This banished thoughts of Europe and brought an end of season position of thirteenth. Though disappointing at the finish, it was City's highest final placing since 1908-09 and their fourth best overall.

Cheesley had his benefit match on 27 November, when his previous club Norwich City provided the opposition and won 6-3.

City played sixteen friendlies during this campaign. These included a 2-0 success against Bristol Rovers at Eastville in a benefit for Frankie Prince, a 0-0 home draw with Moscow Dynamo, and an end of season tour of North America. A 1-1 draw against Vancouver Whitecaps was followed with an 8-3 success over Vancouver Island and a 1-2 defeat versus Portland Timbers.

In the Gloucestershire Senior Professional Cup, City maintained their good record in the competition. They clinched their fourth successive win against Bristol Rovers in the final, having beaten their arch rivals 3-2 in 1975-76, 1-0 in 1976-77, and 3-0 in 1977-78. This time goals from Gow and Mann clinched a 2-0 away win in front of 6,661 fans on 15 May for City to claim the Cup for the 46th time.

By this time, the youth policy so ably nurtured by Sillett had been allowed to wither as Dicks had given few first-team chances to the talented youngsters in the reserves. The 'stiffs' finished eighth in the Football Combination this season, following on from placings of fifth, tenth and eighteenth respectively in the three previous years. The lack of opportunity for home produced talent following Sillett's departure in 1974 had its effect in the FA Youth Cup. Apart from reaching the fifth round in 1975-76, where they lost 1-6 in a replay at Newcastle, the Youths made little headway in the competition. They reached only the third round in 1976-77 and 1977-78. It was even worse in 1978-79 as they were blown away 1-5 at the first time of asking by Bristol Rovers.

Match of the Season 1978-79

Bristol City 5 Coventry City 0

Division 1, 26 December 1978

Both City and Coventry were in the top half of the table at the time of this Boxing Day clash, but the Sky Blues, who had been hoping to put an end to a run of poor form away from home, were no match for the rampant Robins. City provided their fans with the perfect Christmas present as they notched up their record top-flight score, which extended Coventry's miserable winless away run to eight matches, including a 1-7 mauling at West Brom.

As City turned on the style after half-time, their previous best score in this division should have been easily surpassed, but the heroics of the Sky Blues custodian Les Sealey thwarted their endeavours. Fortunately, a poor Coventry side were unable to find the net themselves, so enabling City's 5-1 home victory over Nottingham Forest in 1910-11 to be supplanted in the club's records.

Did You Know?

At half-time in the Wolves home game in Nov 1998 the two mascots came to blows on the pitch. This was better than the game, which City lost 1-6.

The season proved to be the zenith of City's brief four-year flirtation with the elite, and this match was probably the team's best all-round performance. The first half of the campaign had seen City become an established First Division force with wins on their travels at Burnden Park, Old Trafford, and Portman Road, as well beating the likes of Liverpool and Aston Villa at Ashton Gate. The progress made was such that the team were challenging for a place in European competition right up to early April, giving little indication of the troubles that lay ahead.

City's side in 1978-79 still contained many of their promotion-winning side of 1975-76, but to this had been added the skill and experience of Hunter, Cormack and Royle. All three played a full part in City's thrilling display against Coventry, but Royle was the star with his hat-trick increasing his total goals haul for the season to seven.

Surprisingly, despite appearing in all City's remaining fixtures, Royle did not find the back of the net again this campaign. Lack of goals and a poor disciplinary record eventually wrecked the club's European ambitions. For their part, despite this heavy defeat, Coventry went on to achieve their third highest top-flight placing, finishing in tenth spot, whilst City ended a disappointing thirteenth after the promise of so much more.

3

DECLINE & FALL 1979-1984

LEAGUE DIVISION 1	**1979-80**
Division 1	20th (Relegated)
League Cup	4th Round
FA Cup	4th Round

Whilst many fans were worried about the loss of Norman Hunter, who in June had turned down City's offer of a two-year contract in favour of joining Barnsley as player-coach, most thought of City as an established top-flight club at this stage. Further Leeds links were severed with the departure of Terry Cooper on a free-transfer to join Bristol Rovers, but with the signing of midfielder Tony Fitzpatrick from St Mirren for a club record £250,000 in July optimism was high that City would build on their previous campaign's success and perhaps claim a European place.

Despite gaining only one point from their opening game, at home to Leeds, this optimism did not appear misplaced as the 23,331 fans present were treated to a vibrant game and an outstanding strike by City's Finnish international Pertti Jantunen. Adding to the general air of a club going places was the issue of a vastly improved programme, and at the end of the season this publication was a deserved winner of the 'Programme of the Year' award, winning all five categories – (i) most improved (ii) best value for money (iii) most attractive cover (iv) best in Division One (v) best in the League. Quite a difference from 1999–2000 when we find City's poor quality effort to be strangely at odds with the brilliant publication put together by Bristol Rovers, despite both programmes being printed by Bristol City's media department.

A 1-3 midweek defeat at Coventry tempered hopes somewhat, but a 2-0 win at Villa Park – clinched by Ritchie's late penalty – followed by a 2-0 home success over Wolves, shifted City up to sixth. Despite suffering only four defeats in their first fourteen League games, City were not playing well and though Dicks took the plaudits when he became the longest serving current manager –

rather crassly being photographed on the pitch behind his desk – the failure to adopt a vigorous 'buy and sale' policy, or bring on the youngsters, was coming home to roost. The loss of Collier, who became the first player to exercise his right under freedom of contract when joining Coventry in the summer of 1979, affected City's judgement to such an extent that ridiculously lengthy contracts were given out to mediocre players of insufficient ability to raise the club's stature. Not surprisingly, perhaps, complacency set in and City rapidly tumbled into the relegation zone once the limited abilities of their side were cruelly exposed in a 0-3 League Cup defeat at Nottingham Forest in November.

Most fans fatalistically accepted City's ultimate fate when Micky Channon's 15-yard drive for Southampton brought defeat at Ashton Gate four days before Christmas. On Boxing Day City dropped into the relegation zone for the first time when they found themselves at the wrong end of a 3-0 scoreline at West Brom. Destined not to climb out of the bottom three throughout the rest of the season, they nevertheless raised hopes with their best ever win against top-flight opposition. It came in the FA Cup, when Derby County were thrashed 6-2 at Ashton Gate.

January was otherwise a sad month. It saw the death at the age of 56 of old-time City favourite Cyril Williams, who was killed in a car smash in Somerset. A 0-3 home defeat by Ipswich provoked much anti-Dicks feeling, which resulted in the police having to break up a demonstration in the officials' car park after the match.

Only one win in eighteen matches from early November made relegation almost inevitable, but City's fate was not settled until the penultimate game on 29 April – a 2-5 defeat at Southampton. Paradoxically, a 0-0 draw in the final game at Spurs raised City up to twentieth, a position which would have brought safety but for the introduction of three-up, three-down, seven years previously.

So ended City's second spell in the top division and whilst many of the fans who journeyed to White Hart Lane for the final game were resigned to not getting back quickly, it is doubtful that even in their worst ever dreams they envisaged the nightmare that was to unfold. To the surprise of many, Alan Dicks and his assistant Tony Collins were awarded new five-year contracts, with the manager mouthing reassurances about his team doing well in 1980-81.

The season's only success came in the Anglo-Scottish Cup, but Dicks blew City's chances of reclaiming the cup by fielding under-strength sides in the two-legged final against old rivals St Mirren. In the preliminary stages a 4-0 win at Birmingham had augured well and a 0-0 draw at Plymouth followed by a 1-0 home success over Fulham left City group winners. In the quarter-finals Partick Thistle were beaten 3-1 over two legs, and though Morton escaped with a 2-2 draw at Ashton Gate, City turned the tables in the semi-final second leg, winning 1-0 at Cappielow.

A Howard Pritchard goal in the dying seconds enabled City to take the Gloucestershire Cup for the fifth successive year, before the curtain was brought down on a miserable season with a 1-3 defeat against Derek Dougan's XI in Merrick's benefit match.

In the Youth Cup a 7-1 away success over Torquay was followed by a 6-0 away demolition of Port Vale, before City came unstuck at Ashton Gate in January when Middlesbrough won 2-1.

The club's worsening financial problems were manifest in a new record loss of £161,223 being declared. Season ticket sales continued to fall, only 5,373 being sold compared to 6,807 in 1978-79, but price increases brought only a slight drop in receipts from £236,058 to £230,896. Whereas in 1978-79 season tickets for all seats had been £45, in 1979-80 centre seats in both stands cost £55, whilst wing seats in the Grandstand cost £50 compared to £45 in the Dolman.

Match of the Season 1979-80

Bristol City 2 Leeds United 2

Division 1, 18 August 1979

In a season that was to end in relegation, highlights were few and far between. Nevertheless, the optimism of the fans that the previous season's results could be equalled or bettered was reflected by the club itself, whose marketing strategy prospered under the direction of Tony Rance. In addition to the much improved, award-winning match programme, the introduction of pre-match entertainment in the form of the Bristol City cheerleaders in 1977-78 and novelties such as staging women's lacrossse at the home game with Nottingham Forest – when the English beat a Combined Scottish & Welsh side 15-3 – did much to raise the club's profile.

A crowd of just over 23,000 for the visit of Leeds were treated to a ding-dong struggle, the highlight of which was Jantunen's 20-yard drive into the Open End goal to put City 2-1 in front. Unfortunately, Alan Curtis, Leeds' new signing from Swansea, enjoyed a dream debut and he notched his second goal of the game to deprive City of a win eight minutes from time.

But this bright draw ushered in a false dawn. Eighth at the end of September, a run of fourteen games for City yielded just nine points and pushed them down into the drop-zone. Goalscoring was a persistent problem. Joe Royle, for example, despite his heading ability in laying on the chances, struggled to score goals.

LEAGUE DIVISION 2	**1980-81**
Division 2	21st (Relegated)
League Cup	2nd Round
FA Cup	5th Round

A low-key pre-season underlined City's diminished status: sandwiched between draws at Poole and Swindon, the Robins could muster only a 1-0 win over tiny Barnstaple. This hardly offered much encouragement for a successful season. Nor did City's first competitive results of the new campaign. They found themselves eliminated in the group stage of the Anglo-Scottish Cup, following a 1-1 home draw with Notts County and a 0-1 defeat at Orient.

And as for misplaced hopes of a rapid return to the top flight, these were soon dispelled when City failed to win any of their first nine games. The departure of Joe Royle to Norwich shortly before the opening fixture left a gap in attack that was never filled. Come May, with City finishing the season with less goals than points, it was not surprising that relegation was the outcome, or that City's measly 29 goals scored marked the 1980-81 side, in the days of two points for a win, as the club's worst ever in the scoring stakes.

Given such a record, it is surprising City did not finish bottom. An even poorer Rovers team – ironically in a season when they shared Ashton Gate for five games early on, following the destruction by fire of Eastville's South Stand – prevented such ignominy and gave Bristol soccer the dubious distinction of being the first provincial city ever to provide two teams being relegated from the same division together. Strangely enough, just nine years later the two clubs were to provide the reciprocal, becoming the first outside London to be promoted from the same division at the same time.

Manager Alan Dicks had seemed bullish at the start of the season, insisting he had a good enough squad to make an impact in the promotion race, but a 0-1 home defeat by Swansea on 6 September brought Dicks' long reign to an end: he was sacked two days later. Tony Collins (chief scout 1967-72 and assistant manager 1976-80) and first-team coach Ken Wimshurst acted as caretakers before Bob Houghton took over on a three-year contract worth £25,000 per annum on 29 September.

Initially, it seemed that City had pulled off a remarkable coup in obtaining the services of a man who had guided Swedish club Malmo to the European Cup final in 1979, when they lost 0-1 to Nottingham Forest, as well winning the Swedish League and Cup four times since 1974. Houghton brought in Roy Hodgson as his assistant and early home wins over Luton and Newcastle suggested City had stumbled upon a dream ticket, but this took no account of the club's rapidly worsening financial position, which was to scupper long-term progress. In the short-term, however, £100,000 was found to bring in giant Swedish international keeper Jan Moller from Houghton's former club.

Following a vibrant attacking performance against Luton in Houghton's first home match in charge, the fans grew increasingly frustrated by the new manager's defensive inclinations. Just two goals in a barren run of nine League games between 20 December and late February that yielded just one solitary win left City fighting a rearguard action to maintain their status. That battle was lost, with but two more wins chalked up before the end of the season.

Gates slumped, and with many players enjoying lengthy contracts negotiated in First Division days the club was not just fighting against a second relegation, but was soon to be embroiled in a struggle for their very survival. The coffers saw little benefit from City's short-lived participation in the League Cup – Birmingham winning 2-1 on aggregate – but progress in the FA Cup kept the wolf from the door for a while. A 2-0 win over Derby was followed by a 5-0 goal-bonanza over Carlisle before the Robins were knocked out at the fifth round stage by Nottingham Forest.

Desperate times call for desperate remedies. Welcome revenue was generated by the staging of cricket at the ground for the first time since Bedminster's departure in 1912. In September a crowd of 7,925 were in attendance to see a Rest of the World cricket XI beat an England side, but this did little to stem losses, which this season amounted to £491,969. The average home attendance almost halved from 18,932 to 9,765, whilst the number of season ticket holders was slashed from 5,373 to 2,943. Not surprisingly, by the time of the AGM in November 1981, the club was on its knees financially. An organisation known as 'Friends of Bristol City' had been formed a month previously, following a statement that the club owed debts in excess of £700,000.

The fight to reinstate Robert Hobbs flared up again, but at a shareholders meeting in December the rebel group, led by Lionel Amos and supported by Leslie Kew, Frederick Matthews, D Squires and J Drinkwater, withdrew their challenge when they accepted that they could not prevail. However, nine days later, Stephen Kew, who had been chairman for the three-and-a-half years since the overthrow of Hobbs, stood down, though he remained on the board. Long-time City supporter Archie Gooch, who had been on the board for less than a year, then took over the helm for what was to prove to be the most desperate time in the club's history.

Public interest in the annual contest for the Gloucestershire Cup continued to dwindle. The attendance for this season's final –

having attained a high of 20,097 in 1954-55 – dropped to a new low of 2,558 at Eastville on 5 May. The dramatic drop in local interest was unexpected, as it was not until 1978-79 that crowds dropped below five figures for the first time since 1965-66. Mabbutt's extra-time goal took City to within sight of their record of seven successive trophy wins notched up between 1905-06 and 1911-12.

The Reserves had a poor season, dropping to seventeenth in the Football Combination, though reaching the semi-finals of the Somerset Premier Cup.

Match of the Season 1980-81

Nottingham Forest 2 Bristol City 1

FA Cup, 5th Round, 14 February 1981

City's unexpected FA Cup run started at the Baseball Ground, when many thought Derby would avenge their 2-6 hammering in the previous year's competition. But keeper John Shaw was in superb form as City hung on for a goalless draw, and then won the replay 2-0, thanks to Tom Ritchie's inspired performance. In the next round City were unable to supply the killer finish despite being on top at Carlisle, but they had no such trouble in the replay when five goals without reply clinched a meeting with defending European Cup holders Nottingham Forest, who had beaten Bolton and Manchester United to reach this stage.

Almost 27,000 spectators assembled at the City Ground, where they saw City almost pull off a shock victory against a Forest side possibly suffering the effects of a midweek trip to Japan where they lost 0-1 to Nacional in the World Club Championship final. Kevin Mabbutt coolly stroked a goal just prior to half-time, and despite all Forest's pressure it was not until seven minutes from time that John Robertson's debatable penalty turned the tide. Ian Wallace then deprived City of a replay that would have proved a welcome boost to their depleted coffers, turning the ball in during a goalmouth scramble for a late winner.

Sadly, City's stirring FA Cup form was not translated into their League performances. Forest also had their disappointments as they exited the competition in the next round when losing a replay at Ipswich 0-1. Having already lost their grip on the European Cup, seventh place in the First Division meant Forest did not qualify for Europe in 1981-82.

LEAGUE DIVISION 3	**1981-82**
Division 3	23rd (Relegated)
League Cup	3rd Round
FA Cup	4th Round

At long last City found their man when a fee of £150,000 secured the services of centre-forward Mick Harford from Newcastle. No doubt the introduction of three points for a win was partly responsible for the club pursuing the services of a proven goalscorer, but Harford, despite his valiant endeavours, could not compensate for deficiencies elsewhere in City's team. Behind the scenes, changes amongst the backroom staff had seen the appointment of Alex Lockhart as physiotherapist and club doctor S Dasgupta took up his new duties for the home win over Plymouth.

The fans expected Third Division stability at the very least, but as the financial crisis came to a head relegation paled into insignificance in the face of threats to the club's very survival. The outcome was a season that ended with City having the dubious distinction of being the first club ever to tumble from the First to the Fourth Division in successive seasons. Although suffering just one defeat in the opening five games, the following nineteen fixtures yielded only three further wins. Rob Newman's 20-yard free-kick clinched a 1-0 success at Walsall in February, but by then much had happened to change the composition of City's line-up.

The club's chronic bank-balance necessitated the transfer of Kevin Mabbutt to Crystal Palace in September, with Welsh international centre-half Terry Boyle coming in part-exchange. Clive Whitehead, who was on an eleven-year contract said to be worth £550 per week, went to West Brom in November. There was even talk of Bob Houghton moving on early in the season. It had been rumoured that he had been offered the position of manager of the Swedish national side, but he chose to tough it out at Ashton Gate until a 1-3 home defeat by Wimbledon on 2 January caused him to throw in the towel. His assistant, Roy Hodgson, took over on a caretaker basis, but he had little opportunity of demonstrating his considerable managerial ability, which was gained when in charge of Swedish club Halmstad.

Following the announcement of the club's £700,000 plus debt, various rescue packages, including the formation of 'Friends of Bristol City', were established. But despite Park Furnishers becoming the club's first sponsors – when their name was emblazoned across the front of City's shirts in the home game against Southend – in November, by the turn of the year the situation was so bad that closure appeared imminent. A run in the FA Cup produced much needed revenue, but the decision to bring forward the kick-off time for the second round clash with Northampton to 7pm because of City's staff party had unforeseen consequences. The tie saw one of the club's lowest ever home attendances in the competition – just 2,901. The gate for the meeting with First Division Aston Villa in the next round was much better, but even so City's share of the £45,000 receipts, from 20,279 spectators, was but a drop in the ocean in the sea of debt in which they were immersed.

With the Receivers at the door and the club estimated to be insolvent with liabilities of £850,000, it was widely thought that the following week's game at Newport would be the club's last, despite the attempts by local businessmen Deryn Coller (Park Furnishers) and Ken Sage (Alusage) to save the rather long-in-the-tooth Bristol Babe. Their plan was to re-launch the club with a £1 million share-issue under a new organisation known as Bristol City (1982) plc. This scheme was initially dependent on the acceptance of a redundancy package by eight players (the so-called Ashton Gate Eight) who were on high wages and long contracts. These players – Chris Garland (who returned to play on a match-by-match basis in 1982-83), Peter Aitken, Jimmy Mann, Julian Marshall, Geoff Merrick, David Rodgers, Gerry Sweeney and Trevor Tainton – were understandably aggrieved about being offered only one-third of their entitlement, but following the intervention of Gordon Taylor (Secretary of the Professional Footballers Association) they eventually agreed to accept an improved redundancy offer (raised from £58,000 to £80,000, plus the guarantee of a testimonial match).

The new organisation took over in a temporary capacity the following day, though the now-defunct City retained the players' registration and ownership of the ground. Hodgson was left with an unenviable task, but the fans responded with admirable support as the embryonic organisation began their existence with a home draw with promotion-chasing Fulham on 6 February.

Apart from Moller, Boyle, Harford and Shaw, the remaining players were mainly raw youngsters, hence the reason for City's old nickname of the Babes being heard again. Financial restraints and shortage of players precipitated the disbandment of City's Reserve side, which resigned from the Football Combination in February.

Hodgson, aided by his new assistant Colin Toal and chief scout Richard Dinnis, bolstered the squad by the loan signings of defender Aiden McCaffery from Bristol Rovers, and midfielders Ray Gooding (Coventry) and Les Carter (Crystal Palace). In the event, the Football League, preoccupied by City's transfer debts, would not sanction the renewal of McCaffery and Gooding's monthly contracts, and they soon returned from whence they came. It was of little surprise that City were unable to escape from the jaws of relegation, especially given the March transfers of Moller to Toronto Blizzards for £85,000 and Harford to Birmingham for £125,000.

The fate of the new administration hung in the balance however, as everything hinged on a share issue in April, which was only successful at the last due to injection of money from local businessmen, plus further investment from the interim board members. Bristol City plc was finally up and running on 30 April, when it dispensed with the services of caretaker boss Hodgson and put Youth team manager Gerry Sharpe in control for what little of the season remained. The stadium was purchased for the new plc for £565,000 on 7 May.

The team fared well under Sharpe's direction, only losing once in six outings, but the directors were unimpressed. They settled on ex-City player and former Bristol Rovers manager Terry Cooper as their choice to kick-start City's revival, after conducting interviews with both him and Sharpe, as well as Stuart Morgan (Weymouth), Frank Burrows (ex-Portsmouth) and ex-City forward Joe Royle.

On the eve of the Argentine invasion of the Falkland Islands, Cooper, having persuaded Doncaster boss Billy Bremner to release him from his playing contract, inherited a club bereft of many players. Free-transfers were granted to Les Carter, Billy Down, Peter Devine, Jon Economou, Allan Hay, David Mogg, John Shaw, Gary Smith, Mark Smith and Steve Wheery.

What then of The Ashton Gate Eight, who were the recipients of a special benefit match played on 24 March, when 6,020 fans turned up to see Southampton beat Ipswich Town 2-1? Each of these sacrificial lambs found other clubs with whom to play out the season. Sweeney, after a brief spell at Trowbridge Town joined up with Aitken at York, Garland and Merrick went to Hong Kong to play for Carolina Hills, Mann turned out for Barnsley, Rodgers initially went to Torquay, along with Tainton, before moving to Lincoln, whilst Marshall went to Blackburn. After the winding up of the old club it was reported that these players shared £82,750, such sum including the receipts of the special match referred to above.

The change of regime terminated the Park Furnishers agreement, their name last being emblazoned across City's chests in the Newport game. It was not until the 0-1 home defeat by Brentford in March that the traditionalists had to put up with their favourites' shirts again being tarnished in such a way. Hirerite's sponsorship would last for more than eight years, until 1990-91. They were superseded by Thorn for three seasons, who were in turn followed by Dry Blackthorn 1993-94, Auto Windscreen's 1994-1996, Sanderson's Computer Equipment 1996-1999, and DAS 1999-2000.

Did You Know?

In February 1976 City entertained Southampton, who played in yellow shirts. No 9 Peter Osgood's shirt was a much brighter yellow than his team-mates'.

Match of the Season 1981-82

Bristol City 0 Fulham 0

Division 3, 6 February 1982

This fixture will always be remembered by City fans as the game they thought they would never see. Just seven days earlier a large exodus of supporters flocked over the Severn Bridge to Newport fearing that they could be witnessing City's last match, as the burden of ever increasing debt left the club facing closure. The tide of debt had to be stemmed and the salvage plan was subject to eight players accepting a redundancy package before midday on Tuesday, 2 February. As the drama unfolded in the full glare of the television and press cameras at the Dragonara Hotel, the players accepted an improved package. This left Roy Hodgson the task of fielding a side to turn out against promotion-chasing Fulham.

Relief at City's survival almost doubled the attendance from the previous home game, and the fans gave tremendous support to a basically young and inexperienced side that did duty at Ashton Gate on this day. Debuts were given to Wayne Bray – a 17-year-old midfielder who had won seven England schoolboy caps and was the youngest member of the Bristol Boys team that won the English Schools Trophy two years previously; Jon Economou, a 20-year-old Londoner who had waited three years for his chance; and 18-year-old Wiltshire lad Rob Newman. With the glare of publicity still on the club, television cameras recorded scenes and interviews with supporters in the crowd. As for the new directors, they wore red bowler hats, which they tossed to the fans in acknowledgement of having succeeded with part one of the rescue plan.

On the day, the Bristol Babes more than held their own against their experienced opponents. Unfortunately, the upsurge in enthusiasm was unable to sustain City for the rest of the season, and they were doomed to relegation well before the end of the campaign. Fulham, though, had cause to rue the points lost in this game as they ultimately cost them promotion.

LEAGUE DIVISION 4	**1982-83**
Division 4	14th
League Cup	2nd Round
FA Cup	1st Round

The first AGM of the new administration was held at the Colston Hall on 21 June 1982. The new board was named as follows: Des Williams (chairman), Les Kew (vice-chairman), Bob Boyd, Deryn Coller, Bob Marshall, Oliver Newland and Ivor Williams.

The money raised from the share issue had barely been enough to purchase the assets from the old company, so frugality was the word at Ashton Gate where the directors paid personally for both their drinks and those of their visitors. In such a difficult time new boss Cooper was to prove the ideal man to take the club forward. He worked tirelessly in the summer to put a team together with the limited finances at his disposal. He persuaded the directors to sanction the appointment as his assistant of Clive Middlemass, who had been a colleague at Leeds and managed Workington for two years before linking up with Cooper at Bristol Rovers. Cost cutting measures during the season ended the lengthy associations of Gerry Sharpe and Commercial Manager Jim Evans, after periods of 21 and nineteen years respectively. The board charged the Supporters Club £10,000 rent for their premises in the Grandstand, and the executive 51 Club was renamed the Directors' Club.

Cooper did well to secure the free-transfer services of 23-year-old striker Glyn Riley from Barnsley and 30-year-old winger Alan Crawford from Chesterfield, not to mention persuading Tom Ritchie to return from Sunderland to his old stomping ground. With a small playing staff of fifteen, Cooper scoured the local non-league scene, from where he picked up 22-year-old Simon Panes (top-scorer for Western League Melksham the previous season) on a short part-time contract. Of the ten players given free-transfers at the end of the previous campaign, John Shaw and Jon Economou were re-signed on fresh terms. Kevin Slabber's broken leg in a reserve game left Cooper keeping his fingers crossed that goalkeeper Shaw stayed clear from injury as the club could not afford to sign another keeper. Twins Nyere and Omele Kelly joined as youth players, while their elder brother Errington arrived from Bristol Rovers during the season. Nyere became City's then youngest ever player at the age of sixteen years, 244 days (until ousted by Marvin Brown in 1999) when coming on as an 82nd-minute substitute in a 1-3 defeat at Hartlepool on 16 October.

Cooper's confidence in his side making an immediate return to the Third Division was to prove misplaced. Ironically, the board fretted over the prospect of having to pay out more than £10,000 in promotion bonuses and took out insurance to guard against such an eventuality. Friendly wins at Bridport and Cheltenham Town preceded City's participation in the newly established Football League Trophy. Despite a home win over Torquay, losses at Exeter and Newport meant City bowed out at the group stage.

Although finding themselves in the Fourth Division for the first time in their history, City's form was initially encouraging. In the first match, at home to Hull, Russell Musker notched his first goal for the Robins with a 20-yard spectacular after Riley had marked his debut with the club's first ever goal in the Fourth Division. City lost Musker's services when he broke a leg in a 1-2 League Cup defeat at Swindon on 31 August. That was also the day former chairman Robert Hobbs died, aged 75, at his Salcombe home. A 2-2 League draw at Tranmere four days later kept hopes high, before a 1-4 mauling at Crewe set the alarm bells ringing.

Another mauling was not long in coming. This time City went down 1-7 at Northampton, a result which had Cooper eating his words about instant promotion. He revised his long-term objectives, saying 'it could take three years to get promotion'. Nor was this as bad as it was going to get. Crewe's win at Halifax on 29 October dumped City to 92nd place in the Football League. They could go no lower. On this occasion the ignominy did not last long. The point earned from a goalless draw at Aldershot the following day took City off the floor, but a 0-1 defeat at Rochdale on 4 December – when Andy Llewellyn made his debut at the age of sixteen years, 281 days – saw City hit rock bottom again. Another single-goal defeat at Chester kept City there, but a 2-2 draw at Bury took them up a place, and gradual improvement over the rest of the campaign brought an eventual finishing position of fourteenth. For this they were indebted to a nine-match unbeaten run of five wins and four draws in the spring.

It was the signing of centre-half Forbes Phillipson-Masters from Plymouth in November – following Boyle's transfer to Newport, to save on his £400 per week wages – which provided the cornerstone to City's recovery. The newcomer brought much needed stability to the defence with his no-nonsense approach. Peter Johnson from Newcastle also impressed at full-back during his run of 21 consecutive matches in a four-month loan stay, his wages being met by supporters' contributions.

In the League Cup, City overcame their first leg deficit against fellow Fourth Division Swindon by winning the home tie 2-0. This was rewarded by a two-leg clash with First Division Sheffield Wednesday. City had it all to do after conceding two early goals in the first leg at Ashton Gate, which they lost 1-2. But at Hillsborough in the return they put up a gritty display to level the tie on aggregate before going out in extra-time. City showed less resolve in the FA Cup, going out in the first round at Third Division Orient when, despite full-back Johnson opening the scoring with a fierce shot from the edge of the area, they were overwhelmed 1-4.

In the Gloucestershire Cup, City were unable to return to their winning ways. Hoping to avenge the 0-1 home defeat that ended their run of six straight victories the previous season, City were disappointed to lose 1-2 at Eastville on 21 September.

Following City's resignation from the Football Combination the previous February, the Reserves now found themselves competing in the Western League for the first time since 1964-65. This time they had to start in the lower section, but City were unable to make any impact and ended the season in thirteenth place.

The FA Youth Cup saw a slight improvement on the displays of the two previous seasons when the team had been eliminated at the first time of asking. After beating Plymouth 2-1 in a replay to avenge their defeat of the year before, City lost by the same score against Bristol Rovers, this following a 1-1 home draw seven days previously.

At the AGM in December the accounts were declared for the partial financial year of 1981-82, as well as those for 1982-83. The figures for 1982-83 showed a profit of £2,391, which was no doubt helped by the staging of a Rolling Stones Concert at Ashton Gate in June 1982. The 35,123 rock fans who turned out for the occasion produced the anomaly of Ashton Gate's largest crowd in the history of the club under the new organisation. The loss of £60,672 revealed for 1981-82 included the £43,649 cost of the share issue.

Match of the Season 1982-83

Bristol City 4 Wimbledon 2

Division 4, 23 October 1982

When the season began, City fans hoped that their club's fortunes would take a turn for the better. But it was nearly all gloom and doom throughout the first half of the campaign.

With only one win from the opening eleven League games, this surprise success over previously unbeaten Wimbledon lifted the gloom somewhat for City's hard-pressed supporters. Top of the table Dons, seeking a club record seventh straight League win, were surprisingly defensive at the outset. 'Boring Wimbledon' is the chant, before Alan Nicholls sparked City's superlative display when

Did You Know?

City keeper Ray Cashley scored past his opposite number, Hull's Wealands, from over 95 yards in September 1973. The goal put City 2-1 up.

heading in Crawford's cross. Dave Bassett's boys attempted to adopt a more expansive approach, but City took control. With player-boss Cooper and midfielder Jon Economou pulling the strings, two strikes by Riley had the game virtually won by half-time.

After the break the game was more even and Wimbledon climbed back into contention with a goal by John Leslie, before Riley – perhaps inspired by the prankster who put a dead mouse in his boot before the game – completed his first League hat-trick. Despite Dean Thomas's late penalty, City gained a deserved success over one of their relegation companions of the previous season. The only blot on the afternoon was the 70th-minute sending off of City's ex-Wimbledon man Steve Galliers.

City's shock victory did not prevent Wimbledon from easily winning the Fourth Division Championship. In doing so they established a new record of 98 points, after finishing the season with a 22-game unbeaten run, and three years later found themselves among the elite. For City, their surprise win did not spark an upturn in fortunes, though improved form in the New Year acted as a platform for promotion in 1983-84.

LEAGUE DIVISION 4	**1983-84**
Division 4	4th (Promoted)
League Cup	1st Round
FA Cup	3rd Round

Surprise was expressed when Cooper's first signing for the new season was revealed as Howard Pritchard, who had previously played for the club before moving to Swindon. He came on a free-transfer and was a revelation. A vastly improved player from the one who left Ashton Gate three years previously, Pritchard was to provide the wing thrust that was to play a major part in City's promotion. Other signings saw Cooper bring in free-transfer players in 23-year-old striker John Kerr from Tranmere and the excellent central defender Bruce Halliday from Bury, whilst another raid on the Western League produced Shepton Mallet's Gary Marshall.

During the season Musker moved to Gillingham for a £7,500 fee after having a spell on loan with Exeter, and Kerr was to decamp to Stockport, whilst in the boardroom Cooper became a co-opted member and Bob Boyd was replaced by Mike Fricker. Amongst the back room staff a reshuffle saw Mike Gibson, one of the greatest goalkeepers in City's history, promoted to reserve team manager, whilst club Secretary John Lillington, who severed a 16-year association with the club when resigning in November, was replaced by ex police sergeant and erstwhile Birmingham supporter Bob Twyford, aged 45, who commenced his duties on 19 January 1984.

Despite the absence of Rob Newman, who missed the first two matches due to suspension, and the loss of Alan Nicholls with a broken leg in a pre-season match, City opened with a 4-0 win over Mansfield at Ashton Gate, but early form was patchy. Bundled out of the League Cup by Oxford, City found themselves unable to gain any consolation in the Gloucestershire Cup when losing to Bristol Rovers for the third season in a row on 20 September. Suddenly fortunes changed, and four successive wins that started with a 5-0 home League win over Torquay United four days later, not only shot City into second place, but earnt them a £250 prize for being the Division's top scorers in September.

On top of the table for the first time thanks to a Paul Stevens goal against York on 18 October, City failed to maintain their form, despite the signing of 29-year-old Kenny Stroud from Newport County, who was sent off in his second game in a 0-1 defeat Blackpool on 1 November. Four successive defeats saw City slip to seventh, before Kerr's goal brought a 1-0 win at Darlington to halt the sequence.

The intervention of the FA Cup brought a meeting with the famous Corinthian Casuals, played on the equally famous Champion Hill ground of Dulwich Hamlet. A goalless draw in south-east London brought the amateurs to Ashton Gate on 23 November when Pritchard's hat-trick helped bring about a 4-0 win and set up a mouth-watering prospect of an away match with Bristol Rovers in the second round. Third Division Rovers took the lead in front of a 14,396 crowd paying receipts of £31,809, but after Ritchie had levelled matters, Martin Hirst, a 21-year-old Bristol University geography student, found the net with a late winner for a famous City victory over the old enemy.

The following round brought a magnificent display against Notts County in a 2-2 draw at Meadow Lane on 8 January, but in the replay in front of the largest attendance (16,107) since City's reformation, the First Division club came out on top 2-0. At this time in the League, City were in the midst of a nine-match unbeaten run that ended with a 0-1 defeat at Plainmoor on 11 February when they were third place, during which time Cooper received the award as Bell's Fourth Division Manager of the Month at City's 2-1 home win over Wrexham on 21 January. A 1-3 defeat at Exeter on 22 February in the first round of the Associate Members Cup was City's fourth game without a win, but a 2-1 home victory over Aldershot three days later was the start of a run-in that only produced two defeats in 16 games as City clinched the promotion prize.

The transfer deadline signings of winger Keith Curle from Torquay for £10,000, and striker Trevor Morgan for a similar amount from Bournemouth were crucial, especially that of the experienced Morgan, who played in all City's remaining games. They both made their debuts in the 1-1 draw with York on 3 March as City embarked on the thrilling last third of the season, which was unfortunately marred by the behaviour of their hooligan brigade in a 0-2 defeat at Reading on 7 April. Cooper, who had bravely acted as peacemaker, was so disgusted by the actions of City's mad minority that he threatened to resign.

Morgan's two goals in a 2-1 win at Sealand Road on 7 May clinched promotion when it was estimated that City fans accounted for more than 3,000 of Chester's 4,013 crowd. This success completed City's programme with them in third place, but by the time other clubs had caught up with their fixtures they had to settle for a final placing of fourth. The Reserves made a memorable season a cause for a double celebration as they won the First Division of the Western League to gain promotion to the Premier. This success was reflected in the club's balance sheet, a profit of £31,089 being revealed at the AGM held in the Supporters Club on 13 December 1984.

Match of the Season 1983-84

Bristol Rovers 1 Bristol City 2

FA Cup, 2nd Round, 10 December 1983

In a promotion season there are many highlights, and this was certainly the case in 1983-84. Despite manager Cooper's attempts to dampen the expectations of City fans at the start of the campaign, it was expected that promotion would be won. An exciting team, capable of scoring goals and defending strongly, was just the combination required for City to begin the climb back.

The promotion challenge brought a steady rise in attendances, culminating in a crowd of more than 12,000 who saw the 1-0 win over Swindon that put City on the brink of promotion in their last home game. Although promotion brought great joy to the City fans, the result that gave them their greatest satisfaction was achieved in the second round of the FA Cup when local rivals Bristol Rovers were beaten on their home ground at Eastville.

When the draw was made many thought the Rovers were favourites by virtue of their superior Third Division status, the first time in four previous pairings in the competition that the Rovers had been the higher status club. However, what many overlooked was the fact that the Rovers had never won on their own ground in these meetings. Rovers were in the Southern League when they beat Football League newcomers City 3-2 in a replay at St John's Lane in 1901-02. When they pulled off a famous 4-3 victory at Ashton Gate in 1957-58, they were the more successful Second Division club, but by the time of Second Division City's 2-1 replay win at Eastville in 1967-68 Rovers had dropped back to the Third Division. The 1945-46 competition was unique in the annals of the FA Cup, as it was the only time it has operated as a two-legged tournament. Fortunately City took advantage to gain their only home success over the Rovers in the tournament, winning 4-2 at Ashton Gate, before clinching a double with a 2-0 success at Eastville a week later.

This latest clash with the Rovers attracted a 14,396 crowd to Eastville, who paid receipts of £31,809. After a goalless first half, they saw Archie Stephens give the Rovers a 50th-minute lead with one of his typically brave headers in front of the massed ranks of City fans on the open Muller Road terrace. Terry Cooper then came on as substitute in place of Alan Crawford and City began to dictate

Did You Know?

Gerry Gow missed four penalty-kicks for City in season 1972-73. Of those matches, City won 1, drew 1, and lost the other two by a single goal.

the play. Anguished when Glyn Riley fired against a post, the City fans were joyful on 78 minutes as Tom Ritchie cracked in a fine equaliser. As the minutes passed a replay looked ever more likely, but City kept up the offensive and whilst Martyn Hirst's mis-hit 89th-minute winner was rather fortunate, there was no denying that the success it brought was fully deserved.

In the next round City put on a fine display against First Division Notts County at Meadow Lane to achieve a 2-2 draw, before going out of the competition 0-2 in a replay at Ashton Gate. The Rovers went on to only narrowly miss promotion by finishing in fifth place, whilst revenge over City in the FA Cup wasn't long in coming. The very next season the extraordinary sequence of away successes in the competition continued with Rovers coming back from conceding an early goal to deservedly gain a 3-1 victory in the second round at Ashton Gate on 8 December 1985.

Despite the players sharing more than £30,000, the club's finances considerably improved as a result of promotion, and were also helped by the £17,700 receipts from Billy Graham's Crusade at Ashton Gate, when 250,000 attended over an eight-day period in May 1984. The fans as always paid the price with season tickets in the Grandstand increasing from £65 to £75, whilst match day rates went up by 50p to £4 and ground admission for both the Open and the Covered Ends also increased by the same amount to £2.

4

RECOVERY
1984-1989

LEAGUE DIVISION 3	**1984-85**
Division 3	5th
League Cup	2nd Round
FA Cup	2nd Round

Promotion meant Terry Cooper's contract was extended for two years. Following the release of full-back Gary Williams on a free-transfer, he set about strengthening his side. His main target was Darlington's talented goalscoring winger Alan Walsh. The Quakers wanted £85,000 for their star player, who had scored almost 100 goals in 250 games for his hometown club. Cooper offered just £10,000, and an independent tribunal allowed Cooper to get away with daylight robbery by setting a paltry £18,000 fee on 27-year-old Walsh, who was destined to be one of the best ever players to wear a City shirt. Another top capture was 30-year-old Bobby Hutchinson on a free from Tranmere. A bruised instep suffered in a 3-3 draw at Hereford in a pre-season friendly meant Hutchinson did not appear in the first team again until November, coming on as substitute at Doncaster, when Newman sustained the broken shin which kept him out of action for over three months.

With Curle having been sent off in City's 6-2 friendly win at Cheltenham, it was a depleted side that opened the League season with a 2-0 home win over Wigan, but at least the contract disputes with Riley, Ritchie and Paul Stevens had been resolved. Cooper had little choice but to give 17-year-old Lee Rogers his debut in defence, and include himself as substitute. Though inconsistent, early form was encouraging and an exhilarating 3-0 home win over the Rovers pushed City up into third place. Cooper then swooped to sign 27-year-old Steve Neville from Exeter for £12,000, with Morgan moving in the opposite direction. For three months it did not look like money well spent, as Neville struggled to find his goal touch. He broke his drought in his thirteenth game by netting both goals in City's win at Brentford.

The departure of Ritchie to team up with former colleague Gerry Gow at Yeovil was a shock. Another crowd favourite nearing the end of an illustrious City career was keeper Shaw. Concern over his form led Cooper to blood 20-year-old local lad Mike Hooper, who made his League debut in a 2-1 home win over Lincoln. The former England Boys keeper, a part-timer studying English at Swansea University, impressed enough to keep his place for the following week's FA Cup-tie against Bristol Rovers. This time his inexperience proved costly. City lost 1-3, whereupon Shaw was briefly restored until Keith Waugh arrived on loan from Sheffield United. As Cooper was unwilling to pay the £25,000 fee required to make the transfer permanent, Ian Leigh was borrowed from Bournemouth. He lasted just one game before Shaw was restored for the rest of the season. Shaw was given a free transfer at the end of the campaign, moving to Exeter. He was replaced, ironically, by Keith Waugh, whom Cooper now managed to sign on a free transfer.

A 0-1 defeat at Reading in December pushed City down to tenth, but a pulsating 4-3 home win over Plymouth on Boxing Day, followed by a 1-0 success over Burnley, carried City into the New Year on a wave of optimism. Defeat at Hull sullied the mood, and further setbacks at the hands of Walsall and Rotherham saw City fast losing touch with the pacesetters. It required Neville's first goals to restore morale, and a run of five straight wins hauled City up to fourth. By this time Cooper had strengthened his squad with the free transfer signing of 23-year-old centre-half Mark Hughes from Swansea, and on transfer deadline day spent £30,000 to purchase 27-year-old Wigan forward Steve ('Rambo') Johnson.

Hooliganism reared its ugly head when Millwall were the visitors in early March. In scenes worse than those witnessed at Reading the previous season, seats were ripped up in the Dolman Stand, causing £2,500 worth of damage, whilst outside the ground a young City fan needed 67 stitches after being slashed. Secretary Bob Twyford was so sickened by the violence that he handed in his resignation – he was eventually replaced by Jean Harrison – stating that as a former police sergeant he could not be associated with a game which attracted so many ugly characters. Following a meeting with senior police chiefs, steps were immediately taken to sort out the main trouble-spots in the ground, and the decision was taken to install close-circuit television in the summer. When leaders Bradford City arrived the week after the Millwall mayhem, an extension to the players tunnel was in place, and the police presence doubled. Unaccompanied teenagers were denied entry to the Dolman Stand.

Losing 0-1 at Plymouth on 5 April was a promotion blow, but the real damage was done eight days later at Eastville. In a match ruined by the gale-force wind blowing towards the Muller Road End, City's decision to kick against the storm in the first half betrayed a negative attitude that the Rovers exploited to win 1-0. Despite suffering only one further defeat in the remaining eight games, the damage had been done and City had to be satisfied to finish in fifth place, six points behind third-placed Hull.

In the League Cup, City disposed of Newport 5-1 on aggregate and were rewarded with a meeting with First Division West Ham in the second round. A thriller at Ashton Gate ended 2-2, with City feeling aggrieved that they did not take a lead into the second leg. At Upton Park, after holding the Hammers until half-time, a second-half collapse brought about City's biggest ever defeat in the competition – 1-6.

The FA Cup first round produced a hard-fought tie at Fisher Athletic, but Riley's early strike was enough to take City through. A winning run in the Freight Rover Trophy saw Hereford beaten 2-1 on aggregate in the first round and Port Vale dispatched 2-1 at Ashton Gate. Walsh's penalty was not enough in the Southern Area quarter-final at Ashton Gate, when just 3,167 crowd saw Newport win 2-1. City's last chance to claim some silverware this campaign disappeared with the Gloucestershire Cup, which was again moved back to the end of the season. At Eastville on 21 May Walsh's penalty took the contest into extra-time, but City lost 1-3.

The Reserves also came close to winning something. Their first season in the Premier Division of the Western League, following promotion, saw them finish third. They also reached the semi-finals of the Somerset Premier Cup. In the FA Youth Cup, City were unable to improve on the previous season's first round 1-3 knock-out at home to Plymouth, losing at the first stage 0-4 at Reading.

City's promotion almost doubled the number of season tickets sold, from 1,287 to 2,073, and with average home League gates increasing from 7,287 to 8,507, it was not surprising that finances remained buoyant. A profit of £46,156 was declared at the AGM.

Match of the Season 1984-85

Bristol City 2 Bradford City 0

Division 3, 9 March 1985

City went into this game on a high, following a 4-1 away success at Bolton. Even so, the table-topping Yorkshire side were expected to provide a stern test, despite the loss of the suspended midfielder Greg Abbott. Cancer victim 18-year-old Roger Crook, who was ferried by ambulance to the game, was among the 9,222 crowd who

Did You Know?

At Queen's Park Rangers in April 1977 the rain was so torrential that City's Geoff Merrick had to rescue a dog from a large puddle.

appreciated Bradford's attacking inclinations in an open game. Howard Pritchard found himself unmarked to head the Robins' opener midway through the first half. On two other occasions the right-winger went close – being denied by the crossbar either side of the interval – whilst Bradford were unfortunate when Don Goodman's header thudded against a post. Alan Walsh made sure of the points thirteen minutes from time, his typically fierce right-foot shot from the edge of the penalty area clinching a vital win. Hughes was named Man of the Match, his performance in stifling Bradford's Northern Ireland striker Bobby Campbell earning the plaudits of Terry Cooper, who went so far as to tip him for future Welsh honours.

Despite this victory – which lifted the Robins to fifth – being part of a five-match winning sequence, City were unable to make an impression in the promotion race. The fact that they were unable to improve on their position only served to demonstrate the calibre of the promotion candidates. Bradford were an outstanding side, and they soon shook off the effects of this defeat. They went on to win a total of 28 games and clinch the Championship with 94 points, four better than runners-up Millwall. For Roger Crook, though, there was no happy ending: he died a few days after the match.

LEAGUE DIVISION 3	**1985-86**
Division 3	9th
League Cup	1st Round
FA Cup	2nd Round

City started the new season as second favourites for the Third Division Championship, but before the campaign kick-off Ashton Gate welcomed illustrious visitors in two friendlies. Manchester United beat City 1-0 in front of a 6,707 crowd, and a week later 8,182 spectators witnessed a 3-3 draw with Liverpool.

Newcomers for City included Brian Williams, signed on a free-transfer from Bristol Rovers, and another ex-Rovers man, Gary Emmanuel from Swindon Town. The fans, though, were indignant about this increasing Rovers connection. Williams was sent off in the League curtain-raiser against Walsall at Ashton Gate, whilst Emmanuel was barracked. A 1-5 League Cup defeat at Hereford and a 0-5 hammering at Bournemouth put paid to Emmanuel's short Ashton Gate career. He was soon on his way to Swansea, but Williams would go on and establish himself in the City side for two seasons before moving to Shrewsbury.

Conceding goals at an alarming rate early on in the season, City suffered four straight League defeats and, not surprisingly, found themselves bottom of the table. Heads rolled, among them centre-half Hughes, who had been outstanding the previous season. Cooper slated him for being overweight, and Hughes soon departed for a bargain £3,000 to Tranmere, for whom he went on to give noble service for many years. It was not until 7 September that City obtained their initial League victory. Pritchard's second-half header against Wigan launched City on a seven-match unbeaten run that lifted them up to eighteenth.

A break from League action saw Ashton Gate stage an Under-21 International in October. Only 3,826 turned up to see England beat Turkey 3-0. A week later a 3-6 shocker at Bury saw City at sixes and sevens. Ex-Cardiff midfielder David Tong made his debut in a 3-0 win over a poor Wolves side at the end of the month, a result which sparked a sequence of fifteen games with just three defeats. Strangely, those three losses came one after the other in early December, the first of which being a 1-2 home defeat by Exeter in the FA Cup. City returned to winning ways with a spirited 2-0 success over Plymouth on Boxing Day.

Victories over Doncaster and Rotherham ensured a bright start to 1986, and, apart from successive defeats at Derby and Wolves, City maintained their form throughout the coming months. Keeper John Vaughan came in on loan from West Ham when a back injury ruled out Waugh for two games in early March. Bristol Rovers were beaten 2-0 at Ashton Gate at the end of the month, but in the last Eastville derby before Rovers' relocation Neville's goal was sufficient only to ensure a 1-1 draw. Topsy-turvy end of season form saw City eventually finish ninth. They notched their best victory of the season at Bolton, winning 4-0, before immediately succumbing by the same score at Plymouth.

Ample consolation for a mediocre League season was found in the Freight Rover Trophy, in which City reached Wembley for the first time. In the preliminary competition things didn't look promising. City started with a goalless home draw against Plymouth in January, but a 2-1 win at Walsall two weeks later put City top of their three-club group. They enjoyed the luck of the draw in the knock-out stages, reaching the semi-finals with home wins over Northampton (3-2) and Gillingham (3-0). At this stage supporters were still largely apathetic, as seen by crowds of just 3,038 for the visit of Northampton and 5,707 for Gillingham. But all this changed for the two-legged regional final. In the first game at Hereford, in front of 7,608 spectators, it looked as though City were re-living nightmares of that 1-5 League Cup thrashing early in the season. This time they kept the margin of defeat down to 0-2, but that still left themselves a mountain to climb in the return three days later.

The second leg at Ashton Gate kept the 11,558 fans enthralled, as Hereford battled for their lives. Following a goalless first half, City's hopes seemed to be ebbing away. It took Riley's header, which slipped through the Hereford keeper's fingers after 62 minutes to get City on the move, and within minutes Pritchard saw his effort deflected into the Hereford net by the unfortunate Mike Pejic. Undismayed, Hereford were unlucky when Ian Wells hit the bar with a fierce shot, and shortly before the end of normal time Chris Price shot narrowly wide.

The visitors often looked the more likely winners in extra-time and Paul Maddy should have won it for them three minutes from time, when unmarked in the penalty area and with the goal at his mercy. Waugh dived to his left to parry Maddy's powerful shot. It was not until the dying seconds that Neville clinched the game for City. He calmly controlled Hutchinson's knock-down from Walsh's cross from the left before steering in his 25th goal of the season. The 3-2 aggregate win set up an appointment with Northern Section winners Bolton Wanderers in the national final.

An estimated 30,000 City fans travelled to Wembley on 24 May. Despite the electric atmosphere, both sets of fans made sure that it was dubbed the 'friendly final'. City had one last-minute injury scare when David Harle complained of a strained hamstring, but he

Did You Know?

Joe Royle's four goals on his City debut in November 1977 meant that the 4-1 victory over Middlesbrough was City's biggest win of the season.

recovered to be named in City's line-up. Bolton had slight doubts over Tony Caldwell and Mark Came, but they too came through to take their place at Wembley.

Match of the Season 1985-86

Bristol City 3 Bolton Wanderers 0

Freight Rover Trophy final, 24 May 1986

To reach a Wembley final for the first time in City's history has to be the highlight of this or any other season, even though it was in a relatively minor competition restricted to Third and Fourth Division teams. Unfairly dubbed the 'Mickey Mouse Cup', it provided many City fans with the highlight of their time in watching a club that had rarely lived up to its potential.

A competition for the Associate member clubs of the Football League had first come into being in 1933-34, and continued up until World War II. It was not until 1981-82 that it was revamped as the Group Cup, being known as the Football League Trophy the following year, then the Associate Members Cup. It was the coming of sponsorship that saw it renamed the Freight Rover Trophy in 1984-85, when the final was played at Wembley for the first time.

Having finished nine places above Bolton, and having done the double over the Trotters in the League, City were the form favourites to win their first Wembley final. Pre-match pessimists, though, were quick to remind everyone that experience and tradition counted for much at Wembley. The famous Wanderers had only lost once in five previous appearances at the Twin Towers, while their player-manager Phil Neal had played more games at Wembley than he had at Bolton's Burnden Park!

Early arrivals were treated to pre-match entertainment which included a 15-minute each-way game between old-timers which not surprisingly ended goalless:

MIKE MORRIS'S TV AM ROBINS XI: Ray Cashley; Gary Imlach, Jim Ferguson, Gerry Gow, Terry Mancini, Bobby Moore, George Best, Tony Currie, Bobby Gould, Richard Keys, Chris Garland.
GORDON TAYLOR'S P.F.A. TROTTERS XI: Peter Bonetti; Brendon Batson, Fred Eyre, Graham Kelly, Dave Webb, Bill McMurdo, Alan

Hudson, Frank Worthington, Malcolm Macdonald, Stan Bowles, Gordon Taylor.

The final itself was a credit to the Third Division. Bolton had the best of the opening half-hour, with George Oghani bringing a fine save from Keith Waugh and Tony Caldwell hitting the crossbar. The City fans, who formed the majority of the 54,502 crowd, erupted just before the interval when Bobby Hutchinson challenged Bolton keeper Simon Farnworth for Keith Curle's free-kick and the ball fell kindly for Riley to score from eleven yards. Despite the skill of former Scottish international Asa Hartford in midfield, Bolton had no answer to City's resolute display after the break. Howard Pritchard scored number two when Steve Neville's 73rd-minute shot was parried, and Neville capped his Man of the Match display by crossing the ball from the left for Riley to head in City's third.

City's share of the £286,281 Wembley receipts helped produce the profit of £72,937 announced at the AGM in December 1986. The club was further rewarded when taking possession of the winner's prize of a £15,000 minibus. Thousands of Bristolians took to the streets to acclaim their heroes, who made a three-hour open-topped bus tour on the Monday following the game.

Twelve months later City got through to Wembley again, but this time lost in a penalty shoot-out after a 1-1 draw with Mansfield. Bolton's Wembley experience appears not to have served them well. A year later they were relegated to Division Four.

BRISTOL CITY: Waugh, Newman, Williams, Curle, Moyes, Riley, Pritchard, Hutchinson, Harle, Walsh, Neville.
BOLTON: Farnworth; Scott, Phillips, Sutton, Came (Bell), Thompson, Neal, Oghani, Caldwell, Hartford, Gavin.
REFEREE: G Tyson.

LEAGUE DIVISION 3	**1986-87**
Division 3	6th
League Cup	2nd Round
FA Cup	3rd Round

Prospects for 1986-87 were hampered in the summer when star winger Pritchard rejected a new two-year deal and was sold to Gillingham for £22,500. Johnson was also on the move, going to Scunthorpe for £12,500. Newcomers included 6ft 4in Paul Fitzpatrick on a free from Bolton and Gary Hamson from Leeds, though the big captures were 27-year-old Barnsley winger Gordon Owen and 30-year-old centre-half John MacPhail from York. Owen cost £30,000, but MacPhail was obtained for a bargain £14,500 – Cooper once more exploiting the League Tribunal system, after being unable to agree a fee with York boss Denis Smith.

Despite MacPhail being unfit to play until the end of October, the season started well. City were unbeaten in their opening six games, which included two grand tussles with Bournemouth in the League Cup. Walsh's volley produced a 1-0 win at Dean Court, but in the second leg City needed Riley's extra-time volley to take them through after Steve Aylott's opener for the Cherries. A 3-0 League win at Chesterfield had City up in second place, but after losing 0-1 at Doncaster in their next game, the loss of Neville's goalscoring touch began to take its toll. Despite 3-0 wins at Chester and Fulham, defeats at Bournemouth and Blackpool shunted City down to eighth by the time they opened their FA Cup campaign. Southern League VS Rugby proved stubborn opponents, as City gained a flattering 3-1 home success to set up a home derby with Conference club Bath City in round two.

With work to replace the Covered End roof continuing, a boring tie was only enlivened by Paul Bodin's late strike to earn Bath a replay. Despite the fact that Bath now shared their Twerton Park home with Bristol Rovers, police concerns meant the replay was again staged at Ashton Gate. This time a richly entertaining game saw Marshall run the Bath rearguard ragged to engineer a 3-0 win. The visit of Second Division Plymouth in the third round elicited much interest, and a crowd larger than the official figure of 16,943 was thought to be present to witness a rousing 1-1 draw. It took extra-time to separate the sides in the replay before City went down 1-3, thereby missing out on mouth-watering tie at First Division leaders Arsenal.

Following successive defeats against Rotherham and Notts County in November, four wins and a draw kept City handily placed in the League, until Gary Smart's late winner for Bristol

Rovers set the New Year off to a losing start. Further defeats at Rotherham and Wigan sent Terry Cooper delving into the transfer market. Harle and Hamson had already been sold to Scunthorpe and Port Vale respectively, whilst Trevor Morgan had returned to Ashton Gate. Having watched one of British soccer's outstanding strikers play in Southampton's Reserves, Cooper persuaded his former Leeds colleague Joe Jordan to join City on a month's loan.

Making his debut in a 5-0 drubbing of Doncaster, the 35-year-old Jordan bagged his first City goals in his second match, in the Freight Rover Trophy. City had commenced their defence of the trophy by topping a group that included Exeter and Bristol Rovers and then beating Southend 1-0 at home in the first round. Jordan's goals came in a 3-0 home win over Brentford. City's luck held in the next round as Gillingham were beaten 2-0 at Ashton Gate to send them into a two-legged tie with Fourth Division Aldershot, who had gone ten games unbeaten. In the first leg, goals by Jordan and Newman secured a 2-1 win at a packed Recreation Ground. Six days later a 16,371 crowd were at Ashton Gate to see City win 2-0.

In the League, though, despite the capture of Steve Galliers on loan from Wimbledon, and Jim Harvey, for whom Cooper paid Hereford £20,000, City were erratic. A shock home defeat by a well-organised Brentford looked to have dashed all hopes of a play-off place, but slip-ups by the other contenders enabled City to reach the final day of the campaign in fifth place. It was now that their luck changed. City's old problems from the penalty spot returned with a vengeance, depriving them not only of a place in the play-offs, but also the Freight Rover Trophy.

First, that critical last League match. After taking an early lead against Swindon through Morgan's header, City were unable to turn their pressure into further goals. They paid the price midway through the second half when Peter Coyne's mis-hit volley brought Swindon level. Shortly before the final whistle Jordan was tripped in the area but Owen drove his spot-kick wide of the Covered End goal. This, coupled with Gillingham's home win over Bolton, sent City down to sixth. That would have been good enough today to earn a play-off place, but in 1986-87 the quartet comprised teams finishing third, fourth and fifth, plus the club finishing one above the relegation places in Division Two.

Looking for solace in the Freight Rover Trophy final at Wembley City were cruelly disappointing against Mansfield. Though Neville had not recovered from a broken leg sustained four months earlier at Wigan, City were at full strength with the recall of Walsh and Riley. They were favourites against opponents who had finished four places and sixteen points adrift of them. The previous season

Did You Know?

The best goal ever scored by an opponent at Ashton Gate? Probably that by Liverpool's Steve Heighway in 1978. He beat three players in a 70-yard run.

Cooper had let assistant-boss Clive Middlemass lead the team out, but this time it was the turn of long-serving scout Jock Rae. City's team was: Waugh, Newman, Williams, Moyes, MacPhail, Llewellyn (Fitzpatrick), Owen, Walsh (Curle), Riley, Marshall, Jordan.

City, wearing white even though there wasn't a colour clash, could not match the standards of the previous year. Mansfield took control and Man of the Match Keith Cassells centred for Kevin Kent to hammer the Stags ahead in front of a 58,586 crowd. Three minutes from time Riley slammed in an equaliser. Extra-time brought no further goals, so for the first time ever a Wembley final was decided by a penalty shoot-out.

City had the advantage of going first, and Williams, Newman, MacPhail and Curle put their kicks away. Cassells missed Mansfield's second, but strikes by Mark Kearney, Ian Stringfellow and Gary Pollard kept them in the hunt. With City 4-3 up they needed only to net their fifth kick to retain the trophy. Wretchedly, Owen's blaster flew off keeper Kevin Hitchcock's boot and over the bar. Kent dispatched his kick for the Stags to take the contest into sudden death. This didn't take long, as Moyes saw his effort saved, whilst Tony Kenworthy made no mistake for Mansfield.

Wembley receipts of £324,592 enabled City to declare a £156,925 profit at their AGM in December 1987, the figure boosted by season ticket revenue increasing from £78,885 to £83,806.

The Reserves also had a successful season, improving on their ninth place in the Western League in 1985-86 to finish third. In their second season of the South West Counties League they did even better, taking the Championship after finishing eighth the previous season. In the Somerset Premier Cup they equalled last year's accomplishment in reaching the semi-finals.

Match of the Season 1986-87

Bristol City 1 Swindon Town 1

Division 3, 9 May 1987

This was a disappointing season for City fans who had anticipated a return to Division Two. City had flattered to deceive throughout the campaign, just doing enough to keep hopes alive of a promotion play-off place, thanks to a good home record that saw only three defeats. Away from home it was a different tale: City's reasonable total of seventeen points up to the New Year was followed by a meagre return of twelve points from their subsequent twelve games.

As the season entered its decisive phase, City had looked odds-on gaining a play-off place, but a spell of only three wins in nine games left them needing victory against Swindon in their final match to be sure of taking part. The fact that the Moonrakers were only playing for their pride, having already qualified for the play-offs, convinced the 19,201 crowd – the biggest at Ashton Gate since the advent of the new company – that their supposedly more motivated team would easily secure the required victory.

They were to be proved wrong. Despite controlling the early play and going in front in the twelfth minute thanks to Morgan's glancing header from Owen's chip, City lost control of the game to Swindon's neat possession football. Even though Marshall's lob hit the Swindon crossbar and Newman was denied by Fraser Digby's fine save, it came as no surprise when, after 66 minutes, Swindon equalised. Llewellyn conceded a needless free-kick, from which Joe Jordan's misdirected headed clearance fell to the unmarked Peter Coyne, whose mis-hit volley went in off a post. Ultimately, however, the fate of City's season was decided by Cooper's decision to take off regular penalty taker Brian Williams. Minutes later, Jordan was supposedly tripped in the area.

Scuffles ensued as Swindon bitterly contested the penalty decision. Confusion reigned amongst the City players as to who should take the kick. Owen bravely volunteered, even though he had failed from the spot at Middlesbrough in the League and at home to Brentford in the Freight Rover Trophy. His concentration was not helped by the kick being delayed as the referee sought to calm the jostling that broke out amongst the players. To the dismay of City's fans, Owen placed his shot wide.

In the thirteen minutes that remained City threw everything at Swindon. Marshall had a shot cleared off the line by Mark Jones, and keeper Digby pulled off a fine save to keep out Newman's volley. In the end, though, Swindon might even have won. In the dying seconds Moyes' handball inside the area was punished by a free-kick outside.

Swindon went on to deservedly gain promotion, beating Gillingham 2-0 in the play-off final, after disposing of Wigan 3-2 on aggregate in the semi-finals. City were left to rue on the loss of too many points against inferior opposition over the season, and the fact that their relentless siege on the Walsall goal in their penultimate game failed to secure the win that would have assured a play-off berth.

LEAGUE DIVISION 3	**1987-88**
Division 3	5th
League Cup	1st Round
FA Cup	2nd Round

So near, yet so far. A hectic season saw Terry Cooper's reign end and Joe Jordan's begin. The new manager inspired City to the final of the play-offs. Despite Cooper's earlier comment that apart from seeking to permanently sign on-loan midfielder Steve Galliers (he signed for £37,500) he would not need to add to his playing staff, this wasn't how things turned out. It was musical chairs at Ashton Gate. The comings and goings started before a ball was kicked. A tribunal fixed fee of £27,500 bought Tony Caldwell from Bolton. £18,000 was recouped from Sunderland when MacPhail joined up with his old York boss Denis Smith. A small fee brought Port Vale's Russell Bromage to replace Brian Williams, who moved to Second Division Shrewsbury. Trevor Morgan joined Bolton for £16,000.

The fans, like the manager, were confident of promotion, but were jolted by City's failure to avenge their Freight Rover defeat in the opening game, losing 0-2 at Mansfield. A run of nine League games unbeaten put the world to rights. City were top of the pile after beating Chesterfield 2-1. It was not such a happy story in the League Cup, as City lost 3-5 on aggregate to Swindon in the first round.

With Riley on loan at Torquay, and Harvey joining Tranmere for £20,000, City's run ended with a 0-3 reverse at Northampton, when Galliers and Fitzpatrick were sent off. A 3-2 home win over Southend, followed by a 4-1 success at Grimsby, did not put a halt to the transfer merry-go-round. Curle was sold to Reading for a club record fee of £150,000, and captain Moyes joined Shrewsbury for £25,000. Cooper paid £22,000 to Doncaster for defender Glenn Humphries – who marked his debut with a 38-second own-goal in City's 1-4 defeat at Rotherham – £55,000 for striker Carl Shutt from Sheffield Wednesday, and £50,000 to Charlton for centre-half John Pender. Livewire Shutt was an instant hit, scoring twice on his debut and netting eleven goals in his first twelve games. Pender, though, was sent off as his new side crashed 2-4 at Blackpool. Form slumped and City endured six League games without a win until York were beaten 3-2 in mid-December.

Success of sorts was achieved in the FA Cup, when Caldwell, who had not settled, bagged the goal that brought a flattering home win over Beazer Homes League Aylesbury, when 18-year-old reserve keeper Mark Coombe made his only first-team appearance for City. With Waugh fit to reclaim his position from loan keeper

Mark Prudhoe (Walsall), City's luck ran out in the second round. A 0-1 home defeat by Torquay provoked shouts for Cooper's head. With assistant manager Clive Middlemass having left to take charge at Carlisle, Jordan took over as Cooper's right-hand man, whilst ex City favourite Alan Crawford, who had been at Western League Bristol Manor Farm, was appointed youth coach.

Cooper bounced back, earning the Third Division Manager of the Month award on the back of four wins and a draw up to the turn of the year, which hoisted City from twelfth to fourth. The movement of players continued, though, with Owen going on loan to Hull, before joining Mansfield for £35,000, while keeper John Vaughan was loaned from West Ham for his second spell at Ashton Gate. Winger Ralph Milne was another loan signing, but City found £50,000 to pay for him – Milne marking his debut with a clean strike in a 3-2 home win over Bury. Caldwell was loaned to Chester, and Micky Tanner transferred to Bath, whilst another £50,000 paid for the services of Steve McClaren from Derby. This proved to be the manager's last throw of the dice, as City were by then off the pace in eighth spot and out of the newly-named Sherpa Van Trophy. Having qualified second in their group, they lost 0-1 at Aldershot.

After a 0-2 defeat at Southend on 11 March, the directors met to consider Cooper's future, and his last match in charge was the following Wednesday night's Gloucestershire Cup clash with Bristol Rovers at Ashton Gate. City won 3-1 in front of 2,278 fans, as they completed a strange double in the competition, after having clinched the delayed 1986-87 final with a 2-1 success in front of just 1,376 fans in the first Twerton Park derby during December.

When Jordan took temporary charge, there were no recriminations from Cooper, only sadness that he was leaving a club where he had enjoyed every minute. With only eleven games in which to prove himself, the caretaker boss was handicapped by having Newman and Humphries suspended, whilst illness and injury ruled out Bromage, Shutt and himself. A goalless draw at Fulham got Jordan's show on the road. His first venture into the transfer market saw Reading striker Colin Gordon arrive on a month's loan. A penalty by the big fair-haired marksman, and a strike by Neville that ended his 23-week barren spell, forged a 2-0 home win over Rotherham. Aldershot were beaten by the same score, but though a 0-1 defeat at Chester seemed to have dashed City's promotion hopes, Jordan's never-say-die spirit lifted his team to five wins and a draw in their last seven games. Gordon's late goal in the final match clinched a play-off place.

Jordan was rewarded with a two-year contract before the play-offs started. City's fifth position brought them a two-legged semi-final with Sheffield United, who had finished third from bottom in the Second Division. At Ashton Gate, 25,335 fans saw Walsh notch the only goal just before half-time. In the second leg three days later, Shutt, replacing the injured Neville, shattered his hometown club by giving City the lead. United levelled on the night when Colin Morris looped a header over Waugh, but City's defence stayed firm thereafter to condemn the Blades to relegation.

City's opponents in the two-legged final were Walsall, who had beaten Notts County 4-2 on aggregate in the other semi-final. The first match was at Ashton Gate, when many of the 25,128 crowd were confident of a City win. Though Neville was fit to return, City were weakened by Gordon's return to Reading. Jordan had been unwilling to pay the £70,000 demanded for his transfer.

Walsh duly put City ahead from a free-kick, but a cruel equaliser – Andy Llewellyn's clearance struck Waugh and rebounded into the net for an own-goal in the 63rd minute – changed the complexion of the game. Two strikes by Republic of Ireland international David Kelly appeared to give Walsall what looked like an unassailable advantage. The story of City's extraordinary 2-0 win in the second leg, which meant the contest went to a third game, is taken up in Match of the Season.

In those days play-offs took no account of the away-goals rule. With the two teams finishing 3-3 on aggregate, this was just as well, as otherwise City would have gone out. A third fixture was therefore required. This also took place at Fellows Park, on 30 May, a Bank Holiday, which encouraged 4,000 City fans to make the trip. The venue had been decided not by the toss of a coin but by a penalty shoot-out, which City lost. Neither the players nor the fans were perturbed by this return to the Midlands, as they thought they had the measure of Walsall. But they reckoned without their old nemesis, Kelly. City trailed by three goals after just nineteen minutes, and Kelly completed his hat-trick to tie up a 4-0 success for the Saddlers. This amounted to City's heaviest defeat in almost three years. To add salt to the wound, Shutt was sent off shortly before the final whistle for fouling keeper Fred Barber.

Unfortunately, both the home and away games with Walsall were marred by thugs, who again tarnished City's name. The 1-3 defeat at Ashton Gate was too much to stomach for some City fans, who went on the rampage, fighting a pitched battle with police in Ashton Park and smashing the windscreens of dozens of cars. At Fellows Park there were forty arrests. Whilst some fans appeared to have justifiable complaints at the heavy handed methods, there was no excuse for the mindless thugs who overturned police vans as they fought with the local constabulary.

Did You Know?

After losing four games on the trot early in 1979, Alan Dicks took his players for a short holiday in Torremolinos. They came home and lost their fifth!

Match of the Season 1987-88

Walsall 0 Bristol City 2

Division 3, Play-Off final, 2nd leg, 28 May 1988

Having lost the play-off home leg 1-3, few City fans were persuaded by Jordan's insistence that the remaining promotion place was still up for grabs. The small band of optimists pointed to Jordan's motivational qualities, which had steered City into a play-off spot when the side looked out of contention. Jordan even picked himself to play his first full game for five months.

Jordan's battlers did not let a matter of a two-goal deficit deter them at Fellows Park, and by the end it was Walsall who were grateful to earn another chance. City's inspired players were a yard quicker to the ball and could well have brought the aggregate scores level in the opening fourteen minutes. Milne forced a fine save from Fred Barber and Walsh crashed a close-range volley against a post. Later, Shutt shot inches wide and Walsh curled a free-kick just too high as the home side were penned back by a stream of attacks. Just when it seemed that City's dominance would go unrewarded, Newman rose on the half-hour to glance Walsh's corner over the line, despite Craig Shakespeare's desperate clearance.

A half-time pep talk revived Walsall slightly, and Waugh did well to deflect David Kelly's drive for a corner. Galliers then made a goal-line clearance to deny Phil Hawker, before Shutt levelled the aggregate scores with a low drive in the 66th minute. Both sides created and wasted chances in the time remaining.

With no provision for extra-time or away goals, the promotion decider would go to a third game, the venue to be determined by a penalty shoot-out. Willie Naughton put the Saddlers ahead, but Barber blocked Walsh's reply. Trevor Christie fired Walsall two up before Newman put City on the scoresheet. Shakespeare then made it 3-1, at which point Milne's effort was saved. It was left to David Kelly to secure that ill-fated second meeting at Fellows Park.

Promotion backfired on Walsall boss Tommy Coakley and his assistant, former City favourite Gerry Sweeney. The Saddlers were not strong enough to cope with higher-grade football and were headed for instant relegation. Coakley and Sweeney lost their jobs before the season was out.

LEAGUE DIVISION 3	**1988-89**
Division 3	11th
League Cup	Semi-Final
FA Cup	3rd Round

The general consensus was that there would be no stopping City now. But that was not how things turned out. Poor form in the League even saw Jordan's job on the line, but, like Dicks before him, Jordan was rescued by City's Cup performances.

In the FA Cup, City recorded the greatest number of replays in their history, requiring *four* attempts to dispose of Aldershot in the second round, after beating Southend in round one. Although their sixth match in the competition, at Hartlepool, saw the team go out 0-1, Ashton Alf wasn't unduly concerned as City were still going strong in the League Cup.

That Wembley trail started modestly, as in both legs of the first round against Exeter the Robins scored once without reply. A 4-2 win at the Manor Ground shattered Second Division Oxford's eight-season, 27-match unbeaten home record in the League Cup. A 2-0 second-leg success booked City a home tie with Second Division Crystal Palace. An early three-goal salvo destroyed Palace, and further progress looked assured when the luck of the draw paired City with Fourth Division Tranmere. A formality it might have been on paper, but in real life Tranmere made things extremely difficult. Shutt's strike on the half-hour mark was all that separated the sides at the finish.

Faced with Second Division Bradford City in the quarter-finals, many fans expected the Robins to bow out. Bradford had accounted for Everton in the previous round, so the virtually-retired Jordan recalled himself to City's colours. He won the Man of the Match award for an inspirational display at Valley Parade, Walsh's early strike taking City through to the semi-finals for the second time in their history.

Few gave City a prayer against the might of Brian Clough's Nottingham Forest, but in the first leg on the banks of the Trent it took an unfortunate own-goal by John Pender four minutes from time to deny City an epic giant-killing cup win. City's goalscoring hero was 19-year-old Paul Mardon, whose name didn't even appear in the match programme. He had put City in front midway through the second half with a 15-yard drive for his first senior goal.

City's brave performance earned the media spotlight, and the second leg at Ashton Gate on Sunday, 26 February was shown live on ITV. The wind and rain spoilt the game as a spectacle, but the occasion is taken up in Match of the Season.

Did You Know?

John Palmer is City's briefest ever substitute. At Torquay in March 1983 he shook hands with the departing Paul Williams when the ref blew for time.

In the Sherpa Van Trophy, City's interest disappeared at the first round stage. After qualifying in second place from their Group games – which included a 0-1 reverse at Bristol Rovers – they were slaughtered at Molineux, where Wolves won 3-0. A similar scoreline had also been City's fate at Twerton Park at the start of the season, when Bristol Rovers secured the Gloucestershire Cup in front of just 1,664 fans on 17 August.

With numerous changes in personnel during the close season, both on and off the pitch, perhaps it was not surprising that League form was indifferent. Departures included Neville, who returned to Exeter as player-coach, and Marshall to Carlisle, both for £10,000 tribunal fees. Jimmy Lumsden, previously assistant to Eddie Gray at Leeds, joined City in a similar capacity, whilst physiotherapist Alex Lockhart departed for private practice. Former Everton and Chelsea midfielder Gary Stanley took up the offer of a contract after impressing whilst on trial, and striker Scott McGarvey arrived from Grimsby in exchange for Caldwell. Neither Stanley or McGarvey would prove to be a success, but John Bailey was an instant hit with his sense of fun and skilful play. The 31-year-old had been released by Newcastle three months previously, and, impressing during a trial, signed permanent forms.

Keeper Waugh's early season injury saw City borrow ex-Bristol Rover Tim Parkin from Sunderland, before Andy Leaning (27) was signed for £10,000 from Sheffield United after a period on loan. Jordan was no less active in the transfer market than Cooper had been, and it was not long before £35,000 was changing hands to secure the services of 24-year-old Mark Gavin from Bolton. Money was recouped by Fitzpatrick moving to Carlisle for £40,000. Then came the astonishing swoop by Manchester United. Few could believe that the famous Reds considered Ralph Milne to be worth £170,000. But this failed to take account of Alex Ferguson's Aberdeen years, when Dundee United's Milne was one of the brightest lights in Scottish football. Milne did enough damage to Aberdeen over the years to ensure that Ferguson marked his card. It must also be admitted that the right-winger looked a far better player at Old Trafford than he ever did at Ashton Gate.

A 1-5 home defeat by Fulham in early October was one low spot. Another was Bristol Rovers' victory on 2 January that plunged City into a trough of four successive League defeats. Tony Shepherd, on loan from Celtic, made his debut in that game against Rovers, which City lost 0-1 in front of the biggest Ashton Gate crowd for almost nine years. Notwithstanding the stirring League Cup run, the manager's position was still under review when City lost 1-2 at home to Blackpool on 15 April, but a Bob Taylor hat-trick three days later helped City to a 6-1 thrashing of Huddersfield and eased the weight on Jordan's shoulders.

Taylor became an Ashton Gate hero, a real snip at £175,000 from Leeds, while Shutt, valued at £50,000, was a makeweight in the deal. Taylor made his debut in a 1-1 draw at Bristol Rovers, forming an instant understanding with the marauding Robbie Turner, for whom City paid Wimbledon £45,000 in late January. The Taylor-Turner spearhead would drive City to promotion in 1989-90.

Many felt that City's final position of eleventh was unsatisfactory. The fact that Bristol Rovers reached the play-offs did not make things easier for Jordan. There were many occasions when Jordan's managerial capabilities were questioned, but four wins from City's last six games gave promise of better times ahead.

Match of the Season 1988-89

Bristol City 0 Nottingham Forest 1

League Cup, semi-final, 2nd leg, 26 February 1989

This was City's second semi-final appearance in the League Cup, which started life in 1960-61. The advent of sponsorship saw it being named the Milk Cup in 1982-83, then the Littlewoods Cup 1986-87, Rumbelows Cup 1990-91, Coca-Cola Cup 1992-93 and its current incarnation as the Worthington Cup in 1998-99.

The tie stood at 1-1 after the first leg. With Forest boss Brian Clough banished from the touchline following an incident in the previous round, Gary Parker shattered City's dreams at Ashton Gate with a goal six minutes from the end of extra-time to keep Forest on course for a unique Wembley hat-trick. For City it was a heartbreaking conclusion to a game of high drama for the partisan West Country crowd of almost 30,000.

For most the game it appeared that Keith Waugh had returned to haunt Clough, as he thwarted the Forest attack with many fine saves. Waugh was an impressionable 5-year-old on the Roker Park terraces when Clough suffered the collision with Bury's goalkeeper which put paid to his playing career. Now the unemotional Clough sat poker-faced alongside his chairman Maurice Roworth as Waugh defied Forest to merit his Man of the Match award. Waugh more than anyone else almost earned gallant City a replay at Villa Park.

However, Parker's late goal should take nothing away from Jordan's braves, who came within a coat of paint of reaching Wembley. With less than a minute of normal time remaining, Alan Walsh blasted a shot against Steve Sutton's right-hand post at the Covered End. For a split second the City players thought they were Wembley bound, but the ball flew off the post to Steve Hodge, who was happy to hack it away for a corner.

The match was played in driving rain and on a glue-pot pitch. After a nervy opening, City laid siege to the Forest citadel in the first 45 minutes and were perhaps unfortunate not to be in front at the interval. It was a different story in the second half. It was virtually one-way traffic, as Forest unleashed their onslaught. City survived thanks to Waugh, and once extra-time was under way the introduction of Carl Shutt for Mark Gavin allowed City to re-impose themselves as the dominate force.

Failure to take their chances proved costly. Forest, who had sealed a place at Wembley the previous Wednesday in the Simod Cup, secured their return trip when Webb crossed from the right for Parker to fire his 12-yard shot into the roof of the Open End net. A minute later Parker almost made it two, rifling another effort against the crossbar.

At the end Clough allowed himself a smile as he advised Jordan to be careful and kissed him on the cheek. Doubtless Clough smiled even more when his team beat Luton 3-1 in the final, not to mention annexing the Simod Cup (a competition for the top two divisions of the Football League) with a 4-3 success against Everton. Forest were unable to make it a unique Wembley treble: their FA Cup bid ended in the semi-final. Liverpool beat them after both clubs had endured the traumas of Hillsborough.

Despite the extra revenue generated by their cup exploits, City's financial situation took a turn for the worse, with a loss of £185,354 as against a profit of £106,877 the previous year. Season ticket sales increased from £90,725 to £102,219, but average home League attendances fell 1,697 to 8,121.

The Reserves were unable to retain their hold on the South West Counties League Cup, which they had won the previous campaign. In the League though, they improved on their 1987-88 showing by three places to finish fourth. The Youths continued their general poor form in the FA Youth Cup that characterised the 1980s, during which they never progressed past the second round. This time they lost 2-3 at home to Plymouth, having beaten Bristol Rovers 3-1 at Ashton Gate in front of 270 spectators.

5

LOST OPPORTUNITIES 1989-1994

LEAGUE DIVISION 3	**1989-90**
Division 3	2nd (Promoted)
League Cup	1st Round
FA Cup	5th Round

With the loss of crowd favourite Alan Walsh to Turkish club Besiktas for £45,000, Jordan set about rebuilding the side for a promotion challenge. The board allowed him substantial funds to spend, and spend he did, though additional revenue was generated by the sale of Galliers to Maidstone for £20,000. McClaren moved to Oxford in a straight swap for Gary Shelton. Gillingham's lightning-fast winger David Smith was snapped up for £75,000, midfielder Paul Wimbleton (Cardiff) cost £60,000, and £175,000 was found to sign the cultured David Rennie from Leeds.

City also needed a new goalkeeper. Waugh was unhappy with his new terms and moved to Coventry for a tribunal-fixed fee of £40,000. Ronnie Sinclair came from Leeds on a free transfer, but it was Leaning who played in goal when City opened the League season with a 1-1 draw at Bury, after losing the Gloucestershire Cup final at home to Bristol Rovers. A modest start was not helped by the loss of Bailey with a fractured toe in the second match against Birmingham. A 4-5 aggregate defeat by Reading in the League Cup increased the pressure on Jordan, but September was a good month, with victories over Blackpool, Cardiff and Shrewsbury and a goalless home draw with Bristol Rovers. A 0-6 hammering in a top of the table clash at Tranmere took the icing off the cake somewhat, but City still lay fourth.

In October young striker Nigel Hawkins moved to Blackpool for £17,500, while Bailey's 25-yarder at Crewe brought City their fourth win in six games played that month. Welsh International striker Andy Jones arrived on a month's loan, but despite his useful performances the board blocked a proposed £125,000 transfer. Goals from Turner and the prolific Taylor earned the 2-0 win at Walsall that took City to the top for the first time, but failure to win another League game until mid-December saw them tumble down to sixth.

In the FA Cup, City experienced no such problem. After beating Conference club Barnet in the first round, victories over Fulham and Swindon earned a mouth-watering clash with Chelsea. Receipts of £97,780 were generated by the 24,535 crowd that crammed into Ashton Gate to witness the shock of the fourth round. Gavin's late strike clinched a sensational 3-1 win, capitalising on Turner's two-goal haul and an inspirational display by Sinclair between the posts. City's fame spread far and wide, even bringing new supporters from Scandinavia who formed their own Supporters Club. Sadly, despite being presented with a plum home tie with Fourth Division Cambridge United in the next round, City were unable to progress to the last eight. Taken aback by the quality of Cambridge's football in a goalless draw at Ashton Gate, City lost out after another marathon contest. Taylor's rasping drive in the replay earned an extra-time 1-1 draw, but after losing the toss for choice of venue, City were humiliated 1-5 back at the Abbey Stadium.

Though City lost out in the Leyand Daf Cup, 0-1 at home to Notts County in January, League form had picked up. A 4-0 success at Birmingham allowed City to reclaim top spot, and despite home defeats by Reading and Tranmere the course seemed set not just for promotion, but a long-awaited championship. Paul Miller had come on loan from Wimbledon, and Wimbleton was sold to Shrewsbury for £60,000. Seeking further reinforcements, in early March Jordan paid Millwall £50,000 for 28-year-old striker Dean Horrix.

Horrix played just three games. Tragedy struck following a 1-0 win at Shrewsbury. After a night out with friends, Horrix was a passenger in a car driven by his wife that hit a tree. Mrs Horrix escaped with a damaged hand. Her husband died instantly.

The tragedy stunned the club, but made the players even more determined to win promotion. The team could do little wrong, as a run of fourteen undefeated games kept them looking down on the rest. Despite the shrewd signing of Nicky Morgan from Stoke, plus the capture of Junior Bent from Huddersfield and Iain Ferguson on loan from Hearts, the side was stuttering without Taylor. The striker had pulled a hamstring after claiming a hat-trick in a 4-1 home demolition of Crewe. He attempted a comeback at Bolton, but his season was finished. It was this game at Burnden Park that ultimately cost City the championship. Their 0-1 defeat on what was normally considered one of their lucky grounds opened the door to the relentlessly pursuing Bristol Rovers.

As luck would have it, the penultimate game of the season was against Rovers at Twerton Park four days later. Despite the championship being at stake, City put on a gutless show, as Rovers swept to a 3-0 victory and took over at the top with a two-point lead. Whilst a 4-0 home win over Walsall in the final game ensured promotion, it could not compensate for the Twerton defeat. Rovers won 3-0 at Blackpool to secure the championship.

The promotion drive boosted City's League average attendance to 11,544. This, coupled with the revenue generated by their FA Cup exploits, yielded an annual profit of £68,550. Receipts of £66,633 were produced by City's biggest home League gate – 19,483 for the Walsall promotion-clincher.

The Reserves did their bit to convince the fans that City were on the up. They won the South West Counties League Cup, but finished third in the League and were knocked out at the semi-final stage of the Somerset Professional Cup.

Match of the Season 1989-90

Bristol Rovers 3 Bristol City 0

Division 3, 2 May 1990

It often appeared that there was a jinx on this fixture. Throughout Rovers' ten-season sojourn at Twerton Park from 1986-87, adverse weather necessitated a change to the scheduled date on no fewer than three occasions, whilst a Grandstand fire – alleged to have been started by City hooligans – forced postponement in 1990-91. Who knows, the result of this vital championship fixture might have been different if it had been played on its original date of 3 February, when a waterlogged pitch brought cancellation.

Historically, City held the advantage in League derbies with 26 wins against eighteen for the Rovers, ten of these wins coming at Eastville. At what became known as Fortress Twerton, however, City rarely gave a good account of themselves. It would not be until the most recent derby played on this ground seven years later that City broke their duck in the League. None of this bothered City fans unduly; they expected victory, knowing that a win was vital to ensure Rovers did not snatch the title at City's expense.

Apart from a 1-3 defeat at Notts County in April, Rovers had not tasted defeat in the League since going down 1-2 at Brentford in January. Twenty games had produced 45 points to put them hot on the heels of City, whose 0-1 defeat at Bolton in the previous game now offered Rovers the chance to assume top spot. Conversely for City, it meant that their fate was still in their hands. A City win would not only clinch promotion, but also ensure they finished as champions.

Did You Know?

At Plymouth in April 1985, the local constabulary prevented 700 City fans from attending the game. Their train was detained in a railway siding.

Twerton was packed with 9,813 excited fans, paying receipts of £29,950, on a warm sunny evening. Rovers' physical team quickly seized the initiative. City were back-peddling from the start and appeared to have no idea how to cope with the muscular presence of Devon White. Apart from Mark Gavin's mis-hit cross-shot in the first half and Robbie Turner's header past the post in the second, City lacked conviction. It was no surprise they fell behind midway through the first half, when Man of the Match White capitalised on Andy Llewellyn's slip to convert David Mehew's cross. Carl Saunders set up White to fire in the second from ten yards after 55 minutes. Seven minutes later referee Roger Dilkes ruled out Mehew's header, when Phil Purnell's fierce drive was handled on the line by Llewellyn, but Ian Holloway netted the resultant penalty to tie up Rovers' deserved success.

Regrettably, with the Rovers fans in good voice with the strains of 'Goodnight Irene' reverberating around the ground, some of City's so-called fans appeared unable to countenance defeat. Disturbances broke out as a few hot-heads sought to get the match abandoned. The referee was encouraged to continue by the sportsmanlike attitude of both teams, with City captain Rob Newman telling him – 'You keep the game going, and we'll keep going for you'. City boss Joe Jordan is also to be commended, preventing the situation from getting out of hand by walking round the ground and confronting the unruly City fans.

Defeat denied City the championship, but not promotion, which was secured against Walsall three days later.

LEAGUE DIVISION 2	**1990-91**
Division 2	9th
League Cup	2nd Round
FA Cup	3rd Round

With Bristol having erased the shame of being the first provincial City to have both its sides relegated from the same division in the same season by reversing the process, local interest was intense as the new campaign approached. City embarked on a tour of Scotland and the North for their pre-season preparations. Ayr, Clydebank and Carlisle were duly beaten. Revenge of sorts was achieved against an under-strength Bristol Rovers side, when City's 4-1 win secured the Gloucestershire Cup at Twerton Park. Pre-season preparations were concluded with a 1-1 home draw with Crystal Palace and a 2-0 success over Aston Villa in Newman's benefit.

The League campaign commenced at Ashton Gate, when City fought back from a half-time deficit to beat Blackburn 4-2. City's side included new signings Louie Donowa from Ipswich (£45,000), Andy May from Huddersfield (£90,000), as well as their major capture – Welsh International centre-half Mark Aizlewood, who cost £125,000 from Bradford City. Missing was Wayne Allison – who had joined City from Watford, plus a £100,000 cheque, as make-weight in a deal that saw Gavin move in the opposite direction – and Murray Jones, who arrived on a free from Crystal Palace. Also on the move was Turner, who joined Plymouth for £150,000, and Pender who in mid-October joined Burnley for £70,000.

Allison made his debut at West Brom, as substitute in City's 2-2 draw in the first round of the League Cup, but Jones was destined never to break into the first team. A 1-0 extra-time win in the second leg carried City through to a two-legged meeting with First Division Sunderland. A stirring performance at Roker earned a 1-0 win thanks to Morgan's header, but in the return leg City equalled their record 1-6 defeat in the competition.

The debacle against Sunderland coincided with City's assistant boss Lumsden's appointment as manager. Though Joe Jordan had signed a three-year contract in the summer, he resigned on 19 September to take over at Hearts in place of Alex McDonald. Three successive games were won during the period of Lumsden's temporary control, and it was perhaps unfortunate that – no sooner had he put pen to paper – City should feature in a game in which they were punished for every mistake. City's involvement in the Full Members (Zenith Data Systems) Cup did not last long, though they were perhaps unfortunate to go out 2-3 in a penalty shoot-out, at the end of a 1-1 extra-time draw at Oxford.

In the League, matters had taken a turn for the worse after City's 1-0 home win over Newcastle United in late September. The next four games yielded only one point, from a 1-1 home draw with West Ham, which kicked off at 11.30am. Despite a 2-1 success at Millwall, performances were still erratic. With Lumsden in hospital, his assistant Tony Taylor was in charge when City beat Hull 4-1 at home to record their best win of the season. Losses to Port Vale, Oxford and Charlton prompted Lumsden to make his first major signing. He paid £200,000 to Rotherham for full-back Martin Scott, who made his debut in a 1-1 home draw with Sheffield Wednesday. Other moves at the turn of the year saw Murray, after a spell on loan with Doncaster, joining Exeter for £30,000, Chris Honor going on loan to Swansea, whilst Humphries was sold to Scunthorpe for £55,000.

There was no New Year's joy for City. A 0-2 defeat at Barnsley heralded five straight losses in January, including a 1-2 exit from the FA Cup at Norwich. The 2-3 defeat at Twerton Park dumped City down to thirteenth, their lowest position of the season. Morgan ended his goal drought in the next game to inspire a 2-0 home win over West Brom. This sparked a run of three successive victories that fostered hopes of a play-off place. The Gulf War was raging when City beat Oxford 3-1, but the game was marred by the death of club chairman Des Williams with a heart attack.

Donowa's late goal that secured a 1-0 home win against Bristol Rovers set off a four-match unbeaten run and hoisted City into a play-off position. But 0-1 and 1-4 defeats at West Ham and Portsmouth in late March ultimately proved fatal to City's promotion hopes and dropped them down to eighth. All hope was finally extinguished when Teddy Sheringham's hat-trick at Ashton Gate brought Millwall a 4-1 win. When the curtain came down on the season City lay ninth, a satisfactory placing on their return to the Second Division.

For older City fans, there was a treat to be savoured on the ground of Bristol Manor Farm at the Creek, where Newman's highly successful benefit season ended with a special match. His City XI drew 2-2 with a Bristol City 1976 XI in front of 500 spectators, who saw goals from Donowa and Newman matched by strikes from Fear and Cheesley.

With the average home League attendance rising to 13,495, and season ticket sales doubling from £122,165 to £250,235, City's profits increased to a new record of £424,172.

The Reserves also did well, finishing as Champions of the South West Counties, as well as winning the League Cup and the Somerset Premier Cup.

Did You Know?

In 1988 City fans did not believe Alex Ferguson would pay £170,000 for Ralph Milne. But when with Dundee United, Milne caused havoc to Ferguson's Aberdeen.

Match of the Season 1990-91

Bristol City 1 Bristol Rovers 0

Division 2, 5 March 1991

It might even be unique statistically, but this was the season when *both* derby fixtures had to be re-arranged. The Stand fire at Twerton forced postponement of City's away game on 19 September, whilst snow and ice prevented the match at Ashton Gate going ahead on 12 February.

The Rovers won the re-arranged game at Twerton, which kicked-off at midday on 26 January, and were hoping to achieve a League double over City, even though such a feat was rare in the 36 seasons of Bristol derbies. Only twice had the Rovers managed it, whilst City's record was not much better, notching only four such 'doubles' since the two sides first met in the Football League in 1922-23.

Lying one point ahead of Rovers in the table, and with a game in hand, City were both the favourites and the form side. They had won three of their previous four games and the majority of the 22,269 fans – paying receipts of £102,821.50 – for this Tuesday evening match expected a home win. History, though, was against City. Their last home League victory over the Rovers had been back in March 1986, when the result was 2-0.

City's hero in 1991 was Louie Donowa, a late replacement for the injured David Smith. It was his goal that denied Rovers an eleventh successive unbeaten game in League derbies. Just two minutes from time he latched onto a through-ball, and though keeper Brian Parkin blocked his first effort, the ball popped up for Donowa to stoop to head it into the empty net. The late goal was a real sickener for Rovers, especially for Ian Holloway. When Andy Reece had been sent tumbling by Andy Leaning, Holloway's spot-kick was saved.

Donowa had justified his selection with a strong running display which gave Rovers' left-back Vaughan Jones a torrid time. Geoff Twentyman's marshalling qualities were a key factor in the early stages as Rovers weathered City's opening 20-minute blitz. Nicky Morgan was thrice thwarted by the woodwork, but committed Rovers were resilient and came back well in a thrilling match, which was capably refereed by Ron Groves. City managed seven shots on target and five off, against five and nine for the Rovers, whilst the corner count was to the advantage of the homesters 8-4.

At the final whistle the City fans were in raptures, their displays of celebration more reminiscent of promotion than just winning a match, even though it was against the old enemy. The only disquieting note of a memorable night were the jeers of a small number of Rovers fans during the minute's silence held in memory of City chairman Des Williams, whose heart attack had claimed his life ten days previously.

City's win broke the mould, for in subsequent seasons the Ashton Gate club re-established their former supremacy, notching up six more League derby successes, including three away, whilst Rovers have won but twice.

LEAGUE DIVISION 2	**1991-92**
Division 2	17th
League Cup	2nd Round
FA Cup	5th Round

The season started well enough with City second in the table after going unbeaten for the first five games. These included a 1-0 home win over promotion favourites Blackburn, but a run of six matches that yielded just two points saw City plummet to eighteenth after losing 1-4 at Derby on 5 October.

This was not what Ashton Alf was expecting. Confidence had been high in the close season that City would put together a promotion challenge, though the loss of the versatile Newman to Norwich for £600,000 after he had netted a cool £100,000 from his benefit year caused some disquiet. Other concerns revolved around the development of Ashton Gate in the summer, a consequence of the Taylor Report's requirement for all-seater stadiums. The cost of extending the Grandstand roof, both length and widthways, to enable it to join up with the Covered End, plus the installation of 9,000 seats, came to £670,000. The work was partly funded by the Football Trust, City's outlay being a modest £260,000. Many fans were unhappy at losing the standing terraces at the Covered End. Nor did it help when it was realised that the seats provided in this part of the ground had no backs. Fortunately the Open End was still available to those who wished to stand, a facility that remained available until the building of the Atyeo Stand in 1994 converted Ashton Gate into an all-seater stadium.

As well as the departure of Newman, others to seek pastures new included Honor, Donowa and Mardon. It was the supposed delights of the Scottish League that attracted Honor, as he joined Airdrie for £20,000, whilst Donowa and Mardon shot up the M5 to Birmingham, who paid £50,000 and £60,000 respectively. Among the new intake of players were Rochdale keeper Keith Welch, who cost £200,000, as well as free-transfer signings Gerry Harrison and Gus Caesar from Watford and Cambridge United respectively. All except Caesar were in the side that beat Bristol Rovers 3-2 in the Gloucestershire Cup final at Ashton Gate on 7 August.

The next local derby also went in City's favour: City won 3-1 in a Football League Cup, second round tie at Twerton. Sadly, the Robins did not have long to savour their victory. The return leg at Ashton Gate ended in a 2-4 extra-time defeat, which sent Rovers through on away goals. Erratic League form and Taylor's scoring drought forced Lumsden to buy and sell. He signed striker Terry Connor from Swansea for £192,000 and defender Russell Osman for

Did You Know?

At Aldershot in 1989, terracing behind the goal had to be evacuated because of faulty power cables. A case of more 'live wires' off the pitch than on it.

£60,000 from Southampton, and sold unsettled winger David Smith to Plymouth for £185,000. The void out on the wing was later filled by the return of Gavin from Watford for a cut-price £65,000.

Leaving aside a 1-2 home defeat by First Division Southampton in the second round of the Full Members (Zenith Data Systems) Cup, City put together a seven-match unbeaten run. It began with a 1-0 home win over Watford and ended with a 1-3 defeat at Middlesbrough, where Osman was sent off. But thereafter it was free-fall all the way, with only a 3-0 home League win over Port Vale to take the mind off relegation. The gloom was not lightened by the selling of crowd favourite Taylor to West Brom for £300,000, following the departures of Caesar to Airdrie for £30,000 and goalkeeper Sinclair to Stoke for £25,000.

Fortunately, the fans had the diversion of the FA Cup to take their minds off City's League predicament. This included its share of giant-killing, as well as an outstanding performance at Leicester. Against First Division Wimbledon in the third round at Ashton Gate, Warren Barton's late own-goal gave City a fortunate replay, which was won by May's swerving long-range drive. In the next round at Filbert Street, City's new boy, Polish International Jacki Dziekanowski, signed from Celtic for £250,000, turned in a performance that had Match of the Day commentator John Motson drooling. The draw for the fifth round took City to Nottingham Forest, where they lost 1-4.

A 1-2 defeat at Charlton meant City had not won in the League for seven games. At this point Lumsden was dismissed and Mark Aizlewood, Russell Osman and Gary Shelton took over as joint caretaker managers until ex-York and Sunderland boss Denis Smith was appointed on 9 March. It was not until Smith's third match in charge that City's long winless run, which by then had extended to eleven games, came to an end. Dziekanowski's two strikes was sufficient for a City side, strengthened by signing of Andy Cole on loan from Arsenal, to beat Wolves 2-0 at Ashton Gate.

With the further capture of Leroy Rosenior on a free from West Ham, City's new-look side embarked on an eight-match unbeaten run that lifted them to safety. A 2-1 home win over Ipswich ensured survival, whereupon the season petered out with three losses. In the last game, at Watford, City's record £250,000 buy Ray Atteveld from Everton, together with Aizlewood and Allison, were sent off.

The excitement of the final couple of months sustained average home League attendances at a relatively healthy 11,479. But despite the transfer of Rennie to Birmingham for £120,000 late in the season, a deficit of £659,284 was declared.

The Reserves won the South West Counties League for the second successive season but were unable to retain their hold on the League Cup or the Somerset Premier Cup, exiting at the quarter-final stage of both tournaments The Youths reached the third round of the FA Youth Cup for the first time since 1979-80, beating Swindon and Epsom & Ewell before losing 0-3 at Southend.

Match of the Season 1991-92

Bristol City 2 Ipswich Town 1

Division 2, 18 April 1992

A season that started with so much promise degenerated into a relegation battle. The coming of new boss Denis Smith sparked hopes of salvation with his astute signings of Andy Cole and Leroy Rosenior, and his ability to cultivate the talents of Jacki Dzienkanowski. City's unbeaten run of eight games, of which five were won, between 17 March and 18 April, enabled them to claw themselves clear of the trap-door.

This game against Ipswich was the last in this unbeaten run. City needed the points to be sure of saving their status. The enthusiasm of City's fans was such that older supporters' minds turned to the second half of the 1966-67 season, when the coming of Chris Crowe and Hugh McIlmoyle sparked a revival.

It was thought that the clash with League leaders Ipswich would give an indication as to just how far City had progressed under their new manager, and the fans were not disappointed. Yet again the brilliant skills of Dziekanowski were displayed at their very best, and in harness with the electrifying pace of Cole, City more than matched their visitors.

Goalkeeper Keith Welch was rarely troubled as City's deadly duo Rosenior and Cole turned up trumps once more. Rosenior volleyed in the opener late in the first half; then Cole doubled City's lead in the 53rd minute after waltzing past three defenders. It was not until the closing stages that Ipswich made a fist of it, via the penalty spot, after Matt Bryant had brought down Chris Kiwomya.

For City, this result meant that they staved off relegation. In a sense it was a pity, for they now returned to their losing ways. For Ipswich, this reverse was but a blip in their march to the title, which they won by four points from Middlesbrough.

LEAGUE DIVISION 1	**1992-93**
Division 1 (New Style)	15th
League Cup	2nd Round
FA Cup	3rd Round

City's record fee of £250,000 for Atteveld did not linger in the record books for long. In July Cole was signed from Arsenal for double that amount as Denis Smith set about rebuilding for the new season. At the time the manager was hugely popular and many City fans were of the opinion that they at last had a man in charge with the charisma and the talent to take City forward. The love-affair with the new boss did not last, of course. His implementation of a defensive formation that suited neither the players nor the fans quickly brought disillusionment. So did the acquisition of centre-half David Thompson from Millwall, in exchange for Andy May, and full-back Brian Mitchell on a free from Bradford City. Once the new season began to unfold it was clear that City were back to their familiar role of strugglers.

An upheaval to the structure of the English game saw the formation of the FA Premier League, which meant that all lower divisions were upgraded. City were now a First Division club once more, though in reality the goalposts had been moved. The top clubs had long been agitating for more control, becoming ever more greedy. A breakaway was stifled in the mid-1980s, but this time, in collusion with the FA, it was successful. With the Football League's loss of their top twenty-two clubs, the rest of the competition was restructured with the remaining three divisions having their status enhanced and all their clubs becoming full members.

City's goals flowed in the League opener against Portsmouth, though keeper Leaning looked out of sorts with the requirements of the new back-pass rule. They flowed again in the first round of the League Cup, when City notched up a 5-1 win over Third Division Cardiff. Sadly, such games were the exception. Perhaps the fans should have been forewarned by a 1-2 defeat at the hands of Bristol Rovers in the Gloucestershire Cup final at Twerton Park on 5 August, but a 2-1 home friendly win against Chelsea three days later suggested all was well.

With the demise of the Full Members Cup, the Anglo-Italian Cup, which had been contested in the late 1960s and early 70s, was revamped in its place. City beat Watford 1-0 at home and then drew 1-1 at Luton to qualify for European competition for the first time.

This venture was less than successful, as City could not manage to beat any of their four Italian opponents. Both home games were lost, 0-2 to Cosenza and 1-2 to Reggiana. Away, City did slightly better, losing 3-4 at Pisa before bowing out with a 2-2 draw at Cremonese.

In domestic competition, heavy defeats by West Ham, Newcastle and Brentford, not to mention being knocked out the League Cup 3-5 on aggregate by Sheffield United, set alarm bells ringing at Ashton Gate. City's defence looked unable to adapt to the sweeper system. Danish international Bjorn Kristensen was borrowed from Newcastle but was unable to prevent a humiliating 0-4 defeat in the televised local derby at Twerton in mid-December. Some cheer came when Leroy Rosenior turned out for Sierra Leone in a goal-less draw against Toga in the African Nations Cup, but the chill of an English winter gripped City in a vice: the team was sinking like a stone.

Smith changed tactics: he abandoned the sweeper system and restored to wingers, but by the time the FA Cup came round City had gone seven League games without a win and were wallowing down in eighteenth spot. The Cup offered no relief – a 0-2 defeat at Luton was made worse by the expulsion of Scott. This was the final straw for City's board. The next day Smith was dismissed, and player-coach Russell Osman given temporary control.

Osman did not offer instant solutions, and most City fans were resigned to relegation, but slowly but surely he turned things round. The captures of Glenn Pennyfather from Ipswich and Stuart Munro (Blackburn) were crucial, and their debuts were marked by a shock 3-2 success at Portsmouth. This, though, was a false dawn and the fans had to suffer a five-match winless run before the next victory. City's forgotten man Nicky Morgan took over from Andy Cole, who had been transferred to Newcastle for a record £1.75 million the day before. It was Morgan who clinched a 1-0 win at Birmingham with a looping header. Brian Tinnion was then signed from Bradford City for a tribunal fee of £180,000, making his debut in a 1-2 defeat at Swindon. Mark Shail, a 25-year-old central defender who cost £40,000 from Yeovil, saw his first action when coming on as substitute in the 0-0 home draw with Derby.

Former favourites Gerry Sweeney and Clive Whitehead joined Osman's coaching staff and with a new crew at the helm City slowly climbed to safety. The team notched important wins over Watford, Grimsby, Bristol Rovers and Wolves to move up to fourteenth with five matches left. In contrast to the previous season, this time City remained unbeaten in their final matches, but the fact that four of those games were drawn meant an end of season position of fifteenth. Osman was rewarded with a three-year managerial contract, which he signed on 1 May. Many supporters, though, were critical of City's defensively orientated tactics under their new boss, and after the final game, against Brentford, ex-City great John Atyeo remarked: 'We may have stayed up, but at what cost for the future?' And City won the match 4-1!

None of this deterred the fans turning up six days later to support a special benefit for ex-City favourite Chris Garland, who was suffering from Parkinson's disease. The visit of Manchester United attracted a crowd of 21,716; the game ended 3-3.

The sale of Andy Cole had a predictable effect on the balance sheet as City announced a profit of £517,481 for the season. That figure included an increase in season ticket revenue from £311,452 to £325,799.

Back in the Football Combination for the first time in nine years, the Reserves had a less than successful season. They finished seventeenth and in the Somerset Premier Cup they were knocked out in round one. The Youths did better, reaching the fifth round of the FA Youth Cup after enjoying home advantage in every round. They overcame Bristol Rovers, Epsom & Ewell, Swansea, and Swindon before losing 3-4 to Norwich.

Match of the Season 1992-93

Bristol City 4 Brentford 1

Division 1, 8 May 1993

A season which again saw City flirting with relegation, culminated with this, their best win of the campaign after a run of just two defeats in thirteen games. With Brentford needing all three points to be sure of retaining their status, a better than average crowd of 12,695, including an estimated 3,000 Bees fans from West London, converged on Ashton Gate on a blustery Saturday afternoon.

Fears that Osman's side might take things easy were dispelled by City's blistering start. Attacking the Covered End, Mark Gavin and Gary Shelton exposed the Brentford defence after six minutes with a quick exchange of passes before City's No 8 set up Leroy Rosenior to score at the near post. Mark Aizlewood had a header cleared off the line by Kenny Sansom, and Rosenior hit a shot just over before Wayne Allison doubled City's advantage on 29 minutes. Gary Shelton's aggression forged the opening for Allison, on the right-hand side of the box, to fire home an angled drive.

Goals scored had replaced goal-difference to separate sides level on points, and after the break the Bees adopted a cavalier approach to try to snatch something from the game. City's keeper Keith Welch had to be alert to tip over Keith Millen's 47th-minute header, but Gary Blissett's 29th goal of the season was their sole reward. He

Did You Know?

The Bristol local press introduced colour photos in December 1989. The first home game to feature colour photos was versus Rotherham. But it ended 0-0!

headed in from almost on the goal-line on 57 minutes, after Marcus Gayle's header came back off the bar. By then, though, Rosenior had further increased City's tally, as two minutes earlier he had punished slack defending. Latching onto Mark Shail's through-ball he curled a delightful right-footed shot inside Gerry Peyton's left-hand post.

City's counter-attacks met with virtually no resistance, and it was no surprise when Rosenior notched the fourth hat-trick of his career with a typical poacher's strike, when Tinnion's shot was only half-saved. The only surprise was that this ended the scoring. In the remaining 23 minutes Allison and Junior Bent spurned inviting opportunities to rattle up a massive win.

Apart from isolated spells, Brentford failed to show the spirit necessary to prevent a return from whence they had come just twelve months previously. They looked strangely uncoordinated, and Bees manager Phil Holder was moved to comment after the game that his players could not handle the pressure.

The cycle, though, was to turn full circle four years later, when the Second Division play-offs saw Brentford beat City in both legs of the semi-final. Alas, Brentford lost to Crewe in the play-off final.

LEAGUE DIVISION 1	**1993-94**
Division 1	13th
League Cup	1st Round
FA Cup	5th Round

The close-season signings of 29-year-old Ian Baird (£295,000) from Hearts and 27-year-old Liam Robinson (£130,000) from Bury did little to suggest that the goalscoring void created by Andy Cole's departure would be easily filled. A 1-1 home draw with Bristol Rovers in the Gloucestershire Cup, which the old enemy won 5-3 in a penalty shoot-out, followed by a 1-2 defeat by Cape Town Spurs six days later, was not encouraging. Few fans were surprised when City lost their League opener 1-3 at Wolves.

Goals from Baird and Allison brought a merited home success over Crystal Palace (the eventual champions) a week later, but only one more win in the next six games left City floundering in twentieth spot after a 0-0 draw at Portsmouth. By then City were already out of both cup competitions organised by the Football League.

In the League Cup, all looked set fair with a 1-0 win at Swansea, but in the return leg the Swans surprised everyone but themselves by winning 2-0. In the Anglo-Italian Cup, City failed to qualify from their group after losing 1-3 at Portsmouth. Fortunately, matters improved in the FA Cup, but more of that later.

Back in the League, a fourteen-game run with only two defeats took City up to eighth place by early December, but the football was anything but entertaining. Boardroom matters, in fact, took centre stage. The resignation of director Ivor Williams, who sold his five percent holding of foundation shares to the Supporters Club for £35,000, brought to public attention boardroom disagreements that had been smouldering for some eighteen months. With the announcement on 18 May 1993 of an FA Inquiry into monies claimed by City from the Football Trust for ground improvements, it became clear that rebels were waiting to strike.

These rebels, calling themselves the Reform Group, officially launched their bid for power on 30 September, and issued their blueprint for the future – 'The Way To Win' – five days later. This group consisted of board member Mike Fricker, Deryn Coller (a recent board member), Peter Burchill, John Clapp and David Russe. The literature explained that Coller had resigned from the board the previous March because he could no longer countenance what he claimed were financial irregularities which, due to block voting, he was powerless to prevent. Fricker did not resign, as he felt he had a duty to protect those who had brought to his attention the matters that led to the Inquiry.

Did You Know?

When City gained promotion in 1989-90, Bob Taylor became the first player since John Atyeo to score 30 goals a season – 27 in the League, 7 in cups.

Matters came to a head with an EGM at the Whitchurch Sports Centre on 12 November. About 1,000 small shareholders were present to decide the fate of the opposing parties, but in truth many appeared to be unimpressed by both factions. Particular concerns were voiced that, despite the Reform Group's declared objectives of City attaining Premiership status within five years, and winning a major trophy to gain entry to European competition within ten, no concrete proposals were put forward for the injection of cash. Hard decisions had to made, and for many the clinching factor was the fact that the FA had announced on that very day the result of their Inquiry.

The Inquiry had culminated in a seven-hour hearing at the Park Hotel, London, on 9 November. A three-man commission, headed by Southampton Vice-Chairman Keith Wiseman, supported by Alan Turvey (a divisional member from Hayes) and Barry Bright (Kent FA) interviewed Chairman Les Kew and took evidence from a range of City officials, as well as the floodlight contractor. The outcome went against City, who were fined £40,000 (£30,000 suspended for two years).

In this context it was not surprising that the Reform Group won the power struggle. The Chairman and three directors were voted off the board, Mike Fricker was re-elected, and four new members elected. David Russe was named as the new Chairman, with Fricker as his deputy. Supporters Club Chairman Garry Williams was co-opted as a member and a statement was issued: 'We must now start the task of rebuilding bridges ... of uniting this great club, its staff and its supporters, so that we can surge forward to one common goal.'

Ironically, though City had been eighth when the new regime assumed power, the team had slipped to thirteenth by the season's end, playing football that was anything but exciting and entertaining – which had been promised. Manager Osman, who had found himself in an unenviable position during the boardroom upheavals, called upon a record 38 players in all competitions during the campaign. He was willing to give chances to players released by other clubs, such as Marvin Harriott (Barnsley) and Scott Partridge (Bradford City), as well as blooding youngsters and bargain signings like Zimbabwean international Henry McKop (£15,000 from Bonner Sport in Germany).

It was in the FA Cup that City gave their fans something to shout about. Their win at Liverpool was almost on par with the victory over Leeds twenty years earlier. This time the team's headline-making win would not have the same effect on the club's fortunes, even though it was followed by a 4-0 success at Stockport in the fourth round before City went out to Charlton 0-2 in a replay at the Valley in round five.

At the end of the season, City set off on a three-match eleven day tour of Zimbabwe, further afield than their first foreign trip in 1946 when they sailed across the North Sea to Denmark. City were unbeaten in Africa, winning one and drawing two matches.

League attendances were a cause of mounting concern. Not even City's epic win at Anfield sparked a resurgence, for just 8,171 turned up for the visit of Tranmere eleven days later. The Cup run did, however, alleviate City's financial plight. At the AGM in December 1994 a profit of £59,680 was announced.

City's reserve strength was not encouraging. The second team finished twentieth in the Football Combination, though they did reach the third round of the Somerset Premier Cup. The Youths in the FA Youth Cup went out in the second round to Aston Villa, after winning 1-0 at Reading in round one.

Match of the Season 1993-94

Liverpool 0 Bristol City 1

FA Cup, 3rd Round replay, 25 January 1994

For a club with a less than impressive Cup pedigree, triumphs of this magnitude did not occur very often. City achieved just fifteen acts of giant-killing over top-flight opposition during 88 previous seasons of FA Cup action – Middlesbrough (1903), Bolton (1903 & 1979), Arsenal (1905 & 1920), Bury (1909), Liverpool (1910), Bradford City (1920), Portsmouth (1935), Southampton (1967), Leeds (1974), Derby (1980), Chelsea (1990), Wimbledon (1992), plus a fourth round, first leg win over Brentford in 1946.

The sequence of cup ties against Liverpool in January 1994 was special for Bristol City for the simple reason that the players outperformed the Premier League superstars in all three games.

The original tie at Ashton Gate had come to a premature halt through floodlight failure after 65 minutes. A 20,612 crowd had seen Wayne Allison's 39th-minute glancing header cancel out Ian Rush's side-footed early opener. The re-arranged fixture eleven days later brought 21,718 back to Ashton Gate, encouraged by admission prices being reduced. Both sides made changes – Liverpool bringing in Steve McManaman for Stig Bjornebye, and City replacing Ian Brown with Junior Bent, and filling the void left by the suspended Matt Bryant with Andy Llewellyn. The score and scorers were the same as in the first game: Rush prodded in from close-range midway through the second half and Allison levelled when sweeping in a right-footed effort at the far post.

Playing in their purple and green change strip, and roared on by more than 7,000 travelling fans, City were unchanged for the Anfield replay. Liverpool brought in Steve Harkness for Julian Dicks and Mark Walters for Robbie Fowler.

To hold Liverpool's all-stars at Ashton Gate twice was one thing, but to beat them in their own back yard was tantamount to mission impossible. In fairness, this was not the Liverpool team of old. Manager Graeme Souness was under much pressure on account of his side's indifferent League form, and if ever there was a time to humble the Reds, this was it.

Liverpool had their chances. City did well to survive an amazing goalmouth scramble midway through the first half, but by the end of ninety minutes the home team were well beaten. City turned in a superlative performance and deserved more than Brian Tinnion's 67th-minute curler past Bruce Grobbelaar. Rob Edwards, Liam Robinson and Tinnion all squandered first-half chances as Liverpool's defence was pulled apart by the pace of Allison and Bent. As for the much-vaunted Liverpool attack – for whom Rush needed one goal to equal Denis Law's FA Cup record of 41 – they were closely marshalled by City's defence.

McManaman switched wings to try his luck against Llewellyn, and John Barnes dropped into midfield, but to no avail as City sustained the pressure after the break. Grobbelaar was lucky to stay on the pitch when he handled outside the box to prevent Bent connecting with Dave Martin's through-ball. Four minutes later Bent blazed over with another inviting opportunity. Even after Tinnion's goal, chances continued to come City's way, but they were not taken, denying City a score-line that would have more realistically demonstrated their superiority on the day.

Upon the final whistle the Kop rose to salute City's heroes as they undertook a lap of honour. It was a sensational night for all connected with Bristol City Football Club, but not for Souness, for whom this defeat was the last straw. Two days later he resigned, to be succeeded in the Anfield hot-seat by his assistant Roy Evans.

Despite the hope that this great victory would propel City onward and upward, it was not to be. In the Cup, victory over Stockport was followed by defeat to Charlton in the fifth round. In the League, City would be relegated one season later.

6

RE-VAMP 1994-1999

LEAGUE DIVISION 1	**1994-95**
Division 1	23rd (Relegated)
League Cup	2nd Round
FA Cup	4th Round

As a consequence of the Atyeo Stand at the Open End of the ground, Osman had to look for free-transfer signings. He acquired during the close season 31-year-old keeper Phil Kite (Cardiff) and midfielders Rod McAree (a 20-year-old from Liverpool) and 21-year-old Colin Loss from Gresley Rovers. This did not augur well for the coming campaign.

The new stand, on which work had commenced in March 1994, was used for the first time in August, when Port Vale were the visitors, but it was not fully functional until six weeks later when FA Chairman Sir Bert Millichip performed the opening ceremony. This Stand was named in honour of Bristol City great John Atyeo, who had scored 350 goals in 645 appearances for the club, as well as grabbing five in his six England games. Sadly, John was no longer alive to appreciate the honour – he had died in June 1993. With both the main stands – Dolman in 1970 and Williams in 1992 – being named after directors, it was fitting that another City great, Billy Wedlock (26 England caps between 1907 and 1914), should be similarly honoured. The Covered End was named after him in 1996.

After pre-season away games against Wimborne (1-1), Clandown (8-0), Petersfield (7-1) and Bath (3-2) – as well as a 1-3 home defeat by Tottenham – the serious business got underway with the Gloucestershire Cup final on 3 August. The first ninety minutes were thrill-less and goalless. No extra-time was played, so the contest was settled by a penalty shoot-out. Rovers won it by the extraordinary score of 11-10, after City's keeper Keith Welch failed to score past his opposite number.

In the League Cup, City could not muster a goal in either of their first round ties with Notts County, going out 0-4 on aggregate.

City enjoyed more success in the FA Cup. After a goalless home draw with Stoke, the floodgates opened in the replay at the Victoria ground as City notched up a 3-1 extra-time victory, which earned them a home clash with Premiership side Everton. This, though, was as good as it got. The Toffees won 1-0 at Ashton Gate on 29 January, in front of a 19,816 crowd which paid club record receipts of £174,231.

By then, one manager had gone and other arrived. City's disastrous start, with only four wins in eighteen League and Cup games had ex-City player Chris Garland warning in the *Western Daily Press* that 'The Club has the sniff of doom'. He complained that the directors were forcing Osman to work with his hands tied behind his back by not generating funds for him to spend on players.

Osman's sacking on 14 November, following a 0-3 defeat at Sheffield United nine days earlier, split the fans. Many felt that he had had a raw deal. Former chairman Les Kew suggested it was Osman's support for the former board that was responsible for his dismissal. Others, mindful of Osman's dour tactics and the limited opportunities he had given to crowd favourite Dziekanowski, felt the sacking warranted. Joe Jordan assumed his duties the following day, but this too divided supporters. Many could not forgive Jordan for having walked out on the club four years earlier when he joined Hearts.

Jordan began his second term in charge with a thrilling 3-2 home win over Swindon, but a sequence of six defeats left City deep in the relegation mire by Christmas. A 3-1 home success over Stoke on 27 December stopped the rot, but with only one League win during January, City were unable to improve on their 23rd placing. Despite the signings of Gary Owers from Sunderland (a £750,000 part-exchange deal for Martin Scott), Martin Kuhl from Derby for £300,000, and Richard Dryden for £200,000 from Birmingham, form remained wretched. With only four more League wins in the final eighteen games it was little wonder that City were relegated. The only surprise was that City did not finish bottom – an even worse Notts County side propped up the table some five points below. For those fans taking the wider perspective, relegation was almost predictable. This had, after all, been the fifth season since promotion, demonstrating once again that a five-year cycle often shaped City's history.

Off the pitch, finances were worsening. A loss of £766,945 (compared to a £59,680 profit in 1993-94) was declared at a much delayed AGM, held in May 1996, though the number of season tickets holders had surprisingly increased from 2,185 (£298,983) to 2,365 (£367,248).

Did You Know?

During the home defeat by Notts Co in Dec 1995, each time a City substitution was made comedians in the crowd held up every number between 1 and 11.

Perhaps it was a consequence of the building of the Atyeo Stand, but after it was completed the state of City's pitch began to give cause for concern. So much so that the Reserves had to play on Clevedon Town's ground at the Hand Stadium. Eleven Football Combination games took place at this venue. The Reserves improved on their previous season's showing to finish fifteenth, as well as reaching the semi-finals of the Somerset Premier Cup before losing 0-2 to Bath City. In the FA Youth Cup, City's youngsters did well to progress through to the fifth round, where they put up a brave display before succumbing 1-2 to Tottenham Hotspur in front of a 1,089 Ashton Gate crowd.

The stars of this otherwise miserable season were undoubtedly Bristol City Women's Football team, who played in the South West Region Women's Football League Division One. They won the Championship, the League Cup and the Pat Sowden Cup, but missed out on promotion to the National League by losing a play-off 2-3 at Leyton Orient. City's Ladies were also the giant-killers of the Women's FA Cup. Unfortunately, Liverpool proved too strong in the semi-final, winning 5-0 on Mangotsfield's Cossham Street ground.

Match of the Season 1994-95

Bristol City 3 Swindon Town 2

Division 1, 20 November 1994

Highlights were few and far between in a season which brought a return to the nether reaches. Everything had seemed so different when Joe Jordan made a hero's return to Ashton Gate, inspiring City to this win over West Country rivals Swindon Town.

The upturn in mood at the club was palpable. Upon the final whistle of this dazzling televised spectacular it was as though the National Lottery had been won, leaving City's success-starved fans feeling like millionaires. Having notched up only five goals in their preceding ten games, City's second-half play in this contest was a revelation. Following a goalless opening half, Junior Bent got the show going in the 54th minute, reacting quickest when Swindon keeper Frazer Digby parried Wayne Allison's curling 25-yarder. Two minutes later Allison was on the scoresheet himself, drilling Scott

Partridge's pass into the bottom corner of the net. Keith Scott lifted Swindon with an almost immediate response, scooping the ball past Phil Kite after Paul Bodin had played him into the area. The see-saw swung City's way again just after the hour, as Bent's industry and commitment produced a cross which gave Allison a simple tap-in. It was not until the final minute that Swindon's Scott, looking yards offside, gave the margin of victory an unfair slant by forcing the ball over the line at his second attempt.

The euphoria of Jordan's return did not endure. City never recovered from the effects of losing the next six games. For Swindon, this defeat ended manager John Gorman's reign. He joined City as Jordan's assistant, but his replacement in the Swindon hot-seat – Steve McMahon – was unable to prevent the Wiltshire team taking the drop with City.

LEAGUE DIVISION 2	**1995-96**
Division 2	13th
League Cup	2nd Round
FA Cup	1st Round

When a club is relegated they often react by being in the following season's promotion chase. City, though, buck the trend. Apart from the early 1920s this has not been their experience, and it certainly was not in 1995-96, when at one stage they looked distinctly likely to suffer a second successive demotion. It was only in the second half of the season that the fans accepted that the team had the ability to keep out of the relegation zone. A run of seven matches with only one defeat, culminating in a 2-0 win at Brighton, even had City up in eleventh spot.

An unforeseen consequence of the building of the Atyeo Stand was the rapid deterioration of the Ashton Gate pitch. It was re-laid during the summer, but with the new surface needing time to bed down, this meant the cancellation of the 99th Gloucestershire Senior Professional Cup final. All pre-season friendlies had to be played away from home, too, except that with Chelsea. A crowd of 10,422 were attracted to Ashton Gate for this meeting with the Premiership side. They were rewarded by Phil Barber's 72nd-minute goal that allowed City to recover from a 0-1 first-half deficit.

With City's losing streak continuing on their return to the re-designated Second Division, pressure on the board intensified. Chairman David Russe resigned in September and his successor, Mike Fricker, faced the harsh truths of the club losing money and support. Despite the welcome sharp-shooting of David Seal, City won only one of their opening ten League games. City were next to bottom, before a welcome 4-0 home win over Hull was achieved on 14 October.

The £175,000 signing of Darren Barnard from Chelsea, and improved performances from Paul Agostino, turned things around. City began to put some form together, though it would not be until the New Year that the side began to gel. Stirring performances by Brian Tinnion and Matt Hewlett in a 1-1 draw at Wycombe in mid-December sparked an upturn in fortunes, as City only lost eight of their remaining 26 games. Paul Agostino's superb header at Twerton Park in March helped City to their first ever League win on that ground, in what to date has proved to be last local derby played there. Further victories against Wrexham, Hull and Rotherham carried City to the safety of mid-table.

City's finances were boosted by the team's pairing with Premier Division Newcastle in the second round of the League Cup, after

Did You Know?

City's most painful defeat of the 1990s? Probably in 1991 when they led Rovers 4-1 over two legs in the Rumbelows Cup. Yet City somehow lost!

they had required penalties to dispose of Colchester at the first hurdle. A 15,952 Ashton Gate crowd saw City slaughtered 0-5 by Kevin Keegan's Premiership leaders, but an improved showing in the second leg at St James' Park enabled City to hold their heads high, despite a 1-3 defeat. There was little joy or revenue to be had from the FA Cup. City went down to a first round home replay defeat by Bournemouth, despite largely dominating the action. In the cup competition for the League minnows (Auto Windscreens Shield) City lost their opening group game 0-3 at Oxford, but a 2-0 home win over Barnet was enough to clinch a meeting with Shrewsbury in the first round. No goals in 120 minutes at Gay Meadow meant a penalty shoot-out, which City lost 6-7.

Proposals to revive City's flagging fortunes were put forward in December by recently appointed director Scott Davidson. Along with fellow directors John Clapp and Bob Neale, Davidson was joined by successful local businessman John Laycock to head a new group willing to take control. The deal was concluded in March 1996. This was followed by a share issue in the summer. Fans responded by paying £457,080 for 4,854 supporters' shares, as well as purchasing season tickets, joining the new membership scheme, and participating in other fund-raising ventures. This did not prevent a loss of £686,071 being declared for the season at the AGM.

In the Football Combination, City Reserves finished thirteenth, whilst in the Somerset Premier Cup they lost 0-1 at home to Mangotsfield United at the semi-final stage. The Youths meanwhile suffered their record defeat in the FA Youth Cup when they were annihilated 0-7 by Crystal Palace on Wimbledon's old Plough Lane ground in front of a meagre gathering of 104 hardy fans.

Match of the Season 1995-96

Bristol Rovers 2 Bristol City 4

Division 2, 16 March 1996

Victory in a local derby is always cause for celebration, and City's success in this game at the adopted home of the Rovers at Twerton Park in the City of Bath was no exception. Since Rovers moved there in 1986 it had not been a happy hunting ground for City, who had failed to bag a win in seven League visits. In such circumstances

Did You Know?

After the game with WBA in April 1995 a Portaloo caught fire. The flames spread to the Covered End. The drama was more exiting than the match.

victory was therefore extremely sweet, but it was made even sweeter by the fact that it was the last derby, to date, played at this venue.

The Rovers, managed by John Ward, who would later steer City to promotion, started as favourites. But they went behind early on when Kevin Nugent squeezed the ball through keeper Andy Collett's legs. A crowd of almost 9,000 were treated to a thrilling contest that could have gone either way after Rovers' Andy Gurney fired a 16-yarder into the far corner of the net. Matt Hewlett's right-footed shot from eighteen yards, deflected in off Paul Miller, gave City the advantage on the stroke of half-time.

Shortly after the interval Rovers' Marcus Stewart saw his low shot ruled out through Peter Beadle being offside, and City took advantage seven minutes later. Martin Kuhl swept a pass out to Junior Bent on the right, and the winger's floated cross to the far-post was met Paul Agostino, who headed into the Rovers net. The other half of City's Aussie duo then made victory certain. Substitute David Seal met Hewlett's through-ball with a delightful chip that well and truly laid to rest the Twerton hoodoo. Billy Clarke's almost immediate response could not sway the final outcome.

Thus City won the 80th League derby. The overall record now read as follows: P80 W30 D27 L23 F115 A96. This was not to be a productive season for either club, the Rovers finishing tenth, three places and ten points above City. It was only the 25th occasion since the two clubs first met in the League in 1923 that the red and whites had finished lower than their rivals.

LEAGUE DIVISION 2	**1996-97**
Division 2	5th (play-off semi-finals)
League Cup	2nd Round
FA Cup	3rd Round

Ongoing problems with the Ashton Gate pitch saw it being re-laid yet again, this time properly, at a cost of £180,000. It looked in mint condition for City's Open Day on 21 July and was ready to stage the 99th Gloucestershire Senior Professional Cup final two weeks later. A late goal by Shaun Goater, City's new £150,000 signing from Rotherham, was enough to give City a 1-0 win over Bristol Rovers in what was probably the last such contest. Neither club was keen to carry on this local tradition, which had commenced back in 1887-88, though they agreed that their Reserves should compete for the Gloucestershire Senior Challenge Cup, which had been contested by the clubs in the north of the county since 1936-37.

Come May it was unfortunate that City concluded their official Centenary season without any other trophy. Reaching the promotion play-offs, things looked bright when they were paired with a Brentford side that appeared to have gone off the boil. The Bees, though, came good at the right time, beating City 2-1 in both legs.

An inauspicious opening to the season had brought only one win from the first five games, including a 3-3 draw at Torquay in the League Cup. The debut of former QPR winger Greg Goodridge, who cost just £50,000, brought Ashton Gate to its feet as City grabbed a 5-0 win over Luton. The signing of the inspirational Shaun Taylor from Swindon for £100,000 in early September lit the spark under City's season.

After beating Torquay by the barest margin in the second leg of the League Cup, City had the daunting task of facing First Division leaders Bolton in round two. Following a goalless draw at Ashton Gate, few gave City a chance at Burnden Park, but a goal from Owers kept City in the hunt, and it needed extra-time before Bolton eventually won 3-1.

In the League, City only lost four out of twenty games by the time the third round of the FA Cup came around. Wins against Swansea and St Albans took them to Chesterfield. A feeble display was answered by a 0-2 defeat to a side destined to become only the fifth lower division club to reach the semi-finals – a fact that, to City fans, served only to demonstrate what might have been. Also in January City's venture into the Auto Windscreens Shield got under away. While Owers' goal was enough to win their first round tie at Swansea, Goater's strike at Watford was not enough to avert a 1-2 defeat.

Did You Know?

When Sunderland won 6-1 in the Rumbelows Cup in 1990, it was City's worst home defeat since 1949. But Sunderland had 7 shots on target: City had 10!

Dismissal from the cups affected League form, and seven of the next thirteen games were lost. Among the successes during this otherwise barren spell was a 2-1 victory over Bristol Rovers on their Memorial ground home which they shared with Bristol Rugby Club. The small group of selected City fans had to travel by arranged transport from Ashton Gate, but the inconvenience was forgotten as goals by Agostino and Goater earned the win. Jordan was unable to bathe in the glow of victory for long: losing the next two games brought the curtain down on his second managerial spell at the club.

Jordan's sacking was no surprise as he had been under pressure all season. It was widely predicted that had the team lost at Millmoor in mid-September he would have been dismissed there and then. Rotherham duly went two goals up, but Owers saved the manager's bacon with a 25-yarder followed by an easy header.

Former Rovers boss John Ward was selected as Jordan's replacement. Ward was at the time assistant to Adrian Heath at Burnley, but no obstacles were put on his leaving and he took over at Ashton Gate four days after Jordan's dignified departure. Ward had easily topped the local *Evening Post* poll for the fans' choice as boss, ahead of such names as Gary Mabbutt, David Webb, Mel Machin, Sammy McIlroy and John Rudge.

In the interim, coach Gerry Sweeney took charge for City's visit to Crewe, where he oversaw a 2-1 win. Ward's first match in charge brought a 0-1 home defeat by Gillingham, but he roused his troops for an assault on the play-offs, the semi-finals of which were secured thanks to five successive wins.

The first leg with Brentford was played at a monsoonal Ashton Gate, when City were caught cold by Brentford's adventurous start. Marcus Bent went close for the visitors when his shot shaved a post, and his eighth-minute overhead kick needed a smart save from Welch. It was no surprise when Paul Smith gave Brentford the lead six minutes later by ramming in a shot to Welch's right. City clawed their way back into contention with a glancing header from Owers that went in off a post, but on the half-hour Rob Taylor restored Brentford's advantage by flicking in a header from Gus Hurdle's cross. This ended the scoring, though City felt they had cause to rue referee Uriah Rennie's readiness to let the game flow – despite several bone-crunching challenges – as they had three penalty appeals turned down.

The second leg was at Griffin Park three days later. To City's credit they were up for it, no doubt encouraged by Brentford's poor home form of late. On top throughout the first period, City levelled on aggregate shortly after the break when Barnard's fierce cross-shot found the corner of the net. Not long afterwards Goater might have put City ahead overall, but he failed to make proper contact with a free header. City paid dearly for the miss when Rob Taylor beat Welch with a curler on 67 minutes, and Marcus Bent ensured Brentford's participation in the final by stealing in front of Rob Edwards to fire the decisive goal.

There would be no happy ending for the Bees, who lost the Wembley final to a first-half goal to Crewe.

The Reserves' eighteenth position was above the relegation trap-door of the Football Combination, but that did not prevent them being removed from the competition, along with Bristol Rovers, Bournemouth, Cardiff and Swansea. Other clubs apparently did not relish all the travelling involved to the West Country.

In the Football Combination League Cup, City Reserves failed to qualify from their group, but they reached the final of the Somerset Premier Cup, losing 1-2 at Yeovil. The youngsters in the FA Youth Cup could do no better than win 2-1 at Leyton Orient, before losing their home match against Bournemouth 2-3.

The AGM reported a loss of £387,672, though the number of season tickets sold increased from 1,884 to 3,092.

Match of the Season 1996-97

Bristol City 2 Chesterfield 0

Division 2, 30 April 1997

A run of bad results in March brought four defeats in five games and marked the end of the road for manager Joe Jordan. His replacement, John Ward, performed wonders to take City to the play-offs.

Ward appeared undeterred by the 0-1 home loss by Gillingham that saw City down in ninth place. He engendered a new spirit in the club, both with the fans as well as the players, and a five-match undefeated spell left City poised to clinch a play-off berth. All they needed to do in this, their penultimate League fixture, was beat Chesterfield. A crowd in excess of 16,000 were lured to Ashton Gate for this vital game against the FA Cup giant-killers, who a few weeks earlier had been robbed of a place in the final by woeful refereeing, and who were themselves looking for a win to keep alive their own play-off hopes.

City tore into their opponents from the first whistle and Shaun Goater twice went close before he opened the scoring in the seventh minute, courtesy of his reliable right boot. Darren Barnard's centre had looked too deep, but Gary Owers' first-time knock-back left City's top scorer free to smash home from six yards. City were in no mood to sit back on their lead, and they had their fans in good voice as they continued to press home their attacks.

Chesterfield's Kevin Davies, subject to a £350,000 bid by City earlier in the year, rarely threatened. Instead it was giant striker Andy Morris who caused most problems. Keith Welch did well to tip his 30-yarder over for a corner before City doubled their lead. In the 38th minute Goater's attempted cross from the corner of the six-yard box was adjudged to have been handled by defender Sean Dyche, and Darren Barnard sent former City keeper Andy Leaning the wrong way from the spot.

Gary Owers almost made it three: his cheeky lob had the back-peddling keeper at full-stretch to tip the ball over. Goater then saw his back-heeled effort cleared off the line by Jonathan Howard as City ended the first half in as much control as anyone could remember at the halfway stage of a major game. It was low tempo thereafter, as City were content to protect their lead, but great were the scenes at the final whistle as the fans celebrated as though promotion had already been achieved.

The euphoria was not to last. City's winning impetus was lost with a 0-2 defeat in the final League fixture at Wycombe three days later. Brentford took full advantage in the play-offs.

LEAGUE DIVISION 2	**1997-98**
Division 2	2nd (Promoted)
League Cup	2nd Round
FA Cup	2nd Round

Following the late run to make the play-offs the previous season, the fans' confidence of success this term was shared by the bookies, who installed City among the promotion favourites. The signings of wing-back Mickey Bell from Wycombe for £150,000, defender Sean Dyche (£275,000 Chesterfield), as well as strikers Colin Cramb (£250,000 Doncaster) and Steve Torpey (£400,000 Swansea) upped expectations. Despite early hiccups that sparked demonstrations against the team's style of play, a tactical rethink by boss Ward set City on their way to a return to the First Division. Promotion was achieved with aplomb, with some five games remaining. The only disappointment in the minds of supporters was the sale of ace striker Shaun Goater to Manchester City on the eve of the transfer deadline. His departure was reckoned to be the major factor that denied the club the championship.

League action commenced at sun-drenched Grimsby, where Torpey's crisp shot on the turn put City ahead. A sickening clash of heads shortly afterwards ended his involvement, and Grimsby came back strongly. Keith Welch pulled off vital saves, but was powerless to stop Tommy Widdrington's equaliser. With Ward keeping faith with his preferred 5-3-2 formation for the first home game, the fans were not best pleased, despite a 2-0 success over Blackpool.

For the time being Ward persisted with his unpopular system, but it brought only one win from the subsequent five games. The fans erupted in protest after witnessing a dire 1-1 draw with Bournemouth which dumped City in nineteenth place. At first, Ward was content to tinker with the problem – introducing mercurial winger Greg Goodridge for the next game, a 3-0 home win over Luton – but he was not ready to jettison the 5-3-2 philosophy. It was not until three matches later, at half-time in the home match with York, that he finally switched to 4-4-2.

With the team suffering just one defeat in seven matches since mid-September, the fans were in good heart with a goalless draw at Walsall, but a 2-0 win at Millwall heralded even better fortunes, as City embarked on their longest winning run since their promotion campaign of 1905-06.

A run of nine successive victories (eight in the League) was ended only by a 0-1 reverse at Bournemouth in the FA Cup. A 1-1 draw in the top of the table clash at Watford a week later enabled City to maintain their long unbeaten League tag. Victories over

Chesterfield and Millwall then extended this run to eleven games before City were shot down at Craven Cottage by big spending Fulham at the end of the year.

Undeterred, City responded with a 4-1 home thrashing of rivals Grimsby, a result that took City to the top for the first time. City's reign was short: a goalless home draw with Northampton knocked them off their perch, but it was not until a three-match winless spell in February that alarm bells started ringing, especially as they had scored only three goals in six games.

It took Mickey Bell's second-half penalty to get the show back on the road in an otherwise mediocre performance at York. A 2-0 home win over Bristol Rovers that took City back to the top in mid-March convinced the sceptics that promotion was within the team's grasp. However, it was not until Grimsby's failure to win at Wycombe on 10 April that the dream was realised.

In the meantime, the decision to accept Manchester City's £500,000 offer for Shaun Goater was clearly taken over Ward's head. He brought in Oldham's Sean McCarthy and Jason Roberts from Wolves on loan. With McCarthy taking over from Goater, City's away fixture with Wycombe looked like being pivotal to the team's promotion chances. City responded well, with Cramb's two strikes earning a nail-biting 2-1 victory.

City's next fixture was at Oldham, in front of the Sky cameras. Roberts played from the start, but despite scoring and playing his part in City's win, he was back on the bench for the fixture with Carlisle. Disillusioned, he headed off without permission to play for Grenada in an international tournament, as a consequence of which Ward made the mistake of discounting him from his future plans. A 1-0 home win over Carlisle disguised the loss of this fine prospect. But as City toiled with the less mobile McCarthy up front, a mere four points from their last five games cost them dear. In mitigation, City could point to Lady Luck deserting them when a fierce equalising 'goal' by Adam Locke (a free-transfer signing from Colchester) was disallowed at Burnley. In the circumstances, it was just as well that Grimsby lent a helping hand at Wycombe.

Whilst the Championship was beyond recall, nothing could hide the fact that this had been a great season. A League double over Bristol Rovers, not to mention a 2-1 aggregate success over them in the League Cup, followed by a 2-1 home win over Premiership Leeds, meant City had some prized scalps under their belts. In the Auto Windscreens Shield, City beat Millwall before losing at Bournemouth. The Cherries were the only blot on City's season. Thrice City lost at Dean Court, whilst at Ashton Gate in the League Steve Robinson's late goal earned Bournemouth a deserved point.

Did You Know?

At Millwall in 1997 Shaun Goater started with a brace on his teeth and a face swollen on one side. Millwall ensured he got a whack on the other side too.

To celebrate a remarkable season, thousands of fans took to the streets on 3 May to applaud their heroes on an open-top bus tour of the city. It concluded with a civic reception at the Council House, where the players were presented with the Runners-Up Shield and medals. The occasion took a bizarre twist when they were given the wrong medals, receiving those earmarked for the First Division runners-up. Nor were the team the only ones at Bristol City with something to celebrate. Groundsman Steve Drew scooped the coveted Groundsman of the Year award for the Second Division.

With the demise of the Gloucestershire Senior Professional Cup, City Reserves contested what had been the northern competition (Gloucestershire Senior Challenge Cup). Overcoming Cheltenham via a penalty shoot-out, they demolished Bristol Rovers 6-0 (Cramb scoring all six), before beating Forest Green Rovers 2-1 in the Ashton Gate final in front of 590 spectators. The Reserves also annexed the South West Trophy League Championship, beating Bristol Rovers 3-0 in the two-legged final. The Youths disposed of Torquay and Swansea in the FA Youth Cup, but found Arsenal too strong in the third round, losing 1-3.

Match of the Season 1997-98

Bristol City 1 Watford 1

Division 2, 13 April 1998

City blew it in this Easter Monday game. They badly needed to win to pull the rug from under Watford's relentless surge for the Championship. You would not have sensed the urgency, though, as City performed as though a second draw with the Hornets this season would be good enough. Lack of ambition is always corrosive, and the City players would have to pay heavily for theirs.

Sure, City had some excuses. They lost inspirational captain Shaun Taylor in the 37th minute with knee ligament damage that was to sideline him for almost twelve months. They had also lost star striker Shaun Goater, in his case by being sold a month previously. But attitute is everything, and City demonstrated that they lacked that priceless commodity on a pudding of a pitch that two days earlier had been cut up badly by the England Monarchs American Football team.

No quarter was given during the early exchanges in front of the division's largest crowd of the season. City forced two early corners and twice went close to scoring, but having weathered the storm Watford stepped up a gear and began to impose themselves. Tommy Mooney had Watford's best chance of the first half, but his effort was cleared off the line by Louis Carey.

After the break, Colin Cramb went close for City when his back-header hit the bar, but Watford hit back and Peter Kennedy's left-footed effort was blocked by Keith Welch. City were not so fortunate on 64 minutes when Alan Hazan's cross was met by a fierce close-range strike by Kennedy. Welch saved, but Jason Lee thumped in the rebound. Four minutes later City levelled thanks to Welsh international Rob Edwards, who steered the ball home from inside the six-yard box. Though City enjoyed territorial control for the rest of the game they never looked capable of bagging a winner. For Watford, the point clinched promotion and set them on course for the Championship.

In the next game at Chesterfield, Brian Tinnion had to take over between the sticks in place of the injured Welch. City's 0-1 defeat left Watford a point behind with a game in hand. With both clubs winning their penultimate fixtures, the destination of the title went to the wire. The Hornets won a potentially difficult game at Fulham, while City failed against mid-table Preston at Deepdale. Yet again a Championship had been tossed away.

The following season Watford demonstrated their worth, gaining promotion to the Premier League via the play-offs. City meanwhile returned from whence they came. Their players proved unequal to the demands of the higher level, though the club did not exactly help matters when ridding themselves of their popular and successful manager and bringing in Benny Lennartsson in his place.

LEAGUE DIVISION 1	**1998-99**
Division 1	24th (Relegated)
League Cup	2nd Round
FA Cup	3rd Round

Many City fans spent the summer dreaming of further promotion as the club splashed out on new players, helped by the financial input of former City Chairman Archie Gooch, who returned to the board after a sixteen-year absence. The new intake included Ade Akinbiyi (a club record fee of £1.2 million from Gillingham), Tony Thorpe (£800,000 Fulham), Carl Hutchings (£130,000 Brentford), Julian Watts (a free from Leicester), Danish international Soren Andersen (£410,000 Aalborg), and Moldovan international Ivan Tistimetanu (£500,000 FC Zimbru). The only player to move on was Gary Owers, who signed for Notts County.

Despite all this new blood, City's early form was disappointing. With hindsight, perhaps the 0-5 pre-season maulings at the hands of Aalborg and Borussia Monchengladbach should have alerted the club that it was not going to be easy to build on the previous season's promotion.

A 2-2 draw in the opening Division One game, at home to Oxford, was fair reward, but the rot started in the next game, when a last-minute equaliser at Queens Park Rangers robbed City of two points. Despite beating Shrewsbury 7-4 on aggregate to progress to the second round of the Worthington Cup, it was not until 26 September, when Crewe were annihilated 5-2 at Ashton Gate, that City gained their first three-point haul – in the process avenging Crewe's Worthington Cup victory a few days previously.

In the meantime, manager John Ward was showing increasing signs of desperation. Following the 1-3 defeat at Ipswich he went on record as saying that he was running out of alternatives. Thinking he needed help, the club appointed 55-year-old Swedish coach Benny Lennartsson as Director of Coaching, who took up his duties on 28 October. His appointment came as a surprise to the shareholders who had attended City's AGM just six days previously, when a loss of £312,799 was declared for season 1997-98 – despite an increase in the number of season ticket holders to 5,500.

Ward, who had been asked by the board back in September to come up with some suitable candidates for the new coaching position, had recommended the ex-Queens Park Rangers manager Ray Harford. The board, in its infinite wisdom, decided that they preferred a continental coach. With the impending announcement of Lennartsson's appointment, Ward felt that he had no option other than to resign.

Did You Know?

When City lost 0-4 at Bury in 1996, disgusted fans were barred from leaving 30 minutes early. One of them phoned local radio about being imprisoned!

Ward's final match in charge was a thrilling 2-1 Ashton Gate win over Bolton, when City's vibrant play gave every indication of a return to form. But all this had been scattered to the winds by the time of Lennartsson's first game at Bradford City eight days later. City's motorway journey north on the Friday before the game lasted nine hours, but there could be no excuse for the team's lack of application on the pitch, which resulted in a 0-5 whitewash. Sadly, such displays became the norm, even though Lennartsson tried his best to convince the fans that City were getting better.

The 1-6 home thrashing by Wolves in the next game undermined confidence even further, and despite a fortunate 2-0 win over a Sheffield United side missing eight regulars – which brought Lennartsson his first success – City rarely threatened to escape from the jaws of relegation. The diversion of the FA Cup brought another meeting with Everton, who by coincidence had won at Ashton Gate during City's last relegation season four years previously. This time Everton doubled their victory margin to 2-0, with City paying a heavy price for missing their chances.

Another last-minute goal prevented City taking all three points that their play at West Brom would have deserved, but the real damage was done by an injury to their Moldovan international Ivan Tistimetanu, which was to keep him out for the rest of the season. With Welch out of form and – following City's 2-4 defeat at Birmingham in late November – out of favour, the services of Bo Andersen, touted as one of the best continental keepers, was secured from Lyngby. In the event, the useful form of reserve Steve Phillips kept the Dane out in the cold until the end of March. By then, City had virtually thrown in the towel, though the loan signing of David Howells from Southampton had helped concoct a mini-revival. His super strike against Port Vale helped the team to a 2-0 win and sparked two further victories off the cuff. Nine points from three games, but City needed more of the same. A 0-1 loss at Bolton left the club without a prayer. Following three successive defeats, a debut goal by Lorenzo Pinamonte against Norwich at least allowed City to bow out of the First Division on a winning note.

Paradoxically, a season that ended in relegation also saw City field a club record number of six full internationals. These were Rob Edwards (Wales), Greg Goodridge (Barbados), Soren Andersen

(Denmark), Ivan Tistimetanu (Moldova), Jim Brennan (Canada) and Vilmos Sebok (Hungary). City reserve Jehad Muntasser had even represented Libya. Vilmos, who had been signed for £200,000 from Ujpest Dozsa, notched a hat-trick in Hungary's 5-0 home win over Liechtenstein in March, and also played in the away draw in Slovakia and in the 1-1 draw with England in Budapest.

In the midst of City's gloom, fans were for a while distracted by news of the club's plans to relocate to a new stadium on the site of the old Whitchurch Airport at Hengrove Park. With the proposed cost of redeveloping Ashton Gate estimated to be in the region of £25 million, the City board calculated that it would be more cost effective to build a new stadium elsewhere. With that in mind, an approach was made to the Bristol City Council about the feasibility of finding an alternative home. The Council put forward Hengrove Park as a suitable venue, upon which the club formally confirmed their interest.

However, whilst the proposed new ground has been earmarked as a possible World Cup venue, should England secure the 2006 nomination, there is still – as of January 2000 – no indication as to whether planning permission for this stadium will be granted. If that remains the case by the end of the 1999-2000 season, Bristol City will remain at Ashton Gate and commence the first phase of redevelopment with a proposed £15 million West Stand to replace the Williams Grandstand.

Season 1998-99 also marked the first season of City's Youth Academy, as part of the new FA School of Excellence scheme. Their Under-19 side finished sixth, whilst the Under-17s were runners-up in their League, but lost 1-2 at Sunderland in the third round of the FA Youth Cup. The Reserves, who played a series of friendlies throughout the season, were knocked out at the semi-final stage of the Gloucestershire Senior Challenge Cup. At the end of the season a City Under-20 side took part in the Groningen Championships, but after failing to qualify for the semi-finals from their group they were cheered by having won the Fair Play Award.

Match of the Season 1998-99

Sunderland 1 Bristol City 1

Division 1, 8 September 1998

Having won promotion and invested heavily in new players during the summer, City fans were upbeat. In the event, this miserable campaign mirrored that of 1923-24, when relegation followed promotion in the shortest possible time.

As early as September it was evident City faced hard times, but against championship favourites Sunderland at the Stadium of Light they at least upset a few pundits. City's surprise draw suggested that the happy hunting they often enjoyed at Sunderland's old Roker Park (four wins and seven draws in nineteen visits) might well have been transferred to the Wearsider club's new home.

The facilities at the Stadium of Light, compared to those at Ashton Gate, were enough in themselves to give City an inferiority complex. And this is how it came across in this live game on Sky TV. Without a win in their opening six games, City were overrun as John Ward's defensive ploy – leaving Ade Akinbiyi alone up front – seemed sure to bring disaster. Keith Welch's inspired display of goalkeeping kept Sunderland at bay. Welch even saved Kevin Phillips' 24th-minute spot-kick, but by then City trailed 0-1. Welch had been helpless to prevent Phillips's opener – a first-time shot into the roof of the net for his sixth goal of the season.

City's slight improvement after the break at least created some half-chances, but Welch was still by far the busier keeper. With time running out, most of City's travelling support seemed satisfied that the margin of defeat was at least respectable. But substitute Soren Andersen had other ideas. Collecting a pass from Mickey Bell on the left, Andersen swivelled and hammered in an unstoppable shot past Sunderland keeper Thomas Sorensen. It brought City their luckiest and most unexpected point of the season.

Whilst this slight setback did not deflate Sunderland, who dropped only six points at home all season on their way to the Championship, the result did nothing to encourage the Robins. Ward watched from afar as City finished bottom of the League.

7

IN A RUT
1999-2005

LEAGUE DIVISION 2	**1999-2000**
Division 2	9th
League Cup	2nd Round
FA Cup	3rd Round

Despite the club giving the impression that they would be sticking by Lennartsson, it was no surprise when a new manager was appointed, on 5 July, though the choice provoked howls of protest. This was partly due to his connections with Bristol Rovers, for whom he boasted an eight-year playing career, but mainly because of concerns over the inglorious football his sides had been known to play. Ex-Gillingham and Bournemouth boss Tony Pulis, sacked by the Gills five days earlier, was apparently the man supporters were asked to believe would take City onward and upward.

Graffiti condemning the ugly football they might have to endure was soon dubbed on walls near Ashton Gate, but with Pulis demonstrating a welcome trait of seemingly telling things the way they were, most fans were optimistic of a quick return to Division One. Even the bookmakers had the Robins marked as second favourites. 'Shape up or ship out' was Pulis's maxim.

With City having adopted the now-familiar squad numbering system, a defensive approach in the first half of the League opener at Reading's Madejski Stadium did little to endear Pulis to City's long-suffering travelling fans. As the team struggled throughout the early part of the season, criticism intensified. However, the bullish attitude adopted by Pulis at the club's AGM (in the sports hall of St George Community School on 28 October) won over most of the 500 shareholders present. Chairman Scott Davidson ignored one supporter's comments that City's football was the worse he had seen in fifteen years of supporting the club, whilst many felt, as was voiced by another fan, that what had been a fantastic club under Ward had 'lost it big-time'. The directors explained their reasons for hiving the ground and stadium at Ashton Gate into a separate subsidiary company, whilst a record loss of £2,352,643 was revealed in respect of the club's workings for the year ending 31 May 1999.

The sale of Akinbiyi – despite previous contrary assurances – to Wolves for a record Football League fee of £3.5 million was a blow, as was that of Canadian international wing-back Jim Brennan to Forest for £1.5 million. His loss was covered by the presence of Mickey Bell but the signings of Steve Jones from Charlton (£500,000) and ex-Rover Peter Beadle (£200,000) from Notts County did little to fill the hole left by Akinbiyi's departure, after returning from international duty for Nigeria, when injury cost him a cap.

Tistimetanu made a welcome return from his long lay-off following injury, and much was expected from loanee 20-year-old Tommy Black from Arsenal, who debuted in a goalless home draw against Wycombe Wanderers as Man of the Match.

Though City ended the first half of season undefeated on their own ground, spectators endured some terrible home displays. Eight draws and fifteen goals scored in twelve games tells its own story. On their travels, two wins and eleven goals didn't enhance prospects for the second half of the campaign. Highlights were few and far between, the laying of the Bournemouth hoodoo in the FA Cup being the most laudable achievement, though City's best form was reserved for the 0-0 derby against Rovers. Another 'highlight' was a World Cup match at Ashton Gate. This, though, was for the Rugby Union code when, on 3 October, New Zealand beat Tonga 45-9 in front of a 22,000 crowd.

Apart from the Auto Windscreens Shield, City's cup interests ended quickly. In the League Cup, City succumbed to Nottingham Forest. This season, for the first and only time, the 3rd round of the FA Cup was scheduled for December not January, and saw City lose 0-1 at Sheffield Wednesday.

Against this background, many fans felt relief when in January Pulis left to become manager at Portsmouth. Chief Scout Tony Fawthrop, aided by David Burnside and Leroy Rosenior, took over in a caretaker capacity. Restoring Tony Thorpe to the side brought an impressive victory at Bournemouth, and it wasn't until 4 March that City suffered their first League defeat of 2000, when third-placed Millwall's 4-1 win shattered play-off hopes. Substitute Brian Tinnion shone in the 2-2 home draw with Stoke to get City back on track, but whilst four wins and a draw from their last seven games secured a ninth-place finish, the Reds were well short of a play-off spot, some eighteen points off the pace.

The Auto Windcreens Shield proved to be the season's saving grace. City opened up by beating Cheltenham 3-1 on 12 January and followed this with a 4-1 penalty shoot-out success following a

1-1 draw at home to Bournemouth. Victories over Reading and Exeter carried City through to a final with Stoke at Wembley.

Fawthrop was rewarded by being appointed manager on 6 May, a decision that exposed a rift in the seven-man City board. Split 4-3, Chairman Scott Davidson said he would have preferred the club to have set their sights a bit higher. Hardly a ringing endorsement for the new manager, but worse was to come with allegations of Fawthorp being a director of a failed company with debts of £200,000. After just twenty days in charge, he quit, citing family considerations, to become the club's football co-ordinator. Davidson was ousted as chairman and was replaced by John Laycock.

The Reserves did well in the Avon Insurance Combination Championship, but finished fifth, seven points behind winners Millwall. Success came in the Somerset Premier Cup, with Bath beaten 3-2 in the final at Clevedon's Town ground at the Hand Stadium. In the FA Academy, City reached the play-offs at Under-19 level, after finishing Group D in third place. They then lost on penalties to Manchester United after a 1-1 draw. In the Under-17 League they did even better, finishing runners-up to Arsenal before a 2-1 victory over Spurs took them into the second round of the play-offs, when they lost 2-3 to Leicester. In the FA Youth Cup, City reached the third round after disposing of Forest Green Rovers 4-0 and Plymouth 2-1, before going out 1-2 at Manchester City. The 30th season of the FA Women's Cup saw City beat Oxford and Corfe Hills United 3-2 and 5-4 respectively, before losing 0-2 at home to Tottenham.

Match of the Season 1999-2000

Stoke City 2 Bristol City 1

Auto Windscreens Shield final, 16 April 2000

This was one of the last games at Wembley before the demolition of the famous twin towers. Tinnion was unable to reproduce the form he displayed in the recent Ashton Gate League meeting between the sides, but it was a good final, exemplified by the humour exhibited between opposing fans. Stoke were keen to win in memory of the recently deceased Sir Stanley Matthews, whilst City were keen to make up for dropping out of play-off contention.

Stoke gave impetus to their promotion quest by winning at Wembley for the second time in eight years. City, who had claimed their third final appearance, had cause for complaint over Stoke's winner – a quickly taken free-kick reminiscent of England's leveller, headed in by Hurst, in the 1966 World Cup final.

Did You Know?

The 75,057 crowd at Wembley for the 1999-2000 Auto Windscreens Shield is the largest ever gathering to watch a match involving Bristol City.

Lack of interest in the early rounds has often been compensated by good crowds at the finals of a tourney which started life as the Associate Members Cup, before various sponsorship deals saw it periodically renamed. Today's 75,057 gathering had only been bettered by the 80,841 who attended the Wolves v Burnley clash twelve seasons earlier.

City, in gold and black as Stoke turned out in their traditional red and white stripes, found themselves under early pressure. On 28 minutes Tinnion sent Aaron Brown free, to no avail, and four minutes later Andrew Jordan's clearance unluckily found Stoke's Graham Kavanagh, who skipped around Scott Murray and Louis Carey before burying the ball into the net.

In the second half Murray felt he should have had a penalty, and Paul Holland's thunderbolt was turned over before the equaliser came in the 74th minute. Tinnion's corner was met by the inrushing Holland, the ball flying in off Damian Spencer, who had come on seven minutes earlier for the injured Brown.

For a spell City looked the more likely winners. Spencer spurned two good chances – nodding wide at the back post from Murray's cross and then, when Thorpe passed back to him in acres of space, tried to finish spectacularly but ended up on his backside.

After conceding a free-kick, Carey had his back to the ball, back-chatting referee Kevin Lynch, when Mickael Hansson lifted the ball over for Kavanagh, whose flick on was steered home for the winning goal by Peter Thorne in the 82nd minute.

Stoke fan Sue Forster commented: 'City will complain about the winner, but it was just quick thinking on our part. I think they were more annoyed at themselves for dozing off. City did play well and it was a good game. They probably did have the better of the second-half, but we took our chances.'

City: Mercer; Carey (Amankwaah 86), Bell, Jordan, Millen, Tinnion; Murray, Holland, Thorpe, Beadle, Brown A (Spencer 67).

Stoke: Ward; Hansson, Clarke; Mohan, Gunnarsson, O'Connor; Gudjonsson, Kavanagh, Lightbourne (Iwelumo 89), Thorne, Gunnlaugsson (Dryden 61).

City claimed swift revenge, of sorts, when, for the second time, Ashton Gate's Steve Drew was named Division Two's top groundsman, beating off the challenge of Stoke City and Oxford United.

LEAGUE DIVISION 2	**2000-01**
Division 2	9th
League Cup	1st Round
FA Cup	5th Round

The resignation from the Board of former chairman Scott Davidson, as well as directors John Clapp and Bob Neale, coincided with the appointment of Danny Wilson (ex-Barnsley and Sheffield Wednesday) as manager on 28 June. Pledging to play attractive, passing and winning football, it was a message to delight City's long-suffering fans. As it turned out, they were not to be disappointed, even though the season was a rollercoaster affair, delighting, confusing and, at times, frustrating.

The usual round of friendlies, which saw Nottingham Forest beaten 3-2 in front of a 4,499 Ashton Gate crowd on 26 July got the new regime under way. Defeats at Dorchester and Chester and at home to Charlton and Wimbledon had the fans fearing the worst, especially as goalkeeper Billy Mercer's continuing injury problems had him ruled out. Alan Miller arrived on loan from Blackburn, and with new signings Mark Lever from Grimsby and £600,000 striker Lee Peacock (Manchester City), goals from Tony Thorpe and Paul Holland set the campaign off with victory at the Racecourse.

Four straight League defeats (three at home) were ended by a 0-0 draw at Oldham, sparking a fifteen-match unbeaten run. Scott Murray's goal at Oxford kept City off the foot of the table, and Bournemouth's Gareth O'Connor's winner postponed a first home win until 21 October – 4-0 over high-fliers Reading – marred by the broken ankle sustained by Dani Rodrigues, City's on-loan signing from Southampton. With Wilson fielding an weakened side that saw substitute Darren Jones make his only first-team appearance, the run ended with a 0-3 LDV Vans Trophy loss at Plymouth.

Beating Bury 4-1 in early December lifted City into the top six for the first time, but a 1-2 home defeat to Brentford – the third of four unsuccessful attempts against the Bees this season – and losses at Northampton and Stoke dented promotion hopes. The play-offs remained within reach, however, and an unbeaten run of six League games had City clinging onto sixth place, thanks to goals from Lee Peacock and Keith Millen which secured the double over Wrexham on 13 February.

Brentford were next up, and with the inevitable result. City were on the downward spiral once more. A 0-4 drubbing at Colchester didn't help, and it took a 2-1 home win over Millwall to steady the ship. It was too late, however, despite only three defeats in their last ten games, and City had to be content with finishing ninth.

Did You Know?

By 2007, although City have been promoted on ten occasions, they have only managed four championships – the last of which was as long ago as 1954-55.

In the League Cup, the pairing with Brentford meant that few fans were surprised by City's eventual exit after a 2-2 home draw, but the FA Cup brought more interest and a little bit of drama. After Tony Thorpe brought City success at Chesterfield, where the Third Division side had only lost once previously this season, there was back-stage drama prior to the second-round home 3-1 win over Conference side Kettering. On his way to the game, City keeper Steve Phillips wrote off his sports car in a crash at Pensford. But, more importantly, a young boy in the other vehicle was hospitalised with facial injuries. A shaken Phillips was given a lift to Ashton Gate, where his poor clearance led to the visitors opening the scoring. Second-half goals from Lee Peacock, Simon Clist and Tony Thorpe got City out of the mire.

In the next round, a 2-0 win at Huddersfield avenged the semi-final defeat by the Terriers in 1920. Luck was on City's side against Conference visitors Kingstonian in the fourth round, with Thorpe's last-minute goal earning a replay. At the Kingsmead Stadium it took Murray's soft-daisy-cutter to save City's blushes in front of the Sky television cameras and book a place in the fifth round for the first time since 1989. Despite playing some decent football at Filbert Street, City lacked the punch to challenge Premiership Leicester and lost 0-3.

City's reserve action took place in the Avon Insurance Combination, where they finished seventeenth out of 25. In the Gloucestershire Senior Challenge Cup, the Reserves reached the final, held over to the start of the following campaign, when they lost 0-1 at Cinderford. In the FA Academy, City finished bottom at Under-19 and Under-17 level. They did no better in the FA Youth Cup, losing 0-1 at Swansea in the first round. In the Women's FA Cup, City won 6-1 at Oxford before losing 0-4 at home to Bristol Rovers, who reached the semi-finals.

The season brought an end to the indoor bowls in the Dolman stand, a great loss for many of Bristol's green bowlers, who included ex-City player Pete McCall, who represented England for four years in the sport. With the departure of David Burnside, who had been responsible for the setting up of City's Academy system, Tony Fawthrop took over as Academy Director from the renowned ex-West Bromwich Albion star, who many will recall for his ball-juggling skills during the 1960s.

Match of the Season 2000-01

Bristol City 6 Cambridge United 2

Nationwide League Division 2, 1 January 2001

After suffering back-to-back defeats, City replied with this thumping New Year's Day win at home to Cambridge, but the losers were a tad unlucky.

In the early stages City gave little hope to their fans looking for a cure for their New Year hangovers. Matt Hill was fortunate when referee Scott Mathieson failed to spot his handling of John Hansen's cross, and shortly afterwards Paul Connor fired wide after City had got themselves into a right mess. Mickey Bell had hearts in mouths with a sliced clearance across the face of his own goal, and keeper Steve Phillips did well to beat away Hansen's raking drive. City were also indebted to Louis Carey for heading off the line from former Rovers striker John Taylor.

All this was forgotten as Brian Tinnion swept the ball wide to Scott Murray, who brought the ball down before finding the corner of the net with a vicious low shot. Unfortunately, the celebrations died almost as quickly as they had begun, as Hanson's ball was knocked on by Taylor for Paul Wanless to steer a looping headed equaliser.

Thankfully, the second half started better than the first. Tinnion's ball over the top released Murray to fire into the roof of the net from an acute angle. Incredibly, Cambridge again equalised – Taylor's cross from the left finding Paul Connor, who headed past Phillips. Fortunately, when Simon Clist was upended in the box by Tom Cowan, Thorpe made no mistake with the spot-kick – 3-2.

City's defensive failings were still apparent, and the home crowd sighed with relief when Connor fired over. But then Cambridge needlessly conceded a throw in, from which Brown's deep cross was volleyed in by Thorpe.

The visitors really were finished eight minutes from time when their keeper, Lionel Perez, only partially clawed out Brown's effort and Thorpe pounced to claim his second Ashton Gate hat-trick of the season. For the U's, matters got even worse when Perez was given his marching orders for handling on the edge of his own area. Peter Beadle flicked the resultant free-kick up for Tinnion to volley past reserve keeper Shaun Marshall to complete a bizarre afternoon's entertainment.

LEAGUE DIVISION 2	**2001-02**
Division 2	7th
League Cup	2nd Round
FA Cup	1st Round

A 0-1 loss at Kidderminster got the pre-season friendlies off to a poor start, and despite wins at Hereford and Yeovil, further defeats at Exeter and at home to Southampton didn't auger well.

Hardly an omen for success, City deciding to play in all red, which never served them well on previous occasions. True to form, they missed out on the play-offs, five points behind Huddersfield. The season was not without its merits, though the disappointing conclusion at Bloomfield Road tended obscure much of what had gone before.

With Tinnion and Thorpe in top form in an opening day 3-0 win at Northampton, which sparked a seven-match unbeaten run, fans optimistically talked of promotion. Unfortunately, despite showing grit and resilience to match their obvious flair and attacking dynamism, the team often flopped when the heat was on. The decision to relegate top-scorer Thorpe to the bench, following his mid-season bombshell that he would leave in the summer, didn't help City's promotion aspirations.

The London Road drubbing on 22 September raised concerns, but fears were quelled by a brilliant performance in beating Tranmere at the Gate, when first-half goals by Thorpe and Steve Jones took City up to third. A 0-1 defeat by Wycombe on 20 October was City's first at home, but it was the following month that the alarm bells really started to ring with losses against Brighton and Reading, as well as being bundled out of the FA Cup by Third Division strugglers Leyton Orient.

Apart from a 0-1 Boxing Day defeat by Port Vale on their frozen pitch, a period of consistency then followed. This saw progress in the LDV Vans trophy with a 2-0 win at Southend and a 2-1 home success over Peterborough. Livewire Matt Hill celebrated the birth of his first child with a goal in City's televised win at Swindon, but Northampton turned the formbook upside down by winning 3-1 at Ashton Gate. Further misery came with City being deprived of a place in the LDV Vans final by goalkeeper Lionel Perez, who inspired Cambridge to a 2-0 victory on 9 March.

For the crucial run in, striker Christian Roberts was signed from Exeter, which could hardly compensate for the loss of never-say-die Hill and the guile of Tinnion, through a knee injury and suspension respectively. A late goal by Brighton at the Withdean was hard to take, but hopes were raised with a 2-0 success over Bury. Sadly, the

1-5 thrashing at Blackpool, which saw many City fans exiting in disgust at half-time, was the final straw.

In the final analysis, placing the club's aspirations on the shoulders of young and inexperienced players backfired, but to blame them would be unfair as the seniors were often found wanting at crucial stages. Indeed, the emergence of Danny Coles and the progress made by Hill and Joe Burnell, as well as Tommy Doherty's return to form, gave hope for the future.

Some fans insisted that the club lacked ambition, whilst others like Tim Davey, the *Bristol Evening Post* columnist, were inwardly angry about City's failure to achieve any shred of success.

Perhaps City were hoping for funds from ITV Digital, which started transmitting live Football League matches at the start of the season. As we know, the project foundered, leaving many clubs in financial difficulties, on 30 April.

City continued to post massive losses, though quite why this should be – with the ground staging an Under-17 international, as well as rugby and other events such as *Gig at the Gate* on 25 May, when Headliners Blue and Spandau Ballet were among the performers – the limited information given in the accounts never makes clear. In subsequent years others, such as Elton John, Neil Dymond and Rod Taylor performed at the Gate, which also hosted top-flight rugby as well as annual firework displays.

In the Avon Insurance Combination, City's Reserves finished well down in 19th place, though they were destined to win both the League Cup and the Gloucestershire Senior Challenge Cup, the finals of which were held over to the following season when Luton were beaten 3-0 in the former and Cirencester Town 6-0 in the latter.

In the FA Academy Under-19 League, City finished three off the bottom of Group B with 32 points. They fared even worse in the Under-17 League – only goal-difference prevented them claiming the wooden spoon in Group A from Reading. The FA Youth Cup saw a 2-1 victory over Lowestoft Town and a 3-0 win at Potters Bar before City's youths were bundled out 0-5 at Ipswich.

The tenth season of women's football since the formation of a National League in 1992-93 saw City gain promotion after running away with the Championship of the South-West Combination, but after winning 9-1 at Bournemouth and then beating Reading 5-1 in the Women's Cup, they suffered the indignity of losing 2-6 at home to Bristol Rovers. They also lost to the Rovers, 1-4, in the final Gloucestershire Cup at Oaklands Park, Almondsbury. Another honour did come their way though, for their reserves who won the Gloucestershire County League.

Did You Know?

Tony Thorpe's 28 minute hat-trick for City at Northampton in 2001-02 was reported as being the quickest ever known at the start of a season.

Match of the Season 2001-02

Bristol City 3 Bristol Rovers 0

LDV Vans Trophy, Southern Area semi-final, 9 January 2002

Bristol derbies are seldom one-sided affairs, despite City enjoying the upper hand in recent seasons after several hard-fought and often uninspiring encounters. This, however, was different. Even though City were pre-match favourites, few die-hards fans would have expected the old enemy to be overcome so easily, with no little panache in front of 17,367 Ashton Gate crowd.

Both sides emerged to firecrackers and the sort of din that makes Bristol derbies such special occasions, the 3,000 Rovers fans massed behind the goal in the Wedlock Stand giving as good as they got. It wasn't enough, however, as City outfought and outplayed their rivals almost from the kick-off. For everyone decked out in blue and white it most have been embarrassing to see their heroes brought to earth with such a bump, following on from their sensational FA Cup victory at Premiership Derby the previous Sunday.

After Rovers forced a corner in the opening seconds, the City keeper became little more than a spectator. Scott Murray mesmerised Trevor Challis and Mike Trought with a weaving fourth-minute run that ended with the wing-back dragging his shot wide. Aaron Brown also got the chance to demonstrate his speed, one surging run leaving the Rovers skipper Lewis Hogg for dead before forcing a corner, and another a cross that saw Tommy Doherty connect with a glancing off-target header.

With Mickey Bell pushing forward outside Brown on the left, it was all City, especially as their tenacious defenders kept Nathan Ellington and Kevin Gall under wraps. The breakthrough came on the half-hour. Striker Lee Matthews, still short of full-match fitness, gathered possession on the left before charging towards goal and finishing with a right-footed shot that flew in off a post.

Even at this stage a Rovers recovery seemed improbable, whist a second City goal seldom looked far away. Ellington, Rovers' hat-trick hero at Derby, raised derisory cheers when his flat drive almost struck the corner flag. Cautions for Dwayne Plummer and Trevor Challis for fouls on Matthew Hill and Murray respectively illustrated Rovers' frustrations before City doubled their advantage.

Right on the interval Joe Burnell won a midfield tussle that saw the ball break to Matthews, who motored goalwards and again finished emphatically, this time with a left-footer into the far corner.

Four minutes into the second half City's victory was tied up when Matthews caused havoc on the edge of the box and set up Bell, who cut inside before firing a beauty high into the net with his less-favoured right foot. City kept up the pressure and the 68th-minute booking of substitute Martin Cameron completed a night of misery for the Rovers.

City: Phillips; Amankwaah, Hill; Burnell, Coles, Doherty (Tinnion 50); Murray (Rodrigues 83), Matthews, Peacock, Brown A, Bell (Lever 71).

Rovers: Howie; Smith, Challis; Foran, Trought, Hogg; Plummer, Shore, Gall (Bubb 75), Ellington, Ommel (Cameron 64).

Referee: David Crick (Surrey).

LEAGUE DIVISION 2	**2002-03**
Division 2	3rd (play-off semi-finals)
League Cup	1st Round
FA Cup	3rd Round

Those who waited until the start of the campaign to purchase their season tickets found themselves paying £288 for the Atyeo Stand and £340 for the Williams and Dolman. This was about 20 per cent more than the price offered at the end of the previous season.

Pre-season friendlies saw a 0-1 defeat by Yeovil on Dorchester's ground and a 0-3 loss at home to Ipswich. A 1-1 draw at Tiverton, as well as 1-0 and 5-0 successes at Exeter and Hereford respectively had City ready for the big kick-off.

Blackpool, who had often proved troublesome over recent years, were first up. A home crowd of 11,891 compared badly with City's post-war record attendance of 42,594 when Blackpool visited in the FA Cup in 1958-59. Then they had silky skills and Stanley Matthews, now they were brawn and muscle. Fittingly, their strong-arm tactics failed them. They had two players sent off and lost to goals from Lee Peacock and Scott Murray.

Defeats followed at Brentford and Wigan before City got into gear. However, on 14 September, thanks in part to a wonder strike by Lee Matthews at Cheltenham, they occupied an automatic promotion spot. Two days later John Laycock stood down as chairman and was replaced by Stephen Lansdown.

Losses at Oldham and Queens Park Rangers dropped City down to ninth, before a nineteen-match unbeaten run (fourteen League, two FA Cup, three LDV Vans Trophy) carried the team through the rest of 2002 and up to second. It might have been different had the weather not intervened when City were losing at home to Notts County on 2 November. Anyway, a 1-2 loss at Wycombe put City on skid row for eight matches and it wasn't until 22 February that the next win came, 2-1 at Northampton.

The catalyst for change came in the shape of ex-Manchester United striker Mark Robins, who City signed on loan from Rotherham. He inspired a revival during his one-month spell and it was unfortunate that, due to Rotherham's goalscoring problems, he wasn't allowed to extend his time at Ashton Gate. Even so, with only five points dropped in City's last eight games an automatic promotion spot was almost claimed. It was the 1-1 draw at Crewe and the 0-2 defeat at Chesterfield in the penultimate game that did for City's chances. The dismissal of Tony Butler and Aaron Brown certainly didn't help City's cause at Saltergate, where they were beaten by two goals in the dying minutes.

Did You Know?

City have one of the best records in what was originally known as the Associate Members Cup. Four times finalists, they won the trophy in 1985-86 and 2002-03.

In the play-offs for the first time since 1996-97, City were confronted by Cardiff in the semi-final. Given that City hadn't lost a Severnside derby for 32-years, the fans were confident of success, but were less optimistic after Cardiff's 1-0 win at Ninian Park. At Ashton Gate, Wilson's side proved unable to find the net when it mattered most. Despite topping 100 goals through the season, a goalless draw ensued.

A disappointing outcome, but a successful campaign for all that, especially in the cups. Losing 0-1 in the first round of the League Cup to Oxford, City rattled up double figures in the FA Cup – 7-0 at Heybridge Swifts and 3-1 at Harrogate Railway – to set up a trip to Leicester's new Walkers Stadium. City spurned the chances to win this oddly low-key cup-tie and succumbed 0-2.

In the LDV Vans Trophy, though it took a 112th-minute 'golden goal' by Danny Coles to secure victory at Boston on 13 November. Wins over Wycombe, Bournemouth, and Cambridge followed, before Carlisle provided the opposition in the final at Cardiff's Millennium Stadium. City were clear favourites, as Carlisle were struggling near the bottom of Division Three. In fact, City struggled in front of a 50,913 crowd on 6 April before late goals from Lee Peacock and substitute Liam Rosenior brought success.

In the Avon Insurance Combination, City's reserves finished seventh, nine points behind champions Crystal Palace. Their best chance of silverware came in the Gloucestershire Senior Cup, but after reaching the final they crashed to a 0-1 defeat at Mangotsfield United. Former City striker David Seal scored the winner from the spot, but it was the 32nd-minute sending off of Liam Rosenior by Premiership referee Steve Dunn that did for City's chances. In the FA Academy Under-19 League, City finished bottom of Group C. They performed better at Under-17 level, finishing sixth. In the FA Youth Cup, a 5-3 first round success over Swansea ushered in a 0-1 defeat at Cambridge United.

The Women's contingent finished third in the Southern Division, seventeen points behind champions Bristol Rovers, who clinched a place in the top flight for the first time. In the Womens FA Cup the Millwall Lionesses were dispatched 2-0 before City lost 3-4 on penalties to Oldham Curzon following a 1-1 draw. Granted a place in the Women's Premier League Cup – which started in 1992-93 – City lost 2-5 at home to Aston Villa in the preliminary round.

Match of the Season 2002-03

Mansfield Town 4 Bristol City 5

Nationwide League Division 2, 23 November 2002

City have been involved in amazing games over the years, but this must surely take the biscuit. With just four minutes remaining at Field Mill, the Robins staged the mother of all fightbacks to turn a 2-4 deficit into a most unlikely victory.

In the first half there was little indication of what was to come, though Scott Murray's rapid leveller, after Wayne Corden had side-stepped Steve Phillips to rifle in the opener, set the tempo. With Christian Roberts chipping City ahead soon after the change-around it was disappointing to see them concede a soft equaliser when defender Mark Lever – who City released in the summer – nodded the ball back for Iyseden Christie to finish from close range.

It was the Stags' award of a penalty, after Liam Lawrence fell over Coles' outstretched leg, that sparked the frantic finale. Whilst manager Danny Wilson had no complaints over the award, the City players were incensed. In the ensuing skirmish the referee first produced yellow cards, then red to dismiss midfielder Lee Williamson. The excitement continued with Steve Phillips saving Wayne Corden's spot kick, only for the same player to ram home the loose ball to make it 3-2. It appeared all up for City when Christie finished off a strong run with yet another fierce finish.

Mansfield were rocked by City's 81st-minute introduction of super-sub Leroy Lita, fresh from his two goals in the FA Cup demolition of Heybridge Swifts, and they hacked at everything as the ball pinged around their box. Lita, after being felled for Brian Tinnion's successful spot-kick, struck in the fourth minute of added time, but City were not yet done. There was still time for Roberts to blast home for a memorable victory. Euphoria for the City fans who stayed to the end, but hard luck on the many who had left early.

'Leroy is a natural,' said boss Danny Wilson. 'He is a very positive player and with his pace, as well as that of Mickey Bell, Murray and Roberts, we'll always create chances. Christian's strike to round off our terrific comeback was tremendous.'

Tempers frayed after the final whistle. Mansfield boss Stuart Wakiss, captain Neil Moore and midfielder Liam Lawrence were red-carded for subjecting referee Eddie Iderton to foul and abusive language about the extent of added time.

The *Bristol Evening Post's* Simon Parkinson noted: 'It's hard to say that City deserved this remarkable win – their forwards grabbed the headlines and not the boys at the back, who had a rare off day.'

LEAGUE DIVISION 2	**2003-04**
Division 2	3rd (play-off losing finalists)
League Cup	3rd Round
FA Cup	2nd Round Replay

A City side comprising first-teamers and reserves started the pre-season with a 4-0 win over a North & West Wilts XI at Devizes FC. Goalless draws with Leeds (home) and Team Bath (away) preceded a 5-2 win at Forest Green. Losing 0-1 at Millwall lowered the mood, but not as much as the 2-6 home thrashing by Real Mallorca.

In view of City's frequent five-yearly 'promotion and relegation cycles' it was anticipated that this would be one of those good years. Sadly, it turned out to be nearly, but not quite, though many blamed the negative tactics of Danny Wilson in the play-off final for that. Against opponents beaten 4-1 at the Withdean six months earlier it was all so unnecessary, but City should have garnered enough points to go up automatically.

The bookies almost got in right: City were joint third promotion favourites with Brighton, behind Queens Park Rangers and Sheffield Wednesday. Only the Owls failed to live up to their billing, finishing sixteenth. The surprise package were Plymouth, whose title winning odds were 20/1.

City's cause wasn't helped by the departure of player of the year Scott Murray, sold to Reading for £650,000, though he would return on transfer deadline day. Others moving on were the experienced Peter Beadle to Brentford and promising youngster Liam Rosenior, out of contract, to Fulham. Also missing from City's early games was Aaron Brown, serving a seven-match ban for successive dismissals at the end of last season.

The ranks were boosted, however, by Scottish Under-21 striker Lee Miller (£300,000 from Falkirk). With Aussie Luke Wilkshire (£250,000 from Middlesbrough) also on board, season ticket sales reached a new high of 8,000. The season started with a bang.

All seemed right with the world after a 5-0 home win over Notts County. Four days later the 5,807 crowd at the League-Cup tie with Swansea were treated to extra-time, the sending-off of Swans' Brad Maylett, and three more City goals. Extra-time was also needed against First Division Watford – a header from Miller clinching victory. Next up were Southampton, but in front of a 17,408 crowd City were unable to prevent the Premiership visitors winning 3-0.

City's early League form wasn't impressive, and they were fined £2,500 for having six players booked in a 1-2 defeat at Colchester, but home wins over Grimsby, Tranmere and Swindon, as well as at Plymouth of all places on 30 September served to keep City going.

Sadly, Plymouth extracted small revenge by dumping City out of the LDV Vans Trophy 0-4 at Home Park.

The FA Cup saw the Reds pitted against one of the famous old names of football in Bradford Park Avenue, who had lost their Football League place to Cambridge United in 1970. At their Horsfall Stadium a cup shock by the UniBond League side looked on the cards but, in front of Sky TV cameras, City recovered to win 5-2 – the same score as on their last visit to Park Avenue in 1962-63.

Wins over Brighton (4-1 away) and Barnsley (2-1 home) took City up to sixth, but before the Tykes returned in the FA Cup a 0-1 loss at Blackpool had City slipping again. They exited the FA Cup in an Oakwell replay, but a 1-0 win at Stockport sparked a renaissance. Eleven straight League wins: the tenth saw City top the pile for the first time thanks to Aaron Brown's late winner at Grimsby. 'The Reds could only lose it now,' was the consensus. Even the most pessimistic of fans believed promotion was in reach.

Unfortunately, three games short of equalling their own League record of fourteen successive wins, City looked to settle for a draw at a weakened Sheffield Wednesday and were undone by Graeme Lee's last-gasp winner. Four defeats in six March games wrecked hopes of automatic promotion, though the return of Murray and the short-term signing of Tony Rougier kept City in the play-off hunt. With just one loss in their last seven fixtures, they finished just a point behind runners-up Queens Park Rangers. The winning momentum carried City past Hartlepool in the semi-finals, only to fall flat in the play-off final at the sunkissed Millennium Stadium. They became the first ever Bristol City side to miss promotion after winning nine or more successive League games.

William Johnson in *The Daily Telegraph* summed up the day's events, paraphrasing Churchill: 'Never in the field of human conflict have so many witnessed so few moments of genuine excitement as in this laboured play-off triumph for battling Brighton over boring Bristol City'. Neither side was in any mood for expansive football and penalties always looked likely. In the event, Brighton got their reward from the spot 36 minutes early. Leon Knight, who had rattled City's bar with a first-half free-kick, took the kick after Chris Iwelumo forced Danny Coles into a desperate lunge.

Quite why City played so negatively is a mystery, but the fact that Wilson did not even have Leroy Lita on the bench suggests more than tension was responsible Many felt Wilson had been unduly influenced by last season's promotion of Wigan on the back of a strong defence. Ultimately, it was lack of goals that cost him his job. A sad end for the manager who had won the January award as Second Division Manager of the Month.

Did You Know?

The City side of 2003-04 became the first in the club's history not to gain promotion after winning nine or more successive League games in a season.

A notable season nevertheless. In conceding 37 League goals, City's defence was not only the best in the division but equal-best, with Third Division Champions Doncaster, in the whole Football League. City's 2-1 win at Notts County in January saw Brian Tinnion join a select band of City players – John Atyeo, Trevor Tainton and Tom Ritchie - in making 500 appearances. With Danny Wilson's reign ending on 5 June, Tinnion was appointed player-manager, with Keith Millen as his assistant.

The Academy saw an exciting development. As part of the Government's flagship educational programme, it became a lead commercial sponsor and moved location to the former St George Community School. On the pitch, it was the wooden spoon for the Under-19s, and the Under-17s finished just three off the bottom.

The Reserves, despite defaulting at Swansea through late postponement, did better, ending up fourth in the Wales & West Division of the Pontin's Holiday Combination. They also won the Somerset Professional Cup for the seventh time by beating Brislington 5-0. Having reached the final of the Gloucestershire Senior Challenge Cup, it was disappointing for the Reserves once again to find it held over until the following season. It was worth the wait, however, as City beat Rovers 5-2 to notch up their third success in the competition. In the FA Youth Cup, a 4-2 victory over Plymouth and a 7-2 hammering of Cheltenham took the youngsters into the third round, where they lost 0-3 at Stoke.

A great campaign for the Women's side, who clinched a place in the top-flight for the first time. Their 6-0 win over AFC Wimbledon at Oaklands Park, Almondsbury, on 2 May, brought them the Southern Division Championship ahead of Southampton Saints. In the FA Women's Cup they were unable to match Bristol Rovers – who reached the semi-finals – losing 0-3 at home to Reading Royals in the third round. In the Premier League Cup, City fell at the first hurdle, 1-3 at Leeds, but came from behind to beat Rovers 3-1 to lift the Gloucestershire FA Women's Challenge Cup for the first time.

For the supporters, the season didn't end until 5 June, when the 'Fans Forum derby' took place. Following the success of last season's inaugural meeting, which City won on penalties at the Memorial Ground, this time Gareth Walbyoff's left-footed strike from just inside the penalty area secured victory for the Rovers eighteen minutes from time at Ashton Gate.

Match of the Season 2003-04

Bristol City 2 Hartlepool 1

Play-off semi-final, 2nd Leg, 19 May 2004

Having drawn the away leg, City were favourites in this live Sky television offering. However, facing opponents with the division's best away record, nobody underestimated little Hartlepool. The visitors, seeking their first-ever play-off success, snuffed out City for much of the game, though the homesters' cause was not helped by leading scorer Lee Peacock limping off in the 31st minute after being floored by Mike Nelson.

Hartlepool's Richie Humphreys fired over from 30 yards in the first minute, and City survived another scare when Eifion Williams was denied by a last-ditch clearance from Danny Coles. At the other end Brian Tinnion crossed for Lee Peacock, but the Scot couldn't get his head to the ball. Six minutes prior to the interval, Adam Boyd cut inside to hit the base of the post. Hartlepool kept up the pressure in the second half and it was no surprise when they went ahead on 63 minutes – Williams crossing from the right for young midfielder Anthony Sweeney to head in unmarked.

Roberts, Doherty, Rougier and Murray all had attempts to level, but with time running out it appeared that City were to be exiting the play-offs at the same stage as last year. Fortunately, Roberts turned up trumps in a great four-minute spell. In the 88th minute the Welshman supplied the cross for Marc Goodfellow to arrow in an headed equaliser, then, in the second minute of added-time, Roberts beat two defenders before hammering a left-foot shot into the Atyeo Stand net.

Ashton Gate has experienced many euphoric moments down the years, but few to compare with the end of this game. Ecstatic supporters spilled onto the pitch when Premiership official Graham Poll blew his whistle to conclude the action. For the fans who danced and sang on the field it must have seemed that the Robins were destined for promotion. Unfortunately real life seldom pans out like a good story and City were destined for disappointment in the final, despite the efforts of psychologist Brian Jones.

Probably the most disappointed fan at the Millennium Stadium was 35-year-old Jer Boon, who had cycled to every City first-team game, home and away, throughout the season. Having clocked up 7,000 miles and raised £3,000 for the Breast Cancer Campaign, it was a pity that his final ride was for such a disappointing occasion.

LEAGUE ONE	**2004-05**
League One	7th
League Cup	2nd Round
FA Cup	1st Round

The goals flowed in the pre-season friendlies – 4-1 at Newport, 9-1 at Clevedon, 1-0 at Kidderminster, 3-0 at Yeovil, and 4-0 at Forest Green, before a 0-0 draw at home to Portsmouth in Brian Tinnion's benefit and a 1-3 home loss by WBA brought City back to earth.

The maxim 'Never mind the quality, feel the width' comes to mind as the Football League rebranded 'Division Two' as 'League One', regardless of it still being the third tier of English Football, and City were playing there for the sixth successive season. Perhaps the 50th anniversary of the club's last divisional triumph (in Division Three South) would be auger well for another.

Louis Carey's departure for Coventry was a blow, but he would return in the New Year as City slipped out of play-off contention. A stuttering start brought a home draw with promoted Torquay and it wasn't until late August that the first win arrived – 4-1 over bogey side Brentford. Sadly, the Bees would win the return as well as get the upper hand in the FA Cup.

A 3-1 success at Wrexham on 20 November took City into a play-off position, only for Sheffield Wednesday to win 4-1 at the Gate. Despite just three wins from the following thirteen games, City had only dropped to seventh by mid-February, thought a win at Colchester a week later saw them slip to ninth. Three wins and two draws in the last five games left City just a point adrift of the play-offs, giving a false impression of what had really been a difficult campaign.

The need for a combative central defender was often apparent, but this was frequently masked by the attacking prowess of Steve Brooker and Leroy Lita. With Chelsea coincidentally clinching their first Championship since 1954-55, it was a pity City were unable to follow suit, but the real disappointment was the decline of Tommy Doherty. The Northern Ireland international, last season's Player of the Year, was stripped of the captaincy in February as his form fell away and he fell out with the manager. This, however, was but one manifestation of dressing room unrest that contributed to City's lack of achievement.

Failing to beat Doncaster in the final home game cost a play-off place, on the day the club's new mascot was revealed – Scrumpy the Robin replaced the City CAT, which had derived from the City Away Travel Service (CATS). Despite going back to their roots in reviving the robin, it didn't herald a return of City's old signature tune 'When the Red, Red, Robin Goes Bob, Bob, Bobbing Along' – a tradition still maintained by Charlton. Commemorative bricks in City's new 5,200-seater stand could be bought for £35. With work scheduled to start in July, it was expected to be the swansong of the Wedlock cover.

Funding, however, was a problem. The project was put on hold, but, with the following season's decision to redevelop part of the 52-year-old Williams Stand and form the 'Premier Club', there were fears that a cheaper option might eventually be erected. With many fans facing being deprived – by the well-heeled brigade – of seats occupied for many years, it was hardly surprising that dissent ensued. Indeed, one long-standing supporter, frequently heard on Geoff Twentyman's Radio Bristol Friday night's sports phone-in, vowed never to go to Ashton Gate again.

In the LDV Vans Trophy, Paul Heffernan's early goal took care of Peterborough, then the MK Dons were defeated 2-1 before City succumbed to Sam Parkin's close-range effort at Swindon. In the Wales & West Division of the Pontin's Holiday Combination, the Reserves finished fifth. The FA Academy League saw the merging of the Under-19 and Under-17 levels into Under-18s, and City were only kept off the bottom of Group B by goal-difference. In the FA Youth Cup, City reached the fourth round by disposing of Bridgwater 3-0, Sutton United 4-1 and Rotherham 3-1, only to lose 1-3 at Leyton Orient.

The City Women found their top-flight status impossible to maintain, but their second-string took the Southern Division Two title. In the Women's Cup, City lost 0-6 at home to Everton, who reached the final at Upton Park where, in front of an 8,567 crowd, they lost 0-1 to Charlton. The City Ladies were also found wanting in the Premier League Cup, losing out 1-4 to Arsenal in the second round after a 2-1 victory at Chelsea in the first. It didn't get much better in the Gloucestershire FA Women's Challenge Cup as two first-half goals allowed Bristol Rovers to secure the trophy for the sixth time in eight seasons.

Whilst City had built up a record 9,000 season-ticket fan-base, the disappointments of the campaign considerably reduced the numbers renewing for 2005-06. Despite identical early-bird rates to that offered last year – £275 for the Atyeo Stand, £325 and £350 (Dolman) and £325 (Williams) – the frustrations of the season took their toil with the number of season ticket sales declining to 7,700. Nevertheless it was a good total, but perhaps an early warning of the long-awaited and much-needed backlash over the exorbitantly high cost of attending soccer matches which came to fruition with many empty seats in the Premiership in 2006-07.

Did You Know?

The City Cat mascot derived from the City Away Travel Service (CATS), but at the end of 2004-05 the more appropriate Scrumpy the Robin took over.

Match of the Season 2004-05

Bristol City 2 Everton 2

Carling Cup, 2nd Round, 22 September 2004

City, seeking to avenge a home 0-5 League Cup hammering in 1967-68, have rarely fared well against Everton, though some will recall an unlucky FA Cup defeat in 1994-95. Whilst City have twice reached the semi-finals, the competition has hardly been one to set the pulses of Ashton Gate fans racing. This time, courtesy of overcoming Wycombe, the fans were in for a rare treat as City's bravado performance brought about a memorable match.

Premiership Everton grabbed first-half goals thanks to Duncan Ferguson's spot-kick, after Danny Coles had handled, and Nick Chadwick's heading in Gary Nashsmith's free-kick on half-time. Undismayed, City came out to attack the Atyeo end. Scott Murray sent in a low cross-shot that fizzed into the net off of the boot of Everton defender Alan Stubbs. Three minutes later Tommy Doherty found Christian Roberts, who sent the ball into the middle where Leroy Lita rifled home. City pilled on the pressure, but five minutes from time a penalty was awarded against Jamie Smith for his challenge on James McFadden. Phillips came into his own with a remarkable double save. Having leapt to beat out McFadden's spot-kick, he reacted to parry his follow-up header over the bar. Seconds later Phillips was at it again, saving Jospeh Yobo's header, before twice rescuing City early in extra-time.

It was City's turn to threaten in the second half of extra-time, but Everton keeper Richard Wright prevented Lita's curling free-kick from drifting past him. Thus it was all down to the penalty shoot-out, which Murray started by thumping home for City. Phillips then saved Steve Watson's effort, only for Lita to send his penalty wide. Tim Cahill levelled for Everton before Paul Heffernan's effort, which made it 2-1, was matched by Stubbs. Lee Miller and then Kevin Campbell were both successful to keep the scores level, only for Danny Coles to be denied by the crossbar. It was down to Lee Carsley to drill home the final kick as City bowed out, frustrated and dejected, but far from disgraced.

8

CHANGE FOR THE BETTER 2005-2007

LEAGUE ONE	**2005-06**
League One	9th
League Cup	1st Round
FA Cup	1st Round

The pre-season friendlies saw big wins at Hereford and Bath City, a 1-1 draw with Tamworth at Lilleshall, a 1-0 (Grant Smith) win over Rovers at the Memorial Stadium, a 3-3 draw at Cheltenham, and a 7-0 victory at Exeter. Commercial manager Richard Gould – son of ex-City striker Bobby – departed to become Chief Executive with Somerset County Cricket Club.

With last season's transfers of Matt Hill to Preston, Danny Coles (Hull), Tommy Doherty (Queens Park Rangers) and Leroy Lita (Reading) for fees totalling £1,475 million, and close-season departures of Paul Heffernan to Doncaster and Lee Miller to Dundee United, City's team was much changed. But with top striker Marcus Stewart on board, alongside former Sunderland club-mate Michael Bridges, hopes for a good campaign were high.

Yet one hundred years after City's best ever season, for a while this looked like being the worst. Whilst the appointment of Harry Thickett from within had proved an unqualified success in 1905-06, last year's elevation of Brian Tinnion began to look particularly unwise. With City playing ragged and passionless football, a 1-7 humbling in early September at Swansea was the last straw. Even so, the supporters couldn't help but feel for their forlorn manager, alone on the pitch after the game.

The following day saw a parting of the ways, and Tinnion was gone. Other departures saw John Laycock resign from the board, just five days after the death of former chairman Archie Gooch.

Gary Johnson, who had masterminded Yeovil's rise from the Conference to League One, was the board's choice to succeed Tinnion. The former Latvian national manager immediately oversaw a 3-2 win at Brentford, but this masked a deeper malaise. Following a 1-0 home win over Tranmere, a club record nine successive defeats (seven League, one FL Trophy, one FA Cup) ensued (broken only by the 3-1 home win over Skonto Riga behind closed doors).

After a gap of 21 seasons, a return to the bottom division looked inevitable. Fortunately, Johnson gave an early demonstration of his mettle with an impressive display at what could well have been a difficult AGM on 30 November.

Following an unlucky home defeat by Bradford City, the horrific sequence was ended by a 2-0 success against high-flying Huddersfield. Johnson made full use of loan players, which made nonsense of the transfer window system forced on the Football League this season – four years after being introduced into the Premiership. The fans anxiously awaited the January transfer window, but in the event, the manager concentrated on what he had, looking for winners and weeding out some of the rest. City shot up the table and just missed out on a play-off place

It was the signings of David Noble from Boston and Bas Savage (Coventry), both initially on loan, plus the capture of former Woking goalkeeper Adriano Basso and season-long loanee from Fulham Liam Fontaine, that turned the campaign around. The Brazilian Basso, despite his wayward kicking, proved to be a brilliant keeper, but the fans didn't know what to make of gangly Savage, possessed of surprising skill for one so tall. He earned a cult following at the Gate but – unable to add to his solitary League goal – few were surprised by his summer release. The sour chemistry between self-confessed City fan Marcus Stewart and Johnson saw the former Premiership striker loaned to Preston, before eventually signing for Yeovil in the January 2007 transfer window.

Coinciding with City's record losing sequence came the launch of the Bristol City Supporters Trust at the Dolman Exhibition Hall at Ashton Gate on 28 November. A gala night saw BBC soccer pundit Jonathan Pearce in attendance, plus a video-link message from City fan Richard Scudamore, the Premier League Chief Executive. Support was also offered by Dan Levy of Stockport County's Trust, as well Jacqui Forster of Supporters Direct. One thousand City fans turned up. The contest to pick a 'dream team' from the ex-players in attendance to match that chosen by club historian David Woods and Tom Hopegood resulted in the following eleven: Mike Gibson; Gerry Sweeney, Shaun Taylor, Jackie White, Geoff Merrick; Jantzen Derrick, Rob Newman, Alan Walsh; Brian Clark, John Galley, Bobby (*Shadow*) Williams.

City's horrendous kit was made worse by black numbers, which had often coincided with poor seasons. Fortunately, neither the new manager nor the players were affected by negative thoughts.

Did You Know?

City's worst ever run of defeats occurred during the 2005-06 season, when they lost nine competitive games in a row (7 League, 1 Football League Trophy, 1 FA Cup).

The corner started to be turned with the demise of Bristol's Saturday night sports paper – the *Green 'Un* – on 19 December. Becoming instead a free supplement in Monday's edition of the *Evening Post* from 9 January, the void was filled the following season by *Your Sport*, but this folded after just 27 issues.

In the Wales & West Division of the Pontin's Holiday Combination, the Reserves finished fourth. In the FA Academy Under-19 League, City finished third in Group B. Looking to prosper in the FA Youth Cup, after overcoming Bristol Rovers (5-3) and Gillingham (2-1) City were instead beaten 0-1 at home by Bolton. In Women's football, City almost regained their place in the top flight, but after finishing as runners-up to Cardiff in the Southern Division they lost out on away goals after drawing 5-5 on aggregate in a two-legged play-off with Sunderland. The Premier League Cup saw the City ladies succumb 0-5 at Arsenal.

Match of the Season 2005-06

Bristol City 2 Huddersfield Town 0

Coca-Cola League One, 10 December 2005

Despite City's improved display in losing to Bradford City four days earlier, only the super optimist believed that City's nine-game losing run was about to end against high-flying Huddersfield. The team desperately needed a good start, and Scott Murray provided it. A late replacement for the injured Wilkshire, Murray took Orr's cross in his stride, though his left-footed shot was helped on its way by a slight deflection.

Defending from the front, City were in Yorkshire faces right from the off. Huddersfield's strike-force of Pawal Abbott and Andy Booth got little change from a back four that never wavered. On the few occasions that Town were permitted a sight of goal, they found themselves thwarted by City keeper Adriano Basso.

David Cotterill finally banished the blues with a super swish of his right boot. The goal guaranteed victory, sent spirits soaring with the quality of the strike, and consigned a run of defeats to the dustbin. The Welsh Under-21 international embarked on a run from the centre-circle that left two defenders trailing before a wrong-footing shimmy allowed a slide-rule finish.

LEAGUE ONE	**2006-07**
League One	2nd
League Cup	1st Round
FA Cup	4th Round Replay

City's board doubled in size with the addition of Colin Sexstone and Roger Pearce. For Chief Executive Sexstone, it was a reward for his hard work since joining from Gloucestershire County Cricket Club in 2001. A pre-season tour of Latvia brought wins over Skonto Riga (2-1) and Jurmala (2-0), and a 1-1 draw with Olympic.

With City reverting to their traditional red shirts and white shorts, after five seasons in all red, the vibes felt good. Even the players were bold about winning the divisional championship. As the season panned out, the 1-0 opening-day victory over Scunthorpe – the best side to visit Ashton Gate all season – turned out to be crucial, for it ushered in four successive defeats which might otherwise have been five. Fearing a repetition of the previous season's early woes, the fans feared the worse at Northampton. Shown live on Sky, matters didn't look good at half-time, with the score 1-1 and Bradley Orr sent off for head-butting his own captain, Louis Carey. Dave Cotterill inspired a 3-1 win and brought about the winger's £2 million transfer to Premiership Wigan. City had begun their climb, and a 3-1 home success over Chesterfield took them into a play-off position.

All this was commendable, given the loss of key players. Steve Brooker, Bradley Orr, Dave Partridge and Scott Brown attended court on 1 September to answer charges relating to last October's drunken brawl, all but Brown receiving custodial sentences. Welsh international Partridge, on loan at Leyton Orient, was jailed for two months, Brooker and Orr for 28 days, Brown having to do 100 hours community service. Brown played his part in City's recovery, scoring in next day's 1-0 win over Brighton. Later he was surprisingly transferred to Cheltenham, only to break his leg during Town's 1-0 Ashton Gate success.

On completing their sentences, the shamed players were welcomed back, but Brooker was plagued by injury and his contribution was much missed. Defender Orr continued to shine, reminiscent of Gordon Parr many years earlier. Quite how the irate City fan during the visit of Huddersfield singled out Orr to wave his fist at is a mystery, because of all City's players Orr could never be faulted for lack of commitment. However, it perhaps says something about today's confused morality that, in contrast to the earlier attitude adopted by the club to their errant players, the misguided fan was reportedly banned from the Gate for life.

City kept up the pressure but rarely looked convincing. Lack of fire-power was a problem, although a 3-0 success at Oldham raised hopes, especially as it took their unbeaten run to eighteen games. Unfortunately, City were unable to equal their post-war record as the next game brought a 0-1 home defeat by lowly Cheltenham. Doubts were then raised by a 0-1 loss at leaders Scunthorpe, which a lucky 1-1 home draw with Huddersfield did little to disperse.

The manager unwisely took exception to comments made by upset fans at that game. 'Be positive or stay away' was his message, but Johnson would have been better advised to look at the reasons for the fans' discontent. Coming in the week that saw 'the Ashton Gate Eight' honoured by the Bristol City Supporters Trust, the manager might have reflected that some of those critical fans had dug deep to save the club in 1982. Pressure of a different kind surfaced near the end of the season against Swansea. Johnson went onto the pitch to take the ball off Izzy Iriekpen who was preventing City from taking a free-kick. It was actually quite funny, but the City manager was consigned to the stand.

The City bard, Gareth Calway, summed up the situation with a poem, which appeared in the *Western Daily Press* of 8 April:

We are West Country blokes, We have humble-grumble hopes.
We make self-deprecatory jokes. We are always on the ropes.
When we win we think it's a hoax. Our striker bursts through – and then croaks.

Now we are really so close, To those dizzy second tier slopes,
As second to those country folks, From Scunthorpe (who aren't such dopes).

We deserve some master-strokes, And this man who's managed to coax
A side that goes second and copes, Has been sent off for wanting it most

More than time-wasters and soft yolks, Dressed in black who think they're popes,
And turn crucial games into soaps.

Our Big City team always gropes, While many a lesser team lopes,
But this one could be the toast "Promotion – and Championship hosts!"

And we're hymning it deep in our throats, And we don't want it gone up in smokes. Gary gets to its heart, and stokes. Don't send him off – hug him close.

Despite the lack of goals and frequent off-key performances, the side displayed tremendous resilience. Elimination from the Johnson's Paint Trophy, 0-1 over two-legs to League Two Bristol Rovers, was a blow, especially as it cost City an appearance in the final at the Millennium Stadium, but they compensated by winning five successive League games. Then a hiccup. A midweek home defeat by lowly Bradford City, saw the visitors grab their first win in ten games.

Did You Know?

City's manager 'tackled' Swansea's Izzy Iriekpen, who was delaying a Reds free-kick. Gary Johnson was banished to the stand but escaped further punishment.

Despite the indignity of losing to the Rovers, 35-year-old City supporter Brian Flynn was so touched by the plight of eighteen-year-old Rovers fan Jamie Cooper – seriously injured by mortar bombs in Basra – that he raised funds for a helicopter to fly Jamie to Cardiff for the final. With Rovers Chairman Geoff Dunford offering free tickets, all sides combined to help the Royal Green Jacket see his favourites lose 2-3 to Doncaster at the Millennium Stadium.

For City, whilst goals proved hard to come by in the League, they flowed in the FA Cup, although a 1-0 win at Conference club York gave little indication of what was to come. The second round saw City beat Gillingham 4-3 to avenge their only post-war defeat by a non-League side (as Gillingham were) in 1947-48. Championship Coventry were next up: a 3-3 draw was followed by a 2-0 success at the Ricoh Arena that cost Coventry boss Micky Adams his job. In the fourth round Premiership Middlesbrough cruised into a 2-0 half-time lead, but Richard Keogh's back-header and Scott Murray's wonder strike brought a replay in front of the live television cameras at the Riverside. One goal apiece after 90 minutes, 2-2 after extra-time, but Boro nicked it 5-4 on penalties. The fourteen goals City scored in six FA Cup-ties contrasted with just 63 (their lowest total since 2003-04) from their League engagements.

On the day Scunthorpe clinched promotion, all three other automatic promotion hopefuls also won. City's 2-0 home win over Yeovil kept them four points ahead of Forest and five in front of Blackpool. Whilst a good position to be in, City's poor scoring record left them vulnerable to any Forest surge.

It was a long time coming, but Gary Johnson won the Manager of the Month award for the first time – March's seven League games earning sixteen points. The post-award blues then struck. A 0-0 home draw with Swansea marked City's third consecutive home game without a win, and was followed by defeat at Gillingham. With just two points and a single goal from three games, City's promotion challenge might have imploded. Forest were also wobbling, but Blackpool were coming up fast on the rails.

With three games to go there was drama at Carlisle. Adriano Basso was out with a damaged knee. With reserve keepers Chris Weale and Sean Thomas also injured, City were permitted a seven-day emergency loan of John Ruddy from Everton. It didn't auger well against opponents with five successive wins.

With City conceding an early goal, the doomsday scenario loomed large, but in first-half injury-time McCombe powered home a header to spark a 3-1 win. It didn't much matter that Forest won 3-0 to bring their goal difference to within one of City's. Promotion was just one win away. Many fans expected it to be clinched at Millwall and two thousand travelled to the New Den in anticipation, only to miss much of the game through late arrival. A bad day got even worse with a 0-1 defeat.

Now City had to beat already relegated Rotherham, victims of a ten-point deduction. Noble's volley calmed the nerves, and when he doubled the advantage the relief was palpable. After an hour it was 3-1 and there were no more scares in store. The crowd invaded the pitch at the end. Whilst it was a pity that it wasn't in celebration of a championship, it was a great day for Bristol City and a great weekend for both Bristol clubs. Rovers won at Hartlepool to claim a League Two play-off spot, and went on to steal some of City's thunder by securing promotion at the new Wembley.

On the Sunday following City's final game the players embarked on *The Matthew* – a replica of the vessel in which John Cabot sailed to Newfoundland in 1497 – for a trip up the Avon past the *SS Great Britain* to the Arnolfini. Transferring to an open-top bus they then toured the city prior to a civic reception at the Council House.

Among the players released was Andy Smith, who had failed to score in 35 games for Preston, Stockport, Motherwell, Cheltenham and Bristol City. After seven years as a professional at Ashton Gate, Craig Woodman was another on his way, together with midfielder Danny Wring.

So ended an amazing season, though the fact that for the first time in four years no City player was nominated for the PFA side justified the sense that, player for player, City were short of being the best in the Division. On the other hand, the outstanding form of goalkeeper Adriano Basso, captain Louis Carey and centre-half Jamie McCombe (voted Player of the Season), makes it particularly surprising that not one of these was selected by their fellow professionals. It is to Gary Johnson that the credit belongs for putting City back on an upward path. Transforming the club round in less than two years, with a record of P99, W48, D21, L30, F146, A108, is no mean achievement.

As usual, the fans paid for the success by facing ticket price rises of 30-40%. At least, for the first time in fourteen years season tickets would be issued for the Wedlock Stand, whose good acoustics heightens the atmosphere. In the FA Youth Cup, City reached the fifth round, losing to Arsenal on penalties. The Women's side finished sixth, but joined with Team Bath some months later.

With the Chairman promising City fans a stadium to be proud of, work began at the end of the season on upgrading Ashton Gate. An investment of £500,000 on an initial phase of improvements saw the remaining 4,000 wooden seats in the Dolman Stand being replaced by red plastic seating identical to that in the lower tier, and the pitch being relayed.

Match of the Season 2006-07

Bristol City 1 Nottingham Forest 1

Coca-Cola League One, 31 March 2007

City, who reverted back to 4-2-4 after a couple of months of playing 3-5-2, produced one of their best displays in this vital clash. It was not enough to make home advantage count against third-placed Forest, so the gap remained four points with seven games left.

Whilst City had won a penalty shoot-out on the banks of the Trent in the Johnson's Paint Trophy earlier in the season, they were seeking their first League win over the former European Champions since 1974. Grant Holt's stooping header threatened to plunge the City's season into despair, but Bradley Orr fired the ball into the roof of the Wedlock end net after Forest keeper Paul Smith could only parry Cole Skuse's shot.

Making headlines for the right reasons, the 23-year-old Scouser deserved his moment in the spotlight. Only his third goal in 118 City appearances, it was without doubt his most important. There was a growing sense that this would be City's time, as Johnson had forged a side in his own image – feisty and resilient in equal measure and unwilling to concede an inch. Their second-half onslaught saw Louis Carey thunder a header wide, Lee Johnson going close with a dipper, whilst Steve Brooker let fly from eighteen yards. Even substitute Phil Jevons unleashed an angled shot which the keeper stuck out a boot to divert wide.

For Forest's part, they scarcely created a chance after taking the lead and paid a high price for missing out on victory. Consigned to the end of season play-offs, all seemed well with a 2-0 win at Yeovil in the first-leg of their semi-final, but astonishingly they succumbed 2-5 after extra-time at home, to lose out on a final with Blackpool.

Playmaker Brian Tinnion in action during City's 0-3 FA Cup defeat at Filbert Street (February 2001)

Action from the Freight Rover Trophy final versus Mansfield at Wembley (May 1987)

City celebrate their Millennium Stadium LDV final success against Carlisle (April 2003)

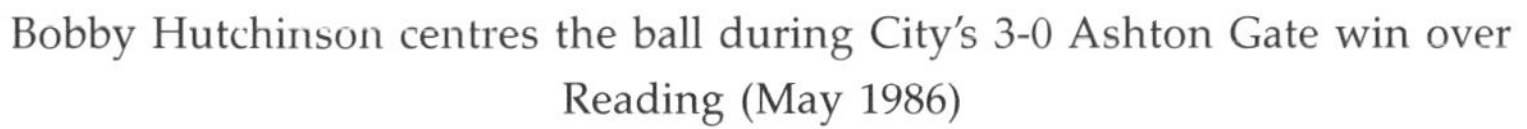

Bobby Hutchinson centres the ball during City's 3-0 Ashton Gate win over Reading (May 1986)

Marcus Stewart 2005-06

Mick Harford celebrates at Newport's Somerton Park
It ended 1-1 (January 1982)

Swansea's Izzy Iriekpen voices his pleasure to City boss Gary Johnson (April 2007)

Mick Harford heads in City's Somerton Park equaliser (January 1982)

Action from City's 4-2 derby success at Twerton Park (March 1996)

These shares became worthless following City's financial crisis of 1982

No. 2452 -10- **Shares.**

The Bristol City Football Club, Limited,

INCORPORATED UNDER THE COMPANIES' ACTS.

Capital £110,000 **Divided in 110,000 Shares of £1 each**

This is to Certify *that* D. M. WOODS

of 46 LOWER REDLAND ROAD, REDLAND, BRISTOL 6.

is the Registered Proprietor of TEN *Fully Paid Shares of £1 each, numbered* -32256- *to* -32265- *inclusive in The Bristol City Football Club, Limited, subject to the Memorandum and Articles of Association, and the Rules and Regulations of the said Club.*

Given under the Common Seal of the said Club,

this THIRTY FIRST *day of* OCTOBER 1978

Directors.

Secretary.

This Certificate must be produced at the Company's Office in the event of Transfer.

The City squad celebrate promotion (April 1998)

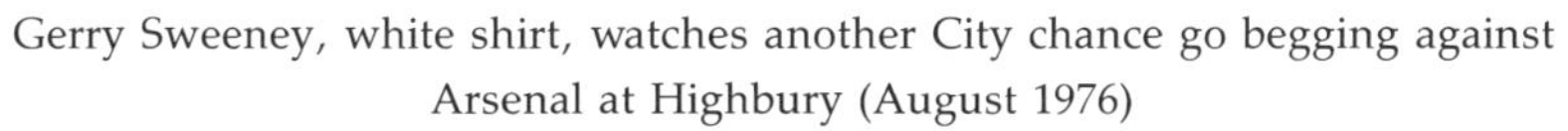

Gerry Sweeney, white shirt, watches another City chance go begging against Arsenal at Highbury (August 1976)

Shaun Taylor, City's inspirational captain (1997-98)

The joyous Ashton Gate scene after promotion was secured by beating Rotherham United (May 2007)

Greg Goodridge, a tricky and skilful winger, whose long throw-ins were often a considerable asset to the City side (1998-99)

Paul Cheesley powerfully heads City into the lead at Oxford (January 1976)

Scott Murray celebrates a Lee Matthews cracker against the Rovers in the LDV trophy (January 2002)

City's promotion winning squad of 1975-76

Steve Brooker celebrates one of his many goals (2004-05)

An amusing interlude during the game versus Hull at Boothferry Park (February 1968)

The City players celebrate winning the Anglo-Scottish Cup (December 1977)

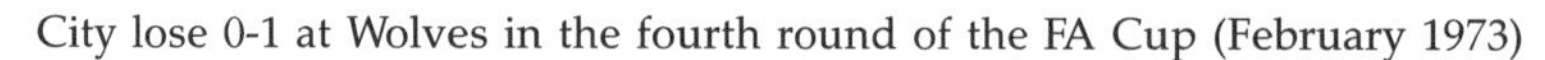

City lose 0-1 at Wolves in the fourth round of the FA Cup (February 1973)

Jamie McCombe (centre) and captain Louis Carey, the rocks at the heart of City's parsimonious defence (2006-07)

City boss Tony Fawthrop leads his side out at Wembley for the Auto Windscreens Shield final versus Stoke (April 2000)

Darren Barnard opens the scoring from the penalty spot against Wrexham (April 1997)

Peterborough's David Seaman saves from Tom Ritchie. City won 1-0 (February 1983)

Ace goalscorer Shaun Goater, who departure to Maine Road cost City the 1997-98 Second Division Championship

Glenn Humphries clears against Sheffield United in the play-offs (May 1988)

Leeds keeper David Harvey casts a forlorn figure in the Ashton Gate fog.
This First Division game was abandoned at half-time (December 1976)

The squad of 1978-79 that took Bristol City to their highest top flight position in 70 years

Guide to Seasonal Summaries

Col 1: Match number (for league fixtures); Round (for cup-ties).
e.g. 4R means 'Fourth round replay.'

Col 2: Date of the fixture and whether Home (H), Away (A), or Neutral (N).

Col 3: Opposition.

Col 4: Attendances. Home gates appear in roman; Away gates in *italics*.
Figures in **bold** indicate the largest and smallest gates, home and away.
Average home and away attendances appear after final league match.

Col 5: Respective league positions of City and opponents after the game.
City's position appears on the top line in roman.
Their opponents' position appears on the second line in *italics*.
For cup-ties, the division and position of opponents is provided.
e.g. 2:12 means the opposition are twelfth in Division 2.

Col 6: The top line shows the result: W(in), D(raw), or L(ose).
The second line shows City's cumulative points total.

Col 7: The match score, City's given first.
Scores in **bold** show City's biggest league win and heaviest defeat.

Col 8: The half-time score, City's given first.

Col 9: The top line shows City's scorers and times of goals in roman.
The second line shows opponents' scorers and times of goals in *italics*.
A 'p' after the time of a goal denotes a penalty; 'og' an own-goal.
The third line gives the name of the match referee.

Team line-ups: City line-ups appear on top line, irrespective of whether they are home or away. Opposition teams are on the second line in *italics*.
Players of either side who are sent off are marked !
City players making their league debuts are displayed in **bold**

Substitutes: Names of substitutes appear only if they actually took the field.
A player substituted is marked *
A second player substituted is marked ˆ
A third player substituted is marked "
These marks indicate the sequence of substitutions.

N.B. For clarity, all information appearing in *italics* relates to opposing teams.

No	Date		Att	Pos	Pt	F-A	H-T	Scorers, Times, and Referees	1	2	3	4	5	6	7	8	9	10	11	12 sub used
1	H	HUDDERSFIELD			L	2-3	1-1	Crowe 3, McIlmoyle 58	Gibson	Ford	Briggs	Parr	Connor	Low	Derrick	Crowe	McIlmoyle	Quigley	Peters	
	19/8		18,148		0			*Ellam 18, Nicholson 47, Harper 51*	*Oldfield*	*Parkin*	*Catlin*	*Nicholson*	*Ellam*	*Meagan*	*McHale*	*Shaw*	*Harper*	*Dobson*	*Hill*	
								Ref: R Paine	After the day's quickest score, when Crowe finishes off a superb four-man move, City are stunned by Town's fight-back in an all-action game. A typical McIlmoyle header hauls City back into game, but are unable to equalise, even squandering a 70th-min pen as Ford's effort hits post.											
2	H	QP RANGERS			L	0-2	0-1		Gibson	Ford	Briggs	Parr	Connor	Low	Derrick*	Crowe	McIlmoyle	Quigley	Peters	Bush
	22/8		20,228		0			*Leach 11, 77*	*Springett*	*Clement*	*Harris*	*Keen*	*Keetch*	*Hazell*	*Lazarus*	*Morgan I*	*Allen*	*Leach*	*Morgan R*	
								Ref: E Jennings	City are outclassed by weakened opponents who include four reserves. Rangers, twice thwarted by the post in the five mins leading up to half-time, are indebted to Leach. He drives in left-wing centre before clinching victory over pathetic City by deftly heading in cross from the right.											
3	A	IPSWICH		21	L	**0-5**	0-2		Gibson	Ford	Briggs	Parr	Connor	Low	Savino	Crowe	McIlmoyle	Quigley	Peters	
	26/8		*13,702*	*2*	0			*Brogan 8, 14, 68, Hegan 57, Viljoen 75*	*Hancock*	*Carroll*	*Houghton*	*Jefferson*	*Baxter*	*Boulton*	*Spearritt*	*Hegan*	*Baker**	*Viljoen*	*Brogan*	*McNeil*
								Ref: R Tinker	City's rearguard, often exposed by smaller opponents, are given a harassing time. Unbeaten Ipswich canter to an easy win after Brogan's fine angled shot from the left puts them ahead. Crowe is denied towards the finish, his header from a Savino free-kick being cleared off the line.											
4	A	QP RANGERS		21	L	1-3	1-0	McIlmoyle 8	Gibson	Ford	Briggs	Parr	Connor	Low	Savino	Bush	McIlmoyle	Quigley	Peters	
	29/8		*15,448*	*3*	0			*Morgan I 48, Allen 49, Morgan R 89*	*Kelly*	*Clement**	*Harris*	*Keen*	*Hunt*	*Hazell*	*Lazarus*	*Morgan I*	*Allen*	*Leach*	*Morgan R*	*Watson*
								Ref: R Spittle	McIlmoyle's left-foot shot, in off the far post, from the edge of the penalty area is scant reward for City's first-half performance. Quigley is the star with display of perpetual motion, but blatant defensive errors by Gibson & Ford within 55 secs in second half give Rangers the advantage.											
5	H	CARLISLE		20	W	1-0	1-0	Jacobs 35	Gibson	Jacobs	Briggs	Quigley	Connor	Low	Peters	Crowe	McIlmoyle	**Tainton***	Bartley	Down
	2/9		13,842	*16*	2				*Ross*	*Neil*	*Caldwell*	*McConnell*	*Passmoor*	*McCarron*	*Saville**	*Garbutt*	*Carlin*	*Balderstone*	*Sharp*	*Murray*
								Ref: K Burns	City are well on top against defensive opponents, but numerous wasted opportunities – notably by Crowe and McIlmoyle – restrict their first victory of the season to a solitary strike. Jacobs latched onto a poor clearance to net from ten yards with a left-foot shot for his first-ever goal.											
6	H	MIDDLESBROUGH		19	D	0-0	0-0		Gibson	Jacobs	Briggs	Quigley	Connor*	Low	Savino	Crowe	McIlmoyle	Tainton	Peters	Bush
	5/9		13,216	*17*	3				*McPartland*	*Butler*	*Jones*	*Gates*	*Rooks*	*Horner*	*Masson*	*Crossan*	*O'Rouke*	*Hickton*	*Chadwick*	
								Ref: V Batty	Quigley is again the star performer, holding City's depleted injury-hit side together after Connor, Low and Jacobs suffer early knocks. Boro supply most of the skill and are somewhat unfortunate not to win. Gibson, back to somewhere near his best form, does much to deny them.											
7	A	BLACKBURN		21	L	0-2	0-0		Gibson	Jacobs	Briggs	Parr	Low	Tainton	Derrick	Quigley	McIlmoyle	Crowe	Peters	
	9/9		*14,621*	*2*	3			*Connelly 61, Ferguson 64p*	*Blacklaw*	*Newton*	*Wilson*	*Clayton*	*Coddington*	*Rogers*	*Ferguson*	*Helliwell*	*Anderson*	*Darling*	*Connelly*	
								Ref: J Taylor	City are forced on the defensive throughout by opponents who miss many chances. Helliwell seizes on a poor clearance and slips ball through to Connelly to shoot opener. Low elbows Anderson off ball to concede the penalty. Rogers is booked for retaliation after being held by Quigley.											
8	H	BLACKPOOL		22	L	2-4	1-2	Quigley 28, Derrick 88	Gibson	Jacobs	Briggs	Parr	Connor	Low	Crowe	Derrick	McIlmoyle	Quigley	Peters	
	16/9		13,191	*3*	3			*Ingram 26, 86, Skirton 42, 87*	*Taylor*	*Armfield*	*Mowbray*	*Milne*	*James*	*McPhee*	*Skirton*	*Craven*	*Ingram*	*Green*	*Oates*	
								Ref: C Nicholls	City's defence falters badly in front of the Match of the Day cameras. Skirton's final goal for the Seasiders is right out of the top drawer. He completes a fine left-side run by cutting in and firing home at the Open End. Derrick slams in game's final goal with ill-concealed annoyance.											
9	A	MILLWALL		21	D	1-1	1-1	Crowe 23	Gibson	Jacobs	Briggs	Quigley	Connor	Bush	Crowe	Garland	Derrick	Down	Peters*	Ford
	23/9		*12,121*	*10*	4			*Dunphy 30*	*Leslie*	*Gilchrist*	*Burnett*	*Jones*	*Kitchener*	*Wilson*	*Possee**	*Dunphy*	*Hunt*	*Weller*	*Armstrong*	*Welsh*
								Ref: W Handley	Crisis club City, under the control of caretaker boss Les Bardsley following the sacking of Fred Ford, take an early lead. Crowe crashes in a fierce drive from the right into the far corner, before Dunphy fashions Millwall's skilful equaliser from 15 yards through a crowded goalmouth.											
10	H	HULL		19	D	3-3	3-3	Garland 4, Bush 24, Sharpe 32	Gibson	Ford	Briggs	Quigley	Connor	Parr	Crowe	Garland	Bush	Sharpe	Derrick	
	30/9		11,630	*21*	5			*Houghton 2, 44p, Chilton 27*	*Swan*	*Butler D*	*Lees**	*Jarvis*	*Pettit*	*Simpkin*	*Young*	*Wagstaff*	*Chilton*	*Houghton*	*Butler F*	*Wilkinson*
								Ref: J Clarke	This defensive, error-ridden thriller ignites from the off. The Tigers take an early lead as Houghton punishes Parr's poor headed clearance to net from the edge of the penalty area, but Garland crashes home an early equaliser from Crowe's right-wing centre for his first League goal.											

No	Venue	Opponent	Att	Pos	Pts	F-A	H-T	Scorers, Times, and Referees	1	2	3	4	5	6	7	8	9	10	11	12 sub used
11	A	CRYS PALACE		22	L	0-2	0-0		Gibson	Ford	Briggs	Quigley	Connor	Parr*	Crowe	Garland	Bush	Sharpe	Tainton	Savino
7/10			*19,938*	*1*	5			*Kember 63, Woodruff 77*	*Jackson J*	*Sewell*	*Presland*	*Payne*	*McCormick*	*Bannister*	*Light*	*Kember*	*White*	*Woodruff*	*Jackson C**	*Long*
								Ref: R Kirkpatrick	City, watched by their new manager Alan Dicks, hold their own against Palace until caught out by Cliff Jackson's inswinging corner from the right. McCormick nods the ball back across the box for Kember to head in. City's comeback hopes are ended by Woodruff's chip over Gibson.											
12	H	CARDIFF		20	D	1-1	0-1	Crowe 57	Gibson	Ford	Briggs	Quigley	Connor	Parr	Peters	Crowe	Bush	Derrick	Bartley	
14/10			15,609	*17*	6			*Brown 42*	*Wilson*	*Coldrick*	*Ferguson*	*Clarke*	*Murray*	*Harris*	*Jones*	*Brown*	*King*	*Toshack*	*Bird*	
								Ref: G Hill	The swirling wind proves troublesome for City, who find themselves deservedly behind when Brown beats Parr to the ball and finds the corner of the net from eight yards. Bartley's inswinging corner from the right brings the equaliser, Crowe heading home from almost on the goal-line.											
13	A	PORTSMOUTH		21	L	0-2	0-1		Gibson	Ford	Briggs	Quigley	Connor	Parr	Derrick	Sharpe	Bush	Garland*	Peters	Low
21/10			*21,278*	*3*	6			*Jennings 21, Ford 89 (og)*	*Milkins*	*Pack*	*Ley*	*Smith*	*Tindall*	*Harris*	*McCann*	*Pointer*	*Hiron*	*Kellard*	*Jennings*	
								Ref: G Roper	With Alan Dicks having completed his duties with Coventry, his City career starts with this defensive-orientated display that reaps what it deserves. Jennings volleys home his ninth strike of the season early on and, at the death, Ford's own-goal completes the misery of City fans.											
14	A	ROTHERHAM		21	L	0-1	0-0		Gibson	Briggs	**Davis**	**Wimshurst**	Connor	Parr	Derrick	Crowe	Garland*	Quigley	Bartley	Sharpe
4/11			***5,938***	*20*	6			*Chappell 80*	*Hill*	*Wilcockson*	*Burgin*	*Rabjohn**	*Hazelden*	*Tiler*	*Pring*	*Galley*	*Sheffield*	*Hodgson*	*Crickmore*	*Chappell*
								Ref: R Egan	City, with £12,000 signing Ken Wimshurst from Southampton, pay dearly for missing many opportunities against the Millers. A centre from Charlie Crickmore, Rotherham's £20,000 signing from Gillingham, causes confusion in the City goalmouth and sub Chappell forces the ball in.											
15	H	DERBY		21	W	1-0	0-0	Garland 68	Gibson	Briggs	Davis	Wimshurst	Connor	Parr	Derrick	Crowe	Garland	Quigley	Bartley	
10/11			15,919	*7*	8				*Matthews*	*Wright*	*Hopkinson*	*Webster**	*McFarland*	*Saxton*	*Hughes*	*Durban*	*O'Hare*	*Hector*	*Waller*	*Barker*
								Ref: T Locket	A case of the pot calling the kettle black as Dicks complains of Derby's ultra-defensive tactics. City's team of furies give the home crowd their first glimmer of hope for many weeks. Garland flings himself boldly forward to head superbly into the top corner to bring a deserved success.											
16	A	PLYMOUTH		20	W	1-0	1-0	Connor 44	Gibson	Briggs	Davis	Wimshurst	Connor	Parr	Derrick	Crowe	Garland	Quigley	Bartley	
18/11			*11,179*	*22*	10				*Dunne*	*Everitt*	*Baird*	*Piper*	*Nelson*	*Hore*	*Davey*	*Bickle*	*Peacock*	*Neale*	*Harrison*	
								Ref: K Walker	The 200 or so City fans in the crowd are overjoyed as their favourites achieve their fourth successive victory at Home Park. City's centre-half is the hero as he goes up for Crowe's inswinging corner; the ball ending up in the net as Connor's header hits Mike Everitt on the shoulder.											
17	H	CHARLTON		21	L	0-2	0-0		Gibson	Briggs	Davis	Wimshurst	Connor	Parr	Derrick	Crowe	Garland	Quigley	Bartley	
25/11			12,567	*17*	10			*Went 46p, Gregory 51*	*Wright*	*Curtis*	*Kinsey*	*Moore*	*Went*	*Reeves*	*Campbell*	*Tees*	*Gregory*	*Booth*	*Peacock*	
								Ref: H Davey	Peacock hits a post for Charlton early on as City struggle to settle down in an entertaining game. Went puts visitors in front with a disputed pen after Parr plays the ball cleanly away from Gregory, who later scores with an angled shot from the left. Quigley is booked in the last minute.											
18	A	PRESTON		20	W	1-0	1-0	Garland 10	Gibson	Briggs*	Davis	Wimshurst	Connor	Parr	Crowe	Sharpe	Garland	Quigley	Bartley	Bush
2/12			*10,127*	*18*	12				*Kelly*	*Ross*	*Ritchie*	*Smith*	*Singleton*	*McNab*	*Lee*	*Spavin**	*Forrest*	*Lyall*	*Temple*	*Gemmill*
								Ref: V Batty	Garland atones for an earlier miss to put City ahead at Deepdale as Parr's misplaced shot finds him free to clip the ball into the top corner. City spurn chances to increase advantage in the first half and are forced to defend after the break. Davis is booked in 70th minute for fouling Lee.											
19	H	NORWICH		20	L	0-2	0-1		Gibson	Parr	Davis	Wimshurst	Connor	Bush	Crowe	Sharpe*	Garland	Quigley	Bartley	Low
5/12			13,444	*6*	12			*Bryceland 35, Curran 90*	*Keelan*	*Stringer*	*Mullett*	*Lucas*	*Brown*	*Sharpe*	*Foggo*	*Bryceland*	*Manning*	*Curran*	*Kenning*	
								Ref: A Dimond	City are doubly unfortunate on 30 minutes after the ref disallows Bartley strike and awards penalty for Stringer's handball. Sharpe's kick hits the bar. Dominant City are left to rue missed opportunities. Norwich capitalise on Wimshurst's slip and then a breakaway move to win the game.											
20	A	HUDDERSFIELD		20	W	3-0	1-0	Galley 30, 71, 77	Gibson	Parr	Briggs	Wimshurst	Connor	Bush	Crowe	Garland	**Galley**	Quigley	Bartley	
16/12			*12,071*	*14*	14				*Oldfield*	*Parkin*	*Catlin**	*Nicholson*	*Mielczarets*	*Meagan*	*Shaw*	*Dobson*	*Worthington*	*Hill*	*Harper*	*Legg*
								Ref: G Robinson	A magnificent hat-trick debut by John Galley, a £25,000 signing from Rotherham some two weeks previously when his leg was in plaster. He hammers in an unstoppable left-foot shot for the opener, then a perfectly placed left-foot effort, before picking up a rebound to seal a great win.											
21	H	IPSWICH		20	D	1-1	1-0	Galley 17	Gibson	Parr	Briggs	Wimshurst	Connor	Bush	Crowe	Garland	Galley	Quigley	Bartley	
22/12			17,628	*5*	15			*Baxter 71*	*Hancock*	*Carroll*	*Houghton*	*Jeferson*	*Baxter*	*Viljoen*	*Spearritt*	*Hegan*	*Wigg**	*Hunt*	*Brogan*	*Woods*
								Ref: R Prichard	City's chapter of penalty woes continues with their third consecutive miss as Crowe blasts wide in the 63rd min after Galley had been brought down by Baxter. Galley is unfortunate to have his soaring header struck off shortly after putting City ahead when he nudged ball over line.											

No	Date		Att	Pos	Pt	F-A	H-T	Scorers, Times, and Referees	1	2	3	4	5	6	7	8	9	10	11	12 sub used
22	A	BIRMINGHAM		20	L	1-4	0-1	Wimshurst 60 [Vowden 90]	Gibson	Parr	Briggs	Wimshurst	Connor	Bush	Crowe*	Garland	Galley	Quigley	Peters	Derrick
	26/12		40,429	1	15			Briggs 45 (og), Leggatt 53, Bridges 83,	Herriot	Murray	Green	Wylie	Sleeuwenh'k	Beard	Bridges	Vincent	Pickering	Vowden	Leggatt	
								Ref: W Gow	City have but one chance in the first half, when Crowe's shot hits the foot of a post. It takes Wimshurst's headed goal to herald relief from siege conditions; but City's revival is ended by a late goal-burst from the League's most prolific attack. Briggs and Quigley are both booked.											
23	H	BIRMINGHAM		20	W	3-1	1-0	Crowe 43, Galley 47, 84	Gibson	Parr	Briggs	Wimshurst	Connor	Bush	Derrick	Crowe	Galley	Quigley	Peters	
	30/12		23,493	3	17			Vincent 62	Herriot	Murray	Martin	Wylie	Sleeuwenh'k	Beard	Bridges	Vincent	Pickering	Vowden	Leggatt	
								Ref: J Osborne	After outplaying Birmingham in the first half, City fully deserve the lead that Crowe gives them as he slides the ball home. Galley's rocket from the edge of the area doubles the advantage, but the Robins are restricted to breakaways after the Blues register in a goalmouth scramble.											
24	A	CARLISLE		19	D	0-0	0-0		Gibson	Parr	Briggs	Wimshurst	Connor	Bush	Derrick	Crowe	Galley	Quigley	Peters	
	6/1		8,261	14	18				McPartland	Neil	Caldwell	McConnell	Garbutt	Marshland	Rudge	Murray	McIlmoyle*	Balderstone	McVitie	Passmoor
								Ref: P Baldwin	Carlisle, without a win for seven matches, exert early pressure on an icy pitch. McIlmoyle's header is cleared off the line by Briggs before City respond midway through the first half when Galley's header hits the crossbar. McPartland makes a superb save from Galley to deny City a win.											
25	H	BLACKBURN		19	D	0-0	0-0		Gibson	Jacobs	Parr	Wimshurst	Connor	Bush	Derrick	Crowe	Galley	Quigley	Peters	
	13/1		19,900	7	19				Blacklaw	Newton	Wilson	Shaples	Coddington	Hole	Ferguson	Rogers	Gilliver*	Darling	Connelly	Mulvaney
								Ref: W Castle	Derrick misses two first-half chances as both teams find it tough going in the Ashton Gate mud. Ref makes several controversial decisions after the break and Quigley receives his third booking of the season in the 72nd min. Galley is thwarted right at the end by Ferguson's great tackle.											
26	A	BLACKPOOL		19	D	1-1	0-1	Galley 59	Gibson	Jacobs*	Parr	Wimshurst	Connor	Bush	Derrick	Crowe	Galley	Quigley	Peters	Garland
	20/1		13,032	3	20			Skirton 38p	Taylor	Armfield	Thompson	Milne	Rowe	McPhee	Skirton*	Green	Ingram	Oates	Suddick	Craven
								Ref: K Burns	Skirton, a former Ashton Gate amateur, puts Blackpool ahead from the penalty spot with a power shot to Gibson's right, after Jacobs brought down Green. In a high-standard game of many incidents, Galley runs in unchallenged at the far post to head past Taylor for City's equaliser.											
27	H	MILLWALL		20	L	0-2	0-2		Gibson	Parr	Briggs	Wimshurst	Connor	Bush	Garland	Crowe	Galley	Quigley	Peters	
	3/2		14,673	8	20			Conlon 28, Possee 43	Leslie	Gilchrist	Cripps	Jones	Kitchener	Burnett	Possee	Weller	Conlon	Neil	Jacks	
								Ref: J Lewis	Defensively-minded Millwall achieve a smash and grab win. Conlon bursts through to shoot home from eight yards shortly after Quigley was booked for obstructing the taking of a Lions free-kick. Possee completes the scoring, touching Conlon's speculative 30-yarder over the line.											
28	A	HULL		20	L	2-4	1-0	Galley 33, 69	Gibson	Parr	Briggs	Wimshurst	Connor	Bush	Derick	Garland	Galley	Quigley	Crowe	
	10/2		12,596	17	20			Wagstaff 49, 51, 58, Butler I 50	McKechnie	Banks	Butler D	Greenwood	Wilson	Simpkin	Houghton*	Wagstaff	Chilton	Davidson	Butler I	Henderson
								Ref: T Pallister	After a minute's silence for the Hull trawler disaster, a poor first half is enlivened by Galley's typical header and efforts to capture a dog. Three quick strikes alters things after the break. Immediately after Galley spurns an easy chance, a fierce Wagstaff drive secures Hull's fourth goal.											
29	H	CRYS PALACE		19	W	2-1	2-0	Galley 10, Wimshurst 43	Gibson	Jacobs	Briggs	Wimshurst	Connor	Parr	Derrick	Garland	Galley	Quigley	Crowe	
	24/2		13,083	14	22			Woodruff 83	Jackson J	Sewell	Bannister	Payne	Stephenson	McCormick	Lazarus	Kember	White	Woodruff	Tomkins	
								Ref: J Carr	City, in dire need of points, make a great start. A superb goal from Galley, who hooks in on the turn from eight yards, is followed by Wimshurst running Crowe's through-ball past Jackson. Palace come more alive after the break, but only reward is when Woodruff converts White's pass.											
30	H	ASTON VILLA		19	D	0-0	0-0		Gibson	Jacobs	Briggs	Wimshurst	Connor	Parr	Derrick	Garland	Galley	Quigley	Crowe	
	27/2		17,138	15	23				Dunn	Bradley	Wright	Park	Chatterley	Deakin	Roberts	Mitchinson	Woodward	Godfrey	Anderson	
								Ref: A Jones	Galley, thrice thwarted by Villa's reserve keeper, is the only City forward to have any genuine goal attempts in a disappointing match. Villa, basing everything on defence, are but a pale shadow of their great sides of the past. Anderson wastes their only chance when he bursts through.											
31	A	CARDIFF		19	W	1-0	0-0	Galley 66	Gibson	Jacobs	Briggs	Wimshurst	Connor	Parr	Crowe	Garland	Galley	Quigley	Peters	
	2/3		15,334	16	25				Davies	Derrett	Ferguson	Clarke	Murray	Harris	Jones	Clark	King	Toshack	Lea	
								Ref: D Lyden	Cardiff appear preoccupied with next Wednesday's European Cup match v Moscow Torpedo. Thus assisted, City are able to achieve their first victory over their Welsh opponents in ten seasons. A poor game is settled by Galley, who heads Peters' floated free-kick into the roof of the net.											

No	Venue	Opponent	Pos	Res	FT	HT	Scorers, Times, Referees	1	2	3	4	5	6	7	8	9	10	11	12
32	H	PORTSMOUTH	18	W	3-0	1-0	Harris 28 (og), Garland 75, Galley 84	Gibson	Jacobs	Briggs	Wimshurst	Connor	Parr	Crowe	Garland	Galley	Quigley	Peters	
	16/3	16,085	*4*	27				*Milkins*	*Pack*	*Ley*	*Smith*	*Tindall*	*Harris*	*McCann*	*Trebilcock*	*Hiron*	*Kellard*	*Jennings*	
							Ref: J Finney	City are gifted the lead in a game spoilt by the windy conditions. Crowe's curling centre provokes Harris to head into his own net. Pompey's comeback attempt is ended by a fine solo goal by Garland, running through from inside his own half, before Galley's header wraps things up.											
33	A	NORWICH	19	L	2-3	1-1	Quigley 44, Garland 53	Gibson	Jacobs	Briggs	Wimshurst	Connor	Parr	Crowe	Garland	Galley	Quigley	Peters	
	23/3	*13,634*	*7*	27			*Manning 14, 89, Crickmore 76*	*Vasper*	*Stringer*	*Black*	*Lucas*	*Brown*	*Allcock*	*Foggo*	*Anderson*	*Manning*	*Curran*	*Crickmore*	
							Ref: G McCabe	Vasper is caught off his line as Garland finds the net with a hopeful hook from the by-line as Allock attempts to let the ball run out. Gibson requires treatment after a controversial equaliser, before the Canaries clinch all the points with Manning's brilliant header from Foggo's corner.											
34	H	ROTHERHAM	19	L	0-1	0-1		Gibson	Jacobs	Briggs	Wimshurst	Connor	Parr	Crowe	Garland	Galley	Quigley	Peters	
	29/3	19,783	*20*	27			*Downes 5*	*Hill*	*Swift*	*Hague*	*Quinn*	*Watson D*	*Tiler*	*Chappell*	*Haselden*	*Downes**	*Storrie*	*Bentley*	*Shepherd*
							Ref: D Nippard	A hard, physical, vital relegation encounter against Tommy Docherty's defensively-organised side. Tiler and Hague receive bookings, but the game's 44 fouls are evenly distributed. City fail to match the Millers at the start and Downes rises above Connor for the game's only goal.											
35	H	BOLTON	19	D	1-1	1-0	Hatton 31 (og)	Gibson	Jacobs	Briggs	Wimshurst	Connor	Parr	Crowe	Garland	Galley	Derrick	Peters*	Bush
	2/4	**11,047**	*12*	28			*Greaves 53*	*Hopkinson*	*Cooper*	*Farrimond*	*Williams*	*Hulme*	*Hatton D*	*Rimmer*	*Byrom*	*Greaves*	*Lennard*	*Taylor*	
							Ref: B Homewood	Derrick, replacing the injured Quigley, is City's star man early on before fading in the second-half snowstorms. His right-wing cross forces Hatton to head into his own net. City are on the attack throughout, but Bolton level in a breakaway when Greaves hooks in from Taylor's pass.											
36	A	DERBY	19	L	1-3	0-1	Briggs 82	Gibson	Jacobs	Briggs	Wimshurst	Connor	Parr	Derrick	Garland	Galley	Bush*	Quigley	Bartley
	6/4	*16,028*	*12*	28			*Hector 42p, Barker 73, 81*	*Boulton*	*Webster*	*Richardson*	*Stewart*	*McFarland*	*Hopkinson*	*Durban*	*Barker*	*O'Hare*	*Hector*	*Hinton*	
							Ref: T Hill	Briggs turns in Bartley's left-wing corner for his first-ever League goal, but by then County had the game won. Two goals for Barker, his second a screamer that goes in off the bar. O'Hare goes in goal for seven first-half minutes, whilst after the break Hector blasts a penalty wide.											
37	H	PLYMOUTH	19	W	2-0	0-0	Galley 51, 87	Gibson	Jacobs	Briggs	Wimshurst	Connor	Parr	Derrick	Garland	Galley	Bush*	Quigley	Crowe
	13/4	17,076	*22*	30				*Dunne*	*Sillett*	*Sullivan*	*Hore*	*Saxton*	*Etheridge*	*Bickle*	*Burnside*	*Tedesco*	*Piper*	*Reynolds*	
							Ref: M Sinclair	City squander many first-half opportunities, but Galley benefits from better service after the break when City abandon their 4-3-3 plan. The centre-forward heads in Jacobs' cross as City take lead and makes the game safe with a 15-yard shot from in off the post from Derrick's pass.											
38	A	BOLTON	20	L	0-1	0-1		Gibson	Jacobs	Briggs	Wimshurst	Connor	Parr	Derrick	Garland	Galley	Crowe	Quigley	
	17/4	*7,289*	*14*	30			*Greaves 17*	*Hopkinson*	*Ritson*	*Farrimond*	*Williams*	*Hulme*	*Hatton D*	*Wharton*	*Hill*	*Greaves*	*Bromley*	*Taylor*	
							Ref: T Pallister	Expensive blunders by City's two most reliable players prove costly. Galley, goalscorer extraordinaire, proves his fallibility by missing two simple chances, whilst Gibson makes one of his rare errors. He gifts Greaves an easy header when letting a centre slip through his fingers.											
39	A	CHARLTON	20	W	2-1	2-0	Crowe 8, Galley 29	Gibson	Jacobs	Briggs	Wimshurst	Connor	Bush	Derrick	Garland	Galley	Crowe	Quigley	
	23/4	*11,756*	*19*	32			*Gregory 69*	*Wright*	*Keirs*	*Kinsey*	*Campbell*	*Went*	*Reeves*	*Hince*	*Tees**	*Treacy*	*Gregory*	*Peacock*	*Stenson*
							Ref: E Jennings	In-form Charlton, with three points from relegation rivals over Easter, prove vulnerable to quick thrusts through the middle. Crowe's fierce shot gives City an early lead and then Galley's mis-hit shot strikes Went and rolls in to put City in command over one of their bogey sides.											
40	H	PRESTON	19	W	**4-1**	2-1	Galley 15, Garland 17, Crowe 51,	Gibson	Jacobs	Briggs	Wimshurst	Connor	Bush	Derrick	Garland	Galley	Crowe	Quigley	
	27/4	16,935	*20*	34			*Irvine 40* [Wimshurst 58]	*Kelly*	*Patrick*	*Ross*	*Smith*	*Hawkins*	*Knighton*	*Temple*	*Irvine*	*Charnley*	*McNab*	*Gemmill*	
							Ref: B Daniel	Requiring one point to be safe from relegation, City are surprised as Irvine heads Preston back into the match from a Gemmill corner. They then storm to their best win of the season with strikes from Crowe, who draws out Kelly before slotting home, and a great shot by Wimshurst.											
41	A	ASTON VILLA	19	W	4-2	3-2	Derrick 10, Crowe 19, Garland 20,	**Watling**	Jacobs	Briggs	Wimshurst	Connor	**Merrick**	Derrick	Crowe	Garland*	Quigley	Bartley	Bush
	4/5	*15,301*	*15*	36			*Godfrey 4, Chatterley 12* [Bush 54]	*Withers*	*Edwards*	*Aitken*	*Chatterley*	*Turnbull*	*Deakin*	*Rudge*	*Mitchinson*	*Greenhaigh*	*Godfrey*	*Anderson*	
							Ref: H Richards	With relegation pressure lifted, City storm to their first-ever victory over Villa at their 19th attempt, despite being without the injured Gibson and Galley. Both sides are committed to an attacking policy. Bush sets the seal on a great win with a thundering 15-yarder into the top corner.											
42	A	MIDDLESBROUGH	19	L	1-2	0-1	Garland 87	**Mahoney**	Jacobs	Briggs	Wimshurst	Connor	Parr	Derrick	Crowe	Garland	Quigley	Bartley	
	11/5	*12,684*	*6*	36			*Webb 4, 81*	*Whigham*	*Smith*	*Jones*	*Crossan*	*Rooks*	*Spraggon*	*Chadwick*	*McMordie*	*Webb*	*Hickton*	*Lugg*	
	Home	Away					Ref: K Styles	City bring in another keeper for his debut, but he is overshadowed by Stan Webb. This match, a pale shadow of the FA Cup clashes between the sides, is settled by Webb, who marks his debut by forcing the ball over the line from six yards. He then clinches the points with a header.											
Average	15,935	14,417																	

LEAGUE DIVISION 2 (CUP-TIES) Manager: Fred Ford ⇨ Alan Dicks SEASON 1967-68

League Cup					F-A	H-T	Scorers, Times, and Referees	1	2	3	4	5	6	7	8	9	10	11	12 sub used
2	H	EVERTON	21	L	0-5	0-2	*[Brown 68]*	Gibson	Jacobs	Briggs	Parr	Low	Bush	Derrick	Crowe	McIlmoyle	Sharpe	Peters	
13/9		*22,054*	*1:8*				*Kendall 5, 63, Royle 44, Hurst 58,*	*West*	*Wright*	*Brown*	*Kendall*	*Labone*	*Harvey*	*Young*	*Ball*	*Royle*	*Hurst*	*Temple*	
							Ref: J Yates	City are given a soccer lesson by a superb Everton team, whose keeper does not have a shot to save until the 82nd minute. Kendall's first goal is scored from 16 yards, but his second finishes off the best move of the night. He picks his spot after a passage of play involving eight passes.											

FA Cup																			
3	H	BRISTOL ROV	19	D	0-0	0-0		Gibson	Parr	Briggs	Wimshurst	Connor	Bush	Derrick	Crowe	Galley	Quigley	Peters	
27/1		*37,237*	*3:19*					*Taylor L*	*Hillard*	*Munro*	*Williams J*	*Taylor S*	*Stone*	*Jarman*	*Jones W*	*Biggs*	*Mabbutt*	*Jones R*	
							Ref: H New	A big letdown after all the hype. Incidents to excite a strangely quiet, near-capacity crowd are few and far between as City fail to exploit the gulf in status between the sides. Crowe's clever play produces a chance but Laurie Taylor dives to his left to keep out Galley's right-foot drive.											
3R	A	BRISTOL ROV	19	W	2-1	2-1	Crowe 37, Galley 38	Gibson	Parr	Briggs	Wimshurst	Connor	Bush	Derrick*	Crowe	Galley	Quigley	Peters	Garland
30/1		*30,157*	*3:19*				*Taylor S 28*	*Taylor L*	*Hillard*	*Munro*	*Williams J*	*Taylor S*	*Stone*	*Jarman**	*Jones W*	*Plumb*	*Mabbut*	*Jones R*	*Ronaldson*
							Ref: H New	What a difference three days make. A rip-roaring contest with City riding their luck as Rovers' twice hit a post and Parr clears off the line from Ronaldson. After going behind to Stuart Taylor's header, Crowe equalises with a great cross-shot, and then Galley heads in to clinch victory.											
4	A	MIDDLESBROUGH	20	D	1-1	1-1	Garland 38	Gibson	Jacobs	Briggs	Wimshurst	Connor	Parr	Derrick	Garland	Galley	Quigley	Crowe	
17/2		*29,086*	*11*				*Parr 8 (og)*	*Whigham*	*Horner*	*Jones*	*Masson**	*Gates*	*Spraggon*	*Kear*	*Horsfield*	*Hickton*	*Crossan*	*Downing*	*McNeil*
							Ref: D Lyden	A hard-fought contest that brings bookings for Galley, Jacobs and Crossan. City fight back well after Parr deflects Horsfield's weak shot past Gibson. Derrick is unfortunate with his deft effort disallowed for offside. Garland earns a replay with a fierce shot from Wimshurst's free-kick.											
4R	H	MIDDLESBROUGH	20	W	2-1	2-0	Connor 4, Galley 27	Gibson	Jacobs	Briggs	Wimshurst	Connor	Parr	Derrick	Garland	Galley	Quigley	Crowe*	Peters
20/2		21,771	*11*				*Hickton 78*	*Whigham*	*Jones*	*Worthington*	*Masson*	*Gates*	*Spraggon*	*Kear*	*Horsfield*	*Hickton*	*Crossan**	*McNeill*	*Chadwick*
							Ref: D Lyden	City take early control as a headed goal by Connor from Crowe's inswinging corner is followed by a strike to grace any occasion. A wonderful move between Wimshurst and Derrick produces a chip forward to Galley who rises to head home. Hickton's fine shot leads to nailbiting finish.											
5	A	LEEDS	19	L	0-2	0-2		Gibson	Jacobs	Briggs	Wimshurst	Connor	Parr	Sharpe	Garland	Galley	Quigley	Crowe	
9/3		*45,227*	*1:2*				*Jones 34, Lorimer 45*	*Sprake !*	*Reaney*	*Cooper*	*Bremner*	*Charlton*	*Hunter*	*Greenhoff*	*Lorimer*	*Jones*	*Giles**	*Hibbitt*	*Madeley*
							Ref: A Dimond	A hard-fought, tough encounter boils over after the break. Bookings for Garland, Hibbitt and Wimshurst, whilst Sprake is sent off for punching Garland. City's great spirit isn't reflected in a scoreline which is given an unfair spin by Lorimer's 20-yard screamer into the top of the net.											

		Home					Away					
	P	W	D	L	F	A	W	D	L	F	A	Pts
1 Ipswich	42	12	7	2	45	20	10	8	3	34	24	59
2 QP Rangers	42	18	2	1	45	9	[illegible]	6	8	22	27	58
3 Blackpool	42	12	6	3	33	16	[illegible]	4	5	38	27	58
4 Birmingham	42	12	6	3	54	21	[illegible]	8	6	29	30	52
5 Portsmouth	42	13	6	2	43	18	[illegible]	7	9	25	37	49
6 Middlesbro	42	10	7	4	39	19	[illegible]	5	9	21	35	46
7 Millwall	42	9	10	2	35	16	[illegible]	7	9	27	34	45
8 Blackburn	42	13	5	3	34	16	[illegible]	6	12	22	33	43
9 Norwich	42	12	4	5	40	30	[illegible]	7	10	20	35	43
10 Carlisle	42	9	9	3	38	22	[illegible]	4	12	20	30	41
11 Crys Palace	42	11	4	6	34	19	3	7	11	22	37	39
12 Bolton	42	8	6	7	37	28	5	7	9	23	35	39
13 Cardiff	42	9	6	6	35	29	4	6	11	25	37	38
14 Huddersfield	42	10	6	5	29	23	3	6	12	17	38	38
15 Charlton	42	10	6	5	43	25	2	7	12	20	43	37
16 Aston Villa	42	10	3	8	35	30	5	4	12	19	34	37
17 Hull	42	6	8	7	25	23	6	5	10	33	50	37
18 Derby	42	8	5	8	40	35	5	5	11	31	43	36
19 BRISTOL CITY	42	7	7	7	26	25	6	3	12	22	37	36
20 Preston	42	8	7	6	29	24	4	4	13	14	41	35
21 Rotherham	42	7	4	10	22	32	3	7	11	20	44	31
22 Plymouth	42	5	4	12	26	36	4	5	12	12	36	27
	924	219	128	115	787	516	[illegible]	128	219	516	787	924

Odds & ends

Double wins: (2) Plymouth, Preston.
Double loses: (3) QP Rangers, Rotherham, Norwich.

Won from behind: (1) Aston Villa (a).
Lost from in front: (4) Huddersfield (h), QP Rangers (a), Hull (a), Norwich (a).

High spots: Exciting 3-3 home draw with Hull on 30 September.
Beating Bristol Rovers on way to 5th Round of the FA Cup.
John Galley's hat-trick at Leeds Road on his City debut.
Vital win at the Valley on 20 April.
City's first-ever victory over Aston Villa at their 19th attempt.

Low spots: Dismissal of Fred Ford.
Outplayed by Everton in the League Cup.
Losing 0-5 at Ipswich on 26 August.
Blackpool's 4-2 success at Ashton Gate.
Losing a bruising encounter against Rotherham at Ashton Gate.

Player of the year: John Quigley.
Ever-presents: (0).
Hat-tricks: (1) John Galley.
Leading scorer: John Galley (18).

	Appearances						Goals			
	Lge	*Sub*	LC	*Sub*	FAC	*Sub*	**Lge**	LC	FAC	**Tot**
Bartley, Danny	**12**	*1*								
Briggs, Alec	**39**		1		5		**1**			**1**
Bush, Terry	**20**	*6*	1		2		**2**			**2**
Connor, Jack	**41**				5		**1**		1	**2**
Crowe, Chris	**38**	*1*	1		5		**7**		1	**8**
Davis, Richard	**6**									
Derrick, Jantzen	**27**	*1*	1		4		**2**			**2**
Down, Dickie	**1**	*1*								
Ford, Tony	**8**	*1*								
Galley, John	**21**				5		**16**		2	**18**
Garland, Chris	**29**	*1*			3	*1*	**8**		1	**9**
Gibson, Mike	**40**		1		5					
Jacobs, Trevor	**21**		1		3		**1**			**1**
Low, Gordon	**8**	*2*	1							
McIlmoyle, Hugh	**8**		1				**2**			**2**
Mahoney, Mike	**1**									
Merrick, Geoff	**1**									
Parr, Gordon	**36**		1		5					
Peters, Lou	**22**		1		2	*1*				
Quigley, John	**41**				5		**2**			**2**
Savino, Ray	**3**	*1*								
Sharpe, Gerry	**5**	*1*	1		1		**1**			**1**
Tainton, Trevor	**4**									
Watling, Barry	**1**									
Wimshurst, Ken	**29**				5		**3**			**3**
(own-goals)							**2**			**2**
25 players used	**462**	***16***	**11**		**55**		**48**		**5**	**53**

No	Date	Att	Pos	Pt	F-A	H-T	Scorers, Times, and Referees	1	2	3	4	5	6	7	8	9	10	11	12 sub used
1	A FULHAM			L	0-1	0-1		Gibson	Jacobs	Briggs	Wimshurst	Connor	Parr	Crowe	Garland	Galley	**Kellard**	Bartley	
	10/8	*16,572*		0			*Gilroy 8*	*Seymour*	*Ryan*	*Dempsey*	*Matthewson*	*Callaghan*	*Brown*	*Haynes**	*Conway*	*Large*	*Gilroy*	*Barrett*	*Pentecost*
							Ref: T Dawes	Fulham, seeking a quick return to Division One, take an early lead when Joe Gilroy slides in a Johnny Haynes pass. City have as much of the play as Fulham in the sunny conditions and should have levelled on the hour when Jacobs fired wide. Bookings for Kellard and Gilroy.											
2	H SHEFFIELD UTD			D	1-1	0-0	Galley 68	Gibson	Briggs	Merrick	Wimshurst	Connor	Parr	Crowe	Garland	Galley	Kellard	Derrick	
	17/8	19,280		1			*Addison 60p*	*Hodgkinson*	*Badger*	*Shaw*	*Munks*	*Mallender*	*Wagstaff B*	*Woodward*	*Carlin*	*Addison*	*Currie*	*Reece*	
							Ref: K Wynn	Interest seldom flags in this game, in which City's enthusiasm counters United's greater skill. After Briggs handles to concede a penalty, City level when Galley finishes off Wimshurst's through-ball with a thunderous twelve-yard left-foot drive. Mallender booked for kicking Galley.											
3	H BOLTON		13	D	2-2	1-1	Garland 29, Galley 72	Gibson	Jacobs	Merrick*	Wimshurst	Connor	Parr	Crowe	Garland	Galley	Kellard	Derrick	Briggs
	20/8	17,353	*6*	2			*Wharton 39, 86*	*Hopkinson*	*Ritson*	*Farrimond*	*Williams*	*Hulme*	*Hatton*	*Wharton*	*Hill*	*Greaves*	*Bromley*	*Taylor*	
							Ref: M Sinclair	An exciting game, which features much good football. Terry Wharton brushes off Derrick's challenge to whip in Bolton's late equaliser and rob City of the win their play deserved. Garland heads in a brilliant opening goal after Bolton are caught out by Wimshurst's quick free-kick.											
4	A BLACKPOOL		14	D	2-2	2-1	Garland 34, Kellard 37	Gibson	Jacobs	Briggs	Wimshurst	Connor	Parr	Crowe	Garland	Galley	Kellard	Derrick	
	24/8	*15,767*	*7*	3			*Milne 17, Green 66*	*Taylor*	*Armfield*	*Mowbray*	*Milne*	*James*	*McPhee*	*Skirton*	*Green*	*White*	*Suddick*	*Hutchison*	
							Ref: K Burns	After missing two easy chances, it is third-time lucky for Garland at Bloomfield Road as his swerving left-foot shot equalises Milne's headed opener. Kellard's 20-yarder gives City the advantage at the interval, but Green races through from the halfway line to fire in a great leveller.											
5	A ASTON VILLA		16	L	0-1	0-0		Gibson	Jacobs	Briggs	Wimshurst	Connor	Parr	Crowe*	Garland	Galley	Kellard	Sharpe	Bush
	26/8	*17,685*	*15*	3			*Woodward 73*	*Dunn*	*Wright*	*Aitken*	*Edwards*	*Turnbull*	*Park*	*Ferguson*	*Mitchinson*	*Woodward*	*Godfrey*	*Rudge**	*Greenhaigh*
							Ref: J Osborne	City, on top in the first half, are exasperated by Villa's time-wasting and audacious possession football after the break. Villa are unfortunate when Ferguson's fine shot hits the post, but gain reward when Woodward runs through to score with ease after Godfrey dispossesses Parr.											
6	H BLACKBURN		16	W	1-0	1-0	Galley 37	Gibson	Jacobs	Briggs	Wimshurst	Connor	Parr	Crowe	Garland	Galley	Kellard	Sharpe	
	31/8	19,787	*6*	5				*Blacklaw*	*Newton*	*Wilson*	*Mulvaney*	*Coddington*	*Hole*	*Metcalfe*	*Rogers*	*Martin*	*Darling*	*Connelly*	
							Ref: J Yates	City's great team effort secures their first win of the season. In an absorbing match Blackburn display most of the poise and skill, but Sharpe is the master of England's Keith Newton. A brilliant Garland header enables Galley to shoot home and take Blackburn's unbeaten record.											
7	A HULL		15	D	1-1	0-0	Galley 73	Gibson	Jacobs	Briggs	Wimshurst	Connor	Parr	Tainton*	Garland	Galley	Kellard	Sharpe	Bush
	7/9	*12,309*	*14*	6			*Chilton 56*	*McKechnie*	*Banks*	*Beardsley*	*Pettit*	*Wilson*	*Greenwood*	*Jarvis**	*Wagstaff*	*Chilton*	*Simpkin*	*Butler I*	*Houghton*
							Ref: F Cowen	Chilton shoots Hull ahead to punish City for squandering their better chances. Garland, after being brought down, extends City's series of spot-kick failures to five as his tame 53rd-minute effort is easily saved, and shortly afterwards Wimshurst rolls his acute-angled shot against a post.											
8	H DERBY		17	D	0-0	0-0		Gibson	Jaobs	Briggs	Wimshurst	Connor	Parr	Crowe	Garland	Galley	Kellard	Sharpe	
	4/9	15,850	*13*	7				*Green*	*Webster*	*Robson*	*Durban*	*McFarland*	*Mackay*	*Walker*	*Carlin*	*O'Hare*	*Hector*	*Hinton*	
							Ref: R Tinkler	An action-packed contest that has everything except goals. Garland leads Dave Mackay a merry dance and might well have scored twice, but for the brilliance of keeper Les Green. Referee Ray Tinkler (Boston) is a replacement for the indisposed Peter Hayward of Bournemouth.											
9	A MILLWALL		16	D	2-2	1-1	Wimshurst 44, Garland 72	Gibson	Jacobs	Briggs	Wimshurst	Connor	Parr	Sharpe	Garland	Galley	Kellard	Bush	
	16/9	*13,079*	*3*	8			*Cripps 43, Jones 71*	*King*	*Brown*	*Cripps*	*Jones*	*Kitchener*	*Burnett*	*Weller*	*Jacks*	*Conlon*	*Dunphy*	*Possee*	
							Ref: W Castle	City survive to achieve their sixth draw in an action-packed thriller at Cold Blow Lane. Twice the Lions lead, thanks to a Cripps header and a Jones shot, but on each occasion City level almost from the kick-off. Wimshurst lashes in from 15 yards, and Garland heads in a Briggs cross.											
10	A OXFORD		16	D	0-0	0-0		Gibson	Jacobs	Briggs	Wimshurst	Connor	Parr	Sharpe	Garland*	Galley	Bush	Kellard	Derrick
	21/9	*13,123*	*14*	9				*Barron*	*Lucas*	*Beavon*	*Atkinson R*	*Kyle*	*Clarke*	*Sloan*	*Atkinson G*	*Gaston*	*Evanson**	*Harrington*	*Bullock*
							Ref: R Paine	City make hard work in claiming a point against opponents reduced to ten men on 69 minutes. Harrington follows earlier casualty Evanson, in being carried off with a suspected fractured leg. Referee fails to spot City substitute Derrick wearing the No 8 shirt throughout the second half.											

No	Date	Opponent	Att	Pos	Res/Pts	F-A	H-T	Scorers, Times, and Referees	1	2	3	4	5	6	7	8	9	10	11	12 sub used
11	H	CARDIFF		17	L	0-3	0-0		Gibson	Jacobs	Briggs	Wimshurst	Connor	Parr	Sharpe	Garland	Galley	Bush*	Kellard	Derrick
	28/9		**20,632**	*6*	9			*King [illegible]5, Toshack 73, Jones 78*	*Davies*	*Derrett*	*Bell*	*Sutton*	*Murray*	*Harris**	*Jones*	*Clark*	*King*	*Toshack*	*Lea*	*L-Phillips*
								Ref: T Hall	City, unfortunate when a Briggs shot hits the bar just before the break, are surprised by King's brilliant 25-yard strike that puts the visitors ahead. Toshack's header then doubles their advantage, before Jones fires in a 25-yard rocket to set the seal on Cardiff's impressive success.											
12	A	CHARLTON		18	D	0-0	0-0		Gibson	Jacobs	Briggs	Wimshurst	Connor	Parr	Sharpe	Garland	Bush	Kellard	Derrick	
	5/10		*15,394*	*1*	10				*Wright*	*Curtis*	*Kinsey*	*Campbell*	*Keirs*	*Reeves*	*Hince*	*Treacy*	*Gregory*	*Moore*	*Peacock**	*Went*
								Ref: M Fussey	City's defence is kept fully extended by top of the table Charlton at the Valley after boss Dicks ignores the claims of Crowe to replace the injured Galley. Kellard and Briggs both make goal-line clearances to deny the Haddicks, who also twice hit the woodwork in the first half.											
13	H	ASTON VILLA		17	W	1-0	0-0	Kellard 70	Gibson	Jacobs	Briggs	Wimshurst	Connor	Parr	Sharpe	Crowe	Galley	Kellard	Derrick	
	8/10		15,199	*21*	12				*Dunn*	*Wright*	*Aitken*	*Edwards*	*Turnbull*	*Hole*	*Ferguson**	*Godfrey*	*Greenhaigh*	*Broadbent*	*Anderson*	*Martin*
								Ref: M Kirkhof	City show few ideas to counter negative tactics, as they lack the players to supply pace down the flanks. Connor does well to clear Ferguson's 55th-minute shot off the line, before Kellard's terrific right-foot drive from the edge of the area secures City's first-ever home win over Villa.											
14	H	BIRMINGHAM		17	D	0-0	0-0		Gibson	Jacobs*	Briggs	Wimshurst	Connor	Parr	Sharpe	Crowe	Galley	Kellard	Derrick	Bush
	12/10		19,578	*15*	13				*Herriot*	*Martin*	*Green*	*Wylie*	*Robinson*	*Beard*	*Hockey*	*Greenhoff*	*Vowden*	*Page*	*Vincent*	
								Ref: A Oliver	Despite the absence of goals the football is of a constant high standard. Birmingham play an open game, but their high scoring attack is mainly restricted to long shots. In contrast City create many opportunities, but are denied by their own poor finishing and Jim Herriot's good form.											
15	A	CRYS PALACE		17	L	1-2	1-0	Sharpe 17	Gibson	Ford	Briggs	Wimshurst	Connor	Parr	Tainton	Sharpe	Galley	Kellard	Derrick	
	19/10		*15,033*	*6*	13			*Woodruff 70, Lazarus 78*	*Jackson J*	*Hoy*	*Loughlan*	*Bannister*	*McCormick*	*Blyth**	*Lazarus*	*Kember*	*Jackson C*	*Woodruff*	*Taylor*	*Sewell*
								Ref: E Jennings	Against the shock League Cup conquerors of Leeds, City take a deserved lead. Sharpe jabs the ball in from six yards after Jackson fails to hold a low-angle drive. Gibson has no chance with Woodruff's shot from the edge of the area, but City claim foul as Lazarus notches winner.											
16	H	PORTSMOUTH		16	D	2-2	0-1	Sharpe 56, Galley 72	Gibson	Ford	Briggs	Wimshurst	Connor	Parr	Tainton	Sharpe	Galley	Kellard	Derrick	
	26/10		16,071	*17*	14			*Pointer 44, McCann 47*	*Milkins*	*Youlden*	*Ley*	*Smith*	*Tindall*	*Harris*	*Pointer*	*McCann*	*Haydock**	*Trebilcock*	*Travers*	*Jennings*
								Ref: R Challis	Former England forward Ray Pointer stabs in McCann's cross to give defensive-minded Pompey the lead. After McCann forces the ball over the line, attack-minded City do well to fight back. Sharpe nods ball over the advancing Milkins and later Galley shoots in from eight yards.											
17	H	HUDDERSFIELD		18	L	0-1	0-1		Gibson	Ford	Briggs	Wimshurst	Connor	Parr	Sharpe	Garland	Galley	Kellard	Derrick	
	9/11		13,738	*4*	14			*Smith S 36*	*Poole*	*Smith A*	*Legg*	*Nicholson*	*Ellam*	*Cherry*	*Smith S*	*Lawson*	*Aimson*	*McGill*	*Dobson*	
								Ref: B Daniels	City are unchanged following the midweek friendly at Morton. Despite Garland shooting against a post on 34 minutes, City are unimpressive and give young keeper Poole little to do. After McGill's good play, Stephen Smith fires in a great 20-yard shot for Huddersfield's winner.											
18	A	PRESTON		19	L	0-1	0-0		Gibson	Jacobs	Briggs*	Wimshurst	Connor	Parr	Sharpe	Garland	Galley	Bush	Kellard	Derrick
	16/11		*12,325*	*8*	14			*Gemmill 69*	*Kelly*	*Ross*	*Ritchie*	*McNab*	*Hawkins*	*Knighton*	*Temple*	*Spavin**	*Irvine*	*Ingram*	*Gemmill*	*Hughes*
								Ref: R Harper	City are fortunate that the referee ignores Preston's three penalty appeals as their defensive policy comes unstuck. Gemmill crashes the ball in from close range midway through the second half to bring Preston their deserved success. Kelly saves well from Garland near the call of time.											
19	H	NORWICH		18	L	0-1	0-1		Gibson	Ford	Jacobs	Bush*	Connor	Parr	**Skirton**	Sharpe	Galley	Kellard	Derrick	Tainton
	23/11		13,824	*16*	14			*O'Donnell 4*	*Keelan*	*Stringer*	*Butler*	*Howhall*	*Mallender*	*Anderson*	*Foggo*	*O'Donnell*	*Manning*	*Curran*	*Crickmore*	
								Ref: W Handley	City play with little conviction and the crowd react with ironic cheers on the infrequent times the ball reaches the wing. With £15,000 Alan Skirton from Blackpool making his debut, City fail to recover after Manning's short pass allows O'Donnell to shoot in from 16 yards.											
20	A	CARLISLE		20	L	0-3	0-1		Gibson	Jacobs	Davis	Wimshurst	Connor	Parr	Skirton	Sharpe	Galley	Kellard	Derrick	
	30/11		*9,263*	*13*	14			*Murray 8, McVitie 50, McIlmoyle 75*	*Ross*	*McConnell*	*Caldwell*	*Ternent*	*Passmoor*	*Garbutt*	*Barton*	*Murray*	*McIlmoyle*	*Balderstone*	*McVitie*	
								Ref: T Hill	City's much-improved performance flounders due to the alert keeping of Alan Ross and some poor finishing. A deceptive scoreline is completed by headers from McVitie and McIlmoyle, after Murray had veered past Connor to drive in a low 18-yarder for Carlisle's opener.											
21	A	MIDDLESBROUGH		21	L	1-4	0-2	Sharpe 88 *[McMordie 60]*	Gibson	Jacobs	Briggs	Wimshurst*	Connor	Parr	Skirton	Sharpe	Galley	Bush	Kellard	Tainton
	3/12		*18,038*	*2*	14			*Hickton 19, 41p, Downing 56,*	*Whigham*	*Smith*	*Jones*	*Spraggon*	*Rooks*	*Kinnell*	*Chadwick*	*Hickton*	*Horsfield*	*McMordie*	*Downing*	
								Ref: H Davey	After their praiseworthy attacking policy at Carlisle, City's return to a defensive strategy is suicidal. Hickton, who was unmarked when he lobbed in the opener, nets from the spot after being tripped by Kellard. Boro' are denied top spot by Sharpe, who fires in from 20 yards.											

No	Venue	Opponent / Date	Att	Pos	Pt	Res	F-A	H-T	Scorers, Times, and Referees	1	2	3	4	5	6	7	8	9	10	11	12 sub used
22	H	BURY		20		W	2-1	1-0	Skirton 17, Galley 50	Gibson	Jacobs	Briggs	Wimshurst	Connor	Parr	Skirton	Sharpe	Galley	Kellard	Bartley	
		7/12	**9,664**	*18*	16				*Collins 72*	*Ramsbottom*	*Parnell*	*Saile*	*Kerr*	*Turner*	*Lindsay*	*Farrell*	*Jones*	*Towers*	*Collins*	*Grundy*	
									Ref: C Nicholls	On a dry, cold afternoon, Bury cause City all manner of problems after Collins hits magnificent 25-yard screamer into the top corner of the net. Connor clears a Towers flick off the line as City somewhat fortuitously hold onto to the advantage gained by headers from Skirton and Galley.											
23	A	BIRMINGHAM		20		L	0-2	0-2		Gibson	Jacobs	Briggs	Wimshurst	Connor	Parr	Skirton	Sharpe	Galley	Kellard	Derrick*	Bartley
		14/12	*18,958*	*17*	16				*Pickering 1, 15*	*Herriot*	*Martin*	*Green*	*Wylie*	*Robinson*	*Page*	*Greenhoff*	*Hockey*	*Pickering*	*Vincent**	*Summerill*	*Murray*
									Ref: A Morrisey	Pickering beats Gibson with a dipping 20-yarder to put the Blues in front after only 39 seconds, and later doubles their advantage when sliding in a deflection off Connor. In the second half Briggs clears Summerill's effort off the line as City continue to fight a rear-guard action.											
24	H	CHARLTON		19		W	2-0	0-0	Sharpe 70, Skirton 73	Gibson	Jacobs	Briggs	Wimshurst*	Connor	Parr	Skirton	Sharpe	Galley	Kellard	Bartley	Bush
		26/12	17,427	*6*	18					*Wright*	*Curtis*	*Kinsey*	*Campbell*	*Went*	*Reeves*	*Gregory*	*Booth*	*Tees*	*Moore*	*Peacock*	
									Ref: I Jones	On a chilly, windy Boxing Day the wing play of Skirton and Bartley inspire City to a convincing win over promotion-chasing Charlton. Bartley centres on the run for Sharpe to head in, and then Skirton outpaces Kinsey to net with a cross-shot into the far corner of the Open End goal.											
25	A	PORTSMOUTH		20		D	1-1	0-1	Galley 89	Gibson	Jacobs	Briggs	Wimshurst	Connor	Parr	Skirton	Sharpe*	Galley	Kellard	Bartley	Derrick
		28/12	*19,529*	*13*	19				*Brown 4*	*Milkins*	*Pack*	*Ley*	*Smith*	*Hand*	*Youlden*	*McCann*	*Pointer*	*Brown*	*Bromley*	*Jennings*	
									Ref: J Finney	For City, who turn out in all white, Gibson – in his white jockey cap, green jersey and maroon tracksuit trousers – is the height of sartorial elegance. Brown puts Pompey ahead when Gibson can only push out Pointer's shot, but City get a deserved late leveller thanks to Galley.											
26	H	MIDDLESBROUGH		19		W	3-0	2-0	Sharpe 28, Galley 37, 70	Gibson	Jacobs	Briggs	Wimshurst	Connor	Parr	Skirton	Garland	Galley	Kellard	Sharpe	
		11/1	13,696	*6*	21					*Whigham*	*Gates*	*Smith*	*Spaggon**	*Rooks*	*Kinnell*	*Chadwick*	*Hickton*	*Horsfield*	*McMordie*	*Downing*	*Laidlaw*
									Ref: B Homewood	City are unable to break their penalty hoodoo after Garland is pushed by Gates. Another change of kicker, but the result the same, as Whigham dives to his right to save Skirton's 71st-minute shot. Galley takes advantage of Kinnell's missed kick to waltz ball in for City's second goal.											
27	A	HUDDERSFIELD		20		L	1-4	0-4	Galley 85	Gibson	Jacobs	Briggs	Wimshurst	Connor	Parr	Skirton	Garland	Galley	Kellard	Sharpe	
		18/1	*9,059*	*8*	21				*Nic'son 10, Aimson 19, Dobs'n 33p, 42*	*Poole*	*Smith A*	*Legge*	*Nicholson*	*Ellam*	*Cherry*	*Dobson*	*Lawson*	*Aimson*	*McGill*	*Hill*	
									Ref: D Laing	City, after being outplayed at Leeds Road, improve after the break and gain consolation with a late Galley header. Nicholson and Aimsom shoot early goals for the Town, before a harsh pen seals City's fate, when Connor is adjudged to have held down Aimson in going for a centre.											
28	A	CARDIFF		20		L	0-3	0-2		Gibson	Jacobs	Briggs	Wimshurst*	Connor	Parr	Skirton	Garland	Galley	Kellard	Sharpe	Bush
		25/1	*26,210*	*3*	21				*Clark 18, 44, King 61*	*Davies*	*Carver*	*Bell*	*Sutton*	*Murray*	*Derrett*	*Jones*	*Clark*	*Lea*	*Toshack*	*King*	
									Ref: H New	City are outplayed by promotion-chasing Cardiff at Ninian Park, where former favourite Brian Clark scores twice. Lea is given offside when he nods in, but no such problem when Clark slides the ball home shortly after. City are well beaten by the time King heads in Toshack's chip.											
29	H	PRESTON		19		W	2-1	0-0	Sharpe 47, Galley 69	Gibson	Jacobs	Briggs	Wimshurst	Connor	Parr	Skirton	Garland	Galley	Kellard	Sharpe	
		[illegible]/2	13,419	*17*	23				*Lee 55*	*Kelly*	*Ross*	*McNab**	*Spark*	*Cranston*	*Heppolette*	*Temple*	*Spavin*	*Ingram*	*Knighton*	*Lee*	*Hawkins*
									Ref: T Reynolds	Sharpe turns in Garland's centre to give the City a deserved lead at an unusual-looking Ashton Gate, where the spectators are restricted to three sides because of the demolition work for the new stand. Galley runs in City's winner after Lee's low shot produces North End's equaliser.											
30	H	CARLISLE		19		W	3-0	0-0	Garland 47, 55, Sharpe 51	Gibson	Jacobs	Briggs	Wimshurst	Connor	Parr	Skirton	Garland	Galley	Kellard	Sharpe	
		15/2	13,785	*11*	25					*Ross*	*Marsland*	*Caldwell*	*Ternant*	*Passmoor*	*Garbutt*	*Barton*	*Murray*	*McIlmoyle*	*Balderstone*	*McVitie*	
									Ref: K Wynn	Carlisle are unable to improve their impressive away record, despite their superior play prior to half-time. City stun the Cumbrians with quick goals after the break. Skirton's good play gives Garland time and space to stroke the ball home, and then sets up Sharpe's near-post header.											
31	[illegible]	CRYS PALACE		19		D	1-1	1-0	Connor 9	Gibson	Jacobs	Briggs	Wimshurst	Connor	Parr	Skirton	Garland	Galley	Kellard	Sharpe	
		22/2	14,695	*6*	26				*Woodruff 49*	*Jackson*	*Sewell*	*Loughan*	*Hoy*	*McCormick*	*Blyth*	*Lazarus*	*Kember*	*Woodruff*	*Dawkins**	*Taylor T*	*Taylor C*
									Ref: L Callaghan	John Jackson denies City in the first half, except when Connor hurls himself forward to head in from Garland. The tactical substitution of a defender for an attacker at the break changes the complexion of the game. Clive Taylor sets up Woodruff's right-footed strike from 16 yards.											

No	Venue	Opponent	Pos	Res	Score	HT	Scorers, Times, Referees	1	2	3	4	5	6	7	8	9	10	11	12
32	H	FULHAM	18	W	**6-0**	4-0	Garl[illegible]6, 85, Ryan 27 (og), Skirton 38p,	Gibson	Jacobs	Briggs	Wimshurst	Connor	Parr	Skirton	Garland	Galley	Kellard	Sharpe	
	1/3	15,715	*22*	28			[Sharpe, 44, Galley 88]	*Williamson*	*Cohen*	*Ryan*	*Tranter*	*Matthews'n**	*Horne*	*Jones*	*Lloyd*	*Dear*	*Haynes*	*Brown*	*Earle*
							Ref: Thomas	A St David's Day spectacular on a cold, windy afternoon at Ashton Gate as relegation-threatened Fulham are overwhelmed. At last City break their pen hoodoo, after Williamson grabs Garland around the legs. Skirton ends City's two-year barren spell with a kick to the keeper's right.											
33	A	SHEFFIELD UTD	19	L	1-2	0-1	Sharpe 55	Gibson	Jacobs	Briggs	Wimshurst	Connor	Parr	Skirton	Garland	**Broomfield**	Kellard	Sharpe	
	8/3	*14,887*	*9*	28			*Salmons 15, Tudor 64*	*Hodgkinson*	*Badger*	*Heaton*	*Hemsley*	*Colquhoun*	*Powell*	*Woodward*	*Currie*	*Tudor*	*Salmons*	*Reece*	
							Ref: J Taylor	Alan Hodgkinson, who marks his 500th League appearance by being captain for the day, is not much troubled by City's attack in a poor game. After Sharpe shoots in from a corner to level a drive by Salmons, the contest is settled by Tudor, who reacts quickest to stab home a loose ball.											
34	H	BLACKPOOL	18	D	1-1	1-0	Galley 34	Gibson	Jacobs	Briggs	Wimshurst	Connor	Parr	Skirton	Garland	Galley	Kellard	Sharpe	
	15/3	16,060	*11*	29			*Suddick 67*	*Taylor*	*Armfield*	*Bentley*	*Craven*	*James*	*McPhee*	*Brown*	*Green*	*White*	*Milne*	*Suddick*	
							Ref: R Challis	A gift Blackpool equaliser, as Suddick has the simple task of shooting into an empty net after Gibson fails to hold Parr's back-pass. City deservedly take the lead when an alert Galley runs in at the far post to slide home a Garland cross-shot that appeared to be going wide.											
35	A	BLACKBURN	17	W	3-1	1-1	Galley 33, 73, Derrick 62	Gibson	Jacobs	Briggs	Wimshurst	Connor	Parr	Skirton*	Garland	Galley	Kellard	Derrick	Bartley
	22/3	*7,566*	*14*	31			*Martin 13*	*Blacklaw*	*Kopel*	*Wilson**	*Newton*	*Coddington*	*Mulvaney*	*Metcalfe*	*Martin*	*Fryatt*	*Rogers*	*Connelly*	*Darling*
							Ref: D Corbett	Against a Blackburn side including new signing Frank Kopel, City pull off their first away win of the season. After Martin's early header, City equalise when the ball rebounds off a post and ends up in the net via Galley's shins. Derrick's superb left-foot 20-yarder is a goal all the way.											
36	A	NORWICH	17	D	1-1	0-0	Kellard 69p	Gibson	Jacobs	Briggs	Wimshurst	Connor	Parr	Derrick	Garland	Galley	Kellard	Sharpe	
	26/3	*8,682*	*16*	32			*Foggo 52*	*Vasper*	*Stringer*	*Butler*	*Howshall*	*Mallender*	*Forbes*	*Foggo*	*Bennett*	*Conlon*	*Lucas*	*Crickmore**	*Anderson*
							Ref: K Markham	Disgust at a pathetic display by players and officials alike elicits angry protests from the fans. Cushions are hurled from the stands at the end of this bore of a game. Derrick is unlucky to have his 15th-min header struck off, but a late tackle on Sharpe brings City their penalty equaliser.											
37	H	HULL	15	D	1-1	1-0	Connor 41	Gibson	Jacobs	Briggs	Wimshurst	Connor	Parr	Derrick	Garland	Galley	Kellard	Sharpe	
	29/3	13,105	*12*	33			*Jarvis 73*	*McKechnie*	*Banks*	*Beardsley*	*Jarvis*	*Pettit*	*Simpkin*	*Greenwood**	*Lord*	*Wilkinson*	*Wagstaff*	*Butler I*	*Butler D*
							Ref: K Walker	A game littered with mistakes on a hard surface, with City's square defence frequently catching the Tigers offside. Connor, at the near post, heads Kellard's corner just inside the far post, but Hull equalise when a defender deflects a Jarvis shot, from the edge of the area, over the line.											
38	A	BOLTON	17	L	0-1	0-1		Gibson	Jacobs	Briggs	Wimshurst	Connor	Parr	Crowe	Garland	Galley	Kellard*	Derrick	Tainton
	7/4	*8,172*	*19*	33			*Byrom 38*	*Hopkinson*	*Cooper*	*Farrimond*	*Williams*	*Hulme*	*Marsh*	*Wharton*	*Greaves*	*Byrom*	*Rimmer*	*Phillips*	
							Ref: J Hunting	City are made to pay for their one defensive lapse against a Bolton side with only one win from their previous 15 games. Byrom does the damage by supplying the second header to Cooper's free-kick after Wharton is fouled. Hopkinson does well to tip over Galley's overhead kick.											
39	H	MILLWALL	18	D	0-0	0-0		Gibson	Jacobs	Briggs	Wimshurst	Connor	Parr	Skirton	Garland	Galley	Kellard	Sharpe	
	8/4	14,382	*6*	34				*Standen*	*Brown B*	*Burnett*	*Jacks*	*Kitchener*	*Dorney*	*Possee*	*Jones*	*Peterson*	*Bolland*	*Dunphy*	
							Ref: D Lloyd	An undistinguished end to the Easter holiday as City fail to take their chances in a moderate encounter. The chapter of wasted opportunities begins as early as the third minute when Sharpe shoots wide of an open goal and ends in the dying seconds as Galley's snap-shot hits the post.											
40	H	OXFORD	17	W	2-0	0-0	Galley 74, 85	Gibson	Ford	Briggs	Wimshurst	Connor	Parr	Skirton	Garland	Galley	Kellard	Sharpe	
	12/4	11,457	*20*	36				*Barron*	*Beavon*	*Gladwin*	*Atkinson R*	*Clarke*	*Higgins**	*Sloan*	*Shuker*	*Skeen*	*Atkinson G*	*Harrington*	*Hatch*
							Ref: J Lewis	City do most of the attacking in the first half, but the nearest they come to a goal is when Clarke almost puts into his own net with a back pass to Barron. United, with the advantage of the wind, look more dangerous after the break, but Galley's two late shots clinch City's victory.											
41	A	BURY	15	W	2-1	1-1	Galley 36, Sharpe 68	Gibson	Jacobs	Briggs	Kellard	Connor	Parr	Skirton	Garland	Galley	Sharpe	Bartley*	Wimshurst
	15/4	***6,020***	*21*	38			*Arrowsmith 16*	*Forrest*	*Parnell*	*Tilley*	*Anderson*	*Turner*	*Parry*	*Farrell*	*Collins**	*Arrowsmith*	*Kerr*	*Grundy*	*Jones*
							Ref: M Fussey	After Bury go ahead with a superb volley, Galley's header and a cracking shot by Sharpe condemn the Shakers to relegation. Arrowsmith is left to rue missing an open goal in the second min and having a 15th-minute pen saved by Gibson, after Connor had handled on the goal-line.											
42	A	DERBY	16	L	**0-5**	0-3	*[Hector 88]*	Watling	Jacobs	Briggs	Wimshurst	Connor	Parr	Skirton	Garland	Bartley	Kellard	Sharpe	
	19/4	***31,644***	*1*	38			*Durban 17, 32, 44, Hinton 54,*	*Green*	*Webster*	*Robson*	*Durban*	*McFarland*	*Mackay*	*McGovern*	*Carlin*	*O'Hare*	*Hector*	*Hinton*	
	Home	Away					Ref: F Cowan	Footballer of the Year Dave Mackay carries the Championship trophy as Derby take the field. The rampaging Rams go in front when Durban heads in after Kellard had cleared off the line. Watling punches Hinton's fierce 79th-minute pen over the bar after O'Hare is tackled by Briggs.											
Average	15,463	14,729																	

League Cup					F-A	H-T	Scorers, Times, and Referees	1	2	3	4	5	6	7	8	9	10	11	12 sub used
1	H	NEWPORT		W	2-0	1-0	Galley 36, Garland 48	Gibson	Jacobs	Briggs	Wimshurst	Connor	Parr	Derrick	Garland*	Galley	Kellard	Bartley	Bush
14/8		9,763						*Weare*	*Williams D*	*Wilson*	*Cooper*	*Wood*	*Rowland*	*McClelland*	*Hill*	*Buck*	*Jones*	*Thomas*	
							Ref: T Lockett	Newport looked quite capable of emulating Swansea's shock victory at Eastville the previous evening, until a wonder goal quells their spirit. Garland turns as he is falling on the by-line and hits the ball into goal off the far post. Kellard's chip to Galley produces City's headed opener.											
2	H	MIDDLESBROUGH	16	W	1-0	0-0	Galley 84	Gibson	Jacobs	Briggs	Wimshurst	Connor	Parr	Crowe	Garland	Galley	Kellard	Sharpe	
4/9		13,918	*5*					*Whigham*	*Smith*	*Jones*	*Gates*	*Rooks*	*Myton*	*Kear*	*McMordie*	*Hickton*	*Horsfield**	*Downing*	*Chadwick*
							Ref: R Paine	An unexpected win for City as triumph turns into tragedy for Willie Whigham. Lauded for saving Wimshurt's seventh-min pen, after Sharpe is tripped by Smith, he later gifts Galley an easy tap-in, when failing to complete an easy catch. Boro's defensive tactics reap a just reward.											
3	A	LEEDS	16	L	1-2	0-1	Garland 70	Gibson	Jacobs	Briggs*	Wimshurst	Connor	Parr	Bush	Garland	Galley	Crowe	Kellard	Derrick
25/9		*16,359*	*1:1*				*Johanneson 40, Jones 63*	*Sprake*	*Reaney*	*Cooper*	*Bremner*	*Madeley*	*Gray*	*O'Grady*	*Lorimer*	*Jones*	*Giles*	*Johanneson*	
							Ref: S Kayley	City are often mesmerised by a brilliant Leeds side. Bremner's pass inside of Briggs allows Johanneson to crash the ball in from ten yards, but the Peacocks relax after Jones volleys in their second. City make belated efforts to save the game after Garland rams in from Crowe's pass.											

FA Cup																			
3	A	WEST HAM	20	L	2-3	1-1	Galley 11, Skirton 88	Gibson	Jacobs	Briggs	Wimshurst	Connor	Parr	Skirton	Garland	Galley	Kellard	Sharpe	
4/1		*32,526*	*1:6*				*Peters 15, 64, Hurst 52*	*Ferguson*	*Bonds*	*Charles*	*Cushley*	*Stephenson*	*Moore*	*Redknapp*	*Boyce*	*Hurst*	*Lindsay*	*Peters*	
							Ref: E Jennings	All-action City shock the Hammers with their high standard of play. Peters heads in West Ham's equaliser from Redknapp's corner after Galley, looking suspiciously offside, turns Skirton's centre over the line. Hurst hooks the ball over Gibson to put the Hammers in front.											

	Home						Away					
	P	W	D	L	F	A	W	D	L	F	A	Pts
1 Derby	42	16	4	1	43	16	10	7	4	22	16	63
2 Crys Palace	42	14	4	3	45	24	8	8	5	25	23	56
3 Charlton	42	11	8	2	39	21	7	6	8	22	31	50
4 Middlesbro	42	13	7	1	36	13	[illegible]	4	11	22	36	49
5 Cardiff	42	13	3	5	38	19	7	4	10	29	35	47
6 Huddersfield	42	13	6	2	37	14	[illegible]	6	11	16	32	46
7 Birmingham	42	13	3	5	52	24	[illegible]	5	11	21	35	44
8 Blackpool	42	9	8	4	33	20	[illegible]	7	9	18	21	43
9 Sheffield Utd	42	14	4	3	41	15	[illegible]	7	12	20	35	43
10 Millwall	42	10	5	6	33	23	[illegible]	4	10	24	26	43
11 Hull	42	10	7	4	38	20	[illegible]	9	9	21	32	42
12 Carlisle	42	10	5	6	25	17	[illegible]	5	10	21	32	42
13 Norwich	42	7	6	8	24	25	[illegible]	4	9	29	31	40
14 Preston	42	8	8	5	23	19	[illegible]	7	10	15	25	39
15 Portsmouth	42	11	5	5	39	22	[illegible]	9	11	19	36	38
16 BRISTOL CITY	42	9	9	3	30	15	2	7	12	16	38	38
17 Bolton	42	8	7	6	29	26	4	7	10	26	41	38
18 Aston Villa	42	10	8	3	22	11	2	6	13	15	37	38
19 Blackburn	42	9	6	6	30	24	4	5	12	22	39	37
20 Oxford	42	8	5	8	21	23	4	4	13	13	32	33
21 Bury	42	8	4	9	35	33	3	4	14	16	47	30
22 Fulham	42	6	7	8	20	28	1	4	16	20	53	25
	924	230	129	103	733	452	1 3	129	230	452	733	924

Odds & ends

Double Wins: (2) Blackburn, Bury.
Double Losses: (2) Cardiff, Huddersfield.

Won from behind: (2) Blackburn (a), Bury (a).
Lost from in front: Crystal Palace (a).

High spots: The fine FA Cup performance at Upton Park.
3-0 home win v Middlesbrough on 11 January.
Demolition of Fulham 6-0 at Ashton Gate.
The all-action play of Bobby Kellard.
Beating Bristol Rov 5-0 (a) in the Gloucestershire Cup Final on 28 Apr.

Low spots: Only scoring five goals in twelve League games from 21 September to 3 December.
Negative tactics at Middlesbrough that reap their just reward.
Pathetic performance, devoid of skill or effort, at Norwich.
Annihilation by the Champions at Derby.

Player of the year: Bobby Kellard.
Ever-presents: (3) Jack Connor, Bobby Kellard, Gordon Parr.
Hat-tricks: (0).
Leading scorer: John Galley (22).

	Appearances						Goals			
	Lge	*Sub*	LC	*Sub*	FAC	*Sub*	Lge	LC	FAC	Tot
Bartley, Danny	**6**	*2*	1							
Briggs, Alec	**39**		3		1					**1**
Broomfield, Ian	**1**									
Bush, Terry	**7**	*5*	1	*1*						
Connor, Jack	**42**		3		1		**2**			**2**
Crowe, Chris	**10**		2							
Davis, Richard	**1**									
Derrick, Jantzen	**16**	*4*	1	*1*			**1**			**1**
Ford, Tony	**5**									
Galley, John	**39**		3		1		**19**	2	1	**22**
Garland, Chris	**31**		3		1		**6**	2		**8**
Gibson, Mike	**41**		3		1					
Jacobs, Trevor	**37**		3		1					
Kellard, Bobby	**42**		3		1		**3**			**3**
Merrick, Geoff	**2**									
Parr, Gordon	**42**		3		1					
Sharpe, Gerry	**36**		1		1		**10**			**10**
Skirton, Alan	**21**				1		**3**		1	**4**
Tainton, Trevor	**3**	*3*								
Watling, Barry	**1**									
Wimshurst, Ken	**40**	*1*	3		1		**1**			**1**
(own-goals)							**1**			
21 players used	**462**	***15***	**33**	***2***	**11**		**46**	**4**	**2**	**52**

No	Date	Att	Pos	Pt	F-A	H-T	Scorers, Times, and Referees	1	2	3	4	5	6	7	8	9	10	11	12 sub used
1	H WATFORD			W	1-0	1-0	Galley 32	Gibson	Jacobs	**Drysdale**	**Clarke**	**Rooks**	Parr	Skirton	Garland	Galley	Kellard	Sharpe	
	9/8	19,362		2				*Walker*	*Welbourne*	*Williams*	*Eddy*	*Garvey*	*Lees*	*Scullion*	*Hale*	*Garbett*	*Green*	*Lewis**	*Sinclair*
							Ref: A Jones	For their first-ever Second Division game, Watford have Endean and Walley suspended. Green's shot hits the post for the Hornets on 27 mins, while shortly after Eddy clears Galley's effort off the line. A fine move ends with Galley's superb header that is worthy of winning any game.											
2	A HULL			L	0-2	0-0		Gibson	Jacobs	Drysdale	Clarke	Rooks	Parr	Skirton	Garland*	Galley	Kellard	Derrick	Bush
	16/8	*10,170*		2			*Chilton 79, Blampey 84*	*McKechnie*	*Banks**	*Butler D*	*Jarvis*	*Barker*	*Simpkin*	*Blampey*	*Wagstaff*	*Chilton*	*Houghton*	*Butler I*	*Wilkinson*
							Ref: S Kayley	City are rather fortunate in the 14th minute when Chilton is ruled to have pushed his way past Rooks and Parr before firing in a superb goal. Coming more into the contest after the break, City are undone when Wagstaff's brilliant run down the right leaves Chilton a simple tap-in.											
3	H CARDIFF		18	L	0-2	0-0		Gibson	Jacobs	Drysdale	Merrick	Rooks	Parr	Skirton	Garland	Galley	Kellard*	Sharpe	Connor
	23/8	23,237	*6*	2			*Clark 74, Bird 82p*	*Davies*	*Carver*	*Bell*	*King*	*Murray*	*Harris*	*Jones*	*Clark*	*Lea*	*Toshack*	*Bird*	
							Ref: M Sinclair	The nearest to a goal, in the opening 45 incident-packed mins of this game, are when a shot by Lea and a header by Galley hit the woodwork. Clark breaks the deadlock by heading in Bird's corner at the near post and then Parr's blatant unnecessary handball gifts Cardiff their penalty.											
4	A SHEFFIELD UTD		19	L	1-2	1-2	Tainton 20	Gibson	Jacobs	Drysdale	Merrick*	Connor	Parr	Tainton	Garland	Galley	Derrick	Sharpe	Clarke
	26/8	*15,539*	*2*	2			*Connor 4 (og), Tudor 15*	*Hodgkinson*	*Badger*	*Heaton*	*Barlow*	*Colquhoun*	*Powell*	*Woodward*	*Addison*	*Tudor*	*Currie*	*Reece*	
							Ref: W Castle	Injury again disrupts the career of the luckless Merrick as he dislocates his left elbow in the 32nd minute. United are rampant after Connor flicks the ball into his own net and Tudor's header, but Tainton shoots in off the far post to inspire a fight-back that has the Blades hanging on.											
5	A HUDDERSFIELD		20	L	0-3	0-2		Gibson	Briggs	Drysdale	**Menmuir***	Rooks	Bush	Skirton	Garland	Galley	Derrick	Sharpe	Tainton
	30/8	*10,206*	*3*	2			*Hoy 19, Briggs 37 (og), Dobson 70*	*Poole*	*Clarke*	*Hutt*	*Nicholson*	*Ellam*	*Cherry*	*Hoy*	*Lawson*	*Worthington*	*McGill*	*Dobson*	
							Ref: R Johnson	After Worthington's low centre is flicked in by Hoy, City concede their third own-goal of the campaign as Lawson's effort strikes Briggs on the head before trickling over the line. Dobson looks yards offside when receiving ball from McGill, before driving the third goal past Gibson.											
6	H PRESTON		20	D	0-0	0-0		Gibson	Briggs	Drysdale	Tainton	Rooks	Parr	Skirton	Garland	Galley	Derrick	Sharpe	
	6/9	13,740	*17*	3				*Kelly*	*Ross*	*Ritchie*	*Heppolette*	*Hawkins*	*McNab*	*Wilson*	*Irvine*	*Ingram*	*Gemmill*	*Lee*	
							Ref: A Oliver	Garland is unfortunate in the 43rd minute when his left-foot shot from Sharpe's pull-back is disallowed for offside against the winger. City create and waste many chances in the first half, but find Preston more resolute after the break as the game drifts along in a rather aimless way.											
7	A MIDDLESBROUGH		21	L	0-2	0-2		Gibson	Briggs	Drysdale	Tainton	Rooks	Parr	Skirton	Garland	Galley	Derrick	Kellard	
	13/9	*14,513*	*11*	3			*Downing 3, Smith A 45*	*Short*	*Smith A*	*Jones*	*Smith G*	*Gates*	*Spraggon*	*Lugg*	*McMordie*	*Webb*	*Hickton*	*Downing*	
							Ref: R Matthewson	Alec Smith foils City's spirited first-half comeback by firing in from ten yards when Drysdale fails to clear. After Downing's magnificent six-yard header from Lugg's free-kick, City are frustrated by their own poor finishing as they sink into a relegation position for the first time.											
8	H NORWICH		21	W	4-0	1-0	Galley 2, 64, Skirton 62, Bartley 80	Gibson	Ford	Drysdale	Tainton	Rooks	Parr	Skirton	Garland	Galley	Kellard	Derrick*	Bartley
	20/9	11,879	*14*	5				*Keelan*	*Stringer*	*Butler*	*Mallender*	*Forbes*	*Anderson*	*Foggo*	*Bryceland*	*Silvester*	*Bennett*	*Howshall**	*Crickmore*
							Ref:R Darlington	Galley's simple headed goal, as Keelan and Forbes miss Ford's long centre, inspires City. The substitution of Derrick (City's best player) is greeted with much booing and slow hand-clapping, before Skirton shoots into the corner of the net from twelve yards two minutes later.											
9	H CHARLTON		18	W	**6-0**	2-0	Skirton 2, 58, Galley 24, 65, 87, [Bartley 88]	Gibson	Ford*	Drysdale	Tainton	Rooks	Parr	Skirton	Garland	Galley	Kellard	Bartley	Briggs
	23/9	15,098	*14*	7				*Burns*	*Curtis*	*Kinsey*	*Campbell*	*Keirs*	*Reeves*	*Kenning*	*Gilchrist*	*Crawford*	*Moore*	*Peacock*	
							Ref: C Thomas	This surely can't last as City take their goal tally to ten in two matches. After Skirton nods the ball back, Galley hits a tremendously powerful ten-yard volley for City's opener. Charlton's harassed defenders are relieved to hear the final whistle as City receive the acclaim of their fans.											
10	A MILLWALL		18	D	1-1	1-1	Standen 22 (og)	Gibson	Briggs	Drysdale	Wimshurst	Rooks	Bush	Skirton	Garland	Galley	Tainton	Kellard	
	27/9	*11,406*	*21*	8			*Possee 7*	*Standen*	*Nicholls*	*Cripps*	*Dorney*	*Kitchener*	*Burnett*	*Possee*	*Dunphy*	*Weller*	*Bolland**	*Alder*	*Neil*
							Ref: K Wynn	Jim Standen, playing his first game after finishing cricket with Worcestershire, gives City a helping hand. In his attempt to deal with Kellard's corner, he only succeeds in putting the ball in his own net. Possee's delicate header from Burnett's free-kick gives the Lions an early lead.											

No	Date	Opponent / Att	Pos	Pts	Result	F-A	H-T	Scorers, Times, and Referees	1	2	3	4	5	6	7	8	9	10	11	12 sub used
11	H	BIRMINGHAM	15		W	2-0	0-0	Garland 86, Galley 90	Gibson	Ford	Drysdale	Tainton	Rooks	Parr	**Spiring***	Garland	Galley	Kellard	Bartley	Wimshurst
	4/10	18,694	*13*	10					*Herriot*	*Martin*	*Thompson*	*Beard*	*Robinson*	*Pendrey*	*Murray*	*Hockey*	*Hateley*	*Vincent*	*Summerill*	
								Ref: V Batty	In a game largely confined to midfield, both sides find it difficult to make progress. Garland, thwarted on 17 minutes as his powerful header is saved, makes a breakthrough near the end. He fires in his first goal of the season, before Galley's header secures a third-successive home win.											
12	H	HULL	12		W	3-1	1-0	Garland 23, Skirton 52, Galley 86	Gibson	Ford	Drysdale	Tainton	Rooks	Parr	Skirton	Garland	Galley	Kellard	Bartley	
	7/10	18,132	*13*	12				*Chilton 54*	*McKechnie*	*Banks*	*Butler D*	*Pettit*	*Barker*	*Simpkin*	*Wilkinson*	*Lord*	*Chilton**	*Houghton*	*Butler I*	*Greenwood*
								Ref: R Kirkpatrick	After Chilton heads enterprising Hull back into the game, City have reason to be relieved when the popular referee Roger Kirkpatrick penalises Pettit for handling Kellard's cross. Unfortunately Skirton drives his spot-kick well wide and it needs Galley's late header to clinch the points.											
13	A	PORTSMOUTH	12		D	0-0	0-0		Gibson	Ford	Drysdale	Tainton	Rooks	Parr	Skirton	Garland	Broomfield	Kellard	Bartley	
	11/10	*14,900*	*18*	13					*Milkins*	*Travers*	*Ley*	*Pointer*	*Hand*	*Harris*	*Trebilcock*	*McCann*	*Hiron*	*Bromley*	*Jennings*	
								Ref: B Daniels	Against a Pompey side seeking to improve on their dismal return of just three points at home this season, City's decision to extend their attacking football to away games is understandable. Unfortunately glaring misses by Broomfield and Skirton means a goalless afternoon.											
14	A	LEICESTER	15		L	0-2	0-1		Gibson	Ford	Drysdale	Wimshurst	Rooks	Parr	Skirton	Garland	Galley	Tainton	Kellard	
	18/10	*25,954*	*5*	13				*Fern 32, Glover 87*	*Shilton*	*Rodrigues*	*Nish*	*Roberts*	*Sjoberg*	*Cross*	*Farrington*	*Fern*	*Brown*	*Gibson*	*Glover*	
								Ref: K Styles	City revert to a defensive line-up with Wimshurst as sweeper. Just after Galley's header is ruled offside, Brown twice suffers as his 73rd-min shot is disallowed and later the officials fail to note his header is over the line. Fern climbs above three defenders to head in Farrington's cross.											
15	H	CARLISLE	15		D	0-0	0-0		Gibson	Ford	Drysdale	Tainton	Rooks	Parr	Skirton	Garland	Galley	Kellard	Bartley	
	25/10	15,161	*7*	14					*Ross*	*Hemstead*	*Caldwell*	*Passmoor*	*Winstanley*	*Balderstone*	*Barton*	*Brown*	*Hatton*	*Ternent*	*Murray*	
								Ref: G Hartley	Garland is unlucky early on when his 18-yard left-foot shot on the turn crashes against the bar. Carlisle illustrate, with their neat football, why they are so highly placed in the table, but they are fortunate to survive a second-half barrage. At the death Tainton slices a good chance wide.											
16	A	BOLTON	15		L	1-3	0-1	Sharpe 80	**Wilson**	Jacobs	Drysdale	Wimshurst	Rooks	Parr	Skirton	Sharpe	Garland	Tainton	Kellard*	Merrick
	1/11	*6,757*	*16*	14				*Rooks 36 (og), Byrom 65, Wharton 78*	*Hopkinson*	*Ritson*	*Hallows*	*Williams*	*Hurley*	*Marsh*	*Wharton*	*Byrom*	*Greaves*	*Rimmer*	*Taylor*	
								Ref: R Capey	City never really recover after Rooks pokes the ball past loan keeper Wilson, just two minutes after Parr had cleared Byrom's shot off the line. Sharpe's low 15-yard drive elicits a belated City response, after Byrom's narrow-angled shot and Wharton's stab in from Drysdale's back-pass.											
17	H	ASTON VILLA	13		W	1-0	1-0	Skirton 44	Gibson	Jacobs	Drysdale	Tainton	Rooks	Parr	Skirton	Garland	Bush	Kellard	Bartley	
	8/11	16,165	*22*	16					*Phillips*	*Wright*	*Aitken*	*Hole*	*Edwards*	*Rioch N*	*McMahon*	*Godfrey*	*Martin**	*Rioch B*	*Anderson*	*Simmonds*
								Ref: H New	Mike Gibson has to have a pain-killing injection in his left shoulder before making a welcome return to the City team. On a blustery afternoon the standard of play is poor, but Skirton's powerful header gives City the lead. In the dying moments Bush's thundering drive hits the crossbar.											
18	H	OXFORD	13		W	2-0	1-0	Garland 18, Bartley 83	Gibson	Jacobs	Drysdale	Tainton	Rooks	Parr	Skirton*	Garland	Bush	Kellard	Bartley	Sharpe
	11/11	**10,698**	*14*	18					*Barron*	*Lucas*	*Gladwin*	*Smithson*	*Clarke*	*Shuker**	*Evanson*	*Atkinson G*	*Skeen*	*Harrington*	*Atkinson R*	*Thompson*
								Ref: E Wallace	Gibson is City's saviour as his superb performance prevents the always likely prospect of a shock result. Garland, named as deputy keeper just before the start, has an inspired 15-minute period during which time he has two shots saved as well as registering with a gem of a header.											
19	H	QP RANGERS	10		W	2-0	1-0	Bush 29, Garland 78	Gibson	Jacobs	Drysdale	Tainton*	Rooks	Parr	Skirton	Garland	Bush	Kellard	Bartley	Sharpe
	15/11	18,893	*3*	20					*Kelly*	*Watson*	*Harris*	*Hunt*	*Mobley**	*Hazell*	*Bridges*	*Leach*	*Clarke F*	*Marsh*	*Clarke C*	*Clement*
								Ref: K Wynn	City demonstrate that they are really on the up with this win over high-flying Rangers, who do not really threaten until the last quarter. Bush times his jump to perfection when sending a dropping header over Kelly, and Garland effortlessly slots the ball home after taking a return pass.											
20	A	BLACKBURN	11		D	3-3	1-1	Sharpe 12, 75, Bush 49	Gibson	Jacobs	Drysdale	Wimshurst	Rooks	Parr	Sharpe	Garland	Bush	Kellard	Bartley	
	22/11	*13,307*	*2*	21				*Darling 2, Rogers 69, Martin 82p*	*Blacklaw*	*Kopel*	*Wilson*	*Hunter*	*Mulvaney*	*Knighton*	*Connelly*	*Metcalfe*	*Martin*	*Rogers*	*Darling*	
								Ref: R Paine	After Darling's powerful ten-yard opener and Sharpe's equalising shot, City have to thank Gibson for maintaining parity until half-time. Bush heads City in front just after the break, but Parr's handball enables Rovers to obtain the very least they deserve, as Martin nets from the spot.											
21	H	BLACKPOOL	9		W	2-1	1-0	Rooks 35, Sharpe 74	Gibson	Jacobs	Drysdale	Tainton	Rooks	Parr	Sharpe	Garland	Bush	Kellard	Bartley	
	29/11	14,818	*8*	23				*Hutchison 85*	*Thomson*	*Armfield*	*Mowbray*	*McPhee*	*James*	*Hatton*	*Brown**	*Rowe*	*Pickering*	*Suddick*	*Hutchison*	*Bentley*
								Ref: B Homewood	City, who are in command throughout, have the ball in the Blackpool net in the 27th minute, but Sharpe is ruled offside. Rooks times his jump perfectly to head in Bartley's corner, and Sharpe coolly drives the ball in from eight yards before Hutchison hooks in Suddick's cross in reply.											

No	Date		Att	Pos	Pt	F-A	H-T	Scorers, Times, and Referees	1	2	3	4	5	6	7	8	9	10	11	12 sub used
22	A	SWINDON		9	D	1-1	1-0	Burrows 25 (og)	Gibson	Jacobs	Drysdale	Tainton	Rooks	Parr	Skirton	Garland	Galley	Kellard	Bartley	
	6/12		*23,522*	*6*	24			*Horsfield 72*	*Downsboro'*	*Thomas*	*Trollope*	*Butler*	*Burrows*	*Harland*	*Heath*	*Smart*	*Horsfield*	*Noble*	*Rogers*	
								Ref: T Reynolds	City are given a gift lead as Downsborough takes too many steps after fielding Skirton's centre. From the free-kick Kellard chips to the far post where Burrows running in sends the ball powerfully into his own goal. Horsfield drives in a low left-foot shot for Swindon's equaliser.											
23	H	MIDDLESBROUGH		9	D	0-0	0-0		Gibson	Jacobs	Drysdale	Tainton	Rooks	Parr	Skirton	Garland	Galley	Sharpe	Bartley	
	13/12		15,290	*10*	25				*Whigham*	*Smith A*	*Jones*	*Smith G*	*Gates*	*Spraggon*	*Downing*	*Laidlaw*	*McIlmoyle*	*Hickton*	*Allen*	
								Ref: D Corbett	No sparkle at Ashton Gate where City, who take half-an-hour before getting in a shot, make little impression on Middlesbrough's defence. Bartley misses their best opportunity, stabbing the ball wide following a good move involving Skirton, Tainton and Jacobs near the end.											
24	H	HUDDERSFIELD		10	L	1-2	1-1	Skirton 43	Gibson	Jacobs	Drysdale	Tainton	Rooks	Parr	Skirton	Garland	Galley*	Sharpe	Bartley	Bush
	27/12		20,541	*3*	25			*Rooks 7 (og), Worthington 84*	*Poole*	*Clarke*	*Hutt*	*Nicholson*	*Ellam*	*Cherry*	*Smith*	*Lawson*	*Worthington*	*McGill*	*Chapman*	
								Ref: J Lewis	Another Rooks own-goal as the ball ends up in the top corner of the net after he juts out his foot to deal with Smith's shot. Worthington's 25-yard screamer clinches the Terriers win following City's leveller when Skirton rams the ball over the line after Poole pushes out Galley's shot.											
25	A	CARDIFF		11	L	0-1	0-0		Gibson	Jacobs	Drysdale	Tainton	Connor	Parr	Skirton	Garland	Bush	Sharpe	Bartley	
	29/12		*18,479*	*4*	25			*Toshack 90*	*Davies*	*Carver*	*Bell*	*Sutton*	*Murray*	*Woodruff*	*King*	*Clark*	*Harris*	*Toshack*	*Bird*	
								Ref: D Pugh	Toshack's first goal in ten games, an injury-time header from Woodruff's long centre, ends brave City's defensive battle. On a snow-covered surface City do not create much, though Bush should have scored instead of shooting wide from eight yards with only five minutes remaining.											
26	A	NORWICH		11	L	**1-4**	0-1	Garland 52	Gibson	Jacobs	Drysdale	Tainton	Rooks	Merrick	Skirton	Garland	Bush	Sharpe	Bartley*	Wimshurst
	10/1		*6,523*	*13*	25			*Silvester 26, 90, Conlon 50, 56*	*Vasper*	*Butler*	*Black*	*Stringer*	*Forbes*	*Lucas*	*Briggs*	*Conlon*	*Silvester*	*Paddon*	*Fogo*	
								Ref: F Nicholson	In front of the lowest Carrow Road attendance for twelve years, Silvester drives the ball in from eight yards, after Gibson parries Conlon's header. Jacobs is lying injured when Conlon heads the Canaries further in front, but Garland registers with a cross-shot shortly afterwards.											
27	H	MILLWALL		11	D	1-1	1-1	Bush 12	Gibson	Jacobs	Drysdale	Wimshurst	Rooks	Parr	Sharpe	Garland	Bush	Kellard	Bartley*	Tainton
	17/1		13,133	*19*	26			*Dunphy 43*	*King*	*Brown*	*Cripps*	*Dorney*	*Kitchener*	*Burnett*	*Possee*	*Dunphy*	*Weller*	*Bolland*	*Neil*	
								Ref: N Burtenshaw	Bartley follows up to make sure Bush's early shot crosses the line, but City are made to pay for not taking their chances as Dunphy disposes Parr to shoot Millwall's equaliser. After King makes an excellent save to deny Bush just after the break, Millwall take control for long periods.											
28	A	PRESTON		11	W	1-0	1-0	Sharpe 44	Gibson	Jacobs	Drysdale	Wimshurst	Rooks	Parr	Skirton*	Garland	Bush	Kellard	Sharpe	Tainton
	24/1		*11,045*	*20*	28				*Kelly*	*Ross*	*Ritchie*	*Heppolette*	*McNab*	*Spark*	*Lee*	*Spavin*	*Hawkins*	*Gemmill*	*Clark*	
								Ref: H Williams	Making his Preston debut Clive Clark, signed for £25,000 from QPR, is denied by an offside decision after netting early in the second half. City achieve their first away win of the season as Sharpe heads into an open net after interplay between Bush and Garland splits Preston apart.											
29	A	BIRMINGHAM		11	D	2-2	1-1	Bush 22, Skirton 82	Gibson	Jacobs	Drysdale	Wimshurst	Rooks	Parr	Skirton	Garland	Bush	Kellard	Sharpe	
	31/1		*20,421*	*13*	29			*Summerill 32, Vincent 66*	*Herriot*	*Martin*	*Thomson*	*Page*	*Robinson*	*Beard*	*Murray*	*Vincent*	*Hateley*	*Hockey*	*Summerill*	
								Ref: M Sinclair	Birmingham make the most of an escape when a 27th-minute shot by Rooks is disallowed. Summerill takes the ball round Gibson and Parr's tackle to run in an equaliser to Bush's gentle header. Skirton forces home City's late equaliser after Vincent had scored direct from a corner.											
30	H	PORTSMOUTH		9	W	3-0	1-0	Bush 34, 87, Sharpe 89	Gibson	Jacobs	Drysdale	Wimshurst	Rooks	Parr	Skirton	Garland	Bush	Kellard	Sharpe	
	7/2		13,831	*12*	31				*Milkins*	*Hand*	*Travers*	*Pointer*	*Harris**	*Munks*	*McCann*	*Storrie*	*Hiron*	*Bromley*	*Jennings*	*Ley*
								Ref: D Lyden	Portsmouth's packed midfield stifle City's attack as well as providing a platform for their neat approach play. Bush nets from ten yards with a left-foot shot on the turn, but City are hard pressed to keep Pompey at bay until the centre-forward turns in Garland's pass for his second goal.											
31	A	WATFORD		11	L	0-2	0-1		Gibson	Jacobs	Drysdale	Wimshurst	Rooks	Parr	Skirton	Garland	Bush	Kellard	Sharpe	
	14/2		*12,744*	*19*	31			*Garbett 26, Lugg 74p*	*Walker*	*Welbourne*	*Williams*	*Lugg*	*Lees*	*Whalley*	*Scullion*	*Garbett*	*Endean*	*Packer*	*Owen*	
								Ref: A Green	City, after making a bright start at snow-covered Vicarage Road, are rocked by Garbett's header from Owen's cross. Williams clears Skirton's header off the goal-line straight after the break, but all City's efforts are in vain as Gibson brings down Garbett to concede a 74th-minute pen.											

32	A	ASTON VILLA		10	W	2-0	0-0	Connor 69, Sharpe 70	Gibson	Jacobs	Drysdale	Wimshurst	Connor	Parr	Skirton	Garland	Bush	Kellard	Sharpe	
	21/2		***26,870***	*22*	33				*Dunn*	*Wright*	*Aitken*	*Hole*	*Curtis*	*Tiler*	*Godfrey**	*Chatterley*	*Lochhead*	*Rioch B*	*Anderson*	*Martin*
								Ref: [illegible] Sinclair	City are much the better side as Villa offer little in the way of attacking threat. Chatterley saves Villa when he heads Skirton's chip off the line, but the respite is short as a min later Connor's first-time shot from 15 yards finds the net. Sharpe completes the scoring by slipping the ball in.											
33	H	LEICESTER		12	D	0-0	0-0		Gibson	Jacobs	Drysdale	Wimshurst	Rooks	Parr	Skirton	Garland	Bush	Kellard	Sharpe	
	28/2		17,044	*9*	34				*Shilton*	*Woollett*	*Nish*	*Roberts*	*Sjoberg*	*Cross*	*Farrington*	*Fern*	*Brown**	*Matthews*	*Glover*	*Rodrigues*
								Ref: [illegible] Batty	A typical all-action display by Bobby Kellard, booked for the fifth time last week, gives reason for Leicester boss Frank O'Farrell to raise his £30,000 bid. A few seconds before half-time Skirton's headed goal is disallowed as Sharpe, the supplier of the pass, is adjudged offside.											
34	H	BLACKBURN		9	W	4-0	2-0	Bush 4, 57, Sharpe 38, Kellard 84	Gibson	Jacobs	Drysdale	Wimshurst	Rooks*	Parr	Skirton	Garland	Bush	Kellard	Sharpe	Tainton
	7/3		12,683	*10*	36				*Blacklaw*	*Eccles*	*Wilson*	*Hunter*	*Mulvaney**	*Knighton*	*Metcalfe*	*Goodwin*	*Martin*	*Calloway*	*Connelly*	*Hill*
								Ref: [illegible] Osborne	Rovers seeking to add to their solitary success at Ashton Gate in 1909 are easily defeated. Improved wing play brings first-half headed goals for Bush and Sharpe, whilst after the break Bush takes deliberate aim for City's third, and Kellard drives in from the region of the penalty spot.											
35	A	BLACKPOOL		10	L	0-1	0-0		Gibson	Jacobs	Drysdale	Wimshurst	Rooks	Parr	Skirton	Garland	Bush	Kellard	Sharpe	
	14/3		*13,657*	*3*	36			*Bentley 86*	*Thomson*	*Armfield*	*Mowbray*	*Bentley*	*James*	*Hatton*	*Burns**	*Craven*	*Pickering*	*Suddick*	*Hutchison*	*Brown*
								Ref: A Bone	After Sharpe's seventh-min miskick in front an open goal, City find themselves restricted to breakaways as Blackpool assert themselves. In the second half City's policy of playing high balls down the middle is unproductive and Bentley's tremendous 25-yarder gives Pool the points.											
36	A	OXFORD		11	L	0-2	0-1		Gibson	Jacobs	Drysdale	Wimshurst	Connor	Parr	Skirton	Garland	Bush	Kellard	Sharpe	
	18/3		*9,086*	*13*	36			*Lewis 30, 72*	*Barron*	*Lucas*	*Gladwin*	*Smithson*	*Clarke*	*Thompson**	*Sloan*	*Atkinson R*	*Skeen*	*Lewis*	*Atkinson G*	*Clayton*
								Ref: C Nicholls	Pathetic City succumb to goals from free-kicks as Lewis twice slams the ball in. Skirton nets what appeared to be a valid equaliser, but Sharpe is marginally offside. Kellard's uncharacteristic quiet performance is likely due disciplinary concerns should he pick up another booking.											
37	H	SWINDON		11	D	3-3	0-1	Galley 46, Sharpe 67, Kellard 76p	Gibson	Jacobs	Drysdale	Wimshurst	Rooks	Parr	Skirton*	Garland	Galley	Kellard	Sharpe	Bush
	21/3		**24,905**	*6*	37			*Horsfield 8, 57, Wimshurst 84 (og)*	*Downsboro'*	*Thomas*	*Trollope*	*Butler*	*Burrows*	*Harland*	*Smith*	*Smart*	*Horsfield*	*Noble*	*Rogers*	
								Ref: J Hunting	Swindon's third goal is unlucky for Wimshurst as the ball strikes him and goes into the net after Horsfield misses a cross. City take the lead for the only time in an enthralling match after Thomas attempts to punch the ball over the bar. Kellard beats the keeper with a kick to his right.											
38	H	BOLTON		11	D	2-2	1-0	Kellard 41p, Sharpe 86	Mahoney	Jacobs	Drysdale	Wimshurst	Rooks	Parr	Skirton	Garland	Galley	Kellard	Sharpe	
	27/3		17,298	*16*	38			*Hulme 73, Byrom 85*	*Boswell*	*Ritson*	*Marsh**	*Williams*	*Hulme*	*Rimmer*	*Wharton*	*Byrom*	*Hunt*	*Greaves*	*Taylor*	*Farrimond*
								Ref: E Jennings	Just 30 seconds after Byrom shoots low into the net, Sharpe rams in City's late equaliser. Offside cuts short Bolton's celebrations when Hunt fires in on six minutes, and City take the lead with a penalty, after Boswell holds Sharpe. Bolton level as Hulme smashes in a poor clearance.											
39	A	QP RANGERS		10	D	2-2	1-0	Jacobs 3, Bush 86	Mahoney	Jacobs	Drysdale	Wimshurst	Rooks	Connor	Tainton	Spiring	Galley*	Kellard	Sharpe	Bush
	28/3		*11,017*	*8*	39			*Bridges 50, Francis 55*	*Spratley*	*Watson*	*Harris*	*McGovern*	*Mobley*	*Hazell*	*Bridges*	*Francis*	*Leach*	*Marsh*	*Ferguson*	
								Ref: H Davey	Jacobs' centre is misjudged by Spratley and the ball goes into the far corner of the net for City's early lead. Bush heads in Tainton's high cross for a late equaliser after Rangers take charge. Francis takes careful aim for his goal, while Bridges fires in a shot that goes under Mahoney.											
40	A	CARLISLE		11	L	1-2	1-2	Jacobs 26	Mahoney	Jacobs	Drysdale	Wimshurst*	Rooks	Parr	Tainton	Spiring	Bush	Kellard	Sharpe	Skirton
	31/3		***6,219***	*12*	39			*Brown 13, McVitie 16*	*Ross*	*Hemstead*	*Davis*	*Ternent*	*Garbutt*	*Peddelty*	*McVitie*	*Barton*	*Brown*	*Hatton*	*Balderstone*	
								Ref: K Styles	City's defence is badly at fault as Brown's weak header trickles in the net for Carlisle's opener, and then McVitie runs through to shoot home. Jacobs fires in from 25 yards to gain some reward for a spirited reply, that had caused Garbutt to head a cross onto his own post shortly before.											
41	H	SHEFFIELD UTD		13	L	0-1	0-1		Gibson	Jacobs	Drysdale	Tainton	Rooks	Parr	Skirton	Spiring*	Bush	Kellard	Sharpe	Derrick
	4/4		11,159	*4*	39			*Colquhoun 37*	*Hodgkinson*	*Badger*	*Flynn*	*Addison*	*Colquhoun*	*Powell*	*Woodward*	*Currie*	*Tudor*	*Salmons*	*Reece*	
								Ref: A Morrissey	City are rescued from their lethargy when Colquhoun heads in from Woodward's corner. They dominate the play, but are left to rue many missed chances and appeals for a penalty when Sharpe is brought down by Powell in the box. Tudor blasts United's best chance over the bar.											
42	A	CHARLTON		14	L	1-2	0-1	Garland 88	Gibson	Jacobs	Drysdale	**Gow**	Rooks	Parr	Tainton	Garland	Bush	Kellard	Sharpe	
	14/4		*15,972*	*20*	39			*Campbell 13, Treacy 50*	*Wright*	*Curtis*	*Kinsey*	*Moore*	*Keirs*	*Reeves*	*Kenning*	*Treacy*	*Riddick*	*Campbell*	*Peacock**	*Gregory*
	Home		Away					Ref: N Burtenshaw	With Kellard seeking a transfer, Rooks takes over as City captain. Campbell's eight-yard shot and Treacy's superb header enable Charlton to maintain their status. Garland heads in from Kellard's free-kick at the death, but earlier Bush can only find the post from a similar situation.											
Average	16,274		14,205																		

League Cup			Att	Pos	Res	F-A	H-T	Scorers, Times, and Referees	1	2	3	4	5	6	7	8	9	10	11	12 sub used
1	A	EXETER			D	1-1	0-0	Kellard 72	Gibson	Jacobs	Drysdale	Clarke	Rooks	Parr	Skirton	Garland	Bush	Kellard	Sharpe	
		13/8	*8,003*					*Banks 74*	*Shearing*	*Crawford*	*Blain*	*Balson*	*Sharples*	*Newman*	*Corr*	*Giles*	*Banks*	*Mitten*	*Walker*	
								Ref: T Reynolds	Giles hits the bar as the Grecians bustling play forces City into an abundance of errors. Kellard's soft shot from the edge of the penalty area puts City ahead, but Exeter obtain a deserved equaliser when Banks runs through onto Newman's perfect pass to slip the ball past Gibson.											
1F	H	EXETER		15	W	3-2	2-0	Rooks 6, Kellard 30, Sharpe 69	Gibson	Jacobs	Drysdale	Merrick	Rooks	Parr	Skirton	Garland	Galley	Kellard	Sharpe	
		19/8	10,924	*4:23*				*Corr 57, Parr 83 (og)*	*Shearing*	*Crawford*	*Blain*	*Giles*	*Newman*	*Parker*	*Corr*	*Banks*	*Wingate*	*Mitten*	*Walker*	
								Ref: W Gow	Exeter show that their cup reputation is no myth after a Rooks header and Kellard's diagonal shot give City early control. Banks creates panic in the City defence and Corr finds the net after three shots had been cleared. Parr slams ball into own net to set up a nail-biting finale.											
2	H	LEICESTER		20	D	0-0	0-0		Gibson	Briggs	Drysdale	Tainton	Rooks	Parr	Skirton	Garland	Galley	Derrick	Sharpe	
		2/9	15,883	*4*					*Shilton*	*Rodrigues*	*Houghton*	*Nish*	*Sjoberg*	*Cross*	*Brown*	*Fern*	*Lochhead*	*Roberts*	*Glover*	
								Ref: I Jones	Garland and Tainton are denied by the woodwork in the first half as City generally dominate last season's FA Cup finalists in this fluent game. Briggs is fortunate ten minutes before time as a linesman spots his handball in the penalty area, but decides to put his flag down again.											
2R	A	LEICESTER		20	D	0-0	0-0		Gibson	Briggs	Drysdale	Tainton	Rooks	Parr	Skirton	Garland	Galley	Derrick	Sharpe*	Spiring
		10/9	*20,797*	*2*		*aet*			*Shilton*	*Rodrigues*	*Houghton*	*Nish*	*Harrison*	*Manley*	*Gibson*	*Fern*	*Lochhead*	*Mackay**	*Glover*	*Tewley*
								Ref: A Jones	City are unable to turn their superiority over a Leicester side, missing five regulars, into goals. Sharpe, after an earlier header is cleared off the line, should have ended the drought just before half-time, but from a perfect position lifts his shot over the bar. Garland is booked for dissent.											
2	A	LEICESTER		21	L	1-3	1-1	Galley 5	Gibson	Briggs	Drysdale	Tainton	Rooks	Parr	Skirton	Garland	Galley	Kellard	Bartley	
RR		15/9	*12,600*	*2*				*Lochhead 13, 52, 59*	*Shilton*	*Rodrigues*	*Houghton*	*Nish*	*Sjoberg*	*Cross*	*Matthews*	*Fern*	*Lochhead*	*Brown*	*Glover*	
								Ref: E Jennings	Leicester rediscover their form in this 2nd replay at Filbert Street after City go ahead when Galley taps in Skirton's cross. Lochhead whips in Rodrigues' fierce cross for the equaliser and goes on to complete a hat-trick by shooting in from Fern's low cross and Brown's headed pass.											

FA Cup			Att	Pos	Res	F-A	H-T	Scorers, Times, and Referees	1	2	3	4	5	6	7	8	9	10	11	12 sub used
3	A	CHESTER		11	L	1-2	0-1	Skirton 70	Gibson	Jacobs	Drysdale	Tainton	Connor	Parr	Skirton	Garland	Bush	Sharpe	Bartley	
		3/1	10,030	*4:9*				*Webber 3, Dearden 89*	*Carling*	*Cheetham*	*Birks**	*Sutton*	*Turner*	*Bradbury*	*Dearden*	*Spence*	*Webber*	*Draper*	*Provan*	*Edwards*
								Ref: H Williams	City pay the cost of seemingly settling for a replay after unmarked Skirton's headed response to Webber's opening eight-yard header. City, who find Chester's bustling tactics difficult to handle, play one short for five minutes in the first half after Bush collides with Carling.											

		Home						Away					
		P	W	D	L	F	A	W	D	L	F	A	Pts
1	Huddersfield	42	14	6	1	36	10	10	6	5	32	27	60
2	Blackpool	42	10	9	2	25	16	10	4	7	31	29	53
3	Leicester	42	12	6	3	37	22	[illegible]	7	7	27	28	51
4	Middlesboro	42	15	4	2	36	14	[illegible]	6	10	19	31	50
5	Swindon	42	13	7	1	35	17	[illegible]	9	8	22	30	50
6	Sheffield Utd	42	16	2	3	50	10	[illegible]	3	12	23	28	49
7	Cardiff	42	12	7	2	38	14	[illegible]	6	9	23	27	49
8	Blackburn	42	15	2	4	42	19	[illegible]	5	11	12	31	47
9	QP Rangers	42	13	5	3	47	24	[illegible]	6	11	19	33	45
10	Millwall	42	14	4	3	38	18	[illegible]	10	10	18	38	44
11	Norwich	42	13	5	3	37	14	[illegible]	6	12	12	32	43
12	Carlisle	42	10	6	5	39	28	[illegible]	7	10	19	28	41
13	Hull	42	11	6	4	43	28	[illegible]	5	12	29	42	41
14	BRISTOL CITY	42	11	7	3	37	13	[illegible]	6	13	17	37	39
15	Oxford	42	9	9	3	23	13	[illegible]	6	12	12	29	39
16	Bolton	42	9	6	6	31	23	[illegible]	6	12	23	38	36
17	Portsmouth	42	8	4	9	39	35	[illegible]	5	11	27	45	35
18	Birmingham	42	9	7	5	33	22	[illegible]	4	15	18	56	33
19	Watford	42	6	8	7	26	21	[illegible]	5	13	18	36	31
20	Charlton	42	7	8	6	23	28	[illegible]	9	12	12	48	31
21	Aston Villa	42	7	8	6	23	21	[illegible]	5	15	13	41	29
22	Preston	42	7	6	8	31	28	[illegible]	6	14	12	35	28
		924	241	132	89	769	438	[illegible]	132	241	438	769	924

Odds & ends

Double wins: (1) Aston Villa
Double losses: (3) Cardiff, Sheffield Utd, Huddersfield.

Won from behind: (0).
Lost from in front: (0).

High spots: Beating Norwich 4-0 at Ashton Gate.
Beating Charlton 6-0 at Ashton Gate.
Doing the double over Aston Villa.
Exciting 3-3 draws with Blackburn (a) and Swindon (h).
Beating Blackburn 4-0 at Ashton Gate.
Beating Bristol Rovers 2-1 (h) in the Gloucestershire Cup Final.

Low spots: Losing 0-1 at Chester in the FA Cup.
Losing 0-2 at Oxford.

Player of the year: Dickie Rooks.
Ever-presents: (1) Brian Drysdale.
Hat-tricks: (1) John Galley.
Leading scorer: Gerry Sharpe (11).

	Appearances						Goals			
	Lge	*Sub*	LC	*Sub*	FAC	*Sub*	Lge	LC	FAC	Tot
Bartley, Danny	**16**	*1*	1		1		**3**			**3**
Briggs, Alec	**4**	*1*	3							
Broomfield, Ian	**1**									
Bush, Terry	**22**	*4*	1		1		**9**			**9**
Clarke, Malcolm	**2**	*1*	1							
Connor, Jack	**5**	*1*			1		**1**			**1**
Derrick, Jantzen	**6**	*1*	2							
Drysdale, Brian	**42**		5		1					
Ford, Tony	**7**									
Galley, John	**20**		4				**9**	1		**10**
Garland, Chris	**39**		5		1		**6**			**6**
Gibson, Mike	**38**		5		1					
Gow, Gerry	**1**									
Jacobs, Trevor	**31**		2		1		**2**			**2**
Kellard, Bobby	**35**		3				**3**	2		**5**
Mahoney, Mike	**3**									
Menmuir, Billy	**1**									
Merrick, Geoff	**3**	*1*	1							
Parr, Gordon	**38**		5		1					
Rooks, Dickie	**38**		5				**1**	1		**2**
Sharpe, Gerry	**28**	*2*	4		1		**10**	1		**11**
Skirton, Alan	**34**	*1*	5		1		**7**		1	**8**
Spiring, Peter	**4**			*1*						
Tainton, Trevor	**25**	*4*	3		1		**1**			**1**
Wilson, Bob	**1**									
Wimshurst, Ken	**18**	*2*								
(own-goals)							**2**			**2**
26 players used	**462**	***19***	**55**	***1***	**11**		**54**	**5**	**1**	**60**

LEAGUE DIVISION 2

Manager: Alan Dicks

SEASON 1970-71

No	Date			Att	Pos	Pt	F-A	H-T	Scorers, Times, and Referees	1	2	3	4	5	6	7	8	9	10	11	12 sub used
1		H	SUNDERLAND			W	4-3	2-1	Sharpe 14, 86, Skirton 44, Wimsh'st 63	Gibson	Jacobs	Drysdale	Wimshurst	Rooks	Parr	Skirton*	Garland	Galley	Gow	Sharpe	Tainton
	15/8			17,584		2			*Kerr 16, Baker72, 74*	*Montgomery*	*Irvin*	*Harvey*	*Todd*	*Heslop*	*McGiven*	*Park*	*Kerr*	*Baker*	*Porterfield*	*Hughes*	
									Ref: K Walker	A thrill a second clash in which skill far outweighs brawn, despite two bookings for each side. Jacobs is given a torrid afternoon by Hughes, but Sharpe secures the points for City after weathering much pressure in closing stages, following Baker's fine volley from the edge of the box.											
2		A	CHARLTON			D	1-1	0-1	Galley 82	Gibson	Jacobs*	Drysdale	Wimshurst	Rooks	Parr	Skirton	Garland	Galley	Gow	Sharpe	Tainton
	22/8			*10,460*		3			*Peacock 18*	*Wright*	*Curtis*	*Kinsey*	*Moore*	*Keirs*	*Reeves*	*Davies**	*Treacy*	*Gregory*	*Campbell*	*Peacock*	*Riddick*
									Ref: C Robinson	Galley stabs in Skirton's cross from the right to reward City's much improved second-half performance. Charlton highlight City's defensive shortcomings as Curtis clips a long ball through the middle for Peacock to steal in on the left and hook the ball first time over Gibson's head.											
3		H	CARDIFF		4	W	1-0	0-0	Sharpe 89	Gibson	Jacobs	Drysdale	Wimshurst	Rooks	Parr	Skirton	Garland*	Galley	Gow	Sharpe	Tainton
	29/8			**24,969**	*5*	5				*Parsons P*	*Carver*	*Bell*	*Sutton*	*Murray*	*Harris*	*Clark*	*Gibson*	*Woodruff*	*Toshack*	*King*	
									Ref: G Kew	City achieve their first home success over the Bluebirds in eight games. Sharpe hammers in Tainton's cross from the right to end jinx. As usual, Woodruff's long throws cause problems, but Rooks and Parr are in fine form. Bookings for Gow in first half and Ian Gibson after the break.											
4		A	LEICESTER		11	L	**0-4**	0-4	*[Nish 44p]*	Gibson	Jacobs	Drysdale	Wimshurst	Rooks	Parr	Skirton	Tainton	Galley	Gow	Sharpe	
	2/9			*20,435*	*5*	5			*Farrington 20, Kellard 21, Brown 34,*	*Shilton*	*Whitworth*	*Nish*	*Kellard*	*Sjoberg*	*Cross*	*Farrington*	*Matthews*	*Stringfellow**	*Brown*	*Glover*	*Fern*
									Ref: R Johnston	Seeking their first home success, Leicester start nervously against City. Skirton has a searing left-foot volley disallowed for barging his way past Cross before Leicester gain confidence with two quick goals. Nish completes City's rout with a penalty after Rooks fouled Stringfellow.											
5		A	SHEFFIELD UTD		8	D	3-3	1-0	Galley 27, 50, Gow 63	Gibson	**Stacey**	Drysdale	Wimshurst	Connor	Parr	Skirton	Garland	Galley	Gow	Sharpe	
	5/9			*15,097*	*19*	6			*Woodward 66, Dearden 72, Tudor 89*	*Hodgkinson*	*Badger*	*Hemsley*	*Powell*	*Colquhoun*	*Salmons*	*Woodward*	*Barnwell**	*Dearden*	*Currie*	*Reece*	*Tudor*
									Ref: B. Homewood	Woodward's scorching 20-yarder sparks United's fightback in a thrill a minute game in which City squander a three-goal lead. City twice clear shots off the line before taking the lead in their third attack, when Alan Hodgkinson is punished for dropping a cross under Galley's challenge.											
6		H	HULL		8	D	3-3	2-1	Garland14, Skirton 22, 57	Gibson	Stacey	Drysdale	Wimshurst	Connor	Parr	Skirton	Garland	Galley	Gow	Sharpe	
	12/9			12,978	*3*	7			*Chilton 44, 49, Butler 74*	*McKechnie*	*Beardsley*	*De Vries**	*Wilkinson*	*Neill*	*Simpkin*	*Lord*	*Greenwood*	*Chilton*	*Wagstaff*	*Butler*	*Pearson*
									Ref: B Daniels	City sparkle until Gibson's short free-kick out of defence lets the visitors back into the game. Despite going ahead again, City become a nervy shambles and Hull gain a deserved share of the spoils when Wagstaff's chip from the right is delightfully flicked in at the near post by Butler.											
7		A	QP RANGERS		12	L	1-2	0-0	Garland 49	Gibson	Stacey	Drysdale	Wimshurst	Connor	Parr	Skirton	Garland*	Galley	Gow	Sharpe	Tainton
	19/9			*13,367*	*17*	7			*Marsh 68, Bridges 70*	*Parkes*	*Hazell*	*Clement*	*Venables*	*Hunt*	*Sibley*	*Bridges*	*Francis*	*Saul*	*Marsh*	*Ferguson*	
									Ref: T Dawes	Garland takes a pass in his stride and smashes a left-footer high into net as City confirm their superiority at Loftus Road. Defensive errors then bring defeat. Marsh is left free at the far post to head in a right-wing centre; then Bridges beats the offside trap to flick a through ball into goal.											
8		H	BLACKBURN		12	D	1-1	0-0	Skirton 59	Gibson	Stacey	Drysdale	Wimshurst	Rooks	Parr	Skirton	Garland	Galley	Gow	Sharpe	
	23/9			14,019	*19*	8			*Conlon 67*	*Jones*	*Kopel*	*Wilson*	*Hunter*	*Mulvaney*	*Knighton*	*Conlon*	*Russell*	*Goodwin*	*Rogers*	*Kerr*	
									Ref: J Hunting	City get the slow handclap from disgruntled fans as they hit rock bottom form against defensive opponents. Skirton takes advantage of City's only real chance with a crisp drive past the advancing Jones, but Blackburn respond. Conlon gets past Drysdale and levels with a fierce shot.											
9		H	BIRMINGHAM		7	W	2-1	0-0	Galley 74, Sharpe 75	Gibson	Stacey	Drysdale	Wimshurst	Rooks	Parr	Skirton	Garland	Galley	Gow	Sharpe	
	29/9			15,979	*17*	10			*Summerill 77*	*Kelly*	*Martin*	*Pendrey*	*Hockey*	*Hynd*	*Robinson*	*Francis**	*Vowden*	*Latchford R*	*Vincent*	*Summerill*	*Thomson*
									Ref: L Callaghan	City respond to Brum's physical approach with an aggressive second-half display. Surprisingly, only Gow is booked, and that was for abusive language. City's opener is credited to Galley, whose shot hits a post and rolls along the line before Martin nets the ball whilst trying to clear.											
10		A	LUTON		11	L	0-3	0-2		Gibson	Stacey	Drysdale	Wimshurst*	Rooks	Parr	Skirton	Garland	Galley	Gow	Sharpe	Tainton
	3/10			*15,992*	*3*	10			*MacDonald 17, 33, Slough 55*	*Read*	*Ryan John*	*Slough*	*Hoy*	*Nicholl*	*Moore*	*Ryan Jim*	*Court*	*MacDonald*	*Keen*	*Givens**	*Busby*
									Ref: A Jones	City suffer a comprehensive defeat as MacDonald scores twice, his second a classic header to finish off Jim Ryans's cross, to take his tally to seven. On the attack from the outset, Luton take the lead when Gibson diverts the ball into MacDonald's path when saving Keen's strong shot.											

No	Date	Venue	Opponent	Att	Pos	Pts	Res	FT	HT	Scorers, Times, and Referees	1	2	3	4	5	6	7	8	9	10	11	12
11	10/10	H	OXFORD	16,027	14		L	**0-4**	0-1	[Smithson 70p]	Gibson	Stacey	Drysdale	Tainton	Rooks	Parr	Skirton	Garland	Broomfield	Gow	Sharpe	
					3	10				*Atkinson 2, Evanson 55, 65,*	*Kearns*	*Lucas*	*Shuker*	*Smithson*	*Clarke*	*Thompson*	*Sloan*	*Atkinson G*	*Skeen*	*Clayton*	*Evanson*	
										Ref: R Matthewson	City are unable to hold an eager Oxford side who take an early lead, when Atkinson punishes a static defence by deftly flicking Lucas' long diagonal ball into the corner of the net. Smithson completes City's rout by converting a penalty, awarded when Gibson grabs Sloan's legs.											
12	17/10	A	SUNDERLAND	*17,335*	17		L	0-1	0-1		Gibson	Stacey	Drysdale	Wimshurst	Rooks	Parr	Skirton	Garland	Galley	Gow*	Sharpe	Tainton
					9	10				*McGiven 30*	*Montgomery*	*Malone**	*Irvin*	*Todd*	*Pit*	*McGiven*	*Porterfield*	*Kerr*	*Baker*	*Harris*	*Hughes*	*Park*
										Ref: R Lee	City, in all white, demonstrate much energy in attack and tightness in defence by playing in a 4-3-3 formation. Sharpe blasts wide from ten yards before Sunderland score. Kerr's centre from the left is played back by Hughes, for McGiven to send in an unstoppable 18-yarder.											
13	20/10	A	MIDDLESBROUGH	*16,651*	20		L	0-1	0-0		Gibson	Stacey*	Drysdale	Wimshurst	Rooks	Parr	**Fear**	Garland	Galley	Tainton	Sharpe	Merrick
					8	10				*Hickton 84*	*Whigham*	*Maddren*	*Jones G*	*Smith*	*Gates*	*Spraggon*	*Mills*	*McMordie**	*McIlmoyle*	*Hickton*	*Laidlaw*	*Webb*
										Ref: W Johnson	A tough unrelenting struggle in the wind and rain at Ayresome Park as City adopt a 4-4-2 formation. Hickton denies City any reward for much wholehearted effort when he heads in from a disputed free-kick. Luckless Stacey, booked earlier for handball, is carried off with ankle damage.											
14	24/10	A	BOLTON	*7,749*	21		L	0-1	0-0		Gibson	Drysdale	Merrick	Wimshurst	Rooks	Parr	Skirton	Garland	Tainton	Gow	Sharpe	
					13	10				*Williams 86*	*Boswell*	*Ritson*	*Farrimond*	*Williams G*	*Hurley*	*Hulme*	*Taylor*	*Byrom*	*Fletcher*	*Rimmer*	*Phillips*	
										Ref: D Lyden	A scrappy game as City again utilise a 4-4-2 formation. Bolton are jeered by their fans just prior to their late goal. Taylor's ball into the middle is back-headed by Fletcher for Williams to stride forward unchallenged to net from eight yards. Parr is booked for fouling Fletcher from behind.											
15	31/10	H	SHEFFIELD WED	13,093	21		L	1-2	0-0	Broomfield 82	Gibson	Drysdale	Merrick	Wimshurst	Connor	Parr	Skirton	Broomfield	Galley*	Tainton	Sharpe	Gow
					14	10				*Prendergast 54, Sissons 71*	*Grummitt*	*Rodrigues**	*Wilcockson*	*Thompson*	*Ellis*	*Pugh*	*Sinclair*	*Prendergast*	*Warboys*	*Todd*	*Sissons*	*Craig*
										Ref: R Capey	City hold early initiative in an incident-packed game, but a chapter of misses leads to a loss of momentum after half-time. Parr's poor defensive header sets up Craig's high centre, which Prendergast heads through Gibson's arms. A goalmouth scramble allows Broomfield to score at last.											
16	7/11	A	SWINDON	*16,678*	20		L	1-2	0-0	Gilroy 66	Gibson	Drysdale	Merrick	Wimshurst	Rooks	**Rodgers**	Garland	Broomfield	Galley	Tainton	Sharpe	
					12	10				*Horsfield 72, Noble 90*	*Jones*	*Thomas*	*Trollope*	*Butler*	*Blick*	*Harland*	*Smith*	*Smart*	*Horsfield*	*Noble*	*Rogers*	
										Ref: R Kirkpatrick	Rodgers marks his City debut with a booking, while an alert linesman averts strife as Swindon are awarded a 63rd-minute 'goal'. The aptly named Mr Handy prevails to ensure the decision is changed to a corner. Noble blasts in Horsfield's centre for Swindon's injury-time winner.											
17	14/11	H	WATFORD	11,100	20		W	**3-0**	2-0	Broomfield 2, Wimshurst 39, Sharpe 84	Gibson	Drysdale	Merrick	Wimshurst	Rooks	Rodgers	Garland	Broomfield	Galley	Tainton	Sharpe	
					17	12					*Walker*	*Welbourne*	*Williams*	*Eddy*	*Lees*	*Walley*	*Scullion*	*Wigg*	*Endean*	*Packer*	*Woods**	*Garbett*
										Ref: M Fussey	Despite missing many chances, City end a run of seven-successive League defeats. Broomfield latches onto a ball played over Watford's defence to net from eight yards, Wimshurst smashes in a crisp left-foot drive, and Sharpe forces ball over line after his initial shot is blocked.											
18	21/11	A	MILLWALL	*9,173*	20		L	0-2	0-2		Gibson	Drysdale	Merrick	Gow	Rooks	Rodgers*	Garland	Broomfield	Galley	Tainton	Sharpe	Parr
					11	12				*Cripps 23, Allder 42*	*King*	*Brown B*	*Cripps*	*Dorney*	*Kitchener*	*Burnett*	*Bridges*	*Dunphy*	*Bolland*	*Possee*	*Allder*	
										Ref: K Burns	City lose composure after going behind when Cripps finishes off Brown's cross from the right with a diving header. Hesitancy between Gibson and Rooks then doubles the deficit as Allder runs between them to deposit the ball in an empty net. Bookings for Drysdale and Garland.											
19	23/11	H	CARLISLE	13,561	19		W	2-1	0-0	Galley 83, Gow 86	Gibson	Jacobs	Drysdale	Tainton	Rooks	Rodgers*	Sharpe	Broomfield	Galley	Gow	Bartley	Merrick
					7	14				*Hatton 55*	*Ross*	*Hemstead**	*Davis*	*Ternent*	*Winstanley*	*Sutton*	*Martin*	*Barton*	*Hatton*	*Owen*	*Balderstone*	*Kinsella*
										Ref: A Morrisey	With vouchers being issued for the Spurs cup-tie, the crowd is smaller than expected. Gow secures the points with a 20-yard screamer, but Carlisle take a deserved lead through Hatton, who manages to evade Gibson's attempts at a rugby tackle. Ternent is booked for pushing the ref.											
20	5/12	A	ORIENT	*6,250*	19		D	1-1	0-1	Sharpe 80	Gibson	Jacobs	Drysdale	Wimshurst	Rooks	Parr	Skirton	Garland*	Galley	Gow	Sharpe	Tainton
					20	15				*Riddick 11*	*Goddard*	*Jones*	*Rofe*	*Bennett*	*Mancini*	*Allen*	*Lazarus*	*Riddick*	*Fairbrother*	*Dyson*	*Brabrook**	*Bullock*
										Ref: M Kerhof	City obtain a deserved point on a heavy pitch, that makes passing difficult, when Skirton's back-header is hooked low into the corner of the net by Sharpe. Orient's goal is a simple affair: Riddick heads in from Brabrook's cross. A four-man move ends with Skirton heading onto the bar.											
21	12/12	H	NORWICH	10,637	20		L	0-1	0-1		Gibson	Jacobs*	Drysdale	Wimshurst	Rooks	Parr	Skirton	Garland	Galley	Gow	Sharpe	Tainton
					7	15				*Silvester 37*	*Keelan*	*Payne*	*Black*	*Stringer*	*Forbes*	*Briggs*	*Livermore*	*Silvester*	*Howard*	*Padden*	*Foggo*	
										Ref: R Barker	Dominant City fall to a Canaries smash and grab win that is inspired by Keelan's great display. Norwich are unlucky on 63 mins to be given an indirect free-kick instead of a Ken Foggo score, but in a rare breakaway Silvester heads Foggo's cross high into the net to Gibson's right.											

No	Date		Att	Pos	Pt	F-A	H-T	Scorers, Times, and Referees	1	2	3	4	5	6	7	8	9	10	11	12 sub used
22	H	CHARLTON		20	D	2-2	0-2	Rooks 56, Sharpe 58p	Gibson	Jacobs	Drysdale	Wimshurst	Rooks	Parr*	Skirton	Garland	Galley	Gow	Sharpe	Tainton
	19/12		**10,187**	*22*	16			*Plumb 2, 23*	*Wright*	*Curtis*	*Bruck*	*Kenning*	*Went*	*Shipperley**	*Davies*	*Treacy*	*Plumb*	*Bond*	*Peacock*	*Reeves*
								Ref: I Smith	Ex Bristol Rover Dickie Plumb is denied a hat-trick on 67 minutes when his left-footer hits a post. City suffer early shocks in this bottom of the table clash, but Rooks' header brings them back into the game. The penalty trickles in after hitting underside of bar and twice bouncing on line.											
23	A	BIRMINGHAM		20	L	0-2	0-2		Gibson	Jacobs*	Drysdale	Wimshurst	Rooks	Parr	Skirton	Spiring	Garland	Gow	Sharpe	Tainton
	9/1		*15,292*	*14*	16			*Taylor 16, Latchford R 45*	*Latchford D*	*Martin*	*Hockey*	*Page*	*Hynd*	*Robinson*	*Campbell**	*Bowker*	*Latchford R*	*Summerill*	*Taylor*	*Thwaites*
								Ref: G Jones	Following a minute's silence in memory of the Ibrox disaster victims, and replacement of a broken corner flag, City are denied on five minutes when Spiring's strike is disallowed because of free-kick taken prior to the ref's signal. Bob Latchford is also unlucky, hitting bar near the end.											
24	H	MIDDLESBROUGH		20	L	0-2	0-1		Gibson	Drysdale	Merrick	Gow	Rodgers	Parr	Skirton	Garland	Galley	Derrick*	Sharpe	Broomfield
	16/1		10,535	*6*	16			*Hickton 25, Parr 80 (og)*	*Whigham*	*A Smith*	*Jones*	*Moody*	*Gates*	*Spraggon*	*Downing*	*McMordie*	*McIlmoyle*	*Hickton*	*Laidlaw*	
								Ref: C Nicholls	Chants of 'Dicks must go' greet Derrick's substitution shortly after Parr's unlucky own-goal. Gibson prevents a heavy defeat as City have Sharpe stretchered off on 87 mins following McMordie's tackle. Strikes by Gow and Laidlaw are disallowed on 15 and 67 mins respectively.											
25	A	CARLISLE		20	L	1-2	1-1	Galley 14	**Cashley**	Jacobs	Drysdale	Wimshurst	Rooks	Parr	Fear	Gow	Galley	Merrick	Garland*	Tainton
	30/1		*7,764*	*6*	16			*Hatton 19, Owen 74*	*Ross*	*Davis*	*Gorman*	*Ternant*	*Winstanley*	*Sutton*	*Murray*	*Martin*	*Owen*	*Hatton*	*Balderstone*	
								Ref: S Kayley	Cashley makes a confident start to his League career behind an uncertain defence. He has no chance with Owen's header from Gorman's cross from the left, but is caught off his line by Hatton's magnificent 25-yarder. Galley heads his hundredth League goal, after a great run by Fear.											
26	H	ORIENT		21	D	0-0	0-0		Cashley	Tainton	Drysdale	Wimshurst	Rooks	Parr	Spiring	Garland	Galley	Gow	Fear	
	6/2		11,423	*18*	17				*Goddard*	*Jones*	*Rofe*	*Bennett*	*Mancini*	*Allen*	*Lazarus**	*Brisley*	*Bullock*	*Dyson*	*Fairbrother*	*Riddick*
								Ref: V Batty	Fairbrother proves a real handful to City, who find control difficult on a well-sanded pitch in this relegation clash. City improve after the break and have a Wimshurst chip, as well as a Rooks header, cleared off line by Mancini, whilst Drysdale deals likewise with Dyson's inswinger.											
27	A	NORWICH		21	L	2-3	2-0	Galley 15, Fear 26	Cashley	Tainton	Drysdale	Wimshurst	Rooks	Parr	Spiring	Garland*	Galley	Merrick	Fear	Broomfield
	13/2		*10,513*	*8*	17			*Silvester 56, Anderson 65, Bennett 68*	*Keelan*	*Payne*	*Black*	*Stringer*	*Forbes*	*Anderson*	*Livermore*	*Silvester*	*Bennett*	*Paddon*	*Foggo*	
								Ref: N Paget	Galley takes advantage of the strong wind to net with a superb 35-yard lob as City are well on top before the break. It's a different tale after the interval. Norwich storm back with the wind to their advantage and Anderson, involved in all three of their goals, scores with a low cross-shot.											
28	H	MILLWALL		19	W	3-2	2-0	Wimshurst 14, Gow 45, Fear 76	Cashley	Tainton	Drysdale	Wimshurst	Rooks	Parr	Spiring	Broomfield	Garland	Gow	Fear	
	20/2		10,578	*11*	19			*Cripps 47, Bridges 54*	*King*	*Brown B*	*Cripps*	*Dorney*	*Kitchener*	*Garner*	*Brown S**	*Bolland*	*Bridges*	*Dunphy*	*Allder*	*Neill*
								Ref: I Jones	City field their youngest forward line as Wimshurst's 20-yarder slips through King's fingers for a gift lead and Gow forces home a low shot. Fear scores City's winner after the Lions' fightback, Cripps, later booked, flicking in from a free-kick and Bridges heading in at the near post.											
29	A	SHEFFIELD WED		20	L	0-2	0-2		Cashley	Tainton	Drysdale	Wimshurst*	Rooks	Parr	Spiring	Broomfield	Garland	Gow	Fear	Merrick
	27/2		*12,347*	*12*	19			*Prendergast 11, 39*	*Grummitt*	*Todd*	*Burton*	*Thompson*	*Prophett*	*Pugh*	*Sinclair*	*Craig*	*Sunley*	*Prendergast*	*Sissons*	
								Ref: C Robinson	City, after missing four good chances, allow Wednesday to go ahead. Cashley is at fault, allowing Prendergast's header to slip beneath him, but is blameless later when his wonder save presents Prendergast with his second goal. Garland is booked in the 43rd minute for abusive language.											
30	H	BOLTON		19	D	1-1	1-1	Garland 40	Gibson	Tainton	Drysdale	Wimshurst	Rooks	Parr	Skirton	Garland	Galley	Gow	Bartley	
	6/3		10,550	*20*	20			*Waldron 18*	*Clarke*	*Ritson*	*McAllister*	*Waldron*	*Rimmer !*	*Greaves*	*Hallows*	*Byrom*	*Hulme*	*Seddon*	*Manning*	
								Ref: A Oliver	The Trotters score first as Rooks lays injured in the area, Alan Waldron shooting low into goal from ten yards. Garland looks offside as he lobs the ball in on the turn to equalise. Bookings for Roy Greaves and Garland, whilst Warwick Rimmer is sent off on 75 mins for fouling Garland.											
31	A	PORTSMOUTH		19	D	1-1	1-0	Garland 18	Gibson	Jacobs	Drysdale	Wimshurst	Rodgers	Parr	Tainton	Garland	Galley	Gow	Bartley	
	10/3		*8,676*	*17*	21			*Hand 76*	*Milkins*	*Smith*	*Youlden**	*Hand*	*Blant*	*Munks*	*Piper*	*Pointer*	*Hiron*	*Bromley*	*Jennings*	*Trebilcock*
								Ref: C Thomas	City have their defensive tactics breached by Hand, whose shot is deflected away from Gibson. An illegally taken free-kick rules out Garland's superb soaring header, but three minutes later the striker gets his reward, collecting Tainton's through pass to slip the ball past Milkins.											

No	Date	Opponent	Att	Pos	Pts	Res	HT	Scorers, Times, and Referees	1	2	3	4	5	6	7	8	9	10	11	subs used
32	A	WATFORD		19	W	**3-0**	0-0	Gow [illegible]3, Garland 66, Galley 83	Gibson	Jacobs	Drysdale	**Wilson**	Parr	**Hill**	Tainton	Garland	Galley	Wimshurst	Gow	
	13/3		*12,288*	*18*	23				*Edmonds*	*Butler*	*Williams*	*Garbett*	*Lees*	*Walley*	*Scullion*	*Welbourne*	*Wigg*	*Eddy*	*Farley**	*Woods*
								Ref: R Matthewson	With loan signings Hill and Wilson in their ranks, City settle down after a negative start. Gow is at the near post to finish off a cross. Then Garland scores with a left-foot shot before Galley's superb solo run from the centre-circle, during which he beats three men, seals City's win.											
33	H	SWINDON		19	W	2-1	0-0	Gow [illegible]7, Galley 53	Gibson	Jacobs	Drysdale	Wilson	Parr	Hill	Tainton	Garland	Galley	Wimshurst	Gow	
	20/3		17,310	*10*	25			*Horsfield 64*	*Downsboro'*	*Thomas*	*Trollope*	*Butler*	*Burrows*	*Harland*	*Peplow*	*Gough*	*Horsfield*	*Noble*	*Rogers*	
								Ref: F Nicholson	Swindon are outplayed on a quagmire of a pitch. Wilson supplies the midfield drive often lacking this season, while Tainton gives Trollope cause to regret passing a last-minute fitness test. Gow's header and Galley's shot earn goals before Parr's error allows Swindon a ray of hope.											
34	H	SHEFFIELD UTD		19	L	0-1	0-1		Gibson	Jacobs	Drysdale	Wilson	Parr	Hill	Tainton	Garland	Galley	Wimshurst*	Gow	Fear
	27/3		14,999	*2*	25			*Currie 14*	*Hope*	*Badger*	*Hemsley*	*Barlow*	*Colquhoun*	*Hockey*	*Woodward*	*Ford**	*Dearden*	*Currie*	*Reece*	*Salmons*
								Ref: G Hill	A linesman denies City a 27th-minute equaliser, ruling that Gow unfairly won the ball before chipping into goal from almost on the by-line. United are full value for their win, secured by Currie, who accepts a return ball from Dearden to run into the area and score with great aplomb.											
35	A	CARDIFF		19	L	0-1	0-1		Gibson	Jacobs	Drysdale	Wilson	Rooks	Hill	Tainton	Garland	Galley	Wimshurst	Gow	
	3/4		***24,638***	*2*	25			*Wimshurst 4 (og)*	*Eadie*	*Carver*	*Bell*	*Sutton*	*Murray*	*Phillips*	*King*	*Gibson**	*Warboys*	*Woodruff*	*Bird*	*Harris*
								Ref: J Hunting	City make a mockery of their lowly position and dominate proceedings, but are unable to convert any of their many chances. Cardiff offer little threat, except in breakaways, but are gifted victory by Wimshurst, who deflects the ball off his head when challenging for a cross from the left.											
36	H	LUTON		19	W	3-2	0-2	Rooks 59, Garland 64, 66	Cashley	Jacobs	Drysdale	Wilson	Rooks	Hill*	Tainton	Garland	Galley	Wimshurst	Gow	Merrick
	9/4		18,846	*4*	27			*Busby 23, MacDonald 43*	*Read*	*Ryan John*	*Slough*	*Givens*	*Nicholl*	*Moore*	*Ryan Jim*	*Busby*	*MacDonald*	*Keen*	*Anderson**	*Goodeve*
								Ref: D Nippard	Great entertainment, superb attacking football by both sides. City's two-goal 90-second burst climaxes a contest that has everything. Luton's opening goal is perfection, as Busby finishes off MacDonald's right-wing cross. Garland hammers home the ball from the left to clinch the win.											
37	H	PORTSMOUTH		18	W	2-0	1-0	Garland 30, Tainton 85	Cashley	Jacobs	Drysdale	Wilson	Rooks	Merrick	Tainton	Garland	Galley*	Wimshurst	Gow	Fear
	10/4		14,663	*17*	29				*Standen*	*Youlden*	*Travers*	*Hand*	*Blant*	*Munks*	*Piper*	*Storrie*	*Hiron*	*Bromley*	*Jennings*	
								Ref: A Hart	A quiet afternoon for Cashley against defensively-minded opponents in this vital relegation clash. Garland slides the ball home from a Rooks header to put City ahead. After the break, Gow has a low drive disallowed for offside, but great play by Fear lays on a goal for Tainton.											
38	A	HULL		18	L	0-1	0-0		Cashley	Jacobs	Drysdale	Wilson	Rooks	Merrick	Tainton	Garland	Galley*	Wimshurst	Gow	Parr
	12/4		*22,178*	*4*	29			*Banks 58*	*McKechnie*	*Banks*	*Beardsley*	*Wilkinson*	*Neill*	*Houghton*	*Knighton*	*Lord*	*Chilton*	*Wagstaff*	*Butler*	
								Ref: W Castle	Cashley, playing over Easter due to Gibson dislocating a finger at Cardiff, saves a penalty given for Gow tripping Chilton. Despite Hull's fifth-successive failure from the spot, Cashley blocking Knighton's kick, they win this mediocre contest thanks to Banks' tame shot finding the net.											
39	A	OXFORD		19	L	0-1	0-0		Cashley	Jacobs	Drysdale	Wilson	Rooks	Parr*	Tainton	Fear	Galley	Merrick	Gow	Bartley
	17/4		*8,902*	*12*	29			*Clarke D 67*	*Kearns*	*Lucas*	*Shuker*	*Roberts*	*Clarke C*	*Evanson*	*Clarke D*	*Atkinson G*	*Skeen*	*Cassidy*	*Clayton*	
								Ref: D Pugh	Oxford have the ball in City's net just after the start. Tainton volleys home on 39 minutes, but both efforts are disallowed for offside. Derek Clarke rises high above the advancing Cashley to head the only goal; but City's relegation fears are eased with news of Blackburn's defeat.											
40	H	QP RANGERS		19	D	0-0	0-0		Cashley	Tainton	Drysdale	Wilson	Rooks	Hill	Fear	Garland	Galley*	Merrick	Gow	Skirton
	24/4		12,522	*12*	30				*Parkes*	*Watson*	*Gillard*	*Hunt*	*Evans*	*Hazell*	*Francis*	*Venables*	*Clement*	*Marsh*	*Saul*	
								Ref: C Fallon	Clement leads Rangers' attack in place of the injured McCulloch. City are reinforced by the return of Hill and Garland, though ankle problems forces the withdrawal of Jacobs. An uneventful contest apart from flashes of Marsh's skill, with neither side demonstrating much penetration.											
41	H	LEICESTER		19	L	0-1	0-0		Cashley	Jacobs	Drysdale	Wilson	Rooks	Merrick	Tainton	Spiring*	Garland	Fear	Gow	Skirton
	27/4		16,103	*1*	30			*Brown 89*	*Shilton*	*Whitworth*	*Nish*	*Kellard*	*Sjoberg**	*Cross*	*Farrington*	*Brown*	*Fern*	*Carlin*	*Manley*	*Stringfellow*
								Ref: W Gow	Ebullient Bobby Kellard, much missed this season since his transfer, celebrates fulfilment of his ambition of reaching the top flight as Leicester clinch the title. Brown lashes in Kellard's right-wing corner for the injury-time winner. Wilson was booked 57 mins for throwing the ball away.											
42	A	BLACKBURN		19	D	2-2	2-0	Galley 8, 27	**Bond**	Jacobs	Drysdale	Gow	Rooks	Hill	Tainton	Garland*	Galley	Broomfield	Fear	**Menmuir**
	1/5		***3,971***	*21*	31			*Hunter 56, Rogers 70*	*Jones*	*Goodwin*	*Kopel*	*Hunter*	*Fazackerley*	*Wilson**	*Metcalfe*	*Conlon*	*Pickering*	*Parkes*	*Rogers*	*Eccles*
	Home	Away						Ref: V James	Blackburn, doomed to Associate Member status for the first time, look dead and buried at the interval. Injury-hit City introduce 17-year-old Len Bond, who distinguishes himself on several occasions. Rovers deserve the draw, achieved by Hunter's header and Rogers' fine low shot.											
Average	14,174	13,131																		

League Cup					F-A	H-T	Scorers, Times, and Referees	1	2	3	4	5	6	7	8	9	10	11	12 sub used
2	A	ROTHERHAM	7	D	0-0	0-0		Gibson	Jacobs	Drysdale	Wimshurst	Connor	Parr	Skirton	Garland	Galley	Gow	Sharpe*	Tainton
8/9		7,384	3:8					*Tunks*	*Houghton*	*Leigh*	*Bettany*	*Watson*	*Swift*	*Brogden*	*Hague*	*Phillips**	*Bentley*	*Mullen*	*Lill*
							Ref: K Howley	Dogged defending by Connor and Parr on a night of cup shocks keep City in the competition against keen young Rotherham forwards. Garland is guilty of the 'miss of the season' after rounding the keeper in the second minute. Leigh appears from nowhere to clear the ball off the line.											
2R	H	ROTHERHAM	7	W	4-0	1-0	Skirton 26, Gow 54, Garland 55, 83	Gibson	Jacobs*	Drysdale	Wimshurst	Connor	Parr	Skirton	Garland	Galley	Gow	Sharpe	Tainton
15/9		9,403	3:11					*Tunks*	*Houghton*	*Leigh*	*Bettany*	*Swift*	*Hague*	*Brogden*	*Fantham*	*Womble*	*Bentley*	*Mullen**	*Warnock*
							Ref: R Burns	Bettany hits a post for the visitors shortly before Skirton heads City in front. After the break, Gow's harmless shot deceives Tunks and then the move of the match sees Chris Garland running 40 yards to head in. A cool chip from Garland seals a rather flattering scoreline for City.											
3	A	BLACKPOOL	11	W	1-0	1-0	Sharpe 24	Gibson	Stacey	Drysdale	Tainton	Rooks	Parr	Skirton	Garland	Galley*	Gow	Sharpe	Broomfield
7/10		10,877	1:21					*Thomson*	*Armfield*	*Mowbray*	*Hatton*	*James*	*Alcock*	*Burns*	*Suddick*	*Craven**	*Hutchison*	*Coleman*	*McNicholas*
							Ref: H Williams	City's first away cup win over top-flight opposition for 61 years. Teamwork, with every player working for each other, forms the basis of City's shock success. Blackpool are decisively beaten as Sharpe spurns numerous opportunities to add to his header from Skirton's perfect cross.											
4	A	LEICESTER	21	D	2-2	1-1	Garland 17, Sharpe 72	Gibson	Drysdale	Merrick	Wimshurst	Rooks	Parr	Skirton	Garland*	Broomfield	Tainton	Sharpe	Gow
28/10		21,577	3				*Farrington 27, Nish 76p*	*Shilton*	*Whitworth*	*Nish*	*Manley*	*Sjoberg*	*Cross*	*Farrington*	*Brown A*	*Stringfellow*	*Kellard*	*Glover*	
							Ref: D Pugh	Shilton secures Leicester an undeserved replay. Inspired City twice ahead, but the Filberts respond with a 25-yard shot and a disputed pen after Parr cuts across Manley. City's second is the goal of the game, Sharpe finishing a 40-yard dribble with a shot into far corner. Rooks is booked.											
4R	H	LEICESTER	21	W	2-1	1-0	Rodgers 15, Wimshurst 104	Gibson	Drysdale	Merrick	Wimshurst	Rodgers	Parr	Skirton*	Broomfield	Galley	Tainton	Sharpe	Gow
3/11		16,575	1		aet		*Nish 82p*	*Shilton*	*Whitworth*	*Nish*	*Manley*	*Sjoberg*	*Cross*	*Farrington*	*Fern*	*Stringfellow**	*Kellard*	*Glover*	*Brown A*
							Ref: W Gow	City demonstrate much courage and determination as Leicester take the tie into extra-time with a late equaliser. Rodgers hits a tremendous shot which cannons off Sjoberg and into the net. Leicester take the initiative in the second half, but City win in extra-time with a well-taken goal.											
QF	A	FULHAM	20	D	0-0	0-0		Gibson	Drysdale	Merrick	Wimshurst	Rooks	Rodgers	Garland	Broomfield	Galley	Tainton	Sharpe	
17/11		16,281	3:1					*Seymour*	*Pentecost*	*Callaghan*	*Brown Stan*	*Matthewson*	*Dunne*	*Moreline**	*Halom*	*Earle*	*Lloyd*	*Barrett*	*Morton*
							Ref: J Taylor	City are on top at rain-soaked Craven Cottage but squander many opportunities. Sharpe hits a post at the Cottage end on eight minutes. There is nearly a spectacular 30-yard up and under own-goal by Matthewson, who chased Gibson's goal-kick whilst under pressure from Broomfield.											
QF R	H	FULHAM	20	W	1-0	1-0	Sharpe 31p	Gibson	Drysdale	Merrick	Gow	Rooks	Parr	Skirton	Garland*	Galley	Tainton	Sharpe	Broomfield
24/11		23,230	3:1					*Seymour*	*Pentecost*	*Callaghan*	*Brown Stan*	*Matthewson*	*Dunne*	*Horne*	*Halom*	*Earle*	*Lloyd*	*Barrett*	
							Ref: J Taylor	Fulham chairman, comedian Tommy Trinder, sums up City's performance with his well-known catchphrase 'you lucky people'. Few would disagree as City are outplayed. Brown's trip on Skirton yields a penalty, but Fulham are denied justice of a similar award just before the end.											
SF 1	H	TOTTENHAM	20	D	1-1	0-0	Skirton 56	Gibson	Jacobs	Drysdale	Wimshurst	Rooks	Parr	Skirton	Garland	Galley	Gow	Sharpe	
16/12		30,201	1:3				*Gilzean 72*	*Jennings*	*Kinnear*	*Knowles*	*Mullery*	*England*	*Beal*	*Gilzean*	*Perryman*	*Chivers*	*Peters*	*Pearce*	
							Ref: N Burtenshaw	City are thwarted by Gilzean's immaculate far-post header, rounding off Peters' pinpoint pass. Wimshurst controls the midfield as the game opens up in the second half. City score with Jennings out of position when Beal's clearance hits Peters and rolls obligingly into Skirton's path.											
SF 2	A	TOTTENHAM	20	L	0-2	0-0		Gibson	Jacobs	Drysdale	Wimshurst	Rooks	Parr	Skirton*	Garland	Sharpe	Gow	Spiring	Tainton
23/12		29,982	1:4		aet		*Chivers 98, Pearce 111*	*Jennings*	*Kinnear*	*Knowles*	*Mullery*	*England**	*Beal*	*Gilzean*	*Perryman*	*Chivers*	*Peters*	*Neighbour*	*Pearce*
							Ref: K Burns (City lost 1-3 on aggregate)	A brave show by City as a costly error of judgement by Gibson grants Spurs a breakthrough goal. Advancing too soon to Knowles' free-kick, he is exposed as Chivers heads in. City's best chance falls to Sharpe, a fraction late as Tainton's cross presents an open goal on 51 minutes.											

FA Cup																			
3	A	SOUTHAMPTON	20	L	0-3	0-0		Cashley	Parr	Drysdale	Wimshurst*	Rooks	Rodgers	Tainton	Garland	Broomfield	Gow	Sharpe	Merrick
11/1		24,131	1:8				*O'Neil 72, Davies 79, 85*	*Martin*	*Kirkup*	*Hollywood*	*Fisher*	*McGrath*	*Gabriel*	*Paine*	*Channon*	*Davies*	*O'Neil*	*Jenkins**	*Byrne*
							Ref: C Nicholls	Tenacious City give the Saints many anxious moments as Cashley has a debut to remember, making many fine saves, incuding a 69th-minute penalty after Rooks' handball. He dives right to hold Mick Channon's kick, but Southampton undismayed, respond with three late strikes.											

		Home						Away					
	P	W	D	L	F	A	W	D	L	F	A	Pts
1 Leicester	42	12	7	2	30	14	[illegible]	6	4	27	16	59
2 Sheffield Utd	42	14	6	1	49	18	[illegible]	8	6	24	21	56
3 Cardiff	42	12	7	2	39	16	[illegible]	6	7	25	25	53
4 Carlisle	42	16	3	2	39	13	[illegible]	10	7	26	30	53
5 Hull	42	11	5	5	31	16	[illegible]	8	5	23	25	51
6 Luton	42	12	7	2	40	18	[illegible]	6	9	22	25	49
7 Middlesbro	42	13	6	2	37	16	[illegible]	8	9	23	27	48
8 Millwall	42	13	5	3	36	12	[illegible]	4	11	23	30	47
9 Birmingham	42	12	7	2	30	12	[illegible]	5	11	28	36	46
10 Norwich	42	11	8	2	34	20	[illegible]	6	11	20	32	44
11 QP Rangers	42	11	5	5	39	22	[illegible]	6	10	19	31	43
12 Swindon	42	12	7	2	38	14	[illegible]	5	13	23	37	42
13 Sunderland	42	11	6	4	34	21	[illegible]	6	11	18	33	42
14 Oxford	42	8	8	5	23	23	3	6	9	18	25	42
15 Sheffield Wed	42	10	7	4	32	27	2	5	14	19	42	36
16 Portsmouth	42	9	4	8	32	28	1	10	10	14	33	34
17 Orient	42	5	11	5	16	15	4	5	12	13	36	34
18 Watford	42	6	7	8	18	22	4	6	11	20	38	33
19 BRISTOL CITY	42	9	6	6	30	28	1	5	15	16	36	31
20 Charlton	42	7	6	8	28	30	1	8	12	13	35	30
21 Blackburn	42	5	8	8	20	28	1	7	13	17	41	27
22 Bolton	42	6	5	10	22	31	1	5	15	13	43	24
	924	225	141	96	697	444	[illegible]	141	225	444	697	924

Odds & ends

Double wins: (1) Watford.
Double losses: (5) Leicester, Oxford, Middlesbrough, Sheffield Wed, Norwich.

Won from behind: (2) Carlisle (h), Luton (h).
Lost from in front: (4) QP Rangers (a), Swindon (a), Carlisle (a), Norwich (a).

High spots: Goals galore in thrilling game against Sunderland at Ashton Gate on the opening day of the season.
Great fight-back to beat Luton 3-2 at Ashton Gate.
Debut of Hill and Wilson in 3-0 success at Vicarage Road.
Reaching the semi-final of the League Cup.
Beating Blackpool 1-0 at Bloomfield Road in the League Cup.

Low spots: Gerry Sharpe's career-ending injury against Middlesbrough.
Losing in the semi-final of the League Cup.
Losing 0-4 against Oxford at Ashton Gate.
Finishing League programme by playing five games without a win.
Lack of goals, City failing to score in 18 League games.

Player of the year: Brian Drysdale.
Ever-presents: (1) Brian Drysdale.
Hat-tricks: (0).
Leading scorer: John Galley (12).

	Appearances						Goals			
	Lge	*Sub*	LC	*Sub*	FAC	*Sub*	Lge	LC	FAC	Tot
Bond, Len	**1**									
Bartley, Danny	**3**	*1*								
Broomfield, Ian	**9**	*2*	3	*2*	1		**2**			**2**
Connor, Jack	**4**		2							
Cashley, Ray	**11**				1					
Derrick, Jantzen	**1**									
Drysdale, Brian	**42**		9		1					
Fear, Keith	**10**	*2*					**2**			**2**
Galley, John	**36**		7				**12**			**12**
Garland, Chris	**38**		8		1		**8**	3		**11**
Gibson, Mike	**30**		9							
Gow, Gerry	**37**	*1*	6	*2*	1		**5**	1		**6**
Hill, Brian	**7**									
Jacobs, Trevor	**21**		4							
Menmuir, Billy		*1*								
Merrick, Geoff	**13**	*4*	4			*1*				
Parr, Gordon	**31**	*2*	8		1					
Rodgers, David	**6**		2		1			1		**1**
Rooks, Dickie	**33**		6		1		**2**			**2**
Sharpe, Gerry	**24**		9		1		**7**	3		**10**
Spiring, Peter	**6**		1							
Skirton, Alan	**20**	*2*	8				**4**	2		**6**
Stacey Steve	**9**		1							
Tainton, Trevor	**26**	*11*	5	*2*	1		**1**			**1**
Wilson, Les	**10**									
Wimshurst, Ken	**34**		7		1		**3**	1		**4**
26 players used	**462**	***26***	**99**	***6***	**11**	***1***	**46**	**11**		**57**

LEAGUE DIVISION 2 — Manager: Alan Dicks — SEASON 1971-72

No	Date		Att	Pos	Pt	F-A	H-T	Scorers, Times, and Referees	1	2	3	4	5	6	7	8	9	10	11	12 sub used
1	H	MILLWALL			D	3-3	2-2	Gow 3, Sweeney 13, Garland 73	Cashley	Wimshurst	Drysdale	**Emanuel**	Rooks	Merrick	Tainton	Garland*	Galley	**Sweeney**	Gow	Fear
	14/8		12,612		1			*Dunphy 17, Possee 23, Bolland 74*	*King*	*Brown*	*Cripps**	*Dorney*	*Kitchener*	*Burnett*	*Possee*	*Bolland*	*Bridges*	*Dunphy*	*Allder*	*Coxhill*
								Ref: J Taylor	An exciting game as Cashley blunders to let Millwall back into contention. He lets Eamonn Dunphy's gentle free-kick through his fingers and fails to come off line as Derek Possee fires the equaliser. Gow scored the first with a right-foot shot after beating three defenders in a solo run.											
2	A	SHEFFIELD WED			W	**5-1**	3-0	Galley 12, 26, 65, Emanuel 37,	Cashley	Wimshurst	Drysdale	Emanuel	Rooks	Merrick	Tainton	Garland*	Galley	Sweeney	Gow	Fear
	21/8		*12,724*		3			*Prendergast 89* [Garland 63]	*Grummitt*	*Rodrigues*	*Burton*	*Prophett*	*Holsgrove**	*Pugh*	*Sinclair*	*Craig*	*Downes*	*Prendergast*	*Sissons*	*Thompson*
								Ref: G Hill	Galley sparks off City's biggest away win for five years when finishing off a four-man move with a shot into the top corner. A brilliant display against mediocre opponents, whose only consolation is a strike at the death, when Mike Prendergast heads in from Ken Burton's centre.											
3	H	MIDDLESBROUGH		2	W	2-1	2-0	Wimshurst 2, Garland 29p	Cashley	Wimshurst	Drysdale	Emanuel	Rooks	Merrick	Tainton	Garland	Galley	Sweeney	Gow	
	28/8		16,474	*19*	5			*Maddren 71*	*Whigham*	*Maddren*	*Jones*	*Stiles*	*Boam*	*Spraggon*	*Downing*	*Hickton*	*McMordie*	*Vincent*	*Laidlaw**	*Mills*
								Ref: H Hackney	Bill Maddren's magnificent strike sets up a nail-biting finish after City take an early two-goal lead. Wimshurst nets with a poor free-kick and Garland puts away pen after John Vincent's handball. Bookings for Gow, Emanuel and Nobby Stiles as ref adheres to clampdown directive.											
4	H	CARDIFF		1	W	2-0	1-0	Galley 20, Gow 46	Cashley	Wimshurst	Drysdale	Emanuel	Rooks	Merrick	Tainton	Garland	Galley	Sweeney	Gow	
	31/8		**23,525**	*20*	7				*Eadie*	*Carver*	*Bell*	*Sutton*	*Murray*	*Phillips*	*Gibson*	*Clark*	*Hoy*	*Warboys*	*Foggon*	
								Ref: J Hunting	Table-topping City put on a superb show after Cardiff dominate the early stages. Against the run of play, City take the lead as Galley hooks the ball into the roof of the net after side-stepping a defender. Gow then sets the seal on a fine success by driving home Tainton's cross.											
5	A	BURNLEY		2	D	1-1	0-0	Galley 49	Cashley	Wimshurst	Drysdale	Emanuel	Rooks	Merrick	Tainton	Fear*	Galley	Sweeney	Gow	Spiring
	4/9		*13,634*	*7*	8			*Bellamy 47*	*Mellor*	*Docherty*	*Cliff*	*Bellamy**	*Waldron*	*Dobson*	*Thomas*	*West*	*Fletcher*	*Casper*	*Kindon*	*Collins*
								Ref: T Dawes	A lively game in the brilliant sunshine, but not a rough one despite the booking of five players. Galley is unfortunate on 14 minutes when his header is disallowed for offside, but he equalises Arthur Bellamy's shot from the edge of the box, by heading in Wimshurst's high lob.											
6	H	HULL		1	W	4-0	2-0	Galley 8, 79, Fear 38p, Gow 81	Cashley	Wimshurst	Drysdale	Emanuel	Rooks	Merrick	Tainton	Fear	Galley	Sweeney	Gow	
	11/9		16,659	*10*	10				*McKechnie*	*Banks*	*De Vries*	*Wilkinson*	*Greenwood*	*Knighton*	*Lord*	*Houghton*	*Pearson*	*Wagstaff*	*O'Riley**	*Simpkin*
								Ref: S Kaley	City celebrate Alan Dicks' award as Bells Manager of the Month as Galley heads in Tainton's cross and then Fear punishes Francis Banks handball with a confident penalty. After the break, Galley is on target with a tap-in before Gow's header completes a handsome victory.											
7	A	BIRMINGHAM		2	L	0-1	0-1		Cashley	Wimshurst	Drysdale	Emanuel*	Rooks	Merrick	Tainton	Fear	Galley	Sweeney	Gow	Spiring
	18/9		*28,745*	*9*	10			*Latchford 40*	*Kelly D*	*Martin*	*Pendrey*	*Page**	*Hynd*	*Robinson*	*Campbell*	*Francis*	*Latchford R*	*Phillips*	*Taylor*	*Smith*
								Ref: A Oliver	City lose their unbeaten record against superior opponents in a fast, attractive game. Tenacious defending restrict Birmingham to Bob Latchford's headed goal, so leaving City to rue the referee's decision not to award penalty when Tainton was clearly fouled just after half-time.											
8	H	NORWICH		4	L	0-1	0-0		Cashley	Wimshurst	Drysdale	Emanuel*	Rooks	Merrick	Tainton	Fear	Galley	Sweeney	Gow	Spiring
	25/9		18,768	*1*	10			*Stringer 48*	*Keelan*	*Payne*	*Butler*	*Stringer*	*Forbes*	*Anderson*	*Howard*	*Silvester*	*Livermore*	*Paddon*	*Foggo**	*Briggs*
								Ref: R Armstrong	City find the Norwich defence in fine form in this top-of-the-table clash. David Stringer poaches the points for the Canaries, latching onto Merrick's poor clearance to blast in from six yards. City are denied by Kevin Keelan's superb display and Gerry Butler clearing off the line.											
9	H	BLACKPOOL		2	W	4-0	1-0	Galley 24, Tainton 62, Wimshurst 67,	Cashley	Wimshurst	Drysdale	Emanuel	Rooks	Merrick	Tainton	Spiring	Galley	Sweeney	Gow	
	23/9		20,352	*12*	12			[Gow 87p]	*Ramsbottom*	*Hatton*	*Fuschillo*	*Booth*	*Alcock*	*Suddaby*	*Ainscow*	*Green*	*James*	*Suddick*	*Wann*	
								Ref: C Nicholls	Blackpool are unlucky as a slip by debutant Paul Fuschillo allows Galley to score from a narrow angle, whilst Dennis Wann hits the bar early in each half. Terry Alcock's foul concedes a penalty after Tainton's 25-yarder and Wimshurst's free-kick had increased City's advantage.											
10	A	SWINDON		2	W	1-0	0-0	Spiring 79	Cashley	Wimshurst	Drysdale	Emanuel	Rooks	Merrick	Tainton	Spiring	Galley	Sweeney	Gow	
	2/10		*21,595*	*15*	14				*Downsboro'*	*Thomas*	*Trollope*	*Butler*	*Burrows*	*Mackay**	*Peplow*	*Harland*	*Jones C*	*Noble*	*Rogers*	*Bunkell*
								Ref: N Burtenshaw	Spiring's fierce right-foot volley from Tainton's cross secures City's win in a defensive-orientated contest. Neither side exhibit much control in the sweltering heat, though early on Don Rogers posed his usual threat. Merrick heads out Joe Butler's thunderous shot just prior to the break.											

No	H/A	Date / Opponent	Att	Pos	Pt	F-A	H-T	Scorers, Times, and Referees	1	2	3	4	5	6	7	8	9	10	11	12 sub used
11	H	WATFORD		2	W	2-1	1-0	Spiring 38, Galley 53	Cashley	Wimshurst	Drysdale	Emanuel	Rooks	Merrick	Tainton	Spiring	Galley	Sweeney	Gow	
		9/10	18,100	*19*	16			*Lindsay 82*	*Walker*	*Butler*	*Williams*	*Welbourne*	*Baxter*	*Lees*	*McGettigan*	*Eddy*	*Wigg*	*Lindsay*	*Franks*	
								Ref: N Paget	City are shocked midway through the first half as Ron Wigg hits the bar, but gain reward for their almost constant attacking when Spiring nudges in Drysdale's cross. Watford's adoption of a more offensive approach after the break pays off when Lindsay's shot creeps into the net.											
12	A	MILLWALL		3	L	1-3	1-1	Spiring 38	Cashley	Wimshurst	Drysdale	Emanuel	Rooks	Merrick	Tainton*	Spiring	Galley	Sweeney	Gow	Fear
		16/10	*14,041*	2	16			*Merrick 2 (og), Bridges 79, Bolland 85*	*King*	*Brown*	*Cripps*	*Dorney*	*Kitchener*	*Burnett*	*Bridges*	*Dunphy*	*Smethurst*	*Bolland*	*Possee*	
								Ref: R Capey	A disastrous start as Merrick heads into his own goal whilst attempting to clear Eamonn Dunphy's free-kick, but Spiring levels with a superb shot. City are unfortunate on 77 mins when Sweeney hits the post, but succumb to a Barry Bridges' header and Gordon Bolland's 30-yarder.											
13	A	PORTSMOUTH		3	D	1-1	0-0	Spiring 82	Cashley	Wimshurst	Drysdale	Emanuel	Rooks	Merrick	Tainton	Spiring	Galley	Sweeney	Gow	
		20/10	*12,575*	*11*	17			*Ley 57*	*Milkins*	*Smith*	*Ley*	*Hand*	*Youlden*	*Munks*	*Piper*	*Reynolds*	*Hiron*	*McCann*	*Trebilcock*	
								Ref: B Daniels	City's pattern-weaving display has Portsmouth all a dither, especially in the first half. George Ley puts Pompey in front from a free-kick after Rooks is penalised for pushing Ray Hiron, but City deservedly equalise with Spiring's powerful drive after Gow dribbles past three defenders.											
14	H	ORIENT		3	W	5-3	1-3	Rooks 35, Spiring 52, Galley 55, 90, [T'nton 71]	Cashley	Wimshurst	Drysdale	Emanuel	Rooks	Merrick	Tainton	Spiring	Galley	Sweeney	Gow	
		23/10	17,772	*18*	19			*B'wyer 19, 42, Brisley 26*	*Goddard*	*Allen*	*Rofe*	*Dyson*	*Hoadley*	*Harris*	*Lazarus*	*Brisley*	*Bullock*	*Bennett*	*Bowyer*	
								Ref: E Jolly	City stage a remarkable recovery in this pulsating affair. Rooks' header brings City back into the match after Orient's great start with Ian Bowyer heading in and a 20-yarder from Terry Brisley. A sensational Galley volley levels matters and Tainton lashes ball in to put City ahead.											
15	A	CHARLTON		4	L	0-2	0-1		Cashley	Wimshurst	Drysdale	Emanuel*	Rooks	Merrick	Tainton	Spiring	Galley	Sweeney	Gow	Fear
		30/10	*10,101*	*18*	19			*Hunt 14, Treacy 60*	*Dunn*	*Reeves*	*Warman*	*Bond*	*Went*	*Shipperley*	*Davies*	*Treacy*	*Hunt*	*Rogers*	*Peacock*	
								Ref: R Perkin	Wimshurst finds his lack of pace exploited as an out-of-sorts City succumb to lowly Charlton. Peter Hunt, playing his first game of the season, gives City an early jolt with his low shot, and after the break Ray Treacy's glancing near-post header finishes off Dennis Bond's corner.											
16	H	FULHAM		5	L	1-2	0-2	Galley 82	Gibson	Wimshurst	Drysdale	Emanuel*	Rooks	Merrick	Tainton	Spiring	Galley	Sweeney	Gow	Jacobs
		6/11	17,295	*17*	19			*Barrett 26, Cross 40*	*Webster*	*Fraser*	*Callaghan*	*Brown*	*Matthewson*	*Richardson*	*Conway*	*Cross*	*Earle*	*Lloyd*	*Barrett*	
								Ref: R Lee	Roger Cross heads in Jimmy Conway's centre just prior to the interval, but offside deprives Fulham of reward for the move of the match. Gibson saves City from a heavy defeat as they are often exposed through the middle. Galley rises majestically to head in Tainton's cross.											
17	A	QP RANGERS		7	L	0-3	0-1		Gibson	Wimshurst	Drysdale	Emanuel	Rooks	Merrick	Tainton	Spiring	Galley	Sweeney	Gow	
		13/11	*14,898*	*3*	19			*O'Rouke28, Merrick 73 (og), Marsh 90*	*Parkes*	*Clement*	*Hazell*	*Saul*	*Mancini*	*Hunt*	*Morgan*	*Francis*	*Leach*	*Marsh*	*O'Rouke*	
								Ref: R Crabb	Rodney Marsh, with one of his infamous dives, wins penalty in the last moments. Gibson goes left to save Marsh's kick, but from the resulting corner the Rangers star man hooks the ball home. Rangers counter the Wimshurst-Tainton alliance as City's play is spoilt by poor passing.											
18	H	CARLISLE		7	L	**1-4**	1-3	Gow 3	Gibson	Jacobs	Drysdale	Emanuel	Rooks	Merrick	Tainton	Wimshurst	Fear*	Sweeney	Gow	Parr
		19/11	13,017	*12*	19			*Barton 20, Bowles 42, Owen 44, 88*	*Ross*	*Hemstead*	*Gorman*	*Ternent*	*Winstanley*	*Sutton*	*Barton*	*Martin*	*Owen*	*Bowles*	*Balderstone**	*Davis*
								Ref: H Davey	Carlisle, superior in midfield and lethal in attack, win this game much as they please after Gow nets at the third attempt. Frank Barton cuts through for the equaliser and then fine approach play between Chris Balderstone and Bobby Owen allows Stan Bowles to shoot them ahead.											
19	A	SUNDERLAND		9	D	1-1	0-1	Wilson 75	Gibson	Wimshurst	Drysdale	Emanuel*	**Bruton**	Merrick	Tainton	Gow	Broomfield	Wilson	Sweeney	Parr
		27/11	15,655	*5*	20			*Pitt 39*	*Montgomery*	*Malone*	*Coleman*	*Harvey*	*Pitt*	*Chambers*	*McGiven*	*Kerr*	*Watson*	*Hughes*	*Tueart*	
								Ref: G Jones	Former England star Jackie Milburn accepts the consensus view of this being a bore. Wilson, playing his first game since signing permanently from Wolves, is City's saviour. He puts the finishing touch to a move with Broomfield after Ritchie Pitt's strong shot puts Sunderland ahead.											
20	H	LUTON		10	D	0-0	0-0		Gibson	Wimshurst	Drysdale	Wilson	Rooks	Merrick	Tainton	Spiring	Broomfield	Sweeney	Gow*	Bruton
		4/12	*12,921*	*14*	21				*Read*	*Ryan John*	*Slough*	*Keen*	*Nicholl*	*Moore*	*Anderson*	*Court*	*Halom*	*Givens*	*Hindson*	
								Ref: C Robinson	City's punchless attack is easily controlled by the dominant form of John Moore and Chris Nicholl, whilst at the other end Gibson brings off many fine saves. Don Givens and John Ryan are unfortunate to be booked for tackles much milder than many others unpunished in the game.											
21	A	OXFORD		9	D	0-0	0-0		Gibson	Wimshurst	Drysdale	Bruton	Rooks	Merrick	Tainton	Wilson	Broomfield	Sweeney	**Griffin**	
		11/12	*8,264*	*17*	22				*Burton**	*Lucas*	*Shuker*	*Roberts*	*Clarke C*	*Evanson*	*Skeen*	*Flemimg*	*Clarke D*	*Cassidy*	*Aylott*	*Clayton*
								Ref: K Styles/Bent	The loss of Ray Burton – injured bringing down Broomfield – transforms the game into a thriller. Masterly display by Gibson thwarts Oxford as they lay siege to City's goal. Linesman Bent takes over from the injured referee for the last five mins. Bookings for Burton and Dick Lucas.											

No	Date	Opponent	Att	Pos	Pt	F-A	H-T	Scorers, Times, and Referees	1	2	3	4	5	6	7	8	9	10	11	12 sub used
22	H	BURNLEY		11	L	0-2	0-0		Gibson	Wimshurst	Drysdale	Gow	Bruton	Merrick	Tainton	Wilson	Rooks	Sweeney	**Burnside***	Griffin
	18/12		12,909	*6*	22			*Fletcher 58, 90*	*Mellor*	*Docherty*	*Thomson*	*Bellamy*	*Waldron*	*Dobson*	*Thomas*	*West*	*Fletcher*	*Kindon*	*James*	
								Ref: W. Castle	Unmerciful barracking for skipper Wimshurst as City's makeshift side are subjected to much pressure by high-scoring Burnley. The playing of Rooks at centre-forward and the introduction of Burnside is not a success. Steve Kindon's electrifying run sets up Paul Fletcher's second goal.											
23	A	PRESTON		11	L	0-1	0-1		Gibson	Wimshurst	Drysdale	Wilson	Rooks	Merrick	Tainton	Spiring	Galley	Sweeney	Gow	
	27/12		*19,738*	*7*	22			*Lyall 1*	*Kelly*	*McMahon*	*McNab*	*Bird*	*Hawkins*	*Spavin**	*Spark*	*Clark*	*McIlmoyle*	*Lyall*	*Ingram*	*Tarbuck*
								Ref: H Hackney	Peter Doherty, now assistant at Deepdale, admits his old club are unlucky to lose. City blitz the Preston goal for the entire second half, but are unable to recover from George Lyall's 45-second shoulder-high shot that Gibson knocks against the bar for Hugh McIlmoyle to nudge in.											
24	H	BIRMINGHAM		10	W	1-0	1-0	Galley 15	Gibson	Wimshurst	Drysdale	Wilson	Bruton	Merrick	Tainton	Spiring	Galley	Sweeney	Gow	
	1/1		17,457	*7*	24				*Latchford D*	*Carroll*	*Pendrey*	*Page*	*Hynd*	*Harland*	*Campell*	*Francis*	*Latchford R*	*Hatton*	*Summerill*	
								Ref: R Crabb	City are back to their best in this all-action contest with a display of non-stop running in the first half. Galley's 15-yard textbook header is one of his finest goals, whilst Gibson is outstanding after the break when Birmingham wrest control. Page, Pendrey and Tainton are booked.											
25	A	MIDDLESBROUGH		11	L	0-1	0-0		Gibson	Wimshurst	Drysdale	Wilson	Bruton	Merrick	Tainton	Spiring	Galley	Sweeney	Gow	
	8/1		*13,117*	*7*	24			*Downing 59*	*Platt*	*Craggs*	*Stone*	*Madren*	*Boam*	*Gates*	*Downing*	*McMordie*	*Mills*	*Hickton*	*Laidlaw*	
								Ref: R Matthewson	A poor match, devoid of thrills, on a cold, grey day at Ayresome Park, as City offer little in the way of attacking enterprise. Derrick Downing's 25-yarder benefits from a deflection off Bruton's foot to sail over Gibson's head and into the net. Gow heads off the line to save City early on.											
26	A	BLACKPOOL		15	L	0-1	0-1		Gibson	Jacobs	Drysdale	Wilson	Bruton	Merrick	Gow	Spiring*	Galley	Sweeney	Bartley	Tainton
	22/1		*9,923*	*12*	24			*Suddick 7*	*Burridge*	*Hatton**	*Bentley*	*Suddaby*	*James*	*Simpkin*	*Burns*	*Suddick*	*Dyson*	*Lennard*	*Hutchison*	*Ainscow*
								Ref: C Howell	Merrick leads City for the first time and after winning the toss finds himself much involved as Blackpool exert heavy pressure. Gibson is unsighted as Alan Suddick's ten-yard volley beats him at the near post. Jacobs is booked for his 87th-minute foul on Tommy Hutchison.											
27	H	PORTSMOUTH		14	D	1-1	1-1	Galley 21	Bond	Jacobs	Drysdale	Gow	Bruton	Merrick	Tainton	Wilson	Galley	Sweeney	Bartley	
	29/1		10,949	*15*	25			*Bruton 35 (og)*	*Milkins*	*Smith*	*Collins*	*Wilson*	*Hand*	*Blant*	*Piper*	*Reynolds*	*Trebilcock*	*Ley*	*Jennings*	
								Ref: B Homewood	City employ two orthodox wingers for the first time this season. Galley's shot finds the net after hitting John Collins and John Milkins, whilst Nicky Jennings' hard-hit centre canons in off Bruton. City are much relieved at the death as Norman Piper's strike is disallowed for handball.											
28	A	ORIENT		18	L	0-2	0-1		Bond	Jacobs	Drysdale	Emanuel	Rodgers	Merrick	Tainton	Wilson	Galley	Sweeney	Gow*	Parr
	12/2		*13,272*	*16*	25			*Bullock 34, 51*	*Bowtell*	*Hoadley*	*Rofe*	*Bennett*	*Harris*	*Allen*	*Fairbrother*	*Dyson*	*Bullock*	*Walley*	*Bowyer*	
								Ref: N Paget	A phantom whistler helps Orient's success in bog-like conditions. City stop as Ian Bowyer nods the ball back across goal for Mike Bullock to head home. Peter Allen's flighted chip sets up Bullock for another scoring header, while near the end Bowyer's strike is disallowed for offside.											
29	H	CHARLTON		16	W	2-0	2-0	Galley 32, Tainton 39	Cashley	Jacobs	Drysdale	Emanuel	Rooks	Merrick	Tainton	Spiring	Galley	Sweeney	Bartley	
	19/2		**10,207**	*18*	27				*Dunn*	*Jones*	*Warman*	*Bond*	*Went*	*Shipperley*	*Davies*	*Treacy**	*Hunt*	*Rogers*	*Flanagan*	*Barnard*
								Ref: J Williams	Galley's near-post header and a five-yard effort by Tainton give City a well-deserved success. Against poor opposition, City's all-round supremacy is difficult to fault. The calm efficiency of Merrick and the commanding form of Rooks means a trouble-free afternoon for Cashley.											
30	A	FULHAM		17	L	0-2	0-0		Cashley	Jacobs	Drysdale	Wilson	Rooks	Merrick	Tainton	Spiring	Galley	Sweeney	Bartley	
	23/2		*9,276*	*20*	27			*Callaghan 86, Earle 89*	*Mellor*	*Moreline*	*Callaghan*	*Brown*	*Matthewson*	*Richardson*	*Conway*	*Cross*	*Earle*	*Lloyd*	*Barrett*	
								Ref: R Toseland	Cashley's outstanding performance is unable to prevent Fulham, with Peter Mellor making his debut, obtaining a deserved success. John Conway's corner is headed on into the middle, where Fred Callaghan has time to stumble over the ball, before lashing it in from seven yards.											
31	H	QP RANGERS		15	W	2-0	0-0	Rodgers 64, Galley 69	Cashley	Jacobs	Drysdale	Emanuel	Rodgers	Merrick	Tainton	Spiring	Galley	Gow	Bartley	
	4/3		11,105	*6*	29				*Parkes*	*Clement*	*Gillard*	*Hazell*	*Mancini*	*Hunt*	*O'Rourke*	*Francis*	*McCulloch*	*Marsh**	*Busby*	*Leach*
								Ref: R Toseland	Rangers are reduced to being a very ordinary side when Rodney Marsh limps out of the action with a pulled muscle. Cashley's great save from John O'Rourke after five minutes and Emanuel's stirring midfield display keep City in the game, before Rodgers heads in Bartley's cross.											

No	Venue / Date	Opponent / Att	Pos	Res / Pts	F-A	H-T	Scorers, Times, and Referees	1	2	3	4	5	6	7	8	9	10	11	12
32	A	WATFORD	11	W	2-0	1-0	Bartley 5, Galley 80	Cashley	Jacobs	Drysdale	Emanuel	Rodgers	Merrick	Tainton	Spiring	Galley	Gow	Bartley	
	11/3	*5,384*	*22*	31				*Walker*	*Butler*	*Williams*	*Lugg*	*Franks*	*Eddy*	*McGettigan**	*Wigg*	*Morrisey*	*Lindsay*	*Welbourne*	*Kenning*
							Ref: D Laing	Watford's smallest crowd for six years have little to excite them. City, who create little, go ahead from a free-kick as Rodgers and Spiring create an opening in Watford's defensive wall. Gow steps over the ball and Bartley follows up to place his shot into the corner of the net.											
33	H	SHEFFIELD WED	10	W	1-0	1-0	Spiring 39	Cashley	Jacobs	Drysdale	Emanuel	Rodgers	Merrick	Tainton	Spiring	Galley	Gow	Bartley	
	18/3	12,568	*16*	33				*Grummitt*	*Thompson*	*Clements*	*Prophett*	*Holsgrove*	*Pugh*	*Sinclair*	*Craig*	*Joicy*	*Sunley*	*Sissons*	
							Ref: B Daniels	Cashley dives to his right to save Tommy Craig's spot-kick after the break. Bookings for Dave Clements, Alan Thompson and Gow, but the ref errs – perhaps suffering from the earlier effects of being pole-axed – in not awarding the Owls another pen when Jacobs blatantly trips Sunley.											
34	A	HULL	10	D	1-1	0-1	Tainton 55	Cashley	Jacobs	Drysdale	Emanuel	Rodgers	Merrick	Tainton*	Spiring	Galley	Gow	Bartley	Sweeney
	25/3	*11,700*	*18*	34			*Wagstaff 28*	*McKechnie*	*Banks*	*De Vries*	*Kaye*	*Neill*	*Knighton*	*McGill*	*Lord*	*Pearson*	*Wagstaff*	*Butler**	*Greenwood*
							Ref: E Jolly	Three remarkable saves by Cashley, including Ian Butler's point-blank header, in the ten minutes leading up to half-time. City then begin to dictate a game that was slipping away from them following Ken Wagstaff's 25-yard cross-shot. Tainton lashes in an angled drive to equalise.											
35	H	SWINDON	8	W	1-0	0-0	Galley 88	Cashley	Jacobs	Drysdale	Emanuel	Rodgers	Merrick	Tainton	Spiring	Galley	Gow	Bartley	
	31/3	21,496	*14*	36				*Downsboro'*	*Thomas*	*Trollope*	*Bunkell*	*Burrows*	*Butler*	*Hubbard*	*Smart*	*Horsfield*	*Noble*	*Rogers*	
							Ref: C Thomas	City are so much on top in this game that even centre-half Rodgers squanders two scoring opportunities. It is not until the dying minutes that their great display gets its reward with Galley's memorable 15-yard volley. A booking for Joe Butler, who brings down Spiring on 59 minutes.											
36	H	PRESTON	7	W	4-1	1-1	Spiring 8, Tainton 82, Emanuel 87, [Galley 90]	Cashley	Jacobs	Drysdale	Emanuel	Parr	Merrick	Tainton	Spiring	Galley	Gow	Bartley	
	1/4	12,562	*14*	38			*Tarbuck 1*	*Kelly*	*McMahon*	*Connor*	*Bird*	*McNab*	*Spavin*	*Heppolette*	*Young**	*McIlmoyle*	*Lamb*	*Tarbuck*	*Hughes*
							Ref: I Jones	Spiring runs in at the far post to put away Galley's flick-on from a free-kick to level matters after Tarbuck's 25-yard drive past the motionless Cashley on just 35 seconds. An untidy game, but Tainton's left-foot drive and headers from Emanuel and Galley secure City's healthy win.											
37	A	NORWICH	7	D	2-2	0-1	Sweeney 84, Gow 88p	Cashley	Jacobs	Drysdale	Emanuel	Parr*	Merrick	Tainton	Spiring	Galley	Gow	Bartley	Sweeney
	4/4	***34,914***	*1*	39			*Cross 24, Bone 70*	*Kelan*	*Payne*	*Black*	*Stringer*	*Forbes*	*Briggs*	*Livermore*	*Bone*	*Cross*	*Paddon*	*Foggo*	
							Ref: R Kirkpatrick	An inspired substitution brings City a share of the spoils in front of the best Carrow Road crowd of the season. Sweeney nets with a fine header from Bartley's cross. Norwich were fortunate with their opener, as Cross was played on by Parr, but no dispute over Jim Bone's classic header.											
38	A	CARLISLE	9	L	0-2	0-1		Cashley	Jacobs	Drysdale	Emanuel	Bruton	Merrick	Tainton*	Spiring	Galley	Gow	Bartley	Sweeney
	8/4	*6,596*	*6*	39			*Owen 14, Gorman 50*	*Clarke*	*Davis*	*Gorman*	*Ternent*	*Winstanley*	*Delgardo*	*Barton*	*Martin*	*Owen*	*Bowles*	*Webb**	*Hegarty*
							Ref: W Hall	Carlisle, even without the services of Chris Balderstone and Ray Train, are much the better side. Bobby Owen puts the Cumbrians ahead as he steers in a rebound after Cashley's error. Then John Gorman's speculative lob finds the net after the keeper pushes up under the crossbar.											
39	H	SUNDERLAND	8	W	3-1	0-1	Gow 69p, Drysdale 86, Galley 90	Cashley	Jacobs*	Drysdale	Emanuel	Bruton	Merrick	Tainton	Spiring	Galley	Gow	Bartley	Sweeney
	15/4	*12,178*	*5*	41			*Kerr 19*	*Forster*	*Malone*	*Coleman*	*Horswill*	*Pitt*	*Porterfield*	*McGiven*	*Kerr*	*Watson*	*Lathan*	*Tueart**	*Hughes*
							Ref: R Perkin	Spiring falls over his own feet to gain a penalty as lucky City restore parity. Impressive Sunderland fully deserved the lead gained by Bobby Kerr's neat shot, but City snatch an unlikely victory with two late strikes. Drysdale lashes in a fine shot for his first goal for the club.											
40	A	LUTON	10	D	0-0	0-0		Cashley	Sweeney	Drysdale	Emanuel	Bruton	Merrick	Tainton	Spiring	Galley	Gow	Bartley	
	22/4	*8,329*	14	42				*Barber*	*Slough*	*Shanks*	*Keen*	*Garner*	*Moore*	*Wainwright*	*Halom*	*Givens*	*Ryan John*	*Hindson*	
							Ref: R Challis	A typical end-of-season affair in which City have the better chances. Spiring spurns two chances to break the deadlock and is unlucky with a first-half shot which Keith Barber touches onto the crossbar. The Luton pair of Don Givens and John Ryan are the best of the visiting players.											
41	A	CARDIFF	8	W	3-2	2-1	Spiring 10, 65, Gow 20p	Cashley	Sweeney	Drysdale	Emanuel	Rodgers	Merrick	Tainton	Spiring	Galley	Gow	Bartley	
	26/4	*17,227*	*19*	44			*Warboys 32, Woodruff 83*	*Irvin*	*Carver*	*Pethard*	*Sutton*	*Murray*	*Phillips*	*Gibson*	*Clark*	*Woodruff*	*Warboys*	*King*	
							Ref: D Nippard	Cashley makes his fourth-successive penalty stop in the 18th min to deny Ian Gibson after Drysdale fouled Alan Warboys. He then brings off a super save from Peter King's header near the end. City make no mistake with their penalty after Tainton was blatantly tripped by Mel Sutton.											
42	H	OXFORD	8	W	4-2	2-1	Galley 26, 41, Gow 53p, Sweeney 65	Cashley	Sweeney	Drysdale	Emanuel	Rodgers	Merrick	Tainton	Spiring	Galley	Gow	Bartley	
	29/4	10,793	*15*	46			*Clarke 16p, Cassidy 81*	*Burton*	*Lucas*	*Shuker*	*Roberts*	*Smithson*	*Thompson**	*Sloan*	*Atkinson G*	*Clarke D*	*Cassidy*	*Aylott*	*Skeen*
	Home	Away					Ref: C Robinson	City end the season in confident style to celebrate skipper Merrick's 21st birthday. The midfield skills of Emanuel and Gow bring a seventh-successive home success after falling behind to Derek Clarke's penalty. Rodgers is booked for third time this season after bust-up with Clarke.											
	Average 15,225	14,367																	

League Cup					F-A	H-T	Scorers, Times, and Referees	1	2	3	4	5	6	7	8	9	10	11	12 sub used
1	A	PLYMOUTH		L	0-1	0-0		Cashley	Wimshurst	Drysdale	Emanuel*	Rooks	Merrick	Tainton	Fear	Galley	Sweeney	Gow	Spiring
	17/8	*11,248*					*Hinch 48*	*Furnell*	*Davey*	*Harris*	*Hore*	*Darke*	*Provan*	*Brown*	*Allen*	*Hinch*	*Latcham*	*Hutchins*	
							Ref: P Walters	City are easily the best side in the first half, but miss two clear-cut opportunities before Argyle score. The referee turns down City's protest that Cashley was fouled when colliding with Hinch in going for Ronnie Brown's corner. Steve Davey and Galley are booked in a 67th-min fracas.											

FA Cup																			
3	A	PRESTON	11	L	2-4	2-1	Spiring 25, Wilson 37	Gibson	Wimshurst	Drysdale	Wilson	Rooks*	Merrick	Tainton	Spiring	Galley	Sweeney	Gow	Bruton
	15/1	*13,619*	*9*				*Lyall 34, Ingram 81, Clark 84, 87*	*Kelly*	*McMahon*	*McNab*	*Bird*	*Hawkins*	*Spavin*	*Heppolete*	*Clark*	*McIlmoyle*	*Lyall*	*Ingram*	
							Ref: V James	The gamble on Rooks' fitness fails as City crumble to North End's late onslaught after Spiring's bad back-pass led to Gerry Ingram's 81st-min equaliser. City are in total charge early on as Spiring ghosts in to score and then Wilson's header nullifies George Lyall's unstoppable volley.											

	Home						Away					
	P	W	D	L	F	A	W	D	L	F	A	Pts
1 Norwich	42	13	8	0	40	16	[illegible]	7	6	20	20	57
2 Birmingham	42	15	6	0	46	14	[illegible]	12	5	14	17	56
3 Millwall	42	14	7	0	38	17	[illegible]	10	6	26	29	55
4 QP Rangers	42	16	4	1	39	9	[illegible]	10	7	18	19	54
5 Sunderland	42	11	7	3	42	24	[illegible]	9	6	25	33	50
6 Blackpool	42	12	6	3	43	16	[illegible]	1	12	27	34	47
7 Burnley	42	13	4	4	43	22	[illegible]	2	12	27	33	46
8 BRISTOL CITY	42	14	3	4	43	22	[illegible]	7	10	18	27	46
9 Middlesbro	42	16	4	1	31	11	[illegible]	4	14	19	37	46
10 Carlisle	42	12	6	3	38	22	[illegible]	3	13	23	35	43
11 Swindon	42	10	6	5	29	16	[illegible]	6	10	18	31	42
12 Hull	42	10	6	5	33	21	[illegible]	4	13	16	32	38
13 Luton	42	7	8	6	25	24	[illegible]	10	8	18	24	38
14 Sheffield Wed	42	11	7	3	33	22	[illegible]	5	14	18	36	38
15 Oxford	42	10	8	3	28	17	[illegible]	6	13	15	38	38
16 Portsmouth	42	9	7	5	31	26	[illegible]	6	12	28	42	37
17 Orient	42	12	4	5	32	19	[illegible]	5	14	18	42	37
18 Preston	42	11	4	6	32	21	[illegible]	8	12	20	37	36
19 Cardiff	42	9	7	5	37	25	[illegible]	7	13	19	44	34
20 Fulham	42	10	7	4	29	20	[illegible]	3	16	16	48	34
21 Charlton	42	9	7	5	33	25	[illegible]	2	16	22	52	33
22 Watford	42	5	5	11	15	25	[illegible]	4	17	9	50	19
	924	249	131	82	760	434	[illegible]	131	249	434	760	924

Odds & ends

Double wins: (4) Sheffield Wed, Cardiff, Swindon, Watford.
Double losses: (2) Fulham, Carlisle.

Won from behind: (4) Orient (h), Preston (h), Sunderland (h), Oxford (h).
Lost from in front: (1) Carlisle (h).

High spots: Winning 5-0 at Hillsborough on 21 August.
Great fightback to beat Orient on 23 October
Sparkling early-season form.

Low spots: Early exit in both cup competitions.
A heavy home defeat v Carlisle on 19 November.
Losing to Bristol Rov (h) 2-4 in the first penalty shoot-out to decide the Gloucestershire Cup Final.

Player of the year: Geoff Merrick.
Ever-presents: (2) Bryan Drysdale; Geoff Merrick.
Hat-tricks: John Galley (1).
Leading scorer: John Galley (22).

	Appearances						Goals			
	Lge	*Sub*	LC	*Sub*	FAC	*Sub*	Lge	LC	FAC	Tot
Bartley, Danny	**16**						1			1
Bond, Len	**2**									
Broomfield, Ian	**3**									
Bruton, David	**10**	*1*				*1*				
Burnside, David	**1**									
Cashley, Ray	**29**		1							
Drysdale, Brian	**42**		1		1		1			1
Emanuel, John	**33**		1				2			2
Fear, Keith	**5**	*4*	1				1			1
Galley, John	**37**		1		1		22			22
Garland, Chris	**4**						3			3
Gibson, Mike	**11**				1					
Gow, Gerry	**39**		1		1		9			9
Griffin, Kevin	**1**	*1*								
Jacobs, Trevor	**15**	*1*								
Merrick, Geoff	**42**		1		1					
Parr, Gordon	**2**	*3*								
Rodgers, David	**8**						1			1
Rooks, Dickie	**24**		1		1		1			1
Spiring, Peter	**28**	*3*		*1*	1		9		1	10
Sweeney, Gerry	**33**	*4*	1		1		3			3
Tainton, Trevor	**41**	*1*	1		1		5			5
Wilson, Les	**11**				1		1		1	2
Wimshurst, Ken	**25**		1		1		2			2
24 players used	**462**	***18***	**11**	***1***	**11**	***1***	**61**		**2**	**63**

No Date	Att	Pos	Pt	F-A	H-T	Scorers, Times, and Referees	1	2	3	4	5	6	7	8	9	10	11	12 sub used
1 A BRIGHTON			D	1-1	1-1	Bartley 42	Cashley	Wilson	Drysdale	Emanuel	Rodgers	Merrick	Tainton	Spiring	Galley	Gow	Bartley	
12/8	*16,823*		1			*Irvine 28*	*Powney*	*Templeman*	*Spearritt*	*Murray*	*Gall*	*Goodwin*	*Napier K*	*Beamish**	*Irvine*	*Bromley*	*O'Sullivan*	*Lutton*
						Ref: T Dawes	Hardly the normal opening day conditions as City take a deserved point at a wet Goldstone Ground after newly-promoted Brighton go ahead. Irvine was at the far post to head in from a Napier corner, but Bartley is City's saviour as he hooks home a glorious volley from twelve yards.											
2 H MILLWALL			D	2-2	1-1	Gow 20, Spiring 84	Cashley*	Wilson	Drysdale	Ritchie	Rodgers	Merrick	Tainton	Spiring	Galley	Gow	Bartley	Sweeney
19/8	15,648		2			*Wood 43, Smethurst 48*	*King*	*Brown*	*Burnett*	*Dorney*	*Kitchener*	*Bolland*	*Brown S*	*Smethurst*	*Wood*	*Possee*	*Allder*	
						Ref: R Armstrong	Galley goes in goal as Cashley sustains a gashed ankle whilst making a 38th-minute save from Wood. Millwall take control whilst facing ten men up to the interval and it takes an unstoppable left-foot shot by Spiring to earn City a share of the spoils. Bookings for Brown and Burnett.											
3 A SWINDON		16	L	1-2	1-1	Spiring 44	Cashley	Wilson	Drysdale	Ritchie	Rodgers	Merrick	Tainton	Spiring	Galley	Gow	Bartley	
26/8	*15,552*	*13*	2			*Peplow 23, 84*	*Downsboro*	*Thomas*	*Trollope*	*Buler*	*Burrows*	*Potter*	*Peplow*	*Bunkell**	*Treacy*	*Hubbard*	*Rogers*	*Howell*
						Ref: K Styles	A tale of goalkeeping errors. Downsborough allows himself to be distracted by Tainton's challenge to set up Spiring to lash the ball in for City's equaliser, whilst a tragic error gifts Swindon victory. Peplow's gentle lob from the edge of the area slips through Cashley's hands.											
4 A HULL		18	L	0-2	0-1		Cashley	Sweeney	Drysdale !	Ritchie	Rodgers	Merrick	Tainton	Spiring*	Galley	Gow	Bartley	Broomfield
29/8	*8,867*	*15*	2			*Pearson 32, Holme 75*	*Wealands*	*Banks*	*De Vries*	*Wilkinson*	*Kaye*	*Knighton*	*Lord*	*McGill**	*Pearson*	*Holme*	*Butler*	*Houghton*
						Ref: C Howell	A hectic opening sees McGill lose two teeth in a challenge with Rodgers and then Drysdale is sent off for remarks to a linesman. Pearson's magnificent volley gives the Tigers the lead, but City play well and are on top in the second half until Holme profits from a Rodgers error.											
5 H SHEFFIELD WED		22	L	1-2	0-1	Gow 51	Cashley	Sweeney	Drysdale	Emanuel	Rodgers	Merrick	Tainton	Spiring*	Galley	Gow	Bartley	Ritchie
2/9	12,373	*3*	2			*Joicey 22, 80*	*Grummitt*	*Rodrigues*	*Clements*	*Swan**	*Holsgrove*	*Craig*	*Sunley*	*Eustace*	*Joicey*	*Prendergast*	*Sissons*	*Henderson*
						Ref: C Nicholls	City almost incessantly attack in the opening half, but it is Wednesday who profit as Joicey registers with a six-yard header from Sunley's cross. Gow blasts the ball into net to level shortly after squandering a penalty awarded for Clements' push on Tainton. His soft kick was saved.											
6 A ORIENT		18	W	2-0	1-0	Spiring 28, Galley 73	Cashley	Wilson	Sweeney	Ritchie	Bruton	Merrick	Tainton	Spiring	Galley	Gow	Bartley	
9/9	***4,482***	*21*	4				*Goddard*	*Arber*	*Hoadley*	*Bennett*	*Harris*	*Allen*	*Fairbrother*	*Brisley**	*Bullock*	*Downing*	*Bowyer*	*Riddick*
						Ref: R Capey	Orient are mesmerised by City's speed and accuracy. Gow is robbed of a score as ball is over line before Goddard clears on six minutes and shortly after Tainton's shot hits post. Bowyer fails with last minute penalty, hitting bar with re-taken kick after having his first effort saved.											
7 H MIDDLESBROUGH		17	D	1-1	1-0	Spiring 27	Cashley	Wilson	Sweeney	Ritchie	Rodgers	Merrick	Tainton	Spiring	Galley	Gow	Bartley	
16/9	12,185	*15*	5			*McMordie 55*	*Platt*	*Craggs*	*Spraggon*	*Stiles*	*Boam*	*Maddren*	*McMordie*	*Mills*	*Smith*	*Hickton*	*Jones*	
						Ref: H Davey	Quick-thinking Spiring puts City in the lead following Tainton's free-kick. He moves round Stiles to meet Craggs' header from Tainton's free-kick to hammer a shot into the far corner. Middlesbrough are unlucky not to gain more than a draw, secured by McMordie's lob from 12 yards.											
8 A QP RANGERS		16	D	1-1	1-0	Spiring 15	Cashley	Wilson	Sweeney	Emanuel	Rodgers	Merrick	Tainton	Spiring	Broomfield	Gow	Ritchie	
13/9	*11,586*	*8*	6			*Francis 68*	*Parkes*	*Clement*	*Watson*	*Venables*	*Evans*	*Hazell*	*Busby*	*Francis*	*McCulloch*	*Bowles*	*Givens*	
						Ref: K Walker	Rangers boss Gordon Jago is generous with his praise for City, following this tense and exciting game. Against unbeaten opponents, City start with a brilliant 25-yard goal and finish with Cashley making a fine save to prevent Francis adding to his equaliser from Busby's cross.											
9 A CARDIFF		13	W	3-1	2-1	Gow 10p, Galley 12, Drysdale 70	Cashley	Wilson	Drysdale	Emanuel	Rodgers	Merrick	Tainton	Broomfield	Galley	Gow	Sweeney	
23/9	*14,102*	*22*	8			*Bell 22p*	*Irvin*	*Carver*	*Bell*	*Kellock*	*Murray*	*Powell*	*Gibson*	*Clark*	*Woodruff*	*Phillips*	*Reece*	
						Ref: A Oliver	Cardiff are soon in trouble against dominant City. Powell trips Broomfield to concede a penalty, which Gow tucks away to the keeper's right. Then Galley, looking offside, drives the ball in. Tainton's handball lets Cardiff back into the contest, but Drysdale's low drive secures the win.											
10 H FULHAM		13	D	1-1	0-1	Gow 69	Cashley	Wilson	Drysdale	Emanuel	Rodgers	Merrick	Tainton	Broomfield*	Galley	Gow	Sweeney	Ritchie
26/9	14,210	*14*	9			*Earle 24*	*Mellor*	*Cutbush*	*Callaghan*	*Mullery*	*Went*	*Dunne*	*Conway**	*Earle*	*Mitchell*	*Lloyd*	*Barrett*	*Richardson*
						Ref: F Barrett	City are much relieved to share points with impressive Fulham. City's defence is all at sea when Earle knocks in Lloyd's cross. Peter Mellor makes a magnificent save from Gow's 65th-minute penalty, but City notch their equaliser shortly after when Gow nudges in Tainton's cross.											

No	Date	Opponent	Att	Pos	Pt	Res	F-A	H-T	Scorers, Times, and Referees	1	2	3	4	5	6	7	8	9	10	11	12 sub used
11	H 30/9	HUDDERSFIELD	12,644	14 *11*	10	D	0-0	0-0		Cashley	Wilson	Drysdale	Emanuel	Rodgers	Merrick	Tainton*	Spiring	Galley	Gow	Sweeney	Ritchie
										Wood	*Clarke*	*Hutt*	*Pugh*	*Dolan*	*Nicholson*	*Smith D*	*Barry*	*Gowling*	*Lawson**	*Chapman*	*Fairclough*
									Ref: A Hart	Alan Dicks laments that City are not positive enough, so it is surprising that he waits until the 74th minute to introduce Ritchie in place of Tainton. Huddersfield's well-organised defence offers no way through, though Galley heads against the bar as City up the tempo near the end.											
12	A 7/10	PORTSMOUTH	*9,475*	10 *16*	12	W	3-0	1-0	Sweeney 5, 62, Emanuel 57	Cashley	Wilson	Drysdale	Emanuel	Rodgers	Merrick	Tainton	Spiring*	Galley	Gow	Sweeney	Ritchie
										Milkins	*Smith*	*Wilson*	*Hand*	*Stephenson*	*Munks*	*Piper*	*Reynolds*	*Hiron*	*McCann*	*Lewis**	*Price*
									Ref: R Toseland	Still without a victory at home, City gain their third win away. Wilson clears off the line in the final seconds to deny Emanuel, but City's midfielder has already had the satisfaction of registering with a terrific strike that bulges the back of the net before keeper Milkins could move.											
13	H 14/10	NOTT'M FOREST	13,861	11 *12*	13	D	1-1	0-0	Gow 81	Cashley	Wilson	Drysdale	Emanuel	Rodgers	Merrick	Tainton	Ritchie*	Galley	Gow	Sweeney	Bartley
									Fraser 66	*Barron*	*Hindley*	*Gemmell*	*Serella*	*Cottam*	*Fraser*	*Lyall*	*Robertson*	*Chapman*	*Richardson*	*Buckley*	
									Ref: J Williams	City stretch their unbeaten run to eight games. Forest play the better football in the first half, but do not take lead until after the interval, when Cashley is caught off his line by Fraser from 20 yards. Merrick's long punt produces the leveller as Gow runs through to net from ten yards.											
14	A 21/10	OXFORD	*10,182*	8 *11*	15	W	2-0	2-0	Gow 10p, Galley 39	Cashley	Wilson	Drysdale	Emanuel	Rodgers	Merrick	Tainton*	Spiring	Galley	Sweeney	Gow	Bartley
										Burton	*Lucas*	*Shuker*	*Roberts*	*Clarke C*	*Evanson**	*Sloan*	*Skeen*	*Clarke D*	*Curran*	*Aylott*	*Bray*
									Ref: R Challis	City obtain their first-ever goal at the Manor Ground. A debatable handling offence by Roberts allows Gow, who has missed two kicks this season, to drive the ball to Burton's right. Oxford boss Gerry Summers lays the blame for an ill-tempered game on referee Ron Challis.											
15	H 28/10	LUTON	13,562	11 *4*	15	L	0-1	0-1		Cashley	Wilson	Sweeney	Emanuel*	Bruton	Merrick	Ritchie	Spiring	Galley	Gow	Bartley	Fear
									Faulkner 12	*Barber*	*Ryan John*	*Thomson*	*Anderson*	*Faulkner*	*Garner*	*Ryan Jim*	*Slough*	*Halom*	*Hindson*	*Aston*	
									Ref: R Lee	City's late desperate attempts to equalise are thwarted as Keith Barber makes brilliant saves from Bartley and Galley. Luton, superbly prompted by Peter Anderson, deserve the points secured by John Faulkner from Jim Ryan's corner. Bookings for Anderson and John Ryan.											
16	A 4/11	FULHAM	*8,982*	13 *10*	15	L	**1-5**	1-2	Galley 27 *[Strong 70]*	Cashley	Wilson	**Ritchie S**	Ritchie T	Rodgers	Merrick*	Tainton	Spiring	Galley	Gow	Sweeney	Fear
									Earle 8, Mer'k 16 (og), Mitchell 54, 85,	*Mellor*	*Cutbush**	*Callaghan*	*Mullery*	*Went*	*Dunne*	*Strong*	*Earle*	*Mitchell*	*Lloyd*	*Barrett*	*Carlton*
									Ref: R Raby	Debutant Steve Ritchie's poor clearance sets up Earle for a soft early goal. Despite Galley's stupendous drive, City's attempt to add to their remarkable away record is wrecked by defensive errors, and Fulham are able to turn on the style after Mitchell avails himself of such largesse.											
17	H 11/11	QP RANGERS	12,570	14 *2*	15	L	1-2	1-2	Galley 24	Cashley	Jacobs	Wilson	Sweeney	Rodgers	Merrick	Tainton	Spiring*	Galley	Gow	Bartley	Emanuel
									Givens 10, 29	*Parkes*	*Clement*	*Watson*	*Venables*	*Evans*	*Hazell*	*Thomas*	*Francis*	*Leach*	*Bowles*	*Givens*	
									Ref: M Kerkhof	Silly defensive errors continue to mar City performances as Cashley is punished for his failure to deal with Don Givens' early cross. Galley skilfully prods in his first home goal of the season, but Givens gives Merrick the slip to head in a Dave Thomas corner for the winner.											
18	A 14/11	HUDDERSFIELD	*5,962*	13 *14*	17	W	1-0	0-0	Fear 67	Cashley	Jacobs	Wilson	Emanuel	Rodgers	Merrick	Tainton	Fear	Galley	Gow	Sweeney	
										Pierce	*Clarke*	*Hutt*	*Pugh*	*Lyon*	*Dolan*	*Fairclough*	*Smith S*	*Gowling*	*Dungworth*	*Chapman**	*Smith D*
									Ref: E Wallace	Huddersfield, down to ten men with Gowling off injured for the final five minutes, are outplayed. Fear chips in magnificently from 25 yards for his goal, while Rodgers sees his drive hit a post. Tainton is booked for dissent, whilst Emanuel is similarly punished for his tackle on Dolan.											
19	A 13/11	BLACKPOOL	*8,341*	14 *5*	17	L	0-3	0-2		Cashley	Jacobs	Wilson	Emanuel	Rodgers	Merrick	Tainton	Fear	Galley	Gow	Sweeney	
									Alcock 4, Dyson 25, Suddick 65	*Burridge*	*Hatton*	*Bentley*	*Alcock*	*Suddaby*	*Lennard*	*Buns*	*Suddick*	*Rafferty*	*Dyson*	*Ainscow*	
									Ref: V Batty	City are punished for their mistakes as Blackpool control proceedings at Bloomfield Road. Fear is denied by Burridge's fine save midway through the second half, but by then the Pool are 3-0 ahead. Alan Suddick moves in quickly to score after Cashley and Merrick collide.											
20	H 25/11	SUNDERLAND	10,666	11 *20*	19	W	1-0	0-0	Galley 83	Bond	Wilson	Drysdale	Emanuel	Rodgers*	Merrick	Tainton	Fear	Galley	Gow	Sweeney	Spiring
										Montgomery	*Malone*	*Coleman*	*Horswill*	*Watson*	*Porterfield*	*Kerr*	*Hughes*	*Lathan*	*Chambers*	*Tueart*	
									Ref: R Crabb	The tactical 67th-min substitution of Rodgers proves to be a masterstroke. Spiring's alertness lays on a chance for Galley to divert the ball over the line for City's first home win of the season, while Bond pulls off some smart saves to deny cultured Sunderland the point they deserve.											
21	A 2/12	CARLISLE	*6,526*	10 *15*	21	W	2-1	1-0	Spiring 35, Fear 59	Bond	Sweeney	Drysdale	Emanuel	Bruton	Merrick	Tainton	Spiring	Galley	Gow	Fear	
									Owen 88	*Ross*	*Derrett*	*Gorman*	*O'Neill*	*Winstanley*	*Tiler*	*Train*	*Martin*	*Owen*	*Balderstone*	*Laidlaw*	
									Ref: A Jones	City earn the plaudits for an outstanding display. Carlisle boss Alan Ashman salutes them as the best team in the Division. Owen forces the ball in near the end, but City hold on to the points created by Spiring's headed opener and a 15-yard low shot that zips in by star man Fear.											

No	Date	Att	Pos	Pt	F-A	H-T	Scorers, Times, and Referees	1	2	3	4	5	6	7	8	9	10	11	12 sub used
22	H BURNLEY		12	L	0-1	0-1		Bond	Sweeney	Drysdale	Emanuel	Bruton	Merrick	Tainton	Spiring*	**Gould**	Gow	Fear	Wilson
	16/12	15,334	*1*	21			*Dobson 4*	*Stevenson*	*Docherty*	*Newton*	*Dobson*	*Waldron*	*Thomson*	*Nulty*	*Caster*	*Fletcher*	*Collins*	*James*	
							Ref: B Daniels	An unhappy debut for Bobby Gould as he is booked for fouling Colin Waldron, who seldom gives him a chance. Burnley are the best side seen at Ashton Gate so far this season and fully deserve their win, despite Drysdale's protests that he cleared Colin Dobson's header off the line.											
23	A PRESTON		13	D	3-3	2-3	Gould 23, Tainton 34, Ritchie 83	Bond	Wilson	Drysdale	Emanuel*	Rodgers	Merrick	Tainton	Fear	Gould	Gow	Sweeney	Ritchie
	23/12	*7,704*	*7*	22			*McMahon 1, Bruce 16, Tarbuck 37*	*Kelly*	*McMahon*	*Connor*	*Bird*	*Hawkins*	*Sparrow*	*Wilson*	*Spark*	*McIlmoyle*	*Tarbuck*	*Bruce*	
							Ref: R Perkin	A thriller from the start as John McMahon scores with a 25-yarder after twelve seconds before any City player touches the ball. Gould sparks a fight-back with an unstoppable cross-shot from Fear's centre, but City are fortunate as Dave Wilson's 30-yarder hits bar just before half-time.											
24	H CARDIFF		11	W	1-0	0-0	Gow 65p	Cashley	Wilson	Drysdale	Ritchie	Rodgers	Merrick	Tainton	Fear	Gould	Gow	Sweeney	
	26/12	**20,490**	*20*	24				*Irwin*	*Dwyer*	*Bell*	*Phillips*	*Morgan R*	*Morgan P*	*Kellock*	*McCullough*	*Woodruff*	*Vincent*	*Reece**	*Showers*
							Ref: J Yates	Referee John Yates is Santa Claus as he awards City a penalty when Gould appears to pull back Ritchie Morgan. Cardiff boss Jimmy Scoular calls it 'the biggest act of robbery since the theft of the crown jewels,' after Gow whipped in the spot-kick low beyond Bill Irwin's right hand.											
25	A MILLWALL		13	L	0-3	0-2		Cashley	Wilson	Drysdale	Ritchie	Rodgers*	Merrick	Tainton	Fear	Gould	Gow	Sweeney	Spiring
	30/12	*9,707*	*15*	24			*Wood 12, Possee 34, 48*	*King*	*Brown B*	*Cripps*	*Dorney*	*Kitchener*	*Burnett*	*Possee*	*Dunphy*	*Wood*	*Bolland*	*Allder*	
							Ref: W Castle	City's dangerous breaks come to nought as their high crosses into the box are food and drink for Barry Kitchener, and Millwall are well set for victory by half-time. Alf Wood nudges in from a floated free-kick and then Derek Possee turns and hammers a great shot into the top corner.											
26	H SWINDON		10	W	3-0	2-0	Gould 15, Fear 40, Emanuel 89	Bond	Sweeney	Drysdale	Emanuel	Rodgers	Merrick	Tainton	Spiring	Gould	Gow	Fear*	**Hall**
	6/1	12,481	*16*	26				*Allan*	*Thomas*	*Trollope*	*Bunkell*	*Burrows*	*Potter*	*Jenkins*	*Howells**	*Treacy*	*Noble*	*Butler*	*Peplow*
							Ref: K Wynn	Bobby Gould gives the team talk, after which his characteristically energetic play inspires City to their most convincing home display of the season. Swindon offer little after Gould fired City ahead, and then Fear cracks in from a 20-yard free-kick, before Emanuel blasts in the third.											
27	H ORIENT		11	D	2-2	0-1	Merrick 47, Gow 90	Bond	Sweeney	Drysdale	Emanuel	Rodgers	Merrick	Tainton	Spiring	Gould	Gow	Bartley	
	27/1	11,766	*19*	27			*Allen 12, Queen 88*	*Goddard*	*Hoadley*	*Wall*	*Allen*	*Harris*	*Bennett*	*Downing*	*Brisley*	*Bowyer*	*Queen*	*Heppolette*	
							Ref: R Toseland	Orient look anything but relegation candidates early on as Peter Allen finishes with a 20-yard shot high into the net. A messy game isn't helped by an inconsistent ref who, as well as issuing deserved cautions to Phil Hoadley and Drysdale, books Peter Wall, Gerry Queen and Gould.											
28	A MIDDLESBROUGH		12	L	1-2	0-0	Emanuel 64	Cashley	Sweeney	Drysdale	Emanuel	Bruton	Merrick	Tainton	Spiring	Gould	Gow	Bartley*	Ritchie
	10/2	*8,511*	*7*	27			*Hickton 61, Boam 85*	*Platt*	*Craggs**	*Spraggon*	*Gates*	*Boam*	*Maddren*	*McMordie*	*Mills*	*Smith*	*Hickton*	*Souness*	*Brine*
							Ref: M Lowe	Bruton comes close to obtaining his first-ever goal when heading just over in the 8th minute. Emanuel stars, and his equalising drive into the far corner inspires City for a while, but Stuart Boam settles the issue for Boro, the ball going in off his shoulder after his header had hit the bar.											
29	H BRIGHTON		11	W	3-1	1-1	Tainton 8, Ritchie 77, Spiring 89	Cashley	Sweeney	Drysdale	Emanuel	Bruton	Merrick	Tainton	Spiring	Gould	Gow*	Bartley	Ritchie
	17/2	11,116	*22*	29			*O'Sullivan 4*	*Hughes*	*Templeman*	*Spearritt*	*Bromley*	*Piper*	*Goodwin*	*Bridges*	*Murray*	*Beamish**	*O'Sullivan*	*Towner*	*Howell*
							Ref: T Bosi	City wear black armbands in memory of former favourite 'Ginger' Peacock, who died during the week. Peter O'Sullivan slots home from eight yards, but Tainton soon equalises as he finishes off Spiring's sliced shot. Gould was unlucky on 65 mins as his shot was disallowed for offside.											
30	A BURNLEY		10	D	1-1	0-1	Ritchie 65	Bond	Sweeney	Drysdale	Emanuel	Rodgers	Merrick	Tainton	Ritchie	Gould	Gow	Fear	
	24/2	*13,630*	*1*	30			*Dobson 7*	*Stevenson*	*Cliff*	*Newton*	*Dobson*	*Waldron*	*Thomson*	*Nulty*	*Casper*	*Fletcher*	*Collins*	*James*	
							Ref: G Hill	Keeper Alan Stevenson prevents a deserved away success as City outplay Burnley in midfield. Bond is at fault early on as he fails to react quickly enough to Martin Dobson's 25-yarder, but Ritchie, after hitting a post in the first half, notches the equaliser by heading in Fear's cross.											
31	H PORTSMOUTH		11	W	3-1	2-0	Gow 10, 60, Fear 32	Bond	Sweeney	Drysdale	Emanuel	Rodgers	Merrick	Tainton	Ritchie	**Woods**	Gow	Fear	
	3/3	11,002	*14*	32			*Hiron 81*	*Milkins*	*Wilson*	*Collins*	*Hand*	*Stephenson*	*Munks*	*Foggo*	*Piper*	*Hiron*	*Kellard*	*Jennings**	*Lewis*
							Ref: A Jones	Despite another penalty miss by Gow, as his 50th-min kick hits the inside of the post, City's young side storm to another victory over Pompey. Woods has an impressive debut, whilst good play between Fear and Tainton allows star man Gow to squeeze the ball in from a narrow angle.											

No / Date	Venue	Opponent / Att	Pos	Res / Pts	F-A	H-T	Scorers, Times, and Referees	1	2	3	4	5	6	7	8	9	10	11	12
32	A	NOTT'M FOREST	11	L	0-1	0-1		Bond	Sweeney	Drysdale	Emanuel	Rodgers*	Merrick	Tainton	Ritchie	**Gillies**	Gow	Fear	Woods
10/3		*8,680*	*12*	32			*Galley 45*	*Barron*	*Hindley*	*Winfield*	*Chapman*	*Serella*	*Fraser*	*McIntosh*	*Robertson*	*O'Neill*	*Galley*	*Lyall*	
							Ref: R Armstrong	Erstwhile hero John Galley sends City to defeat in the second minute of first-half injury-time, bursting between Sweeney and Rodgers to score with a left-foot shot from twelve yards. City take the game forward impressively, but they offer little in the way of shots to trouble Forest.											
33	A	SHEFFIELD WED	12	L	2-3	0-0	Gould 52, Ritchie 85	Bond	Sweeney	Drysdale	Emanuel	Rodgers	Merrick	Tainton*	Ritchie	Gillies	Gow	Gould	Fear
14/3		*13,635*	*4*	32			*Joicey 66, 87, Sunley 68*	*Grummitt*	*Rodrigues*	*Mullen*	*Prophet*	*Thompson*	*Craig*	*Henderson*	*Coyle*	*Joicey*	*Sunley*	*Sissons**	*Potts*
							Ref: R Capey	Gould's powerful shot from Emanuel's pass allows City to be in a better position than when this fixture was originally postponed after 55 mins on 20 Jan. Unfortunately, Merrick thrice slips to set up Wednesday's goals, and despite Ritchie firing in a late equaliser City are defeated.											
34	H	OXFORD	12	D	0-0	0-0		Cashley	Sweeney	Drysdale	Emanuel	Rodgers	Merrick	Tainton*	Ritchie	Gillies	Gow	Gould	Fear
17/3		11,177	*8*	33				*Thomas*	*Lucas*	*Shuker*	*Roberts*	*Lowe*	*Skeen*	*Gough*	*Fleming*	*Cassidy*	*Curran*	*Aylott*	
							Ref: J Goggins	Apart from an early effort by Gillies, whose left-foot lob just clears the bar, only Hugh Curran looks likely to break the deadlock. His neat flick midway through the first half is disallowed for offside. He then blasts over the bar from four yards in the 84th minute for the miss of the game.											
35	A	LUTON	11	W	3-1	0-1	Gow 47, Gillies 55, Fear 68	Cashley	Sweeney	Drysdale	Emanuel	Rodgers	**Collier**	Fear	Ritchie	Gillies	Gow	Gould	
24/3		*7,102*	*9*	35			*Garner 34*	*Horn*	*Ryan John*	*Thomson*	*Shanks*	*Garner*	*Moore*	*Ryan Jim**	*Anderson*	*Busby*	*Hindson*	*Ashton*	*Fern*
							Ref: J Wrennall	City turn the game on its head with a great display after the break. John Aston gave City the run around early on, but Gow's hooked equaliser from five yards inspires a comeback. Gillies opens his scoring account with a truly great goal, an unstoppable angled drive from fully 25 yards.											
36	H	ASTON VILLA	10	W	3-0	1-0	Gillies 24, Gould 65, 70	Cashley	Sweeney	Drysdale	Emanuel	Rodgers	Merrick	Fear	Ritchie	Gillies	Gow	Gould	
27/3		15,654	*5*	37				*Cumbes*	*Rioch N*	*McDonald*	*Rioch B*	*Nicholl*	*Turnbull*	*McMahon*	*Brown*	*Evans !*	*Vowden*	*Lochead*	
							Ref: G Kew	Another superb strike by Gillies – a perfectly-judged header from Ritchie's chip – sets Emanuel-inspired City on the way to a convincing win. Unfortunately, the referee deprives City of some of the credit by sending off Alun Evans for dissent, as well as booking three other Villains.											
37	A	SUNDERLAND	8	D	2-2	0-1	Merrick 59, Emanuel 89	Cashley	Sweeney	Drysdale	Emanuel	Rodgers	Merrick	Fear	Ritchie	Gillies	Gow	Gould	
31/3		***33,255***	*13*	38			*Merrick 35 (og), Watson 52*	*Montgomery*	*Malone*	*Gutherie*	*Horswill*	*Pitt*	*Young*	*Kerr*	*Hughes*	*Watson*	*Porterfield*	*Tueart*	
							Ref: L Hayes	Merrick's never-say-die attitude, after being at fault for both of Sunderland's goals, typifies City's fighting performance He heads home from Fear's corner to inspire a fightback, which is completed near the end by Emanuel's 25-yard equaliser. Bookings for Emanuel and Denis Tueart.											
38	H	CARLISLE	7	W	**4-1**	3-1	O'Neill 14 (og), Rodgers 20, Gow 27p, [Gould 81]	Cashley	Sweeney	Drysdale	Emanuel	Rodgers	Merrick	Fear	Ritchie	Gillies*	Gow	Gould	Tainton
7/4		**10,588**	*17*	40			*Laidlaw 5*	*Ross*	*Carr*	*Gorman*	*O'Neill*	*Winstanley*	*Tiler*	*Martin*	*Train*	*Owen*	*Balderstone**	*Laidlaw*	*Ternent*
							Ref: A Lees	Carlisle, requiring four points to be safe from relegation, have the tonic of an early goal. Joe Laidlaw bursts through to net with a crisp drive, but City level as Les O'Neill lobs ball into his own goal and then go on to improve their Watney Cup prospects with three more scoring strikes.											
39	A	ASTON VILLA	9	L	0-1	0-0		Cashley	Sweeney	Drysdale	Emanuel	Rodgers*	Merrick	Fear	Ritchie	Gillies	Gow	Gould	Tainton
14/4		*19,545*	*3*	40			*Rioch 76*	*Cumbes*	*Ross*	*Robson*	*Brown*	*Nicholl*	*Rioch N*	*McMahon*	*Little*	*Lochhead*	*Vowden*	*Hamilton*	
							Ref: D Nippard	'I've had enough,' says Gerry Gow, as his injury-time spot-kick is his fourth failure of the season. Jimmy Cumbes dives to his left to make a good save to deprive City of a point they don't deserve. Villa should have won by a five or six-goal margin, but are let down by poor finishing.											
40	H	BLACKPOOL	8	W	3-0	2-0	Gould 10, Emanuel 12, Fear 68	Cashley	Sweeney	Drysdale	Emanuel	Rodgers*	Merrick	Fear	Ritchie	Gillies	Gow	Gould	Tainton
21/4		11,537	*5*	42				*Wood*	*Hatton*	*Bentley*	*Alcock*	*James*	*Suddaby*	*Burns*	*Suddick*	*Rafferty*	*Dyson*	*Ainscow**	*Lennard*
							Ref: C Nicholls	City get back on course for Watney Cup qualification, though Blackpool make most of the running. Ritchie's dazzling footwork sets up Gould to score with a diving header and then Emanuel registers with one of his 25-yard specials, before Fear rolls ball into net to end City's anxieties.											
41	H	PRESTON	7	W	2-1	1-0	Merrick 27, Fear 49	Cashley	Sweeney	Drysdale	Emanuel	Collier	Merrick	Fear	Ritchie	Gillies	Gow	Gould	
23/4		10,799	*19*	44			*Bruce 77*	*Brown*	*McMahon*	*Snookes*	*Bird*	*Hawkins*	*Spark*	*Wilson**	*Lamb*	*McIlmoyle*	*Bruce*	*Young*	*Baxter*
							Ref: F Bassett	The referee gets the bird from City fans as Gow's perfect shot into the far corner on the hour is disallowed because Bobby Gould was offside. Alex Bruce runs 40 yards before scoring with a great solo effort, but City's star, Fear, has Preston in a perpetual tangle with his range of skills.											
42	H	HULL	5	W	2-1	0-0	O'Neill 79 (og), Gould 83	Cashley	Sweeney	Drysdale	Emanuel	Collier*	Merrick	Fear	Ritchie	Gillies	Gow	Gould	Tainton
28/4		11,066	*13*	46			*Pearson 68*	*McKechnie*	*Banks*	*De Vries*	*Kay*	*Neill*	*Knighton*	*McGill*	*Lord*	*Pearson*	*Greenwood*	*Wagstaff*	
Home		Away					Ref: C Thomas	A drab match is brought alive by Pearson's superb 25-yard volley for the Tigers. City's need for Watney Cup goals prompts Dicks to bring on Tainton with 28 mins left, and the gamble pays off with victory when Gould shoots in. Bookings for Merrick and Hull captain Ken Knighton.											
Average 12,892		11,542																	

League Cup			F-A	H-T	Scorers, Times, and Referees	1	2	3	4	5	6	7	8	9	10	11	12 sub used
2 A WEST HAM	22	L	1-2	0-1	Galley 89	Cashley	Wilson	Drysdale	Sweeney	Rodgers*	Merrick	Tainton	Spiring	Galley	Gow	Ritchie	Broomfield
6/9	*17,688 1:12*				*McDowell 44, Best 85*	*Grotier*	*McDowell*	*Lampard*	*Bonds*	*Taylor*	*Moore*	*Tyler*	*Best*	*Holland*	*Brooking*	*Robson*	
					Ref: N Paget	Galley excels as centre-half after the loss of Rodgers following a clash of heads with Billy Bonds. John McDowell fires in a tremendous shot to put the Hammers in front and then Clyde Best hammers in a 20-yard drive, before City gain a deserved reward thanks to Galley scoring header.											

FA Cup			F-A	H-T	Scorers, Times, and Referees	1	2	3	4	5	6	7	8	9	10	11	12 sub used
3 A PORTSMOUTH	10	D	1-1	0-0	Gould 90	Bond	Sweeney	Drysdale	Emanuel	Rodgers	Merrick	Tainton	Spiring	Gould	Gow	Fear*	Hall
13/1	*15,177 17*				*Piper 63*	*Horn*	*Wilson*	*Collins*	*Hand*	*Stephenson*	*Munks*	*Piper*	*Reynolds*	*Hiron*	*Kellard*	*Jennings*	
					Ref: R Crabb	A perfectly-placed linesman awards Gould's headed equaliser in the dying seconds as Pompey claim ball hasn't crossed the line. City, on top in the first half, are made to pay for missed chances when Norman Piper's banana shot floats over the defensive wall to nestle in the top corner.											
3R H PORTSMOUTH	10	W	4-1	1-0	Gould 27, Tainton 74, Sweeney 84,	Bond	Sweeney	Drysdale	Emanuel	Rodgers	Merrick	Tainton	Spiring	Gould	Gow	Bartley	
16/1	16,699 *17*				*Hiron 86* [Gow 89p]	*Horn*	*Wilson*	*Collins**	*Smith*	*Hand*	*Munks*	*Piper*	*Reynolds*	*Hiron*	*Kellard*	*Price*	*Lewis*
					Ref: R Crabb	City overwhelm Pompey with a brilliant display, though Gow admits to impeding Graham Horn (booked for his protests) as Gould heads in. Tainton's header doubles City's advantage, whilst Gow's penalty after David Munks had fouled Tainton cancels out Ray Hiron's late header.											
4 A WOLVES	11	L	0-1	0-1		Cashley	Sweeney	Drysdale	Emanuel	Rodgers*	Merrick	Tainton	Spiring	Gould	Gow	Bartley	Ritchie
3/2	*30,849 1:8*				*Richards 45*	*Parkes*	*Taylor*	*McAlle*	*Shaw*	*Munro*	*Jefferson*	*McCalliog*	*Sunderland*	*Richards*	*Dougan*	*Wagstaffe*	
					Ref: A Grey	An enthralling cup clash well controlled by Alf Grey, despite early bookings for Derek Jefferson, Gould and Ritchie. City are unfortunate to lose, as they do well to overcome losing Rodgers with a hamstring injury. John Richards scores right on the interval with a low cross-shot.											

Abandoned League Fixture			F-A	H-T	Scorers, Times, and Referees	1	2	3	4	5	6	7	8	9	10	11	12 sub used
A SHEFFIELD WED	11		0-0	0-0		Bond	Sweeney	Drysdale	Emanuel	Rodgers	Merrick	Tainton	Spiring	Gould	Gow	Bartley	
20/1	*11,195 8*					*Springett*	*Rodriques*	*Clements*	*Thompson*	*Holsgrove*	*Craig*	*Henderson*	*Coyle*	*Sunley*	*Prendergast*	*Sissons*	
(Abandoned 55 mins due to snow & ice)					Ref: J Williams	'The pitch was unplayable,' said City coach John Sillett. With the snow not stopping, it was somewhat surprising that it took so long before the game was abandoned, this just three minutes after John Sissons had his cross-shot struck off because Mick Prendergast had strayed offside.											

		Home					Away					
	P	W	D	L	F	A	W	D	L	F	A	Pts
1 Burnley	42	13	6	2	44	18	11	8	2	28	17	62
2 QP Rangers	42	16	4	1	54	13	[illegible]	9	4	27	24	61
3 Aston Villa	42	12	5	4	27	17	[illegible]	9	6	24	30	50
4 Middlesbro	42	12	6	3	29	15	[illegible]	7	9	17	28	47
5 BRISTOL CITY	42	10	7	4	34	18	[illegible]	5	9	29	33	46
6 Sunderland	42	12	6	3	35	17	[illegible]	6	10	24	32	46
7 Blackpool	42	12	6	3	37	17	[illegible]	4	11	19	34	46
8 Oxford	42	14	2	5	36	18	[illegible]	5	11	16	25	45
9 Fulham	42	11	6	4	32	16	[illegible]	6	10	26	33	44
10 Sheffield Wed	42	14	4	3	40	20	[illegible]	6	12	19	35	44
11 Millwall	42	12	5	4	33	18	[illegible]	5	12	22	29	42
12 Luton	42	6	9	6	24	23	[illegible]	2	10	20	30	41
13 Hull	42	9	7	5	39	22	[illegible]	5	11	25	37	40
14 Nott'm Forest	42	12	5	4	32	18	[illegible]	7	12	15	34	40
15 Orient	42	11	6	4	33	18	[illegible]	6	14	16	35	36
16 Swindon	42	8	9	4	28	23	[illegible]	7	12	18	37	36
17 Portsmouth	42	7	6	8	21	22	[illegible]	5	11	21	37	35
18 Carlisle	42	10	5	6	40	24	[illegible]	7	13	10	28	34
19 Preston	42	6	8	7	19	25	[illegible]	4	12	18	39	34
20 Cardiff	42	11	4	6	32	21	[illegible]	7	14	11	37	33
21 Huddersfield	42	7	9	5	21	20	[illegible]	8	12	15	36	33
22 Brighton	42	7	8	6	32	31	[illegible]	5	15	14	52	29
	924	232	133	97	722	434	[illegible]	133	232	434	722	924

Odds & ends

Double wins: (3) Cardiff, Portsmouth, Carlisle.
Double losses: (1) Sheffield Wed.

Won from behind: (4) Brighton (h), Luton (a), Carlisle (h), Hull (h).
Lost from in front: (1) Sheffield Wed (a).

High spots: Drawing 1-1 at Turf Moor on 24 February.
Beating Aston Villa 3-0 at Ashton Gate on 27 March.
Great early away form with six wins and three draws from the opening 13 games.
Beating Swindon 3-0 at Ashton Gate on 6 January.
Bobby Gould's last-minute goal in the FA Cup at Fratton Park.
Beating Bristol Rov 5-3 on penalties to win the Gloucestershire Cup on 1 May.

Low spots: Failure to win a home match until 25 November.
Losing 1-5 at Fulham on 4 November.
Unlucky 0-1 defeat v Wolves in the FA Cup.

Player of the year: John Emanuel.
Ever-presents: (1) Geoff Merrick.
Hat-tricks: (0).
Leading scorer: Gerry Gow (13).

	Appearances						Goals			
	Lge	*Sub*	LC	*Sub*	FAC	*Sub*	**Lge**	LC	FAC	**Tot**
Bartley, Danny	**12**	*2*			2		**1**			**1**
Bond, Len	**10**				2					
Broomfield, Ian	**3**	*1*		*1*						
Bruton, David	**6**									
Cashley, Ray	**32**		1		1					
Collier, Gary	**3**									
Drysdale, Brian	**34**		1		3		**1**			**1**
Emanuel, John	**33**	*1*			3		**5**			**5**
Fear, Keith	**20**	*4*			1		**7**			**7**
Galley, John	**20**		1				**6**	1		**7**
Gillies, Donny	**11**						**2**			**2**
Gould, Bobby	**19**				3		**8**		2	**10**
Gow, Gerry	**42**		1		3		**12**		1	**13**
Hall, Colin		*1*				*1*				
Jacobs, Trevor	**3**									
Merrick, Geoff	**41**		1		3		**3**			**3**
Ritchie, Tom	**24**	*7*	1			*1*	**4**			**4**
Ritchie, Steve	**1**									
Rodgers, David	**34**		1		3		**1**			**1**
Spiring, Peter	**20**	*2*	1		3		**7**			**7**
Sweeney, Gerry	**39**	*1*	1		3		**2**		1	**3**
Tainton, Trevor	**33**	*4*	1		3		**2**		1	**3**
Wilson, Les	**21**	*1*	1							
Woods, Eddie	**1**	*1*								
(own-goals)							**2**			**2**
24 players used	**462**	***25***	**11**	***1***	**33**	***2***	**63**	**1**	**5**	**69**

No	Date	Att	Pos	Pt	F-A	H-T	Scorers, Times, and Referees	1	2	3	4	5	6	7	8	9	10	11	12 sub used
1	H BOLTON			W	1-0	1-0	Gould 7	Cashley	Sweeney	Merrick	Emanuel	Rodgers	Collier	Tainton	Ritchie	Gould	Gow	Fear*	Gillies
	25/8	13,665		2				*Siddall*	*McCallister*	*Dunne*	*Rimmer*	*Jones P*	*Nicholson**	*Byrom*	*Jones G*	*Greaves*	*Lee*	*Phillips*	*Waldron*
							Ref: J Bent	This dour struggle is decided early on when the ball rolls slowly into the net after Paul Jones' clearance cannons off Gould. City are not direct enough and, whilst they have two penalty appeals turned down after the break, it is newly promoted Bolton who create the better chances.											
2	A ORIENT			W	1-0	0-0	Rodgers 88	Cashley	Sweeney	Merrick	Emanuel	Rodgers	Collier	Tainton	Ritchie	Gould	Gow	Fear	
	1/9	*7,216*		4				*Goddard*	*Hoadley**	*Downing*	*Allen*	*Linton*	*Walley*	*Fairbrother*	*Brisley*	*Bullock*	*Queen*	*Payne*	*Fisher*
							Ref: R Armstrong	Refusing to leave the pitch with a badly cut eyebrow, Rodgers is City's hero as he heads in from Fear's free-kick. Cashley should have been beaten early on by both Barry Fairbrother and Terry Brisley, but City, with much the best of the action thereafter, fully merit their success.											
3	H LUTON		9	L	1-3	1-2	Gould 39p	Cashley	Sweeney	Merrick	Emanuel	Rodgers*	Collier	Tainton	Ritchie	Gould	Gow	Fear	Drysdale
	8/9	12,208	*6*	4			*Aston 2, Ryan John 4, Finney 48*	*Horn*	*Shanks*	*Thomson*	*Anderson*	*Faulkner*	*Garner*	*Ryan Jim*	*Ryan John*	*Butlin*	*Finney*	*Aston*	
							Ref: R Perkin	City's early season euphoria is quickly shattered by Luton's quick one-two. A push on Tainton allows Gould to atone from the spot for having sliced wide of an open goal, but Tom Finney's great twelve-yard volley ties up a deserved success for the vastly superior Hatters.											
4	A SWINDON		2	W	1-0	1-0	Gould 7	Cashley	Sweeney	Drysdale	Emanuel	Rodgers	Merrick	Tainton	Ritchie	Gould	Gow	Fear	
	11/9	*14,222*	*7*	6				*Allan*	*Thomas*	*Trollope*	*Stroud*	*Burrows*	*Butler*	*Moss*	*McGovern**	*Treacy*	*Legg*	*Jenkins*	*Bunkell*
							Ref: R Toseland	With an imaginative and skilful display City, in their all-white strip, canter to an easy win over previously unbeaten Swindon. Jimmy Allen pulls off many fine saves to keep City at bay, but even he is powerless when the game's first corner is headed on for Gould to hook the ball in.											
5	A PRESTON		4	D	1-1	0-1	Fear 78	Cashley	Sweeney	Drysdale	Emanuel	Rodgers*	Merrick	Tainton	Ritchie	Gould	Gow	Fear	Gillies
	15/9	*10,790*	*16*	7			*Young 20*	*Kelly*	*McMahon*	*McNab*	*Baxter*	*Hawkins*	*Stiles*	*Lamb*	*Bruce*	*Holden*	*Burns**	*Young*	*Morley*
							Ref: J Taylor	Trailing to Neil Young's brilliant 15-yard header, City have Cashley to thank for keeping them in the game. Faced by only ten men after Preston's 75th-minute loss of Alan Kelly with a shoulder injury, Fear takes advantage of Stuart Baxter's keeping to head in a Gillies cross.											
6	H HULL		1	W	3-1	0-1	Ritchie 47, Cashley 55, Gould 82	Cashley	Sweeney	Drysdale	Emanuel	Rodgers	Merrick	Tainton	Ritchie	Gould	Gow	Fear	
	18/9	10,711	*19*	9			*Pearson 24*	*Wealands*	*Banks*	*De Vries*	*Kaye*	*Deere*	*Blampey*	*McGill*	*Lord*	*Pearson*	*Wagstaff*	*Greenwood*	
							Ref: B Daniels	Cashley emerges as City's unlikely goal-scoring hero, following Ritchie's headed equaliser to Stuart Pearson's tap in. The Tigers' slick play counts for nought as Cashley's 95-yard 2ft clearance finds the net and then Gould shoots in a rebound to raise City to the top of the table.											
7	H SHEFFIELD WED		1	W	2-0	1-0	Gould 17, Fear 65	Cashley	Sweeney	Drysdale	Emanuel	Rodgers	Merrick	Tainton	Ritchie	Gould	Gow	Fear	
	22/9	13,829	*17*	11				*Springett*	*Rodrigues*	*Shaw*	*Thompson*	*Holsgrove*	*Craig T*	*Potts*	*Sunley*	*Joicey*	*Prendergast*	*Knighton*	
							Ref: D Turner	Fear's rounding of Peter Springett to shoot in City's second goal produces much protest. Just as well that Owls boss Derek Dooley intervenes to usher his players away from the referee as Bristol Channel's video of the game proves that Fear was onside when collecting the through ball.											
8	A MIDDLESBROUGH		2	L	0-2	0-0		Cashley	Sweeney	Drysdale	Emanuel	Rodgers	Merrick	Tainton	Ritchie*	Gould	Gow	Fear	Gillies
	29/9	*17,069*	*1*	11			*Murdoch 60, Armstrong 84*	*Platt*	*Craggs*	*Spraggon*	*Maddren*	*Boam*	*Souness*	*Murdoch*	*Mills*	*Hickton*	*Foggon*	*Armstrong*	
							Ref: J Wrennal	Boro' look much the better side in this top of the table clash against ultra-defensive City. After surviving a first-half hammering City can only admire Bobby Murdoch's thundering 20-yard drive, and then concede top place on goal average as David Armstrong breaks clear to shoot in.											
9	A HULL		4	L	1-2	0-2	Rodgers 78	Cashley	Sweeney	Drysdale	Emanuel	Rodgers	Merrick	Tainton	Ritchie	Gould*	Gow	Fear	Gillies
	2/10	*7,235*	*12*	11			*Greenwood 5, Wagstaff 37*	*Wealands*	*Banks*	*De Vries*	*Kaye*	*Deere*	*Blampey*	*McGill*	*Lord*	*Pearson*	*Wagstaff**	*Greenwood*	*Hawley*
							Ref: H Davey	Lethargic City's defensive shortcomings bring skilful Hull their deserved success. After Roy Greenwood's speculative cross-shot from the right strikes Drysdale before going in off a post, the failure of Rodgers to effect a simple clearance allows Ken Wagstaff to shoot home.											
10	H WEST BROM		6	D	1-1	1-1	Gould 31	Cashley*	Sweeney	Drysdale	Emanuel	Rodgers	Merrick	Tainton	Ritchie	Gould	Gow	Fear	Gillies
	6/10	14,325	*17*	12			*Brown T 25*	*Latchford*	*Nisbet*	*Merrick*	*Cantello*	*Wile*	*Robertson*	*Hartford*	*Brown T*	*Brown A*	*Shaw*	*Johnston*	
							Ref: D Nippard	After heading in an equaliser to Tony Brown's flicked in opener, Gould takes over in goal when Cashley sustains an arm injury just after the interval. A rough game, with Emanuel playing on with a cracked jaw, sees City twice hit the post, whilst offside rules out a Tony Brown effort.											

No	Venue	Opponent	Att	Pos	Res / Pts	FT	HT	Scorers, Times, and Referees	1	2	3	4	5	6	7	8	9	10	11	12
11	A	MILLWALL		4	W	2-0	0-0	Gould 68, Whitehead 69	Bond	Tainton	Drysdale	Sweeney	Collier	Merrick	**Whitehead**	Ritchie	Gould	Gow	Gillies	
13/10			*7,543*	*20*	14				*King*	*Brown*	*Cripps*	*Dorney*	*Kitchener*	*Burnett*	*Bolland*	*Clark*	*Wood*	*Dunphy*	*Hill*	
								Ref: J Williams	After a poor first half City click into top gear with a display of non-stop attacking action. Gould is on hand to calmly slot in a rebound when Gillies shoots against a post, then Whitehead crowns a sparkling debut by running through to collect a through pass and beat the keeper.											
12	A	ASTON VILLA		3	D	2-2	2-1	Fear 25, Ritchie 32	Bond	Tainton	Drysdale	Sweeney	Collier	Merrick	Whitehead*	Ritchie	Gould	Gow	Fear	Gillies
20/10			*26,918*	*4*	15			*Little 20, Graydon 49*	*Cumbes*	*Gidman*	*Aitken*	*Hockey*	*Nicholl*	*Ross*	*Graydon*	*Brown*	*Evans*	*Vowden**	*Little*	*Morgan*
								Ref: V James	Following Brian Little's headed opener, errors by the Villa custodian reward attack-minded City's fight-back. Jimmy Cumbes, late in getting down to Fear's shot, is at fault again when he drops the ball for Ritchie to tap in. Ray Graydon's 30-yard screamer caps a compelling contest.											
13	H	SWINDON		2	W	1-0	1-0	Fear 3	Bond	Tainton	Drysdale	Sweeney	Collier	Merrick	Whitehead	Ritchie	Gould	Gow	Fear	
23/10			14,474	*20*	17				*Allan*	*Thomas*	*Butler*	*Dixon**	*Burrows*	*Stroud*	*Moss*	*McGovern*	*Treacy*	*Legg*	*Jenkins*	*Collins*
								Ref: B Homewood	Swindon boss Les Allen is of the opinion that City are promotion bound, following the completion of an accomplished double over his side. After Fear spurts through the middle to head in Drysdale's free-kick, Swindon's dogged defending restricts City to the barest winning margin.											
14	H	BLACKPOOL		4	L	0-1	0-0		Bond	Tainton	Drysdale	Sweeney	Rodgers	Merrick	Whitehead*	Ritchie	Gould	Gow	Fear	Gillies
27/10			13,896	*11*	17			*Dyson 62*	*Burridge*	*Curtis*	*Bentley*	*Alcock*	*James*	*Suddaby*	*Burns*	*Suddick*	*Dyson*	*Hatton*	*Walsh*	
								Ref: W Gow	City coach John Sillett berates his players for Blackpool's decisive goal, as a sloppy pass, a wild tackle, and failure to guard the far post, allows Keith Dyson to put away a low cross. In truth though it is the homesters' failure to turn their dominance into goals that costs them the points.											
15	A	FULHAM		5	L	1-2	0-0	Tainton 83	Bond	Sweeney	Drysdale	Emanuel*	Rodgers	Merrick	Tainton	Ritchie	Gould	Gow	Fear	Gillies
3/11			*9,613*	*13*	17			*Conway 52, Busby 56*	*Webster*	*Cutbush*	*Slough*	*Mullery*	*Went*	*Lacy*	*Conway J'n*	*Earle*	*Busby*	*Lloyd*	*Barrett*	
								Ref: D Richardson	In front of the Big Match cameras City are forced to adopt a more positive approach after Bond drops a cross for John Conway's opening goal. Tainton hammers in City's late reply, but by then Viv Busby had steered Fulham into clear water following Steve Earle's 50-yard mazy run.											
16	H	CRYS PALACE		9	L	0-1	0-1		Bond	Tainton	Drysdale	Sweeney	Rodgers	Merrick	Whitehead*	Ritchie	Gould	Gow	Gillies	Fear
10/11			15,488	*22*	17			*Whittle 24*	*Hammond*	*Mulligan*	*Wall*	*Walley*	*Barry*	*Jeffries**	*Cooke*	*Possee*	*Swindlehurst*	*Taylor P*	*Rogers*	*Whittle*
								Ref: G Hill	City fans should be inured against results such as this, as yet again they find themselves as the fall guys. In front of the Match of the Day cameras Alan Whittle's low shot earns Palace, thanks to Paul Hammond's acrobatic goalkeeping display, their first League win of the season.											
17	H	SUNDERLAND		8	W	2-0	0-0	Sweeney 68, Gillies 88	Bond	Tainton	Merrick	Sweeney	Rodgers	Collier	Whitehead	Ritchie	Gillies	Gow	Fear*	Emanuel
17/11			14,965	*10*	19				*Montgomery*	*Malone*	*Bolton*	*Horswill*	*Watson*	*Ashurst**	*Kerr*	*Belfitt*	*Halom*	*Porterfield*	*Tueart*	*Hughes*
								Ref: D Civil	Champagne show as the FA Cup holders are overrun by what is, with an average age of 21.5 years, probably City's youngest-ever side. Gillies' pull back allows Sweeney to hammer City ahead, and just before time Gillies finishes off a 50-yard run with a perfect shot into the net.											
18	A	CARLISLE		9	L	1-2	1-1	Ritchie 37	Bond	Tainton	Merrick	Sweeney	Rodgers	Collier	Whitehead*	Ritchie	Gillies	Gow	Emanuel	Drysdale
24/11			***6,020***	*8*	19			*Winstanley 15, O'Neill 74*	*Ross*	*Carr*	*Gorman*	*O'Neill*	*Winstanley*	*Ternent*	*Martin*	*Balderstone*	*Owen*	*Clarke**	*Laidlaw*	*Train*
								Ref: H Hackney	Following a mishap on the way to Carlisle, when the team coach was forced to swerve, Sweeney is only passed fit after having his cut eye stitched. Ritchie shoots in from Whitehead's centre, but his two spurned chances after the break are costly as Les O'Neill's low shot is decisive.											
19	H	NOTTS CO		10	D	2-2	1-1	Gillies 35, Fear 68	Bond	Tainton	Merrick	Sweeney	Rodgers	Collier	Whitehead*	Ritchie	Gillies	Gow	Fear	Emanuel
1/12			10,436	*3*	20			*Masson 42p, Mann 59*	*McManus*	*Brindley*	*Worthington*	*Masson*	*Needham*	*McVay*	*Nixon**	*Randall*	*Bradd*	*Probert*	*Mann*	*Vinter*
								Ref: G Kew	After dominating the first half and being rewarded with a magnificent 25-yard strike by Gillies, City are unlucky to not be ahead at the break. Don Masson's penalty is rough justice for Rodgers who appears to be pushed in the back before involuntarily handling County's free-kick.											
20	A	PORTSMOUTH		11	L	0-1	0-0		Bond	Tainton	Merrick	Sweeney	Rodgers	Collier	Whitehead	Ritchie	Gillies	Gow	Fear	
8/12			*13,178*	*15*	20			*Davies 56*	*Milkins*	*Roberts*	*Collins*	*Piper*	*Went*	*Manley*	*Marinello*	*Kellard*	*Davies*	*Reynolds*	*Mellows*	
								Ref: A Hart	The hire of a generator for the duration of the power dispute ensures return to a 3pm kick-off. Ron Davies' 20-yard volley wins the game for Pompey, but City are unfortunate. Denied a 51st-min pen when Fear's shot is diverted, Sweeney's late left-foot effort is disallowed for offside.											
21	A	CARDIFF		9	W	1-0	0-0	Gillies 78	Bond	Sweeney	Merrick	Emanuel	Rodgers	Collier	Tainton	Ritchie	Gillies	Gow	Fear	
15/12			*9,368*	*18*	22				*Irwin*	*Dwyer*	*Bell*	*Powell*	*Murray*	*Woodruff*	*Farrington*	*McCulloch*	*Reece*	*Smith**	*Phillips*	*Anderson*
								Ref: R Kirkpatrick	'A travesty of a match' is Cardiff boss Frank O'Farrell's opinion of this lamentable affair. Gillies atones for a first-half miskick in front of an open goal, by running in and driving the ball past Bill Irwin giving City a win that their hard, determined tackling just about deserves for them.											

LEAGUE DIVISION 2

Manager: Alan Dicks

SEASON 1973-74

No	Date	Opponent	Att	Pos	Pt	F-A	H-T	Scorers, Times, and Referees	1	2	3	4	5	6	7	8	9	10	11	12 sub used
22	H	MIDDLESBROUGH		9	D	1-1	0-1	Gillies 58	Bond	Sweeney	Merrick	Emanuel	Rodgers*	Collier	Tainton	Ritchie	Gillies	Gow	Fear	**Durrell**
	22/12		13,116	*1*	23			*Mills 6*	*Platt*	*Creamer*	*Spraggon*	*Souness*	*Boam*	*Maddren*	*Murdoch*	*Mills*	*Hickton*	*Foggon*	*Armstrong*	
								Ref: C Thomas	Clive Thomas is at the centre of controversy in awarding City a free-kick instead of a pen following David Armstrong's 61st-minute handball offence, which clearly takes place inside the area. Gillies punishes David Mills for his 45-yard back-pass with a great shot into the far corner.											
23	A	OXFORD		13	L	**0-5**	0-2	*[Cassidy 47, Clarke C 60]*	Bond	Sweeney	Merrick	Emanuel	Rodgers	Collier	Tainton	Ritchie	Gillies	Gow	Fear*	Durrell
	26/12		*7,742*	*18*	23			*Atkinson G 13, 80, Curran 38,*	*Burton*	*Lucas*	*Shuker*	*Roberts*	*Clarke C*	*Evanson*	*Clarke D*	*Atkinson G*	*Cassidy*	*Curran*	*Aylott*	
								Ref: M Sinclair	The City defence is found wanting as four of Oxford's goals come from set pieces. Graham Atkinson puts the U's ahead with a shot that goes in off Rodgers. All City can offer, as they suffer their worst defeat since April 1969, is a late effort from Emanuel which is headed off the line.											
24	A	LUTON		13	L	0-1	0-1		Bond	Tainton	Drysdale	Sweeney	Collier	Merrick	Fear	Ritchie*	Gillies	Gow	Durrell	**Griffin**
	29/12		*11,398*	*3*	23			*Anderson 37*	*Horn*	*Shanks*	*Thomson*	*Anderson*	*Faulkner*	*Garner*	*Ryan Jim*	*Husband*	*Butlin*	*West*	*Aston*	
								Ref: K Burns	Again City are caught out by a set piece, this time Peter Anderson is unmarked almost on the penalty spot to register with a looping header from skipper Bobby Thomson's free-kick. Bond makes a magnificent 57th-min save in pushing Barry Butlin's shot on the turn round the post.											
25	H	ORIENT		14	L	0-2	0-0		Bond	Tainton	Drysdale	Sweeney	Collier	Merrick	Gillies	**Hunt**	**Cheesley**	Gow	Durrell	
	1/1		19,126	*2*	23			*Collier 65 (og), Merrick 83 (og)*	*Goddard*	*Boyle*	*Roffey*	*Allen**	*Hoadley*	*Walley*	*Fairbrother*	*Brisley*	*Bullock*	*Heppolette*	*Downing*	*Payne*
								Ref: W Castle	A pointless three-match holiday programme extinguishes City's promotion hopes. Bond brings off many fine saves to frustrate a skilful Orient side, but even he cannot prevent deflections from Terry Brisley's free-kick and Derek Downing's cross bringing the visitors deserved success.											
26	H	PRESTON		13	D	0-0	0-0		Cashley	Collier	Drysdale	Sweeney	Rodgers	Merrick	Tainton	Ritchie	Cheesley	Gow	Gillies*	Hunt
	12/1		11,450	*16*	24				*Brown*	*McMahon*	*McNab*	*Sadler*	*Baxter*	*Bird*	*Treacy*	*Hawkins*	*Holden*	*Burns*	*Bruce*	
								Ref: R Challis	City's inability to break down Preston's defensive line-up results in a dull game. A tally of 39 free-kicks to City and 29 against says much, and it is disappointing that Preston boss Bobby Charlton declares himself as being satisfied that his side's work rate gets them a share of the spoils.											
27	A	BOLTON		15	L	1-2	1-2	Hunt 3	Cashley	Collier	Drysdale	Sweeney	Rodgers	Merrick	Tainton	Ritchie	Cheesley*	Gillies	Hunt	Griffin
	20/1		*23,614*	*18*	24			*Merrick 9 (og), Greaves 35*	*Siddall*	*Ritson*	*McAllister*	*Allardyce*	*Jones P*	*Nicholson*	*Byrom*	*Jones G**	*Greaves*	*Whatmore*	*Thompson*	*Olinyk*
								Ref: P Partridge	Hunt's left-foot volley from 20 yards gets City's first Sunday game off to a good start, but defensive errors and a shot-shy attack bring defeat. Merrick heads Sam Allardyce's cross into his own net, whilst failure to close down Roy Greaves allows him to shoot in from 25 yards.											
28	H	CARDIFF		14	W	3-2	1-2	Tainton 5, Sweeney 75p, 90	Cashley	Sweeney	Drysdale	Gow	Collier	Merrick	Tainton	Ritchie	Gillies	Cheesley*	Hunt	Rodgers
	2/2		24,487	*15*	26			*Phillips 16, McCulloch 27*	*Irwin*	*Dwyer*	*Bell*	*Impey*	*Murray*	*Villars*	*Farrington*	*McCulloch*	*Phillips*	*Carlin*	*Anderson*	
								Ref: K Baker	In front of a large crowd obtaining vouchers for the Leeds cup-tie, City gain a late winner when Sweeney heads back in Gary Bell's clearance off the line. Earlier Sweeney, with his short two step run, had netted his first League penalty following Don Murray's manhandling of Ritchie.											
29	A	SHEFFIELD WED		15	L	1-3	1-1	Ritchie 29	Cashley	Collier	Drysdale	Gow	Rodgers	Merrick	Tainton	Ritchie	Gillies	Sweeney	Hunt*	Cheesley
	10/2		*15,784*	*19*	26			*Joicey 12, Henderson 58, Shaw 82*	*Ferguson*	*Cameron*	*Knighton*	*Thompson*	*Eustace**	*Shaw*	*Henderson*	*Sunley*	*Joicey*	*Craig*	*Potts*	*Coyle*
								Ref: R Porterhouse	City show little to worry Leeds in this poor show. Apart from Ritchie's waist-high volley equaliser, City are unable to counter the simple, but effective, play of their opponents. The speed of Tommy Potts sets up the Owls' opener, as his low centre hits Brian Joicey's leg and bounces in.											
30	A	WEST BROM		16	D	2-2	1-1	Hunt 17, Tainton 55	Cashley	Sweeney	Drysdale	Gow	Collier	Merrick	Tainton	Ritchie	Fear	Gillies	Hunt	
	23/2		*18,928*	*5*	27			*Wile 21, Astle 72*	*Latchford*	*Nisbet*	*Thompson*	*Cantello*	*Wile*	*Robertson*	*Johnston*	*Brown T*	*Astle*	*Hartford*	*Glover*	
								Ref: A Morrisey	A memorable free-kick routine puts City in front as Gillies flicks the ball up for Hunt, who lets it bounce once, before letting fly with a left-foot volley. Tainton is lucky when his mis-hit 12-yarder trickles in, but City have to settle for a point as Albion register with a couple of headers.											
31	H	MILLWALL		13	W	**5-2**	1-1	Fear 5, 62, 64, Jones 58 (og),	Cashley	Sweeney	Drysdale	Gow	Collier	Merrick*	Tainton	Ritchie	Fear	Gillies	Hunt	Rodgers
	26/2		9,605	*12*	29			*Smethurst 12, Hill 50* [Tainton 73]	*King*	*Brown*	*Jones*	*Dorney*	*Kitchener*	*Allder*	*Bolland*	*Clark*	*Wood*	*Smethurst*	*Hill*	
								Ref: R Crabb	A remarkable game of seven goals, with not a header among them, as City put on a super show after falling behind to Gordon Hill's brilliant overhead kick. Fear completes City's first hat-trick in two years, following on from an own-goal equaliser when Eddie Jones lofts the ball in.											

No	Date	Opponent	Att	Pos	Pts	Res	F-A	H-T	Scorers, Times, and Referees	1	2	3	4	5	6	7	8	9	10	11	12 sub used
32	H 2/3	OXFORD	**25,904**	14 *19*	30	D	0-0	0-0		Cashley	Sweeney	Drysdale	Gow	Collier	Rodgers	Tainton	Ritchie	Fear	Gillies	Hunt	
									Ref: Yates	*Burton*	*Light*	*Shuker*	*Roberts*	*Clarke C*	*Briggs*	*Gough*	*Atkinson*	*Curran*	*Clarke D*	*Aylott*	
										Again the lure of cup-tie vouchers swells the crowd, but most of the entertainment is before the start when Dicks receives his award as the February Manager of the Month. In a dreary bore of a game, the nearest thing to a goal is Steve Aylott's 27th-minute chip that hits the bar.											
33	H 16/3	ASTON VILLA	12,759	16 *15*	30	L	0-1	0-0		Cashley	Sweeney	Drysdale	Gow	Collier	Merrick	Tainton	Ritchie	Fear	Gillies	Hunt	
									Morgan 70 Ref: A Robinson	*Cumbes*	*Gidman*	*Aitken*	*McMahon*	*Nicholl*	*Turnbull*	*Little*	*Ross*	*Morgan*	*Hamilton*	*Leonard*	
										City suffer a cup hangover as they fail to pose any problems for Villa. Cashley's boob costs City a share of the points, as he drops Chris Nicholl's 55-yard free-kick to set up Sammy Morgan's easy tap-in. A poor game, littered with poor passing and a general lack of desire.											
34	A 19/3	BLACKPOOL	*7,710*	16 *5*	31	D	2-2	2-1	Emanuel 30, Gow 39	Cashley	Sweeney	Drysdale	Gow	Collier	Merrick	Tainton	Ritchie	Fear	Gillies	Emanuel	
									James 18, Davies 48 Ref: J Hough	*Burridge*	*Hatton*	*Bentley*	*Alcock*	*James*	*Suddaby*	*Burns*	*Suddick*	*Davies*	*Evanson**	*Ainscow*	*Walsh*
										As well as thundering in an equaliser to Glyn James' headed opener, Emanuel's inspiring midfield display boosts City in an all-action game at Bloomfield Road. City should have won after Gow shoots in from three yards, but Wynn Davies seizes on defensive indecision to tap home.											
35	A 23/3	CRYS PALACE	*16,840*	16 *21*	31	L	1-3	0-0	Whitehead 69	Cashley	Sweeney	Drysdale	Gow	Collier	Merrick	Tainton	Ritchie*	Fear	Gillies	Emanuel	Whitehead
									Possee 60, 67, Rogers 63p Ref: R Lee	*Hammond*	*Mulligan*	*Jump*	*Johnson*	*Barry*	*Blyth*	*Jeffries*	*Possee*	*Whittle*	*Rogers*	*Taylor P*	
										City's only response to Palace's goal rush is a Ritchie half-volley that hits a post and Whitehead's climbing far-post header to Tainton's cross. Palace clinch a double over City with two headed goals from Derek Possee and a Don Rogers pen after Emanuel brings down Alan Whittle.											
36	H 30/3	FULHAM	10,946	16 *8*	31	L	0-1	0-0		Cashley	Sweeney	Drysdale	Gow	Collier	Rodgers	Tainton	Ritchie	Fear*	Gillies	Emanuel	Whitehead
									Mullery 74 Ref: P Reeves	*Mellor*	*Cutbush*	*Strong*	*Moore*	*Lacy*	*Dunne*	*Conway Jim*	*Mullery*	*Busby*	*Lloyd*	*Barrett*	
										Beware the Ides of March, a warning that has gone unheeded by City, who have failed to win a single game during the past month. Fulham celebrate manager Alec Stock's 57th birthday with a double over City when Alan Mullery hooks the ball in from Bobby Moore's free-kick.											
37	H 6/4	CARLISLE	**9,570**	16 *5*	33	W	2-0	1-0	Cheesley 31, Gillies 75	Cashley	Sweeney	Drysdale	Gow	Collier	Merrick	Tainton*	Hunt	Cheesley	Gillies	Emanuel	Fear
									Ref: J Taylor	*Ross*	*Carr*	*Winstanley*	*McCartney*	*Green*	*Balderstone*	*Martin*	*Train*	*Owen*	*Clarke*	*Laidlaw*	
										Against a skilful Carlisle side Cheesley obtains his first City goal with a magnificent 15-yard header from Tainton's free-kick. After Cashley makes a brilliant save to keep out Bobby Owen's close-in effort, Gillies relieves City's relegation fears with a cross-shot into the far corner.											
38	H 12/4	NOTT'M FOREST	13,125	16 *9*	35	W	1-0	1-0	Cheesley 5	Cashley	Sweeney	Drysdale	Gow	Collier	Merrick	Tainton	Ritchie	Cheesley*	Gillies	Emanuel	Fear
									Ref: R Toseland	*Peacock*	*O'Kane*	*Serella*	*Chapman*	*Cottam*	*Richardson**	*McKenzie*	*Lyall*	*Martin*	*Galley*	*Bowyer*	*Dennehy*
										City should have had more than Cheesley's low drive to show for their early supremacy, before the loss of their scorer just before the break allows Forest to take control. Cashley brings down Duncan McKenzie to concede a penalty, but George Lyall blasts the kick high and wide.											
39	A 13/4	SUNDERLAND	***28,884***	16 *7*	37	W	2-1	1-1	Ritchie 2, Emanuel 79	Cashley	Sweeney	Drysdale	Gow	Collier	Merrick	Tainton	Ritchie	Fear	Gillies	Emanuel	
									Longhorn 21 Ref: K McNally	*Montgomery*	*Malone*	*Bolton*	*Longhorn*	*Watson*	*Belfitt*	*Kerr*	*Hughes*	*Halom*	*Porterfield**	*Towers*	*Ashurst*
										Cashley makes two fantastic saves to preserve Ritchie's 80-second headed opener, but he has no chance with Dennis Longhorn's overhead kick. With the keeper prostrate, following a collision with Dave Watson, Emanuel silences the Roker Roar with his 30-yarder into an open net.											
40	A 16/4	NOTT'M FOREST	*12,756*	15 *8*	38	D	1-1	0-0	Ritchie 50	Cashley	Sweeney	Drysdale	Gow	Collier	Merrick	Tainton	Ritchie	Fear	Gillies	Emanuel	
									McKenzie 48 Ref: P Willis	*Peacock*	*O'Kane*	*Winfield*	*Chapman*	*Cottam*	*Jackson*	*McKenzie*	*Lyall*	*Galley*	*McIntosh*	*Bowyer*	
										Cashley's world-class save from Ian Bowyer's twelve-yard 88th-minute thunderbolt allows City to complete an unbeaten Easter. After Duncan McKenzie brings the game to life, by smashing John Galley's through-ball into the net, Ritchie levels when Fear heads on Drysdale's free-kick.											
41	H 20/4	PORTSMOUTH	11,143	16 *14*	38	L	0-2	0-1		Cashley	Sweeney	Drysdale	Gow	Collier	Merrick	Tainton	Ritchie	Fear	Gillies*	Emanuel	Hunt
									Davies 12, Stewart 77 Ref: T Bosi	*Best*	*Roberts*	*Wilson*	*Hand*	*Went*	*Stephenson*	*Marinello*	*Kellard*	*Davies*	*Piper*	*Stewart*	
										Despite mustering only three shots, Pompey achieve their first away win of the season. Collier's failure to clear gifts Ron Davies his low drive, and whilst City have their chances, it is Peter Marinello's great run and perfect pass that sets up Andy Stewart's unstoppable 15-yard clincher.											
42	A 27/4	NOTTS CO	*6,991*	16 *10*	38	L	1-2	0-2	Gillies 84	Cashley	Sweeney	Drysdale	Gow	Rodgers	Merrick	Tainton	Gillies	Cheesley*	Fear	Emanuel	Whitehead
									Rodgers 11 (og), Bradd 42 Ref: A Gray	*McManus*	*Brindley*	*O'Brien*	*Masson*	*Stubbs*	*Bolton*	*Randall*	*McVay*	*Needham*	*Bradd*	*Probert*	
	Average	Home 14,058	Away 13,325							The players' inability to master a bumpy pitch and stiff breeze results in a poor match. Rodgers amazingly jabs the ball into his own net and an abysmal offside trap allows Les Bradd to waltz the ball home, before Fear's left-flank run and cross allows Gillies to shoot in from ten yards.											

League Cup					F-A	H-T	Scorers, Times, and Referees	1	2	3	4	5	6	7	8	9	10	11	12 sub used
2	A	SCUNTHORPE	6	D	0-0	0-0		Bond	Sweeney	Drysdale	Gow	Collier	Merrick	Tainton*	Ritchie	Gould	Gillies	Fear	Woods
9/10		*4,418 4:18*						*Barnard*	*Lynch*	*Welbourne*	*Simpkin*	*Barker*	*Davidson*	*Houghton*	*Pilling*	*Collier*	*Keeley*	*Warnock*	
							Ref: J Hunting	Safety-first City only create two opportunities, one in each half. Fear should have given Geoff Barnard no chance early on, but his shot was smothered, then Ritchie's header elicits a brilliant save. Outplayed for most of the tie, City are indebted to their defence for replay survival.											
2R	H	SCUNTHORPE	4	W	2-1	0-1	Fear 77, Sweeney 80	Bond	Tainton	Drysdale	Sweeney	Collier	Merrick	Whitehead	Ritchie	Gould	Gow	Gillies*	Fear
16/10		7,837 *4:17*					*Welbourne 45*	*Barnard*	*Lynch*	*Welbourne*	*Simpkin*	*Barker*	*Miney*	*Houghton*	*Pilling*	*Fletcher*	*Keeley*	*Warnock*	
							Ref: T Reynolds	At last City overcome their Scunthorpe hoodoo, but not without a fright. It takes Fear's 67th-minute appearance off the subs bench to provide the spark to overcome Don Welbourne's headed opener. Fear levels with a brilliant chip over the Iron's wall, and Sweeney shoots in winner.											
3	H	COVENTRY	4	D	2-2	1-1	Gould 10, 52	Bond	Sweeney	Drysdale	Emanuel	Rodgers	Merrick	Tainton	Ritchie	Gould	Gow	Fear*	Gillies
30/10		19,196 *1:7*					*Smith 22, Cartwright 69*	*Glazier*	*Coop*	*Holmes*	*Mortimer*	*Parker*	*Dugdale*	*Smith*	*Alderson*	*Stein*	*Cartwright*	*Hutchison*	
							Ref: A Oliver	Gould is robbed of a likely hat-trick as the referee turns down a clear penalty when he is shoved by Alan Dugdale just four minutes from the end of this spectacular cup-tie. Gould twice puts City ahead with hard-hit drives, but two headed replies allow Coventry to survive for a replay.											
3R	A	COVENTRY	5	L	1-2	1-2	Whitehead 42	Bond	Tainton	Drysdale	Sweeney	Rodgers	Merrick	Whitehead	Ritchie	Gould	Gow	Gillies*	Fear
6/11		*13,049 1:10*					*Alderson 20, Stein 32*	*Glazier*	*Coop*	*Holmes*	*Mortimer*	*Philpotts*	*Dugdale*	*Cartwright*	*Alderson*	*Stein*	*McGuire*	*Hutchison*	
							Ref: A Oliver	City earn the praise, but not the spoils, as they make an honourable exit. 'What a prospect' says Coventry boss Joe Mercer of Whitehead, who gains reward for his teasing, tormenting and tantilising display when firing in from the edge of the area to haul City back into the game.											

FA Cup					F-A	H-T	Scorers, Times, and Referees	1	2	3	4	5	6	7	8	9	10	11	12 sub used
3	H	HULL	14	D	1-1	1-1	Merrick 18	Bond	Tainton	Drysdale	Fear	Collier	Merrick	Griffin	Ritchie	Gillies	Gow	Durrell*	Emanuel
5/1		8,968 *9*					*Galvin 20*	*Wealands*	*Banks*	*McGill*	*Galvin*	*Deere*	*Burnett*	*Holme*	*Lord*	*Pearson*	*Wagstaff*	*Greenwood*	
							Ref: R Crabb	Just 90 seconds after Merrick heads City in front, Bond drops a simple cross to allow Chris Galvin to prod in Hull's equaliser. Content to settle for a replay, the Tigers are fortunate just before the call of time when Gow shoots over the top after Jeff Wealands gifts an easy chance.											
3R	A	HULL	14	W	1-0	0-0	Tainton 54	Cashley	Tainton	Drysdale	Sweeney	Collier	Merrick	Rodgers	Ritchie	Gillies	Gow	Woods	
8/1		*5,340 9*						*Wealands*	*Banks*	*McGill*	*Galvin*	*Deere*	*Burnett*	*Holme*	*Lord*	*Hemmerman*	*Wagstaff*	*Greenwood*	
							Ref: V James	City never stop harrying and chasing against opponents who appear to give up after Gow's cross sets up Tainton to blast in from eight yards. Denied two possible penalties in the first half, City are fortunate to escape conceding one in the last minute when Tainton pulls Chris Galvin.											
4	A	HEREFORD	15	W	1-0	1-0	Merrick 17	Cashley	Collier	Drysdale	Sweeney	Rodgers	Merrick	Tainton	Ritchie	Gillies*	Cheesley	Hunt	Fear
26/1		*17,431 3:16*						*Hughes*	*Radford*	*Naylor**	*McLaughlin*	*Jones*	*Tavener*	*Redrobe*	*Tyler*	*Hinch*	*Evans*	*Rudge*	*Jenkins*
							Ref: E Jolly	Playing against the wind and driving rain, as well as the slope, in the first half, City are fortunate when Ronnie Radford is penalised despite his shirt being pulled. From Hunt's chipped in free-kick from near the left corner flag, Merrick is at the far post to shoot in with his trusty left foot.											
5	H	LEEDS	16	D	1-1	0-1	Fear 65	Cashley	Sweeney	Drysdale	Gow	Collier	Merrick	Tainton	Ritchie	Fear	Gillies	Hunt	
16/2		37,141 *1:1*					*Bremner 42*	*Harvey*	*Yorath*	*Cherry*	*Bremner*	*McQueen*	*Hunter*	*Lorimer*	*Jordan*	*Jones*	*Giles**	*Madeley*	*Clarke*
							Ref: J Taylor	Leeds are fortunate to survive to face Fear again after City's talented striker had led them a merry dance. He lobs in a great equaliser to Billy Bremner's 25-yarder, as well as hitting the bar in the first half with a great shot on the turn, and laying on chances for Tainton and Gillies.											
5R	A	LEEDS	16	W	1-0	0-0	Gillies 73	Cashley	Sweeney	Drysdale	Gow	Collier	Merrick	Tainton	Ritchie*	Fear	Gillies	Hunt	Rodgers
19/2		*47,182 1:1*						*Harvey*	*Cherry*	*Cooper*	*Bremner*	*Ellam*	*Hunter*	*Lorimer*	*Clarke*	*Jones*	*Giles**	*Madeley*	*Jordan*
							Ref: J Taylor	Unlike the first meeting, this time it is Leeds who are the dominant side. City's desperate rearguard action is akin to the Siege of the Alamo, but after the post denies Peter Lorimer on 60 minutes, it is like the Relief of Mafeking for a while when Gillies shoots in his left-footed winner.											
QF	H	LIVERPOOL	16	L	0-1	0-0		Cashley	Sweeney	Drysdale	Gow	Collier	Rodgers	Tainton	Ritchie	Fear	Gillies	Hunt*	Emanuel
9/3		37,671 *1:2*					*Toshack 48*	*Clemence*	*Smith*	*Lindsay*	*Thompson*	*Cormack*	*Hughes*	*Keegan*	*Hall*	*Heighway**	*Toshack*	*Callaghan*	*Boersma*
							Ref: D Turner	In the quarter-finals for the first time since 1920, City at 25-1 make the 5-2 favourites work hard for their success. Until John Toshack shoots in from ten yards, the ball falling into his path when Rodgers fails to deal with Kevin Keegan's cross, there is little to choose between the sides.											

		Home						Away					
	P	W	D	L	F	A	W	D	L	F	A	Pts
1 Middlesbro	42	16	4	1	40	8	11	7	3	37	22	65
2 Luton	42	12	5	4	42	25	[illegible]	7	7	22	26	50
3 Carlisle	42	13	5	3	40	17	[illegible]	4	10	21	31	49
4 Orient	42	9	8	4	28	17	[illegible]	10	5	27	25	48
5 Blackpool	42	11	5	5	35	17	[illegible]	8	7	22	23	47
6 Sunderland	42	11	6	4	32	15	[illegible]	3	10	26	29	47
7 Nott'm Forest	42	12	6	3	40	19	[illegible]	9	9	17	24	45
8 West Brom	42	8	9	4	28	24	[illegible]	7	8	20	21	44
9 Hull	42	9	9	3	25	15	[illegible]	8	9	21	32	43
10 Notts Co	42	8	6	7	30	35	[illegible]	7	7	25	25	43
11 Bolton	42	12	5	4	30	17	[illegible]	7	11	14	23	42
12 Millwall	42	10	6	5	28	16	[illegible]	8	9	23	35	42
13 Fulham	42	11	4	6	26	20	[illegible]	6	10	13	23	42
14 Aston Villa	42	8	9	4	33	21	[illegible]	6	10	15	24	41
15 Portsmouth	42	9	8	4	26	16	5	4	12	19	46	40
16 BRISTOL CITY	42	9	5	7	25	20	5	5	11	22	34	38
17 Cardiff	42	8	7	6	27	20	2	9	10	22	42	36
18 Oxford	42	8	8	5	27	21	2	8	11	8	25	36
19 Sheffield Wed	42	9	6	6	33	24	3	5	13	18	39	35
20 Crys Palace	42	6	7	8	24	24	5	5	11	19	32	34
21 Preston*	42	7	8	6	24	23	2	6	13	16	39	31
22 Swindon	42	6	7	8	22	27	1	4	16	14	45	25
	924	212	143	107	665	441	1 7	143	212	441	665	923

* 1 pt deducted

Odds & ends

Double wins: (4) Swindon, Millwall, Sunderland, Cardiff.
Double loses: (4) Luton, Fulham, Crystal Palace, Portsmouth.

Won from behind: (3) Hull (h), Cardiff (h), Millwall (h).
Lost from in front: (1) Bolton (a).

High spots: Cashley's goal at Ashton Gate against Hull on 18 Sep.
Ernie Hunt's goal at the Hawthorns on 23 February.
Keith Fear's hat-trick against Millwall on 26 February.
Both FA Cup games against Leeds.
FL Cup game against Coventry at Ashton Gate on 30 October.

Low spots: Losing to Crystal Palace at Ashton Gate on 10 November.
Being annihilated at Oxford on 26 December.
Failure to beat Liverpool in the FA Cup.
Losing 0-2 against Bristol Rovers in the Gloucestershire Cup on 29 Apr.

Player of the Year: Gerry Gow.
Ever-presents: (1) Trevor Tainton.
Hat-tricks: (1) Keith Fear.
Leading scorer: Keith Fear (10).

	Appearances						Goals			
	Lge	*Sub*	LC	*Sub*	FAC	*Sub*	Lge	LC	FAC	Tot
Bond, Len	**15**		4		1					
Cashley, Ray	**27**				5		**1**			**1**
Cheesley, Paul	**7**	*1*			1		**2**			**2**
Collier, Gary	**31**		2		6	*2*				
Drysdale, Brian	**32**	*2*	4		6					
Durrell, Joe	**2**	*2*			1					
Emanuel, John	**24**	*2*	1			*2*	**2**			**2**
Fear, Keith	**32**	*3*	2	*2*	4	*1*	**8**	1	1	**10**
Gillies, Donny	**28**	*8*	3	*1*	6		**6**		1	**7**
Gould, Bobby	**16**		4				**7**	2		**9**
Gow, Gerry	**41**		4		5		**1**			**1**
Griffin, Kevin		*2*			1					
Hunt, Ernie	**9**	*2*			4		**2**			**2**
Merrick, Geoff	**40**		4		5				2	**2**
Rodgers, David	**26**	*2*	2		3	*1*	**1**			**1**
Ritchie, Tom	**39**		4		6		**6**			**6**
Sweeney, Gerry	**42**		4		5		**3**	1		**4**
Tainton, Trevor	**42**		4		6		**5**		1	**6**
Whitehead, Clive	**9**	*3*	2				**2**	1		**3**
Woods, Eddie				*1*	1					
(own-goals)							**1**			**1**
20 players used	**462**	*27*	**44**	*4*	**66**	*6*	**47**	**5**	**5**	**57**

No	Date		Att	Pos	Pt	F-A	H-T	Scorers, Times, and Referees	1	2	3	4	5	6	7	8	9	10	11	12 sub used
1	A	NOTT'M FOREST			D	0-0	0-0		Cashley	Sweeney	Drysdale	Gow	Rodgers	Merrick	Tainton	**Mann**	Gillies	Cheesley	Whitehead	
	17/8		*11,339*		1				*Peacock*	*O'Kane*	*Richardson*	*Chapman*	*Cottam*	*Jones*	*Dennehy*	*Lyall*	*Martin**	*Robertson*	*Bowyer*	*Woodcock*
								Ref: J Rice	Poor entertainment as City are happy to settle for a point against Forest, for whom Miah Dennehy's cross-shot hits the inside of a post early on. Midway through the second half Cheesley's great 30-yard strike is booked for the top corner, but Dennis Peacock pulls off a superlative save.											
2	H	ORIENT			D	0-0	0-0		Cashley	Sweeney	Drysdale	Gow	Collier	Merrick	Tainton	Ritchie*	Gillies	Cheesley	Whitehead	Mann
	24/8		10,985		2				*Jackson*	*Fisher*	*Roffey*	*Hoadley*	*Harris*	*Walley**	*Fairbrother*	*Heppolette*	*Bullock*	*Queen*	*Possee*	*Downing*
								Ref: D Nippard	A combination of missed chances, misfortune and inspired keeping by John Jackson prevents a rout at Ashton Gate. City produce a brilliant display of passing football, but the promise of goals never materialises as Orient, missing five regulars, hang on to snatch an unlikely point.											
3	A	OLDHAM		21	L	0-2	0-0		Cashley	Sweeney	Drysdale	Gow	Collier	Merrick	Tainton	Ritchie	Gillies	Cheesley	Whitehead*	Hunt
	31/8		*9,860*	*11*	2			*Jones 46, Cashley 47 (og)*	*Ogden*	*Wood*	*Whittle*	*Blair*	*Mulvaney*	*Bailey*	*Garwood*	*Bell*	*Jones*	*Robins*	*Groves*	
								Ref: R Clay	City's tale of woe in front of goal continues, as shortly after Sweeney puts a 57th-minute penalty wide, Hunt is unlucky with a neatly headed effort that is disallowed. Cashley is at fault for the Latics' second, as he cannot stop himself trying to save Maurice Whittle's indirect free-kick.											
4	H	BOLTON		14	W	2-1	1-1	Gillies 33, Drysdale 79	Cashley	Sweeney	Drysdale	Gow	Collier	Merrick	Tainton	Ritchie	Gillies	Fear	Emanuel	
	7/9		**9,300**	*11*	4			*Ritson 32*	*Siddall*	*Ritson*	*Dunne*	*Nicholson*	*Jones P*	*McAllister*	*Byrom*	*Jones G**	*Greaves*	*Whatmore*	*Thompson*	*Taylor*
								Ref: A Turvey	A freak goal wins this game after John Ritson drives in Tony Dunne's cross to put the Trotters in front. Gillies shoots in from Fear's chip for the leveller, but Barry Siddall keeps City out until Drysdale's long shot is taken over the keeper's head and into the net by the gale-force wind.											
5	A	CARDIFF		10	W	1-0	0-0	Fear 46	Cashley	Sweeney	Drysdale	Gow	Collier	Merrick	Whitehead	Ritchie	Gillies	Fear	Emanuel	
	14/9		*8,858*	*22*	6				*Healey*	*Larmour*	*Pithard*	*Villars*	*Murray*	*Phillips*	*McInch*	*Charles*	*Showers*	*Reece**	*Anderson*	*Attley*
								Ref: J Hunting	Cardiff are unlucky not to take an early lead as Derek Showers heads in from Willie Anderson's free-kick. The referee orders the kick to be re-taken as Jimmy McInch had returned to the pitch without permission. City though are full value for their success, obtained by Fear's header.											
6	H	SOUTHAMPTON		7	W	2-0	1-0	Sweeney 15, Merrick 56	Cashley	Sweeney	Drysdale	Gow	Collier	Merrick	Whitehead	Ritchie	Gillies	Fear	Emanuel	
	21/9		15,708	*20*	8				*Turner*	*Mills*	*Peach*	*Fisher*	*Bennett*	*Blyth*	*O'Brien**	*Channon*	*Osgood*	*Gilchrist*	*Steele*	*Stokes*
								Ref: T Bosi	City's positive, attacking football should have brought more than two goals, whilst the Saints are unhappy about their three strikes that are struck off. After Sweeney shoots City ahead, Merrick ties up the points as his 40-yard free kick, which is meant as a cross, ends up in the net.											
7	H	YORK		7	D	0-0	0-0		Cashley	Sweeney	Drysdale	Gow	Collier	Merrick	Whitehead	Ritchie	Gillies	Fear	Emanuel	
	24/9		11,867	*9*	9				*Crawford*	*Hunter*	*Oliver*	*Holmes*	*Swallow*	*Topping*	*Lyons*	*Cave*	*Seal*	*Jones**	*Wann*	*Hinch*
								Ref: D Civil	When Whitehead blasts the ball in off the crossbar in the 42nd minute, it doesn't seem to matter that the ref changes his mind after first giving a goal. It is surely only a matter of time, but the goals just don't come as Graeme Crawford and the woodwork frustrate all of City's efforts.											
8	A	MILLWALL		13	L	0-1	0-0		Cashley	Sweeney	Drysdale	Gow	Collier	Merrick	Whitehead	Ritchie	Gillies*	Fear	Emanuel	**Brolly**
	28/9		***5,750***	*18*	9			*Dorney 51*	*King*	*Brown B*	*Jones*	*Donaldson*	*Kitchener*	*Dorney*	*Bolland*	*Saul*	*Smethurst**	*Allder*	*Hill*	*Wood*
								Ref: A Robinson	On an uneven pitch City are robbed as the referee disallows Ritchie's 80th-minute in off his thigh equaliser, claiming he had played the ball with his arm. Well on top early on, City go behind when Alan Dorney out jumps two defenders to head powerfully into the top corner.											
9	A	SHEFFIELD WED		13	D	1-1	0-0	Merrick 57	Cashley	Sweeney	Drysdale	Gow	Collier	Merrick	Tainton	Ritchie	Gillies	Fear	Emanuel	
	5/10		*10,318*	*21*	10			*Holsgrove 50*	*Springett*	*Rodrigues*	*Shaw*	*Dowd*	*Holsgrove*	*Knighton*	*Potts*	*Harvey*	*Joicey*	*Craig*	*Sunley**	*Prudham*
								Ref: R Matthewson	Luckless Gillies heads against the post and then fails in front of an open goal in the three minutes leading up to the interval. City, who hardly allow Wednesday a chance, can do nothing about John Holsgrove's cracking drive, but Merrick salvages a point by heading in Fear's chip.											
10	H	SUNDERLAND		12	D	1-1	0-1	Gow 77	Cashley	Sweeney	Drysdale	Gow	Collier	Merrick	Tainton	Ritchie	Gillies*	Fear	Emanuel	Whitehead
	12/10		13,084	*2*	11			*Halom 32*	*Montgomery*	*Malone*	*Bolton*	*Moncur*	*Watson*	*Porterfield*	*Kerr*	*Hughes*	*Halom*	*Robson*	*Towers*	
								Ref: K Baker	Classy Sunderland are knocked out of their first-half stride by a City side whose all-action display after the interval is crowned by Gow's 20-yd free-kick equaliser. The Wearsider's boss Bob Stokoe is less than happy though, as he claims that his defence was still lining up their wall.											

No	Venue	Opponent	Pos	Res	F-A	H-T	Scorers, Times, Referees	1	2	3	4	5	6	7	8	9	10	11	12
11	A	FULHAM	11	D	1-1	1-0	Fear	Cashley	Sweeney	Drysdale	Gow	Collier	Merrick	Tainton	Ritchie	Cheesley	Fear	Emanuel	
19/10		*8,960*	*8*	12			*Mullery 57*	*Mellor*	*Cutbush*	*Strong*	*Mullery*	*Lacy*	*Moore*	*Conway Jim*	*Slough*	*Busby*	*Lloyd*	*Barrett*	
							Ref: R Kirkpatrick/P White	Fear gives impressive City the lead when stroking the ball in, but they are made to pay for their lack of a killer touch as Alan Mullery's 22-yard thunderbolt crashes past Cashley. After sustaining a back injury earlier in the half, the referee is replaced by the senior lineman in the 71st min.											
12	A	OXFORD	15	L	0-2	0-0		Cashley	Sweeney	Drysdale	Whitehead	Collier	Merrick	Tainton	Ritchie	Fear	Cheesley	Emanuel	
23/10		*5,772*	*13*	12			*Heron 57, Sims 69*	*Milkins*	*Light*	*Shuker*	*Roberts*	*Clarke C*	*Briggs*	*Aylott*	*Fleming*	*Clarke D*	*Sims*	*Heron**	*Bray*
							Ref: R Crabb	What a let down! Just when City are beginning to look the part they flop. Against hard-chasing opponents, City are fortunate the score does not match last season's drubbing. Cashley lets John Sims' overhead slip through his fingers after earlier being beaten by Brian Heron's header.											
13	H	NOTTS CO	10	W	3-0	0-0	Sweeney 78p, Mann 81, Cheesley 88	Cashley	Sweeney	Drysdale	Mann	Collier	Merrick	Tainton	Ritchie	Fear	Cheesley	Emanuel	
26/10		10,343	*15*	14				*Brown*	*Brindley*	*O'Brien*	*Masson*	*Needham*	*Stubbs*	*Carter*	*Probert !*	*Bradd*	*Mann*	*Scanlon*	
							Ref: C Newsome	City never look back after Sweeney nets from the spot when Brian Stubbs brings down Ritchie, though the sending off of Eric Probert, for protesting too much over the penalty, obviously helps. City have the luck early on when Ian Scanlon, faced by an empty net, hits the post.											
14	A	PORTSMOUTH	6	W	1-0	0-0	Gow 65	Cashley	Sweeney	Drysdale	Gow	Collier	Merrick	Tainton	Ritchie	Fear	Mann	Emanuel	
2/11		*9,596*	*20*	16				*Best*	*Roberts*	*Wilson*	*Piper*	*Went*	*Stephenson*	*Marinello*	*Reynolds*	*Stewart*	*Hand**	*Mellows*	*Foggo*
							Ref: M Taylor	Gow saves City's blushes after their early impressive display fails to produce any goals. Pushed back on defensive after the break, Gow's right-foot 25-yard drive completely beats David Best in the Pompey goal. City's numerous back-passes during the closing stages win few friends.											
15	H	OXFORD	5	W	3-0	0-0	Mann 47, Merrick 54, Ritchie 76	Cashley	Sweeney	Drysdale	Gow	Collier	Merrick	Tainton	Ritchie	Fear	Mann	Emanuel	
5/11		10,036	*14*	18				*Milkins*	*Light*	*Shuker*	*Roberts*	*Evanson*	*Briggs*	*Aylott*	*Fleming*	*Clarke D*	*McCulloch*	*Sims*	
							Ref: B Homewood	Gow ensures his 200th appearance is an occasion to remember with his whiplash tackling and accurate passing. Although failing to score he has major roles in the build-up to Mann's crisp low-shot, and Merrick's header. After a mediocre start, City are brilliant after the interval.											
16	H	MANCHESTER U	4	W	1-0	1-0	Emanuel 31	Cashley	Sweeney	Drysdale*	Gow	Collier	Merrick	Tainton	Ritchie	Fear	Mann	Emanuel	Cheesley
9/11		28,104	*1*	20				*Stepney*	*Forsyth*	*Houston*	*Greenhoff*	*Sidebottom*	*Buchan*	*Macari*	*McIlroy*	*Pearson*	*McCalliog*	*Daly**	*Graham*
							Ref: A Hart	Ritchie's stirring display reduces United to a state of panic, though it is Emanuel who secures the points by firing in as Fear's shot is cleared off the line. Tommy Docherty is surely joking with his comment that 'City were the most defensive home side United had played this season'.											
17	A	WEST BROM	4	L	0-1	0-1		Cashley	Tainton	Sweeney	Gow	Collier	Merrick	Whitehead*	Ritchie	Fear	Mann	Emanuel !	Cheesley
16/11		*11,936*	*6*	20			*Mayo 22*	*Osborne*	*Nisbet*	*Wilson*	*Trewick*	*Wile*	*Rushbury*	*Glover*	*Shaw*	*Mayo*	*Hughes*	*Johnston !*	
							Ref: A Morrisey	Little goes right at the Hawthorns as City's attempts to counter Mayo's shot into an open goal, after the ball rebounds off the referee, are twice thwarted by the post. Emanuel receives his marching orders in the 79th minute, when retaliating against Willie Johnston, who is also sent off.											
18	H	BLACKPOOL	7	L	0-1	0-1		Cashley	Tainton	Sweeney	Gow	Collier	Merrick	Gillies	Ritchie	Fear*	Griffin	Emanuel	Whitehead
23/11		11,584	*9*	20			*Hatton 35p*	*Burridge*	*Hatton*	*Harrison !*	*Curtis*	*Hart*	*Suddaby*	*Evans*	*Ainscow*	*Parker*	*Bentley*	*Evanson**	*Alcock*
							Ref: G Kew	Despite their blistering, all-action football after the break City's long-time need for a striker is even more obvious. Unfortunately it is all try and not enough skill and Blackpool are able to maintain the advantage given them by Hatton's spot-kick, following Merrick's push on Tony Evans.											
19	A	HULL	8	L	0-1	0-1		Cashley	Sweeney	Merrick	Gow	Rodgers	Collier	Tainton	Ritchie	Fear*	Mann	Emanuel	Gillies
30/11		*9,612*	*5*	20			*Lord 14*	*Wealands*	*Banks*	*De Vries*	*Galvin**	*Croft*	*Blampey*	*McGill*	*Lord*	*Wood*	*Wagstaff*	*Hawley*	*Greenwood*
							Ref: D Turner	A poor game, decided by Malcolm Lord's brilliant chip as Cashley is punished for his tendency to stand well off his line. The absence of a consistent striker grows more serious by the week, though Fear's is unlucky to have his 33rd-minute hook shot disallowed for handball.											
20	H	ASTON VILLA	8	W	1-0	1-0	Mann 28	Cashley	Sweeney	Merrick	Gow*	Rodgers	Collier	Tainton	Ritchie	Cheesley	Griffin	Mann	Whitehead
7/12		13,390	*7*	22				*Cumbes*	*Robson*	*Aitken*	*Ross*	*Nicholl*	*Brown*	*Graydon*	*Little B*	*Little A*	*Hamilton*	*Carrodus*	
							Ref: B Daniels	Ex Rover Ray Graydon is the butt of the crowd's barracking as City hang onto Mann's headed goal, which is their only on-target effort. With Griffin in agony with badly bruised ribs and Ritchie hobbling with a knee injury, the superb play of Collier and Rodgers keeps Villa at bay.											
21	H	NOTT'M FOREST	7	W	1-0	1-0	Cheesley 32	Cashley	Collier	Drysdale	Sweeney	Rodgers	Merrick	Tainton	Ritchie	Cheesley	Griffin	Mann	
14/12		10,006	*13*	24				*Middleton*	*O'Kane*	*Greenwood*	*Chapman*	*Jones*	*Richardson*	*Dennehy*	*Martin**	*Butlin*	*Bowyer*	*O'Neill*	*Robertson*
							Ref: J Taylor	Cheesley caps his best display of the season with a great volley as he causes all manner of problems for Forest in the first half. After the break though, it is different and it takes all the best endeavours of the League's most parsimonious defence to hang on to achieve back-to-back wins.											

No	Date		Att	Pos	Pt	F-A	H-T	Scorers, Times, and Referees	1	2	3	4	5	6	7	8	9	10	11	12 sub used
22	A	NORWICH		8	L	2-3	2-1	Ritchie 41, Mann 42	Cashley	Collier	Drysdale	Sweeney	Rodgers	Merrick	Tainton	Ritchie	Cheesley	Griffin*	Mann	Durrell
	21/12		*16,981*	*3*	24			*Suggett 16, Boyer 65, 67*	*Keelan*	*Machin*	*Sullivan*	*Morris*	*Forbes*	*Stringer*	*Miller*	*MacDougall*	*Boyer*	*Suggett*	*Powell**	*Steele*
								Ref: A Porter	Norwich are all at sea after being hit by City's two-goal 90-second blitz, but Cheesley's miss in firing wide when clean through a minute before the break lets them off the hook. Cashley is at fault as Colin Suggett gets Norwich off to a good start by scoring directly from a corner.											
23	H	CARDIFF		8	D	0-0	0-0		Cashley	Sweeney	Drysdale	Mann	Collier	Merrick	Tainton	Ritchie	Cheesley	Fear	Durrell	
	26/12		12,484	*18*	25				*Irwin*	*Dwyer*	*Pethard*	*Buchanan*	*Morgan*	*Larmour*	*Reece*	*Smith*	*Showers*	*Whitham*	*Anderson*	
								Ref: R Toseland	A poor game as both sides suffer a Christmas hangover, but Cardiff end their long losing sequence in Severn derbies. Durrell is robbed of a winner five minutes from time when his volley from the edge of the penalty area is disallowed due to an offside decision against Sweeney.											
24	A	BRISTOL ROV		5	W	4-1	0-1	Fear 58, 90, Mann 72, Tainton 77	Cashley	Sweeney	Drysdale	Mann	Collier	Merrick	Tainton	Ritchie	Fear	Cheesley	Durrell*	Griffin
	28/12		*20,911*	*14*	27			*Fearnley 26*	*Sheppard*	*Bater*	*Parsons*	*Aitken*	*Taylor*	*Prince*	*Fearnley*	*Coombes*	*Warboys*	*Staniforth**	*Britton*	*Jones*
								Ref: G Hill	Rovers fail to take full advantage of the gale-force wind at their backs in the first half, and Gordon Fearnley's opener from a suspiciously offside position is never going to be enough. For City it is a different story after the break and Fear's great 25-yard volley ties up great win.											
25	A	ASTON VILLA		6	L	0-2	0-1		Cashley	Sweeney	Drysdale	Mann	Collier	Merrick	Tainton	Ritchie	Fear	Cheesley*	Durrell	Whitehead
	11/1		*22,422*	*4*	27			*Little 35, Hamilton 83*	*Cumbes*	*Robson*	*Aitken*	*Ross*	*Nicholl*	*McDonald*	*Graydon*	*Little B*	*Leonard*	*Hamilton*	*Pimblett*	
								Ref: R Challis	Jim Cumbes, who has only one save to make, needs the services of a team-mate to clear Ritchie's last-minute volley off the line. Brian Little's curved 20-yarder puts Villa ahead, and after the floored Fear's penalty appeal is ignored, Ian Hamilton nudges home Ray Graydon's cross.											
26	H	HULL		6	W	2-0	1-0	Collier 11, Gillies 75	Cashley	Sweeney	Drysdale	Emanuel	Collier	Merrick	Tainton	Mann	Fear	Gillies	Brolly	
	18/1		10,423	*11*	29				*Wealands*	*Banks*	*Daniel*	*Galvin*	*Deere*	*Burnett !*	*McGill*	*Lord*	*Wood*	*Grimes*	*Greenwood*	
								Ref: J Yates	Collier heads in from Brolly's free-kick for his first senior goal. Following the sending off of Dennis Burnett ten minutes later for bringing down Fear, who only had the keeper to beat, City are often frustrated by their hard-working opponents, until Gillies turns in Fear's cross.											
27	A	MANCHESTER U		5	W	1-0	0-0	Gillies 90	Cashley	Sweeney	Drysdale	Emanuel	Collier	Merrick	Tainton	Mann	Fear	Gillies	Brolly	
	1/2		***47,118***	*1*	31				*Stepney*	*Forsyth*	*Houston*	*Daly**	*James*	*Buchan*	*Morgan*	*McIlroy*	*Baldwin*	*Macari*	*McCalliog*	*Young*
								Ref: M Lowe	A first-half bomb warning adds to the frenzied atmosphere of this clash. The closest United come to a goal is an early 30-yarder by Steve James that hits the crossbar, but for City Gillies hooks the ball low into the Stretford End net in the third min of injury time to clinch victory.											
28	H	PORTSMOUTH		5	W	3-1	0-1	Stephenson 49 (og), Sweeney 51, [Gillies 63]	Cashley	Sweeney	Drysdale	Emanuel	Collier	Merrick	Tainton	Mann	Fear	Gillies	Brolly	
	8/2		13,804	*18*	33			Hiron 38	*Best*	*Roberts*	*Hand*	*Piper*	*Went*	*Stephenson*	*Marinello*	*Lewis**	*Graham*	*Hiron*	*Mellows*	*Foggo*
								Ref: J Bent	Pompey's attack-minded approach is deserving of a better fate, but City at last find some goalscoring form. Ray Hiron's low drive puts the visitors in front, but Alan Stephenson's deflection of Fear's free-kick into his own net sets up City for scoring shots by Sweeney and Gillies.											
29	A	BLACKPOOL		6	L	0-2	0-2		Cashley	Sweeney	Drysdale	Emanuel	Collier	Merrick	Tainton	Mann	Gillies	Cheesley	Brolly	
	15/2		*8,687*	*5*	33			*Ainscow 27, Bentley 43*	*Burridge*	*Curtis*	*Harrison*	*Hart*	*Alcock*	*Hatton*	*Walsh*	*Ainscow*	*Davies*	*Bentley*	*Evanson*	
								Ref: K Styles	The instructions of Blackpool manager Harry Potts for his players to attack the Second Division's best defence from the outset pays dividends. Collier's weak back-pass lets Alan Ainscow in to flick the ball past Cashley, whilst a poor clearance sees Bill Bentley fire in from 22 yards.											
30	H	WEST BROM		5	W	2-1	0-1	Sweeney 64p, Fear 79	Cashley	Sweeney	Drysdale	Emanuel	Collier	Merrick	Tainton	Mann	Gillies	Fear	Brolly	
	22/2		14,180	*8*	35			*Shaw 12*	*Osborne*	*Thompson*	*Wilson*	*Cantello*	*Robertson*	*Rushbury*	*Shaw*	*Brown T*	*Mayo**	*Hughes*	*Johnston*	*Trewick*
								Ref: C Thomas	The finest game at Ashton Gate so far this season as City recover from David Shaw's stabbed-in opener from Willie Johnston's free-kick. Fear is the catalyst of City's deserved success. He is tripped by David Rushbury for Sweeney's penalty, and then scores with a stunning 18-yard chip.											
31	H	OLDHAM		5	W	3-1	2-0	Wood 21 (og), Brolly 24, Fear 88	Cashley	Sweeney	Drysdale	Emanuel	Collier	Merrick	Tainton	Mann	Gillies	Fear	Brolly	
	1/3		12,461	*18*	37			*Robins 90*	*Ogden*	*Wood*	*Whittle*	*Edwards**	*Hicks*	*Holt*	*McVitie*	*Bell*	*Robins*	*Chapman*	*Groves*	*Branagan*
								Ref: T Bune	City swamp Oldham with a scintillating first-half display. Emanuel is unlucky with a 19th-min shot that finds the net, as the referee orders the free-kick to be retaken. Ian Wood heads into his own goal to open the scoring, though the full-back protests later that Fear also got a touch.											

No	H/A	Opponent	Pos	Res	F-A	H-T	Scorers, Times, and Referees	1	2	3	4	5	6	7	8	9	10	11	12
32	A	YORK	6	L	0-1	0-1		Cashley	Sweeney	Drysdale	Emanuel	Collier	Merrick	Tainton	Mann	Gillies*	Fear	Brolly	Ritchie
	8/3	*7,567*	*14*	37			*Pollard 43*	*Crawford*	*Calvert*	*Oliver*	*Holmes*	*Woodward*	*Topping*	*Lyons*	*Cave*	*Seal*	*Jones*	*Pollard*	
							Ref: A Hamil	City lose ground in the promotion race as their all out second-half attacks fail to bring any reward. Mann is unlucky ten minutes from time with a superb shot which cannons off the angle of bar and post. Brian Pollard fires in the only goal when Cashley pushes out Jimmy Seal's header.											
33	H	MILLWALL	5	W	2-1	1-0	Fear 35, Mann 80	Cashley	Sweeney	Drysdale	Emanuel	Collier	Merrick	Tainton	Mann	Gillies	Fear	Brolly	
	15/3	12,393	*19*	39			*Clark 89*	*King*	*Donaldson*	*Moore*	*Dorney*	*Kitchener*	*Saul*	*Hazell*	*Jones*	*Clark*	*Summerill*	*Smethurst**	*Kelly C*
							Ref: W Gow	The loss of Eddie Jones with an ankle injury following Merrick's 62nd-minute tackle inspires ten-man Millwall's battling second-half display. Clark's tap in gives the Lions some reward, but by then City have the points as Mann's 20-yard scorcher adds to Fear's prodded in opener.											
34	A	BOLTON	5	W	2-0	1-0	Gillies 32, Ritchie 71	Cashley	Sweeney	Drysdale	Emanuel	Collier	Merrick	Tainton	Mann	Gillies	Ritchie	Brolly	
	22/3	*11,387*	*8*	41				*Siddall*	*Ritson*	*Dunne*	*Greaves*	*Jones P*	*Allardyce*	*Byrom*	*Curran**	*Lee*	*Reid*	*Thompson*	*Whatmore*
							Ref: C Seel	Frustrated with the award of a free-kick instead of a penalty when clearly brought down inside the area, Gillies gets his revenge 21 minutes later by heading in Brolly's cross. City's tenacious midfield display is the basis of their victory, which is assured by Ritchie's six-inch tap in.											
35	A	SOUTHAMPTON	3	W	1-0	1-0	Gillies 40	Cashley	Sweeney	Drysdale	Emanuel	Collier	Merrick	Tainton	Mann	Gillies	Ritchie	Brolly	
	28/3	*21,019*	*13*	43				*Turner*	*Andruszewski*	*Peach*	*Holmes*	*Bennett*	*Blyth*	*McCalliog**	*Channon*	*Osgood*	*Steele*	*Stokes*	*Crabbe*
							Ref: G Kew	City move into a promotion spot with the aid of rather lucky goal as the ball soars high over the keeper when Tainton's free-kick hits Gillies on the shoulder. Southampton are outplayed throughout as City's committed display brings them a deserved first-ever League success at the Dell.											
36	H	NORWICH	5	L	0-1	0-1		Cashley	Sweeney	Drysdale	Emanuel*	Collier	Merrick	Tainton	Mann	Gillies	Fear	Brolly	Gow
	29/3	22,118	*4*	43			*Suggett 17*	*Keelan*	*Butler*	*Powell*	*Morris*	*Forbes*	*Stringer*	*McGuire*	*MacDougall*	*Boyer*	*Suggett*	*Peters*	
							Ref: J Hunting	Tired City stumble against a classy Norwich side, who did not play yesterday. The Canaries show class and composure under City's almost ceaseless, but often punchless pressure. Colin Suggett drives in the decider after Ted MacDougall hooks back Phil Boyer's deep cross.											
37	H	BRISTOL ROV	5	D	1-1	0-1	Sweeney 77	Cashley	Sweeney	Drysdale	Emanuel*	Collier	Merrick	Tainton	Mann	Gillies	Ritchie	Brolly	Gow
	1/4	**28,953**	*19*	44			*Collier 33 (og)*	*Eadie*	*Jacobs*	*Bater*	*Aitken**	*Day*	*Prince*	*Stephens*	*Smith*	*Warboys*	*Staniforth*	*Dobson*	*Stanton*
							Ref: D Nippard	Another wasteful City performance as they are unable to translate their superiority into goals. After Colin Dobson's centre ends up in the net via Collier's shoulder, it takes Wilf Smith's misguided back-pass to give Sweeney the chance to slot in City's late equaliser from seven yards.											
38	A	NOTTS CO	4	W	2-1	1-1	Gillies 34, 65	Cashley	Sweeney	Drysdale	Emanuel	Collier	Merrick	Tainton	Mann	Gillies	Ritchie	Gow	
	5/4	*7,227*	*13*	46			*Probert 19*	*Brown*	*Brindley*	*O'Brien*	*McVay*	*Needham*	*Benjamin*	*Carter*	*Randall*	*Bradd*	*Probert*	*Scanlon*	
							Ref: P Partridge	Mann's free-roving role behind the front-runners has County in knots. Eric Probert finds a gap in City's defensive wall to put the Magpies, ahead, but Gillies twice heads in to keep promotion prospects alive, though Tainton admits his 35-yard pass for the last was really a shot.											
39	H	SHEFFIELD WED	5	W	1-0	0-0	Fear 78	Cashley	Sweeney	Drysdale	Gow	Collier	Merrick	Tainton	Mann*	Gillies	Ritchie	Brolly	Fear
	12/4	12,514	*22*	48				*Fox*	*Cameron*	*Knighton*	*Mullen*	*Dowd*	*Shaw*	*Potts*	*Harvey*	*Ferguson*	*Henson*	*Joicey*	
							Ref: C Newsome	Near the end of this tension-filled game Fear is relieved that the referee takes an amused view of his act of supplication on being pulled up for taking a quick free-kick. Wednesday's stubborn defensive display is overcome by Fear's outrageous skill as he backheels in Tainton's cross.											
40	A	ORIENT	5	L	0-1	0-1		Cashley	Sweeney	Drysdale	Gow	Collier	Merrick	Tainton	Mann	Gillies	Ritchie	Emanuel*	Fear
	15/4	*6,486*	*11*	48			*Possee 39*	*Jackson*	*Fisher*	*Grealish*	*Bennett*	*Gray**	*Walley*	*Cunningham*	*Possee*	*Bullock*	*Queen*	*Heppolette*	*Roeder*
							Ref: L Shapter	A muddy pitch stifles City's talents in a match which exceeds its finishing time by some twelve minutes due to floodlight failure near the end. City do not create many chances and they lose ground in the promotion race as Derek Possee, who is well offside, rams in Glen Roeder's pass.											
41	A	SUNDERLAND	5	L	**0-3**	0-1		Cashley	Sweeney	Drysdale	Emanuel	Collier	Merrick	Tainton	Mann	Gillies	Ritchie	Fear*	Brolly
	19/4	*30,530*	*3*	48			*Bolton 43, Robson 64, Belfitt 88*	*Montgomery*	*Malone*	*Guthrie*	*Moncur*	*Watson*	*Bolton*	*Kerr*	*Hughes*	*Belfitt*	*Robson*	*Towers*	
							Ref: E Wallace	The problem of poor finishing that has dogged City all season is the only difference between the sides at Roker Park. City are frustrated when Ritchie's twenty-yard drive is kept out by a post shortly before Joe Bolton opens the scoring with a weak drive which somehow beats Cashley.											
42	H	FULHAM	5	W	3-1	0-1	Ritchie 54, Sweeney 58p, Gillies 85	Cashley	Sweeney	Drysdale	Gow	Collier	Merrick	Tainton	Ritchie	Gillies	Fear	Whitehead	
	26/4	11,538	*9*	50			*Barrett 20*	*Mellor*	*Cutbush*	*Fraser*	*Mullery*	*Lacy*	*Moore*	*Scrivens*	*Dowie**	*Busby*	*Lloyd*	*Barrett*	*Bullivant*
	Home	Away					Ref: J Taylor	City's game against the FA Cup finalists is marred by second-half crowd disturbances and a dart throwing incident which halts play. Against attractive opponents Ritchie's powerful header sparks City's stirring revival before the misguided antics of the few spoil things for the many.											
Average	14,061	13,921																	

League Cup					F-A	H-T	Scorers, Times, and Referees	1	2	3	4	5	6	7	8	9	10	11	12 sub used
1	H	CARDIFF		W	2-1	1-0	Sweeney 30, Merrick 56	Cashley	Sweeney	Drysdale	Gow	Collier	Merrick	Tainton	Mann	Gillies	Cheesley	Whitehead*	Ritchie
19/8			8,813				*McInch 74*	*Irwin*	*Pethard*	*Charles*	*Phillips*	*Murray*	*Smith*	*Villars*	*Showers*	*Reece**	*McInch*	*Anderson*	*Impey*
							Ref: K Burns	City chalk up their seventh-successive win over the Welshmen, who are flattered by the narrow scoreline. Sweeney jabs City ahead when Gillies has his shot pushed out by Bill Irwin, and Merrick's trusty left foot doubles the advantage before Jimmy McInch fires in Cardiff's reply.											
2	A	CRYS PALACE	14	W	4-1	0-1	Sweeney 54p, Gow 60, Whiteh'd 84,	Cashley	Sweeney	Drysdale	Gow	Collier	Merrick	Tainton*	Ritchie	Gillies	Fear	Emanuel	Whitehead
10/9			*16,263*	*3:9*			*Whittle 11p* [Gillies 89]	*Hammond*	*Barry*	*Jump*	*Johnson*	*Jeffries*	*Blyth*	*Lindsay*	*Whittle*	*Swindleh'rst**	*Chatterton*	*Tayler*	*Rogers*
							Ref: R Challis	Sweeney makes amends for giving away Palace's penalty when fisting the ball off the line, by netting City's spot-kick opener after Fear is nudged from behind by Derek Jeffries. Following Gow's 30-yard drive in off the post, City go on to their biggest away win for three years.											
3	H	LIVERPOOL	13	D	0-0	0-0		Cashley	Sweeney	Drysdale	Gow	Collier	Merrick	Tainton*	Ritchie	Gillies	Fear	Emanuel	Whitehead
8/10			25,753	*1:2*				*Clements*	*Smith*	*Lindsay*	*Lawler*	*Boersma*	*Hughes*	*Keegan*	*Hall*	*Heighway*	*Kennedy*	*Callaghan*	
							Ref: R Perkin	Visions of a Cup upset flash through City minds just two minutes from the end of this impressive team performance. Fear cleverly slips in front of Tommy Smith to collect a superb Gillies through-pass, but Ray Clemence advances swiftly to divert the ball off target with his knee.											
3R	A	LIVERPOOL	11	L	0-4	0-1		Cashley	Sweeney	Drysdale	Gow	Collier	Merrick	Tainton	Ritchie	Cheesley	Fear*	Emanuel	Whitehead
16/10			*23,694*	*1:1*			*Heighway 39, 76, Kennedy 49, 82*	*Clements*	*Smith*	*Lindsay*	*Lawler*	*Boersma*	*Hughes*	*Keegan*	*Cormack*	*Heighway*	*Kennedy*	*Callaghan*	
							Ref: R Perkin	Steve Heighway heralds City's departure from the Cup with an unstoppable 18-yarder after exchanging two passes in a breathtaking run. The final scoreline is rather unfair to City who take the offensive early on, but are gradually worn down by their opponents impressive covering.											

FA Cup																			
3	A	SHEFFIELD UTD	5	L	0-2	0-1		Cashley	Sweeney	Drysdale	Mann	Collier	Merrick	Tainton	Ritchie	Fear*	Cheesley	Durrell	Griffin
4/1			*20,163*	*1:14*			*Dearden 16, Currie 90*	*Brown*	*Badger*	*Hemsley*	*Nicholl*	*Franks*	*Eddy*	*Woodward*	*Speight**	*Dearden*	*Currie*	*Field*	*Bradford*
							Ref: R Matthewson	City produce plenty of good football against top-flight United, but lack the finishing ability to turn their dash into goals. Bill Dearden's brave header to Tony Currie's angled shot gives United an early lead, but it isn't until the dying seconds that Currie kills City off with his 20-yarder.											

		Home					Away					
	P	W	D	L	F	A	W	D	L	F	A	Pts
1 Manchester U	42	17	3	1	45	12	9	6	6	21	18	61
2 Aston Villa	42	16	4	1	47	6	[illegible]	4	8	32	26	58
3 Norwich	42	14	3	4	34	17	6	10	5	24	20	53
4 Sunderland	42	14	6	1	41	8	5	7	9	24	27	51
5 BRISTOL CITY	42	14	5	2	31	10	[illegible]	3	11	16	23	50
6 West Brom	42	13	4	4	33	15	[illegible]	5	11	21	27	45
7 Blackpool	42	12	6	3	31	17	[illegible]	11	8	7	16	45
8 Hull	42	12	8	1	25	10	[illegible]	6	12	15	43	44
9 Fulham	42	9	8	4	29	17	[illegible]	8	9	15	22	42
10 Bolton	42	9	7	5	27	16	[illegible]	5	10	18	25	42
11 Oxford	42	14	3	4	30	19	[illegible]	9	11	11	32	42
12 Orient	42	8	9	4	17	16	[illegible]	11	7	11	23	42
13 Southampton	42	10	6	5	29	20	[illegible]	5	11	24	34	41
14 Notts Co	42	7	11	3	34	26	[illegible]	5	11	15	33	40
15 York	42	9	7	5	28	18	[illegible]	3	13	23	37	38
16 Nott'm Forest	42	7	7	7	24	23	[illegible]	7	9	19	32	38
17 Portsmouth	42	9	7	5	28	20	3	6	12	16	34	37
18 Oldham	42	10	7	4	28	16	[illegible]	8	13	12	32	35
19 Bristol Rov	42	10	4	7	25	23	2	7	12	17	41	35
20 Millwall	42	8	9	4	31	19	2	3	16	13	37	32
21 Cardiff	42	7	8	6	24	21	2	6	13	12	41	32
22 Sheffield Wed	42	3	7	11	17	29	2	4	15	12	35	21
	924	232	139	91	658	378	[illegible]	139	232	378	658	924

Odds & ends

Double wins: (5) Bolton, Southampton, Notts Co, Portsmouth, Manchester U.

Double losses: (2) Blackpool, Norwich.

Won from behind: (6) Bolton (h), Bristol Rov (a), Portsmouth (h), West Brom (h), Notts Co (a), Fulham (h).

Lost from in front: (1) Norwich (a).

High spots: Doing the double over Manchester U.

Beating Bristol Rov 4-1 at Eastville on 28 December.

Beating Crystal Palace 4-1 at Selhurst Park in the FL Cup on 10 Sep.

Winning 1-0 at Southampton on 28 March.

Low spots: Losing 0-1 at home to Norwich on 29 March.

Losing 1-2 against Bristol Rov (a) in the Gloucestershire Cup on 29 Apr.

Player of the year: Gary Collier.

Ever-presents: (3) Ray Cashley, Geoff Merrick, Gerry Sweeney.

Hat-tricks: (0).

Leading scorer: Donnie Gillies (10).

	Appearances						Goals			
	Lge	*Sub*	LC	*Sub*	FAC	*Sub*	**Lge**	LC	FAC	**Tot**
Brolly, Mike	**13**	*2*					**1**			**1**
Cashley, Ray	**42**		4		1					
Cheesley, Paul	**13**	*2*	2		1		**2**			**2**
Collier, Gary	**41**		4		1		**1**			**1**
Drysdale, Brian	**38**		4		1		**1**			**1**
Durrell, Joe	**3**	*1*			1					
Emanuel, John	**31**		3				**1**			**1**
Fear, Keith	**29**	*2*	3		1		**8**			**8**
Gillies, Donnie	**28**	*1*	3				**9**	1		**10**
Gow, Gerry	**22**	*2*	4				**2**	1		**3**
Griffin, Kevin	**4**					*1*				
Hunt, Ernie		*1*		*1*						
Mann, Jimmy	**29**	*1*	1		1		**6**			**6**
Merrick, Geoff	**42**		4		1		**3**	1		**4**
Ritchie, Tom	**32**	*1*	3	*1*	1		**4**			**4**
Rodgers, Dave	**5**									
Sweeney, Gerry	**42**		4		1		**6**	2		**8**
Tainton, Trevor	**38**		4		1		**1**			**1**
Whitehead, Clive	**10**	*4*	1	*3*				1		**1**
(own-goals)							**2**			**2**
19 players used	**462**	***17***	**44**	***4***	**11**	***1***	**47**	**6**		**53**

No	Date		Att	Pos	Pt	F-A	H-T	Scorers, Times, and Referees	1	2	3	4	5	6	7	8	9	10	11	12 sub used
1	H	BOLTON			W	1-0	0-0	Sweeney 62p	Cashley	Sweeney	Drysdale	Gow	Collier	Merrick	Tainton	Ritchie	Mann	Cheesley	Brolly	
	16/8		10,510		2				*Siddall*	*Ritson*	*Dunne*	*Greaves*	*Jones P*	*Walsh*	*Byrom*	*Curran*	*Jones G*	*Reid*	*Thompson*	
								Ref: M Taylor	A poor City performance brings an unlikely win thanks to a twice-taken penalty, following the up-ending of Mann by Paul Jones. After referee rules that Sweeney's saved first kick be retaken due to Tony Dunne's encroachment, City's full-back takes full advantage of his second chance.											
2	H	SUNDERLAND			W	3-0	2-0	Brolly 7, Mann 9, 68	Cashley	Sweeney	Emanuel	Gow	Collier	Merrick	Tainton	Ritchie	Mann	Cheesley	Brolly	
	19/8		12,199		4				*Swinburne*	*Ashurst*	*Bolton*	*Longhorn*	*Clarke*	*Moncur*	*Kerr*	*Holden*	*Halom*	*Robson*	*Porterfield**	*Gibb*
								Ref: C White	Brolly's crisp six-yard shot sparks the best display so far of Dicks' managerial reign as Sunderland are shattered by City's class, skill and pace. Ashton Gate has never been a lucky venue for the Wearsiders, but it is doubtful that they have ever suffered a more comprehensive defeat here.											
3	A	HULL		3	L	**1-3**	0-2	Ritchie 47	Cashley	Sweeney	Emanuel	Gow	Collier	Merrick	Tainton	Ritchie	Mann	Cheesley	Brolly	
	23/8		*5,076*	*5*	4			*Greenwood 26, 31, Fletcher 73*	*Wealands*	*Banks*	*De Vries*	*Galvin*	*Croft**	*Roberts*	*Grimes*	*Lord*	*Wood*	*Fletcher*	*Greenwood*	*McGill*
								Ref: C Seel	City fail to show much form as they suffer their first League defeat of the season. Cashley is caught in no-man's land by Roy Greenwood's angled chip, but can do nothing when Peter Fletcher cheekily lobs the ball over his shoulder before turning and firing in an explosive volley.											
4	A	SOUTHAMPTON		7	L	**1-3**	0-2	Gow 87	Cashley	Sweeney	Emanuel	Gow	Collier	Merrick	Tainton	Ritchie	Mann	Cheesley	Brolly*	Gillies
	26/8		*16,833*	*1*	4			*Stokes 16, 90, Peach 28*	*Middleton*	*Rodrigues*	*Steele*	*Holmes*	*Bennett*	*Blyth*	*O'Brien*	*Channon*	*Stokes*	*McCalliog*	*Peach*	
								Ref: B Daniels	Bobby Stokes hammers in a last-minute strike to end Bristol City's late fight back that almost secured a point. Mann is thwarted by a post and Emanuel shoots over from four yards, whilst in between City get some reward as Gow finishes off a superb move between Ritchie and Gillies.											
5	H	BRISTOL ROV		6	D	1-1	1-1	Cheesley 19	Cashley	Sweeney	Drysdale	Gow	Collier	Merrick	Tainton	Ritchie	Mann	Cheesley	Brolly	
	30/8		17,940	*14*	5			*Bannister 3*	*Eadie*	*Smith*	*Williams*	*Aitken*	*Taylor*	*Prince*	*Stephens**	*Pulis*	*Warboys*	*Bannister*	*Evans*	*Fearnley*
								Ref: R Matthewson	After Bruce Bannister's deft footwork turns in Alan Warboy's off-target shot, Bristol City recover to dominate matters. It is no surprise when Cheesley slides in the equaliser from Tainton's through-ball, but thereafter Jim Eadie's inspired form prevents any alteration to the score-line.											
6	A	BLACKBURN		5	W	2-1	0-0	Sweeney 57p, Mann 79	Cashley	Sweeney	Drysdale	Gow	Collier	Merrick	Tainton	Ritchie	Mann	Cheesley	Brolly	
	6/9		*10,381*	*9*	7			*Parkes 54*	*Jones*	*Heaton*	*Burgin*	*Metcalfe**	*Hawkins*	*Fazackerley*	*Beamish*	*Oates*	*Hickman*	*Parkes*	*Martin*	*Hoy*
								Ref: J Yates	Despite depriving Blackburn of their unbeaten record, Dicks is far from happy with his side's performance. After Tony Parkes' 15-yard cross-shot gives Rovers the lead, it takes Sweeney's well-hit penalty, following Andy Burgin's trip on Cheesley, to get City turning on the style.											
7	H	OXFORD		1	W	4-1	1-0	Cheesley 22, 85, Ritchie 68, 73	Cashley	Sweeney*	Drysdale	Gow	**Harding**	Merrick	Tainton	Ritchie	Gillies	Cheesley	Brolly	Emanuel
	12/9		10,373	*15*	9			*Tait 86*	*Milkins*	*Light*	*Shuker*	*Bodell*	*Clarke C*	*Jeffrey*	*McGrogan*	*Duncan*	*Clarke D*	*Foley**	*Aylott*	*Tait*
								Ref: K Salmon	City soar to the top of affairs against a bewildered Oxford side still seeking their first away win in over a year. City's non-stop running pays off as Cheesley heads in the opener, and whilst Derek Clarke's header hits the bar for United shortly after, it is mainly one-way traffic thereafter.											
8	A	CHELSEA		4	D	1-1	1-1	Cheesley 41	Cashley	Gillies	Drysdale	Gow	Collier	Merrick	Tainton	Ritchie	Mann	Cheesley	Brolly	
	20/9		*18,644*	*8*	10			*Garner 25*	*Sherwood*	*Harris*	*Hay*	*Stanley*	*Droy*	*Dempsey*	*Britton*	*Wilkins R*	*Bason*	*Hutchinson*	*Garner !*	
								Ref: G Kew	City let ten-man Chelsea off the hook by settling for point after the 76th-minute dismissal of Bill Garner for his trip on Cashley. A game of some promise early on, as Cheesley nets from 15 yards to equalise Garner's header, degenerates into a physical shambles with five bookings.											
9	H	BLACKPOOL		4	W	2-0	2-0	Cheesley 20, Gow 43p	Cashley	Gillies	Drysdale	Gow	Collier	Merrick	Tainton	Ritchie	Mann	Cheesley*	Brolly	Whitehead
	27/9		**10,246**	*9*	12				*Wood*	*Curtis**	*Bentley*	*Hart*	*Suddaby*	*Hatton*	*Ronson*	*Suddick*	*Walsh*	*Ainscow*	*Moore*	*Harrison*
								Ref: J Bent	City dominate the first half, but shortly after Cheesley fires into the far corner of the net from just inside the box to give them the lead, Paul Hart is unlucky when his header hits a post. Gow is fortunate with his weak spot-kick that beats George Wood, after Bill Bentley fells Ritchie.											
10	A	NOTTS CO		5	D	1-1	0-0	Mann 59	Cashley	Gillies	Drysdale	Gow	Collier	Merrick	Tainton	Ritchie	Mann	Cheesley	Brolly	
	4/10		*10,802*	*2*	13			*Needham 68*	*McManus*	*Richards P*	*O'Brien*	*Bolton*	*Needham*	*Stubbs*	*Carter**	*Probert*	*Bradd*	*McVay*	*Scanlon*	*Vinter*
								Ref: R Lewis	Mann's drive is brilliantly cleared off the goal-line by David McVay just before half-time, but he is not to be denied for long. County concede for the first time this season in a home League match. Mann shoots the ball in from 15 yards, after Cheesley deliberately leaves Gow's cross.											

No	Date	Opponent	Att	Pos	Res	Pts	F-A	H-T	Scorers, Times, and Referees	1	2	3	4	5	6	7	8	9	10	11	12
11	A	OLDHAM		2	W		4-2	1-1	Mann 14, Gillies 70, Cheesley 79,	Cashley	Gillies	Drysdale	Gow	Collier	Merrick	Tainton	Ritchie	Mann	Cheesley	Brolly*	Whitehead
	7/10		*9,552*	*7*		15			*Whittle 35p, Jones 49* [Whiteh'd 83]	*Ogden*	*Branagan*	*Whittle*	*Wood*	*Hicks*	*Holt*	*Bell*	*Jones**	*Robins*	*Chapman*	*Groves*	*Young*
									Ref: R Perkin	Mann runs round keeper Chris Ogden to slip in the opener, but Oldham take the lead with a penalty and a free-kick as Merrick twice brings down George Jones. Cheesley's headed goal is lauded as the best of the season as City's refreshing attacking policy brings a well-merited win.											
12	H	CHARLTON		2	W		**4-0**	2-0	W'head 26, Gow 37p, Cheesl'y 74, 78	Cashley	Gillies	Drysdale	Gow	Collier	Merrick	Tainton	Ritchie	Mann	Cheesley	Whitehead	
	11/10		12,659	*13*		17				*Tutt*	*Penfold*	*Warman*	*Bowman*	*Giles*	*Young*	*Powell*	*Hales*	*Flanagan*	*Hunt*	*Berry*	
									Ref: T Reynolds	Gow's penalty, after Cheesley is brought by down Peter Hunt, is a vast improvement on his Blackpool effort. Graham Tutt is sent the wrong way as he cracks the ball to the keeper's right at the East End. The move of the match ends with Cashley's tap-in to conclude the day's scoring.											
13	A	YORK		1	W		4-1	3-0	Cheesley 1, 31, 55p, Ritchie 41	Cashley	Gillies	Drysdale	Gow	Collier	Merrick	Tainton	Ritchie	Mann	Cheesley	Whitehead	
	18/10		***5,073***	*21*		19			*Cave 65*	*Crawford*	*Oliver*	*Downing*	*Cave*	*Swallow*	*Topping*	*Pollard*	*Holmes**	*Seal*	*Lyons*	*McMordie*	*Hunter*
									Ref: J Butcher	A memorable match for Cheesley, who notches City's first hat-trick for 20 months as his mis-hit pen finds a way through Graeme Crawford's legs. He gets off the mark by smashing in from 18 yards, then adds another with a diving header at the far post to put away Whitehead's cross.											
14	H	WEST BROM		2	L		0-2	0-0		Cashley	Gillies*	Drysdale	Gow	Collier	Merrick	Tainton	Ritchie	Mann	Cheesley	Whitehead	Sweeney
	25/10		19,133	*14*		19			*Brown A 70, Brown T 88*	*Osborne*	*Mulligan*	*Wilson*	*Cantello*	*Wile*	*Robertson*	*Martin*	*Brown T*	*Brown A*	*Giles*	*Johnston*	
									Ref: G Trevett	A well-organised Baggies side inflict City's first home League defeat of the season. Alastair Brown beats three men in a run from midfield before firing the opener into the far corner, then Tony Brown's perfect low-shot from the right makes sure of ending City's short stay at the top.											
15	A	LUTON		2	D		0-0	0-0		Cashley	Gilies	Drysdale	Gow	Collier	Merrick	Tainton	Ritchie	Mann	Cheesley	Whitehead	
	1/11		*11,446*	*12*		20				*Barber*	*Ryan John*	*Thomson*	*Chambers*	*Faulkner*	*Futcher P*	*Ryan Jim**	*King*	*Anderson*	*West*	*Aston*	*Husband*
									Ref: H Davey	City improve on last week's performance, but after spurning their chances they are fortunate to survive Luton's revival. Unlucky when Mann's 30-yard dipper hits the bar on 54 minutes, City are indebted to Cashley for getting his fingertips to Andy King's cracking drive near the end.											
16	H	ORIENT		3	D		0-0	0-0		Cashley	Gillies	Drysdale	Gow	Collier	Merrick	Tainton	Ritchie	Mann	Cheesley	Whitehead*	Fear
	7/11		14,553	*11*		21				*Jackson*	*Fisher*	*Grealish*	*Bennett*	*Hoadley*	*Walley*	*Cunningham*	*Roeder*	*Queen*	*Mooney*	*Heppolette*	
									Ref: D Turner	'City are the best team we have played' says Orient boss George Petchey, but such words are of little consolation. Frustrated by Orient's battling midfield, City's third-successive scoring blank raises concerns. Only Cheesley poses a threat, twice being thwarted by great saves.											
17	A	NOTT'M FOREST		3	L		0-1	0-1		Cashley	Gillies	Drysdale	Gow	Collier	Merrick	Tainton	Ritchie	Mann	Cheesley	Whitehead*	Sweeney
	15/11		*11,582*	*12*		21			*Butlin 6*	*Middleton*	*Anderson*	*Clark*	*McGovern*	*Chapman*	*Richardson*	*Robertson*	*O'Neill*	*O'Hare*	*Butlin*	*Bowyer*	
									Ref: P Partridge	The goal drought continues as despite City's second-half domination they cannot counter Barry Butlin's perfectly-placed shot from a narrow angle. Forest boss Brian Clough opines that City deserved a point, but for all their pressure after the break they only create two real chances.											
18	H	YORK		3	W		4-1	2-1	Ritchie 21, 36, 72, Merrick 78	Cashley	Sweeney	Drysdale	Gow	Collier	Merrick	Tainton	Ritchie	Mann	Cheesley*	Whitehead	Fear
	22/11		11,228	*22*		23			*Seal 42*	*Crawford*	*Creamer*	*Woodward*	*McMordie*	*Swallow*	*Topping*	*Lyons**	*Holmes*	*Seal*	*Hinch*	*Downing*	*Hosker*
									Ref: A Glasson	In front of the Match of the Day viewers City end their goal drought in fine style against attack-minded opponents. Ritchie grabs his first-ever hat-trick, cashing in on centre-half Barry Swallow's mistakes for two of his goals, after getting off the mark by heading in Mann's centre.											
19	A	FULHAM		2	W		2-1	2-0	Ritchie 11, 26	Cashley	Sweeney	Drysdale*	Gow	Harding	Merrick	Tainton	Ritchie	Mann	Cheesley	Fear	**McNeill**
	29/11		*11,400*	*7*		25			*Mullery 90p*	*Mellor*	*Fraser*	*Strong*	*Mullery*	*Howe*	*Moore*	*Dowie*	*Conway*	*Busby*	*Slough*	*Barrett*	
									Ref: J Taylor	Not a lucky venue for City in the past, the fates are with them this time as they survive a terrific pounding. Fulham's only reward is a last min pen when Alan Slough is up-ended, but by then Ritchie had run from the halfway line for City's opener and added another with a fine header.											
20	H	CARLISLE		3	D		0-0	0-0		Cashley	Sweeney	Drysdale	Gow	Collier	Merrick	Tainton	Ritchie	Mann	Cheesley	Fear	
	6/12		12,446	*19*		26				*Ross*	*Carr*	*Gorman*	*Train*	*Green*	*Parker*	*McCartney*	*Martin*	*Clarke**	*Barry*	*McVitie*	*Laidlaw*
									Ref: R Crabb	Carlisle's disciplined defence seems more like Hadrian's Wall to City's frustrated forwards. Ross saves the Cumbrians near the finish with a great dive to his left to keep out Mann's thundering 35-yarder, but it is not all one way as McVitie and Martin miss easy second-half chances.											
21	H	HULL		3	W		3-0	1-0	Ritchie 30, Mann 53, Cheesley 90	Cashley	Sweeney	Drysdale	Gow	Collier	Merrick	Tainton	Ritchie	Mann	Cheesley	Fear	
	13/12		10,361	*14*		28				*Wealands*	*Daniel*	*Banks*	*Galvin*	*Croft*	*Roberts*	*Grimes*	*Gibson**	*Wood*	*Fletcher*	*Greenwood*	*Hawley*
									Ref: B Perkin	Playing their best football of the year in this brilliant win, City go into the second half of the season firmly entrenched in a promotion place, with a lead of four points over Notts County. Cheesley ends his seven-match goal drought by heading in Fear's corner in the last seconds.											

No	Date		Att	Pos	Pt	F-A	H-T	Scorers, Times, and Referees	1	2	3	4	5	6	7	8	9	10	11	12 sub used
22	A	BOLTON		3	L	0-1	0-0		Cashley	Sweeney	Drysdale	Gow	Collier	Merrick	Tainton	Ritchie	Mann*	Cheesley	Fear	Brolly
	20/12		*19,164*	*2*	28			*Whatmore 80*	*Sidall*	*Ritson*	*Dunne*	*Greaves*	*Jones P*	*Allardyce*	*Waldron*	*Whatmore*	*Jones G*	*Reid*	*Smith**	*Byrom*
								Ref: R Toseland	'A cracking match that would not have disgraced the First Division' is the verdict of Bolton boss Ian Greaves. A rousing tussle, with both sides committed to attack, is settled by a wretched defensive error. Neil Whatmore rolls the ball in after intercepting Collier's weak back-pass.											
23	H	PLYMOUTH		3	D	2-2	1-1	Merrick 35, Collier 58	Cashley	Sweeney	Drysdale	Gow	Collier	Merrick	Tainton	Ritchie	Mann	Cheesley*	Fear	Whitehead
	26/12		*21,471*	*18*	29			*Mariner 27, 48*	*Aleksic*	*Darke*	*Burrows*	*Sutton*	*Green*	*Delve*	*Randell*	*Johnson*	*Mariner*	*Rafferty*	*McAuley*	
								Ref: D Wallace	A thrilling clash in which the 13th-minute loss of Cheesley with a strained back possibly explains City's inept finishing. Paul Mariner shows how to do it with a brilliant flicked header and a superb shot on the turn, though Merrick's goal is also a gem as he heads in Fear's free-kick.											
24	A	PORTSMOUTH		3	W	1-0	1-0	Ritchie 8	Cashley	Sweeney	Drysdale	Gow	Collier	Merrick	Tainton	Ritchie	Mann	Brolly	Fear	
	27/12		*14,315*	*22*	31				*Lloyd*	*Lawler*	*Mellows*	*Roberts*	*Went*	*Cahill*	*Eames*	*Piper*	*Foster*	*Reynolds*	*McGuinness**	*Hand*
								Ref: B Daniels	Pompey look anything but relegation candidates as City cling onto Ritchie's early effort when he ran through the middle to shoot in. Pity then that Fear shot a 5th-min chance wide from just two yards, as otherwise City fans may then not have had to suffer such a nerve-racking finale.											
25	A	OXFORD		3	D	1-1	1-0	Cheesley 5	Cashley	Sweeney	Drysdale	Gow	Collier	Merrick	Tainton	Ritchie	Mann	Cheesley	Fear	
	10/1		*7,594*	*20*	32			*Clarke C 73*	*Burton*	*Taylor*	*Shuker*	*Lowe*	*Clarke C*	*Jeffrey**	*Houseman*	*Aylott*	*Clarke D*	*McCulloch*	*Briggs*	*Foley*
								Ref: T Bune	It is so easy at the start as Cheesley heads in Gow's perfect cross, but thereafter Cashley is the hero with many great saves. Colin Clarke's header takes a deflection for United's deserved leveller, but Peter Houseman is unlucky with his last-minute effort being ruled offside.											
26	H	BLACKBURN		2	W	1-0	1-0	Mann 6	Cashley	Sweeney	Drysdale	Gow	Collier	Merrick	Tainton	Ritchie	Mann	Brolly	Fear	
	17/1		*12,168*	*19*	34				*Jones*	*Wilkinson*	*Wood*	*Metcalfe*	*Hawkins*	*Fazackerley*	*Mullen**	*Oates*	*Svarc*	*Parkes*	*Wagstaffe*	*Hird*
								Ref: K Ridden	With only Mann's miskicked shot from five yards to show for all their domination, City face the possibility of yet another anxious finale. Loan signing Dave Wagstaffe (Wolves), brings Blackburn back into the contest after the break, but City manage to successfully match their efforts.											
27	A	PLYMOUTH		2	D	0-0	0-0		Cashley	Sweeney	Drysdale	Gow	Collier	Merrick	Tainton	Ritchie	Mann	Brolly	Fear	
	24/1		*17,887*	*11*	35				*Aleksic*	*Darke*	*Burrows*	*Horswill*	*Green*	*Delve*	*Randell**	*Sutton*	*Mariner*	*Rafferty*	*McAuley*	*Johnson*
								Ref: T Bosi	Cashley finds darts and a knife in his goal area before the game starts, but thankfully unruly spectators do not cause problems during play. Argyle are constantly thwarted, as City create few friends with their defensive approach and do not manage so much as a single shot on target.											
28	H	SOUTHAMPTON		2	D	1-1	1-0	Ritchie 32	Cashley	Sweeney	Drysdale	Gow	Collier	Merrick	Tainton	Ritchie	Mann	Cheesley	Fear	
	7/2		22,316	*6*	36			*Holmes 77*	*Turner*	*Rodrigues*	*Peach*	*Holmes*	*Blyth*	*Steele*	*Fisher*	*Channon*	*Osgood*	*McCalliog*	*Stokes*	
								Ref: D Reeves	On Match of the Day again, City's brilliant first-half play is rewarded as Ritchie stabs in Cheesley's low cross. Peter Osgood, distinctively clad in a brighter yellow than his colleagues, inspires the Saints as Nick Holmes nets with an easy shot to extend their unbeaten run to 13 games.											
29	A	ORIENT		1	W	1-0	0-0	Ritchie 74	Cashley	Sweeney	Drysdale	Gow	Collier	Merrick	Tainton	Ritchie	Mann	Cheesley*	Fear	Gillies
	14/2		*5,785*	*15*	38				*Jackson*	*Fisher**	*Payne*	*Grealish*	*Hoadley*	*Walley*	*Cunningham*	*Queen*	*Bullock*	*Heppolette*	*Possee*	*Allder*
								Ref: K Baker	Shortly after offside rules out Cheesley's tap-in, Ritchie's near-post header takes City back to the top of the table. Orient run out of steam near the end, having been out of action for a month due to an influenza epidemic, though Laurie Cunningham forces Cashley to save his late effort.											
30	H	NOTT'M FOREST		3	L	0-2	0-1		Cashley	Sweeney	Drysdale	Gow	Collier	Merrick	Tainton	Ritchie	Mann	Cheesley	Fear*	Gillies
	21/2		15,302	*12*	38			*Curran 17, O'Hare 50*	*Wells*	*O'Kane**	*Clark*	*McGovern*	*Chapman*	*Bowyer*	*Curran*	*O'Neill*	*O'Hare*	*Butlin*	*Robertson*	*McCann*
								Ref: R Lewis	Terry Curran's pace and the skills of John O'Hare and Martin O'Neill cause City many problems as they are repeatedly carved apart by their slick opponents. Curran shoots in from twelve yards to open the scoring, and O'Hare delicately steers the ball past Cashley to tie matters up.											
31	H	OLDHAM		1	W	1-0	1-0	Cheesley 5	Cashley	Sweeney	Drysdale	Gow	Collier	Merrick	Tainton	Ritchie	Mann	Cheesley	Whitehead	
	24/2		14,631	*8*	40				*Platt*	*Wood*	*Whittle*	*Bell*	*Edwards*	*Holt*	*Blair*	*Shaw*	*Hicks*	*Chapman*	*Groves*	
								Ref: B James	City's second-half jitters return, but fortunately Oldham can only manage one shot on target. Cheesley, who could have notched a hat-trick in the first eight minutes, secures the points with his early header, but after Tainton's 30-yarder hits the post five minutes later, the game declines.											

No		Date	Opponent	Att	Pos	Pts	Res	F-A	H-T	Scorers, Times, and Referees	1	2	3	4	5	6	7	8	9	10	11	12
32	H		LUTON		1		W	3-0	0-0	Ritchie 54, 57, Cheesley 71	Cashley	Sweeney	Drysdale	Gow	Collier	Merrick	Tainton	Ritchie	Gillies	Cheesley	Whitehead	
		6/3		15,872	7	42					*Barber*	*Ryan John*	*Buckley*	*Chambers*	*Faulkner*	*Futcher P*	*Husband*	*King*	*Futcher R*	*West*	*Fuccillo**	*Aston*
										Ref: Hough	Cashley's stunning 52nd-minute save to keep out Ron Futcher's header is the turning point after Gow's first-half penalty had crashed against the bar. Ritchie's two well-taken shots give City the initiative, while Cheesley's unstoppable drive is a tonic to their influenza-weakened side.											
33	A		CHARLTON		1		D	2-2	0-0	Gow 31, Sweeney 83	Cashley	Sweeney	Drysdale	Gow	Collier	Merrick	Tainton	Ritchie	Gillies	Cheesley*	Whitehead	McNeill
		12/3		12,711	12	43				*Berry 64, Young T 66*	*Wood*	*Berry*	*Young D*	*Young T*	*Giles*	*Curtis*	*Powell*	*Hales*	*Hope*	*Peacock*	*Flanagan*	
										Ref: L Burden	City ride their luck at the Valley where Charlton striker Derek Hales has efforts struck off for offside in the 15th and 70th mins. City make all the running though and Gow deservedly puts them ahead with a perfectly-placed low shot, but it takes Sweeney's rasping drive to save a point.											
34	A		WEST BROM		1		W	1-0	1-0	Sweeney 45	Cashley	Sweeney	Drysdale	Gow	Collier	Merrick	Tainton	Ritchie	Gillies	Cheesley	Whitehead*	Mann
		17/3		26,278	5	45					*Osborne*	*Mulligan*	*Robson*	*Brown T*	*Wile*	*Robertson*	*Martin*	*Cantello**	*Mayo*	*Giles*	*Johnston*	*Brown A*
										Ref: M Sinclair	The City hordes who swelled the Hawthorns crowd on St Patrick's Day are convinced that City are promotion bound after this pulsating clash. Alastair Brown and John Wile see their shots cannon off the woodwork in the final few minutes as City hang onto Sweeney's drive.											
35	H		FULHAM		1		D	0-0	0-0		Cashley	Sweeney	Drysdale	Gow	Collier	Merrick	Tainton	Ritchie	Gillies	Cheesley	Whitehead	
		20/3		19,546	12	46					*Mellor*	*Cutbush*	*Strong*	*Mullery*	*Lacy*	*Howe*	*Mitchell*	*Conway*	*Busby*	*Slough*	*Barrett*	
										Ref: A Morrissey	Jaded-looking City play out a dreary draw, but increase their hold at the top of the table to four points. Fulham's packed midfield holds City at bay, though Sweeney on running through to net near the end is frustrated as his effort is disallowed due to Whitehead being given offside.											
36	A		SUNDERLAND		1		D	1-1	0-0	Sweeney 47	Cashley	Sweeney	Drysdale	Gow	Collier	Merrick	Tainton	Ritchie	Gillies	Cheesley*	Whitehead	Mann
		23/3		**38,395**	2	47				*Holden 85*	*Montgomery*	*Malone*	*Bolton*	*Train*	*Ashurst*	*Moncur*	*Kerr*	*Hughes*	*Holden*	*Robson*	*Greenwood*	
										Ref: R Lee	Mel Holden's late headed equaliser which preserves Sunderland's 13-month unbeaten home record, is likely to prove costly for City in their Championship quest. Sweeney's right-foot rocket shot that finishes off a brilliant seven-pass move is worthy of earning more than a point.											
37	A		CARLISLE		1		W	1-0	1-0	Gow 16p	Cashley	Sweeney	Drysdale	Gow	Collier	Merrick	Tainton	Ritchie	Gillies	Fear*	Whitehead	Mann
		27/3		7,563	18	49					*Ross*	*Carr*	*Gorman*	*O'Neill**	*Green*	*Owen*	*Lathan*	*Bonnyman*	*Clarke*	*Laidlaw*	*Martin*	*McVitie*
										Ref: K Styles	After missing four open-goal opportunities Ritchie is much relieved as City manage to hang onto Gow's penalty, awarded after Bill Green pulls back Whitehead. In truth Carlisle offer little threat, though Cashley does well to divert Joe Laidlaw's ten-yard drive just before the break.											
38	A		BLACKPOOL		1		L	1-2	1-1	Ritchie 4	Cashley	Sweeney	Drysdale	Gow	Collier	Merrick	Tainton	Ritchie	Gillies	Cheesley*	Whitehead	Mann
		3/4		8,273	10	49				*Moore 42, Walsh 77*	*Wood*	*Hatton*	*Bentley*	*McEwan*	*Suddaby*	*Alcock*	*Evanson*	*Suddick*	*Walsh*	*Ainscow*	*Moore*	
										Ref: G Courtney	City's zest for attack brings an early reward as Ritchie shoots them ahead with a shot on the run from 14 yards, but their defence is awry when Kevin Moore taps in Pool's equaliser. Missed chances prove costly as Micky Walsh heads in keeper George Wood's 90-yard clearance.											
39	H		CHELSEA		2		D	2-2	1-1	Ritchie 6, 74	Cashley	Sweeney	Drysdale	Gow	Collier	Merrick	Tainton	Ritchie	Gillies	Cheesley	Whitehead*	Mann
		10/4		25,319	11	50				*Swain 43, Stanley 75*	*Bonnetti*	*Harris*	*Wilkins G*	*Stanley*	*Wicks*	*Hay*	*Britton*	*Wilkins R*	*Finnieston*	*Swain*	*Lewington*	
										Ref: J Hunting	The Match of the Day cameras are at Ashton Gate for the third time this season as Kenny Swain's spectacular 20-yard chip equalises Ritchie's tapped-in opener. Another Ritchie tap-in restores City's advantage, but Gary Stanley secures Chelsea's deserved point by heading past Cashley.											
40	A		BRISTOL ROV		1		D	0-0	0-0		Cashley	Sweeney	Drysdale	Gow	Collier	Merrick	Tainton	Ritchie	Gillies	Cheesley	Whitehead	
		13/4		26,480	16	51					*Eadie*	*Williams*	*Bater*	*Day*	*Taylor*	*Prince*	*Stephens*	*Smith*	*Warboys*	*Bannister*	*Britton*	
										Ref: T Reynolds	Jim Eadie denies City, with saves from Tainton and Whitehead being rated world class by his boss Don Megson. Whilst the Rovers fail to muster a shot on target, a draw is fair result for a tension-racked game made even more difficult by a none-too-even ground and a tricky breeze.											
41	H		PORTSMOUTH		2		W	1-0	1-0	Whitehead 3	Cashley	Sweeney	Drysdale	Gow	Collier	Merrick	Tainton	Ritchie	Gillies	Cheesley	Whitehead	
		20/4		**27,394**	22	53					*Figgins*	*Ellis*	*Roberts*	*Denyer*	*Cahill*	*Eames*	*McGuinness*	*Piper*	*Graham*	*Kamara*	*Mellows*	
										Ref: B Homewood	Whitehead's glorious right-foot shot from ten yards clinches City's return to the elite for the first time since 1911. Already-relegated Pompey prove tougher opponents than expected as further goals to ease the tension refuse to come. At the whistle City's delirious fans invade the pitch.											
42	H		NOTTS CO		2		L	1-2	0-1	Whitehead 74	Cashley	Sweeney	Drysdale	Gow	Collier	Merrick	Tainton	Ritchie	Gillies*	Cheesley	Whitehead	Mann
		24/4		24,614	7	53				*O'Brien 15, Benjamin 73*	*McManus*	*Richards*	*O'Brien*	*Smith*	*Needham*	*Stubbs*	*McVay*	*Sims*	*Bradd*	*Mann*	*Scanlon**	*Benjamin*
		Home		Away						Ref: A Turvey	The promotion celebrations are soured as a competitive and skilful County bring City back to reality. O'Brien stuns Cashley with his 30-yard volley into the top corner of the net and whilst Whitehead prods in for City, it is too late as Benjamin's header had added to County's haul.											
Average		16,204		14,059																		

League Cup					F-A	H-T	Scorers, Times, and Referees	1	2	3	4	5	6	7	8	9	10	11	12 sub used
2	A	WEST HAM	5	D	0-0	0-0		Cashley	Sweeney	Drysdale	Gow	Collier	Merrick	Tainton	Ritchie	Mann !	Cheesley	Brolly*	Gillies
	9/9		*19,837 1:2*					*Day*	*McDowell*	*Lampard*	*Bonds*	*Taylor T*	*Lock*	*Holland**	*Paddon*	*Jennings*	*Brooking*	*Robson*	*Ayris*
							Ref: A Robinson	Reduced to ten men for the last half-hour gritty City hold the Hammers at Upton Park. Mann is the villain as he fells Billy Jennings with a crisp punch to earn his sending-off, whilst Cashley is the hero by saving Graham Paddon's 64th-min spot-kick following Merrick's handball.											
2R	H	WEST HAM	4	L	1-3	1-0	Cheesley 19	Cashley	Sweeney	Drysdale	Gow	Collier	Merrick	Tainton	Ritchie	Mann	Cheesley	Brolly*	Gillies
	24/9		19,849 *1:3*				*Brooking 72, Best 75, Taylor A 78*	*Day*	*McDowell*	*Lampard*	*Bonds*	*Taylor T*	*Lock*	*Taylor A*	*Paddon*	*Best*	*Brooking*	*Holland*	
							Ref: A Robinson	City dominate the first hour, but fail to take their chances. After Ritchie is brought down in the 32nd minute, Sweeney's double miss from the spot turns the game. Tommy Taylor's encroachment gives Sweeney another chance, but Mervyn Day dives to his right to pull off a fine save.											

FA Cup																			
3	A	COVENTRY	3	L	1-2	0-1	Brolly 78	Cashley	Sweeney	Drysdale	Gow	Collier	Merrick	Tainton	Ritchie	Mann	Brolly	Fear	
	3/1		*15,653 1:14*				*Cross 14, Merrick 74 (og)*	*Blyth*	*Coop*	*Brogan*	*Craven*	*Dugdale*	*Holmes*	*Cartwright*	*Green**	*Cross*	*Murphy*	*Hutchison*	*Oakley*
							Ref: A Robinson	Despite Fear shooting against the bar at the start, Coventry dominate the first half, but after the break the tables are turned. Tainton is denied an obvious 71st-min pen on being sent tumbling, but whilst Brolly registers with a screamer, Merrick's headed own-goal keeps City out of the hat.											

		Home					Away					
	P	W	D	L	F	A	W	D	L	F	A	Pts
1 Sunderland	42	19	2	0	48	10	[illegible]	6	10	19	26	56
2 BRISTOL CITY	42	11	7	3	34	14	[illegible]	8	5	25	21	53
3 West Brom	42	10	9	2	29	12	[illegible]	4	7	21	21	53
4 Bolton	42	12	5	4	36	14	[illegible]	7	6	28	24	52
5 Notts Co	42	11	6	4	33	13	[illegible]	5	8	27	28	49
6 Southampton	42	18	2	1	49	16	[illegible]	5	13	17	34	49
7 Luton	42	13	6	2	38	15	[illegible]	4	11	23	36	48
8 Nott'm Forest	42	13	1	7	34	18	[illegible]	11	6	21	22	46
9 Charlton	42	11	5	5	40	34	[illegible]	7	10	21	38	42
10 Blackpool	42	9	9	3	26	22	[illegible]	5	11	14	27	42
11 Chelsea	42	7	9	5	25	20	[illegible]	7	9	28	34	40
12 Fulham	42	9	8	4	27	14	4	6	11	18	33	40
13 Orient	42	10	6	5	21	12	3	8	10	16	27	40
14 Hull	42	9	5	7	29	23	5	6	10	16	26	39
15 Blackburn	42	8	6	7	27	22	4	8	9	18	28	38
16 Plymouth	42	13	4	4	36	20	[illegible]	8	13	12	34	38
17 Oldham	42	11	8	2	37	24	2	4	15	20	44	38
18 Bristol Rov	42	7	9	5	20	15	4	7	10	18	35	38
19 Carlisle	42	9	8	4	29	22	3	5	13	16	37	37
20 Oxford	42	7	7	7	23	25	4	4	13	16	34	33
21 York	42	8	3	10	28	34	2	5	14	11	37	28
22 Portsmouth	42	4	6	11	15	23	5	1	15	17	38	25
	924	229	131	102	684	422	[illegible]	131	229	422	684	924

Odds & ends

Double wins: (4) Blackburn, Oldham, York, Portsmouth.
Double losses: (1) Nott'm Forest.

Won from behind: (2) Blackburn (a), Oldham (a).
Lost from in front: (1) Blackpool (a).

High spots: Beating York 4-1 at Ashton Gate.
Winning 1-0 v West Brom at the Hawthorns.
Brilliant display v Hull at Ashton Gate.
Clinching promotion with a 1-0 home success over Portsmouth.
Beating Bristol Rov (h) 3-2 in the Gloucestershire Cup Final on 4 May.

Low spots: Losing out on the Championship due to a poor end of season. run that saw six points dropped in the last five games.

Player of the Year: The Whole Team.
Ever presents: (5) Ray Cashley, Gerry Gow, Geoff Merrick, Tom Ritchie, Trevor Tainton.
Hat-tricks Paul Cheesley (1), Tom Ritchie (1).
Leading scorer: Tom Ritchie (18).

	Appearances						Goals			
	Lge	*Sub*	LC	*Sub*	FAC	*Sub*	Lge	LC	FAC	Tot
Brolly, Mike	**14**	*1*	2		1		**1**		1	**2**
Cashley, Ray	**42**		2		1					
Cheesley, Paul	**38**		2				**15**	1		**16**
Collier, Gary	**40**		2		1		**1**			**1**
Drysdale, Brian	**39**		2		1					
Emanuel, John	**3**	*1*								
Fear, Keith	**13**	*2*			1					
Gillies, Donnie	**22**	*3*		*2*			**1**			**1**
Gow, Gerry	**42**		2		1		**5**			**5**
Harding, Steve	**2**									
McNeil,		*2*								
Mann, Jimmy	**30**	*6*	2		1		**7**			**7**
Merrick, Geoff	**42**		2		1		**2**			**2**
Ritchie, Tom	**42**		2		1		**18**			**18**
Sweeney, Gerry	**32**	*2*	2		1		**5**			**5**
Tainton, Trevor	**42**		2		1					
Whitehead, Clive	**19**	*3*					**4**			**4**
17 players used	**462**	***20***	**22**	***2***	**11**		**59**	**1**	**1**	**61**

No	Date	Att	Pos	Pt	F-A	H-T	Scorers, Times, and Referees	1	2	3	4	5	6	7	8	9	10	11	12 sub used
1	A ARSENAL			W	1-0	0-0	Cheesley 65	Cashley	Sweeney	Drysdale	Gow	Collier	Merrick	Tainton	Ritchie	Mann	Cheesley	Whitehead	
	21/8	41,082		2				Rimmer	Rice	Nelson	Ross	O'Leary	Simpson	Ball	Armstrong	MacDonald	Radford	Cropley*	Storey
							Ref: G Kew	City fans are in dreamland as their favourites make a winning return to the top flight. Full of running, poise and flair, City outclass Arsenal, but squander many excellent chances until Whitehead's cross sets up Cheesley to ram an eight-yard header into the net to clinch a famous victory.											
2	H STOKE			D	1-1	0-0	Gillies 49	Cashley	Sweeney	Drysdale	Gow	Collier	Merrick	Tainton	Ritchie	Mann	Cheesley*	Whitehead	Gillies
	24/8	25,316		3			Smith 86	Shilton	Dodd	Pejic	Mahoney	Smith	Bloor	Salmons	Greenhoff	Conroy	Hudson	Crooks*	Bowers
							Ref: D Lloyd	A phantom turnstile perhaps as an attendance of 32,537 is originally announced? A great City performance as they overcome the early loss of Cheesley after colliding with Peter Shilton. A poor back-pass allows Gillies to shoot past Shilton, but Denis Smith heads in Stoke's equaliser.											
3	A NEWCASTLE		8	D	0-0	0-0		Cashley	Sweeney	Drysdale	Gow	Collier	Merrick	Tainton	Ritchie	Mann	Gillies	Whitehead	
	28/8	31,775	5	4				Mahoney	Nattrass	Kennedy	Hudson	Bird	Nulty	Bar'wclough	Oates	Cannell	Tudor	Craig T*	Howard
							Ref: D Richardson	Unable to match their peerless approach work with any finishing power, City are denied top spot as their penalty appeals, after John Bird's chopping down of Ritchie, are ignored. The Magpies offer little and their futile efforts bring a chorus of slow handclapping from their fans.											
4	H SUNDERLAND		2	W	4-1	3-1	Mann 30, Tainton 34, Ritchie 42, [Gillies 56]	Cashley	Sweeney	Drysdale	Gow	Collier	Merrick	Tainton	Ritchie*	Mann	Gillies	Whitehead	Fear
	4/9	20,865	17	6			Robson 41	Swinburne	Ashurst	Bolton	Towers	Clarke	Moncur	Kerr	Hughes	Greenwood	Robson	Train	
							Ref: J Taylor	City equal their highest-ever League position as Sunderland are mesmerised. Bryan Robson's splendid cross-drive is the visitors' only response as Mann's tremendous 23-yarder, Tainton's half-volley, Ritchie's header, and Gillies' low shot from 20 yards bring City a scintillating success.											
5	A MANCHESTER C		7	L	1-2	0-2	Fear 85	Cashley	Sweeney	Drysdale	Gow	Collier	Merrick	Tainton	Ritchie*	Mann	Gillies	Whitehead	Fear
	11/9	35,891	3	6			Tueart 27, Barnes 28	Corrigan	Docherty	Donachie	Doyle	Watson	Conway	Barnes	Kidd	Royle	Hartford	Tueart	
							Ref: R Perkin	A cold windy afternoon at Maine Road as Dennis Tueart chips Cashley for the opener, and then Peter Barnes leaves defenders floundering before finishing with a low cross-shot. Fear calmly slots in Whitehead's pull-back, but it is too late for City, who top the Fair Play League.											
6	H WEST HAM		5	D	1-1	1-0	Fear 10	Cashley	Sweeney	Drysdale	Gow	Collier	Merrick	Tainton	Fear	Mann	Gillies	Whitehead	
	18/9	28,535	20	7			Taylor A 69	Day	Coleman	Lampard*	Bonds	Green	Taylor T	Jennings	Paddon	Taylor A	Brooking	Holland	McGiven
							Ref: L Burden	The PG Tips performing chimps do their act before the match, but as they depart, the idiots fighting in the Covered End take over. Ten-man West Ham overcome the loss of Pat Holland with a broken shin just before half-time to gain a well-merited point when Alan Taylor shoots in.											
7	A EVERTON		10	L	0-2	0-0		Cashley	Sweeney	Drysdale	Gow	Collier	Merrick	Tainton	Ritchie	Mann	Gillies	Whitehead	
	25/9	25,761	6	7			Dobson 72, Latchford 88	Davies	Darracott	Jones	Lyons	McNaught	Hamilton	King	Dobson	Latchford	Goodlass	Telfer	
							Ref: R Newsome	City are badly missing their injured striker Paul Cheesley. A skilful midfield display, but City never look like pulling back Martin Dobson's header and Bob Latchford's shot, though Dai Davies was forced to make a brilliant save to keep out Garry Collier's first-half shot on the turn.											
8	H IPSWICH		16	L	1-2	0-1	Tainton 53	Cashley	Sweeney	Drysdale	Gow	Collier	Merrick	Tainton	Ritchie	Mann	Gillies*	Whitehead	Fear
	2/10	21,022	8	7			Whymark 32, Osborne 72	Cooper	Burley	Mills	Talbot	Hunter	Beattie	Osborne	Gates*	Bertschin	Whymark	Woods	Lambert
							Ref: T Spencer	Playing with stitches in his face following a nightclub incident, Cashley's shaky display hands the points to cultured Ipswich. Failure to call gifts Bertschin the chance to slot the ball in, then, after Tainton's 25-yard equaliser, his weak punch allows Roger Osborne to head the winner.											
9	H LEICESTER		19	L	0-1	0-0		Bond	Sweeney	Drysdale	**Bain**	Collier	Merrick*	Tainton	Ritchie	Mann	Gillies	Whitehead	Fear
	16/10	19,746	10	7			Worthington 59	Wallington	Whitworth	Rofe	Kember	Sims	Woollett	Weller	Sammels	Worthington	Alderson	Garland	
							Ref: L Shapter	Leicester have the greater skill and deserve Frank Worthington's winner when he slides in a simple chance after Chris Garland's sits on the ball in a mêlée. Bond impresses in goal for punchless City, whilst debutant Bain takes the eye with his unruffled play and cultured passing.											
10	A ASTON VILLA		20	L	1-3	1-0	Ritchie 26	Bond	Sweeney	Drysdale	Gow*	Collier	Rodgers	Tainton	Ritchie	Mann	Gillies	Whitehead	McNeill
	23/10	37,094	2	7			Nicholl 52, Gidman 65, Graydon 80	Burridge	Gidman	Smith	Phillips	Nicholl	Mortimer	Graydon	Little	Gray	Cropley	Carrodus	
							Ref: R Kirkpatrick	A gripping match at Villa Park is turned upside down by Bond's groin muscle strain shortly after Ritchie's eight-yarder puts City in front. Villa take the points with headed goals from Chris Nicholl and John Gidman, and a great twelve-yard shot on the turn from Ray Graydon.											

No	Venue / Date	Opponent / Att	Pos	Pts	Res	HT	Scorers, Times, and Referees	1	2	3	4	5	6	7	8	9	10	11	subs used
11	H	BIRMINGHAM	20	L	0-1	0-0		**Shaw**	Gillies	Drysdale	Sweeney	Collier	Merrick	Tainton	Ritchie	Mann	Cheesley	Whitehead	
	26/10	21,474	*10*	7			*Burns 71*	*Latchford*	*Rathbone*	*Page*	*Emmanuel*	*Gallagher*	*Pendrey*	*Jones*	*Francis*	*Burns*	*Hibbitt*	*Connolly*	
							Ref: R Crabb	The crowd look to Cheesley to restore City's fortunes, but he plainly isn't fit after his serious injury sustained against Stoke nine weeks ago. Keeper Shaw looks impressive on his debut, but in being unable to hold a Trevor Francis drive, sets up Kenny Burns to run the ball in.											
12	A	DERBY	20	L	0-2	0-1		Shaw	Sweeney	Merrick	Bain	Collier	**Hunter**	Tainton	Ritchie	Mann	Gillies	Whitehead	
	30/10	*22,252*	*17*	7			*George 17, Hector 83*	*Moseley*	*Thomas*	*Newton*	*Macken*	*McFarland*	*Todd*	*Powell*	*King*	*Rioch*	*George**	*James*	*Hector*
							Ref: T Bosi	England international Norman Hunter (Leeds £40,000) adds authority to City's defence, despite being booked in the 32nd minute for his late tackle on Charlie George. County deservedly take the points thanks to George's clever header, and Kevin Hector's perfect volley.											
13	H	COVENTRY	20	D	0-0	0-0		Shaw	Gillies	Merrick	Sweeney	Collier	Hunter	Tainton	Ritchie	Mann	Fear	Whitehead	
	6/11	17,306	*15*	8				*Blyth*	*Coop*	*McDonald*	*Yorath*	*Lloyd*	*Holmes*	*Beck*	*Murphy*	*Ferguson*	*Powell*	*Hutchison*	
							Ref: C Thomas	Only Ritchie manages to cause Jim Blyth any problems early on, but after the break the rapport between Merrick, with his overlapping play, and Fear gets City moving. Unfortunately, despite a five-fold increase in the shots ratio, City have to settle for a draw as the goals don't come.											
14	A	TOTTENHAM	19	W	1-0	0-0	Fear 84	Shaw	Gillies	Merrick	Sweeney	Collier	Hunter	Tainton	Ritchie	Mann	Fear	**Cormack**	
	13/11	*28,795*	*20*	10				*Jennings*	*Naylor*	*Gorman*	*Hoddle*	*Young*	*Osgood*	*Conn*	*Perryman*	*Duncan*	*Pratt*	*Taylor*	
							Ref: K Baker	In the day's only First Division game City easily contain Spurs, but despite the presence of Peter Cormack (Liverpool £50,000), offer little in attack themselves. City only manage one shot on target, but this is enough to clinch their unlikely win as Fear slides in Merrick's low cross.											
15	H	NORWICH	17	W	3-1	2-0	Ritchie 34, Cormack 40, Sweeney 47p	Shaw	Gillies	Merrick*	Sweeney	Collier	Hunter	Tainton	Ritchie	Fear	Cormack	Whitehead	Mann
	20/11	19,243	*18*	12			*Boyer 79*	*Keelan*	*Ryan*	*Sullivan*	*Paddon*	*Jones*	*Powell*	*Neighbour*	*Osgood*	*Boyer*	*Suggett*	*Peters*	
							Ref: A Robinson	Shortly after Ritchie knocks the ball over the line following a goalmouth scramble, Cormack celebrates his home debut with an easy tap-in. Phil Boyer gives Shaw no chance with his close-in shot, but by then Jim Ryan's holding of Ritchie had brought City the reward of a penalty.											
16	A	LIVERPOOL	19	L	1-2	1-1	Ritchie 25	Shaw	Gillies	Merrick	Sweeney	Collier	Hunter	Tainton	Ritchie	Fear*	Cormack	Whitehead	Mann
	27/11	***44,323***	*1*	12			*Keegan 45, Jones 56*	*Clemence*	*Neal*	*Jones*	*Thompson*	*Kennedy*	*Hughes*	*Keegan*	*McDermott*	*Heighway*	*Toshack*	*Callaghan*	
							Ref: G Nolan	Beaten, but not disgraced at Anfield, where Ritchie gives Liverpool a jolt with an early lob over Ray Clemence. Denied a pen when Joey Jones floors Ritchie, City are rocked by Kevin Keegan's headed equaliser just two mins later. Jones fires in from 25 yards for Pool's hard-earned win.											
17	H	MIDDLESBROUGH	19	L	1-2	0-1	Merrick 48	Shaw	Gillies	Merrick	Sweeney	Collier*	Hunter	Tainton	Fear	Garland	Cormack	Whitehead	Mann
	18/12	**15,145**	*9*	12			*Armstrong 24p, Brine 53*	*Platt*	*Craggs*	*Cooper*	*Souness*	*Boam*	*Maddren*	*McAndrew*	*Mills*	*Brine*	*Wood**	*Armstrong*	*Boersma*
							Ref: R Perkin	A pre-match Christmas Concert and a half-time circus display fails to attract the fans, who will have to watch Match of the Day. Merrick gets his revenge for a disputed penalty, when he is adjudged to have tripped David Mills, by equalising with a low left-foot shot from twelve yards.											
18	A	WEST BROM	19	D	1-1	0-0	Ritchie 59	Shaw	Gillies	Merrick	Sweeney	Collier	Hunter	Tainton	Ritchie	Garland*	Cormack	Whitehead	Fear
	27/12	*30,497*	*10*	13			*Cross 53*	*Osborne*	*Mulligan*	*Robson*	*Brown T*	*Wile*	*Robertson*	*Martin*	*Treacy*	*Cross*	*Trewick*	*Johnston*	
							Ref: A Jones	A hard-earned point by methodical City at the Hawthorns. Ray Treacy heads against the bar for Albion in the 29th minute, but it isn't until after the break that the goals come. After David Cross heads the Baggies in front, Ritchie knocks in Whitehead's cross for City's equaliser.											
19	A	MANCHESTER U	20	L	1-2	1-0	Fear 4	Shaw	Gillies	Merrick	Sweeney	Collier	Hunter	Tainton	Fear	Garland	Cormack*	Whitehead	Gow
	13/1	*43,051*	*9*	13			*Pearson 48, Greenhoff B 80*	*Stepney*	*Nicholl*	*Houston*	*McIlroy*	*Greenhoff B*	*Buchan*	*Coppell*	*Greenhoff J*	*Pearson*	*Macari*	*Hill*	
							Ref: A Hamil	An absorbing contest, in which Fear heads City in front from Whitehead's cross. Dispute over both United goals as Gillies complains of being pushed in the back when Stuart Pearson headed in, while Lou Macari is seemingly offside when Brian Greenhoff deflects in United's winner.											
20	H	ARSENAL	20	W	2-0	1-0	Cormack 22, 63	Shaw	Gillies	Merrick	Sweeney	Collier	Hunter	Tainton	Fear	Garland	Cormack	Whitehead	
	22/1	25,905	*5*	15				*Rimmer*	*Rice*	*Nelson*	*Storey*	*O'Leary*	*Simpson*	*Hudson*	*Brady*	*MacDonald*	*Stapleton*	*Rostron*	
							Ref: M Baker	Breathtaking City complete the double over a skilful, but goal-shy Arsenal. Cormack is denied a hat-trick as Jimmy Rimmer pulls off a magnificent 81st-minute save to keep out his header, but the keeper had no chance with his headed opener or his shot into the net off the bar.											
21	H	NEWCASTLE	20	D	1-1	0-0	Garland 83	Shaw	Gillies	Merrick	Sweeney	Collier	Hunter	Tainton	Fear	Garland	Cormack	Whitehead*	Gow
	5/2	22,995	*8*	16			*Burns 68*	*Mahoney*	*Nattrass*	*Kennedy*	*Cassidy*	*McCaffery*	*Nulty*	*Bar'wclough*	*Cannell**	*Burns*	*Gowling*	*Blackhall*	*Oates*
							Ref: D Civil	Justice is satisfied, given that Garland appeared to have dived, as ex City player Mike Mahoney saves Sweeney's weak penalty just before half-time. Mickey Burns puts Newcastle in front with a superb backheader, but Garland levels by sliding in his first goal since returning to City.											

No	Date		Att	Pos	Pt	F-A	H-T	Scorers, Times, and Referees	1	2	3	4	5	6	7	8	9	10	11	12 sub used
22	A	SUNDERLAND		20	L	0-1	0-0		Shaw	Gillies	Merrick	Sweeney	Collier	Hunter	Gow	Ritchie	Garland	Cormack	Whitehead	
	11/2		*21,407*	*22*	16			*Holden 59*	*Siddall*	*Henderson*	*Bolton*	*Towers**	*Clarke*	*Ashurst*	*Kerr*	*Elliot*	*Holden*	*Lee*	*Rowell*	*Arnott*
								Ref: E Garner	City are the fall guys in this vital relegation clash as not only do Sunderland achieve their first win in 13 League and Cup matches, but they notch their first goal in 1,017 mins of play. Mel Holden does well to nod in Bobby Kerr's deep centre between Shaw and the near post.											
23	H	MANCHESTER C		18	W	1-0	0-0	Garland 51	Shaw	Gillies	Merrick*	Sweeney	Collier	Hunter	Gow	Fear	Garland	Cormack	Whitehead	Tainton
	19/2		27,018	*3*	18				*Corrigan*	*Clements*	*Donachie*	*Doyle*	*Watson*	*Power*	*Owen*	*Kidd*	*Royle*	*Hartford*	*Tueart*	
								Ref: C White	Hunter for England is the cry after an almost faultless display that inspires City to climb out of the bottom three for the first time this year. His chipped free-kick allows Garland to hammer home the only goal from eight yards to end Manchester City's 17-match unbeaten run.											
24	A	WEST HAM		20	L	0-2	0-1		Shaw	Gillies	Merrick	Sweeney	Collier	Hunter	Gow	Fear	Garland*	Cormack	Whitehead	Tainton
	26/2		*29,713*	*18*	18			*Bonds 27p, Merrick 60 (og)*	*Day*	*Bonds*	*Lampard*	*Otulakowski*	*Green*	*Lock*	*Taylor*	*Radford*	*Devonshire*	*Brooking*	*Jennings*	
								Ref: A Turvey	Sweeney's header and a fierce shot on the turn by Gillies are the only efforts to trouble Mervyn Day. A lacklustre game is decided by Billy Bonds' penalty, after Gow sends Alan Taylor sprawling, and Merrick's own-goal as Shaw partially saves Alan Devonshire's cross.											
25	H	EVERTON		21	L	1-2	1-1	Cormack 2p	Shaw	Gillies	Merrick	Sweeney	Collier	Hunter	Gow	Fear*	Garland	Cormack	Whitehead	Ritchie
	5/3		21,108	*15*	18			*Latchford 45, Gillies 68 (og)*	*Lawson*	*Jones*	*Pejic*	*Lyons*	*McNaught*	*King*	*Hamilton*	*Dobson*	*Latchford*	*McKenzie*	*Goodlass*	
								Ref: D Turner	Despite the tonic of Cormack's early penalty at the Open End following Andy King's trip on Whitehead, City fade badly after Bob Latchford's headed equaliser. Gillies firmly steers Latchford's cross into his own net to tie up Everton's deserved success ahead of their League Cup Final.											
26	A	IPSWICH		22	L	0-1	0-0		Shaw	Gillies	Merrick	Sweeney	Collier	Hunter	Ritchie	Mann	Garland	Cormack	Whitehead	
	12/3		*24,548*	*2*	18			*Wark 59p*	*Cooper*	*Burley*	*Mills*	*Talbot*	*Hunter*	*Tibbott*	*Osborne*	*Wark**	*Mariner*	*Whymark*	*Woods*	*Gates*
								Ref: K Baker	City have keeper Shaw to thank for keeping them in this contest, but he can do little about John Wark's penalty after Paul Mariner is brought down by Hunter. Ipswich boss Bobby Robson succinctly sums up City's performance viz – 'they competed all the way, but lacked penetration'.											
27	H	DERBY		22	D	2-2	0-2	Sweeney 63, Fear 85	Shaw	Gillies	Merrick	Sweeney	Collier	Hunter	Mann	Ritchie	Garland*	Gow	Whitehead	Fear
	15/3		18,552	*18*	19			*Daly 28, Hales 34*	*Boulton*	*Langan*	*Webster*	*Daly*	*Daniel*	*Todd*	*Powell*	*Hector*	*Hales*	*George*	*James*	
								Ref: B Daniels	Gillies' switch to centre-forward after the break sparks City's recovery. Derby, so impressive early on when Gary Daly volleyed in from 25 yards, are made to pay for their complacent attitude in the second half. Sweeney's 25-yard shot on the run and Fear's drive earn City's point.											
28	H	QP RANGERS		20	W	1-0	0-0	Collier 78	Shaw	Gillies	Merrick	Sweeney	Collier	Hunter	Tainton	Mann	Fear	Gow	Whitehead	
	19/3		21,956	*15*	21				*Parkes*	*Clement*	*Gillard*	*Hollins*	*McLintock*	*Webb*	*Eastoe*	*Cunningham*	*Masson*	*Bowles**	*Givens*	*Shanks*
								Ref: A Robinson	The brilliance of both keepers restricts the goals in this action-packed thriller. Phil Parkes has no chance as Collier's 12-yard shot on the turn secures City's valuable win, but the game is marred when Stan Bowles sustains a broken ankle on falling awkwardly three minutes from time.											
29	A	LEICESTER		19	D	0-0	0-0		Shaw	Gillies	Merrick	Sweeney	Collier	Hunter	Tainton	Mann	Fear	Gow	Whitehead	
	26/3		*16,454*	*6*	22				*Wallington*	*Whitworth*	*Rofe**	*Kember*	*Woollett*	*May*	*Birchenall*	*Sammels*	*Worthington*	*Alderson*	*Earle*	*Yates*
								Ref: R Capey	Despite the extra shooting practice put in by Fear and Gillies during the week City fail to score for the tenth time this season. This game should have been won with ease, but the fact that only five of City's 16 goal attempts were on target suggests further practice is necessary.											
30	H	ASTON VILLA		20	D	0-0	0-0		Shaw	Gillies	Merrick	Sweeney	Collier	Hunter	Tainton	Mann	Fear*	Gow	Whitehead	Garland
	2/4		27,276	*8*	23				*Burridge*	*Gidman*	*Robson*	*Young*	*Nicholl*	*Mortimer*	*Deehan*	*Little*	*Gray*	*Cropley*	*Carrodus*	
								Ref: D Nippard	City made most of the first-half running, but it takes Sweeney's goal-line clearance to prevent Villa snatching an undeserved 43rd-minute lead. Despite their overall dominance, City create little apart from headers from Gillies and Hunter, which are cleared off the line by John Robson.											
31	H	WEST BROM		20	L	1-2	0-1	Fear 58p	Shaw	Gillies	Merrick	Sweeney	Collier	Hunter	Tainton	Mann	Fear	Gow	Whitehead	
	5/4		23,474	*5*	23			*Hunter 2 (og), Cross 51*	*Godden*	*Mulligan*	*Statham*	*Martin*	*Wile*	*Robertson*	*Robson*	*Cunningham*	*Cross*	*Giles*	*Johnston*	
								Ref: L Shapter	After Hunter steers Derek Statham's cross into his own net, City squander many chances before David Cross shows how to finish with a low cross-drive. Fear's penalty gets City back into the game, but muffs a second spot-kick 13 mins from time when his weak effort is easily saved.											

No	Venue	Opponent	Pos	Res	F-A	H-T	Scorers, Times, Referees	1	2	3	4	5	6	7	8	9	10	11	12
32	A	BIRMINGHAM	22	L	**0-3**	0-2		Shaw	Gillies	Merrick	Sweeney	Collier	Hunter	Tainton	Mann*	Fear	Gow	Whitehead	Garland
9/4		*19,626*	*12*	23			*Francis 11p, 23, 89p*	*Montgomery*	*Calderwood*	*Pendry*	*Kendall*	*Gallagher*	*Want*	*Jones*	*Francis*	*Burns*	*Hibbitt*	*Connolly*	
							Ref: R Chadwick	Ex England boss Alf Ramsay, now a Birmingham director, pays City a back-handed compliment in that 'they play too much football'. City gain no reward for outplaying the Blues after the break and Merrick's handball gifting Trevor Francis his hat-trick recalls first-half nightmares.											
33	H	TOTTENHAM	22	W	1-0	0-0	Cormack 66p	Shaw	Sweeney	Merrick	Gow	Collier	Hunter	Tainton	Ritchie	Garland*	Cormack	Whitehead	Fear
12/4		27,568	*21*	25				*Daines*	*Naylor*	*Holmes**	*Pratt*	*Osgood*	*Perryman*	*Jones*	*Hoddle*	*Armstrong*	*McNab*	*Taylor*	*Keeley*
							Ref: C Thomas	Cormack hands City a lifeline as he sends the keeper the wrong way to put his spot-kick into the right-hand side of the Covered End goal after Terry Naylor floors Whitehead. A well-deserved win for City who are now just two points behind Tottenham with a game in hand.											
34	A	NORWICH	22	L	1-2	1-1	Cormack 40	Shaw	Sweeney	Merrick	Gow	Collier	Hunter	Tainton	Ritchie	Gillies*	Cormack	Whitehead	Mann
16/4		*17,839*	*13*	25			*Peters 11, Reeves 84*	*Keelan*	*Ryan*	*Sullivan*	*Suggett*	*Jones*	*Powell*	*Neighbour**	*Reeves*	*Gibbins*	*Steele*	*Peters*	*Evans*
							Ref: L Hayes	City's enterprising approach work is again wasted by lack of striking power. Martin Peters drives in from 25 yards for the Norwich opener, but after Cormack shoots in City's leveller, Kevin Reeves latches onto Colin Sullivan's impeccable through-ball to knock in a late winner.											
35	A	STOKE	22	D	2-2	1-0	Ritchie 40, Garland 67	Shaw	Sweeney	Merrick	Gow	Collier	Hunter	Tainton	Ritchie*	Garland	Cormack	Whitehead	Fear
20/4		***12,277***	*16*	26			*Smith 56, Bloor 68*	*Shilton*	*Dodd*	*Marsh*	*Mahoney*	*Smith*	*Bloor*	*Robertson*	*Salmons*	*Tudor*	*Crooks*	*Rugglero*	
							Ref: K Styles	Headers by Ritchie and Garland double City's previous best away scoring return this season. Shaw is responsible for both Stoke equalisers, being stranded when Denis Smith heads in Geoff Salmons' inswinger, he is again at fault when Alan Bloor's header squeezes beneath him.											
36	A	QP RANGERS	22	W	1-0	0-0	Ritchie 64	Shaw	Sweeney	Merrick	Gow	Collier	Hunter	Tainton	Ritchie	Garland	Cormack	Whitehead	
26/4		*14,576*	*16*	28				*Parkes*	*Clement*	*Gillard*	*Hollins*	*McLintock*	*Webb*	*Eastoe*	*Francis*	*Masson**	*Kelly*	*Givens*	*Thomas*
							Ref: M Taylor	City turn in a tenacious display against an over-elaborate Rangers side at muddy Loftus Road to claim their first away win in just over five months as Ritchie slides in Garland's pass. Merrick raises a laugh from the rain-drenched fans by rescuing a dog from a large puddle.											
37	A	LEEDS	22	L	0-2	0-1		Shaw	Sweeney	Merrick	Gow	Collier	Hunter	Tainton	Ritchie	Garland	Cormack*	Whitehead	Fear
30/4		*21,461*	*10*	28			*Thomas 9, Gray E 47*	*Stewart*	*Stevenson*	*Gray F*	*Cherry*	*McQueen*	*Madelay*	*Thomas*	*McGhie*	*Jordan**	*Currie*	*Gray E*	*Harris*
							Ref: G Nolan	It looks like the end as this passionless display leaves City three points from safety. Sweeney's suicidal square ball across the edge of his own penalty area sets up Gwyn Thomas to shoot in a debut goal, and later Eddie Gray is at the near post to tap in Gordon McQueen's headed pass.											
38	H	MANCHESTER U	22	D	1-1	1-0	Garland 6	Shaw	Sweeney	Merrick	Gow !	Collier	Hunter	Tainton	Ritchie*	Garland	Gillies	Whitehead	Mann
7/5		28,864	*6*	29			*Greenhoff J 50p*	*Stepney*	*Nicholl*	*Houston**	*Jackson*	*Greenhoff B*	*Buchan*	*Coppell*	*Greenhoff J*	*McCreery*	*Macari*	*Albiston*	*McIlroy !*
							Ref: R Toseland	Utd boss Tommy Docherty is unhappy about City's physical approach, though Stuart Houston 23rd-min departure with a broken leg is due to an awkward fall. After Garland slides the ball in, Whitehead and Ritchie both hit the woodwork before Collier's high kick concedes a penalty.											
39	H	LEEDS	21	W	1-0	0-0	Garland 69	Shaw	Sweeney	Merrick	Mann	Collier	Hunter	Tainton	Ritchie	Garland	Gillies	Whitehead	
10/5		23,335	*10*	31				*Stewart*	*Stevenson*	*Hampton*	*Cherry*	*McQueen*	*Madeley*	*Thomas**	*McNiven*	*Gray F*	*Currie*	*Gray E*	*Harris*
							Ref: T Bune	No sign of the fog that caused this fixture to be abandoned at half-time on 4 December when the score was tied at 0-0. Garland turns in his best display of the season, and he is rewarded by hammering in a twelve-yard left-foot drive from Merrick's free-kick for City's deserved winner.											
40	A	MIDDLESBROUGH	22	D	0-0	0-0		Shaw	Sweeney	Merrick*	Mann	Collier	Hunter	Tainton	Ritchie	Cormack	Gillies	Whitehead	Gow
14/5		*14,849*	*10*	32				*Platt*	*Craggs*	*Bailey*	*Souness*	*Boam*	*Maddren*	*McAndrew*	*Mills*	*Wood**	*Hedley*	*Armstrong*	*Boersma*
							Ref: K Walmsley	The presentation of a silver salver to Jack Charlton to mark the end of his four-year reign as Middlebrough boss is the highlight of a dreadful match. City obtain their first point at Ayresome Park for 68 years, thanks to the crossbar which keeps out a 55th-minute lob from David Mills.											
41	H	LIVERPOOL	19	W	2-1	1-1	Garland 43, 75	Shaw	Gillies	Sweeney	Gow	Collier	Hunter	Tainton	Ritchie	Garland	Mann	Whitehead	
16/5		**37,265**	*1*	34			*Johnson 30*	*Clemence*	*Neal*	*Lindsay*	*Smith*	*Kennedy*	*Hughes*	*Callaghan*	*Case*	*Fairclough*	*Johnson*	*McDermott*	
							Ref: K Burns	Following his diving header to finish off Whitehead's low diagonal pass, Garland gives City a First Division lifeline. He takes full advantage as Ray Clemence pushes the ball onto his head. A great win over the League Champions, who took the lead from David Johnson's header.											
42	A	COVENTRY	18	D	2-2	0-1	Gow 54, Gillies 79	Shaw	Gillies	Sweeney	Gow	Collier	Hunter	Tainton	Ritchie	Garland	Mann	Whitehead*	Cormack
19/5		*36,892*	*19*	35			*Hutchison 15, 52*	*Sealey*	*Oakey*	*McDonald*	*Yorath*	*Holton*	*Coop*	*Beck*	*Wallace*	*Ferguson*	*Powell*	*Hutchison*	
	Home	Away					Ref: R Challis	City gain the necessary point to ensure First Division survival, but against opponents seeking a win to preserve their status it is a close run thing. Recovering from a 0-2 deficit City have Coventry on the ropes, but news of Sunderland's defeat leaves both sides content with a point.											
Average	23,522	27,151																	

League Cup					F-A	H-T	Scorers, Times, and Referees	1	2	3	4	5	6	7	8	9	10	11	12 sub used
2	A	COVENTRY	8	L	0-1	0-1		Cashley	Sweeney	Drysdale	Gow	Collier	Merrick	Tainton	Ritchie	Mann	Gillies	Whitehead	
31/8		*13,878*	*18*				*Ferguson 41*	*Blyth*	*Coop*	*McDonald*	*Craven*	*Holmes*	*Dugdale*	*Cartwright*	*Yorath*	*Ferguson*	*Beck*	*Murphy*	
							Ref: D Reeves												

Despite City's early exit from the League Cup, the fans rise at the end to acclaim their performance. Dominant City rain in 26 goal attempts (twelve on target) compared with Coventry's five (three). Mick Ferguson heads high into the net from eight yards to break City's hearts.

FA Cup					F-A	H-T	Scorers, Times, and Referees	1	2	3	4	5	6	7	8	9	10	11	12 sub used
3	A	IPSWICH	19	L	1-4	0-3	Fear 66	Shaw	Gillies	Merrick	Sweeney	Collier	Hunter	Tainton	Ritchie	Fear	Cormack	Whitehead	
8/1		*25,139*	*2*				*Mariner 16, 37, Whymark 42, Gates 82*	*Cooper*	*Burley*	*Mills*	*Talbot*	*Roberts*	*Beattie*	*Osborne*	*Wark*	*Mariner*	*Whymark**	*Woods*	*Gates*
							Ref: J Hunting												

An inglorious exit as City's defensive attitude costs them dear. Paul Mariner's 20-yard chip to put Ipswich two up is the goal of the match, but his opening header isn't bad either. Fear slides in Tainton's cross for City's sole response as Ipswich extend their unbeaten run to 15 games.

Abandoned League Fixture					F-A	H-T	Scorers, Times, and Referees	1	2	3	4	5	6	7	8	9	10	11	12 sub used
	H	LEEDS	19	-	0-0	0-0		Shaw	Gillies	Merrick	Sweeney	Collier	Hunter	Tainton	Ritchie	Garland	Cormack	Whitehead	
4/12		31,400	*9*					*Harvey*	*Reaney*	*Hampton*	*Cherry*	*McQueen*	*Gray F*	*Lorimer*	*Hankin*	*Jordan*	*Stevenson*	*Gray E*	
		(Abandoned at half-time due to fog)					Ref: B Daniels												

Garland headed a Whitehead cross against the bar shortly before the break, but the biggest Ashton Gate crowd in eleven years cannot see much as the fog came down to obscure much of what was going on. It was hardly surprising, therefore, when the game was abandoned at half-time.

	Home						Away					
	P	W	D	L	F	A	W	D	L	F	A	Pts
1 Liverpool	42	18	3	0	47	11	5	8	8	15	22	57
2 Manchester C	42	15	5	1	38	13	6	9	6	22	21	56
3 Ipswich	42	15	4	2	41	11	7	4	10	25	28	52
4 Aston Villa	42	17	3	1	55	17	5	4	12	21	33	51
5 Newcastle	42	14	6	1	40	15	4	7	10	24	34	49
6 Manchester U	42	12	6	3	41	22	6	5	10	30	40	47
7 West Brom	42	10	6	5	38	22	6	7	8	24	34	45
8 Arsenal	42	11	6	4	37	20	5	5	11	27	39	43
9 Everton	42	9	7	5	35	24	5	7	9	27	40	42
10 Leeds	42	8	8	5	28	26	7	4	10	20	25	42
11 Leicester	42	8	9	4	30	28	4	9	8	17	32	42
12 Middlesbro	42	11	6	4	25	14	3	7	11	15	31	41
13 Birmingham	42	10	6	5	38	25	3	6	12	25	36	38
14 QP Rangers	42	10	7	4	31	21	3	5	13	16	31	38
15 Derby	42	9	9	3	36	18	0	10	11	14	37	37
16 Norwich	42	12	4	5	30	23	2	5	14	17	41	37
17 West Ham	42	9	6	6	28	23	2	8	11	18	42	36
18 BRISTOL CITY	42	8	7	6	25	19	3	6	12	13	29	35
19 Coventry	42	7	9	5	34	26	3	6	12	14	33	35
20 Sunderland	42	9	5	7	29	16	2	7	12	17	38	34
21 Stoke	42	9	8	4	21	16	1	6	14	7	35	34
22 Tottenham	42	9	7	5	26	20	3	2	16	22	52	33
	924	240	137	85	753	430	85	137	240	430	753	924

Odds & ends

Double wins: (3 Arsenal, Tottenham, QP Rangers.
Double losses: (3) Everton, Ipswich, Birmingham.

Won from behind: (1) Liverpool (h).
Lost from in front: (4) Aston Villa (a), Liverpool (a), Manchester U (a), Everton (h).

High spots: Beating Arsenal 1-0 at Highbury.
Destroying Sunderland 4-1 at Ashton Gate.
Winning 1-0 v Queens Park Rangers (a).
Coming from behind to beat Liverpool 2-1 at Ashton Gate.
Drawing 2-2 at Coventry to stay up.
Beating Bristol Rov (a) 1-0 in the Gloucestershire Cup Final on 24 May.

Low spots: Losing 0-2 at Leeds.
Succumbing to Ipswich (a) 1-4 in the FA Cup.
Paul Cheesley's injury v Stoke (h) that ended his promising career.

Player of the year: Norman Hunter.
Ever-presents: (2) Gary Collier, Gerry Sweeney.
Hat-tricks: (0).
Leading scorers: Keith Fear (7), Chris Garland (7).

	Appearances						Goals			
	Lge	*Sub*	LC	*Sub*	FAC	*Sub*	Lge	LC	FAC	Tot
Bain, John	**2**									
Bond, Len	**2**									
Cashley, Ray	**8**		1							
Cheesley, Paul	**3**						**1**			**1**
Collier, Gary	**42**		1		1		**1**			**1**
Cormack, Peter	**19**	*1*			1		**6**			**6**
Drysdale, Brian	**11**		1							
Fear, Keith	**17**	*9*			1		**6**		1	**7**
Garland, Chris	**19**	*2*					**7**			**7**
Gillies, Donny	**36**	*1*	1		1		**3**			**3**
Gow, Gerry	**27**	*3*	1				**1**			**1**
Hunter, Norman	**31**				1					
McNeill, Brian		*1*								
Mann, Jimmy	**25**	*5*	1				**1**			**1**
Merrick, Geoff	**39**		1		1		**1**			**1**
Ritchie, Tom	**29**	*1*	1		1		**7**			**7**
Rodgers, David	**1**									
Shaw, John	**32**				1					
Sweeney, Gerry	**42**		1		1		**2**			**2**
Tainton, Trevor	**36**	*2*	1		1		**2**			**2**
Whitehead, Clive	**41**		1		1					
21 players used	**462**	***25***	**11**		**11**		**38**		**1**	**39**

LEAGUE DIVISION 1 — Manager: Alan Dicks — SEASON 1977-78

No	Date		Att	Pos	Pt	F-A	H-T	Scorers, Times, and Referees	1	2	3	4	5	6	7	8	9	10	11	12 sub used
1	H	WOLVES			L	2-3	1-1	Cormack 37p, 57p	Shaw	Gillies	Merrick	Gow	Collier	Hunter	Tainton	Ritchie	Garland	Cormack	Whitehead	
	20/8		25,291		0			*Carr 20p, Sunderland 65, Patching 73*	*Parkes*	*Palmer*	*Daly*	*Daley*	*Parkin*	*McAlle*	*Patching*	*Carr*	*Richards*	*Kindon*	*Sunderland*	
								Ref: R Crabb	A game of four penalties possibly creates a record of sorts, though Alan Sunderland has to finish off Willie Carr's spot-kick when it hits the bar. Newly-promoted Wolves dominate the midfield and Martin Patching shoots Steve Daley's cross low into the net to tie up their deserved win.											
2	A	NOTT'M FOREST			L	0-1	0-0		Shaw	Sweeney	Merrick*	Gow	Collier	Hunter	Tainton	Ritchie	**Mabbutt**	Cormack	Whitehead	Mann
	23/8		*21,743*		0			*Withe 82*	*Middleton*	*Anderson*	*Clark*	*McGovern*	*Lloyd*	*Burns*	*O'Neill*	*Bowyer*	*Withe*	*Woodcock*	*Robertson*	
								Ref: A Jenkins	City's ultra-defensive display in deploying two sweepers gives 18-year-old Mabbutt few chances to shine on his debut. Forest, who manage five shots on target compared to City's none, are kept at bay until John Robertson's free-kick is headed in by John Withe from ten yards.											
3	A	LEICESTER		18	D	0-0	0-0		Shaw	Sweeney	Merrick	Gow	Collier	Hunter	Tainton	Ritchie	Mabbutt	Cormack	Whitehead	
	27/8		*17,011*	*10*	1				*Wallington*	*Whitworth*	*Rofe*	*Kember*	*Sims*	*Woollett*	*Alderson*	*Sammels*	*Worthington*	*Kelly*	*Weller*	
								Ref: B Daniels	City's weak finishing, only one shot on target, prevents an improved performance not producing more than a draw. Lucky when Jon Sammels twice hits the post within a minute early on, City pay for their good fortune when two pen appeals, following fouls on Whitehead, are ignored.											
4	H	ASTON VILLA		17	D	1-1	0-1	Mabbutt 80	Shaw	Sweeney	Merrick	Gow	Collier	Hunter	Tainton	Ritchie*	Mabbutt	Cormack	Whitehead	Mann
	3/9		22,359	*16*	2			*Little 21*	*Rimmer*	*Gregory*	*Robson*	*Mortimer*	*McNaught*	*Phillips*	*Deehan*	*Little*	*Grey*	*Cropley*	*Carrodus*	
								Ref: D Smith	Villa start the brighter and it is no surprise when Brian Little flicks the ball into the net over Shaw's head, after dashing past Sweeney to take Frank Carrodus' pass in his stride. Mabbutt's superb header from Whitehead's cross is scant reward for City's second-half domination.											
5	A	NORWICH		19	L	0-1	0-0		Shaw	Sweeney	Merrick	Gow	Collier	Hunter	Tainton	Garland*	Mabbutt	Cormack	Whitehead	Mann
	10/9		***12,836***	*9*	2			*Gibbins 86*	*Keelan*	*Ryan*	*Sullivan*	*Machin*	*Jones*	*Powell*	*Neighbour*	*Reeves*	*Busby**	*Suggett*	*Davies*	*Gibbins*
								Ref: P Richardson	City's well-organised defensive display comes to naught as substitute Roger Gibbins heads in Jimmy Neighbour's deep pass from the right for the Canaries' late winner. Tony Powell's 34th-minute trip on Whitehead just outside the penalty area deprives City of their best scoring chance.											
6	H	WEST HAM		17	W	3-2	2-1	Mabbutt 8, Ritchie 24, 66	Shaw	Sweeney	Gillies	Gow	Collier	Hunter	Tainton	Ritchie	Mabbutt	Cormack	Whitehead	
	17/9		21,344	*20*	4			*Robson 7, Pike 87*	*Day*	*Lampard*	*Brush*	*Holland*	*Taylor T*	*Lock*	*Taylor A*	*Robson*	*Curbishley*	*Brooking*	*Devonshire**	*Pike*
								Ref: L Burden	Demonstrating a refreshing attacking tendency, City do well to beat a fluent West Ham side. After Mabbutt heads in to equalise Pop Robson's long-distance opener, Ritchie's 20-yard shot and second-half tap-in put City in charge, until Geoff Pike's late header brings an anxious finale.											
7	A	MANCHESTER C		18	L	0-2	0-1		Shaw	Gillies	Sweeney	Gow	Collier	Hunter	Tainton	Ritchie	Mabbutt	Cormack*	Whitehead	Mann
	24/9		*41,897*	*1*	4			*Barnes 24, Owen 76*	*Corrigan*	*Clements*	*Doyle*	*Owen*	*Watson*	*Booth*	*Barnes*	*Channon*	*Kidd*	*Hartford*	*Power*	
								Ref: R Perkin	After the goal feast in a 4-6 defeat by an England XI on Tuesday, City's attack is off target against the League leaders at Maine Road. Mabbutt admits that he should have scored at least four as wasteful City are punished by a Peter Barnes stab-in and Gary Owen's crisp low 20-yard shot.											
8	H	QP RANGERS		18	D	2-2	1-2	Tainton 31, Cormack 60p	Shaw	Gillies	Sweeney	Mann	Collier	Hunter	Tainton	Ritchie	Mabbutt	Cormack	Whitehead	
	1/10		20,641	*13*	5			*Masson 8, Eastoe 15*	*Parkes*	*Clement*	*Gillard**	*Hollins*	*Needham*	*Abbott*	*Eastoe*	*Busby*	*Masson*	*Bowles*	*Givens*	*Williams*
								Ref: A Lees	A brilliant contest as City recover from Don Masson's left-footed opener and Peter Eastoe's easy tap-in. Tainton is the hero with his first goal for a year, a cracking shot from 20 yards, giving City hope, and winning the penalty when sent tumbling by Ron Abbott's clumsy challenge.											
9	H	LEEDS		17	W	3-2	1-1	Ritchie 21, Mabbutt 65, Hunter 79	Shaw	Gillies	Sweeney	Mann	Collier	Hunter	Tainton	Ritchie	Mabbutt	Cormack	Whitehead	
	8/10		25,514	*8*	7			*Hankin 20, 84*	*Stewart*	*Cherry*	*Gray F*	*Lorimer*	*McQueen*	*Madeley*	*Gray E*	*Hankin*	*Jordan*	*Currie*	*Graham*	
								Ref: A Glasson	Yet another memorable match as City respond to Ray Hankin's first-time drive from the edge of the penalty area. Ritchie coolly eludes Dave Stewart to tuck in an immediate leveller, and Hunter sets the seal on City's success by lashing the ball home through a crowded goalmouth.											
10	A	EVERTON		18	L	0-1	0-1		Shaw	Gillies	Sweeney	Mann	Collier	Hunter	Tainton	Ritchie	Mabbutt	Cormack	Whitehead*	Gow
	15/10		*39,230*	*3*	7			*King 24*	*Wood*	*Jones*	*Pejic*	*Lyons*	*Higgins*	*Buckley**	*King*	*Dobson*	*Latchford*	*Pearson*	*Telfer*	*Darracott*
								Ref: M Lowe	City put up a brave fight at Goodison after Everton threaten to overwhelm them in the first half. Keeper Shaw performs wonders for City, but he is caught out when Bob Latchford's failure to control the ball sets up Andy King for a 20-yard snap-shot that flies in off the inside of a post.											

No	Venue	Opponent	Att	Pos	Pts	F-A	H-T	Scorers, Times, and Referees	1	2	3	4	5	6	7	8	9	10	11	12
11	H	ARSENAL		18	L	0-2	0-1		Shaw	Gillies	Sweeney	Gow	Collier	Merrick	Tainton	Ritchie	Mabbutt	Mann	Whitehead	
22/10			24,864	*8*	7			*Rix 45, MacDonald 90*	*Jennings*	*Rice*	*Nelson*	*Price*	*Young*	*Simpson*	*Brady*	*Hudson*	*MacDonald*	*Stapleton*	*Rix*	
								Ref: K Baker	Alan Dicks blames reaction to Wednesday's stormy encounter at Hibs in the Anglo-Scottish Cup as part of the reason for Arsenal's first away win of the season. Shaw is caught in no man's land by Graham Rix's chip, and Gow's back-pass sets up Malcolm MacDonald to roll the ball in.											
12	A	CHELSEA		20	L	0-1	0-0		Shaw	Sweeney	Merrick	Gow*	Collier	Hunter	Tainton	Ritchie	Gillies	Cormack	Mann	Whitehead
29/10			*22,313*	*17*	7			*Aylott 55*	*Bonetti*	*Harris*	*Wilkins G*	*Britton*	*Droy*	*Wicks*	*Aylott**	*Wilkins R*	*Langley*	*Swain*	*Cooke*	*Walker*
								Ref: P Reeves	City squander their chances at Stamford Bridge where the lively Gillies is unlucky in having a shot cleared off the line as well as being denied by the crossbar. Chelsea are outplayed, but still pocket the points as Charlie Cooke's cross sets up Trevor Aylott to head in their winner.											
13	A	NEWCASTLE		20	D	1-1	0-0	Gillies 78	Shaw	Sweeney	Merrick	Gow	Collier	Hunter	Tainton	Ritchie	Mabbutt*	Gillies	Mann	Whitehead
5/11			*23,321*	*21*	8			*Martin 74*	*Hardwick*	*Nattrass*	*Barker*	*Walker*	*Bird*	*Blackley*	*Barrowclough*	*Martin*	*Burns*	*Gowling*	*Craig*	
								Ref: N Glover	Shortly after Dennis Martin heads in for a makeshift Newcastle side, Gillies nets City's first away goal of the season with a twelve-yard drive through a crowded goalmouth. On top early on, City's best chance is spurned by Mann, who shoots straight at the keeper when clean through.											
14	H	DERBY		19	W	3-1	2-1	Ritchie 32, 45, Gillies 56	Shaw	Sweeney	Merrick	Gow	Collier	Hunter	Tainton	Ritchie	Mabbutt	Gillies	Whitehead	
12/11			20,196	*18*	10			*Rioch 14*	*Middleton*	*Langan*	*Nish*	*Rioch*	*McFarland*	*Todd*	*Powell*	*Hector*	*Hughes*	*Masson*	*Ryan*	
								Ref: B Homewood	Great entertainment, following a minute's silence before the kick-off in respect of Harry Dolman, who died on Wednesday. Ritchie heads in two superb goals to celebrate his 200th game, and Gillies ties up City's success with great 30-yard strike to rival Bruce Rioch's opening effort.											
15	A	LIVERPOOL		19	D	1-1	1-1	Gow 27	Shaw	Sweeney	Merrick	Gow	Collier	Hunter	Tainton	Ritchie	Mabbutt	Mann	Gillies	
19/11			*41,053*	*6*	11			*Dalglish 13*	*Clemence*	*Neal*	*Jones*	*Thompson*	*Kennedy*	*Hughes*	*Dalglish*	*Fairclough*	*Heighway*	*Toshack*	*Callaghan*	
								Ref: A Hamil	Gow's tremendous 30-yard volley gives City heart after Kenny Dalglish's low 16-yard shot had put Liverpool ahead with his first goal in eight games. City, for whom Hunter is inspired, turn in one of their best-ever defensive performances as Pool gain their first point in four games.											
16	H	MIDDLESBROUGH		18	W	**4-1**	2-1	Royle 11, 27, 59, 83	Shaw	Sweeney	Merrick	Gow	Collier	Hunter	Tainton	Ritchie	**Royle**	Gillies	Whitehead*	Cormack
26/11			20,536	*13*	13			*Mills 43*	*Cuff*	*Craggs*	*Cooper*	*Souness*	*Boam*	*Ramage*	*Mahoney*	*Mills*	*Ashcroft*	*McAndrew*	*Armstrong**	*Cummins*
								Ref: A Robson	Joe Royle's remarkable City debut nearly doesn't happen as, following a mix up over transfer forms, he is only cleared to play on the morning of the match. Four goals from four chances, a header followed by a right-footed effort, then two left-footers, guarantees him instant cult status.											
17	A	COVENTRY		17	D	1-1	0-1	Ritchie 79	Shaw	Sweeney	Merrick	Cormack	Collier	Hunter	Tainton	Ritchie	Royle	Gillies	Whitehead	
3/12			*22,307*	*5*	14			*Ferguson 32*	*Blyth*	*Oakey*	*McDonald*	*Yorath*	*Holton*	*Coop*	*Nardiello*	*Wallace*	*Ferguson*	*Powell*	*Hutchison*	
								Ref: K Salmon	City all but overwhelm high-riding Coventry, but glaring misses mean they have to be satisfied with a point. Mick Ferguson drives in from eight yards to put the Sky Blues ahead, but not long after Royle is thwarted by the post, Ritchie taps in as Jim Blyth spills the No 9's shot.											
18	H	IPSWICH		14	W	2-0	1-0	Tainton 5, Gillies 86	Shaw	Sweeney	Merrick	Gow	Collier	Hunter	Tainton	Ritchie	Royle*	Gillies	Whitehead	Mabbutt
10/12			24,375	*11*	16				*Cooper*	*Mills*	*Tibbott*	*Talbot*	*Hunter*	*Osman*	*Gates*	*Viljoen*	*Mariner*	*Wymark*	*Woods*	
								Ref: D Reeves	Having won the Anglo-Scottish Cup on Monday with a 3-2 aggregate win over St Mirren, City extend their unbeaten League run to six games. Tainton's 25-yarder and a late header from Gillies, make up for Paul Cooper diving to his right to save Sweeney's ninth-minute spot-kick.											
19	A	DERBY		16	L	0-1	0-1		Shaw	Sweeney	Merrick	Gow	Collier	Hunter	Tainton	Ritchie	Royle	Gillies	Whitehead	
17/12			*21,802*	*12*	16			*Todd 24*	*Middleton*	*Langan*	*Nish**	*Daly*	*McFarland*	*Todd*	*Curran*	*Hughes*	*Masson*	*George*	*Ryan*	*Powell*
								Ref: M Baker	Royle is robbed of a goal to celebrate his £90,000 transfer from Man City. The referee adjudges that he fouls Colin Todd before coming away with the ball and chipping a brilliant 40th-min right-foot shot over John Middleton. Derby are fortunate to win courtesy of Todd's easy tap-in.											
20	H	WEST BROM		15	W	3-1	0-1	Gow 60, Ritchie 65, 75	Shaw	Sweeney	Merrick	Gow	Collier	Hunter	Tainton	Ritchie	Royle	Gillies	Whitehead*	Mabbutt
26/12			29,292	*6*	18			*Brown T 3*	*Godden*	*Mulligan*	*Statham*	*Brown T*	*Wile*	*Robertson*	*Martin*	*Brown A*	*Regis**	*Robson*	*Johnston*	*Cunninghm*
								Ref: T Reynolds	Ritchie leaves no room for doubt with his 20-yard strike in the 75th minute, after earlier turning Hunter's long-range drive into the net. Tony Brown bursts through on his own for Albion, but Royle frustrates City's first-half efforts to equalise by lofting his spot-kick into the crowd.											
21	A	BIRMINGHAM		16	L	0-3	0-0		Shaw	Gillies	Sweeney	Gow	Collier	Merrick	Tainton	Ritchie	Royle	Mabbutt	Cormack	
27/12			*24,110*	*18*	18			*Gallagher 48, Towers 66, Francis 76*	*Montgomery*	*Calderwood*	*Pendrey*	*Towers*	*Howard*	*Gallagher*	*Page**	*Francis*	*Bertschin*	*Hibbitt*	*Dillion*	*Connolly*
								Ref: D Lloyd	Joe Gallagher fires in Birmingham's first goal in five games, shortly after Ritchie's shot is struck-off because Royle is offside. City, unlucky with Collier's goal claim following a mêlée, are finished off by Trevor Francis, who runs from the halfway line for his 100th League goal.											

No	Date			Att	Pos	Pt	F-A	H-T	Scorers, Times, and Referees	1	2	3	4	5	6	7	8	9	10	11	12 sub used
22		H	NOTT'M FOREST		17	L	1-3	0-2	Mabbutt 72	Shaw	Sweeney	Merrick	Gow	Collier	Hunter	Tainton	Ritchie	Royle	Gillies*	Mann	Mabbutt
	31/12			**31,506**	*1*	18			*Needham 12, W'dcock 26, O'Neill 58*	*Shilton*	*Anderson*	*Barrett*	*McGovern*	*Needham*	*Burns*	*O'Neill*	*Gemmill*	*Withe*	*Woodcock*	*Robertson*	
									Ref: L Shapter	Mabbutt shoots in and also hits the bar near the end as City stage a mini-revival during the final 20 minutes. It is too late however as John Needham's header, Tony Woodcock's cool shot, and Martin O'Neill's great run had put superior Forest on course for their eighth away win.											
23		A	WOLVES		18	D	0-0	0-0		Shaw	Sweeney	Gillies	Gow	Collier	Merrick	Tainton	Ritchie	Royle	Mabbutt	Mann	
	2/1			*25,283*	*15*	19				*Bradshaw*	*Palmer*	*Parkin*	*Daley*	*Hazell*	*McAlle*	*Hibbitt*	*Carr*	*Richards*	*Bell*	*Black*	
									Ref: J Worrall	Stylish City gain a deserved draw at Molineux. Royle is robbed by the linesman who rules Mabbutt is offside as his 20-yarder dips over Paul Bradshaw in the fifth minute, whilst Wolves are unlucky when Alan Black hits a post and Gillies clears off the line from Norman Bell.											
24		H	LEICESTER		17	D	0-0	0-0		Shaw	Sweeney	Merrick	Gow	Collier	Hunter	Tainton	Ritchie	Royle	Mabbutt	Whitehead	
	14/1			19,458	*22*	20				*Wallington*	*Williams*	*Rofe*	*Kelly*	*Sims*	*Webb*	*Goodwin*	*Earle*	*Smith*	*Salmons*	*Armstrong*	
									Ref: C Downey	The Ashton Gate pitch presents a sorry spectacle to Match of the Day viewers as it is a morass of sand, mud and peat, following yesterday's decision to protect the surface in case of frost. Royle misses City's three best chances, but a draw is a fair result for a dull, unexciting game.											
25		A	ASTON VILLA		18	L	0-1	0-0		Shaw	Sweeney	Merrick	Gow	Collier	Hunter	Tainton	Ritchie	Royle	Gillies*	Whitehead	Mann
	28/1			*29,676*	*10*	20			*Deehan 80*	*Rimmer*	*Gidman*	*Smith*	*Phillips*	*McNaught*	*Mortimer*	*Craig*	*Little*	*Deehan*	*Cowans*	*Carrodus*	
									Ref: R Lewis	John Deehan punishes wasteful City with an easy paced shot from 20 yards after wrong footing Hunter. A combination of Jimmy Rimmer's excellent goalkeeping and abysmal finishing, notably by Ritchie, Royle and Gillies, make City's superior performance count for naught.											
26		H	NORWICH		17	W	3-0	3-0	Ritchie 10, Royle 13, Whitehead 15	Shaw	Sweeney	Merrick	Gow	Collier	Hunter	Mann	Ritchie	Royle	Cormack	Whitehead	
	4/2			**16,993**	*10*	22				*Keelan*	*Bond*	*Sullivan*	*Ryan*	*Jones*	*Powell*	*Maguire*	*Suggett*	*Gibbins*	*Reeves**	*Peters*	*Neighbour*
									Ref: R Crabb	Royle notches his first goal since his debut, a simple tap-in after Whitehead's fierce low-hit centre cannons off David Jones. The pitch, which cuts up badly, is blamed for curtailing City's breathtaking opening following Whitehead's rasping left-foot drive into the top corner of the net.											
27		A	MANCHESTER U		15	D	1-1	1-1	Cormack 42	Shaw	Sweeney	Merrick	Gow	Collier*	Hunter	Mann	Ritchie	Royle	Cormack	Whitehead	Tainton
	8/2			***43,457***	*11*	23			*Hill 28p*	*Roche*	*Nicholl*	*Albiston*	*McIlroy*	*Houston*	*Buchanan**	*Coppell*	*Jordan*	*Pearson*	*Macari*	*Hill*	*Greenhoff J*
									Ref: C Seel	The magnificent seven (six City) is the bookings tally, among whom are Ritchie and Cormack who dispute the award of Gordon Hill's penalty following Merrick's heading duel with Joe Jordan. Cormack side-steps two players before crashing in City's deserved equaliser from six yards.											
28		A	WEST HAM		14	W	2-1	1-1	Mann 45, Royle 62	Shaw	Sweeney	Merrick	Gow	Rodgers	Hunter	Mann	Ritchie	Royle	Cormack	Whitehead	
	11/2			*19,934*	*19*	25			*Robson 13*	*Day*	*McDowell*	*Lampard*	*Bonds*	*Taylor T*	*Green*	*Devonshire*	*Robson*	*Cross*	*Brooking*	*Hales**	*Taylor A*
									Ref: C Thomas	City have reserve centre-half David Rodgers to thank for their first away win of the season. He outjumps everyone in the Hammers' penalty area to set up Royle to head in the decisive goal, after Mann had equalised with one of his typical power drives from all of 25 yards.											
29		H	MANCHESTER C		12	D	2-2	2-1	Royle 1, 6	Shaw	Sweeney	Merrick	Gow*	Rodgers	Hunter	Mann	Ritchie	Royle	Cormack	Whitehead	Tainton
	17/2			25,416	*2*	26			*Kidd 23, Shaw 70 (og)*	*Corrigan*	*Clements*	*Donnachie*	*Booth*	*Watson*	*Owen*	*Channon*	*Bell*	*Kidd*	*Harford*	*Barnes*	
									Ref: A Glasson	Royle has the visitors in a spin, as not only does he notch a 45-second header and a great strike, but also brings a great save out of Joe Corrigan as well as hitting the post. Man City's fight-back gains a deserved point when Tommy Booth's shot hits the post and rebounds in off Shaw.											
30		A	QP RANGERS		13	D	2-2	0-1	Gow 53, Sweeney 60	Shaw	Sweeney	Merrick	Gow	Rodgers	Hunter	Tainton	Ritchie	Royle	Mann	Whitehead	
	25/2			*17,051*	*20*	27			*Bowles 17p, Busby 49*	*Parkes*	*Clement*	*Gillard*	*Hollins*	*Howe*	*Abbott*	*Shanks*	*Busby*	*James*	*Bowles*	*Givens*	
									Ref: M Sinclair	Stan Bowles registers with his second spot-kick attempt after Shaw is adjudged to have moved when he fires high over the bar. Gow, unlucky with a 24th-minute shot cleared off the line and a 48th-minute effort that hits the bar, gets City back in the game when squeezing the ball in.											
31		A	LEEDS		11	W	2-0	0-0	Ritchie 53, Gillies 82	Shaw	Sweeney	Merrick	Gow	Rodgers	Hunter	Tainton	Ritchie	Royle	Mann	Whitehead*	Gillies
	4/3			*24,830*	*6*	29				*Harvey*	*Reaney**	*Hampton*	*Flynn*	*Cherry*	*Madeley*	*Gray F*	*Thomas*	*Currie*	*Clarke*	*Graham*	*Parkinson*
									Ref: T Farley	Merrick's vital goal-line clearance to prevent Arthur Graham from scoring, just after the interval, is the game's turning point. Royle is a real handful as City complete a double over Leeds. He sets up Ritchie's half-volley as well as laying on the pass for Gillies to fire in from ten yards.											

32	H	EVERTON	12	L	0-1	0-1		Shaw	Sweeney	Merrick	Gow	Rodgers	Hunter	Tainton	Ritchie	Royle	Mann	Whitehead*	Gillies
11/3		25,614	*2*	29			*Ross 45*	*Wood*	*Jones*	*Pejic*	*Lyons*	*Kenyon*	*Ross*	*King*	*Dobson*	*Latchford*	*McKenzie**	*Thomas*	*Telfer*
							Ref: A Robinson	Despite almost constant pressure Trevor Ross's 25-yard strike in first-half injury-time brings City's six match unbeaten run to a halt. Luckless City have two penalty appeals turned down, while two of Everton's three bookings are for professional fouls that prevent clear runs on goal.											
33	A	ARSENAL	13	L	**1-4**	1-4	Tainton 32 *[Price 23]*	Shaw	Sweeney	Merrick	Gow	Rodgers	Hunter	Tainton	Ritchie	Royle	Mann	Whitehead	
18/3		*28,163*	*4*	29			*Stapleton 11, 38, Sunderland 15,*	*Jennings*	*Rice*	*Nelson*	*Price*	*O'Leary*	*Young*	*Brady*	*Sunderland**	*MacDonald*	*Stapleton*	*Hudson*	*Rix*
							Ref: C Maskell	City are pleased to escape with only a 1-4 drubbing following Arsenal's opening three-goal salvo. Tainton's right-foot shot from the edge of the penalty area is City's sole reply to Frank Stapleton's six-yard shot, Alan Sunderland's searing drive and David Price's deft header.											
34	H	CHELSEA	11	W	3-0	2-0	Cormack 27p, Gow 38, Rodgers 80	Shaw	Sweeney	Merrick	Gow	Rodgers	Hunter	Tainton !	Ritchie	Royle*	Cormack	Mann	Gillies
21/3		20,062	*15*	31				*Bonetti*	*Locke*	*Harris*	*Britton*	*Droy !*	*Wicks*	*Finnieston**	*Swain*	*Langley*	*Lewington*	*Hay*	*Garner*
							Ref: L Burden	Tainton's 83rd-min dismissal for kicking at Steve Wicks, and Micky Droy's departure two mins later for a savage tackle on Ritchie mars an otherwise thrilling game. Droy's push on Ritchie gifts Cormack his pen, before Gow's delightful chip and a Rodgers header seals City's win.											
35	H	BIRMINGHAM	12	L	0-1	0-1		Shaw	Sweeney !	Merrick	Gow	Rodgers	Hunter	Mann	Ritchie	Gillies	Cormack	Whitehead*	Mabbutt
25/3		21,434	*15*	31			*Francis 31*	*Montgomery*	*Calderwood*	*Pendry*	*Towers*	*Gallagher*	*Howard*	*Page*	*Francis*	*Bertschin*	*Hibbitt**	*Connolly*	*Broadhurst*
							Ref: A Turvey	Despite the sending off of Sweeney for kicking Tony Towers, and the booking of six players (four City), it is not a bad-tempered affair. Trevor Francis secures the Blues victory with a left-foot drive, but Ritchie is unlucky to have his shot disallowed at the death for a dubious handball.											
36	A	WEST BROM	13	L	1-2	1-0	Hunter 42	Shaw	Gillies	Merrick	Gow	Rodgers	Hunter	Tainton	Ritchie	Royle*	Cormack	Mann	Mabbutt
27/3		*23,741*	*8*	31			*Johnston 62, Brown 89*	*Godden*	*Mulligan*	*Statham*	*Brown T*	*Wile*	*Robertson*	*Martin*	*Cunningham*	*Regis*	*Trewick*	*Johnston*	
							Ref: N Midgley	After taking the lead from Hunter's free-kick, City are made to pay the price for slack marking. Willie Johnston intercepts Shaw's short goal-kick to level matters, then Tony Brown cuts in front of Rodgers to lift a through ball into the net from twelve yards for Albion's late winner.											
37	H	NEWCASTLE	14	W	3-1	1-0	Nulty 18 (og), Ritchie 49, Hunter 53	Shaw	Sweeney	Merrick	Gow	Rodgers	Hunter	Tainton	Ritchie	Royle	Cormack	Mann	
1/4		17,142	*22*	33			*Barrowclough 84*	*Mahoney*	*Nattrass*	*Kennedy*	*Barton*	*Bird**	*Blackhall*	*Barrowclough*	*Burns*	*Nulty*	*McGhee*	*Walker*	*Scott*
							Ref: D Civil	Shaw's failure to get his hands to Micky Burns' 36th-minute chipped free-kick is fortuitous as unbeknown to the players the award was indirect. Hunter stars for City with his hard cross ending up in the net off Geoff Nulty, and then getting on the scoresheet with a 15-yard volley.											
38	A	MIDDLESBROUGH	15	L	0-2	0-1		Shaw	**Stevens**	Gillies	Gow	Rodgers	Merrick	Mann	Ritchie	Royle	Cormack	Whitehead*	Mabbutt
8/4		*14,667*	*14*	33			*Ramage 43, Cummins 76*	*Brown*	*Craggs*	*Bailey*	*Mahoney*	*Boam*	*Ramage*	*Mills*	*Cummins*	*Shearer*	*McAndrew*	*Armstrong*	
							Ref: N Ashley	Shaw is pelted by stones and pieces of glass ten minutes from the end, by which time defensive-minded City are already well beaten. Yorkshire fast bowler Alan Ramage prods home Boro's first from ten yards, then Stan Cummins doubles the advantage when Shaw spills a free-kick.											
39	H	LIVERPOOL	15	D	1-1	0-1	Cormack 74	Shaw	Gillies	Merrick	Gow	Rodgers	Hunter	Tainton*	Ritchie	Royle	Cormack	Mann	Mabbutt
15/4		31,244	*4*	34			*Heighway 28*	*Clemence*	*Neal*	*Smith*	*Thompson*	*Kennedy*	*Hughes*	*Dalglish*	*Case*	*Heighway*	*McDermott*	*Souness*	
							Ref: T Bune	A goal that will be remembered for years to come is the accolade as Steve Heighway beats Hunter, Merrick and Shaw in a 70-yard solo run before putting the ball in an open net. After shooting high and wide from a 41st-min penalty, Cormack fires in a left-foot half volley equaliser.											
40	A	IPSWICH	16	L	0-1	0-0		Shaw	Sweeney	Merrick	Gow !	Rodgers	Hunter	Tainton	Ritchie	Royle	Cormack*	Mann	Mabbutt
22/4		*22,579*	*15*	34			*Mills 64*	*Cooper*	*Burley*	*Mills*	*Talbot*	*Hunter*	*Osman*	*Osborne*	*Wark*	*Mariner*	*Geddis*	*Woods*	
							Ref: B Daniels	After Gow's 82nd-min sending off for retaliation following a Russell Osman foul, City nearly save a point when Tainton hits the bar. A poor game, in which Ipswich's thoughts appear focussed on next week's FA Cup Final, is settled by a 20-yarder from the right foot of Mick Mills.											
41	H	MANCHESTER U	16	L	0-1	0-0		Shaw	Sweeney	Merrick	Mann	Rodgers	Hunter	Tainton	Ritchie	Royle	Cormack*	Whitehead	Mabbutt
25/4		26,035	*10*	34			*Pearson 50*	*Roche*	*Albiston*	*Houston*	*McIlroy*	*McQueen*	*Nicholl*	*Coppell*	*Jordan*	*Pearson*	*Grimes*	*Greenhoff B*	
							Ref: T Spencer	Substitute Mabbutt twice almost snatches a goal after coming on for the last twelve minutes, but United hold on to Stuart Pearson's deft back-header that finishes off Ashley Grimes' chipped free-kick. City miss their chances, but in truth are outplayed by much superior opponents.											
42	H	COVENTRY	15	D	1-1	0-0	Royle 61	Shaw	Sweeney	Merrick	Gow	Rodgers	Hunter	Tainton	Ritchie	Royle	Mann	Whitehead*	Mabbutt
29/4		21,191	*7*	35			*Wallace 63*	*Blyth*	*Roberts*	*McDonald*	*Yorath*	*Osgood*	*Coop*	*Green**	*Wallace*	*Ferguson*	*Powell*	*Hutchison*	*Beck*
Average	Home 23,357	Away 25,572					Ref: A Gunn	The chances go begging at Ashton Gate, where Shaw's agile display has the Coventry strikers shaking their heads in exasperation. Royle ends his goal famine to rifle City ahead with a right-footed shot from ten yards, but Ian Wallace quickly equalises with a looping header.											

League Cup	Att	Pos	Res	F-A	H-T	Scorers, Times, and Referees	1	2	3	4	5	6	7	8	9	10	11	12 sub used
2 H STOKE		18	W	1-0	1-0	Mabbutt 9	Shaw	Sweeney	Merick	Gow*	Collier	Hunter	Tainton	Ritchie	Mabbutt	Cormack	Whitehead	Gillies
29/8	11,877	*2:7*					*Shilton*	*Dodd*	*Marsh*	*Kendall*	*Smith*	*Bloor*	*Goodwin*	*Richardson*	*Gregory*	*Waddington*	*Crooks*	
						Ref: M Sinclair	Much prone to over elaboration and sloppy defending, City are fortunate that Stoke are unable to take advantage. Ritchie's determined run, outside of Alan Bloor, to the by-line sets up City's passage to the next round – his chip allowing Mabbutt to head in from seven yards.											
3 A WREXHAM		18	L	0-1	0-0		Shaw	Gillies	Sweeney	Gow	Collier	Merrick	Tainton	Ritchie	Fear*	Mann	Whitehead	Bain
26/10	*10,183*	*3:4*				*Shinton 52*	*Davies*	*Evans*	*Dwyer*	*Davis*	*Roberts*	*Thomas*	*Shinton*	*Sutton*	*Lyons*	*Whittle*	*Cartwright*	
						Ref: B Martin	City are thoroughly outplayed by Third Division opponents who twice hit the woodwork. Scarcely able to move out of their own half due to the sheer pace of Wrexham's attacks, City succumb just after the interval when Bobby Shinton neatly heads in Graham Whittle's cross.											

FA Cup	Att	Pos	Res	F-A	H-T	Scorers, Times, and Referees	1	2	3	4	5	6	7	8	9	10	11	12 sub used
3 H WREXHAM		18	D	4-4	2-2	Mabbutt 6, 89, Ritchie 13, Cormack 83	Shaw	Sweeney	Gillies*	Gow	Collier	Merrick	Tainton	Ritchie	Royle	Mabbutt	Mann	Cormack
7/1	19,644	*3:1*				*Shi'n 18, 68, M'ick 23 (og), McNeil 54*	*Davies*	*Hill*	*Dwyer*	*Davis*	*Roberts*	*Thomas*	*Shinton*	*Sutton*	*McNeil*	*Whittle*	*Griffiths*	
						Ref: R Perkin	City snatch a last-gasp replay as Mabbutt sweeps in a low shot in the final minute. The first six goals are all headers, including Merrick's own-goal to bring Wrexham level. The Welshmen control the game thereafter, until Cormack jabs the ball home to inspire City's late comeback.											
3R A WREXHAM		18	L	0-3	0-3		Shaw	Sweeney	Gillies	Gow	Collier	Merrick	Tainton	Ritchie	Royle	Mabbutt	Cormack	
9/1	*15,614*	*3:1*				*McNeil 25, Whittle 31, Thomas 45*	*Davies*	*Hill*	*Dwyer*	*Davis*	*Cegielski*	*Thomas*	*Shinton*	*Sutton*	*McNeil**	*Whittle*	*Griffiths*	*Lyons*
						Ref: R Perkin	City are fortunate to escape with only a three-goal beating as Bobby Shinton squanders two second-half pens. Dixie McNeil's header, Graham Whittle's scorching 18-yarder and a Mike Thomas' chip complete yet another humiliating visit to the Racecourse ground for Bristol City.											

	P	W	D	L	F	A	W	D	L	F	A	Pts
		Home					Away					
1 Nott'm Forest	42	15	6	0	37	8	10	8	3	32	16	64
2 Liverpool	42	15	4	2	37	11	9	5	7	28	23	57
3 Everton	42	14	4	3	47	22	8	7	6	29	23	55
4 Manchester C	42	14	4	3	46	21	6	8	7	28	30	52
5 Arsenal	42	14	5	2	38	12	7	5	9	22	25	52
6 West Brom	42	13	5	3	35	18	5	9	7	27	35	50
7 Coventry	42	13	5	3	48	23	5	7	9	27	39	48
8 Aston Villa	42	11	4	6	33	18	7	6	8	24	24	46
9 Leeds	42	12	4	5	39	21	6	6	9	24	32	46
10 Manchester U	42	9	6	6	32	23	7	4	10	35	40	42
11 Birmingham	42	8	5	8	32	30	8	4	9	23	30	41
12 Derby	42	10	7	4	37	24	4	6	11	17	35	41
13 Norwich	42	10	8	3	28	20	1	10	10	24	46	40
14 Middlesbro	42	8	8	5	25	19	4	7	10	17	35	39
15 Wolves	42	7	8	6	30	27	5	4	12	21	37	36
16 Chelsea	42	7	11	3	28	20	4	3	14	18	49	36
17 BRISTOL CITY	42	9	6	6	37	26	2	7	12	12	27	35
18 Ipswich	42	10	5	6	32	24	1	8	12	15	37	35
19 QP Rangers	42	8	8	5	27	26	1	7	13	20	38	33
20 West Ham	42	8	6	7	31	28	4	2	15	21	41	32
21 Newcastle	42	4	6	11	26	37	2	4	15	16	41	22
22 Leicester	42	4	7	10	16	32	1	5	15	10	38	22
	924	223	132	107	741	490	107	132	223	490	741	924

Odds & ends

Double wins: (2 West Ham, Leeds.

Double losses: (4) Nott'm Forest, Everton, Arsenal, Birmingham.

Won from behind: (5) West Ham (h), Leeds (h), Derby (h), West Brom (h), West Ham (a).

Lost from in front: (2) West Brom (a), Wolves (h).

High spots: Beating West Ham 3-2 at Ashton Gate on 17 September.

A memorable encounter with Leeds at Ashton Gate on 8 October.

Four goals for Joe Royle on his debut v Middlesbrough on 26 Nov.

Beating Hibernian (h) 5-3 in the Anglo-Scottish Cup on 1 November.

Winning the Anglo-Scottish Cup 3-2 on aggregate v St Mirren.

Beating Bristol Rov (h) 3-0 in the Gloucestershire Cup Final on 2 May.

Low spots: First-half annihilation by Arsenal at Highbury on 18 March.

Losing to Wrexham in both the FA and the FL Cup.

Player of the Year: Norman Hunter.

Ever-presents (1) John Shaw.

Hat-tricks: (1) Joe Royle.

Leading scorer: Tom Ritchie (12).

	Appearances						**Goals**			
	Lge	*Sub*	LC	*Sub*	FAC	*Sub*	**Lge**	LC	FAC	**Tot**
Bain, John				*1*						
Collier, Gary	**27**		2		2					
Cormack, Peter	**25**	*1*	1		1	*1*	**6**		1	**7**
Fear, Keith			1							
Garland, Chris	**2**									
Gillies, Donnie	**24**	*3*	1	*1*	2		**4**			**4**
Gow, Gerry	**37**	*1*	2		2		**4**			**4**
Hunter, Norman	**38**		1				**3**			**3**
Mabbutt, Kevin	**16**	*10*	1		2		**4**	1	2	**7**
Mann, Jimmy	**26**	*5*	1		1		**1**			**1**
Merrick, Geoff	**37**		2		2					
Ritchie, Tom	**41**		2		2		**11**		1	**12**
Rodgers, David	**15**						**1**			**1**
Royle, Joe	**26**				2		**8**			**8**
Shaw, John	**42**		2		2					
Stevens, Paul	**1**									
Sweeney, Gerry	**38**		2		2		**1**			**1**
Tainton, Trevor	**36**	*2*	2		2		**3**			**3**
Whitehead, Clive	**31**	*2*	2				**2**			**2**
(own-goals)							**1**			**1**
19 players used	**462**	*24*	**22**	*2*	**22**	*1*	**49**	**1**	**4**	**54**

No	Date		Att	Pos	Pt	F-A	H-T	Scorers, Times, and Referees	1	2	3	4	5	6	7	8	9	10	11	12 sub used
1	A	BOLTON			W	2-1	0-1	Mann 64, Ritchie 86	Shaw	Sweeney	**Cooper**	Mann	Rodgers	Hunter	Tainton	Ritchie	Royle	Cormack	Garland	
	19/8		*21,355*		2			*Gowling 32*	*McDonagh*	*Nicholson*	*Walsh*	*Greaves*	*Jones P*	*Allardyce**	*Morgan*	*Whatmore*	*Gowling*	*Worthington*	*Train*	*Dunne*
								Ref: R Perkin	City's commitment to a more attacking policy bears early fruit as Ritchie's dribble past three defenders ends with him slotting home a late winner. Newly-promoted Bolton deserve Alan Gowling's fierce opener, but after Mann fires in from almost 25 yards City take control.											
2	H	NORWICH			D	1-1	0-1	Cormack 66p	Shaw	Sweeney	Cooper	Mann	Rodgers	Hunter	Tainton	Ritchie	Royle	Cormack	Garland*	Whitehead
	22/8		19,968		3			*Ryan 45p*	*Keelan*	*Bond*	*Sullivan*	*Ryan John*	*Hoadley*	*Powell*	*Neighbour*	*Reeves*	*Chivers*	*Robson*	*Peters*	
								Ref: M Baker	Hunter has a nightmare first half, getting booked for a foul on Kevin Reeves and then tripping Jimmy Neighbour to concede Norwich's pen. Whitehead peps City, but it takes the rather lucky award of a spot-kick to level matters after Mann's hopeful shot had hit Phil Hoadley's hand.											
3	H	ASTON VILLA		5	W	1-0	0-0	Rodgers 66	Shaw	Sweeney	Gillies	Mann	Rodgers	Hunter	Tainton	Ritchie	Royle	**Pritchard**	Whitehead	
	26/8		23,881	*6*	5				*Rimmer*	*Gidman*	*Smith*	*Evans A*	*McNaught*	*Mortimer*	*Shelton**	*Little*	*Gregory*	*Cowans*	*Carrodus*	*Shaw G*
								Ref: T Spencer	City's new-look side, with Whitehead operating at left-back and Sweeney in midfield, play with greater fluency than in their previous two games. Teenager Pritchard has an outstanding debut and it is from his cross that Rodgers runs in from a deep position to head in City's winner.											
4	A	WOLVES		7	L	0-2	0-1		Shaw	Sweeney	Gillies	Mann	Rodgers	Hunter	Tainton	Ritchie	Royle*	Gow	Whitehead	Cormack
	2/9		*16,121*	*19*	5			*Rodgers 13 (og), Hibbitt 85*	*Bradshaw*	*Daniel*	*Palmer*	*Parkin*	*Berry*	*McAlle*	*Hibbitt*	*Carr*	*Richards*	*Bell*	*Daley*	
								Ref: R Chadwick	Rodgers sets Wolves on the way to their first win of the season, glancing Willie Carr's cross off of his head into the net. Despite controlling midfield City fail to create many chances, though Paul Bradshaw has to be at his best in the closing seconds to save Gow's close-range shot.											
5	A	TOTTENHAM		12	L	0-1	0-1		Shaw	Sweeney	Gillies	Mann	Rodgers	Hunter	Tainton	Ritchie	Royle	Gow	Whitehead	
	9/9		*34,035*	*15*	5			*Rodgers 19 (og)*	*Daines*	*McAllister*	*Gorman*	*Holmes*	*Lacy*	*Perryman*	*Villa*	*Ardiles*	*Lee*	*Pratt*	*Taylor*	
								Ref: C Maskell	Woeful finishing prevents City benefiting from their classy approach play as Spurs are often outplayed. It is City who turn on the Argentinian style soccer for the Match of the Day viewers, but Rodgers gifts Tottenham the points, flicking the ball into the net for yet another own-goal.											
6	H	SOUTHAMPTON		8	W	3-1	1-1	Rodgers 21, Ritchie 74, 88	Shaw	Sweeney	Gillies	Gow	Rodgers	Hunter	Tainton	Ritchie	Royle*	Cormack	Mabbutt	Mann
	16/9		21,795	*12*	7			*Holmes 40*	*Wells*	*Golac*	*Peach*	*Williams*	*Nicholl*	*Waldron*	*Ball*	*Boyer*	*MacDougall**	*Holmes*	*Curran*	*Hayes*
								Ref: A McDonald	Four bookings for City and one for Southampton as petulance predominates in the oppressive heat. In a game of few chances it is curious that all the shots on target produce goals. Rodgers opens the scoring with a powerful header that bounces down over the line after hitting the bar.											
7	A	IPSWICH		6	W	1-0	0-0	Ritchie 66p	Shaw	Sweeney	Gillies	Gow	Rodgers	Hunter	Tainton	Ritchie	Royle	Mann	Mabbutt	
	23/9		*19,054*	*18*	9				*Cooper*	*Burley*	*Mills*	*Talbot*	*Osman*	*Beattie*	*Wark*	*Muhren*	*Mariner*	*Whymark**	*Woods*	*Brazil*
								Ref: B Daniels	The only surprise is that it takes a spot-kick to decide this game as City carve out a host of chances with Mabbutt (twice) and Mann being thwarted by the woodwork. Ritchie places his first-ever penalty low to Paul Cooper's left following on from Kevin Beattie's tug on Mabbutt.											
8	H	EVERTON		5	D	2-2	2-1	Gow 4, Hunter 23	Shaw	Sweeney	Gillies	Gow	Rodgers	Hunter	Tainton	Ritchie	Royle	Mann	Mabbutt	
	30/9		22,502	*2*	10			*Latchford 11, 67*	*Wood*	*Todd*	*Pejic*	*Lyons*	*Wright*	*Ross*	*King*	*Dobson*	*Latchford*	*Walsh*	*Thomas !*	
								Ref: L Shapter	City lose their way after David Thomas is sent off for dissent when the referee refuses penalty claims following Sweeney's 51st-minute handball. Bob Latchford rescues a point for Everton by hammering the ball into the net when Mickey Walsh's header rebounds off the post.											
9	A	QP RANGERS		9	L	0-1	0-0		Shaw	Sweeney	Gillies	Gow	Rodgers	Hunter	Tainton	Ritchie	Royle	Mann	Whitehead	
	7/10		*15,707*	*15*	10			*Busby 90*	*Parkes*	*Shanks*	*Gillard*	*Hollins*	*Howe*	*Cunningham*	*Eastoe*	*Francis*	*Harkouk**	*Bowles*	*McGee*	*Busby*
								Ref: M Taylor	City's unwillingness to settle for a point costs them dear in the dying seconds as they are caught out by a Rangers counter attack. Don Shanks' centre is missed by two defenders and Peter Eastoe heads the ball back for Martyn Busby to fire in a low drive past Shaw from 20 yards.											
10	H	NOTT'M FOREST		11	L	1-3	1-2	Ritchie 11p	Shaw	Sweeney	Gillies*	Gow	Rodgers	Hunter	Tainton	Ritchie	Royle	Mann	Mabbutt	Whitehead
	14/10		26,947	*3*	10			*Birtles 4, Robertson 25p, 54p*	*Shilton*	*Anderson*	*Clark*	*McGovern*	*Lloyd*	*Burns*	*O'Neill*	*Gemmill*	*Birtles*	*O'Hare*	*Robertson*	
								Ref: C Thomas	A magnificent game, but City are unable to stop Forest extending their record unbeaten run to 36 games, despite twice hitting the woodwork and dominating the corner count 19-2. Garry Birtles scores the only goal from open play when shooting in a left-footed opener from ten yards.											

No	Venue	Opponent / Date	Att	Pos	Res / Pts	F-A	H-T	Scorers, Times, and Referees	1	2	3	4	5	6	7	8	9	10	11	12
11	A	MANCHESTER U		9	W	3-1	1-0	Mabbutt 11, 50, 88	Shaw	Sweeney	Gillies	Gow	Rodgers	Hunter	Tainton	Ritchie	Royle	Mann	Mabbutt	
		21/10	*47,211*	*6*	12			*Greenhoff J 70*	*Roche*	*Albiston*	*Houston*	*McIlroy**	*McQueen*	*Buchan*	*Coppell*	*Greenhoff J*	*Jordan*	*Macari*	*Grimes*	*Greenhoff B*
								Ref: J Butcher	Mabbutt breaks his away scoring duck in style by firing in a hat-trick. City give United's collection of stars a lesson in team work at Old Trafford where Shaw saves Jimmy Greenhoff's controversial penalty after Tainton is harshly adjudged to have pushed Sammy McIlroy.											
12	H	ARSENAL		11	L	1-3	1-2	Rodgers 29	Shaw	Sweeney	Gillies	Gow	Rodgers	Hunter	Tainton	Ritchie	Whitehead	Mann*	Mabbutt	Bain
		28/10	26,958	*7*	12			*Brady 15, 60p, Stapleton 27*	*Jennings*	*Rice*	*Nelson*	*Price*	*O'Leary**	*Young*	*Brady*	*Gatting*	*Stapleton*	*Heeley*	*Rix*	*Walford*
								Ref: A Hamil	With Royle out with a groin strain his heading ability is sorely missed as City's attack fails to function. Liam Brady provides the best display of individual artistry seen for years at Ashton Gate, and it's his fall on being challenged by Hunter that produces the spot-kick that kills City off.											
13	A	MIDDLESBROUGH		11	D	0-0	0-0		Shaw	Sweeney	Gillies	Gow	Rodgers	Hunter	Tainton	Ritchie	Royle	Bain	Mabbutt	
		4/11	20,461	*14*	13				*Stewart*	*Craggs*	*Bailey*	*Mahoney*	*Boam*	*McAndrew*	*Proctor*	*Mills*	*Hodgson*	*Burns*	*Armstrong*	
								Ref: P Richardson	A poor game at Ayresome Park, where City are unlucky in the 27th minute when Royle has his full-blooded header struck off for climbing over Stuart Boam. City's defence deals easily with Boro's efforts to extend their three-match winning run, but offer little in attack themselves.											
14	H	BOLTON		10	W	4-1	1-1	Ritchie 45, Royle 57, 58, Rodgers 84	Shaw	Sweeney	Gillies	Gow	Rodgers	Hunter	Tainton	Ritchie	Royle	Bain*	Mabbutt	Whitehead
		11/11	18,608	*19*	15			*Walsh 4*	*McDonagh*	*Nicholson*	*Dunne**	*Greaves*	*Walsh*	*Smith*	*Morgan*	*Reid*	*Gowling*	*Worthington*	*McNab*	*Whatmore*
								Ref: A Robinson	Royle opens his goal account for the season with a crisp 18-yarder that Peter Nicholson deflects into the net. Mike Walsh punishes lax marking to head Bolton into an early lead, but City's aggression and team work make victory inevitable following Ritchie's deftly nodded equaliser.											
15	A	ASTON VILLA		12	L	0-2	0-0		Shaw	Sweeney	Gillies	Gow	Rodgers	Hunter	Tainton	Ritchie	Royle !	Bain*	Mabbutt	Whitehead
		18/11	*27,621*	*7*	15			*Deehan 58, Cowans 70*	*Rimmer*	*Gidman*	*Williams*	*Evans**	*McNaught*	*Mortimer*	*Shelton*	*Linton*	*Deehan*	*Cowans*	*Gregory*	*Gibson*
								Ref: N Glover	City lose the midfield battle as John Deehan's great hooked shot and an 18-yard low cross-shot by Gordon Cowans enable Villa to collect their first home win since the opening day of the season. Royle's punch at Allan Evans in the 76th minute results in his first dismissal in 13 years.											
16	H	WOLVES		12	L	0-1	0-0		Shaw	Sweeney	Gillies	Gow	Rodgers	Hunter	Tainton	Ritchie	Mabbutt	Mann*	Whitehead	Cormack
		21/11	18,295	*21*	15			*Daley 89*	*Bradshaw*	*Palmer*	*Parkin*	*Daniel*	*Hazell*	*Berry*	*Hibbitt*	*Carr*	*Bell*	*Eves*	*Daley*	
								Ref: D Lloyd	Steve Daley gives new Wolves manager John Barnwell a flying start as he rifles in a left-footed shot past Shaw in the last minute. Ritchie and Mabbutt force Paul Bradshaw to pull off some early saves, but in a poor game City's attack again fails to function properly without Royle.											
17	A	BIRMINGHAM		13	D	1-1	1-0	Mabbutt 26	Shaw	Sweeney	Gillies	Gow	Rodgers	Hunter	Tainton	Ritchie	Royle	Mann	Mabbutt	
		25/11	*21,152*	*21*	16			*Tarantini 69*	*Freeman*	*Tarantini*	*Dennis*	*Towers**	*Gallagher*	*Page*	*Dillon*	*Buckley*	*Givens*	*Calderwood*	*Fox*	*Barrowclough*
								Ref: B Martin	£250,000 Argentinian full-back Alberto Tarantini rescues a point for bottom club Birmingham as he heads in from Steve Fox's perfect corner. City outplay the Blues, but are unable to add to Mabbutt's opener, when he backheaded Mann's cross past the helpless Neil Freeman.											
18	H	DERBY		11	W	1-0	0-0	Gillies 84	Shaw	Sweeney	Gillies	Gow	Rodgers	Hunter	Tainton !	Ritchie	Royle	Mann	Mabbutt	
		2/12	18,096	*12*	18				*Middleton*	*Langan*	*Buckley*	*Daly*	*McFarland**	*Moreland*	*Carter*	*Powell*	*Duncan*	*Caskey*	*Clarke*	*Hill*
								Ref: L Burden	It takes the 75th-minute sending off of Tainton, after kicking Jonathan Clarke, to spark City into action. Gillies snatches the points with a long shot that is deflected beyond the reach of John Middleton. Derby never look like adding to their single away success in the past twelve months.											
19	A	LEEDS		11	D	1-1	1-1	Royle 23	Shaw	Sweeney	Gillies	Gow	Rodgers	Hunter	Mann	Ritchie	Royle	Cormack	Mabbutt	
		9/12	*22,529*	*9*	19			*Flynn 28*	*Harvey*	*Cherry*	*Stevenson*	*Flynn*	*Hart*	*Madeley*	*Gray E*	*Hankin*	*Thomas*	*Currie*	*Harris*	
								Ref: N Midgley	After Royle shoots them ahead, City are indebted to their back four as Leeds take control. Shaw has no chance as Brian Flynn fires in from the edge of the pen area, but thereafter City soak up the pressure and almost notch a winner as Ritchie and Royle both waste breakaway chances.											
20	H	LIVERPOOL		11	W	1-0	0-0	Royle 77	Shaw	Sweeney	Gillies	Gow	Rodgers	Hunter	Tainton	Ritchie	Royle	Cormack	Mann*	Whitehead
		16/12	28,347	*1*	21				*Clemence*	*Neal*	*Kennedy A*	*Thompson*	*Kennedy R*	*Hansen*	*Dalglish*	*Case*	*Heighway**	*McDermott*	*Souness*	*Johnson*
								Ref: K Salmon	Old Evertonian Royle nudges memories of Merseyside derby days as he shakes off Liverpool's tight marking to hook City's match clincher into the net. City finish as deserved winners on a surface better suited to their quick-tackling display, than to Liverpool's one-touch football.											
21	A	CHELSEA		10	D	0-0	0-0		Shaw	Sweeney	Gillies	Gow	Rodgers	Hunter	Tainton	Ritchie	Royle	Cormack	Whitehead	
		23/12	*19,867*	*22*	22				*Iles*	*Harris*	*Stride*	*Nutton*	*Wicks*	*Bumstead*	*Stanley*	*McKenzie*	*Osgood*	*Langley*	*Britton*	
								Ref: H Robinson	Without a win in seven games, and beaten 2-7 at Middlesbrough last Saturday, Chelsea prove to be stubborn opponents as they deny City their first-ever win at Stamford Bridge. The Pensioners supply plenty of speed and bustle in the first half, but after the break City take control.											

No	Date		Att	Pos	Pt	F-A	H-T	Scorers, Times, and Referees	1	2	3	4	5	6	7	8	9	10	11	12 sub used
22	H	COVENTRY		7	W	**5-0**	2-0	Royle 17, 21, 50, Ritchie 52	Shaw	Sweeney	Gillies	Gow	Rodgers	Hunter	Tainton	Ritchie	Royle	Cormack	Whitehead	
	26/12		23,335	*9*	24			[Cormack 74]	*Sealey*	*Coop*	*McDonald*	*Blair*	*Holton*	*Osgood*	*Hunt*	*Wallace*	*Thompson*	*Powell*	*Hutchison*	
								Ref: A Glasson	Keeper Les Sealey performs miracles to keep the score down, but is unable to stop Royle's hat-trick. Ritchie's perfect pass sets up Royle to shoot in with clinical ease, then follows a stylish volley, before his header puts City well on the way to achieving their best ever top-flight win.											
23	H	MANCHESTER C		7	D	1-1	1-0	Ritchie 9	Shaw	Sweeney	Gillies	Gow	Rodgers	Hunter*	Tainton	Ritchie	Royle	Cormack	Whitehead	Mann
	30/12		25,693	*15*	25			*Futcher R 66*	*Corrigan*	*Ranson*	*Donachie*	*Power*	*Watson*	*Futcher P*	*Channon*	*Owen*	*Futcher R*	*Hartford*	*Barnes*	
								Ref: D Reeves	City's 100th top-flight win is denied by opponents who have now gone eleven games without a win. Keeper Joe Corrigan is fortunate as three shots are repelled by his woodwork, but after Ritchie's header puts City in front, Ron Futcher's looping header saves the Maine Road men.											
24	A	WEST BROM		7	L	1-3	1-2	Cormack 22p	Shaw	Sweeney	Gillies	Gow	Rodgers	Collier	Tainton	Ritchie	Royle*	Cormack	Whitehead	Mann
	1/1		*31,738*	*2*	25			*Brown A 10, 82, Wile 43*	*Godden*	*Batson*	*Statham*	*Brown T*	*Wile*	*Robertson*	*Robson*	*Brown A*	*Regis*	*Cantello*	*Cunningham*	
								Ref: K Styles	Albion's new multi-studded astro-boots enable them to make a nonsense of the Siberian conditions at the Hawthorns. Alistair Brown fires the Baggies ahead, but Cormack levels with a twice-taken penalty, after Ritchie's header had been punched off the line by Brendon Batson.											
25	H	TOTTENHAM		7	D	0-0	0-0		Shaw	Sweeney	Gillies	Gow	Rodgers	Hunter	Tainton	Ritchie	Royle	Cormack	Whitehead	
	13/1		29,122	*9*	26				*Kendall*	*Holmes*	*McAllister*	*Villa*	*Lacy*	*Perryman*	*Pratt*	*Ardiles*	*Lee*	*Jones*	*Taylor*	
								Ref: P Reeves	Referee Peter Reeves is criticised by both managers for allowing this parody of a match to take place. Spurs' Argentinian pair Osvaldo Ardiles and Ricardo Villa are the only players able to master the icy conditions, and the nearest to a goal is Colin Lee's header which hits the crossbar.											
26	H	IPSWICH		7	W	3-1	2-0	Whitehead 19, Tainton 26, Gow 89	Shaw	Sweeney	Cooper	Gow	Rodgers	Collier	Tainton	Mabbutt	Royle	Cormack	Whitehead	
	3/2		17,599	*14*	28			*Mariner 90*	*Cooper*	*Mills*	*Tibbott*	*Parkin**	*Osman*	*Butcher*	*Wark*	*Muhren*	*Mariner*	*Whymark*	*Woods*	*Geddis*
								Ref: C Newsome	After this impressive win the talk is of City gaining a place in Europe next term. Rodgers receives the plaudits of Ipswich boss Bobby Robson for reducing the Ipswich attack to virtual impotence. Whitehead volleys City in front, shortly after Shaw had pulled off two remarkable saves.											
27	A	EVERTON		7	L	**1-4**	1-1	Whitehead 10	Shaw	Sweeney	Cooper	Gow	Rodgers	Hunter	Tainton	Ritchie	Royle	Cormack	Whitehead	
	10/2		*29,116*	*3*	28			*King 33, 65, 68, Wright 70*	*Wood*	*Robinson*	*Higgins*	*Lyons*	*Wright*	*Ross*	*Todd*	*Dobson*	*Latchford*	*King*	*Thomas*	
								Ref: G Owen	City, who outplay Everton for long spells, are made to pay for not making the most of their greater opportunities after Whitehead slams in Gow's mis-hit shot. Andy King heads in Everton's leveller and completes a hat-trick by shooting in two of his three further chances.											
28	A	SOUTHAMPTON		7	L	0-2	0-2		Shaw	Sweeney	Cooper	Gow	Rodgers	Hunter	Tainton	Ritchie*	Royle	Cormack	Whitehead	Mabbutt
	20/2		*19,845*	*10*	28			*Hayes 9, Holmes 29*	*Gennoe*	*Golac*	*Peach*	*Baker*	*Nicholl*	*Waldron*	*Ball*	*Boyer*	*Hayes*	*Holmes*	*Curran*	
								Ref: B Homewood	Mabbutt's two glaring misses during his half-hour substitute appearance probably cost City a point. Hunter's 100th City game is marred by conceding the free-kick which led to Nick Holmes blasting the Saints into a two-goal lead, and a 38th-min booking for a foul on Austin Hayes.											
29	A	NOTT'M FOREST		7	L	0-2	0-2		Cashley	Sweeney	Cooper	Gow	Rodgers	Collier	Tainton	Ritchie	Royle	Cormack*	Mabbutt	Mann
	24/2		*28,008*	*6*	28			*Needham 7, Birtles 15*	*Shilton*	*Anderson*	*Clark*	*McGovern*	*Lloyd*	*Needham*	*O'Neill**	*Gemmill*	*Birtles*	*Woodcock*	*Robertson*	*Francis*
								Ref: D Richardson	Alan Dicks' ban on his players arguing with the referees backfires in this game as David Needham is palpably offside as he heads in Tony Woodcock's chip. Cashley does well on his return to the side, but he is powerless as Garry Birtles heads in John Robertson's magnificent cross.											
30	H	MANCHESTER U		10	L	1-2	1-0	Gow 18	Cashley	Sweeney	Gillies	Gow	Collier	Hunter	Tainton	Garland	Royle	Mann	Whitehead	
	3/3		24,583	*7*	28			*Ritchie 53, McQueen 76*	*Bailey*	*Nicholl*	*Albiston*	*McIlroy*	*McQueen*	*Buchan*	*Coppell*	*Greenhoff J*	*Ritchie*	*Grimes*	*Thomas*	
								Ref: A Robinson	Cashley's injury just after the break costs City this game as his left arm is virtually useless following Andy Ritchie's shoulder charge. It is doubtful that a fit Cashley would have prevented Utd's well-struck equaliser, but he would certainly have stopped Gordon McQueen's header.											
31	A	ARSENAL		13	L	0-2	0-2		Shaw	Sweeney	Gillies	Gow*	Collier	Hunter	Tainton	Garland	Royle	Mann	Whitehead	Ritchie
	10/3		*24,288*	*3*	28			*Rix 31, Stapleton 43*	*Jennings*	*Rice*	*Nelson*	*Talbot*	*O'Leary*	*Walford*	*Brady*	*Heeley**	*Stapleton*	*Price*	*Rix*	*McDermott*
								Ref: H Robinson	A sunshine break in Torremolinos fails to change City's fortunes as they succumb to a fifth successive League defeat. The adoption of a 4-4-2 formation for the first time this season, even though a more adventurous policy is adopted at half-time, suggests they get what they deserve.											

No / Date	Venue	Opponent / Att	Pos	Res / Pts	F-A	H-T	Scorers, Times, and Referees	1	2	3	4	5	6	7	8	9	10	11	12
32	H	MIDDLESBROUGH	14	D	1-1	0-0	Gow 56	Shaw	Sweeney	Gillies	Gow	Rodgers	Hunter	Tainton	Ritchie	Royle	Mabbutt	Whitehead	
17/3		**13,559**	*16*	29			*Armstrong 83*	*Platt*	*Craggs*	*Johnson*	*Mahoney*	*Boam*	*McAndrew*	*Hodgson*	*Proctor*	*Ashcroft*	*Burns**	*Armstrong*	*Jankovic*
							Ref: C Downey	With the Match of the Day cameras again at Ashton Gate, City show to a painful degree their now chronic incapacity to finish off uninspired opposition. Fortunate to have only conceded Gow's low cross-shot, Boro' steal a point with David Armstrong's crisp left-footed drive.											
33	A	NORWICH	14	L	0-3	0-3		Shaw	Sweeney	Gillies	Gow	Rodgers	Hunter	Tainton	Ritchie	Royle*	Mabbutt	Whitehead	Cormack
24/3		***13,238***	*9*	29			*Neighbour 9, Evans 26, Reeves 31*	*Hansbury*	*Bond*	*Davies**	*McGuire*	*Hoadley*	*Powell*	*Neighbour*	*Reeves*	*Robson*	*Paddon*	*Evans*	*Symonds*
							Ref: A Cox	Playing against a strong wind at the start, City's elementary blunders allow Norwich to shoot in all three of their goals. City never look capable of taking a point off the draw specialists, and boss Dicks flies off to Holland to check on the form of Ajax's mercurial winger Geert Meijer.											
34	H	BIRMINGHAM	14	W	2-1	1-0	Meijer 5, Garland 89	Shaw	Sweeney	Cooper	Gow	Rodgers	Hunter	Mann	Ritchie	Royle*	Mabbutt	**Meijer**	Garland
31/3		16,453	*21*	31			*Gallagher 47*	*Freeman*	*Page*	*Dennis*	*Towers*	*Gallagher*	*Tarantini*	*Ainscow*	*Broadhurst*	*Givens**	*Dillion*	*Barrowclough*	*Calderwood*
							Ref: M Sinclair	A Dutch treat as City's new £92,000 signing gets his English career off to a great start with a left-footed shot into the far right-hand corner of the Open End goal. After Joe Gallagher heads the Blues level, Garland clinches City's first win in eight with a great 20-yard banana shot.											
35	H	QP RANGERS	11	W	2-0	0-0	Mabbutt 55, 68	Shaw	Sweeney	Cooper	Mann	Rodgers	Hunter	Tainton	Ritchie	Royle	Mabbutt	Meijer	
3/4		16,671	*20*	33				*Richardson*	*Clement*	*Wallace*	*Roeder*	*Howe*	*Hollins*	*Shanks**	*Busby*	*Walsh*	*McGee*	*Goddard*	*Allen*
							Ref: D Lloyd	Meijer again excels with his varied crosses and telling through balls, but Derek Richardson smothers his low drive to prevent him getting on the scoresheet. Cooper's forays down the left contribute to City's dominating display, which is rewarded by Mabbutt twice shooting in.											
36	A	DERBY	9	W	1-0	0-0	Ritchie 79	Shaw	Sweeney	Cooper	Gow	Rodgers	Hunter	Mann	Ritchie	Royle	Mabbutt*	Meijer	Whitehead
7/4		*17,090*	*18*	35				*Middleton*	*Langan*	*Buckley*	*Daly**	*Webb*	*Wicks*	*Carter*	*Powell*	*Greenwood*	*Moreland*	*Crawford*	*Caskey*
							Ref: D Clarke	A stamina-sapping game on a morass of a pitch, covered with 100 tons of sand – Derby boss Tommy Docherty claiming it was done without his knowledge - to dry out the waterlogged surface. Ritchie's far-post header to Meijer's cross is fitting testament to City's great durability.											
37	H	CHELSEA	7	W	3-1	0-0	Rodgers 50, Mabbutt 66, Meijer 68	Shaw	Sweeney	Cooper	Gow	Rodgers	Hunter	Mann*	Ritchie	Royle	Mabbutt	Meijer	Whitehead
10/4		19,784	*22*	37			*Langley 60p*	*Borota*	*Wilkins G*	*Stride*	*Bannon*	*Droy*	*Nutton*	*Harris*	*Wilkins R*	*Aylott*	*Langley*	*Fillery*	
							Ref: A Seville	City notch up their fourth win in ten days over the basement clubs. Rodgers breaks the deadlock by blasting the ball in after every other player fails to read the referee's excellent advantage following a push on Royle, but Chelsea level from the spot after Ritchie sends Fillery sprawling.											
38	A	COVENTRY	8	L	2-3	0-3	Mabbutt 76, Gow 88	Shaw	Sweeney	Cooper	Gow	Rodgers*	Hunter	Mann	Ritchie	Royle	Mabbutt	Meijer	Whitehead
14/4		*17,681*	*7*	37			*Powell 5p, Hutchison 7, Hunt 29*	*Sealey*	*Roberts*	*McDonald*	*Yorath**	*Holton*	*Coop*	*Nardiello*	*Blair*	*Hunt*	*Powell*	*Hutchison*	*Hagan*
							Ref: K Hackett	City take over the mantle of superiority after the break, but run out of time in their efforts to equalise. Cooper is stunned to concede Powell's pen after going up for the ball with Brian Roberts, but no dispute over Steve Hunt's spectacular overhead that puts Coventry firmly in control.											
39	H	WEST BROM	9	W	1-0	0-0	Mabbutt 69	Shaw	Sweeney	Whitehead	Gow	Collier	Hunter	Tainton	Ritchie	Royle	Mabbutt	Meijer	
17/4		**30,191**	*2*	39				*Godden*	*Batson*	*Statham*	*Mills*	*Wile*	*Robertson*	*Robson*	*Brown A*	*Regis*	*Cantello*	*Cunningham*	
							Ref: J Martin	Albion look anything but possible champions as they exhibit little of the flair that has made them such an outstanding team. City claim the points that their dominating display deserves, when Mabbutt follows up to stab in a rebound after Tony Godden palms out his free-header.											
40	A	LIVERPOOL	9	L	0-1	0-1		Shaw	Sweeney	Whitehead	Gow*	Collier	Hunter	Tainton	Ritchie	Royle	Mabbutt	Meijer	**Jantunen**
21/4		*43,191*	*1*	39			*Dalglish 6*	*Clemence*	*Neal*	*Kennedy A*	*Thompson*	*Kennedy R*	*Hansen*	*Dalglish*	*Case*	*Johnson**	*McDermott*	*Souness*	*Heighway*
							Ref: P Partridge	With only one win in their previous five meetings Liverpool, who were beginning to view City encounters with some apprehension, are a trifle fortunate to win this one. An untidy goal settles the issue as Kenny Dalglish pounces on David Johnson's mis-kick to slide the ball in.											
41	H	LEEDS	11	D	0-0	0-0		Shaw	Sweeney	Whitehead	Gow	Collier	Hunter	Tainton	Ritchie	Royle	Mabbutt	Meijer	
28/4		26,041	*5*	40				*Harvey*	*Hird*	*Gray F*	*Hampton !*	*Hart*	*Cherry*	*Harris*	*Hankin*	*Madeley*	*Gray E*	*Graham*	
							Ref: L Burden	Mabbutt reacts angrily to Leeds boss Jimmy Adamson's comment that Peter Hampton's 69th-minute over the top tackle did not warrant him being sent off. A typically poor end of the season game is only notable by the presentation of a silver salver to Norman Hunter by City fans.											
42	A	MANCHESTER C	12	L	0-2	0-1		Shaw	Sweeney	Whitehead	Gow	Collier	Hunter	Tainton	Ritchie	Royle	Mabbutt*	Meijer	Mann
5/5		*29,739*	*15*	40			*Deyna 41, Hartford 83*	*Corrigan*	*Reid*	*Donachie*	*Henry*	*Watson*	*Bell*	*Channon*	*Deyna*	*Silkman*	*Hartford*	*Power*	
Home / Average 22,306		Away / 24,717					Ref: T Mills	City outplay the Blues at Maine Road, but fail miserably in front of goal after producing some of their best approach play of the season. Kazru Deyna side-steps Shaw to clip the ball into an open goal and then Asa Hartford ties up Man City's flattering win with a 15-yard low drive.											

LEAGUE DIVISION 1 (CUP-TIES) Manager: Alan Dicks SEASON 1978-79

League Cup					F-A	H-T	Scorers, Times, and Referees	1	2	3	4	5	6	7	8	9	10	11	12 sub used
2	H	CRYS PALACE	5	L	1-2	0-1	Ritchie 54	Shaw	Sweeney	Gillies	Mann	Rodgers	Hunter	Tainton	Ritchie	Royle*	Pritchard	Whitehead	Garland
	29/8	10,924	*2:6*				*Murphy 16, Swindlehurst 82*	*Burridge*	*Hinshelwood*	*Sansom*	*Chatterton*	*Cannon*	*Gilbert*	*Murphy*	*Nicholas*	*Swindlehurst*	*Elwiss*	*Hilaire*	
							Ref: A Glasson	Woeful City are made to pay for squandering two good early chances as Jerry Murphy fires the Glaziers in front. Ritchie's jabbed-in equaliser makes up for offside disallowing his shot two minutes earlier, but David Swindlehurst's firm header brings a deserved success for the Palace.											

FA Cup					F-A	H-T	Scorers, Times, and Referees	1	2	3	4	5	6	7	8	9	10	11	12 sub used
3	H	BOLTON	7	W	3-1	0-0	Gow 62, Rodgers 65, Ritchie 82	Shaw	Sweeney	Gillies	Gow	Rodgers	Hunter	Tainton	Ritchie	Royle	Cormack	Whitehead	
	9/1	17,392	*17*				*Smith 64*	*McDonagh*	*Nicholson*	*Dunne*	*Greaves*	*Jones P*	*Walsh*	*Morgan*	*Smith*	*Gowling*	*Worthington*	*McNab*	
							Ref: L Shapter	City clear the third-round hurdle for the first time in four years after Gow sparks the game into life with a right-footed shot past Jim McDonagh. Brian Smith gives Bolton hope as he nips in for a fine solo goal, but Rodgers side-foots the ball home almost immediately.											
4	A	CRYS PALACE	7	L	0-3	0-1		Shaw	Sweeney	Gillies	Gow	Rodgers	Hunter !	Tainton	Ritchie !	Royle	Cormack*	Whitehead	Mann
	29/1	*21,463*	*2:1*				*Nicholas 21, Fenwick 55, Kember 87*	*Burridge*	*Hinshelwood*	*Sansom*	*Kember*	*Cannon*	*Gilbert*	*Nicholas*	*Murphy*	*Swindlehurst*	*Fenwick*	*Walsh*	
							Ref: K McNally	Ref Kevin McNally is criticised for sending off Hunter and Ritchie in the 52nd and 88th mins respectively, as well as booking four other players as City make an inglorious exit. Kenny Sansom lays on the decisive second goal for Terry Fenwick to steer into the corner of the net.											

	P	W	D	L	F	A	W	D	L	F	A	Pts
		Home					Away					
1 Liverpool	42	19	2	0	51	4	11	6	4	34	12	68
2 Nott'm Forest	42	11	10	0	34	10	10	8	3	27	16	60
3 West Brom	42	13	5	3	38	15	11	6	4	34	20	59
4 Everton	42	12	7	2	32	17	5	10	6	20	23	51
5 Leeds	42	11	4	6	41	25	7	10	4	29	27	50
6 Ipswich	42	11	4	6	34	21	9	5	7	29	28	49
7 Arsenal	42	11	8	2	37	18	6	6	9	24	30	48
8 Aston Villa	42	8	9	4	37	26	7	7	7	22	23	46
9 Manchester U	42	9	7	5	29	25	6	8	7	31	38	45
10 Coventry	42	11	7	3	41	29	3	9	9	17	39	44
11 Tottenham	42	7	8	6	19	25	6	7	8	29	36	41
12 Middlesbro	42	10	5	6	33	21	5	5	11	24	29	40
13 BRISTOL CITY	42	11	6	4	34	19	4	4	13	13	32	40
14 Southampton	42	9	10	2	35	20	3	6	12	12	33	40
15 Manchester C	42	9	5	7	34	28	4	8	9	24	28	39
16 Norwich	42	7	10	4	29	19	0	13	8	22	38	37
17 Bolton	42	10	5	6	36	28	2	6	13	18	47	35
18 Wolves	42	10	4	7	26	26	3	4	14	18	42	34
19 Derby	42	8	5	8	25	25	2	6	13	19	46	31
20 QP Rangers	42	4	9	8	24	33	2	4	15	21	40	25
21 Birmingham	42	5	9	7	24	25	1	1	19	13	39	22
22 Chelsea	42	3	5	13	23	42	2	5	14	21	50	20
	924	209	144	109	716	501	109	144	209	501	716	924

Odds & ends

Double wins: (3) Bolton, Ipswich, Derby.
Double losses: (3) Wolves, Nott'm Forest, Arsenal.

Won from behind: (2) Bolton (a), Bolton (h).
Lost from in front: (2) Everton (a), Manchester U (h).

High spots: Winning 3-1 at Old Trafford on 21 October.
Beating Coventry (h) 5-0 (City's record top-flight win).
Hammering Bristol Rov (h) 6-1 in the Anglo-Scottish Cup on 5 August.
Winning 2-0 at Eastville to secure the Gloucestershire Cup on 15 May.

Low spots: Poor form after the turn of the year that saw the chance of
European qualification slip from City's grasp.
Losing to Crystal Palace in both the FA and the League Cup.

Player of the year: Gerry Gow.
Ever-presents: (1) Gerry Sweeney.
Hat-tricks: (2) Kevin Mabbutt, Joe Royle.
Leading scorer; Tom Ritchie (11).

	Appearances						Goals			
	Lge	*Sub*	LC	*Sub*	FAC	*Sub*	**Lge**	LC	FAC	**Tot**
Bain, Jimmy	**3**	*1*								
Cashley, Ray	**2**									
Collier, Gary	**9**									
Cooper, Terry	**11**									
Cormack, Peter	**14**	*3*			2		**3**			**3**
Garland, Chris	**4**	*1*		*1*			**1**			**1**
Gillies, Donnie	**27**		1		2		**1**			**1**
Gow, Gerry	**38**				2		**5**		1	**6**
Hunter, Norman	**39**		1		2		**1**			**1**
Jantunen, Pertti		*1*								
Mabbutt, Kevin	**26**	*1*					**9**			**9**
Mann, Jimmy	**23**	*5*	1			*1*	**1**			**1**
Meijer, Geert	**9**						**2**			**2**
Pritchard, Howard	**1**		1							
Ritchie, Tom	**39**	*1*	1		2		**9**	1	1	**11**
Rodgers, David	**36**		1		2		**5**		1	**6**
Royle, Joe	**40**		1		2		**7**			**7**
Shaw, John	**40**		1		2					
Sweeney, Gerry	**42**		1		2					
Tainton, Trevor	**37**		1		2		**1**			**1**
Whitehead, Clive	**22**	*8*	1		2		**2**			**2**
21 players used	**462**	***21***	**11**	***1***	**22**	***1***	**47**	**1**	**3**	**51**

LEAGUE DIVISION 1 Manager: Alan Dicks SEASON 1979-80

No Date	Att	Pos	Pt	F-A	H-T	Scorers, Times, and Referees	1	2	3	4	5	6	7	8	9	10	11	12 sub used
1 H LEEDS			D	2-2	1-1	Ritchie 34p, Jantunen 65	Shaw	Sweeney	Whitehead	Gow	Rodgers	Merrick	**Fitzpatrick**	Ritchie	Mabbutt	Jantunen	Meijer	
18/8	23,331		1			*Curtis 9, 82*	*Harvey*	*Hird*	*Stevenson*	*Flynn*	*Parkinson*	*Hampton*	*Curtis*	*Cherry*	*Hankin*	*Harris*	*Graham*	
						Ref: D Lloyd	After an uneasy opening City settle down to play some polished football. Ex Swansea striker Alan Curtis has a dream debut for Leeds as he fires in both of his chances. Keith Parkinson pushes Ritchie in the back for his penalty, whilst Jantunen nets with an unstoppable 20-yard drive.											
2 A COVENTRY			L	1-3	1-1	Ritchie 37p	Shaw	Sweeney	Whitehead	Gow	Rodgers*	Merrick	Fitzpatrick	Ritchie	Mabbutt	Jantunen	Meijer	Tainton
21/8	*19,208*		1			*English 24, Powell 63p, Hutchison 83*	*Blyth*	*Jones*	*McDonald*	*Blair*	*Holton*	*Gillespie*	*Hutchison*	*English*	*Ferguson*	*Powell*	*Hunt**	*Hateley*
						Ref: N Ashley	Tom English jabs Coventry ahead, but City equalise after David Jones brings down Finnish international Jantunen. The ball hits Merrick's arm to gift Coventry their penalty kick, but few can argue with the final result as the Sky Blues have a shots on target advantage of eleven to two.											
3 A ASTON VILLA	11	W	2-0	1-0		Mabbutt17, Ritchie 89p	Shaw	Tainton	Whitehead	Gow	Sweeney	Merrick	Fitzpatrick	Ritchie	Mabbutt*	Jantunen	Royle	Mann
25/8	*25,526*	*13*	3				*Rimmer*	*Swain*	*Gibson*	*Evans*	*McNaught*	*Williams*	*Morley*	*Little**	*Deehan*	*Cowans*	*Shelton*	*Linton*
						Ref: G Nolan	City's slick football before the interval is replaced by resolute defending after the break. Mabbutt nips in to head in the opener, then with Villa down to ten men following the loss of the injured Gary Williams, Ritchie easily scores from the spot after being brought down by Ivor Linton.											
4 H WOLVES		6	W	2-0	1-0	Gow 8, Royle 72	Shaw	Tainton	Whitehead	Gow	Sweeney	Merrick	Fitzpatrick	Ritchie	Royle	Jantunen	Mabbutt	
1/9	19,428	*8*	5				*Bradshaw*	*Palmer*	*Parkin*	*Daniel*	*Berry*	*Hughes*	*Hibbitt*	*Carr*	*Rafferty*	*Clarke*	*Patching*	
						Ref: J Martin	Despite being over-run City's patched-up defence keeps a clean sheet for a third successive League and Cup match. Wolves are frustrated by Shaw's great display between the sticks and their own poor finishing, as City take the points with easy open goal shots for Gow and Royle.											
5 A IPSWICH		10	L	0-1	0-0		Shaw	Tainton	Whitehead	Gow	Sweeney	Merrick	Fitzpatrick	Ritchie	Royle	Jantunen*	Mabbutt	Cormack
8/9	*16,878*	*6*	5			*Woods 53*	*Cooper*	*Burley*	*Mills*	*Osborne*	*Osman*	*Butcher*	*Wark*	*Muhren*	*Mariner**	*Brazil*	*Woods*	*Gates*
						Ref: K Salmon	Arnold Muhren gives a lesson in first-time passing as City's outplayed midfield gets bogged down. Three magnificent saves by Shaw keep City in with a chance of saving the game, but the unequal deadlock is broken when George Burley's cross sets up Clive Woods to shoot in.											
6 H STOKE		10	D	0-0	0-0		Shaw	Tainton	Whitehead	Gow	Sweeney	Merrick	Fitzpatrick	Ritchie	Royle*	Mann	Mabbutt	Meijer
15/9	16,917	*14*	6				*Johns*	*Evans*	*Scott*	*Irvine*	*Smith*	*Doyle*	*Dodd*	*Heath*	*O'Callaghan*	*Crooks*	*Richardson*	
						Ref: C Thomas/R Gifford	Sweeney is the crowd's scapegoat for City's lacklustre display against a Stoke side who field an extra defender in place of ex Rovers' forward Paul Randall. The only entertainment is a pulled calf muscle that causes the referee to hand over to Roger Gifford after just two minutes.											
7 H NOTT'M FOREST		10	D	1-1	1-0	Mann 35	Shaw	Tainton	Whitehead	Gow	Sweeney	Merrick	Fitzpatrick	Ritchie*	Mabbutt	Mann	Cormack	Royle
22/9	22,767	*2*	7			*Mills 72*	*Shilton*	*Anderson*	*Gray*	*McGovern*	*Lloyd*	*Burns*	*Mills*	*O'Hare*	*Birtles*	*Woodcock*	*Robertson*	
						Ref: M Baker	City create little against a Forest side who miss a host of chances, but Mann's cannonball shooting almost brings an unlikely victory. He puts City ahead with a stupendous 35-yarder that dumbfounds Peter Shilton, then hits the bar from 25 yards, before Gary Mills shoots in for Forest.											
8 A EVERTON		8	D	0-0	0-0		Shaw	Tainton	Whitehead	Gow	Sweeney	Merrick	Fitzpatrick	Ritchie*	Royle	Mann	Mabbutt	**Hay**
29/9	*24,733*	*12*	8				*Wood*	*Barton**	*Bailey*	*Lyons*	*Higgins*	*Ross*	*Hartford*	*Stanley*	*King*	*Kidd*	*Eastoe*	*Wright*
						Ref: G Napthine	A more adventurous approach might well have secured both points against a laboured Everton side seeking their first home win of the season. Royle puts in a hard-working performance against his old club, but it is skipper Gow who wastes City's best chance by shooting over the bar.											
9 A LIVERPOOL		12	L	**0-4**	0-3	*[McDermott 80]*	Shaw	Tainton	Whitehead	Gillies	Sweeney	Merrick	Fitzpatrick	Ritchie	Royle	Jantunen*	Mabbutt	Cormack
6/10	*38,213*	*8*	8			*Johnson 4, Dalglish 31, Kennedy R 35,*	*Clemence*	*Neal*	*Kennedy A*	*Thompson*	*Kennedy R*	*Hansen*	*Dalglish*	*Case*	*Johnson*	*McDermott*	*Souness*	
						Ref: P Partridge	Liverpool take control of their 3,000th League game when David Johnson is free to head in Alan Kennedy's free-kick, but 16 minutes later Ritchie's header forces Ray Clemence to pull off a great save. Over-run in midfield before the break, City recover in a more even second half.											
10 H COVENTRY		10	W	1-0	0-0	Ritchie 58	Shaw	Sweeney	Whitehead	Gow	Rodgers	Merrick	Fitzpatrick	Ritchie	Royle	Mann	Tainton	
9/10	15,300	*12*	10				*Sealey*	*Coop*	*McDonald*	*Gooding*	*Holton*	*Gillespie*	*Nardiello*	*Wallace*	*Hutchison*	*Powell*	*Hunt*	
						Ref: A Cox	City, who have yet to put a fluent game together this season, are again unconvincing as Ritchie's low left-foot drive brings a rather lucky win. Dicks defends his 4-4-2 line-up as being necessary to tighten the defence, but City's clean sheet owes more to their opponents' poor finishing.											

No	Venue / Date	Opponent / Att	Pos	Res / Pts	F-A	H-T	Scorers, Times, and Referees	1	2	3	4	5	6	7	8	9	10	11	12
11	H	MANCHESTER U	11	D	1-1	1-1	Rodgers 38	Shaw	Sweeney	Whitehead	Gow	Rodgers*	Merrick	Fitzpatrick	Ritchie	Royle	Mann	Tainton	Mabbutt
	13/10	**28,305**	1	11			Macari 21	Bailey	Nicholl	Albiston	McIlroy	McQueen	Buchan	Grimes	Wilkins	Coppell	Macari	Thomas	
							Ref: A Gunn	City are unfortunate in not being able to add to their first-half score when Rodgers stabbed in the equaliser, as Utd run out of steam. In the final ten mins both Mann and Ritchie hit the bar, whilst Mann has two shots scrambled off the line, and Gary Bailey makes a great save from Royle.											
12	A	CRYS PALACE	13	D	1-1	0-0	Royle 67	Shaw	Sweeney	Whitehead	Gow*	Rodgers	Merrick	Fitzpatrick	Ritchie	Royle	Mann	Tainton	Mabbutt
	20/10	27,499	3	12			Cannon 79p	Burridge	Hinshelwood	Sansom	Nicholas	Cannon	Gilbert	Murphy	Kember	Walsh	Flanagan	Hilaire	
							Ref: J Sewell	Vince Hilaire robs City of both points with a theatrical fall that gives Palace a controversial second penalty, 27 minutes after Shaw had saved Mike Flanagan's earlier effort. Royle's goal, which is brilliantly lobbed over the advancing John Burridge, is deserving of being a winner.											
13	H	ARSENAL	16	L	0-1	0-0		Shaw	Sweeney	Whitehead	Mabbutt	Rodgers	Merrick	Fitzpatrick	Ritchie	Royle	Mann	Tainton	
	27/10	22,927	8	12			Sunderland 66	Jennings	Rice	Nelson	Talbot	O'Leary	Young	Brady	Sunderland	Stapleton	Hollins	Rix	
							Ref: D Civil	Alan Sunderland consigns City to their first home defeat in 15 matches, effortlessly stabbing in a rebound after Shaw blocks his first effort. Arsenal are the more accomplished side as City only put their game together during the final 20 minutes when Mabbutt wastes two chances.											
14	A	LEEDS	11	W	**3-1**	1-1	Mabbutt 20, 51, Merrick 54	Shaw	Sweeney	Whitehead	Mabbutt	Hay	Merrick	Fitzpatrick	Ritchie	Royle	Mann	Tainton	
	3/11	17,377	17	14			Gray 1	Lukic	Cherry	Stevenson	Hampton*	Hart	Madeley	Chandler	Entwhistle	Hankin	Curtis	Gray	Harris
							Ref: K Walmsley	Despite Eddie Gray driving in the opener after just 28 seconds, City gain a comprehensive win at Elland Road and move to within six points of the top of the table. A trio of headers clinches the points in front of a restless crowd who chant for the sacking of Leeds boss Jimmy Adamson.											
15	H	DERBY	15	L	0-2	0-2		Shaw	Sweeney	**Kenyon**	Mabbutt	Hay*	Merrick	Fitzpatrick	Ritchie	Royle	Mann	Tainton	Meijer
	10/11	16,943	19	14			Moreland 34, Duncan 44	McKellar	Langan	Buckley	Clark	McCaffery	Osgood	Emery	Powell	Duncan	Davies	Moreland	
							Ref: L Shapter	Inept City are killed off just before half-time with Vic Moreland's header and a toe-poke from John Duncan bringing Derby their first away win in 16 games. City's switch to all-out attack, on Meijer's appearance after the break, alters little as the Derby keeper hasn't a save to make.											
16	A	MIDDLESBROUGH	16	L	0-1	0-0		Shaw	Sweeney	Gillies	Tainton	Rodgers	Merrick	Fitzpatrick	Ritchie	Mabbutt*	Mann	Garland	Pritchard
	17/11	14,517	7	14			Armstrong 71	Platt	Craggs	Peters	Nattrass	Ashcroft	McAndrew	Cochrane	Bell	Hodgson	Burns	Armstrong	
							Ref: K McNally	Boro' captain Tony McAndrew is lucky not to be sent off in the 23rd min for a dreadful tackle on Mabbutt, who is replaced at half-time. City, who play attractive football without really threatening, are killed off when David Armstrong finishes his 40-yard dash with a low cross-shot.											
17	H	MANCHESTER C	14	W	1-0	1-0	Rodgers 29	Shaw	Sweeney	Whitehead	Gow	Rodgers	Merrick	Fitzpatrick	Tainton*	Royle	Mann	Garland	Ritchie
	24/11	18,549	13	16				Corrigan	Ranson	Donachie	Bennett	Caton	Stepanovic	Henry	Daley	Robinson	Power !	Deyna	
							Ref: D Hutchinson	Tony Fitzpatrick, City's record £250,000 signing from St Mirren, is the star of this exciting game as his classic cross sets up Rodgers to head the only goal. Manchester skipper Paul Power is sent off for foul and abusive language in the 79th minute following an offside dispute.											
18	A	BOLTON	14	D	1-1	0-0	Rodgers 47	Shaw	Sweeney	Whitehead	Gow	Rodgers	Merrick	Fitzpatrick	Tainton	Royle	Mann	Garland	
	1/12	**12,074**	22	17			Greaves 90	McDonagh	Nicholson	Burke	Greaves	Jones	Walsh	Morgan	Whatmore	Dowling*	Cantello	McNab	Carter
							Ref: J Bray	Poetic justice perhaps after City have a lucky escape in the 84th minute when the referee waves play-on as Peter Nicholson is felled in the area. In the third minute of injury-time Ray Greaves shoots in Bolton's leveller from eight yards, with City appealing that Nicholson is offside.											
19	H	TOTTENHAM	17	L	1-3	0-1	Ritchie 84p	Shaw	Sweeney	Whitehead	Gow	Rodgers	Merrick	Fitzpatrick	Tainton	Royle	Garland	Meijer*	Ritchie
	8/12	25,090	6	17			Miller 21, Hoddle 72p, 90	Daines	Hughton	Miller	Pratt	Smith	Perryman	Ardiles	Jones	Lee	Hoddle	Villa	
							Ref: D Letts	Talk of relegation is in the air as City are outclassed and over-run. Osvaldo Ardiles appears to take a dive for Spurs' penalty, but he lays on the goal of the match at the death, as he twists and turns past three men before setting up Hoddle to finish off his classic cross with a diving header.											
20	A	NORWICH	19	L	0-2	0-1		Shaw	Sweeney	Whitehead	Gow	Rodgers*	Merrick	Fitzpatrick	Tainton	Royle	Ritchie	Garland	Cormack
	15/12	11,657	5	17			Taylor 25, Robson 46	Keelan	Bond	Downs	Ryan	Brown	Jones	Mendham*	Taylor	Robson	Paddon	Peters	Lythgoe
							Ref: G Flint	Another poor performance as City slither to defeat on the first really heavy pitch of the season. Defensive blunders are City's undoing as a poor header by the concussed Rodgers leads to Alan Taylor shooting in the first goal, then Cormack's back-pass gifts Keith Robson the second.											
21	H	SOUTHAMPTON	19	L	0-1	0-0		Shaw	Sweeney	Whitehead	Gow	Kenyon	Merrick	Fitzpatrick	Tainton	Royle	Ritchie	Mann*	Mabbutt
	21/12	14,185	5	17			Channon 53	Wells	Golac	Peach	Williams	Watson	Nicholl	Ball	Boyer	Channon	Holmes	Hebberd	
							Ref: D Reeves	Mabbutt is robbed of a clear scoring opportunity in the 86th minute when he is grabbed around the waist by Chris Nicholl, who only receives a yellow card for his professional foul. On a snow-covered pitch Southampton deserve the points gained by Mike Channon's 15-yard drive.											

No	Date		Att	Pos	Pt	F-A	H-T	Scorers, Times, and Referees	1	2	3	4	5	6	7	8	9	10	11	12 sub used
22	A	WEST BROM		20	L	0-3	0-0		Shaw	Sweeney	Whitehead	Gow	Kenyon	Merrick	Fitzpatrick	Tainton	Royle	Mabbutt	Mann*	Meijer
	26/12		19,490	16	17			Owen 75, Barnes 80, 89	Godden	Batson	Pendrey	Trewick	Wile	Robertson	Robson	Deehan	Regis	Owen	Barnes	
								Ref: R Toseland	'The best three goals I've ever had scored against me' is Shaw's praise for the Albion strikers. Gary Owen's 25-yard chip is followed by Peter Barnes' two goals, a left-footed flick after a 50-yard dribble, and a ferocious low drive after another fine scamper down the touchline.											
23	H	ASTON VILLA		20	L	1-3	0-0	Gow 75p	Shaw	Sweeney	Whitehead	Gow	Rodgers	Merrick	Pritchard	Tainton	Mabbutt	Mann	Garland	
	29/12		18,799	6	17			Shaw 51, 54, 76	Rimmer	Swain	Gibson	Ormsby	McNaught	Mortimer	Bremner	Little	Donovan	Cowans	Shaw	
								Ref: D Hedges	City play much good football, but they are unable to finish off the chances that Pritchard supplies from the wing. Gary Shaw's second goal for Villa is a magnificent 35-yard strike, but he is lucky with his first that goes in off his neck following a corner, as his namesake is impeded.											
24	H	BRIGHTON		20	D	2-2	1-0	Gow 23p, 71p	Shaw	Tainton	Whitehead	Gow	Rodgers	Merrick	Pritchard	Fitzpatrick	Mabbutt*	Mann	Garland	Ritchie
	1/1		19,896	18	18			Clarke 55, Rodgers 75 (og)	Moseley	Gregory	Williams	Horton	Foster	Stevens	Ryan	Ward	Clarke	Lawrenson	O'Sullivan	
								Ref: M Robinson	City create the greater number of chances, but Rodgers slices Peter Ward's cross into his own net to enable Brighton to sustain their revival of 13 points from the last nine games. Whitehead causes panic with his overlaps and he is twice scythed down for Gow to slot in from the spot.											
25	A	WOLVES		20	L	0-3	0-1		Shaw	Tainton	Whitehead	Gow	Rodgers	Merrick	Pritchard	Fitzpatrick*	Ritchie	Mann	Garland	Sweeney
	12/1		18,835	12	18			Gray 17, Richards 75, Daniel 89	Bradshaw	Palmer	Parkin	Daniel	McAlle	Berry	Atkinson	Carr	Gray	Richards	Thomas	
								Ref: R Chadwick	The message is clear – buy or be relegated as the best City can manage in this game is Garland's 25-yarder that hits the post in the 84th min. A brilliant 22-yard chip by John Richards is the goal of the game, while the impressive Peter Daniel finishes off the best move of the match.											
26	H	IPSWICH		20	L	0-3	0-1		Shaw	Tainton	Whitehead	Gow	Rodgers	Sweeney	Pritchard	Fitzpatrick	Royle	Jantunen	Garland	
	19/1		15,004	5	18			Gates 42, Brazil 73, Mariner 87	Cooper	Burley	Mills	Thijssen	Osman	Butcher	Wark	Muhren	Mariner	Brazil	Gates	
								Ref: J Warner	Alan Brazil's outstanding strike as he turns inside two defenders before zipping a shot into the far corner of the net is the turning point, just six mins after Garland's crisp low left-footed effort hits the base of the far post. Paul Mariner's shot through Shaw's legs completes City's demise.											
27	A	STOKE		20	L	0-1	0-0		Shaw	Gillies	Whitehead	Tainton	Rodgers	Kenyon	Pritchard	Fitzpatrick	Ritchie*	Sweeney	Garland	**Doyle**
	2/2		14,510	19	18			Rodgers 56 (og)	Fox	Evans	Johnson	Irvine	Smith	Dodd	Heath	Richardson	Chapman	Crooks	Cook	
								Ref: M Lowe	Whilst Rodgers unluckily diverts Garth Crook's pull-back into his own goal, City can have few complaints over losing this vital encounter. Stoke have three goals disallowed, including Paul Richardson's successful 62nd-min spot-kick having to be retaken due to encroachment.											
28	A	NOTT'M FOREST		20	D	0-0	0-0		Cashley	Sweeney	Whitehead	Tainton	Rodgers	Merrick	Pritchard	Fitzpatrick	Royle	Ritchie	Doyle	
	9/2		23,421	6	19				Shilton	Anderson	Gunn	McGovern	Lloyd	Burns	O'Neill	Bowles	Birtles	George	Robinson	
								Ref: D Owen	A massed defence and a gluey surface combine to frustrate Forest, who are never able to demonstrate their prime attacking quality of pace. City offer little in attack, though Peter Shilton denies Royle a goal, and then when Rodgers' header beats him, Bryn Gunn heads clear.											
29	H	EVERTON		20	W	2-1	0-1	Ritchie 58, Rodgers 68	Cashley	Sweeney	Whitehead	Gow	Rodgers	Merrick	Pritchard	Fitzpatrick	Royle	Ritchie	Tainton	
	19/2		16,317	19	21			Ross 45	Hodge	Gidman	Bailey	Wright	Lyons	Ross	Megson	Eastoe	Hartford	Kidd	McBride	
								Ref: C Downey	City demonstrate great resolve in overcoming the setback of conceding Trevor Ross's gloriously angled shot right on half-time, after Royle and Tainton had both been denied by the post. Pritchard's cross sets up Ritchie's headed equaliser, then Rodgers hooks in to clinch the points.											
30	A	MANCHESTER U		20	L	**0-4**	0-3		Cashley	Sweeney	Whitehead	Gow	Rodgers	Merrick	Pritchard	Fitzpatrick	Royle*	Ritchie	Tainton	Mabbutt
	23/2		**43,329**	2	21			Jordan 7, 48, McIlroy 39, Mer'k 43 (og)	Bailey	Nicholl	Houston	McIlroy	McQueen*	Buchan	Coppell	Wilkins	Jordan	Macari	Grimes	Ritchie
								Ref: G Tyson	On Match of the Day City look like title contenders with their neat, composed football. United though have Joe Jordan, and he arrives at the far post to head home after Ashley Grimes' corner had been deflected, and completes the scoring with an arrogant header from a Grimes cross.											
31	H	CRYS PALACE		20	L	0-2	0-0		Cashley	Sweeney	Whitehead	Gow	Rodgers	Merrick	Pritchard	Fitzpatrick	Royle	Ritchie*	Tainton	Mabbutt
	1/3		16,549	10	21			Nicholas 57, Flanagan 87	Fry	Hinshelwood	Sansom	Nicholas	Cannon	Gilbert	Murphy	Francis	Walsh	Flanagan	Hilaire	
								Ref: V Callow	City waste their opportunities before Peter Nicholas sets Palace on the way to both points by shooting in a loose ball after Vince Hilaire muffs his kick. Neither side show much in the way of First Division quality as Mike Flanagan heads in to complete Palace's rather flattering success.											

No	Date	Opponent	Att	Pos	Res	Pts	F-A	H-T	Scorers, Times, and Referees	1	2	3	4	5	6	7	8	9	10	11	12
32	A	ARSENAL		20	D		0-0	0-0		Cashley	Sweeney	Whitehead	Mann	Gillies	Merrick	Mabbutt	Fitzpatrick	Royle	Ritchie	Tainton	
	1[illegible]/3		*21,559*	*4*		22				*Jennings*	*Devine*	*Nelson*	*Talbot*	*O'Leary*	*Young*	*Brady*	*Vaersen*	*Stapleton*	*Price*	*Rix*	
									Ref: R Challis	Joe Royle, thrice denied by Pat Jennings in the first half, remains optimistic that City can still beat the drop. It is really a point gained at Highbury as it is Arsenal who create most of the chances. City are indebted to Cashley's agility and courage as he keeps the Gunners at bay.											
33	H	LIVERPOOL		21	L		1-3	0-1	Mabbutt 63	Cashley	Sweeney	Whitehead	Mann	Gillies	Merrick	Mabbutt	Fitzpatrick	Royle	Ritchie	Tainton	
	15/3		27,523	*1*		22			*Kennedy R 5, Dalglish 55, 89*	*Clemence*	*Neal*	*Kennedy A*	*Thompson*	*Kennedy R*	*Hansen*	*Dalglish*	*Case*	*Johnson*	*McDermott*	*Souness*	
									Ref: R Lewis	Flawless Liverpool turn on the style as City are outclassed in front of the Match of the Day cameras. Pool's shot on sight policy unsettles City, and Ray Kennedy opens the scoring with a fine shot from the edge of the box. Mabbutt's hooked shot from Royle's header is City's sole reply.											
34	A	DERBY		21	D		3-3	2-1	Ritchie 20, 28p, Mann 58	Cashley	Sweeney	Whitehead	Mann	Gillies	Merrick	Fitzpatrick	Ritchie	Royle	Mabbutt	Tainton	
	22/3		*17,020*	*20*		23			*Biley 45, 48, 54p*	*McKellar*	*Langan*	*Buckley*	*Powell S*	*McFarland*	*Osgood*	*Emery**	*Powell B*	*Biley*	*Swindlehurst*	*Emson*	*McCaffery*
									Ref: T Farley	Merrick claims loss of balance in bringing down Dave Swindlehurst for County's penalty, whilst City's spot-kick follows Keith Osgood's felling of Mabbutt. Ritchie nets the opener with a shot from 15 yards, and Mann completes the action with an untypically close-range effort.											
35	H	WEST BROM		21	D		0-0	0-0		Cashley	Sweeney	Whitehead*	Gow	Rodgers	Merrick	Fitzpatrick	Ritchie	Royle	Mabbutt	Mann	Tainton
	5/4		16,873	*10*		24				*Godden*	*Batson*	*Cowdrill*	*Moses*	*Wile*	*Robertson*	*Robson*	*Deehan*	*Regis*	*Owen*	*Barnes*	
									Ref: L Burden	The Baggies unbeaten seven-match run comes under threat at Ashton Gate, and they are visibly shaken by City's second-half verve. Gow is in brilliant form in City's midfield, but again the finish is missing as the home fans protest with banners advocating change of management.											
36	A	BRIGHTON		21	W		1-0	0-0	Ritchie 52	Cashley	Sweeney	Whitehead	Gow	Rodgers	Merrick	Fitzpatrick	Ritchie	Royle	Mann	Pritchard	
	7/4		*23,115*	*17*		26				*Moseley*	*Gregory*	*Williams*	*Horton*	*Foster*	*Ryan*	*McNab*	*Wood*	*Clarke**	*Lawrenson*	*O'Sullivan*	*Suddaby*
									Ref: C Maskell	With Derby losing at Coventry and Man City dropping another home point, Ritchie's side-footer from five yards renews hope of escaping relegation. A poor game, but with Gow and Whitehead limping, City do well to become only the second side to win at the Goldstone this year.											
37	H	BOLTON		21	W		2-1	1-0	Ritchie 39p, Mann 60	Cashley	Sweeney	Whitehead	Gow	Rodgers	Merrick	Fitzpatrick	Ritchie	Royle	Mann	Pritchard*	Tainton
	12/4		14,270	*22*		28			*Allardyce 75*	*McDonagh*	*Graham*	*Bennett*	*Hoggan*	*Jones*	*Walsh*	*Nowak*	*Whatmore**	*Carter*	*Wilson*	*Reid*	*Allardyce*
									Ref: C Newsome	City's best run of the season, six points from four games, keeps survival hopes alive, but Bolton's failure to win condemns them to relegation. Gow's chip hits Paul Jones on the arm for City's spot-kick, then Mann finds his range again from long distance to double City's advantage.											
38	A	MANCHESTER C		21	L		**1-3**	0-3	Rodgers 69	Cashley	Sweeney	Whitehead	Gow	Rodgers	Merrick	Fitzpatrick	Ritchie	Royle	Mann	Pritchard*	Tainton
	13/4		*32,745*	*17*		28			*Robinson 13, Denya 32, Tueart 40*	*Corrigan*	*Ranson*	*Reid*	*Futcher*	*Caton*	*Power*	*Henry*	*Daley*	*Deyna*	*Tueart*	*Robinson*	
									Ref: P Reeves	City squander all but one of their chances, whilst the Blues convert theirs. Rodgers heads in from Merrick's free-kick, but by then seven good opportunities had been spurned. Man City are fortunate with their opener as Mick Robinson knocks the ball down with hand before slotting in.											
39	H	MIDDLESBROUGH		20	W		3-1	1-1	Royle 12, Ritchie 48, 88	Cashley	Sweeney	Whitehead	Mann	Rodgers	Merrick	Pritchard	Fitzpatrick	Royle	Ritchie	Tainton	
	22/4		**12,013**	*10*		30			*Armstrong 4*	*Stewart*	*Craggs*	*Bailey*	*Johnston*	*Ashcroft**	*Angus*	*Cochrane*	*Proctor*	*Hodgson*	*Jankovic*	*Armstrong*	*Hedley*
									Ref: A Glasson	City are fortunate not to find themselves beyond redemption before Royle opens their account with a fierce volley. Shortly after David Armstrong's headed opener, City are relieved when their nervously conceded own-goal is struck off due to an earlier offside infringement.											
40	H	NORWICH		21	L		2-3	0-1	Rodgers 65, Ritchie 88	Cashley	Sweeney	Whitehead	Gow	Rodgers	Merrick*	Fitzpatrick	Ritchie	Royle	Mann	Pritchard	Tainton
	26/4		16,596	*15*		30			*Robson 25, 74, Peters 46*	*Hansbury*	*Bond*	*Symonds*	*Barham*	*McDowell*	*Jones*	*Woods*	*Fashanu*	*Robson*	*Paddon*	*Peters*	
									Ref: A Seville	Ritchie makes some recompense for his spot-kick failure after just 25 seconds, with a late tap-in, but by then it is too late as City's top-flight status hangs by a thread. Injury reduces City to ten men in the 78th minute, following Justin Fashanu's head-butt on the unfortunate Rodgers.											
41	A	SOUTHAMPTON		21	L		2-5	0-0	Mabbutt 68, 70	Cashley	Sweeney	Whitehead	Gow	Gillies	Tainton	Fitzpatrick	Ritchie*	Royle	Mann	Pritchard	Mabbutt
	29/4		*16,309*	*8*		30			*Boyer 46, 51, 66, Hayes 50, [Channon 84]*	*Wells*	*Golac*	*Waldron*	*Williams S*	*Watson*	*Nicholl*	*Hebberd*	*Boyer*	*Channon*	*Holmes*	*Hayes**	*Rogers*
									Ref: M Bidmead	City are sent sliding out of the First Division by Soton's blitz at the start of the second half. Phil Boyer heads in to start the rot, and then fires home twice more to grab his third hat-trick of the season. Mabbutt responds for City with a close-range shot, and a ferocious 18-yarder.											
42	A	TOTTENHAM		20	D		0-0	0-0		Shaw	Sweeney	Whitehead	Gow	Hay	Merrick	Fitzpatrick*	Ritchie	Royle	Mann	Mabbutt	Gillies
	3/5		*23,585*	*14*		31				*Daines*	*Hughton*	*Miller*	*Hazard*	*McAllister*	*Perryman*	*Ardiles*	*Jones*	*Falco*	*Hoddle*	*Galvin*	
		Home	Away						Ref: M Scott	Already doomed City only have themselves to blame for not bowing out with a win, even though they have cause to thank the woodwork for repelling a Glenn Hoddle effort. Mabbutt misses City's best chance, as with only Barry Daines to beat his lob falls the wrong side of the post.											
Average		18,932	21,981																		

League Cup					F-A	H-T	Scorers, Times, and Referees	1	2	3	4	5	6	7	8	9	10	11	12 sub used
2:1	H	ROTHERHAM	11	W	1-0	1-0	Ritchie 38p	Shaw	Tainton	Whitehead	Gow	Sweeney	Merrick	Fitzpatrick	Ritchie	Royle	Jantunen	Meijer	
28/8		6,981	*3:7*					*Mountford*	*Forrest*	*Tiler*	*Rhodes*	*Green*	*Breckin*	*Gooding*	*McEwan*	*Gwyther*	*Fern*	*Finney*	
							Ref: A Robinson	After a one minute silence in memory of Lord Mountbatten, murdered by an IRA bomb, the Millers prove difficult to beat. It takes John Breckin's push on Ritchie for City to gain an advantage, the striker creating an English football record with penalties in four successive games.											
2:2	A	ROTHERHAM	6	D	1-1	0-1	Mabbutt 87	Shaw	Tainton	Whitehead	Gow	Sweeney	Merrick	Fitzpatrick	Ritchie	Royle	Jantunen	Mabbutt	
4/9		*7,327*	*3:1*				*Fern 31*	*Mountford*	*Forrest*	*Tiler*	*Rhodes*	*Green*	*Breckin*	*Gooding*	*McEwan*	*Gwyther*	*Fern*	*Finney*	
							Ref: M Scott (City won 2-1 on aggregate)	Mabbutt's late headed goal from Jantunen's wickedly curved cross takes City through to the next round, two minutes after a hairline offside decision had ruled out Gerry Forrest's shot. City are fortunate not to concede any more than Rodney Fern's tap-in, as they are often over-run.											
3	A	PETERBOROUGH	10	D	1-1	0-1	Gow 76	Shaw	Tainton	Whitehead	Gow	Sweeney	Merrick	Fitzpatrick	Ritchie	Mabbutt	Mann	Cormack*	Royle
26/9		*7,067*	*4:7*				*Parkinson 44*	*Waugh*	*Carmichael*	*Phillips*	*Chard*	*Smith*	*Foster*	*Gynn*	*Kellock*	*Quow*	*Robson*	*Parkinson*	
							Ref: M Peck	Royle's verve and mobility in a 20-minute substitute appearance saves City, as he heads down Sweeney's cross for Gow to lob the ball in from 20 yards. Although both Mabbutt and Gow hit the woodwork in the first half, Andy Parkinson's cross-shot deservedly gives Posh the lead.											
3R	H	PETERBOROUGH	8	W	4-0	2-0	Jantunen 1, Royle 22, 82, Mabbutt 88	Shaw	Sweeney	Whitehead	Gow*	Hay	Merrick	Fitzpatrick	Tainton	Royle	Jantunen	Mabbutt	Meijer
2/10		9,125	*4:5*					*Waugh*	*McVay*	*Phillips*	*Chard*	*Smith**	*Foster*	*Gynn*	*Kellock*	*Parkinson*	*Robson*	*Carmichael*	*Guy*
							Ref: A Selville	Jantunen's 25-yarder that puts City ahead after just 55 seconds, sparks a vintage first-half display that sees Sweeney hitting the bar and Royle heading in from Fitzpatrick's long pass. After the break though, Posh's great spirit has City hanging on until two late strikes ease the tension.											
4	H	NOTT'M FOREST	16	D	1-1	0-1	Sweeney 86	Shaw	Sweeney	Whitehead	Mabbutt	Rodgers*	Merrick	Fitzpatrick	Ritchie	Royle	Mann	Tainton	Hay
30/10		25,695	*2*				*O'Hare 29*	*Shilton*	*Anderson*	*Gray*	*McGovern*	*Lloyd*	*Burns*	*O'Hare*	*Francis*	*Birtles*	*Woodcock*	*Robertson*	
							Ref: C Downey	Sweeney's acute-angled chip is a great finale to a pulsating cup-tie. John O'Hare stumbles the ball into the net for Forest's untidy goal after City's fine start had been disrupted by a seven-minute delay in bringing on Hay, following the early departure of Rodgers with a broken nose.											
4R	A	NOTT'M FOREST	15	L	0-3	0-2		Shaw	Sweeney	Kenyon	Mabbutt	Hay	Merrick	Fitzpatrick	Ritchie	Royle*	Mann	Tainton	Gillies
14/11		20,462	*3*				*O'Neill 12, Anderson 43, W'dcock 60*	*Shilton*	*Anderson*	*Gray*	*McGovern*	*Lloyd*	*Needham*	*O'Neill**	*Francis*	*Birtles*	*Woodcock*	*Robertson*	*Bowyer*
							Ref: J Worrall	City are devoid of ambition and never offer a threat as Forest take their unbeaten League Cup run to 21 games. Viv Anderson's first-time hook shot into the top corner of the net is the best of the goals as the European Champions outclass City, who can only manage two shots on target.											

FA Cup																			
3	H	DERBY	20	W	6-2	3-0	G'land, 6, 85, P'd 12, 61, W'head 39, [Mann 88]	Shaw	Tainton	Whitehead	Gow	Rodgers	Merrick	Pritchard	Fitzpatrick	Ritchie	Mann	Garland	
5/1		13,384	*21*				*Davies 84, Daly 87*	*McKellar*	*Emery*	*Buckley*	*Daly*	*Powell S*	*Osgood*	*Clark**	*Powell B*	*Greenwood*	*Davies*	*Moreland*	*Emson*
							Ref: D Civil	Goals galore as City notch up their record Cup win over top-flight opposition. Pritchard's return to the side works wonders, notching two goals himself, a stab in and a fierce shot into the roof of the net, as well having sent over the corner for Garland to head in City's opener.											
4	H	IPSWICH	20	L	1-2	1-1	Whitehead 38	Shaw	Tainton	Whitehead	Gow	Rodgers	Merrick*	Pritchard	Fitzpatrick	Mabbutt	Sweeney	Garland	Doyle
26/1		19,608	*5*				*Wark 45, Mariner 87*	*Cooper*	*Burley*	*Mills*	*Thijssen*	*Osman*	*Butcher*	*Wark*	*Muhren*	*Mariner*	*Brazil*	*Gates*	
							Ref: T Bune	City pay the penalty for missed chances as Shaw fumbles Frans Thijssen's mis-hit shot to present Paul Mariner with his late winner. Ipswich ride their luck at times, but John Wark's equaliser is pure magic as Mike Mills' left-wing run and cross ends with a perfect diving header.											

		Home						Away					
		P	W	D	L	F	A	W	D	L	F	A	Pts
1	Liverpool	42	15	6	0	46	8	10	4	7	35	22	60
2	Manchester U	42	17	3	1	43	8	7	7	7	22	27	58
3	Ipswich	42	14	4	3	43	13	8	5	8	25	26	53
4	Arsenal	42	8	10	3	24	12	10	6	5	28	24	52
5	Nott'm Forest	42	16	4	1	44	11	4	4	13	19	32	48
6	Wolves	42	9	6	6	29	20	10	3	8	29	27	47
7	Aston Villa	42	11	5	5	29	22	5	9	7	22	28	46
8	Southampton	42	14	2	5	53	24	4	7	10	12	29	45
9	Middlesbro	42	11	7	3	31	14	5	5	11	19	30	44
10	West Brom	42	9	8	4	37	23	2	11	8	17	27	41
11	Leeds	42	10	7	4	30	17	3	7	11	16	33	40
12	Norwich	42	10	8	3	38	30	3	6	12	20	36	40
13	Crys Palace	42	9	9	3	26	13	3	7	11	15	37	40
14	Tottenham	42	11	5	5	30	22	4	5	12	22	40	40
15	Coventry	42	12	2	7	34	24	4	5	12	22	42	39
16	Brighton	42	8	8	5	25	20	3	7	11	22	37	37
17	Manchester C	42	8	8	5	28	25	4	5	12	15	41	37
18	Stoke	42	9	4	8	27	26	4	6	11	17	32	36
19	Everton	42	7	7	7	28	25	2	10	9	15	26	35
20	BRISTOL CITY	42	6	6	9	22	30	3	7	11	15	36	31
21	Derby	42	9	4	8	36	29	2	4	15	11	38	30
22	Bolton	42	5	11	5	19	21	0	4	17	19	52	25
		924	228	134	100	722	437	100	134	228	437	722	924

Odds & ends

Double wins: (0).
Double losses: (4) Ipswich, Liverpool, Norwich, Southampton.

Won from behind: (3) Leeds (a), Everton (h), Middlesbrough (h).
Lost from in front: (0).

High spots: Drawing 2-2 with Leeds at Ashton Gate on 18 August.
Winning 3-1 at Elland Road on 3 November.
Beating Derby 6-2 in the FA Cup on 5 January.
Beating Bristol Rov (h) 1-0 in the Gloucestershire Cup Final on 6 May.

Low spots: Relegation.
Losing 2-3 at home to Norwich on 26 April.
Lack of ambition in 0-3 FL Cup defeat at Nott'm Forest.
Losing 1-5 on aggregate v St Mirren in the Final of the Anglo-Scottish Cup.

Player of the year: Geoff Merrick.
Ever-presents: (0).
Hat-tricks: (0).
Leading scorer: Tom Ritchie (14).

	Appearances						Goals			
	Lge	*Sub*	LC	*Sub*	FAC	*Sub*	**Lge**	LC	FAC	**Tot**
Cashley, Ray	**14**									
Cormack, Peter	**1**	*3*	1							
Doyle, Ian	**1**	*1*				*1*				
Fitzpatrick, Tony	**41**		6		2					
Garland, Chris	**10**				2				2	**2**
Gillies, Donnie	**7**	*1*		*1*						
Gow, Gerry	**31**		4		2		**4**	1		**5**
Hay, Alan	**3**	*1*	2	*1*						
Jantunen, Pertti	**7**		3				**1**	1		**2**
Kenyon, Roger	**4**		1							
Mabbutt, Kevin	**21**	*6*	5		1		**13**	2		**15**
Mann, Jimmy	**28**	*1*	3		1		**3**		1	**4**
Meijer, Geert	**3**	*3*	1	*1*						
Merrick, Geoff	**39**		6		2		**1**			**1**
Pritchard, Howard	**15**	*1*			2				2	**2**
Ritchie, Tom	**35**	*3*	5		1		**6**	1		**7**
Rodgers, David	**26**		1		2		**6**			**6**
Royle, Joe	**34**	*1*	5	*1*			**3**	2		**5**
Shaw, John	**28**		6		2					
Sweeney, Gerry	**40**	*1*	6		1			1		**1**
Tainton, Trevor	**34**	*5*	6		2					
Whitehead, Clive	**40**		5		2				2	**2**
22 players used	**462**	*27*	**66**	*4*	**22**	*1*	**37**	**8**	**7**	**52**

LEAGUE DIVISION 2 — Manager: Dicks ⇨ Bob Houghton — SEASON 1980-81

No	Date		Att	Pos	Pt	F-A	H-T	Scorers, Times, and Referees	1	2	3	4	5	6	7	8	9	10	11	12 sub used
1	A	PRESTON			D	1-1	0-0	Mann 54	Cashley	Sweeney	Hay	Tainton	Rodgers	Merrick*	Whitehead	Fitzpatrick	Mabbutt	Ritchie	Mann	Garland
	16/8		*6,293*		1			*Elliott 59*	*Tunks*	*Taylor*	*Cameron*	*Burns*	*Baxter*	*Blackley*	*Bell*	*Coleman*	*Elliott*	*Potts*	*McGhee*	
								Ref: M Scott	After four seasons of top-flight struggle, City are given a sharp reminder that life is likely to be no easier at this level. Poor defensive play and an attack that is handled with consummate ease by Preston make City's gaining of a point, thanks to Mann's 25-yarder, somewhat of a miracle.											
2	H	WEST HAM			D	1-1	1-1	Ritchie 15	Cashley	Sweeney	**Baddeley**	Tainton	Rodgers*	Merrick	Fitzpatrick	Mabbutt	Ritchie	Mann	Whitehead	Garland
	19/8		14,001		2			*Cross 19*	*Parkes*	*Stewart*	*Brush*	*Bonds*	*Martin*	*Devonshire*	*Holland*	*Goddard*	*Cross*	*Brooking*	*Pike*	
								Ref: D Lloyd	Trevor Brooking writes off City's chances of being promotion contenders. Ritchie stabs City ahead as they play with style, but the Hammers equalise as Rodgers is injured. City are lucky when Paul Goddard's strike is disallowed for offside as West Ham take control after half-time.											
3	H	BRISTOL ROV		12	D	0-0	0-0		Cashley	Sweeney	Whitehead	Tainton	Gow	Merrick	Fitzpatrick	Mabbutt	Ritchie	Mann	Pritchard	
	23/8		**16,612**	*20*	3				*Thomas*	*Gillies*	*Bater*	*Mabbutt*	*Hughes*	*Lee*	*McCaffery*	*Bar'wclough*	*Williams*	*Bates*	*Penny**	*Pulis*
								Ref: B Daniels	The hot sunshine takes the steam out of this derby clash. Rovers get the point they came for with an ultra-defensive performance. Apart from occasional Gary Mabbutt inspired breaks, City are not troubled, but despite almost constant attacking are lost for ideas to beat Martin Thomas.											
4	A	WATFORD		18	L	0-1	0-0		Cashley	Sweeney	Whitehead	Gow	Hay	Merrick	Tainton	Ritchie	Mabbutt	Mann	Pritchard*	Garland
	30/8		*10,759*	*14*	3			*Patching 78*	*Steele*	*Henderson*	*Jackett*	*Patching*	*Sims*	*Bolton*	*Blissett*	*Poskett*	*Jenkins*	*Train*	*Rostron*	
								Ref: K Hackett	Mistakes at both ends by Alan Hay prove costly. He hesitates too long on his own line as Martin Patching rushes forward to prod in and then shoots over the bar in the final move of the game. Awful City are outclassed by a Watford side putting in 21 shots on goal to City's mere three.											
5	H	SWANSEA		21	L	0-1	0-1		Cashley	Sweeney	Whitehead	Gow	Hay	Merrick	Tainton	Ritchie	Mabbutt	Doyle	Garland*	Pritchard
	6/9		9,761	*7*	3			*James L 21*	*Stewart*	*Attley*	*Hadziabdic*	*Mahoney*	*Stevenson*	*Phillips*	*Giles*	*James R*	*James L*	*Charles*	*Robinson**	*Waddle*
								Ref: R Challis	The City fans turn on chairman Stephen Kew and manager Alan Dicks after another anaemic display. Playing without direction or spark, they are outplayed by a more skilful Swansea. Leighton James, the game's most talented player, curls a 20-yard shot into the net for the only goal.											
6	A	SHEFFIELD WED		22	L	1-2	1-1	Ritchie 37	Cashley	Sweeney	Hay	Tainton	Rodgers	Merrick	Fitzpatrick	Gow	Whitehead	Ritchie	Mabbutt	
	13/9		*15,260*	*6*	3			*Pearson 40, King 53*	*Bolder*	*Blackhall*	*Grant*	*Smith*	*Pickering*	*King*	*Taylor*	*Johnson*	*Owen**	*Pearson*	*Mellor*	*Campbell*
								Ref: B Hill	City, under caretaker boss Ken Wimshurst, are deprived of a point in an indifferent game as Cashley concedes a bizarre goal. Jeff King's effort from 20 yards is going wide before taking deflections off Tainton and then Rodgers to trickle in. A debut goal for 17-year-old John Pearson.											
7	H	NOTTS CO		22	L	0-1	0-0		Cashley	Sweeney	Hay	Tainton	Rodgers !	Merrick	Mann	Gow	Whitehead	Ritchie	Mabbutt	
	20/9		8,253	*3*	3			*Masson 82*	*Avrmovic*	*Benjamin*	*O'Brien*	*Kelly**	*Kilcline*	*Richards*	*McCulloch*	*Masson*	*Harkouk !*	*Hunt*	*Hooks*	*Wood*
								Ref: K Salmon	Rodgers, after being twice booked, is sent off in the 71st min for the first time in his career. Paul Hooks always troubles City with his pace and he sets up County's winner for Don Masson to blast in from 18 yards. Rachid Harkouk is dismissed for violent conduct with two minutes left.											
8	A	QP RANGERS		22	L	0-4	0-2		Cashley	Tainton	Sweeney	Gow	Whitehead	Merrick	Mann	Fitzpatrick	Mabbutt	Ritchie	Pritchard*	**Smith**
	27/9		*8,551*	*17*	3			*Neal 15, 70, Langley 44, Shanks 72*	*Woods*	*McCreary*	*Gillard*	*Waddock*	*Wicks*	*Roeder*	*Neal*	*Shanks*	*Langley*	*Currie*	*Burke*	
								Ref: J Hunting	The Robins still seek their first win of the season as fellow relegation strugglers Rangers tear holes in their 3-4-3 formation. City win the first-half corner count 10-1, but in a game which could easily have produced a dozen goals, they are again let down by their wayward finishing											
9	A	GRIMSBY		22	L	0-1	0-0		Cashley	Sweeney	Hay	Gow	Rodgers*	Merrick	Tainton	Fitzpatrick	Ritchie	Mabbutt	Whitehead	Mann
	4/10		*8,781*	*14*	3			*Drinkell 80*	*Batch*	*Czuczman*	*Crosby*	*Waters*	*Wiggington*	*Moore K*	*Ford*	*Kilmore**	*Drinkell*	*Mitchell*	*Cummimg*	*Brolly*
								Ref: N Midgley	Mabbutt blames himself for ruining new boss Bob Houghton's first game in charge. Just two minutes from the end of this colourless encounter he glides his careful shot wide of the far post. Kevin Drinkell powers in a magnificent header from former City player Mike Brolly's corner.											
10	H	LUTON		21	W	2-1	0-1	Ritchie 58p, Mabbutt 63	Cashley	Sweeney	Hay	Gow	Whitehead	Merrick	Tainton	Fitzpatrick	Mabbutt	Ritchie	Smith	
	7/10		7,571	*16*	5			*Saxby 38*	*Findlay*	*Stephens*	*Donaghy*	*Grealish*	*Saxby*	*Price*	*Hill*	*Stein*	*Harrow*	*West*	*Moss*	
								Ref: C Newsome	City obtain their first win of the season after a poor first-half display. Luton play neat football and Cashley does well to keep them out before Mike Saxby thumps home a rebound. A controversial penalty changes the game and City secure victory when Mabbutt scores from close in.											

No / Date	Venue	Opponent	Att	Pos	Res / Pts	F-A	H-T	Scorers, Times, and Referees	1	2	3	4	5	6	7	8	9	10	11	12 sub used
11	H	NEWCASTLE		21	W	2-0	0-0	Ritchie 71, 89p	Cashley	Sweeney	Hay	Gow	Whitehead	Merrick	Tainton	Fitzpatrick	Mabbutt	Ritchie	Smith	
11/10			10,468	9	7				*Carr*	*Kelly*	*Davies*	*Martin*	*Boam*	*Mitchell*	*Shoulder**	*Wharton*	*Shinton*	*Rafferty*	*Hibbitt*	*Cartwright*
								Ref: D Reeves	Houghton cites looking through old videos as the key to sparking a revival. He changes City's style so as to get the ball forward quicker as Newcastle's unbeaten seven-match run is ended. Ritchie scores with a rocket header and then nets a penalty after the best move of the game.											
12	A	BOLTON		21	D	1-1	1-1	Mabbutt 19	Cashley	Sweeney	Hay	Gow	Whitehead	Merrick	Tainton	Fitzpatrick	Mabbutt	Ritchie	Smith	
18/10			*8,988*	14	8			*Gowling 17*	*Poole*	*Graham*	*Nicholson*	*Cantello*	*Jones*	*Walsh*	*Reid*	*Carter*	*Gowling*	*Kidd*	*Burke*	
								Ref: T Morris	Youngster Gary Smith misses two great chances as City have to settle for a point. The homesters look a dreadfully poor side, but go ahead as Alan Gowling tucks away Mike Carter's cross. City respond immediately as Mabbutt nets with a superb side-foot volley from Tainton's pass.											
13	A	WREXHAM		21	L	0-1	0-0		Cashley	Sweeney	Hay	Gow	Whitehead	Merrick	Tainton	Fitzpatrick	Mabbutt	Ritchie	Smith*	Garland
21/10			***4,179***	12	8			*McNeil 80p*	*Davies*	*Hill*	*Jones*	*Davis*	*Cegleiski*	*Carrodus*	*Fox*	*Sutton*	*McNeil*	*Vinter*	*Cartwright*	
								Ref: J Bray	A drab game which always looked likely to be settled with a penalty. Dreadful City only muster one shot on target and Mabbutt is fortunate to remain on the field after a bad tackle. Tainton concedes spot-kick on being adjudged to have climbed on Mike Vinter's shoulders to head clear.											
14	H	DERBY		21	D	2-2	1-0	Mabbutt 34, 70	Cashley	Sweeney	Hay	Mann*	Whitehead	Merrick	Tainton	Fitzpatrick	Mabbutt	Ritchie	Garland	Smith
25/10			12,049	8	9			*Wilson 86, Emson 90*	*Jones*	*Emery*	*Buckley*	*Sheridan*	*Powell S*	*Osgood*	*Skivington**	*Clark*	*Biley*	*Hector*	*Emson*	*Wilson*
								Ref: A Robinson	A nightmare conclusion for City, as lapses of concentration allow Derby to poach two goals at the death. Mabbutt picks up Steve Emery's poor back-pass to put City ahead and then doubles the advantage to volley in Tainton's cross, before Merrick's pass-back sets up the shock finish.											
15	A	ORIENT		21	L	1-3	1-1	Mabbutt 13	Cashley	Sweeney	Hay	Mann	Whitehead	Merrick	Tainton	Fitzpatrick	Mabbutt	Ritchie	Garland	
1/11			*4,698*	7	9			*Chiedozie 12, Parsons 69, Moores 87*	*Day*	*Fisher*	*Roffey*	*Taylor*	*Gray*	*Parsons*	*Chiedozie*	*Moores*	*Mayo*	*Bowles*	*Margerrison*	
								Ref: C Maskell	City look impressive with their crisp counter-attacking, but are let down by lack of height in defence. The injured Rodgers is sorely missed as Orient fling everything high into the box. City's efforts to draw level are curtailed by Ian Moores, who skilfully flicks in with his back to goal.											
16	H	BLACKBURN		20	W	2-0	0-0	Garland, 47 Tainton 85	Cashley	Sweeney	Hay	Mann	Whitehead	**Marshall**	Tainton	Fitzpatrick	Mabbutt*	Ritchie	Garland	Pritchard
8/11			9,026	5	11				*Butcher*	*Branagan*	*Rathbone*	*Parkes*	*Keeley*	*Fazackerley*	*Brotherston*	*McKenzie*	*Garner*	*Speight*	*Stonehouse*	
								Ref: L Shapter	Sparkling attacking play by City against opponents willing to play open football produces great entertainment for the fans. Garland impresses and fully deserves his headed goal from Whitehead's free-kick. Tainton ties up the points as he cuts inside to whip his shot into the far corner.											
17	A	WEST HAM		21	L	**0-5**	0-2	*[Brooking 72, Cross 85]*	Cashley	Sweeney	Hay	Mann	Marshall	Merrick	Tainton*	Fitzpatrick	Whitehead	Ritchie	Pritchard	Smith
11/11			***25,210***	1	11			*Goddard 11, 89, Martin 16,*	*Parkes*	*Stewart*	*Lampard*	*Bonds*	*Martin*	*Devonshire*	*Holland*	*Goddard*	*Cross*	*Brooking*	*Pike*	
								Ref: J Martin	City are overwhelmed in midfield by the supremely-talented Hammers, especially after the withdrawal of Tainton in the 69th minute. Smith has no chance to adjust to the pace of the game and within three minutes Trevor Brooking puts the result beyond doubt with a close-range shot.											
18	H	PRESTON		21	D	0-0	0-0		Cashley	Sweeney	Hay	Mann	Marshall	Whitehead	Tainton	Fitzpatrick*	Garland	Ritchie	Pritchard	Merrick
15/11			8,467	13	12				*Tunks*	*Westwell*	*McAteer*	*Burns*	*Baxter*	*Blackley*	*Bell*	*Coleman**	*Elliott*	*Bruce*	*McGee*	*Taylor*
								Ref: M Baker	Preston offer little as an attacking force, whilst their keeper Roy Tunks performs miracles to keep City at bay. Pritchard picks up a booking for returning to the field after treatment without the ref's permission. 'Bristol City are too good to go down,' says North End boss Nobby Stiles.											
19	A	CAMBRIDGE		21	L	1-2	0-2	Mann 90	Cashley	Sweeney	Hay	Mann	Marshall	Whitehead	Tainton	Fitzpatrick	Garland	Ritchie	Pritchard	
22/11			*4,922*	8	12			*Lyons 18, 40*	*Key*	*Donaldson*	*Murray*	*Smith*	*Fallon*	*Gibbins*	*O'Neil*	*Spriggs*	*Reilly*	*Lyons*	*Christie*	
								Ref: K Baker	City are flattered by the scoreline as Mann's goal from close range gives them an undeserved reward for a dismal performance. This rather dull game is only enlivened by two goals from John Lyons who shoots home from twelve yards before his header puts the game out of City's reach.											
20	H	OLDHAM		21	D	1-1	0-1	Fitzpatrick 53	Cashley	Sweeney	Hay	Whitehead	Rodgers	Merrick*	Tainton	Fitzpatrick	Mabbutt	Ritchie	Garland	Pritchard
29/11			8,485	20	13			*Heaton 43*	*Platt*	*Hoolickin**	*Blair*	*Keegan*	*Clements*	*Hurst*	*Heaton*	*Futcher*	*Steel*	*Palmer*	*Atkinson*	*Sinclair*
								Ref: T Spencer	A well-organised offside-trap frustrates City, who rue Mabbutt's early failure to score with only the keeper to beat. Oldham are dangerous on the break and Paul Heaton runs clear to beat Cashley, before Fitzpatrick snaps up his first City goal after Mabbutt's left-foot volley hits the bar.											
21	A	SHREWSBURY		21	L	0-4	0-1	*[Edwards 87]*	Shaw	Sweeney	Hay	**Aitken**	Rodgers	Marshall	Tainton	Fitzpatrick	Mabbutt	Ritchie	Whitehead	
6/12			*4,435*	14	13			*Biggins 39, Tong 63, Atkins 72,*	*Wardle*	*King*	*Larkin*	*Turner**	*Griffin*	*Keay*	*Tong*	*Atkins*	*Biggins*	*Petts*	*Cross*	*Edwards*
								Ref: A Challinor	City are made to pay dearly for wasting chances created by their skilful, penetrative football. Ian Atkins creates Shrewsbury's opening goals, before scoring himself. City's misfortune is complete as Edwards blasts home the fourth, straight after Aitken's shot was headed off the line.											

No	Date	Att	Pos	Pt	F-A	H-T	Scorers, Times, and Referees	1	2	3	4	5	6	7	8	9	10	11	12 sub used
22	H BOLTON		21	W	**3-1**	1-1	Mabbutt 4, 47, Aitken 72	Shaw	Sweeney	Hay	Aitken	Rodgers	Marshall	Tainton	Fitzpatrick	Mabbutt	Ritchie	Whitehead*	Garland
	13/12	7,850	*12*	15			*Gowling 15p*	*Poole*	*Graham*	*McElhinney*	*Wilson*	*Jones*	*Brennan*	*Nicholson**	*Whatmore*	*Hoggan*	*Kidd*	*Gowling*	*Thomas*
							Ref: D Hutchinson	City maintain their dominance over opponents seeking to add to their only win at Ashton Gate as long ago as 1904. Alan Gowling equalises for Bolton from the spot after Shaw fells him, but his second-half error results in Aitken chipping in a brilliant goal to keep the City fans happy.											
23	A NEWCASTLE		21	D	0-0	0-0		Shaw	Sweeney	Hay	Aitken	Rodgers	Marshall	Tainton	Fitzpatrick	Mabbutt	Ritchie	Garland*	Pritchard
	20/12	*14,131*	*13*	16				*Carr*	*Carney*	*Johnson*	*Martin*	*Boam*	*Mitchell*	*Shinton*	*Trewick*	*Waddle*	*Shoulder*	*Wharton*	
							Ref: C Seel	Bob Houghton reckons his side will be out of the bottom three by the end of January, but the evidence of this miserable match, against a poor Newcastle side without a goal in four games, suggests he is somewhat over optimistic. At least, City manage to end a run of five away defeats.											
24	H CARDIFF		21	D	0-0	0-0		**Moller**	Sweeney	Hay	Aitken	Rodgers	Marshall	Tainton	Fitzpatrick	Mabbutt !	Ritchie	Garland	
	26/12	15,039	*18*	17				*Healey*	*Jones !*	*Roberts*	*Hughes*	*Pontin*	*Dwyer*	*Lewis*	*Kitchen*	*Stevens*	*Ronson*	*Buchanan*	
							Ref: R Lewis	Poor holiday fare with defences in control. Swedish international keeper Jan Moller demonstrates why City spent £120,000 on him with a late stop from Gary Stevens. Two sendings off right on half-time, Linden Jones for his bad tackle on Mabbutt and the City player for retaliation.											
25	A CHELSEA		21	D	0-0	0-0		Moller	Sweeney	Hay	Aitken	Rodgers	Marshall	Tainton	Fitzpatrick	Garland*	Ritchie	Pritchard	Smith
	27/12	*18,514*	*3*	18				*Borota*	*Locke*	*Rofe*	*Bumstead*	*Pates*	*Chivers*	*Hutchings**	*Fillery*	*Lee*	*Mayes*	*Rh's-Brown*	*Walker*
							Ref: J Warner	City's teenage striker Garry Smith misses a great chance in the dying seconds of securing a first-ever win at Stamford Bridge. With only the keeper to beat, he delays too long and fails to get in a shot. City have the better chances in an even contest, but are let down by poor finishing.											
26	H CAMBRIDGE		21	L	0-1	0-1		Moller	Sweeney	Hay	Aitken	Rodgers	Marshall	Tainton	Fitzpatrick	Mabbutt	Ritchie	Pritchard	
	10/1	9,869	*11*	18			*Marshall 5 (og)*	*Key*	*Donaldson*	*Murray*	*Smith*	*Fallon*	*Finney*	*Streete*	*Spriggs*	*Reilly*	*Taylor*	*Christie*	
							Ref: H King	Misunderstanding between Moller and Marshall floor City as the centre-half heads into the empty net as the keeper comes out. Cambridge, making their first visit to Ashton Gate, put up a great defensive performance for the remaining 85 mins to end City's six-match unbeaten run.											
27	H WATFORD		21	D	0-0	0-0		Shaw	Sweeney	Hay	Aitken	Rodgers	Marshall	Tainton	Fitzpatrick	Mabbutt	Ritchie*	Pritchard	**Chandler**
	17/1	8,982	*14*	19				*Sherwood*	*Rice*	*Harrison*	*Taylor*	*Sims*	*Jackett*	*Callaghan*	*Blissett*	*Armstrong*	*Train*	*Poskett*	
							Ref: N Ashley	Watford manager Graham Taylor is forthright in stating that the windy conditions were too much for all 22 players. Coronation Street's Peter Adamson is among the crowd that see this poor advert for the skill of the combatants. Once again City fail to make the most of their chances.											
28	A BRISTOL ROV		21	D	0-0	0-0		Shaw	Sweeney	Hay	Aitken	Rodgers*	Marshall	Tainton	Fitzpatrick	Mabbutt	Mann	Whitehead	Pritchard
	31/1	*10,087*	*22*	20				*Kite*	*Gillies*	*Jones*	*Cooper*	*Hughes*	*Emmanuel*	*Bar'wclough*	*Williams G*	*Lee*	*Randall*	*Mabbutt*	
							Ref: R Toseland	If not exactly a non-event, two disciplined defences make sure there are no dynamics to excite Eastville's largest and noisiest crowd of the season. City's elation at securing a point is tempered by the fact that Rodgers suffers a broken leg in a 54th-min collision with Vaughan Jones.											
29	H SHEFFIELD WED		21	W	1-0	0-0	Pritchard 49	Moller	Stevens	Sweeney	Aitken	Marshall	**Nicholls**	Tainton	Mann	Mabbutt	Pritchard	Whitehead	
	7/2	11,494	*10*	22				*Bolder*	*Blackhall*	*Grant*	*Smith*	*Shirtliff*	*Sterland*	*Mirocevic*	*Johnson**	*Leman*	*McCulloch*	*Curran*	*Pearson*
							Ref: D Vickers	Wednesday play superbly after half-time, but are beaten when Pritchard touches home a ball from Sweeney, just a minute after Marshall had his strike disallowed. Sweeney gets back quickly to make the goal-line save of the season to head over Andy McCulloch's powerful shot.											
30	H QP RANGERS		21	L	0-1	0-0		Moller	Stevens	Hay	Aitken	Marshall	Nicholls	Tainton	Fitzpatrick	Mabbutt	Mann*	Whitehead	Pritchard
	21/2	11,036	*8*	22			*Waddock 59*	*Burridge*	*Shanks*	*Gillard*	*Fenwick*	*Wicks*	*Hazell**	*Langley*	*King*	*Stainrod*	*Currie*	*Silkman*	*Waddock*
							Ref: M Heath	City fans, given leaflets before the game asking them to purchase ten-year season tickets for £500, are hardly encouraged by this display as the home strikers are easily contained. Substitute Gary Waddock procures the points for the visitors with a superb volley from almost 25 yards.											
31	A NOTTS CO		21	L	1-2	1-2	Nicholls 37	Moller	Stevens	Hay	Aitken	Marshall	Nicholls	Tainton	Fitzpatrick	Mabbutt	Pritchard	Whitehead	
	28/2	*7,609*	*2*	22			*O'Brien 3p, Christie 15*	*Avramovic*	*Benjamin*	*O'Brien*	*Kelly**	*Kilcline*	*Richards*	*McCulloch*	*Masson*	*Christie*	*Hunt*	*Hooks*	*Harkouk*
							Ref: P Willis	The referee sets the City on their way to defeat with a controversial re-take decision for encroachment after Moller saved Ray O'Brien's low shot to his left. City go on to give one of their best displays of the season after Nicholls shoots in, but customary poor finishing lets them down.											

No Date	H/A	Opponent	Att	Pos	Pt	F-A	H-T	Scorers, Times, and Referees	1	2	3	4	5	6	7	8	9	10	11	12
32	H	GRIMSBY		21	D	1-1	0-1	Cumming 75 (og)	Moller	Stevens	Hay	Aitken	Marshall	Nicholls	Tainton	Mann	Mabbutt	Pritchard*	Whitehead	Smith
10/3			6,898	*5*	23			*Cumming 12*	*Batch*	*Moore D*	*Crombie*	*Waters*	*Wigginton*	*Moore K*	*Brolly*	*Whymark*	*Drinkell*	*Mitchell*	*Cumming*	
								Ref: D Civil	City fail to get the breaks they deserve in the mud as they are denied by the brilliance of Grimsby keeper Nigel Batch. He foils City's almost incessant attacks, until colleague Bob Cumming, scorer of the opener with a crisp drive, beats him whilst being put under pressure by Tainton.											
33	A	LUTON		21	L	1-3	1-2	Pritchard 8	Moller	Stevens	Hay	Aitken	Marshall	Whitehead	Tainton*	Fitzpatrick	Mabbutt	Pritchard	Smith	Mann
14/3			*8,745*	*7*	23			*White 24, 35, Moss 75p*	*Findlay*	*Stephens*	*Donaghy*	*Grealish*	*Saxby*	*Price*	*Hill*	*Stein*	*White*	*Antic*	*Moss*	
								Ref: L Burden	Jake Findlay is lucky to stay on the pitch as Tainton is robbed of almost certain goals by blatant professional fouls. Pritchard punishes him for the first infraction by firing home the resultant 25-yard free-kick, but City are incensed in not being given a 42nd-min penalty for his second.											
34	A	SWANSEA		21	D	0-0	0-0		Moller	Stevens	Hay	Aitken	Marshall	Sweeney	Tainton	Fitzpatrick	Mabbutt	Pritchard	Whitehead	
17/3			*10,832*	*7*	24				*Stewart*	*Evans*	*Hadziabdic*	*Rajkovic*	*Charles*	*Stevenson*	*Craig*	*James R*	*Curtis**	*James L*	*Mahoney*	*Robinson*
								Ref: A Hamil	City's inability to take chances continues to be their downfall. Swansea-born Marshall gives his best display for City, while the immaculate control of Mabbutt, the speed of Whitehead and the surging thrusts of Fitzpatrick and Aitken give promise of goals that do not materialise.											
35	H	WREXHAM		21	L	0-2	0-1		Moller	Stevens	Hay	Aitken	Marshall	Sweeney	Tainton	Fitxpatrick	Mabbutt	Pritchard	Whitehead	
21/3			6,948	*15*	24			*Carrodus 45, Fox 77*	*Davies*	*Hill*	*Dwyer*	*Jones*	*Cegleiski*	*Carrodus*	*Fox*	*Arkwright*	*Vinter*	*Buxton*	*Cartwright*	
								Ref: C Thomas	City's hopes of avoiding relegation are buried in the Ashton mud as they give their worst display for more than ten years. Injury-hit Wrexham, missing Mel Sutton and Dixie McNeil, make most of their few chances after defensive hesitation lets in Frank Carrodus to bundle the ball in.											
36	A	DERBY		21	L	0-1	0-0		Moller	Stevens	Hay	Aitken	Marshall	Sweeney	Tainton	Fitzpatrick*	Mabbutt	Smith	Chandler	Mann
28/3			*14,798*	*5*	24			*Swindlehurst 69*	*Jones*	*Emery*	*Buckley*	*Powell S*	*McFarland*	*Powell B*	*Wilson*	*Hector*	*Duncan*	*Swindlehurst*	*Emson*	
								Ref: D Richardson	City fail to score for the 22nd time this season as again their stylish approach play does not produce any reward. David Swindlehurst shoots in from Paul Emson's pull-back for Derby, whilst City boss Houghton laments the fact that scoring chances fell to the wrong players on his side.											
37	H	ORIENT		21	W	**3-1**	0-0	Hay 56, Mann 63, Mabbutt 73	Moller	Stevens	Hay	Aitken	Marshall	Sweeney	Tainton	Mann	Mabbutt	Smith	Chandler	
4/4			6,201	*12*	26			*Jennings 78*	*Day*	*Fisher*	*Roffey*	*Taylor T*	*Gray*	*Moores*	*Chidozie**	*Bowles*	*Jennings*	*Hughton*	*Taylor P*	*Mayo*
								Ref: C Newsome	City find their goalscoring form in the second half as they achieve their first win in nine games. A comedy of errors for City's third as Bobby Fisher loses possession in the area to present an easy chance. Mabbutt heads home after Tainton stumbles and balloons the ball into the air.											
38	A	BLACKBURN		21	L	0-1	0-0		Moller	Stevens	Hay	Aitken	Marshall	Sweeney	Tainton	Fitzpatrick	Mabbutt	Mann	Chandler	
11/4			*9,970*	*3*	26			*Burke 56*	*Arnold*	*Branagan*	*Rathbone*	*Kendall*	*Keeley*	*Fazackerley*	*Garner*	*Crawford*	*Lowey*	*Burke*	*Speight*	
								Ref: G Courtney	City more than match promotion-chasing Blackburn in soccer skills, but again are unable to turn pressure into goals. Hay's mistake gifts Rovers a corner from which Marshall Burke nets with a close-range header to leave City some five points from safety with just four games left.											
39	H	CHELSEA		21	D	0-0	0-0		Moller	Stevens	Hay	Aitken	Marshall	Sweeney	**Musker**	Fitzpatrick	Mabbutt	Mann	Chandler	
18/4			10,011	*9*	27				*Borota*	*Chivers*	*Pates*	*Bumstead*	*Droy**	*Nutton*	*Driver*	*Fillery*	*Lee*	*Mayes*	*Hutchings*	*Locke*
								Ref: A Glasson	Peter Borota looks like a clown with his acrobatics and frying pan gloves, but he has the last laugh. He prevents City from turning one of their most creative displays of the season into victory with many outstanding saves. Locke clears a shot off the line, the only time Borota was beaten.											
40	A	CARDIFF		21	W	3-2	1-1	Mabbutt 39, Mann 58, 90	Moller	Stevens	Hay	Aitken	Marshall	Sweeney	Musker*	Fitzpatrick	Mabbutt	Mann	Chandler	Tainton
20/4			*5,575*	*20*	29			*Grapes 7, Kitchen 70*	*Healey*	*Jones*	*Sullivan*	*Grapes*	*Pontin*	*Dwyer*	*Lewis*	*Kitchen*	*Stevens*	*Ronson*	*Micallef*	
								Ref: M Baker	Cardiff obtain a fortunate equaliser as ref ignores offside flag, but justice is done at the death. Mann's sensational 35-yard injury-time free-kick earns City their first away win for a year as well as rekindling hopes of Second Division survival. Bookings for Phil Dwyer, Hay and Mabbutt.											
41	H	SHREWSBURY		21	D	1-1	1-0	Mann 15	Moller	Stevens	Whitehead*	Aitken	Marshall	Sweeney	Musker	Tainton	Mabbutt	Mann	Chandler	Smith
25/4			**6,042**	*14*	30			*Cross 49*	*Wardle*	*King*	*Leonard*	*Turner*	*Griffin*	*Keay*	*Tong*	*Atkins*	*Dungworth*	*Biggins**	*Cross*	*Bates*
								Ref: C Downey	Moller is at fault as he concedes a goal on losing the ball to John Dungworth, but his blushes are saved by the referee, who incorrectly assumes he has been fouled. A poor showing by City, who went in front with a trademark Mann goal, a 20-yard left-foot thunderbolt into the top corner.											
42	A	OLDHAM		21	L	0-2	0-0		Moller	Stevens	**Williams**	Aitken	Marshall	Sweeney	Tainton	Musker	Mabbutt	Mann*	Chandler	Smith
2/5			*4,785*	*15*	30			*Wylde 48, Heaton 49*	*McDonnell*	*Sinclair*	*Blair*	*Keegan*	*Clements*	*Futcher*	*Wylde*	*Heaton*	*Steel*	*Palmer*	*Atkinson*	
Average	Home 9,765		Away 9,863					Ref: R Bridges	City make the early running, Chandler causing the Latics defence many problems, but fall apart as Oldham banish their relegation fears after the break. Roger Wylde is put clear to slip the ball in, and then Paul Heaton is there to snap a chance from a shot Moller could only half save.											

League Cup				F-A	H-T	Scorers, Times, and Referees	1	2	3	4	5	6	7	8	9	10	11	12 sub used
2:1 A BIRMINGHAM	12	L		1-2	0-1	Ritchie 70	Cashley	Sweeney	Whitehead	Tainton	Gow	Merrick	Fitzpatrick*	Ritchie	Mabbutt	Mann	Pritchard	Hay
26/8	*12,163*	*1:7*				*Ainscow 23, Gemmill 49p*	*Wealands*	*Langan*	*Dennis*	*Curbishley*	*Gallagher*	*Todd*	*Ainscow*	*Bertschin*	*Worthington*	*Gemmill*	*Dillion*	
						Ref: D Richardson	A controversial penalty award against Sweeney sparks City's display of passion and quality as Birmingham are outplayed in the second half. Ritchie heads in from Gow's cross to pull back a goal, but Birmingham hang onto the advantage of Alan Ainscow's twelve-yard cross-shot.											
2:2 H BIRMINGHAM	18	D		0-0	0-0		Cashley	Sweeney	Whitehead	Gow	Hay	Merrick	Tainton	Ritchie	Mabbutt	Doyle*	Garland	Jantunen
2/9	6,955	*1:13*					*Wealands*	*Langan*	*Dennis*	*Curbishley*	*Gallagher*	*Todd*	*Ainscow*	*Bertschin*	*Worthington*	*Gemmill*	*Dillion*	
						Ref: M Bidmead (City lost 1-2 on aggregate)	City, adopting a 4-2-4 formation, start with verve and enthusiasm. Early missed chances upset their attacking plan and they just fade away as Birmingham take control. The cheers of City fans when Jantunen is brought on, turn to boos when they realise that young Doyle is taken off.											

FA Cup				F-A	H-T	Scorers, Times, and Referees	1	2	3	4	5	6	7	8	9	10	11	12 sub used
3 A DERBY	21	D		0-0	0-0		Shaw	Sweeney	Hay	Aitken	Rodgers	Marshall	Tainton	Fitzpatrick	Mabbutt	Garland	Pritchard	
3/1	*19,071*	*5*					*Jones*	*Emery*	*Richards*	*Clark**	*McFarland*	*Ramage*	*Powell S*	*Hector*	*Biley*	*Swindlehurst*	*Emson*	*Reid*
						Ref: D Lloyd	John Shaw keeps the 400-1 outsiders in the Cup, making two brilliant saves to stop Kevin Hector and Alan Biley. A typical cup-tie, full of commitment and endeavour, but lacking much in the way of goalmouth incidents. Bookings for Alan Ramage, Roy McFarland and Hay.											
3R H DERBY	21	W		2-0	1-0	Mabbutt 18, Ritchie 54	Shaw	Sweeney	Hay	Aitken	Rodgers	Marshall	Tainton	Fitzpatrick	Mabbutt	Ritchie	Pritchard	
7/1	13,649	*5*					*Jones*	*Emery*	*Richards*	*Clark*	*Osgood*	*Ramage*	*Powell S*	*Hector*	*Biley*	*Swindlehurst*	*Reid**	*Emson*
						Ref: D Lloyd	A confident win by City, who are inspired by a star performance by Ritchie. A tenacious run down the left by Pritchard sets up a cross for Mabbutt to drive in from 20 yards. Derby only have a couple of opportunities before Ritchie ensures passage to the last 32 with a simple tap-in.											
4 A CARLISLE	21	D		1-1	0-1	Mabbutt 49	Moller	Sweeney	Hay	Aitken	Rodgers	Marshall	Tainton	Fitzpatrick	Mabbutt	Ritchie*	Whitehead	Pritchard
24/1	*10,057*	*3:23*				*Coady 38*	*Swinburne*	*Haigh*	*Coady*	*McDonald*	*Houghton*	*Parker*	*Coughlin*	*Campbell*	*Bannon**	*Beardsley*	*Staniforth*	*Hamilton*
						Ref: D Richardson	City are well on top, especially in the second half when they threaten to take Carlisle apart. A replay would have been unnecessary if chances had been taken; though Moller is called upon to make a great save when Gordon Staniforth's shot is deflected by Marshall in the 81st minute.											
4R H CARLISLE	21	W		5-0	0-0	Mabbutt 47, 59, Ritchie 66p, 70 [Mann 79]	Moller	Sweeney	Hay	Aitken	Rodgers	Marshall	Tainton*	Fitzpatrick	Mabbutt	Ritchie	Whitehead	Mann
28/1	12,801	*3:23*					*Swinburne*	*Haigh*	*Coady*	*McDonald*	*Houghton*	*Parker*	*Coughlin*	*Campbell*	*Bannon*	*Beardsley*	*Staniforth**	*Hamilton*
						Ref: D Richardson	Mabbutt opens the floodgates, though he spurns a hat-trick opportunity for Sunderland-bound Ritchie to mark his farewell appearance with a penalty. Carlisle's best chance occurs in the final minute, but the long arms of Moller deny Paul Bannon when he looks almost certain to score.											
5 A NOTT'M FOREST	21	L		1-2	1-0	Mabbutt 40	Moller	Stevens	Sweeney	Aitken	Marshall	Nicholls	Tainton	Mann	Mabbutt	Pritchard	Whitehead	
14/2	*26,732*	*1:8*				*Robertson 83p, Wallace 88*	*Shilton*	*Anderson*	*Gray F*	*Gray S*	*Burns*	*Gunn*	*Mills*	*Wallace*	*Francis*	*Walsh*	*Robertson*	
						Ref: K Walmsley	Forest, out of sorts following their midweek trip to Japan, are rescued by a late Houdini act. City look likely giant-killers when Mabbutt coolly strokes the ball home, but a debatable pen against Marshall turns the tide. Ian Wallace nets in a goalmouth scramble to deprive City of a replay.											

		P	W	D	L	F	A	W	D	L	F	A	Pts
			Home					Away					
1	West Ham	42	19	1	1	53	12	9	9	3	26	17	66
2	Notts Co	42	10	8	3	26	15	8	9	4	23	23	53
3	Swansea	42	12	5	4	39	19	6	9	6	25	25	50
4	Blackburn	42	12	8	1	28	7	4	10	7	14	22	50
5	Luton	42	10	6	5	35	23	8	6	7	26	23	48
6	Derby	42	9	8	4	34	26	6	7	8	23	26	45
7	Grimsby	42	10	8	3	21	10	5	7	9	23	32	45
8	QP Rangers	42	11	7	3	36	12	4	6	11	20	34	43
9	Watford	42	13	5	3	34	18	3	6	12	16	27	43
10	Sheffield Wed	42	14	4	3	38	14	3	4	14	15	37	42
11	Newcastle	42	11	7	3	22	13	3	7	11	8	32	42
12	Chelsea	42	8	6	7	27	15	6	6	9	19	26	40
13	Cambridge	42	13	1	7	36	23	4	5	12	17	42	40
14	Shrewsbury	42	9	7	5	33	22	2	10	9	13	25	39
15	Oldham	42	7	9	5	19	16	5	6	10	20	32	39
16	Wrexham	42	5	8	8	22	24	7	6	8	21	21	38
17	Orient	42	9	8	4	34	20	4	4	13	18	36	38
18	Bolton	42	10	5	6	40	27	4	5	12	21	39	38
19	Cardiff	42	7	7	7	23	24	5	5	11	21	36	36
20	Preston	42	8	7	6	28	26	3	7	11	13	36	36
21	BRISTOL CITY	42	6	10	5	19	15	1	6	14	10	36	30
22	Bristol Rov	42	4	9	8	21	24	1	4	16	13	41	23
		924	217	144	101	668	405	101	144	217	405	668	924

Odds & ends

Double wins: (0).
Double losses: (4) Notts Co, QP Rangers, Wrexham, Cambridge.

Won from behind: (2) Luton (h), Cardiff (a).
Lost from in front: (2) Sheffield Wed (a), Luton (a).

High spots: Beating Bolton 3-1 at Ashton Gate on 13 December.
Winning 3-2 at Ninian Park on 20 April.
Beating Carlisle 5-0 in the FA Cup.
Reaching the 5th Round of the FA Cup.
Beating Bristol Rov (a) 1-0 in the Gloucestershire Cup Final on 5 May.

Low spots: Losing 0-5 at West Ham on 11 November.
Low spots: Scoring fewer goals (29) than points (30).
Relegation to the Third Division.

Player of the Year: Kevin Mabbutt.
Ever-presents: (0).
Hat-tricks: (0).
Leading scorer: Kevin Mabbutt (14).

	Appearances						Goals			
	Lge	*Sub*	LC	*Sub*	FAC	*Sub*	Lge	LC	FAC	Tot
Aitken, Peter	**22**				5		**1**			**1**
Baddeley, Kevin	**1**									
Cashley, Ray	**20**		2							
Chandler, Ricky	**7**	*1*								
Doyle, Ian	**1**		1							
Fitzpatrick, Tony	**34**		1		4		**1**			**1**
Garland, Chris	**10**	*5*	1		1		**1**			**1**
Gow, Gerry	**11**		2							
Hay, Alan	**36**		1	*1*	4		**1**			**1**
Jantunen, Perti		*1*		*1*						
Mabbutt, Kevin	**38**		2		5		**9**		5	**14**
Mann, Jimmy	**22**	*3*	1		1	*1*	**6**		1	**7**
Marshall, Julian	**26**				5					
Merrick, Geoff	**17**	*1*	2							
Moller, Jan	**17**				3					
Musker, Russell	**4**									
Nicholls, Alan	**4**				1		**1**			**1**
Pritchard, Howard	**15**	*6*	1		3	*1*	**2**			**2**
Ritchie, Tom	**27**		2		3		**5**	1	3	**9**
Rodgers, David	**14**				4					
Shaw, John	**5**				2					
Smith, Gary	**7**	*7*								
Stevens, Paul	**14**				1					
Sweeney, Gerry	**33**		2		5					
Tainton, Trevor	**40**	*1*	2		5		**1**			**1**
Whitehead, Clive	**31**		2		3					
Williams, Gary	**1**									
(own-goals)							**1**			**1**
27 players used	**462**	*25*	**22**	*2*	**55**	*2*	**29**	**1**	**9**	**39**

No	Date		Att	Pos	Pt	F-A	H-T	Scorers, Times, and Referees	1	2	3	4	5	6	7	8	9	10	11	12 sub used
1	A	CARLISLE			D	2-2	0-2	Harford 58, Mann 81	Moller	Stevens	Merrick	Mann	Rodgers	Marshall	Tainton	Musker	Mabbutt	**Harford**	**Devine**	
	29/8		*3,924*		1			*Lee 5, Robson 43*	*Swinburne*	*Ashurst*	*Rushberry**	*Cody*	*Houghton*	*Parker*	*Coughlin*	*Campbell*	*Lee*	*Robson*	*Crabbe*	*Bannon*
								Ref: A Robinson	City recover after a nightmare first half at Brunton Park. Rob Lee is unmarked as he heads home and then, just before the break, Pop Robson nips in between City's tall defenders to nod in Carlisle's second. Harford, City's £150,000 signing, sparks comeback with a glancing header.											
2	H	DONCASTER			D	2-2	2-0	Mabbutt 39, Harford 44	Moller	Stevens	Merrick	Mann	Rodgers	Marshall	Tainton	Musker	Mabbutt	Harford	Devine	
	5/9		6,996		2			*Dawson 81, Mell 89*	*Boyd*	*Russell*	*Dawson*	*Snodin*	*Lally*	*Dowd*	*Pugh*	*Harle*	*Warboys*	*Lister**	*Mell*	*Douglas*
								Ref: A Seville	Two late blunders by Rodgers, shortly after Harford's header hits the post, cost City their first three-point haul in a game they dominate. His failure to cut out a centre gives Richard Dawson an easy chance, and a weak back-pass sets up Stewart Mell to lob the ball over Moller.											
3	A	FULHAM		19	L	1-2	1-0	Mann 9	Moller	Stevens	Hay	Mann	Rodgers	Merrick	Tainton	Musker	Harford	Mabbutt	Devine	
	12/9		*4,196*	*12*	2			*Davies 65, Brown 90*	*Peyton*	*Hopkins*	*Strong*	*Beck*	*Brown*	*Gale*	*Davies*	*Wilson*	*Coney*	*O'Sullivan*	*Lewington*	
								Ref: I Borrett	Fulham control the midfield and keep the City defence under almost constant pressure. Mann produces City's only shot on target when his blockbuster free-kick produces an early lead, while Roger Brown's superb injury-time header presents a deserving winner to the Cottagers.											
4	H	NEWPORT		13	W	2-1	0-1	Mann 58, 86	Moller	Stevens	Sweeney	Aitken	Rodgers	Marshall	Tainton	Mann	Mabbutt	Harford	Hay	
	19/9		8,021	*2*	5			*Aldridge 30*	*Kendall*	*Elsey*	*Lees*	*Davies*	*Oakes*	*Bailey*	*Vaughan*	*Johnson*	*Gwyther*	*Aldridge**	*Moore*	*Tynan*
								Ref: D Vickers	Passions run high as the ref allows City's free-kick equaliser, despite having blown for an encroachment. Moller's save from Gwyther's spot-kick just before half-time is the turning point, and Mann's spectacular 25-yard winning drive into the top corner knocks County off top spot.											
5	H	PLYMOUTH		6	W	3-2	1-2	Harford 2, Nicholls 61, Mann 72	Moller	Stevens	Sweeney	Aitken	Rodgers*	Nicholls	Tainton	Mann	Mabbutt	Harford	Hay	Musker
	22/9		7,383	*23*	8			*Sims 15, Hodges 32*	*Crudgington*	*Nisbet*	*Uzzell*	*Harrison*	*Foster*	*Cooper*	*Hodges*	*Kemp*	*Sims*	*Randell*	*Dennis**	*Murphy*
								Ref: H Taylor	Plymouth's failure to put up a defensive wall allows Mann to save City's blushes with a stunning 35-yard free-kick. City are fortunate as they never look like getting back into game after previously goalless Argyle snatch the lead with a John Sims header and a tap in by Kevin Hodges.											
6	A	PORTSMOUTH		13	L	0-2	0-1		Moller	Stevens	Sweeney	Aitken	Rodgers	Nicholls	Tainton	Mann	Mabbutt	Harford	Hay	
	26/9		*10,203*	*11*	8			*Tait 6, Berry 86*	*Knight*	*McLaughlin*	*Viney*	*Kamara*	*Aizlewood*	*Ellis*	*Hummerman*	*Doyle*	*Rafferty*	*Berry*	*Tait*	
								Ref: M James	A terrible performance by City, as they fall to Mick Tait's header and Steve Berry's mis-hit 30-yard shot from the left touchline that dips into the top corner. Harford puts himself about in the manner of an old fashioned centre-forward, but he needs a supply of good quality crosses.											
7	A	GILLINGHAM		15	D	1-1	0-0	Harford 77	Moller	Stevens	Hay	Aitken	Rodgers	Nicholls	Tainton	Mann	Mabbutt	Harford	Musker	
	29/9		*3,887*	*17*	9			*Price 60*	*Hillyard*	*Sitton*	*Ford*	*Bruce*	*Weatherly*	*Bowman*	*Adams*	*Duncan*	*Tydeman**	*Lee*	*Price*	*Sharpe*
								Ref: K Salmon	Harford's looping header from Stevens' right-wing cross underlines just what a dangerous striker he is with the right service. Unfortunately in this dismal match such service is in short supply and City are somewhat fortunate to respond to Kenny Price's freak ricochet from a clearance.											
8	H	WALSALL		20	L	0-1	0-1		Moller	Stevens	Hay	Aitken	Rodgers	Whitehead	Tainton	Mann	Mabbutt	Harford	Musker	
	3/10		6,049	*4*	9			*Penn 3*	*Green*	*Macken*	*Mower*	*Beech*	*Serella*	*Hart**	*Rees*	*Waddington S*	*Penn*	*Buckley*	*Caswell*	*Loveridge*
								Ref: L Burden	The Saddlers, who have not conceded an away League goal this season, take an early lead. Don Penn is at the near post to put away Mark Rees' cross. City are unlucky when Mabbutt clears the bar with a 17th-minute penalty, but Walsall deserve to avenge their recent cup defeat.											
9	H	PRESTON		19	D	0-0	0-0		Moller	Stevens	Hay	Aitken	Rodgers	Sweeney	Musker	Mann	Mabbutt	Harford	Whitehead	
	10/10		5,454	*22*	10				*Litchfield*	*Coleman*	*McAteer*	*Clark*	*Booth*	*O'Riordan*	*Kelly*	*Buckley*	*Bruce*	*Anderson**	*Dunn*	*Farnelly*
								Ref: L Shapter	In front of the Match of the Day cameras Whitehead demonstrates much of his old guile and pace, but City are nearly made to pay for not making the most of their early domination. Preston almost snatch a late victory, but John Kelly squanders his chance of a debut goal.											
10	A	OXFORD		20	L	0-1	0-1		Moller	Stevens	Hay	Aitken	Rodgers	Sweeney	Devine	Mann	Mabbutt	Harford	Whitehead	
	17/10		*4,087*	*11*	10			*Cassells 45p*	*Burton*	*Doyle*	*Fogg*	*Jeffrey*	*Wright*	*Shotton*	*Jones**	*Foley*	*Cassells*	*Thomas*	*Smithers*	*Kearns*
								Ref: J Moules	Following Fred Ford's death yesterday, this fixture is somewhat appropriate. Oxford's match-winning pen is a travesty as Andy Thomas falls to the ground without any contact being made. City attack relentlessly after the break, having eight shots on target, but the goals don't come.											
11	H	READING		17	W	2-0	0-0	Devine 54, Tainton 79	Moller	Stevens	Hay	Aitken	Rodgers	Sweeney	Tainton	Mann	Harford	Devine	Whitehead	
	20/10		5,178	*10*	13				*Fearon*	*Williams*	*Lewis*	*Wood*	*Hicks*	*Hetzke**	*Earles*	*Dixon*	*Heale*	*Beavon*	*Sanchez*	*Kearney*
								Ref: H King	City produce their most fluent football of the season as Harford wins everything in the air. After the speedy Devine slots home his first League goal, City hit a purple patch and Tainton, Whitehead, Aitken and Harford all go close before Tainton sweeps in a deflection at the far post.											

No	Venue	Opponent / Date	Att	Pos	Res / Pts	F-A	H-T	Scorers, Times, Referees	1	2	3	4	5	6	7	8	9	10	11	12 sub used
12	A	LINCOLN		16	W	2-1	2-0	Harford 33, 39	Moller	Stevens	Tainton	Aitken	Rodgers	Sweeney	Devine	Mann	Mabbutt	Harford	Whitehead	
		24/10	*3,819*	*18*	16			*Bell 60*	*Naylor*	*Thompson*	*McVay*	*Cockerill*	*Peake*	*Carr*	*Commack**	*Shipley*	*Hobson*	*Cunningham*	*Bell*	*Gilbert*
								Ref: K Walmsley	As well as heading both goals for City's first away win of the season, Mick Harford picks up a statuette for helping Lincoln to promotion last term. The Imps deserved their goal, as seconds earlier the ref awarded them a free-kick instead of allowing Tony Cunningham's brilliant lob.											
13	H	CHESTERFIELD		15	D	0-0	0-0		Moller	Stevens	Williams	Aitken	Rodgers	**Boyle**	Tainton	Mann	Harford	Devine	Whitehead	
		31/10	8,110	*3*	17				*Turner*	*Turk*	*O'Neill*	*Wilson*	*Green*	*Ridley*	*Windridge**	*Henderson*	*Bonnyman*	*Kowaiski*	*Crawford*	*Walker*
								Ref: A Ward	Terry Boyle has an outstanding debut after signing from Crystal Palace in a swap deal that saw Kevin Mabbutt move the other way. Much skill and good play by both sides belies the scoreline and causes City boss Bob Houghton to bemoan the introduction of three-points-for-a-win.											
14	A	MILLWALL		17	L	0-2	0-1		Moller	Stevens	Williams	Aitken	Rodgers	Boyle	Tainton	Mann	Harford	Devine	Chandler	
		3/11	*5,002*	*4*	17			*Boyle 43 (og), West 60*	*Gleasure*	*Martin*	*Warman*	*Chatterton*	*Allardyce*	*Slough*	*Hayes*	*Anderson*	*McKenna*	*Horrix*	*West*	
								Ref: J Deakin	Boyle puts his crisp header into the wrong net from Alan West's free-kick, while another West shot hits Aitken on his knee before going in. It could have been worse for a City side too stereotyped and predictable as Millwall miss a 41st-min penalty which Nick Chatterton blasts wide.											
15	A	BRENTFORD		14	W	1-0	0-0	Harford 82	Moller	Stevens	Williams	Aitken	Rodgers	Boyle	Tainton	Mann	Harford	Devine	Chandler	
		7/11	*6,758*	*15*	20				*McKellar*	*Salman*	*Tucker*	*McNichol*	*Whitehead*	*Hurlock*	*Kamara*	*Bowen*	*Johnson**	*Bowles*	*Roberts*	*Booker*
								Ref: A Gunn	Brentford boss Fred Callaghan is scathing of City's negative tactics just five days after the departing Whitehead criticised Houghton as being too defensively minded. City, after hardly mustering an attack in the first half, obtain a late winner when Harford heads in Devine's corner.											
16	H	SOUTHEND		17	L	0-2	0-0		Moller	Stevens	Williams	Aitken	Rodgers	Boyle	Tainton	Mann*	Harford	Devine	Musker	Sweeney
		14/11	6,310	*8*	20			*Cusack 79p, Pennyfather 90*	*Keeley*	*Stead*	*Yates*	*Pennyfather*	*Moody*	*Cusack*	*Gray**	*Poutney*	*Spence*	*Mercer*	*Nelson*	*Greaves*
								Ref: D Hutchinson	Keith Mercer insists he is no cheat on being awarded a penalty. He refutes City players' allegations that he dived following a Rodgers tackle outside the box. Southend, the better side throughout, make sure of their success when Glenn Pennyfather's half-hit shot trickles over the line.											
17	H	BURNLEY		19	L	2-3	1-1	Mann 16p, Garland 52	Moller	Stevens	Williams	Aitken	Rodgers	Boyle	Devine	Mann	Harford	Garland	Musker	
		28/11	5,255	*20*	20			*Young 3, McGee 77, 90p*	*Stevenson*	*Laws*	*Wharton*	*Cassidy*	*Overson*	*Phelan*	*Dobson*	*Steven**	*Hamilton*	*McGee*	*Young*	*Potts*
								Ref: C Thomas	Two decisions by referee Clive Thomas, in his last League season, decide this enthralling contest. City are denied a valid claim for an 85th-minute penalty, whilst Burnley's, five minutes later, is given to enable them to obtain due reward for their fine display of one-touch football.											
18	A	SWINDON		20	D	0-0	0-0		Moller	Stevens	Williams	Aitken	Boyle	Nicholls	Devine	Mann	Chandler	Harford	Tainton	
		5/12	*7,236*	*19*	21				*Allan*	*Baddeley*	*Williams*	*Hughes*	*Lewis*	*Graham*	*Emmanuel*	*Carter*	*Rowland*	*Rideout*	*Pritchard*	
								Ref: J Martin	City's young defenders emerge with credit from this game, in which the attackers of both sides are devoid of ideas. Mann breaks clear in the last minute, but his left-foot shot flashes just wide. Howard Pritchard missed Swindon's best chance on five mins when his header hit the bar.											
19	A	BRISTOL ROV		21	L	0-1	0-1		Moller	Stevens	Williams	Aitken	Rodgers	Boyle	Tainton	Mann	Chandler	Harford	Devine	
		29/12	***12,155***	*8*	21			*McCaffery 4*	*Thomas*	*Jones*	*Williams B*	*McCaffery*	*Parkin*	*Mabbut*	*Barrett**	*Gillies*	*Penny*	*Slatter*	*Williams D*	*Stephens*
								Ref: T Bune	Rovers end 18 years of City dominance in League encounters in an exciting clash that sees Archie Stephens hit a post as well as having his header cleared off the line. Aidan McCaffery is Rovers' hero, as he beats Moller with a low drive from Timmy Parkin's flick on from a corner.											
20	H	WIMBLEDON		21	L	1-3	1-1	Stevens 45	Moller	Stevens	Williams	Aitken	Boyle	Nicholls	Tainton	Mann	Chandler	Harford	Devine*	Sweeney
		2/1	4,781	*23*	21			*Ketteridge 38, Lazarus 63, 77*	*Beasant*	*Clement*	*Thomas*	*Smith*	*Morris*	*Downes*	*Ketteridge*	*Leslie*	*Lazarus*	*Hodges*	*Joseph*	
								Ref: K Barrett	City disintegrate completely in the second half and suffer a humiliating defeat to end Houghton's Ashton Gate reign. Stevens gets his first League goal for City, who thrice hit the woodwork, but they are torn apart by Francis Joseph, who sets up two of Wimbledon's strikes.											
21	H	HUDDERSFIELD		20	D	0-0	0-0		Moller	Stevens	Williams	Aitken	Boyle	Nicholls	Tainton	Mann	Chandler*	Harford	Musker	Garland
		16/1	5,142	*8*	22				*Taylor*	*Brown*	*Burke*	*Stanton*	*Sutton*	*Hanvey*	*Lillis*	*Kennedy*	*Fletcher*	*Hotte*	*Cowling*	
								Ref: A Hamil	It takes the 75th-minute appearance of sub Garland to wake City up and he is deprived of a penalty near the end when he falls over the keeper's arm. A poor game, after which Terriers boss Mike Buxton says 'if any of my players are happy with their play I will throw them off the coach'.											
22	A	NEWPORT		21	D	1-1	1-1	Harford 16	Moller	Stevens	Williams	Aitken	Boyle*	Sweeney	Tainton	Mann	Chandler	Harford	Musker	Hay
		30/1	*5,915*	*17*	23			*Vaughan 12*	*Kendall*	*Lees*	*Relish*	*Davies*	*Oakes*	*Johnson*	*Vaughan*	*Elsey*	*Aldridge**	*Waddle*	*Moore*	*Tynan*
								Ref: C White	The City fans who travel to Newport fearing it might be the club's final game are rewarded by players who give their all in a match they should have won. Nigel Vaughan drives in a low shot to put County ahead, but City equalise as Harford glances Mann's corner past Mark Kendall.											
23	H	FULHAM		22	D	0-0	0-0		Moller	Stevens	Hay	**Newman***	Williams	Nicholls	Musker	**Bray**	Chandler	Harford	**Economou**	**Smith**
		6/2	9,312	*2*	24				*Peyton*	*Lock*	*Strong*	*O'Driscoll*	*Brown*	*Gale*	*Tempest*	*Wilson*	*Coney*	*O'Sullivan*	*Lewington*	
								Ref: M Heath	A triumph for the club given up for dead earlier in the week, as they never look remotely in danger of losing against high-riding Fulham. Denuded by the departure of the Ashton Gate Eight, the Bristol Babes match Fulham for skill and often outplay them with their enthusiasm.											

LEAGUE DIVISION 3

Manager: Houghton ⇨ Hodgson ⇨ Sharpe

SEASON 1981-82

No	Date		Att	Pos	Pt	F-A	H-T	Scorers, Times, and Referees	1	2	3	4	5	6	7	8	9	10	11	12 sub used
24	A	PLYMOUTH		22	L	1-2	0-1	Chandler 71	Moller	Stevens	Hay	Newman	Williams	Nicholls	Musker	Bray	Chandler	Harford	Economou	
	9/2		*5,260*	*11*	24			*Cook 38, Hodges 64*	*Crudgington*	*Nisbet*	*Uzzell*	*Harrison*	*James*	*Cooper*	*Hodges*	*Cook*	*Sims*	*Randell*	*Rogers*	
								Ref: G Napthine	Moller stands between Plymouth and an avalanche of goals at Home Park. He makes eight outstanding saves as Plymouth mount incessant pressure and even gets a hand to Jeff Cook's opener. City's only respite is when Chandler gets his first League goal with a great solo effort.											
25	A	WALSALL		22	W	1-0	1-0	Newman 34	Moller	Stevens	Hay	Newman	Williams	Nicholls	Musker	Bray	Chandler	Harford	Economou*	Smith
	13/2		*4,020*	*8*	27				*Green*	*Macken**	*Mower*	*Beechr*	*Serella*	*Hart*	*Reest*	*Lowrey*	*Penn*	*Buckley*	*Cashwell*	*Round*
								Ref: T Mills	Walsall's aggressive tactics are condemned by City boss Roy Hodgson as the Babes bring off the Third Division shock result of the day. City's goal by Newman is reminiscent of those by Mann before his enforced departure – a 20-yard free-kick that the Walsall keeper does not see.											
26	H	PORTSMOUTH		22	L	0-1	0-0		Moller	Stevens	Williams	Newman	**McCaffery**	Nicholls	Musker	**Carter**	Chandler	Harford	Hay	
	20/2		9,407	*16*	27			*Rafferty 80*	*Knight*	*McLaughlin*	*Bryant*	*Barnard*	*Aizlewood**	*Garner*	*Hammerman*	*Rafferty*	*Gregory*	*Bason*	*Crown*	*Bartlett*
								Ref: M Baker	City play attractive, fluent football in a one-sided game, but are unable to put their chances away. Pompey make City pay as a poor back-pass by Nicholls gives Bill Rafferty the solitary goal. Newman and Chandler are both unfortunate with efforts which came back off the woodwork.											
27	H	EXETER		22	W	3-2	2-1	Harford 17, 30, Chandler 82	Moller	Stevens	Williams	Newman*	McCaffery	Nicholls	Musker	Carter	Chandler	Harford	Hay	Economou
	23/2		6,617	*18*	30			*Roberts 29, Rogers P 81*	*Bond*	*Mitchell**	*Sparrow*	*Rogers M*	*Foster*	*Roberts L*	*Fisher*	*Rogers P*	*Kellow*	*Delve*	*Pullar*	*Pratt*
								Ref: D Reeves	Against the most entertaining side in the country, whose 26 League games have produced 105 goals, City are imperiously driven forward by Musker. City's opener is their best goal for years, as Chandler's cross from the right is headed in with the speed of a bullet by Mick Harford.											
28	A	PRESTON		18	W	3-1	1-1	McCaffery 45, Bray 50, Harford 90	Moller	Stevens	Williams	Bray	McCaffery	Nicholls	Musker*	Carter	Chandler	Harford	Hay	Newman
	27/2		*6,424*	*22*	33			*Kelly 23*	*Hodge*	*Taylor**	*McAteer*	*Bell*	*Booth*	*O'Riordan*	*Kelly*	*McGee*	*Elliott*	*Naughton*	*Bruce*	*Anderson*
								Ref: G Courtney	Three superb goals, stern defending and a large amount of luck brings a vital win. Preston monopolise the play, but City have all the breaks after John Kelly scores from twelve yards in a goalmouth scramble. Bray notches his first City goal as his 35-yarder loops over the keeper.											
29	H	OXFORD		21	L	0-2	0-0		Moller	Stevens	Williams	Bray	McCaffery	Nicholls	**Gooding**	Carter	Chandler	Harford	Hay	
	6/3		8,155	*4*	33			*Shotton 50, Kearns 83*	*Burton*	*Doyle*	*Farr*	*Jeffery*	*Briggs*	*Shotton*	*Brock*	*Foley*	*Cassells**	*Thomas*	*Seacole*	*Kearns*
								Ref: A Robinson	City fail to adjust to the muddy conditions as Oxford's greater skill and direct approach brings about a disappointing defeat. Carter is denied his first League goal by Roy Burton's great save on 15 mins. Oxford give new manager Jim Smith a great start with a slick second-half display.											
30	A	READING		21	L	1-3	0-0	Dixon 62 (og)	Moller	Stevens	Williams	Bray	McCaffery	Nicholls	Musker	Carter	Chandler	Gooding*	Hay	Newman
	10/3		*3,552*		33			*Dixon 54, 86, Beavon 56*	*Fearon*	*Williams J*	*White*	*Webb*	*Hicks*	*Hetzke*	*Beavon*	*Earles*	*Dixon*	*Sanchez*	*Donnellan**	*Lewis*
								Ref: V Callow	City's lightweight side are again found out by the muddy conditions. Reading's Kerry Dixon ends a barren eight-match spell with a bizarre hat-trick. A cracking drive is followed by a headed own-goal, before finishing with a shot from the right past the badly-positioned Moller.											
31	H	LINCOLN		22	L	0-1	0-1		Moller	Stevens	Hay	Newman	McCaffery	Williams	Bray	Carter	Chandler	Gooding	Economou	
	13/3		6,570	*5*	33			*Cunningham 35*	*Felgate*	*Carr*	*Turner P*	*Cockerill*	*Peake*	*Thompson*	*Shipley*	*Turner W*	*Hobson*	*Cunningham*	*Hibbard*	
								Ref: D Civil	Lincoln extend their unbeaten run to ten games with a sweetly hit left-foot shot from 12 yards. Moller blames a long-standing shoulder injury for failing to keep a clean sheet in his final game, but it is doubtful that any keeper would have been able to save Tony Cunningham's strike.											
32	A	CHESTERFIELD		22	L	0-1	0-0		Shaw	Stevens	Hay	Newman	Williams	Nicholls	Musker	Bray	Carter	Harford	Economou	
	20/3		*4,240*	*1*	33			*Wilson 68*	*Turner*	*Stirk*	*O'Neill*	*Wilson*	*Green**	*Pollard*	*Windridge*	*Henderson*	*Bonnyman*	*Ridley*	*Crawford*	*Athersych*
								Ref: N Glover	City are made to pay for their misses against top of the table Chesterfield. Harford hits the post with his shot when clean through in the 55th minute, and then Economou and Bray spurn good chances before Danny Wilson settles the game for the Spireites with a spectacular 20-yarder.											
33	H	BRENTFORD		22	L	0-1	0-0		Shaw	Stevens	Hay	Newman*	Williams	Nicholls	Musker	Bray	Chandler	Carter	Economou	Boyle
	27/3		6,243	*7*	33			*Bowen 67*	*McKellar*	*McNicholl*	*Hill*	*Salman*	*Whitehead*	*Hurlock*	*Kamara !*	*Johnson*	*Bowen*	*Bowles*	*Roberts*	
								Ref: D Lloyd	City's lack of experience shows against a Brentford side reduced to ten men early on. Chandler is unfortunate when hitting the woodwork twice in the second half, but Keith Bowen makes no mistake and steers the ball into a vacant net after a mix up between Shaw and Boyle.											
34	A	SOUTHEND		22	L	0-3	0-0		Shaw	Stevens	Williams	Musker	Boyle	Nicholls !	Economou*	Bray	Chandler	Carter	Hay	Newman
	3/4		*3,416*	*9*	33			*Greaves 68, 75, Phillips 73p*	*Cawston*	*Stead*	*Yates*	*Pountney*	*Moody*	*Hadley*	*Greaves*	*Phillips*	*Nelson**	*Mercer*	*Otulakowski*	*Spence*
								Ref: A Ward	City look capable of taking a point from this undistinguished game until Nicholls gets involved in an off-the-ball incident with Steve Phillips to gift Southend their penalty. Danny Greaves heads Southend in front and then punishes slack marking at a free-kick to coolly slot in their third.											

No	Date	Venue	Opponent	Att	Pos	Pts	Res	F-A	H-T	Scorers, Times, and Referees	1	2	3	4	5	6	7	8	9	10	11	12
35	6/4	H	CARLISLE	4,329	22	34	D	1-1	0-1	Chandler 79	Shaw	Stevensr	Williams	Musker	Boyle	Nicholls	Bray	Chandler	Newman	Carter	Hay	
					3					*Lee 8*	*Swinburn*	*Parker*	*Rushbury*	*Larkin*	*Ashurst*	*Craig*	*Ritchie*	*Haigh*	*Robson*	*Lee*	*Stainiforth*	
										Ref: M Robinson	A battling City performance as Hodgson's decision to field a more attacking formation presents Carlisle with a dream start. Dave Rushbury's cross-field pass sets up Bob Lee's angled drive, but Chandler makes up for his open-goal miss against Southend by lobbing in the equaliser.											
36	10/4	A	EXETER	*4,580*	22	34	L	0-4	0-2		Shaw	Stevens	Williams	Musker	Boyle	Nicholls	Bray	Chandler	Newman	Carter*	Hay	Economou
					15					*Kellow 29, 65p, Pratt 41, Rogers P 76*	*Bond*	*Rogers M*	*Sparrow*	*Giles*	*Foster*	*Roberts P*	*Pratt*	*Rogers P*	*Kellow*	*Delve*	*Hatch*	
										Ref: D Hedges	Enterprising Exeter take their League goals total to 60 with a clinical demolition of City who, whilst lively in midfield, show little confidence in attack. After Kellow's diving header puts Exeter ahead, Pratt seizes on a Williams slip as he attempts to control Shaw's short throw-out.											
37	12/4	H	BRISTOL ROV	**11,451**	22	34	L	1-2	0-1	Bray 66	Shaw	Stevens	Williams	Musker	Boyle	Nicholls	Bray	Chandler	Newman*	Economou	Hay	Devine
					13					*Williams D 3, Randall 54*	*Kite*	*Jones*	*Slatter*	*Randall*	*Parkin*	*Bailey*	*Barrett*	*Williams D*	*Stephens**	*Mabbutt*	*Williams G*	*McCaffery*
										Ref: R Lewis	Rovers are fortunate to hang on in an incident-packed derby following Bray's carefully placed 20-yarder. City have eight shots on target to three for the Rovers, but they have no one to match the ability of David Williams, who finds the corner of the net with a sweet 25-yard drive.											
38	17/4	H	SWINDON	6,929	23	34	L	0-3	0-1		Shaw	Stevens	Hay	Musker	Boyle	Williams	Devine*	Bray	Chandler	Carter	Economou	Newman
					21					*Pritchard 25, Emmanuel 49, 62*	*Allan*	*Henry**	*Baddeley*	*Emmanuel*	*Lewis*	*Stroud*	*Pritchard*	*Carter*	*Rideout*	*Greenwood*	*Graham*	*Quinn*
										Ref: J Bray	City hit a new low as they illustrate to their dwindling band of fans that they are not good enough to retain their status. Fatal hesitation by Williams allows Howard Pritchard to shoot Swindon ahead, while Gary Emmanuel twice runs through City's defence to add a couple more.											
39	21/4	A	CHESTER	***1,210***	22	35	D	0-0	0-0		Shaw	Stevens	Hay	Musker	Boyle	Nicholls	Williams	Bray*	Chandler	Carter	Economou	Devine
					24						*Millington*	*Cottam*	*Burns*	*Storton*	*Zelem*	*Blackwell*	*Sutcliffe*	*Jones*	*Allen*	*Ludlam*	*Henderson*	
										Ref: N Wilson	Shaw keeps City in the game by saving John Allen's thundering drive and a Bryn Jones header in the first half, as well as coming off his line to deny Peter Henderson after the break. City could have stolen the points as four clear chances go begging in the last five minutes.											
40	24/4	A	BURNLEY	*7,063*	23	35	L	0-2	0-0		Shaw	Stevens	Hay	Musker	Boyle	Nicholls	Williams	Devine	Chandler	Carter*	Economou	Newman
					5					*Laws 60, Dobson 80*	*Stevenson*	*Laws*	*Wharton*	*Cassidy*	*Overson*	*Holt*	*Dobson*	*Steven*	*Hamilton*	*McGee*	*Young*	
										Ref: G Owen	Manager Hodgson is proud of his side after an outstanding effort reaps no reward because of continued failings in front of goal. City miss chances before Brian Laws hammers in a low cross to put Burnley ahead. Martin Dobson seals the points by turning the ball over the line.											
41	1/5	H	GILLINGHAM	4,183	23	38	W	2-1	1-0	Williams 41, Economou 85	Shaw	Williams	Hay	Musker	Boyle	Nicholls	Economou	Devine	Chandler	Stevens	Carter	
					11					*Lee 75*	*Hillyard*	*White*	*Adams*	*Bruce*	*Weartherly*	*Shaw**	*Powell*	*Tydeman*	*Grewcock*	*Cascarino*	*Lee*	*Sage*
										Ref: T Spencer	A carnival atmosphere at Ashton Gate as three days after the announcement that the future of the club has been secured, City achieve their first win in 13 games. City, under caretaker boss Gerry Sharpe, benefit with both Williams and Economou scoring their first goals for the club.											
42	4/5	A	HUDDERSFIELD	*3,468*	23	38	L	**0-5**	0-3	*Boyle 3 (og), Cowling 11, Robins 29, [Stanton 62, Wilson 88]*	Shaw	Williams	Hay	Musker	Boyle	Nicholls	Economou	Devine	Chandler	Stevens	Carter*	Newman
					14						*Cox*	*Brown*	*Burke*	*Stanton*	*Valentine*	*Hanvey*	*Lillis*	*Kennedy*	*Robins*	*Wilson*	*Cowling*	
										Ref: M Scott	City's relegation is assured as their adventurous approach is spoilt by wretched defending. Boyle deflects in Micky Kennedy's corner, while hesitation by Williams allows Dave Cowling to head into the vacant net. Then Stevens gifts Huddersfield their fifth goal with a poor back-pass.											
43	3/5	A	WIMBLEDON	*2,114*	23	39	D	0-0	0-0		Shaw	Stevens	Hay	Musker	Williams	Nicholls	Bray	Devine	Chandler	Newman	Economou	
					22						*Beasant*	*Leslie*	*Armstrong*	*Smith*	*Morris*	*Downes*	*Thomas*	*Joseph*	*Hodges*	*Evans*	*Belfield**	*Ketteridge*
										Ref: D Axcell	Wimbledon have the better chances, with Francis Joseph hitting the post early on and John Leslie having a 67th-minute strike disallowed for offside. Chandler, with two more misses, continues his run of bad luck, while Williams mars much excellent play with his casual attitude.											
44	12/5	H	MILLWALL	**3,404**	23	42	W	**4-1**	2-1	Newman 22, 35p, Chandler 55, 65	Shaw	Williams	Hay	Musker	Boyle	Nicholls	Bray*	Stevens	Chandler	Newman	Economou	Smith
					8					*Dibble 45*	*Gleasure*	*Roberts*	*Robinson*	*Chatterton*	*Kitchener**	*Allardyce*	*Massey*	*Shinton*	*Horrix*	*Dibble*	*West*	*Hayes*
										Ref: C Newsome	Shaw inspires City to their best win of the season as he leaps to his left to save Nicky Chatterton's 49th-minute spot-kick. Newman takes Peter Gleasure by surprise with a 20-yarder for the first goal, and Chandler holds off two defenders as he controls a 40-yard pass to net on 55 minutes.											
45	15/5	H	CHESTER	4,475	23	45	W	1-0	1-0	Chandler 39	Shaw	Williams*	Hay	Musker	Boyle	Nicholls	Bray	Stevens	Chandler	Newman	Economou	Smith
					24						*Millington*	*Dean*	*Raynor*	*Zelam*	*Cottam*	*Ludlam*	*Allen*	*Williams**	*Simpson*	*Jones*	*Henderson*	*Blackwell*
										Ref: A Glasson	Poor finishing as well as acrobatic goalkeeping by Grenville Millington prevents a more convincing win. Boyle cracks a header against the bar and Economou's cracking drive hits the post. A great winning goal as Chandler wins the ball in the centre-circle and runs through to stroke in.											
46	18/5	A	DONCASTER	*4,252*	23	46	D	2-2	0-2	Thompson 81, Chandler 84	Shaw	Stevens	**Down**	Musker	Boyle	Hay	Economou	Bray*	Chandler	Newman	Smith	**Thompson**
					19					*Snodin 5, 20*	*Humphries S*	*Allanson**	*Russell*	*Lister*	*Humphries G*	*Wigginton*	*Pugh*	*Liddell*	*Mell*	*Snodin*	*Little*	*Douglas*
		Home	Away							Ref: R Bridges	A touch of deja-vu, but this time it is Doncaster who suffer as City hit back with two late goals to snatch a draw. Despite conceding two opportunist strikes, City fight back to dominate the second half. Thompson caps his debut with a well-struck goal from the edge of the area.											
Average		6,511	5,077																			

League Cup			Att	Pos	Res	F-A	H-T	Scorers, Times, and Referees	1	2	3	4	5	6	7	8	9	10	11	12 sub used
1:1	H	WALSALL			W	2-0	2-0	Harford 28, Mann 44	Moller	Stevens	Merrick	Mann	Rodgers	Marshall	Tainton	Musker	Mabbutt	Harford	Devine	
1/9			3,944						*Green*	*Macken*	*Mower*	*Beech*	*Serella*	*Hart*	*Waddington S*	*Caswell*	*Penn*	*Buckley*	*Preece*	
								Ref: D Letts	Moller's brilliant save – his arm seeming to stretch to push Alan Buckley's 63rd-min header round the post – frustrates a Walsall side who create many chances. Mann unleashes one of his long-distance thunderbolts to give City a healthy advantage to take into the second leg.											
1:2	A	WALSALL		19	L	0-1	0-0		Moller	Stevens	Sweeney	Aitken	Rodgers	Merrick*	Musker	Mann	Mabbutt	Harford	Hay	Devine
15/9			*2,830*	*22*				*Penn 84*	*Green*	*Macken*	*Mower**	*Beech*	*Serella*	*Hart*	*Rees*	*Waddington S*	*Penn*	*Buckley*	*Caswell*	*Round*
								Ref: K Hackett (City won 2-1 on aggregate)	A nerve-jangling finale after Hay shoots at the keeper to waste an early chance for City. Walsall get a late lifeline when Don Penn runs the ball in from what looks like an offside position. City are then reduced to kick-anywhere tactics and are rather fortunate to survive to make progress.											
2:1	A	CARLISLE		19	D	0-0	0-0		Moller	Stevens	Hay	Aitken	Rodgers	Sweeney	Whitehead	Mann	Mabbutt	Harford	Musker	
6/10			*4,111*	*7*					*Swinburne*	*Parker*	*Rushbury*	*Haigh*	*Ashurst*	*Larkin*	*Coughlin*	*Beardsley*	*Lee*	*Crabbe**	*Staniforth*	*Hamilton*
								Ref: D Owen	City's non-stop running prevents Carlisle, who had won their four previous home games, from settling. The Cumbrians set out at a frantic pace, but by the finish City look the more likely winners. Mabbutt misses City's best chance, when slicing a close range shot on 37 minutes.											
2:2	H	CARLISLE		16	W	2-1	0-1	Rodgers 49, Mann 89p	Moller	Stevens	Tainton	Aitken	Rodgers	Sweeney	Devine	Mann	Mabbutt	Harford	Whitehead	
27/10			5,220	*7*				*Staniforth 35p*	*Swinburne*	*Parker*	*Rushbury*	*Campbell*	*Ashurst*	*Larkin*	*Crabbe*	*Robson*	*Lee*	*Beardsley*	*Staniforth*	
								Ref: A Robinson (City won 2-1 on aggregate)	'Poetic justice' says David Rodgers, as the ref gives City a controversial last-minute penalty. Whitehead admits that Tony Larkin's challenge on him was perfectly fair, whilst Rodgers, who had volleyed in City's equaliser, is adamant that Dave Rushbury blatantly dived for his award.											
3	A	QP RANGERS		14	L	0-3	0-2		Moller	Stevens	Williams	Aitken	Rodgers	Boyle	Tainton	Mann	Harford	Devine	Musker	
10/11			*9,215*	*2:3*				*Flanagan 8, Stainrod 40, Allen 47*	*Burridge*	*Gregory*	*Fenwick*	*Wilkins*	*Hazell*	*Roeder*	*Micklewhite*	*Flanagan**	*Allen*	*Stainrod*	*Gillard*	*Stewart*
								Ref: J Bray	On the artificial surface at Loftus Road, Stevens complains he has been pushed out of City's wall when Mike Flanagan fires in. Impressive Rangers make sure of passage to the fourth round with a cracking shot by Simon Stainrod and Clive Allen's header either side of half-time.											

FA Cup			Att	Pos	Res	F-A	H-T	Scorers, Times, and Referees	1	2	3	4	5	6	7	8	9	10	11	12 sub used
1	H	TORQUAY		17	D	0-0	0-0		Moller	Stevens	Williams	Aitken	Rodgers	Boyle	Tainton	Mann	Harford	Devine	Chandler	
20/11			5,221	*4:8*					*O'Keefe*	*Jones*	*Pethard*	*Brown*	*Wilson*	*Larmour*	*Fell*	*Lawrence*	*Cooper*	*Rioch*	*Sermanni*	
								Ref: L Burden	Struggling City find no relief in the FA Cup as Torquay offer most of the ideas in a dull first-round tie. Further disappointment for Chandler, who is still waiting to score his first City goal. He had an effort disallowed at Brentford and quite rightly two ruled out for offside in this clash.											
1R	A	TORQUAY		17	W	2-1	0-0	Mann 62, 81	Moller	Stevens	Williams	Aitken	Rodgers	Boyle	Tainton	Mann	Harford	Devine	Musker	
25/11			*4,334*	*4:8*				*Lawrence 69*	*O'Keefe*	*Jones*	*Pethard*	*Brown*	*Wilson*	*Larmour*	*Bowker*	*Lawrence*	*Cooper*	*Rioch*	*Sermanni*	
								Ref: L Burden	Mann's explosive shooting earns City passage through to the second round in a thrilling replay. Torquay, with eleven shots on target compared to City's three, threaten to run riot. Moller though, is in outstanding form, but even he can do nothing about United's brilliant headed equaliser.											
2	H	NORTHAMPTON		20	W	3-0	1-0	Tainton 24, Harford 64, 85	Moller	Stevens	Williams	Aitken	Rodgers	Boyle	Tainton	Mann	Chandler	Harford	Devine	
15/12			2,901	*4:24*					*Poole*	*Saunders*	*Saxby*	*Brady*	*Gage*	*Sandy*	*Coffill*	*Buchanan*	*Heeley*	*Phillips*	*Mahoney**	*Alexander*
								Ref: A Hamil	A poor game in which Tainton nets with a 20-yarder and Harford has a superb header disallowed. Northampton fall away after Mark Heeley's shot is judged not to have crossed the line. Harford strikes with a header and then a firm shot after seizing on Gary Saxby's poor back-pass.											
3	A	PETERBOROUGH		21	W	1-0	0-0	Chandler 64	Moller	Stevens	Williams	Aitken	Boyle	Nicholls	Tainton	Mann	Chandler	Harford	Musker	
6/1			*6,811*	*4:6*					*Freeman*	*Butler*	*Collins*	*Gynn*	*Smith*	*Rodaway*	*Syrett*	*Kellock*	*Cooke*	*Massey**	*Chard*	*Cliss*
								Ref: B Stevens	Chandler's first goal in senior football makes him worth his weight in gold to hard up City. The former England Schoolboy International shoots past Neil Freeman after swivelling on Harford's headed pass. Posh are on top in the first half and Phil Chard hits City's post in the second min.											
4	H	ASTON VILLA		22	L	0-1	0-0		Moller	Stevens	Williams	Aitken	Boyle	Sweeney	Tainton	Mann	Garland*	Harford	Musker	Chandler
23/1			20,279	*1:16*				*Shaw 78*	*Rimmer*	*Swain*	*Gibson*	*Evans*	*Williams*	*Mortimer*	*Blair*	*Shaw*	*Withe*	*Cowans*	*Morley*	
								Ref: B Hill	On top in the first half and given more space than by Third Division sides, City play neat and constructive football against top flight Villa, but are not particularly threatening in attack. Gary Shaw is fortunate with the only goal as Aitken's shin deflects his mis-hit shot past Moller.											

		Home						Away					
		P	W	D	L	F	A	W	D	L	F	A	Pts
1	Burnley	46	13	7	3	37	20	8	10	5	29	25	80
2	Carlisle	46	17	4	2	44	21	6	7	10	21	29	80
3	Fulham	46	12	9	2	44	22	9	6	8	33	29	78
4	Lincoln	46	13	7	3	40	16	8	7	8	26	24	77
5	Oxford	46	10	8	5	28	18	9	6	8	35	31	71
6	Gillingham	46	14	5	4	44	26	6	6	11	20	30	71
7	Southend	46	11	7	5	35	23	7	8	8	28	28	69
8	Brentford	46	8	6	9	28	22	11	5	7	28	25	68
9	Millwall	46	12	4	7	36	28	6	9	8	26	34	67
10	Plymouth	46	12	5	6	37	24	6	6	11	27	32	65
11	Chesterfield	46	12	4	7	33	27	6	6	11	24	31	64
12	Reading	46	11	6	6	43	35	6	5	12	24	40	62
13	Portsmouth	46	11	10	2	33	14	3	9	11	23	37	61
14	Preston	46	10	7	6	25	22	6	6	11	25	34	61
15	Bristol Rov *	46	12	4	7	35	28	6	5	12	23	37	61
16	Newport	46	9	10	4	28	21	5	6	12	26	33	58
17	Huddersfield	46	10	5	8	38	25	5	7	11	26	34	57
18	Exeter	46	14	4	5	46	33	2	5	16	25	51	57
19	Doncaster	46	9	9	5	31	24	4	8	11	24	44	56
20	Walsall	46	10	7	6	32	23	3	7	13	19	32	53
21	Wimbledon	46	10	6	7	33	27	4	5	14	28	48	53
22	Swindon	46	9	5	9	37	36	4	8	11	18	35	52
23	BRISTOL CITY	46	7	6	10	24	29	4	7	12	16	36	46
24	Chester	46	2	10	11	16	30	5	1	17	20	48	32
		1104	258	155	139	827	594	139	155	258	594	827	1499

* deducted 2 pts

Odds & ends

Double wins: (0).
Double losses: (5) Portsmouth, Oxford, Southend, Burnley, Bristol Rov.

Won from behind: (3) Newport (h), Plymouth (h), Preston (a).
Lost from in front: (2) Fulham (a), Burnley (h).

High spots: The ability of Mick Harford.
The survival of Bristol City.
City's fine end-of-season run under caretaker manager Gerry Sharpe.

Low spots: Losing to Bristol Rov in the Gloucestershire Cup as well as succumbing twice in the League.
The financial crisis.
Further relegation.

Player of the Year: Mick Harford.
Ever-presents: (1) Paul Stevens.
Hat-tricks: (0).
Leading scorer: Mick Harford (14).

	Appearances						Goals			
	Lge	*Sub*	LC	*Sub*	FAC	*Sub*	**Lge**	LC	FAC	**Tot**
Aitken, Peter	**19**		5		4					
Boyle, Terry	**22**	*1*	1		5					
Bray, Wayne	**19**						**2**			**2**
Carter, Les	**16**									
Chandler, Ricky	**30**				3	*1*	**7**		1	**8**
Devine, Peter	**19**	*2*	3	*1*	3		**1**			**1**
Down, Billy	**1**									
Economou, Jon	**17**	*2*					**1**			**1**
Garland, Chris	**1**	*1*			1		**1**			**1**
Gooding, Ray	**3**									
Harford, Mick	**30**		5		5		**11**	1	2	**14**
Hay, Alan	**33**	*1*	2							
Mabbutt, Kevin	**11**		4				**1**			**1**
McCaffery, Aidan	**6**						**1**			**1**
Mann, Jimmy	**22**	*6*	5		5		**6**	2	2	**10**
Marshall, Julian	**3**				1					
Merrick, Geoff	**3**		2							
Moller, Jan	**31**		5		5					
Musker, Russell	**32**	*1*	4		3					
Newman, Rob	**15**	*6*					**3**			**3**
Nicholls, Alan	**27**				1		**1**			**1**
Rodgers, David	**18**		5		3			1		**1**
Shaw, John	**15**									
Smith, Mark	**1**	*4*								
Stevens, Paul	**46**		5		5		**1**			**1**
Sweeney, Gerry	**8**	*2*	3		1					
Tainton, Trevor	**19**		3		5		**1**		1	**2**
Thompson, Steve		*1*					**1**			**1**
Whitehead, Clive	**6**		2							
Williams, Gary	**33**		1		5		**1**			**1**
(own-goals)							**1**			**1**
30 players used	**506**	***27***	**55**	***1***	**55**	***1***	**40**	**4**	**6**	**50**

No	Date		Att	Pos	Pt	F-A	H-T	Scorers, Times, and Referees	1	2	3	4	5	6	7	8	9	10	11	12 sub used
1	H	HULL			W	2-1	1-0	Riley 38, Musker 75	Shaw	Stevens	Williams G	Newman	Boyle	**Riley**	Economou	Musker	Cooper	Ritchie	**Crawford**	
	28/8		4,853		3			Flounders 85	Norman	Swann	Thompson	Richards	Skipper	Booth	Marwood	Askew*	Whitehurst	Mutrie	Roberts G	Flounders
								Ref: K Cooper	Musker chooses the right time to get his first City goal, his 20-yard spectacular coming as Hull look likely to snatch an equaliser to cancel out Riley's thunderous opener. Billy Whitehurst hits the post for the Tigers on 69 mins, but Flounders' stunning header is the least they deserve.											
2	A	TRANMERE			D	2-2	0-2	Ritchie 49, 51	Shaw	Stevens	Newman	Williams G	Boyle	Riley	Economou	Bray	Cooper	Ritchie	Crawford	
	4/9		1,528		4			Hamilton 24, Kerr 39	Endersby	Burgess	Mooney*	Parry	Hamilton	Williams J	Powell	Hutchinson	Kerr	Mungall	Griffiths	Ferguson
								Ref: P Tyldsley	City's only chance in the first half is Crawford's cross-shot that hits the bar, shortly after Bryan Hamilton's 25-yarder puts Tranmere ahead. Coach Clive Middlemass masterminds City's stirring fight-back and Ritchie is denied a hat-trick winner when his shot is cleared off the line.											
3	A	CREWE		14	L	1-4	0-1	Ritchie 46p	Shaw	Stevens	Newman	Williams G	Boyle	Riley	Economou*	Bray	Cooper	Ritchie	Crawford	Thompson
	7/9		1,409	18	4			Evans 2p,63, Moore 68, Craven 77	Smith	Moore	Bowers	Salathiel	Scott	Palios	Haselgrave	Sutton	Goodwin	Evans	Craven	
								Ref: R Banks	'We forgot the basics' laments boss Cooper as City fall apart, despite Ritchie's dubious pen equalising Crewe's similarly contentious award. Clive Evans is unmarked as he heads in from a corner to restore Crewe's lead and further errors see them obtain their first win in 14 games.											
4	H	BLACKPOOL		15	D	0-0	0-0		Shaw	Stevens	Newman	Williams G	Boyle	Riley	Economou*	Cooper	Bray	Ritchie	Crawford	Chandler
	11/9		5,340	13	5				Hesford	Simmonite	Brockbank	Deary	Hetzke	Serella	Noble	Hockaday	Stewart	Pashley	Butler	
								Ref: A Crickmore	Ritchie, who once set a British record of scoring with a penalty in four successive matches, accepts the blame for letting the points slip from City's grasp in this game. Ritchie's 76th-min spot-kick hits the outside of the post after Dave Serella is harshly penalised for a tackle on Riley.											
5	A	NORTHAMPTON		21	L	**1-7**	0-3	Riley 80 [Denyer 89]	Shaw	Stevens	Newman	Williams G	Boyle	Riley	Chandler*	Bray	Cooper	Ritchie	Thompson	Crawford
	19/9		2,967	11	5			Massey 17, 52, Syrett 27, 34, 46, 90,	Freeman	Brady	Phillips	Gage	Burrows	Heeley*	Saunders	Saxby	Syrett	Massey	Buchanan J	Denyer
								Ref: K Salmon	A totally undisciplined performance produces one of City's most humiliating defeats. John Shaw is left cruelly exposed time and time again by abysmal marking. Dave Syrett, with one goal in his previous five appearances, avails himself of two free headers and two close-range shots.											
6	H	SCUNTHORPE		21	L	0-2	0-0		Shaw	Stevens	Nicholls	Williams G	Boyle	Riley	Newman*	Economou	Cooper	Ritchie	Crawford	**Panes**
	25/9		4,025	6	5			O'Berg 55, Parkinson 75	Neenan	Keeley	Pointon	Fowler	Boxall	Hunter	O'Berg	Angus	Duncan	Telfer*	Leman	Parkinson
								Ref: T Holbrook	Scunthorpe maintain their League hoodoo over City at Ashton Gate with a fierce 12-yard shot by Paul O'Berg and Noel Parkinson's brilliant volley. City, turning out in shirts without the sponsor's name, rue Riley's three missed chances and Newman's shot being hooked off the line.											
7	H	TORQUAY		22	L	0-1	0-1		Shaw	Stevens	Williams G	Nicholls	Boyle	Economou	Thompson	Newman	Ritchie	Riley	Crawford*	Panes
	28/9		**3,318**	3	5			Gallagher 2	Horne	Doyle	Smith	Wilson	Wigginton	Brown	Grapes	Steeples*	Cooper	Anderson	Gallagher	Rioch
								Ref: B Norman	Problems in the laundry department perhaps as City again play in plain shirts. Bruce Rioch is far and away the best player on view in a match threatened by a first-half cloudburst, as Torquay, with eight shots on target compared to City's four, are deserving winners of a dull game.											
8	A	PETERBOROUGH		23	L	0-3	0-2		Shaw	Stevens*	**Johnson**	Williams G	Boyle	Riley	Economou !	Thompson	Panes	Ritchie	Newman	Chandler
	2/10		2,739	17	5			Benjamin 15, Gynn 22, 84	Seaman	Quow	Collins	Firm	Gynn	Rodaway	Slack	Linton*	Cooke	Benjamin	Chard	Cliss
								Ref: K Baker	City suffer their fourth successive defeat after an enforced chocolate lunch when the team coach breaks down on way to the game. The Posh are presented with an easy win by City's sloppy first-half display and the 43rd-minute sending off of Economou for swearing at a linesman.											
9	H	YORK		22	D	2-2	1-1	Crawford 8, Chandler 61	Shaw	Newman	Johnson	Nicholls	Boyle	Bray	Economou	Thompson	Chandler	Riley	Crawford	
	9/10		3,730	13	6			Byrne 41, Ford 82	Jones	Evans	Dawson	Sbragia	Crosby	Hood	Pollard	Ford	Walwyn	Byrne	Senior*	Busby
								Ref: C Thomas	This thriller, encouraged by the referee's exemplary use of the advantage rule, produces a fair result as York have 17 shots (twelve on target) compared with City's 18 (eight). Many fans miss the start of the second half as the break is shortened to enable York to catch the 5.14pm train.											
10	A	HARTLEPOOL		23	L	1-3	1-2	Riley 34	Shaw	Newman	Johnson	Nicholls	Ritchie	Riley	Cooper	Williams G	Chandler	Thompson*	Crawford	**Kelly N**
	16/10		1,449	11	6			Bird 15, Lawrence 35p, Dobson 69	Watson	Brown	Stimpson	Lowe	Bird	Linighan A	Bainbridge	Dobson	Linacre	Lawrence	Barker	
								Ref: J Key	City, denied a 50th-min equaliser when Newman's free-kick hits the bar and bounces down over the line, are made to pay for missed chances. All of Pool's goals are from dead-ball situations and their high balls into the box highlight City's need for a commanding central defender.											
11	A	HALIFAX		23	D	2-2	1-2	Ritchie 42, Newman 50	Shaw	Newman	Johnson	Nicholls	Boyle	Riley	Cooper	Ritchie	Chandler	Williams G	Crawford	
	19/10		1,465	19	7			Davison 27, 36	Smelt	Nobbs	Goodman	Evans	Smith	Hendrie	Wood*	Davison	Spooner	Nuttall	Ward	Hallybone
								Ref: M Scott	An alert linesman flags vigorously to catch referee's attention that Newman's header from Crawford's corner had crossed the line before being cleared by Keith Nobbs. Bobby Davison seizes on errors by Ritchie and then Williams to net with two shots to take his season's tally to nine.											

No	Date	Venue	Opponent	Att	Pos	Pts	F-A	H-T	Scorers, Times, and Referees	1	2	3	4	5	6	7	8	9	10	11	12 sub used
12		H	WIMBLEDON		22	W	4-2	3-0	Nicholls 31, Riley 34, 44, 68	Shaw	Newman	Johnson	Nicholls	Boyle	Riley	Economou	Ritchie	Chandler	Cooper	Crawford	
	23/10			4,744	*2*	10			*Leslie 66, Thomas 87p*	*Beasant*	*Peters*	*Thomas*	*Gage*	*Tagg**	*Morris*	*Evans*	*Ketteridge*	*Leslie*	*Downes*	*Hodges*	*Galliers !*
									Ref: D Civil	City turn the form book upside down to take the League's last unbeaten record. Riley, shocked to find a mouse in his boot, scores the first hat-trick of his career. Boring Wimbledon is the chant, until they play a more expansive game after Nicholls heads in Crawford's cross.											
13		A	ALDERSHOT		23	D	0-0	0-0		Shaw	Newman	Johnson	Nicholls	Boyle	Riley	Economou	Thompson	Cooper	Chandler	Crawford	
	30/10			*2,826*	*8*	11				*Johnson*	*Andruszewski*	*Gillard*	*Scott*	*Wooler*	*Jopling*	*Sanford*	*Banton*	*Goddard*	*McDonald*	*Brodie*	
									Ref: B Hill	A ragged, disjointed City display that is only brightened by the flank play of Johnson and the midfield skills of Newman. Boss Cooper is critical of the officials for disallowing Thompson's 44th-minute volley from Johnson's pull-back, because Chandler is in an offside position.											
14		H	CHESTER		21	D	0-0	0-0		Shaw	Newman	Johnson	Nicholls	Boyle	Cooper	Riley	Economou	Thompson*	Chandler	Crawford	Williams G
	2/11			4,215	*12*	12				*Salmon*	*Bradley*	*Needham*	*Storton*	*Zelem*	*Dean*	*Sloan*	*Blackwell*	*Thomas*	*Ludlam*	*Cooke*	
									Ref: L Shapter/K Deane	A dismal encounter whose only highlight is referee Lester Shapter's pulled muscle bringing about his replacement by senior linesman Ken Deane for the second half. Cooper's misplaced pass gifts John Thomas a 71st-minute chance to break deadlock, but Shaw makes a great save.											
15		H	STOCKPORT		21	D	2-2	0-0	Riley 58, Chandler 64	Shaw	Newman	Johnson	Nicholls	Boyle	Riley	Economou	Williams G	Cooper	Chandler*	Crawford	Kelly N
	6/11			4,648	*18*	13			*Quinn 65, Newman 69 (og)*	*Lloyd*	*Rutter*	*Sherlock*	*Emerson*	*Bowles*	*Thorpe*	*Williams*	*Phillips*	*Quinn*	*Park*	*Coyle*	
									Ref: C Downey	Brian Lloyd denies 16-year-old Nyrere Kelly a story-book home debut as he spreads to block the youngster's 85th-minute effort. Newman slams Tony Coyle's low cross into own net for Stockport's leveller to end twelve minutes of hectic action that has warmed the frozen fans.											
16		A	MANSFIELD		22	D	1-1	1-0	Riley 21	Shaw	Newman	Johnson	Nicholls	Stevens	Riley	Economou	Williams G	Ritchie	Cooper	Crawford	
	13/11			*2,035*	*10*	14			*Newman 79 (og)*	*Arnold*	*Blackhall*	*Kennedy*	*Woodhead**	*Ayre*	*Calderwood*	*Matthews*	*Caldwell*	*Waddle*	*Hutchinson*	*Nicholson*	*Dungworth*
									Ref: D Owen	A bad day for Newman who is made to pay for his good fortune of staying on the pitch after bringing down Dave Caldwell in the 54th minute. He touches ball over line as Shaw fails to hold Gary Nicholson's cross to deprive City of their first away win and then finds his wallet stolen.											
17		H	COLCHESTER		23	L	0-2	0-1		Shaw	Stevens	Johnson	Nicholls	**Phill-Masters**	Riley	Newman	Thompson	Cooper	Chandler*	Crawford	Kelly N
	27/11			4,371	*6*	14			*Bremner 27, Allinson 85*	*Walker*	*Ward*	*Coleman**	*Longhorn*	*Wignall*	*Hunter*	*Allinson*	*Osborne*	*McDonough*	*Bremner*	*Leslie*	*Adcock*
									Ref: T Bune	Phillipson-Masters has an unhappy debut, but Nicholls is at fault with United's opener. Glaring misses by Riley, Chandler and Kelly as well as Mike Walker's superb goalkeeping prevent City getting back into the game. Ian Allinson gives a lesson in finishing to complete City's misery.											
18		A	ROCHDALE		24	L	0-1	0-0		Shaw	**Llewellyn**	Johnson	Nicholls	Phill-Masters	Riley	Newman	Thompson	Chandler	Cooper	Crawford	
	4/12			*1,307*	*19*	14			*Farrell 75*	*Pearce*	*Keenan*	*Snookes*	*Farrell*	*McElhinney**	*Nicholson*	*Thompson D*	*Greaves*	*Hilditch*	*Wellings*	*Hamilton*	*Weir*
									Ref: A Challinor	Peter Farrell puts City at the bottom of the League as he rises unmarked to send in a looping header over Shaw, who captains the side in Ritchie's absence. The goal is a tragedy for City's improved defence, in which Phillipson-Masters, Nicholls and Cooper are outstanding.											
19		A	CHESTER		24	L	0-1	0-0		Shaw	Llewellyn	Johnson	Nicholls	Phill-Masters	Riley	Newman	Thompson	Panes*	Cooper	Crawford	Garland
	1[illegible]/12			***1,306***	*9*	14			*Cooper 55 (og)*	*Salmon*	*Lean*	*Lane*	*Storton*	*Bradley*	*Johnson*	*Williams**	*Cooke*	*Thomas*	*Ludlam*	*Wilson*	*Zelem*
									Ref: D Allison	Garland, signed on non-contract forms, makes a successful return to City's side by playing the last half-hour in place of Panes. A spectacular own-goal settles a poor match. Cooper swings his right foot at Clive Wilson's angled low drive and the ball crashes into the top corner.											
20		A	BURY		23	D	2-2	0-0	Chandler 61, Crawford 66	Shaw	Cooper	Johnson	Nicholls	Phill-Masters	Economou	Ritchie	Newman	Riley	Chandler	Crawford	
	13/12			*2,196*	*1*	15			*Madden 46, Parker 48*	*Brown*	*Gardner*	*Bramhall*	*Halliday*	*Davies*	*Gore*	*Hilton**	*Madden*	*Parker*	*Jakub*	*Firth*	*Potts*
									Ref: J Lovatt	Against top of the table Bury the goal-shy City attack at long last find some form. Chandler, revelling in the ankle-deep snow, puts City back in the game with a glancing header from Cooper's well-flighted free-kick. The 50th-minute injury of Paul Hilton is the turning point of the game.											
21		H	PORT VALE		23	L	1-3	0-1	Phillipson-Masters 55	Shaw	Newman	Johnson	Nicholls	Phill-Masters	Riley*	Cooper	Ritchie	Economou	Chandler	Crawford	Garland
	27/12			6,852	*5*	15			*Armstrong 44, Moss 56, Newton 61*	*Siddall**	*Tartt*	*Bromage*	*Hunter*	*Sproson*	*Cegielski*	*Fox*	*Moss*	*Newton*	*Greenhoff*	*Armstrong*	*Ridley*
									Ref: A Glasson	Despite a purposeful opening, City rarely seem likely to break down the visitors' uncompromising defence. Terry Armstrong's 25-yarder puts Vale ahead with their only shot of the first half. Wayne Cegielski takes over in goal for final three minutes as Barry Siddall is stretchered off.											
22		A	HEREFORD		22	W	3-1	3-1	Chandler 5, 11, Kelly N 40	Shaw	Newman	Johnson	Nicholls	Phill-Masters	Garland	Kelly N	Ritchie	Cooper	Chandler	Crawford	
	28/12			*3,548*	*23*	18			*McNeil 12*	*Powell*	*Price*	*Bray*	*Hicks*	*Pejic*	*Musial*	*Harvey*	*Lane*	*Phillips*	*McNeil*	*White*	
									Ref: A Seville	The boot is on the other foot as City benefit from Hereford's woeful finishing to gain their first away win in 23. Chandler claims the goal that puts City on course for three vital points when his touch to Ritchie's shot deceives Andy Powell. The Bulls have 22 shots to just seven by City.											
23		H	SWINDON		22	D	1-1	0-0	Riley 89	Shaw	Newman	Johnson	Nicholls	Phill-Masters	Cooper	Kelly N	Ritchie	Garland	Chandler*	Crawford	Riley
	1/1			**8,927**	*4*	19			*Pritchard 64*	*Allan*	*Baverstock*	*Baillie*	*Emmanuel !*	*Lewis*	*Graham*	*Pritchard*	*Batty*	*Rideout*	*Rowland*	*Barnard*	
									Ref: M Robinson	Gary Emmanuel is sent off after protesting at City's equaliser, when Nicholls appeared to kick the ball out of the keeper's hands for Riley to tap the ball in. Ritchie has his shirt on back-to-front in the first half after a hurried twelfth-min change as City have two No 7s on the pitch.											

No	Date		Att	Pos	Pt	F-A	H-T	Scorers, Times, and Referees	1	2	3	4	5	6	7	8	9	10	11	12 sub used
24	A	DARLINGTON		22	D	2-2	2-2	Chandler 9, Garland 44	Shaw	Williams G	Johnson	Nicholls	Phill-Masters*	Riley	Garland	Ritchie	Cooper	Chandler	Crawford	Newman
	3/1		*1,425*	*21*	20			*Walsh 14, 35*	*Cuff*	*Liddle*	*Young*	*Smith*	*Rhodes*	*Kamara*	*Gilbert*	*McLean*	*Honour*	*Walsh*	*McFadden*	
								Ref: D Scott	Garland slides in Chandler's angled ball to level matters after Alan Walsh naps a pair with his 20-yard free-kick before coolly slotting home a through ball. Facing a gale-force wind after the break City defend well and come closest to a winner, but Pat Cuff saves Newman's header.											
25	A	HULL		23	L	0-1	0-0		Shaw	Williams G	Johnson	Nicholls	Phill-Masters	Riley	Garland	Ritchie	Cooper	Chandler	Crawford	
	15/1		***6,835***	*1*	20			*Mutrie 79*	*Davies*	*Swann*	*Askew*	*Roberts D*	*Skipper*	*Booth*	*Marwood*	*McClaren*	*Whitehurst**	*Mutrie*	*Roberts G*	*McNeil*
								Ref: T Mills	Forbes Phillipson-Masters, due to sign permanently for City next week, collects his eighth booking of the season as a backs to the wall display almost frustrates the Tigers. Following a free-kick, Les Mutrie gives Shaw no chance with his shot from Peter Skipper's headed pass.											
26	H	TRANMERE		21	W	1-0	0-0	Riley 55	Shaw	Williams G	Johnson	Nicholls	Newman	Riley	Ritchie	Chandler	Economou	Garland	Crawford	
	18/1		3,776	*20*	23				*Endersby*	*Mungall*	*Burgess*	*Mooney*	*Hamilton**	*Oliver*	*Powell*	*Aspinall*	*Kerr*	*Brown O*	*Griffiths*	*Woods S*
								Ref: J Martin	Cooper's shrewd positional switch of Chandler to midfield so as to allow Riley to revert to attack brings City their first home success for three months. Tranmere are outplayed for long periods and City deserve more than the one goal scored by Riley's unstoppable eight-yard volley.											
27	H	NORTHAMPTON		21	L	1-3	1-2	Ritchie 41p	Shaw	Williams G	Johnson	Nicholls	Newman	Riley	Ritchie	Garland*	Economou	Chandler	Crawford	Cooper
	22/1		4,874	*15*	23			*Phillips 21, Syrett 36, Massey 50*	*Freeman*	*Tucker*	*Phillips*	*Gage*	*Brady*	*Coffill*	*Saunders*	*Patching*	*Muir*	*Syrett*	*Massey*	
								Ref: R Lewis	Neil Freeman, in his farewell performance before joining the police, thwarts City with a string of outstanding saves. Ritchie gives City some hope with a penalty after Peter Coffill's rash tackle on Johnson, but Steve Massey finishes off a lovely move to clinch the points for Town.											
28	A	SCUNTHORPE		23	D	1-1	0-0	Nicholls 49	Shaw	Newman	Williams G	Nicholls	Phill-Masters	Riley	Ritchie	Garland	Economou	Chandler	Crawford	
	5/2		*3,624*	*5*	24			*Parkinson 82*	*Neenan*	*Oates*	*Pointon*	*Boxall*	*Baines*	*Hunter*	*O'Berg*	*Cammack*	*Mann*	*Parkinson*	*Leman*	
								Ref: A Hamil	City's loss of Peter Johnson, who returns to Newcastle following a three-month loan spell, is compensated by Phillipson-Masters' availability after serving his suspension. Scunthorpe, including old City favourite Jimmy Mann, gain a draw with Noel Parkinson's 20-yard free-kick.											
29	H	PETERBOROUGH		21	W	1-0	1-0	Ritchie 38p	Shaw	Newman	Williams G	Nicholls	Phill-Masters	Riley	Ritchie	Economou	Cooper	Musker	Crawford	
	12/2		3,922	*12*	27				*Seaman*	*Winters*	*Collins*	*Gynn*	*Firm*	*Slack*	*Clarke*	*Rodaway*	*Cooke*	*Benjamin*	*Chard*	
								Ref: L Burden	Musker makes a successful return to first-team action after over five months out with a broken leg. He provides midfield authority behind Ritchie and Riley. There is little between the sides, but a handball by John Winters allows Ritchie to put away the match-winning penalty.											
30	H	HALIFAX		18	W	**3-0**	2-0	Ritchie 15, Cooper 37, Economou 71	Shaw	Newman	Williams G	Nicholls	Phill-Masters	Riley*	Cooper	Ritchie	Economou	Musker	Crawford	Chandler
	15/2		3,403	*10*	30				*Smelt*	*Nobbs*	*Wood*	*Evans*	*Smith*	*Hendrie*	*Ward*	*Kendall**	*Allatt*	*Nuttall*	*Staniforth*	*Goodman*
								Ref: B Daniels	Ritchie's low 18-yard shot past Lee Smelt sets up City's escape from the re-election zone. Playing delightful one-touch football on a freezing pitch they dominate opponents boasting six wins from their seven previous games. Dave Evans claims the last touch in City's other goals.											
31	A	YORK		20	L	0-3	0-0		Shaw	Newman	Williams G	Nicholls	Phill-Masters	Riley	Ritchie	Economou*	Chandler	Musker	Crawford	Bray
	19/2		*2,879*	*8*	30			*Byrne 62, 86, Pollard 85p*	*Jones*	*Evans*	*Hay*	*Sbragia*	*Smith*	*Hood*	*Ford*	*Crosby*	*Walwyn*	*Byrne*	*Pollard*	
								Ref: J Hough	City's chance of saving anything from this game is destroyed when, with the ball having already been cleared, Williams trips Keith Walwyn to concede a senseless penalty. City are unable to contrive a single shot on target against a York side achieving their tenth successive home win.											
32	H	HARTLEPOOL		17	W	2-0	1-0	Ritchie 7p, Economou 47	Shaw	Newman	Williams G	Nicholls	Phill-Masters	Riley	Ritchie	Economou	Cooper	Musker	Crawford	
	26/2		4,207	*21*	33				*Blackburn*	*Brown*	*Stimpson*	*Robinson*	*Barker*	*Linighan A*	*Lowe*	*Smith*	*Dobson*	*Lawrence**	*Linacre*	*Langridge*
								Ref: J Bray	City are lucky when Riley's early tumble results in a penalty, from which Ritchie gives keeper Eddie Blackburn no chance. A poor game in which Hartlepool only create one clear chance. Newman's 50-yard run ends with a perfect through-ball for Economou to score from ten yards.											
33	A	WIMBLEDON		20	L	1-2	0-2	Kelly E 47	Shaw	Newman	Williams G	Nicholls	Phill-Masters	Riley	Ritchie	Economou	**Kelly E**	Musker	Crawford	
	5/3		*2,591*	*3*	33			*Newman 25 (og), Leslie 30*	*Beasant*	*Peters*	*Sparrow*	*Barnett*	*Smith*	*Hatter**	*Evans*	*Belfield*	*Leslie*	*Hodges*	*Gage*	*Fishenden*
								Ref: M Dimblebee	New signing Errington Kelly inspires a battling second performance with a superb angled drive just after the break. Kelly makes his presence felt right from the start with a spectacular overhead kick, but City are on the rack when Newman slices Gary Barnett's cross into his own net.											
34	H	ALDERSHOT		20	W	2-0	1-0	Crawford 42, Riley 52	Shaw	Newman	Williams G	Nicholls	Phill-Masters	Riley	**Smith**	Kelly E*	Cooper	Economou	Crawford	Llewellyn
	12/3		4,281	*16*	36				*Johnson*	*Andruszewski*	*Gillard*	*Briley*	*Whitlock*	*Jopling*	*Shrubb*	*Banton*	*Goddard*	*McDonald*	*Robinson**	*Lucas*
								Ref: A Hamil	City, without Ritchie who is suffering from food poisoning, struggle early on. Phillipson-Masters draws the defence for Crawford to head in from Newman's free-kick, then Nigel Smith's raking pass to the left-wing allows Crawford to send in a perfect cross for Riley to head in.											

No	Date	Opponent	Att	Pos	Pts	F-A	H-T	Scorers, Times, and Referees	1	2	3	4	5	6	7	8	9	10	11	12
35	A 18/3	STOCKPORT		21	D	2-2	1-1	Riley 17, Ritchie 70	Shaw	Llewellyn	Williams G	Nicholls	Newman	Riley	Economou !	Ritchie	**Williams P***	Cooper	Crawford	**Palmer**
			2,036	*14*	37			*Power 18, Emerson 55*	*Lloyd*	*Rutter*	*Sherlock*	*Emerson*	*Sword*	*Thorpe*	*Williams*	*Phillips*	*Coyle*	*Power*	*Smith*	
								Ref: F Roberts	Riley's goal, a glancing header which strikes a defender, is City's only effort on target in the first half, whilst Shaw has to make six saves in the same period. Dean Emerson's well-struck shot gives County a well-deserved lead, but depleted City fight back well for a headed equaliser.											
36	A 20/3	TORQUAY		17	W	2-0	1-0	Crawford 8, Riley 74	Shaw	Newman	Williams G	Nicholls	Phill-Masters	Riley	Economou	Ritchie	Williams P*	Cooper	Crawford	Palmer
			3,209	*13*	40				*Horn*	*Smith*	*Young*	*Wilson*	*Little*	*Rioch*	*Jones*	*James*	*Bishop*	*Anderson*	*Gallagher*	
								Ref: C Thomas	Phillipson-Masters inspires City to their best away performance of the season. Plain sailing as Crawford heads in Riley's cross and later returns the compliment with a through-ball for Riley to coolly lob in. The shortest sub appearance on record as Palmer only has time to shake hands.											
37	H 26/3	MANSFIELD		15	W	3-1	0-1	Riley 54, Williams P 61, Crawford 83	Shaw	Newman	Williams G	Nicholls	Phill-Masters	Riley*	Ritchie	Williams P	Cooper	Economou	Crawford	Palmer
			4,945	*12*	43			*Caldwell 34*	*Arnold*	*Blackhall*	*Kearney*	*Rhodes*	*Bird**	*Calderwood*	*Woodhead*	*Bell*	*Dungworth*	*Caldwell*	*Reynolds*	*Kennedy*
								Ref: T Spencer	Paul Williams from Western League side Ottery St Mary, lauded as the most exciting Ashton Gate prospect in years, caps his home debut by stabbing Cooper's cross over the line. Mansfield, with three regulars missing, are swept aside in the second half after dominating the first.											
38	H 2/4	HEREFORD		15	D	1-1	1-1	Ritchie 41	Shaw	Llewellyn	Williams G	Nicholls	Phill-Masters	Riley	Ritchie	Williams P	Cooper	Bray*	Crawford	Palmer
			6,278	*24*	44			*Phillips 33*	*Wilmot*	*Price*	*Bartley*	*Larkin*	*Pejic !*	*Maddy*	*Harvey*	*Lane*	*Phillips*	*Carter*	*White*	
								Ref: B Stevens	Hereford look likely winners until Mel Pejic's 68th-min dismissal for foul on Crawford. Stewart Phillips' sweet left foot shot puts the visitors ahead shortly after Gary Williams hits the post. Ritchie finishes off Crawford's clever pass for City's leveller and later the post denies Riley.											
39	A 4/4	PORT VALE		15	D	1-1	1-1	Riley 33	Shaw	Newman	Williams G	Nicholls	Phill-Masters	Riley	Bray	Ritchie	Cooper	Williams P	Crawford	
			6,573	*4*	45			*Armstrong 21*	*Siddall*	*Tartt*	*Bromage*	*Hunter*	*Ridley*	*Cegielski*	*Fox*	*Steel*	*Newton*	*Lawrence M**	*Armstrong*	*Earle*
								Ref: A Robinson	Gary Williams and Wayne Bray, often criticised in the past for their casual approach, inspire City's heroic performance on a quagmire pitch. Terry Armstrong seizes on ball stuck in the mud to put Vale in front, but City respond with Riley's looping header from Bray's curling cross.											
40	H 9/4	ROCHDALE		15	D	0-0	0-0		Shaw	Newman	Williams G	Nicholls	Phill-Masters	Riley	Bray*	Williams P	Cooper	Economou	Crawford	Kelly N
			4,780	*22*	46				*Crawford*	*Keenan*	*Carr*	*Farrell*	*Higgins*	*Williams*	*Thompson D*	*Greenhoff B*	*French*	*Greenhoff J*	*Hilditch*	
								Ref: D Hedges	For the first time in many months the shouts of rubbish are heard as City fail to beat mediocre Rochdale. City waste many chances, making 18 goal attempts compared to Rochdale's six. Boss Cooper confronts a disgruntled fan in a vain attempt to encourage cheers rather than the jeers.											
41	A 16/4	BLACKPOOL		14	W	4-1	1-1	Hetzke 9 (og), Ritchie 59p, Riley 65, [Crawford 70]	Shaw	Newman	Williams G	Nicholls	Phill-Masters	Riley	Economou	Ritchie	Cooper	Williams P	Crawford	
			2,209	*16*	49			*McNiven 24*	*Hesford*	*Bardsley*	*Pritchett*	*Deary*	*Hetzke*	*Greenall*	*Hockaday*	*McNiven*	*Stewart*	*Noble**	*Pashley*	*Bamber*
								Ref: D Shaw	Ritchie's successful spot-kick, after Colin Greenall brings down Riley, changes the course of the game. After Steve Hetzke's 30-yard volley into his own net, David McNiven heads in Pool's leveller and then Terry Pashley hits the crossbar as City struggle to remain on equal terms.											
42	H 23/4	BURY		15	W	2-1	0-1	Breckin 56 (og), Nicholls 64	Shaw	Newman	Williams G	Nicholls	Phill-Masters	Riley	Ritchie	Williams P	Cooper*	Economou	Crawford	Kelly E
			5,230	*4*	52			*Johnson 2*	*Brown*	*Gardner*	*Breckin*	*Hilton M*	*Bramhall*	*Halliday*	*Cantello**	*Madden*	*Johnson*	*Jakub*	*Potts*	*Parker*
								Ref: J Deakin	The fates are again kind to the City as, following Steve Johnson's spectacular overhead kick to give Bury an early lead, they equalise when David Brown, John Breckin and Paul Williams collide in going for Riley's cross. Nicholls secures the points for the City with a simple tap-in.											
43	A 29/4	COLCHESTER		15	L	1-3	1-2	Ritchie 43p	Shaw	Newman	Williams G	Nicholls	Phill-Masters	Riley	Ritchie	Williams P	Kelly E*	Economou	Crawford	Palmer
			2,196	*5*	52			*Allinson 35p, Bowen 38, McDonaugh 88*	*Walker*	*Cook**	*Packer*	*Leslie*	*Wignall*	*Coleman*	*Allinson*	*Osborne*	*Bowen*	*Adcock*	*Hull*	*McDonaugh*
								Ref: T Ward	A harsh spot-kick award as keeper Shaw is adjudged to have tripped Ian Allinson heralds the end of City's nine-match unbeaten run. Despite getting back into the contest when Ritchie nets from a penalty after Riley is fouled, City's uninspired midfield make things easy for the U's.											
44	H 2/5	DARLINGTON		15	D	2-2	1-2	Crawford 14 Phillipson-Masters 86	Shaw	Newman	Williams G	Cooper	Phill-Masters	Ritchie	Kelly E*	Riley	Williams P	Economou	Crawford	Palmer
			4,877	*17*	53			*Todd 18, Kamara 24*	*Barber*	*Kamara*	*Liddle*	*Smith*	*Barton*	*Wakefield*	*Honour*	*McLean*	*Todd*	*Walsh*	*Young*	
								Ref: K Barratt	Darlington keeper Fred Barber takes the glory in an open, free-flowing game. Despite restricting the Quakers to two shots, the City have to rely on a mis-hit volley from Phillipson-Masters to save a point after Alan Kamara had jinked his way through for a spectacular solo goal.											
45	H 7/5	CREWE		13	W	2-1	0-0	Newman 76, 89	Shaw	Newman	Williams G	Nicholls	Cooper	Crawford	Ritchie	Smith*	Economou	Palmer	Riley	Llewellyn
			4,785	*23*	56			*Chapman 61*	*Smith*	*Brady*	*Bowers*	*Edwards*	*Scott*	*Hart*	*Haselgrave*	*Chapman*	*Waller*	*Walker*	*Cliss*	
								Ref: M James	Newman's fine volley and glancing header in the closing stages secures City's rather fortunate win. Crewe waste a second-minute pen when Nigel Walker blasts well wide after Economou's handball, but bedraggled City look out of it when Daryl Chapman heads the visitors in front.											
46	A 14/5	SWINDON		14	L	0-2	0-1		Shaw	Llewellyn	Williams G	Nicholls	Palmer	Bray*	Ritchie	Economou	Cooper	Williams P	Crawford	**Jones**
			5,313	*8*	56			*Barnard 39, Pritchard 71*	*Stevens*	*Baillie*	*Baddeley*	*Batty*	*Henry*	*Graham*	*Pritchard*	*Barnard*	*Quinn*	*Rowland*	*Blackler*	
	Home		Away					Ref: L Shapter	Palmer is frustrated by the post in the early stages and then after the interval Paul Batty clears his header off the line. Barnard shoots Swindon ahead and then the impressive Pritchard, who earlier had hit the woodwork, puts the game beyond City's grasp with a superb cross-shot.											
Average	4,799		2,768																	

LEAGUE DIVISION 4 (CUP-TIES) Manager: Terry Cooper SEASON 1982-83

Milk Cup				F-A	H-T	Scorers, Times, and Referees	1	2	3	4	5	6	7	8	9	10	11	12 sub used
1:1 A	SWINDON		L	1-2	0-1	Boyle 80	Shaw	Stevens	Newman	Williams G	Boyle	Riley	Economou	Musker*	Cooper	Ritchie	Crawford	Bray
	31/8	*3,736*				*Rideout 11p, 89*	*Allan*	*Henry*	*Baddeley*	*Emmanuel*	*Lewis*	*Graham*	*Pritchard**	*Hughes*	*Rideout*	*Rowland*	*Barnard*	*Carter*
						Ref: J Deakin	A gritty City display after Cooper is lucky not to be sent off for his handling offence that gifts Swindon their penalty, and the loss of Musker with a broken ankle. Boyle equalises with a looping back-header, but Rideout's magnificent 35-yard drive gives Swindon a 2nd leg advantage.											
1:2 H	SWINDON	15	W	2-0	2-0	Boyle 29, Ritchie 43	Shaw	Stevens	Newman	Williams G	Boyle	Cooper	Riley	Chandler	Bray	Ritchie	Thompson	
	14/9	3,786 *10*					*Allan*	*Henry**	*Baddeley*	*Emmanuel*	*Lewis*	*Graham*	*Pritchard*	*Hughes*	*Rideout*	*Rowland*	*Barnard*	*Quinn*
						Ref: A Robinson (City won 3-2 on aggregate)	Boyle's powerful header into the top corner sparks a rousing battle. Ritchie is full of praise for the referee who overrules the linesman to allow his goal after forcing ball through keeper's hands. 'The ball was never in the keeper's possession so I had every right to go for it' says Ritchie.											
2:1 H	SHEFFIELD WED	23	L	1-2	0-2	Newman 78	Shaw	Newman	Williams G	Nicholls	Boyle	Riley	Bray	Economou	Chandler*	Thompson	Crawford	Panes
	4/10	4,458 *2:3*				*Taylor 2, 6*	*Bolder*	*Sterland*	*Bailey*	*Smith*	*Lyons*	*Shelton*	*Megson**	*Taylor*	*Bannister*	*Owen*	*Simmons*	*Pickering*
						Ref: D Hedges	City again self-destruct, before Newman's twelve-yard thunderbolt gives some hope for the second leg. Williams' poor back-pass gifts Kevin Taylor the simplest of goals and debutant Tony Simmons is given too much room as he sends over a cross for Taylor to volley in his second.											
2:2 A	SHEFFIELD WED	22	D	1-1	0-0	Chandler 64	Shaw	Newman	Thompson*	Nicholls	Boyle	Riley	Economou	Ritchie	Chandler	Cooper	Crawford	Kelly N
	26/10	7,920 *2:1*		*aet*		*Taylor 109*	*Bolder*	*Sterland*	*Bailey*	*Smith*	*Lyons*	*Shirtliff P R**	*Megson*	*Taylor*	*Bannister*	*McCulloch*	*Owen*	*Pickering*
						Ref: N Midgeley (City lost 2-3 on aggregate)	Gallant City, reduced to ten men with the loss of the limping Ritchie 23 mins before the end, put up a heroic performance. Chandler volleys in a rebound to bring the aggregate scores level, but Kevin Taylor ends City's hopes in extra-time with a delightful chip to leave Shaw stranded.											

FA Cup				F-A	H-T	Scorers, Times, and Referees	1	2	3	4	5	6	7	8	9	10	11	12 sub used
1 A	ORIENT	22	L	1-4	1-3	Johnson 17	Shaw	Stevens	Johnson	Nicholls	Newman	Riley	Economou	Ritchie*	Williams G	Cooper	Crawford	Thompson
	20/11	2,772 *3:21*				*Foster 20, Godfrey 28, 38, Sussex 70*	*Day*	*Roffey*	*Peach*	*Foster*	*Cunningham*	*Donn*	*Osgood*	*Godfrey*	*Houchen*	*Sussex*	*Taylor*	
						Ref: M James	Johnson, with a glorious shot from the edge of the area, scores only the second goal of his career, but confusion with Ritchie off injured in the 20th min leaves City down to ten men when Orient equalise. Colin Foster latches onto Tony Cunningham's free-kick to scramble the ball in.											

		Home						Away					
	P	W	D	L	F	A	W	D	L	F	A	Pts
1 Wimbledon	46	17	4	2	57	23	12	7	4	39	22	98
2 Hull	46	14	8	1	48	14	11	7	5	27	20	90
3 Port Vale	46	15	4	4	37	16	11	6	6	30	18	88
4 Scunthorpe	46	13	7	3	41	17	10	7	6	30	25	83
5 Bury	46	15	4	4	43	20	8	8	7	31	26	81
6 Colchester	46	17	5	1	51	19	7	4	12	24	36	81
7 York	46	18	4	1	59	19	4	9	10	29	39	79
8 Swindon	46	14	3	6	45	27	5	8	10	16	27	68
9 Peterborough	46	13	6	4	38	23	4	7	12	20	29	64
10 Mansfield	46	11	6	6	32	26	5	7	11	29	44	61
11 Halifax	46	9	8	6	31	23	7	4	12	28	43	60
12 Torquay	46	12	3	8	38	30	5	4	14	18	35	58
13 Chester	46	8	6	9	28	24	7	5	11	27	36	56
14 BRISTOL CITY	46	10	8	5	32	25	3	9	11	27	45	56
15 Northampton	46	10	8	5	43	29	4	4	15	22	46	54
16 Stockport	46	11	8	4	41	31	3	4	16	19	48	54
17 Darlington	46	8	5	10	27	30	5	8	10	34	41	52
18 Aldershot	46	11	5	7	40	35	1	10	12	21	47	51
19 Tranmere	46	8	8	7	30	29	5	3	15	19	42	50
20 Rochdale	46	11	8	4	38	25	0	8	15	17	48	49
21 Blackpool	46	10	8	5	32	23	3	4	16	23	51	49
22 Hartlepool	46	11	5	7	30	24	2	4	17	16	52	48
23 Crewe	46	9	5	9	35	32	2	3	18	18	39	41
24 Hereford	46	8	6	9	19	23	3	2	18	23	56	41
	1104	283	142	127	915	587	127	142	283	587	915	1512

Odds & ends

Double wins: (0).
Double losses: (2) Northampton, Colchester.

Won from behind: (3) Mansfield (h), Bury (h), Crewe (h).
Lost from in front: (0).

High spots: Beating Wimbledon 4-2 at Ashton Gate on 23 October.
Drawing 2-2 at Bury on 18 December to move off the bottom.

Low spots: Heavy defeat at Northampton on 19 September.
Reaching the bottom of the League on losing at Rochdale on 4 Dec.
Losing 1-2 v Bristol Rovers (a) in the Gloucestershire Cup on 21 Sep.

Player of the year: Glyn Riley.
Ever-presents: (1) John Shaw.
Hat-tricks: (1) Glyn Riley.
Leading scorer: Glyn Riley (16).

	Appearances						Goals			
	Lge	*Sub*	LC	*Sub*	FAC	*Sub*	Lge	LC	FAC	Tot
Boyle, Terry	**14**		4					2		**2**
Bray, Wayne	**9**	*1*	2	*1*						
Chandler, Ricky	**20**	*3*	3				**6**	1		**7**
Cooper, Terry	**37**	*1*	3		1		**1**			**1**
Crawford, Alan	**44**	*1*	3		1		**7**			**7**
Economou, Jon	**34**		3		1		**2**			**2**
Garland, Chris	**7**	*2*					**1**			**1**
Johnson, Peter	**20**				1				1	**1**
Jones, Mark		*1*								
Kelly, Errington	**4**	*1*					**1**			**1**
Kelly, Nyrere	**2**	*4*		*1*			**1**			**1**
Llewellyn, Andy	**5**	*2*								
Musker, Russell	**6**		1				**1**			**1**
Newman, Rob	**42**	*1*	4		1		**3**	1		**4**
Nicholls, Alan	**39**		2		1		**3**			**3**
Palmer, John	**2**	*6*								
Panes, Simon	**2**	*2*		*1*						
Phill-Masters, Forbes	**25**						**2**			**2**
Riley, Glyn	**43**	*1*	4		1		**16**			**16**
Ritchie, Tom	**37**		3		1		**12**	1		**13**
Shaw, John	**46**		4		1					
Smith, Nigel	**2**									
Stevens, Paul	**10**		2		1					
Thompson, Steve	**10**	*1*	3			*1*				
Williams, Gary	**35**	*1*	3		1					
Williams, Paul	**11**						**1**			**1**
(own-goals)							**2**			**2**
26 players used	**506**	*28*	**44**	*3*	**11**	*1*	**59**	**5**	**1**	**65**

No	Date		Att	Pos	Pt	F-A	H-T	Scorers, Times, and Referees	1	2	3	4	5	6	7	8	9	10	11	12 sub used
1	H	MANSFIELD			W	4-0	2-0	Crawford 13, 42, Riley 49, 87	Shaw	Stevens	Williams G	Phill-Masters	**Halliday**	Riley	Pritchard	Ritchie	**Kerr***	Musker	Crawford	Williams P
	27/8		5,759		3				*Arnold*	*Whitworth*	*Kearney*	*Matthews*	*Foster*	*Calderwood*	*Barrowclough*	*Hutchinson*	*Dungworth**	*Caldwell*	*Lowery*	*Woodhead*
								Ref: H King	Mansfield boss Ian Greaves says City are a different class than the Stags in this one-sided game. Riley is unfortunate when his shot hits the post in the 85th minute, but he makes no mistake shortly after to net from 16 yards after racing onto a splendid pass by substitute Paul Williams.											
2	A	BURY			L	1-2	1-2	Kerr 8	Shaw	Stevens	Williams G	Phill-Masters	Halliday	Riley	Pritchard	Ritchie	Kerr*	Musker	Crawford	Williams P
	3/9		*2,015*		3			*Madden 19, 23*	*Brown*	*Gardner*	*Pashley*	*Coleman*	*Hilton P*	*Bramhall*	*Potts**	*Madden*	*Entwhistle*	*Jakub*	*Carrodus*	*Spence*
								Ref: J Key	Despite Kerr's header slipping through David Brown's hands, City are second best before the break. Bury equalise with a shot that owes something to a deflection off Halliday, but Craig Madden's winning header is all his own work. No reward for City's second-half dominance.											
3	A	COLCHESTER		7	D	0-0	0-0		Shaw	Newman	Williams G	Phill-Masters	Halliday	Riley*	Pritchard	Ritchie	Kerr	Stevens	Crawford	Williams P
	6/9		*2,120*	*3*	4				*Chamberlain*	*Cook*	*Farrell*	*Hadley*	*Wignall*	*Houston*	*Groves*	*Osborne*	*Bowen*	*Adcock*	*Hull*	
								Ref: M James	City end the U's 100 per cent record, but bore the spectators in the process. Colchester, with top scorer Allinson having been sold to Arsenal, lack the fire-power to trouble a blanket defence. They have two shots on goal, whilst City are scarcely any better in mustering just one more.											
4	H	HARTLEPOOL		6	W	2-0	0-0	Pritchard 46, Riley 53	Shaw	Newman	Williams G*	Phill-Masters	Halliday	Economou	Pritchard	Ritchie	Kerr	Riley	Crawford	Stevens
	10/9		5,310	*22*	7				*Blackburn*	*Brown*	*Wilson*	*Buckley*	*Linighan A*	*Weir*	*Lowe*	*Whitfield*	*Waddle**	*Johnson*	*Robinson*	*Staff*
								Ref: D Reeves	Pritchard looks for a penalty when toppled by Alan Weir, but leaps to his feet on hearing no whistle to strike the ball past a stunned Eddie Blackburn. Hartlepool's negative tactics so infuriate Economou that he takes off his shirt to hand it to former Everton player Mick Buckley.											
5	A	WREXHAM		7	L	1-3	0-1	Crawford 75	Shaw	Newman	Williams G	Halliday	Phill-Masters	Riley	Pritchard	Stevens	Williams P*	Economou	Crawford	Musker
	16/9		*1,731*	*8*	7			*Edwards 21, Gregory 52, Hunt 89*	*Wardle*	*King*	*Cunnington*	*Hunt*	*Coleman*	*Keay*	*Wright*	*Evans*	*Edwards*	*Gregory*	*Heath*	
								Ref: D Allison	Ex City keeper Bob Wardle, on a month's loan from Liverpool, derives special satisfaction in beating his old club. City have 70 per cent of the possession, but give away silly goals. Halliday fails to block Dave Gregory's cross and Andy Edwards shoots home in Wrexham's first attack.											
6	H	TORQUAY		6	W	**5-0**	1-0	Crawford 41, 59, 66, Riley 64, Ritchie 81p	Shaw	Stevens	Williams G	Halliday	Phill-Masters	Riley	Pritchard	Ritchie	Kerr	Economou	Crawford	
	24/9		**5,266**	*24*	10				*Turner*	*Collins*	*Holmes*	*Sheridan*	*Little*	*Carr*	*Hughes*	*Pugh*	*Bishop**	*Sims*	*Anderson*	*Fifield*
								Ref: L Robinson	'Too many players were trying to score' is Cooper's comment. An alert linesman signals that Crawford's header is over the line as City open their account. A push on Economou condemns Torquay to their second successive 0-5 away defeat as Ritchie makes no mistake from the spot.											
7	H	READING		4	W	3-1	0-1	Ritchie 61, Pritchard 63, 88	Shaw	Stevens	Williams G	Halliday	Phill-Masters	Riley	Pritchard	Ritchie	Kerr*	Economou	Crawford	Cooper
	27/9		6,322	*17*	13			*Senior 15*	*Judge**	*Williams*	*White*	*Beavon*	*Hicks*	*Wood*	*Price*	*Horrix*	*Senior*	*Sanchez*	*Crown*	*Matthews*
								Ref: J Deakin	Cooper's vintage half-hour show lifts City to a hard-earned win. Ritchie replies to Trevor Senior's headed opener, when unwittingly deflecting Steve Wood's clearance. Laurie Sanchez, replacing the injured Alan Judge on 65 minutes, is beaten by Pritchard's header from Cooper's chip.											
8	A	HEREFORD		2	W	2-0	1-0	Ritchie 42, Kerr 64	Shaw	Stevens	Williams G	Halliday	Phill-Masters	Riley	Pritchard	Ritchie	Kerr	Economou	Crawford	
	1/10		*5,943*	*5*	16				*Rose*	*Price*	*Leonard*	*Hicks*	*Pejic*	*Delve*	*Harvey*	*Emery**	*Phillips*	*Kearns*	*Black*	*Beacock*
								Ref: K Baker	Ritchie's headed goal is City's only shot on target in the first half as Crawford is withdrawn to a deeper role to strengthen the defence. Much relieved when John Delve's 53rd-minute header is disallowed for offside, City break quickly for Pritchard to cross for Kerr to hook the ball in.											
9	H	HALIFAX		2	W	3-0	3-0	Riley 1, Crawford 15, Kerr 42	Shaw	Stevens	Williams G	Halliday	Phill-Masters	Riley	Pritchard	Ritchie	Kerr	Economou*	Crawford	Cooper
	8/10		6,698	*19*	19				*Smelt*	*Nobbs*	*Wood*	*Evans**	*Smith !*	*Hendrie*	*Nuttall*	*Mell*	*Staniforth*	*Kendall*	*Ward*	*Cook*
								Ref: J Martin	City celebrate the award of a £250 cheque for being the Fourth Division's top scorers last month as Riley shoots in on 44 seconds. City are unable to capitalise after the break against opponents handicapped by the 53rd-min sending-off of Tom Smith for a professional foul on Riley.											
10	A	TRANMERE		2	L	0-2	0-1		Shaw	Stevens	Williams G	Halliday	Phill-Masters	Riley	Pritchard	Ritchie	Kerr	Economou*	Crawford	Cooper
	14/10		*2,520*	*3*	19			*Williams G 21, Halliday 59 (og)*	*Davies*	*McMahon*	*Burgess*	*Parry*	*Mungall*	*Williams J**	*Ferguson*	*Aspinall*	*Hilditch*	*Brown*	*Williams G*	*Hamilton*
								Ref: M Peck	City dominate the early play, but on falling behind to Gary Williams' 25-yarder they are often outplayed. Mark Hilditch fires against a post shortly before Halliday heads an own-goal. Les Parry is unfortunate to concede a 78th-min penalty for handball, but Ritchie's kick is saved.											
11	H	YORK		1	W	1-0	1-0	Stevens 39	Shaw	Stevens	Williams G	Halliday*	Phill-Masters	Riley	Pritchard	Ritchie	Kerr	Economou	Crawford	Cooper
	18/10		10,888	*2*	22				*Astbury*	*Evans*	*Hay !*	*Sbragia*	*MacPhail*	*Senior*	*Ford*	*Crosby*	*Walwyn**	*Byrne*	*Pollard*	*Busby*
								Ref: K Cooper	Former City player Alan Hay is sent off for dissent shortly after the only goal – a superb move between Stevens and Kerr ending with an angled drive. Halliday goes off injured following his early crunching tackle on Keith Walwyn, but the striker bravely plays on for an hour.											

No	Venue	Opponents / Date	Att	Pos	Res / Pts	FT	HT	Scorers, Times, Referees	1	2	3	4	5	6	7	8	9	10	11	12
12	A	ALDERSHOT		1	L	0-1	0-1		Shaw	Stevens	Williams G	Newman !	Phill-Masters	Riley	Pritchard	Ritchie	Kerr*	Economou	Crawford	Cooper
		22/10	*3,195*	*17*	22			*Lawrence 12*	*Coles*	*Shrubb*	*Mazzon*	*Briley**	*Ampofo*	*Jopling*	*Lucas*	*Banton*	*Lawrence*	*McDonald*	*Burvill*	*O'Sullivan*
								Ref: D Axcell	Riley fails with two good chances, but in between these misses Les Lawrence gives Aldershot the lead with a simple tap-in. City, up against it following Newman's 41st-minute dismissal for a tackle on Dale Banton, are unfortunate when Crawford's header hits the bar near the end.											
13	H	PETERBOROUGH		2	L	0-1	0-0		Shaw	Stevens	Williams G	Halliday	Phill-Masters	Riley	Pritchard	Ritchie	**Stroud**	Economou*	Crawford	Newman
		29/10	7,380	*6*	22			*Buchanan 75*	*Seaman*	*Chard*	*Imlach*	*Benjamin*	*Wile*	*Slack*	*Pike*	*Tydeman*	*Hankin*	*Waddle*	*Clarke**	*Buchanan*
								Ref: J Worrall	A woeful City performance as Terry Cooper, who has just been appointed to the board, admits that there is not much chance of signing a proven goalscorer. Substitute David Buchanan settles a poor game in Posh's favour, meeting Ian Benjamin's cross with a firm diving header.											
14	A	BLACKPOOL		6	L	0-1	0-1		Shaw	Stevens	Newman	Halliday	Phill-Masters	Riley*	Pritchard	Ritchie	Stroud !	Williams P	Crawford	Williams G
		1/11	*4,344*	*5*	22			*Windridge 19*	*Siddall*	*Bardsley*	*Ferns*	*Rodaway*	*Hetzke*	*Greenall*	*Windridge*	*Mercer*	*Stewart !*	*Deary*	*McNiven*	
								Ref: N Ashley	After Steve Hetzke's handball, Pritchard is left to rue his early penalty miss. Barry Siddall easily saves the half-hit shot and shortly after Dave Windridge shoots in from 20 yards. Paul Stewart on 74 minutes and Stroud shortly after are both sent off for second bookable offences.											
15	H	DONCASTER		7	L	1-2	1-1	Stroud 25	Shaw	Stevens	Williams G	Halliday*	Phill-Masters	Riley	Pritchard	Ritchie	Stroud	Williams P	Crawford	Economou
		5/11	6,145	*3*	22			*Kowalski, 7, Harle 68*	*Boyd*	*Russell*	*Harle*	*Snodin I*	*Lister*	*Humphries*	*Miller*	*Moss*	*Douglas*	*Kowalski*	*Snodin G*	
								Ref: A Buksh	After the shock of Andy Kowalski's opening volley, City monopolise possession. Shaw is fortunate not to be sent off after bringing down Ernie Moss on 55 minutes, but Doncaster snatch an unlikely victory when David Harle is on hand to tap in after Shaw saves from the No 8.											
16	A	DARLINGTON		5	W	1-0	0-0	Kerr 67	Shaw	Stevens	Williams G	Halliday	Phill-Masters	Riley*	Pritchard	Ritchie	Stroud	Economou	Williams P	Kerr
		12/11	*1,888*	*21*	25				*Barber*	*Craggs*	*Johnson*	*Honour**	*Smith*	*Barton*	*Cartwright*	*Todd*	*Davies*	*Walsh*	*McLean*	*Wakefield*
								Ref: A Challinor	Kerr heads in Pritchard's cross at the far post to end City's sequence of four defeats. City are forced to weather much early Darlington pressure as Alan Walsh causes many problems, but are not further troubled until John Craggs long-range effort hits the crossbar near the end.											
17	H	CHESTERFIELD		4	W	2-0	0-0	Ritchie 53p, Pritchard 59	Shaw	Stevens	Williams G	Halliday	Newman	**Hirst**	Pritchard	Ritchie	Stroud	Kerr	Williams P*	**Marshall**
		26/11	5,835	*16*	28				*Brown J*	*Kendal*	*O'Neill**	*Scrimgeour*	*Stimpson*	*Bellamy*	*Birch*	*Spooner*	*Newton*	*Clayton*	*Baines*	*Klug*
								Ref: D Vickers	Ritchie turns the game for a depleted City without five regulars. He scores with a perfectly-placed penalty after being floored when cleverly beating Barrie Stimpson. Chesterfield are unlucky when Steve Spooner's 18th-minute shot is ruled out for offside against John Clayton.											
18	A	NORTHAMPTON		7	L	0-1	0-1		Shaw	Stevens	Williams G	Halliday !	Newman	Hirst	Pritchard	Ritchie	Stroud	Kerr	Riley*	Cooper
		3/12	2,823	*10*	28			*Belfon 18*	*Gleasure*	*Tucker*	*Mundee*	*Gage*	*Lewis*	*Burrows*	*Jeffrey*	*O'Neill*	*Austin*	*Belfon**	*Hayes*	*Muir*
								Ref: A Ward	Despite much excellent play City lack the killer touch in front of goal, though Hirst is unfortunate when his shot is cleared off the line on the half-hour mark. Halliday is sent off near the end for a second caution in a minute as City strive to counter Frankie Belfon's fierce drive.											
19	A	ROCHDALE		7	W	1-0	0-0	Pritchard 86	Shaw	Stevens	Williams G	Newman	Phill-Masters	Hirst	Pritchard	Ritchie	Stroud	Riley	Crawford*	Cooper
		17/12	*1,501*	*20*	31				*Conroy*	*Greenhoff B*	*Chapman*	*Farrell*	*Williams*	*Doyle*	*Higgins*	*Hamilton*	*Johnson*	*Allatt**	*Thompson D*	*Griffiths*
								Ref: R Nixon	Pritchard seizes on Bill Humphries' sliced clearance to shoot in from 15 yards for City's late winner. With only one previous home defeat this season Rochdale are fortunate when Stroud's ferocious drive hits a post, but it is City's poor finishing that nearly lets them off the hook.											
20	H	STOCKPORT		4	W	3-1	2-0	Riley 20, Crawford 37, Stroud 52	Shaw	Stevens	Williams G	Halliday	Phill-Masters	Stroud	Pritchard	Ritchie*	Hirst	Riley	Crawford	Cooper
		26/12	9,246	*13*	34			*Sword 85*	*Salmon*	*Putter*	*Sherlock*	*Emerson*	*Bowles*	*Thorpe*	*Williams*	*Jones*	*Quinn*	*Sword*	*Evans*	
								Ref: T Spencer	Riley bounces back to form following the birth of his first child earlier this month. He sets City on course for a convincing win with a close-range shot. Stockport's attempts to spring the offside trap are frequently exposed and it is no surprise when Stroud is free to crash in a drive.											
21	A	CREWE		5	D	2-2	1-2	Ritchie 10p, Pritchard 55	Shaw	Stevens	Williams G	Halliday	Phill-Masters	Stroud	Pritchard	Ritchie	Hirst*	Riley	Crawford	Cooper
		28/12	*3,457*	*15*	35			*Crabbe 14, King 44p*	*Naylor*	*Brady*	*Bowers*	*King*	*Scott*	*Hart*	*Pullar**	*Crabbe*	*Waller*	*Leonard*	*Cliss*	*Edwards*
								Ref: D Richardson	City are run ragged in the first half after Bowers fouls Pritchard to concede Ritchie's pen. Crabbe's 20-yard chip puts Crewe level and then they take the lead after Phillipson-Masters brings down Waller. City's stirring second-half fight-back is rewarded by Crawford's fine volley.											
22	H	CHESTER		3	W	4-2	0-1	Craword 60, Stevens 76, Ritchie 81, [Riley 86]	Shaw	Stevens	Williams G	Halliday	Phill-Masters	Riley	Pritchard	Ritchie	Hirst*	Stroud	Crawford	Cooper
		31/12	7,565	*24*	38			*Camden 2, Brett 87*	*Harrington*	*Evans*	*Blackwell*	*Brett*	*Zelem !*	*Holden*	*Allen*	*Storton*	*Camden*	*Elliott*	*Sutcliffe !*	
								Ref: T Bune	Brett's late goal is Chester's only shot of the second half after their X-certificate tackling gifts City victory following the dismissal of Zelem and Sutcliffe either side of half-time. Harrington is unlucky with City's leveller, knocking the ball into the net after blocking Crawford's shot.											
23	H	WREXHAM		6	W	2-1	1-0	Ritchie 9p, Crawford 79	Shaw	Stevens	Williams G	Halliday	Phill-Masters	Stroud	Pritchard	Ritchie	Hirst*	Riley	Crawford	Cooper
		21/1	6,444	*18*	41			*Gregory 89p*	*Millington*	*King*	*Cunnington*	*Hunt*	*Heath*	*Keay*	*Wright*	*Arkwright*	*Steel*	*Gregory*	*Salathiel*	
								Ref: J Moules	Crawford celebrates heading in City's second goal, but to many fans it appears that Pritchard's head supplied the last vital touch as they both try to force home a ball that had cannoned off the crossbar. Ritchie's penalty follows on from a handball that deprives Riley of a goal.											

CANON LEAGUE DIVISION 4 — Manager: Terry Cooper — SEASON 1983-84

No	Date		Att	Pos	Pt	F-A	H-T	Scorers, Times, and Referees	1	2	3	4	5	6	7	8	9	10	11	12 sub used
24	A	SWINDON		4	D	1-1	0-0	Riley 83	Shaw	Stevens	Williams G	Halliday	Phill-Masters	Stroud	Pritchard	Ritchie	Riley	Hirst*	Crawford	Cooper
	24/1		*6,692*	*16*	42			*Quinn 51*	*Andrews*	*Henry*	*Baddeley*	*Batty*	*Gibson*	*Rowland*	*Hockaday*	*Emmanuel*	*Quinn*	*Nelson*	*Barnard*	
								Ref: C Downey	Riley's superbly-struck volley from the edge of the penalty area earns City a precious point from a match that appeared lost. Injury-hit Swindon raise their game in the derby atmosphere and on-loan keeper Ian Andrews has an inspired League debut. Jimmy Quinn hooks in a fine volley.											
25	A	HARTLEPOOL		4	D	2-2	1-2	Riley 32, Pritchard 67	Shaw	Stevens	Williams G	Halliday	Phill-Masters	Stroud	Pritchard	Ritchie	Riley	Hirst	Crawford*	Cooper
	28/1		*1,881*	*24*	43			*Dobson 4, Staff 12*	*Blackburn*	*Smithies*	*Barker*	*Hogan*	*Linighan A*	*Linighan D*	*Kennedy*	*Linacre J*	*Robinson D*	*Dobson*	*Staff*	
								Ref: D Allison	Financially-threatened Hartlepool deserve more for their early domination than Paul Dobson's bicycle kick and Paul Staff's rifle shot. Hirst shoots in from the corner of the area before Pritchard secures City's fortunate draw after running through to slip the ball past Eddie Blackburn.											
26	H	BURY		3	W	3-2	1-0	Ritchie 41p, Riley 59, Crawford 72	Shaw	Stevens	Williams G	Newman	Phill-Masters	Stroud	Pritchard	Ritchie	Hirst	Riley	Crawford	
	31/1		7,770	*11*	46			*Hilton 58, Jakub 68*	*Butcher*	*Gardner*	*Pashley*	*Park*	*Hilton P*	*Bramhall*	*White*	*Madden*	*Entwhistle**	*Jakub*	*Deacy*	*Carrodus*
								Ref: A Robinson	Bury are content to defend in numbers until Paul Hilton's ill-judged tackle on Ritchie produces a penalty opener. Hilton atones for his error by heading in Terry Pashley's cross, whilst Crawford is all on his own as he shoots City's winner. Nick Deacy limps off in the closing stages.											
27	H	HEREFORD		3	W	1-0	1-0	Crawford 42	Shaw	Stevens	Williams G	Newman	Phill-Masters	Stroud	Pritchard	Ritchie	Hirst*	Riley	Crawford	Cooper
	4/2		7,222	*21*	49				*Rose*	*Emery*	*Dalziel**	*Hicks*	*Pejic*	*Larkin*	*Hendie*	*Harvey*	*Phillips*	*Kearns*	*Butler*	*Bray*
								Ref: C Thomas	Cooper only has £20,000 to spend after City make hard work of this win. Superb saves by Kevin Rose keeps the Bulls (only one win in their previous 16 games) in with a chance. Ian Dalziel lies injured as Pritchard sets up Crawford to head in at the far post for City's first double.											
28	A	TORQUAY		3	L	0-1	0-0		Shaw	Stevens	Williams G	Halliday	Phill-Masters	Stroud	Pritchard	Ritchie	Newman	Hirst	Crawford*	Cooper
	11/2		*4,309*	*13*	49			*Sims 70*	*Turner*	*Pugh*	*Anderson*	*Carr*	*Impey*	*Lennox*	*Hughes*	*Curle*	*Bishop*	*Sims*	*Barnes*	
								Ref: V Callow	City exert much early pressure in a game which is a fine advertisement for basement soccer, but Shaw brings their ten-match unbeaten League run to an end. His mistimed punch from Brian Hughes' corner gifts John Sims his match-winning header to please new boss Dave Webb.											
29	H	BLACKPOOL		3	D	1-1	0-1	Stroud 80	Shaw	Stevens	Williams G	Halliday	Phill-Masters	Stroud	Pritchard	Ritchie	Hirst*	Newman	Crawford	Cooper
	14/2		7,599	*7*	50			*Hetzke 33*	*Pierce*	*Moore*	*Ferns*	*Rodaway*	*Hetzke*	*Walsh*	*Britton*	*Mercer*	*Stewart*	*Windridge*	*McNiven**	*Dyer*
								Ref: D Hedges	City dominate the second half in their attempts to equalise Steve Hetzke's 20-yard free-kick, but the flow of the game is effected by the award of 43 free-kicks for mainly petty offences. Blackpool at last fail to clear one of City's 14 corners and Stroud rifles a superb shot in off the post.											
30	A	PETERBOROUGH		5	L	**1-4**	1-1	Crawford 23	Shaw	Stevens	Williams G	Halliday	Phill-Masters	Stroud	Pritchard	Ritchie	Newman	Hirst	Crawford*	Cooper
	18/2		*3,356*	*8*	50			*Waddle 33, 81, Hankin 46, Worrall 70*	*Seaman*	*Chard*	*Imlach*	*Beech*	*Wile*	*Firm*	*Benjamin*	*Tydeman*	*Hankin*	*Waddle*	*Worrall*	
								Ref: A Gunn	City skipper Tom Ritchie admits, after this defeat, that City may not have a strong enough squad to go up. Crawford shoots City ahead, but defensive errors allow the Posh to take charge. Gary Worrall, on loan from Manchester United, strikes a magnificent goal from a narrow angle.											
31	H	ALDERSHOT		4	W	2-1	2-1	Ritchie 20p, Riley 24	Shaw	Stevens	Newman	Halliday	Phill-Masters	Stroud	Pritchard	Ritchie	Riley	Hirst	Cooper	
	25/2		7,140	*5*	53			*Lawrence 44*	*Coles*	*Shrubb*	*Gillard*	*Briley*	*Souter*	*Jopling*	*Burvill*	*Banton*	*Lawrence*	*McDonald*	*Mazzon*	
								Ref: L Shapter	Ian Gillard and Don Souter complain of being punched and kicked by City fans as they leave the pitch after this vital promotion clash. Riley produces two flashes of inspiration to win the game. He topples dramatically for Ritchie's penalty, then nets with an 18-yarder into the corner.											
32	A	YORK		3	D	1-1	0-0	Morgan 79	Shaw	Stevens	Newman	Halliday	Phill-Masters	Stroud	Pritchard	Ritchie	Riley	**Morgan**	**Curle**	
	3/3		*5,096*	*1*	54			*Phillipson-Masters 46 (og)*	*Jones*	*Senior*	*Hay*	*Sbragia*	*MacPhail*	*Hood*	*Ford*	*Crosby*	*Walwyn*	*Byrne*	*Pearce*	
								Ref: I Hendrick	Trevor Morgan, City's new £10,000 striker from Bournemouth, maintains his remarkable scoring-debut sequence. He stoops to head in from Pritchard's free-kick to level matters after Phillipson-Masters has the misfortune to deflect John Byrne's vicious cross into his own net.											
33	A	DONCASTER		3	L	0-1	0-1		Shaw	Stevens	Newman	Halliday	Phill-Masters	Stroud	Pritchard	Ritchie	Morgan	Riley*	Curle	Hirst
	6/3		*4,954*	*2*	54			*Douglas 4*	*Peacock*	*Yates*	*Breckin*	*Snodin I*	*Harle*	*Humphries*	*Miler**	*Moss*	*Douglas*	*Kowalski*	*Snodin G*	*Woods*
								Ref: A Robinson	City never look like ending Doncaster's 15-match unbeaten run after Colin Douglas handles the ball before shooting in. Stevens clears a header off the line after the break, but City are unlucky in the 24th minute with the award of a free-kick on the edge of the box instead of a penalty.											
34	H	DARLINGTON		5	W	1-0	0-0	Morgan 84	Shaw	Stevens	Newman	Halliday	Phill-Masters	Stroud	Pritchard	Ritchie	Riley	Morgan	Curle	
	10/3		7,046	*18*	57				*Barber*	*Craggs*	*Johnson*	*Gilbert*	*Smith*	*Barton*	*Cartwright*	*Todd*	*Hannah*	*Wilson*	*McLean**	*Honour*
								Ref: D Letts	According to City's full-backs, John Hannah's 58th-min free-header from Kevin Todd crosses the line before Shaw claws the ball out. A goal then would have been rough justice for City who gain a late winning reward for their almost constant attacking with Morgan's right-foot volley.											

No	H/A	Opponent	Att	Pos	Res	F-A	H-T	Scorers, Times, Referees	1	2	3	4	5	6	7	8	9	10	11	12
35	H	ROCHDALE		4	D	1-1	0-1	Riley 80	Shaw	Stevens	Newman	Halliday	Phill-Masters	Stroud	Pritchard	Ritchie	Riley	Morgan	Curle*	Hirst
	13/3		7,101	*21*	58			*O'Connor 43*	*Conroy*	*Oates*	*Chapman*	*Reid*	*McMahon*	*Williams*	*Thompson D*	*Hamilton*	*O'Connor*	*Allatt*	*Griffiths*	
								Ref: R Lewis	Enterprising Rochdale belie their lowly position against inept City. Malcolm O'Connor's rasping drive puts the visitors ahead, and they are unlucky on 72 mins when Vernon Allatt's header is struck off for pushing. Riley's heads in City's equaliser and later the post denies Pritchard.											
36	A	HALIFAX		4	W	2-1	0-0	Pritchard 48, Riley 76	Shaw	Stevens	Newman	Halliday	Phill-Masters	Stroud	Pritchard	Ritchie	Morgan	Riley	Curle	
	17/3		**1,204**	*21*	61			*Evans 89*	*Smelt*	*Kendall*	*Wood*	*Evans*	*Smith*	*Hendrie*	*Gallagher B*	*Little*	*Staniforth*	*Cook**	*Ward*	*Mell*
								Ref: J Lovatt	Pritchard opens the scoring with a coolly-executed volley and creates the second with a brilliant pass to Riley. A first half littered with offsides is best forgotten, but after the break City's defence is in control until a twice-taken free-kick by David Evans is deflected off Riley into the net.											
37	H	TRANMERE		4	D	1-1	0-0	Morgan 85	Shaw	Stevens	Newman	Halliday	Phill-Masters	Stroud*	Pritchard	Ritchie	Riley	Morgan	Hirst	Cooper
	24/3		6,613	*9*	62			*Hutchinson 49*	*Davies*	*Higgins*	*Burgess*	*Philpotts*	*Williams G*	*Palios*	*Ferguson*	*Aspinall*	*Hilditch*	*Hutchinson*	*Goodlass*	
								Ref: D Burgess	Tranmere boss Bryan Hamilton tips City for promotion after his impressive side take a deserved point. Rovers punish Newman's indecision as Mark Hilditch crosses for Bobby Hutchinson to hammer in, but City equalise when Cooper's measured pass sets up Morgan's low drive.											
38	A	MANSFIELD		3	W	1-0	0-0	Newman 56	Shaw	Stevens	Newman	Halliday	Phill-Masters	Stroud	Pritchard	Ritchie	Riley	Morgan	Hirst	
	27/3		*1,828*	*23*	65				*Hitchcock*	*Woodhead*	*Whitworth*	*Lowery*	*Ayre*	*Foster*	*Barrowclough*	*Matthews*	*Juryeff*	*Caldwell*	*Nicholson**	*Calderwood*
								Ref: D Shaw	Newman clips a curling right-foot free-kick round Mansfield's wall to clinch a City victory far more emphatic than the score suggests. Re-election-threatened Mansfield look the poorest side City have faced this season, but Shaw has to be alert to parry Tony Lowery's low shot.											
39	H	COLCHESTER		2	W	4-1	1-0	Ritchie 26p, 63, Riley 67, 81	Shaw	Stevens	Newman	Halliday	Phill-Masters	Stroud	Pritchard	Ritchie	Riley	Morgan	Hirst	
	31/3		6,612	*9*	68			*Wignall 78*	*Chamberlain*	*Cook*	*Phillips**	*Hedman*	*Wignall*	*Houston*	*Groves*	*Osborne*	*Bowen*	*Adcock*	*Leslie*	*Hadley*
								Ref: M Heath	Despite Ritchie's penalty, after another of Riley's theatrical falls, City's play is racked with tension before a bout of one-touch football allows Ritchie to score with a low shot. In a rare U's raid Steve Wignall nets with a superb header, but Riley fires in to ensure City have the final say.											
40	A	READING		2	L	0-2	0-2		Shaw	Stevens	Newman	Halliday	Phill-Masters	Stroud	Pritchard	Ritchie	Riley	Morgan	Hirst*	Cooper
	7/4		***8,780***	*3*	68			*Sanchez10, Horrix 36*	*Judge*	*Williams*	*Richardson*	*Price*	*Hicks*	*Wood*	*White*	*Horrix*	*Senior*	*Sanchez*	*Crown*	
								Ref: D Vickers	A day of shame for so called City fans as terrace violence leads to the game being held up for 15 mins in the second half. Reading are good value for their win secured by a Lawrie Sanchez shot and Dean Horrix's freak effort. His attempted cross curls over Shaw's head into the net.											
41	H	NORTHAMPTON		2	W	4-1	1-1	Crawford 32, 58, Riley 83, Ritchie 87p	Shaw	Stevens	Newman	Halliday	Phill-Masters	Stroud	Pritchard	Ritchie	Riley	Morgan	Crawford*	Cooper
	14/4		6,655	*16*	71			*O'Neill 44p*	*Gleasure*	*Lewis*	*Forster*	*Gage*	*Burrows**	*Hayes !*	*Jeffrey*	*O'Neill*	*Mundee*	*Austin*	*Muir*	*Belfon*
								Ref: K Cooper	Crawford's return, after knee-ligament trouble, inspires an impressive win on a day other promotion rivals Aldershot and Blackpool falter. The referee, finding cause to book six players, aids City's cause by sending off Austin Hayes in the 23rd minute for his second bookable offence.											
42	H	CREWE		2	W	2-1	2-0	Hirst 29, Pritchard 31	Shaw	Stevens	Newman	Hirst	Phill-Masters	Stroud	Pritchard	Ritchie	Riley	Morgan	Crawford	
	17/4		8,184	*14*	74			*Leonard 61*	*Naylor*	*Davies*	*Edwards*	*King*	*Scott*	*Hart*	*Cliss*	*Bishop*	*Waller*	*Leonard**	*Williams*	*Thomas*
								Ref: E Scales	Hirst puts himself in good heart for his geography degree finals next month with his first League goal. A sweetly-struck volley from the edge of the penalty area helps City overcome battling Crewe for whom Mark Leonard scores after latching onto Ian Bishop's hopeful through-ball.											
43	A	STOCKPORT		2	D	0-0	0-0		Shaw	Stevens	Newman	Halliday	Phill-Masters	Stroud	Pritchard	Ritchie	Riley	Morgan	Hirst	
	21/4		*2,645*	*13*	75				*Salmon*	*Thorpe*	*Rutter*	*Emerson*	*Sword*	*Bowles*	*Williams*	*Evans*	*Kerr*	*Taylor*	*Coyle*	
								Ref: D Scott	City fans are sure City are promotion bound as they chant 'going up, going up' after this exciting draw at Edgeley Park. Although there are no goals, this is one of the best games seen at Stockport this season. Action swings from end to end with goalmouth thrills coming thick and fast.											
44	A	CHESTERFIELD		3	D	1-1	0-0	Phillipson-Masters 78	Shaw	Stevens	Newman	Halliday	Phill-Masters	Stroud	Pritchard	Ritchie	Riley*	Morgan	Hirst	Curle
	28/4		2,975	*14*	76			*Kendal 77*	*Brown J*	*Bellamy*	*Brown N*	*Kendal*	*Baines*	*Hunter*	*Brown P*	*Scrimgeour*	*Newton*	*Klug*	*O'Neill*	
								Ref: K Baker	In a lacklustre encounter, without the competitive spirit expected, giant centre-half Phillipson-Masters pops up with his first goal of the season to push City closer to promotion. His header from Newman's free-kick cancels out Steve Kendal's shot from a suspiciously-offside position.											
45	H	SWINDON		3	W	1-0	0-0	Pritchard 46	Shaw	Stevens	Newman	Halliday	Phill-Masters	Stroud	Pritchard	Ritchie	Riley	Morgan	Crawford	
	5/5		**12,810**	*16*	79				*Endersby*	*Henry*	*Baillie*	*Batty*	*Baddeley*	*Graham*	*Barnard*	*Emmanuel*	*Quinn*	*Hockaday*	*Nelson*	
								Ref: B Stevens	City celebrate Cooper signing a new two-year contract with this derby win, that has the fans erroneously thinking that promotion had been achieved. Swindon dominate the first half, but City take control after Pritchard crashes in Crawford's pass to finish off a brilliant move.											
46	A	CHESTER		3	W	2-1	1-0	Morgan 32, 87	Shaw	Stevens	Newman	Halliday	Phill-Masters	Stroud	Pritchard	Ritchie	Riley	Morgan	Crawford	
	7/5		*4,013*	*24*	82			*Zelem 81*	*Harrington*	*Dixon*	*Lane*	*Williams M*	*Zelem*	*Elliott*	*Allen*	*Sanderson*	*Coy*	*Wharton**	*Brett*	*Bulmer*
		Home	Away					Ref: P Scott	Needing a point to secure promotion City live up to Cooper's pledge in going for a win at Sealand Road. Morgan's low drive from a free-kick punishes Chester for up-ending Pritchard, and he slots home the winner after Peter Zelem had silenced the 3,000 City fans with his header.											
Average		7,287	3,447																	

Milk Cup					F-A	H-T	Scorers, Times, and Referees	1	2	3	4	5	6	7	8	9	10	11	12 sub used
1:1	A	OXFORD		D	1-1	0-1	Riley 86	Shaw	Stevens	Williams G	Halliday	Phill-Masters	Riley	Pritchard	Ritchie	Kerr*	Musker	Crawford	Williams P
	31/8	*3,924*					*Brock 16*	*Hardwick*	*Hinshelwood*	*Grant*	*Thomas**	*Briggs*	*Shotton*	*Lawrence*	*Whatmore*	*Biggins*	*Hebberd*	*Brock*	*Vinter*
							Ref: E Scales	Kevin Brock takes advantage of a rebound to put disappointing Oxford in front after Shaw's great block of an Andy Thomas shot. Halliday is City's star man with an almost faultless display at the back. Riley smashes home City's deserved equaliser following Musker's corner.											
1:2	H	OXFORD	7	L	0-1	0-1		Shaw	Newman	Williams G	Halliday	Phill-Masters	Riley	Pritchard	Ritchie*	Kerr	Economou	Crawford	Williams P
	12/9	5,163	*3:6*				*Thomas 1*	*Hardwick*	*Hinshelwood*	*McDonald*	*Thomas*	*Briggs*	*Shotton*	*Lawrence*	*Vinter**	*Biggins*	*Hebbard*	*Brock*	*Barnett*
							Ref: L Burden (City lost 1-2 on aggregate)	An impressive first-half display by the City, despite being caught napping after just 16 secs when Andy Thomas races clear to shoot past Shaw. Oxford, denied a 25th-min pen when Phillipson-Masters handles the ball, take control after the break following Ritchie's exit due to injury.											

FA Cup					F-A	H-T	Scorers, Times, and Referees	1	2	3	4	5	6	7	8	9	10	11	12 sub used
1	A	CORINTHIAN CAS	5	D	0-0	0-0		Shaw	Stevens	Williams G	Halliday	Newman	Kerr	Pritchard	Ritchie	Williams P	Economou*	Hirst	Cooper
	19/11	*2,118*	*IL*					*Chapman*	*Rulton*	*Stevenson*	*Coldspring*	*Bateman*	*Pardew*	*Armitt*	*Green*	*Merron*	*Gray*	*Watson*	
	(at Dulwich H'let)						Ref: M James	City are made to fight for survival against the famous amateurs in this tie played on the Champion Hill ground of Dulwich Hamlet. Casuals skipper Peter Bateman puts an early chance over the bar and they put on the pressure straight after the break, before City turn the tide.											
1R	H	CORINTHIAN CAS	5	W	4-0	2-0	Riley 7, Pritchard 20, 46, 55,	Shaw	Stevens	Williams G	Halliday	Newman	Economou*	Pritchard	Ritchie	Riley	Kerr	Stroud	Cooper
	23/11	5,339	*IL*					*Chapman*	*Rulton*	*Stevenson*	*Coldspring*	*Cleaver*	*Pardew*	*Armitt*	*Green*	*Merron**	*Gray*	*Watson*	*Bateman*
							Ref: M James	Riley calms any City worries with an early tap-in after Ritchie's shot hits the post. Casuals bow out of the Cup in the best tradition of gracious losers as Pritchard notches the second hat-trick of his career. Bernie Merron insists on shaking hands with City players when being substituted.											
2	A	BRISTOL ROV	8	W	2-1	0-0	Ritchie 78, Hirst 89	Shaw	Stevens	Williams G	Halliday	Phill-Masters	Stroud	Pritchard	Ritchie	Hirst	Riley	Crawford*	Cooper
	10/12	*14,396*	*3:2*				*Stephens 50*	*Kite*	*Slatter*	*Williams B*	*Bater*	*Parkin*	*McCaffery*	*Holloway*	*Williams G*	*Stephens*	*Randall**	*Barrett*	*White*
							Ref: K Baker	Hirst's mis-hit shot from Riley's pull-back earns City a deserved victory at Eastville Stadium. City refuse to be dismayed after Archie Stephens puts the Rovers ahead with magnificent header. Riley hits the post before Ritchie cracks in a fine equaliser after swivelling to lose his marker.											
3	A	NOTTS CO	6	D	2-2	1-1	Crawford 3, Ritchie 64	Shaw	Stevens	Williams G	Halliday	Phill-Masters	Riley	Pritchard	Ritchie	Stroud	Hirst	Crawford*	Cooper
	8/1	*11,042*	*1:20*				*Christie 34p, 49*	*McDonagh*	*Goodwin*	*Worthington*	*Richards*	*Hunt*	*Kilcline*	*O'Neill*	*Clarke*	*Christie*	*Harkouk**	*Chiedozie*	*McCulloch*
							Ref: N Glover	City's superb performance belies their lowly status. Crawford is free at the far post to head in Pritchard's cross for an early lead. County level with a penalty after Rachid Harkouk appears to dive, but City are denied a similar award in the 75th minute when Ritchie is brought down.											
3R	H	NOTTS CO	3	L	0-2	0-0		Shaw	Stevens	Williams G	Halliday	Phill-Masters	Riley	Pritchard	Ritchie	Stroud	Hirst	Crawford*	Cooper
	10/1	16,107	*1:20*				*Kilcline 48, McCulloch 73*	*McDonagh*	*Goodwin*	*Worthington*	*Richards*	*Hunt*	*Kilcline*	*O'Neill*	*McCulloch*	*Christie*	*Harkouk*	*Chiedozie*	
							Ref: N Glover	The fans who are undeterred by price increases of up to 40 per cent receive poor reward as City are muscled out of the Cup. Pritchard is controversially ruled offside on hammering home Ritchie's pass shortly after Brian Kilcline bundles the ball in off a post to put Notts ahead.											

		Home						Away					
	P	W	D	L	F	A	W	D	L	F	A	Pts
1 York	46	18	4	1	58	16	13	4	6	38	23	101
2 Doncaster	46	15	6	2	46	22	9	7	7	36	32	85
3 Reading	46	17	6	0	51	14	5	10	8	33	42	82
4 BRISTOL CITY	46	18	3	2	51	17	6	7	10	19	27	82
5 Aldershot	46	14	6	3	49	29	8	3	12	27	40	75
6 Blackpool	46	15	4	4	47	19	6	5	12	23	33	72
7 Peterborough	46	15	5	3	52	16	3	9	11	20	32	68
8 Colchester	46	14	7	2	45	14	3	9	11	24	39	67
9 Torquay	46	13	7	3	32	18	5	6	12	27	46	67
10 Tranmere	46	11	5	7	33	26	6	10	7	20	27	66
11 Hereford	46	11	6	6	31	21	5	9	9	23	32	63
12 Stockport	46	12	5	6	34	25	5	6	12	26	39	62
13 Chesterfield	46	10	11	2	34	24	5	4	14	25	37	60
14 Darlington	46	13	4	6	31	19	4	4	15	18	31	59
15 Bury	46	9	7	7	34	32	6	7	10	27	32	59
16 Crewe	46	10	8	5	35	27	6	3	14	21	40	59
17 Swindon	46	11	7	5	34	23	4	6	13	24	33	58
18 Northampton	46	10	8	5	32	32	3	6	14	21	46	53
19 Mansfield	46	9	7	7	44	27	4	6	13	22	43	52
20 Wrexham	46	7	6	10	34	33	4	9	10	25	41	48
21 Halifax	46	11	6	6	36	25	1	6	16	19	64	48
22 Rochdale	46	8	9	6	35	31	3	4	16	17	49	46
23 Hartlepool	46	7	8	8	31	28	3	2	18	16	57	40
24 Chester	46	7	5	11	23	35	0	8	15	22	47	34
	1104	285	150	117	932	573	117	150	285	573	932	1506

Odds & ends

Double wins: (5) Mansfield, Hereford, Halifax, Darlington, Chester.
Double losses: (2) Peterborough, Doncaster.

Won from behind: (2) Reading (h), Chester (h).
Lost from in front: (2) Bury (a), Peterborough (a).

High spots: Achieving promotion.
Beating York 1-0 at Ashton Gate on 18 October.
Winning 2-1 at Chester to clinch promotion on 7 May.
Overcoming Bristol Rov in the FA Cup.

Low spots: Heavy defeat at Peterborough.
Losing FA replay v Notts County (h) 0-2.
Losing 2-3 v Bristol Rov (h) in the Gloucestershire Cup Final on 20 Sep.

Player of the year: Howard Pritchard.
Ever presents: (2) Howard Pritchard, John Shaw.
Hat-tricks: (2) Alan Crawford, Howard Pritchard.
Leading scorer: Glyn Riley (18).

	Appearances						Goals			
	Lge	*Sub*	LC	*Sub*	FAC	*Sub*	Lge	LC	FAC	Tot
Cooper, Terry	**1**	*20*				*5*				
Curle, Keith	**5**	*1*								
Crawford, Alan	**31**		2		3		**15**		1	**16**
Economou, Jon	**11**	*1*	1		2					
Halliday, Bruce	**41**		2		5					
Hirst, Martyn	**22**	*2*			4		**1**		1	**2**
Kerr, John	**13**	*1*	2		2		**4**			**4**
Marshall, Gary		*1*								
Morgan, Trevor	**15**						**5**			**5**
Musker, Russell	**2**	*1*	1							
Newman, Rob	**29**	*1*	1		2		**1**			**1**
Phill-Masters, Forbes	**44**		2		3		**1**			**1**
Pritchard, Howard	**46**		2		5		**10**		3	**13**
Riley, Glynn	**42**		2		4		**16**	1	1	**18**
Ritchie, Tom	**45**		2		5		**12**		2	**14**
Shaw, John	**46**		2		5					
Stevens, Paul	**45**	*1*	1		5		**2**			**2**
Stroud, Ken	**34**				4		**3**			**3**
Williams, Gary	**29**	*1*	2		5					
Williams, Paul	**5**	*3*		*2*	1					
19 players used	**506**	***33***	**22**	***2***	**55**	***5***	**70**	**1**	**8**	**79**

No		Date	Att	Pos	Pt	F-A	H-T	Scorers, Times, and Referees	1	2	3	4	5	6	7	8	9	10	11	12 sub used
1	H	WIGAN			W	2-0	0-0	Riley 60, 84	Shaw	Stevens	Newman	**Rogers**	Phill-Masters	Hirst	Pritchard	Riley	Morgan	**Walsh**	Crawford	
		25/8	8,122		3				*Tunks*	*Butler*	*Comstive*	*Kelly*	*Cribley*	*Methven*	*Bailey*	*Barrow*	*Johnson*	*Lowe !*	*Langley**	*Bruce*
								Ref: M James	Wigan's David Lowe is sent off after swinging an elbow in frustration at the control City apprentice Lee Rogers exhibits over him on his debut. Clever running into space after the interval exposes the ponderous Wigan defence and the irrepressible Riley twice heads in.											
2	A	NEWPORT			D	0-0	0-0		Shaw	Stevens	Newman	Rogers	Phill-Masters	Hirst	Pritchard	Riley	Morgan*	Walsh	Crawford	Curle
		1/9	*5,279*		4				*Plumley*	*Jones*	*Matthewson*	*Reid*	*Saxby*	*Boyle*	*Carter*	*Pulis*	*Kent*	*Chamberlain**	*Lewis*	*Green*
								Ref: R Lewis	City weather much pressure and old adversary Tony Pulis is convinced that Newport will not let them off the hook again in next week's League Cup match. Roy Carter has his shot disallowed just before half-time, while sub Phil Green later sends a diving header against a post.											
3	H	SWANSEA		10	D	2-2	1-1	Walsh 16p Crawford 66	Shaw	Stevens	Newman	Rogers	Halliday	Hirst	Pritchard	Riley*	Morgan	Walsh	Crawford	Curle
		8/9	8,700	*23*	5			*Mardenborough 21, Saunders 70*	*Rimmer*	*Evans*	*Marustik*	*Lewis*	*Stevenson*	*Richardson*	*Saunders*	*Robinson*	*Richards*	*Mardenboro'**	*Pascoe*	*Rajkovic*
								Ref: D Vickers	Swansea, who have not won an away match for two seasons, almost end this run as Shaw has to make a fine save from Chris Marustik ten mins from time. Dean Saunders handles the ball to concede a penalty, but the striker makes amends by shooting in the Swans' second equaliser.											
4	A	CAMBRIDGE		6	W	3-2	1-1	Walsh 8, Newman 72, Crawford 74	Shaw	Stevens	Newman	Rogers	Halliday	Hirst	Pritchard	Riley	Morgan	Walsh	Crawford	
		15/9	*2,444*	*21*	8			*Moyes 36, Greaves 69*	*Branagan*	*Clark*	*Beattie*	*Fallon*	*Moyes*	*Daniels*	*Cartwright**	*Massey*	*Cooke*	*Comfort*	*Pyle*	*Greaves*
								Ref: J Ball	City maintain their unbeaten record in sensational style in this thrill-a-minute clash. Trailing 1-2 after Danny Greaves' debut goal, Newman crashes in a stunning right-foot volley from the edge of the penalty area, and then Crawford slides in the winner under Keith Branagan's body.											
5	A	DERBY		8	L	0-1	0-1		Shaw	Stevens	Newman	Halliday	Phill-Masters	Hirst	Pritchard	Riley*	Morgan	Walsh	Crawford	Curle
		19/9	*11,314*	*11*	8			*Wilson 32*	*Steele*	*Palmer*	*Buckley*	*Powell*	*Hindmarch*	*Burns*	*Taylor*	*Wilson*	*Davison*	*Hooks*	*Robertson*	
								Ref: E Scales	The referee incurs City's wrath by failing to spot Rob Hindmarch's blatant handball right on half-time and disallowing Pritchard's 77th-minute shot. Kevin Wilson, the League's top scorer, shoots the only goal, firing in from the edge of the area on collecting Kevin Taylor's through-ball.											
6	H	ORIENT		7	W	3-2	1-1	Newman 15, Walsh 47, Crawford 78	Shaw	Stevens	Newman	Halliday	Phill-Masters	Hirst	Pritchard	Riley	Morgan	Walsh	Crawford	
		22/9	6,941	*23*	11			*Silkman 24, Cornwell 88*	*Wilmot*	*Hales*	*Stride*	*Corbett*	*Foster*	*Banfield*	*Silkman*	*Brooks*	*Sussex*	*Cadette**	*Godfrey*	*Cornwell*
								Ref: L Shapter	The fans jeer every square ball as City concentrate on slowing down the pace and keeping possession in the second half. Despite the boost of Newman's early scoring volley, City struggle to find any rhythm before the break. Orient level with Barry Silkman's shot from a narrow angle.											
7	A	WALSALL		10	L	**1-4**	0-1	Walsh 54	Shaw	Stevens	Newman	Halliday	Phill-Masters	Hirst	Pritchard	Riley	Morgan	Walsh	Crawford	
		29/9	*4,754*	*13*	11			*Kelly 3, 65, O'Kelly 61p, Bamber 73*	*Cherry*	*Hart*	*Mower*	*Shakespeare*	*Brazier*	*Hawker**	*Handysides*	*O'Kelly*	*Bamber*	*Kelly*	*Childs*	*Jones*
								Ref: J McAulay	In the ascendancy after Walsh turns in Hirst's pass for an equaliser, City are sunk by a disputed pen. Richard O'Kelly makes no mistake from the spot as heated protests that Gary Childs took a blatant dive fall on deaf ears. David Kelly notches Walsall's third with a well-judged chip.											
8	H	ROTHERHAM		10	L	0-1	0-1		Shaw	Stevens	Newman	Curle	Phill-Masters	Hirst	Pritchard	Riley	Morgan	Walsh	Crawford	
		2/10	6,586	*7*	11			*Birch 38p*	*Mimms*	*Forrest*	*Mitchell*	*Trusson*	*Johnson*	*Pickering*	*Birch*	*Gooding*	*Dungworth*	*Simmons*	*Kilmore*	
								Ref: M Cotton	It's not City's night as offside rules out efforts by Newman in the 69th minute and Morgan at the death, as well as being twice thwarted by the woodwork. After Stevens up-ends Kevin Kilmore with a clumsy tackle, Shaw is sent the wrong way by Alan Birch's penalty decider.											
9	A	YORK		9	W	2-0	1-0	Morgan 38, Walsh 71	Shaw	Stevens	Newman	Curle	Phill-Masters	Hirst*	Pritchard	Ritchie	Morgan	Walsh	Riley	Cooper
		6/10	*4,890*	*2*	14				*Jones*	*Evans*	*Hay*	*Sbragia*	*MacPhail*	*Haslegrave*	*Ford*	*Hood**	*Walwyn*	*Byrne*	*Nicholson*	*Atkinson*
								Ref: G Aplin	John Shaw provides the perfect answer to his critics with a brilliant display against the previously-unbeaten League leaders. He dives to his left to keep out John MacPhail's 19th-min spot-kick after Curle is harshly penalised for handball. Walsh ties up City's victory with a fierce volley.											
10	H	GILLINGHAM		8	W	2-0	1-0	Riley 13, Morgan 59	Shaw	Stevens	Newman	Curle	Phill-Masters	Riley	Pritchard	Ritchie	Morgan	Walsh	Crawford	
		13/10	7,088	*7*	17				*Hillyard*	*Hinnigan*	*Sage*	*Oakes*	*Johnson*	*Shaw*	*Robinson*	*Shearer*	*Leslie**	*Mehmet*	*Cascarino*	*Weatherly*
								Ref: A Selville	Exhilarating City are fortunate with Riley's headed opener as Phillipson-Masters gets away with chopping down John Leslie in the build-up. Morgan heads in from a kneeling position at the Open End, before Mark Weatherly has his 20-yard drive disallowed by an offside decision.											
11	A	BRADFORD C		5	D	1-1	0-1	Pritchard 50	Shaw	Stevens	Newman	Curle	Phill-Masters	Riley*	Pritchard	Ritchie	Morgan	Walsh	Stroud	Crawford
		20/10	*4,569*	*4*	18			*Campbell 12*	*McManus*	*Cherry*	*Withe*	*McCall*	*Jackson*	*Evans*	*Hendrie*	*Goodman*	*Campbell*	*Abbot*	*Ellis*	
								Ref: D Richardson	A point is City's just reward for a sterling second-half fight-back. Bobby Campbell's volley is all the Bantams have to show for their early dominance and the City, with the wind behind them after the break, draw level as Pritchard bundles the ball over the line from Walsh's corner.											

No	H/A	Opponent / Date	Att	Pos	Res / Pts	FT	HT	Scorers, Times, and Referees	1	2	3	4	5	6	7	8	9	10	11	12 sub used
12	H	BOLTON		4	W	3-2	2-2	Pritchard 2, Walsh 41p, 73	Shaw	Stevens	Newman	Phill-Masters	Curle	Stroud	Pritchard	Ritchie	Morgan	Walsh	Crawford	
		23,10	7,713	*16*	21			*Foster 19, Oghani 22*	*Farnworth*	*Borrows*	*Phillips*	*Joyce*	*Berry*	*Valentine*	*Thompson*	*Chandler*	*Oghani*	*Foster*	*Bell*	
								Ref: J Bray	George Oghani's close-range volley puts lively Bolton in front, after Pritchard's left-foot curler gives the homesters a dream start. A lucky win for City, courtesy of a harsh penalty decision for Peter Valentine's tackle on Pritchard and Walsh's free-kick slipping from Farnworth's grasp.											
13	A	MILLWALL		6	D	1-1	0-0	Morgan 69	Shaw	Llewellyn	Newman	Curle	Phill-Masters	Riley	Pritchard	Ritchie	Morgan	Walsh	Stroud	
		27/10	*7,039*	*1*	22			*Lovell 87*	*Sansome*	*Stevens*	*Roffey*	*Brisley*	*Smith*	*Cusack*	*Lowndes*	*Bremner*	*McLeary**	*Lovell*	*Otulakowski*	*Neal D*
								Ref: B Hill	City come close to ending Millwall's unbeaten record. After battling to stay on terms in the first half, Morgan stabs the ball home to give City the lead. Steve Lovell, denied by the woodwork on 66 minutes, chests down Dave Cusack's cross to drive in the Lions' late equaliser.											
14	H	BRENTFORD		7	D	1-1	0-0	Walsh 67	Shaw	Llewellyn	Newman	Curle	Phill-Masters	Riley	Pritchard	Ritchie	Morgan	Walsh	Stroud	
		3 11	7,674	*8*	23			*Kamara 69*	*Swinburne*	*Fisher*	*Murray*	*Roberts P*	*Salman*	*Hulock*	*Kamara*	*Booker*	*Cassells*	*Alexander*	*Roberts G*	
								Ref: R Gifford	Brentford keeper Trevor Swinburne has an inspired game, but he is unable to do anything about Walsh's vicious left-foot shot from the edge of the area. Chris Kamara makes the most of a free header to level matters, just after Curle had cleared Keith Booker's header off the line.											
15	A	DONCASTER		8	D	1-1	0-0	Walsh 62	Shaw	Llewellyn	Newman*	Curle	Phill-Masters	Riley	Pritchard	Ritchie	Morgan	Walsh	Stroud	**Hutchinson**
		6/11	*3,947*	*5*	24			*Harle 85*	*Peacock*	*Russell*	*Yates*	*Snodin I*	*Philliben*	*Brown T*	*Buckley*	*Butterworth*	*Douglas*	*Harle*	*Snodin G*	
								Ref: N Wilson	Hutchinson's long-awaited City debut, after an instep injury, comes two months late and about an hour too soon! Lacking match practice, he replaces the injured Newman as early as the 19th minute. Another Walsh special puts City ahead, but David Harle taps in a simple equaliser.											
16	H	BRISTOL ROV		3	W	3-0	1-0	Stroud 10, Riley 50, 62	Shaw	Llewellyn	Halliday	Phill-Masters	Curle	Riley	Pritchard	Ritchie	Morgan	Walsh	Stroud	
		10/11	**18,675**	*7*	27				*Cashley*	*Slatter*	*Williams B*	*Williams G*	*Parkin*	*McCaffery*	*Holloway*	*Williams D*	*Stephens*	*Randall**	*Bater*	*O'Connor*
								Ref: A Ward	City score with their first three shots on target. Stroud's blistering right-foot volley from the edge of the area puts City in front, while Riley twice shoots in to punish Rovers for switching to a sweeper system. An Archie Stephens 87th-min header forces Shaw to make his only save.											
17	A	PRESTON		8	L	2-3	1-1	Riley 9, Phillipson-Masters 54	Shaw	Llewellyn*	Halliday	Curle	Phill-Masters	Riley	Pritchard	Ritchie	Morgan	Walsh	Stroud	Hutchinson
		24/11	*3,912*	*18*	27			*Naughton 22, Houston 81, Jones M 88*	*Litchfield*	*Jones M*	*McAteer*	*Jones D*	*Welsh*	*Clark*	*McGee*	*Gray*	*Johnson*	*Naughton*	*Houston*	
								Ref: T Mills	North End snatch an improbable victory with two goals in the final nine minutes. Andy McAteer's centre appears to curve out before Graham Houston forces the ball over the line and then Mark Jones shoots in from an acute angle. In the dying seconds Morgan fires against the bar.											
18	H	LINCOLN		6	W	2-1	2-0	Walsh 9, Ritchie 21	**Hooper**	Llewellyn	Halliday	Phill-Masters	Curle	Riley	**Neville**	Ritchie*	Hutchinson	Walsh	Stroud	Crawford
		1/12	7,270	*18*	30			*Strodder 88*	*Naylor*	*Redfearn*	*McCarrick*	*Shipley*	*Walker*	*Thompson*	*McGinley*	*Turner P*	*Hobson*	*Jack*	*Mair**	*Strodder*
								Ref: N Butler	Cooper complains of poor vocal support following this lacklustre game. The similar styles of Neville and Riley produce a lack of balance in attack. Gordon Mair heads against the bar for Lincoln before Gary Strodder exploits Hooper's weakness on crosses to head in from a corner.											
19	A	BOURNEMOUTH		8	L	1-2	1-1	Riley 1	Shaw	Llewellyn	Halliday	Curle	Phill-Masters	Riley	Pritchard	Neville	Hutchinson	Walsh	Stroud	
		15/12	*4,987*	*9*	30			*Graham 10, Savage 81*	*Smeulders*	*Nightingale*	*Savage*	*Williams*	*Brown*	*Howlett*	*O'Driscoll*	*Russell*	*Graham*	*Thompson*	*Morrell*	
								Ref: C Downey	City outplay Bournemouth, but are unable to add to Riley's 48-second opener. He shoots from a rebound after John Smeulders blocks Neville's effort. Milton Graham guides in the Cherries' equaliser from 25 yards, six mins after a marginal offside decision had ruled out Riley's header.											
20	A	READING		10	L	0-1	0-0		Shaw	Llewellyn	Rogers	Curle	Phill-Masters	Riley	Pritchard	Neville	Hutchinson	Walsh	Stroud	
		22/12	*4,101*	*13*	30			*White 76*	*Westwood*	*Williams*	*Richardson*	*Beavon**	*Hicks*	*Wood*	*Duncan*	*Juryeff*	*Senior*	*White*	*Crown*	*Horrix*
								Ref: D Brazier	Fans cite the transfer of Trevor Morgan as a reason for City's recent slump, but the truth is that many players are out of form. City improve after a dismal first half, but Reading take the points. Mark White volleys into an empty net after Shaw is beaten in the air by Trevor Senior.											
21	H	PLYMOUTH		8	W	4-3	3-2	Hutchinson 19, 36, Walsh 26, 87p	**Waugh**	Llewellyn	Rogers	Phill-Masters	Curle	Pritchard	Hutchinson	Stroud	Walsh	Riley	Neville	
		26/12	10,402	*17*	33			*Tynan 24, 42, 53*	*Crudgington*	*Nisbet*	*Goodyear !*	*Harrison*	*Ham*	*Rogers*	*Hodges*	*Cooper*	*Summerfield*	*Staniforth*	*Tynan*	
								Ref: M Robinson	This action-packed match is settled by a dubious penalty as Pritchard makes the most of Gordon Staniforth's innocuous challenge. Argyle, for whom Clive Goodyear is sent off on 78 mins for a second bookable offence, fail to capitalise on Tommy Tynan's stunning hat-trick shot.											
22	H	BURNLEY		7	W	1-0	0-0	Pritchard 88	Waugh	Stevens	Llewellyn	Curle	Phill-Masters	Riley	Pritchard	Neville*	Hutchinson	Walsh	Stroud	Ritchie
		29/12	8,282	*20*	36				*Hansbury*	*Palmer*	*Hampton*	*Phelan*	*Kennedy*	*Hird*	*Grewcock*	*Malley*	*Lawrence**	*Biggins*	*Hutchison*	*Devine*
								Ref: K Miller	A different Burnley than normal as their defensive tactics produce a dreary game. Many disgruntled spectators had already headed for home when Hutchinson flicks on Walsh's corner and Pritchard is at the far post to head in a late winner as Neville still seeks his first City goal.											
23	A	HULL		8	L	1-2	1-1	Riley 6	Waugh	Llewellyn	Stevens	Curle	Phill-Masters	Riley	Pritchard	Neville	Hutchinson*	Walsh	Stroud	Crawford
		1/1	*9,753*	*2*	36			*Whitehurst 16, McEwan 58p*	*Norman*	*McNeil*	*Pearson*	*Swann*	*Skipper*	*McEwan*	*Flounders*	*McClaren*	*Whitehurst**	*Askew*	*Ring*	*Williams N*
								Ref: A Robinson	The referee's insistence of blowing his whistle for virtually every challenge explains the ridiculously high total of 59 free-kicks. The official incurs City's wrath in regard to Hull's penalty, ruling that Waugh holds down Andy Flounders. Riley shoots in on the turn to put City ahead.											

CANON LEAGUE DIVISION 3 — Manager: Terry Cooper — SEASON 1984-85

No	Date			Att	Pos	Pt	F-A	H-T	Scorers, Times, and Referees	1	2	3	4	5	6	7	8	9	10	11	12 sub used
24		H	CAMBRIDGE		7	W	3-0	1-0	Pritchard 31, Walsh 57, Riley 73	Shaw	Stevens*	Llewellyn	Curle	Phill-Masters	Riley	Pritchard	Neville	Hutchinson	Walsh	Stroud	Crawford
	26/1			6,547	*24*	39				*Branagan*	*Fallon*	*Bennett*	*Lockhart*	*Moyes*	*Osgood*	*Comfort*	*Sinton*	*McDonough*	*Pyle*	*Finney**	*Daniels*
									Ref: T Spencer	After an enforced winter break Bobby Hutchinson takes over as the City captain, following Tom Ritchie's move to Yeovil. Pritchard's volley puts City ahead in a dull first half, but after the break Walsh's vicious twelve-yarder and Riley's close-range header finish off poor opposition.											
25		H	WALSALL		10	L	1-2	0-1	Walsh 80	**Leigh**	Stevens	Llewellyn	Curle	Phill-Masters*	Riley	Pritchard !	Neville	Hutchinson	Walsh	Stroud	Crawford
	2/2			7,240	*13*	39			*Kelly 5, Shakespeare 67*	*Cherry*	*Caswell*	*Hawker*	*Shakespeare*	*Brazier*	*Hart*	*Handysides*	*Kelly*	*Elliott S*	*O'Kelly*	*Childs*	
									Ref: D Hedges	City are reduced to ten men for the last two minutes when Pritchard is sent off for a retaliatory kick on Phil Hawker. Loan keeper Leigh has a nightmare start when Kelly shoots in as he fails to hold a simple back-pass. Magnificent strike by Craig Shakespeare from a disputed free-kick.											
26		A	ORIENT		8	W	1-0	0-0	Walsh 77	Shaw	Stevens	Llewellyn	Curle	Phill-Masters	Riley	Pritchard	Neville	Hutchinson	Walsh	Stroud	
	9/2			*2,754*	*21*	42				*Wilmot*	*Hales**	*Castle*	*Cunningham*	*Foster*	*Silkman*	*Godfrey*	*Harvey*	*Jones*	*Donnellan*	*Corbett*	*Sussex*
									Ref: M James	Walsh strikes with a typical opportunist effort, shooting in from ten yards, to stifle Orient's comeback hopes. City adapt well on a snowbound pitch. Neville and Hutchinson have first-half efforts cleared off the line, but after the break Kevin Godfrey's shot strikes Llewellyn on the line.											
27		A	ROTHERHAM		8	L	1-2	1-1	Riley 31	Shaw	Stevens	Llewellyn	Curle	Phill-Masters	Riley	Hirst*	Neville	Hutchinson	Walsh	Stroud	**Hughes**
	16/2			*4,901*	*2*	42			*Simmons 38, Stevens 72 (og)*	*Mimms*	*Forrest*	*Mitchell*	*Trusson*	*Johnson*	*Crosby*	*Birch*	*Gooding*	*Richardson*	*Simmons*	*Kilmore**	*Dungworth*
									Ref: K Redfern	Stevens is horrified as the ball loops into the net when his foot deflects Ian Richardson's cross for Rotherham's winner. The Millers impress as both teams play attractive football, and they equalise Riley's whiplash shot on the turn, when Tony Simmons picks his spot with a low volley.											
28		A	BRENTFORD		7	W	2-1	2-1	Neville 9, 27	Shaw	Stevens	Newman	Curle	Hughes	Riley	Pritchard	Neville	Hutchinson	Walsh	Stroud	
	23/2			*4,526*	*17*	45			*Booker 26*	*Phillips*	*Fisher*	*Murray*	*Roberts P*	*Wignall*	*Hurlock*	*Kamara*	*Torrance**	*Booker*	*Salman*	*Cooke*	*Lynch*
									Ref: J Ashworth	At long last Steve Neville opens his Bristol City goal account. He is unmarked when heading in Walsh's free-kick and then doubles his tally on shooting in from six yards. After spurning a hat-trick opportunity, Neville should have been awarded a penalty when held by Steve Wignall.											
29		H	DERBY		6	W	3-0	2-0	Riley 14, Marshall 33, Crawford 82	Shaw	Stevens	Newman	Curle	Hughes	Riley*	**Marshall**	Neville	Hutchinson	Walsh	Stroud	Crawford
	26/2			8,727	*13*	48				*Steele*	*Blades*	*Buckley*	*Powell**	*Pratley*	*Streete*	*Micklewhite*	*Christie*	*Davison*	*Lewis*	*Robertson*	*Hooks*
									Ref: D Reeves	Sparkling City outplay big-spending Derby. Walsh, unfortunate when he hits his 64th-minute thunderous indirect free-kick into the roof of the net, supplies the crosses for headed goals by Marshall and Crawford. The non-stop running of Neville and Riley give Derby a busy night.											
30		H	MILLWALL		6	L	0-1	0-0		Shaw	Stevens	Newman	Curle	Hughes	Riley*	Pritchard	Neville	Hutchinson	Walsh	Stroud	Marshall
	2/3			10,875	*3*	48			*Lovell 88*	*Sansome*	*Stevens*	*Hinshelwood*	*Briley*	*Smith*	*Cusack*	*Lowndes*	*Fashanu*	*Chatterton*	*Lovell*	*Otulakowski*	
									Ref: T Holbrook	Alan Walsh and Keith Curle will have nightmares about this crushing blow to City's promotion hopes. Walsh's pen is saved by Paul Sansome after Neville is chopped down by Nicky Chatterton, while Curle is caught out of position when Steve Lovell lobs in Millwall's late winner.											
31		A	BOLTON		6	W	4-1	3-0	Neville 5, 43, 68, Riley 17	Shaw	Stevens	Newman	Curle	Hughes	Riley	Pritchard	Neville	Hutchinson	Walsh	Stroud	
	5/3			*3,774*	*15*	51			*Joyce 48*	*Farnworth*	*Borrows*	*Phillips*	*Joyce*	*Came*	*Deakin*	*Oghani*	*Chandler*	*Evans*	*Caldwell*	*Bell*	
									Ref: C Seel	Neville looks offside when put clear by Riley's header to shoot in the opening goal, but no doubt about his tap-in and a later header for the third League hat-trick of his career. In an all-action first half Walsh has a goal disallowed for pushing and Stroud clears a header off the line.											
32		H	BRADFORD C		5	W	2-0	1-0	Pritchard 22, Walsh 77	Shaw	Stevens	Newman	Curle	Hughes	Riley	Pritchard	Neville*	Hutchinson	Walsh	Stroud	Marshall
	9/3			9,222	*1*	54				*Harvey*	*Cherry**	*Withe*	*McCall*	*Jackson*	*Evans*	*Hendrie*	*Goodman*	*Campbell*	*Singleton*	*Ellis*	*Holmes*
									Ref: H King	Bradford City are undone by their attack-minded approach. Pritchard is unmarked to head home Neville's cross, and is then denied by the crossbar either side of half-time. Don Goodman's header hits the post for Bradford after the break, but Walsh fires in to tie up a vital win.											
33		A	GILLINGHAM		5	W	3-1	1-0	Hutchinson 36, 63, Neville 84	Shaw	Stevens	Newman	Curle	Hughes	Riley	Pritchard	Neville	Hutchinson	Walsh	Stroud	
	16/3			*6,369*	*3*	57			*Cascarino 68*	*Fry*	*Sage*	*Hinnigan**	*Oakes*	*Musker*	*Shaw*	*Cochrane*	*Shearer*	*Robinson*	*Mehmet*	*Cascarino*	*Weatherly*
									Ref: J Martin	Hutchinson's two headed goals cap an inspired performance by the City skipper. In heavy snow after the interval Gillingham prove vulnerable to City's fast breaks. Tony Cascarino volleys the Gills back into the match, but Neville breaks clear to settle the issue with his cool finish.											
34		H	YORK		4	W	1-0	1-0	Walsh 18	Shaw	Stevens	Newman	Curle	Hughes	Riley	Pritchard	Neville	Hutchinson	Walsh	Stroud	
	23/3			8,655	*11*	60				*Jones*	*Senior*	*Hay*	*Hood*	*MacPhail*	*Haslegrave**	*Pearce*	*Banton*	*Butler*	*Crosby*	*Nicholson*	*Richards*
									Ref: J Moules	York, without six first choice players, contain out-of-touch City with ease. The match is settled by a controversial goal as both Hutchinson, early in the build-up, and Walsh, at the finish look offside. Even the referee looks long and hard at the linesman before allowing Walsh's shot.											

35	H	DONCASTER		4	W	1-0	1-0	Riley 25	Shaw	Stevens	Newman	Curle	Hughes	Riley	Pritchard	Neville*	Hutchinson	Walsh	Stroud	**Johnson**
	30/3		7,965	*13*	63				*Peacock*	*Russell*	*Snodin G**	*Snodin I*	*Brown T*	*Kowalski*	*Butterworth*	*Deans*	*Douglas*	*Travis*	*Lister*	*Philliben*
								Ref: D Vickers	With the pitch covered by pools of water the referee calls a temporary halt to proceedings on 22 minutes as heavy rain continues to fall. Riley gives Dennis Peacock no chance with his firm downward header. Doncaster improve in the second half and give City some anxious moments.											
36	A	PLYMOUTH		5	L	0-1	0-0		Shaw	Stevens	Newman	Curle	Hughes	Riley*	Pritchard	Neville	Hutchinson	Walsh	Stroud	Johnson
	5/4		*9,959*	*15*	63			*Staniforth 79*	*Crudgington*	*Nisbet*	*Uzzell*	*Coughlin*	*McElhinney*	*Burrows*	*Rogers*	*Hodges*	*Tynan*	*Staniforth*	*Goodyear*	
								Ref: M Robinson	Police prevent 700 City fans seeing this contest as a late arriving train is ordered into a siding after early skirmishes on the terraces. Gordon Staniforth settles the game by netting a rebound. A fractional offside decision rules out Newman's tap-in, and Curle's volley hits the crossbar.											
37	H	HULL		4	W	2-0	0-0	Johnson 46, Pritchard 79	Shaw	Stevens	Newman	Curle	Hughes	Riley	Pritchard	Johnson	Hutchinson	Walsh	Stroud	
	8/4		11,964	*2*	66				*Norman*	*Swann*	*Pearson*	*Williams N**	*Skipper*	*McEwan*	*Flounders*	*McClaren*	*Whitehurst*	*Askew*	*Jobson*	*Saville*
								Ref: T Bune	A firm downward header from Pritchard's cross allows Steve Johnson, City's £20,000 signing from Wigan, to mark his first full appearance with a goal. City's dazzling play deserves more than just another score, when Pritchard nips in front of a defender to shoot in Johnson's header.											
38	A	BRISTOL ROV		5	L	0-1	0-0		Shaw	Stevens	Newman	Curle	Hughes	Riley*	Pritchard	Johnson	Hutchinson	Walsh	Stroud	Neville
	13/4		***12,957***	*6*	66			*Holloway 67*	*Green*	*Slatter*	*Williams B*	*Bater*	*Parkin*	*Jones*	*Holloway*	*Raynor*	*Randall*	*Bannon*	*O'Connor*	
								Ref: M Dimblebee	City's ridiculous decision to play against the gale-force wind after winning the toss costs them this game. The Rovers, undeterred by the conditions after the break, punish City's offside tactics. Mark O'Connor breaks clear from a free-kick and crosses for Ian Holloway to shoot in.											
39	H	PRESTON		5	W	**4-0**	2-0	Riley 13, 87, Walsh 32p, 70	Shaw	Stevens	Newman	Curle	Hughes	Riley	Pritchard*	Johnson	Hutchinson	Walsh	Stroud	Neville
	20/4		6,937	*20*	69				*Campbell*	*Farrelly*	*Jones M*	*Gibson*	*Atkins*	*Clark*	*Kelly*	*Houghton**	*Twentyman*	*Brazil*	*Houston*	*Johnson*
								Ref: D Letts	A controversial penalty gives City the lead after Bob Atkins is adjudged to have climbed on Pritchard's back. Man of the match Walsh fails to heed referee's signal when he blasts in an indirect free-kick, but makes amends after the interval when he breaks from halfway to shoot home.											
40	A	WIGAN		5	D	2-2	1-0	Johnson 38, Walsh 81p	Shaw	Llewellyn	Newman	Curle !	Hughes	Neville	Pritchard	Johnson	Hutchinson	Walsh	Hirst	
	23/4		*2,423*	*17*	70			*Bennett 75, Walsh 80*	*Tunks*	*Butler*	*Knowles*	*Kelly*	*Walsh*	*Methven*	*Lowe*	*Aspinall W'rren*	*Newell*	*Jewell**	*Langley*	*Bennett*
								Ref: J Key	After Johnson's magnificent ten-yard volley, City concede the initiative by committing unnecessary petty fouls. Curle is sent off for butting Kevin Langley just prior to Steve Walsh forcing in a rebound for Wigan. Colin Methven handles a harmless through-ball for the pen equaliser.											
41	A	LINCOLN		4	D	1-1	0-1	Johnson 60	Shaw	Llewellyn	Newman	Curle	Hughes	Riley	Neville	Johnson	Hutchinson	Walsh	Stroud	
	27/4		***1,908***	*19*	71			*Thompson 31*	*Naylor*	*McCarrick*	*Collins*	*Redfearn*	*North M*	*Thompson*	*McGinlay*	*Shipley*	*Hobson*	*Thomas*	*Mair*	
								Ref: A Selville	With Millwall only drawing at Burnley, City miss a great chance of making up ground in the promotion race. Steve Thompson's lobbed header puts the Imps in front and it takes Johnson's curling and dipping free-kick to save City from an embarrassing defeat against a poor opposition.											
42	H	NEWPORT		4	W	2-1	1-1	Riley 41, Newman 75	Shaw	Llewellyn	Newman	Curle	Hughes	Riley	Neville	Johnson*	Hutchinson	Walsh	Stroud	Hirst
	30/4		**5,952**	*17*	74			*Chamberlain 45*	*Kendall*	*Jones*	*Relish**	*Pulis*	*Boyle*	*Matthewson*	*Kent*	*Emmanuel*	*Cooper*	*Kellow*	*Chamberlain*	*Giles*
								Ref: G Napthine	City gain revenge for last Thursday's Freight Rover Cup defeat. Newman's thunderous 30-yarder settles this dull contest. Newport, who fail to force a single corner, score with their only shot on target. Neville Chamberlain shoots after Steve Cooper had headed the ball over the keeper.											
43	H	BOURNEMOUTH		4	W	2-0	1-0	Marshall 45, Riley 61	Shaw	Llewellyn	Newman	Curle	Hughes	Riley	Neville	Marshall	Hutchinson	Walsh	Stroud*	Hirst
	4/5		7,083	*11*	77				*Smeulders*	*Nightingale*	*Savage*	*Beck*	*Lewis*	*Schiavi*	*Shaw*	*Russell*	*Rafferty*	*Thompson*	*Morrell*	
								Ref: P Vanes	The Cherries' keeper John Smeulders has a nightmare. He is deceived by Marshall's 25-yarder which bounces up to strike him on the arm before rolling into the net, and later carries the ball outside the area to concede a free-kick, which he punches straight onto Riley's head.											
44	A	BURNLEY		4	W	1-0	0-0	Neville 78	Shaw	Llewellyn	Newman	Curle	Hughes	Riley	Hirst	Neville	Hutchinson	Marshall*	Stroud	Halliday
	3/5		*4,570*	*23*	80				*Hansbury*	*Scott*	*Hampton*	*Phelan*	*Overson*	*Hird*	*Grewcock**	*Rhodes*	*Taylor*	*Biggins*	*Hutchison*	*Miller*
								Ref: P Willis	Neville hammers in a scorching half-volley to keep alive City's faint promotion hopes. Burnley are restricted to long-range shots in the first half, but manage to exert more pressure on City's defence after the break. On going ahead City bring on sub Halliday to boost their midfield.											
45	H	READING		4	L	2-3	2-1	Neville 7, Riley 33	Shaw	Llewellyn	Newman	Halliday	Hughes	Riley	Pritchard	Neville	Hutchinson	Walsh*	Stroud	Hirst
	1/5		7,038	*9*	80			*Newman 26 (og), Horrix 60, Gilkes 72*	*Westwood*	*Williams*	*Ritchardson*	*Beavon*	*Hicks*	*Wood*	*Burvill*	*White*	*Peters*	*Horrix*	*Christie**	*Gilkes*
								Ref: L Shapter	City's back four are cruelly exposed by a slick Reading side. Neville obtains his first home goal when jabbing in Riley's perfect pass. Mike Gilkes rounds Shaw to slot in Reading's winner, but by then news of the Bradford City disaster at Valley Parade was diverting public attention.											
46	A	SWANSEA		5	D	0-0	0-0		Shaw	Llewellyn	Newman	Halliday	Hughes	Riley	Pritchard*	Neville	Hutchinson	Walsh	Hirst	Stroud
	17/5		*11,187*	*20*	81				*Rimmer*	*Lewis*	*Sullivan*	*Price*	*Stevenson*	*Marustik*	*Turner*	*Parlane*	*Waddle*	*McHale*	*Pascoe*	
Average	Home 8,507		Away 5,753					Ref: J Bray	City retain sole possession of their unwanted record as the Swans gain the point necessary to save them from sliding from the First to the Fourth in consecutive seasons. A magnificent, exciting game, in which keepers Jimmy Rimmer and Shaw play at the top of their form.											

Milk Cup						F-A	H-T	Scorers, Times, and Referees	1	2	3	4	5	6	7	8	9	10	11	12 sub used
1:1	H	NEWPORT			W	2-1	1-1	Crawford 34, Riley 73	Shaw	Stevens	Newman	Rogers	Phill-Masters	Hirst	Pritchard	Riley	Morgan	Walsh	Crawford	
	28/8		5,644					*Chamberlain 13*	*Jones G*	*Jones L*	*Matthewson*	*Reid*	*Boyle*	*Saxby*	*Lilygreen**	*Chamberlain*	*Carter*	*Kent*	*Lewis*	*Green*
								Ref: H Taylor	An entertaining match to which Newport fully contribute with their slick passing. County take the lead with a controversial goal as Neville Chamberlain's shot cannons off the underside of the crossbar, but City draw level with Crawford's glancing header from Pritchard's cross.											
1:2	A	NEWPORT		6	W	3-0	2-0	Morgan 17, 37, Riley 69	Shaw	Stevens	Newman	Rogers	Halliday	Hirst	Pritchard	Riley	Morgan*	Walsh	Crawford	Curle
	4/9		*3,276*	*17*					*Kendall*	*Jones L*	*Matthewson*	*Reid**	*Boyle*	*Saxby*	*Carter*	*Pulis*	*Kent*	*Green*	*Lewis*	*Lilygreen*
								Ref: J Martin (City won 5-1 on aggregate)	Scintillating City storm into the second round with a blend of aggression and skill that could upset any club in the competition. Morgan is razor sharp as he lobs in the first goal and then registers again with a thunderous 25-yarder. Riley rounds Mark Kendall to tie up a convincing win.											
2:1	H	WEST HAM		7	D	2-2	2-2	Morgan 20, Walsh 33	Shaw	Stevens	Newman	Halliday	Phill-Masters	Hirst	Pritchard	Riley	Morgan	Walsh	Crawford	
	25/9		15,609	*1:7*				*Cottee 28, Walford 37*	*McAlister*	*Stewart*	*Walford*	*Allen*	*Martin*	*Gale*	*Bonds*	*Goddard*	*Cottee*	*Dickens*	*Pike*	
								Ref: V Callow	City are unlucky not to be taking a lead into the return leg as the Hammers are outplayed after the break. Surprisingly all the goals come before the interval. Steve Walford notches West Ham's second equaliser with a 30-yarder after Morgan opens the scoring with a real pile-driver.											
2:2	A	WEST HAM		9	L	1-6	1-1	Walsh 34p *[Whitton 68, Walford 78]*	Shaw	Stevens	Newman	Masters	Curle	Riley	Pritchard	Ritchie*	Morgan	Walsh	Crawford	Smith
	9/10		*11,376*	*1:5*				*Cottee 24, 75, Goddard 48, 56,*	*McAlister*	*Stewart*	*Walford*	*Allen*	*Martin*	*Gale*	*Whitton*	*Goddard*	*Cottee*	*Bonds**	*Pike*	*Barnes*
								Ref: K Baker (City lost 3-8 on aggregate)	City are hit by West Ham's remarkable resurgence after confidently taking the game forward before the break. Walsh's penalty equaliser, after Ray Stewart palms the ball over the bar, rewards City's thoughtful play, but Paul Goddard's brilliant 25-yarder changes everything.											

FA Cup																				
1	A	FISHER ATH		6	W	1-0	1-0	Riley 9	Shaw	Llewellyn	Halliday	Curle	Phill-Masters	Riley	Pritchard	Ritchie	Morgan	Walsh	Stroud	
	17/11		*2,000*	*SLP:8*					*Bowtell*	*Davis*	*Collins**	*Sharp*	*Shinners*	*Dark*	*Lewington*	*Murrock*	*Dennehy*	*Sansom*	*Bayram*	*Chambers*
								Ref: M Bodenham	It looks easy as Riley has time and space to shoot an early goal, but Fisher come back strongly. Despite Morgan heading against the bar, Fisher refuse to be overawed. Dave Sansom's 36th-minute low drive forces Shaw to make a good save and by the end City are glad to have survived.											
2	H	BRISTOL ROV		6	L	1-3	1-3	Halliday 4	Hooper	Llewellyn	Halliday	Curle	Phill-Masters	Riley	Pritchard	Hirst*	Hutchinson	Walsh	Stroud	Ritchie
	8/12		19,367	*7*				*O'Connor 8, Randall 18, 42*	*Cashley*	*Slatter**	*Williams B*	*Bater*	*Parkin*	*McCaffery*	*Holloway*	*Williams D*	*Stephens*	*Randall*	*O'Connor*	*Williams G*
								Ref: A Robinson	City off to a fine start as Halliday heads in from Walsh's exquisitely chipped free-kick, but Mark O'Connor gets his head to Ian Holloway's cross to loop an equaliser over the flat-footed Hooper. Rovers coast to an easy win after Paul Randall twice shows his pace to slide the ball in.											

		Home						Away				
	P	W	D	L	F	A	W	D	L	F	A	Pts
1 Bradford City	46	15	6	2	44	23	13	4	6	33	22	94
2 Millwall	46	18	5	0	44	12	8	7	8	29	30	90
3 Hull	46	16	4	3	46	20	9	8	6	32	29	87
4 Gillingham	46	15	5	3	54	29	10	3	10	26	33	83
5 BRISTOL CITY	46	17	2	4	46	19	7	7	9	28	28	81
6 Bristol Rov	46	15	6	2	37	13	6	6	11	29	35	75
7 Derby	46	14	7	2	40	20	5	6	12	25	34	70
8 York	46	13	5	5	42	22	7	4	12	28	35	69
9 Reading	46	8	7	8	31	29	11	5	7	37	33	69
10 Bournemouth	46	16	3	4	42	16	3	8	12	15	30	68
11 Walsall	46	9	7	7	33	22	9	6	8	25	30	67
12 Rotherham	46	11	6	6	36	24	7	5	11	19	31	65
13 Brentford	46	13	5	5	42	27	3	9	11	20	37	62
14 Doncaster	46	11	5	7	42	33	6	3	14	30	41	59
15 Plymouth	46	11	7	5	33	23	4	7	12	29	42	59
16 Wigan	46	12	6	5	36	22	3	8	12	24	42	59
17 Bolton	46	12	5	6	38	22	4	1	18	31	53	54
18 Newport	46	9	6	8	30	30	4	7	12	25	37	52
19 Lincoln	46	8	11	4	32	20	3	7	13	18	31	51
20 Swansea	46	7	5	11	31	39	5	6	12	22	41	47
21 Burnley	46	6	8	9	30	24	5	5	13	30	49	46
22 Orient	46	7	7	9	30	36	4	6	13	21	40	46
23 Preston	46	9	5	9	33	41	4	2	17	18	59	46
24 Cambridge	46	2	3	18	17	48	2	6	15	20	47	21
	1104	274	136	142	889	614	142	136	274	614	889	1520

Odds & ends

Double wins: (6) Cambridge, Orient, York, Gillingham, Bolton, Burnley.
Double losses: (3) Walsall, Rotherham, Reading.

Won from behind: (2) Cambridge (a), Bolton (h).
Lost from in front: (5) Preston (a), Bournemouth (a), Hull (a), Rotherham (a), Reading (h).

High spots: The skilful play of Alan Walsh.
3-0 win over Bristol Rov at Ashton Gate on 10 November.
Beating Hull 2-0 at Ashton Gate on 8 April.

Low spots: Missing out on promotion.
Succumbing to an Ian Holloway strike at Eastville on 13 April.
Losing to Bristol Rov in both the FA and the Gloucestershire Cup.

Player of the year: Alan Walsh.
Ever-presents: (0).
Hat-tricks: (1) Steve Neville.
Leading scorer: Alan Walsh (22).

	Appearances						Goals			
	Lge	*Sub*	LC	*Sub*	FAC	*Sub*	Lge	LC	FAC	Tot
Cooper, Terry		*10*								
Crawford, Alan	**10**	*6*	4				**4**	1		**5**
Curle, Keith	**37**	*3*	1	*1*	2					
Halliday, Bruce	**11**	*1*	2		2				1	**1**
Hirst, Martyn	**13**	*3*	3		1					
Hooper, Mike	**1**				1					
Hughes, Mark	**19**	*1*								
Hutchinson, Bobby	**29**	*2*			1		**4**			**4**
Johnson, Steve	**6**	*2*					**3**			**3**
Leigh, Ian	**1**									
Llewellyn, Andy	**22**				2					
Marshall, Gary	**3**	*2*					**2**			**2**
Morgan, Trevor	**17**		4		1		**3**	3		**6**
Neville, Steve	**26**	*2*					**8**			**8**
Newman, Rob	**34**		4				**3**			**3**
Phill-Masters, Forbes	**25**		3		2		**1**			**1**
Pritchard, Howard	**39**		4		2		**6**			**6**
Riley, Glynn	**44**		4		2		**18**	2	1	**21**
Ritchie, Tom	**10**	*1*	1		1	*1*	**1**			**1**
Rogers, Lee	**6**		2							
Shaw, John	**41**		4		1					
Smith Gary				*1*						
Stevens, Paul	**30**		4							
Stroud, Kenny	**34**	*1*			2		**1**			**1**
Walsh, Alan	**45**		4		2		**20**	2		**22**
Waugh, Keith	**3**									
26 players used	**506**	*34*	**44**	*2*	**22**	*1*	**74**	**8**	**2**	**84**

No	Date		Att	Pos	Pt	F-A	H-T	Scorers, Times, and Referees	1	2	3	4	5	6	7	8	9	10	11	12 sub used
1	H	WALSALL			L	2-3	1-1	Walsh 7p, Neville 87	Waugh	Llewellyn	**Williams B !**	Curle	Hughes	Riley	Marshall*	Hutchinson	**Emmanuel**	Neville	Walsh	Johnson
	17/8		7,196		0			*Cross 27, Daley 50, O'Kelly 88p*	*Cherry*	*Hart*	*Mower*	*Shakespeare*	*Brazier*	*Hawker*	*Handysides*	*Cross*	*O'Kelly*	*Elliott*	*Daley**	*Childs*
								Ref: J Deakin	The loss of Williams on half-time for his second bookable offence, as well as the 87th-minute departure of the injured Johnson adds to City's woes as they are outplayed by the slick Saddlers. Emmanuel palms away Steve Elliott's header to present Walsall with their spot-kick winner.											
2	A	BOURNEMOUTH			L	**0-5**	0-4		Waugh	Llewellyn	Newman	Curle	Hughes	Hutchinson	Emmanuel	Williams B	Johnson	Walsh	Neville	
	24/8		*4,969*		0			*Clarke 1, 9, 89, Russell 7, 40*	*Smeulders*	*Heffernan*	*Sulley*	*Newson*	*Brown*	*Nightingale*	*O'Driscoll*	*Russell*	*Clarke*	*Thompson*	*Morrell*	
								Ref: A Ward	City's much maligned defence only holds out for 45 seconds before Colin Clarke fires in from Colin Russell's pass. Three down in just nine minutes, City make a spirited recovery but a long ball down the right exposes Hughes, and Clarke runs through to complete his hat-trick.											
3	H	GILLINGHAM		24	L	1-2	1-0	Hutchinson 40	Waugh	Llewellyn	Newman	Curle	Rogers	Hutchinson	Pritchard	Williams B	Johnson	Walsh	Neville*	Riley
	26/8		5,883	*14*	0			*Cascarino 48, 87*	*Hillyard*	*Sage*	*Elsey*	*Oakes*	*Weatherly**	*Shaw*	*Cochrane*	*Shearer*	*Collins*	*Musker*	*Cascarino*	*Byrne*
								Ref: M Robinson	A vast improvement, but Llewellyn's mis-hit back-pass puts Tony Cascarino clean through to shoot in Gillingham's late winner. City dominate matters, but only Hutchinson's fine drive manages to evade Ron Hillyard, despite having ten on-target efforts, compared to Gillingham's three.											
4	A	ROTHERHAM		24	L	0-2	0-1		Waugh	Llewellyn	Newman	Curle	Rogers	Hirst*	Pritchard	Hutchinson	Johnson	Walsh	Neville	Marshall
	31/8		*3,255*	*10*	0			*Forrest 12, Tynan 57p*	*O'Hanlon*	*Forrest*	*Dungworth*	*Trusson**	*Smith*	*Pickering*	*Birch*	*Martin*	*Tynan*	*Simmons*	*Emerson*	*Gooding*
								Ref: R Nixon	City's slump continues at Millmoor, with their worst display yet. After Steve Forrest bursts unchallenged into the penalty area to fire in, only Waugh's bravery and poor Rotherham finishing keeps the score down, until Hirst's trip on Alan Birch produces Tommy Tynan's penalty.											
5	H	WIGAN		23	W	1-0	0-0	Pritchard 68	Waugh	Llewellyn	Newman	Curle	Rogers	Williams B	Pritchard	Hutchinson	Johnson	Neville*	Walsh	Riley
	7/9		5,673	*6*	3				*Stewart*	*Butler*	*Knowles*	*Jewell**	*Beesley*	*Methven*	*Lowe*	*Aspinall*	*Newell*	*Langley*	*Griffiths*	*Cook*
								Ref: M Reed	City's tremendous attitude and commitment brings a well-deserved victory over high-flying Wigan. After gaining no reward for a superb opening, Pritchard grabs the spoils with a prodigious leap to meet Walsh's looping cross and send a well-directed header past Billy Stewart.											
6	A	CARDIFF		20	W	3-1	1-0	Walsh 44, 77, Pritchard 85	Waugh	Llewellyn	Newman	Curle	Rogers	Williams B	Pritchard	Hutchinson	Johnson*	Walsh	Neville	Riley
	14/9		*4,412*	*17*	6			*Withey 74*	*Rees*	*McLoughlin*	*Carver*	*Gibbins*	*Ford*	*Mullen*	*Gummer*	*Farrington*	*Vaughan*	*Withey*	*Giles**	*Micallef*
								Ref: V Callow	Pritchard stakes his claim for further Welsh international honours with a sparkling display at Ninian Park. Pritchard's flick to Llewellyn sets up Walsh to shoot in at the far-post, then Waugh is the hero as he saves Jimmy Mullen's poorly-struck spot-kick after Curle's 68th-min handball.											
7	H	DERBY		20	D	1-1	1-0	Newman 36	Waugh	Llewellyn	Newman	Curle	Rogers	Williams B	Pritchard	Hutchinson	Riley	Walsh	Neville*	Marshall
	17/9		7,750	*12*	7			*Davison 57*	*Wallington*	*Street*	*Buckley*	*Williams*	*Hindmarch*	*MacLaren*	*Micklewhite*	*Christie*	*Davison*	*McClaren*	*Chandler*	
								Ref: D Hedges	City lose their way after the interval, only putting in two shots as Derby up the pace. Newman, City's hero before the break with a well-placed header, is the villain for County's equaliser as he allows Gary Micklewhite to float over a perfect far-post cross for Bobby Davison to nod in.											
8	A	YORK		19	D	1-1	0-1	Pritchard 74	Waugh	Llewellyn	Newman	Curle	Rogers	Williams B	Pritchard	Hutchinson	Riley*	Walsh	Neville	Marshall
	21/9		*3,904*	*11*	8			*MacPhail 45p*	*Astbury*	*Senior**	*Hay*	*McAughtrie*	*MacPhail*	*Haslegrave*	*Ford*	*Mills*	*Walwyn*	*Houchen*	*Canham*	*Gabbiadini*
								Ref: J Hough	Pritchard's volley over the bar is City's only first-half effort, as Waugh's push on Keith Houchen allows John MacPhail to put York ahead from the spot. City's spirited revival after the break is rewarded by Pritchard who is able to pick his spot with a header from Marshall's cross.											
9	H	BLACKPOOL		16	W	2-1	1-1	Neville 24, Pritchard 73	Waugh	Llewellyn	Newman	Curle	Rogers	Williams B	Pritchard	Hutchinson	Riley*	Walsh	Neville	Johnson
	28/9		6,570	*12*	11			*O'Keefe 16*	*O'Rouke*	*Moore*	*Walsh**	*Conroy*	*Law*	*Greenall*	*Davies*	*Deary*	*Stewart*	*O'Keefe*	*Dyer*	*Stonehouse*
								Ref: A Robinson	Blackpool are deservedly caught out by their well-drilled offside trap as the referee decides to ignore a belated flag for Walsh to cross for Pritchard to head in City's winner. Pool's over-physical approach wins few friends, but Eamon O'Keefe's 25-yard volley is much appreciated.											
10	A	NEWPORT		18	D	1-1	0-0	Neville 72	Waugh	Llewellyn	Newman	Curle	Rogers	Williams B	Pritchard	Hutchinson	Johnson*	Walsh	Neville	Riley
	1/10		*3,776*	*16*	12			*Boyle 89*	*Kendall*	*Pulis*	*Jones P*	*Reck*	*Peacock*	*Boyle*	*Mardenboro'**	*Lewis*	*James*	*Staniforth*	*Gill*	*Tyler*
								Ref: H Taylor	Neville gathers Walsh's 70-yard pass and outstrips two defenders before slotting the ball past the advancing Mark Kendall. A superb goal to put City ahead, but the advantage is wasted as failure of their offside trap leaves Terry Boyle all alone to head in Peter Jones' long free-kick.											
11	H	CHESTERFIELD		18	D	0-0	0-0		Waugh	Llewellyn*	Newman	Curle	Rogers	Williams B	Pritchard	Hutchinson	Johnson	Walsh	Neville	Riley
	5/10		6,416	*13*	13				*Marples*	*Scrimgeour*	*O'Neill*	*Batty*	*Baines*	*Hunter*	*Reid*	*Moss*	*Walker*	*Henderson*	*Williamson*	
								Ref: M James	Unimaginative City offer precious little against unyieldingly defensive opposition. Derbyshire wicket-keeper Chris Marples saves the few efforts that come his way, while Shaun O'Neill almost snatches a shock win for the Spireites with a cross that Williams clears off the line.											

No	Date	Venue	Opponent	Att	Pos	Res	Pt	F-A	H-T	Scorers, Times, and Referees	1	2	3	4	5	6	7	8	9	10	11	12
12		A	NOTTS CO		19	L		0-4	0-2		Waugh	Rogers	Newman	Curle	**Moyes**	Williams B !	Pritchard	Hutchinson	Johnson*	Walsh	Neville	Riley
	12/10			*4,332*	*5*		13			*Hunt 22, 29, 60, McParland 70*	*Leonard*	*Richards*	*Clarke*	*Benjamin*	*Sims*	*Yates*	*McParland**	*Goodwin*	*Young*	*Waitt*	*Hunt*	*Daws*
										Ref: C Trussell	County's 6ft 5in tall striker Mick Waitt gives City's defence, with new centre-half David Moyes, a torrid time. Three headed flicks, two from near-post corners, lay on three of County's goals as poor City, with Williams sent off in the 78th min for kicking David Hunt, slump to defeat.											
13		H	DARLINGTON		17	W		1-0	0-0	Walsh 64	Waugh	Rogers	Newman	Curle	Moyes	Williams B	Pritchard	Hutchinson	Riley	Walsh	Neville	
	19/10			5,873	*24*		16				*Barber*	*Evans*	*Morgan*	*Tupling*	*Green*	*Pallister*	*Roberts*	*Poskett**	*Aldred*	*MacDonald*	*McLean*	*Airey*
										Ref: M Cotton	Walsh answers his critics with a moment of match-winning brilliance as his 25-yard curling free-kick hits the back of the net. In a game that produces little in the way of ill feeling, despite the abundant goalmouth action, referee Malcolm Cotton astonishingly books seven players.											
14		A	BURY		18	L		3-6	0-1	Walsh 47p, Neville 58, Riley 60	Waugh	Rogers	Newman*	Curle	Moyes	Williams B	Pritchard	Hutchinson	Riley	Walsh	Neville	Johnson
	22/10			*2,460*	*12*		16			*Dobson 37p, 81, Beckford 46, White 59,*	*Butcher*	*Dixon*	*Pashley*	*Bramhall*	*Valentine*	*Dobson*	*White*	*Madden*	*Beckford*	*Jakub*	*Young*	
										Ref: F Roberts *[Young 72, Madden 89]*	Cooper blames his side for throwing the match away by not closing the game up after Riley had headed City level at 3-3. Bury, who lost their previous game 0-5 at Blackpool, manage 16 shots on target to City's six, but in the first half it was the Robins who created the better chances.											
15		H	WOLVES		16	W		3-0	2-0	Riley 2, Hutchinson 40, Walsh 85p	Waugh	Llewellyn	Newman	Curle	Rogers	Riley	Pritchard	Hutchinson	**Tong**	Walsh	Neville	
	26/10			7,138	*23*		19				*Barrett*	*Herbert*	*Barnes*	*Streete*	*Clarke*	*Stoutt*	*Purdie*	*Ryan*	*Ainscow*	*King*	*Wassell**	*Chapman*
										Ref: A Buksh	How the mighty have fallen as Wolves produce what must rank as one of their poorest-ever displays at Ashton Gate. Walsh's penalty, after Neville had been floored by Nicky Clarke, completes the scoring, but City have only themselves to blame in not managing more than three.											
16		A	DONCASTER		14	D		1-1	1-0	Riley 7	Waugh	Llewellyn	Newman	Curle	Rogers	Riley	Pritchard	Hutchinson	Tong	Walsh	Neville	
	2/11			*2,871*	*11*		20			*Brown 59*	*Rhodes*	*Deans**	*Rushbury*	*Humphries*	*Brown T*	*Cusack*	*Buckley*	*Douglas*	*Butterworth*	*Harle*	*Dobbin*	*Travis*
										Ref: A Robinson	City, who demonstrate that they can play with flair and creativity away from home without sacrificing defence, are let down by their strikers. Riley heads in Neville's cross, but golden opportunities are spurned before Tony Brown nods the ball over the line for Doncaster's equaliser.											
17		A	LINCOLN		15	D		1-1	1-1	Neville 37	Waugh	Llewellyn	Newman	Curle	Rogers	Riley	Pritchard	Hutchinson	Tong	Walsh	Neville	
	5/11			***1,379***	*20*		21			*Redfearn 28*	*Judge*	*McNeil*	*McCarrick*	*Redfearn*	*Strodder*	*Measham**	*Toman*	*Turner*	*Latchford*	*McGinley*	*Ward*	*Richards G*
										Ref: L Dilkes	City's offside trap again proves costly as their cavalry charge at a Lincoln free-kick leads to Curle's clearance rebounding into the net off of Neil Redfearn. Neville rescues City's point as he slams Pritchard's low cross into an empty net, after Alan Judge is drawn out of position.											
18		H	BRENTFORD		16	D		0-0	0-0		Waugh	Llewellyn	Newman	Curle	Rogers	Riley	Pritchard	Hutchinson	Tong	Walsh*	Neville	Johnson
	9/11			6,598	*10*		22				*Phillips*	*Salman*	*Murray*	*Evans*	*Wignall*	*Hurlock*	*Lynch*	*Cooke !*	*Booker*	*Butler*	*Torrance*	
										Ref: M Scott	Curle denies uncompromising Brentford's quest for victory by blocking George Torrance's goal-bound shot in the dying moments. Lucky not to concede a 57th-minute spot-kick as Robbie Cooke goes tumbling, Curle is the victim a minute later as the No 8 is sent off for lashing out.											
19		A	SWANSEA		14	W		3-1	2-1	Hutchinson 38, 40, Walsh 50	Waugh	Llewellyn	Newman	Curle	Rogers	Riley	Pritchard	Hutchinson	Tong	Walsh	Neville	
	23/11			*4,414*	*23*		25			*Harrison 20*	*Rimmer*	*Hough*	*Sullivan*	*Gibbins*	*Harrison*	*Emmanuel*	*McHale*	*Randell*	*McCarthy*	*Waddle*	*Budd**	*Melville*
										Ref: A Seville	After Chris Harrison gives crisis club Swansea the lead with a looping header, City are fortunate to be ahead at the break. Hutchinson adds to his close-in effort by turning sharply and blasting past Jimmy Rimmer and the near post from an unbelievably acute angle.											
20		H	BOLTON		12	W		2-0	1-0	Riley 9, Neville 85	Waugh	Llewellyn	Newman	Curle	Rogers	Riley	Pritchard	Hutchinson	Tong	Walsh	Neville	
	30/11			6,251	*18*		28				*Farnworth*	*Joyce*	*Scott*	*Rudge*	*Came*	*Sutton*	*Fitzpatrick*	*Oghani !*	*Caldwell*	*Hartford*	*Bell**	*Walker*
										Ref: N Butler/D Delaney	David Delaney, who replaces the injured Noel Butler in the 23rd minute, sends off George Oghani eight minutes later for kicking Waugh. City, for whom Walsh and Pritchard are denied by the woodwork, add to Riley's early 18-yarder when Neville taps in Walsh's powerful low cross.											
21		A	READING		13	L		0-1	0-0		Waugh	Llewellyn	Newman	Curle	Rogers	Riley !	Moyes	Hutchinson	Tong	Walsh	Neville	
	14/12			*5,785*	*1*		28			*Gilkes 84*	*Westwood*	*Peters*	*Bailie*	*Beavon*	*Hicks*	*Wood*	*Rogers*	*Horrix*	*Senior*	*Bremner*	*Gilkes*	
										Ref: I Hemley	'Is this game for men or not?' opines boss Terry Cooper as City have six players booked and Riley sent off in the 75th minute after a fracas with Dean Horrix. City cope well against Reading's pressurising style, but eventually succumb as Michael Gilkes hits home Bremner's cross.											
22		H	BOURNEMOUTH		13	L		1-3	1-0	Hutchinson 11	Waugh	Llewellyn	Newman	Curle	Rogers	Riley	Pritchard	Hutchinson	Tong	Walsh	Neville	
	21/12			5,621	*16*		28			*Heffernan 65, Howlett 73, Newson 78*	*Leigh*	*Heffernan*	*Sulley*	*Newson*	*Brown*	*Beck*	*O'Driscoll*	*Howlett*	*Clarke*	*Thompson*	*Morrell*	
										Ref: R Lewis	Everyone dressed as Father Christmas is allowed in free, but most of the goodwill on the terraces disappears in the second half as Walsh fires a penalty against the post. Gary Howlett delivers the killer-blow with a superbly struck 30-yard shot which sails on the wind into the top corner.											
23		H	PLYMOUTH		12	W		2-0	2-0	Walsh 7p, Neville 37	Waugh	Llewellyn	Newman	Curle	Moyes	Riley	Pritchard	Hutchinson	Tong	Walsh	Neville	
	26/12			8,296	*5*		31				*Crudgington*	*Nisbet*	*Cooper L*	*Goodyear*	*McElhinney*	*Summerfield*	*Hodges**	*Coughlin*	*Cooper S*	*Clayton*	*Nelson*	*Rawbotham*
										Ref: D Vickers/J Carter	A Boxing Day feast of attacking football as City make a mockery of their poor League position. Kevin Summerfield's rash challenge on Pritchard allows Walsh to score from the spot, then Neville heads in to double the advantage, before the injured ref is replaced at half-time.											

No	Date		Att	Pos	Pt	F-A	H-T	Scorers, Times, and Referees	1	2	3	4	5	6	7	8	9	10	11	12 sub used
24	A	GILLINGHAM		12	D	1-1	0-0	Newman 77	Waugh	Newman	Williams B	Curle	Moyes	Rogers	Pritchard	Hutchinson	Tong	Walsh	Neville	
	28/12		*4,672*	*8*	32			*Cascarino 88*	*Hillyard*	*Sage*	*Elsey*	*Oakes*	*Weatherly*	*Hinnigan*	*Byrne*	*Shrearer*	*Robinson**	*Mehmet*	*Cascarino*	*Musker*
								Ref: D Reeves	'We're like a Christmas Club' says Cooper as City let victory slip in the dying minutes. Moyes deflects Tony Cascarino's low shot into the net to level Newman's headed opener, after Waugh's brilliant 25th-minute penalty save from Dave Mehmet had kept City level at the break.											
25	H	DONCASTER		12	W	4-1	1-0	Pritchard 6, Walsh 50p, 70, Neville 72	Waugh	Newman	Williams B	Curle	Moyes	Marshall	Pritchard	Hutchinson	Tong	Walsh	Neville	
	7/1		*5,385*	*7*	35			*Douglas 65*	*Rhodes*	*Stead*	*Holmes**	*Humphries*	*Flynn*	*Cusack*	*Buckley*	*Douglas*	*Joyce*	*Woods*	*Brown T*	*Dobbin*
								Ref: G Ashby	After Colin Douglas volleys in following Waugh's weak punch, Walsh ends Doncaster's stubborn resistance with a breathtaking 70th-minute acute-angled shot. For a side near the top of the table Doncaster offer little, though City are somewhat flattered by the margin of their success.											
26	H	ROTHERHAM		12	W	3-1	2-0	Williams 34, Walsh 38, Neville 49	Waugh	Newman	Williams B	Curle	Moyes	Marshall	Pritchard	Hutchinson	Tong	Walsh	Neville	
	11/1		6,672	*13*	38			*Tynan 52*	*O'Hanlon*	*Barnsley*	*Dungworth*	*Gooding*	*Smith**	*Pickering*	*Birch*	*Emerson*	*Tynan*	*Simmons*	*Pugh*	*Eley*
								Ref: H King/L Loosemore	Referee Howard King's replacement by Les Loosemore in the 20th minute enlivens a dull first half in which Williams' deflection of Tony Tynan's clearance and Walsh's 15-yard prod-in put City in charge. After the break Tynan's crisp half-volley gives Rotherham some reward.											
27	A	WALSALL		12	L	1-2	1-0	Neville 36	Waugh	Newman	Williams B	Curle	Moyes	Llewellyn	Pritchard*	Hutchinson !	Tong	Walsh	Neville	Riley
	18/1		*4,952*	*6*	38			*Cross 53p, Elliott 66*	*Cherry*	*Gunn*	*Hawker*	*Shakespeare*	*Brazier*	*Hart*	*Childs*	*Cross*	*Daley**	*Elliott*	*Naughton*	*Kelly*
								Ref: D Scott	Cheating players, loutish fans and pathetic refereeing at Fellows Park in the week that the Popplewell report is produced. The alert Neville shoots City ahead as the keeper fumbles Walsh's effort, but the game turns as Hutchinson is sent off for protesting Cross's dive for the penalty.											
28	H	CARDIFF		12	W	2-1	2-1	Neville 23, Marshall 36	Waugh	Newman	Williams B	Curle	Moyes	Riley	Marshall	Hutchinson	Tong	Walsh	Neville	
	25/1		7,541	*20*	41			*Wheeler 34*	*Smelt*	*Marustik*	*Giles*	*Ford*	*Stevenson*	*Mullen*	*Christie**	*Vaughan*	*Wheeler*	*Farrington*	*Micallef*	*McLoughlin*
								Ref: T Holbrook	A patchy performance as Neville fires in from Curle's long free-kick to give City an early lead, before Paul Wheeler heads in the Bluebirds equaliser. Riley's accurate cross sets up Marshall to restore City's advantage, but Lee Smelt performs heroics to prevent any further addition.											
29	A	WIGAN		10	D	1-1	0-1	Newman 68	Waugh	Newman	Williams B	Curle	Moyes	Riley	Llewellyn	**Tanner***	Tong	Walsh	Neville	Marshall
	1/2		*3,402*	*4*	42			*Cook 39*	*Tunks*	*Butler*	*Knowles*	*Kelly**	*Cribley*	*Methven*	*Lowe*	*Barrow*	*Jewell*	*Langley*	*Cook*	*Aspinall*
								Ref: K Redfern	Three brilliant saves by Roy Tunks from Walsh preserve Wigan's invincible home record. Williams clears off the line early on, before Paul Cook's thunderous drive puts Wigan in front. Marshall's introduction has an immediate impact as Newman heads in from his right-wing cross.											
30	H	BURY		9	W	4-1	1-1	Riley 29, 67, Neville 47, Walsh 48	Waugh	Newman	Williams B	Curle	Moyes	Riley	Marshall	Hutchinson	Tong	Walsh	Neville	
	4/2		5,074	*21*	45			*Madden 33*	*Hughes*	*Dixon*	*Pashley*	*Robinson*	*Valentine*	*Hill*	*Harris**	*Madden*	*Cross*	*Jakub*	*Young*	*Bramhall*
								Ref: C Downey	Walsh celebrates his new contract with a vicious left-foot drive from twelve yards as City take Bury apart after the break. Riley is the star with his two strikes, evading a scything tackle to shoot in the opener, and then controlling the ball on his chest before firing into the roof of the net.											
31	H	YORK		9	D	2-2	1-1	Moyes 1, Neville 70	Waugh	Llewellyn	Williams B	Curle	Moyes	Riley	Marshall	Hutchinson	Tong	Walsh	Neville	
	22/2		6,392	*12*	46			*MacPhail 44p, Canham 89*	*Leaning*	*Senior*	*Hood*	*McAughtrie*	*MacPhail*	*Mills*	*Ford*	*Banton**	*Walwyn*	*Haslegrave*	*Canham*	*Butler*
								Ref: J Deakin	York deserve their leveller before the break thanks to John MacPhail's pen after Williams handles Keith Walwyn's header on the line. Neville sprints 40 yards to head in Walsh's cross with a diving header, but Tony Canham's mis-hit 25-yard swerver destroys City's promotion hopes.											
32	A	BLACKPOOL		10	L	1-2	0-1	Bryant 66	Waugh*	Llewellyn	Williams B	Curle	Moyes	Riley	**Bryant**	Hutchinson	Tong	Walsh	Neville	Marshall
	1/3		*3,366*	*8*	46			*Butler 8, Deary 63p*	*O'Rouke*	*Moore*	*Walsh*	*Conroy*	*Law*	*Greenall*	*Britton*	*Deary*	*Stewart*	*Butler**	*Dyer*	*O'Keefe*
								Ref: J Lloyd	Marshall demonstrates his versatility between the sticks as Waugh's earlier back injury forces the keeper's 42nd-min departure. He has no chance with Pool's controversial pen following Moyes' supposed handball, but Bryant celebrates his City debut with a brilliant half-volley.											
33	H	NEWPORT		8	W	3-1	1-0	Walsh 11, Marshall 83, Curle 89	**Vaughan**	Llewellyn	Williams B	Curle	Moyes	Riley	Marshall	Hutchinson*	Tong	Walsh	Neville	Johnson
	4/3		**4,395**	*18*	49			*Mardenborough 52*	*Kendall*	*Pulis*	*Jones P*	*Berry*	*Carter*	*Boyle*	*Mardenboro'*	*Relish**	*Gill*	*Staniforth*	*Lewis*	*Peacock*
								Ref: J Moules	Curle celebrates yesterday's birth of his first child with a blistering 70-yard dribble to take him past the challenges of Tony Pulis and Peter Jones and side-foot in City's memorable last-minute goal. On top in the first half, City register with their only second-half shots on target.											
34	A	CHESTERFIELD		9	D	0-0	0-0		Vaughan	Llewellyn	Williams B	Curle	Moyes	Riley	Marshall	Hutchinson	Newman	Walsh	Neville	
	8/3		*2,547*	*15*	50				*Marples*	*Hewitt*	*O'Neill*	*Spooner**	*Baines*	*Hunter*	*Brown P*	*Moss*	*Williamson*	*Henderson*	*Scrimgeour*	*Caldwell*
								Ref: I Hemley	On the evidence of this season's meetings, games with Chesterfield should carry a warning to fans in that they could be bored to death. In following Reading's 4-2 win at Saltergate on Tuesday, John Duncan's side adopt a rigid defensive approach throughout the whole game.											

No	Date	Opponent	Att	Pos	Pt	F-A	H-T	Scorers, Times, and Referees	1	2	3	4	5	6	7	8	9	10	11	subs used
35	H	NOTTS CO		7	W	3-0	1-0	Walsh 45, Moyes 72, Riley 88	Waugh	Llewellyn	Williams B	Curle	Moyes	Riley	Marshall	Hutchinson	Newman	Walsh	Neville	
	15/3		5,701	*9*	53				*Mimms*	*Smalley*	*Richards*	*Benjamin*	*Sims*	*Yates*	*Barnes*	*Goodwin*	*Waitt*	*Harkouk**	*Hunt*	*McParland*
								Ref: R Gifford	County, who came equipped to spoil with five men strung out across the back, and an efficient offside trap, do not force Waugh to make a save until three minutes from time. Walsh's low deflected shot breaks the deadlock, and Riley's lunge at a low centre seals City's success.											
36	A	DERBY		7	L	0-2	0-2		Waugh	Llewellyn	Williams B	Curle	Moyes	Riley	Marshall*	Hutchinson	Newman	Walsh !	Neville	Pritchard
	19/3		*11,113*	*3*	53			*Gregory 27, Christie 45*	*Steele*	*Blades*	*Buckley*	*Williams*	*Pratley*	*MacLaren*	*Micklewhite*	*Christie*	*Davison*	*Gregory*	*Chandler*	
								Ref: M Reed	Walsh receives his marching orders for the first time in his career for protesting over Trevor Christie's high tackle as the No 8 goes on to score off the inside of the post just before half-time. Derby's expensive side deserve their win which was set up by John Gregory's twelve yard opener.											
37	A	WOLVES		10	L	1-2	0-0	Walsh 62	Waugh	Llewellyn	Williams B	**Underhill**	Moyes	Riley	Marshall	Hutchinson	Newman	Walsh	Neville*	Pritchard
	22/3		*3,696*	*24*	53			*Mutch 69, Edwards 90*	*Barrett*	*Palmer*	*Barnes*	*Streete*	*Zelem*	*Purdie*	*Lockhart*	*Holmes*	*Mutch*	*Edwards D*	*Chapman*	
								Ref: P Willis	In a swirling wind City have the skill, but lack commitment against a poor Wolves side. Walsh's left-footed shot from twelve yards should have set City on the victory road, but Dean Edwards volleys Wolves' winner at the death, after Andy Mutch had levelled from an acute angle.											
38	H	BRISTOL ROV		9	W	2-0	1-0	Neville 26, Walsh 71	Waugh	Llewellyn	Williams B	Curle	Moyes	Riley	Pritchard	Hutchinson	**Harle***	Walsh	Neville	Newman
	29/3		**12,171**	*16*	56				*Green*	*Scales*	*Bater*	*Tanner*	*Parkin*	*Jones*	*Francis**	*Penrice*	*Morgan*	*White*	*Stevenson*	*Purnell*
								Ref: K Cooper	Despite almost total possession City find chances hard to come by as the Rovers' defence battles manfully to stem the tide. City's opener is lucky as Vaughan Jones' headed clearance rebounds off Neville, but no fluke about Walsh's turn and 15-yard angled drive that ties matters up.											
39	H	LINCOLN		10	D	1-1	0-1	Neville 48	Waugh	Llewellyn	Williams B	Curle	Bryant	Riley	Pritchard	Hutchinson	Harle	Marshall	Neville	
	5/4		5,375	*19*	57			*White 16*	*Swinburne*	*Hodson*	*Redfearn*	*White*	*West**	*Strodder*	*McInnes*	*Turner*	*Gamble*	*Kilmore*	*Mair*	*Toman*
								Ref: R Bridges	Trevor Swinburne frustrates City with a string of great saves after Bryant's failure to cut out a through-ball allows Devon White to run through and fire past Waugh. Neville slams in City's equaliser from close range, but the nearest to a winner is Riley's disallowed 55th-min header.											
40	A	BRENTFORD		9	W	2-1	2-1	Riley 30, Pritchard 38	Waugh	Llewellyn	Williams B	Curle	Moyes	Riley	Pritchard	Hutchinson	Harle	Marshall*	Neville	Newman
	13/4		*3,701*	*11*	60			*Millen 17*	*Phillips*	*Salman*	*Murray*	*Millen*	*Wignall*	*Booker*	*Holloway*	*Sinton*	*Butler*	*Cooke*	*Burke**	*Lynch*
								Ref: M Heath	City's fine attacking performance is rewarded courtesy of a corner flag from which a rebound allows Marshall to cross for Pritchard's sweetly-timed volley. Defensive problems persist though, and the Bees take the lead as Keith Millen rises high to plant a firm header past Waugh.											
41	H	SWANSEA		11	L	0-1	0-0		Waugh	Llewellyn	Williams B	Curle	Moyes	Riley*	Pritchard	Hutchinson	Harle	Walsh	Neville	**Moore**
	19/4		6,013	*22*	60			*Price 80*	*Hughes*	*Lewis*	*Sullivan*	*Price P*	*Gibbins*	*Emmanuel*	*Hutchison*	*Pascoe*	*McHale*	*Waddle*	*Hough*	
								Ref: D Vickers	The diminutive Moore cheers up the City fans with his touches after coming on for the last 22 minutes of a match that leaves boss Cooper speechless. Neville's 54th-minute curler that hits the bar is City's best effort as Swansea take the points with Paul Price's 15-yard low drive.											
42	A	BRISTOL ROV		10	D	1-1	0-0	Neville 74	Waugh	Llewellyn	Williams B	Curle	Moyes	Riley	Pritchard	Hutchinson	Harle	Walsh	Neville	
	22/4		*9,922*	*16*	61			*Scales 80*	*Green*	*Scales*	*England*	*Tanner**	*Parkin*	*Jones*	*Francis*	*Penrice*	*Morgan*	*White*	*Purnell*	*Noble*
								Ref: L Shapter	Ron Green's heroics in keeping out Moyes' point-blank header come to naught as Neville latches onto the rebound to put City deservedly in front. Fittingly, though, John Scales' fierce cross-shot ensures that it is Rovers who have final say as the curtain descends on Eastville derbies.											
43	A	BOLTON		9	W	**4-0**	2-0	Riley 19, Neville 31, 54, Llewellyn 67	Waugh	Llewellyn	Williams B	Curle	Moyes	Riley	Pritchard	Newman	Harle	Walsh	Neville	
	26/4		*4,493*	*16*	64				*Farnworth*	*Scott*	*Phillips*	*Sutton*	*Came*	*Bell*	*Darby*	*Oghani*	*Entwhisle*	*Hartford*	*Gavin*	
								Ref: J Ashworth	Newman stars with his long probing passes in an action-packed second half that contains 23 of the game's 29 shots on target. Llewellyn completes the scoring with his first League goal. Taking a return pass from Riley on the edge of the box he coolly beats Simon Farnworth.											
44	A	PLYMOUTH		9	L	0-4	0-1		Waugh	Llewellyn	Williams B	Curle	Moyes	Riley	Pritchard	Newman	Harle	Walsh	Neville	
	29/4		***24,888***	*2*	64			*Tynan 32, 64, Nelson 54, Coughlin 61*	*Crudgington*	*Nisbet*	*Cooper L*	*Goodyear*	*McElhinney*	*Matthews*	*Hodges*	*Coughlin*	*Tynan*	*Summerfield*	*Nelson*	
								Ref: J Deakin	Cooper's prediction of an exciting shoot-out between two attacking sides is made to look a sick joke as City can only manage one worthwhile goal attempt. Tommy Tynan wins everything in the air, but he uses his feet to set Argyle on course to clinching promotion with an easy opener.											
45	H	READING		9	W	3-0	3-0	Neville 7, Walsh 34p, 40p	Waugh	Llewellyn	Williams B	Newman	Moyes	Riley	Pritchard	Hutchinson	Harle	Walsh	Neville	
	3/5		7,814	*1*	67				*Westwood*	*Williams*	*Richardson*	*Beavon*	*Peters*	*Wood*	*Hurlock*	*Horrix*	*Senior*	*White*	*Rogers*	
								Ref: M James	City's sizzling soccer makes a mockery of the League table as only Gary Westwood saves the Champions from a landslide. Hutchinson heads down Llewellyn's free-kick for Neville to open the scoring, whilst Gary Peters up-ends Neville for the first penalty and handles for the second.											
46	A	DARLINGTON		9	D	1-1	0-1	Riley 60	Waugh	Llewellyn	Williams B	Curle	Moyes	**Honor**	Marshall	Newman	Tanner	Walsh	Neville*	Riley
	15/5		*1,615*	*13*	68			*Roberts 44*	*Astbury*	*Aldred*	*Ward*	*Tupling*	*Green*	*Lloyd*	*Roberts*	*Woodcock*	*Airey*	*McLean*	*Robinson*	
	Home	Away						Ref: M Peck	Following Curle's innocuous 85th-minute tackle, Waugh saves both Dave McLean's first spot-kick, and Dave Woodcock's effort. Walsh sets up City's goal by putting Riley clear to shoot into the net between two defenders, after Alan Roberts had slotted in Darlington's easy opener.											
	Average 6,600	5,214																		

Milk Cup

			Pos	Res	F-A	H-T	Scorers, Times, and Referees	1	2	3	4	5	6	7	8	9	10	11	12 sub used
1:1	A	HEREFORD		L	1-5	0-3	Johnson 77	Waugh	Llewellyn	Williams B	Curle	Hughes	Riley	Marshall*	Hutchinson	Emmanuel	Neville	Walsh	Johnson
21/8		*2,449*					*K'rns 1, Price 15, H'vey 42p, Ph'lps 60, 78*	*Rose*	*Price*	*Dalziel*	*Halliday*	*Cegielski*	*Pejic*	*Harvey*	*Delve*	*Phillips*	*Kearns*	*Butler*	
							Ref: K Barratt												

Clinical finishing by Hereford as they notch up their first victory over City, after taking the lead in just 41 secs following Riley's back-pass. Incredibly City have more shots and force three times as many corners as Hereford, but defensive frailties highlight the need for new blood.

			Pos	Res	F-A	H-T	Scorers, Times, and Referees	1	2	3	4	5	6	7	8	9	10	11	12 sub used
1:2	H	HEREFORD	24	W	2-0	1-0	Johnson 6, Hutchinson 83	Waugh	Llewellyn	Newman	Curle	Rogers	Williams B*	Pritchard	Hutchinson	Johnson	Walsh	Neville	Marshall
3/9		2,373	*4:11*					*Rose*	*Price*	*Dalziel*	*Halliday*	*Pejic*	*Cegielski*	*Harvey*	*Maddy*	*Phillips*	*Kearns*	*Butler*	
							Ref: R Gifford (City lost 3-5 on aggregate)												

City win back their respect as only keeper Kevin Rose comes between them and a sensational recovery. Hope is rekindled early on as Johnson heads in from Williams' pass, but despite incessant pressure, City's only further reward is Hutchinson's late flick in from Pritchard's cross.

FA Cup

			Pos	Res	F-A	H-T	Scorers, Times, and Referees	1	2	3	4	5	6	7	8	9	10	11	12 sub used
1	A	SWINDON	16	D	0-0	0-0		Waugh	Llewellyn	Newman	Curle	Rogers	Riley	Pritchard	Hutchinson	Tong	Walsh	Neville	
17/11		*10,468*	*4:7*					*Allen*	*Henry*	*Ramsey*	*Barnard*	*Cole*	*Calderwood*	*Rowland*	*Hall**	*Gordon*	*Wade*	*Hockaday*	*Gardiner*
							Ref: K Miller												

Cup football at its best with a feast of open attacking football and countless near misses at both ends. Whilst City have the edge with ten shots on target, compared to Swindon's three, they have cause to be thankful to Newman for clearing an in-swinging corner off the goal-line.

			Pos	Res	F-A	H-T	Scorers, Times, and Referees	1	2	3	4	5	6	7	8	9	10	11	12 sub used
1R	H	SWINDON	16	W	4-2	1-0	Neville 26, 57, 60, Riley 77	Waugh	Llewellyn	Curle	Rogers	Newman	Pritchard	Hutchinson	Tong	Walsh	Riley	Neville	
20/11		8,979	*4:7*				*Ramsey 46, Barnard 52*	*Allen*	*Henry*	*Cole*	*Calderwood*	*Ramsey*	*Roberts*	*Rowland**	*Barnard*	*Hockaday*	*Gordon*	*Wade*	*Hall*
							Ref: K Miller												

Another magnificent Cup battle, but this time the game has everything. Goals aplenty, near misses – Brian Wade hitting a post in the tenth minute – Waugh's penalty save from Andy Rowland midway through the second half, and two strong City appeals for spot-kick awards.

			Pos	Res	F-A	H-T	Scorers, Times, and Referees	1	2	3	4	5	6	7	8	9	10	11	12 sub used
2	H	EXETER	12	L	1-2	1-1	Walsh 17p	Waugh	Llewellyn*	Newman	Curle	Rogers	Riley	Pritchard	Hutchinson	Tong	Walsh	Neville	Williams B
7/12		8,052	*4:18*				*Kellow 25, Crawford 60*	*Shaw*	*Jackson*	*Viney*	*McNichol*	*McCaffery*	*Marker*	*Ling*	*Harrower**	*Kellow*	*Keough*	*Crawford*	*Pratt*
							Ref: H King												

Alan Crawford admits that his stunning 15-yard winner that shocks his former team-mates was a hit and hope effort. Aidan McCaffery pulls back Riley to give away the penalty, but City's failure to clear Jim McNichol's free-kick allows Tony Kellow to net a close-range leveller.

		P	W	D	L	F	A	W	D	L	F	A	Pts
			Home					Away					
1	Reading	46	16	3	4	39	22	13	4	6	28	29	94
2	Plymouth	46	17	3	3	56	20	9	6	8	32	33	87
3	Derby	46	13	7	3	45	20	10	8	5	35	21	84
4	Wigan	46	17	4	2	54	17	6	10	7	28	31	83
5	Gillingham	46	14	5	4	48	17	8	8	7	33	37	79
6	Walsall	46	15	7	1	59	23	7	2	14	31	41	75
7	York	46	16	4	3	49	17	4	7	12	28	41	71
8	Notts Co	46	12	6	5	42	26	7	8	8	29	34	71
9	BRISTOL CITY	46	14	5	4	43	19	4	9	10	26	41	68
10	Brentford	46	8	8	7	29	29	10	4	9	29	32	66
11	Doncaster	46	7	10	6	20	21	9	6	8	25	31	64
12	Blackpool	46	11	6	6	38	19	6	6	11	28	36	63
13	Darlington	46	10	7	6	39	33	5	6	12	22	45	58
14	Rotherham	46	13	5	5	44	18	2	7	14	17	41	57
15	Bournemouth	46	9	6	8	41	31	6	3	14	24	41	54
16	Bristol Rov	46	9	8	6	27	21	5	4	14	24	54	54
17	Chesterfield	46	10	6	7	41	30	3	8	12	20	34	53
18	Bolton	46	10	4	9	35	30	5	4	14	19	38	53
19	Newport	46	7	8	8	35	33	4	10	9	17	32	51
20	Bury	46	11	7	5	46	26	1	6	16	17	41	49
21	Lincoln	46	7	9	7	33	34	3	7	13	22	43	46
22	Cardiff	46	7	5	11	22	29	5	4	14	31	54	45
23	Wolves	46	6	6	11	29	47	5	4	14	28	51	43
24	Swansea	46	9	6	8	27	27	2	4	17	16	60	43
		1104	268	145	139	941	609	139	145	268	609	941	1511

Odds & ends

Double wins: (2) Cardiff, Bolton.
Double losses: (2) Walsall, Bournemouth.

Won from behind: (3) Blackpool (h), Swansea (a), Brentford (a).
Lost from in front: (5) Walsall (h), Gillingham (h), Bournemouth (a), Walsall (a), Wolves (a).

High spots: Winning 3-1 at Cardiff on 14 September.
Beating Plymouth 2-0 at Ashton Gate on 26 December.
Beating Bury 4-1 on 4 February.
Winning 4-0 at Bolton on 26 April.
Beating Hereford 3-0 in the Freight Rover Trophy on 9 May.
Winning the Freight Rover Trophy at Wembley Stadium by beating Bolton 3-0 on 24 May.
Beating Bristol Rov 1-0 in the Gloucestershire Cup Final on 9 Sep.

Low spots: Losing 0-5 at Bournemouth on 24 August.
Losing 3-6 at Bury on 22 October.
Losing at Hereford 1-5 in the FL Cup.
Losing at Hereford 0-2 in the Freight Rover Trophy on 6 May.

Player of the year: Bobby Hutchinson.
Ever-presents (1) Steve Neville.
Hat-tricks: (1) Steve Neville.
Leading scorer: Steve Neville (22).

	Appearances						Goals			
	Lge	*Sub*	LC	*Sub*	FAC	*Sub*	Lge	LC	FAC	Tot
Bryant, Richard	**2**						**1**			**1**
Curle, Chris	**44**		2		3		**1**			**1**
Emmanuel, Gary	**2**		1							
Harle, David	**8**									
Hirst, Martyn	**1**									
Honor, Chris	**1**									
Hughes, Mark	**2**		1							
Hutchinson, Bobby	**42**		2		3		**5**	1		**6**
Johnson, Steve	**8**	*5*	1	*1*				2		**2**
Llewellyn, Andy	**38**		2		3		**1**			**1**
Marshall, Gary	**14**	*5*	1	*1*			**2**			**2**
Moore, Gordon		*1*								
Moyes, David	**27**						**2**			**2**
Newman, Rob	**37**	*2*	1		3		**3**			**3**
Neville, Steve	**46**		2		3		**19**		3	**22**
Pritchard, Howard	**32**	*2*	1		3		**6**			**6**
Riley, Glyn	**33**	*8*	1		3		**10**		1	**11**
Rogers, Lee	**21**		1		3					
Tanner, Michael	**2**									
Tong, David	**19**				3					
Underhill, Graham	**1**									
Vaughan, John	**2**									
Walsh, Alan	**44**		**2**		**3**		**18**		**1**	**19**
Waugh, Keith	**44**		**2**		**3**					
Williams, Brian	**36**		**2**			*1*	**1**			**1**
25 players used	**506**	*23*	**22**	*2*	**33**	*1*	**69**	**3**	**5**	**77**

No	Date		Att	Pos	Pt	F-A	H-T	Scorers, Times, and Referees	1	2	3	4	5	6	7	8	9	10	11	12 sub used
1	H	BURY			D	2-2	2-2	Hutchinson 17, Moyes 33	Waugh	Llewellyn	Newman	Curle	Moyes	Riley	**Owen**	Hutchinson	Harle	Walsh	Neville	
	23/8		8,239		1			*Taylor 18, Greenwood 43*	*Hughes*	*Ross*	*Pashley*	*Flynn*	*Valentine*	*Young*	*Robinson A*	*Butler*	*Taylor*	*Jakub*	*Greenwood*	
								Ref: M Dimblebee	Gordon Owen, a £30,000 capture from Barnsley, wastes no time making an impression as it's his corners which bring City's goals. Yet twice, after Hutchinson's sprints for his superbly-headed opener, Bury ruthlessly exploit all too familiar defensive frailties to wipe out City's lead.											
2	A	GILLINGHAM			D	1-1	1-1	Hamson 32	Waugh	Newman	Llewellyn	Curle	Moyes	Riley	Owen	Hutchinson	Harle	Walsh	**Hamson**	
	30/8		*4,185*		2			*Shearer 45*	*Hillyard*	*Haylock*	*Elsey*	*Pearce*	*Weatherly*	*Hinnigan*	*Pritchard**	*Shearer*	*Robinson*	*Collins*	*Cascarino*	*Eves*
								Ref: M Bodenham	Moyes enjoys his physical battle with Tony Cascarino, as City gain a deserved point at the Priestfield Stadium. Cooper complains that the linesman had already signalled time in the first half before Howard Pritchard's corner leads to David Shearer shooting in from close range.											
3	H	WIGAN		9	W	2-1	1-1	Walsh 34, Moyes 83	Waugh	Llewellyn	Newman	Curle	Moyes	Riley	Owen	Hutchinson*	Harle	Walsh	Hamson	**Fitzpatrick**
	6/9		6,730	*23*	5			*Griffiths 43*	*Tunks*	*Butler*	*Knowles*	*Hamilton*	*Cribley*	*Beesley*	*Lowe*	*Thompson*	*Jewell*	*Cook**	*Griffiths*	*Hilditch*
								Ref: A Buksh	Moyes silences the chants of City's irate fans as he rises unchallenged at the far post to meet Walsh's corner and send an unstoppable header past Roy Tunks. City are fortunate to garner full points with an indifferent performance after Walsh's quick turn and shot had put them ahead.											
4	A	CHESTERFIELD		2	W	3-0	1-0	Owen 32, Newman 53, Harle 86	Waugh	Llewellyn	Newman	Curle	Moyes	Riley	Owen	Hutchinson	Harle	Walsh	Hamson	
	13/9		*2,605*	*15*	8				*Brown J*	*Hewitt*	*Williamson*	*Bellamy*	*Scrimgeour*	*Reid*	*Kendall*	*Moss*	*Walker*	*Henderson*	*Coyle**	*Kowalski*
								Ref: J McAulay	City find their form at last with 90 minutes of incisive attacking football. Waugh saves Brian Scrimgeour's 62nd-minute pen after Curle fells Ernie Moss, but by then City are already two in front, Owen shooting in the opener from a free-kick and Newman nodding home a rebound.											
5	A	DONCASTER		7	L	0-1	0-0		Waugh	Llewellyn	Newman	Curle	Moyes	Riley	Owen	Hutchinson	Harle	Walsh	Hamson*	Neville
	17/9		*2,236*	*4*	8			*Dobbin 46*	*Rhodes*	*Stead*	*Rushbury*	*Redfearn*	*Brown*	*Cusack*	*Russell*	*Dobbin*	*Woods*	*Clayton*	*Burke*	
								Ref: M Scott	City fail their physical at Belle Vue as rugged Doncaster deservedly take the points. Waugh pulls off a string of fine saves to keep City in contention, and it is rough justice that he should be caught too far off his line as Jim Dobbin's 30-yarder sails over his head and into the net.											
6	H	CARLISLE		5	W	3-0	2-0	Moyes 17, Walsh 32, 49	Waugh	Llewellyn	Williams B	Curle	Moyes	Riley	Owen	Hutchinson	Harle*	Walsh	Neville	Newman
	20/9		7,040	*18*	11				*Endersby*	*Haigh*	*McCartney*	*Wright*	*Saunders**	*Halsall*	*Baker*	*Cooke*	*Poskett*	*Bishop*	*Worrall*	*Lynam M*
								Ref: K Cooper	Walsh and Owen have a field day as Carlisle's formation, with both full-backs tucked into the middle, leaves plenty of space on the flanks. Walsh lays on the cross for Moyes to head in at the far post, before getting in on the scoring stakes himself by twice shooting in easy chances.											
7	A	BOURNEMOUTH		7	L	0-2	0-0		Waugh	Llewellyn	Williams B	Curle	Moyes !	Riley	Owen	Hutchinson	Harle	Walsh	Neville	
	27/9		*5,975*	*2*	11			*Savage 58p, 89p*	*Peyton*	*Williams*	*Morrell*	*Savage*	*Newson*	*Whitlock*	*O'Driscoll*	*Howlett*	*Richards*	*O'Connor*	*Puckett*	
								Ref: D Hedges	The dismissal of Moyes for arguing over the late penalty sparks crowd unrest, the referee calling a slightly premature halt to the proceedings as the fans spill onto the pitch. Williams' foul on Sean O'Driscoll gifts the first penalty, whilst Moyes' tackle on Carl Richards brings the second.											
8	H	DARLINGTON		9	D	1-1	0-0	Newman 64	Waugh	Llewellyn	Williams B	Curle	Moyes	Riley*	Owen	Hutchinson	Harle	Walsh	Neville	Newman
	30/9		6,667	*14*	12			*Mills 82*	*Astbury*	*Evans*	*Morgan*	*Hine*	*Green*	*Lloyd*	*Roberts A*	*Ward*	*Currie*	*Mills*	*Robinson*	
								Ref: K Miller	Newman shows neat control to break the deadlock against defensive opponents. Accepting the ball from Hutchinson he steers in a shot from the edge of the area, before City's charity show leaves Cooper fuming as Owen's misplaced pass leads to David Mills lashing in the equaliser.											
9	A	CHESTER		7	W	3-0	1-0	Harle 16, Hamson 57, Neville 84	Waugh	Newman	Williams B	Curle	Moyes	Hamson	Owen	Hutchinson	Harle	Walsh	Neville	
	4/10		*2,819*	*21*	15				*Stewart*	*Greenough*	*Lane*	*Holden*	*Abel*	*Butler*	*Kelly*	*Barrow*	*Richardson*	*Houghton**	*Graham*	*Rimmer*
								Ref: R Guy	David Harle, sent off ten times in his career, shows he is much more than his reputation suggests. He opens the scoring with a superb first-time volley, supplies the cross for Hamson to tap in the second, and is involved in the build-up as Neville notches City's third with a diving header.											
10	H	YORK		5	W	3-0	0-0	Walsh 67, 87, Neville 72	Waugh	Llewellyn	Williams B	Curle	Newman	Hamson	Owen	Hutchinson*	Harle	Walsh	Neville	Marshall
	11/10		7,951	*8*	18				*Leaning*	*Senior*	*McKenzie*	*Sbragia*	*McAughtrie*	*Hood*	*Ford*	*Banton*	*Gabbiadini**	*Mills*	*Canham*	*Butler*
								Ref: K Burge	City's switch to a 4-2-4 pattern following Hutchinson's ankle injury sparks a revival after an atrocious first half. John Atyeo, making his first visit to Ashton Gate in a decade, is impressed as Walsh registers with tremendous 25-yard drive, and a great shot on the turn from close in.											
11	H	MIDDLESBROUGH		9	D	2-2	2-2	Walsh 13, 19p	Waugh	Newman	Williams B	Rogers	**MacPhail**	Hamson	Owen*	Marshall	Harle	Walsh	Neville	Riley
	25/10		8,800	*2*	19			*Slaven 25, Laws 36*	*Pears*	*Laws*	*Cooper*	*Mowbray*	*Parkinson*	*Pallister*	*Slaven*	*Stephens*	*Hamilton*	*Gill*	*Ripley*	
								Ref: J Martin	Walsh gives City the lead with an unstoppable volley, and then registers from the spot after Neville is brought down, before Bernie Slaven seizes on a poor back-pass to get Boro' back into the game. Brian Laws levels with a 35-yard free-kick that takes a deflection off of Walsh.											

No / Date	Venue	Opponent	Att	Pos	Res / Pts	F-A	H-T	Scorers, Times, and Referees	1	2	3	4	5	6	7	8	9	10	11	12
12	A	BLACKPOOL		10	L	0-1	0-0		Waugh	Newman	Williams B	Rogers	MacPhail	Hamson	Llewellyn	Marshall*	Harle	Walsh	Neville !	Riley
1/11			4,370	4	19			*Butler 75*	*Siddall*	*Davies*	*Walsh*	*Law*	*Methven*	*Deary*	*Mayes*	*Thompson**	*Stewart*	*Dyer*	*Taylor*	*Butler*
								Ref: P Tyldesley	City cut out their defensive frailties at the expense of their attack. Unfortunately Neville's dismissal for a kick at Mike Walsh just before the break undermines much effort. Brian Butler's twenty-yarder strikes Hamson as he attempts to close down, and the ball is deflected past Waugh.											
13	H	MANSFIELD		10	D	0-0	0-0		Waugh	Newman	Williams B	Rogers	MacPhail	Riley	Marshall*	Hamson	Harle	Walsh	Neville	**Withey**
4/11			**6,407**	8	20				*Hitchcock*	*Graham*	*Logan*	*Lowery*	*Foster*	*Kenworthy*	*Kent*	*Kearney*	*Stringfellow*	*Cassells*	*McKernon*	
								Ref: J Moules	City's uninspired display illustrates how much the zest and enthusiasm of the injured Hutchinson is missed. Kevin Hitchcock saves the Stags after the interval when City at last put their game together, but he is fortunate that MacPhail's 50th-minute header is disallowed for offside.											
14	A	FULHAM		8	W	3-0	2-0	Neville 15, 88, Walsh 28p	Waugh	Newman	Williams B	Moyes	MacPhail	Riley	Hamson	Hutchinson	Harle	Walsh	Neville	
8/11			4,459	17	23				*Vaughan*	*Marshall*	*Hopkins*	*Scott**	*Oakes*	*Parker*	*Barnett*	*Hoddy*	*Coney*	*Kerrins*	*Davies*	*Achampong*
								Ref: K Barratt	It is thanks to Waugh that Fulham's blistering start is contained. Neville volleys in the opener, then a fortunate penalty after the ball rears up to hit Dean Coney's hand puts City in control. Another Walsh penalty is saved, but Neville coolly steers in City's final goal six minutes later.											
15	H	ROTHERHAM		9	L	0-1	0-1		Waugh	Newman	Williams B	Moyes	MacPhail	Riley	Marshall	Hutchinson	Harle*	Walsh	Withey	Owen
22/11			6,756	22	23			*Pugh 26*	*O'Hanlon*	*Dungworth*	*Crosby*	*Gooding*	*Warburton*	*Slack*	*Pugh*	*Williams*	*Evans*	*Haycock*	*Douglas*	
								Ref: R Wiseman	Millers' boss and ex City favourite Norman Hunter has a good day after receiving a rousing reception from the Ashton Gate fans. Just before a hailstorm makes conditions farcical, a reverse-pass by Gareth Evans sends Daral Pugh through City's square defence to prod the ball home.											
16	A	NOTTS CO		11	L	0-2	0-2		Waugh	Newman	Williams B	Moyes	MacPhail	Hamson	Owen	Hutchinson	Fitzpatrick	Walsh	Neville	
29/11			3,987	4	23			*Goodwin 7, McParland 13*	*Leonard*	*Smalley*	*Davis*	*Thompson*	*Yates*	*Benjamin*	*McParland*	*Goodwin*	*Waitt*	*Kevan*	*Clarke*	
								Ref: P Don	City beat themselves at the outset as David Clarke's cross glances off Mark Goodwin to spin gently past Waugh, and then the infamous offside trap fails again for Ian McParland to shoot home. Mick Leonard makes a fine save as Walsh fails from the spot for the fourth successive time.											
17	A	NEWPORT		9	W	1-0	1-0	Neville 21	Waugh	Newman	Williams B	Moyes	MacPhail	Hamson	Owen	Hutchinson	Fitzpatrick	Walsh	Neville	
2/12			3,205	20	26				*Kendall*	*Jones L*	*Jones P*	*O'Shea*	*Berry*	*Mullen**	*Mardenboro'*	*Gibbins*	*Carter*	*Staniforth*	*Lewis*	*Vinter*
								Ref: M Cotton	After a wretched November, City bounce back on the promotion trail with a slender but deserved success at Somerton Park. City's much-maligned defence does well to withstand Newport's late rally as they hang on to Neville's early goal, when he turned in Walsh's low cross.											
18	A	SWINDON		7	W	2-1	0-1	Neville 52, 87	Waugh	Newman	Williams B	Moyes	MacPhail	Marshall	Owen*	Hutchinson	Fitzpatrick	Walsh	Neville	Riley
14/12			7,637	6	29			*White 25*	*Digby*	*Henry*	*Hockaday*	*Jones*	*Franklin*	*Calderwood*	*Bamber*	*Kamara*	*White*	*Gilligan**	*Barnard*	*Wade*
								Ref: M Reed	Even Neville is not sure how his mis-hit 87th-min shot reached the back of the net as the ball trickled through a muddy goalmouth and over the line via a post. A lucky goal perhaps, but certainly a deserved reward for Cooper's brave policy of attacking the Railwaymen with two wingers.											
19	H	BOLTON		6	W	4-1	2-1	Neville 18, Riley 40, Newm'n 48, Walsh 70	Waugh	Newman	Williams B	Moyes	MacPhail	Riley	Marshall	Hutchinson*	Fitzpatrick	Walsh	Neville	Llewellyn
20/12			8,028	14	32			*Elliott 7*	*Salmon*	*Neal*	*Phillips*	*Joyce*	*Came*	*Scott*	*Caldwell*	*Thompson*	*Elliott*	*Hartford*	*Gavin*	
								Ref: B Hill	As so often with Bolton's visits to Ashton Gate the entertainment is first class. The Trotters are let down by their finishing after Steve Elliott heads them in front. Steve Thompson has his pen saved by Waugh with the score at 3-1, then Walsh adds City's fourth with a right-foot drive.											
20	A	PORT VALE		6	D	0-0	0-0		Waugh	Newman	Williams B	Moyes	MacPhail	Marshall	Riley	Hutchinson	Fitzpatrick	Walsh	Neville	
26/12			4,168	24	33				*Williams A*	*Banks*	*Bromage*	*Walker*	*Hazell*	*Sproson*	*Smith*	*Earle*	*Jones*	*Bowden*	*Hamson*	
								Ref: V Callow	No chance of skilful football on a quagmire pitch at Vale Park. After a bright start when City swarmed all over the bottom club, it is Vale who create the better chances with Paul Smith squandering a clear opportunity and Waugh doing well to save Ray Walker's low 25-yard drive.											
21	H	WALSALL		7	W	2-1	0-1	MacPhail 63p, Fitzpatrick 66	Waugh	Newman	Williams B	Moyes	MacPhail	Riley	Marshall	Curle !	Fitzpatrick	Walsh	Neville	
27/12			10,193	10	36			*Kelly 7*	*Barber*	*Dornan*	*Mower*	*Shakespeare*	*Forbes*	*Hart*	*Train**	*Cross*	*Kelly*	*Christie*	*Naughton*	*Hawker*
								Ref: K Cooper	City show great spirit after going behind to David Kelly's volley and having Curle sent off in the 36th minute for his wild challenge on Fred Barber. Fitzpatrick runs clear to slot in the winner after Neville, who has a late strike disallowed for offside, appeared to dive for the penalty.											
22	H	BRISTOL ROV		7	L	0-1	0-0		Waugh	Newman	Williams B	Moyes	MacPhail	Marshall	Riley*	Curle	Fitzpatrick	Walsh	Neville	Hutchinson
1/1			17,122	14	36			*Smart 87*	*Carter*	*Jones*	*Scales*	*Weston**	*Twentyman*	*Carr*	*Dryden*	*Smart*	*Morgan*	*Mehew*	*Tanner*	*Micallef*
								Ref: J Deakin	Gary Smart makes City pay for wasting their chances as he settles this derby with a superb 20-yard strike. City dominate the play, but Rovers demonstrate much resolve, especially when David Mehew takes over in goal from the injured Tim Carter for the last 15 mins of the first half.											
23	A	ROTHERHAM		7	L	0-2	0-0		Waugh	Newman	Williams B	Moyes	MacPhail	Riley	Curle	Hutchinson	Fitzpatrick*	Walsh	Neville	Marshall
3/1			3,170	14	36			*Evans 54, Campbell 65*	*Newcombe*	*Douglas*	*Crosby*	*Gooding*	*Dungworth*	*Green*	*Pugh*	*Williams*	*Evans*	*Trusson*	*Campbell*	
								Ref: G Tyson	City go down to their second defeat in the three days since Cooper was named Third Division manager of the month. After the galling derby defeat, City fall to a moderate Millers side, who score twice on the break with a Gareth Evans volley and Winston Campbell's close-range shot.											

No	Date		Att	Pos	Pt	F-A	H-T	Scorers, Times, and Referees	1	2	3	4	5	6	7	8	9	10	11	12 sub used
24	A	WIGAN		8	L	**1-3**	1-2	Walsh 25	Waugh	Newman	Williams B	Moyes	MacPhail	Fitzpatrick	Marshall	Curle	Morgan	Walsh	Neville*	Riley
	24/1		*3,092*	*7*	36			*Hilditch 38, Campbell 44, 75*	*Tunks*	*Hamilton*	*Knowles*	*Cook*	*Cribley*	*Holden*	*Hilditch*	*Thompson*	*Campbell*	*Jewell*	*Griffiths*	
								Ref: T Holbrook	All zip goes out of the City side with Neville's 42nd-min departure with a broken leg following Andy Holden's crunching tackle. Walsh heads City in front, but Bobby Campbell nets with a fierce shot and an easy header, after Mark Hilditch had turned in a rebound to bring Wigan level.											
25	H	CHESTERFIELD		8	W	1-0	0-0	Walsh 55	Waugh	Curle	Williams B	Moyes	MacPhail*	Newman	Marshall	Morgan	Fitzpatrick	Walsh	Owen	Riley
	31/1		*6,426*	*12*	39				*Marples*	*Hewitt*	*Rogers*	*Bellamy*	*Bloomer*	*Reid*	*Coyle*	*Airey*	*Caldwell*	*Henderson*	*Greaves**	*Bernadeau*
								Ref: A Gunn	An inept display against a side crushed 0-3 by lowly Rochdale in the Freight Rover Trophy just four days ago cannot be explained away by an icy pitch. Managing only two shots on target in one of the worst games in living memory, City secure victory with Walsh's low 15-yard drive.											
26	H	DONCASTER		7	W	**5-0**	2-0	Walsh 17, 68, 88, Owen 34, Newman 47	Waugh	Newman	Williams B	Moyes	MacPhail	Curle	Owen	Fitzpatrick*	Morgan	Walsh	**Jordan**	Tanner
	7/2		8,982	*10*	42				*Rhodes*	*Stead*	*Brown**	*Redfearn*	*Humphries*	*Cusack*	*Russell*	*Miller*	*Gaynor*	*Clayton*	*Burke*	*Holmes*
								Ref: J Ireland	Jordan breathes new life into City's season with a memorable debut that inspires everyone around him. Walsh nets his fourth career hat-trick, his first for City all shot in with typical aplomb, whilst a similar finish by Owen and a header from Newman completes City's nap hand.											
27	A	CARLISLE		5	W	2-1	2-0	Morgan 9, Jordan 30	Waugh	Llewellyn	Williams B	Curle	Moyes	Morgan	Owen	Jordan	Fitzpatrick	Walsh	Newman	
	14/2		*2,500*	*24*	45			*McGarvey 66p*	*Nixon*	*Lomax*	*Gorman*	*Haigh*	*Wright**	*Halsall*	*Baker*	*Cooke*	*McGarvey*	*Bishop*	*Worrall*	*Poskett*
								Ref: P Harrison	Morgan strikes the sweetest of right-foot volleys to set City on course for their third successive League win. Jordan heads in to double the advantage, but Carlisle (nine shots on target to City's four) take control after Williams concedes the spot-kick for bringing down John Cooke.											
28	H	BOURNEMOUTH		4	W	2-0	1-0	Newson 29 (og), Owen 77p	Waugh	Newman	Williams B	Curle	Llewellyn	Moyes	Owen	Galliers	Morgan	Walsh	Jordan	
	21/2		14,538	*2*	48				*Peyton*	*Newson*	*Morrell*	*O'Connor*	*Williams*	*Whitlock*	*O'Driscoll*	*Pulis*	*Aylott*	*Richards**	*Cooke*	*Heffernan*
								Ref: P Wright	The tension is palpable as City show they now have the steel, as well as the flair, to win promotion. A significant victory over the impressive Cherries comes courtesy of Mark Newson's errors, as he heads Llewellyn's free-kick into his own net, then fells Owen to concede the penalty.											
29	A	DARLINGTON		7	D	0-0	0-0		Waugh	Newman	Williams B	Moyes	Llewellyn	Curle	Owen	Fitzpatrick	Morgan	Walsh	Jordan	
	28/2		***2,044***	*23*	49				*Astbury*	*Evans*	*Morgan**	*Hine*	*Lloyd*	*Robinson*	*Tupling*	*Ward*	*Currie*	*MacDonald*	*Riley*	*Davis*
								Ref: K Walmsley	Cooper says 'the result defies belief' as City fail to exploit their complete dominance. A string of brilliant Mike Astbury saves, Phil Lloyd's goal-line clearance, and Walsh twice shooting against the woodwork, sums up City's frustration as the visitors fail to get a shot on target.											
30	H	BLACKPOOL		5	W	3-1	3-1	Walsh 26, Newman 36, Fitzpatrick 43	Waugh	Newman	Williams B	Moyes	Llewellyn	Curle	Owen	Fitzpatrick	Morgan	Walsh	Jordan	
	3/3		10,980	*7*	52			*Stewart 34*	*Siddall*	*Matthews*	*McAteer*	*Law*	*Methven*	*Deary*	*Davies*	*Thomson*	*Stewart*	*Madden*	*Taylor*	
								Ref: K Baker	The deadlock breaking 30-yard bender that leaves Barry Siddall motionless in the Open End goal is described by Walsh as the best free-kick he has ever taken. Paul Stewart skilfully shoots in Blackpool's equaliser, but Newman restores City's advantage by forcing in Walsh's header.											
31	A	MIDDLESBROUGH		5	L	0-1	0-1		Waugh	Newman	Williams B	Moyes	Llewellyn	Curle	Owen	Fitzpatrick*	Morgan	Walsh	Jordan !	Riley
	7/3		***10,220***	*3*	52			*Mowbray 35*	*Pears*	*Coyle*	*Cooper*	*Mowbray*	*Parkinson*	*Kernaghan*	*Slaven*	*Stephens*	*Hamilton*	*Gill*	*Hodgson !*	
								Ref: D Hutchinson	An ill-tempered battle with Jordan's 70th-min sending off being followed 13 mins later by the dismissal of David Hogdson for kicking Curle in the stomach. Owen spurns City's best chance of equalising Tony Mowbray's header, shooting wide from the spot just before half-time.											
32	H	NEWPORT		5	W	4-0	2-0	Morgan 23, Jordan 26, Newman 84 [Williams 87p]	Waugh	Newman	Williams B	Moyes	Llewellyn	Curle	Owen	Tanner	Morgan	Walsh*	Jordan	Marshall
	14/3		9,137	*22*	55				*Freestone*	*Jones L*	*Lewis*	*Berry*	*Carter**	*Compton*	*Giles*	*Gibbins*	*Staniforth*	*Mills*	*Millett*	*Mardenboro'*
								Ref: T Ward	Another goal to remember as Newman brightens up a dull second half with a curving right-foot volley that finds the corner of the Covered End net. Williams completes the scoring with his first City pen after his short centre had struck Newport player-manager John Lewis on the arm.											
33	A	BRENTFORD		6	D	1-1	1-0	Owen 27	Waugh	Newman	Williams B	Moyes	Llewellyn	Curle	Owen	Tanner !	Morgan	Walsh	Jordan	
	17/3		*4,051*	*15*	56			*Maddy 46*	*Phillips*	*Perryman*	*Murray*	*Millen*	*Droy*	*Maddy*	*Carroll*	*Sinton*	*Cooke*	*Stevens*	*Turner*	
								Ref: M Bodenham	City are lucky to survive Tanner's 85th-minute dismissal for his attempt to butt Paul Maddy. In the second half it is only desperate defending and good luck that keeps Brentford at bay, after Maddy's shot on the turn had levelled Owen's close-range opener from Jordan's astute header.											
34	A	YORK		6	D	1-1	0-1	Tanner 48	Waugh	Newman	Williams B	Moyes	Llewellyn	Curle*	Owen	Tanner	Morgan	Walsh	Riley	Marshall
	21/3		*2,874*	*20*	57			*Canham 3*	*Leaning*	*McKenzie*	*Senior*	*Pickering*	*McAughtrie*	*Haslegrave*	*Ford*	*Gabbiadini**	*Walwyn*	*Mills*	*Canham*	*Hood*
								Ref: A Robinson	Though Owen is robbed of a winner by a linesman failing to note that his 53rd-minute shot is well over the line before Tony Canham hooks clear, City's inept performance scarcely deserves the point earned by Tanner's speculative 30-yarder after Canham had headed York in front.											

No	H/A	Opponent / Date	Att	Pos	Res	Pts	F-A	H-T	Scorers, Times, and Referees	1	2	3	4	5	6	7	8	9	10	11	12
35	H	CHESTER		6	W		1-0	0-0	Morgan 70	Waugh	Newman	Williams B	Moyes	Llewellyn	Fitzpatrick	Owen	Tanner	Morgan	Walsh	Riley	
		28/3	8,230	*15*		60				*Stewart*	*Greenough*	*Woodthorpe*	*Fazackerley*	*Abel*	*Butler**	*Kelly*	*Barrow*	*Rimmer*	*Houghton*	*Graham*	*Croft*
									Ref: D Vickers	Waugh preserves City's points by stopping Ricky Greenough's curler in the dying mins, as well keeping his side in the game midway through the second half with the save of the season from Graham Abel's perfectly-struck shot. Morgan out-jumps his marker to head in City's winner.											
36	A	BURY		5	W		2-1	2-1	Morgan 13, Owen 37	Waugh	Newman	Williams B	Moyes	Llewellyn	Fitzpatrick	Owen*	Honor	Morgan	Walsh	Jordan	Marshall
		31/3	*2,200*	*13*		63			*Greenwood 19*	*Farnworth*	*Hill*	*Fairbrother*	*Hart*	*Valentine*	*Higgins*	*Harris**	*Hoyland*	*Greenwood*	*McIlroy*	*Lee*	*Robinson L*
									Ref: N Ashley	City survive a second-half onslaught to take the points earned by Morgan's headed opener, and Owen's dream volley, after Greenwood's power header had brought the Shakers level. 'A match of First Division standard' says Sammy McIlroy who inspires a skilful Bury side.											
37	H	FULHAM		5	D		0-0	0-0		Waugh	Newman	Williams B	MacPhail	Llewellyn	Fitzpatrick*	Owen	**Harvey**	Morgan	Walsh	Jordan	Honor
		4/4	8,551	*20*		64				*Vaughan*	*Parker*	*Carr*	*Lewington*	*Oakes*	*Hicks*	*Barnett*	*Hopkins*	*Coney*	*Pike*	*Elkins*	
									Ref: J Bray	Fulham show great resolve following a 0-6 humiliation at the hands of Port Vale in their previous game. City's promotion drive comes off the rails as they adapt poorly to the conditions posed by the incessant rain. Walsh fails to connect with their one real chance just four yards out.											
38	A	MANSFIELD		7	L		0-2	0-0		Waugh	Newman	Williams B	Moyes	MacPhail	Llewellyn	Owen	Harvey	Morgan	Walsh	Jordan	
		11/4	*2,888*	*9*		64			*Kearney 68p, 75*	*Hitchcock*	*Graham*	*Kenworthy*	*Lowery*	*Foster*	*Pollard*	*Kent*	*Danskin**	*Stringfellow*	*Cassells*	*Kearney*	*Anderson*
									Ref: J Watson	City hit a new low at windswept Field Mill, where the Mansfield goalie is untroubled until five minutes from time. MacPhail insists that the ball hits his chest for the penalty, but there is no doubt that his deflection of a Keith Cassells centre sets up Mark Kearney's headed second.											
39	A	BRISTOL ROV		7	D		0-0	0-0		Waugh	Newman	Williams B	Moyes	MacPhail	Llewellyn	Marshall	Galliers	Morgan	Walsh	Jordan	
		18/4	*4,695*	*21*		65				*Bradshaw*	*Jones*	*Rushbury*	*Cawley*	*Twentyman*	*Tanner*	*Purnell*	*Penrice*	*Turner**	*Meacham*	*Hibbitt*	*Scales*
									Ref: J Key	Those that stay away get it right as the lowest-ever attendance for a Bristol derby in the League watches this passionless encounter. The only excitement comes just before the end when Jeff Meacham's shot is disallowed as Gary Penrice lets the ball run over the line before crossing.											
40	H	PORT VALE		7	W		1-0	1-0	Walsh 10	Waugh	Newman	Williams B	Moyes	MacPhail	Llewellyn	Owen	Galliers	Riley	Walsh*	Jordan	Marshall
		20/4	8,669	*13*		68				*Williams A*	*Webb*	*Bromage*	*Walker*	*Hazell*	*Sproson*	*Smith*	*Earle*	*Jones**	*Beckford*	*Maguire*	*Bowden*
									Ref: M Dimblebee	After Walsh cleverly makes space in a crowded penalty area before curling a left-footer past Alex Williams, City often look second best against Vale. It takes skipper Williams' last ditch 79th-minute challenge on the clean through John Bowden to save the points for City.											
41	H	GILLINGHAM		6	W		2-0	2-0	Williams 19p, Marshall 32	Waugh	Newman	Williams B	Moyes	MacPhail	Llewellyn	Owen	Galliers	Riley	Marshall	Jordan	
		22/4	10,260	*7*		71				*Kite*	*Haylock*	*Pearce*	*Berry*	*Weatherly*	*Gernon*	*Robinson*	*Shearer*	*Lovell**	*Elsey*	*Cascarino*	*Pritchard*
									Ref: H King	The Gills dispute Williams' penalty as Irvin Gernon is caught out by Riley's turn, but there is no argument about City's early superiority against promotion rivals. Marshall gives Paul Haylock a nightmare opening, and the lively winger's firm header doubles City's advantage.											
42	A	BOLTON		6	D		0-0	0-0		Waugh	Newman	Williams B	Moyes	MacPhail	Llewellyn	Owen*	Galliers	Riley	Marshall	Jordan	Curle
		25/4	*4,414*	*19*		72				*Felgate*	*Neal*	*Scott*	*Joyce*	*Sutton*	*Came*	*Caldwell*	*Brookman*	*Elliott*	*Hartford*	*Gavin**	*Stevens*
									Ref: M Robinson	City's promotion quest is likely to end in failure because of an unexpected inability to hit the back of the net. Another Waugh clean sheet should have been enough to ensure victory against relegation-haunted Bolton, but despite constant pressure City only create two good chances.											
43	H	BRENTFORD		7	L		0-2	0-0		Waugh	Newman	Williams B	Moyes	MacPhail	Llewellyn	Marshall	Galliers	Riley	Walsh*	Jordan	Curle
		28/4	9,050	*11*		72			*Carroll 73, Blissett 86*	*Phillips*	*Joseph*	*Murray*	*Millen*	*Droy**	*Perryman*	*Carroll*	*Sinton*	*Cooke*	*Blissett*	*Turner*	*Nogan*
									Ref: G Ashby	A nightmare for City as Steve Perryman's well-organised side notch up a deserved success. Robbie Carroll's well-struck drive puts the Bees ahead, and then, shortly after Jordan heads against the bar, Gary Blissett puts the game beyond City's grasp by taking the ball round Waugh.											
44	H	NOTTS CO		5	W		3-1	1-1	Marshall 30, Jordan 73, Morgan 82	Waugh	Newman	Williams B	Moyes	MacPhail	Llewellyn	Owen	Galliers	Morgan	Marshall	Jordan	
		2/5	9,189	*6*		75			*McParland 44*	*Leonard*	*Smalley*	*Davis*	*Kevan*	*Hunt*	*Benjamin**	*McParland*	*Goodwin*	*Young*	*Campbell*	*Thompson*	*Clarke*
									Ref: K Burge	Aggrieved City are roused from their slumbers just after the break when their penalty appeals, after Marshall is tripped by Mike Leonard, fall on deaf ears. Jordan puts them ahead with a brilliant diving header, and then slips a well-weighted pass for Morgan to neatly slot the ball in.											
45	A	WALSALL		5	D		1-1	0-0	Morgan 88	Waugh	Newman	Williams B	Moyes	MacPhail	Llewellyn	Owen	Galliers	Morgan	Marshall*	Jordan	Curle
		4/5	*7,683*	*8*		76			*Kelly 74*	*Barber*	*Taylor*	*Mower*	*Shakespeare*	*Forbes*	*Hart*	*Childs*	*Cross*	*Kelly*	*Christie*	*Hawker*	
									Ref: W Flood	With Marshall again being denied a clear penalty, as well as Fred Barber's heroics, it takes Morgan's late header to keep play-off hopes on course. Walsall go ahead in a rare breakaway when David Kelly puts in a shot that loops over Waugh, after taking a deflection off of Williams.											
46	H	SWINDON		6	D		1-1	1-0	Morgan 12	Waugh	Newman	Williams B*	Moyes	MacPhail	Llewellyn	Owen	Galliers	Morgan	Marshall	Jordan	Curle
		9/5	**19,201**	*3*		77			*Coyne 66*	*Digby*	*Hockaday*	*King*	*Jones*	*Parkin*	*Calderwood*	*Bamber*	*Kamara*	*Quinn**	*Coyne*	*Berry*	*Ramsey*
		Home	Away						Ref: D Reeves	City's ambitions are in tatters as Owen's late penalty miss allows Gillingham (1-0 winners over Bolton) to oust them from a play-off place. Morgan's glancing header gets City off to a good start, then Marshall hits the bar before Peter Coyne's mis-hit volley brings Swindon level.											
Average		9,441	4,151																		

Littlewoods Cup			F-A	H-T	Scorers, Times, and Referees	1	2	3	4	5	6	7	8	9	10	11	subs used
1:1 A BOURNEMOUTH		W	1-0	0-0	Walsh 46	Waugh	Llewellyn	Newman	Curle	Moyes	Riley	Owen	Hutchinson	Harle	Walsh	Hamson	
26/8	*2,631*					*Peyton*	*Pulis*	*Morrell*	*Savage*	*Heffernan*	*Whitlock*	*O'Driscoll*	*Howlett*	*Aylott*	*Richards*	*Puckett*	
					Ref: N Butler	Walsh's magnificent volley, struck on the turn, from the edge of the penalty area draws the acclaim; but City's defence also deserve credit for responding to the Bury game criticism with a clean sheet. Bournemouth manage five shots on target, whilst City are only able to muster two.											
1:2 H BOURNEMOUTH		D	1-1	0-0	Foley 97	Waugh	Llewellyn	Newman	Curle	Moyes	Riley	Owen	Hutchinson	Harle*	Walsh	Hamson^	Fitzpat'k/Marshall
2/9	4,776		aet		*Aylott 60*	*Peyton*	*Pulis*	*Morrell**	*Heffernan*	*Whitlock*	*Savage*	*O'Driscoll*	*Howlett*	*Aylott*	*Richards*	*Puckett*	*Lewis*
					Ref: H King (City won 2-1 on aggregate)	With yesterday's death of Ivor Guy, many fans think that something akin to his 70-yarder at Ninian Park during the war will be necessary to crack Bournemouth's resistance. In the event however Riley saves City's blushes with a close-in volley from Owen's right-wing cross.											
2:1 H SHEFFIELD UTD	5	D	2-2	1-2	Neville 15, Walsh 87p	Waugh	Llewellyn	Williams B	Curle	Moyes	Riley*	Owen	Hutchinson	Neville	Walsh	Fitzpatrick	Marshall
23/9	8,366 *2:4*				*Morris 33p, Foley 39*	*Burridge*	*Barnsley*	*Pike*	*Arnott*	*Stancliffe*	*Smith*	*Morris*	*Frain*	*Dempsey*	*Foley*	*Beagrie**	*Withe*
					Ref: L Shapter	A thrilling cup-tie that lives up to all expectations as slick Sheffield outplay City in the first half, yet at the end they are hanging on for dear life. Both teams complain about harshly-awarded penalties, after Neville's 30-yard chip over a stranded John Burridge had put City ahead.											
2:2 A SHEFFIELD UTD	7	L	0-3	0-1		Waugh	Llewellyn	Williams B	Curle	Moyes	Hamson	Owen	Hutchinson*	Harle	Walsh	Neville^	Newman/Withey
7/10	*5,587 2:9*				*Foley 33, Morris 57, Dempsey 86*	*Burridge*	*Barnsley*	*Pike*	*Dempsey*	*Stancliffe*	*Eckhardt^*	*Morris*	*Frain*	*Withe**	*Foley*	*Beagrie*	*Wigley/Smith*
					Ref: H Taylor (City lost 2-5 on aggregate)	United's Colin Morris, best man at Waugh's wedding, runs through onto Steve Foley's pass to slot in the killer goal as City fail to match their 1st leg form. United's other goals are two long-range efforts, Foley's 22-yard left-foot volley, and Mark Dempsey's angled drive from 25 yards.											

FA Cup																	
1 H V S RUGBY	8	W	3-1	0-0	Marshall 74, Hutchinson 82, Walsh 89	Waugh	Newman	Williams B	Moyes	MacPhail	Riley	Hamson*	Hutchinson	Harle	Walsh	Withey	Marshall
15/11	7,069 *SL*				*Lane 57p*	*Marsden*	*Potter*	*Ferns*	*Lane*	*Geddes**	*Martin*	*Ingram*	*Flannagan*	*Norris*	*Conway*	*Draper*	*Gardener*
					Ref: K Cooper	Keith Cooper's excellent application of the advantage rule prevents impressive VS Rugby claiming the greatest result of their 30-year history. City's blushes are saved as the referee waves play on when Marshall rides a scything tackle to hammer a 25-yard swerver past Ian Marsden.											
2 H BATH CITY	9	D	1-1	0-0	Neville 59	Waugh	Newman	Williams B	Moyes	MacPhail	Marshall	Owen	Hutchinson	Fitzpatrick	Walsh	Neville	
6/12	10,053 *VC*				*Bodin 88*	*Mogg*	*England*	*Bodin*	*Sherwood*	*Fulbrook*	*Barton*	*O'Donnell*	*Adams^*	*Grimshaw*	*Crawford**	*Payne*	*Stevens/Shaw*
					Ref: A Seville	A dull local derby in which City, performing in new kit with a white hoop across their red jersey, have the edge. Neville injects some life into the proceedings by hammering the ball past David Mogg, but Paul Bodin replies with a fine volley (Bath's only shot on target) to earn a replay.											
2R A BATH CITY	9	W	3-0	1-0	Owen 34p, 86, Neville 80	Waugh	Newman	Williams B	Moyes	MacPhail	Marshall	Owen	Hutchinson	Fitzpatrick	Walsh	Neville	
9/12	9,058 *VC*					*Mogg*	*England*	*Sherwood*	*Stevens*	*Fulbrook*	*Barton*	*O'Donnell*	*Adams**	*Grimshaw*	*Bodin*	*Payne*	*Shaw*
(At Ashton Gate)					Ref: A Seville	Marshall runs Bath ragged in this richly entertaining replay. After David Mogg is adjudged to have tripped Walsh for the spot-kick opener, City go on to a deserved success with Neville side-footing in Marshall's cross, and Owen's shot being deflected into the net off Paul Stevens.											
3 H PLYMOUTH	7	D	1-1	0-0	Riley 56	Waugh	Newman	Williams B	Moyes	MacPhail	Marshall	Riley	Llewellyn	Fitzpatrick	Walsh	Neville	
10/1	16,943 *2:5*				*Summerfield 49*	*Crudgington*	*Nisbet*	*Cooper L*	*Goodyear*	*McElhinney**	*Matthews*	*Hodges*	*Coughlin*	*Tynan*	*Summerfield*	*Nelson*	*Brimacombe*
					Ref: J Martin	Fitzpatrick's fluffed header at the end of a second half of rousing action, deprives City of Cup glory. In front of a crowd which appears to be much larger than the official figure of 16,943, Riley shoots in City's leveller, after Kevin Summerfield's angled drive had put Argyle in front.											
3R A PLYMOUTH	7	L	1-3	0-0	Marshall 108	Waugh	Newman	Williams B	Moyes	MacPhail	Tanner*	Riley	Llewellyn	Fitzpatrick	Walsh	Neville	Marshall
19/1	*14,142 2:5*		aet		*Summerfield 94, Nelson 109, Tynan 118*	*Crudgington*	*Nisbet*	*Uzzell*	*Goodyear*	*McElhinney**	*Matthews^*	*Hodges*	*Coughlin*	*Tynan*	*Summerfield*	*Nelson*	*Bur'ws/Row'm*
					Ref: R Gifford	After Kevin Summerfield's lashed-in opener, Marshall's slammed in atonement for shooting wide from a glorious opportunity in the dying minutes of normal time, is in vain as Waugh's error in allowing a tame Gary Nelson shot to slide under his body puts City out of the Cup.											

		Home						Away					
		P	W	D	L	F	A	W	D	L	F	A	Pts
1	Bournemouth	46	19	3	1	44	14	10	7	6	32	26	97
2	Middlesbro	46	16	5	2	38	11	12	5	6	29	19	94
3	Swindon *	46	14	5	4	37	19	11	7	5	40	28	87
4	Wigan	46	15	5	3	47	26	10	5	8	36	34	85
5	Gillingham	46	16	5	2	42	14	7	4	12	23	34	78
6	BRISTOL CITY	46	14	6	3	42	15	7	8	8	21	21	77
7	Notts Co	46	14	6	3	52	24	7	7	9	25	32	76
8	Walsall	46	16	4	3	50	27	6	5	12	30	40	75
9	Blackpool	46	11	7	5	35	20	5	9	9	39	39	64
10	Mansfield	46	9	9	5	30	23	6	7	10	22	32	61
11	Brentford	46	9	7	7	39	32	6	8	9	25	34	60
12	Port Vale	46	8	6	9	43	36	7	6	10	33	34	57
13	Doncaster	46	11	8	4	32	19	3	7	13	24	43	57
14	Rotherham	46	10	6	7	29	23	5	6	12	19	34	57
15	Chester	46	7	9	7	32	28	6	8	9	29	31	56
16	Bury	46	9	7	7	30	26	5	6	12	24	34	55
17	Chesterfield	46	11	5	7	36	33	2	10	11	20	36	54
18	Fulham	46	8	8	7	35	41	4	9	10	24	36	53
19	Bristol Rov	46	7	8	8	26	29	6	4	13	23	46	51
20	York	46	11	8	4	34	29	1	5	17	21	50	49
21	Bolton **	46	8	5	10	29	26	2	10	11	17	32	45
22	Carlisle	46	7	5	11	26	35	3	3	17	13	43	38
23	Darlington	46	6	10	7	25	28	1	6	16	20	49	37
24	Newport	46	4	9	10	26	34	4	4	15	23	52	37
		1104	260	156	136	859	612	136	156	260	612	859	1500

* promoted after play-offs
** relegated after play-offs

Odds & ends

Double wins: (4) Chesterfield, Carlisle, Chester, Newport.
Double losses: (1) Rotherham.

Won from behind: (3) Swindon (a), Bolton (h), Walsall (h).
Lost from in front: (1) Wigan (a).

High spots: Superb game with Bolton at Ashton Gate on 20 December.
Jordan's debut against Doncaster on 7 February.
Newman's volley against Newport at Ashton Gate on 14 March.
Beating Bristol Rov 3-0 in the Freight Rover Trophy on 16 December.
Reaching Wembley for the second consecutive year.

Low spots: Gary Smart's superb strike that brings Bristol Rov their victory at Ashton Gate on 1 January.
Failure to beat Swindon on 9 May costing City a Play-Off place.
Losing the Freight Rover Trophy Final to Mansfield in the first ever penalty shoot-out at Wembley Stadium.

Player of the year: Rob Newman.
Ever-presents: Keith Waugh.
Hat-tricks: (1) Alan Walsh.
Leading scorer: Alan Walsh (19).

	Appearances						Goals			
	Lge	*Sub*	LC	*Sub*	FAC	*Sub*	Lge	LC	FAC	Tot
Curle, Keith	**24**	*4*	4							
Fitzpatrick, Paul	**18**	*1*	1	*1*	4		**2**			**2**
Galliers, Steve	**9**									
Harle, David	**15**		3		1		**2**			**2**
Hamson, Gary	**12**		3		1		**2**			**2**
Harvey, Jimmy	**2**									
Honor, Chris	**1**	*1*								
Hutchinson, Bobby	**18**	*1*	4		3		**1**		1	**2**
Jordan, Joe	**19**						**3**			**3**
Llewellyn, Andy	**30**	*1*	4		2					
MacPhail, John	**26**				5		**1**			**1**
Marshall, Gary	**18**	*6*		*2*	3	*2*	**2**		2	**4**
Morgan, Trevor	**19**						**7**			**7**
Moyes, David	**41**		4		5		**3**			**3**
Neville, Steve	**19**	*1*	2		4		**8**	1	2	**11**
Newman, Rob	**43**	*2*	2	*1*	5		**6**			**6**
Owen, Gordon	**34**	*1*	4		2		**5**		2	**7**
Riley, Glyn	**22**	*6*	3		3		**1**	1	1	**3**
Rogers, Lee	**3**									
Tanner, Mike	**4**	*1*			1		**1**			**1**
Walsh, Alan	**41**		4		5		**16**	2	1	**19**
Waugh, Keith	**46**		4		5					
Williams, Brian	**41**		2		5		**2**			**2**
Withey, Graham	**1**	*1*		*1*	1					
(own-goals)							**1**			**1**
24 players used	**506**	***26***	**44**	***5***	**55**	***2***	**63**	**4**	**9**	**76**

No	Date		Att	Pos	Pt	F-A	H-T	Scorers, Times, and Referees	1	2	3	4	5	6	7	8	9	10	11	subs used
1	A	MANSFIELD			L	0-2	0-2		Waugh	Llewellyn	**Bromage**	Moyes	Newman	Tanner	Marshall	Fitzpatrick^	**Caldwell***	Walsh	Jordan	**Owen**/Harvey
	15/8		_5,441_		0			_Cassells 9, Stringfellow 20_	_Hitchcock_	_Graham_	_Kearney_	_Lowery_	_Foster_	_Coleman_	_Kent_	_Hodges*_	_Stringfellow_	_Cassells_	_Charles_	_Chambers_
								Ref: J McAuley	City lack the sparkle and pace to live up to their pre-match boast to avenge their Wembley defeat. After Keith Cassells latches onto a through ball to fire the Stags in front, his mis-hit shot catches City's defence flat-footed and Ian Stringfellow is on hand to tuck away an easy chance.											
2	H	PRESTON			W	3-1	1-0	Owen 12, 53, Walsh 49p	Waugh	Llewellyn	Bromage	Moyes	Newman	Tanner	Marshall	Fitzpatrick	Owen	Walsh	Jordan	
	22/8		7,655		3			_Brazil 82_	_Brown_	_Branagan^_	_Bennett_	_Atkins_	_Jones_	_Allardyce_	_Miller_	_Swann_	_Lowery_	_Brazil_	_Rathbone*_	_Worth'gton/Wrightson_
								Ref: D Vickers	Owen's skill tears North End apart after an early slice of luck when his free-kick is cruelly deflected past David Brown. Jordan's exquisite pass sets up Walsh's pen after Fitzpatrick is sent sprawling, but failure of City's notorious offside trap allows Gary Brazil to head in for Preston.											
3	A	BRENTFORD		7	W	2-0	0-0	Newman 60p, Owen 85	Waugh	Llewellyn	Bromage	Moyes	Newman	Tanner	Neville	Fitzpatrick	Owen	Walsh	Jordan	
	29/8		_4,328_	_21_	6				_Phillips_	_Joseph_	_Murray_	_Millen_	_Lee_	_Feeley_	_Smith_	_Sinton_	_Cooke_	_Blissett_	_Carroll*_	_Perryman_
								Ref: H King	The result is better than the performance, but at least City improve on their dreadfully boring first-half display. Neville's clip by Colin Lee allows Newman to send Gary Phillips the wrong way from the spot, before Owen side-foot's in Llewellyn's low cross to make victory secure.											
4	H	PORT VALE		3	W	1-0	0-0	Neville 89	Waugh	Llewellyn	Bromage	Moyes	Newman	Tanner	Marshall^	Fitzpatrick	Owen	Walsh*	Jordan	Neville/Caldwell
	31/8		8,716	_13_	9				_Williams_	_Webb_	_Pearson_	_Banks*_	_Hazell_	_Sproson_	_Maguire_	_Earle_	_Jones_	_Beckford_	_Hamson^_	_Finney/Hooper_
								Ref: P Don	Whilst Vale dominate the proceedings like last year, Andy Jones' 39th-minute header against the bar is the nearest they come to gaining any reward. Neville capitalises on Bob Hazell's one mistake to volley in City's late steal past Alex Williams from the edge of the penalty area.											
5	A	BURY		4	D	1-1	1-1	Neville 32	Waugh	Llewellyn	Bromage	Moyes	Newman	Tanner	Neville	Fitzpatrick	Caldwell	Walsh	Jordan	
	5/9		_2,376_	_9_	10			_Hoyland 10_	_Hughes_	_Hill_	_Pashley_	_Hoyland_	_Valentine_	_Hart_	_Lee^_	_Greenwood*_	_Taylor_	_McIlroy_	_Brotherston_	_Colville/Higgins_
								Ref: F Roberts	City are on the rack until Jordan's class turn and pass sets-up Neville to shoot a leveller past Phil Hughes. Unfortunately Jordan heads wide in front of an open goal on 75 minutes, and Bury hang onto a point gained by Jamie Hoyland's 25-yard opener that took a deflection off Newman.											
6	H	BRISTOL ROV		7	D	3-3	1-1	Walsh 38, Fitzpatrick 65, Moyes 73	Waugh	Llewellyn	Bromage	Moyes	Newman	**Galliers**	Marshall	Fitzpatrick	Neville	Walsh	Jordan	
	12/9		14,746	_14_	11			_Jones 9, Reece 58, Holloway 83_	_Carter_	_Alexander_	_Tanner_	_Hibbitt_	_Twentyman_	_Jones_	_Holloway_	_Reece_	_White_	_Penrice_	_Purnell_	
								Ref: K Barratt	Six of the best in a derby-day spectacular as City have cause to rue three other efforts that are disallowed. Vaughan Jones shoots Rovers ahead from a free-kick, but Marshall's right-wing scamper and perfect cross sets up Walsh to head in City's impressive equaliser at the far post.											
7	A	WALSALL		7	D	1-1	0-0	Llewellyn 81	Waugh	Llewellyn	Bromage	Moyes	Newman	Galliers	Owen	Fitzpatrick	Neville	Walsh	Jordan	
	15/9		_6,425_	_3_	12			_Kelly 86_	_Barber_	_Dornan_	_Taylor_	_Shakespeare_	_Forbes_	_Hart_	_Goodwin_	_Cross_	_Kelly_	_Christie_	_Jones P_	
								Ref: H Taylor	City should have been able to hold onto the lead that Llewellyn gives them with a spectacular 35-yard left-foot shot that dips perfectly into the top corner of Fred Barber's net. Unfortunately David Kelly whips inside of Bromage to notch Walsall's leveller with a superb low cross-shot.											
8	A	NOTTS CO		5	W	1-0	0-0	Newman 63p	Waugh	Llewellyn	Bromage	Moyes	Newman	Galliers	Owen	Fitzpatrick	Neville	Walsh	Jordan	
	19/9		_5,705_	_3_	15				_Leonard_	_Smalley_	_Fairclough_	_Kevan_	_Yates_	_Hart_	_Mills_	_McParland_	_Birtles_	_Pike_	_Lund*_	_Thompson_
								Ref: M Bailey	City have to thank their defence for a determined performance at Meadow Lane to keep Notts at bay. Newman's penalty clinches the points, following Paul Hart's curtailment of Owen's scamper through County's rearguard, and thereafter City have much the better of the contest.											
9	H	GILLINGHAM		6	D	3-3	1-2	Owen 27, 66, Fitzpatrick 60	Waugh	Llewellyn	Bromage	Moyes	Newman	Galliers	Neville	Fitzpatrick	Owen	Walsh	Jordan*	Caldwell
	26/9		10,080	_5_	16			_Lovell 9, Smith 14, Elsey 61_	_Kite_	_Haylock_	_Pearce_	_Quow_	_West_	_Greenall_	_Pritchard_	_Shearer^_	_Lovell*_	_Elsey !_	_Smith D_	_Berry/Eves_
								Ref: P Wright	Karl Elsey's header is the best goal of this exciting game, but shortly after he was sent off for a minor brush with Fitzpatrick. The Gills hang on for a deserved point when Neville smashes the rebound against a post after Newman blasts a controversial 80th-min pen straight at Phil Kite.											
10	H	CHESTERFIELD		1	W	2-1	1-0	Owen 39, Newman 63	Waugh	Llewellyn	Bromage	Moyes	Newman	Galliers	Neville	Fitzpatrick	Owen*	Walsh	Jordan	Caldwell
	29/9		9,080	_16_	19			_Waller 65_	_Muggleton_	_Rogers_	_Henderson_	_Bradshaw_	_Benjamin_	_Wood_	_Coyle_	_Reid_	_Waller_	_Caldwell_	_Bloomer_	
								Ref: K Burge	With Walsh ripping Chesterfield to shreds it looked as though the visitors might be heading for a repeat of their recent 0-10 humiliation at Gillingham. Chances are scorned however and City have to be satisfied that Owen's blaster and Newman volley's take them top of the table.											
11	A	NORTHAMPTON		5	L	0-3	0-1		Waugh	Llewellyn	Bromage	Moyes	Newman	Galliers !	Neville	Fitzpatrick !	Owen^	Walsh	Jordan*	Marshall/Caldwell
	3/10		_6,234_	_1_	19			_Chard 6, 59, Bunce 77_	_Gleasure_	_Reed_	_Logan_	_Chard_	_Wilcox_	_McPherson_	_Bunce_	_Benjamin_	_Gilbert_	_Morley_	_McGoldrick_	
								Ref: K Morton	Whilst Fitzpatrick is unlucky to be sent off in the 62nd min for his mistimed tackle, the same cannot be said for Galliers nine mins earlier who argues with the ref. Phil Chard seals City's fate with a header that has Waugh well beaten, after earlier registering with a 20-yard free-kick.											

No	Venue	Opponent / Date	Att	Pos	Pts	F-A	H-T	Scorers, Times, and Referees	1	2	3	4	5	6	7	8	9	10	11	subs used
12	H	SOUTHEND		3	W	3-2	1-1	Newman 40p, 87, Fitzpatrick 66	Waugh	Curle	Bromage	Moyes	Newman	Galliers	Marshall*	Fitzpatrick	Owen	Walsh^	Jordan	Neville/Llewellyn
		10/10	8,606	*23*	22			*Robinson 36, McDonough 47*	*Steele*	*Martin*	*Johnson*	*Burrows*	*Westley*	*Hall*	*Robinson*	*Pennyfather*	*Nogan*	*McDonough*	*Ling*	
								Ref: P Danson	Cooper's instructions for Newman to move forward for the last seven minutes pays off as he drills in a narrow angled 15-yarder to defeat an impressive Southend side. A good day for Newman as David Martin's trip on Moyes allowed him to shoot in City's earlier spot-kick leveller.											
13	A	GRIMSBY		3	W	4-1	4-0	Newman 3, 27, Neville 39, Jordan 40	Waugh	Llewellyn	Bromage	Moyes	Newman	Tanner	Marshall*	Curle	Owen	Neville	Jordan	Walsh
		17/10	*3,100*	*17*	25			*McGarvey 80*	*Sherwood*	*Toale*	*Agnew*	*Turner*	*Slack*	*Burgess*	*Watson*	*Robinson*	*Walsh**	*O'Riordan*	*McGarvey*	*Grocock*
								Ref: E Parker	Jordan's diving header caps City's most clinical display of finishing in a long time, as well as bringing to end the leanest spell of his illustrious career. After going ahead when Newman's mis-hit shot from ten yards finds the corner of the net, City's movement off the ball is a revelation.											
14	H	SUNDERLAND		6	L	0-1	0-1		Waugh	Llewellyn	Bromage	Moyes	Newman	Galliers^	Neville	Curle	Owen	Walsh*	Jordan	Caldwell/Tanner
		20/10	15,387	*1*	25			*Owers 1*	*Hesford*	*Kay*	*Agboola*	*Corner*	*MacPhail*	*Owers*	*Cornforth**	*Doyle*	*Gates*	*Gabbiadini*	*Atkinson^*	*Lemon/Gray*
								Ref: M Reed	On his return to Ashton Gate, John MacPhail gives an almost faultless performance in the heart of the Sunderland defence. He contributes to a superb defensive display that deservedly takes the Rokerites to the top of the table, thanks to Gary Owers putting away a rebound off Waugh.											
15	A	ROTHERHAM		6	L	**1-4**	1-3	Caldwell 14	Waugh	Llewellyn	Bromage	Moyes	Newman	**Humphries**	Tanner^	Fitzpatrick*	Owen	Caldwell	Jordan	Walsh/Honor
		24/10	*3,397*	*15*	25			*Humphries 1 (og), Airey 20, 85, Evans 30*	*O'Hanlon*	*Douglas*	*Scott*	*Grealish**	*Dungworth*	*Green*	*Pugh*	*Williams*	*Evans*	*Airey*	*Campbell*	*Haycock*
								Ref: J Rushton	Humphries has a nightmare City debut, stooping to head a Colin Douglas cross into his own goal after just 38 seconds. Caldwell's first-time shot from Tanner's chip brings City level, but United ruthlessly exploit aerial weakness, where Moyes is no match for the powerful Carl Airey.											
16	A	BLACKPOOL		8	L	2-4	1-1	Shutt 21, 51	Waugh	Newman	Bromage	Humphries	**Pender !**	Galliers	Owen	Fitzpatrick	**Shutt**	Marshall	Jordan	
		3/11	*3,140*	*13*	25			*Morgan 1, Taylor 59, Madden 88, 90p*	*Siddall*	*Davies**	*Morgan*	*Bradshaw*	*Methven*	*Deary*	*Cunningham*	*Madden*	*Walwyn*	*McAteer*	*Taylor*	*Lancashire*
								Ref: K Redfern	A pulsating, rough and tumble match is ultimately decided by Pender's 87th-minute sending off for hauling back Mark Taylor. After Steve Morgan gets the match off to a dramatic start by shooting in from 25 yards after just 76 seconds, Shutt marks his debut by heading City level.											
17	A	ALDERSHOT		14	L	1-2	0-1	Shutt 68	**Prudhoe**	Llewellyn	Bromage	Humphries	Pender	Galliers	Owen	Newman	Shutt	Marshall*	Neville	Walsh
		7/11	*4,324*	*18*	25			*Langley 30, Berry 90*	*Coles*	*Berry*	*Phillips*	*Roberts*	*Anderson*	*Wignall*	*Ring**	*Langley*	*Johnson*	*McDonald*	*Burvill*	*Riley*
								Ref: P Foakes	City might be thought unlucky to lose in injury-time for the second successive game, but they are their own worst enemies. They miss enough chances (ten on target efforts compared to three for the Shots) to have won at a canter, whilst a poor back-pass gifts Tommy Langley his goal.											
18	H	CHESTER		12	D	2-2	1-2	Newman 44, Shutt 68	Prudhoe	Llewellyn	Bromage	Humphries	Newman	Galliers	Owen*	Fitzpatrick	Shutt	Neville	Marshall	Jordan
		21/11	8,103	*10*	26			*Rimmer 23p, 38*	*Stowell*	*Greenough*	*Woodthorpe*	*Fazackerley*	*Lundon*	*Abel*	*Maddy*	*Barrow*	*Rimmer*	*Bennett*	*Croft**	*Painter*
								Ref: J Moules	Ricky Greenough's foul on Bromage sparks City's revival as Newman follows up his penalty, which Mike Stowell tips onto the post, to tap-in the rebound. Shutt's superb header brings City level, then he has a shot kicked off the line, before a late Neville header almost brings victory.											
19	A	WIGAN		13	D	1-1	1-0	Walsh 20	Prudhoe	Llewellyn	Bromage	Humphries	Pender	Galliers	Newman	Fitzpatrick	Shutt	Walsh	Jordan	
		28/11	*2,879*	*9*	27			*Holden 49*	*Hughes*	*Butler*	*Knowles*	*Hamilton*	*Beesley*	*Holden*	*Senior*	*Pilling*	*Campbell*	*Jewell**	*Cook*	*Ainscow*
								Ref: J Watson	Jordan celebrates his first game as assistant boss by helping City regain lost pride following their abject display in the 1-3 Freight Rover defeat at Wolves. Walsh's header rewards City's early dominance, but their defence has to show its mettle after Andy Holden's lashed-in leveller.											
20	H	YORK		12	W	3-2	2-1	Galliers 8, 47, Fitzpatrick 32	Waugh	Honor	Newman	Humphries	Pender	Galliers	Owen	Fitzpatrick	Shutt	Walsh*	Neville	Jordan
		12/12	6,235	*24*	30			*Banton 9, 63*	*Smallwood*	*Hood^*	*Johnson*	*Wilson*	*Whitehead*	*Tuthill**	*Mills*	*Bradshaw*	*Helliwell*	*Banton*	*Canham*	*Himsworth/Clegg*
								Ref: G Ashby	Galliers answers his critics by picking his spot to put City ahead, and then netting what proves to be the winner with a tame shot that slides under the keeper's body. City are hard pressed in the closing stages after hesitant defending had allowed Dale Banton to shoot past Waugh.											
21	H	FULHAM		6	W	**4-0**	3-0	Shutt 28, 31, 38, 81	Waugh	Honor !	Newman	Humphries	Pender	Galliers	Owen	Fitzpatrick*	Shutt	Walsh	Neville	Llewellyn
		15/12	**6,150**	*5*	33				*Stannard*	*Langley*	*Thomas*	*Lewington*	*Eckhardt*	*Hicks*	*Skinner**	*Wilson*	*Rosenior*	*Davies*	*Walker !*	*Pike*
								Ref: P Vanes	Honor has the sympathy after a 50th-minute fracas with Clive Walker results in them both being sent off, but Shutt has the glory. After his ten minute hat-trick, he side-foots a rebound past a grounded Jim Stannard to become the first City player in ten years to net four goals in a game.											
22	A	DONCASTER		5	W	2-1	1-1	Walsh 32, Shutt 82	Waugh	Honor	Newman	Humphries	Pender	Galliers	Tanner	Fitzpatrick*	Shutt	Walsh	Neville	Llewellyn
		19/12	*1,819*	*23*	36			*Deane 10*	*Rhodes*	*Stead*	*Miller*	*Raffell*	*Burke**	*Brannigan*	*James*	*Kinsella*	*Deane^*	*Turnbull*	*Kimble*	*Flynn/Chamberlain*
								Ref: N Midgley	Under new boss Dave Mackay, Doncaster hold the early initiative as Brian Deane heads in Garry Kimble's cross and Lee Turnbull rattles the bar, before Walsh's stunning volley gets City into the game. Shutt slams in the winner after Pender's point-blank header is blocked on the line.											
23	A	GILLINGHAM		5	D	1-1	1-0	Newman 23p	Waugh	Honor	Newman	Humphries	Pender	Galliers	Fitzpatrick	Tanner^	Shutt	Walsh	Neville*	Jordan/Llewellyn
		26/12	*6,261*	*11*	37			*Smith 54*	*Kite*	*Haylock*	*Pearce*	*Peacock*	*West*	*Greenall*	*Pritchard*	*Eves**	*Lovell^*	*Elsey*	*Smith D*	*Weatherly/Cooper*
								Ref: D Vickers	After Phil Kite concedes a pen for his foul on Shutt, Newman fools the keeper with a side-footed spot-kick rather than his normal blaster. Dave Smith's leveller is the highlight of a lively game, an unstoppable 25-yarder into the roof of City's net from Gavin Peacock's tapped free-kick.											

No	Date		Att	Pos	Pt	F-A	H-T	Scorers, Times, and Referees	1	2	3	4	5	6	7	8	9	10	11	subs used
24	H	BRIGHTON		4	W	5-2	3-0	P'der 20, N'man 31, Fitzpr'k 42, Walsh 82	Waugh	Honor*	Newman	Humphries	Pender	Galliers	Marshall^	Fitzpatrick	Shutt	Walsh	Neville	Llewellyn/Jordan
	28/12		16,058	*5*	40			*Nelson 53, Wood 76* [Jordan 89]	*Keeley*	*Brown*	*Dublin*	*Jasper*	*Rougvie*	*Gatting*	*Nelson*	*Trusson*	*Bremner*	*Wilkins*	*Wood*	
								Ref: K Burge	Superb entertainment as City end Brighton's unbeaten 17-match run. Walsh, who starts the rout with a pinpoint free-kick to set-up Pender's headed opener, kills off Brighton's fight-back with a stunning shot from 25 yards, before producing a perfect cross for Jordan's late header.											
25	H	BRENTFORD		7	L	2-3	0-3	Shutt 53, Galliers 65	Waugh	Llewellyn	Newman	Humphries	Pender	Galliers	Marshall*	Tanner	Shutt	Walsh	Neville	Jordan
	1/1		12,877	*6*	40			*Blissett 19, 20, Sinton 39*	*Phillips*	*Joseph*	*Stanislaus*	*Millen*	*Evans*	*Jones**	*Turner*	*Sinton*	*Birch*	*Blissett*	*Rix*	*Perryman*
								Ref: J Deakin	The Brentford jinx strikes as Boss Cooper is announced as Bell's Manager of the Month for December. Yet again away success over the Bees is not matched by victory at Ashton Gate, where the highlight of City's spirited second-half display is a crisp volley from the inspired Galliers.											
26	A	PRESTON		8	L	0-2	0-1		Waugh	Llewellyn	Bromage	Humphries	**Mardon**	Galliers	**Hawkins***	Newman	Shutt	Walsh	Neville^	Tanner/Jordan
	9/1		*5,729*	*19*	40			*Rathbone 8, Brazil 62*	*Brown*	*Rathbone**	*Bennett*	*Atkins*	*Chapman*	*Allardyce*	*Mooney*	*Swann*	*Ellis*	*Brazil*	*Joyce*	*Miller*
								Ref: T Simpson	On Preston's artificial pitch City soon find themselves behind when Waugh badly misjudges Mick Rathbone's free-kick. Despite the advantage of a strong wind after the break, Gary Brazil's side-foot into the corner of the net from twelve yards leaves City a well-beaten side at the finish.											
27	H	NOTTS CO		8	W	2-1	0-1	Walsh 57, Jordan 76	Waugh	Honor	Bromage	Mardon^	Pender	Galliers	Marshall*	Newman	Shutt	Walsh	Neville	Jordan/Llewellyn
	16/1		9,558	*2*	43			*Lund 12*	*Leonard*	*Smalley*	*Withe*	*Kevan*	*Yates*	*Birtles*	*Mills^*	*McParland*	*Lund*	*Pike**	*Thorpe*	*Fairclough/Barnes*
								Ref: P Durkin	Jordan's diving header ends County's twelve match unbeaten run after City had been outplayed in the first half. A linesman's flag denies Newman a 20th-min volleyed equaliser to Gary Lund's stroked-in opener, but Walsh eventually levels after the break with a rare headed goal.											
28	H	BURY		8	W	3-2	0-1	Galliers 51, Milne 56, Walsh 74	Vaughan	Honor	Bromage	Mardon	Pender	Galliers	**Milne**	Newman	Shutt	Walsh	Neville	
	6/2		9,158	*10*	46			*Valentine 12, Hoyland 57*	*Farnworth*	*Hill*	*Pashley*	*Hoyland*	*Valentine**	*Higgins*	*Lee^*	*Robinson*	*Taylor*	*Fairbrother*	*Bishop*	*Hart/Greenwood*
								Ref: M Bodenham	Milne's arrogant side-foot volley is candidate for goal of the season as City turn on the style after their dismal first-half showing. Enterprising Bury are a yard quicker than the City before the interval and thoroughly deserving of Peter Valentine's looping header that puts them in front.											
29	H	WALSALL		7	D	0-0	0-0		Vaughan	Llewellyn	Bromage	Mardon	Pender	Galliers*	Milne	Newman	Shutt	Walsh	Neville^	Honor/Caldwell
	9/2		8,545	*3*	47				*Barber*	*Jones M*	*Mower*	*Shakespeare*	*Forbes*	*Hart*	*Jones P*	*Goodwin*	*Christie**	*Kelly*	*Naughton*	*O'Kelly*
								Ref: D Reeves	The gale force wind ruins this encounter with gusts ripping sheeting off the Dolman Stand and bending the corner flags double. City have nine shots on target, whilst Walsall manage just one, but the nearest to a goal is Shutt's early drive which Craig Shakespeare clears off the line.											
30	A	BRIGHTON		7	L	2-3	0-1	Walsh 65, Caldwell 82	Vaughan	Llewellyn	Bromage	Mardon	Pender	Honor	Milne	Newman	Shutt*	Walsh	Neville	Caldwell
	13/2		*8,782*	*5*	47			*Nelson 7, 55, Rougvie 54*	*Keeley*	*Brown*	*Dublin*	*Curbishley*	*Rougvie*	*Gatting*	*Nelson*	*Trusson*	*Bremner*	*Wilkins*	*Crumplin*	
								Ref: J Carter	Battling bravely against the driving wind and rain to keep the half-time deficit to Gary Nelson's volley, City allow Albion to blast in a quick double just after the break. Walsh shoots in from Newman's pass to inspire a fight-back, but more is needed than Caldwell's side-footed effort.											
31	H	MANSFIELD		8	L	1-2	1-2	Foster 36 (og)	Waugh	Honor	Bromage	Mardon	Pender	**McClaren**	Milne	Newman	Caldwell	Walsh	Neville*	Marshall
	20/2		9,528	*16*	47			*Kent 3, Graham 29*	*Hitchcock*	*Graham*	*Ryan*	*Lowery**	*Foster*	*Coleman*	*Owen*	*Kenworthy*	*Kent*	*Cassells*	*Charles*	*Garner*
								Ref: J Lloyd	Don't despair! Steve McClaren (£50,000 ex Derby) has the class to put City back in the promotion race according to Norman Hunter. In this game though, their defence errs to let Kevin Kent shoot into an open net and then allowing Mike Graham to tap in from Waugh's palm out.											
32	H	NORTHAMPTON		9	D	2-2	1-2	Walsh 13, Reed 85 (og)	Waugh	Llewellyn	Honor	Humphries	Pender	McClaren	Milne	Newman	Caldwell	Walsh	Neville*	Marshall
	27/2		8,578	*6*	48			*Adcock 38, Chard 42*	*Gleasure*	*Reed*	*Wilson*	*Donald*	*Wilcox*	*Slack*	*Singleton*	*Longhurst**	*Gilbert*	*Adcock*	*Chard*	*McGoldrick*
								Ref: R Wiseman	McClaren comments that he has never seen four more weirder goals than those conceded by City in this game and last week against Mansfield. Tony Adcock prods in Northampton's first when Llewellyn fails to clear, then City's defence is all at sea as Phil Chard heads in the second.											
33	A	CHESTERFIELD		8	W	4-1	2-1	Milne 15, Caldwell 27, Walsh 63,	Waugh	Llewellyn	Honor	Humphries	Pender	McClaren	Milne	Newman	Caldwell	Walsh	Galliers	
	1/3		***1,657***	*19*	51			*Phillips 35* [Pender 68]	*Brown J*	*Rogers*	*McGeeney*	*Wood*	*Benjamin*	*Hunter*	*Coyle*	*Phillips*	*Waller**	*Arnott*	*Eley^*	*Morris/Bloomer*
								Ref: P Harrison	Galliers returns from suspension to breathe new life into City's promotion challenge. Milne's fine low shot gets City off to a good start, and then Caldwell side-foots in a low cross, before Steve Phillips turns in a rebound after Waugh had pushed Les Hunter's header against a post.											
34	H	GRIMSBY		8	D	1-1	0-0	Walsh 76	Waugh	Llewellyn	Newman	Humphries	Pender	McClaren	Milne	Shutt*	Caldwell	Walsh	Galliers^	Neville/Honor
	5/3		8,343	*21*	52			*O'Riordan 65*	*Sherwood*	*Dixon*	*Agnew*	*Cunnington*	*Burgess*	*Jobling*	*Robinson*	*Saunders**	*North^*	*O'Riordan*	*McGarvey*	*McDermott/Stubbs*
								Ref: M James	City's fourth successive home match without a victory makes nonsense of promotion talk. It's sheer torture for the fans who bear witness to lethargic City's worst display of the season, their only consolation being Walsh's superbly struck equaliser to Don O'Riordan's headed opener.											

No Date		Opponent Att	Pos	Res Pts	F-A	H-T	Scorers, Times, and Referees	1	2	3	4	5	6	7	8	9	10	11	subs used
35	A	SOUTHEND	8	L	0-2	0-1		Waugh	Llewellyn	Newman	Humphries	Pender	McClaren	Milne*	Galliers	Caldwell	Honor	Neville^	Marshall/Fitzpatrick
11/3		3,562	22	52			*Crown 24, Westley 49*	*Steele*	*O'Shea*	*Johnson*	*Westley*	*Martin*	*Butler*	*Brush*	*Hall*	*Crown*	*McDonough**	*Neal*	*Ling*
							Ref: D Hedges	Southend, who have only kept one clean sheet in home in the League this season, hardly come under threat, as David Crown's shot on the turn, and Shane Westley's header bring them easy success. Newman's vicious half-volley ten minutes from time is City's only worthwhile attempt.											
36	A	FULHAM	8	D	0-0	0-0		Waugh	Llewellyn	Honor	Mardon	Pender	McClaren	Milne	Galliers	Fitzpatrick	Walsh*	Neville	Caldwell
19/3		4,896	11	53				*Stannard*	*Eckhardt*	*Elkins*	*Skinner*	*Oakes*	*Hopkins*	*Barnett^*	*Scott*	*Marshall*	*Achampong*	*Walker**	*Hoddy/Gore*
							Ref: V Callow	With Joe Jordan replacing Terry Cooper as manager following Tuesday night's 3-1 Gloucestershire Cup success, City manage their first clean sheet in seven League games. City demonstrate plenty of commitment, but lack the cutting edge to take advantage of a weakened Fulham side.											
37	H	ROTHERHAM	7	W	2-0	0-0	Gordon 57p, Neville 89	Waugh	Llewellyn	Honor	Humphries	Pender	McClaren	Milne	Galliers	**Gordon***	Walsh	Neville	Marshall
26/3		7,517	18	56				*Crichton*	*Douglas*	*Crosby*	*Grealish*	*Johnson !*	*Green*	*Buckley*	*Pepper*	*Wylde**	*Haycock*	*Dungworth^*	*Airey/Mendonca*
							Ref: P Foakes	Nigel Johnson's miserable afternoon culminates in his being sent off for felling McClaren, after earlier tripping Neville to concede Gordon's spot-kick. Neville ends his 23-week goal drought, and seals City's deserved success, by racing clear to blast a fierce shot past Paul Crichton.											
38	H	ALDERSHOT	7	W	2-0	1-0	Milne 38, Walsh 85	Waugh	Llewellyn	Newman	Humphries	Pender	McClaren	Milne*	Galliers	Gordon^	Walsh	Neville	Bromage/Shutt
2/4		8,712	19	59				*Lange*	*Berry*	*Barnes D*	*Joseph*	*Smith*	*Wignall*	*Bedford*	*Langley*	*Riley*	*Ring**	*Burvill*	*Anderson*
							Ref: J Moules	Walsh's speculative hook-shot into the top corner lends some sanity to the scoreline after City had been frustrated by their own poor finishing and Aldershot's offside tactics. Milne spurned two good chances before driving in a 20-yard opener after Lange pushed out Neville's shot.											
39	A	CHESTER	7	L	0-1	0-1		Waugh	Llewellyn	Newman	Humphries	Pender	McClaren	Milne	Galliers !	Gordon	Walsh	Neville*	Shutt
4/4		2,858	15	59			*Bennett 7*	*Stewart*	*Butler*	*Lundon*	*Fazakerley*	*Abel*	*Lightfoot*	*Lowey*	*Barrow*	*Bennett*	*Croft*	*Graham*	
							Ref: J Penrose	City's ill discipline and their unreliable offside trap seriously damage play-off aspirations. Their defence is in disarray early on when McClaren trips Milton Graham as he cuts into the area, then eight minutes from time Galliers is sent off following his protests over a blocked free-kick.											
40	H	BLACKPOOL	7	W	2-1	1-0	McClaren 25, Gordon 66p	Waugh	Llewellyn	Newman	Humphries	Pender	McClaren	Milne	Galliers	Gordon	Walsh	Neville	
9/4		6,460	12	62			*Taylor 50*	*Siddall*	*Matthews*	*Morgan**	*Coughlin*	*Methven*	*Walsh*	*Deary*	*Rooney*	*Walwyn*	*Cunningham*	*Taylor^*	*Bradshaw/Madden*
							Ref: I Hemley	McClaren stars in City's midfield, much like old favourite Bobby Etheridge whose death at the age of 54 was announced this week. After Neville is thrice denied by Barry Siddall's point-blank saves, City's early frustration is relieved as McClaren's shot finds the back of the net.											
41	A	BRISTOL ROV	7	L	0-1	0-0		Waugh	Llewellyn	Newman	Humphries	Pender	McClaren	Milne*	Galliers	Gordon	Walsh	Neville	Jordan
12/4		5,947	14	62			*Penrice 48*	*Martyn*	*Alexander*	*Twentyman*	*Clark*	*Mehew*	*Jones*	*Holloway*	*Reece*	*White*	*Penrice*	*Purnell*	
							Ref: R Groves	After a first half dominated by City's greater individual class, the Rovers better teamwork receives its reward after the break. Gary Penrice settles this derby with a coolly-taken shot in the heat of a goalmouth scramble, but is later unlucky to have a 20-yard side-foot effort struck-off.											
42	A	PORT VALE	8	D	1-1	0-0	Newman 80	Waugh	Llewellyn	Bromage	Humphries	Mardon	McClaren	Milne	Neville	Gordon*	Walsh	Newman	Shutt
18/4		2,671	11	63			*Mills 57*	*Grew*	*Webb*	*Hughes*	*Walker*	*Hazell*	*Sproson*	*Ford*	*Earle*	*Riley*	*Beckford*	*Mills*	
							Ref: T Mills	A ding-dong struggle, in which Llewellyn twice clears off the line, while McClaren's shot is rebuffed by a post, ends all square. Simon Mills' opening shot takes a wicked deflection, but Newman celebrates being captain for the first time by heading in City's deserved equaliser.											
43	A	SUNDERLAND	8	W	1-0	1-0	Gordon 18	Waugh	Llewellyn	Newman	Humphries	Pender	McClaren	Milne	Galliers	Gordon*	Walsh	Neville^	Shutt/Bromage
23/4		**18,225**	1	66				*Carter*	*Hardwick*	*Gray*	*Ord*	*MacPhail*	*Owers*	*Lemon*	*Pascoe*	*Gates**	*Gabbiadini*	*Armstrong^*	*Bertschin/Doyle*
							Ref: D Shaw	Jackie Milburn rates City's defensive display at Roker Park to be the best he has ever seen. Apart from breakaways it's all hands to the pumps – Llewellyn twice kicking off the line – as City hang onto to the advantage gained by Gordon's stoop to head in from Milne's cross.											
44	H	WIGAN	7	W	4-1	2-1	Neville 13, Galliers 43, Marshall 70, [Jordan 75]	Waugh	Llewellyn	Bromage	Newman	Pender	McClaren	Milne	Galliers	Shutt	Walsh^	Neville*	Jordan/Marshall
30/4		7,340	6	69			*Jewell 30*	*Hughes*	*Senior^*	*Knowles*	*Hamilton*	*McEwan*	*Beesley*	*Thompson D*	*Thompson C**	*Piling*	*Jewell*	*Butler*	*Cook/Campbell*
							Ref: D Elleray	With victory vital to both sides City dramatically revive their play-off prospects by taking their chances in an entertaining game, whilst Wigan waste theirs. Following Paul Jewell's headed equaliser, Galliers runs from the halfway-line and restores City's lead with a delightful chip.											
45	A	YORK	6	W	1-0	0-0	Milne 87	Waugh	Llewellyn	Bromage	Newman	Pender	McClaren	Milne	Galliers	Shutt*	Marshall	Neville^	Jordan/Fitzpatrick
2/5		2,620	24	72				*Endersby*	*McMillan*	*Johnson*	*Clegg*	*Tutill*	*McKenzie*	*Howlett*	*Bradshaw*	*Helliwell*	*Staniforth*	*Himsworth*	
							Ref: C Trussell	Milne's exquisite late chip rewards City's commitment in a game where they have enough chances to have won many times over. Marshall's 16th-minute header hits both crossbar and post, whilst offside rules out Neville's shot and Shutt fires over an open net from just four yards.											
46	H	DONCASTER	5	W	1-0	0-0	Gordon 79	Waugh	Llewellyn	Newman	Humphries	Pender	McClaren	Milne	Galliers	Gordon	Walsh	Neville*	Jordan
7/5		**18,373**	24	75				*Samways*	*Miller*	*Brevett*	*Robinson L*	*Robinson R*	*Raffell*	*Kinsella^*	*Turnbull*	*Deane*	*Chamberlain*	*Kimble**	*Rankine/Holmes*
Home Average 9,818		Away 4,886					Ref: P Vanes	The nerves are jangling for players and fans alike at Ashton Gate, where City eventually clinch a play-off place after Gordon has his 62nd-minute penalty saved by Mark Samways. Gordon makes amends by shooting into an empty net after his lunge robs Samways of the ball.											

Littlewoods Cup

Littlewoods Cup			F-A	H-T	Scorers, Times, and Referees	1	2	3	4	5	6	7	8	9	10	11	subs used
1:1 A SWINDON		L	0-3	0-0		Waugh	Llewellyn	Bromage	Moyes	Newman	Tanner	Marshall*	Fitzpatrick	Owen !	Walsh	Jordan	Neville
18/8	*6,807*				*Quinn 65, 68, 85*	*Digby*	*O'Regan*	*King*	*Kamara*	*Parkin*	*Calderwood*	*Kelly*	*Gittens**	*Quinn*	*Bamber*	*Barnard*	*Henry*
					Ref: A Buksh	City earn the first-half applause for their quality football, but fail to capitalise as they are twice thwarted by the woodwork. After the break Owen's dismissal is soon followed by Town's opener as Jimmy Quinn makes up for blazing a spot-kick over the bar with a close-range shot.											
1:2 H SWINDON		W	3-2	3-1	Owen 9, 12, Tanner 26	Waugh	Llewellyn	Bromage	Moyes	Newman	Tanner	Marshall^	Fitzpatrick	Owen	Walsh	Jordan*	Neville/Caldwell
25/8	7,013				*Bamber 25, Berry 54p*	*Digby*	*O'Regan*	*King*	*Kamara*	*Parkin*	*Calderwood*	*Coyne**	*Berry*	*Quinn*	*Bamber*	*Barnard*	*Henry*
					Ref: K Cooper (City lost 3-5 on aggregate)	Fraser Digby's 19th-minute save from Walsh's spot-kick concludes a brilliant opening spell in which Swindon are torn apart. The bar keeps out an early Moyes effort before Owen registers with a header and a 25-yarder before he is also denied by the woodwork in the 18th minute.											

FA Cup

FA Cup			F-A	H-T	Scorers, Times, and Referees	1	2	3	4	5	6	7	8	9	10	11	subs used
1 H AYLESBURY UTD	14	W	1-0	0-0	Caldwell 62	**Coombe**	Llewellyn	Bromage	Humphries	Pender	Galliers	Owen	Newman	Shutt	Walsh*	Caldwell	Marshall
14/11	8,263 *BHLP*					*Garner*	*Robinson*	*James*	*Hackett*	*Hutter*	*Botterill*	*McBean**	*Duggan*	*Hercules*	*Phillips*	*Harthill*	*Davie*
					Ref: D Hutchinson	Aylesbury, missing two key players through suspension, embarrass City without quite having the ability to pull off a shock victory. Peter McBean and Cliff Hercules both squander open-goal opportunities, before Caldwell heads in City's winner from Owen's perfect far-post cross.											
2 H TORQUAY	13	L	0-1	0-0		Waugh	Honor	Bromage	Humphries	Pender	Galliers	Fitzpatrick*	Newman	Shutt	Walsh	Jordan^	Marshall/Neville
5/12	9,027 *4:4*				*Caldwell 85*	*Allen*	*McNichol*	*Pearce*	*Haslegrave*	*Cole*	*Impey*	*Dawkins*	*Lloyd*	*Caldwell*	*Loram*	*Dobson*	
					Ref: K Barratt	Following Wednesday's success in beating the Rovers in the delayed 1986-87 Gloucestershire Cup Final, City find Torquay a much tougher proposition. The fans chant for Cooper's head as United notch up a deserved success when Dave Caldwell heads in Mark Loram's centre.											

Play-offs

Play-offs			F-A	H-T	Scorers, Times, and Referees	1	2	3	4	5	6	7	8	9	10	11	subs used
SF 1 H SHEFFIELD UTD		W	1-0	1-0	Walsh 43	Waugh	Llewellyn	Newman	Humphries	Pender	McClaren	Milne	Galliers	Gordon*	Walsh	Neville^	Shutt/Jordan
15/5	25,335					*Benstead*	*Wilder*	*Powell*	*Webster*	*Stancliffe*	*Barnsley*	*Heatherston^*	*Withe**	*Cadette*	*Downes*	*Beagrie*	*Philliskirk/Pike*
					Ref: J Martin	City's attractive approach play is too often marred by poor centres. Waugh is the busier of the two goalkeepers, but Walsh's blistering far-post volley gives City an important advantage which could have been better if he had not been denied by the woodwork just after the half-time break.											
SF 2 A SHEFFIELD UTD		D	1-1	1-0	Shutt 17	Waugh	Llewellyn	Newman	Humphries	Pender	McClaren	Milne	Galliers	Gordon*	Walsh	Shutt^	Jordan/Marshall
18/5	*19,066*				*Morris 47*	*Benstead*	*Powell*	*Pike*	*Webster*	*Stancliffe*	*Barnsley**	*Morris*	*Cadette*	*Williams*	*Downes*	*Beagrie*	*Agana*
					Ref: G Courtney	Llewellyn saves City with goal-line clearances. On top before the break, Walsh is unlucky when his long-range free-kick hits a post, but Shutt's stooping header does the trick. After the break, though, it is a different story when Waugh is beaten by a spectacular volley from his best man.											
F:1 H WALSALL		L	1-3	1-0	Walsh 38	Waugh	Llewellyn	Newman	Humphries	Pender	McClaren	Milne	Galliers	Shutt	Walsh	Neville*	Jordan
25/5	25,128				*Waugh 63 (og), Kelly 79, 90*	*Barber*	*Taylor*	*O'Kelly**	*Shakespeare*	*Forbes*	*Goodwin*	*Hawker*	*Hart*	*Christie*	*Kelly*	*Naughton*	*Jones M*
					Ref: J Worrall	All City have to show for their first-half dominance is Walsh's long-range free-kick. A fortunate equaliser for the Saddlers when Llewellyn's clearance strikes Waugh and rebounds over the line, but the final goal is a gem. David Kelly finishes off his great 50-yard run with fine aplomb.											
F:2 A WALSALL		W	2-0	1-0	Newman 30, Shutt 66	Waugh	Llewellyn	Newman	Humphries	Pender	McClaren	Milne	Galliers	Shutt*	Walsh	Jordan	Caldwell
28/5	*13,941*					*Barber*	*Taylor*	*Dornan*	*Shakespeare*	*Forbes*	*Goodwin*	*Hawker*	*Hart*	*Christie*	*Kelly*	*Naughton*	
					Ref: G Tyson	Walsh is unlucky with an early volley that crashes against a post, but Newman's header brings the reward that City's attacking play deserves. After the break Shutt's low drive levels the aggregate score, but Walsall win the penalty shoot-out 4-1 to secure home advantage for the replay.											
F:R A WALSALL		L	0-4	0-3		Waugh	Llewellyn	Newman	Humphries	Pender	McClaren	Milne	Galliers	Shutt !	Walsh	Jordan	
30/5	*13,007*				*Kelly 11, 17, 63, Hawker 19*	*Barber*	*Taylor*	*Dornan^*	*Shakespeare*	*Forbes*	*Goodwin**	*Hawker*	*Hart*	*Christie*	*Kelly*	*Naughton*	*Jones M/Sanderson*
					Ref: G Courtney	Few would have predicted this defensive collapse just when it mattered most. David Kelly started the rot when shooting into an unguarded net, whilst Phil Hawker is also left free to head in from a corner. Shutt receives his marching orders for a punch at Walsall's keeper just before time.											

		Home					Away					
	P	W	D	L	F	A	W	D	L	F	A	Pts
1 Sunderland	46	14	7	2	51	22	13	5	5	41	26	93
2 Brighton	46	15	7	1	37	16	8	8	7	32	31	84
3 Walsall *	46	15	6	2	39	22	8	7	8	29	28	82
4 Notts Co	46	14	4	5	53	24	9	8	6	29	25	81
5 BRISTOL CITY	46	14	6	3	51	30	7	6	10	26	32	75
6 Northampton	46	12	8	3	36	18	6	11	6	34	33	73
7 Wigan	46	11	8	4	36	23	9	4	10	34	38	72
8 Bristol Rov	46	14	5	4	43	19	4	7	12	25	37	66
9 Fulham	46	10	5	8	36	24	9	4	10	33	36	66
10 Blackpool	46	13	4	6	45	27	4	10	9	26	35	65
11 Port Vale	46	12	8	3	36	19	6	3	14	22	37	65
12 Brentford	46	9	8	6	27	23	7	6	10	26	36	62
13 Gillingham	46	8	9	6	45	21	6	8	9	32	40	59
14 Bury	46	9	7	7	33	26	6	7	10	25	31	59
15 Chester	46	9	8	6	29	30	5	8	10	22	32	58
16 Preston	46	10	6	7	30	23	5	7	11	18	36	58
17 Southend	46	10	6	7	42	33	4	7	12	23	50	55
18 Chesterfield	46	10	5	8	25	28	5	5	13	16	42	55
19 Mansfield	46	10	6	7	25	21	4	6	13	23	38	54
20 Aldershot	46	12	3	8	45	32	3	5	15	19	42	53
21 Rotherham**	46	8	8	7	28	25	4	8	11	22	41	52
22 Grimsby	46	6	7	10	25	29	6	7	10	23	29	50
23 York	46	4	7	12	27	45	4	2	17	21	46	33
24 Doncaster	46	6	5	12	25	36	2	4	17	15	48	33
	1104	255	153	144	869	616	144	153	255	616	869	1503

* promoted after play-offs
** relegated after play-offs

Odds & ends

Double wins: (4) Notts County, Chesterfield, York, Doncaster.
Double losses: (1) Mansfield.

Won from behind: (5) Southend (h), York (h), Doncaster (a), Notts County (h), Bury (h).
Lost from in front: (1) Blackpool (a).

High spots: An exciting derby with Bristol Rov on 12 September.
Carl Shutt's four-goal haul v Fulham on 15 December.
Beating Brighton 5-2 at Ashton Gate on 28 December.
Ralph Milne's goal against Bury at Ashton Gate on 6 February.
An exciting 1-0 win against Doncaster to clinch a play-off place.
Beating Sheffield Utd 1-0 at Ashton Gate on 15 May in the 1st leg of the play-off semi-final.
Hanging on to a 1-1 draw at Bramhall Lane on 18 May in the 2nd Leg of the play-off semi-final.
Beating Walsall (a) 2-0 in the 2nd Leg of the play-off final on 28 May.
Beating Bristol Rov (a) 2-1 on 2 Dec in the delayed1986-87 Glos Cup final, and winning this season's competition 3-1 (h) on 15 March.

Low spots: Losing 1-4 at Rotherham on 24 October.
Losing 0-1 against Bristol Rov on 12 April.
Losing 1-3 (h) v Walsall on 25 April in the 1st leg of the play-off final.
Losing 0-4 at Fellows Park on 30 May in the replay of the play-off Final.

Player of the year: Alan Walsh.
Ever-presents (0).
Hat-tricks: (1) Carl Shutt.
Leading scorer: Alan Walsh (12) (Note: Not including play-offs).

	Appearances						Goals			
	Lge	*Sub*	LC	*Sub*	FAC	*Sub*	Lge	LC	FAC	Tot
Bromage, Russell	**28**	*2*	2		2					
Caldwell, Tony	**8**	*8*		*1*	1		**3**		1	**4**
Coombe, Mark					1					
Curle, Keith	**3**									
Fitzpatrick, Paul	**22**	*2*	2		1		**5**			**5**
Galliers, Steve	**35**				2		**5**			**5**
Gordon, Colin	**8**						**4**			**4**
Harvey, Jimmy		*1*								
Hawkins, Nigel	**1**									
Honor, Chris	**14**	*3*			1					
Humphries, Glenn	**24**				2					
Jordan, Joe	**17**	*11*	2		1		**4**			**4**
Llewellyn, Andy	**36**	*6*	2		1		**1**			**1**
McClaren, Steve	**16**						**1**			**1**
Mardon, Paul	**8**									
Marshall, Gary	**13**	*6*	2			*2*	**1**			**1**
Milne, Ralph	**19**						**4**			**4**
Moyes, David	**15**		2				**1**			**1**
Neville, Steve	**37**	*3*		*2*		*1*	**5**			**5**
Newman, Rob	**44**		2		2		**11**			**11**
Owen, Gordon	**17**	*1*	2		1		**6**	2		**8**
Pender, John	**28**				2		**2**			**2**
Prudhoe, Mark	**3**									
Shutt, Carl	**18**	*4*			2		**10**			**10**
Tanner, Mike	**10**	*2*	2					1		**1**
Vaughan, John	**3**									
Walsh, Alan	**39**	*3*	2		2		**12**			**12**
Waugh, Keith	**40**		2		1					
(own-goals)							**2**			**2**
27 players used	**506**	***52***	**22**	***3***	**22**	***3***	**77**	**3**	**1**	**81**

BARCLAYS LEAGUE DIVISION 3

Manager: Joe Jordan

SEASON 1988-89

No	Date		Att	Pos	Pt	F-A	H-T	Scorers, Times, and Referees	1	2	3	4	5	6	7	8	9	10	11	subs used
1	A	NOTTS CO			D	0-0	0-0		Waugh	Llewellyn	Bromage	Humphries	Pender	McClaren	Milne*	Galliers	Newman	Walsh	Caldwell	Honor
	27/8		*6,285*		1				*Leonard*	*Norton*	*Withe*	*O'Riordan*	*Yates*	*Law*	*Mills*	*McParland**	*Birtles*	*Pike*	*Thorpe*	*Lund*
								Ref: K Morton	Mindful of Jordan's efforts to sign a new keeper, Waugh has one of those rare days when everything goes right. He pulls off a string of spectacular saves to keep impressive County at bay, and has luck on his side with his one error, as Galliers is on hand to clear off the line.											
2	H	CHESTERFIELD			W	4-0	1-0	Walsh 43, 71, Newman 51p, Llewellyn 63	Waugh	Llewellyn	Bromage	Mardon	Pender	McClaren*	Newman	Galliers	Shutt	Walsh	Hawkins	Fitzpatrick
	3/9		7,547		4				*Brown*	*Hewitt*	*McGeeney**	*Henderson*	*Rogers*	*Hunter^*	*Eley*	*Arnott*	*Waller*	*Morris*	*Thompson*	*Bloomer/Wood*
								Ref: H King	City's exhilarating display provides proof that Jordan's policy of playing five at the back is not necessarily a negative tactic. Walsh twice registers with headers, popping up unmarked for the opener, and then finishing off Shutt's pin-point cross to complete City's emphatic win.											
3	A	CHESTER		11	L	0-2	0-0		Waugh	Llewellyn	Bromage	Mardon	Pender	McClaren	Newman	Galliers	Shutt*	Walsh	**McGarvey**	Milne
	10/9		*2,831*	*2*	4			*Lightfoot 66, Dale 85*	*Stewart*	*Glenn*	*Woodthorpe*	*Hinnigan*	*Abel*	*Lightfoot*	*Jakub*	*Barrow*	*Benjamin*	*Johnson*	*Newhouse**	*Dale*
								Ref: M Peck	McGarvey's hopes of making an impressive debut are dashed by Chester's impressive trio of uncompromising central defenders. City fail to match Chester's endeavour, and they concede their first goal in the 426th min of the season when Chris Lightfoot heads in from close range.											
4	H	PRESTON		12	D	1-1	1-1	Bromage 14	**Carter**	Llewellyn^	Bromage	Mardon	Pender	McClaren	Milne*	Galliers	Newman	Walsh	McGarvey	Shutt/Honor
	17/9		7,913	*19*	5			*Rathbone 44*	*Brown*	*Rathbone*	*McAteer*	*Atkins*	*Jones*	*Allardyce*	*Miller*	*Joyce*	*Ellis*	*Brazi*	*Patterson*	
								Ref: I Hemley	Jordan's refashioned defence looks decidedly creaky and it is thanks to on-loan keeper Tim Carter that City salvage a point. After Bromage stabs in McGarvey's pass, Mick Rathbone catches City cold, meeting Andy McAteer's cross at the far post to shoot past Carter from ten yards.											
5	A	BLACKPOOL		12	D	2-2	2-1	McGarvey 32, 39	Carter	Llewellyn	Bromage	Newman	Pender	McClaren	Milne*	Galliers	Shutt	Walsh	McGarvey	Hawkins
	20/9		*3,412*	*20*	6			*Davies 30, Taylor 78*	*Siddall*	*Burgess*	*Morgan*	*Deary*	*Methven*	*Elliott*	*Davies*	*Cunningham*	*Garner^*	*Coughlin**	*Taylor*	*Thompson/Walwyn*
								Ref: G Aplin	City sparkling attack is let down by some sloppy defending at Bloomfield Road. Blackpool go ahead against the run of play when Mike Davies steals in to beat Carter from eight yards, but McGarvey twice shoots in to put City ahead, before Mark Taylor heads in Pool's late equaliser.											
6	H	PORT VALE		16	L	0-1	0-1		Carter	Llewellyn	Bromage	Newman	Pender	McClaren	Milne	Galliers	Shutt*	Walsh	McGarvey	Hawkins
	24/9		7,235	*2*	6			*Walker 6*	*Grew*	*Webb*	*Hughes*	*Walker*	*Mills*	*Sproson*	*Ford*	*Earle*	*Futcher*	*Beckford*	*Rley*	
								Ref: R Lewis	Ron Futcher who opted to join ambitious Vale in preference to City looks to have made the right choice on the evidence of this game. City's defence stands off to watch as Ray Walker, after getting the luck of the bounce at the edge of the penalty area, strides forward to beat Carter.											
7	H	SWANSEA		12	W	2-0	1-0	Walsh 31, Milne 77	**Leaning**	Llewellyn	Bromage	Newman*	Pender	McClaren	Milne	Galliers	Shutt^	Walsh	Hawkins	Mardon/McGarvey
	1/10		7,786	*17*	9				*Wilmot*	*Hough*	*Legg*	*Melville**	*Knill*	*James*	*Thornber*	*Raynor*	*Allon^*	*Bodak*	*Lewis*	*D'Auria/Love*
								Ref: L Shapter	Swansea have cause to be aggrieved when Walsh's lethal left-foot breaks the deadlock, as two minutes earlier Paul Raynor was penalised for a foul on Leaning after bundling the ball in the net. Milne heads in to make victory certain, and Walsh crashes a late volley against the crossbar.											
8	A	GILLINGHAM		7	W	1-0	1-0	Gavin 1	Leaning	Llewellyn	Bromage*	Newman	Pender	McClaren	**Gavin**	Galliers	McGarvey	Walsh	Hawkins^	Mardon/Jordan
	4/10		*2,966*	*20*	12				*Kite*	*Burley*	*Haylock*	*Peacock*	*Clarke*	*Walker*	*Perry*	*Quow**	*Lovell*	*Weatherly*	*Smith D*	*Cooper*
								Ref: D Axcell	City are under siege for much of this poor match after Gavin takes just 85 seconds to celebrate his debut by shooting low past Phil Kite. The Gills are twice thwarted by the bar and then denied by McClaren's goal-line clearance, whilst Gavin and Walsh hit the woodwork for City.											
9	H	FULHAM		11	L	**1-5**	0-2	Newman 85p *[Marshall 80]*	Leaning	Llewellyn^	Mardon	Newman	Pender	McClaren	Gavin	Galliers	McGarvey*	Walsh	Hawkins	Jordan/Humphries
	8/10		8,160	*6*	12			*Peters 18, Sayer 35, 86, Eckhardt 56*	*Stannard*	*Peters*	*Langley*	*Wilson*	*Eckhardt*	*Thomas*	*Marshall*	*Skinner*	*Sayer*	*Gordon**	*Barnett*	*Mauge*
								Ref: R Gifford	City have 80% of the possession and loads of chances, but Fulham score from all their shots on target. McGarvey heads against the bar and misses three other chances before Leaning's handling offence outside the area allows Andy Peters to shoot in Fulham's opener from a free-kick.											
10	A	HUDDERSFIELD		11	W	1-0	0-0	Walsh 85	Leaning	Llewellyn^	**Bailey**	Humphries	Pender	McClaren	Newman	Galliers	Shutt*	Walsh	Jordan	McGarvey/Mardon
	15/10		*5,952*	*16*	15				*Hardwick*	*Trevitt*	*Hutchings*	*May*	*O'Doherty*	*Mitchell*	*O'Regan*	*Winter*	*Withe*	*Maskell*	*Bent**	*Marsden*
								Ref: A Dawson	Any doubts to Walsh's right to merit a place amongst City's greats are dispelled by his superlative strike that settles this game. He gathers a clearance beyond the halfway line and spurts clear of the Terriers' defence to sweep a perfect low 20-yard shot into the far corner of the net.											
11	A	NORTHAMPTON		7	W	3-1	0-1	Milne 52, McGarvey 73, 90,	Leaning	Newman	Bailey	Humphries	Pender	McClaren	Milne	Galliers	McGarvey	Walsh	Gavin*	Jordan
	22/10		*3,668*	*17*	18			*McGoldrick 45*	*Gleasure*	*McGoldrick*	*Thomas*	*Donald*	*Flexney*	*McPherson*	*Singleton*	*Reed**	*Gilbert*	*Adcock*	*Sandeman^*	*Johnson/Wilson*
								Ref: J Lloyd	Playing in borrowed blue shirts City notch up their first win at Northampton since 1961. After Eddie McGoldrick easily shoots in from Tony Adcock's pass, City make their dominance count with Milne's ten-yard equaliser being followed by two simple tap-ins from McGarvey.											

No	H/A	Opponent	Att	Pos	Pt	F-A	H-T	Scorers, Times, and Referees	1	2	3	4	5	6	7	8	9	10	11	subs used
12	H	ALDERSHOT		8	D	1-1	0-1	McGarvey 65	Waugh	Newman	Bailey	Humphries	Pender	McClaren	Milne	Galliers	McGarvey	Walsh	Jordan*	Shutt
	25/10		8,685	*24*	19			*Burvill 20*	*Lange*	*Berry*	*Barnes*	*Burvill*	*Smith*	*Wignall*	*Phillips*	*Riley*	*Claridge*	*McDonald*	*Randall*	
								Ref: A Seville	After four successive away wins in League and Cup, City's display against bottom of the table Aldershot is disappointing. Glyn Riley cleverly creates the opening for Glen Burvill to shoot the visitors in front, but after the break McGarvey heads in Newman's cross to save a point.											
13	A	MANSFIELD		11	D	2-2	2-1	McGarvey 30, Walsh 38	Waugh	Newman	Bailey	Humphries	Pender	McClaren	Milne	Galliers	McGarvey*	Walsh	Gavin	Shutt
	29/10		*3,808*	*10*	20			*Kent 24, Charles 63*	*Cox*	*McKernon*	*Ryan*	*Kent*	*Foster*	*Coleman*	*Owen*	*Kearney*	*Hodges*	*Cassells**	*Charles*	*Stringfellow*
								Ref: A Flood	City are absolutely brilliant in the first half as McGarvey's header and Walsh's vicious right-foot drive bring about recovery from Kevin Kent's drilled-in opener. Steve Charles, though, levels with a close-range volley after the break to reward Mansfield for their great resilience.											
14	H	BOLTON		9	D	1-1	1-0	Newman 10	Waugh	Llewellyn	Bailey	Humphries	Pender	McClaren	Milne	Newman	Shutt*	Walsh	Gavin	McGarvey
	5/11		8,809	*12*	21			*Morgan 58*	*Felgate*	*Brown*	*Cowdrill*	*Savage**	*Brookman*	*Winstanley*	*Crombie*	*Thompson*	*Morgan*	*Stevens*	*Darby*	*Storer*
								Ref: J Carter	Trevor Morgan returns to give his former team-mates a lesson in the art of scoring goals after dominant City fail to add to Newman's drilled-in opener. He has just one opportunity, breaking clear to hammer in a low-drive that Waugh can only deflect into the bottom corner of the net.											
15	H	WOLVES		12	L	0-1	0-0		Waugh	Newman	Bailey	Humphries	Pender	McClaren*	Milne	Galliers	Shutt^	Walsh	Gavin	Llewellyn/McGarvey
	8/11		11,336	*1*	21			*Mutch 89*	*Kendall*	*Bellamy*	*Venus*	*Streete*	*Robertson*	*Robinson*	*Thompson*	*Downing*	*Bull*	*Mutch*	*Dennison*	
								Ref: G Ashby	The utterly absorbing contest between two well-matched sides, each managing five shots on target, is settled at the death. Andy Mutch is given space to score with an overhead as City's static defence allows the ball, from Robert Dennison's right-wing corner, to bounce in front of goal.											
16	A	WIGAN		10	W	1-0	0-0	Gavin 76	Waugh	Newman	Bailey	Humphries	Pender	**Stanley***	McGarvey^	Galliers	Shutt	Walsh	Gavin	Llewellyn/Hawkins
	12/11		*2,675*	*20*	24				*Adkins*	*Senior*	*Tankard*	*Hamilton !*	*Beesley*	*McEwan*	*Thompson*	*Butler*	*Entwhistle*	*Diamond*	*Rimmer*	
								Ref: A Wilkie	With Milne transferred to Man Utd for £170,000, City have difficulty in breaking down a side reduced to ten men. David Hamilton is sent off as early as the eighth min for his tackle on Galliers, but City have to repel unlikely Wigan pressure before Gavin volleys in his ten-yard winner.											
17	A	SHEFFIELD UTD		12	L	0-3	0-1		Waugh	Stanley	Bailey	Humphries	Newman	McClaren	McGarvey*	Galliers	Shutt	Walsh	Gavin	Hawkins
	26/11		*11,248*	*2*	24			*Deane 12, 78, Agana 63*	*Benstead*	*Wilder*	*Pike*	*Booker*	*Stancliffe*	*Smith*	*Roberts*	*Todd*	*Agana*	*Deane*	*Bryson*	
								Ref: T Holbrook	United's greater prowess in and around the penalty area brings City's run of away success to an end. After Brian Deane rises unchallenged to head in United's opener, City come close to an equaliser on a number of occasions, before Tony Agana ends all hope with a stunning volley.											
18	H	READING		10	W	2-1	0-1	Walsh 56, Hawkins 77	Waugh	Newman	Bailey	Humphries	Pender	McClaren	McGarvey*	Galliers	Shutt	Walsh	Gavin	Hawkins
	3/12		8,045	*13*	27			*Senior 39*	*Phillips*	*Franklin*	*Richardson*	*Elsey*	*Hicks*	*Whitlock*	*Knight*	*Tait**	*Senior*	*Moran*	*Gilkes*	*Taylor*
								Ref: J Deakin	Backed by a strong wind and driving rain Gavin inspires City's second-half fight-back after surviving Steve Richardson's crunching tackles. He takes on the Reading defence before delivering a perfect cross for Walsh to volley in an equaliser to Trevor Senior's headed opener.											
19	H	CARDIFF		7	W	2-0	1-0	Newman 4, Hawkins 82	Waugh	Newman	Bailey	Humphries*	Pender	McClaren	McGarvey	Stanley	Shutt^	Walsh	Gavin	Llewellyn/Hawkins
	17/12		7,493	*18*	30				*Wood*	*Rodgerson^*	*Platnauer*	*Wimbleton*	*Abraham*	*Boyle*	*Curtis**	*Bartlett*	*Gilligan*	*Gummer*	*Lynex*	*Bater/Wheeler*
								Ref: R Lewis	Newman's majestic shot past George Wood from the edge of the area sets up City's victory in the Severnside derby. Cardiff, unlucky before the break with the award of a free-kick rather than a pen, are finished by a defensive mix-up allowing Hawkins to shoot in City's killer second.											
20	A	BURY		10	L	1-2	1-1	McGarvey 9	Waugh	Honor	Bailey	Newman	Pender	McClaren	McGarvey	Stanley	Shutt*	Walsh	Gavin	Hawkins
	23/12		*3,368*	*4*	30			*Hoyland 22, Robinson 58p*	*Farnworth*	*Hill*	*Bishop*	*Hoyland*	*Valentine*	*Clements*	*Lee*	*Robinson*	*Elliott*	*McIlroy*	*Parkinson*	
								Ref: J Key	Making light of the driving rain in the early stages City take the lead when McGarvey turns neatly on Shutt's cross to hammer the ball home. After Jamie Hoyland had levelled matters with his looping header, Newman brings down David Lee to concede Bury's match-winning penalty.											
21	A	SOUTHEND		9	W	2-1	1-0	McGarvey 7, Walsh 80	Waugh	Honor	Bailey	Newman	Pender	McClaren	McGarvey	Stanley*	Shutt	Walsh	Gavin	Galliers
	31/12		*4,012*	*16*	33			*Bennett 83*	*Sansome*	*Johnson*	*Martin*	*Butler*	*Westley*	*Brush*	*Hall*	*Edinburgh**	*Crown*	*Bennett*	*Ling*	*McDonough*
								Ref: D Hedges	A hard-earned, but deserved victory at Roots Hall, where Pender is dominant at the heart of City's defence. McGarvey pounces as Paul Sansome can only parry a cross, and then Walsh heads in from four yards to double City's advantage, before Southend make their late reply.											
22	H	BRISTOL ROV		10	L	0-1	0-0		Waugh	Honor	Bailey	Newman	Pender	McClaren	McGarvey	Stanley*	Shutt	Walsh	Gavin^	**Shepherd**/Hawkins
	2/1		**23,191**	*5*	33			*Penrice 54*	*Martyn*	*Alexander*	*Twentyman*	*Yates*	*Smith**	*Jones*	*Holloway*	*Reece*	*White*	*Penrice*	*Purnell*	*McClean*
								Ref: J Carter	What used to be mission impossible is not anymore, as the Rovers come to Ashton Gate and conquer with ease. With Liverpool boss Kenny Dalglish watching from the stand, the grounded Devon White sticks out a foot to divert the ball for Gary Penrice to shoot in from 20 yards.											
23	A	CHESTERFIELD		11	L	0-1	0-0		Waugh	Honor	Bailey	Newman	Pender	McClaren	McGarvey*	Shepherd	Gavin	Walsh	Galliers	Jordan
	14/1		*3,488*	*22*	33			*Bloomer 47*	*Cherry*	*Hewitt*	*Prindiville*	*Shaw*	*Brien*	*Rogers*	*Eley**	*Arnott*	*Waller*	*Bloomer*	*Morris*	*MacDonald*
								Ref: T Fitzharris	Jordan will need all his inspirational qualities to raise City for their League Cup quarter-final after this dreary display. Bob Bloomer shoots into an open goal to put the Spirietes ahead, but Walsh's disallowed header is all City can muster for their total domination of the closing stages.											

BARCLAYS LEAGUE DIVISION 3

Manager: Joe Jordan

SEASON 1988-89

No	Date		Att	Pos	Pt	F-A	H-T	Scorers, Times, and Referees	1	2	3	4	5	6	7	8	9	10	11	subs used
24	H	CHESTER		13	L	0-1	0-0		Waugh	Honor	Bailey	Newman	Pender	McClaren	Shepherd	Galliers	Shutt	Walsh*	Gavin	McGarvey
	21/1		9,586	8	33			Johnson 66	Stewart	Butler^	Woodthorpe	Hinnigan	Abel	Lane	Jakub	Barrow	Johnson	Graham*	Dale	Newhouse/Lightfoot
								Ref: J Martin	Ex City forward Steve Johnson shows the aggression so lacking amongst Jordan's featherweight attackers as he heads powerfully past Waugh. Chester, beaten in their three previous games, are fully deserving of their success as they squander several good chances to add to their lead.											
25	A	PRESTON		13	L	0-2	0-0		Waugh	Honor	Bailey	Newman	Pender	McClaren	Galliers	**Turner**	Shutt	Walsh	Gavin	
	28/1		6,091	7	33			Mooney 58, 61	Tunks	Williams N	Rathbone	Jones	Wrightson	Atkins	Mooney	Joyce	Ellis	Brazil	Patterson	
								Ref: T Simpson	City's sixth defeat in seven matches begs the question of whether sufficient members of Jordan's squad have the hunger for success to go with their undoubted ability. On Deepdale's artificial surface Brian Mooney's 20-yarder, and his simple tap-in bring Preston their deserved success.											
26	A	SWANSEA		12	D	1-1	1-0	Turner 15	Waugh	Honor	Bailey	Newman	Pender	Mardon	Galliers	Turner	McGarvey^	Walsh	Stanley*	McClaren/Gavin
	3/2		6,523	3	34			James 86p	Bracey	Lewis	Coleman	Melville	Knill	James	Thornber*	Davies	Phillips	Wade	Hutchison	Hough^/Raynor
								Ref: R Bridges	A hero when volleying past Lee Bracey, Turner turns villain near the end when he prevents City from ending their lean spell. Much of City's hard work goes to waste as Turner gifts Robbie James his fierce pen when jumping with his arm raised to clear Tommy Hutchison's free-kick.											
27	H	GILLINGHAM		11	W	1-0	0-0	Jordan 74	Waugh	Honor	Bailey	Newman	Pender	Mardon	Galliers	**Dolan^**	McGarvey*	Walsh	McClaren	Jordan/Gavin
	11/2		7,319	24	37				Kite	Burley	Stimson	Reeves	Walker	Manuel	O'Shea	Docker	Lovell	Lillis*	Smith D	Shipley
								Ref: M Bodenham	Jordan secures victory as he races clear onto Walsh's pass to smash an unstoppable 20-yarder into the far corner of the net. The Gills threaten whenever David Smith is in possession, and they are unlucky not to secure a penalty when the speedy winger is blatantly tripped by Mardon.											
28	A	FULHAM		13	L	1-3	1-1	McGarvey 27	Waugh	Honor	Bailey	Newman	Pender	Mardon	Dolan	McClaren	Gavin	Walsh	McGarvey*	Stanley
	18/2		4,408	9	37			Walker 8, Davies 50, Marshall 65	Stannard	Langley	Elkins	Skinner	Rougvie	Thomas	Marshall	Scott	Cole*	Davies	Walker	Donnellan
								Ref: M Bailey	Grateful Fulham cash in to end four games without a win as City suffer a Cup hangover. McGarvey neatly heads in an equaliser after Clive Walker had blasted in from an acute angle, but City's motivation fades away after a bout of head tennis ends with John Marshall nodding in.											
29	A	ALDERSHOT		11	W	1-0	1-0	Walsh 32	Waugh	Stanley^	Bailey	Newman	Pender	Shutt	Honor	McClaren	Walsh	Turner	Dolan*	Jordan/Mardon
	21/2		**1,960**	23	40				Lange	Brown	Barnes	Burvill	Smith	Wignall	Stewart	Puckett	Claridge	Mazzon	Randall*	Riley
								Ref: P Foakes	There are more live wires off the pitch than on as the terracing behind one goal has to be evacuated in the first half because of a power cable fault. Walsh's feared left foot settles this poor game, curling a powerful shot round the Aldershot wall after Shutt is tripped 25 yards out.											
30	H	NORTHAMPTON		12	W	3-1	3-0	Shutt 27, Walsh 33, Turner 43	Waugh	Honor	Bailey*	Newman	Pender	Mardon	Llewellyn	McClaren	Shutt	Walsh	Turner	Stanley
	4/3		7,197	16	43			Walsh 85 (og)	Gleasure	Williams	Wilson	Thomas	Bodley^	McPherson	Quow	Collins*	Gilbert	Adcock	Berry	Culpin/Sandeman
								Ref: L Dilkes	After a shaky start Shutt's memorable angled drive into the roof of the net from 25 yards revives City. Robbie Turner wins over the Ashton Gate fans with his all-action display. His challenge setting up Walsh's precision strike, and then heading in Llewellyn's superb far-post cross.											
31	A	BOLTON		14	L	0-2	0-0		Waugh	Honor*	Bailey	Newman	Pender	Mardon	LLewellyn	McClaren	Shutt	Walsh	Turner	Gavin
	11/3		4,423	19	43			Darby 83, 86	Felgate	Brown	Cowdrill	Brookman*	Crombie	Winstanley	Chandler	Thompson	Thomas	Jeffrey	Darby	Storer
								Ref: T Mills	City get what they deserve for offering little more than a packed defence at Burnden Park. Twice Bailey has to hook off the line, whilst Mike Jeffrey hits the post, but Julian Darby's prod-in, and his far-post header deservedly bring Bolton their first win over City in more than 14 years.											
32	H	NOTTS CO		14	L	0-4	0-1		Waugh	Honor	Bailey	Newman	Pender	Mardon	Gavin*	McClaren	Shutt	Walsh	Turner	Galliers
	18/3		6,407	10	43			Barnes 33, 53, O'Riordan 60, Draper 65	Cherry	McStay	Withe	O'Riordan	Yates	Law	Turner	Barnes*	Lund	Pike^	Draper	Thorpe/Fairclough
								Ref: R Gifford	City give a dreadful, passionless display against mid-table County, who are not discouraged by Waugh's saving of Geoff Pike's early penalty. Mark Draper is unmarked as he lashes in the final goal, after Paul Barnes had outpaced City's spread-eagled defence to clip in the opener.											
33	H	MANSFIELD		11	W	2-0	1-0	Newman 27p, 84	Waugh	Honor	Bailey	Humphries	Pender	Newman	Galliers	McClaren*	Hawkins^	Walsh	Turner	Mardon/Jordan
	21/3		5,065	14	46				Cox	McKernon	Kearney	Hodges*	Foster	Coleman	Hathaway	Charles	Kent	Cassells	Ryan	Owen
								Ref: P Vanes	With the game already won Jordan is surprisingly booed as he brings himself on for the exhausted Hawkins. Newman is City's man of the match, netting with a penalty after George Foster whips his legs away, and quelling Mansfield's second-half revival with his late cross-shot.											
34	A	BRISTOL ROV		11	D	1-1	1-1	Walsh 24	Waugh	Honor	Bailey	Humphries^	Pender	Newman	Galliers*	McClaren	**Taylor**	Walsh	Turner	Mardon/Hawkins
	25/3		8,435	5	47			Penrice 26	Martyn	Alexander	Twentyman	Yates	Reece	Jones	Holloway	Bailey	McClean	Penrice	Purnell*	White
								Ref: P Wright	City's joy as Walsh fires in from six yards, is soon cut short by Penrice's shot into an empty net. Geoff Twentyman's goal-line clearance, and keeper Nigel Martyn's save from Newman's 41st-min penalty, prevents City's first League win over Rovers for more than three years.											

No / Date	H/A	Opponent	Att	Pos	Res / Pts	F-A	H-T	Scorers, Times, and Referees	1	2	3	4	5	6	7	8	9	10	11	subs used
35	H	BURY		10	W	3-0	1-0	Turner 44, 63, Taylor 89	Waugh	Honor	Bailey	Humphries	Pender	Newman	McClaren	Mardon	Taylor	Walsh	Turner	
27/3			8,496	*8*	50				*Farnworth*	*Pashley*	*Bishop*	*Hoyland*	*Wassall*	*Clements*	*Lee*	*Robinson*	*Hulme**	*McIlroy^*	*Parkinson*	*Greenwood/Atkin*
								Ref: W Burge	Bury supply the neat football, but it is City who have the killer touch after Newman's 42nd-min pen is saved by Simon Farnworth. Turner is on hand to hammer in City's opener, and then turns up to head in McClaren's cross, before Taylor gets in on the act with an unstoppable drive.											
36	A	CARDIFF		11	D	1-1	0-1	Taylor 79	Waugh	Honor	Bailey	Humphries	Pender	Newman	McClaren	Mardon	Taylor	Walsh	Turner	
1/4			*6,358*	*18*	51			*Platnauer 18*	*Wood*	*Rodgerson*	*Platnauer*	*Morgan*	*Boyle*	*Stevenson*	*Kelly*	*Bater*	*Gilligan*	*Wheeler**	*Lynex*	*Walsh*
								Ref: R Wiseman	Taylor (£225,000 ex Leeds) demonstrates his worth by controlling the ball on his chest, before swivelling to deliver a low-shot that takes the Cardiff keeper by surprise. Waugh keeps City in contention, but even he can do nothing about Nicky Platnauer's deflected free-kick.											
37	A	BRENTFORD		13	L	0-3	0-2		Waugh	Honor	Bailey	Humphries	Pender	Newman	McClaren	Mardon*	Taylor	Walsh	Turner	Galliers
4/4			*4,627*	*11*	51			*Sealy 1, 51, Cockram 30p*	*Parks*	*Buttigieg*	*Stanislaus**	*Bates*	*Evans*	*Cockram*	*Jones*	*Sealy*	*Purdie^*	*Blissett*	*Smillie*	*Pearce/Godfrey*
								Ref: H King	After braving the sleet, snow and swirling winds to reach Griffin Park, the fans have to endure City's disjointed and undisciplined play. Right from the kick-off City are in trouble, the unmarked Tony Sealy shooting in after just twelve seconds, and it is downhill all the way thereafter.											
38	H	SOUTHEND		14	L	0-2	0-1		Waugh	Honor	Bailey	Humphries	Pender	Newman	McClaren*	Bromage	Hawkins	Walsh^	Turner	Mardon/McGarvey
3/4			6,213	*19*	51			*Ling 10, 60*	*Sansome*	*Roberts*	*Johnson*	*Butler*	*Prior*	*Brush*	*Martin*	*Hall*	*Crown*	*McDonough*	*Ling*	
								Ref: J Moules	City, embarrassed by a Southend side fighting to keep clear of relegation, are made to pay for poor marking and lack of concentration. Martin Ling, after being allowed the space in the first half to convert Derek Hall's cross, nips in to rob Bailey and coolly slip the ball past Waugh.											
39	H	BRENTFORD		14	L	0-1	0-0		Waugh	Newman	Bailey	Humphries	Pender	Gavin	McClaren	Bromage	Taylor	Walsh	Turner	
11/4			**4,339**	*9*	51			*Evans 83*	*Parks*	*Feeley*	*Stanislaus**	*Bates*	*Evans*	*Cockram*	*Jones*	*Sealy*	*Purdie^*	*Blissett*	*Smillie*	*Pearce/Godfrey*
								Ref: M Reed	No doubt those missing from the gaping terraces will have thought they did well in skipping this defeat. However City's ten to three shots on target advantage, suggests that Brentford are fortunate that Tony Evans' late header from Allan Cockram's free-kick brings all three points.											
40	H	BLACKPOOL		14	L	1-2	1-0	Taylor 36	Waugh	Newman	Bailey	Humphries	Pender	Gavin	McClaren	Bromage	Taylor	Walsh	Turner*	Hawkins
15/4			5,090	*21*	51			*Walwyn 66, 72*	*Siddall*	*Burgess*	*Matthews**	*Elliott*	*Methven*	*Deary*	*Davies*	*Coughlin*	*Garner*	*Gore*	*Madden*	*Walwyn*
								Ref: R Pawley	Taylor's first-half volley fails to halt City's slump from cup heroes to possible relegation candidates. Keith Walwyn's 61st-minute arrival brings Blackpool their first win in eleven games on a day that 95 fans are crushed to death attending the FA Cup Semi-Final at Hillsborough.											
41	H	HUDDERSFIELD		13	W	**6-1**	5-0	Taylor 2, 16, 27, Walsh 4p, Gavin 15, [McClaren 76]	Waugh	Honor	Bailey	Newman	Pender	Gavin	McClaren	Galliers	Taylor	Walsh	Turner	
18/4			4,542	*9*	54			*Maskell 62*	*Hardwick*	*Trevitt*	*Mitchell*	*May*	*O'Doherty !*	*Duggan*	*Byrne**	*Winter*	*Cecere*	*Maskell*	*Smith*	*McInerney*
								Ref: P Alcock	City's super show follows a minute's silence for the Hillsborough victims. Taylor completes his hat-trick with two low shots, after opening his account with a header and being up-ended for Walsh's penalty. Ken O'Doherty is sent off for his second bookable offence on 82 minutes.											
42	A	PORT VALE		13	W	1-0	0-0	Taylor 59	Waugh	Honor	Bailey	Newman	Pender	Gavin	McClaren	Galliers	Taylor	Walsh	Turner	
21/4			*6,923*	*3*	57				*Grew*	*Mills*	*Hughes*	*Walker*	*Webb*	*Glover*	*Jeffers*	*Earle*	*Jones**	*Beckford*	*Riley*	*Futcher*
								Ref: N Midgley	City would not have been flattered by a four-goal winning margin as Taylor and Turner turn in a brilliant performance at Vale Park. Mark Grew repeatedly comes to Vale's rescue as his defence is torn apart time and again, but he cannot keep out Taylor's firm downward header.											
43	H	WIGAN		13	L	0-1	0-0		Waugh	Honor*	Bailey	Newman	Pender	McClaren	Galliers	Gavin	Taylor	Walsh	Turner^	Humphries/**Eaton**
29/4			5,555	*20*	57			*Tankard 88*	*Adkins*	*Senior*	*Tankard*	*Atherton*	*Beesley*	*Pilling*	*Thompson*	*Rimmer*	*Entwistle*	*Page*	*Griffiths*	
								Ref: G Pooley	Wigan snatch the points, with Allen Tankard's superb 35-yard left-footed late strike, after City had been denied by the woodwork on five occasions. Nigel Adkins' great display between the sticks ensures City's home record is the worst since their relegation season of 1981-82.											
44	A	WOLVES		14	L	0-2	0-1		Waugh	Humphries	Bailey	Newman	Pender	McClaren	Galliers !	Gavin	Taylor	Walsh	Hawkins*	Eaton
1/5			***17,351***	*1*	57			*Bull 35, 89*	*Hansbury*	*Bellamy*	*Thompson*	*Streete*	*Robertson*	*Vaughan*	*Gooding*	*Downing*	*Bull*	*Mutch*	*Dennison*	
								Ref: D Hedges	Galliers' over-the-ball tackle on Steve Bull leaves City a man short from the 65th minute, but they are not finished off until just before time. Bull slams in Andy Mutch's chipped pass for his 49th goal of the season, after earlier scoring with a perfectly-angled shot past Waugh.											
45	A	READING		11	W	2-1	1-1	Turner 43, Pender 60	Waugh	Honor	Bromage	Newman	Pender	McClaren	Galliers	Gavin	Taylor	Walsh	Turner	
5/5			*3,620*	*17*	60			*Hicks 42*	*Francis*	*Jones**	*Richardson*	*Beavon*	*Hicks*	*Whitlock*	*Knight^*	*Elsey*	*Senior*	*Gilkes*	*Payne*	*Williams/Moran*
								Ref: K Cooper	Waugh's 79th-minute save from Stuart Beavon's spot-kick sentences Reading to their sixth successive defeat. After McClaren does well early on to clear off the line, headers from Martin Hicks and Turner keeps things level at the break, before Pender's header secures City's victory.											
46	H	SHEFFIELD UTD		11	W	2-0	0-0	Turner 55, Taylor 75	Leaning	Honor	Bromage	Newman	Pender	McClaren	Galliers	Gavin	Taylor	Walsh	Turner	
13/5			10,769	*2*	63				*Tracey*	*Wilder*	*Pike*	*Moore*	*Stancliffe*	*Carr*	*Roberts*	*Todd**	*Agana*	*Deane*	*Bryson*	*Powell*
Average	Home 8,121		Away 5,410					Ref: M James	A pitch invasion four minutes from the end takes the headlines away from City's win. Turner's volley, and Taylor's follow-up when Simon Tracey parries his first effort, produce a defeat United can live with, as only a massive deficit could have robbed them of automatic promotion.											

Littlewoods Cup				F-A	H-T	Scorers, Times, and Referees	1	2	3	4	5	6	7	8	9	10	11	subs used
1:1 H EXETER			W	1-0	1-0	Newman 6p	Waugh	Llewellyn	Bromage	Humphries*	Pender	McClaren	Milne	Galliers	Newman	Walsh	Caldwell^	Honor/Hawkins
30/8	6,005						*Gwinnett*	*Banks*	*Viney*	*Rogers*	*Taylor*	*Cooper*	*Rowbotham*	*Hiley*	*Langley*	*Neville*	*Harrower*	
						Ref: K Cooper	Exeter are unfortunate to lose to Newman's penalty after Lee Rogers was adjudged to have handled McClaren's cross. The visitors create the better chances in a poor game, Darren Rowbotham and Shaun Taylor going close, before Llewellyn's goal-line clearance robs Richard Cooper.											
1:2 A EXETER			W	1-0	0-0	Walsh 84	Waugh	Llewellyn	Bromage	Mardon	Pender	McClaren	Newman	Galliers	Shutt	Walsh	Jordan*	Milne
7/9	*2,749*						*Gwinnett*	*Banks*	*Viney*	*Rogers*	*Taylor*	*Cooper*	*Rowbotham*	*Hiley*	*Batty*	*Neville*	*Harrower*	
						Ref: V Callow (City won 2-0 on aggregate)	City's tactics to defend their first-leg advantage produces a game as dull as Exeter's sub-standard floodlights. Milne's mazy run creates the perfect opening for Walsh to return to his more normal scoring mode, his trusty left foot confirming City's place in the second round.											
2:1 A OXFORD		16	W	4-2	2-1	Walsh 6, Hawkins 44, Shutt 60, Milne 89	Leaning	Llewellyn	Bromage	Newman	Pender	McClaren	Milne	Galliers	Shutt*	Walsh	Hawkins	Mardon
28/9	*3,705*	*2:12*				*Saunders 28, 65*	*Hucker*	*Bardsley*	*Smart*	*Phillips L*	*Hill*	*Greenall*	*Heath**	*Foyle*	*Saunders*	*Mustoe*	*Rhoades-Br'n*	*Purdie*
						Ref: R Wiseman	City's splendid all-round team performance ends Oxford's eight season (27 game) record of not having been beaten at home in the League Cup. Milne seals City's victory with a cracking 20-yarder past Peter Hucker at the finish of his superb run at Oxford's retreating defence.											
2:2 H OXFORD		13	W	2-0	1-0	Shutt 37, McClaren 58	Leaning	Llewellyn	Humphries	Newman	Pender	McClaren	Gavin^	Galliers	Shutt	Walsh	Jordan*	Hawkins/Mardon
11/10	6,255	*2:10*					*Judge*	*Bardsley*	*Phillips J*	*Phillips L*	*Briggs*	*Greenall*	*Purdie*	*Foyle*	*Saunders*	*Mustoe^*	*Rh'des-Br'n**	*Hill/Heath*
						Ref: B Stevens (City won 6-2 on aggregate)	City are fortunate to survive Oxford's impressive start, but once Jordan abandons his safety-first tactics designed to preserve the first-leg lead things improve. McClaren shoots in from 18 yards after earlier providing the through ball for Shutt's great 15-yard left-foot shot on the run.											
3 H CRYS PALACE		11	W	4-1	3-0	Shutt 12, Milne 19, 22, Walsh 82	Waugh	Newman	Bailey	Humphries	Pender	McClaren	Milne	Galliers	Shutt	Walsh	Gavin	
1/11	12,167	*2:8*				*Pardew 89*	*Parkin*	*Pemberton*	*Hone*	*Pardew*	*Hopkins*	*O'Reilly*	*Refearn*	*Thomas*	*Bright*	*Salako*	*Barber*	
						Ref: J Rushton	Palace are demoralised as City repeat the purple patch they struck at Mansfield with an early three-goal salvo. Shutt's flying header is followed by Milne's double strike, as he registers with a first-time curler around Brian Parkin, before drilling in Walsh's low cross from close range.											
4 H TRANMERE		12	W	1-0	1-0	Shutt 30	Waugh	Stanley	Bailey	Newman	Pender	McClaren	Hawkins	Galliers	Shutt*	Walsh	Gavin	Jordan
29/11	11,110	*4:10*					*Nixon*	*Higgins*	*McCarrick*	*Martindale*	*Moore^*	*Vickers*	*Murray**	*Bishop*	*Steel*	*Muir*	*Mungall*	*Williams/Malkin*
						Ref: A Buksh	Shutt brings the tie to life by finishing with a perfectly-struck right-foot shot after beating a couple of defenders. Tranmere abandon their sweeper system after the break, but City have the chances (six on target, compared to Tranmere's one) without being able to add to their score.											
QF A BRADFORD C		11	W	1-0	1-0	Walsh 2	Waugh	Honor	Bailey	Newman	Pender	McClaren	Galliers	Shepherd	Jordan*	Walsh	Gavin	Shutt
18/1	*15,330*	*2:18*					*Tomlinson*	*Mitchell*	*Abbott**	*Banks^*	*Jackson*	*Evans D*	*Palin*	*Sinnott*	*Ormondroyd*	*Kennedy*	*Leonard*	*Jewell/Oliver*
						Ref: B Hill	Given little chance of succeeding where Everton and Spurs had failed in cup competitions this season, Jordan inspires City's great display at Valley Parade. Walsh's reliable left foot decides the outcome after only 85 seconds, as City's defence restrict Bradford to two on-target shots.											
SF A NOTT'M FOREST		11	D	1-1	0-0	Mardon 65	Waugh	Honor	Bailey	Newman	Pender	Mardon	Galliers	McClaren	Gavin	Walsh	Jordan	
1 15/2	*30,016*	*1:4*				*Pender 86 (og)*	*Sutton*	*Laws*	*Pearce*	*Chettle*	*Wilson*	*Hodge*	*Carr*	*Webb*	*Clough*	*Chapman*	*Parker*	
						Ref: T Holbrook	Despite the handicap of facing one of their bogey teams, City turn in a magnificent backs-to-the-wall performance. Mardon's 15-yard drive should have inflicted Forest's first defeat in 12 games, but Pender turns Neil Webb's flick into his own net to leave the tie neatly balanced.											
SF H NOTT'M FOREST		11	L	0-1	0-0		Waugh	Honor	Bailey	Newman	Pender	Mardon	Galliers	McClaren	Gavin*	Walsh	Jordan	Shutt
2 26/2	28,084	*1:7*		*aet*		*Parker 114*	*Sutton*	*Laws*	*Pearce*	*Walker*	*Wilson*	*Hodge*	*Carr*	*Webb*	*Clough*	*Chapman*	*Parker*	
						Ref: J Worrell (City lost 1-2 on aggregate)	Shown live on ITV this game is marred by the tragic death of drummer Colin Burgess just before the start. An epic struggle in the wind and rain, nearly settled by Walsh's shot against the post at the end of normal time, is resolved by Gary Parker's fierce drive late into extra-time.											

FA Cup							1	2	3	4	5	6	7	8	9	10	11	subs used
1 H SOUTHEND		10	W	3-1	2-0	Walsh 22, McGarvey 32, Shutt, 80	Waugh	Honor	Bailey	Humphries	Pender	Newman	McGarvey	Galliers	Shutt	Walsh	Gavin	
19/11	*7,027*	*21*				*Ling 57*	*Sansome*	*Edinburgh*	*Johnson*	*Martin**	*Westley*	*Hall*	*Clark^*	*Robinson*	*Crown*	*Bennett*	*Ling*	*Smith/Ramsey*
						Ref: M James	It's easy for City until Martin Ling shoots in following Waugh's penalty save. Fortunately Shutt curtails Southend's fight-back by grabbing another of his customary classic cup goals. He arrives at speed to meet Gavin's right-wing cross and send a soaring header into the net.											
2 A ALDERSHOT		10	D	1-1	0-0	Shutt 90	Waugh	Newman	Bailey	Humphries	Pender	McClaren	McGarvey	Galliers*	Shutt	Walsh	Gavin	Stanley
10/12	*3,793*	*4:23*				*McDonald 76p*	*Lange*	*Brown*	*Phillips*	*Burvill*	*Smith*	*Wignall*	*Mazzon**	*Anderson*	*Claridge*	*McDonald*	*Randall*	*Ring*
						Ref: J Borrett	Deep into injury-time Shutt saves City, as his soft header to Walsh's free-kick squirms through Tony Lange's hands and trickles into the net. Ian McDonald, denied by the bar just after half-time, puts Aldershot in front with a controversial penalty after Pender blocks Steve Claridge.											

Rd	Venue	Opponent	Pos	Res	F-A	H-T	Scorers, Times, and Referees
2R	H	ALDERSHOT	10	D	0-0	0-0	
13/12		7,299 4:23			*aet*		Ref: J Borrett
2	A	ALDERSHOT	7	D	2-2	0-1	Shutt 90, Newman 110p
RR 20/12		*3,801 4:23*			*aet*		*Randall 14, Claridge 111* Ref: D Axcell
2R	H	ALDERSHOT	7	W	1-0	1-0	Shutt 10
RR 22/12		6,246 *4:23*					Ref: H King
3	A	HARTLEPOOL	10	L	0-1	0-0	
7/1		*4,033 4:16*					*Baker 70p* Ref: P Jones

Waugh | Newman | Bailey | Humphries | Pender | McClaren | McGarvey | Galliers* | Shutt | Walsh | Gavin | Stanley
Lange | Brown | Phillips | Burvill | Smith | Wignall | Mazzon | Ring | Claridge | McDonald | Randall | Chandler*

Nothing goes right for City, even losing the toss for choice of venue for the second replay. There is plenty of effort, but no one is able to find the telling pass necessary to eliminate an Aldershot side, for whom Steve Claridge strikes the post, belying their lowly League position.

Waugh | Llewellyn^ | Bailey | Newman | Pender | Stanley | McGarvey | Galliers | Hawkins* | Walsh | Gavin | Shutt/Honor
Lange | Brown | Phillips | Ring | Smith | Wignall | Mazzon | Anderson^ | Claridge | McDonald | Randall | Barnes/Chandler*

Shutt's mid-air volley produces a last-gasp equaliser, after Adrian Randall's speculative 35-yard drive had put the Shots in front. In extra-time Claridge drives the ball in to punish City for thinking the tie won with Newman's pen after David Barnes had clattered into the back of Gavin.

Waugh | Honor | Bailey | Newman | Pender | McClaren | McGarvey | Stanley* | Shutt | Walsh | Gavin | Galliers
Lange | Brown | Barnes | Ring | Smith | Wignall | Mazzon | Anderson | Claridge | McDonald | Randall | Chandler*

City's longest-ever cup-tie is settled early on as Honor's deflected cross gives Shutt the time to bring the ball down before blasting it in. Newman completely subdues the dangerous Steve Claridge, and Aldershot are left to rue letting City off the hook in the previous games.

Waugh | Honor | Bailey | Newman | Pender | McClaren | McGarvey* | Shepherd | Shutt | Walsh | Gavin | Jordan
Moverley | Nobbs | McKinnon | Tinkler | Stokes | Baker | Honour | Toman | Borthwick | Grayson | Barratt | Allon*

City stumble out of the FA Cup as their lightweight attack rarely threaten a worthwhile shot at the Victoria ground. Skipper Pender's needless pull on Joe Allon's shirt after the ball had been cleared gifts Pool the penalty that deservedly takes them on a rare visit to the fourth round.

		Home					Away					
	P	W	D	L	F	A	W	D	L	F	A	Pts
1 Wolves	46	18	4	1	61	19	8	10	5	35	30	92
2 Sheffield Utd	46	16	3	4	57	21	9	6	8	36	33	84
3 Port Vale *	46	15	3	5	46	21	9	9	5	32	27	84
4 Fulham	46	12	7	4	42	28	10	2	11	27	39	75
5 Bristol Rov	46	9	11	3	34	21	10	6	7	33	30	74
6 Preston	46	14	7	2	56	31	5	8	10	23	29	72
7 Brentford	46	14	5	4	36	21	4	9	10	30	40	68
8 Chester	46	12	6	5	38	18	7	5	11	26	43	68
9 Notts Co	46	11	7	5	37	22	7	6	10	27	32	67
10 Bolton	46	12	8	3	42	23	4	8	11	16	31	64
11 BRISTOL CITY	46	10	3	10	32	25	8	6	9	21	30	63
12 Swansea	46	11	8	4	33	22	4	8	11	18	31	61
13 Bury	46	11	7	5	27	22	5	6	12	28	45	61
14 Huddersfield	46	10	8	5	35	25	7	1	15	28	48	60
15 Mansfield	46	10	8	5	32	22	4	9	10	16	30	59
16 Cardiff	46	10	9	4	30	16	4	6	13	14	40	57
17 Wigan	46	9	5	9	28	22	5	9	9	27	31	56
18 Reading	46	10	6	7	37	29	5	5	13	31	43	56
19 Blackpool	46	10	6	7	36	29	4	7	12	20	30	55
20 Northampton	46	11	2	10	41	34	5	4	14	25	42	54
21 Southend	46	10	9	4	33	26	3	6	14	23	49	54
22 Chesterfield	46	9	5	9	35	35	5	2	16	16	51	49
23 Gillingham	46	7	3	13	25	32	5	1	17	22	49	40
24 Aldershot	46	7	6	10	29	29	1	7	15	19	49	37
	1104	268	146	138	902	593	138	146	268	593	902	1510

* promoted after play-offs

Odds & ends

Double wins: (4) Gillingham, Huddersfield, Northampton, Reading.
Double losses: (4) Chester, Fulham, Wolves, Brentford.

Won from behind: (3) Reading (h), Reading (a), Northampton (a).
Lost from in front: (2) Bury (a), Blackpool (h).

High spots: 4-[illegible] home success over Chesterfield on 3 Sep tember.
Beating Huddersfield 6-1 at Ashton Gate on 18 April.
Carl Shutt's goal that ends marathon four-game FA Cup battle with Aldershot.
Beating Oxford 4-2 at the Manor Ground in the FL Cup.
Beating Bradford City (a) 1-0 to reach the Semi-Finals of the FL Cup.
Record-breaking seven successive wins to reach the semi-finals of the FL Cup.

Low spots: Losing 0-1 v Bristol Rov at Ashton Gate on 2 January.
Losing 0-3 against Brentford at Griffin Park on 11 April.
Succumbing to a late extra-time goal in the 2nd leg of the FL Cup Semi-Final at Ashton Gate.
Losing 0-3 v Bristol Rov (a) in the Gloucestershire Cup Final on 17 Aug.

Player of the year: Keith Waugh.
Ever-presents: (1) Alan Walsh.
Hat-tricks: ([illegible]).
Leading scorer: Alan Walsh (16).

	Appearances						Goals			
	Lge	*Sub*	LC	*Sub*	FAC	*Sub*	Lge	LC	FAC	Tot
Bailey, John	35		5		6					
Bromage, Russell	13		3				1			1
Caldwell, Tony	1		1							
Carter, Tim	3									
Dolan, Eamonn	3									
Eaton, Jason		*2*								
Fitzpatrick, Paul		*1*								
Galliers, Steve	30	*3*	9		4	*1*				
Gavin, Mark	26	*3*	6		6		3			3
Hawkins, Nigel	7	*10*	2	*2*	1		2	1		3
Honor, Chris	24	*2*	3	*1*	3	*1*				
Humphries, Glenn	20	*2*	3		3					
Jordan, Joe	2	*7*	5	*1*		*1*	1			1
Leaning, Andy	6		2							
Llewellyn, Andy	13	*3*	4		1		1			1
Mardon, Paul	13	*7*	3	*2*				1		1
McClaren, Steve	44	*1*	9		4		1	1		2
McGarvey, Scott	20	*6*			6		9		1	10
Milne, Ralph	10	*1*	3	*1*			2	3		5
Newman, Rob	46		9		6		6	1	1	8
Pender, John	45		9		6		1			1
Shepherd, Tony	2	*1*	1		1					
Shutt, Carl	21	*3*	5	*2*	5	*1*	1	4	4	9
Stanley, Gary	8	*2*	1		2	*2*				
Taylor, Bob	12						8			8
Turner, Robbie	19						6			6
Walsh, Alan	46		9		6		11	4	1	16
Waugh, Keith	37		7		6					
28 players used	**506**	***54***	**99**	***9***	**66**	***6***	**53**	**15**	**7**	**75**

No	Date	Opponent	Att	Pos	Pt	F-A	H-T	Scorers, Times, and Referees	1	2	3	4	5	6	7	8	9	10	11	subs used
1	A	BURY			D	1-1	0-0	Taylor 57	Leaning	Llewellyn	Bailey	**Wimbleton**	Pender	**Rennie**	Gavin^	Newman	Taylor	**Smith**	Turner*	Eaton/Mardon
	19/8		*3,399*		1			*Greenwood 88*	*Farnworth*	*Hill*	*Withe*	*Hoyland*	*Valentine*	*Knill*	*Lee*	*Feeley**	*Cunningham*	*Robinson*	*Parkinson^*	*McIlroy/Greenwood*
								Ref: J Lloyd	City's encouraging display is blotted by lax defending as Nigel Greenwood is unmarked when he curls in Bury's late equaliser. Pender's push deprives Taylor of the fruits of his close-range shot, but within minutes Bailey's pass allows City's No 9 to celebrate with a legitimate strike.											
2	H	BIRMINGHAM			W	1-0	0-0	Taylor 74	Leaning	Llewellyn	Bailey	Wimbleton	Pender	Rennie	Gavin	Newman	Taylor	Smith	**Shelton**	
	26/8		8,938		4				*Thomas*	*Ashley*	*Matthewson*	*Atkins*	*Sproson*	*Overson*	*Peer*	*Bailey*	*Gordon*	*Frain*	*Sturridge**	*Yates*
								Ref: M James	The Brummies look the more effective side, but lack the finishing power as they fail to put away three good first-half chances. Off-form Taylor's match-winning spectacular overhead kick to connect with Newman's headed pass is an early candidate for goal of the season.											
3	A	NORTHAMPTON		15	L	0-2	0-0		Leaning	Llewellyn	Honor	Wimbleton^	Pender	Rennie	Gavin*	Newman	Taylor	Smith	Shelton	Turner/Mardon
	2/9		*4,088*	*10*	4			*Thomas 46, Adcock 89p*	*Gleasure*	*Sandeman*	*Wilson*	*Thomas*	*Wilcox*	*McPherson*	*Quow*	*Collins*	*Donald*	*Adcock*	*Berry*	
								Ref: J Moules	'What a load of rubbish' is the cry from the sizeable contingent of travelling fans at the end of this dismal affair. City cannot manage a single shot on target, whilst sloppy defending loses a chance of a point as Dean Thomas' free-kick finds its way through a gaping hole in City's wall.											
4	H	BLACKPOOL		8	W	2-0	0-0	Wimbleton 50p, Newman 65	Leaning	Llewellyn	Bromage	Wimbleton	Pender	Rennie	Shelton*	Newman	Taylor	Smith	Turner	Gavin
	9/9		7,172	*19*	7				*McIlhargey*	*Burgess*	*Morgan*	*Gore*	*Briggs*	*Methven*	*Wright*	*Thompson*	*Garner*	*Matthews*	*Bradshaw**	*Elliott*
								Ref: R Bigger	Fielding seven back-four players, Pool's defensive intentions come to naught when Colin Methven's push on Taylor produces City's penalty. Jordan's decision to play his first team in the reserves midweek is vindicated as Newman nudges in the second to erase memories of last week.											
5	A	CARDIFF		6	W	3-0	1-0	Shelton 45, Taylor 54, Turner 62	Leaning	Llewellyn	Bromage	Wimbleton	Pender	Rennie	Shelton*	Newman	Taylor	Smith	Turner	Mardon
	16/9		*5,970*	*24*	10				*Wood*	*Rodgerson*	*Daniel*	*Lynex**	*Abraham*	*Perry*	*Curtis*	*Morgan*	*Gilligan*	*Kelly*	*Sendall*	*Fry*
								Ref: K Breen	Shortly after Wimbleton fires his spot-kick against a post, Shelton volleys in to set up a comfortable win. Class and courage are personified by City's strike force, Taylor's brilliant turn and rasping shot demonstrating class, whilst Turner has the courage to net with a fearless header.											
6	H	BRISTOL ROV		5	D	0-0	0-0		Leaning	Llewellyn	Bromage*	Wimbleton	Pender	Rennie	Shelton	Newman	Taylor	Smith^	Turner	Mardon/Gavin
	23/9		17,432	*2*	11				*Martyn*	*Alexander !*	*Twentyman*	*Yates*	*Mehew*	*Jones*	*Holloway*	*Reece*	*White*	*Penrice*	*Wilmott*	
								Ref: J Deakin	City find out yet again that no amount of money can buy the teamwork and organisation that makes the Rovers such a powerful force. Whilst by no means a one-sided contest, the Rovers look the better unit as they overcome Ian Alexander's 34th-min dismissal for his second offence.											
7	H	SHREWSBURY		4	W	2-1	1-0	Taylor 43, 86	Leaning	Llewellyn	Mardon	Wimbleton	Pender	Rennie	Shelton*	Newman	Taylor	Smith	Turner	Gavin
	26/9		9,188	*5*	14			*Purdie 60*	*Perks*	*Green*	*Priest*	*Kelly*	*Pratley*	*Moyes*	*Brown*	*Bell*	*Purdie*	*McGinlay**	*Naughton*	*Griffiths*
								Ref: A Buksh	Shrewsbury live up to their top of the table billing with some slick control and neat passing, but City chase and harry their opponents into submission. Taylor, who lashed in City's opener, clinches the points with a header, after Jon Purdie had earlier slid in Shrewsbury's leveller.											
8	A	TRANMERE		4	L	**0-6**	0-2	*[Bishop 85, 89]*	Leaning	Llewellyn	Mardon	Wimbleton	Pender*	Rennie	Shelton	Newman	Taylor	Smith^	Turner !	Humphries/Gavin
	29/9		*8,977*	*1*	14			*Malkin 40, 41, Rennie 55 (og), Muir 77*	*Nixon*	*Higgins*	*McCarrick*	*Martindale**	*Hughes*	*Vickers*	*Morrissey*	*Harvey*	*Malkin*	*Muir*	*Thomas*	*Bishop*
								Ref: P Danson	An absorbing contest for 40 minutes, becomes an embarrassing rout after Chris Malkin turns in Tony Thomas' cross. Reduced to ten men following Turner's 53rd-minute sending off for elbowing Steve Vickers in the face, City loose Shelton just before the end with a calf strain.											
9	A	BRENTFORD		5	W	2-0	1-0	Wimbleton 35p, Turner 77	Leaning	Llewellyn	Bailey	Wimbleton	Pender	Rennie	Gavin	Newman	Taylor	Smith	Turner	
	7/10		*7,421*	*19*	17				*Parks*	*Bates**	*Fleming*	*Millen*	*Evans*	*Ratcliffe*	*Jones*	*May*	*Holdsworth*	*Blissett^*	*Godfrey*	*Cockram/Cadette*
								Ref: D Hedges	City spoil Brentford's 100th birthday with a deserved victory at Griffin Park. Poor finishing means City have to be satisfied with Wimbleton's penalty following Jamie Bates' push on Smith, and Turner's powerful close-range header, which is fumbled over the line by Tony Parks.											
10	H	SWANSEA		6	L	1-3	1-1	Taylor 15	Leaning	Llewellyn	Bailey	Wimbleton	Pender	Rennie	Gavin	Newman	Taylor	Smith	Eaton	
	14/10		8,794	*18*	17			*Raynor 1, Salako 66, 79*	*Freestone*	*Hough*	*Coleman*	*Melville*	*Boyle*	*James*	*Harris*	*Curtis*	*Hutchison*	*Salako*	*Raynor*	
								Ref: K Barratt	John Salako (on loan from Palace) inspires Swansea to their first away points and goals of the season. Blunders at the back are City's undoing, starting after just 45 seconds as Salako exposes Newman's poor marking with an accurate cross for the unattended Paul Raynor to head in.											
11	H	NOTTS CO		5	W	2-0	1-0	Eaton 16, Short 80 (og)	Leaning	Llewellyn	Bailey	Shelton	Humphries	Rennie	Gavin	Newman	Taylor	Smith*	Eaton	Wimbleton
	17/10		8,331	*12*	20				*Cherry*	*Palmer*	*Platnauer*	*Short*	*Yates*	*Robinson*	*Draper^*	*Turner*	*Lund*	*Barnes*	*Chapman**	*Stant/McStay*
								Ref: L Shapter	City's skilful first-half display is rewarded when Eaton caps a sweeping move, involving half-a-dozen players, with a perfect left-foot shot to open his League account. Under pressure as Notts County hit back, City are much relieved when Gavin's cross cannons in off Craig Short.											

No	Date	Opponent	Att	Pos	Pt	F-A	H-T	Scorers, Times, and Referees	1	2	3	4	5	6	7	8	9	10	11	subs used
12	A	MANSFIELD		8	L	0-1	0-1		Leaning	Llewellyn^	Bailey	Shelton	Humphries	Rennie	Gavin	Newman	Taylor	Smith	Eaton*	Wimbleton/Mardon
	21/10		*2,941*	*18*	20			*Christie 15*	*Cox*	*Hunt*	*Gray*	*Christie*	*Foster*	*O'Riordan*	*Kent*	*Stringfellow*	*Wilkinson*	*Charles*	*Kearney*	
								Ref: T Fitzharris	Such is City's inconsistency they can now manage to look like two different sides in the same match. Impressive after the break, City were fortunate not to have been losing by more than Trevor Christie's easy header at half-time as Steve Charles saw his shot rebound off of a post.											
13	H	WIGAN		6	W	3-0	2-0	Shelton 5, Rennie 41, Turner 65	Leaning	Llewellyn	Bailey	Shelton	Humphries	Rennie	Gavin	Newman	Eaton	Smith*	Turner	**Mellon**
	28/10		**6,365**	*23*	23				*Adkins*	*Senior*	*Tankard*	*Rimmer*	*Atherton*	*Patterson*	*Thompson^*	*Ward**	*Daley*	*Hilditch*	*Griffiths*	*Kelly/Johnson*
								Ref: J Martin	City have to be thankful for Turner's strength and aerial dominance in the howling wind and incessant rain at Ashton Gate. His frustration on heading against the bar after 30 minutes is relieved as he shoots in City's third, after earlier sending over the cross for Rennie's headed goal.											
14	A	CREWE		4	W	1-0	1-0	Bailey 18	Leaning	Llewellyn	Bailey	Shelton	Humphries	Rennie	Gavin	Newman	Taylor	Smith*	Turner	Eaton
	31/10		*3,554*	*21*	26				*Edwards P*	*Murphy*	*Swain*	*Smart*	*Dyson*	*Callaghan^*	*Jaspar*	*Hignett*	*Sussex*	*Clayton**	*Walters*	*Cutler/Fishenden*
								Ref: R Pawley	City's tremendous work rate and resolve, aided and abetted by Leaning's heroics and Bailey's tremendous 25-yarder, bring a hard-earned win at Gresty Road. Andy Sussex is denied by a post, whilst Leaning makes a great one-handed stop to keep out Chris Cutler's eight-yard header.											
15	A	WALSALL		1	W	2-0	1-0	Taylor 6, Turner 65	Leaning	Llewellyn	Bailey	Shelton	Humphries	Rennie	Gavin	Newman	Taylor	Smith	Turner	
	4/11		*5,286*	*20*	29				*Green*	*Wilder*	*O'Hara*	*Lemon*	*Forbes*	*Skipper*	*Kelly*	*Rimmer*	*Bertschin*	*Goodwin**	*Thorpe*	*Saville*
								Ref: T West	City's one blot on an exhilarating performance that takes them to the top of the table is their failure to kill off the game in a one-sided first half. Walsall offer little, though Stewart Rimmer should have equalised Taylor's opening header, before Turner heads in from Gavin's great cross.											
16	H	BOLTON		3	D	1-1	1-1	Newman 10	Leaning	Llewellyn	Bailey	Shelton	Humphries	Rennie	Gavin	Newman	Taylor !	Smith	Turner	
	11/11		11,994	*6*	30			*Brown 33*	*Felgate*	*Brown*	*Cowdrill*	*Comstive*	*Crombie*	*Winstanley*	*Henshaw*	*Thompson*	*Reeves*	*Philliskirk*	*Darby*	
								Ref: M Pierce	With the Berlin Wall coming down last night City find a wall of their own to conquer after Newman's early volley is countered by Phil Brown's low 25-yard drive. A disciplined response to Taylor's 43rd-minute sending off for elbowing Mark Winstanley, allows City to gain a point.											
17	A	READING		4	D	1-1	1-0	Rennie 10	Leaning	Llewellyn	Bailey	Shelton	Humphries	Rennie	Gavin	Newman	Eaton*	Smith	Turner	Wimbleton
	25/11		*5,353*	*14*	31			*Senior 56*	*Francis*	*Jones*	*Richardson*	*Beavon*	*Hicks*	*Whitlock*	*Knight*	*Tait**	*Senior*	*Conroy^*	*Payne*	*Taylor/Moran*
								Ref: H King	City are undone by their failure to put away their host of chances following Rennie's 25-yard drive into the top corner of the Reading net. The absence of the suspended Taylor proves costly as City's appeals for offside go unheeded when Trevor Senior taps in from Lee Payne's cross.											
18	H	ROTHERHAM		6	D	0-0	0-0		Leaning	Llewellyn	Bailey	Shelton	Humphries	Rennie	Gavin	Newman	**Jones**	Smith	Turner	
	2/12		9,509	*2*	32				*O'Hanlon*	*Barnsley*	*Robinson*	*Grealish*	*Johnson*	*Scott*	*Buckley*	*Pepper*	*Williamson*	*Evans*	*Hazel*	
								Ref: A Smith	The advent of colour soccer photos in the local press might not be marked by any goals, but there is plenty to shout about in this finely-balanced contest. Only the finishing lacks quality as both City and Rotherham post their promotion credentials to hold the crowd's interest.											
19	H	ORIENT		3	W	2-1	2-0	Taylor 8, 20	**Sinclair**	Llewellyn	Bailey	Shelton	Humphries	Rennie	Gavin	Newman	Taylor	Smith*	Jones^	Wimbleton/Turner
	16/12		7,486	*14*	35			*Castle 53*	*Heald*	*Sitton*	*Dickenson*	*Beesley*	*Day*	*Hoddle*	*Howard*	*Castle*	*Hull*	*Cooper*	*Pike**	*Nugent*
								Ref: K Cooper	Bob Taylor's two goals in this hard-earned win takes his tally since joining City to 21 in 32 appearances. He is however rather fortunate with his opener as he appears to make contact with Paul Heald instead of the ball when challenging for a defensive header held up in the wind.											
20	A	FULHAM		3	W	1-0	1-0	Taylor 32	Sinclair	Llewellyn	Bailey	Shelton	Humphries	Rennie	Gavin	Newman	Taylor	Smith*	Turner^	Wimbleton/Jones
	26/12		*6,089*	*11*	38				*Stannard*	*Donnellan !*	*Burns*	*Skinner**	*Nebbeling*	*Eckhardt*	*Marshall*	*Scott*	*Sayer^*	*Watson*	*Walker*	*Mauge/Milton*
								Ref: G Pooley	Gavin finds himself branded a cheat at sun-drenched Craven Cottage after Leo Donnellan had been rightly sent off in the 38th min for felling City's winger. Turner's well-timed leap and flicked header sets up Taylor with a typically accurate shot from 18 yards to give City the points.											
21	A	HUDDERSFIELD		3	L	1-2	0-1	Jones 74	Sinclair	Llewellyn	Bailey	Shelton	Humphries	Rennie	Gavin	Newman	Taylor	Smith	Turner*	Jones
	30/12		*7,681*	*5*	38			*Smith 11, Maskell 86*	*Martin*	*Marsden*	*Hutchings*	*May**	*Mitchell*	*Lewis*	*O'Regan*	*Bray*	*O'Connell*	*Maskell*	*Smith*	*Onuora*
								Ref: E Parker	Jones hooks in an equaliser to Mark Smith's 25-yard opener as City dominate after the break, before falling for a late sucker-punch. City pay the penalty for looking for all three points rather than holding out for a draw as Craig Maskell holds off Humphries to fire in Town's winner.											
22	H	PRESTON		3	W	2-1	1-0	Swann 36 (og), Newman 71	Sinclair	Llewellyn	Bailey	Shelton	Humphries	Rennie	Gavin	Newman	Taylor	Smith	Turner*	Wimbleton
	1/1		11,803	*20*	41			*Mooney 85*	*Kelly*	*Williams*	*Bennett*	*Bogie*	*Flynn*	*Hughes*	*Mooney*	*Swann*	*Joyce*	*Patterson*	*Harper*	
								Ref: R Gifford	Jaded City get a boost as Gary Swann's headed flick to Llewellyn's cross sends the ball into the back of the Preston net. Thereafter Alan Kelly's acrobatics keep City at bay, until Newman compensates for his disallowed 69th-minute effort with a ferocious shot from close range.											
23	A	BIRMINGHAM		1	W	4-0	1-0	Taylor 43, 86, Turner 65, Newman 71	Sinclair	Llewellyn	Bailey	Shelton	Humphries	Rennie	Gavin	Newman	Taylor	Smith	Turner	
	13/1		***11,277***	*9*	44				*Thomas*	*Clarkson*	*Frain*	*Atkins*	*Overson*	*Matthewson*	*Bell**	*Bailey*	*Sturridge*	*Gleghorn*	*Langley*	*Hopkins*
								Ref: S Bell	Birmingham, who had previously conceded just five League goals at home, are annihilated by City's breathtaking display. Taylor starts and finishes the rout, netting with a low drive just before the interval, he races between two defenders to nonchalantly stroke in City's fourth.											

No	Date		Att	Pos	Pt	F-A	H-T	Scorers, Times, and Referees	1	2	3	4	5	6	7	8	9	10	11	subs used
24	H	BURY		1	W	1-0	1-0	Smith 35	Sinclair	Llewellyn	Bailey	Shelton	Humphries	Rennie	Gavin	Newman	Taylor*	Smith	Turner	**Miller**
	20/1		10,992	6	47				Kelly	Hill	Clements	Hoyland	Greenall*	Knill	Lee	Robinson	Hulme	Feeley	Withe^	Bishop/Greenwood
								Ref: K Cooper	A minute's silence in memory of the son of City's assistant boss Jimmy Lumsden, precedes this keenly-fought encounter. Newman's 44th-min penalty, which is saved by Gary Peters, prevents City adding to Smith's shot into an empty net, following a poor back-pass by Kenny Clements.											
25	H	CHESTER		1	W	1-0	0-0	Newman 57	Sinclair	Llewellyn	Bailey	Shelton	Humphries	Rennie	Gavin	Newman	Taylor*	Smith	Turner	Miller
	30/1		8,769	15	50				Stewart	Reeves	Woodthorpe	Hinnigan	Lightfoot	Lane	Butler^	Barrow	Abel	Dale*	Croft	Newhouse/Hamilton
								Ref: R Wiseman	After a first half facing a gale-force wind, Newman has the City fans singing in the rain with a goal fit to win any match. As the wind subsides, Shelton touches a short free-kick to Smith, who turns the ball back for Newman to find the top corner of the net with a classic 30-yard shot.											
26	H	CARDIFF		1	W	1-0	1-0	Shelton 4	Sinclair	Llewellyn	Bailey	Shelton	Humphries	Rennie	Gavin	Newman	Taylor*	Mellon^	Turner	Miller/Honor
	10/2		11,982	22	53				Hansbury	Rodgerson	Daniel	Barnard	Abraham	Gibbins	Morgan^	Griffin	Pike	Perry*	Kelly	Lynex/Chandler
								Ref: T Ward	After the bonus of an early goal when Shelton looked suspiciously offside on shooting in from ten yards, City might well have had cause to rue their missed chances. Fortunately though, Jon Morgan does not have any of Shelton's luck, as offside rules out his 67th-minute leveller.											
27	H	READING		1	L	0-1	0-0		Leaning	Llewellyn^	Bailey	Shelton	Humphries	Rennie	Mellon	Newman	Taylor	Smith	Turner*	Eaton/Honor
	24/2		10,616	13	53			Leworthy 70	Francis	Jones	Richardson	Wood	Hicks	Conroy	Gooding	Tait	Senior*	Gilkes	Moran	Leworthy
								Ref: K Morton	City's uninspired display reaps what it deserves against a Reading side who had only won once away in the League before this game. After David Leworthy's six-yard volley puts the Royals in front, Rennie squanders City's chance of a point by spooning his penalty high and wide.											
28	A	CHESTER		1	W	3-0	2-0	Taylor 4, 24, 84	Sinclair	Llewellyn	Bailey	Shelton	Humphries	Rennie	Mellon*	Newman	Taylor^	Smith	**Horrix**	Honor/Eaton
	3/3		**2,502**	15	56				Stewart	Reeves	Woodthorpe	Hinnigan*	Lightfoot	Lane	Butler	Barrow	Dale	Pugh^	Croft	Painter/Danzey
								Ref: I Cruikshanks	New signing Dean Horrix (£50,000 ex Millwall) makes a confident debut, his incisive break and measured cross allowing Taylor to head in the opener from six yards. Chester have their chances, but lack a marksman of Taylor's calibre, who completes his hat-trick with another header.											
29	H	TRANMERE		3	L	1-3	0-1	Shelton 59	Sinclair	Llewellyn	Bailey	Shelton	Humphries	Honor*	Mellon	Newman	Taylor	Smith	Horrix	Jordan
	6/3		14,376	1	56			McCarrick 7, Muir 48, Bishop 50	Nixon	Higgins	McCarrick*	Bishop	Hughes	Vickers	Malkin	Harvey	Steel	Muir	Thomas	Martindale
								Ref: V Callow	Slick Tranmere register their eighth successive win after Mark McCarrick's shot from the edge of the pen area clips Jimmy Harvey's heel and loops into the net. Shelton's neat turn and angled shot is City's sole response to further Rovers goals and Chris Malkin's shot against a post.											
30	A	SHREWSBURY		2	W	1-0	0-0	Smith 87	Sinclair	Llewellyn	Bailey	Shelton	Humphries	Rennie	Mellon*	Newman	Taylor	Smith	Horrix	Honor
	10/3		4,785	14	59				Perks	Green	Lynch	Kelly	Finley	Moyes	Weir	Wimbleton^	Hartford*	McGinlay	Naughton	Melrose/Gorman
								Ref: G Aplin	'We are going up as Champions, I don't know what the panic is about' says John Bailey before this thoroughly deserved success. Smith fires in low past Steve Perks to bring City's reward for their domination of the proceedings, having five shots on target compared to Shrewsbury's one.											
31	A	BLACKPOOL		1	W	3-1	1-0	Taylor 18, 55, Shelton 90	Sinclair	Llewellyn	Bailey	Shelton	Humphries	Rennie	Mellon	Newman	Taylor	Smith	Eaton	
	13/3		3,227	23	62			Brook 47	Wood	Wright*	Morgan	Groves	Methven	Elliott	Gore	Brook	Eyres	Garner	Richards	Davies
								Ref: P Jones	City respond to the death of Dean Horrix in a car crash last Saturday night with a Championship display at Bloomfield Road. Gary Brook's volleyed-in equaliser is but a small interlude in City's domination, and Shelton's swerving low shot into the corner ties up a well-deserved win.											
32	H	BRENTFORD		1	W	2-0	1-0	Gavin 15, Rennie 60	Sinclair	Llewellyn	Bailey	Shelton	Humphries	Rennie	Gavin	Newman	Taylor	Smith*	Mellon	Turner
	17/3		10,813	11	65				Parks	Cousins	Peters	Buttigieg	Evans	Buckle	Gayle*	Godfrey^	Holdsworth	Blissett	Smillie	Cadette/Driscoll
								Ref: A Simmons	Gavin displays his arrogant skills after racing onto Smith's through-ball to outpace Jason Cousins and shoot in the opener. It is just a case of when City would score again, and inevitably Gavin's touch tees up Rennie to fire in a 15-yarder which even Tony Parks is powerless to stop.											
33	A	SWANSEA		1	W	**5-0**	2-0	Taylor 26, 27, 76, Newman 49, Honor 83	Sinclair	Llewellyn	Bailey	Shelton	Humphries*	Rennie	Gavin	Newman	Taylor^	Smith	Turner	Honor/Eaton
	20/3		7,051	16	68				Bracey	Trick	Coleman	Melville	James	Thornber	Harris	Davey*	Curtis	Raynor^	Hutchison	D'Auria/Phillips
								Ref: M Bodenham	City's penchant this season for beating their bogey teams is confirmed by this rare win at the Vetch. 'Champions' chant the massed ranks of the travelling fans as Taylor's hat-trick (an instinctive header sandwiched between two shots) sends City's promotion bid into overdrive.											
34	A	NOTTS CO		1	D	0-0	0-0		Sinclair	Llewellyn	Bailey	Shelton	Humphries*	Rennie	Gavin	Newman	Taylor	Smith	Turner	Honor
	24/3		9,598	4	69				Cherry	Norton	Platnauer	Short	Yates	Robinson	O'Riordan	Turner	Bartlett	Thomas	Johnson	
								Ref: D Scott	It is not often a goalless draw is greeted by scenes of unbridled celebration, but this is what happens amongst the City fans at Meadow Lane. Another giant step towards promotion, but in truth City get much more than they deserve after failing to register a single shot on target.											

No	Venue	Opponent	Att	Pos	Pts	Res	F-A	H-T	Scorers, Times, Referees												
35	H	NORTHAMPTON		1		W	3-1	2-1	Turner 5, Shelton 17, Taylor 61	Sinclair	Llewellyn	Bailey	Shelton	Humphries	Rennie	Gavin	Newman	Taylor*	Smith	Turner	**Ferguson**
27/3			11,965	*23*	72				*Barnes 43*	*Gleasure*	*Chard*	*Wilson*	*Terry*	*Wilcox*	*McPherson**	*Berry*	*Collins*	*Leaburn*	*Barnes*	*Thorpe*	*Donald*
									Ref: K Cooper	Close-range shots from Turner and Shelton make it seem so easy early on, but over-elaboration and sloppy passing allow Northampton to get back into the game. After Bobby Barnes waltzes through unchallenged to score, it needs Taylor's poaching skills to make sure of the points.											
36	H	MANSFIELD		1		D	1-1	0-0	Taylor 87	Sinclair	Llewellyn	Bailey	Shelton	Humphries	Rennie	Gavin	Newman	Taylor	Smith	Turner*	Ferguson
31/3			11,773	*19*	73				*Kearney 70*	*Beasley*	*Murray*	*Kearney*	*Christie*	*Foster*	*Smalley*	*Kent**	*Clarke^*	*Wilkinson*	*Fairclough*	*Charles*	*Hodges/Chambers*
									Ref: T Lunt	After Mark Kearney puts Mansfield in front with a simple six-yard header, Taylor nets his 29th goal of the season to salvage City a point from a game that appeared to be lost. His powerful far-post header finishes off Gavin's cross to deny the Stags their first away win for six months.											
37	A	ROTHERHAM		1		W	2-1	0-1	Johnson 49 (og), Taylor 70	Sinclair	Llewellyn	Bailey	Shelton	Humphries	Rennie	Gavin	Newman	Taylor	Smith*	Ferguson	Honor
3/4			*5,526*	*7*	76				*Buckley 26*	*O'Hanlon*	*Barnsley*	*Robinson*	*Goodwin*	*Johnson*	*Heard**	*Buckley*	*Dempsey*	*Williamson*	*Mendonca^*	*Cash*	*Hazel/Evans*
									Ref: T Holbrook	Taylor chooses the perfect moment to become City's first 30-goal striker since the days of John Atyeo. His brilliant header opens up a seven-point gap at the top of the Third Division after Smith's shot cannons in off Nigel Johnson to equalise Rotherham's deserved chipped-in opener.											
38	A	WIGAN		1		W	3-2	1-1	Smith 15p, Taylor 49, Ferguson 71	Sinclair	Llewellyn	Bailey*	Shelton	Humphries	Rennie	Gavin	Newman	Taylor	Smith	Ferguson	Honor
7/4			*3,331*	*14*	79				*Baraclough 12, Parkinson 64*	*Hughes*	*Senior*	*Tankard*	*Parkinson*	*Atherton*	*Johnson*	*Thompson*	*Patterson*	*Baraclough*	*Hilditch*	*Griffiths**	*Page*
									Ref: A Bennett	With news of the death of the great Peter Doherty (City boss 1958-60) in Blackpool, City are involved in a ding-dong struggle not far away in Wigan. The saving of Smith's second pen in the 18th minute makes things more difficult, but Ferguson fires in a 15-yard angled-shot winner.											
39	H	CREWE		1		W	4-1	3-0	Gavin 12p, Taylor 23, 29, 62	Sinclair	Honor	Llewellyn	Shelton^	Humphries	Rennie	Gavin	Newman	Taylor*	Smith	Ferguson	Turner/Mellon
10/4			13,800	*10*	82				*Murphy 74*	*Greygoose*	*Swain*	*McKearney*	*Smart*	*Callaghan*	*Hignett*	*Jasper*	*Murphy*	*Foreman**	*Gardiner*	*Cutler^*	*Joseph/Jones R*
									Ref: G Pooley	Taylor's brilliant 30-yard volley which completes his hat-trick, takes City's No 9 to the top of the Football League scoring charts. Jordan's shrewd tactical brain halts Crewe's 14-match unbeaten run, but City are concerned over the loss of Taylor with a 67th-min hamstring injury.											
40	A	PRESTON		1		D	2-2	1-1	Morgan 3, Shelton 73	Sinclair	Honor	Llewellyn	Shelton	Humphries	Rennie	Gavin	Newman	**Morgan**	Smith	Ferguson	
14/4			*7,601*	*20*	83				*Flynn 44, Harper 76*	*Kelly*	*Williams*	*Swann*	*McIlroy*	*Flynn*	*Wrightson*	*Mooney*	*Hughes*	*Joyce*	*Atkins**	*Bogie*	*Harper*
									Ref: D Hutchinson	After Nicky Morgan's (£30,000 ex Stoke) early tap-in from Smith's low cross, Preston equalise when Mike Flynn ghosts in at the far post to head over the line. Shelton's free-kick takes a wicked deflection off Gavin to put City back in front, before Harper heads Preston level again.											
41	H	FULHAM		1		W	5-1	2-1	Morgan 36, Smith 41, Newman 57,	Sinclair	Llewellyn	Bailey	Shelton	Humphries	Rennie	Gavin	Newman	Morgan	Smith	Ferguson	
18/4			16,139	*16*	86				Eckhardt 12 [F'guson 60, Shelton 79]	*Stannard*	*Eckhardt*	*Pike*	*Skinner^*	*Newson*	*Thomas*	*Cole**	*Scott*	*Milton*	*Barnett*	*Nebbeling*	*Walker/Davies*
									Ref: H King	Sinclair's collision with Smith sees Jeff Eckhardt swoop onto the loose ball to put Fulham in front, but with both wingers in top form City fight back for victory. Gavin's free-kick against the bar sets up Morgan's superb close-range equaliser, whilst Smith lays City's last goal on a plate.											
42	A	ORIENT		1		D	1-1	0-1	Newman 61	Sinclair	Llewellyn	Bailey	Shelton	Humphries	Rennie	Gavin	Newman	Morgan	Smith	Ferguson*	Turner
21/4			*7,273*	*14*	87				*Howard 32*	*Heald*	*Hales*	*Sitton*	*Beesley*	*Whitbread*	*Baker*	*Howard*	*Nugent*	*Harvey*	*Hull**	*Carter*	*Campbell*
									Ref: G Singh	Orient are kept at bay by Shelton's tireless running and bone-shaking tackles. After Newman's sweet volley counters Terry Howard's twelve-yard drive, out of sorts City are denied a club record equalling 13th away win when Turner's header is disallowed because of a Morgan foul.											
43	H	HUDDERSFIELD		1		D	1-1	0-1	Morgan 52	Sinclair	Llewellyn	Bailey	Shelton	Humphries	Rennie	Gavin	Newman	Morgan	Smith	Ferguson*	Turner
24/4			17,791	*8*	88				*Duggan 19*	*Hardwick*	*May*	*Hutchings*	*Kelly*	*Mitchell*	*Duggan*	*O'Regan*	*Marsden*	*Byrne**	*Maskell*	*Edwards*	*Smith*
									Ref: M James	The champagne remains on ice as City fail to get the win to secure promotion. Boosted by Andy Duggan's header the visitors prove difficult to break down, but Morgan's tap-in, after Gavin's brilliant turn and shot is parried by Steve Hardwick, takes City's unbeaten run to 14 games.											
44	A	BOLTON		1		L	0-1	0-1		Sinclair	Llewellyn	Bailey	Shelton	Humphries	Rennie	Gavin	Newman	Taylor*	Smith	Morgan	Turner
28/4			*11,098*	*6*	88				*Green 32*	*Felgate*	*Brown*	*Cowdrill*	*Green*	*Came*	*Winstanley*	*Storer**	*Thompson*	*Reeves*	*Philliskirk*	*Darby*	*Gregory*
									Ref: T Mills	David Felgate's faultless display between the sticks leaves City's nerves a jangling as Rovers beat Shrewsbury 1-0 to put them just a point behind. Scott Green keeps Bolton's play-off ambitions alive as he cuts inside to unleash a shot which spins viciously to wrong-foot Sinclair.											
45	A	BRISTOL ROV		2		L	0-3	0-1		Sinclair	Llewellyn	Bailey*	Shelton	Humphries	Rennie	Gavin	Newman	Morgan	Smith	Turner^	Honor/Ferguson
2/5			*9,813*	*1*	88				*White 25, 55, Holloway 62p*	*Parkin*	*Alexander*	*Twentyman*	*Yates*	*Mehew*	*Jones*	*Holloway*	*Reece*	*White*	*Saunders*	*Purnell*	
									Ref: L Dilkes	Ex manager Cooper and player Andy Llewellyn confidently predict a City success, but in the event Rovers romp to an easy victory. It's all too much for City's yob element who attempt to bring proceedings to a halt, but Jordan deserves great credit for his efforts to diffuse the situation.											
46	H	WALSALL		2		W	4-0	2-0	Shelton 3, Gavin 38p, Rennie 84,	Sinclair	Llewellyn	Bailey*	Shelton	Humphries	Rennie	Gavin^	Newman	Morgan	Smith	Ferguson	Honor/**Bent**
5/5			**19,483**	*24*	91				[Morgan 86]	*Green*	*Dornan*	*Hawker*	*Smith**	*Forbes*	*Skipper*	*Ford*	*Rimmer^*	*Shaw*	*Taylor*	*O'Hara*	*Bremner/Goldsmith*
	Home		Away						Ref: T Fitzharris	Erroneous news that Rovers had lost at Blackpool had City fans thinking the Championship prize was theirs. It wasn't to be however, but the fans celebrate in scenes reminiscent of 1976, after City's sparkling display was sealed by Rennie's brilliant chip and Morgan's bullet header.											
Average	11,544		6,254																		

League Cup	Att	Pos	Res	F-A	H-T	Scorers, Times, and Referees	1	2	3	4	5	6	7	8	9	10	11	subs used
1:1 H READING			L	2-3	1-2	Wimbleton 42p, Smith 66	Leaning	Llewellyn	Bailey	Wimbleton	Pender	Rennie	Gavin	Newman	Taylor	Smith	Eaton	
22/8	6,318					*Gilkes 15, 29, 80*	*Francis*	*Williams*	*Richardson*	*Beavon*	*Hicks*	*Wood*	*Jones*	*Taylor*	*Senior*	*Gilkes*	*Payne*	
						Ref: K Burge	City's generous defence allows Michael Gilkes the easiest of hat-tricks after he puts Reading in front with a low shot via Trevor Senior's nod-on. Smith smashes in a fierce 25-yarder to cap City's second-half fight-back, but Gilkes has loads of space to shoot home the Royals' winner.											
1:2 A READING			D	2-2	2-0	Taylor 16, 31	Leaning	Llewellyn	Honor	Wimbleton*	Pender	Rennie	Gavin^	Newman	Taylor	Smith	Shelton	Mardon/Eaton
29/8	*4,457*					*Senior 47, Gilkes 62*	*Francis*	*Williams*	*Richardson*	*Beavon*	*Hicks*	*Wood*	*Jones*	*Taylor*	*Senior*	*Gilkes*	*Payne**	*Conroy*
						Ref: P Alcock (City lost 4-5 on aggregate)	Trevor Senior levels the aggregate score from a suspiciously offside position, after Taylor's opening shot and later header had put City in charge. City are denied taking the tie into extra-time by Michael Gilkes' exquisitely-taken shot, and Mardon's failure in front of an open net.											

FA Cup	Att	Pos	Res	F-A	H-T	Scorers, Times, and Referees	1	2	3	4	5	6	7	8	9	10	11	subs used
1 H BARNET		3	W	2-0	2-0	Taylor 21, Turner 41	Leaning	Llewellyn	Bailey	Shelton	Humphries	Rennie	Gavin	Newman	Taylor	Smith*	Turner	Eaton
18/11	7,538	*C:2*					*Guthrie*	*Wilson*	*Stacey*	*Poole*	*Reilly*	*Payne**	*Stein^*	*Murphy*	*Bull*	*Cooper*	*Bodley*	*Clarke/Gridelet*
						Ref: M Bodenham	City need their better finishing ability to beat Conference side Barnet, as the visitors produce the more attractive football. The alert Taylor takes full advantage as Peter Guthrie fumbles Rennie's low drive, whilst Turner volleys in from six yards to finish off Smith's accurate cross.											
2 H FULHAM		6	W	2-1	0-1	Taylor 56, Wimbleton 80p	Sinclair	Llewellyn	Bailey	Wimbleton	Humphries	Rennie	Gavin	Newman	Taylor	Smith	Turner	
9/12	7,662	*12*				*Scott 43*	*Stannard*	*Donnellan*	*Mauge**	*Lenington^*	*Nebbeling*	*Peters*	*Marshall*	*Scott*	*Sayer*	*Watson*	*Langley*	*Skinner/Barnett*
						Ref: D Vickers	A classic cup-tie is settled when Smith's stumble following Leo Donnellan's challenge brings a penalty. City dominate the play, but are made to pay for missed chances when the referee has no doubts about Peter Scott's 25-yard opener that hits the underside bar before bouncing down.											
3 H SWINDON		3	W	2-1	2-1	Taylor 22, Newman 35	Sinclair	Llewellyn	Bailey	Shelton	Humphries	Rennie	Gavin	Newman	Taylor	Smith	Turner	
6/1	17,422	*2:5*				*Shearer 41*	*Digby*	*Kerslake*	*Bodin*	*McLoughlin*	*Calderwood*	*Gittens*	*Jones T**	*Shearer*	*White*	*MacLaren*	*Foley*	*Hockaday*
						Ref: K Burge	This stirring contest is a fine advert for West Country soccer, despite the treacherous underfoot conditions. Taylor waltzes the ball past Fraser Digby to put City ahead, and then tries to lay claim to the second goal when the ball pins about in the box before going in the net off Newman.											
4 H CHELSEA		1	W	3-1	1-0	Turner 4, 52, Gavin 89	Sinclair	Llewellyn	Bailey	Shelton	Humphries	Rennie	Gavin	Newman	Taylor	Smith	Turner	
27/1	24,535	*1:6*				*Wilson 84*	*Beasant*	*Clarke*	*Dorigo*	*Roberts*	*Johnson*	*Monkou**	*McAllister*	*Bumstead*	*Dixon*	*Wilson K*	*Le Saux*	*Lee*
						Ref: D Phillips	Goal-stopper Sinclair and goal-scorer Turner inspire City in this magnificent cup-tie. Two relatively simple goals underline Turner's goal-taking ability, but he also sets up City's third with an exquisite turn and 20-yard shot that is pushed out by Dave Beasant for Gavin to steer in.											
5 H CAMBRIDGE		1	D	0-0	0-0		Sinclair	Llewellyn	Bailey	Shelton	Humphries	Rennie	Gavin	Newman	Taylor	Smith	Turner	
17/2	20,676	*4:12*					*Vaughan*	*Fensome*	*Kimble*	*Bailie**	*Chapple*	*Daish*	*Cheetham*	*Leadbitter*	*Dublin*	*Taylor*	*Philpott*	*O'Shea*
						Ref: S Lodge	City blow their great chance of reaching the Quarter-Finals as they turn in a most disappointing display. It might have been different if Gavin had not been denied by the post early on, but Cambridge are much the better side, impressive in all departments and quicker on the ball.											
5R A CAMBRIDGE		1	D	1-1	0-0	Taylor 94	Sinclair	Llewellyn	Bailey	Shelton	Humphries	Rennie	Gavin	Newman	Taylor	Smith	Turner	
21/2	*9,796*	*4:12*		*aet*		*Dublin 91*	*Vaughan*	*Fensome*	*Kimble*	*Bailie*	*Chapple*	*Daish*	*Cheetham*	*Leadbitter*	*Dublin*	*Taylor*	*Philpott*	
						Ref: S Lodge	Determination sees City survive a memorable night of cut-and-thrust soccer at the Abbey Stadium. John Taylor's cross that hits the woodwork is surprisingly the nearest to a goal until extra-time, when Bob Taylor's rasping drive into the top corner levels Dion Dublin's headed opener.											
5 A CAMBRIDGE		1	L	1-5	0-1	Taylor 75 *[Taylor 72]*	Leaning	Llewellyn	Bailey	Shelton	Humphries	Rennie	Gavin*	Newman	Taylor	Smith	Turner	Mellon
RR 27/2	*9,047*	*4:14*				*Leadbitter 44, Philpott 49, Dublin 51, 68*	*Vaughan*	*Fensome*	*Kimble*	*Bailie**	*Chapple*	*Daish*	*Cheetham^*	*Leadbitter*	*Dublin*	*Taylor*	*Philpott*	*O'Shea/Robinson*
						Ref: J Moules	After losing the toss for venue it is back to the Abbey Stadium where City are blown away after failing to take their first-half chances. Chris Leadbitter's close-range overhead kick opens the scoring, whilst John Taylor's cool 72nd-minute chip completes City's humiliation.											

		P	W	D	L	F	A	W	D	L	F	A	Pts
			Home					Away					
1	Bristol Rov	46	15	8	0	43	14	11	7	5	28	21	93
2	BRISTOL CITY	46	15	5	3	40	16	12	5	6	36	24	91
3	Notts Co *	46	17	4	2	40	18	8	8	7	33	35	87
4	Tranmere	46	15	5	3	54	22	8	6	9	32	27	80
5	Bury	46	11	7	5	35	19	10	4	9	35	30	74
6	Bolton	46	12	7	4	32	19	6	8	9	27	29	69
7	Birmingham	46	10	7	6	33	19	8	5	10	27	40	66
8	Huddersfield	46	11	5	7	30	23	6	9	8	31	39	65
9	Rotherham	46	12	6	5	48	28	5	7	11	23	34	64
10	Reading	46	10	9	4	33	21	5	10	8	24	32	64
11	Shrewsbury	46	10	9	4	38	24	6	6	11	21	30	63
12	Crewe	46	10	8	5	32	24	5	9	9	24	29	62
13	Brentford	46	11	4	8	41	31	7	3	13	25	35	61
14	Orient	46	9	6	8	28	24	7	4	12	24	32	58
15	Mansfield	46	13	2	8	34	25	3	5	15	16	40	55
16	Chester	46	11	7	5	30	23	2	8	13	13	32	54
17	Swansea	46	10	6	7	25	27	4	6	13	20	36	54
18	Wigan	46	10	6	7	29	22	3	8	12	19	42	53
19	Preston	46	10	7	6	42	30	4	3	16	23	49	52
20	Fulham	46	8	8	7	33	27	4	7	12	22	39	51
21	Cardiff	46	6	9	8	30	35	6	5	12	21	35	50
22	Northampton	46	7	7	9	27	31	4	7	12	24	37	47
23	Blackpool	46	8	6	9	29	33	2	10	11	20	40	46
24	Walsall	46	6	8	9	23	30	3	6	14	17	42	41
		1104	257	156	139	829	585	139	156	257	585	829	1500

* promoted after play-offs

Odds & ends

Double wins: (10) Birmingham, Blackpool, Cardiff, Shrewsbury, Brentford, Wigan, Crewe, Walsall, Fulham, Chester.
Double losses: (1) Tranmere.

Won from behind: (3) Rotherham (a), Wigan (a), Fulham (h).
Lost from in front: (0).

High spots: Winning 5-0 at Swansea on 20 March.
Beating Rotherham 2-1 at Millmoor on 3 April.
Beating Wigan at Springfield Park 3-2 on 7 April.
Beating Crewe 4-1 at Ashton Gate on 10 April.
Beating Fulham 5-1 at Ashton Gate on 16 April.
Beating Chelsea 3-1 in the FA Cup.

Low spots: Losing 0-6 at Prenton Park on 29 September.
Losing to Swansea at Ashton Gate on 14 October.
Losing to Bristol Rov 0-5 at Twerton Park on 2 May.
Losing 1-5 against Cambridge in the FA Cup on 27 February.
Losing 1-2 at Ashton Gate v Bristol Rov in the Glos Cup on 8 August.

Player of the Year: Bob Taylor.
Ever-presents: (2) Rob Newman, Andy Llewellyn.
Hat-tricks: (3) Bob Taylor.
Leading scorer: Bob Taylor (34).

	Appearances Lge	*Sub*	LC	*Sub*	FAC	*Sub*	Goals Lge	LC	FAC	Tot
Bailey, John	**38**		1		7		**1**			**1**
Bent, Junior		*1*								
Bromage, Russell	**3**									
Eaton, Jason	**6**	*5*	1	*1*		*1*	**1**			**1**
Ferguson, Iain	**8**	*3*					**2**			**2**
Gavin, Mark	**36**	*4*	2		7		**3**		1	**4**
Honor, Chris	**4**	*10*	1				**1**			**1**
Horrix, Dean	**3**									
Humphries, Glenn	**36**	*1*			7					
Jones, Andy	**2**	*2*					**1**			**1**
Jordan, Joe		*1*								
Leaning, Andy	**19**		2		2					
Llewellyn, Andy	**46**		2		7					
Mardon, Paul	**2**	*5*		*1*						
Mellon, Micky	**7**	*2*				*1*				
Miller,Paul		*3*								
Morgan, Nicky	**7**						**4**			**4**
Newman, Rob	**46**		2		7		**8**		1	**9**
Pender, John	**10**		2			*2*				
Rennie, David	**45**		2		7		**4**			**4**
Shelton, Gary	**43**		1		6		**9**			**9**
Sinclair, Ronnie	**27**				5					
Smith, David	**45**		2		7		**4**	1		**5**
Taylor, Bob	**37**		2		7		**27**	2	5	**34**
Turner, Robbie	**26**	*7*			7		**6**		3	**9**
Wimbleton, Paul	**10**	*6*	2		1		**2**	1	1	**4**
(own-goals)							**3**			**3**
26 players used	**506**	***50***	**22**	***2***	**77**	***4***	**76**	**4**	**11**	**91**

BARCLAYS LEAGUE DIVISION 2

Manager: Jordan ⇨ Jimmy Lumsden

SEASON 1990-91

No	Date		Att	Pos	Pt	F-A	H-T	Scorers, Times, and Referees	1	2	3	4	5	6	7	8	9	10	11	subs used
1	H	BLACKBURN			W	4-2	0-1	Aizlewood 51, Taylor 68, 70, Morgan 72	Sinclair	Llewellyn	**Aizlewood**	**May**	Shelton	Rennie	**Donowa**	Newman	Taylor	Morgan	Smith	
	25/8		13,794		3			*Gayle 25, 55*	*Gennoe*	*Atkins*	*Sulley^*	*Irvine*	*Hill*	*Moran*	*Richardson*	*Millar*	*Stapleton*	*Gayle*	*Shepstone**	*Johnrose/Oliver*
								Ref: A Buksh	Presented with his Golden Boots award, Taylor continues amongst the goals. The lethal marksman transforms the match as City throw off the shackles of their tense and inhibited first-half display. Smith's pace and far-post cross finds Morgan to head in to complete a thrilling victory.											
2	A	SWINDON			W	1-0	1-0	Bent 32	Sinclair	Llewellyn	Aizlewood	May	Shelton	Rennie	Bent	Newman	Taylor	Morgan*	Smith	**Allison**
	2/9		*12,686*		6				*Digby*	*Kerslake*	*Bodin*	*Simpson*	*Calderwood*	*Gittens*	*Jones^*	*Shearer*	*Close**	*MacLaren*	*Foley*	*McLoughlin/Hockaday*
								Ref: V Callow	City confirm early-season optimism with a marvellous display at the County Ground as Jordan counters Swindon's diamond formation by pushing Shelton forward and having May shadow Steve Foley. Taylor's 50-yard pass releases Bent to send a side-foot shot past Fraser Digby.											
3	H	PLYMOUTH		5	D	1-1	1-0	Morgan 16	Sinclair	Llewellyn	Aizlewood	May	Shelton	Rennie	Bent	Newman	Taylor*	Morgan	Smith	Allison
	8/9		14,283	*17*	7			*Thomas 67*	*Wilmot*	*Brown*	*Morgan*	*Marker*	*Burrows*	*Hodges*	*Byrne*	*Fiore*	*Turner*	*Thomas*	*Pickard*	
								Ref: P Jones	Sinclair is City's hero with his fantastic stop from Andy Thomas' close-range header two minutes from time, adding to his exploits in saving a second-min pen. Nicky Marker's failure to control a low cross allows Morgan to prod City ahead, but Thomas fires in an unstoppable leveller.											
4	A	WEST BROM		8	L	1-2	0-2	Newman 85	Sinclair	Llewellyn	Aizlewood	May	Shelton	Rennie	Bent	Newman	Taylor*	Morgan	Smith	Allison
	15/9		*12,081*	*9*	7			*Bannister 38, Harbey 42*	*Naylor*	*Hodson*	*Harbey*	*Robson**	*Bradley*	*Strodder*	*Ford*	*West*	*Bannister*	*McNally*	*Shakespeare*	*Goodman*
								Ref: R Nixon	Jordan's pep talk revives City after their passionless first-half display leaves them trailing to Gary Bannister's volley and Graham Harbey's blistering 20-yarder. Unfortunately Aizlewood's tame 54th-min spot-kick means no reward for City until Newman shoots in from close range.											
5	H	BRIGHTON		8	W	3-1	2-0	Smith 10, Taylor 37, 88	Sinclair	Llewellyn	Aizlewood	May	Shelton	Rennie	Bent	Newman	Taylor	Morgan*	Smith	Allison
	22/9		11,522	*10*	10			*Small 89*	*Digweed*	*Crumplin*	*Chapman*	*Wilkins*	*McCarthy*	*Gatting*	*Nelson**	*Barham*	*Small*	*Codner*	*Walker*	*Byrne*
								Ref: J Lloyd	Following Jordan's shock departure to Hearts, City's entertaining style and attacking flair has Brighton twice clearing off the line and grateful not to concede more. Sinclair's failure to spot Mike Small behind him when he rolls the ball in the area gifts Brighton their late consolation.											
6	H	NEWCASTLE		5	W	1-0	1-0	Smith 22	Sinclair	Llewellyn	Aizlewood	May	Shelton	Rennie	Bent	Newman	Taylor	Morgan	Smith	
	29/9		15,858	*10*	13				*Burridge*	*Scott*	*Bradshaw*	*Aitken*	*Kristensen*	*Ranson*	*Gourley*	*Simpson**	*Quinn*	*McGhee*	*Gallacher^*	*Clark/Robinson*
								Ref: L Shapter	Despite penning Newcastle back with a succession of exciting moves, City fail to add to Smith's powerful drive past John Burridge. The visitors dominate territorially after the break, but Aizlewood and Rennie ensure that their highly-rated strike force barely have a sniff at goal.											
7	A	LEICESTER		9	L	0-3	0-1		Sinclair	Llewellyn	Aizlewood	May	Shelton	Rennie	Bent	Newman	Taylor	Morgan	Smith*	Allison
	3/10		*9,815*	*20*	13			*James 2, Kelly 57, 76*	*Hooper*	*Mauchlen**	*Paris*	*Ramsey*	*Walsh*	*James*	*Wright*	*Reid*	*Oldfield*	*Mills*	*Kelly*	*North*
								Ref: I Borrett	Mike Hooper defies his old club with a masterly display of keeping, after Llewellyn's poor clearance leads to Tony James heading Leicester in front. Paul Ramsey's goal-line clearance also frustrates City, as David Kelly's header and shot makes sure of the points for the Filberts.											
8	A	WOLVES		12	L	**0-4**	0-2		Sinclair	Newman	Aizlewood	May	Shelton	Rennie	Donowa	Humphries*	Taylor	Morgan	Smith	Bailey
	6/10		*17,791*	*6*	13			*Thompson 3, Bull 16, 67, 80*	*Stowell*	*Ashley**	*Thompson*	*Bellamy*	*Hindmarch*	*Downing*	*Steele^*	*Cook*	*Bull*	*Westley*	*Dennison*	*Bennett/McLoughlin*
								Ref: P Don	City are simple meat for the Wolves after Steve Bull's rasping drive cannons off the crossbar for Andy Thompson to head into an open net. Morgan, denied by the post on the half-hour, is denied again with a 51st-minute penalty, and Bull completes his hat-trick with a low drive.											
9	H	WEST HAM		13	D	1-1	0-0	Morgan 63	Leaning	Llewellyn	Bailey	Aizlewood	Shelton	Rennie	May	Newman	Taylor	Morgan	Smith	
	13/10		16,838	*3*	14			*McAvennie 61*	*Miklosko*	*Potts*	*Dicks*	*Foster*	*Martin*	*Parris*	*Bishop*	*Quinn*	*Slater**	*Allen*	*Morley*	*McAvennie*
								Ref: J Deakin	Jimmy Lumsden's decision to re-shuffle his side, with Aizlewood in the central defensive role he prefers, brings stability after three heavy defeats. Ex Hammer Morgan heads in City's equaliser, after Frank McAvennie had been allowed to race through and shoot past Leaning.											
10	H	OLDHAM		13	L	1-2	1-2	Morgan 29	Leaning	Llewellyn	Bailey	Aizlewood	Shelton	Rennie*	May	Newman	Taylor*	Morgan	Smith	Allison/Donowa
	20/10		14,031	*1*	14			*Adams 16, 42*	*Hallworth*	*Warhurst*	*Barlow*	*Henry*	*Barrett*	*Jobson*	*Adams*	*Currie**	*Marshall*	*Redfearn*	*Holden R*	*Moulden*
								Ref: T Ward	The classy Latics win the fans' approval as much for their sportsmanship as their football. Morgan blasts in City's goal from close range, but Neil Adams wins the game for Oldham. His stooping header is followed by a far-post tap-in after Dave Currie outmanoeuvres three defenders.											
11	A	MILLWALL		11	W	2-1	0-1	Horne 57 (og), Aizlewood 83	Sinclair	Llewellyn	Bailey	Aizlewood	Shelton	Rennie	May	Newman	Allison	Morgan*	Smith	Taylor
	24/10		*10,335*	*5*	17			*Waddock 8*	*Horne*	*Stevens*	*Cunningham*	*McCarthy*	*Wood*	*McLeary*	*Carter*	*Waddock*	*Sheringham*	*Rae**	*O'Callaghan*	*Allen*
								Ref: M Bodenham	After hitting the woodwork in the first half, Allison justifies his selection in place of the out-of-form Taylor with a firm header that Brian Horne fumbles in. A thrilling game, played in excellent spirit, is settled by Aizlewood, who steers the ball in through a crowd of defenders											

No Date		Opponent Att	Pos	Pt	F-A	H-T	Scorers, Times, and Referees	1	2	3	4	5	6	7	8	9	10	11	subs used
12	A	PORT VALE	13	L	2-3	1-2	Smith 19p, Allison 84	Sinclair	Llewellyn	Bailey*	Aizlewood	Shelton	Rennie	May	Newman	Allison	Morgan	Smith	Donowa
27/10		7,451	*17*	17			*Walker 1, 25p, Beckford 89*	*Wood*	*Mills S*	*Hughes**	*Walker*	*Aspin*	*Parkin*	*Glover*	*Porter*	*Jepson*	*Beckford*	*Jeffers*	*Cross*
							Ref: A Wilkie	Whilst Lumsden complains over a liberal allocation of injury-time, conceding goals in the first and last minutes against mediocre opposition speaks for itself. Darren Beckford runs in unchallenged to nod in Vale's late winner, not long after Allison had slammed in City's equaliser.											
13	H	WATFORD	11	W	3-2	1-0	Allison 18, 48, Falconer 75 (og)	Sinclair	Llewellyn	Bailey	Aizlewood	Shelton	Rennie	May	Newman	Allison	Morgan*	Smith	Donowa
3/11		11,576	*24*	20			*Porter 55, Holdsworth 70*	*James*	*Gibbs*	*Williams^*	*Porter*	*Holdsworth*	*Dublin*	*Thomas*	*Wilkinson*	*Falconer*	*Devonshire*	*Gavin**	*Harrison/Drysdale*
							Ref: T Holbrook	Allison gets back at his old club with a headed opener and a vicious low-drive from outside the penalty area. Watford looked the more likely victors after Gary Porter's 30-yarder and David Holdsworth's header, but May's cross strikes Willie Falconer on the far post for City's winner.											
14	A	OXFORD	13	L	1-3	1-2	Shelton 44	Sinclair	Llewellyn	Bailey^	Aizlewood	Shelton	Rennie	May	Newman	Allison	Morgan*	Smith	Taylor/Donowa
10/11		6,837	*20*	20			*Simpson 4, 87, Foyle 7*	*Kee*	*Robinson*	*Evans C*	*Lewis*	*Foster*	*Melville*	*Magilton*	*Stein*	*Foyle*	*Nogan**	*Simpson*	*Phillips*
							Ref: G Singh	A give-away as Oxford win a game in which they are second best throughout. After Shelton's dispatch of Allison's pass, Oxford soak up constant pressure and survive countless scares before Paul Simpson makes the game safe with a perfect chip from the edge of the penalty area.											
15	H	HULL	10	W	**4-1**	1-0	May 38, Newman 75, Morgan 88,	Sinclair	Llewellyn	Aizlewood	May	Shelton	Rennie	Bent	Newman	Allison	Morgan	Smith	
17/11		**9,346**	*22*	23			Finnigan 76 [Shelton 89]	*Hesford*	*Brown*	*Jacobs*	*Mail*	*Swan*	*Wilcox*	*Finnigan*	*Payton*	*Bamber**	*Palin*	*McParland*	*Jenkinson*
							Ref: M Bailey	With Tony Taylor in charge, whilst Lumsden is in hospital with disc trouble, City turn on the style after May hits the bar and Smith's 26th-min penalty is saved. Morgan's skilful close-control lays on May's exquisite right-footed opener, and gets in on the act himself with a firm header.											
16	A	IPSWICH	11	D	1-1	0-1	Taylor 88	Sinclair	Llewellyn	Aizlewood	May	Shelton	Rennie	Bent	Newman	Allison*	Morgan	Smith	Taylor
24/11		*9,919*	*12*	24			*Dozzell 20*	*Forrest*	*Yallop*	*Humes*	*Stockwell*	*Gayle*	*Linighan*	*Dozzell*	*Redford*	*Hill*	*Kiwomya*	*Thompson*	
							Ref: J Kirkby	City run Ipswich ragged, particularly in a one-sided second half, though they are fortunate when Neil Thompson blasts a 49th-min pen over the top, after Aizlewood had fisted out Chris Kiwomya's chip. The irrepressible Bent sets up Taylor to notch City's late leveller with a low drive.											
17	H	CHARLTON	13	L	0-1	0-1		Sinclair	Llewellyn	Aizlewood	May	Shelton	Rennie	Bent^	Newman	Taylor	Morgan*	Smith	Humphries/Allison
1/12		10,984	*20*	24			*Lee 44*	*Bolder*	*Pitcher*	*Minto*	*Peake*	*Balmer*	*Caton*	*Lee R*	*Curbishley*	*Dyer*	*Watson*	*Mortimer*	
							Ref: P Durkin	Seldom in recent seasons have City been as comprehensively outplayed as they are in this match. City had the luck on their side in the fourth min, when Paul Mortimer fires against the bar, but Robert Lee makes no mistake just before half-time with a low 18-yard drive past Sinclair.											
18	H	SHEFFIELD WED	12	D	1-1	1-1	Shirtliff 15 (og)	Sinclair	Llewellyn	**Scott**	May	Shelton	Rennie	Bent*	Newman	Taylor	Morgan	Smith	Allison
8/12		11,254	*3*	25			*Wilson 6*	*Pressman*	*Harkes*	*King*	*Palmer*	*Shirtliff*	*Pearson*	*Wilson*	*Sheridan*	*Hirst*	*Francis**	*Worthington*	*Williams*
							Ref: P Tyldesley	Scott (£200,000 ex Rotherham) is voted man of the match by City's 51 Club after producing a goal-line clearance to earn his side a point in the snow and bitter wind. Peter Shirtliff's lunging interception of Smith's hard low-cross only succeeds in turning the ball past his own keeper.											
19	A	BLACKBURN	9	W	1-0	0-0	Newman 47	Sinclair	Llewellyn	Scott	May	Shelton	Rennie	Bent	Newman	Taylor	Morgan	Smith	
15/12		*7,072*	*16*	28				*Grew*	*Atkins*	*Sulley*	*Reid*	*Hill*	*Moran*	*Richardson**	*Millar*	*Stapleton*	*Johnrose*	*Wilcox^*	*Shepstone/Skinner*
							Ref: P Vanes	Newman gives his forwards a lesson in finishing with a firm low-drive from twelve yards that leaves Mark Grew rooted the spot. 'One of these days we are going to score six or seven' is Llewellyn's comment as City's ascendancy produces a quiet afternoon for keeper Sinclair.											
20	A	NOTTS CO	11	L	2-3	1-1	Bent 34, Smith 51	Leaning	Llewellyn	Scott	May	Shelton	Rennie	Bent	Newman	Taylor	Morgan*	Smith	Allison
22/12		*6,586*	*5*	28			*Regis 12, 85, Draper 82*	*Cherry*	*Palmer*	*Harding*	*Short, Craig*	*Yates*	*O'Riordan**	*Thomas*	*Turner*	*Bartlett*	*Regis*	*Draper*	*Johnson*
							Ref: P Foakes	City take Christmas giving too far as Rennie's hesitation allows Dave Regis to latch onto Steve Cherry's long free-kick and score County's impressive winner. A sickening end to a match City should have won as chances were missed after Smith screwed in a low shot past Cherry.											
21	H	PORTSMOUTH	8	W	**4-1**	1-1	Morgan 24, 49, Shelton 71, Rennie 76	Leaning	Llewellyn	Scott	May	Shelton	Rennie	Bent*	Newman	Taylor^	Morgan	Smith	Aizlewood/Allison
26/12		11,892	*22*	31			*Clarke 44*	*Knight*	*Neill*	*Beresford*	*Kuhl*	*Butters*	*Awford*	*Anderton**	*Clarke*	*Whittingham*	*Aspinall^*	*Chamberlain*	*Daniel/Powell*
							Ref: G Williard	The fans who brave the atrocious weather for an 11.30am kick-off are rewarded by the quality play of both sides. Two opportunist strikes by Morgan puts the skids under Pompey, then Shelton's ten-yarder and Rennie's perfectly-struck shot from 30 yards seals City's exciting win.											
22	H	MIDDLESBROUGH	7	W	3-0	1-0	May 20, Morgan 75, Allison 85	Leaning	Llewellyn	Scott	May	Shelton	Aizlewood	Rennie*	Newman	Allison	Morgan	Smith	Donowa
29/12		14,023	*4*	34				*Pears*	*Cooper*	*Phillips*	*Mowbray*	*Coleman*	*Proctor*	*Slaven*	*Mustoe*	*Baird*	*Ripley*	*Hendrie*	
							Ref: G Ashby	The blend of Morgan's deft touches and Allison's raw power prove too much for Boro's defence, as the Second Division's best away side are blitzed. May gets City rolling with a 15-yard hooked shot, then a brilliant Morgan header is followed by Allison coolly side-footing the ball in.											
23	A	BARNSLEY	9	L	0-2	0-2		Leaning	Llewellyn	Scott^	May	Shelton !	Aizlewood	Rennie	Newman	Allison	Morgan*	Smith	Taylor/Donowa
1/1		*8,961*	*6*	34			*Rammell 18, Taggart 26*	*Baker*	*Banks*	*Taggart*	*Fleming*	*Smith*	*Tiler*	*O'Connell*	*Rammell**	*Saville*	*Agnew*	*Archdeacon*	*Deehan*
							Ref: T Fitzharris	Whilst Shelton is harshly dismissed for dissent on being denied a 29th-min free-kick, it is defensive blunders that are responsible for City's defeat. Newman's failure to clear allows Andy Rammell to shoot past Leaning, then Gerry Taggart escapes the attentions of Rennie to head in.											

No	Date		Att	Pos	Pt	F-A	H-T	Scorers, Times, and Referees	1	2	3	4	5	6	7	8	9	10	11	subs used
24	H	SWINDON		9	L	**0-4**	0-1		Leaning	Llewellyn	Scott*	May	Shelton	Aizlewood	Rennie	Newman	Allison	Morgan^	Smith	Donowa/Taylor
	12/1		16,169	12	34			Hazard 38, White 61, 90, Shearer 89	Digby	Kerslake	Bodin	Hazard	Lorenzo	Gittens	Jones	Shearer	White	MacLaren	Foley	
								Ref: B Stevens	Angry City fans look for scapegoats after Leaning stands between Swindon and a victory of record-breaking proportions. By the end it is difficult to work out who is playing where, and Swindon cash in with Duncan Shearer's far-post header and Steve White's opportunist shot.											
25	A	PLYMOUTH		12	L	0-1	0-0		Leaning	Llewellyn	Scott	May	**Bryant**	Aizlewood	Rennie*	Newman	Allison	Morgan	Smith	Donowa
	19/1		8,074	17	34			Robinson 74	Walter	Brown	Morgan	Marker	Burrows	Salman	Barlow	Hodges	Robinson	Adcock	Morrison	
								Ref: R Gifford	Having been fed a diet of fast, attacking soccer in recent seasons, the massed ranks of the City fans are given a rare glimpse of the alternative. Lumsden's decision to field a five-man defence is totally negative as impotent City deservedly go down to Paul Robinson's point-blank header.											
26	A	BRISTOL ROV		13	L	2-3	2-2	Scott 34p, Newman 38	Leaning	Llewellyn	Scott	May	Bryant	Aizlewood	Donowa	Newman	Taylor	Morgan	Smith*	Bent
	26/1		7,054	10	34			Mehew 11, 21, Saunders 63	Kelly	Alexander*	Twentyman	Yates	Mehew	Jones	Holloway	Reece	White	Saunders	Pounder	Bloomer
								Ref: K Barratt	Trailing to David Mehew's double, a shot from twelve yards, followed by a sharp volley, City get back on level terms. Scott's twice-taken pen (both netted) and Newman's dispatch of Donowa's through-ball brings the match alive, which Carl Saunders settles with a nod over the line.											
27	H	WEST BROM		9	W	2-0	1-0	Morgan 14, Taylor 60	Leaning	Llewellyn	Scott	May	Bryant	Aizlewood	Shelton	Newman	Taylor	Morgan*	Smith	Allison
	2/2		11,492	18	37				Rees	Hodson	Anderson	Roberts	Strodder	Raven !	Ford	Goodman	Bannister	Parkin	Shakespeare	
								Ref: J Martin	Although City play with conviction on a difficult snow-covered pitch, Albion look anything but a relegation-threatened side. Morgan's simple tap-in and Taylor's low shot beneath the keeper at the end of a direct run brings City the points, even though Albion fashion twice the chances.											
28	A	HULL		8	W	2-1	0-1	May 48, Newman 53	Leaning	Llewellyn	Scott	May	Bryant	Aizlewood	Shelton	Newman	Taylor	Morgan	Smith*	Donowa
	16/2		**5,212**	24	40			Payton 8	Wright	Norton	Jacobs	De Mange*	Buckley	Shotton	Jenkinson^	Payton	Swan	Palin	Atkinson	Wilcox/Hunter
								Ref: J Watson	Andy Payton punishes City's tentative start by firing in his 19th goal of the season. After the interval man-of-the-match Morgan sets up both City goals with unselfish headers. May's crisp volley and Newman's point-blank shot producing City's fourth away win of the campaign.											
29	H	OXFORD		8	W	3-1	2-1	Shelton 30, 66, Taylor 32	Leaning	Llewellyn	Scott	May	Bryant	Aizlewood	Shelton	Newman	Taylor	Morgan	Smith	
	23/2		10,938	19	43			Nogan 16	Veysey	Robinson	Smart*	Foyle	Foster	Melville	Magilton	Phillips	Lewis^	Nogan	Simpson	Ford/Stein
								Ref: J Deakin	Unaware of the sudden death of Chairman Des Williams, City produce some brilliant football to overcome Lee Nogan's crisp 15-yard opener. Shelton's perfectly-curved shot beyond the reach of Ken Veysey levels matters, then he shoots in the goal of the game to tie up City's success.											
30	A	CHARLTON		9	L	1-2	1-2	Smith 16	Leaning	Llewellyn	Scott	May	Bryant	Aizlewood*	Shelton	Newman	Taylor^	Morgan	Smith	Rennie/Allison
	2/3		5,477	18	43			Dyer 42, 44	Bolder	Pitcher	Reid	Peake	Webster	Kernaghan	Lee R	Grant*	Dyer	Mortimer	Minto	Leaburn
								Ref: P Jones	Careless City are a soft touch at Selhurst Park after failing to add to Smith's weak low-shot which bobbled over the keeper's hands. Bryant's lapse of concentration allows Alex Dyer to run the ball in for the equaliser, and then register with a perfectly-executed chip not long after.											
31	H	BRISTOL ROV		8	W	1-0	0-0	Donowa 88	Leaning	Llewellyn	Scott	May*	Bryant	Aizlewood	Shelton	Newman	Taylor	Morgan^	Donowa	Rennie/Allison
	5/3		**22,269**	11	46				Parkin	Alexander*	Twentyman	Clark	Mehew	Jones	Holloway	Reece	White	Saunders	Pounder	Willmott
								Ref: R Groves	Donowa's first City goal could hardly have come at a better time, as his late stooped header, after Brian Parkin fails to gather his innocuous shot, ends five years of derby blues. Morgan is thrice denied by the woodwork, whilst Leaning saves Ian Holloway's 75th-minute spot-kick.											
32	H	IPSWICH		5	W	4-2	2-1	Taylor 27, 39, Shelton 49, Morgan 70	Leaning	Llewellyn	Scott	May*	Bryant	Aizlewood	Shelton	Newman	Taylor	Morgan	Donowa	Smith
	9/3		11,474	15	49			Dozzell 18, Goddard 75	Forrest	Yallop*	Thompson	Stockwell	Linighan	Palmer	Zondervan	Goddard	Whitton	Dozzell	Milton	Hill
								Ref: H King	Taylor's goal-poaching ability turns the match after Jason Dozzell capitalises on acres of space to send a glorious 25-yard drive past Leaning. A perfectly-placed header and an acrobatic overhead confirms the striker's resurgence of confidence as City move into a play-off position.											
33	H	LEICESTER		5	W	1-0	0-0	Taylor 88	Leaning	Llewellyn	Scott	May	Bryant	Aizlewood	Shelton*	Newman	Taylor	Morgan^	Donowa	Smith/Allison
	12/3		13,297	22	52				Muggleton	North	Gibson^	Mauchlen	Walsh	James	Wright	Ramsey	Oldfield	Mills	Kelly*	Kitson/Reid
								Ref: R Bigger	Jimmy Lumsden admits it is sheer robbery as Taylor volleys in City's late winner after the prone Tony James had played all the City attackers onside. City have Leaning to thank for keeping them in the game, as Leicester create virtually all the clear chances of a disappointing game.											
34	A	NEWCASTLE		5	D	0-0	0-0		Leaning	Llewellyn	Scott	May	Bryant	Aizlewood	Shelton	Newman	Taylor	Morgan^	Smith*	Donowa/Allison
	16/3		13,560	11	53				Burridge	Watson S	Neilson	Aitken	Scott	Kristensen	Hunt	Peacock*	Quinn	Howey^	Brock	O'Brien/McGhee
								Ref: D Phillips	Leaning throws himself to palm away Mike Quinn's 87th-min point-blank header and preserve City a well-deserved point from a drab game. City miss the better chances, both Newman and Morgan firing over, while Taylor and Donowa delayed shooting with the goal at their mercy.											

No	Date	Opponent	Att	Pos	Pts	F-A	H-T	Scorers, Times, and Referees												subs used
35 A	20/3	WEST HAM	22,951	7 / 2	L / 53	0-1	0-0	*Gale 67*	Leaning / *Miklosko*	Llewellyn ! / *Potts*	Scott / *Parris*	May / *Gale*	Bryant / *Foster*	Aizlewood / *Hughton*	Shelton / *Bishop*	Newman / *McAvennie !*	Taylor / *Slater**	Morgan / *Keen*	Donowa* / *Quinn^*	Allison / *Allen/Rosenior*
								Ref: P Alcock	City are impressive at Upton Park, where they match, and often outplay, the Hammers. Tony Gale's brilliant chip from a disputed free-kick settles the match six minutes after the dismissal of Frank McAvennie and Llewellyn, for little more than jostling for position at a throw-in.											
36 H	23/3	WOLVES	15,499	7 / 10	D / 54	1-1	0-0	Bryant 54 / *Dennison 62*	Leaning / *Stowell*	Llewellyn* / *Bennett*	Scott / *Thompson*	May / *Hindmarch*	Bryant / *Clarke*	Aizlewood / *Downing*	Shelton / *Birch*	Newman / *Cook !*	Taylor / *Bull*	Morgan^ / *Mutch*	Donowa / *Dennison*	Bent/Allison
								Ref: M Pierce	City squander a host of chances, including a 29th-minute spot-kick which Scott blazes over the bar, as they fail to capitalise on Paul Cook's dismissal for dissent over the pen award. Bryant's stooping header puts City in front, but Robbie Dennison's 25-yard free-kick levels matters.											
37 A	30/3	PORTSMOUTH	10,417	8 / 20	L / 54	1-4	0-1	Morgan 62 / *Clarke 44, 60, 86p, Whittingham 49*	Leaning / *Knight*	Llewellyn* / *Russell*	Mardon / *Daniel*	May / *Murray*	Bryant / *Butters*	Aizlewood / *Magure*	Shelton / *Wigley*	Newman / *Kuhl^*	Taylor / *Whittingham*	Morgan^ / *Clarke*	Donowa / *Anderton**	Allison/Rennie / *Beresford/Black*
								Ref: D Axcell	Despite creating chances, City's overall performance is disappointing. Donowa's poor finish when clean through early on is costly as Colin Clarke (later to complete his hat-trick with a dubious penalty) sweeps in Ray Daniel's cross to put Portsmouth ahead against the run of play.											
38 H	1/4	NOTTS CO	13,466	7 / 8	W / 57	3-2	1-1	Allison 44, Donowa 76, Shelton 84 / *Johnson 30, O'Riordan 75*	Leaning / *Cherry*	Llewellyn / *Short, Chris*	Mardon / *Paris*	May / *Short, Craig*	Bryant / *Yates*	Aizlewood / *O'Riordan*	Shelton / *Thomas*	Newman / *Turner*	Taylor / *Bartlett*	Morgan* / *Draper*	Donowa / *Johnson*	Allison
								Ref: T Lunt	Shelton's blistering volley keeps City in the promotion race, but it is guts rather than skill which triumphs. County are much the better side in the first half, but City equalise Tommy Johnson's driven-in opener when Allison hammers the ball past Steve Cherry at the second attempt.											
39 A	6/4	MIDDLESBROUGH	13,844	8 / 5	L / 57	1-2	1-1	Taylor 2 / *Ripley 20, 89*	Leaning / *Dibble*	May / *Parkinson*	Scott / *Phillips*	Rennie / *Kernaghan*	Bryant / *Coleman*	Aizlewood^ / *Hendrie*	Shelton / *Slaven**	Newman / *Proctor*	Taylor / *Baird*	Allison / *Mustoe*	Donowa* / *Ripley*	Bent/Mardon / *Walsh*
								Ref: R Nixon	The referee hands the points to lucky Boro' as he fails to spot handball offences in the dying minutes when Colin Walsh keeps out Rennie's shot, and Jimmy Phillips stops Taylor's follow-up effort. Straight away the ball reaches the other end for Stuart Ripley to shoot past Leaning.											
40 H	13/4	BARNSLEY	12,081	7 / 9	W / 60	1-0	1-0	Newman 26	Leaning / *Baker*	Llewellyn / *Dobbin**	Scott / *Taggart^*	May / *Fleming*	Bryant / *Smith*	Mardon / *Tiler*	Shelton / *O'Connell*	Newman / *Rammell*	Taylor / *Saville*	Allison / *Agnew*	Bent / *Archdeacon*	*Deehan/Robinson*
								Ref: D Frampton	The play-off prize still beckons for City after this win, which was more emphatic than the score suggests. Barnsley pack their goalmouth for Shelton's indirect free-kick, which is squared to Newman, whose shot from no more than eight yards finds a gap and whistles low into the net.											
41 A	20/4	OLDHAM	14,086	9 / 2	L / 60	1-2	0-0	Newman 86 / *Marshall 65, Redfearn 83p*	Leaning / *Hallworth*	Llewellyn / *Halle**	Scott / *Barlow*	May* / *Henry*	Bryant / *Barrett*	Aizlewood / *Jobson*	Shelton / *Adams*	Newman / *Warhurst*	Taylor^ / *Marshall*	Allison / *Redfearn*	Mardon / *Holden R*	Bent/Morgan / *Currie*
								Ref: A Dawson	City will not grieve over the synthetic pitch at Boundary Park, which is being removed at the end of the season. After Ian Marshall stoops to head the Latics in front, Mardon is incensed over the penalty award when he is adjudged to have handled whilst clearing a shot off the line.											
42 A	23/4	BRIGHTON	7,738	8 / 6	W / 63	1-0	0-0	Shelton 89	Leaning / *Digweed*	Llewellyn* / *Crumplin*	Scott / *Gatting*	Mardon / *Wilkins*	Bryant / *Pates*	Aizlewood / *Chivers*	Shelton / *Barham*	Newman / *Byrne*	Allison / *Small*	Morgan / *Codner*	Taylor / *Walker*	May
								Ref: R Wiseman	Shelton's carefully-placed shot from Allison's head-down saves City's blushes at the Goldstone Ground, where poor finishing threatened to scupper play-off hopes. Brighton offer little, though John Byrne's deflected shot cannons off the bar with Leaning stranded 13 mins from time.											
43 H	27/4	MILLWALL	16,741	8 / 5	L / 63	1-4	1-0	Morgan 44 / *Sheringham 55, 65, 81, Thompson 60*	Leaning / *Horne*	Llewellyn / *Stevens*	Scott / *Dawes*	Mardon* / *Waddock*	Bryant / *Thompson*	Aizlewood / *McCarthy*	Shelton / *Stephenson*	Newman / *Goodman*	Allison / *Sheringham*	Morgan / *Kerr*	Taylor / *Briley*	Bent
								Ref: P Tyldesley	Naïve defending aids Millwall's second-half fight-back which transforms this vital encounter. Three times City are undone by straightforward corners, as their defence fails to counter David Thompson's havoc-producing long runs and prodigious leaps that yield telling headers.											
44 H	4/5	PORT VALE	11,555	9 / 17	D / 64	1-1	1-0	Rennie 15 / *Earle 78*	Leaning / *Wood*	May / *Mills S*	Scott / *Hughes*	Rennie / *Walker*	Bryant / *Parkin**	Aizlewood / *Aspin*	Shelton / *Kent*	Newman / *Earle*	Allison / *Van der Laan*	Morgan / *Glover*	Taylor* / *Porter*	Donowa / *Millar*
								Ref: P Durkin	With Lumsden persisting with the sweeper system, City pay the price for their failure to put away good chances after Rennie drives a fine shot through a packed defence low into the net. Simon Mills' second attempt at a cross eludes Leaning, and Robbie Earle heads into the top corner.											
45 A	8/5	SHEFFIELD WED	**31,716**	9 / 3	L / 64	1-3	0-1	Allison 71 / *Hirst 34, 63, Francis 54*	Leaning / *Turner*	May / *Nilsson**	Scott / *King*	Renie / *Palmer*	Bryant / *Madden*	Aizlewood / *Anderson*	Shelton* / *Wilson*	Newman / *Sheridan*	Allison / *Hirst*	Morgan / *Francis^*	Bent / *Worthington*	Donowa / *Harkes/Williams*
								Ref: P Harrison	With others dropping points, City need to win their last two games to clinch a play-off place, but they are mere bit players at Hillsborough's promotion party. Allison's glorious 25-yard strike is little consolation for being thoroughly outclassed by a Trevor Francis inspired Owls side.											
46 A	11/5	WATFORD	13,029	9 / 20	W / 67	3-2	0-0	Morgan 48, Newman 53, Donowa 87 / *Wilkinson 57, 65*	Leaning / *James*	Llewellyn / *Gibbs*	Scott / *Soloman*	May / *Ashby*	Bryant / *Roeder**	Aizlewood / *Dublin*	Rennie / *Falconer*	Newman / *Wilkinson*	Allison / *Butler*	Morgan / *Porter*	Smith* / *Nicholas*	Donowa / *Callaghan*
	Home / Average 13,495	Away / 11,421						Ref: J Lloyd	Still in with a slight chance of a play-off place, City find that Donowa's tapped-in winner is of no avail as other results go against them. After enjoying the better of the first half, City's superiority is confirmed by Morgan's shot that is deflected past David James just after the break.											

BARCLAYS DIVISION 2 (CUP-TIES) Manager: Jordan ⇨ Jimmy Lumsden SEASON 1990-91

Rumbelows Cup					F-A	H-T	Scorers, Times, and Referees	1	2	3	4	5	6	7	8	9	10	11	subs used
1:1	A	WEST BROM		D	2-2	1-1	Morgan 30, 47	Sinclair	Llewellyn	Aizlewood	May	Shelton	Rennie	Bent	Newman	Taylor*	Morgan	Smith	Allison
29/8		*8,721*					*Bannister 8, Hackett 84*	*Naylor*	*Hodson*	*Harbey*	*Robson*	*Burgess*	*Strodder*	*Ford*	*Goodman*	*Bannister*	*Bradley**	*Shakespeare*	*Hackett*
							Ref: J Key	After Craig Shakespeare breaks clear to present Gary Bannister with a simple goal, City outplay Albion for long periods. Morgan lashes in a loose ball for the equaliser, and then clips a precise shot over Stuart Naylor, but City are deprived of a win by Gary Hackett's superb volley.											
1:2	H	WEST BROM		W	1-0	0-0	Smith 113	Sinclair	Llewellyn	Aizlewood	May	Shelton	Rennie	Bent	Newman	Taylor	Morgan*	Smith	Allison
5/9		9,851			*aet*			*Naylor*	*Hodson*	*Harbey*	*Robson**	*Burgess*	*Strodder !*	*Ford*	*West*	*Bannister^*	*Bradley*	*Shakespeare*	*Hackett/Foster*
							Ref: R Gifford (City won 3-2 on aggregate)	Smith's rasping extra-time shot settles this cup-tie against ten-man Albion, who had lost Gary Strodder for a second bookable offence seven minutes earlier. Albion's physical approach often has City riding their luck, and Aizlewood is forced to clear Gary Bannister's shot off the line.											
2:1	A	SUNDERLAND	8	W	1-0	1-0	Morgan 18	Sinclair	Llewellyn	Aizlewood	May	Shelton	Rennie	Bent	Newman	Taylor	Morgan	Smith	
25/9		*10,358 1:13*						*Norman*	*Kay*	*Brady**	*Bennett*	*Ball*	*Owers^*	*Bracewell*	*Armstrong*	*Davenport*	*Gabbiadini*	*Hardyman*	*Ord/Hauser*
							Ref: D Phillips	Slick City silence the Roker roar as they outplay Sunderland. The only surprise is that they do not add to Morgan's early goal, when he headed in Taylor's flick-on from Llewellyn's cross. City should have done more with eight shots on target compared to Sunderland's total of two.											
2:2	H	SUNDERLAND	12	L	1-6	1-2	Morgan 5 *[Cullen 77]*	Leaning	Llewellyn	Aizlewood	May	Shelton	Rennie	Donowa	Newman	Taylor*	Morgan	Smith	Allison
9/10		11,776 *1:16*					*Hauser 1, Ball 44, Owers 49, G'dini 65, 82*	*Norman*	*Kay*	*Smith*	*Bennett*	*Ball*	*Owers*	*Bracewell^*	*Armstrong*	*Davenport*	*Gabbiadini*	*Hauser**	*Cullen/Ord*
							Ref: J Martin (City lost 2-6 on aggregate)	City fail to celebrate Lumsden's managerial appointment as they go down to their worst home defeat since Norwich's visit in January 1949. The result somewhat flatters Sunderland (seven shots on target) as City (ten shots on target) are made to pay for defensive shortcomings.											

FA Cup																			
3	A	NORWICH	9	L	1-2	1-1	Allison 41	Leaning	Llewellyn^	Bailey	May	Shelton	Aizlewood	Rennie	Newman	Allison	Taylor*	Smith	Donowa/Bent
5/1		*12,630 1:10*					*Rosario 4, Fleck 70*	*Gunn*	*Culverhouse*	*Bowen*	*Butterworth**	*Polston*	*Crook*	*Gordon*	*Fleck*	*Sherwood*	*Rosario*	*Phillips*	*Goss*
							Ref: R Lewis	After recovering from an unkind goal, when a speculative 25-yard effort by David Phillips strikes Robert Rosario and ends up in the net, City's good football is deserving of a replay. Allison heads City level from Smith's cross, but Robert Fleck's 25-yarder takes the Canaries through.											

		Home					Away					
	P	W	D	L	F	A	W	D	L	F	A	Pts
1 Oldham	46	17	5	1	55	21	8	8	7	28	32	88
2 West Ham	46	15	6	2	41	18	9	9	5	19	16	87
3 Sheffield Wed	46	12	10	1	43	23	10	6	7	37	28	82
4 Notts Co*	46	14	4	5	45	28	9	7	7	31	27	80
5 Millwall	46	11	6	6	43	28	9	7	7	27	23	73
6 Brighton	46	12	4	7	37	31	9	3	11	26	38	70
7 Middlesbro	46	12	4	7	36	17	8	5	10	30	30	69
8 Barnsley	46	13	7	3	39	16	6	5	12	24	32	69
9 BRISTOL CITY	46	14	5	4	44	28	6	2	15	24	43	67
10 Oxford	46	10	9	4	41	29	4	10	9	28	37	61
11 Newcastle	46	8	10	5	24	22	6	7	10	25	34	59
12 Wolves	46	11	6	6	45	35	2	13	8	18	28	58
13 Bristol Rov	46	11	7	5	29	20	4	6	13	27	39	58
14 Ipswich	46	9	8	6	32	28	4	10	9	28	40	57
15 Port Vale	46	10	4	9	32	24	5	8	10	24	40	57
16 Charlton	46	8	7	8	27	25	5	10	8	30	36	56
17 Portsmouth	46	10	6	7	34	27	4	5	14	24	43	53
18 Plymouth	46	10	10	3	36	20	2	7	14	18	48	53
19 Blackburn	46	8	6	9	26	27	6	4	13	25	39	52
20 Watford	46	5	8	10	24	32	7	7	9	21	27	51
21 Swindon	46	8	6	9	31	30	4	8	11	34	43	50
22 Leicester	46	12	4	7	41	33	2	4	17	19	50	50
23 West Brom	46	7	11	5	26	21	3	7	13	26	40	48
24 Hull	46	6	10	7	35	32	4	5	14	22	53	45
	1104	253	163	136	866	615	136	163	253	615	866	1493

* promoted after play-offs

Odds & ends

Double wins: (4) Blackburn, Brighton, Watford, Hull.
Double losses: (2) Oldham, Charlton.

Won from behind: (6) Blackburn (h), Millwall (a), Hull (a), Oxford (h), Ipswich (h), Notts Co (h).
Lost from in front: (4) Charlton (a), Middlesbrough (a), Millwall (h), Notts Co (a).

High spots: Beating Blackburn 4-1 at Ashton Gate on 25 August.
Beating Hull at Ashton Gate 4-1 on 17 November.
Beating Blackburn 1-0 at Ewood Park on 15 December.
Beating Pompey 4-1 at Ashton Gate on 26 December.
Louie Donowa's goal that beats Bristol Rov on 5 March.
Moving into a play-off position after beating Ipswich 4-2 on 9 March.
Winning 1-0 at Sunderland in the FL Cup.
Beating Bristol Rov (a) 4-1 in the Gloucestershire Cup Final on 15 Aug.

Low spots: Missing out on the play-offs.
Losing 0-2 at West Brom on 15 September.
Losing at home to Swindon 0-4 on 12 January.
Bundled out of the FL Cup by Sunderland's 1-6 blitz at Ashton Gate.

Player of the year: Andy Llewellyn.
Ever-presents (1) Rob Newman.
Hat-tricks: (0).
Leading scorer: Nicky Morgan (17).

	Appearances						Goals			
	Lge	*Sub*	LC	*Sub*	FAC	*Sub*	Lge	LC	FAC	Tot
Aizlewood, Mark	41	*1*	4		1		2			2
Allison, Wayne	18	*19*		*3*	1		6		1	7
Bailey, John	6	*1*			1					
Bent, Junior	15	*5*	3			*1*	2			2
Bryant, Matt	22						1			1
Donowa, Louie	11	*13*	1			*1*	3			3
Humphries, Glenn	1	*1*								
Leaning, Andy	29		1		1					
Llewellyn, Andy	42		4		1					
Mardon, Paul	6	*1*								
May, Andy	44	*1*	4		1		3			3
Morgan, Nicky	43	*1*	4				13	4		17
Newman, Rob	46		4		1		8			8
Rennie, David	29	*3*	4		1		2			2
Scott, Martin	27						1			1
Shelton, Gary	43		4		1		8			8
Sinclair, Ronnie	17		3							
Smith, David	32	*2*	4		1		5	1		6
Taylor, Bob	34	*5*	4		1		11			11
(own-goals)							3			3
19 players used	**506**	***53***	**44**	***3***	**11**	***2***	**68**	**5**	**1**	**74**

No	Date	Opponent	Att	Pos	Pt	F-A	H-T	Scorers, Times, and Referees	1	2	3	4	5	6	7	8	9	10	11	subs used
1	A	SOUTHEND			D	1-1	0-1	Taylor 57	**Welch**	Llewellyn	Scott	May	Bryant	Aizlewood	Shelton	Rennie	Allison	Taylor	Smith	
	17/8		*6,720*		1			*Benjamin 32*	*Sansome*	*Austin*	*Powell*	*Martin*	*Edwards*	*Prior*	*Ansah*	*Sussex*	*O'Callaghan**	*Benjamin*	*Angell*	*Tilson*
								Ref: R Lewis	A delayed kick-off to let in the hordes of City fans, who make the atmosphere at Roots Hall like that of a home game. Ian Benjamin clips in a rebound to celebrate Southend's Second Division debut, but Taylor drives a low right-foot shot past Sansome for City's well-earned point.											
2	H	BRIGHTON			W	2-1	1-0	Scott 22, Bryant 66	Welch	Llewellyn	Scott	May	Bryant	Aizlewood	Shelton	Rennie	Allison	Taylor	Smith	
	20/8		11,299		4			*Bissett 87*	*Digweed*	*Crumplin*	*Chapman*	*Wilkins*	*Chivers*	*O'Reilly*	*Iovan^*	*Byrne*	*Wade**	*Codner*	*Walker*	*Barham/Bissett*
								Ref: D Frampton	All seating now at the Covered End, but the fans are on their feet as Scott fires City in front against last season's play-off finalists with a direct free-kick which took a deflection. Bryant's first-time shot has City coasting, until Nicky Bissett's diving header brings Brighton's late response.											
3	H	BLACKBURN		2	W	1-0	1-0	Allison 43	Welch	Llewellyn	Scott	May	Bryant	Aizlewood	Shelton	Rennie	Allison	Taylor*	Smith	Morgan
	24/8		11,317	*21*	7				*Mimms*	*Atkins*	*Sulley*	*Reid*	*Moran*	*Dobson !*	*May*	*Agnew*	*Livingstone**	*Speedie*	*Garner^*	*Gayle/Richardson*
								Ref: R Bigger	Against the promotion favourites, City fully deserve the points their skilful play merits, even though the winning strike is a fluke. Chesting down Shelton's chip and swinging a mighty boot, Allison's resulting miskick totally deceives Bobby Mimms as the ball trickles into the net.											
4	A	PORT VALE		4	D	1-1	0-1	Morgan 67	Welch	Llewellyn	Scott	May	Bryant	Aizlewood	Shelton	Rennie	Allison	Taylor*	Smith	Morgan
	31/8		*7,057*	*10*	8			*Mills S 43*	*Grew*	*Mills S*	*Hughes*	*Walker*	*Aspin*	*Glover*	*Porter*	*Van der Laan*	*Houchen**	*Foyle*	*Swan*	*Mills B*
								Ref: M Reed	Sub Morgan is City's hero as his deft headed deflection makes sure that Mark Grew has no chance of stopping Scott's forceful 30-yard volley. Trailing to an early candidate for 'goal of the season', a perfect 35-yard strike from full-back Simon Mills, Morgan's arrival revives City.											
5	H	BRISTOL ROV		2	W	1-0	0-0	Allison 64	Welch	Llewellyn*	Scott	May	Bryant	Aizlewood	Shelton	Rennie	Allison	Morgan	Smith	Bent
	4/9		**20,183**	*22*	11				*Parkin*	*Boothroyd*	*Twentyman*	*Yates*	*Clark*	*Archer*	*Skinner**	*Reece*	*White*	*Stewart*	*Purnell*	*Saunders*
								Ref: M Bodenham	Geoff Twentyman says 'It was a case of the right place, but the wrong man' after he fails to make his shot count when clean through in the dying seconds. Just as well really, because City's dominant display fully deserved the points secured by Allison's low-shot past Brian Parkin.											
6	A	LEICESTER		5	L	1-2	1-2	Morgan 36	Welch	May	Scott	**Edwards**	Bryant	Aizlewood	Bent*	Rennie	Allison	Morgan	Smith	**Harrison**
	7/9		*17,815*	*2*	11			*Gibson 17, Fitzpatrick 37*	*Poole*	*Mills*	*Platnauer*	*Fitzpatrick*	*Walsh*	*James*	*Oldfield*	*Gibson*	*Wright^*	*Kelly*	*Kitson**	*Russell/Gordon*
								Ref: P Don	Leicester survive a second-half battering to deprive impressive City of their unbeaten record. Ex Robin Paul Fitzpatrick prods in Leicester's winner from close range, after Colin Gibson's 30-yard thunderbolt had been equalised by Morgan's steering in of Rennie's low cross.											
7	H	TRANMERE		5	D	2-2	2-1	Allison 10, Shelton 25	Welch	May	Scott	Edwards	Bryant	Aizlewood*	Shelton	Rennie	Allison	Morgan	Smith	Bent
	14/9		11,235	*9*	12			*Brannan 27, Irons 48*	*Nixon*	*Higgins*	*Brannan*	*Irons*	*Mungall*	*Vickers*	*Morrissey**	*Aldridge*	*Malkin*	*Martindale*	*Thomas*	*Cooper^/McNab*
								Ref: P Vanes	City are ironed out of the full compliment of points as Kenny Irons evades Shelton's lunging tackle to cut in and beat Welch with the most innocuous of shots. Despite Smith having his second-min effort harshly disallowed, a draw is a fair result as Tranmere play some great soccer.											
8	H	MILLWALL		6	D	2-2	1-2	Bryant 44, Scott 86p	Welch	May	Scott	Edwards^	Bryant	**Caesar**	Shelton	Rennie	Allison	Morgan*	Smith	Taylor/Harrison
	17/9		10,862	*22*	13			*McCarthy 34, Colquhoun 35*	*Davison*	*Dawes*	*Cooper*	*Bogie*	*McCarthy*	*Wood*	*Kerr*	*Colquhoun*	*Falco**	*Rae*	*Stephenson*	*Armstrong*
								Ref: C Wilkes	After Taylor is elbowed across his throat, Scott drills a perfect spot-kick into the corner of the net to cap City's comeback. Millwall punish City for their offside tactics when Mick McCarthy volleys in the opener, and then an overlap results in John Colquhoun sliding in another.											
9	A	IPSWICH		10	L	2-4	1-1	Allison 4, Smith 56 *[Goddard 89]*	Welch	Llewellyn	Scott	May	Bryant	Caesar	Shelton	Rennie	Allison	**Connor**	Smith	
	21/9		*9,910*	*2*	13			*Thompson 37, Linighan 65, Kiwomya 87*	*Forrest*	*Johnson**	*Thompson*	*Stockwell^*	*Yallop*	*Linighan*	*Zondervan*	*Goddard*	*Whitton*	*Dozzell*	*Kiwomya*	*Milton/Lowe*
								Ref: A Buksh	When Smith's right-wing free-kick beats everyone to put City 2-1 ahead, Ipswich were being jeered by their own supporters, but by the final whistle it is a different story. After half an hour of frenzied goalmouth action, they acclaim an emphatic victory, despite a missed penalty.											
10	H	PORTSMOUTH		14	L	0-2	0-2		Welch	Llewellyn	Scott	May	Bryant	Caesar^	Shelton*	Rennie	Allison	Morgan	Smith	Edwards/Connor
	28/9		9,830	*7*	13			*Beresford 34, 43p*	*Knight*	*Awford*	*Beresford*	*Burns*	*Symons*	*Butters*	*Neill*	*Chamberlain*	*Clarke**	*Wigley*	*Anderton*	*Powell*
								Ref: D Elleray	It is thanks to Welch (£200,000 ex Rochdale) that the score is kept within tolerable limits. While David Elleray's officious handling does little to aid City's cause, the fact is that even if Lumsden himself had been in charge Pompey's impressive side would still have won at a canter.											
11	A	DERBY		18	L	1-4	0-1	Edwards 74 *[Davison 62, 78]*	Welch	Llewellyn	Scott	May*	Bryant	Aizlewood	Edwards	Rennie	Allison	Connor	Smith	Bent
	5/10		*11,880*	*8*	13			*Aizlewood 17 (og), Micklewhite 47,*	*Shilton*	*Sage*	*Forsyth*	*Williams G*	*Coleman*	*Comyn*	*Micklewhite*	*Ormondroyd*	*Davison*	*Williams P*	*McMinn*	
								Ref: W Flood	Woeful City are a shambles and Derby could easily have doubled their score after Aizlewood helps in Gary Micklewhite's shot. Rob Edwards (£130,000 ex Carlisle) volleys in a consolation, before slack marking allows Bobby Davison to shoot Derby's fourth pass the helpless Welch.											

No	Date	Opponent	Att	Pos	Pts	F-A	H-T	Scorers, Times, and Referees	1	2	3	4	5	6	7	8	9	10	11	subs used
12	H	WATFORD		11	W	1-0	1-0	Connor 43	Leaning	Llewellyn	Scott	May	Caesar	**Osman**	Connor^	Rennie	Allison	Morgan*	Smith	Taylor/Harrison
	12/10		7,882	*20*	16				*James*	*Gibbs*	*Drysdale*	*Dublin*	*McLaughlin*	*Putney*	*Hessenthaler**	*Blissett^*	*Butler*	*Porter*	*Nicholas*	*Bazeley/Devonshire*
								Ref: H King	Russell Osman, on loan from Soton, exudes class, as City find the resolution and luck to turn the tide of recent bad results. Connor's boundless energy and enthusiasm takes him between two defenders to send in a well-struck shot that slips through the grasp of the diving David James.											
13	A	BARNSLEY		8	W	2-1	1-0	May 24, Shelton 80	Leaning	Llewellyn	Scott	May	Caesar	Osman	Shelton	Rennie	Allison	Morgan*	Connor	Taylor
	19/10		*6,566*	*19*	19			*Currie 77*	*Butler*	*Robinson*	*Archdeacon*	*Fleming*	*Saville^*	*Taggart*	*O'Connell*	*Refearn*	*Pearson**	*Currie*	*Rammell*	*Graham/Williams*
								Ref: R Hart	Completely on top in the first half, City have to work hard after the break. Osman pulls off the save of the season with a spectacular diving header to deflect David Currie's 48th-minute shot onto the crossbar, whilst skipper Shelton scores the winner with a perfect 25-yard chip.											
14	H	NEWCASTLE		9	D	1-1	0-1	Taylor 86	Leaning	Llewellyn	Scott	May	Caesar	Osman*	Shelton	Rennie	Taylor	Morgan^	Connor	Smith/Allison
	26/10		8,613	*20*	20			*Clark 13*	*Wright*	*Neilson**	*Stimson*	*O'Brien*	*Scott*	*Maguire*	*Clark*	*Peacock^*	*Howey*	*Hunt*	*Roche*	*Makel/Robinson*
								Ref: D Gallagher	With Ossie Ardilles now manager of Newcastle, City are again confounded by deployment of the diamond formation. Fortunately the Magpies fail to add to Lee Clarke's early strike, and City's improved play after the interval is rewarded by Taylor's powerful header to poach a point.											
15	A	CAMBRIDGE		9	D	0-0	0-0		Leaning	Llewellyn	Scott	Caesar	Bryant	Aizlewood	Shelton	Rennie	Taylor	Allison	Connor	
	2/11		**4,810**	*3*	21				*Vaughan*	*Fensome*	*Kimble*	*Dennis*	*O'Shea*	*Daish*	*Taylor*	*Bailie*	*Dublin*	*Claridge*	*Philpott*	
								Ref: R Shepherd	Only the woodwork and some disappointing finishing by Allison prevents Lumsden pulling off a notable tactical success. Unfortunately, whilst his five man defence frustrates Cambridge's bombardment style, the outcome is a grim spectacle that is no advert for Second Division soccer.											
16	H	PLYMOUTH		9	W	2-0	2-0	Morgan 14, Allison 27	Leaning	Llewellyn	Scott	May	Bryant	Aizlewood !	Shelton	Rennie	Allison	Morgan	Smith	
	5/11		**7,735**	*24*	24				*Wilmot*	*Salman*	*Clement*	*Marker*	*Hopkins*	*Morgan*	*Edworthy*	*Marshall*	*Evans^*	*Fiore*	*Cross**	*Barlow/Scott*
								Ref: K Barratt	With the new lights fully operational for the first time, Aizlewood fails to get away with aiming a head butt at Andy Clement in the 31st minute following a late tackle on Scott. Fortunately Morgan's deft right-footed flick and Allison's ferocious 18-yard drive, already had City in control.											
17	H	SUNDERLAND		9	W	1-0	1-0	Allison 25	Leaning	Llewellyn^	Scott	May	Bryant	Aizlewood	Shelton	Rennie	Allison	Morgan*	Smith	Connor/Osman
	9/11		10,570	*14*	27				*Norman*	*Kay*	*Rogan*	*Bennett*	*Ball*	*Davenport*	*Bracewell^*	*Rush**	*Armstrong*	*Byrne*	*Pascoe*	*Russell/Owers*
								Ref: B Hill	Andy Leaning (Evening Post Player of the Month for October) frustrates classy Sunderland. Allison, who somehow contrives to turn a clear heading chance into a handball offence, manages to keep his composure to put away Morgan's flick-on after his first shot had been parried.											
18	A	OXFORD		10	D	1-1	0-0	Allison 52	Leaning	Llewellyn	Scott	May	Bryant	Aizlewood	Shelton	Rennie	Allison	Connor*	Smith	Taylor
	16/11		*5,780*	*24*	28			*Simpson 60*	*Keeley*	*Robinson*	*Smart*	*Lewis*	*Foster*	*Melville*	*Magilton*	*McClaren*	*Aylott*	*Nogan*	*Simpson*	
								Ref: P Taylor	As the fog descends at the Manor Ground, rumour has it that Rennie clears Steve Foster's late header off the line to save City a point. Allison finds space to slot the ball under John Keeley, but Paul Simpson is allowed to burst through unchallenged and volley powerfully past Leaning.											
19	A	MIDDLESBROUGH		11	L	1-3	1-2	Taylor 40	Leaning	Llewellyn*	Scott	May	Bryant	Osman !	Shelton	Rennie	Allison	Connor^	Smith	Taylor/Caesar
	23/11		*12,928*	*2*	28			*Payton 4, Slaven 30, 59*	*Pears*	*Fleming*	*Phillips*	*Kernaghan*	*Mohan*	*Mustoe*	*Slaven*	*Proctor*	*Wilkinson*	*Payton**	*Ripley*	*Pollock*
								Ref: P Jones	City bounce back to play some great football in the first half after failure of their offside trap allows Andy Payton to race away and slot in the opener. Taylor's header gets City back into the game, but Boro' are resurgent after the break, even before Osman's 64th-minute dismissal.											
20	H	CHARLTON		11	L	0-2	0-1		Leaning	Llewellyn	Scott	Connor*	Bryant	Osman	Shelton	Rennie^	Allison	Taylor	Smith	May/Edwards
	30/11		9,123	*9*	28			*Pardew 22, Gorman 59*	*Bolder*	*Pitcher*	*Minto*	*Pardew !*	*Webster*	*Gatting*	*Lee*	*Bumstead*	*Rosenior*	*Gorman**	*Walsh*	*Leaburn*
								Ref: G Ashby	'What a load of rubbish' is the cry, as, apart from Bryant's 38th-minute shot, which is disallowed for offside, City offer little. Even Alan Pardew's late dismissal for a spitting offence fails to revive City, who produce their most feeble and half-hearted home performance in a long while.											
21	A	GRIMSBY		12	L	1-3	1-1	Rennie 34	Leaning	Llewellyn	Scott	May	Bryant	Caesar	Bent	Rennie	Allison	Taylor	Gavin	
	7/12		*4,866*	*16*	28			*Woods 2, Jones 69, Smith 88*	*Reece*	*Ford*	*Jopling*	*Futcher*	*Agnew*	*Dobbin*	*Childs*	*Gilbert*	*Smith*	*Cockerill**	*Woods*	*Jones*
								Ref: R Poulain	Captain for the first time, Martin Scott distinguishes himself with a cracking shot against the bar, then sets up Rennie's goal with his through-ball, before blundering at the death. With City besieging the Grimsby goal in search of a late equaliser, his misplaced pass sets up Mark Smith.											
22	A	BRISTOL ROV		15	L	2-3	1-2	Rennie 11, Bent 89	Leaning	Llewellyn*	Scott	Osman	Bryant	Aizlewood	May	Rennie	Allison	Taylor	Gavin	Bent
	21/12		*6,306*	*18*	28			*White 44, Pounder 45, Saunders 81*	*Kelly*	*Alexander*	*Twentyman*	*Yates*	*Cross*	*Skinner*	*Mehew*	*Reece*	*White*	*Saunders*	*Pounder*	
								Ref: P Durkin	Leaning protests he is fouled as Devon White transforms this pulsating derby by heading the Rovers level. Within a minute he turns provider as his header sets up Tony Pounder to smash the ball home from ten yards. City's approach play is breathtaking, but alas their finishing is not.											
23	H	SWINDON		16	D	1-1	0-1	Taylor 48	Leaning	Llewellyn	Scott	May	Bryant	Aizlewood	Osman	Rennie	Allison	Taylor	Gavin	
	26/12		14,636	*9*	29			*Shearer 9*	*Hammond*	*Kerslake*	*Jones*	*Ling*	*Calderwood*	*Taylor*	*Hazard^*	*Shearer*	*Simpson*	*MacLaren*	*White**	*Mitchell/Summerbee*
								Ref: R Gifford	After Duncan Shearer turns in the opener, it is like old times as Gavin's determination takes him clear onto Rennie's pass to impudently roll the ball into Taylor's path, for the simplest of equalisers. Swindon, unlucky in being denied two obvious pens, are without a win in nine games.											

No	Date	Opponent	Att	Pos	Pt	F-A	H-T	Scorers, Times, and Referees	1	2	3	4	5	6	7	8	9	10	11	subs used
24	H	PORT VALE		12	W	**3-0**	2-0	Allison 1, Osman 14, Bent 49	Leaning	Llewellyn	Scott*	May^	Bryant	Aizlewood	Osman	Rennie	Allison	Taylor	Gavin	Bent/Edwards
	28/12		9,235	*14*	32				*Grew*	*Mills S*	*Hughes D*	*Williams*	*Aspin*	*Glover*	*Jalink*	*Van der Laan*	*Swan**	*Houchen^*	*Jeffers*	*Mills B/Porter*
								Ref: A Smith	Even though Taylor squanders a hat-trick of chances, as he seeks to re-discover his form of two years ago, Lumsden enthuses over his lively display. An open attractive game, to which Vale contribute much, ignites from the off with Allison shooting in from Llewellyn's low cross.											
25	A	BRIGHTON		13	D	0-0	0-0		Leaning	Llewellyn	Scott	May	Bryant	Aizlewood	Osman	Rennie*	Allison	Taylor	Gavin	Bent
	1/1		*7,555*	*23*	33				*Beeney*	*Crumplin*	*Gallacher*	*Chapman*	*Chivers*	*Bissett*	*Robinson*	*Farrington**	*Gall*	*Codner*	*Walker*	*Meade*
								Ref: G Pooley	Shot-shy City fail to deliver a KO after dominating the game against a Brighton side with only one point from their previous five games. Gavin misses from close in, but Allison is the biggest culprit as his lack of know-how when faced by an advancing keeper again costs City dear.											
26	A	BLACKBURN		14	L	**0-4**	0-3		Leaning	May	Scott	Osman	Bryant	Aizlewood	Edwards	Rennie*	Allison	Taylor^	Gavin	Bent/Morgan
	11/1		*12,964*	*1*	33			*Newell 2, 43, Scott 30 (og), Speedie 74*	*Mimms*	*Brown*	*Wright*	*Cowans*	*Hill*	*Moran^*	*Wilcox*	*Atkins**	*Speedie*	*Newell*	*Sellars*	*Reid/Hendry*
								Ref: A Wilkie	City's sweeper system fails as Blackburn enjoy oceans of space. Scott Sellars makes an 80-yard run to set up Rovers' opener for Mike Newell to shoot in. City respond with Rennie firing against the bar, but Scott concedes the softest of own-goals on stretching for Newell's cross.											
27	H	SOUTHEND		14	D	2-2	0-1	Dziekanowski 67, Powell 77 (og)	Leaning	Caesar	Scott	Osman	Bryant	Aizlewood	May	Edwards*	Morgan	**Dziek'owski**	Gavin	Bent
	18/1		9,883	*2*	34			*Angell 4, Ansah 72*	*Sansome*	*Austin*	*Powell*	*Butler*	*Scully*	*Prior*	*Ansah*	*Cornwell*	*Tilson*	*Benjamin*	*Angell*	
								Ref: I Hemley	Jacki Dziekanowski (City's record signing - £250,000 ex Celtic) makes amends for his failure to put away a first-minute chance by making no mistake when Bent rolls the ball into his path. Gavin claims City's second, but his cut-back from the by-line is deflected in off Chris Powell.											
28	H	BARNSLEY		16	L	0-2	0-0		Leaning	Llewellyn	Scott	May	Bryant	Osman	Bent	Morgan*	Dziekanowski	Aizlewood	Gavin	Mellon
	1/2		9,508	*21*	34			*Archdeacon 68, O'Connell 89*	*Butler*	*Robinson*	*Fleming*	*Smith*	*Taggart*	*Bishop*	*Banks*	*Graham*	*Archdeacon*	*Currie*	*O'Connell*	
								Ref: P Alcock	A hapless City performance conjures up fears of a grim battle for Second Division survival as no-nonsense Barnsley took a stranglehold on a drab encounter. Brendan O'Connell's exquisite curler finishes off City, after Owen Archdeacon had put Barnsley ahead with a low shot.											
29	A	SWINDON		16	L	0-2	0-0		Leaning	Llewellyn	Scott	May	Bryant	Osman	Bent	Aizlewood	Morgan*	Dziekanowski	Mellon	Allison
	4/2		*9,860*	*5*	34			*Jones 51, Shearer 81*	*Hammond*	*Kerslake*	*Bodin*	*Ling*	*Calderwood*	*Taylor*	*Hazard*	*Shearer*	*Jones*	*MacLaren*	*Mitchell*	
								Ref: K Burge	In many ways the two sides are closely matched, but Swindon have a play-maker and a regular scorer, two priceless commodities that City lack. Play-maker Micky Hazard sets up the first goal for Tom Jones to rifle in, whilst marksman Duncan Shearer pops up to nod in the second.											
30	A	NEWCASTLE		18	L	0-3	0-0		Leaning	Llewellyn	Scott	May*	Bryant	Osman	Bent	Rennie	Allison	Dziekanowski	Gavin	Shelton
	8/2		***29,484***	*22*	34			*Kelly 54, 61, O'Brien 55*	*Wright*	*Ranson*	*Stimson*	*O'Brien*	*Scott*	*Neilson*	*Watson*	*Peacock*	*Kelly*	*Wilson**	*Brock*	*Roche*
								Ref: J Parker	City are the supporting cast at St James Park for Kevin Keegan's first-match in charge of the Magpies. Sadly, inept City prove in no mood to change the predictable script after Leaning palms weakly at Steve Watson's corner for David Kelly to head in from point-blank range.											
31	A	CHARLTON		21	L	1-2	1-0	Shelton 43	Welch	Osman	Scott	May	Bryant	Aizlewood	Bent^	Shelton*	Allison	Dziekanowski	Edwards	Mellon/Gavin
	22/2		*5,900*	*8*	34			*Walsh 81, Webster 88*	*Bolder*	*Pitcher*	*Barness*	*Pardew*	*Webster*	*Gatting*	*Lee*	*Bumstead**	*Leaburn*	*Nelson*	*Walsh*	*Gorman*
								Ref: G Singh	Lumsden's luck hits rock bottom at Upton Park, where a City win looks probable until Shelton has to hobble off with a knee injury early in the second half. Colin Walsh curls in a 25-yard free-kick for Charlton's unlikely equaliser, then Simon Webster rifles in a dream volley.											
32	H	GRIMSBY		20	D	1-1	1-0	Aizlewood 43	Welch	Osman	Scott	May	Bryant	Aizlewood	Bent	Edwards	Allison	Morgan	Gavin	
	29/2		8,992	*17*	35			*Woods 80*	*Reece*	*McDermott*	*Jopling*	*Knight*	*Lever*	*Cunnington*	*Childs**	*Gilbert*	*Rees*	*Smith*	*Dobbin^*	*Woods/Agnew*
								Ref: J Brandwood	Lumsden's departure has City's own gang of three in charge, and one of them, Mark Aizlewood, is almost on his knees when heading in Gavin's corner. City give their all, but lack the ability to threaten Grimby's defence. It is no surprise when Neil Woods fires in an equaliser.											
33	A	WOLVES		22	D	1-1	1-1	Osman 42	Welch	Llewellyn	Scott	May	Bryant	Osman	Gavin	Edwards	Dziek'owski*	Allison	**McIntyre^**	Morgan/Mellon
	7/3		*12,542*	*12*	36			*Bull 45*	*Stowell*	*Ashley*	*Venus*	*Bennett*	*Mountfield*	*Downing**	*Birch*	*Cook*	*Bull*	*Mutch*	*Dennison^*	*Rankine/Burke*
								Ref: A Gunn	City are the better side at Molineux, where Edwards is denied by the woodwork, but Wolves have Steve Bull who takes full advantage when Osman slips in the mud. A glorious rocket shot to equalise Osman's low volley takes his record against City to eleven goals from five games.											
34	A	PLYMOUTH		23	L	0-1	0-0		Welch	Llewellyn	Scott	May	Bryant	Osman	Mellon	Edwards	Morgan*	Allison	Gavin	Bent
	10/3		*9,734*	*20*	36			*Marshall 48*	*Wilmot*	*Salman*	*Spearing*	*Van Rossum*	*Marker*	*Morrison*	*Hodges*	*Garner*	*Regis*	*Marshall*	*Morgan*	
								Ref: M Pierce	New manager Denis Smith now knows the full extent of his task to keep City up, as woeful lack of firepower consigns them to a sorry defeat. Allison's 85th-minute looping header, that comes back off the bar, is City's best attempt to redress Dwight Marshall's close-range winner.											

No Date		Opponent / Att		Pos	Res	F-A	H-T	Scorers, Times, and Referees	1	2	3	4	5	6	7	8	9	10	11	subs used
35	H	CAMBRIDGE		23	L	1-2	1-0	Scott 17	Welch	Llewellyn^	Scott	Aizlewood	Bryant	Osman	Mellon*	Edwards	**Cole**	Allison	May	Harrison/Bent
14/3			9,579	*3*	36			*Heathcote 69, Norbury 84*	*Sheffield*	*Clayton**	*Kimble*	*Bailie^*	*Chapple*	*Daish*	*Heaney*	*Dennis*	*Dublin*	*Claridge*	*Leadbitter*	*Norbury/Heathcote*
								Ref: J Deakin	Mellon's glaring 73rd-min miss when Cole lays on an open goal, and Welch's failure to collect a cross six mins from time gift-wrap the points for a Cambridge side lacking several key players. Mick Norbury lashes home the winner when Dion Dublin's header rebounds off the bar.											
36	H	WOLVES		21	W	2-0	0-0	Dziekanowski 84, 87	Welch	Llewellyn	Scott	Aizlewood	Bryant	Osman	Mellon	Edwards*	Cole	Allison	May	Dziekanowski
17/3			11,623	*11*	39				*Stowell*	*Ashley*	*Venus*	*Bennett*	*Mountfield*	*Madden*	*Birch*	*Cook*	*Bull*	*Rankine*	*Thompson**	*Mutch*
								Ref: P Scobie	Pride returns to Ashton Gate as the fans and players unite in turning the tide. Dziekanowski's appearance just after the break triggers off the action and he secures the points with a brilliant 18-yard volley, and then a waltz past keeper Mike Stowell after swapping passes with Cole.											
37	A	SUNDERLAND		20	W	3-1	3-0	Cole 7, Allison 19, 39	Welch	Llewellyn	Scott	Aizlewood	Bryant	Osman	Mellon	Dziek'owski^	Cole	Allison*	May	**Rosenior**/Edwards
21/3			*18,968*	*17*	42			*Atkinson 73*	*Norman*	*Kay*	*Rogan*	*Ball*	*Ord**	*Rush^*	*Bracewell*	*Davenport*	*Armstrong*	*Byrne*	*Atkinson*	*Goodman/Mooney*
								Ref: S Lodge	Taking advantage of a strong wind Cole puts the skids under Sunderland. After lashing his shot against the crossbar, he keeps his cool to head the rebound over Tony Norman. A deserved win for City, Brian Atkinson's amazing 40-yarder for Sunderland no more than a consolation.											
38	H	OXFORD		20	D	1-1	0-0	Dziekanowski 89	Welch	Llewellyn	Scott	Aizlewood	Bryant	Osman^	Mellon*	Dziekanowski	Cole	Allison	May	**Atteveld**/Rosenior
28/3			12,402	*21*	43			*Bannister 73*	*Veysey*	*Smart*	*Williams*	*Lewis*	*Evans*	*Melville*	*Magilton*	*Beauchamp*	*Aylott*	*Durnin**	*Penney*	*Bannister*
								Ref: D Shadwell	Welch has little to do, other than to pick the ball out of the net after Atteveld's (£250,000 ex Everton) careless back-pass had put Gary Bannister clear. City, who force 17 corners, as well as managing eight shots on target, deserve more than Dziekanowski's late point saver.											
39	A	TRANMERE		19	D	2-2	0-0	Cole 71, Rosenior 75	Welch	Llewellyn	Scott	Aizlewood	Bryant	Osman	Mellon	Dziekanowski	Cole^	Allison*	May	Rosenior/Edwards
31/3			*5,797*	*15*	44			*Nolan 53, Steel 70*	*Nixon*	*Higgins*	*Nolan*	*Irons*	*Harvey*	*Vickers*	*Morrissey**	*Aldridge*	*Steel*	*Nevin*	*Thomas*	*Malkin*
								Ref: R Dilkes	Dziekanowski is City's inspiration with his skilful play and direct runs at the Tranmere defence. His slick pass into Cole's stride, enables the Arsenal youngster to slot the ball past Eric Nixon, then his fierce shot on the run is blocked to enable Rosenior to knock in the equaliser.											
40	H	LEICESTER		17	W	2-1	1-1	Rosenior 5, Cole 55	Welch	Llewellyn	Scott	Aizlewood	Bryant	Osman	Mellon	Dziek'owski*	Cole	Rosenior^	May	Edwards/Allison
4/4			13,020	*6*	47			*Oldfield 18*	*Poole*	*Mills*	*Whitlow*	*Hil*	*Walsh*	*Grayson*	*Thompson**	*Oldfield*	*Wright*	*Ormondroyd*	*Gee*	*Russell*
								Ref: G Poll	The skills of Cole, Dziekanowski and Rosenior suggest that Denis Smith's pledge to survive with style is a realistic prospect. Rosenior's power header gets City off to a good start, then Cole's stunning close-in shot ties up the win, after David Oldfield's volley had levelled for Leicester.											
41	H	MIDDLESBROUGH		17	D	1-1	0-1	Cole 66	Welch	Llewellyn^	Scott*	Aizlewood	Bryant	Osman	Mellon	Dziekanowski	Cole	Rosenior !	May	Atteveld/Allison
7/4			12,814	*6*	48			*Hendrie 18*	*Pears*	*Fleming*	*Phillips*	*Kernaghan*	*Mohan*	*Peake*	*Pollock*	*Payton**	*Wilkinson*	*Hendrie*	*Falconer*	*Ripley*
								Ref: J Carter	All the passion and commitment needed to avoid relegation go into City's comeback following Rosenior's 44th-min sending-off for kicking out at Alan Kernaghan. Dziekanowski's exquisite pass inside the full-back allows Cole to cut in from the right and shoot past Steve Pears.											
42	A	MILLWALL		16	W	3-2	0-1	Rosenior 53, 75, Cole 64	Welch	Llewellyn	Scott	Aizlewood	Bryant	Osman*	Mellon	Dziek'owski^	Cole	Rosenior	May	Atteveld/Allison
11/4			*6,989*	*15*	51			*Barber 20, Atteveld 88 (og)*	*Davison*	*Cunningham*	*Dawes*	*Stevens*	*Verveer*	*Cooper**	*Stephenson*	*Goodman^*	*Allen*	*Roberts*	*Barber*	*McGlashan/McGinlay*
								Ref: P Wright	Rosenior's aerial power and work-rate, combined with Cole's pace, direct running and clinical finishing rip the Lions apart. Cole's brilliant back-heel sends Allison galloping into the area to slide the ball sideways for Rosenior to fire in what proves to be City's match-winning goal.											
43	H	IPSWICH		17	W	2-1	1-0	Rosenior 37, Cole 53	Welch	Atteveld	Scott	Aizlewood	Bryant	Osman	Mellon	Dziekanowski	Cole	Rosenior	May	
18/4			16,914	*1*	54			*Whitton 83p*	*Forrest*	*Zondervan*	*Thompson*	*Stockwell^*	*Wark**	*Whelan*	*Milton*	*Goddard*	*Whitton*	*Dozzell*	*Kiwomya*	*Palmer/Johnson*
								Ref: J Martin	Ipswich make a late fight of it following their late pen after Bryant fells Chris Kiwomya, but this is the only time Welch is stretched. City's potent duo turn up trumps again, Rosenior volleying in the opener, and Cole beating three defenders before slotting the ball past Craig Forrest.											
44	A	PORTSMOUTH		17	L	0-1	0-1		Welch	Atteveld	Scott	Aizlewood	Bryant	Osman	Mellon*	Dziekanowski	Cole	Rosenior	May	Allison
20/4			*17,168*	*9*	54			*Wigley 15*	*Knight*	*Awford**	*Daniel*	*McLoughlin*	*Symons*	*Doling*	*Neill*	*Kuhl*	*Powell*	*Aspinall*	*Wigley^*	*Burns/McFarlane*
								Ref: G Ashby	City's bad habits resurface as other results erase relegation fears. Portsmouth without four regulars offer little, yet their promotion hopes are sustained by a gift-goal and City's poor finishing. Steve Wigley taps in Pompey's three-pointer after a mix-up between Osman and Welch.											
45	H	DERBY		17	L	1-2	1-1	Atteveld 44	Welch	Atteveld	Scott	Aizlewood*	Bryant	Osman^	Llewellyn	Dziekanowski	Cole	Allison	May	Edwards/Gavin
25/4			16,751	*3*	54			*Gabbiadini 11, Micklewhite 81*	*Sutton*	*Kavanagh*	*Forsyth*	*Williams P*	*McMinn*	*Comyn*	*Johnson*	*Kitson**	*Gabbiadini*	*Ramage*	*Simpson*	*Micklewhite*
								Ref: K Breen	Whilst City can now match any Second Division side for flair, defensive queries have been raised by recent games. Amid the fizz and sparkle of this richly entertaining game, the ease with which Derby's skilful attackers penetrated early on had Denis Smith scampering to the touchline.											
46	A	WATFORD		17	L	2-5	1-1	Cole 27, 48 *[Bliss'tt 88, Gibbs 89]*	Leaning	Atteveld !	Scott	Aizlewood !	Bryant	Osman	Llewellyn^	Dziek'owski*	Cole	Allison !	May	Mellon/Edwards
2/5			*10,582*	*10*	54			*Drysdale 32, Bazeley 54, Putney 58*	*James*	*Gibbs*	*Drysdale*	*Dublin*	*Holdsworth*	*Ashby**	*Hessenthaler*	*Nogan*	*Bazeley*	*Butler^*	*Putney*	*Blissett/Porter*
	Home		Away					Ref: K Morton	Whilst the officious attitude of Bury St Edmunds ref Kelvin Morton had a major bearing on all three dismissals, the manager needs to act fast to curb City's worrying lack of discipline. Twice Cole turns City's superior play into goals, only for the advantage to be quickly tossed away.											
Average	11,479		10,530																	

Rumbelows Cup						F-A	H-T	Scorers, Times, and Referees	1	2	3	4	5	6	7	8	9	10	11	subs used
2:1	A	BRISTOL ROV	10	W		3-1	2-1	Morgan 6, Smith 38, Allison 75	Welch	Llewellyn	Scott	May	Bryant	Caesar	Shelton*	Rennie	Allison	Morgan	Smith	Edwards
	25/9		5,155	*23*				*Llewellyn 37 (og)*	*Parkin*	*Alexander*	*Twentyman*	*Yates*	*Clark*	*Archer*	*Boothroyd*	*Cross*	*White*	*Saunders*	*Stewart**	*Browning*
								Ref: K Cooper	'We've cracked the derby problem' insists Rennie after this slick City success. With ten shots on target compared to five for the Rovers, City deserve the victory clinched by Smith's volley and Allison's right-footed shot, after the Rovers had equalised Morgan's drilled-in opener.											
2:2	H	BRISTOL ROV	18	L		2-4	1-1	Morgan 14, Smith 114	Welch	Llewellyn	Scott	Harrison^	Bryant*	Aizlewood	Edwards	Rennie	Allison	Morgan	Smith	Bent/Taylor
	8/10		9,880	*21*		*aet*		*White 15, 72, Mehew 85, 92*	*Parkin*	*Alexander**	*Twentyman*	*Yates*	*Cross*	*Skinner*	*Mehew^*	*Reece*	*White*	*Browning*	*Pounder*	*Clark/Purnell*
								Ref: J Deakin (City lost on away goals)	City fans, in dreamland when Morgan's precise shot puts their favourites 4-1 up on aggregate early on, wake up to a nightmare. Resolute Rovers go through on away goals, a fitting reward to their great spirit, after the most famous fight-back in the history of the Bristol derby.											

FA Cup																				
3	H	WIMBLEDON	13	D		1-1	0-1	Barton 88 (og)	Leaning	Llewellyn*	Scott	May	Bryant	Aizlewood	Osman	Rennie	Allison	Taylor	Gavin	Bent
	4/1		12,679	*1:17*				*Fashanu 37*	*Segers*	*McGee*	*Phelan*	*Barton*	*Scales*	*Fitzgerald*	*Newhouse*	*Earle*	*Fashanu*	*Sanchez*	*Anthrobus*	
								Ref: K Cooper	The drama and passion of cup football are conspicuously absent from this game as Wimbledon dominate with their unadventurous, but effective football. Drama at the end though with Warren Barton's attempted clearance flying into his own net to give City a lucky reprieve.											
3R	A	WIMBLEDON	14	W		1-0	1-0	May 10	Leaning	Caesar	Scott	Osman	Bryant	Aizlewood	Bent*	May	Morgan	Edwards	Gavin	Taylor
	14/1		*3,747*	*1:17*					*Segars*	*McGee*	*Phelan*	*Barton*	*Scales*	*Fitzgerald*	*Newhouse*	*Earle*	*Fashanu*	*Sanchez*	*Anthrobus**	*Clarke*
								Ref: K Cooper	A display full of guts and commitment wins City a fierce battle at Selhurst Park. May's low right-foot swerving-drive from 25 yards proves decisive, as despite all of rampaging Wimbledon's pressure (eight shots on target compared to City's three) an equaliser is rarely threatened.											
4	A	LEICESTER	15	W		2-1	1-0	Bent 27, Dziekanowski 58	Leaning	Llewellyn	Scott	May	Bryant	Osman	Bent	Dziekanowski	Morgan*	Aizlewood	Gavin	Allison
	25/1		*19,313*	*5*				*Kitson 87*	*Muggleton*	*Mills*	*Reid*	*Smith*	*Walsh*	*Fitzpatrick**	*Oldfield*	*Thompson*	*Wright*	*Willis*	*Kitson*	*Ward*
								Ref: P Vanes	'He may come from a different country, but at times it looks as if he is from a different planet.' Such is John Motson's comment on Match of the Day as Polish international Dziekanowski scores one goal and makes another with a skilful display on a treacherous Filbert Street pitch.											
5	A	NOTT'M FOREST	19	L		1-4	0-1	Dziekanowski 75 *[Sher'ham 78p]*	Leaning	Llewellyn	Scott	Aizlewood	Bryant	Osman	Bent	Shelton	Allison	Dziekanowski	Edwards	
	15/2		*24,615*	*1:15*				*Llewellyn 4 (og), Clough 47, Pearce 67*	*Crossley*	*Laws*	*Pearce*	*Walker*	*Wassall*	*Keane*	*Crosby*	*Gemmill*	*Clough**	*Sheringham^*	*Black*	*Charles/Glover*
								Ref: N Midgley	Allison is denied a goal by a close offside decision as City recover from a nightmare start, when Roy Keane's shot cannoned off a post onto Llewellyn's shin and into the net. Class tells after the break, Nigel Clough increasing Forest's advantage when Aizlewood fails to hack clear.											

		Home					Away					
	P	W	D	L	F	A	W	D	L	F	A	Pts
1 Ipswich	46	16	3	4	42	22	8	9	6	28	28	84
2 Middlesbro	46	15	6	2	37	13	8	5	10	21	28	80
3 Derby	46	11	4	8	35	24	12	5	6	34	27	78
4 Leicester	46	14	4	5	41	24	9	4	10	21	31	77
5 Cambridge	46	10	9	4	34	19	9	8	6	31	28	74
6 Blackburn *	46	14	5	4	41	21	7	6	10	29	32	74
7 Charlton	46	9	7	7	25	23	11	4	8	29	25	71
8 Swindon	46	15	3	5	38	22	3	12	8	31	33	69
9 Portsmouth	46	15	6	2	41	12	4	6	13	24	39	69
10 Watford	46	9	5	9	25	23	9	6	8	26	25	65
11 Wolves	46	11	6	6	36	24	7	4	12	25	30	64
12 Southend	46	11	5	7	37	26	6	6	11	26	37	62
13 Bristol Rov	46	11	9	3	43	29	5	5	13	17	34	62
14 Tranmere	46	9	9	5	37	32	5	10	8	19	24	61
15 Millwall	46	10	4	9	32	32	7	6	10	32	39	61
16 Barnsley	46	11	4	8	27	25	5	7	11	19	32	59
17 BRISTOL CITY	46	10	8	5	30	24	3	7	13	25	47	54
18 Sunderland	46	10	8	5	36	23	4	3	16	25	42	53
19 Grimsby	46	7	5	11	25	28	7	6	10	22	34	53
20 Newcastle	46	9	8	6	38	30	4	5	14	28	54	52
21 Oxford	46	10	6	7	39	30	3	5	15	27	43	50
22 Plymouth	46	11	5	7	26	26	2	4	17	16	38	48
23 Brighton	46	7	7	9	36	37	5	4	14	20	40	47
24 Port Vale	46	7	8	8	23	25	3	7	13	19	34	45
	1104	262	144	146	824	594	146	144	262	594	824	1512

* promoted after play-offs

Odds & ends

Double wins: (1) Sunderland.
Double losses: (3) Portsmouth, Derby, Charlton.

Won from behind: (1) Millwall (a).
Lost from in front: (4) Ipswich (a), Bristol Rov (a), Charlton (a), Cambridge (h), Watford (a).

High spots: Beating Bristol Rov at home in the League and away in the League Cup.
Beating Wolves 2-0 at Ashton Gate on 17 March.
Winning at Roker Park on 21 March.
Beating Leicester in the FA Cup.
Beating Bristol Rov 3-2 at Ashton Gate in the Gloucestershire Cup on 7 August.

Low spots: Losing 0-4 at Blackburn on 11 January.
Failing to change the script at St James Park on 8 February.
Having three players sent off at Watford on 2 May.
Losing 1-4 against Nott'm Forest in the FA Cup.
Losing on away goals against Bristol Rov in the League Cup.

Player of the year: Martin Scott.
Ever-presents: (1) Martin Scott.
Hat-tricks: (0).
Leading scorer: Wayne Allison (11).

	Appearances						Goals			
	Lge	*Sub*	LC	*Sub*	FAC	*Sub*	Lge	LC	FAC	Tot
Aizlewood, Mark	34		1		4		1			1
Allison, Wayne	37	*6*	2		2	*1*	10	1		11
Atteveld, Ray	4	*3*					1			1
Bent, Junior	7	*10*		*1*	3	*1*	2		1	3
Bryant, Matt	43		2		4		2			2
Caesar, Gus	9	*1*	1		1					
Cole, Andy	12						8			8
Connor, Terry	9	*2*					1			1
Dziekanowsli, Jacki	16	*1*			2		4		2	6
Edwards, Rob	12	*8*	1	*1*	2		1			1
Gavin, Mark	12	*2*			3					
Harrison, Gerry		*4*	1							
Leaning, Andy	20				4					
Llewellyn, Andy	37		2		3					
May, Andy	44	*1*	1		3		1		1	2
McIntyre, Jim	1									
Mellon, Micky	12	*4*								
Morgan, Nicky	15	*4*	2		2		3	2		5
Osman, Russell	30	*1*			4		2			2
Rennie, David	27		2		1		2			2
Rosenior, Leroy	5	*3*					5			5
Scott, Martin	46		2		4		3			3
Shelton, Gary	18	*1*	1		1		3			3
Smith, Dave	17	*1*	2				1	2		3
Taylor, Bob	13	*5*		*1*	1	*1*	4			4
Welch, Keith	26		2							
(own-goals)							2		1	3
26 players used	**506**	***57***	**22**	***3***	**44**	***3***	**56**	**5**	**5**	**66**

No	Date		Att	Pos	Pt	F-A	H-T	Scorers, Times, and Referees	1	2	3	4	5	6	7	8	9	10	11	subs used
1	H	PORTSMOUTH			D	3-3	2-2	Dziekanowski 3, 50, Cole 28	Leaning	**Mitchell**	Scott	**Thompson**	Bryant	Osman	Mellon	Dziekanowski	Morgan*	Cole	Shelton	Harrison
	15/8		15,251		1			*Whittingham 8, 15, 56*	*Knight*	*Awford*	*Powell*	*McLoughlin*	*Symons*	*Russell*	*Neill*	*Chamberlain^*	*Walsh**	*Whittingham*	*Burns*	*Clarke/Dolling*
								Ref: R Gifford	With the advent of the Premier League, the newly-designated 1st Div gets off to a hectic start. Dziekanowski's dipping volley past Alan Knight sets the tone. Cole turns on a brilliant display, but Leaning is undone by the new pass-back ruling as he puts on a decidedly shaky performance.											
2	A	LUTON			W	3-0	1-0	Mellon 13, Dreyer 50 (og), Cole 75	Welch	Mitchell	Scott	Thompson	Bryant	Osman	Mellon	Dziek'owski*	Rosenior	Cole	Shelton^	Harrison/Edwards
	22/8		*7,926*		4				*Petterson*	*Linton*	*James^*	*Kamara*	*Peake*	*Dreyer*	*Claridge*	*Hughes*	*Gray*	*Preece*	*Campbell**	*Oakes/Johnson*
								Ref: R Bigger	Smith is pleased that City's defence, superbly marshalled by Osman, achieves a clean sheet. Cole, described by Luton boss David Pleat as 'an erratic talent, capable of great things', has a hand in all three goals. His quick break and well-timed pass sets up Mellon to shoot in the opener.											
3	H	SUNDERLAND		10	D	0-0	0-0		Welch	Mitchell	Scott	Thompson	Bryant	Aizlewood	Mellon	Dziekanowski	Cole	Rosenior*	Shelton	Allison
	29/8		14,076	*15*	5				*Carter*	*Kay*	*Rogan**	*Owers*	*Butcher*	*Ball*	*Cunnington*	*Goodman*	*Bennett*	*Byrne*	*Ord*	*Davenport*
								Ref: M Bodenham	Against a Sunderland side fielding five central defenders, City, outnumbered in midfield, struggle throughout. Even so Rosenior's first-half header thuds against a post, whilst Thompson's 80th-minute effort appeared over the line after crashing down off the underside of the bar.											
4	A	DERBY		7	W	4-3	1-2	Scott 36p, Bent 75, Comyn 78 (og)	Welch	Mitchell	Scott	Thompson	Bryant	Osman	Mellon	Harrison*	Dziekanowski	Allison	Shelton	Bent
	6/9		*12,738*	*24*	8			*Simpson 10, 12 79* [Allison 88]	*Sutton !*	*Kavanagh*	*Forsyth*	*Pembridge*	*Coleman*	*Wassall*	*Gabbiadini**	*Kitson*	*Johnson^*	*Williams*	*Simpson*	*Micklewhite/Comyn*
								Ref: P Harrison	For incident, controversy and attacking football, this live TV spectacular could hardly have been bettered. Early on it looked a case of how many were Derby going to get, but Steve Sutton's dismissal for pulling at Shelton's shirt to prevent a 35th-minute goal transforms the game.											
5	H	SOUTHEND		8	L	0-1	0-0		Welch	Mitchell	Scott	Thompson	Bryant	Osman	Mellon	Dziekanowski	Allison*	Rosenior	Shelton	Bent
	12/9		9,515	*16*	8			*Benjamin 75*	*Sansome*	*Edwards*	*Powell*	*Cornwell*	*Scully*	*Prior*	*Ansah*	*Martin*	*Locke*	*Benjamin*	*O'Callaghan*	
								Ref: V Callow	City are at their frustrating worst, devoid of ideas and prone to sloppy errors at the back. With Mitchell unable to make any impact on the right, City's wing-back system never looks effective, and they pay the cost as Ian Benjamin bursts through to slide his shot under the diving Welch.											
6	H	WEST HAM		9	L	1-5	0-3	Scott 54 *[Allen C 44, 86]*	Welch	Llewellyn	Scott	Thompson	Bryant	Edwards	Harrison	Dziek'owski*	Rosenior	Cole^	Shelton	Allison/Connor
	15/9		14,094	*5*	8			*Robson 6, Morley 27, 89,*	*Miklosko*	*Breacker*	*Thomas*	*Potts*	*Martin*	*Allen M*	*Robson**	*Butler*	*Morley*	*Allen C*	*Keen*	*Small*
								Ref: J Martin	City's difficulties with the sweeper system are exposed as the slick Hammers hand out shock treatment. For home fans it is painful to watch the ease with which West Ham cruise to a three-goal interval lead, after Mitchell Thomas' cut-back enables Mark Robson to shoot past Welch.											
7	A	NEWCASTLE		12	L	**0-5**	0-2	*[Carr 64, Brock 87]*	Welch	Llewellyn	Scott	Thompson	Bryant	Aizlewood*	**Reid**	Dziek'owski^	Rosenior	Allison	Shelton	Connor/Bent
	19/9		***29,434***	*1*	8			*O'Brien 40, Peacock 44p, 68p,*	*Wright*	*Venison*	*Beresford*	*O'Brien*	*Scott*	*Howey*	*Carr**	*Peacock*	*Kelly*	*Clark*	*Sheedy^*	*Quinn/Brock*
								Ref: T Fitzharris	'That's Geordie Magic' screams the scoreboard as City's humiliation comes to an end. After surviving 40 mins of incessant Magpie pressure, the dam bursts when Liam O'Brien punishes Thompson's innocuous challenge with a glorious 30-yard free-kick that has the net billowing.											
8	H	BARNSLEY		10	W	2-1	1-1	Allison 45, Scott 84p	Welch	Mitchell	Scott	Thompson	Bryant	Edwards	Connor^	Dziekanowski	Allison	Mellon*	Reid	Bent/Harrison
	26/9		8,041	*24*	11			*O'Connell 35*	*Butler*	*Robinson*	*Fleming*	*Taggart !*	*Bishop*	*Redfearn*	*Burton^*	*Archdeacon*	*Pearson*	*Liddell**	*O'Connell*	*Currie/Bullimore*
								Ref: P Durkin	Despite losing the services of Gerry Taggart for wrestling Allison out of a clear sixth-minute scoring opportunity, only Welch stands between Barnsley and a well-deserved victory. Instead, Scott's penalty wins it for City, after Edwards goes down under Mark Robinson's challenge.											
9	A	TRANMERE		13	L	0-3	0-1		Welch	Mitchell	Scott	Thompson	Bryant	Reid^	Connor	Dziekanowski	Allison	Cole	Shelton*	Harrison/Rosenior
	3/10		*5,975*	*5*	11			*Aldridge 38, 71p, Nevin 56*	*Nixon*	*Higgins*	*Brannan*	*Martindale*	*Mungall*	*Vickers*	*Morrissey*	*Aldridge*	*Malkin*	*McNab*	*Nevin*	
								Ref: K Barratt	Smith believes Cole's return, after a month-long knee injury, will soon have City on the road to recovery. City, who show the style, but lack the finish, are caught forward in numbers when John Aldridge gets away to give Scott the slip and thump in an 18-yard opener past Welch.											
10	H	CHARLTON		12	W	2-1	1-1	Dziekanowski 16, Harrison 90	Welch	Mitchell^	Scott	Thompson	Osman	Edwards	Harrison	Dziekanowski	Rosenior	Cole	Shelton*	Reid/Allison
	10/10		9,286	*2*	14			*Leaburn 8*	*Bolder*	*Balmer*	*Minto*	*Pardew**	*Webster*	*Pitcher*	*Leaburn*	*Bumstead*	*Dyer*	*Nelson*	*Grant*	*Warden*
								Ref: J Rushton	Harrison's right-foot rocket from 25 yards, midway through four mins of injury-time, gives City a hard-earned win over previously-unbeaten Charlton. Heads could have dropped after Carl Leaburn's four-yard tap-in, but Dziekanowski sidefoots home Cole's cross from ten yards.											
11	A	CAMBRIDGE		11	L	1-2	0-1	Cole 48	Welch	Mitchell	Bryant	Thompson	Osman*	Edwards	Harrison	Dziekanowski	Rosenior	Cole	Shelton	Allison
	17/10		*3,896*	*18*	14			*Kimble 41p, Ainsworth 84*	*Sheffield*	*Rowett*	*Kimble*	*Fowler*	*Heathcote*	*O'Shea*	*Raynor*	*Ainsworth*	*White*	*Cheetham**	*Philpott*	*Francis*
								Ref: K Morton	City are undone by United's up and under tactics. After Cole's cleverly-angled shot equalised Alan Kimble's pen (Bryant hauling down Mike Cheetham), Gareth Ainsworth heads in from six yards to make City pay for their failure to turn to good account their superior approach play.											

No	Venue	Opponent	Att	Pos	Pts	F-A	H-T	Scorers, Times, and Referees	1	2	3	4	5	6	7	8	9	10	11	subs used
12	H	LEICESTER		11	W	2-1	0-1	Cole 74, Grayson 87 (og)	Welch	Mitchell	Scott	Thompson	Bryant*	Osman	Harrison	Dziekanowski	Rosenior	Cole	Shelton^	Allison/Edwards
	24/10		10,436	*7*	17			*Davison 5*	*Hoult*	*Grayson*	*Whitlow**	*Smith*	*Walsh*	*Hill*	*Oldfield*	*Thompson*	*Davison*	*Ormondroyd*	*Joachim^*	*Gee/Lowe*
								Ref: D Frampton	Dziekanowski's skill is the only source of encouragement in City's display which began disastrously and stuttered to an unlikely triumph. Simon Grayson volleys a spectacular own-goal for City's winner, after Cole's headed equaliser owed something to Russell Hoult's dive.											
13	A	BRENTFORD		15	L	1-5	1-2	Cole 25 *[Blissett 55, 60]*	Welch	Mitchell	Scott	Thompson	Edwards	Osman	Harrison	Dziek'owski^	Rosenior	Cole	Allison*	Connor/Gavin
	31/10		*8,726*	*19*	17			*Millen 17, 47, Chalmers 44,*	*Peyton*	*Statham*	*Hughton*	*Millen*	*Westley*	*Chalmers**	*Luscombe^*	*Manuel*	*Gayle*	*Blissett*	*Smillie*	*Ratcliffe/Jones*
								Ref: P Scobie	A Halloween horror show at Griffin Park, as City's static defence concedes four goals following corners. Reduced to ten men for the last three minutes, when Harrison is injured, City's only consolation, following a bright start, is Cole's waltz around Gerry Peyton for the early leveller.											
14	A	MILLWALL		15	L	1-4	1-4	Cole 43 *[Moralee 29]*	Welch	Bryant	Scott	Thompson	Edwards	Osman	Harrison^	Shelton	Rosenior*	Cole	Gavin	Allison/Bent
	4/11		*5,924*	*7*	17			*Cooper 13, Allen 18, May 24,*	*Keller*	*Cunningham*	*Dawes*	*May*	*Cooper*	*Rae*	*Roberts*	*Moralee**	*Allen*	*Byrne^*	*Barber*	*Dolby/Goodman*
								Ref: R Pawley	City contribute more to this sparkling match than the score suggests, but on-going defensive frailties and poor finishing brings another heavy away defeat. Whilst Cole fails with an open-goal chance early on, Colin Cooper has no such problem when cracking in Millwall's opener.											
15	H	BIRMINGHAM		14	W	3-0	1-0	Rosenior 44, Shelton 47, Cole 87	Welch	Bryant	Scott	Thompson	Edwards	Osman	Harrison	Shelton	Rosenior	Cole	Gavin	
	7/11		10,019	*17*	20				*Sealey*	*Clarkson !*	*Frain*	*Donowa**	*Hicks*	*Matthewson*	*Rodgerson*	*Tait*	*Speedie*	*Sturridge^*	*Rowbotham !*	*Potter/Cooper*
								Ref: P Alcock	City already had the game won when Darren Rowbotham's outburst of dissent over Ian Clarkson's dismissal for a high tackle on Edwards, makes it a double 56th-minute sending off. Headers from Rosenior and Cole, as well as Shelton's close-in shot, brings a well-merited victory.											
16	A	GRIMSBY		15	L	1-2	0-0	Cole 53	Welch	Bryant	Scott	Thompson	Edwards	Mitchell	Harrison	Shelton	Rosenior	Cole	Mellon	
	14/11		*5,651*	*8*	20			*Watson 80, Mendonca 89*	*Beasant*	*McDermott*	*Croft*	*Futcher^*	*Lever**	*Dobbin*	*Watson*	*Gilbert*	*Groves*	*Mendonca*	*Rees*	*Rodger/Woods*
								Ref: J Key	Welch is in top form at Blundell Park, but even he can do nothing about Tommy Watson's gloriously headed equaliser, or the cruelly-deflected late winner, fired home from 25 yards by Clive Mendonca. A cruel return for a battling performance that saw City ahead with Cole's volley.											
17	H	SWINDON		15	D	2-2	1-1	Shelton 44, Rosenior 58	Welch	Mitchell*	Scott	**Kristensen**	Bryant	Osman	Shelton	Dziekanowski	Rosenior	Cole	Edwards	Harrison
	21/11		14,081	*2*	21			*Maskell 32, Summerbee 57*	*Hammond*	*Kerslake*	*Horlock*	*Hoddle**	*Calderwood*	*Taylor*	*Hazard*	*Summerbee*	*Maskell*	*Ling*	*Mitchell*	*White*
								Ref: P Jones	On a rain-soaked pitch City twice battle back from behind and on the number of clear chances created should have won. Swindon's open-passing style, encouraged by the skills of Glenn Hoddle and Micky Hazard, allows Dziekanowski the freedom to fully express his abilities.											
18	H	NOTTS CO		13	W	1-0	0-0	Shelton 89	Welch	Harrison	Scott	Kristensen	Bryant	Osman	Shelton	Dziekanowski	Rosenior*	Cole	Edwards	Allison
	28/11		9,086	*21*	24				*Cherry*	*Palmer*	*Dijkstra*	*Thomas*	*Turner*	*Johnson**	*Wilson*	*Draper^*	*Agana*	*Bartlett*	*Smith*	*O'Riordan/Slawson*
								Ref: M Pierce	Back from their first competitive venture into Europe, a 3-4 defeat at Pisa in the Anglo-Italian Cup, City's defence is more resilient against Notts. Shelton fires in a minute before the end of normal time, but City have to endure seven minutes of injury-time before victory is theirs.											
19	A	WATFORD		13	D	0-0	0-0		Welch	Harrison	Scott	Kristensen	Bryant	Osman	Shelton	Dziek'owski*	Rosenior^	Cole	Edwards	Mellon/Allison
	5/12		*6,746*	*15*	25				*Suckling*	*Putney^*	*Drysdale*	*Dublin*	*Holdsworth*	*Ashby*	*Hessenthaler*	*Willis*	*Charlery*	*Porter**	*Nogan*	*Bazeley/Johnson*
								Ref: I Borrett	Cole is always the brightest spark that threatened to turn City's hard-working team-effort into three points. Unfortunately his finishing doesn't match some brilliant runs and City have to be satisfied with a point from this thrilling encounter to end their long barren spell away from home.											
20	A	BRISTOL ROV		15	L	0-4	0-1	*[Taylor 78]*	Welch	Harrison	Scott	Kristensen	Bryant	Osman	Shelton	Dziekanowski	Rosenior*	Cole	Edwards^	Allison/Gavin
	13/12		*7,112*	*19*	25			*Channing 23, Stewart 65, Saunders 68*	*Parkin*	*Alexander*	*Tillson*	*Yates*	*Hardyman*	*Browning*	*Channing*	*Stewart*	*Taylor*	*Saunders*	*Waddock*	
								Ref: J Martin	Humiliation again for City as Malcolm Allison inspires Rovers to their fifth League derby win since moving to Bath. Now without a victory in seven League visits to Fortress Twerton, City never looked like winning this one after Justin Channing struck a low 30-yard drive past Welch.											
21	H	PETERBOROUGH		17	L	0-1	0-1		Welch	Harrison	Scott	Edwards*	Bryant	Osman	Shelton	Bent	Rosenior^	Cole	Gavin	Mitchell/Allison
	19/12		7,333	*11*	25			*Welsh 28*	*Bennett*	*Luke*	*Robinson*	*Halsall*	*Bradshaw*	*Welsh*	*Sterling*	*Cooper*	*Adcock*	*Philliskirk*	*Ebdon*	
								Ref: P Vanes	The storm clouds are gathering for Denis Smith as City run out of luck. Steve Welsh claims his first League goal when putting away Tony Philliskirk's head-down from a contentious free-kick, then seconds later Rosenior has his effort disallowed for a supposed foul on the keeper.											
22	H	OXFORD		17	D	1-1	1-1	Rosenior 31	Welch	Harrison	Scott	Mitchell	Bryant	Osman	Shelton	Bent	Rosenior*	Cole	Gavin	Allison
	26/12		10,737	*16*	26			*Beauchamp 4*	*Reece*	*Smart*	*Ford*	*Lewis*	*Evans*	*Melville*	*Magilton*	*Beauchamp*	*Penney**	*Cusack*	*Durnin*	*Allen*
								Ref: R Gifford	The police have a lot to answer for as not for the first time the fans are inconvenienced by an early kick-off. However despite the 11.30am start the only thing wrong with the game is City's failure to convert a host of chances. Fortunately though Rosenior is able to head in City's equaliser.											
23	A	WOLVES		18	D	0-0	0-0		Welch	Mitchell	Scott !	Harrison^	Bryant	Osman	Shelton	Bent*	Rosenior	Cole	Gavin	Allison/Dziekanowski
	28/12		*16,419*	*7*	27				*Jones*	*Ashley**	*Edwards*	*Burke*	*Madden*	*Blades*	*Rankine*	*Cook*	*Bull*	*Downing*	*Venus*	*Mutch*
								Ref: A Ward	After dominating the first half it takes all of City's resolve to prise a point from Wolves. Shrugging off Scott's 54th-minute dismissal, City contain the Steve Bull-Andy Mutch alliance, and almost win at the last when Dziekanowski bursts clear to force a smart save from Jones.											

BARCLAYS LEAGUE DIVISION 1

Manager: Smith ⇨ Russell Osman

SEASON 1992-93

No	Date		Att	Pos	Pt	F-A	H-T	Scorers, Times, and Referees	1	2	3	4	5	6	7	8	9	10	11	subs used
24	H	NEWCASTLE		18	L	1-2	1-2	Allison 18	Welch	Harrison^	Scott	Llewellyn	Bryant	Osman	Shelton	Bent*	Allison	Cole	Gavin	Mellon/Aizlewood
	9/1		15,446	*1*	27			*Harrison 20 (og), Scott 31*	*Srnicek*	*Venison*	*Beresford*	*O'Brien*	*Scott*	*Howey*	*Lee*	*Peacock*	*Kelly*	*Clark*	*Sheedy**	*Bracewell*
								Ref: K Burge	City, with ten shots on target compared to Newcastle's two, should have beaten the leaders. Unfortunately the Magpies quickly bounce back from Allison's header. Harrison deflects a cross into his own net, then City's slipshod offside trap fails and Kevin Scott fires in the winner.											
25	A	BARNSLEY		18	L	1-2	0-2	Cole 74	Welch	Llewellyn	Aizlewood	Harrison	Bryant	Osman	Bent*	Shelton	Allison	Cole	Gavin	Rosenior
	16/1		*5,423*	*12*	27			*O'Connell 8, 22*	*Butler*	*Robinson*	*Taggart*	*Fleming*	*Bishop*	*Archdeacon*	*Refearn*	*O'Connell*	*Currie*	*Biggins*	*Rammell*	
								Ref: I Cruikshanks	City are entitled to feel aggrieved by Hartlepool referee Ian Cruikshanks as Cole is denied a blatant fifth-min penalty, and Allison is cynically brought down when clean through after the break. Barnsley take the points with Brendan O'Connell's low shot being followed by his header.											
26	A	WEST HAM		18	L	0-2	0-0		Welch	Atteveld^	Scott	Aizlewood	Bryant	Osman	Shelton	Harrison	Allison	Cole	Gavin*	Dziek'owski/Rosenior
	27/1		*12,118*	*2*	27			*Morley 67, Robson 74*	*Miklosko*	*Breacker*	*Brown*	*Potts*	*Gale*	*Allen M*	*Robson**	*Butler*	*Morley*	*Bunbury^*	*Keen*	*Holmes/Parris*
								Ref: B Hill	The difficult task caretaker boss Russell Osman faces to turn the tide in a miserable season is amply demonstrated at Upton Park where City finish up a well-beaten side. Hard work is not enough as Osman's negative tactics are thwarted by Morley's tap-in and Robson's header.											
27	H	LUTON		19	D	0-0	0-0		Welch	Llewellyn	Scott	Aizlewood	Bryant	Osman^	Shelton*	Dziekanowski	Rosenior	Cole	Harrison	Mellon/Allison
	30/1		8,877	*24*	28				*Chamberlain*	*Dreyer*	*James*	*Johnson*	*Hughes*	*Peake*	*Telfer*	*Williams^*	*Rees**	*Gray*	*Preece*	*Oakes/Benjamin*
								Ref: J Carter	City's failure to beat a Luton side with very little to offer suggests that they are firmly on a relegation course. Dziekanowski is the most creative player, and it is his pass that sends Scott through to fire wide from one of only two chances created by City's first-half dominance.											
28	A	PORTSMOUTH		17	W	3-2	1-1	Shelton 15, Bryant 73, Gavin 83	Welch	Llewellyn	**Munro**	Aizlewood	Bryant	**Pennyfather**	Shelton	Dziekanowski	Allison^	Cole	Harrison*	Gavin/Rosenior
	6/2		*10,675*	*5*	31			*Walsh 8, Whittingham 48*	*Knight*	*Awford*	*Daniel*	*McLoughlin**	*Symons*	*Burns*	*Price !*	*Chamberlain*	*Walsh*	*Whittingham*	*Aspinall^*	*Powell/Russell*
								Ref: P Foakes	The new signings help turn the tide against a side reduced to ten men after 82 mins when Chris Price receives the red card for his desperate foul to stop Cole. Three quality goals, shots by Shelton and Gavin, as well as Bryant's header, bring City their first away success since Sep.											
29	A	SOUTHEND		18	D	1-1	1-1	Cole 16	Welch	Llewellyn	Munro	Aizlewood	Bryant	Pennyfather	Shelton	Dziek'owski*	Allison	Cole	Gavin	Rosenior
	10/2		***3,836***	*23*	32			*Collymore 44*	*Sansome*	*Edwards*	*Hyslop*	*Cornwell*	*Scully*	*Prior*	*Ansah*	*Tilson*	*Jones*	*Collymore*	*Angell*	
								Ref: D Elleray	Only the crowd of below 4,000 is in keeping with a bottom of the table clash as on this form both rampaging Southend and slick City should escape the jaws of relegation. A fair result as Stan Collymore's glorious 15-yarder counters Cole's flick in from Bryant's towering header.											
30	A	SUNDERLAND		20	D	0-0	0-0		Welch	Llewellyn	Munro	Aizlewood	Bryant	Pennyfather	Shelton	Dziekanowski	Allison	Cole	Osman	
	20/2		*17,083*	*17*	33				*Norman*	*Kay*	*Smith**	*Atkinson*	*Butcher*	*Ball*	*Mooney^*	*Goodman*	*Colquhoun*	*Gray, Mike*	*Armstrong*	*Ord/Rush*
								Ref: R Dilkes	Munro (ex Blackburn) caps another solid performance with two crucial interceptions in this dour struggle at Roker Park. A 72nd-min goal-line clearance from Brian Atkinson's header, being followed six minutes later by a point-saving tackle on Don Goodman as he prepares to shoot.											
31	A	CHARLTON		20	L	1-2	1-0	Cole 3	Welch	Llewellyn	Munro	Aizlewood	Bryant	Pennyfather^	Shelton	Dziek'owski*	Allison	Cole	Gavin	Osman/Rosenior
	27/2		*7,261*	*10*	33			*Gorman 78, Gatting 90*	*Salmon*	*Pitcher*	*Gatting*	*Pardew*	*Webster*	*Balmer^*	*Houghton*	*Minto*	*Leaburn*	*Nelson**	*Walsh*	*Gorman/Warden*
								Ref: G Poll	Whilst the result does not go City's way and despite away fans having to pay £14 for admission it is fitting that Charlton have returned to the Valley. For City, though, it is like the Valley of Death as their light brigade is halted by Gatting's headed winner two minutes into injury-time.											
32	H	TRANMERE		21	L	1-3	0-2	Cole 49	Welch	Llewellyn*	Munro	Aizlewood !	Bryant^	Pennyfather	Shelton	Dziekanowski	Scott	Cole	Gavin	Allison/Rosenior
	6/3		8,845	*6*	33			*Malkin 37, 78, Nevin 45*	*Nixon*	*Higgins*	*Brannan !*	*Irons*	*Mungall*	*Vickers**	*Morrissey*	*Martindale*	*Malkin*	*McNab*	*Nevin*	*Hughes*
								Ref: M Pierce	City's attractive play counts for nought as individual errors, and Nixon's saving of Scott's 65th-minute spot-kick, increases relegation fears. Welch, at fault when helping Chris Malkin's header into the net, errs again when he allows Pat Nevin's under-hit shot to sneak inside the post.											
33	H	MILLWALL		21	L	0-1	0-1		Welch	Munro	Scott	Aizlewood^	Bryant	Osman	Shelton	Dziek'owski*	Allison	Cole	Gavin	Rosenior/Harrison
	9/3		8,771	*4*	33			*Barber 26*	*Keller*	*Cunningham*	*Dawes*	*Rae*	*Cooper*	*Stevens*	*Roberts*	*Allen*	*Bogie^*	*Byrne**	*Barber*	*Moralee/Dolby*
								Ref: K Barratt	Cole pledges to score the goals to keep City up after squandering three guilt-edged chances, including a second-half penalty, in this exciting game. Phil Barber's angled drive past the unprotected Welch settles the contest as Kasey Keller is in unbeatable form for Milwall.											
34	A	BIRMINGHAM		20	W	1-0	1-0	Morgan 44	Welch	Munro	Scott	Osman	Bryant	Pennyfather	Shelton	Bent	Rosenior	Morgan	Gavin	
	13/3		15,611	*23*	36				*Catlin*	*Hiley*	*Frain*	*Parris*	*Mardon*	*Matthewson^*	*Moulden*	*Gayle*	*Peschisolido*	*Tait**	*Smith*	*Rodgerson/Fenwick*
								Ref: A Flood	Nicky Morgan, City's forgotten man, is back with a typical skilful performance. He crashes an early volley against the crossbar before sinking Birmingham on the stroke of half-time. Gavin's quickly taken free-kick catches out the home defence and Morgan flights in a looping header.											

No	Date	Opponent	Att	Pos	Res / Pts	F-A	H-T	Scorers, Times, and Referees	1	2	3	4	5	6	7	8	9	10	11	subs used
35	H	WATFORD		20	W	2-1	1-1	Bent 12, Pennyfather 85	Welch	Llewellyn	Scott	Osman^	Bryant	Pennyfather	Harrison	Bent	Rosenior	Morgan	Gavin*	Edwards/Allison
	20/3		8,265	*14*	39			*Charlery 41*	*Suckling*	*Soloman*	*Ashby*	*Dublin*	*Holdsworth*	*Bazeley**	*Hessenthaler*	*Nogan^*	*Furlong*	*Charlery*	*Porter*	*Willis/Lavin*
								Ref: J Lloyd	Morgan again stars as the replacement for the departed Cole, as a welcome change of luck brings to an end City's four-month wait for a home success. Lunging in to block Barry Ashby's attempted clearance, Pennyfather watches the ball rebound into the net for City's late winner.											
36	A	SWINDON		22	L	1-2	0-1	Rosenior 83	Welch	Munro	Scott	Osman	Bryant !	Pennyfather	Shelton	Bent*	Rosenior	Morgan	**Tinnion**	Allison
	24/3		*13,353*	*4*	39			*Marwood 19, Bodin 60p*	*Digby*	*Summerbee*	*Bodin*	*Hoddle*	*Calderwood*	*Taylor*	*Marwood*	*MacLaren*	*Mitchell^*	*Ling**	*White*	*Hunt/Close*
								Ref: D Gallagher	Bryant's dismissal a minute before half-time is a handicap City cannot overcome in a niggly West Country derby. Following Brian Marwood's headed opener and Paul Bodin's pen when Steve White is tripped, the most City can manage is Rosenior's tap-in finish to Tinnion's low cross.											
37	H	GRIMSBY		19	W	1-0	0-0	Morgan 70	Welch	Munro	Scott	Osman	Bryant	Pennyfather	Shelton	Bent	Rosenior	Morgan	Tinnion	
	28/3		**6,755**	*10*	42				*Willmott*	*Croft^*	*Agnew*	*Futcher*	*Rodger*	*Ford*	*Childs*	*Gilbert*	*Groves*	*Mendonca**	*Rees*	*Woods/Daws*
								Ref: K Cooper	Given the pressure of the relegation battle, City's football is more attractive than could have been expected as they notch up a priceless win. The Mariners only come to life after City's star man Morgan had steamed in to finish off Tinnion's perfect cross with a powerful header.											
38	A	NOTTS CO		20	D	0-0	0-0		Welch	Munro	Scott	Osman	Bryant	Pennyfather	Shelton	Bent*	Rosenior	Morgan	Tinnion	Allison
	3/4		*6,634*	*18*	43				*Cherry*	*Short, Chris*	*Johnson*	*Thomas*	*Cox*	*Walker*	*Lund^*	*Draper*	*Wilson**	*Devlin*	*Smith*	*Reeves/Agana*
								Ref: R Lewis	Whilst Osman blames the blustery wind and poor surface for the low quality of the football, no one can accuse this City team of lacking commitment. Tinnion's rasping 30-yard drive, which Steve Cherry does well to save, is City's best effort as they battle to hold onto a point.											
39	H	BRISTOL ROV		15	W	2-1	1-0	Morgan 35, Tinnion 79p	Welch	Munro	Aizlewood	Osman	Bryant	Pennyfather	Shelton	Allison	Rosenior	Morgan	Tinnion	
	6/4		**21,854**	*24*	46			*Taylor 81*	*Kelly*	*Alexander !*	*Tillson*	*Yates*	*Clark*	*Pounder*	*Mehew^*	*Reece*	*Taylor*	*Stewart**	*Waddock*	*Evans/Channing*
								Ref: M Reed	City are deserved winners of a match more memorable for atmosphere rather than the calibre of the football. John Taylor drills in a low shot for Rovers, but City's earlier penalty, after Ian Alexander's sending off for handling Tinnion's goal-bound shot, ultimately proves decisive.											
40	A	OXFORD		17	L	0-2	0-1		Welch	Munro^	Scott	Aizlewood	Thompson	Pennyfather	Shelton	Allison	Rosenior*	Morgan	Tinnion	Bent/Harrison
	10/4		*6,145*	*16*	46			*Druce 30, Beauchamp 66*	*Kee*	*Smart*	*Ford*	*Collins*	*Evans*	*Melville*	*Magilton*	*Beauchamp*	*Cusack*	*Druce**	*Narbett*	*Penney*
								Ref: J Carter	City dominate with their neat possession football, but a generous defence renders all their effort worthless. Welch, caught in no man's land by David Collins' back header, has no chance when his defence parts like the Red Sea to let Joey Beauchamp race through and shoot in off a post.											
41	H	WOLVES		14	W	1-0	0-0	Bent 81	Welch	Osman^	Scott	Aizlewood	Bryant	Pennyfather	Atteveld*	Bent	Allison	Morgan	Tinnion	Harrison/**Fowler**
	12/4		11,756	*9*	49				*Stowell*	*Simkin*	*Venus*	*Downing*	*Mountfield*	*Blades^*	*Thompson*	*Cook*	*Rankine**	*Mutch*	*Dennison*	*Birch/Madden*
								Ref: P Wright	With four of the six injured at Oxford coming off the treatment table, the walking wounded demonstrate the great spirit that is guiding City away from the danger zone. Defensive solidarity is rewarded near the end as Bent squirms between two defenders to shoot in from close range.											
42	A	PETERBOROUGH		15	D	1-1	0-0	Tinnion 50	Welch	Munro	Scott	Aizlewood	Bryant	Osman	Shelton	Harrison	Allison	Morgan*	Tinnion	Atteveld
	17/4		*5,169*	*13*	50			*Barnes 68*	*Bennett*	*Bradshaw*	*Spearing*	*Cooper*	*Greenman*	*Welsh*	*Sterling*	*Ebdon*	*Howarth*	*Philliskirk**	*Barnes*	*Iorfa*
								Ref: J Rushton	After Tony Philliskirk's 25-yard volley hits a post, City are disrupted by Morgan's 26th-minute departure with a dislocated ankle. After the break though it is all City, Tinnion's superb strike puts them in front before Bobby Barnes' hooked volley brings the Posh a surprise equaliser.											
43	H	DERBY		15	D	0-0	0-0		Welch	Osman	Munro	Aizlewood	Bryant	Pennyfather*	Shelton^	Harrison	Allison	Bent	Tinnion	Atteveld/**Shail**
	20/4		8,869	*9*	51				*Taylor*	*Patterson*	*Nicholson*	*Forsyth*	*Short*	*Pembridge*	*Sturridge*	*Kuhl*	*Kitson*	*Gabbiadini*	*Simpson*	
								Ref: D Frampton	Osman's battle-scarred troops, inhibited by injury in every department, not only snuff out Derby's multi-million pound team, but create the better chances. Pennyfather's 25-yard volley crashes against a post, whilst Allison spurns a great opportunity by heading wide from six yards.											
44	H	CAMBRIDGE		16	D	0-0	0-0		Welch	Harrison	Munro	Aizlewood	Bryant	Shail	Shelton	Atteveld^	Allison	Bent*	Tinnion	Rosenior/Edwards
	24/4		8,998	*23*	52				*Filan*	*Heathcote*	*Kimble*	*Raynor*	*Chapple*	*O'Shea*	*Dennis^*	*Claridge*	*Butler*	*Clayton*	*Lyne**	*Rush/Bartlett*
								Ref: K Cooper	The sweeper system didn't work when Smith tried it, and it doesn't work in this game as City do not have the players to make the formation effective. Cambridge have the better of the contest, but mind-numbing boredom such as this will have the fans staying away in their droves.											
45	A	LEICESTER		16	D	0-0	0-0		Welch	Osman	Munro	Aizlewood	Shail	Atteveld	Shelton	Gavin	Allison	Rosenior	Tinnion	
	1/5		*19,294*	*5*	53				*Poole*	*Mills*	*Whitlow*	*Smith*	*Walsh*	*Hill*	*Oldfield*	*Thompson**	*Joachim^*	*Lowe*	*Philpott*	*James/Lewis*
								Ref: A Wilkie	A deserved point, with both sides being denied by the woodwork, guarantees safety and earns Osman the manager's chair. Just two defeats in the last twelve games is impressive, but at what cost as City's style of play is not the sort to encourage any but the most committed spectator.											
46	H	BRENTFORD		15	W	**4-1**	2-0	Rosenior 6, 55, 67, Allison 28	Welch	Llewellyn	Edwards	Aizlewood	Shail	Atteveld	Shelton*	Gavin	Allison	Rosenior^	Tinnion	Harrison/Bent
	8/5		12,695	22	56			*Blissett 57*	*Peyton*	*Statham*	*Sansom*	*Millen*	*Evans*	*Manuel**	*Bennett^*	*Dickens*	*Gayle*	*Blissett*	*Smillie*	*Allon/Ratcliffe*
		Home	Away					Ref: M James	A goal feast against a strangely subdued Bees side requiring a point to stay up. Allison shows that he sometimes knows where the net is as he strides through to guide the ball wide of Gerry Payton, but the star is Rosenior as he scores a hat-trick of goals with not a header among them.											
Average		11,004	10,137																	

Coca-Cola Cup					F-A	H-T	Scorers, Times, and Referees	1	2	3	4	5	6	7	8	9	10	11	subs used
1:1 A CARDIFF			L		0-1	0-1		Welch	Mitchell	Scott	Thompson	Bryant	Edwards	Mellon	Dziekanowski	Rosenior	Cole	Shelton	
18/8	7,708						*Dale 3*	*Grew*	*James*	*Searle*	*Millar*	*Perry*	*Brazil*	*Ramsey*	*Griffith*	*Pike**	*Dale*	*Blake*	*Gibbins*
							Ref: A Smith	Welch's confident handling and assured footwork keeps City's hopes alive, despite Nathan Blake seizing on Mitchell's misplaced pass to lay the winner on a plate for Carl Dale. After weathering an alarmingly shaky opening, Dziekanowski fails to convert City's three best chances.											
1:2 H CARDIFF			W		5-1	3-0	Cole 8, 13, 89, Rosenior 23, Allison 65	Welch	Mitchell	Scott	Thompson	Bryant	Aizlewood	Mellon	Dziekanowski	Cole	Rosenior*	Shelton^	Allison/Harrison
25/8	10,174						*Dale 53*	*Grew*	*James*	*Searle*	*Millar*	*Perry*	*Brazil*	*Gibbins*	*Calloway**	*Bird*	*Dale*	*Blake*	*Baddeley*
							Ref: P Vanes (City won 5-2 on aggregate)	City are absolutely brilliant as they put on one of their best-ever displays. Cole, whose speed off the mark, strength in holding off defenders, and coolness in front of goal, stamp him as a very special player, completes his hat-trick when racing clear and shooting past Mark Grew.											
2:1 H SHEFFIELD UTD		13	W		2-1	2-1	Connor 19, Scott 41p	Welch	Mitchell	Scott	Thompson	Bryant	Edwards	Connor*	Dziekanowski	Allison	Mellon	Shelton	Harrison
22/9	6,932	*P:19*					*Rogers 37*	*Kelly*	*Gage*	*Cowan**	*Gannon*	*Gayle*	*Beesley*	*Bradshaw*	*Rogers*	*Cork^*	*Deane*	*Hodges*	*Hartfield/Bryson*
							Ref: G Poll	Smith abandons the sweeper system, but plays Connor and Edwards in wide midfield roles, instead of answering the call for wingers. City, without five regulars, produce a wholehearted display to claim a Premier Division scalp thanks to Tom Cowan being penalised for handball.											
2:2 A SHEFFIELD UTD		13	L		1-4	1-2	Cole 12 *[Deane 66, 74]*	Welch	Mitchell	Scott	Thompson	Osman	Edwards	Harrison	Rosenior*	Allison	Cole	Shelton^	Dziekanowski/Gavin
7/10	7,588	*P:16*					*Whitehouse 5, Bradshaw 33,*	*Kelly*	*Ward*	*Cowan*	*Gannon*	*Gayle*	*Beesley*	*Bradshaw*	*Rogers*	*Littlejohn*	*Deane*	*Whitehouse**	*Cork*
							Ref: A Wilkie (City lost 3-5 on aggregate)	City always look in with a chance, until Brian Deane ends his ten-match lean spell. After Dane Whitehouse's easy tap-in when Welch fails to hold a low centre, Cole equalises for City with a bullet header, before Carl Bradshaw levels the aggregate scores again with a 20-yard volley.											

FA Cup					F-A	H-T	Scorers, Times, and Referees	1	2	3	4	5	6	7	8	9	10	11	subs used
3 A LUTON		18	L		0-2	0-1		Welch	Harrison	Scott !	Llewellyn	Bryant	Osman	Shelton	Mellon*	Allison	Cole	Gavin^	Rosenior/Aizlewood
19/1	6,094	*22*					*Gray 31, Hughes 82*	*Chamberlain*	*Dreyer*	*James*	*Johnson**	*Hughes*	*Peake*	*Telfer*	*Benjamin^*	*Rees*	*Gray*	*Preece*	*Harvey/Oakes*
							Ref: G Willard	City's season is now at rock bottom after this humiliating surrender at Kenilworth Road. Scott's 70th-min sending-off for hitting out at Phil Gray capped a team effort bereft of skill, cohesion and passion. Ceri Hughes' shot in off the crossbar sealed Luton's passage to the next round.											

			Home					Away				
	P	W	D	L	F	A	W	D	L	F	A	Pts
1 Newcastle	46	16	6	1	58	15	13	3	7	34	23	96
2 West Ham	46	16	5	2	50	17	10	5	8	31	24	88
3 Portsmouth	46	19	2	2	48	9	7	8	8	32	37	88
4 Tranmere	46	15	4	4	48	24	8	6	9	24	32	79
5 Swindon *	46	15	5	3	41	23	6	8	9	33	36	76
6 Leicester	46	14	5	4	43	24	8	5	10	28	40	76
7 Millwall	46	14	6	3	46	21	4	10	9	19	32	70
8 Derby	46	11	2	10	40	33	8	7	8	28	24	66
9 Grimsby	46	12	6	5	33	25	7	1	15	25	32	64
10 Peterborough	46	7	11	5	30	26	9	3	11	25	37	62
11 Wolves	46	11	6	6	37	26	5	7	11	20	30	61
12 Charlton	46	10	8	5	28	19	6	5	12	21	27	61
13 Barnsley	46	12	4	7	29	19	5	5	13	27	41	60
14 Oxford	46	8	7	8	29	21	6	7	10	24	35	56
15 BRISTOL CITY	46	10	7	6	29	25	4	7	12	20	42	56
16 Watford	46	8	7	8	27	30	6	6	11	30	41	55
17 Notts Co	46	10	7	6	33	21	2	9	12	22	49	52
18 Southend	46	9	8	6	33	22	4	5	14	21	42	52
19 Birmingham	46	10	4	9	30	32	3	8	12	20	40	51
20 Luton	46	6	13	4	26	26	4	8	11	22	36	51
21 Sunderland	46	9	6	8	34	28	4	5	14	16	36	50
22 Brentford	46	7	6	10	28	30	6	4	13	24	41	49
23 Cambridge	46	8	6	9	29	32	3	10	10	19	37	49
24 Bristol Rov	46	6	6	11	30	42	4	5	14	25	45	41
	1104	263	147	142	859	590	142	147	263	590	859	1509

* promoted after play-offs

Odds & ends

Double wins: (1) Birmingham.
Double losses: (4) West Ham, Newcastle, Tranmere, Millwall.

Won from behind: (5) Derby (a), Barnsley (h), Charlton (h), Leicester (h), Portsmouth (a).
Lost from in front: (3) Grimsby (a), Newcastle (h), Charlton (a).

High spots: Opening day thriller v Portsmouth.
Winning 1-0 at St Andrews on 13 March.
Beating Bristol Rov 2-1 on 6 April.
A brilliant performance in destroying Cardiff 5-1 in the League Cup.

Low spots: Humiliating 0-5 defeat at Newcastle on 19 September.
Losing 0-4 at Twerton Park on 13 December.
Succumbing to Luton in the FA Cup.
Losing 1-2 away to Bristol Rov in the Final of the Gloucestershire Cup on 5 August.

Player of the year: Keith Welch.
Ever-presents: (0).
Hat-tricks: (1) Leroy Rosenior.
Leading scorer: Andy Cole (16).

	Appearances						Goals			
	Lge	*Sub*	LC	*Sub*	FAC	*Sub*	Lge	LC	FAC	Tot
Aizlewood, Mark	19	*1*	1			*1*				
Allison, Wayne	22	*17*	2	*1*	1		4	1		5
Atteveld, Ray	5	*2*								
Bent, Junior	13	*7*					3			3
Bryant, Matt	41		3		1		1			1
Cole, Andy	29		3		1		12	4		16
Connor, Terry	2	*3*	1					1		1
Dziekanowski, Jacki	24	*2*	3	*1*			3			3
Edwards, Rob	14	*4*	3							
Fowler, Jason		*1*								
Gavin, Mark	16	*3*		*1*	1		1			1
Harrison, Gerry	24	*9*	1	*2*	1		1			1
Kristensen, Bjorn	4									
Leaning, Andy	1									
Llewellyn, Andy	12				1					
Mellon, Micky	7	*3*	3		1		1			1
Mitchell, Brian	15	*1*	4							
Morgan, Nicky	10						3			3
Munro, Stuart	16									
Osman, Russell	33	*1*	1		1					
Pennyfather, Glenn	14						1			1
Reid, Nicky	3	*1*								
Rosenior, Leroy	29	*9*	3			*1*	7	1		8
Scott, Martin	35		4		1		3	1		4
Shail, Mark	3	*1*								
Shelton, Gary	42		4		1		4			4
Thompson, David	17		4							
Tinnion, Brian	11						2			2
Welch, Keith	45		4		1					
(own-goals)							3			3
29 players used	**506**	***65***	**44**	***5***	**11**	***2***	**49**	**8**		**57**

No	Date			Att	Pos	Pt	F-A	H-T	Scorers, Times, and Referees	1	2	3	4	5	6	7	8	9	10	11	subs used
1		A	WOLVES			L	1-3	0-1	Scott 57	Welch	Munro	Scott	Aizlewood	Shail	**Hewlett***	**Wyatt^**	Shelton	**Baird**	**Robinson**	Tinnion	**Kamara**/Allison
	14/8			21,052		0			Bull 9, 87, Mountfield 71	Stowell	Rankine	Venus !	Cook	Mountfield	Blades	Birch	Thomas	Bull	Kelly*	Keen	Regis
									Ref: R Poulain	Fears of a goal avalanche, when Bull fires the opener into the top corner of the net, subside after Wolves fail to put away further good chances before half-time. Scott shoots in City's equaliser, but Welch misses Paul Cook's free-kick and is stranded as Derek Mountfield heads in.											
2		H	CRYS PALACE			W	2-0	0-0	Baird 69, Allison 84	Welch	Munro	Scott	Aizlewood	Shail	Hewlett	Wyatt	Shelton	Baird	Robinson*	Tinnion	Allison
	21/8			12,068		3				Martyn	Humphrey	Coleman	Southgate	Young	Thom	Whyte*	Bowry !	Armstrong	Williams	Rodger^	Shaw/Gordon
									Ref: A Smith	Two superb goals go some way towards masking an often dreary preceding hour as City failed to take advantage of Bobby Bowry's 19th-min sending off for elbowing Shelton. Tinnion, unlucky to have a 72nd-minute lob disallowed, supplies the crosses for both City's headed goals.											
3		A	DERBY		21	L	0-1	0-0		Welch	Munro	Scott	Aizlewood	Shail	Edwards	Bent*	**Brown I**	Baird	Tinnion	Shelton	Allison
	28/8			15,643	7	3			Gabbiadini 68	Taylor	Charles	Forsyth	Kuhl	Short, Craig	Wassall	Harkes	Williams	Kitson	Gabbiadini	Pembridge	
									Ref: P Harrison	Ian Brown (£28,000 ex Chelmsford), who skies over from six yards in the 35th minute, and his City colleagues are left to rue how they didn't get something out of this game. Marco Gabbiadini hammers in John Harkes' square pass to make City pay for wasting a string of chances.											
4		H	SOUTHEND		12	W	2-1	1-0	Tinnion 22p, Osman 57	Welch	Munro	Scott	Harrison	Shail	Osman	Bent	Robinson*	Baird	Tinnion	Edwards	Brown I
	4/9			7,392	4	6			Sussex 71	Sansome	Locke	Powell	Bodley	Edwards	Sussex	Ansah	Payne	Lee*	Otto^	Angell	Hunt/Harding
									Ref: C Wilkes	Osman's decision to dispense with the services of the popular Dziekanowski not only brings down the ire of the Ashton Gate fans on his head, but also results in his headed goal being greeted in stony silence. Tinnion's penalty gives City a huge lift after Adam Locke felled Robinson.											
5		A	OXFORD		19	L	2-4	1-2	Baird 43, 83	Welch	Munro	Scott	Aizlewood !	Shail	Osman*	Bent^	Allison	Baird	Tinnion	Edwards	Gavin/Rosenior
	11/9			5,420	17	6			Allen 11, Magilton 30p, 63p, Dyer 72	Reece	Smart	Ford M	Lewis	Robinson	Rogan	Magilton	Beauchamp*	Cusack^	Penney	Allen	Dyer/Collins
									Ref: J Brandwood	Denis Smith's Oxford side come out on top at the end of this controversial match. David Penney escapes with a booking for his horrific 45th-min foul that sends Bent to hospital, whilst Aizlewood is sent off for bringing down Chris Allen to concede Jim Magilton's second spot-kick.											
6		H	LEICESTER		21	L	1-3	0-2	Scott 87	Welch	Munro	Scott	Aizlewood	Shail	Osman	Robinson*	Allison	Baird	Tinnion	Gavin	Rosenior
	14/9			7,899	6	6			Speedie 1, 89, Walsh 13	Ward	Mills	Whitlow	Carey	Walsh	Hill	Oldfield	Thompson	Speedie	Agnew	Ormondroyd	
									Ref: P Alcock	After David Speedie's 80-sec headed opener and Steve Walsh's lob, City control the play, but are let down by poor finishing. Allison is in his usual wasteful form, but Scott registers from 15 yards before Speedie finishes off his run by drilling in Leicester's late goal past Welch.											
7		H	CHARLTON		20	D	0-0	0-0		Welch	**Borrows**	Munro	Shail	Bryant	Scott*	**Martin**	Allison	Baird	Tinnion^	Gavin	Robinson/Edwards
	18/9			7,484	2	7				Salmon	Pitcher	Minto	Garland*	McLeary	Chapple	Robinson	Newton	Gorman	Grant	Walsh	Balmer
									Ref: G Singh	'Put the blame on me' says Allison. Confronted by an open goal in the 78th min, he delays his shot long enough for the keeper to spring across his line and effect a save. Baird's shot against the post late on sums up City's frustrations against a Charlton side happy to settle for a point.											
8		A	PORTSMOUTH		20	D	0-0	0-0		Welch	Borrows	Munro	Shail	Bryant	Edwards	Martin*	Allison	Baird	Robinson	Gavin	Osman
	25/9			10,702	13	8				Knight	Gittens	Blake*	McLoughlin	Symons	Awford	Neill	Stimson	Durnin	Walsh	Kristensen	Powell
									Ref: G Willard	Fratton Park is no place for the faint hearted, as the new harder-edged City show that they are no longer a side that struggles when the going gets tough. Five players are booked, including City's Borrows, Munro and Edwards, as a well-deserved point is prised from the seaside.											
9		H	BOLTON		15	W	2-0	1-0	Allison 15, Scott 76	Welch	Borrows	Munro	Shail	Bryant	Tinnion	Martin*	Allison	Baird	Robinson^	Scott	Edwards/Gavin
	2/10			7,704	16	11				Branagan	Brown	Phillips	Kelly*	Seagraves	Stubbs !	Lee	McAteer	Thompson^	McGinley	Patterson	Darby/Green
									Ref: M Peck	The team put all thought of a possible boardroom take-over out of their minds. Allison, who heads in City's opener, makes an impressive contribution apart from his usual poor finishing that keeps depleted Bolton (Alan Stubbs sent off 34 mins) in the contest until Scott blasts in.											
10		A	LUTON		8	W	2-0	0-0	Tinnion 54p, Baird 56	Welch	Borrows	Munro	Shail	Bryant	Tinnion*	Martin	Gavin	Baird	Robinson	Scott	Edwards
	5/10			5,956	21	14				Sommer	Johnson	James	Williams	Peake	Dreyer	Telfer	Oakes*	Hartson	Hughes	Harper	Houghton
									Ref: K Morton	City demonstrate that the one place where they do not need to make changes is on the field as the team is now beginning to justify claims of better things. Tinnion shoots in from the spot after Gavin is brought down, then Baird produces the finishing touch to the No 8's low cross.											
11		A	NOTTS CO		10	L	0-2	0-0		Welch	Borrows	Munro	Shail	Bryant	Tinnion	Martin	Gavin*	Baird	Robinson	Scott	Allison
	9/10			6,418	11	14			McSwegan 70p, Draper 79	Cherry	Gallagher	Thomas	Turner	Walker	Palmer	Devlin	Draper	McSwegan	Lund	Legg	
									Ref: T Lunt	Bryant's blunder halts City's revival with a challenge that sends Gary McSwegan sprawling in the box, with the ball still out on the wing. Welch gets his hand to the consequential penalty, but can't keep it out, and he is again beaten by Mark Draper's close-in shot nine mins later.											

No	Date		Att	Pos	Pt		F-A	H-T	Scorers, Times, and Referees	1	2	3	4	5	6	7	8	9	10	11	subs used
12	F	BARNSLEY		15		L	0-2	0-1		Welch	Borrows	Munro	Shail	Bryant	Tinnion	Martin*	Allison	Baird	Rosenior^	Scott	Edwards/Robinson
	16/10		6,923	17	14				*Bryson 35, Refearn 52*	*Watson*	*Fleming*	*Boden*	*Wilson*	*Bishop*	*Anderson*	*O'Connoll**	*Redfearn*	*Bryson*	*Biggins*	*Eaden*	*Liddell*
									Ref: T Holbrook	A black day as City's inept display, against visitors who had lost their four previous games, provokes much barracking of both the players and directors. Baird had a 67th-minute effort disallowed for offside as City succumb to Ian Bryson's 15-yd volley, and Neil Redfearn's 25-yd drive.											
13	F	TRANMERE		13		D	2-2	1-1	Shail 16, Allison 84	Welch	Llewellyn	Munro !	Shail	Bryant	Tinnion	Martin*	Bent^	Baird	Allison	Scott	Edwards/Robinson
	22/10		*7,123*	*1*	15				*Nevin 7, Brannan 63*	*Nixon*	*Higgins*	*Nolan*	*Brannan*	*Irons*	*Garnett*	*Kenworthy**	*Muir*	*Malkin*	*Nevin*	*Thomas*	*Branch*
									Ref: K Leach	City survive Munro's 53rd-minute dismissal for his second bookable offence with a great show of discipline and team spirit. There is hardly a dull moment in this encounter from the moment Pat Nevin's volley hits the back of the net until Allison heads in for City's well-earned point.											
14	[illegible]	SUNDERLAND		12		W	2-0	0-0	Allison 82, Baird 90	Welch	Llewellyn	Munro	Shail	Bryant	Tinnion	Martin*	Bent^	Baird	Allison	Scott	Edwards/Robinson
	30/10		8,162	*14*	18					*Chamberlain*	*Ball*	*Gray, Mart**	*Bennett*	*Melville*	*Owers*	*Atkinson*	*Goodman*	*Gray P*	*Smith M^*	*Armstrong*	*Gray, Mike/Russell*
									Ref: P Danson	Sunderland fade after a bright start, and City should have broken the deadlock well before Allison drove in the opener. Cheers instead of jeers are heard at long last as Baird secures the points by skipping past two challenges before burying the ball in the second minute of injury-time.											
15	[illegible]	BIRMINGHAM		9		W	3-0	1-0	Allison 30, 53, 90	Welch	Llewellyn	Munro	Shail	Bryant	Tinnion	Martin	Bent	Allison	Robinson	Scott	
	2/11		9,192	*10*	21					*Miller*	*Hiley*	*Potter*	*Parris*	*Dryden*	*Fenwick*	*Donowa*	*Shutt*	*Saville**	*Jenkinson*	*Smith*	*Wallace*
									Ref: R Gifford	Allison finds his goal touch to claim his first hat-trick in stunning style as rampant City make it a night to remember. Of City's seven on-target efforts, six come from Allison, including the trio of shots for his hat-trick, whilst the Blues can only manage an early drive straight at Welch.											
16	A	MIDDLESBROUGH		9		W	1-0	1-0	Tinnion 40p	Welch	Llewellyn	Scott	Shail	Bryant	Tinnion	Martin	Bent*	Allison	Robinson	Edwards	Pennyfather
	6/11		*9,687*	*10*	24					*Pears*	*Fleming*	*Liburd*	*Gannon*	*Mohan*	*Whyte*	*Kavanagh^*	*Hignett*	*Wilkinson**	*Mustoe*	*Moore*	*Illman/Barron*
									Ref: A Dawson	City's first win at Ayresome Park since a 2-0 success on 9 Nov 1907 comes courtesy of Tinnion's pen after Robinson was up-ended by Curtis Fleming. Despite all of Middlesbrough's extra possession and pressure they only manage six shots on target compared to City's four.											
17	H	MILLWALL		8		D	2-2	1-0	Allison 38, 59	Welch	Llewellyn	Scott	Shail	Bryant	Tinnion	Martin	Bent*	Robinson	Allison	Edwards	Pennyfather
	13/11		8,416	*10*	25				*Rae 71, Beard 78*	*Keller*	*Cunningham*	*Dolby^*	*Roberts*	*V'n d'n H'we**	*Stevens*	*Rae*	*Huxford*	*Mitchell*	*Goodman*	*Beard*	*Barber/Kennedy*
									Ref: J Rushton	With last night's EGM resolving the boardroom battle in favour of the rebels, the team gets down to the serious business of playing football. After Allison's two strikes, City are stunned by Alex Rae's tap-in and a defensive mix-up that allows Mark Beard to guide the ball past Welch.											
18	A	WATFORD		10		D	1-1	0-1	Martin 76	Welch	Llewellyn	Scott	Shail*	Bryant	Tinnion	Martin	Bent	Robinson	Allison	Edwards	Munro
	20/11		*6,045*	*17*	26				*Soloman 33*	*Suckling*	*Lavin*	*Dublin*	*Johnson*	*Holdsworth*	*Watson*	*Dyer*	*Soloman*	*Charlery*	*Porter*	*Willis*	
									Ref: I Borrett	In a dour first half, City, who offer little apart from a Bent strike which is disallowed, are caught flat-footed when Jason Soloman heads in from Bruce Dyer's cross. Waking from their lethargy after the interval, City equalise when Martin crashes the ball into the roof of the net.											
19	A	PETERBOROUGH		8		W	2-0	2-0	Robinson 8, 37	Welch	Llewellyn	Scott	Munro	Bryant	Tinnion	Martin	Bent	Robinson	Allison	Edwards	
	27/11		*5,084*	*24*	29					*Bennett*	*Greenman*	*McDonald*	*Bradshaw*	*Howarth*	*Welsh*	*Adcock**	*Hackett^*	*McGlashan*	*Ebdon*	*Cooper*	*Furnell/Barnes*
									Ref: A Smith	With their eighth clean sheet in 13 outings and only two defeats in the same period, City are one of the Division's form sides. The irrepressible Robinson twice shows his poacher's instincts to blast in from close range and leave City nicely placed for an assault on the promotion prize.											
20	H	MIDDLESBROUGH		8		D	0-0	0-0		Welch	Llewellyn	Scott	Munro	Bryant	Tinnion*	Martin	Bent^	Robinson	Allison	Edwards	Pennyfather/Brown I
	4/12		8,441	*13*	30					*Pears*	*Fleming*	*Liburd**	*Mustoe*	*Mohan*	*Whyte*	*Stamp*	*Hignett*	*Wilkinson*	*Peake*	*Moore*	*Vickers*
									Ref: G Poll	City are unable to complete a double over a Middlesbrough side without a win in ten games. A frustrating afternoon, but a draw is a fair result, even against a Boro team now without a goal in seven outings, as City lack the guile to break down the visitors' five-man midfield.											
21	A	LEICESTER		10		L	0-3	0-2		Welch	Llewellyn	Scott	Munro	Bryant	Tinnion	Pennyfather	Brown I*	Robinson	Allison	Edwards	Fowler
	11/12		*13,394*	*5*	30				*Speedie 13, 61, Joachim 45*	*Ward*	*Grayson*	*Lewis*	*Coatsworth^*	*Agnew*	*Hill*	*Joachim**	*Thompson*	*Speedie*	*Roberts*	*Philpott*	*Oldfield/Eustace*
									Ref: L Dilkes	Julian Joachim's stunning 25-yarder with the outside of his right foot, sandwiched between David Speedie's sharply taken close-range shots, ends City's eight-match unbeaten run. Speedie's histrionics on being tackled by Pennyfather earns an unwarranted booking for the City man.											
22	H	WOLVES		9		W	2-1	1-0	Allison 30, Brown 73	Welch	Llewellyn	Scott	Munro	Bryant	Tinnion !	Pennyfather	Brown I*	Robinson	Allison	Edwards	Bent
	18/12		15,151	*12*	33				*Kelly 90*	*Stowell*	*Thompson*	*Edwards^*	*Venus*	*Bennett*	*Simkin*	*Dennison*	*Birch*	*Bull*	*Kelly*	*Cook**	*Keen/Rankine*
									Ref: G Ashby	Ian Brown, he of the electric pace, grabs his first League goal when running onto Allison's flick to slide the ball in under the diving keeper. City's superiority is not threatened by Tinnion's harsh 78th-min dismissal until David Kelly fires past Welch in the second min of injury-time.											
23	A	WEST BROM		9		W	1-0	1-0	Tinnion 43	Welch	Llewellyn	Scott	Munro	Bryant	Tinnion	Pennyfather	Brown I	Robinson*	Allison	Edwards	Baird
	27/12		*22,888*	*16*	36					*Lange*	*Burgess*	*Lilwall*	*Mardon*	*Raven*	*Ashcroft*	*Heggs**	*O'Regan*	*Taylor*	*Mellon^*	*Hamilton*	*Donovan/Coldicott*
									Ref: I Cruikshanks	Despite often riding their luck, City's fighting spirit and a composed defensive display brings all three points thanks to Tinnion's shot which takes a deflection off Paul Raven. Welch produces his best display of the season to spoil the day for ex City men, Mellon, Mardon and Taylor.											

No	Date		Att	Pos	Pt	F-A	H-T	Scorers, Times, and Referees	1	2	3	4	5	6	7	8	9	10	11	subs used
24	H	NOTT'M FOREST		11	L	**1-4**	0-0	Edwards 59	Welch	Llewellyn	Scott	Munro	Bryant	Tinnion	Pennyfather	Brown I*	Robinson^	Allison	Edwards	Baird/Martin
	28/12		**20,725**	*8*	36			*Collymore 58, 74, Webb 69, Woan 86*	*Crossley*	*Lyttle*	*Webb*	*Cooper*	*Chettle*	*Stone*	*Phillips*	*Gemmill*	*Bohinen*	*Collymore*	*Woan*	
								Ref: M Pierce	'Stan's the man' as he shows after being kept quiet for nearly an hour. Collymore scores Forest's first and third – a curling power drive –before turning provider to allow Ian Woan time to pick his spot. Edwards tucks away City's sole reply when Mark Crossley spills Allison's header.											
25	A	GRIMSBY		11	L	0-1	0-0		Welch	Llewellyn	Scott	Munro*	Bryant	Pennyfather	Martin	Gavin ^	Baird	Allison	Edwards	Shail/Robinson
	1/1		*5,469*	*17*	36			*Groves 86*	*Crichton*	*McDermott*	*Croft*	*Futcher*	*Handyside*	*Dobbin*	*Ford*	*Gilbert*	*Livingstone*	*Mendonca*	*Groves*	
								Ref: P Jones	City are punished for their one mistake when their flat-footed defence allows Paul Groves the space to fire in Grimsby's winner. Edwards comes closest for City with a volley that thunders against the crossbar, but Grimsby's shots advantage of 10-2 suggests that the best side won.											
26	H	STOKE		12	D	0-0	0-0		Welch	Munro	Scott	Shail	Bryant	Tinnion	Martin	Robinson	Baird*	Allison	Edwards	Brown I
	3/1		11,132	*8*	37				*Marshall*	*Clarkson*	*Sandford*	*Cranson*	*Overson*	*Orlygsson*	*Foley*	*Bannister*	*Regis*	*Butler**	*Gleghorn*	*Gynn*
								Ref: P Durkin	Concerns are growing over City's modest scoring record, and against a Stoke side under the control of Joe Jordan the ball just wouldn't go in. After a dire first half, Robinson's open-goal miss on 73 mins, when Baird headed down Scott's centre, sums up City's frustrations in the rain.											
27	A	BARNSLEY		11	D	1-1	0-1	Scott 50	Welch	Munro	Scott	Shail	Osman	Tinnion	Martin	Bent	Robinson	Allison	Edwards	
	15/1		*5,222*	*23*	38			*Rammell 44*	*Butler*	*Eaden*	*Fleming*	*Wilson*	*Taggart*	*Bishop*	*O'Connell*	*Redfearn*	*Rammell*	*Payton*	*Archdeacon*	
								Ref: N Barry	City's vehement offside protests fall on deaf ears, as Welch's parry of Owen Archdeacon's shot gives Andy Rammell an easy tap-in to put the Tykes in front. No protests over Scott's magnificent equaliser though, his 30-yard drive is still rising when it hits the back of Lee Butler's net.											
28	H	NOTTS CO		11	L	0-2	0-1		Welch	Llewellyn^	Scott	Shail	Munro	Tinnion	Martin	Bent	Robinson*	Allison	Edwards	Rosenior/Pennyfather
	22/1		7,458	*14*	38			*Legg 35, Agana 80*	*Cherry*	*Gannon*	*Sherlock*	*Palmer*	*Foster*	*Turner*	*Devlin*	*Draper*	*Lund*	*Legg*	*Agana*	
								Ref: D Gallagher	Even a magnificent cup tussle with Liverpool cannot raise the level of City's League crowds, and those who stayed away from this affair obviously knew what was coming. County, with only one win on their travels, deservedly win this one with Legg's shot and Agana's header.											
29	H	TRANMERE		11	W	2-0	0-0	Tinnion 74, Allison 84	Welch	Llewellyn	Scott	Shail	Munro	Tinnion	Martin	Pennyfather	Robinson*	Allison	Edwards	Brown I
	5/2		8,171	*5*	41				*Nixon !*	*Higgins*	*Mungall*	*Brannan*	*Hughes*	*O'Brien*	*Morrissey*	*Aldridge*	*Malkin*	*Nevin**	*Thomas*	*Coyne*
								Ref: V Callow	Keeper Eric Nixon's sending off for bringing down Brown sees substitute Danny Coyne first employed to take Tinnion's 20-yard free-kick out of the net. Allison then makes sure that City get the points their play deserves by rounding Coyne and shooting home from a narrow angle.											
30	A	SUNDERLAND		12	D	0-0	0-0		Welch	**Harriott**	Scott	Shail	Munro	Tinnion	Martin^	Pennyfather	Robinson*	Allison	Edwards	Brown I/Bryant
	12/2		*16,696*	*15*	42				*Chamberlain*	*Owers*	*Gray, Mike*	*Ball*	*Ferguson*	*Melville*	*Russell*	*Goodman**	*Gray P*	*Smith M*	*Atkinson*	*Lawrence*
								Ref: R Poulain	Russell Osman believes he has unearthed a diamond in Marvin Harriott, signed on a free from Barnsley. The new arrival certainly sparkled in his first test at Roker Park, being one of the few plus points in a game which, despite the strong wind, fell well below the fans' expectations.											
31	A	CRYS PALACE		13	L	**1-4**	1-1	Shail 21	Welch	Harriott*	Scott	Shail	Bryant	Tinnion	Martin	Munro	Robinson	Allison	Edwards	Brown I
	22/2		*12,417*	*1*	42			*Gordon 25p, Salako 60, Armstrong 73, 84*	*Martyn*	*Humphrey*	*Gordon*	*Southgate*	*Young*	*Coleman*	*Shaw*	*Matthew*	*Armstrong*	*Stewart**	*Salako*	*Whyte*
								Ref: G Willard	On an icy pitch both sides stick commendably to their passing game, and City give as good as they get until Welch's collision with Paul Stewart sees John Salako curl a shot into the net. Shail gets City off to a good start with his header, but then handles to concede the penalty.											
32	A	SOUTHEND		11	W	1-0	1-0	Allison 45	Welch	Harriott	Scott	Shail*	Bryant	Tinnion	Martin	Munro	Robinson	Allison	Edwards	Pennyfather
	26/2		***4,615***	*12*	45				*Sansome*	*Locke*	*Powell*	*Gridelet^*	*Edwards*	*Bressington*	*Hunt*	*Sussex*	*Jones**	*Otto*	*Lee*	*Ansah/Payne*
								Ref: G Poll	'We're good enough for the play-offs' says Robinson, after City's gritty display at Roots Hall. After Gary Jones hits a post early on, Robinson does the work for City's match-winning goal, but after evading the advancing Paul Sansome, it is Allison who shoots in from five yards.											
33	H	DERBY		12	D	0-0	0-0		Welch	Harriott	Scott^	Munro	Bryant	Tinnion	Martin	**Hoyland**	Bent*	Allison	Edwards	**Partridge**/Rosenior
	5/3		8,723	*5*	46				*Taylor*	*Charles*	*Nicholson*	*Kuhl**	*Short*	*Williams*	*Cowans*	*Pembridge*	*Kitson*	*Gabbiadini*	*Ratcliffe*	*Johnson*
								Ref: K Cooper	Bent wastes two chances to end this stalemate, the best being an open goal from six yards, which he volleys over the top on the stroke of half-time. Paul Williams is a major stumbling block to City's efforts, but really they have only themselves to blame for not winning this one.											
34	H	OXFORD		15	L	0-1	0-1		Welch	Harriott	Scott	Hoyland	Bryant	Tinnion	Munro^	Hewlett*	Robinson	Allison	Edwards	Bent/Partridge
	15/3		6,635	*23*	46			*Byrne 31*	*Whitehead*	*Elliott*	*Ford M*	*Ford R*	*Smart*	*Dyer*	*Lewis*	*Beauchamp*	*Moody*	*Byrne*	*Allen*	
								Ref: R Gifford	City's bright start is blighted by their inability to put away their chances, and the longer the game goes on the more static becomes their play. Oxford by contrast take what is on offer, and John Byrne's three-yard header lifts them off the bottom of the table – but they will go down.											

No	Venue	Opponent / Date	Att	Pos	Res / Pts	FT	HT	Scorers, Times, Referees	1	2	3	4	5	6	7	8	9	10	11	12 subs used
35	H	PORTSMOUTH		11	W	1-0	0-0	Allison 54	Welch	Hoyland	Munro	Shail	Bryant	Tinnion	Harriott	Hewlett	Robinson*	Allison	Scott	Baird
	13/3		6,352	*17*	49				*Knight*	*Dobson*	*Stimson*	*McLoughlin*	*Daniel*	*Awford*	*Pethwick^*	*Chamberlain*	*Creaney*	*Wood**	*Russell*	*Powell/Hall*
								Ref: T Holbrook	Osman pleads with City fans to lay off 18-year-old Hewlett, who has become a target of the boo boys due to his languid style. In this game, won by Allison's low shot, he should have notched a hat-trick, but after his first touch lets him down with one opening, he twice shoots wide.											
36	A	BOLTON		14	D	2-2	1-2	Allison 18, 68	Welch	Hoyland	Munro	Shail	Bryant	Tinnion	Harriott	Hewlett	Robinson*	Allison	Scott	**Milsom**
	23/3		*10,221*	*16*	50			*Lee 26, Coyle 44*	*Davison*	*Brown*	*Phillips*	*Kelly*	*Seagraves*	*Stubbs*	*Lee**	*McAteer*	*Coyle*	*Walker^*	*Patterson*	*Green/Winstanley*
								Ref: J Rushton	Allison's brave diving header puts City ahead at Burnden Park, but sloppy defending gives away the advantage. Shots by David Lee and Owen Coyle find the back of Welch's net, before Allison strikes again. Receiving the ball in midfield he ends his 50-yard run with an exquisite shot.											
37	A	STOKE		16	L	0-3	0-1		Welch	Hoyland	Munro*	Shail	Bryant	Tinnion	Harriott	Hewlett^	Martin	Allison	Scott	Milsom !/Robinson
	30/3		*13,192*	*8*	50			*Adams 8, 77, Biggins 54p*	*Prudhoe*	*Butler*	*Sandford*	*Cranson*	*Adams*	*Orlygsson**	*Foley*	*Carruthers*	*Biggins^*	*Clark*	*Walters*	*Gleghorn/Regis*
								Ref: M Reed	Milsom is unlucky to be sent off for his second bookable offence having only been on the field for 13 mins, but by then Stoke had the game won. City's comprehensive defeat is completed by Micky Adams' 30-yarder, after Shail's clumsy tackle had earlier gifted Stoke their penalty.											
38	H	WEST BROM		16	D	0-0	0-0		Welch	Harriott	Scott	Shail	Munro	Tinnion*	Martin	Hewlett	Robinson	Allison	Hoyland	Edwards
	2/4		8,624	*20*	51				*Naylor*	*Burgess*	*Edwards*	*O'Regan*	*Parsley*	*Raven*	*Hunt**	*Hamilton*	*Taylor*	*Donovan*	*Smith*	*Shrodder*
								Ref: P Alcock	City throw away all hopes of a place in the play-off frame, as a blank scoresheet means that whilst they have kept 21 clean sheets this season, they have also failed to hit the net on 17 occasions. Tinnion squanders City's best chance, hitting the post with his penalty kick on 24 minutes.											
39	A	NOTT'M FOREST		16	D	0-0	0-0		Welch	Harriott	Scott	Shail	Munro	Tinnion	Martin	Wyatt	Milsom	Allison	Edwards	
	4/4		***24,162***	*2*	52				*Crossley*	*Lyttle*	*Pearce*	*Cooper*	*Chettle*	*Stone*	*Phillips*	*Bohinen**	*Lee*	*Rosario*	*Black*	*Woan*
								Ref: E Parker	City's defence turns in a quality display to thwart a Forest side, who sorely miss the suspended Stan Collymore. Robert Rosario misses Forest's best chance from just two yards before the break, whilst in the second half Wyatt cuts inside to get a 20-yard shot on target for City.											
40	H	GRIMSBY		14	W	1-0	0-0	Scott 90p	Welch	Harriott	Scott	Shail	Munro	**McKop**	Martin*	Wyatt	Partridge	Allison	Edwards	Hewlett
	3/4		5,480	*12*	55				*Crichton*	*Ford*	*Agnew*	*Handyside*	*Rodger*	*Shakespeare*	*Childs**	*Gilbert*	*Livingstone^*	*Mendonca*	*Groves*	*Croft/Woods*
								Ref: M Pierce	City leave it late to win this game, Scott's penalty at the death ending 380 minutes of goal famine. Before the dramatic finale it appeared that all City's hard work in the heavy rain would go unrewarded, but keeper Paul Crichton's up-ending of Allison ensures a deserved outcome.											
41	A	BIRMINGHAM		15	D	2-2	2-0	Partridge 5, 20	Welch	Harriott	McKop	Munro	Scott	Hewlett	Martin	Wyatt*	Partridge	Allison	Edwards	Robinson
	16/4		*20,316*	*23*	56			*Claridge 60p, Donowa 75*	*Bennett*	*Hiley*	*Rogers*	*Donowa*	*Barnett*	*Daish*	*Ward*	*Claridge*	*De Souza**	*Willis*	*Doherty*	*Shutt*
								Ref: S Lodge	Partridge (ex Bradford City) nicks the ball off Liam Daish to fire in his first League goal, and then finds the net again with an easy tap-in. After Allison brings down Steve Claridge for the penalty, ex City player Louie Donowa saves a point for the Blues with his shot past Welch.											
42	H	LUTON		11	W	1-0	1-0	Edwards 20	Welch	Harriott	Scott	Munro	Robinson	Hewlett	Martin	Wyatt	Partridge	Barclay*	Edwards	Bent
	9/4		**5,350**	*20*	59				*Sommer*	*Linton**	*James*	*Harper*	*Greene*	*Dreyer*	*Telfer*	*Hughes*	*Dixon*	*Aunger^*	*Preece*	*Hartson/Thorpe*
								Ref: M Reed	Whilst Luton manage six on-target efforts compared to City's three, it is the homesters who control the play. After a shapeless start City find their stride, and Robinson twice fires wide before Edwards crashes the ball in from close range, when Juergen Sommer drops Hewlett's corner.											
43	H	WATFORD		13	D	1-1	1-0	Partridge 10	Welch	Harriott	Scott	Shail	Robinson	Munro	Martin	Hewlett	Partridge	Barclay^	Edwards*	Tinnion/Wyatt
	23/4		8,324	*19*	60			*Furlong 51*	*Digweed*	*Lavin*	*Dublin*	*Hessenthaler*	*Foster*	*Millen*	*Mooney*	*Johnson*	*Furlong*	*Porter*	*Drysdale*	
								Ref: M Bodenham	Robinson can still do everything but find the net, his 20-yard shot being parried by Perry Digweed for Partridge to drive in from six yards. Paul Furlong punishes City for their inability to score more against the League's worst defence, lobbing in a deserved equaliser from 18 yards.											
44	A	MILLWALL		13	D	0-0	0-0		Welch	Harriott	Scott	Shail	Munro	Tinnion	Martin	Hewlett^	Partridge*	Bent	Edwards	Robinson/Wyatt
	30/4		*11,189*	*6*	61				*Keller*	*Cunningham*	*Huxford*	*Hurlock*	*Van den H'we*	*Stevens*	*Rae^*	*Allen**	*Moralee*	*Mitchell*	*Roberts*	*Kerr/Berry*
								Ref: K Cooper	Whilst Martin has a good game against his old club, and the diminutive Bent causes all sorts of problems, City do not manage to get a single shot on target at the New Den. Hewlett blasts City's best chance high and wide as their superbly-organised defence claims another clean sheet.											
45	A	CHARLTON		13	L	1-3	1-1	Partridge 40	Welch	Harriott	Scott	Shail	Munro	Tinnion	Martin	Wyatt^	Partridge	Bent	Edwards*	Robinson/McKop
	3/5		*6,713*	*10*	61			*Nelson 45, Chapple 47, Scott 66 (og)*	*Salmon**	*Brown*	*Sturgess*	*Garland*	*McLeary*	*Chapple*	*Bennett*	*Pitcher*	*Leaburn*	*Nelson*	*Robinson^*	*Vaughan/Grant*
								Ref: I Hemley	Scott's deflection of a low cross into his own net completes City's misery at the Valley. Classy one-touch football and Partridge's neat tuck-in from Bent's centre had City in control early on, but Garry Nelson's unstoppable volley in first-half injury-time changes the course of the game.											
46	H	PETERBOROUGH		13	W	**4-1**	2-0	Bent 1, 15, Robinson 46, 78	**Brown W**	Harriott	Scott	Shail	Munro	Tinnion	Martin*	Wyatt^	Partridge	Bent	Edwards	Robinson/McKop
	8/5		7,790	*24*	64			*Furnell 58*	*Cooksey*	*Carter*	*Spearing*	*Williams*	*Howarth*	*Clark*	*McGorry*	*Bradshaw*	*Iorfa*	*McGlashan*	*Brissett**	*Furnell*
		Home	Away					Ref: P Durkin	Wayne Brown (age 17) has a great debut between the sticks as Bent and Robinson find their shooting boots. Robinson takes his League tally to four (all against the Posh) – his lob for City's third being followed by his fierce 25-yard effort that swerves to beat the keeper at his near post.											
Average		8,852	11,288																	

Coca-Cola Cup						F-A	H-T	Scorers, Times, and Referees	1	2	3	4	5	6	7	8	9	10	11	subs used
1:1	A	SWANSEA			W	1-0	0-0	Robinson 46	Welch	Munro	Scott*	Aizlewood	Shail	Hewlett	Wyatt	Shelton	Baird	Robinson	Tinnion	Osman
	17/8		3,746	*2*					*Freestone*	*Clode*	*Cook**	*Walker*	*Harris*	*Pascoe*	*Hodge*	*Bowen*	*Torpey*	*Cornforth*	*Hayes*	*Ford*
								Ref: K Burge	Just when this cup-tie is in danger of falling flat, up pops Robinson to add some fizz. With both teams searching in vain for any pattern to their play the game bursts into life after the break when Robinson races onto Welch's long clearance to shoot past Roger Freestone from ten yards.											
1:2	H	SWANSEA		13	L	0-2	0-1		Welch	Munro	Scott	Aizlewood	Shail	Hewlett^	Wyatt*	Shelton	Baird	Robinson	Tinnion	Allison/Osman
	24/8		4,633	*2:10*				*Bowen 37, 81*	*Freestone*	*Clode*	*Ford*	*Walker*	*Harris*	*Pascoe*	*Chapple*	*Bowen*	*Torpey*	*Cornforth*	*Hayes*	
								Ref: D Frampton (City lost 1-2 on aggregate)	Captain Shail admits that City's display lets the players and the club down as Swansea demonstrate a much greater will to win. Jason Bowen shoots in the opener past Welch, then really celebrates his 21st birthday in style with a classic diving header to finish off Colin Pascoe's cross.											

FA Cup						F-A	H-T	Scorers, Times, and Referees	1	2	3	4	5	6	7	8	9	10	11	subs used
3	H	LIVERPOOL		11	D	1-1	0-0	Allison 72	Welch	Llewellyn	Scott	Shail	Munro	Tinnion	Martin	Bent	Robinson	Allison	Edwards	
	19/1		21,718	*P:6*				*Rush 62*	*Grobbelaar*	*Jones*	*Dicks*	*Nicol*	*Redknapp*	*Ruddock*	*Clough*	*Fowler**	*Rush*	*Barnes*	*McManaman*	*Bjornebye*
								Ref: M Bodenham	With the first match abandoned after 65 minutes due to floodlight failure, prices were reduced, hence receipts in the region of £77K compared to £155K eleven days ago. Allison's close-in shot equalises Rush's toe-poke and at the finish Liverpool are happy to have hung on for a replay.											
3R	A	LIVERPOOL		11	W	1-0	0-0	Tinnion 67	Welch	Llewellyn	Scott	Shail	Munro	Tinnion	Martin	Bent*	Robinson	Allison	Edwards	Pennyfather
	25/1		*36,720*	*P:5*					*Grobbelaar*	*Jones*	*Harkness*	*Nicol*	*Redknapp**	*Ruddock*	*Clough*	*Walters*	*Rush*	*Barnes*	*McManaman*	*Hutchison*
								Ref: M Bodenham	Super City pull off a shock victory at Anfield and receive the accolade of the wonderful Liverpool fans as they complete a lap of honour at the finish. City match their opponents shot for shot, but Tinnion finds the finish with a stunning side-foot effort into the bottom corner of the net.											
4	A	STOCKPORT		11	W	4-0	1-0	Shail 4, Allison 48, 60, 67	Welch	Rosenior	Scott	Shail	Munro	Tinnion	Martin	Pennyfather	Robinson	Allison	Edwards	
	9/2		*7,691*	*3:2*					*Edwards*	*Todd*	*Wallace**	*Frain*	*Flynn*	*Barras*	*Miller^*	*Ward*	*Francis*	*Beaumont*	*Preece*	*James/Connelly*
								Ref: P Vanes	An amazing cup-tie as Stockport's near relentless first-half pressure comes to naught. Allison's hat-trick (a header, followed by two shots) plus Shail's early head-in from Tinnion's centre constitute all City's on target efforts, while Stockport get no return from any of their seven attempts.											
5	H	CHARLTON		13	D	1-1	1-0	Tinnion 12	Welch	Munro	Scott	Shail	Bryant	Tinnion	Martin	Pennyfather*	Robinson	Allison	Edwards	Bent
	19/2		20,416	*3*				*Robson 60*	*Salmon*	*Brown*	*Minto*	*Pardew*	*McLeary*	*Balmer*	*Robson*	*Pitcher*	*Leaburn*	*Grant*	*Nelson*	
								Ref: K Hackett	Most City fans were in high expectation of success against high-flying Charlton, but those with longer memories were apprehensive. Tinnion's 25-yard free-kick around the visitors' wall gets City off to a great start, but they are struggling by the time Mark Robson shoots Charlton level.											
5R	A	CHARLTON		10	L	0-2	0-1		Welch	Munro	Scott	Shail*	Bryant	Tinnion	Martin	Bent	Robinson	Allison	Edwards	Rosenior
	2/3		*8,205*	*2*				*Pitcher 34p, Grant 90*	*Vaughan*	*Brown*	*Minto*	*Pardew*	*Chapple*	*Balmer*	*Robson*	*Pitcher*	*Leaburn*	*Grant*	*Nelson*	
								Ref: V Callow	Despite all the confident talk beforehand, City never get going at the Valley. Darren Pitcher's spot-kick straight down the middle, after Allison brings down Steve Brown, and Kim Grant's late strike take Charlton deservedly through to a quarter-final meeting with Manchester United.											

Abandoned FA Cup-tie						F-A	H-T	Scorers, Times, and Referees	1	2	3	4	5	6	7	8	9	10	11	subs used
3	H	LIVERPOOL		12		1-1	1-1	Allison 39	Welch	Munro	Scott	Shail	Bryant	Tinnion	Martin	Brown I	Robinson	Allison	Edwards	
	8/1		20,612	*P:8*				*Rush 12*	*Grobbelaar*	*Jones*	*Dicks*	*Nicol*	*Ruddock*	*Bjornebye**	*Clough*	*Fowler*	*Rush*	*Barnes*	*Redknapp*	*McManaman*
		(Abandoned due to floodlight failure)						Ref: M Bodenham	Joker Bruce Grobbelaar lit up the gloom after floodlight failure halted matters on 65 minutes. Referring to Allison's goal he said: 'If he had a hair on his head I'd have saved it.' After Ian Rush stroked in Liverpool's opener, City hit back strongly and were full value for their equaliser.											

	Home						Away					
	P	W	D	L	F	A	W	D	L	F	A	Pts
1 Crys Palace	46	16	4	3	39	18	11	5	7	34	28	90
2 Nott'm Forest	46	12	9	2	38	22	11	5	7	36	27	83
3 Millwall	46	14	8	1	36	17	5	9	9	22	32	74
4 Leicester *	46	11	9	3	45	30	8	7	8	27	29	73
5 Tranmere	46	15	3	5	48	23	6	6	11	21	30	72
6 Derby	46	15	3	5	44	25	5	8	10	29	43	71
7 Notts Co	46	16	3	4	43	26	4	5	14	22	43	68
8 Wolves	46	10	10	3	34	19	7	7	9	26	28	68
9 Middlesbro	46	12	6	5	40	19	6	7	10	26	35	67
10 Stoke	46	14	4	5	35	19	4	9	10	22	40	67
11 Charlton	46	14	3	6	39	22	5	5	13	22	36	65
12 Sunderland	46	14	2	7	35	22	5	6	12	19	35	65
13 BRISTOL CITY	46	11	7	5	27	18	5	9	9	20	32	64
14 Bolton	46	10	8	5	40	31	5	6	12	23	33	59
15 Southend	46	10	5	8	34	28	7	3	13	29	39	59
16 Grimsby	46	7	14	2	26	16	6	6	11	26	31	59
17 Portsmouth	46	10	6	7	29	22	5	7	11	23	36	58
18 Barnsley	46	9	3	11	25	26	7	4	12	30	41	55
19 Watford	46	10	5	8	39	35	5	4	14	27	45	54
20 Luton	46	12	4	7	38	25	2	7	14	18	35	53
21 West Brom	46	9	7	7	38	31	4	5	14	22	38	51
22 Birmingham	46	9	7	7	28	29	4	5	14	24	40	51
23 Oxford	46	10	5	8	33	33	3	5	15	21	42	49
24 Peterborough	46	6	9	8	31	30	2	4	17	17	46	37
	1104	276	144	132	864	586	132	144	276	586	864	1512

* promoted after play-offs

Odds & ends

Double wins: (3) Southend, Luton, Peterborough.
Double losses: (3) Oxford, Leicester, Notts County.

Won from behind: (0).
Lost from in front: (2) Crystal Palace (a), Charlton (a).

High spots: Beating Peterborough 4-1 at Ashton Gate on 8 May.
Beating Liverpool in FA Cup Replay at Anfield.
A smash and grab FA Cup win at Stockport.

Low spots: Forest's 4-1 win at Ashton Gate on 28 December.
Floodlight failure at Ashton Gate on 8 January just as City were taking control of FA Cup game v Liverpool.
Losing 0-2 at Charlton in FA Cup 5th Round Replay.
Losing Gloucestershire Cup Final against Bristol Rov 3-5 in penalty shoot-out following 1-1 draw at Ashton Gate on 5 August.

Player of the year: Wayne Allison.
Ever-presents: (0).
Hat-tricks: (2) Wayne Allison.
Leading scorer: Wayne Allison (19).

	Appearances						Goals			
	Lge	*Sub*	LC	*Sub*	FAC	*Sub*	Lge	LC	FAC	Tot
Aizlewood, Mark	5		2							
Allison, Wayne	35	*4*		*1*	5		15		4	19
Baird, Ian	16	*3*	2				5			5
Barclay, Dominic	2									
Bent, Junior	17	*3*			3	*1*	2			2
Borrows, Brian	6									
Brown, Ian	5	*6*					1			1
Brown Wayne	1									
Bryant, Matt	27	*1*			2					
Edwards, Rob	31	*7*			5		2			2
Fowler Jason		*1*								
Gavin, Mark	6	*2*								
Harriott, Marvin	17									
Harrison, Gerry	1									
Hewlett, Matt	11	*1*	2							
Hoyland, Jamie	6									
Kamara, Abdul		*1*								
Llewellyn, Andy	15				2					
McKop , Henry	2	*2*								
Martin, David	33	*1*			5		1			1
Milsom, Paul	1	*2*								
Munro, Stuart	43	*1*	2		5					
Osman, Russell	4	*1*		*2*			1			1
Partridge, Scott	7	*2*					4			4
Pennyfather, Glenn	7	*5*			2	*1*				
Robinson, Liam	31	*10*	2		5		4	1		5
Rosenior, Leroy	1	*4*			1	*1*				
Scott, Martin	45		2		5		5			5
Shail, Mark	35	*1*	2		5		2		1	3
Shelton, Gary	3		2							
Tinnion, Brian	40	*1*	2		5		5		2	7
Welch, Keith	45		2		5					
Wyatt, Mike	8	*2*	2							
31 players used	**506**	***61***	**22**	***3***	**55**	***3***	**47**	**1**	**7**	**55**

ENDSLEIGH LEAGUE DIVISION 1 | Manager: Osman ⇨ Joe Jordan | SEASON 1994-95

No	Date	Opponent	Att	Pos	Pt	F-A	H-T	Scorers, Times, and Referees	1	2	3	4	5	6	7	8	9	10	11	subs used
1	H	SUNDERLAND			D	0-0	0-0		Welch	Harriott	Scott	Shail	Bryant	Fowler	**McAree**	Bent*	**Baird**	Allison	Edwards	Partridge
	13/8		**11,127**		1				*Norman*	*Kubicki*	*Gray, Mart'**	*Bennett*	*Ferguson*	*Melville*	*Owers*	*Goodman*	*Gray P*	*Gray, Mike*	*Ball*	*Atkinson*
								Ref: P Alcock	Thrills and spills aplenty, but no goals in this humdinger. Unfortunately Osman's refreshing decision to opt for attack highlights the same deficiencies as last season. Despite laying almost constant siege on the visitors' goal in the first half, City are still unable to supply the finish.											
2	A	BOLTON			W	2-0	1-0	Baird 25, Allison 68	Welch	Harriott	Scott	Shail	Bryant	Fowler	McAree*	Bent^	Baird	Allison	Edwards	Munro/Partridge
	20/8		*12,127*		4				*Branagan*	*McDonald**	*Phillips*	*McAteer*	*Kernaghan*	*Stubbs*	*Lee*	*Patterson*	*Paatelainen*	*McGinlay^*	*Sneekes*	*Thompson/Coyle*
								Ref: J Watson	City at last demonstrate the art of finishing as they withstand Bolton pressure and hit back on the break. John McGinlay receives the Adidas Golden Boot award for his 33 goals last season, but reputations count for nothing as Allison blasts in from 18 yards to seal City's victory.											
3	H	PORT VALE		7	D	0-0	0-0		Welch	Harriott	Scott	Shail	Bryant	Fowler	**Loss**	Bent	Baird*	Allison^	Edwards	Partridge/**Brown I**
	27/8		8,940	*11*	5				*Musselwhite*	*Sandeman*	*Tankard*	*Porter*	*Griffiths*	*Glover D*	*Kent*	*Van der Laan*	*Foyle*	*Glover L*	*Naylor**	*Burke*
								Ref: G Pooley	On the day that sees the old Open End transformed by the opening of the Atyeo Stand, both teams face a new hazard in Graham Pooley who takes the new FA get-tough directive to heart. He books three players in the first 14 mins and by the end has handed out seven yellow cards.											
4	A	BURNLEY		12	D	1-1	0-1	Allison 89	Welch	Harriott	Scott	Shail	Bryant	Fowler	Loss*	Bent	Baird	Allison	Edwards	Partridge
	30/8		*11,207*	*21*	6			*Robinson 41*	*Beresford*	*Parkinson*	*Vinnicombe*	*Davis*	*Winstanley*	*Joyce*	*Harper*	*Gayle*	*Heath*	*Robinson**	*McMinn*	*Harrison*
								Ref: K Lupton	Allison saves a point for City in the second minute of injury-time with a perfect low drive to Marlon Beresford's left, but this is a game that they should have won. Cruelly robbed of a play-on advantage, City are hit as Liam Robinson's looping header finishes off a counter-attack.											
5	A	CHARLTON		16	L	2-3	0-1	Allison 58, 70	Welch	Harriott	Scott	Shail	Bryant	Fowler	Loss*	Bent	Baird	Allison	Edwards	Partridge
	3/9		*9,019*	*14*	6			*Mortimer 26, Whyte 63, 69*	*Ammann*	*Brown*	*Sturgess*	*Mortimer*	*Chapple*	*McLeary*	*Newton*	*Nelson*	*Garland^*	*Whyte*	*Robson**	*Walsh/Grant*
								Ref: T West	A thrilling finish as Allison hits the inside of a post as well as having a shot ruled out for offside, but City are left to regret not starting in a similar inspiring vein. With two goals apiece in the second half, Paul Mortimer's low 20-yard drive before the break is the crucial difference.											
6	H	NOTTS CO		10	W	2-1	1-1	Bent 16, Scott 54p	Welch	Harriott	Scott	Shail	Bryant	Fowler^	Partridge	Bent	Baird*	Allison	Edwards	Loss/McKop
	10/9		6,670	*21*	9			*Jemson 45*	*Cherry*	*Gallagher*	*Turner*	*Emenalo*	*Johnson*	*Yates*	*Jemson**	*Legg*	*Matthews*	*McSwegan*	*Kuhl*	*Lund*
								Ref: J Brandwood	A game sprinkled with strange refereeing decisions, but City are not complaining about Scott's pen even though Bent was clearly outside the box when brought down. Loss hits the post as City regain the control that was briefly threatened by Nigel Jemson's free-kick equaliser.											
7	H	DERBY		13	L	0-2	0-1		Welch	Harriott	Scott	Shail	Bryant	Fowler*	Partridge	Bent	Baird	Allison	Edwards	Loss
	13/9		8,029	*17*	9			*Kitson 22, Carsley 53*	*Taylor*	*Charles*	*Forsyth*	*Hodge*	*Short*	*Williams*	*Cowans*	*Gabbiadini*	*Kitson**	*Pembridge*	*Carsley*	*Simpson*
								Ref: P Vanes	City come in a poor second against a Derby side expertly marshalled in defence by Paul Williams. The Paul Kitson and Marco Gabbiadini partnership pulls the strings up front, as illustrated by Welch's parry of Gabbiadini's shot, which leaves Kitson a simple tap-in for the opener.											
8	A	SOUTHEND		17	L	1-2	0-1	Baird 82	Welch	Harriott	Scott	Shail	Bryant	Tinnion	Partridge	Bent	Baird	**Simpson**	Edwards	
	17/9		*3,663*	*22*	9			*Thomson 9, Whelan 61*	*Sansome*	*Hone*	*Powell*	*Gridelet**	*Edwards*	*Dublin*	*Willis*	*Whelan*	*Regis*	*Otto*	*Thomson^*	*Tilson/Forester*
								Ref: M Pierce	City have the chances, but can only register with Baird's late shot, whilst Southend make better use of their opportunities. A defensive mix-up allows Andy Thompson to burst through and bury the ball, whilst Ronnie Whelan's 20-yard floated free-kick finds the top corner of City's net.											
9	H	MIDDLESBROUGH		20	L	0-1	0-0		Welch	Harriott	Scott	Shail	Bryant	Tinnion*	McAree	Bent	Baird	Simpson	Edwards	Partridge
	24/9		8,642	*2*	9			*Hendrie 69*	*Pears*	*Cox*	*Fleming*	*Vickers*	*Whyte*	*Hignett*	*Mustoe*	*Pollock*	*Wilkinson*	*Hendrie*	*Moore*	
								Ref: J Lloyd	This latest setback brought more criticism cascading down from the Ashton Gate stands. Conceding daft goals doesn't help, and that was certainly the case when Scott was left on his backside as John Hendrie collected Curtis Fleming's long ball to run in and shoot past Welch.											
10	A	LUTON		17	W	1-0	0-0	Baird 56	Welch	Harriott	Scott	Shail	Bryant	Munro	Simpson	Bent*	Baird	Tinnion	Edwards	Partridge
	1/10		***6,633***	*20*	12				*Sommer*	*James*	*Johnson M*	*Waddock*	*Thomas**	*Peake*	*Telfer*	*Oakes*	*Dixon^*	*Preece*	*Marshall*	*Hughes/Harston*
								Ref: P Foakes	City plunder a win as their only worthwhile attempt on goal condemns the Hatters to their third successive home defeat. A cruel reward for Luton's stylish play as Baird ends City's three-match drought by side-footing in from six yards when Juergen Sommer fails to hold Bent's shot.											
11	H	MILLWALL		13	W	1-0	0-0	Baird 56	Welch	Harriott	Scott	Shail	Bryant	Munro	McAree*	**Seal^**	Baird	Simpson	Tinnion	Partridge/Wyatt
	8/10		7,499	*20*	15				*Carter*	*Cunningham*	*Thatcher*	*Van Blerk*	*McCarthy*	*Roberts*	*Beard^*	*Rae !*	*Kerr*	*Mitchell**	*Kennedy*	*Chapman/Savage*
								Ref: J Rushton	City celebrate with a win after FA chairman Sir Bert Millichip officially opened the Atyeo stand in front of 23 old-timers of the Atyeo era, including the great Geoff Bradford of Bristol Rovers. Whilst Baird's header might not have been up to Atyeo's standard, it is welcome enough.											

No / Date	Venue / Opponent	Att / Pos	Res / Pts	F-A	H-T	Scorers, Times, and Referees	1	2	3	4	5	6	7	8	9	10	11	subs used
12	A READING	15	L	0-1	0-0		Welch	Harriott	Humphries	Shail	Bryant	Munro	Allison	Seal*	Baird	Tinnion	Edwards	Partridge
15/10		9,389 2	15			Gilkes 90	Hislop	Bernal	Kerr	Wdowezyk	Williams	Holsgrave^	Gilkes	Gooding	Quinn	Hartenb'rger*	Osborn	Murphy/Parkinson
						Ref: K Leach	Two minutes of stoppage time had already been played when Michael Gilkes finally got behind City's defence and crashed in a rising shot. A cruel end to a bright City performance that brings their usual quota of chances, including Allison's 81st-minute effort against a goal post.											
13	A GRIMSBY	20	L	0-1	0-0		Welch	Harriott	Humphries	Shail	Bryant	Munro*	Allison	Seal^	Baird	Tinnion	Edwards	McAree/Partridge
22/10		4,024 11	15			Childs 61	Crichton	Croft	Jobling	Handyside	Lever	Groves	Watson	Dobbin	Livingstone	Woods	Shakespeare*	Childs
						Ref: A Dawson	The ironic cheers from the away fans summed up City's performance, as they struggled to reply to Gary Childs' headed goal. Whilst Partridge has a low shot disallowed, City offer little threat to a Grimsby side weakened by injuries and the departure of manager Alan Buckley.											
14	H PORTSMOUTH	21	D	1-1	1-0	Scott 15p	Welch	Harriott	Scott*	Shail	Bryant	Tinnion	Bent^	Partridge	Baird	Allison	Edwards	Munro/Seal
29/10		7,238 14	16			Powell 80	Knight	Gittens	Stimson	Kristensen	Symons	McGrath	Pethick	Preki^	Powell	Creaney*	Dobson	Rees/Hall
						Ref: A Flood	Scott's penalty, after Allison is tripped by keeper Alan Knight, should have made City hungry for goals, but nothing else on target from them for the rest of the match tells its own story. Pompey manage six, and one of them, Darryl Powell's volley, escapes Welch for a deserved point.											
15	H WOLVES	21	L	**1-5**	1-2	Baird 32 [65, 87]	Welch	Munro	Humphries	Shail !	Bryant	Tinnion	Bent*	Seal	Baird	**Paterson**	Edwards	Fowler
1/11		10,401 1	16			Walters 12, Thompson 36p, Kelly 63,	Stowell	Smith	Thompson	Ferguson	Blades	Venus	Walters	Thomas	Bull*	Kelly	Froggatt	Stewart
						Ref: C Wilkes	After Baird crashes the ball into the net for City's stunning equaliser, Shail's sending-off for hauling down Steve Bull and the subsequent penalty changes the course of game. David Kelly continues his remarkable scoring record against City with a hat-trick inside 24 minutes.											
16	A SHEFFIELD UTD	22	L	0-3	0-2		Welch	Harriott*	Humphries	Shail	Bryant	Fowler	Wyatt	Seal^	Baird	Paterson	Edwards	Bent/Partridge
5/11		11,568 15	16			Hartfield 6, Gage 11, Whitehouse 75	Kelly	Gage	Nilsen	Hartfield	Gayle	Marshall	Rogers	Veart^	Starbuck	Blake*	Whitehouse	Hodges/Scott
						Ref: W Burns	The writing's on the wall for City as they are unable to stop United winning their first game in nine. Charlie Hartfield starts the rot with a drive in off the post, then comes Kevin Gage's 30-yard thunderbolt, before Dane Whitehouse shoots in from ten yards to complete an easy success.											
17	H SWINDON	22	W	3-2	0-0	Bent 54, Allison 56, 63	**Kite**	Harriott	Scott	**Hansen**	Bryant	Tinnion	Fowler	Bent	Partridge	Allison	Edwards	
20/11		9,086 15	19			Scott 58, 89	Digby	Robinson	Bodin	Tiler	Kilcline*	MacLaren^	Horlock	Beauchamp	Fjortoft	Mutch	Scott	Murray/O'Sullivan
						Ref: P Wright	Following Osman's sacking, Jordan's second spell in charge commences with this dazzling live TV spectacular. Bent pops in Frazer Digby's parry of Allison's curling 25-yarder for the opening goal, whilst Keith Scott ends the proceedings by forcing the ball in at the second attempt.											
18	A OLDHAM	22	L	0-2	0-0		Kite	Harriott	Scott	Shail	Hansen	Tinnion	Fowler*	Bent	Partridge	Allison	Edwards	McAree
26/11		7,277 16	19			Richardson 47, McCarthy 57	Gerrard	Makin	Pointon	Henry	Jobson	Redmond	Richardson	Ritchie	McCarthy^	Graham	Holden*	Brennan/Banger
						Ref: K Breen	Goal-shy City throw the game away, but where they fail Oldham succeed with two quick-fire efforts for a happy first home game for new boss Graeme Sharp. Lee Richardson sends a rising shot into the roof of City's net, then Sean McCarthy follows up to put in his rebound off the post.											
19	H GRIMSBY	23	L	1-2	0-0	Partridge 60	Welch	**Parris**	Scott	Shail	Bryant	Tinnion	**Watson***	Bent	Partridge	Allison	Edwards	Fowler
3/12		**6,030** 4	19			Gilbert 47, Childs 73	Crichton	Croft	Jobling	Handyside	Lever*	Groves	Childs	Dobbin	Livingstone	Woods^	Gilbert	Rodger/Lester
						Ref: K Cooper	A dream come true for Partridge as he scores against his hometown club with a left-footed shot beyond Paul Crichton's drive. It isn't enough though as Dave Gilbert beats Welch from the edge of the box, and Gary Childs hits an unstoppable volley to secure the points for Grimsby.											
20	A BARNSLEY	23	L	1-2	1-1	Bent 33	Welch	Harriott	Scott	Shail	Hansen	Tinnion	Parris	Bent	Baird	Allison^	Edwards	Partridge
7/12		4,305 6	19			Liddell 32, Archdeacon 84	Butler	Eaden	Fleming	Archdeacon	Taggart	Davis	O'Connell^	Redfearn	Jackson*	Liddell	Sheridan	Payton/Bullock
						Ref: E Wolstenholme	After Bent had slotted in Scott's defence-splitting pass for a quick equaliser to Andy Liddell's close-range shot, City took the game to their highly-placed rivals. Unfortunately Owen Archdeacon fired in a late goal to deprive City of the point that their spirited performance deserved.											
21	H BOLTON	23	L	0-1	0-1		Welch	Harriott	Scott	Shail	Hansen^	Tinnion	Parris	Bent	Baird	Allison*	Edwards	Partridge/Watson
10/12		6,144 4	19			Patterson 1	Branagan	Green	Phillips	McAteer	Coleman	Stubbs	Lee	Sneekes*	Paatelainen	McGinlay	Patterson	Coyle
						Ref: G Singh	City's efforts to keep a clean sheet last just 29 seconds as David Lee's cross is allowed to drift across the area for Mark Patterson to fire in a shot that takes a deflection off Harriott. Without a single shot on target in the first half, City manage two after the break to match Bolton's total.											
22	A SUNDERLAND	23	L	0-2	0-0		Welch	Munro	Scott	Shail	Hansen	Partridge	Parris	Bent	Baird	Allison*	Edwards	Tinnion
17/12		11,661 16	19			Howey 56, 75	Chamberlain	Owers	Kubicki	Bennett	Ball	Melville	Ferguson	Russell	Howey	Smith	Armstrong*	Gray, Mike
						Ref: D Allison	Sunderland, with only one previous home success this season, have the luck on their side to quell City's battling display. The referee fails to spot Lee Howey using his hand to push in Sunderland's opener, then the No 9's shot leaves Welch helpless after taking a deflection off Scott.											
23	A WEST BROM	23	L	0-1	0-0		Welch	Hansen	Munro	Shail	Bryant	Tinnion	Parris	Bent	Baird	Allison*	**Owers**	Partridge
26/12		21,071 18	19			Munro 81 (og)	Naylor	O'Regan	Lilwall	Bradley	Mardon	Edwards	Donovan	Ashcroft	Heggs*	Hunt	Hamilton	Taylor
						Ref: T West	A cruel Boxing Day knockout as all City's hard work is undone by a farcical own-goal. Munro and Lee Ashcroft tussled for the ball, which ricocheted off the City man's shin towards Welch. The keeper completely missed his attempted clearance as the ball rolled on into the goal.											

No	Date		Att	Pos	Pt	F-A	H-T	Scorers, Times, and Referees	1	2	3	4	5	6	7	8	9	10	11	subs used
24	H	STOKE		23	W	3-1	0-0	Bryant 66, Allison 78, 80	Welch	Hansen	Munro	Shail*	Bryant	Tinnion	Parris	Bent	Baird^	Allison	Owers	**Dryden**/Partridge
	27/12		8,500	*11*	22			*Cranson 83*	*Sinclair*	*Butler*	*Sandford*	*Cranson*	*Dreyer^*	*Orlygsson*	*Sigardsson*	*Clarkson*	*Biggins**	*Williams*	*Gleghorn*	*Peschisolido/Shaw*
								Ref: P Vanes	City end a run of six straight defeats with this stylish win. Bryant's unstoppable 30-yarder relieves the tension, then Allison's near-post header finishes off Tinnion's corner, before the No 10 slides in Bent's cross. Stoke's solitary reply comes from Ian Cranson's close-range header.											
25	A	TRANMERE		23	L	0-2	0-2		Welch	Hansen	Munro	Shail	Bryant	Tinnion	**Kuhl**	Bent	Baird	Allison*	Owers	Partridge
	31/12		*7,439*	*3*	22			*Jones 7, Irons 41*	*Nixon*	*Stevens*	*Irons*	*McGreal*	*Higgins*	*O'Brien*	*Morrissey*	*Jones G*	*Malkin*	*Nevin*	*Thomas*	
								Ref: P Richards	After Gary Jones shoots Tranmere ahead from eight yards, City do everything bar score. Nixon is in superb form and does well to keep out a 20-yard pile-driver from Kuhl (£300,000 ex Derby). Kenny Irons completes City's frustrations by nodding in from John Morrissey's cross.											
26	H	WATFORD		23	D	0-0	0-0		Welch	Hansen	Munro	Shail	Bryant	Tinnion	Kuhl	Bent	Baird*	Allison	Edwards	Seal
	2/1		9,423	*9*	23				*Miller*	*Lavin*	*Bazeley*	*Foster*	*Holdsworth*	*Ramage*	*Hessenthaler*	*Gibbs*	*Shipperley*	*Porter*	*Mooney*	
								Ref: J Kirkby	City start the new year with the same old problem. They dominate an unspectacular game on a glue-pot pitch, but are unable their translate their possession into goals. Despite a corner count of 15-5 in their favour, City fail to cause Kevin Miller any real concern before the break.											
27	A	PORTSMOUTH		23	D	0-0	0-0		Welch	Hansen	Munro	Shail*	Bryant	Tinnion	Kuhl	Bent	**Fleck**^	Allison	Owers	Dryden/Baird
	14/1		*8,808*	*19*	24				*Knight*	*Russell*	*Daniel*	*McGrath*	*Symons*	*Butters*	*Pethick*	*Preki*	*Powell*	*Creaney*	*Wood**	*Hall*
								Ref: M Bailey	It's the same old recurring nightmare as again City's domination does not translate itself into goals. Tinnion is unlucky with a 15th-minute free-kick, as his curling left-foot effort from 30 yards hits the post, but throughout the whole game only Fleck manages to get a shot on target.											
28	H	SHEFFIELD UTD		23	W	2-1	0-0	Gayle 55 (og), Shail 75	Welch	Hansen	Dryden	Shail	Bryant	Tinnion	Edwards	Bent	Fleck	Allison*	Owers	Partridge
	21/1		10,211	*6*	27			*Gayle 67*	*Mercer*	*Gage !*	*Nilsen*	*Hartfield*	*Gayle*	*Whitehouse*	*Rogers*	*Veart*	*Starbuck*	*Hodges**	*Scott^*	*Beesley/Flo*
								Ref: P Alcock	Following Kevin Gage's dismissal for kicking out after being fouled by Edwards, the Blades level from Phil Starbuck's resultant free-kick. Brian Gayle bundles the ball in, but Shail becomes City's unlikely scoring hero with a shot from 18 yards to end Utd's ten-match unbeaten run.											
29	H	BARNSLEY		22	W	3-2	0-0	Dryden 53, Bryant 66, Allison 83	Welch	Hansen	Munro	Dryden	Bryant	Tinnion	Kuhl	Bent	Fleck	Allison*	Owers	Baird
	4/2		6,408	*9*	30			*Rammell 48, Wilson 86*	*Watson*	*Eaden*	*Fleming*	*Wilson*	*Shotton*	*Moses*	*O'Connell**	*Redfearn*	*Rammell*	*Liddell*	*Sheridan*	*Bullock*
								Ref: G Singh	After a poor first half, Andy Rammell leaves City's defence trailing to steer in the opener. Allison makes sure of the points with a well-struck shot off the instep which curls in from 20 yards, but Barnsley's player-manager Danny Wilson has the last word with a 25-yard thunderbolt.											
30	A	WOLVES		22	L	0-2	0-1		Welch	Hansen	Munro	Shail	Bryant	Tinnion	Kuhl	Bent	Fleck	Allison*	Owers	Baird
	11/2		***25,451***	2	30			*Dennison 25, Kelly 62*	*Jones*	*Blades*	*Thompson*	*Emblen**	*De Wolf*	*Law*	*Rankine^*	*Kelly*	*Goodman*	*Cowans*	*Dennison*	*Bennett/Mills*
								Ref: M Riley	City create many chances, but waste them all, while Wolves make their limited number count. Robbie Dennison's shot and David Kelly's header do the necessary for the Molineux men, but the nearest City come to a goal is Allison's second-half header that comes back off the bar.											
31	A	SWINDON		20	W	**3-0**	1-0	Bent 7, Fleck 51, Bryant 57	Welch	Hansen	Munro	Shail	Bryant	Tinnion	Kuhl	Bent*	Fleck	Allison	Owers	Baird
	15/2		*9,992*	*21*	33				*Hammond*	*Robinson*	*Murray*	*O'Sullivan*	*Nijholt*	*Thomson**	*Horlock*	*Beauchamp*	*Fjortoft*	*Thorne*	*Ling*	*McMahon*
								J Lloyd	With City's Women's team hogging the limelight after beating Huddersfield 4-3 to reach the Cup semi-finals, the men turn on their own great show to destroy Swindon at the County Ground. Bent is the star as he leads Swindon a merry dance after driving the ball in from eight yards.											
32	H	OLDHAM		20	D	2-2	2-1	Allison 8, 34	Welch	Hansen	Munro	Shail	Bryant*	Tinnion	Kuhl	Bent	Fleck	Allison	Owers^	Dryden/Baird
	18/2		7,851	*13*	34			*Halle 28, Ritchie 82*	*Gerrard*	*Snodin*	*Pointon*	*Henry*	*Moore*	*Redmond*	*Halle*	*Ritchie*	*Banger^*	*Richardson*	*Brennan**	*Holden/McCarthy*
								Ref: G Pooley	Oldham are absolutely brilliant as they give City a soccer lesson in all but the art of finishing. How the Latics didn't win after so completely dominating the second-half action is a mystery, but it is unlikely that City will ever be so comprehensively outplayed at Ashton Gate again.											
33	H	LUTON		21	D	2-2	0-1	Owers 65, Bent 85	Welch	Hansen	Munro	Dryden	Bryant	Tinnion	Kuhl	Bent	Fleck	Allison	Owers	
	25/2		7,939	*10*	35			*Oakes 29, 54*	*Sommer*	*James*	*Johnson M*	*Waddock*	*Thomas*	*Peake*	*Telfer*	*Oakes*	*Dixon*	*Preece**	*Marshall*	*Williams*
								Ref: A Flood	The Hatters appear to be cruising after two long-range goals by Scott Oakes, and Juergen Sommer's save of Tinnion's 43rd-minute penalty. Owers then pulls one back from a seemingly offside position, before Bent salvages a point with a brilliant left-footed shot from twelve yards.											
34	A	MIDDLESBROUGH		21	L	0-3	0-1		Welch	Hansen	Munro	Shail	Bryant^	Tinnion	Kuhl	Bent	Fleck*	Allison !	Owers	Baird/Dryden
	4/3		*17,371*	2	35			*Fuchs 10, 48, 65*	*Miller*	*Cox*	*Whyte*	*Vickers**	*Pearson*	*Blackmore*	*Robson*	*Moreno*	*Fuchs^*	*Mustoe*	*Moore*	*Hignett/Wilkinson*
								Ref: J Parker	City are shown the gap between the top and bottom – and finish a distant second. Allison's controversial dismissal for his 34th-minute challenge on Steve Vickers doesn't help, especially as by then Uwe Fuchs had waltzed around Welch and expertly buried his opener with his right foot.											

No	Date	Opponent	Att	Pos	Pts	FT	HT	Scorers, Times, and Referees	1	2	3	4	5	6	7	8	9	10	11	subs used
35	H	CHARLTON		20	W	2-1	1-0	Kuhl 33, Tinnion 60	Welch	Hansen	Munro	Dryden	Bryant	Tinnion	Kuhl	Bent	Fleck*	Allison	Owers	Baird
	7/3		6,118	*14*	38			*Pardew 90*	*Salmon*	*Brown*	*Stuart**	*Jones*	*Rufus*	*Balmer*	*Robson^*	*Nelson*	*Pardew*	*Whyte*	*Mortimer*	*Leaburn/Robinson*
								Ref: J Holbrook	For a change it is City who supply the killer instinct to move out of the bottom four. Kuhl's long-range effort and Tinnion's angled drive are City's only on-target efforts, whilst all Charlton have to show for their six shots is Alan Pardew's close-range strike in the dying seconds.											
36	A	PORT VALE		21	L	1-2	1-1	Owers 10	Welch	Hansen^	Munro	Dryden	Bryant	Tinnion	Kuhl	Bent	Fleck*	Allison	Owers	Seal/Shail
	11/3		*7,645*	*15*	38			*Scott 7, Naylor 75*	*Musselwhite*	*Sanderman*	*Tankard*	*Porter*	*Aspin*	*Scott*	*Guppy*	*Van der Laan*	*Foyle**	*Naylor*	*Walker*	*Glover*
								Ref: N Barry	Andy Porter's drive is deflected into the net off the head of Kevin Scott to give Vale an early lead, but City dominate the first half after Owers' levels with a perfect chip. It is a different story after the break though, and Ray Walker shoots in from close range to reward ascendant Vale.											
37	H	BURNLEY		21	D	1-1	1-0	Partridge 13	Welch	Hansen	Munro	Dryden	Bryant	Edwards	Kuhl	Bent	Baird	Partridge*	Owers	Wyatt
	18/3		6,717	*24*	39			*Eyres 65*	*Russell*	*Harrison*	*Winstanley*	*Davis*	*Vinnicombe !*	*Randall^*	*Hoyland*	*Thompson*	*Nogan**	*Pender*	*Eyres*	*Robinson/Parkinson*
								Ref: M Pierce	It all looks so easy early on as City, already a goal to the good due to Wayne Russell's clearance rebounding off Partridge, have a further advantage with Chris Vinnicombe's 23rd-min sending-off. A dismal second-half display is punished by David Eyres' shot from close range.											
38	A	NOTTS CO		22	D	1-1	0-0	Baird 63	Welch	Hansen	Munro	Dryden	Bryant	Tinnion	Edwards	Bent	Baird !	Partridge	Owers	
	21/3		*5,692*	*24*	40			*White 78*	*Cherry*	*Mills*	*Short^*	*Russell**	*Forsyth*	*Hogg*	*Devlin*	*White*	*Agana*	*Nichol*	*Legg*	*Turner/Johnson*
								Ref: P Harrison	After Baird supplies the finishing touch to Partridge's half-hit shot, the scourge of Bristol derbies returns to haunt City. Devon White pounces on Steve Nichol's scuffed effort to nod the loose ball into the top corner to save a point for the newly-crowned Anglo-Italian Cup winners.											
39	H	SOUTHEND		21	D	0-0	0-0		Welch	Hansen	Munro*	Dryden	Bryant	Tinnion	Edwards	Bent	Baird	Partridge	Owers	**Flatts**
	25/3		6,159	*16*	41				*Royce*	*Hone*	*Powell*	*Whelan*	*Bodley*	*Edwards*	*Jones G**	*Sussex*	*Hails*	*Tilson*	*Dublin*	*Battersby*
								Ref: J Brandwood	Where is the passion to stop City sliding into the Second Division without even a whimper? There was little sign of it on the pitch as two more points slip away in this instantly-forgettable match. A linesman's flag curtails Baird's 56th-min celebrations after turning in Bent's overhead.											
40	A	DERBY		21	L	1-3	1-2	Allison 41	Welch	Hansen	Munro*	Shail	Dryden	Tinnion	Kuhl	Bent	Baird	Allison	Owers	Flatts
	1/4		*14,555*	*8*	41			*Gabbiadini 6, Williams 15, Wrack 61*	*Hoult*	*Yates**	*Wassall*	*Trollope*	*Kavanagh*	*Williams*	*Harkes*	*Pembridge*	*Mills*	*Gabbiadini*	*Simpson^*	*Wrack/Sturridge*
								Ref: J Kirkby	A 31st birthday to forget for Baird as he squanders his chances, while Derby capitalise on City's poor defending. Shail's slip allowed Marco Gabbiadini in to beat Welch, while both Paul Williams (bullet header) and Darren Wrack (angled shot) are unmarked when scoring their goals.											
41	H	TRANMERE		23	L	0-1	0-1		Welch	Hansen	Munro*	Shail	Dryden	Tinnion	Kuhl	Bent	Flatts	Allison	Owers	Partridge
	8/4		6,723	*2*	41			*Aldridge 39p*	*Nixon*	*Stevens*	*Mungall*	*McGreal*	*Garnett*	*O'Brien*	*Brannan*	*Aldridge*	*Jones G*	*Irons*	*Nevin*	
								Ref: P Vanes	City are left to rue missed chances as they go down to their first home League defeat since early December. After Munro is adjudged to have wrestled Pat Nevin to the ground, John Aldridge incurs the wrath of the crowd with his celebration following his successful spot-kick.											
42	A	STOKE		23	L	1-2	1-1	Shail 18	Welch	Hansen	Munro*	Shail	Dryden	Tinnion	Martin^	Bent	Flatts	Allison	Owers	Baird/Edwards
	15/4		*10,158*	*16*	41			*Andrade 28, Peschisolido 89*	*Sinclair*	*Butler*	*Sigurdsson*	*Wallace*	*Clarkson*	*Orlygsson*	*Allen**	*Downing^*	*Peschisolido*	*Andrade*	*Gleghorn*	*Keen/Carruthers*
								Ref: D Allison	Heartbreak as Paul Peschisolido breaks free of City's square defence to round Welch and shoot in Stoke's last-minute winner. A strike that almost guarantees Stoke's survival, whilst City, now seven points short of safety with just four matches remaining, look beyond all hope.											
43	H	WEST BROM		23	W	1-0	0-0	Bent 80	Welch	Hansen	Munro	Shail	Dryden	Edwards*	Kuhl^	Bent	Flatts	Allison	Owers	Partridge/Martin
	17/4		8,777	*17*	44				*Naylor*	*Burgess*	*Agnew*	*O'Regan*	*Strodder*	*Raven**	*Donovan*	*Coldicott*	*Taylor*	*Hunt*	*Hamilton*	*Smith^/Rees*
								Ref: D Orr	Most of the excitement occurs after the game as fire fighters battle to prevent flames from a portaloo spreading to the Covered End. On the pitch, sub Partridge is City's star man, and it is his low centre which ends up in the net after Bent and Paul Agnew challenge for the ball.											
44	A	WATFORD		23	L	0-1	0-0		Welch	Hansen	Munro^	Shail	Dryden	Flatts	Kuhl	Bent*	Partridge	Allison	Owers	Tinnion/Baird
	22/4		*7,190*	*10*	44			*Phillips 62*	*Miller*	*Lavin*	*Page*	*Holdsworth*	*Millen*	*Ramage*	*Hessenthaler*	*Payne*	*Beadle**	*Porter*	*Phillips*	*Bazeley*
								Ref: S Mathieson	Still in with a chance of survival before this game, City's continuing lack of a killer punch condemns them to the drop. Watford, with five shots on target and ten off-target efforts, also suffer from the same malaise, but Kevin Phillips at least manages to register with a diving header.											
45	H	READING		23	L	1-2	0-1	Tinnion 87	Welch	Hansen^	Munro	Shail	Dryden	Tinnion	Martin	Bryant	Partridge*	Allison	Edwards	Seal/Fowler
	29/4		9,474	*2*	44			*Lovell 18, Nogan 58*	*Hislop*	*Bernal*	*Osborn*	*Wdowczyk**	*Williams*	*McPherson*	*Gilkes*	*Gooding*	*Nogan*	*Lovell*	*Taylor*	*Parkinson*
								Ref: P Wright	Inept, passionless City are easily swept away by Reading after Stuart Lovell puts the Royals in front when deftly heading in Simon Osborn's free-kick. Lee Nogan then gets the final touch to another free-kick, before the disaffected Tinnion shoots City's reply into an empty net.											
46	A	MILLWALL		23	D	1-1	1-1	Allison 26	Welch	Hansen	Munro	Bryant^	Dryden	Partridge*	Martin	Kuhl	Baird	Allison	Edwards	Hewlett/Paterson
	7/5		*8,805*	*12*	45			*Dixon 21*	*Keller*	*Beard*	*Thatcher*	*Roberts*	*Witter*	*Stevens**	*McRoberts^*	*Rae*	*Dixon*	*Oldfield*	*Van Blerk*	*Forbes/Taylor*
	Home		Away					Ref: T West	With the country in nostalgic vein due to the build-up to the 50th-anniversary celebrations of VE Day, City capture some of the old bulldog spirit themselves. Allison seizes on Tony Witter's misplaced headed back-pass to steer in City's leveller to Kerry Dixon's twelve-yard shot.											
Average	8,005		10,220																	

Coca-Cola Cup						F-A	H-T	Scorers, Times, and Referees	1	2	3	4	5	6	7	8	9	10	11	subs used
2:1	H	NOTTS CO		17	L	0-1	0-0		Welch	Herriott	Scott	Shail	Bryant	Tinnion	McAree	Bent	Loss*	Partridge	Edwards	Brown I
20/9			2,546	23				*Devlin 87*	*Cherry*	*Sherlock*	*Murphy*	*Turner*	*Johnson*	*Yates*	*Devlin*	*Legg*	*Lund^*	*McSwegan**	*Simpson*	*Jemson/Agana*
								Ref: P Wright	With City's three blanks in four home outings it is perhaps not surprising that the public mood is reflected in the lowest Ashton Gate League Cup attendance. In this game it is the same old tale as City cannot score, giving County's Andy Legg the chance to show how from 15 yards.											
2:2	A	NOTTS CO		20	L	0-3	0-1		Welch	Munro	Scott	Shail	Paterson	Tinnion	McAree*	Bent^	Baird	Bryant	Edwards	Fowler/Brown I
27/9			*2,721*	*24*				*Jemson 16, Lund 48, 74*	*Cherry*	*Mills*	*Johnson*	*Turner*	*Yates*	*Murphy*	*Devlin*	*Legg*	*Lund*	*Jemson**	*Agana*	*Matthews*
								Ref: G Cain (City lost 0-4 on aggregate)	City's defensive problems are now becoming almost as worrying as those up front. Nigel Jemson gets behind Paterson to control Gary Mills' 40-yard pass on his chest and shoot past Welch from eight yards to destroy any hopes City may have had in overcoming a first-leg deficit.											

FA Cup						F-A	H-T	Scorers, Times, and Referees	1	2	3	4	5	6	7	8	9	10	11	subs used
3	H	STOKE		23	D	0-0	0-0		Welch	Hansen	Munro	Shail	Bryant	Tinnion	Kuhl	Bent	Baird*	Allison	Owers	Partridge
7/1			*9,683*	*12*					*Sinclair*	*Butler*	*Sandford*	*Cranson*	*Overson*	*Orlygsson*	*Clarkson*	*Downing**	*Scott*	*Peschisolido^*	*Gleghorn*	*Sturridge/Sigurdsson*
								Ref: K Cooper	Stoke only seem interested in hanging on for a replay as Owers (£300,000 ex Sunderland) and Kuhl control the midfield in this low-key cup-tie. Partridge nearly supplies the breakthrough as he leaves Ronnie Sinclair floundering, only for Lee Sandford to kick his shot off the line.											
3R	A	STOKE		23	W	3-1	0-1	Bent 71, Baird 93, Tinnion 119	Welch	Hansen	Munro	Shail	Bryant	Tinnion	Kuhl*	Bent	Baird	Allison^	Owers	Edwards/Partridge
18/1			*11,579*	*14*		*aet*		*Scott 17*	*Sinclair*	*Clarkson**	*Sandford*	*Cranson*	*Overson*	*Orlygsson*	*Butler*	*Wallace*	*Scott*	*Peschisolido*	*Gleghorn*	*Carruthers*
								Ref: K Cooper	After a jaded first-half display in which they never look like responding to Keith Scott's back header, City suddenly find the form to leave Stoke trailing in their wake. Bent equalises with a powerful cross shot, and Baird hits the ball on the rise to put City ahead early in extra-time.											
4	H	EVERTON		23	L	0-1	0-0		Welch	Hansen	Munro	Shail	Bryant^	Tinnion	Edwards	Bent	Partridge*	Allison	Owers	Seal/Dryden
29/1			19,816	*P:17*				*Jackson 79*	*Southall*	*Jackson*	*Burrows*	*Horne*	*Watson*	*Unsworth*	*Limpar*	*Parkinson*	*Barlow*	*Rideout*	*Hinchcliffe**	*Stuart*
								Ref: T Holbrook	'We needed all the luck of the Cup to get through' says Everton boss Joe Royle. City should have won, both Partridge and Allison being denied by a post, but Matt Jackson's spectacular 20-yard left-foot volley into the roof of the Covered End goal wins it for the Toffee men.											

		Home					Away					
	P	W	D	L	F	A	W	D	L	F	A	Pts
1 Middlesbro	46	15	4	4	41	19	8	9	6	26	21	82
2 Reading	46	12	7	4	34	21	11	3	9	24	23	79
3 Bolton *	46	16	6	1	43	13	5	8	10	24	32	77
4 Wolves	46	15	5	3	39	18	6	8	9	38	43	76
5 Tranmere	46	17	4	2	51	23	5	6	12	16	35	76
6 Barnsley	46	15	6	2	42	19	5	6	12	21	33	72
7 Watford	46	14	6	3	33	17	5	7	11	19	29	70
8 Sheffield Utd	46	12	9	2	41	21	5	8	10	33	34	68
9 Derby	46	12	6	5	44	23	6	6	11	22	28	66
10 Grimsby	46	12	7	4	36	19	5	7	11	26	37	65
11 Stoke	46	10	7	6	31	21	6	8	9	19	32	63
12 Millwall	46	11	8	4	36	22	5	6	12	24	38	62
13 Southend	46	13	2	8	33	25	5	6	12	21	48	62
14 Oldham	46	12	7	4	34	21	4	6	13	26	39	61
15 Charlton	46	11	6	6	33	25	5	5	13	25	41	59
16 Luton	46	8	6	9	35	30	7	7	9	26	34	58
17 Port Vale	46	11	5	7	30	24	4	8	11	28	40	58
18 Portsmouth	46	9	8	6	31	28	6	5	12	22	35	58
19 West Brom	46	13	3	7	33	24	3	7	13	18	33	58
20 Sunderland	46	5	12	6	22	22	7	6	10	19	23	54
21 Swindon	46	9	6	8	28	27	3	6	14	26	46	48
22 Burnley	46	8	7	8	36	33	3	6	14	13	41	46
23 BRISTOL CITY	46	8	8	7	26	28	3	4	16	16	35	45
24 Notts Co	46	7	8	8	26	28	2	5	16	19	38	40
	1104	275	153	124	838	551	124	153	275	551	838	1503

* promoted after play-offs

Odds & ends

Double wins: (1) Swindon.
Double losses: (6) Derby, Middlesbrough, Reading, Grimsby, Wolves, Tranmere.

Won from behind: (1) Barnsley (h).
Lost from in front: (1) Stoke (a).

High spots: Doing the double over Swindon.
Oldham's brilliant display at Ashton Gate on 18 February.
Beating Stoke 3-1 at Ashton Gate on 27 December.
Winning FA Cup replay at Stoke after extra-time.

Low spots: Wolves 5-1 win at Ashton Gate on 1 November.
Matt Jackson's 20-yard volley that deprives City of an FA Cup upset against Everton.
Losing the Gloucestershire Cup Final 11-10 on penalties v Bristol Rov at Twerton on 3 August.

Player of the year: Matt Bryant.
Ever-presents: (0).
Hat-tricks: (0).
Leading scorer: Wayne Allison (13).

	Appearances						Goals			
	Lge	*Sub*	LC	*Sub*	FAC	*Sub*	Lge	LC	FAC	Tot
Allison, Wayne	**37**				3		**13**			**13**
Baird, Ian	**28**	*9*	1		2		**6**		1	**7**
Bent, Junior	**40**	*1*	2		3		**6**		1	**7**
Brown, Ian		*1*		*2*						
Bryant, Matt	**37**		2		3		**3**			**3**
Dryden, Richard	**15**	*4*				*1*	**1**			**1**
Edwards, Rob	**29**	*1*	2		1	*1*				
Flatts, Mark	**4**	*2*								
Fleck, Robert	**10**						**1**			**1**
Fowler, Jason	**10**	*3*		*1*						
Hansen, Vergard	**29**				3					
Harriott, Marvin	**19**		1							
Hewlett, Matt		*1*								
Humphries, Mark	**4**									
Kite, Phil	**2**									
Kuhl, Martin	**17**				2		**1**			**1**
Loss, Colin	**3**	*2*	1							
McAree, Rodney	**4**	*2*	2							
McKop, Henry		*1*								
Martin, David	**3**	*1*								
Munro, Stuart	**29**	*2*	1		3					
Owers, Gary	**21**				3		**2**			**2**
Parris, George	**6**									
Partridge, Scott	**14**	*19*	1		1	*2*	**2**			**2**
Paterson, Scott	**2**	*1*	1							
Seal, David	**5**	*4*				*1*				
Scott, Martin	**18**		2				**2**			**2**
Shail, Mark	**37**	*1*	2		3		**2**			**2**
Simpson, Fitzroy	**4**									
Tinnion, Brian	**33**	*2*	2		3		**2**		1	**3**
Watson, Kevin	**1**									
Welch, Keith	**44**		2		3					
Wyatt, Mike	**1**	*2*								
(own-goals)							**1**			**1**
33 players used	**506**	***59***	**22**	***3***	**33**	***5***	**42**		**3**	**45**

No	Date		Att	Pos	Pt	F-A	H-T	Scorers, Times, and Referees	1	2	3	4	5	6	7	8	9	10	11	subs used
1	H	BLACKPOOL			D	1-1	1-1	Seal 20	Welch	Hansen	Munro	Dryden	**McLeary**	Kuhl	**Barber**	Bent	**Agostino**	Seal	Partridge	
	12/8		7,617		1			*Quinn 1*	*Capleton*	*Brown R*	*Barlow*	*Lydiate*	*Mellon*	*Bradshaw*	*Quinn**	*Bonner*	*Gouck*	*Ellis*	*Preece*	*Bryan*
								Ref: G Pooley	Rocked by the day's fastest goal on just twelve secs when James Quinn swivelled to send his shot past Welch, City are fortunate not to be three down before Seal's super 25-yard chip settles their nerves. Thereafter City enjoy the greater share of the possession, but can't force a winner.											
2	H	STOCKPORT			W	1-0	1-0	Seal 29	Welch	Hansen	Shail	McLeary	Dryden	Kuhl	Bent	**Armstrong**	Seal	Agostino^	Barber*	Plummer/Partridge
	26/8		7,331		4				*Edwards*	*Connelly*	*Todd*	*Bennett*	*Flynn*	*Gannon*	*Beaumont*	*Ware*	*Helliwell**	*Armstrong*	*Williams^*	*Mike/Eckhard*
								Ref: A D'Urso	This game won't go down as one of the best, but the match-winning strike surely must. Collecting the ball out on the left, Seal strides a couple of spaces before letting fly with a 30-yard right-footed drive which curled and dipped beyond the dive of Neil Edwards and into the top corner.											
3	A	SHREWSBURY		16	L	**1-4**	1-0	Agostino 21 *[Rowbotham 88]*	Welch	Hansen	Shail*	McLeary	Dryden	Kuhl	Bent	Armstrong	Seal	Agostino	Barber^	Bryant/Plummer
	29/8		*2,558*	*18*	4			*Reed 47, Spink 55, Dempsey 57,*	*Clarke*	*Scott*	*Reed*	*Taylor*	*Withe*	*Stewart*	*Berkley*	*Rowbotham*	*Spink*	*Walton*	*Dempsey*	
								Ref: U Rennie	Gay Meadow is anything but a happy place for City as they suffer one of their most humiliating defeats in recent years. After Agostino had swept in Bent's low centre City dominated the first half, but Ian Reed's shot through a crowded penalty area sparks a second-half collapse.											
4	A	PETERBOROUGH		16	D	1-1	0-1	Seal 63	Welch^	Bryant	Munro	McLeary*	Dryden	Kuhl	Bent	Armstrong	Seal	Agostino	Fowler"	Shail/**Kite**/Partridge
	2/9		*4,621*	*19*	5			*Farrell 3*	*Sheffield*	*Williams*	*Rioch*	*Ebdon*	*Breen*	*Heald*	*Le Bihan"*	*Manuel*	*Power**	*Farrell*	*Morrison^*	*M'dale/Carter/McG'sh*
								Ref: M Riley	With Welch being taken to hospital with a back injury in the 81st minute, it is fortunate that Jordan had opted for a keeper on the bench for only the second time this season. Seal conjures up a drive of immense power for City's deserved point following Sean Farrell's angled opener.											
5	H	BRIGHTON		22	L	0-1	0-1		Kite	Bryant	Munro	Shail	Dryden	Kuhl	Bent	Armstrong*	Seal	Agostino"	Fowler^	Owers/Plum'r/P'tridge
	9/9		7,585	*14*	5			*Berry 8*	*Rust*	*Myall**	*Chapman*	*Wilkins*	*Foster*	*McCarthy*	*Storer*	*McDougald*	*Bull"*	*Minton*	*Berry^*	*Smith/Byrne/Andrews*
								Ref: G Singh	'You won't see better football than that in this Division' is the opinion of Brighton boss Liam Brady after watching his side tear City apart. Only one goal, Greg Berry drilling the ball past the unprotected Kite, but it should have been more as City's midfield offered little resistance.											
6	H	BRENTFORD		22	D	0-0	0-0		Kite	Hansen	Edwards	Shail	Bryant	Kuhl	Bent^	Owers	Seal	Agostino*	Armstrong	Partridge/Plummer
	12/9		5,054	*17*	6				*Dearden*	*Statham*	*Grainger*	*McGhee*	*Bates*	*Ashby*	*Mundee*	*Smith*	*Forster*	*Hooker*	*Taylor**	*Asaba*
								Ref: A Wiley	City show more commitment than on Saturday, but the nearest to a goal is early on. Bent must be kicking himself for being caught offside when Armstrong and Seal set him up for an easy tap-in, whilst for Brentford, Nicky Forster put his 35th-minute free header against a post.											
7	A	BRADFORD C		22	L	0-3	0-1		Kite	Hansen	Edwards	Dryden	Bryant	Kuhl	Bent	Owers*	Seal	Starbuck	Armstrong	Agostino
	16/9		*5,165*	*4*	6			*Showler 37, Shutt 62, 66*	*Ward*	*Huxford*	*Jacobs*	*Mitchell*	*Mohan*	*Ford*	*Wright*	*Youlds**	*Ormondroyd*	*Shutt*	*Showler*	*Murray*
								Ref: T Heibron	Woeful City are left in tatters with a display bereft of confidence, imagination, as well as simple ability. Bradford, unfortunate perhaps when Tommy Wright's earlier effort is disallowed for offside, take a lucky lead when Kite allows Paul Showler's shot to spin out of his grasp.											
8	A	NOTTS CO		22	D	2-2	0-0	Agostino 57, Seal 85	**Dykstra**	Hansen	Edwards	Dryden	Bryant	Kuhl	Plummer*	Owers	Baird^	Agostino	Starbuck	Bent/Seal
	23/9		*5,251*	*4*	7			*Legg 49, White 55*	*Ward*	*Gallagher*	*Walker*	*Nichol*	*Strodder*	*Murphy*	*Simpson*	*Galloway**	*White*	*Atkins*	*Legg^*	*Short/Agana*
								Ref: P Taylor	Appealing for offside when Andy Legg runs through, City's defence fails again when Devon White fires in from a narrow angle. Fortunately the Aussies save the day, Seal stabbing in a loose ball to secure a point, after Agostino had earlier held off two challenges to shoot into the net.											
9	H	WYCOMBE		22	D	0-0	0-0		Dykstra	Paterson	Hansen	Bryant	Dryden	Edwards	Owers*	Kuhl	Bent	**Nugent**	Starbuck	Seal
	30/9		5,564	*11*	8				*Hyde*	*Rowbotham*	*Hardyman*	*Howard*	*Cousins*	*Patterson*	*Carroll*	*Brown*	*De Souza*	*Williams**	*Farrell*	*McGavin*
								Ref: J Brandwood	Only Paul Hyde's super save from Bent's volley in the closing seconds denies City the win that their improved play after the break deserved. With Paterson operating as a sweeper, City look solid at the back, and the presence of Nugent adds much needed aggression to the attack.											
10	A	SWINDON		23	L	0-2	0-1		Dykstra	Starbuck	Edwards	Dryden	Bryant	Kuhl	Bent	Owers	Nugent	Paterson*	Barnard	Agostino
	7/10		***12,378***	*1*	8			*O'Sullivan 12, Allison 88*	*Digby*	*Culverhouse*	*Bodin*	*McMahon*	*Seagraves*	*Taylor*	*Robinson*	*O'Sullivan*	*Finney*	*Allison*	*Horlock*	
								Ref: R Gifford	Dykstra makes amends for conceding a 32nd pen when his trailing leg tripped Mark Robinson after winning the ball. He saves Paul Bodin's spot-kick with his legs, but is unable to do anything about either of the close-in shots that put Swindon four points clear at the top of the table.											
11	H	HULL		21	W	**4-0**	1-0	Bent 25, 61, Starbuck 58, Barnard 80	Dykstra	Starbuck*	Edwards	Dryden	Bryant	Kuhl^	Bent	Owers	Nugent	Paterson	Barnard	Agostino/Tinnion
	14/10		5,354	*24*	11				*Wilson*	*Watson*	*Lawford*	*Hobson**	*Humphries*	*Abbott*	*Peacock"*	*Williams*	*Brown^*	*Windass*	*Mann*	*Lee/Fewings/Lowth'pe*
								Ref: P Rejer	The fans chant 'sign him on' as Starbuck ends his month's loan from Sheffield Utd. He nets with a perfectly-angled drive from Bent's pass to put City two up after Hull had threatened in the first half with Linton Brown failing in front an of open goal, as well as being denied by a post.											

No / Date	H/A	Opponent	Att	Pos	Res / Pts	F-A	H-T	Scorers, Times, Referees	1	2	3	4	5	6	7	8	9	10	11	Subs
12	A	YORK		19	W	1-0	1-0	Nugent 24	Dykstra	Paterson !	Edwards	Dryden	Bryant	Kuhl	Bent	Owers	Nugent	Barnard	**Carey***	Shail
21/10			*3,367*	*18*	14				*Warrington*	*McMillan*	*Hall*	*Jordan**	*Tutill*	*Barras*	*Matthews^*	*Williams*	*Barnes*	*Peverall*	*Murty*	*Bushell/Baker*
								Ref: D Allison	Skipper Gary Owers inspires City's victory at Bootham Crescent as York go down to their third defeat in four games since their epic League triumph over Man Utd. Nugent chests down a long through-ball to shoot into one corner of the goal as Andy Warrington dived the other way.											
13	H	WALSALL		21	L	0-2	0-2		Dykstra	Paterson*	Edwards	Dryden	Bryant	Kuhl	Bent	Owers	Nugent	Barnard	Carey^	Agostino/Shail
28/10			6,475	*16*	14			*Houghton 8, Wilson 33*	*Walker*	*Evans^*	*Rogers*	*Viveash*	*Marsh*	*Palmer**	*O'Connor*	*Bradley"*	*Lightbourne*	*Wilson*	*Houghton*	*Watkiss/Ntam'k/B'tter*
								Ref: B Knight	City have the chances, but both Agostino and Owers are denied by the woodwork as their mini-revival comes to an end. Caught on the break when Scott Houghton's low shot finds the back of the net, City succumb again as Kevin Wilson's cracking shot takes a deflection past Dykstra.											
14	H	CHESTERFIELD		18	W	2-1	1-1	Barnard 15, Morris 53 (og)	Dykstra	Paterson	Edwards	Dryden	Bryant	Kuhl	Bent	Owers	Nugent	Barnard	Agostino*	Seal
31/10			**4,408**	*8*	17			*Robinson 6*	*Mercer*	*Rogers*	*Dyche*	*Curtis*	*Williams*	*Law*	*Robinson*	*Davies*	*Roberts**	*Morris^*	*Howard"*	*Hazel/Lormor/Perkins*
								Ref: D Orr	Phil Robinson's unstoppable volley is followed by Barnard's great left-footed shot from a 30-yard free-kick, before Billy Mercer hands the points to City. He completely misses the ball as Andy Morris's sliced skywards clearance bounces down and rebounds into the roof of the net.											
15	A	OXFORD		19	L	0-2	0-0		Dykstra	McLeary^	Shail	Dryden	Bryant	Kuhl	Bent	Owers	Nugent	Barnard	Agostino*	Tinnion/Seal
4/11			*5,665*	*12*	17			*Angel 83, Murphy 90*	*Whitehead*	*Robinson**	*Ford M*	*Smith*	*Elliott*	*Gilchrist*	*Rush^*	*Massey*	*Moody*	*Ford B*	*Angel*	*Beauchamp/Murphy*
								Ref: I Hemley	A calamitous error by Shail ends City's brave resistance. He has plenty of time to deal with Mark Angel's drive that comes back off a post, but pushes the ball straight back to the No 11, who fires in an unstoppable shot. Matt Murphy finishes off City from a narrow angle in injury-time.											
16	H	CARLISLE		20	D	1-1	0-0	Nugent 56	Welch	Carey	Edwards	Dryden	Shail	Kuhl	Bent^	Owers	Nugent	Barnard	Partridge*	Agostino/Plummer
18/11			5,423	*21*	18			*Currie 48*	*Caig*	*Edmondson*	*Gallimore*	*Thorpe*	*Bennett*	*Hayward*	*Prokas*	*Currie*	*Reeves*	*Aspinall**	*Murray*	*Thomas*
								Ref: M Pierce	After ten successive games with a sweeper, City lack the killer touch to take advantage of the greater attacking options that a switch to a flat back four produces. Nugent equalises David Currie's free-kick opener from 30 yards, with a shot that deflects in off Darren Edmondson.											
17	A	ROTHERHAM		18	W	3-2	1-1	Barnard 26, Owers 64, Seal 65	Welch	Carey	Edwards	Bryant	Shail*	Kuhl	Bent	Owers	Nugent	Barnard	Seal^	Dryden/Partridge
25/11			*2,649*	*19*	21			*Goater 20, 84*	*Muggleton*	*Smith*	*Hurst*	*Garner*	*Monington*	*Blades*	*Berry*	*McGlashan*	*Jeffrey*	*Goater*	*Roscoe*	
								Ref: I Cruikshanks	An all-action match that climaxes with Owers' handball gifting Rotherham an 86th-min penalty. Shaun Goater, though, misses his hat-trick as he lifts the rebound over the top after Welch had beaten out his spot-kick. A well-deserved win for City who top the shooting stakes 15-10.											
18	A	CREWE		19	L	2-4	1-0	Nugent 30, Dryden 75 *[Carey 90 (og)]*	Welch	Carey	Edwards	Dryden	Shail	Kuhl	Bent	Owers	Nugent	Barnard	Tinnion	
5/12			*2,977*	*2*	21			*Adebola 60, Booty 61, Lennon 85,*	*Gayle*	*Collins*	*Booty*	*Westwood^*	*Macauley*	*Savage**	*Rivers*	*Murphy*	*Adebola*	*Lennon*	*Edwards*	*Unsworth/Smith*
								Ref: P Richard	A cruel end to a hugely entertaining game after Nugent had slid in City's opener to threaten Crewe's unbeaten home record. In the dying secs Carey turns a cross into his own net shortly after Neil Lennon had fired Crewe into the lead with his drive from just inside the penalty area.											
19	H	NOTTS CO		20	L	0-2	0-1		Welch	Carey	Edwards	Dryden	Shail"	Kuhl	Bent	Owers	Nugent	Barnard^	Seal*	Agost'o/Tin'/McLeary
9/12			5,617	*2*	21			*Strodder 9, White 89*	*Ward*	*Mills*	*Baraclough*	*Turner*	*Strodder*	*Murphy*	*Gallagher^*	*Simpson*	*Devlin*	*Arkins*	*Legg**	*Agana/White*
								Ref: R Gifford	After Gary Strodder gets to Andy Legg's long throw before Welch to head in County's opener, City dominate, but fail to turn their midfield control into goals. The wags in the crowd display their displeasure by holding up every number from 1 to 11 when substitutions are made.											
20	A	WYCOMBE		18	D	1-1	0-1	Tinnion 70	Welch	Carey	Hewlett	McLeary	Bryant	Kuhl	Bent*	Owers	Nugent	Barnard	Tinnion	Agostino
16/12			*4,020*	*9*	22			*Blissett 13*	*Roberts*	*Rowbotham*	*Bell*	*Howard*	*Evans*	*Cousins*	*Carroll*	*Garner**	*De Souza*	*Blissett*	*Farrell*	*McGavin*
								Ref: P Taylor	Instead of collapsing after Dave Farrell's centre is turned in by Gary Blissett, City take a grip on the game which tightens as the match progresses. Tinnion earns a point with one of his best-ever goals – a great 30-yard drive over the outstretched fingers of keeper Ben Roberts.											
21	A	BURNLEY		17	D	0-0	0-0		Welch	Carey	Hewlett	McLeary	Bryant*	Kuhl	Agostino^	Owers	Nugent	Barnard	Tinnion	Paterson/Seal
23/12			*9,327*	*5*	23				*Beresford*	*Brass*	*Vinnicombe**	*Hoyland*	*Winstanley*	*Harrison^*	*Weller*	*Joyce*	*Cooke"*	*Nogan*	*Eyres*	*Adams/McMinn/Swan*
								Ref: K Lynch	Gary Owers has City's best chance just before half-time, but his stumble over Marlon Beresford's outstretched leg allows time for Jamie Hoyland to run back and block his eventual shot. City's stylish display is let down by the fact that they can only muster one shot on target.											
22	H	SWANSEA		17	W	1-0	0-0	Kuhl 90	Welch	Carey	Hewlett^	McLeary	Paterson	Kuhl	Agostino*	Owers	Nugent	Barnard	Tinnion	Seal/Plummer
26/12			6,845	*22*	26				*Freestone*	*Jones*	*Clode*	*Walker*	*Edwards*	*Penney^*	*Hurst**	*Ampadu*	*Torpey*	*Cornforth*	*B'well-E'boro*	*Pascoe/Chapple*
								Ref: J Rushton	After close on a dozen games of flattering to deceive, City at last turn their possession into points, even if it does take until the third minute of injury-time. Kuhl seizes on a half clearance from Tinnion's centre, to squeeze a left-foot shot past Roger Freestone from twelve yards.											
23	A	BOURNEMOUTH		16	D	1-1	1-0	Maskell 39	Welch	Carey	Edwards	McLeary	Paterson	Kuhl	Maskell	Hewlett	Nugent	Barnard*	Tinnion	Bent
6/1			*3,667*	*12*	27			*Morris 52*	*Andrews*	*Young*	*Beardsmore*	*Morris*	*Murray**	*Ndah*	*Holland*	*Robinson*	*Jones^*	*Bailey*	*Brissett*	*Mean/Santos*
								Ref: I Hemley	City are robbed ten minutes from time as the officials fail to note that a header from Edwards was over the line before the ball was cleared. After Tinnion's low centre sets up Maskell for an easy tap-in, Mark Morris is unchallenged when rising high to firmly head past Welch.											

No	Date		Att	Pos	Pt	F-A	H-T	Scorers, Times, and Referees	1	2	3	4	5	6	7	8	9	10	11	subs used
24	H	CREWE		16	W	3-2	2-1	Paterson 4, Nugent 25, 67	Welch	Carey	Edwards	McLeary	Paterson	Kuhl	Maskell	Hewlett	Nugent	Bent	Tinnion	
	13/1		6,790	2	30			*Booty 18, Westwood 59*	*Gayle*	*Collins*	*Booty*	*Westwood*	*Barr*	*Whalley*	*Rivers*	*Murphy^*	*Adebola*	*Lennon*	*Edwards**	*Garvey/Unsworth*
								Ref: M Fletcher	This hugely entertaining encounter is settled entirely against the run of play by Nugent, who buries a superb left-foot shot in the corner of Mark Gayle's net. City's win is entirely down to their resilience as skilful Crewe dominated the play with their measured passing football.											
25	H	BRISTOL ROV		16	L	0-2	0-0		Welch	Carey	Edwards^	McLeary	Paterson	Kuhl	Maskell"	Hewlett*	Nugent	Owers	Tinnion	Bent/B'nard/ Agostino
	16/1		**20,007**	13	30			*Beadle 73, 75*	*Parkin*	*Channing*	*Gurney*	*Browning*	*Clark*	*Tillson*	*Armstrong*	*Miller*	*Stewart*	*Matthew*	*Beadle*	
								Ref: G Singh	Fiasco at the Gate with many thousands, including season ticket holders, locked out. Despite the mayhem, three gates trampled down and fans standing in the aisles, the kick-off is only delayed 15 mins. Peter Beadle's tap-in and superb angled-drive secures a deserved win for Rovers.											
26	A	BLACKPOOL		16	L	0-3	0-1		Welch	Carey	Edwards	McLeary	Paterson	Kuhl	Maskell^	Hewlett*	Nugent !	Owers	Tinnion	Bent/Agostino
	20/1		*4,838*	3	30			*Morrison 34, Ellis 56, Preece 73p*	*Banks*	*Bryan*	*Brown*	*Linighan*	*Mellon*	*Quinn**	*Lydiate*	*Bonner^*	*Morrison*	*Ellis*	*Preece*	*Watson/Gouck*
								Ref: T West	Jordan was unrepentant after his on-pitch protest to the referee following Nugent's 20th-minute sending off for supposedly elbowing Phil Brown in the face. City are often exposed by Mark Bonner, and his cross to Tony Ellis sees the striker up-ended by McLeary for Pool's pen.											
27	A	WREXHAM		17	D	0-0	0-0		Welch	Carey	Edwards	Barnard	Paterson	Kuhl	Maskell*	Hewlett	Nugent	Owers	Tinnion	Agostino
	23/1		*2,673*	10	31				*Marriott*	*Brace*	*Hardy*	*Phillips^*	*Jones B*	*McGregor*	*Skinner*	*Russell**	*Connolly*	*Watkin*	*Hughes*	*Owen/Morris*
								Ref: A Wiley	In sub-zero temperatures at the Racecourse Ground, Paterson is a rock at the heart of City's defence as they weather Wrexham's early storm. After the break City have the best of things, but Owers fires wide from the edge of the box and Agostino screws a twelve-yard effort wide.											
28	H	BOURNEMOUTH		17	W	3-0	2-0	Seal 13, Tinnion 21, Agostino 57	Welch	Carey^	Barnard	McLeary	Bryant	Kuhl	Bent*	Hewlett	Seal	Agostino	Tinnion	Plummer/Hansen
	10/2		6,217	12	34				*Andrews*	*Oldbury**	*Beardsmore*	*Morris*	*Casper*	*Bailey*	*Holland*	*Mean^*	*Jones*	*Robinson*	*Brissett*	*Victory/Santos"/R'son*
								Ref: K Leach	With rival boardroom factions battling for control and City losing £9K per week, at least the thrilling action in this match brings back the smiles. Sandwiched between Seal's stunning volley and Agostino's shot into an open net, Tinnion's head is the unlikely source of City's second.											
29	H	SHREWSBURY		15	W	2-0	0-0	Agostino 70, 89	Welch	Carey	Barnard	McLeary	Bryant	Kuhl	Bent	Hewlett	Seal	Agostino	Tinnion	
	13/2		5,269	10	37				*Edwards*	*Seabury*	*Boden*	*Taylor*	*Whiston*	*Scott*	*Dempsey*	*Stevens*	*Anthrobus*	*Walton*	*Berkley**	*Woods*
								Ref: B Knight	After passing a fitness test on his injured leg an hour before the kick-off, Bent is City's star as he sends in a stream of crosses. Agostino gets on the end of a deep centre to the far post to head City in front, before finding it necessary to use his head again to put away a high spinning ball.											
30	A	BRENTFORD		15	D	2-2	0-1	Agostino 48, Barnard 56	Welch	Carey	Barnard	McLeary	Bryant	Kuhl	Bent*	Hewlett	Seal	Agostino	Tinnion	Owers
	17/2		*5,213*	19	38			*McGhee 35, Taylor 67*	*Dearden*	*Harvey*	*Anderson*	*Hutchings*	*Bates*	*McGhee*	*Canham**	*Smith*	*Forster*	*Bent^*	*Taylor*	*Martin/Omigie*
								Ref: F Stretton	Champagne football from City, but failure to kill off the opposition makes the bubbles go flat. Despite 17 goal attempts City have to be content with Agostino equalising David McGhee's headed opener by side-footing in a rebound, and Barnard curling a 20-yard free-kick into the net.											
31	H	PETERBOROUGH		16	L	0-1	0-0		Welch	Carey	Barnard	McLeary	Bryant	Kuhl	Bent*	Hewlett^	Seal	Agostino"	Tinnion	Plum'r/Owers/Nugent
	20/2		5,014	17	38			*Charlery 55*	*Sheffield*	*Basham*	*Clark*	*Sedgemore*	*Foran*	*Heald*	*Martindale*	*Ebdon*	*Farrell*	*Charlery*	*Carter*	
								Ref: J Brandwood	The errors that made the first half of the season so disappointing return to haunt City as they gift the Posh all three points. Bent and Seal both miss good chances, before Bryant dithers on the ball to allow Ken Charlery to nip in and fire an angled shot into the far corner of the net.											
32	H	BRADFORD C		13	W	2-1	1-0	Seal 20, Kuhl 79	Welch	Carey*	Barnard	McLeary	Bryant	Kuhl	Hewlett	Owers	Tinnion	Agostino	Seal^	Bent/Nugent
	24/2		5,400	11	41			*Wright 64*	*Ward*	*Liburd*	*Brightwell*	*Mohan*	*Kernaghan*	*Mitchell*	*Wright*	*Duxbury*	*Showler**	*Stallard^*	*Murray"*	*O'royd/Jewell/Shutt*
								Ref: P Rejer	Kuhl's powerful header in finishing off Barnard's cross settles this fiercely-contested encounter. A cruel result for Bradford, who were on top throughout most of the match and deservedly levelled Seal's hard-driven opener, when Tommy Wright's lob found the back of the net.											
33	A	BRIGHTON		11	W	2-0	1-0	Kuhl 37, 49	Welch	Owers	Barnard	McLeary	Bryant	Kuhl	Bent	Hewlett	Seal^	Agostino	Tinnion	Nugent
	27/2		*4,739*	23	44				*Rust*	*Myall*	*Chapman*	*Parris*	*Johnson*	*McCarthy*	*Mundee**	*Byrne^*	*Minton*	*Storer*	*McDonald*	*McDougald/Fox*
								Ref: A D'Urso	Kuhl misses out on a hat-trick, but he isn't displeased as previous visits to the Goldstone in his Pompey days twice brought the misery of red cards. His hooked shot from the edge of the box puts City in front, then he is perfectly placed to drill home a loose ball to make sure of victory.											
34	A	SWANSEA		11	L	1-2	0-2	Walker 46 (og)	Welch	Owers	Barnard	McLeary	Bryant	Kuhl	Bent*	Hewlett	Seal	Agostino	Tinnion	Nugent
	2/3		*4,109*	21	44			*Chapple 9, Molby 28*	*Freestone*	*Clode*	*Cook*	*Molby*	*Edwards**	*Ampadu^*	*Hodge"*	*Chapple*	*Torpey*	*Comforth*	*Penney*	*Walker/Coates/Th'mas*
								Ref: G Pooley	Jan Molby, Swansea's player-boss, bestrides this game with a performance that exudes authority, poise and elegance. After Shaun Chapple's stunning 25-yard opener, Molby doubles the Swans' advantage with a free-kick that smashes into the back of the net before Welch can move.											

No	Venue / Date	Opponent	Att	Pos	Pts	F-A	H-T	Scorers, Times, and Referees	1	2	3	4	5	6	7	8	9	10	11	subs used
35	H	BURNLEY		11	L	0-1	0-0		Welch	Owers	Barnard	McLeary	Bryant	Kuhl	Bent^	Hewlett	Seal	Agostino*	Tinnion	Nugent/Fowler
	9/3		6,612	*15*	44			*Nogan 83*	*Beresford*	*Parkinson*	*Vinnicombe*	*Harrison**	*Winstanley*	*Thompson*	*Weller*	*Joyce*	*Smith^*	*Nogan*	*Eyres*	*Hoyland/Robinson*
								Ref: S Bennett	City waste their chances, Seal rattling a post, and then having his 74th-minute spot-kick saved, but Agostino's failure from two yards is by far the worst. He wants the ground to open up as he misses the ball completely with his attempt at an extravagant back-heel just after the interval.											
36	A	BRISTOL ROV		11	W	4-2	2-1	Nugent 9, Hewlett 45, Agostino 60,	Welch	Owers	Barnard	McLeary	Bryant	Kuhl	Bent*	Hewlett	Nugent	Agostino^	Tinnion	Fowler/Seal
	16/3		*8,622*	*7*	47			*Gurney 29, Clarke 86* [Seal 85]	*Collett*	*Gurney*	*Morgan*	*Browning*	*Clark*	*Tillson*	*Sterling*	*Miller*	*Stewart*	*Channing**	*Beadle*	*French*
								Ref: J Rushton	In one of the most entertaining of derbies, City's textbook away performance brings their first League win at Twerton. Hewlett's right-foot shot is deflected past the helpless Andy Collett to change the course of the game, but the pick of the goals is Agostino's stylish header.											
37	A	STOCKPORT		11	D	0-0	0-0		Welch	Owers	Barnard	McLeary	Bryant	Kuhl	Bent*	Hewlett	Nugent	Agostino	Tinnion	Fowler
	13/3		*3,713*	*8*	48				*Edwards*	*Connelly*	*Todd*	*Marsden*	*Flynn*	*Bound*	*Durkan*	*Ware*	*Mutch*	*Armstrong*	*Jeffers*	
								Ref: J Kirkby	At Edgeley Park, City dent Stockport's play-off ambitions with a gutsy display. After Barnard brings a super save out of Neil Edwards, City have lady luck on their side when the lively Alun Armstrong crashes Stockport's best chance against a post a few minutes before half-time.											
38	H	WREXHAM		11	W	3-1	1-0	Nugent 18, 84, Tinnion 62	Welch	Owers	Barnard	McLeary"	Bryant	Kuhl	Bent*	Hewlett	Nugent	Agostino^	Tinnion	Fowler/Seal/Carey
	23/3		6,141	*9*	51			*Connolly 66*	*Marriott*	*McGregor*	*Hardy^*	*Phillips**	*Humes !*	*Jones B*	*Chalk*	*Russell*	*Connolly*	*Jones L*	*Ward*	*Watkin/Hunter*
								Ref: G Barber	With the new board installed, Nugent slips in City's opener after Karl Connolly had been denied by a goal-line clearance nine minutes earlier. Following Connolly's diving header, Nugent's angled shot ties up the points, just prior to Tony Humes' dismissal for his second booking.											
39	H	SWINDON		12	D	0-0	0-0		Welch	Owers	Barnard	McLeary	Bryant	Kuhl	Bent*	Hewlett	Nugent	Agostino	Tinnion	Seal
	30/3		11,370	*2*	52				*Talia*	*Culverhouse*	*Bodin*	*Leitch*	*Allen*	*Taylor*	*Robinson*	*O'Sullivan*	*Thorne*	*Allison*	*Horlock*	
								Ref: I Hemley	City's professional performance that thwarts Swindon suggests that they now have what it takes to be a Second Division force next season. It's all City for the final 20 mins and it takes Paul Bodin's clearance to prevent Seal's lob finding the back of the net shortly before the call of time.											
40	A	HULL		11	W	3-2	0-0	Hewlett 56, Agostino 67, Seal 81	Welch	Owers	Barnard	McLeary	Bryant	Kuhl	Fowler	Hewlett	Nugent	Agostino*	Tinnion	Seal
	2/4		***2,641***	*24*	55			*Gordon 72, Mann 82*	*Carroll*	*Humphries^*	*Graham*	*Wilkinson*	*Allison*	*Quigley*	*Peacock*	*Wharton**	*Fewings*	*Mann*	*Williams*	*Gordon/Lawford*
								Ref: R Poulain	A deserved victory as Seal replaces his compatriot Agostino to lob in City's third goal 13 minutes later. Agostino powers in City's second, after setting up Hewlett to shoot in the opener, but substitute Gavin Gordon tucks away his first senior goal to bring Hull back into the game.											
41	A	WALSALL		12	L	1-2	1-1	Seal 33	Welch	Owers	Carey	McLeary	Bryant	Kuhl	Fowler*	Hewlett	Nugent	Seal^	Tinnion	Bent/Agostino
	6/4		*4,142*	*13*	55			*Nugent 2 (og), Bradley 90*	*Walker*	*Ntamark**	*Daniel*	*Viveash*	*Evans*	*Mountfield*	*Keister*	*Bradley*	*Lightbourne !*	*Wilson*	*Houghton*	*Marsh*
								Ref: A Leake	Nugent's despair as the ball cannons off him into City's net is matched by Tinnion 20 mins later when his spot-kick crashes against the legs of the diving James Walker. Kyle Lightbourne receives his marching orders for time wasting, shortly after Bradley heads in the Sadlers' winner.											
42	H	YORK		12	D	1-1	0-0	Kuhl 56p	Welch	Owers	Barnard	McLeary	Bryant*	Kuhl	Bent^	Hewlett	Seal"	Agostino	Tinnion	Pat'son/Plum'r/B'clay
	8/4		7,512	*19*	56			*Bull 90*	*Kiely*	*McMillan*	*Atkinson*	*Pepper*	*Sharples*	*Barras*	*Murty**	*Jordan*	*Naylor*	*Bull*	*Stephenson^*	*Bushell/Peverall*
								Ref: M Fletcher	Kuhl ends City's penalty jinx as, at their fourth attempt this season, he buries their first successful kick. He celebrates with a marathon run dance of delight, but York snatch a point at the death. City's defence dithers and Gary Bull swivels to crash the ball into the roof of the net.											
43	A	CHESTERFIELD		11	D	1-1	1-0	Owers 19	Welch	Owers	Barnard	McLeary	Paterson	Kuhl	Fowler*	Hewlett	Nugent	Agostino^	Tinnion	Bent/Seal
	13/4		*4,619*	*6*	57			*McDougald 60*	*Beasley*	*Hewitt*	*Dyche*	*Curtis*	*Williams*	*Law*	*Hazel*	*McDougald*	*Lormor*	*Holland*	*Jules*	
								Ref: D Orr	Impressive in the first half when Owers finishes off an interchange of passes with Nugent to hammer an angled shot into the bottom corner of the net, City are shaken by Chesterfield's resurgence after the break. Kuhl twice kicks off the line before Junior McDougald shoots past Welch.											
44	H	OXFORD		13	L	0-2	0-0		Welch	Owers	Barnard	McLeary	Paterson	Kuhl	Bent	Hewlett	Nugent	Agostino^	Fowler*	Plummer/Barclay
	20/4		7,674	*3*	57			*Rush 56, Moody 73*	*Whitehead*	*Robinson*	*Ford M*	*Smith*	*Elliott*	*Gilchrist*	*Rush*	*Gray*	*Moody*	*Beauchamp*	*Massey*	
								Ref: P Rejer	Dennis Smith's Oxford notch up their fourth-successive League win over City. McLeary's error in losing possession turns the game as David Rush pounces to slide in a low-angled shot. Then Paul Moody makes sure of the points with a left-foot volley from Joey Beauchamp's cross.											
45	H	ROTHERHAM		13	W	4-3	1-1	Partridge 15, Agostino 47, 49, Kuhl 79	Welch	Carey	Barnard	Paterson	Bryant	Kuhl	Partridge	Hewlett	Nugent	Agostino	Tinnion	
	27/4		6,101	*15*	60			*Jemson 14, Berry 68, McGlashan 88*	*Clarke*	*Smith*	*Hurst*	*McGlashan*	*Breckin*	*Moore*	*Jemson*	*Bowyer*	*Heyward*	*Goater*	*Roscoe**	*Berry*
								Ref: M Pierce	A thrilling home finale in which Agostino takes the eye with his two goals in City's narrow, but deserved win. He holds off three challengers before slipping in a left-foot shot past Matt Clarke, then follows this with a 25-yard drive which squeezes into the bottom corner of the net.											
46	A	CARLISLE		13	L	1-2	1-2	Robinson 22 (og)	Welch	Carey*	Barnard	Paterson	McLeary	Kuhl	Owers	Hewlett	Nugent	Agostino	Tinnion^	Partridge/Edwards
	4/5		*5,925*	*20*	60			*Conway 10, Hayward 28p*	*Caig*	*Edmondson*	*Robinson*	*Delap*	*Bennett*	*Hayward*	*Thomas*	*Currie**	*Reeves*	*Conway*	*Thorpe*	*McAlindon*
	Home		Away					Ref: S Mathieson	Caught ball-watching as Paul Conway volleys in from six yards, City equalise when Jamie Robinson deflects Paul Agostino's low cross into the net. McLeary's felling of Rod Thomas in the area proves conclusive as City, apart from Owers firing against the crossbar, offer little else.											
Average	7,017		4,908																	

Coca-Cola Cup					F-A	H-T	Scorers, Times, and Referees	1	2	3	4	5	6	7	8	9	10	11	subs used
1:1	A	COLCHESTER		L	1-2	1-2	Seal 2	Welch	Hansen	Munro*	Dryden	McLeary	Kuhl	Barber	Bent	Agostino	Seal	Partridge^	Shail/Fowler
15/8			*2,831*				*Adcock 15, Kinsella 16*	*Emberson*	*Locke*	*Betts*	*McCarthy*	*Caesar*	*Cawley*	*Kinsella*	*English*	*Whitton*	*Adcock*	*Cheetham*	
							Ref: P Taylor	Ever the fall guys, City are Colchester's first victims in the League Cup for twelve years. After Seal's half-volley opener after just 132 secs, Tony Adcock's 20-yard strike, and Munro's deflection of Mark Kinsella's shot leaves City the need to redeem themselves in the second leg.											
1:2	H	COLCHESTER		W	2-1	1-0	Seal 28, 81	Welch	Hansen^	Shail	McLeary	Dryden	Kuhl	Bent	Fowler	Seal	Agostino"	Barber*	Plum'r/Bryant/P'tridge
22/8			3,468		*aet*		*Cheetham 61*	*Emberson*	*Locke*	*Betts*	*McCarthy*	*Caesar*	*Cawley*	*Kinsella*	*English*	*Whitton*	*Adcock**	*Cheetham^*	*Fry/Reinelt*
							Ref: G Barber (City won on penalties 5-3)	A standing ovation for gallant Colchester as they succumb in the penalty shoot-out. Despite a history in such deciders that didn't offer any hope, Kuhl, Dryden, Bent, Bryant and Seal give City a full house, whilst full-back Simon Betts blasts Colchester's third against the crossbar.											
2:1	H	NEWCASTLE	22	L	0-5	0-3	*[Gillespie 46, Lee 85]*	Kite	Hansen	Edwards	Dryden	Bryant	Kuhl	Bent	Plummer*	Seal	Agostino	Munro	Hewlett
19/9			15,952 *P:1*				*Peacock 8, Sellars 22, Ferdinand 31,*	*Hislop**	*Barton^*	*Elliott*	*Fox*	*Peacock*	*Howey*	*Lee*	*Gillespie"*	*Ferdinand*	*Ginola*	*Sellars*	*Srnicek/Hottig'r/W'son*
							Ref: K Burge	After Darren Peacock heads in the Magpies' opener from Scott Sellars' corner, magnificent Newcastle hardly need to break sweat in this easy win. So outclassed are City that even the referee shows compassion as he allows Kite to escape with a booking after handling outside the box.											
2:2	A	NEWCASTLE	22	L	1-3	1-0	Agostino 14	Kite	Hansen	Edwards	Dryden	Bryant	Paterson	Owers	Kuhl	Bent	Seal*	Agostino^	Partridge/Plummer
4/10			*36,357 P:1*				*Barton 48, Albert 55, Ferdinand 65*	*Hislop*	*Hottiger*	*Albert*	*Clark*	*Peacock*	*Watson*	*Barton*	*Brayson^*	*Ferdinand*	*Gillespie*	*Sellars**	*Holland/Crawford*
							Ref: J Kirkby (City lost 1-8 on aggregate)	City rediscover their pride and passion to deservedly lead at the break, courtesy of Agostino's header from Bent's cross. After the interval Newcastle take control and Warren Barton's half-volley – together with headers from Philippe Albert and Les Ferdinand – clinch their success.											

FA Cup																			
1	A	BOURNEMOUTH	19	D	0-0	0-0		Welch	Paterson	Edwards	Dryden	Shail	Kuhl	Bent*	Owers	Nugent	Barnard	Carey	Partridge
11/11			*5,304 11*					*Moss*	*Young*	*Beardsmore*	*Morris*	*Murray*	*Pennock*	*Holland*	*Bailey**	*Jones*	*Fletcher*	*Brissett*	*Robinson*
							Ref: G Barber	The last time Welch left a football field he was flat on his back on a stretcher – this time it should have been shoulder high. In a traditional early-round tie with more puff than poise, Welch's save from Steve Jones' 80th-minute volley to keep City in the Cup was on another plane.											
1R	H	BOURNEMOUTH	20	L	0-1	0-1		Welch	Carey	Edwards	Bryant	Shail	Kuhl	Bent	Owers*	Nugent	Barnard	Seal	Tinnion
21/11			5,069 *10*				*Robinson 5*	*Moss*	*Young*	*Beardsmore*	*Morris*	*Murray*	*Pennock*	*Bailey*	*Robinson*	*Jones*	*Fletcher*	*Brissett**	*Mean*
							Ref: G Barber	A cruel defeat for City who dominate this thrilling replay with 30 goal attempts (eleven on target). Poor finishing, outstanding saves, and sheer bad luck thwart City's attempts to redress Steve Robinson's header as Bournemouth equal a club record of seven successive clean sheets.											

		Home					Away					
	P	W	D	L	F	A	W	D	L	F	A	Pts
1 Swindon	46	12	10	1	37	16	13	7	3	34	18	92
2 Oxford	46	17	4	2	52	14	7	7	9	24	25	83
3 Blackpool	46	14	5	4	41	20	9	8	6	26	20	82
4 Notts Co	46	14	6	3	42	21	7	9	7	21	18	78
5 Crewe	46	13	3	7	40	24	9	4	10	37	36	73
6 Bradford C *	46	15	4	4	41	25	7	3	13	30	44	73
7 Chesterfield	46	14	6	3	39	21	6	6	11	17	30	72
8 Wrexham	46	12	6	5	51	27	6	10	7	25	28	70
9 Stockport	46	8	9	6	30	20	11	4	8	31	27	70
10 Bristol Rov	46	12	4	7	29	28	8	6	9	28	32	70
11 Walsall	46	12	7	4	38	20	7	5	11	22	25	69
12 Wycombe	46	9	8	6	36	26	6	7	10	27	33	60
13 BRISTOL CITY	46	10	6	7	28	22	5	9	9	27	38	60
14 Bournemouth	46	12	5	6	33	25	4	5	14	18	45	58
15 Brentford	46	12	6	5	24	15	3	7	13	19	34	58
16 Rotherham	46	11	7	5	31	20	3	7	13	23	42	56
17 Burnley	46	9	8	6	35	28	5	5	13	21	40	55
18 Shrewsbury	46	7	8	8	32	29	6	6	11	26	41	53
19 Peterborough	46	9	6	8	40	27	4	7	12	19	39	52
20 York	46	8	6	9	28	29	5	7	11	30	44	52
21 Carlisle	46	11	6	6	35	20	1	7	15	22	52	49
22 Swansea	46	8	8	7	27	29	3	6	14	16	50	47
23 Brighton	46	6	7	10	25	31	4	3	16	21	38	40
24 Hull	46	4	8	11	26	37	1	8	14	10	41	31
	1104	259	153	140	840	574	140	153	259	574	840	1503

* promoted after play-offs

Odds & ends

Double wins: (2) Hull, Rotherham.
Double losses: (2) Walsall, Oxford.

Won from behind: (3) Chesterfield (h), Rotherham (a), Rotherham (h).
Lost from in front: (2) Shrewsbury (a), Crewe (a).

High spots: Beating Hull 4-0 at Ashton Gate on 14 October.
Beating Bristol Rov 4-2 at Twerton Park on 16 March.
Winning the penalty shoot-out to beat Colchester in the League Cup.
A brilliant FA Cup replay against Bournemouth at Ashton Gate even though City lose 0-1.

Low spots: A humiliating 1-4 defeat at Gay Meadow on 29 August.
Cancellation of this season's Gloucestershire Cup.

Player of the year: Martin Kuhl.
Ever-presents: (1) Martin Kuhl.
Hat-tricks: (0).
Leading scorer: David Seal (13).

	Appearances						Goals			
	Lge	*Sub*	LC	*Sub*	FAC	*Sub*	**Lge**	LC	FAC	**Tot**
Agostino, Paul	**29**	*11*	4				**10**	1		**11**
Armstrong, Gordon	**6**									
Baird, Ian	**1**									
Barber, Phil	**3**		2							
Barnard, Darren	**33**	*1*			2		**4**			**4**
Barclay, Dominic		*2*								
Bent, Junior	**33**	*7*	4		2		**2**			**2**
Bryant, Matt	**31**	*1*	2	*1*	1					
Carey, Louis	**23**	*1*			2					
Dryden, Richard	**17**	*1*	4		1		**1**			**1**
Dykstra, Sieb	**8**									
Edwards, Rob	**18**	*1*	2		2					
Fowler, Jason	**6**	*4*	1	*1*						
Hansen, Vergard	**7**	*1*	4							
Hewlett, Matt	**27**			*1*			**2**			**2**
Kite, Phil	**3**	*1*	2							
Kuhl, Martin	**46**		4		2		**6**			**6**
McLeary, Alan	**30**	*1*	2							
Maskell, Craig	**5**						**1**			**1**
Munro Stuart	**3**		2							
Nugent, Kevin	**29**	*5*			2		**8**			**8**
Owers, Gary	**34**	*3*	1		2		**2**			**2**
Partridge, Scott	**3**	*6*	1	*2*		*1*	**1**			**1**
Paterson, Scott	**16**	*2*	1		1		**1**			**1**
Plummer, Dwayne	**1**	*10*	1	*2*						
Seal, David	**19**	*11*	4		1		**10**	3		**13**
Shail, Mark	**9**	*3*	1	*1*	2					
Starbuck, Phil	**5**						**1**			**1**
Tinnion, Brian	**28**	*3*				*1*	**3**			**3**
Welch, Keith	**35**		2		2					
(own-goals)							**3**			**3**
30 players used	**508**	***75***	**44**	***8***	**22**	***2***	**55**	**4**		**59**

NATIONWIDE LEAGUE DIVISION 2 — Manager: Jordan ⇨ John Ward — SEASON 1996-97

No	Date		Att	Pos	Pt	F-A	H-T	Scorers, Times, and Referees	1	2	3	4	5	6	7	8	9	10	11	subs used
1	A	GILLINGHAM			L	2-3	0-1	Goater 58, Bent 79	Naylor	Owers	Barnard	McLeary	Edwards	Kuhl	Bent^	Hewlett	Nugent*	Goater	Tinnion	Agostino/Partridge
	17/8		7,212		0			Fortune-West 13, Harris 81, Piper 90	Stannard	Humphrey	Ford	Hessenthaler	Harris	Bryant	Chapman*	Ratcliffe	Fortune-West	Butler"	Onuora^	Puttnam/Bailey/Piper
								Ref: A Butler	Sub Lenny Piper breaks City hearts in the second minute of injury-time when he blasts in the Gills' winner from Denis Bailey's cross. A cruel blow for City whose superiority after the break was confirmed by Goater's low, hard shot past Jim Stannard, and Bent's close-range prod.											
2	H	BLACKPOOL			L	0-1	0-1		Welch	Owers	Barnard	Cundy	Shail	Kuhl	Bent^	Hewlett*	Agostino"	Goater	Tinnion	Carey/Partridge/Nugent
	24/8		9,417		0			Ellis 21	Banks	Bryan	Barlow	Butler	Linighan !	Brabin	Bonner	Mellon !	Quinn^	Ellis"	Philpott*	Dixon/Thorpe/Preece
								Ref: D Orr	With second bookable offences depriving Blackpool of the services of Dave Linighan just after half-time and Micky Mellon seven minutes before the end, it is a mystery how City lost. Despite 17 efforts on goal and a corner count of 13, City cannot level Tony Ellis' low drive.											
3	H	LUTON		15	W	5-0	2-0	Goodridge 11, 51, Nugent 41, Goater 46, [Cundy 63]	Welch	Owers	Barnard	Cundy	Shail	Kuhl	Goodridge^	Carey	Nugent	Goater*	Tinnion	Seal/Partridge
	27/8		7,028	24	3				Feuer	James	Thomas	Waddock	Davis	Patterson	Showler*	Hughes	Oldfield"	Grant^	Thorpe !	Alexander/Fotiadis/Guentchev
								Ref: S Bennett	A five-star debut for Greg Goodridge, who has Luton in constant disarray with his speed down the flanks, and accurate crossing, as well as twice getting on the scoresheet. His left-footed rocket shot from the edge of the box is followed by a right-footed effort from fully 15 yards.											
4	A	BURY		18	L	0-4	0-1		Welch	Owers	Barnard	Cundy	Shail	Kuhl	Goodridge*	Carey	Nugent	Goater	Tinnion	Agostino
	31/8		4,160	3	3			Johnson 35, Carter 48, Jackson 50, [Johnrose 87]	Kiely	West	Reid	Daws	Butler	Jackson	Hughes	Johnson	Matthews*	Johnrose	Carter	Rigby^/Stant
								Ref: K Lynch	After this humiliating defeat a City fan contacted the radio phone-in to complain that he was unable to get out of the ground 30 minutes before time. He had to stay and suffer with the rest as Lennie Johnrose ties up Bury's easy success by heading in Michael Jackson's knock-back.											
5	H	PRESTON		12	W	2-1	1-0	Nugent 17, 79	Naylor	Owers	Barnard	Cundy	Edwards	Kuhl	Goodridge^	Carey	Nugent	Agostino*	Tinnion	Seal/Hewlett
	7/9		8,016	19	6			Kilbane 46	Mimms	Kay	Barrick	McDonald"	Wilcox*	Moyes	Davey	Ashcroft	Saville	Wilkinson	Kilbane^	Kidd/Bryson/Atkinson
								Ref: K Leach	City are the only team in it during the first half, but ride their luck later. Kevin Kilbane's 20-yard drive in off a post brings Preston level, but Nugent kills them off. He adds to his opening close-range shot with another easy effort after Bobby Mimms had clawed out Seal's effort.											
6	A	SHREWSBURY		16	L	0-1	0-0		Naylor	Owers	Edwards*	Cundy	Taylor	Kuhl	Barnard	Carey	Nugent^	Goater	Tinnion	Goodridge/Agostino
	10/9		2,502	7	6			Stevens 76	Gall	Seabury	Nielsen	Spink	Taylor L*	Taylor M	Scott	Stevens	Anthrobus	Evans	Berkley	Rowbotham
								Ref: P Taylor	Is he kidding or not? After another miserable away performance, Shrewsbury boss Fred Davies voices his opinion that City could prove to be the team to catch this season! Punchless City are punished for their profligacy by Ian Stevens who scores with a fierce shot from twelve yards.											
7	A	ROTHERHAM		15	D	2-2	0-0	Owers 65, 80	Naylor	Owers	Barnard	Cundy	Taylor	Hewlett	Goodridge	Carey	Nugent*	Goater	Tinnion	Agostino
	14/9		2,546	24	7			Berry 48, Richardson 56p	Cherry	Smith	Hurst	Garner	Richardson	Breckin	Berry*	Bowyer	Monington	Hayward	Roscoe	McGlashan
								Ref: D Laws	With chairman Davidson voicing his concern over City's performances, things looked black for Jordan when Neil Richardson's penalty, after Naylor brings down Mark Monington, puts Rotherham two up. Owers saves the day with a magnificent 25-yarder, followed by an easy header.											
8	H	WALSALL		13	W	4-1	2-1	Goater 30, 44, Hewlett 73, Goodridge 90	Naylor	Owers	Barnard	Edwards	Taylor	Hewlett	Goodridge	Carey*	Agostino^	Goater	Tinnion	Kuhl/Nugent
	21/9		7,412	22	10			Lightbourne 16	Walker	Ntamark	Viveash	Watson	Marsh	Mountfield	Blake	Bradley	Lightbourne	Wilson	Butler	
								R Harris	'That's for you' Goater tells under-pressure Jordan after leading the goal charge to bury woeful Walsall. After Kyle Lightbourne shoots in with his 20-yard free-kick, Goater settles the nerves with a first-time shot from an Owers cross, and then puts City ahead with an angled drive.											
9	A	BURNLEY		10	W	3-2	1-1	Goater 12, 62, Taylor 79	Naylor	Owers	Barnard	Edwards	Taylor	Hewlett	Goodridge*	Carey	Agostino^	Goater	Tinnion	Kuhl/Nugent
	28/9		9,587	11	13			Gleghorn 44, Weller 55	Beresford	Parkinson*	Vinnicombe	Brass	Winstanley	Hoyland	Weller	Smith	Nogan	Barnes	Gleghorn	Cooke
								M Bailey	A thrill a minute game in which Burnley miss their chances – Weller incredibly hitting the bar from just two yards, and Paul Smith having a goal disallowed. Goater is City's goalscoring hero, an angled drive in off the far post, and a crisp header into the top corner of Burnley's net.											
10	H	BRENTFORD		10	L	1-2	1-1	Goodridge 38	Naylor	Owers	Barnard	Edwards	Taylor	Hewlett	Goodridge	Carey*	Agostino^	Goater	Tinnion	Kuhl/Nugent
	1/10		9,520	1	13			Asaba 12, Edwards 72 (og)	Dearden	Hurdle	Anderson	Ashby	McGhee	Hutchings	Asaba*	Smith	Forster	Abrahams^	Taylor	Harvey/Bent
								Ref: A Wiley	Edwards not only blatantly chops down the rampaging Nick Forster as he surges goalwards, but then succeeds in slicing the same player's header from the resultant free-kick into his own net. Brentford's speed and creativity on the break often expose City's poor defending.											
11	A	CHESTERFIELD		13	D	1-1	0-1	Owers 90	Naylor	Owers	Barnard	Edwards	Taylor	Hewlett	Kuhl*	Carey	Agostino^	Goater	Tinnion	Goodridge/Nugent
	5/10		4,438	4	14			Lormor 21	Leaning	Hewitt	Rogers	Curtis	Law	Dyche	Beaumont	Gaughan^	Lormor	Howard*	Jules	Perkins/Holland
								Ref: E Wolstenholme	Furious Chesterfield players protest that Owers had re-enacted Maradona's hand of God con trick when notching City's injury-time lifesaver. Owers insists it was his head, whilst Nugent claims the goal for himself as he says his header was over the line before Owers followed up.											

No	Date	Venue	Opponent	Att	Pos	Pts	Res	F-A	H-T	Scorers, Times, and Referees	1	2	3	4	5	6	7	8	9	10	11	subs used
12		H	YORK		9		W	2-0	1-0	Nugent 3, Goodridge 47	Naylor	Owers	Barnard	Edwards	Taylor	Hewlett	Goodridge^	**Carey***	Nugent	Goater	Tinnion !	Kuhl/Agostino
	11/10			9,308	_20_	17					_Clarke_	_McMillan_	_Atkinson_	_Pepper*_	_Tutill !_	_Barras_	_Murty_	_Randall^_	_Tolson_	_Bull_	_Stephenson_	_Bushell/Pouton_
										Ref: B Knight	After Goodridge crosses for Nugent to touch home from close range in City's first attack, the chances go begging until City's winger runs 60 yards before shooting past Tim Clarke. Sending offs for Tinnion (retaliation) on 53 mins and Steve Tutill (second booking) during injury-time.											
13		H	WYCOMBE		8		W	3-0	1-0	Agostino 18, Barnard 59, Tinnion 75	Naylor	Owers	Barnard	Edwards	Taylor	Hewlett	Goodridge	Carey	Agostino	Goater	Tinnion	
	15/10			**7,325**	_22_	20					_Parkin !_	_Cousins_	_Bell_	_McCarthy_	_Evans_	_Patterson_	_Carroll_	_Brown_	_Farrell*_	_Williams^_	_McGavin_	_De Souza/Crossley_
										Ref: D Pugh	After Agostino's opening header, City cruise to victory over a poor Wycombe side handicapped by Brian Parkin's 72nd-minute sending off for handling the ball outside the area – Tinnion punishing Parkin's aberration by sending the resultant free-kick past stand-in keeper Stan Brown.											
14		A	PLYMOUTH		9		D	0-0	0-0		Naylor	Owers	Barnard	Edwards	Taylor	Hewlett^	Goodridge*	Carey	Agostino	Goater"	Tinnion	Kuhl/McLeary/Seal
	19/10			_9,645_	_14_	21					_Grobbelaar_	_Billy_	_Williams_	_Mauge_	_Heathcote_	_James_	_Simpson_	_Curran_	_Corazzin*_	_Evans_	_Barlow_	_Illman_
										Ref: P Richards	A third-successive clean sheet for City after this uninspiring West Country clash. Bruce Grobbelaar supplies the entertainment in the Argyle goal, catching balls behind his back and sometimes controlling the ball on his chest. Agostino comes closest for City with a diving header.											
15		H	NOTTS CO		9		W	4-0	4-0	Goater 7, 23, 45, Agostino 17	Naylor	Owers	Barnard	Edwards	Taylor	Hewlett"	Goodridge	Carey	Agostino*	Goater^	Kuhl	Nugent/Seal/Plummer
	26/10			9,540	_22_	24					_Ward_	_Wilder_	_Baraclough_	_Derry_	_Murphy_	_Hogg_	_Gallagher_	_Hunt_	_Battersby*_	_Jones_	_Kennedy_	_Agana_
										Ref: A Bates	In contrast to Goodridge's extravagant somersaults in goal celebration, Goater comes up with a less athletic compromise of taking a camera and snapping his team-mates. After registering with two headers, Goater claims his hat-trick with a firm drive into the back of County's net.											
16		A	BOURNEMOUTH		5		W	2-0	0-0	Barnard 79p, Agostino 82	Naylor	Owers	Barnard	Edwards	Taylor	Kuhl*	Goodridge	Carey	Agostino"	Goater	Brennan^	McLeary/ Partridge/Seal
	29/10			_4,197_	_21_	27					_Marshall_	_Young_	_Beardsmore_	_Coll^_	_Cox_	_Bailey_	_Holland_	_Robinson_	_Fletcher_	_Watson*_	_Dean_	_Brissett/Omoyimni_
										Ref: M Pierce	Barnard keeps his own record intact as City's unbeaten run stretches to six games, and five successive clean sheets. He has never missed from the spot in professional soccer and it is his penalty, after Goater was fouled by Owen Coll, which finally breaks Bournemouth's resistance.											
17		A	STOCKPORT		7		D	1-1	1-0	Blackmore 43	Naylor	Owers	Barnard	Edwards	Taylor	**Blackmore**	Goodridge	Carey	Agostino	Goater*	Brennan^	Seal/Partridge
	2/11			_6,654_	_10_	28				_Bennett 83_	_Jones_	_Connelly_	_Todd_	_Bennett_	_Flynn_	_Dinning_	_Durkan^_	_Marsden_	_Angell_	_Cavaco*_	_Jeffers_	_Mutch/Searle_
										Ref: T Jones	Clayton Blackmore (on loan from Middlesbrough) is City's goal hero, though he admits that Agostino's cross goes in off his shoulder. Defending stoutly after the break, City are caught out as Tom Bennett taps in an easy chance to maintain Stockport's run of late goals.											
18		H	MILLWALL		9		D	1-1	0-0	Barnard 82	Naylor	Owers	Barnard	Edwards	Taylor*	Blackmore	Goodridge^	Carey	Agostino	Goater"	Tinnion	Paterson/Partridge/Seal
	9/11			12,517	_1_	29				_Crawford 77_	_Carter_	_Newman_	_Harle_	_Savage_	_Witter_	_Fitzgerald*_	_Bowry_	_Neill_	_Crawford_	_Dair_	_Hartley_	_Lavin_
										Ref: S Baines	Barnard produces a contender for goal of the season with his floated 20-yard free-kick that earns City a point from this gripping tussle with the leaders. With 14 shots overall compared to Millwall's nine, City possibly deserved more than to equalise Steve Crawford's driven-in opener.											
19		H	PETERBOROUGH		8		W	2-0	1-0	Goater 35, Goodridge 87	Naylor	Owers	Barnard	Edwards	Taylor	Kuhl*	Blackmore	Carey	Agostino^	Goater	Tinnion	Goodridge/Nugent
	23/11			12,312	_21_	32					_Sheffield_	_Boothroyd_	_Clark_	_Ebdon*_	_Heald_	_Bodley_	_O'Connor_	_Payne_	_Carruthers_	_Charlery_	_Houghton^_	_Willis/Rowe_
										Ref: T Lunt	City play well below their best, but eventually win through with a display of persistence and hard work. Goater holds off two defenders as he races through the middle to send the ball over the advancing keeper, then Blackmore sets up Goodridge to clinically fire in an angled shot.											
20		A	NOTTS CO		11		L	0-2	0-0		Naylor	Owers	Barnard	Edwards*	Paterson	Kuhl	Goodridge^	Carey	Agostino"	Nugent	Tinnion	Shail/Hewlett/Seal
	30/11			_4,693_	_22_	32				_Arkins 65, Robinson 75_	_Ward_	_Wilder_	_Baraclough_	_Hogg_	_Strodder_	_Derry_	_Kennedy*_	_Robinson_	_Arkins_	_Jones_	_Finnan_	_Agana_
										Ref: M Fletcher	Despite County's lowly position, City rarely look like extending their unbeaten run to ten games. Unlucky perhaps when Vince Arkins' close-range shot is adjudged to have crossed the line, City are exposed when Phil Robinson bursts through their defence to round Naylor and tap in.											
21		H	WATFORD		11		D	1-1	0-0	Barnard 71p	Naylor	Owers	Barnard	Blackmore	Paterson	Hewlett	Goodridge	Carey	Agostino*	Nugent	Tinnion	Seal
	3/12			9,097	_8_	33				_Noel-Williams 56_	_Miller_	_Gibbs_	_Robinson_	_Palmer_	_Millen_	_Page_	_Bazeley_	_Slater*_	_Noel-Will'ms^_	_Penrice_	_Mooney_	_White/Andrews_
										Ref: G Cain	For all City's crisp, sharp and speedy football, they have to be satisfied with a draw gained by Barnard's penalty, after Gary Penrice brings down Hewlett. A poor reward for their attacking display which produces 22 shots (twelve on target) compared to Watford's ten (three).											
22		H	BRISTOL ROV		10		D	1-1	1-0	Agostino 16	Naylor	Owers	Barnard	Edwards !	Taylor	Hewlett	Goodridge*	Blackmore	Agostino^	Nugent	Tinnion	Carey/Goater
	15/12			**18,642**	_13_	34				_Beadle 90_	_Collett_	_Pritchard_	_Martin_	_Browning_	_Clark"_	_Tillson_	_Holloway_	_Hayfield^_	_Harris_	_Lockwood*_	_Beadle_	_Archer/Cureton/Skinner_
										Ref: D Orr	Violence mars this game on Sky TV as some so-called fans are unable to take victory being snatched from ten-man City's grasp by Peter Beadle's tap-in. City should have had the game well won by then, but squander their chances to add to Agostino's brilliant right-footed strike.											
23		A	WREXHAM		11		L	1-2	0-1	Hewlett 79	Naylor	Owers	Barnard	Paterson	Taylor	Hewlett	Goodridge*	Carey	Agostino	Nugent^	Tinnion	Bent/Goater
	21/12			_4,618_	_5_	34				_Watkin 15p, Hughes 68_	_Marriott_	_McGregor_	_Hardy_	_Hughes_	_Humes_	_Jones B_	_Chalk_	_Owen*_	_Watkin_	_Morris_	_Ward_	_Russell_
										Ref: G Laws	A frustrating afternoon for City as controversial decisions prove costly. Hewlett is twice hard done by, as the referee awards a penalty after he wins the ball cleanly in a tackle on Bryan Hughes, then in the last seconds his point saver is disallowed for a supposed handball offence.											

No	Date		Att	Pos	Pt	F-A	H-T	Scorers, Times, and Referees	1	2	3	4	5	6	7	8	9	10	11	subs used
24	H	SHREWSBURY		9	W	3-2	1-2	Agostino 18, Barnard 57p, Owers 87	Naylor	Owers	Barnard	Edwards^	Taylor	Hewlett	Goodridge*	Carey	Agostino	Goater"	Tinnion	Bent/Kuhl/Nugent
	26/12		9,803	*14*	37			*Stevens 32, Nielsen 45*	*Edwards*	*Seabury*	*Nielsen*	*Spink*	*Taylor*	*Whiston*	*Brown*	*Stevens*	*Anthrobus*	*Evans*	*Dempsey*	
								Ref: R Styles	City rediscover their goal touch, but poor defending keeps the game on a knife-edge right until the end. It takes a fortunate penalty to get City level after Shrewsbury recover from Agostino's headed opener, then Owers clinches the points with a six-yard shot into the top corner.											
25	A	PRESTON		6	W	2-0	1-0	Agostino 17, Goater 66	Naylor	Owers	Barnard	Kuhl	Taylor	Hewlett	Bent	Carey	Agostino	Goater*	Tinnion	Nugent
	28/12		***10,905***	*16*	40				*Mimms*	*Gage**	*Barrick^*	*Davey*	*Kidd*	*Gregan*	*Ashcroft*	*McDonald*	*Reeves*	*Bennett*	*Kilbane*	*Squires/Rankine*
								Ref: T Heilbron	Pace, aggression, invention, allied to superb organisation and steely determination, prove too much for North End. Shots from Agostino and Goater earn City only their fourth win in 31 visits to Deepdale, despite Preston moving up a gear after the break when they forced 13 corners.											
26	H	BURNLEY		4	W	2-1	1-1	Bent 19, Goater 68	Naylor !	Owers	Barnard	Kuhl	Taylor	Hewlett	Bent	Carey	Agostino	Goater*	Tinnion	Paterson
	11/1		10,013	*8*	43			*Smith 36*	*Russell*	*Parkinson^*	*Vinnicombe*	*Harrison*	*Swan*	*Brass*	*Little**	*Smith*	*Cooke*	*Barnes*	*Gleghorn*	*Nogan/Weller*
								Ref: M Halsey	Despite being nonplussed when Paul Smith throws himself at the ball and sends it into the net with a quick flip of his ankle, City recover to take the points. Tinnion is not unduly troubled in goal following Naylor's 77th-minute sending off for bringing down Kurt Nogan outside the box.											
27	A	BRENTFORD		3	D	0-0	0-0		Naylor	Owers	Barnard	**Allen**	Taylor	Hewlett	Bent	Carey*	Agostino	Goater^	Tinnion	Paterson/Nugent
	18/1		*7,606*	*1*	44				*Dearden*	*Hurdle*	*Anderson*	*Ashby*	*Bates*	*McGhee*	*Asaba*	*Smith*	*Forster*	*Statham*	*Taylor*	
								Ref: S Bennett	Paul Allen, signed from Swindon until the end of the season, inspires City to a point in this titanic struggle. The ref Steve Bennett has touchline words with boss Jordan who struggles to contain his fury when City are denied a clear penalty after Bent is dragged down by Ijah Anderson.											
28	H	BOURNEMOUTH		4	L	0-1	0-1		Naylor	Owers	Barnard	Paterson	Taylor	Hewlett	Bent^	Allen	Agostino	Nugent*	Tinnion	Seal/Goodridge
	25/1		10,434	*15*	44			*Cox 42*	*Glass*	*Young*	*Vincent*	*Beardsmore*	*Cox*	*Bailey*	*Holland*	*Robinson**	*Rawlinson*	*Fletcher*	*Brissett*	*Town*
								Ref: A Leake	Shades of City's match at Newport 15 years ago, but this time it is Bournemouth who are possibly playing their last game as the receivers ponder a £4.5 million debt. Ian Cox nips in at the near post to steer in Mark Rawlinson's free-kick to give the South Coast club a deserved win.											
29	A	MILLWALL		3	W	2-0	1-0	Goater 15p, 64	Naylor	Owers	Edwards	Paterson	Taylor	Hewlett	Bent	Allen	Agostino	Goater	Tinnion	
	1/2		*9,158*	*9*	47				*Carter*	*Newman"*	*Rogan*	*Savage^*	*Witter*	*Stevens**	*Neill*	*Bowry*	*Crawford*	*Dair*	*Dolby*	*Harle/Hartley/Sadler*
								Ref: D Pugh	Goater returns to City's frontline wearing a brace to hold his teeth together, a five-stitch repair inside his mouth and swelling on one side of his face. By the end he had another whack on the other side to even things up and two goals, his penalty being followed by a great 15-yard header.											
30	H	STOCKPORT		3	D	1-1	0-1	Goater 46	Naylor	Owers	Barnard	Edwards	Taylor	Hewlett	Bent	Allen*	Agostino	Goater	Tinnion	Kuhl
	7/2		13,186	*8*	48			*Armstrong 26*	*Jones*	*Connelly*	*Todd*	*Bennett*	*Flynn*	*Gannon*	*Durkan**	*Dinning*	*Angell*	*Armstrong*	*Cavoco*	*Nash*
								Ref: A Butler	Stockport show all the qualities that have taken them into the semi-finals of the League Cup and on the fringe of the promotion zone. Alan Armstrong drills the ball into the net to give the Hatters the lead, after Sean Connelly's shot was deflected off the referee straight into his path.											
31	A	PETERBOROUGH		4	L	1-3	0-1	Barnard 83p	Naylor	Owers	Barnard	Edwards	Taylor	Hewlett	Bent	Allen	Agostino*	Goater	Carey^	Nugent/Goodridge
	15/2		*4,221*	*21*	48			*Willis 15, 86, Otto 90*	*Griemink*	*Boothroyd*	*Clark*	*Edwards*	*Heald*	*Ramage*	*Donowa*	*Payne*	*Willis*	*Charlery*	*Otto*	
								Ref: C Finch	Fortunate to get back on terms with Barnard's pen, after Andy Edwards was adjudged to have held down Nugent, City succumb to late goals. Roger Willis exploits poor defending to head in from a flag kick, then Ricky Otto breaks clear and fires a breathtaking shot into the far corner.											
32	H	CREWE		3	W	3-0	0-0	Goater 59, Agostino 86, Westw'd 89 (og)	Naylor	Owers	Barnard	Carey	Taylor	Hewlett	Bent^	Allen	Nugent*	Goater	Tinnion	Agostino/Goodridge
	22/2		11,306	*5*	51				*Kearton*	*Lightfoot*	*Unsworth*	*Westwood*	*Macauley*	*Whalley*	*Garvey*	*Savage*	*Tierney*	*Murphy*	*Barr*	
								Ref: P Taylor	Declining the chance to play for Bermuda in the Caribbean tournament, Goater sets City off on the winning trial with a first-time shot from the edge of the box. Agostino then gets in on the act by firing in the second, before unleashing the shot which Ashley Westwood deflects in.											
33	A	WATFORD		7	L	**0-3**	0-2		Naylor	Owers	Barnard	Carey	Taylor	Kuhl	Bent	Allen	Agostino	Goater	Tinnion*	Goodridge
	1/3		*8,539*	*6*	51			*Phillips 10, 25, 78*	*Miller*	*Gibbs*	*Robinson*	*Easton*	*Millen*	*Page*	*Bazeley*	*Scott**	*Phillips*	*Johnson*	*Penrice*	*Noel-Williams*
								Ref: G Frankland	Pint-sized striker Kevin Phillips' hat-trick, all shot in from close range, rips a giant hole in City's promotion bid. Lacklustre City are hurt by sloppy defending and the skilful play of Darren Bazeley on the right flank. City fail to muster a single shot on target during the second half.											
34	A	WALSALL		8	L	0-2	0-1		Naylor	Owers	Barnard	Carey	Taylor	Edwards	Bent	Allen*	Agostino	Goater^	Brennan	Kuhl/Nugent
	4/3		*4,322*	*6*	51			*Lightbourne 35, 76*	*Walker*	*Ntamark*	*Evans*	*Viveash*	*Marsh*	*Mountfield*	*Thomas*	*Keister*	*Lightbourne*	*Watson**	*Hodge*	*Ricketts*
								Ref: B Coddington	With Walsall desperately hanging onto Kyle Lightbourne's stroked in acute-angled opener, Goater shoots wide with only the keeper to beat. Unfortunately Lightbourne makes his chances count and his powerful header finishes off John Hodge's cross to ensure Walsall's success.											

No		Date	Att	Pos	Pt	F-A	H-T	Scorers, Times, and Referees	1	2	3	4	5	6	7	8	9	10	11	subs used
35	A	BRISTOL ROV		9	W	2-1	1-0	Agostino 30, Goater 72	Naylor	Owers	Barnard	Edwards*	Taylor	Hewlett	Bent	Carey	Agostino	Goater^	Brennan	Paterson/Nugent
		16/3	8,078	20	54			Alsop 80	Collett	Pritchard	Power*	Skinner^	White	Tillson	Holloway	Miller"	Cureton	Martin	Beadle	Bennett/Alsop/Hayfield
								Ref: C Wilkes	City lay on the transportation for the limited number of their supporters with tickets for the first League derby at the Memorial Ground. They see a deserved win for their favourites as Goater's angled shot puts City in control, following Naylor's save of Peter Beadle's 40th-minute pen.											
36	H	ROTHERHAM		9	L	0-2	0-0		Naylor	Owers	Barnard	Paterson	Taylor^	Hewlett*	Bent	Carey	Agostino	Goater	Brennan"	Kuhl/Goodridge/Nugent
		18/3	10,646	23	54			Garner 68, Jean 72	Pilkington	Breckin	Bain	Dillon	Bowman	Roscoe	Berry*	Garner	Hayward	McKenzie	McDougald	Jean
								Ref: A Wiley	It looks black for boss Jordan, as chairman Davidson condemns City's performance as appalling. Against the side with the worst away record, Naylor prevents an even heavier defeat, but he can do nothing about Darren Garner's 25-yard drive that crashes in off the underside of the bar.											
37	A	BLACKPOOL		10	L	0-1	0-0		Naylor	Owers	Barnard	Edwards	Kuhl !	Hewlett*	Bent	Carey	Agostino^	Goater	Brennan	Allen/Nugent
		22/3	4,518	12	54			Preece 53	Banks	Bryan	Barlow	Butler	Linighan	Clarkson	Bonner	Mellon	Quinn !	Ellis*	Preece	Bradshaw
								Ref: D Laws	Prior to Kuhl's injury-time dismissal following his second booking, City fail to make their numerical superiority count, after Jimmy Quinn's 61st-min sending off for elbowing. Naylor saves Quinn's 20th-min pen before a teasing cross allows Andy Preece to toe-poke in the only goal.											
38	A	CREWE		9	W	2-1	1-0	Bent 36, Goater 73	Naylor	Owers	Barnard	Edwards	Paterson	Kuhl	Bent	Carey	Agostino*	Nugent	Allen	Goater
		25/3	3,687	6	57			Westwood 46	Kearton	Smith S	Unsworth	Westwood	Lightfoot	Charnock*	Garvey	Savage	Anthrobus	Murphy	Tierney^	Little/Rivers
								Ref: P Reger	Following Jordan's Monday-night sacking, temporary boss Gerry Sweeney plots this win that rekindles City's promotion hopes. Upset by his omission from the starting line-up, Goater comes off the bench to score the winning goal by finishing off Barnard's cross with a firm header.											
39	H	GILLINGHAM		9	L	0-1	0-0		Welch	Owers	Barnard	Edwards	Paterson	Kuhl	Bent	Carey	Goater*	Nugent	Allen^	Agostino/Hewlett
		29/3	11,276	13	57			Onuora 74p	Stannard	Galloway	Butters	Pennock	Green	Bryant	Hessenthaler	Ratcliffe	Onuora*	Akinbiyi^	Chapman	Bailey/Butler
								Ref: A Bates	New boss John Ward gets off to a disappointing start, as resilient Gillingham take the points at Ashton Gate. Paterson's tug on Iffy Onuora inside the area, enables the No 9 to put away the decisive penalty, as City lack the invention to break down opponents with five at the back.											
40	A	LUTON		9	D	2-2	2-1	Goater 3, Agostino 40	Welch	Owers	Brennan	Shail	Paterson	Kuhl	Hewlett	Carey	Agostino*	Goater^	Allen	Bent/Nugent
		1/4	7,550	3	58			Davis 45, Thorpe 73	Feuer	McGowan*	Thomas	Waddock	Davis	Johnson	Hughes	Alexander	Oldfield"	Thorpe	Guentchev^	Marshall/McLaren/Grant
								Ref: G Singh	Despite Goater giving City the lead from his penalty rebound, and Agostino tapping in Allen's cross to double the advantage, it takes a battling rearguard action to secure a point. Headers by Steve Davis and Tony Thorpe set up a rousing finale with City hanging on for their lives.											
41	H	BURY		8	W	1-0	0-0	Barnard 66	Welch	Owers	Barnard	Shail	Paterson	Edwards	Hewlett^	Carey	Goater*	Agostino	Allen	Nugent/Brennan
		5/4	10,274	1	61				Kiely	West^	Armstrong*	Daws	Lucketti	Woodward	Butler	Randall	Johnson	Johnrose	Jepson	Scott/Carter
								Ref: M Fletcher	Barnard (he of the red boots) keeps a play-off place in sight as he registers with one of City's two shots on target. His left-foot shot into the top corner of Dean Kiely's net from 15 yards, ends Bury's five-match winning run, during which time they hadn't conceded a single goal.											
42	H	WREXHAM		7	W	2-1	1-0	Barnard 30p, Goater 88	Welch	Owers	Barnard	Shail	Paterson	Edwards	Hewlett"	Carey	Goater	Agostino^	Allen*	Plummer/Bent/Seal
		15/4	9,817	10	64			Morris 71	Marriott	McGregor	Jones P*	Phillips	Ridler	Jones B	Bennett^	Russell	Connolly	Skinner	Brammer	Cross/Morris
								Ref: S Baines	City all but end Wrexham's play-off ambitions with this nail-biting win achieved by Goater's looped header into the far corner. City escaped to victory that didn't look likely for much of the second half, when Steve Morris headed the visitors deservedly level from Karl Connolly's cross.											
43	A	YORK		6	W	3-0	1-0	Goater 5, 53, Nugent 47	Welch	Owers	Barnard	Shail	Paterson	Edwards	Hewlett	Carey	Nugent^	Goater*	Kuhl	Bent/Seal
		19/4	3,344	20	67				Warrington	McMillan	Atkinson	Bushell	Sharples	Barras	Stephenson	Tinkler	Tolson	Bull	Gilbert*	Greening
								Ref: A Leake	Sporting an all-white kit, City outclass York to move up into a play-off position. After Goater gives City an early lead with a near-post header from Barnard's centre, it takes the save of the game by Welch in the 43rd min to keep out Neil Tolson's dipping shot from the edge of the box.											
44	H	PLYMOUTH		6	W	3-1	1-1	Barnard 35, 61p, Nugent 75	Welch	Owers	Barnard	Shail	Paterson	Edwards	Hewlett	Carey	Nugent	Goater^	Kuhl*	Tinnion/Agostino
		26/4	15,368	18	70			Williams 17	Dungey	Billy	Williams	Saunders^	Heathcote	Perkins"	Rowbotham	Logan	Littlejohn*	Collins	Mauge	Illman/Clayton/Curran
								Ref: J Kirkby	Plymouth threaten to tear City apart after Paul Williams shoots in off the underside of the bar from four yards, but Barnard's cross ends up in the net for a fortunate equaliser. Barnard puts his spot-kick to the keeper's left as the picture in programme shows his Wrexham pen went right.											
45	H	CHESTERFIELD		5	W	2-0	2-0	Goater 7, Barnard 38p	Welch	Owers	Barnard	Shail	Paterson	Edwards*	Hewlett	Carey	Nugent^	Goater	Kuhl	Tinnion/Agostino
		30/4	16,195	12	73				Leaning	Perkins	Jules	Curtis	Williams	Dyche	Beaumont*	Davies	Morris	Ebdon^	Howard	Rogers/Lormor
								Ref: E Lomas	The fans celebrate as though promotion was already achieved as City clinch a play-off place. Their classy first-half display is rewarded by Goater blasting home from six yards, and Barnard sending Andy Leaning the wrong way from the spot after Sean Dyche's handball offence.											
46	A	WYCOMBE		5	L	0-2	0-2		Welch	Owers	Barnard	Shail	Paterson	Tinnion	Hewlett	Carey	Nugent	Goater*	Kuhl^	Agostino/Goodridge
		3/5	7,240	18	73			Carroll 25, McGavin 45	Parkin	Cousins !	Bell	Kavanagh	McCarthy	Forsyth	Carroll	Scott"	Stallard	McGavin*	Brown^	Read/Evans/Simpson
		Home	Away					Ref: G Cain	With boss Ward winning the Manager of the Month, this flop is disappointing and also worrying with the play-offs on the horizon. Two almost identical long-range efforts had the game well won for Wycombe, when Jason Cousins is sent off for his second booking in the 67th minute.											
Average		10,802	6,062																	

Coca-Cola Cup					F-A	H-T	Scorers, Times, and Referees	1	2	3	4	5	6	7	8	9	10	11	subs used
1:1	A	TORQUAY		D	3-3	0-1	Goater 52, Agostino 69, Partridge 83	Naylor	Owers	Barnard	McLeary	Edwards	Kuhl	Bent^	Hewlett	Nugent*	Goater	Tinnion	Agostino/Partridge
20/8		*2,824*					*Baker 43p, 46, 56*	*Newland*	*Mitchell*	*Barrow*	*McCall^*	*Gittens*	*Watson*	*Oatway*	*Nelson*	*Baker*	*Jack**	*Hancox*	*Adcock/Hawthorne*
							Ref: M Fletcher	A typical poacher's goal for Partridge after Jon Gittens loses control in the box, saves City's blushes. Naylor's challenge on Garry Nelson starts the hectic goal action as the resultant pen is the prelude to Paul Baker's powerful header, before Goater fires in City's reply from close range.											
1:2	H	TORQUAY	18	W	1-0	0-0	Barnard 69	Naylor	Owers	Barnard	Edwards	Paterson	Kuhl^	Goodridge	Carey	Nugent	Goater*	Tinnion	Agostino/Hewlett
3/9		4,513	*3:5*					*Newland*	*Winter*	*Barrow^*	*McCall*	*Gittens*	*Watson*	*Oatway*	*Baker*	*Mitchell**	*Jack*	*Hancox*	*Hathaway/Nelson*
							Ref: G Singh (City won 4-3 on aggregate)	City take a firm grip of the game and rarely look like loosing against poor Torquay. Barnard's right-footed effort that curls into the opposite corner of the net from the edge of the box decides the issue, but later Agostino is unlucky with a stunning header that crashes against the bar.											
2:1	H	BOLTON	15	D	0-0	0-0		Naylor	Owers	Barnard	McLeary	Edwards	Hewlett	Goodridge	Carey*	Agostino	Goater^	Tinnion	Kuhl/Nugent
18/9		6,351	*1:1*					*Branagan*	*McAnespie*	*Phillips*	*Frandsen*	*Taggart*	*Fairclough*	*Johansen*	*Lee**	*Blake*	*McGinlay*	*Thompson*	*Todd*
							Ref: G Pooley	City's hard-working display leaves all to play for in the second leg. With both sides content to shoot from long range, chances are few and far between, though at the death John McGinlay should perhaps have done better than shave a post with his volley from McAnespie's centre.											
2:2	A	BOLTON	13	L	1-3	0-0	Owers 57	Naylor	Owers	Barnard	Edwards	McLeary	Hewlett	Goodridge	Carey	Agostino^	Goater*	Tinnion"	Seal/Nugent/Kuhl
24/9		*6,367*	*1:1*		*aet*		*McGinlay 47, Blake 92, Thompson 107*	*Branagan*	*Bergsson*	*Phillips*	*Frandsen*	*Taggart*	*Fairclough*	*Johansen**	*Lee^*	*Blake"*	*McGinlay*	*Thompson*	*Sellars/Taylor/Todd*
							Ref: R Pearson (City lost 1-3 on aggregate)	Heartbreak at Burnden Park as Nathan Blake's prod-in and Alan Thompson's breakaway in extra-time dump City out of the League Cup. Both sides had their chances to win in normal time, which ended all square, with Owers side-footed curler countering John McGinley's 15-yard shot.											

FA Cup					F-A	H-T	Scorers, Times, and Referees	1	2	3	4	5	6	7	8	9	10	11	subs used
1	A	SWANSEA	9	D	1-1	1-0	Kuhl 45	Naylor	Owers	Barnard	Edwards	Taylor	Kuhl	Goodridge	Carey	Agostino	Goater	Tinnion	
16/11		*5,629*	*3:20*				*Torpey 71*	*Freestone*	*Brown**	*Clode*	*Moreira*	*Edwards*	*Jones*	*Jenkins*	*Penney*	*Torpey*	*Ampadu !*	*Coates^*	*O'Leary/King*
							Ref: A Wiley	A thrilling end-to-end cup-tie sees City ahead at the break thanks to Kuhl's perfectly stroked 25-yard shot into the left corner of the net, secs after Naylor had pushed a close-range shot onto the bar. Torpey earns Swansea a deserved replay with a diving header to Mark Clode's cross.											
1R	H	SWANSEA	8	W	1-0	1-0	Agostino 1	Naylor	Owers	Barnard	Edwards	Taylor*	Kuhl	Goodridge	Carey	Agostino	Goater^	Tinnion	Hewlett/Nugent
26/11		8,017	*3:14*					*Freestone*	*O'Leary*	*Clode**	*Moreira*	*Edwards*	*Jones*	*Heggs*	*Penney*	*Torpey*	*Ampadu*	*Coates*	*Thomas*
							Ref: A Wiley	Agostino strikes for City after just 17 seconds when pouncing on a loose ball 25 yards out and lifting a composed shot over Roger Freestone. Despite all the possession no further goals ensue, Goodridge ending a strong run in the second half by disappointingly shooting wide.											
2	H	ST ALBANS CITY	11	W	9-2	5-0	Goodridge 13, Agostino 22, 41, 48, 77,	Naylor	Owers	Barnard	Kuhl*	Paterson	Hewlett	Goodridge	Carey	Agostino	Nugent	Tinnion	Doherty
7/12		7,136	*IL:17*				*Clark 54, Daly 67*	*Howells*	*Mudd*	*Polston*	*Coleman^*	*Daly*	*Bashir*	*Evans*	*Cobb*	*Howell**	*Haworth"*	*Clark*	*Blackman/Risley/Martin*
							Ref: G Barber [Kuhl 25, Hewlett 42, 56, Nugent 81]	Goals galore at Ashton Gate with eleven in a match equalling that for the 1st round game against Chichester City on Guy Fawkes' day in 1960. This time, though, City allow the opposition to notch two, with Steve Clark and Jon Daly heading in at the Covered End for spirited St Albans.											
3	A	CHESTERFIELD	4	L	0-2	0-0		Naylor	Owers	Barnard !	Kuhl^	Taylor	Hewlett	Bent"	Carey	Agostino	Goater*	Tinnion	Edwards/Nugent/Goodridge
14/1		*5,193*	*7*				*Howard 69, 88*	*Mercer*	*Hewitt*	*Jules*	*Curtis*	*Williams*	*Dyche*	*Davies*	*Holland*	*Lormor*	*Howard*	*Morris*	
							Ref: E Wolstenholme	Naylor is City's hero following Barnard's 18th-min sending off for hauling down Kevin Reeves in front of goal. After Goater puts a lob over the bar as well as the stranded Billy Mercer, Naylor saves all that Chesterfield can offer, until Jon Howard stoops to head in a left-wing centre.											

Play-offs					F-A	H-T	Scorers, Times, and Referees	1	2	3	4	5	6	7	8	9	10	11	subs used
SF 1	H	BRENTFORD		L	1-2	1-2	Owers 28	Welch	Owers	Barnard	Shail	Paterson	Edwards	Hewlett*	Allen	Nugent^	Goater	Kuhl"	Tinnion/ Agostino/Carey
11/5		15,581					*Smith 14, Taylor 30*	*Dearden*	*Hurdle*	*Anderson*	*Statham*	*Bates*	*McGhee*	*Asaba*	*Smith*	*Bent*	*Hutchings*	*Taylor*	
							Ref: U Rennie	At a wet Ashton Gate, it's like turning the clock back twenty years or more as the admirable referee Uriah Rennie allows a real old-fashioned blood and thunder contest. Rob Taylor's nod of the head gives Brentford a deserved win after Owers had glanced in Bristol City's equaliser.											
SF 2	A	BRENTFORD		L	1-2	0-0	Barnard 49	Welch	Owers	Barnard	Shail*	Taylor	Edwards	Hewlett	Allen	Nugent	Goater	Tinnion^	Carey"/ Goodridge/Bent
14/5		*9,496*					*Taylor 67, Bent 78*	*Dearden*	*Hurdle*	*Anderson*	*Hutchings*	*Bates*	*McGhee*	*Dennis**	*Smith*	*Bent*	*Statham*	*Taylor*	*Canham*
							Ref: J Kirkby (City lost 2-4 on aggregate)	City spurn their chances at Griffin Park as they threaten to turn the tables. On top throughout the first half, they are rewarded shortly after the break. Barnard's 15-yard cross-shot finds the net, but Goater misses opportunities and Rob Taylor's curler punishes City for their wastefulness.											

		Home					Away					
	P	W	D	L	F	A	W	D	L	F	A	Pts
1 Bury	46	18	5	0	39	7	6	7	10	23	31	84
2 Stockport	46	15	5	3	31	14	8	8	7	28	27	82
3 Luton	46	13	7	3	38	14	8	8	7	33	31	78
4 Brentford	46	8	11	4	26	22	12	3	8	30	21	74
5 BRISTOL CITY	46	14	4	5	43	18	7	6	10	26	33	73
6 Crewe *	46	15	4	4	38	15	7	3	13	18	32	73
7 Blackpool	46	13	7	3	41	21	5	8	10	19	26	69
8 Wrexham	46	11	9	3	37	28	6	9	8	17	22	69
9 Burnley	46	14	3	6	48	27	5	8	10	23	28	68
10 Chesterfield	46	10	9	4	25	18	8	5	10	17	21	68
11 Gillingham	46	13	3	7	37	25	6	7	10	23	34	67
12 Walsall	46	12	8	3	35	21	7	2	14	19	32	67
13 Watford	46	10	8	5	24	14	6	11	6	21	24	67
14 Millwall	46	12	4	7	27	22	4	9	10	23	33	61
15 Preston	46	14	5	4	33	19	4	2	17	16	36	61
16 Bournemouth	46	8	9	6	24	20	7	6	10	19	25	60
17 Bristol Rov	46	13	4	6	34	22	2	7	14	13	28	56
18 Wycombe	46	13	4	6	31	14	2	6	15	20	42	55
19 Plymouth	46	7	11	5	19	18	5	7	11	28	40	54
20 York	46	8	6	9	27	31	5	7	11	20	37	52
21 Peterborough	46	7	7	9	38	34	4	7	12	17	39	47
22 Shrewsbury	46	8	6	9	27	32	3	7	13	22	42	46
23 Rotherham	46	4	7	12	17	29	3	7	13	22	41	35
24 Notts Co	46	4	9	10	20	25	3	5	15	13	34	35
	1104	264	155	133	759	510	133	155	264	510	759	1501

* promoted after play-offs

Odds & ends

Double wins: (4) Preston, Burnley, York, Crewe.
Double losses: (2) Gillingham, Blackpool.

Won from behind: (4) Walsall (h), Burnley (a), Shrewsbury (h), Plymouth (h).
Lost from in front: (0).

High spots: Greg Goodridge's brilliant display on his debut v Luton (h).
Winning 3-2 at Turf Moor on 28 September.
Beating Bristol Rovers 2-1 on our first visit to the Memorial Ground.
Hammering 9 goals against St Albans in the FA Cup.
Shaun Goater's 81st-minute goal against Bristol Rov at Ashton Gate on 6 August to bring City their 54th win in the Gloucestershire Cup Final.
Winning the Herefordshire Cup by beating Hereford 3-2 on 31 July.

Low spots: Losing at Wycombe on 3 May.
Losing in the semi-finals of the promotion play-offs 2-4 on aggregate against Brentford.
Succumbing 0-2 at Chesterfield in the FA Cup.

Player of the year: Shaun Taylor.
Ever-presents: (1) Gary Owers.
Hat-tricks: (2) Shaun Goater (1), Paul Agostino (1).
Leading scorer: Shaun Goater (24).

	Appearances						Goals			
	Lge	*Sub*	LC	*Sub*	FAC	*Sub*	**Lge**	LC	FAC	**Tot**
Agostino, Paul	**34**	*10*	2	*2*	4		**9**	1	5	**15**
Allen, Paul	**13**	*1*								
Barnard, Darren	**44**		4		4		**11**	1		**12**
Bent, Junior	**17**	*5*	1		1		**3**			**3**
Blackmore, Clayton	**5**						**1**			**1**
Brennan, Jim	**7**	*1*								
Carey, Louis	**40**	*2*	3		4					
Cundy, Jason	**6**						**1**			**1**
Doherty, Tommy						*1*				
Edwards, Rob	**31**		4		2	*1*				
Goater, Shaun	**39**	*3*	4		3		**23**	1		**24**
Goodridge, Greg	**19**	*9*	3		3	*1*	**6**		1	**7**
Hewlett, Matt	**33**	*3*	3	*1*	2	*1*	**2**		2	**4**
Kuhl, Martin	**22**	*9*	2	*2*	4				1	**1**
McLeary, Alan	**1**	*2*	3							
Naylor, Stuart	**35**		4		4					
Nugent, Kevin	**19**	*17*	2	*2*	1	*2*	**6**		1	**7**
Owers, Gary	**46**		4		4		**4**	1		**5**
Partridge, Scott		*6*		*1*				1		**1**
Paterson, Scott	**15**	*4*	1		1					
Plummer, Dwayne		*2*								
Seal, David		*12*		*1*						
Shail, Mark	**10**	*1*								
Taylor, Shaun	**29**				3		**1**			**1**
Tinnion, Brian	**30**	*2*	4		4		**1**			**1**
Welch, Keith	**11**									
(own-goals)							**1**			**1**
26 players used	**506**	***89***	**44**	***9***	**44**	***6***	**69**	**5**	**10**	**84**

No	Date	Venue	Opponent	Att	Pos	Pt	F-A	H-T	Scorers, Times, and Referees	1	2	3	4	5	6	7	8	9	10	11	subs used
1		A	GRIMSBY			D	1-1	1-0	Torpey 27	Welch	Carey	**Bell**	Paterson	Taylor	Edwards	Hewlett	Owers	Goater	**Torpey***	Tinnion	**Cramb^**/Barclay
	9/8			*6,479*		1			*Widdrington 74*	*Davison*	*McDermott*	*Gallimore**	*Handyside*	*Lever*	*Widdrington*	*Donovan*	*Black^*	*Livingstone*	*Nogan*	*Groves*	*Jobling/Woods*
									Ref: G Frankland	Torpey's crisp shot on the turn gets the promotion favourites off to a good start, before a clash of heads brings about the early departure of City's £400,000 signing. Town deservedly equalise when Tommy Widdrington slides the ball in after Welch parries Paul Groves' effort.											
2		H	BLACKPOOL			W	2-0	0-0	Cramb 48, Goater 87	Welch	**Locke**	Bell	Paterson	Taylor	Edwards	Hewlett	Owers	Goater	Cramb*	Tinnion^	Bent/**Tisdale**
	16/8			9,043		4				*Banks*	*Bryan**	*Bradshaw*	*Butler*	*Lydiate*	*Brabin*	*Bonner*	*Clarkson*	*Malkin*	*Philpott*	*Preece*	*Linighan*
									Ref: G Singh	City's 5-3-2 formation is a major talking point amongst the fans, but few complaints in this game as Locke and Bell convincingly go forward. Cramb's firm header from Tinnion's centre gives City the lead, before Goater's poor penalty is pushed round the post by Steve Banks.											
3		A	NORTHAMPTON		10	L	1-2	1-2	Cramb 4	Welch	Carey	Bell	Paterson"	Taylor	Edwards	Hewlett^	Owers	Goater	Cramb*	Tinnion	Torpey/Tisdale/Bent
	23/8			*6,217*	*14*	4			*Seal 23, Gayle 44*	*Woodman*	*Clarkson*	*Frain*	*Sampson*	*Warburton*	*Brightwell*	*Parrish*	*Conway**	*Seal^*	*Gayle*	*Hunter*	*Peer/Heggs*
									Ref: P Taylor	John Ward drops a howler in giving permission for on-loan David Seal to turn out for the Cobblers in this game. After Cramb hooks in from Bell's cross to put City ahead, Seal lobs in Town's leveller, and then rubs further salt in the wound with his pass for John Gayle's winner.											
4		H	WIGAN		6	W	3-0	3-0	Goater 26, 37, 39p	Welch	Carey	Bell	Paterson	Taylor	Edwards*	Hewlett	Owers	Goater"	Cramb	Tinnion^	Langan/Tisdale/Barclay
	30/8			9,255	*15*	7				*Carroll*	*Green*	*Johnson*	*Greenall*	*McGibbon*	*Martinez*	*Lee*	*Jones^*	*O'Connell"*	*Kilford*	*Lowe**	*Saville/Sharp/Warne*
									Ref: M Pierce	Goater, with his fastest hat-trick, and Bell impress as City dominate the first half. Goater heads in from Carey's cross to open his account, and then runs onto Cramb's through-ball, before completing his fifth hat-trick, when he shoots in from the spot after Owers is up-ended.											
5		H	FULHAM		10	L	**0-2**	0-1		Welch	Carey	Bell	Paterson^	Taylor	Edwards	Hewlett*	Owers	Goater	Cramb	Tinnion	Barclay/Locke
	2/9			10,293	*9*	7			*Newhouse 14, Carpenter 79*	*Walton*	*Lawrence*	*Herrera*	*Cullip*	*Smith*	*Blake*	*Newhouse^*	*Hayward*	*Moody"*	*Morgan*	*Cockerill**	*Carpenter/Scott/Brooker*
									Ref: R Harris	Out-of-sorts City are taken to task after a minute's silence in memory of Princess Diana and the Fulham Chairman's son Dodi Fayed. Shortly after Moody hits the bar, Newhouse heads in, whilst Carpenter is on hand to make the game safe when Welch is unable to hold Moody's drive.											
6		A	WREXHAM		17	L	1-2	0-1	Goater 68	Welch	Tisdale	Bell	Paterson	Taylor	Edwards"	Hewlett*	Owers	Goater	Cramb^	Tinnion	Carey/Torpey/Goodridge
	13/9			***3,181***	*16*	7			*Spink 13, Watkin 59*	*Marriott*	*McGregor*	*Hardy*	*Phillips*	*Humes**	*Carey*	*Skinner*	*Owen*	*Connelly*	*Spink^*	*Brammer*	*Jones/Watkin*
									Ref: A Bates	Another flop as Wrexham lead with an opportunist strike by Dean Spink. Welch has to be at his best to keep City in the game, but he cannot prevent Steve Watkin registering with a diving header. Goater's header gives City hope, but despite a hectic finale the equaliser doesn't come.											
7		H	BOURNEMOUTH		19	D	1-1	1-0	Goater 26	Welch	Carey	Bell	Tisdale	Taylor	Edwards	Hewlett	Owers	Goater	Torpey	Tinnion	
	20/9			**8,330**	*7*	8			*Robinson 83*	*Glass*	*Young*	*Vincent*	*Howe*	*Cox*	*Bailey*	*Beardsmore*	*Robinson*	*O'Neill^*	*Fletcher*	*Tomlinson**	*Brissett/Rawlinson*
									Ref: M Fletcher	Boss John Ward is stunned by the jeering reaction of the City fans when Steve Robinson converts Jason Brissett's pass to snatch a point for the Cherries. The critics complain that Ward's system of play is too negative as City are unable to build on Goater's early side-foot strike.											
8		H	LUTON		15	W	3-0	3-0	Bell 5p, Torpey 27, 30	Welch	Locke	Bell	**Dyche**	Taylor	Edwards	Goodridge^	Owers	Torpey	Cramb*	Tinnion	Barclay/Doherty
	27/9			8,509	*23*	11				*Davis K*	*Evers*	*Small*	*White*	*Harvey*	*McLaren*	*Waddock^*	*Davies*	*George**	*Thorpe*	*Oldfield*	*Spring/Kean*
									Ref: E Lomas	Goodridge's return brings back the smiles, though Ward still retains a 5-3-2 formation. The woodwork denies both Taylor and Edwards as well as twice thwarting Goodridge, but Bell's spot-kick, after Cramb is bundled over, and Torpey's header and shot bring a convincing success.											
9		A	GILLINGHAM		19	L	**0-2**	0-2		Welch	Locke	Bell	Dyche	Taylor	Edwards	Goodridge	Owers	Torpey	Doherty*	Tinnion	Goater
	4/10			*6,201*	*7*	11			*Akinbiyi 6, 44*	*Moss*	*Green*	*Butters*	*Smith*	*Ashby*	*Bryant**	*Hessenthaler*	*Ratcliffe*	*Butler"*	*Akinbiyi*	*Corbett^*	*Gall'way/Fort'-West/Onoura*
									Ref: A D'Urso	Welch saves City from a heavy defeat as they are well beaten by Ade Akinbiyi's close-range shot and his well-taken effort on the turn. City, for whom Goodridge fires against a post, again incur the jeers of their fans on the final whistle after being out-battled by robust opponents.											
10		A	SOUTHEND		15	W	2-0	1-0	Bell 34, Hails 56 (og)	Welch	Locke	Bell	Dyche	Taylor	Shail	Doherty^	Owers	Torpey	Cramb*	Tinnion	Goater/Plummer
	11/10			*3,218*	*21*	14				*Royce*	*Hails"*	*Jones*	*Marsh**	*Lewis*	*Perkins*	*Allen*	*Byrne^*	*Rammell*	*Dublin*	*Clarke*	*Gridelet/Coulbault/Thomson*
									Ref: D Orr	With Doherty controlling the midfield, City notch up their first away win of the campaign. After Barnard (£150,000 ex Wycombe) strikes with a brilliant 25-yard free-kick to quell United's bright start, Julian Hails ties up the points for City by slotting Locke's cross past his own keeper.											
11		H	YORK		6	W	2-1	0-1	Cramb 68, Torpey 81	Welch	Locke	Bell	Dyche	Taylor	Shail*	Doherty^	Owers	Torpey	Cramb	Tinnion	Goodridge/Edwards
	17/10			9,568	*8*	17			*Rowe 37*	*Samways*	*McMillan*	*Hall*	*Bushell*	*Reed*	*Barras*	*Murty*	*Tinkler*	*Tolson*	*Rowe*	*Stephenson*	
									Ref: M Halsey	The boo-boys make themselves heard at half-time with City fortunate to be only losing to Rowe's shot, as shortly afterwards Bushell wastes a great chance. Cramb seizes on Reed's attempted back-header to slot in the equaliser and Torpey heads in the winner as City switch to 4-4-2.											

No	Date	Venue	Opponent	Att	Pos	Res	FT	HT	Scorers, Times, and Referees	1	2	3	4	5	6	7	8	9	10	11	Subs used
12	21/10	H	PRESTON	9,039	6 / *11*	W / 20	2-1	0-0	Bell 64p, Goodridge 89	Welch	Locke	Bell	Dyche	Taylor	Edwards	Goodridge	Doherty	Torpey	Cramb	Tinnion	
									Dyche 68 (og)	*Moilanen*	*Parkinson*	*Kidd*	*Murdock*	*Moyes*	*Appleton*	*Cartwright*	*Ashcroft*	*Reeves*	*Rankine*	*Barrick*	
									Ref: R Styles												

Goodridge puts Kidd off balance with his trademark step-over before cutting inside to unleash an unstoppable shot into the top of the net and deprive Preston of a deserved point. Dyche diverts the ball into his own net to make up for City's lucky penalty for an unseen handball offence.

No	Date	Venue	Opponent	Att	Pos	Res	FT	HT	Scorers, Times, and Referees	1	2	3	4	5	6	7	8	9	10	11	Subs used
13	25/10	A	WALSALL	*4,618*	7 / *19*	D / 21	0-0	0-0		Welch	Locke	Bell	Dyche	Taylor	Edwards	Goodridge^	Doherty	Torpey	Cramb*	Tinnion	Goater/Hewlett
										Walker	*Marsh*	*Evans*	*Viveash*	*Mountfield*	*Peron*	*Platt**	*Skinner*	*Keates*	*Watson*	*Hodge*	*Ricketts*
									Ref: C Foy												

City should have won this game after controlling most of the play. Walsall's best effort comes from City's Doherty, whose header from a John Hodge cross has Welch flying to tip the ball onto the crossbar. Taylor comes closest to ending the deadlock with two powerful headers.

No	Date	Venue	Opponent	Att	Pos	Res	FT	HT	Scorers, Times, and Referees	1	2	3	4	5	6	7	8	9	10	11	Subs used
14	29/10	A	MILLWALL	*7,026*	3 / *5*	W / 24	2-0	1-0	Torpey 9, Locke 54	Welch	Locke	Bell	Dyche	Taylor	Edwards	Hewlett	Carey	Torpey	Cramb	Tinnion	
										Spink	*Brown*	*Newman*	*Bowry*	*Law*	*McLeary*	*Black*	*Shaw*	*Wilkinson*	*Grant**	*Allen^*	*Savage/Hockton*
									Ref: F Stretton												

Locke produces a stirring performance at the New Den. Not only does his cross lay on a simple header for the opening goal, but he grabs the other himself with a volley from Tinnion's centre. Hewlett's return to City's side is marred by his missing an open net with an early header.

No	Date	Venue	Opponent	Att	Pos	Res	FT	HT	Scorers, Times, and Referees	1	2	3	4	5	6	7	8	9	10	11	Subs used
15	1/11	H	OLDHAM	10,221	2 / *8*	W / 27	1-0	0-0	Bell 61p	Welch	Locke	Bell^	Dyche	Taylor	Edwards	Hewlett	Carey	Torpey	Cramb*	Tinnion	Goater/Doherty
										Pollitt	*Redmond*	*Serrant*	*Graham*	*Hodgson*	*McNiven"*	*Rush**	*Duxbury*	*McCarthy^*	*Rickers*	*Reid*	*Ritchie/Wright/Hughes*
									Ref: D Crick												

City benefit from a moment of madness by defender Doug Hodgson after withstanding Oldham's aerial bombardment. With no real danger he palms away Tinnion's corner to concede a penalty. Bell sends Mike Pollitt the wrong way to add to Ward's Manager of the Month award.

No	Date	Venue	Opponent	Att	Pos	Res	FT	HT	Scorers, Times, and Referees	1	2	3	4	5	6	7	8	9	10	11	Subs used
16	4/11	A	BRISTOL ROV	7,552	2 / *12*	W / 30	2-1	1-0	Goater 27, 49	Welch	Locke	Brennan	Dyche	Taylor	Edwards	Hewlett	Carey	Torpey	Goater*	Tinnion	Cramb
									Tillson 85	*Collett*	*Pritchard*	*Lockwood*	*Penrice*	*Gayle**	*Tillson*	*Holloway*	*French^*	*Beadle*	*Cureton*	*Hayles*	*White/Alsop*
									Ref: M Bailey												

City could hardly ever win at Twerton, but are developing a liking for the Memorial ground with a third success in as many visits. Goater collects Locke's long ball down the right to shoot in the opener, and his angled drive doubles the advantage before Tillson fires in for Rovers.

No	Date	Venue	Opponent	Att	Pos	Res	FT	HT	Scorers, Times, and Referees	1	2	3	4	5	6	7	8	9	10	11	Subs used
17	8/11	A	BRENTFORD	*6,162*	2 / *24*	W / 33	**4-1**	2-0	Torpey 31, Goater 32, 67, Doherty 77	Welch	Locke	Bell	Dyche	Taylor	Edwards*	Hewlett	Carey	Torpey	Goater	Tinnion	Doherty
									Reina 84	*Dearden*	*Hurdle*	*Anderson*	*Hutchings*	*Bates*	*Oatway*	*McGhee*	*Cockerill**	*Bent*	*Reina*	*Taylor*	*Denys*
									Ref: P Danson												

City spoil the first match for new Brentford boss Mickey Adams. A creative midfield and strong defending against long-ball tactics bring City success. After Doherty shoots in when his first effort rebounds off the keeper, poor marking allows Ricky Reina to head home for the Bees.

No	Date	Venue	Opponent	Att	Pos	Res	FT	HT	Scorers, Times, and Referees	1	2	3	4	5	6	7	8	9	10	11	Subs used
18	18/11	H	PLYMOUTH	10,867	2 / *17*	W / 36	2-1	2-0	Bell 33, 34	Welch	Locke	Bell	Goodridge^	Taylor	Carey	Hewlett	Doherty	Torpey	Goater	Tinnion*	Brennan/Langan
									Corazzin 83	*Sheffield*	*Logan*	*Williams*	*Hodges*	*Mauge*	*Wotton**	*Barlow*	*Jean^*	*Littlejohn*	*Corazzin*	*Billy*	*Saunders/Wilson*
									Ref: A Wiley												

City's one-touch passing style rips Argyle apart in the first half. Goater has an early effort ruled out for offside, while Torpey hits the post and Taylor's header is cleared off the line. Carlo Corazzin shoots in for Plymouth after Bell has secured City's points with two brilliant free-kicks.

No	Date	Venue	Opponent	Att	Pos	Res	FT	HT	Scorers, Times, and Referees	1	2	3	4	5	6	7	8	9	10	11	Subs used
19	22/11	H	WYCOMBE	11,129	2 / *16*	W / 39	3-1	1-0	Hewlett 38, 59, Torpey 67	Welch	Locke*	Bell	Goodridge	Taylor	Carey	Hewlett	Doherty	Torpey	Goater^	Brennan	Langan/Cramb
									Scott 82p	*Taylor*	*Cousins*	*Beeton*	*Ryan*	*Mohan*	*Cornforth**	*Kavanagh*	*Scott*	*Read^*	*McGavin*	*Brown*	*McCarthy/Harkin*
									Ref: K Lynch												

Hewlett replies to his critics by netting a glorious shot from just outside the box, and then notches his second when cutting in from the right to stroke the ball past the diving Martin Taylor. Brennan's handball gives the visitors their late penalty, after Torpey's header has City cruising.

No	Date	Venue	Opponent	Att	Pos	Res	FT	HT	Scorers, Times, and Referees	1	2	3	4	5	6	7	8	9	10	11	Subs used
20	25/11	A	CARLISLE	*5,044*	2 / *24*	W / 42	3-0	1-0	Goater 19, 53, Goodridge 59	Welch	Locke	Bell	Goodridge"	Taylor	Carey	Hewlett	Doherty^	Goater	Cramb	Tinnion*	Brennan/Edwards/Barclay
										Caig	*Barr*	*Boertien*	*Hoyland*	*Prokas*	*Pounewat'y*	*Harrison**	*Anthony*	*Stevens*	*Dobie*	*Wright*	*McAllindon*
									Ref: M Pike												

Goodridge rifles in the rebound as Caig's brilliant save denies Goater a hat-trick. Off-form City have Goater to thank for their eighth win in a row. From point-blank range he fires in Anthony's miscued clearance to add to his precision shot opener which had left the keeper helpless.

No	Date	Venue	Opponent	Att	Pos	Res	FT	HT	Scorers, Times, and Referees	1	2	3	4	5	6	7	8	9	10	11	Subs used
21	2/12	H	BURNLEY	11,136	2 / *22*	W / 45	3-1	0-1	Goodridge 48, 83, Bell 71p	Welch	Locke	Bell	Goodridge	Taylor	Carey	Edwards	Doherty	Goater	Cramb*	Brennan	Barclay
									Barnes 29	*Beresford*	*Brass*	*Vinnicombe^*	*Harrison*	*Blatherwick*	*Moore*	*Waddle**	*Ford*	*Howey*	*Barnes*	*Weller*	*Matthew/Cooke*
									Ref: A Bates												

Burnley surprise City early on and deserve the half-time advantage gained by a Paul Barnes' thunderous half volley. Goodridge puts on a dazzling display to turn the tide, firing in two rockets to beat Marlon Beresford, who needlessly brings down Cramb to concede Bell's penalty.

No	Date	Venue	Opponent	Att	Pos	Res	FT	HT	Scorers, Times, and Referees	1	2	3	4	5	6	7	8	9	10	11	Subs used
22	13/12	A	WATFORD	***16,072***	2 / *1*	D / 46	1-1	0-0	Goater 54	Welch	Locke	Bell	Goodridge	Taylor	Carey	Edwards	Doherty	Goater	Cramb*	Tinnion	Dyche
									Noel-Williams 84	*Chamberlain*	*Gibbs*	*Kennedy*	*Page*	*Millen*	*Palmer*	*Mooney*	*Hyde*	*Lee*	*Johnson*	*Rosenthal**	*Noel-Williams*
									Ref: B Knight												

Noel-Williams' shot takes a deflection to wrong-foot Welch and end City's bid to better their 1905-06 side, who share the League record of 14 successive wins. City take the lead when Doherty's long ball finds Cramb, whose flick on allows Goater to burst clear and shoot into the net.

No	Date	Venue	Opponent	Att	Pos	Res	FT	HT	Scorers, Times, and Referees	1	2	3	4	5	6	7	8	9	10	11	Subs used
23	20/12	H	CHESTERFIELD	11,792	2 / *8*	W / 49	1-0	1-0	Bell 13p	Welch	Locke	Bell	Goodridge^	Taylor	Carey	Edwards	Hewlett	Goater	Cramb*	Tinnion	Murray/Paterson
										Mercer	*Hewitt*	*Jules**	*Beaumont*	*Williams*	*Brackin*	*Wilkinson^*	*Holland*	*Reeves*	*Ebdon*	*Perkins*	*Curtis/Willis*
									Ref: A D'Urso												

City are lucky when Chesterfield hit the bar, but they dominate the first half after Bell's clinical penalty punishes Mark Williams for tugging at Goater's shirt. The Spireites take control after the break, but despite all their possession they rarely look capable of forcing an equaliser.

NATIONWIDE LEAGUE DIVISION 2 — Manager: John Ward — SEASON 1997-98

No	Date		Att	Pos	Pt	F-A	H-T	Scorers, Times, and Referees	1	2	3	4	5	6	7	8	9	10	11	subs used
24	H	MILLWALL		2	W	**4-1**	2-0	Cramb 10, Edwards 17, Tinnion 59,	Welch	Locke	Bell	Goodridge*	Taylor	Carey	Edwards	Doherty	Goater^	Cramb	Tinnion	Murray/Torpey
	26/12		16,128	*6*	52			*Veart 53* [Taylor 68]	*Spink*	*Brown*	*Law*	*Bowry*	*Fitzgerald*	*Savage*	*Newman*	*Neill**	*Shaw*	*Grant*	*Veart*	*Sturgess*
								Ref: R Harris	A large crowd, not deterred by the mid-day kick-off, are thrilled as Cramb finishes off Bell's near-post cross and Edwards heads in Goodridge's long throw. Tinnion's strike from a 30-yard free-kick, and Taylor's header ensure a sparkling City win after Carl Veart shoots in for the Lions.											
25	A	FULHAM		2	L	0-1	0-0		Welch	Locke^	Bell	Goodridge	Taylor	Carey	Edwards	Doherty*	Goater	Cramb	Tinnion	Murray/Torpey
	28/12		*13,275*	*6*	52			*Moody 50*	*Taylor*	*Lawrence*	*Herrera**	*Trollope*	*Coleman*	*Neilson*	*Smith^*	*Bracewell*	*Moody*	*Peschisolido*	*Hayward*	*Cullip/Carpenter*
								Ref: J Robinson	City's 15-game unbeaten League run comes to an end as money-bags Fulham complete the double. City go down fighting, but do not produce much in the way of flowing football. Goater thumps a shot against the bar shortly before Paul Moody's glancing header settles the contest.											
26	H	GRIMSBY		1	W	**4-1**	3-0	Cramb 1, 39, Taylor 5, Goater 47	Welch	Locke*	Bell	Goodridge	Taylor	Carey	Edwards	Doherty^	Goater"	Cramb	Tinnion	Murray/Hewlett/Torpey
	10/1		12,567	*6*	55			*Groves 82*	*Davison*	*McDermott*	*Gallimore*	*Rodger**	*Lever*	*Jobling*	*Donovan*	*Black*	*Livingstone*	*Clare^*	*Groves*	*Burnett/Woods*
								Ref: E Wolstenholme	Cramb's first-time shot from Goodridge's cross goes in off a post on just 17 seconds as City get off to a good start to end Grimby's 13-match unbeaten run. Taylor's bullet header and shots by Cramb and Goater overwhelm the Mariners, before Groves heads in a late response.											
27	A	WIGAN		1	W	3-0	2-0	Doherty 3, Tinnion 23, Goater 71	Welch	Murray	Bell	Goodridge*	Taylor	Carey	Edwards	Doherty	Goater	Cramb^	Tinnion	Hewlett/Torpey
	17/1		*5,078*	*16*	58				*Butler*	*Bradshaw"*	*Morgan*	*Greenall*	*McGibbon^*	*Martinez*	*Lee*	*Rogers*	*Jones*	*Fitzhenry**	*Lowe*	*Smeets/Sharp/Warne*
								Ref: D Laws	Another excellent display by City after pint-sized Doherty heads in from a corner, and Tinnion strokes the ball past Lee Butler, following an exchange of passes with Cramb. After the break, Welch is forced to make three excellent saves, before Goater shoots in from twelve yards.											
28	H	NORTHAMPTON		2	D	0-0	0-0		Welch	Murray	Bell	Goodridge	Taylor	Carey	Hewlett	Doherty	Goater	Cramb*	Tinnion	Torpey
	24/1		14,753	*5*	59				*Woodman*	*Hill*	*Frain*	*Sampson*	*Warburton*	*Brightwell*	*Hunt*	*Dozzell*	*Freestone**	*Gayle*	*Hunter*	*Gibb*
								Ref: D Hine	The scantily-clad England Monarch cheerleaders provide the only entertainment at Ashton Gate as City's new goal-celebration music doesn't get an airing. John Gayle hits the crossbar for the Cobblers, but generally City miss the chances – Hewlett failing from less than a yard.											
29	H	WREXHAM		2	D	1-1	1-0	Goater 5	Welch	Murray	Bell	Goodridge	Taylor	Carey	Edwards	Doherty*	Goater	Cramb^	Tinnion	Hewlett/Torpey
	31/1		11,741	*13*	60			*Roberts 48*	*Marriott*	*McGregor*	*Hardy*	*Phillips*	*Ridler*	*Carey*	*Spink*	*Owen*	*Connelly**	*Roberts*	*Brammer*	*Skinner*
								Ref: P Danson	Wrexham's refreshing display of attacking football gains them a deserved point. Goater's chip over Andy Marriott gets City off to a great start, but after Cramb has a shot cleared off the line play becomes more even. Neil Roberts capitalises on a rare Carey error to slot in the equaliser.											
30	A	BLACKPOOL		2	D	2-2	0-0	Hewlett 66, 77	Welch	Murray	Bell	Goodridge	Taylor	Carey	Edwards	Hewlett	Goater	Cramb*	Tinnion	Torpey
	3/2		*3,724*	*14*	61			*Preece 54, Bent 88*	*Banks*	*Bryan*	*Hills*	*Butler*	*Strong*	*Linighan*	*Bonner*	*Clarkson*	*Malkin**	*Bent*	*Preece*	*Philpott*
								Ref: G Frankland	Junior Bent, renowned for his inability to put the ball in the net whilst at Ashton Gate, breaks City's hearts with a lob that finds the back of the net. A topsy-turvy encounter sees Hewlett's header and shot give City a rather fortunate lead, after Andy Preece had fired Blackpool in front.											
31	A	BOURNEMOUTH		2	L	0-1	0-1		Welch	Murray	Bell	Goodridge*	Taylor	Carey	Edwards	Hewlett	Goater	Torpey^	Tinnion	Locke/Barclay
	7/2		*6,673*	*8*	61			*Fletcher 41*	*Glass*	*Young*	*Vincent*	*Rolling*	*Cox*	*Bailey*	*O'Neill*	*Robinson*	*Warren*	*Fletcher S*	*Brissett**	*Teather*
								Ref: P Rejer	City lose at Dean Court for the third time this season, but whilst they were unfortunate before, this time they get what they deserve. City fail to force Jimmy Glass to make a single testing save as they lose to Steve Fletcher's angled drive after Taylor blocks Christer Warren's shot.											
32	H	GILLINGHAM		2	L	**0-2**	0-0		Welch	Locke^	Bell	Goodridge	Taylor	Owers	Edwards	Hewlett	Goater	Johansen*	Tinnion	Torpey/Murray
	14/2		11,781	*9*	61			*Corbett 48, Southall 71*	*Stannard*	*Corbett*	*Pennock*	*Smith*	*Ashby*	*Butters*	*Hessenthaler*	*Southall*	*Butler"*	*Akinbiyi*	*Galloway**	*Bryant^/Ratcliffe/Onuora*
								Ref: A Hall	After a bright start, City are made to pay for their missed chances, when Iffy Onuora carves his way through to lay on Jim Corbett's opener. Taylor's passing error seals City's fate as the live-wire Onoura capitalises again. His shot rebounds off the post to set up Nicky Southall's shot.											
33	A	LUTON		2	D	0-0	0-0		Welch	Locke	Bell	Goodridge*	Taylor	Carey	Edwards	Hewlett	Goater	Johansen^	Tinnion	Murray/Cramb
	21/2		*6,978*	*21*	62				*Davis K*	*Patterson*	*Thomas*	*Evers^*	*Davis S*	*White*	*Allen C**	*McLaren*	*Oldfield*	*Gray*	*Alexander*	*Fotiadis/Marshall*
								Ref: K Leach	City remain the division's top scorers despite their recent goals scarcity. This time, against opponents with the Second Division's worst home record, they are constantly thwarted by Kelvin Davis as Luton make light of the gap between the teams to play a full part in a close encounter.											
34	A	YORK		2	W	1-0	0-0	Bell 65p	Welch	Locke	Bell	Murray	Taylor	Carey	Edwards	Hewlett*	Goater^	Torpey	Tinnion	Owers/Cramb
	24/2		3,770	*13*	65				*Samways*	*McMillan*	*Murty*	*Bushell*	*Jones*	*Barras*	*Pouton*	*Tinkler*	*Bull**	*Rowe*	*Stephenson*	*Greening*
								Ref: B Coddington	City keep up their good record at Bootham Crescent to end a spell of six games without a win. They are fortunate when Gary Bull heads over shortly before Bell cracks his spot-kick past Mark Samways, who is lucky to escape with a yellow card after bringing down Murray in the box.											

No	Date	Opponent	Att	Pos	Pt	Res	FT	HT	Scorers, Times, and Referees	1	2	3	4	5	6	7	8	9	10	11	subs used
35	H	SOUTHEND		2		W	1-0	1-0	Cramb 44	Welch	Locke	Bell	Murray	Taylor	Carey	Edwards	Doherty*	Torpey	Cramb^	Tinnion	Owers/Johansen
	28/2		12,049	*23*	68					*Royce*	*Hails*	*Dublin*	*Gridelet^*	*Jobson*	*Coleman*	*Maher*	*Jones !*	*Rammell*	*Aldridge**	*Clarke*	*Thomson/Stimson*
									Ref: R Styles	Already-booked Nathan Jones earns himself a red card for his dying swan act in attempting to win a pen when challenged by Murray. Despite a one-man advantage for two thirds of this game, City can only manage a solitary goal, when Cramb's header leaves Simon Royce motionless.											
36	H	BRENTFORD		2		D	2-2	0-1	Torpey 54, Cockerill 61 (og)	Welch	Locke	Bell	Murray	Taylor	Carey	Edwards	Doherty	Torpey	Cramb*	Tinnion	Goater
	3/3		10,398	*22*	69				*Bryan 44, Rapley 79*	*Dearden*	*Hutchings*	*Watson*	*Cullip*	*Cockerill"*	*Hogg*	*Oatway^*	*McGhee*	*Bryan**	*Aspinall*	*Taylor*	*Thompson/Rapley/Canham*
									Ref: J Brandwood	Goater wastes the chance of a 3-1 lead, as he fails to appreciate that receiving the ball from a Brentford defender negates Cramb's offside position. Carl Hutchings' long throw twelve minutes later allows Kevin Rapley to net with an overhead kick to deprive City of two points.											
37	H	BRISTOL ROV		1		W	2-0	1-0	Bell 35p, Goater 59	Welch	Locke	Bell	Murray^	Taylor	Carey	Edwards	Hewlett	Torpey*	Goater	Tinnion	Cramb/Goodridge
	14/3		17,086	*8*	72					*Collett*	*Pritchard*	*Power^*	*Penrice*	*Foster*	*Tillson*	*Holloway*	*Ramasut*	*Beadle*	*Cureton*	*Low**	*Bennett/Hayfield*
									Ref: E Lomas	An appalling first half is redeemed in the eyes of City fans as Goater wins a lucky penalty, when Dave Pritchard is judged to have nudged him in the back. Murray ties up the points when, after chasing a lost cause, he centres for Goater to shoot in his unlikely centre at the near post.											
38	A	PLYMOUTH		2		L	**0-2**	0-0		Welch	Locke	Bell	Murray	Taylor	Carey	Edwards*	Hewlett	Goater	Cramb	Tinnion^	Doherty/Barclay
	21/3		*7,622*	*19*	72				*Saunders 50, Conlon 77*	*Sheffield*	*Collins*	*Williams**	*Saunders*	*Heathcote*	*Wotton*	*Barlow*	*Starbuck*	*Conlon*	*Corazzin^*	*Billy*	*Rowbotham/Phillips*
									Ref: M Fletcher	Home Park has become a bogey ground again after City's sequence of success at this venue in the 1960s. Out-of-sorts City never look like turning the clock back, and they are outplayed as shots by Mark Saunders and Barry Conlon consign them to their eighth League defeat.											
39	A	WYCOMBE		2		W	2-1	1-0	Cramb 41, 84	Welch	Locke	Bell	Goodridge^	Taylor	Carey	Owers	Hewlett*	**McCarthy**	Cramb"	Tinnion	Doherty/Murray/**Roberts**
	28/3		*6,326*	*16*	75				*Harkin 57*	*Taylor*	*Kavanagh*	*Beeton*	*Ryan*	*Cornforth*	*Mohan*	*Carroll^*	*Scott*	*Stallard*	*McGavin**	*Brown*	*Harkin/Reed*
									Ref: R Furnandiz	A spirited performance at Adams Park after the shock sale of Goater. City's first-half display is their sharpest for weeks, as Cramb and loan signing McCarthy link up effectively. Cramb fires in a great 25-yard goal and then poaches City's winner by heading in Tinnion's cross.											
40	A	OLDHAM		1		W	2-1	0-1	Goodridge 52, Roberts 53	Welch	Locke	Brennan*	Goodridge	Taylor	Carey	Owers	Hewlett	Roberts^	Cramb"	Tinnion	Doherty/Murray/Paterson
	31/3		*4,543*	*14*	78				*Rush 23*	*Kelly*	*McNiven"*	*Holt*	*Garnett*	*Boxall*	*Rickers*	*Rush**	*Duxbury*	*Hodgson !*	*Littlejohn^*	*Reid*	*Allott/Tipton/Redmond*
									Ref: D Pugh	In front of the Sky TV cameras, City recover from Matthew Rush's superb strike to all but secure promotion. Goodridge fires in an equaliser after Hewlett's shot is blocked, then Roberts shoots home the winner with some style, before Doug Hodgson is sent off for kicking at Doherty.											
41	H	CARLISLE		1		W	1-0	0-0	Goodridge 53	Welch	Locke	Bell	Goodridge	Taylor	Carey	Owers	Hewlett	McCarthy^	Cramb*	Tinnion	Roberts/Doherty
	4/4		12,578	*23*	81					*Caig*	*Liburd**	*Prokas*	*Thorpe*	*Varty*	*Foster*	*Anthony*	*Pounewat'y*	*Stevens*	*Wright*	*Smart*	*Couzens*
									Ref: M Pierce	An inspired performance by Tony Caig in the swirling wind and torrential rain, but his one error allows City to extend their top of the table advantage to four points as Watford lose 2-3 at Wigan. He allows Goodridge's dipping shot from the edge of the box to slither under his body.											
42	A	BURNLEY		1		L	0-1	0-1		Welch	Locke	Bell	Goodridge	Taylor	Carey	Owers	Hewlett*	McCarthy^	Cramb	Tinnion	Doherty/Murray
	11/4		*10,820*	*22*	81				*Payton 7p*	*Woods*	*Weller*	*Winstanley*	*Harrison*	*Moore*	*Little"*	*Waddle^*	*Mullin*	*Cooke*	*Payton**	*Matthew*	*Vinnicombe/Hoyland/Brass*
									Ref: A Butler	With promotion assured by Grimby's failure to win yesterday, City are unable to capitalise against a committed Burnley side. Carey brings down Glen Little to concede the match-winning penalty, but Locke is unlucky when his great cross-shot in the final minutes is disallowed.											
43	H	WATFORD		1		D	1-1	0-0	Edwards 68	Welch	Locke	Bell	Goodridge"	Taylor*	Carey	Owers	Doherty^	McCarthy	Cramb	Tinnion	Edwards/Hewlett/Murray
	13/4		**19,141**	*2*	82				*Lee 64*	*Chamberlain*	*Gibbs*	*Kennedy*	*Page*	*Millen*	*Mooney*	*Bazeley*	*Hyde*	*Lee*	*Palmer*	*Hazan**	*Noel-Williams*
									Ref: A Wiley	On a pitch bearing evidence of the recent American Football game, City are unable to make home advantage tell against their championship rivals. Jason Lee taps in after Welch is unable to hold Peter Kennedy's drive, but Edwards fires home from close range to salvage a point.											
44	A	CHESTERFIELD		1		L	0-1	0-1		Welch*	Locke	Bell	Goodridge	Edwards	Carey	Owers	Doherty^	McCarthy	Cramb	Tinnion	Paterson/Murray
	18/4		*5,085*	*9*	82				*Williams 43*	*Mercer*	*Hewitt*	*Perkins*	*Curtis*	*Williams*	*Carr**	*Willis*	*Howard*	*Reeves*	*Wilkinson^*	*Beaumont*	*Breckin/Lomas*
									Ref: R Pearson	With Taylor out of action, City run into more trouble at Saltergate, as Welch is forced off early on with a groin injury. Tinnion gives an accomplished, but unorthodox, display between the sticks as City dominate territorially, and is only beaten when Mark Williams volleys in.											
45	H	WALSALL		1		W	2-1	1-1	Owers 3, Tinnion 80	Naylor	Locke	Bell	Goodridge^	Paterson	Carey	Owers	Doherty	McCarthy	Cramb*	Tinnion	Murray/Hewlett
	25/4		15,059	*19*	85				*Tholot 23*	*Walker*	*Evans*	*Marsh*	*Viveash*	*Roper*	*Thomas**	*Ricketts*	*Keister*	*Tholot*	*Porter*	*Hodge*	*Platt*
									Ref: S Mathieson	A great start as Owers heads in, but Locke is forced to clear off the line before Didlier Tholot outstrips the City defence to notch a fine leveller. Goodridge then has to follow Locke's example to keep Walsall at bay, but after the break Tinnion's free-kick brings City a hard-earned win.											
46	A	PRESTON		2		L	1-2	1-2	McCarthy 9	Naylor	Locke	Bell	Goodridge	Edwards	Carey	Owers	Doherty	McCarthy*	Cramb^	Tinnion	Murray/Hewlett
	2/5		*12,067*	*15*	85				*Ashcroft 5, Eyres 10*	*Moilanen*	*Parkinson*	*Barrick*	*McKenna*	*Jackson*	*Gregan*	*Rankine*	*Davey*	*Ashcroft*	*Macken*	*Eyres*	
	Home		Away						Ref: C Foy	With the fate of the championship in their own hands, City lack a cutting edge at Deepdale and lose out as Watford win at Fulham. After Lee Ashcroft's brilliant volley for North End, McCarthy levels by shooting into an open net, but David Eyres is at the far post to end City's hopes.											
Average	11,846		6,858																		

Coca-Cola Cup			F-A	H-T	Scorers, Times, and Referees	1	2	3	4	5	6	7	8	9	10	11	subs used
1:1 H BRISTOL ROV		D	0-0	0-0		Welch	Locke	Bell	Paterson	Taylor	Edwards	Hewlett*	Owers	Goater	Cramb^	Tinnion	Tisdale/Bent
12/8 9,341						*Collett*	*Perry*	*Foster*	*Beadle**	*Gayle*	*Tillson*	*Holloway*	*Penrice*	*Alsop*	*Cureton*	*Hayles*	*Bennett*
					Ref: G Cain	City's early superiority is matched by the Rovers after the break, as they fight out an even contest. Mickey Bell is the star performer, but City's midfield still lacks creativity. Bent's perfect cross sets up City's best chance near the end, but Goater heads tamely straight at Andy Collett.											
1:2 A BRISTOL ROV	10	W	2-1	0-0	Taylor 59, Bent 117	Welch	Locke	Bell	Paterson^	Taylor	Edwards	Hewlett	Owers	Goater	Cramb*	Tinnion	Bent/Carey
26/8 *5,872*	*3*		*aet*		*Alsop 48*	*Collett*	*Perry*	*Pritchard*	*Bennett*	*Gayle*	*Tillson*	*Holloway*	*Penrice*	*Alsop**	*Cureton^*	*Hayles*	*Beadle/Lockwood*
					Ref: P Rejer (City won 2-1 on aggregate)	Outplayed in the first half, City recover to put on one of their best derby displays, after Julian Alsop sends the ball looping into their net. After Taylor's emphatic header takes the tie into extra-time, substitute Bent latches onto a return pass from Owers to burst clear and settle the issue.											
2:1 A LEEDS	17	L	1-3	0-1	Goater 77	Welch	Carey	Bell	Paterson	Taylor	Tisdale	Hewlett	Owers	Goater*	Torpey	Tinnion	Goodridge
17/9 *8,806*	*P:9*				*Wetherall 19, Hasselb'k 69p, Ribeiro 90*	*Martyn*	*Halle*	*Robertson*	*Kelly*	*Radebe*	*Wetherall*	*Hopkin*	*Wallace*	*Hasselbaink**	*Kewell*	*Molenaar*	*Ribeiro*
					Ref: G Poll	After Goater pounces on David Wetherall's woeful back header to slide the ball under former Bristol Rovers keeper Nigel Martyn, a super 30-yard shot by Bruno Ribeiro ends City's hopes. Weatherall is fully involved, as he heads the opener and is fouled by Paterson for the penalty.											
2:2 H LEEDS	15	W	2-1	1-1	Goodridge 41, Taylor 61	Welch	Locke	Bell	Dyche	Taylor	Edwards	Goodridge	Owers	Torpey	Doherty*	Tinnion	Barclay
30/9 10,857	*P:8*				*Hasselbaink 8*	*Martyn*	*Molenaar**	*Robertson*	*Kelly*	*Radebe*	*Wetherall*	*Hopkin*	*Wallace*	*Hasselbaink !*	*Haaland^*	*Bowyer*	*Halle/Lilley*
					Ref: N Barry (City lost 3-4 on aggregate)	Taylor towers above a mêlée of players to plant a bullet header past Nigel Martyn, to give City hope of overturning Leeds' first-leg advantage. Jimmy Hasselbaink shoots past Welch to get United off to a great start, but his 30th-minute sending off for flooring Tinnion aids City's cause.											

FA Cup			F-A	H-T	Scorers, Times, and Referees	1	2	3	4	5	6	7	8	9	10	11	subs used
1 H MILLWALL	2	W	1-0	1-0	Taylor 24	Welch	Locke	Bell	Goodridge*	Taylor	Carey	Hewlett	Doherty	Torpey	Goater	Tinnion	Langan
15/11 8,413	*4*					*Spink*	*Brown*	*Sturgess"*	*Bowry*	*Law*	*McLeary*	*Newman*	*Savage*	*Wilkinson*	*Allen^*	*Doyle**	*Grant/Hockton/Bircham*
					Ref: M Fletcher	City dominate the first half, but are called upon to give a resilient performance after the break, when Millwall make a determined effort to save the game. Goodridge gives a brilliant display of his dribbling skills, but the tie is won by Taylor's unstoppable header from Tinnion's corner.											
2 A BOURNEMOUTH	2	L	1-3	0-1	Cramb 83	Welch	Locke	Bell	Goodridge	Taylor	Carey	Edwards	Tisdale^	Goater	Cramb	Brennan*	Tinnion/Barclay
7/12 *5,687*	*8*				*Carey 14 (og), O'Neill 80, Fletcher 90*	*Glass*	*Young*	*Vincent*	*Howe*	*Cox*	*Bailey*	*Beardsmore**	*Robinson*	*Warren*	*Fletcher*	*O'Neill*	*Rawlinson*
					Ref: M Halsey	In front of the Sky TV cameras City dominate this thrilling cup-tie at Dean Court, but the plucky Cherries give them a lesson in finishing. Jimmy Glass keeps City at bay with a great display between the sticks, and it isn't until near the end that Cramb's diving header beats him.											

		Home					Away					
	P	W	D	L	F	A	W	D	L	F	A	Pts
1 Watford	46	13	7	3	36	22	11	9	3	31	19	88
2 BRISTOL CITY	46	16	5	2	41	17	9	5	9	28	22	85
3 Grimsby *	46	11	7	5	30	14	8	8	7	25	23	72
4 Northampton	46	14	5	4	33	17	4	12	7	19	20	71
5 Bristol Rov	46	13	2	8	43	33	7	8	8	27	31	70
6 Fulham	46	12	7	4	31	14	8	3	12	29	29	70
7 Wrexham	46	10	10	3	31	23	8	6	9	24	28	70
8 Gillingham	46	13	7	3	30	18	6	6	11	22	29	70
9 Bournemouth	46	11	8	4	28	15	7	4	12	29	37	66
10 Chesterfield	46	13	7	3	31	19	3	10	10	15	25	65
11 Wigan	46	12	5	6	41	31	5	6	12	23	35	62
12 Blackpool	46	13	6	4	35	24	4	5	14	24	43	62
13 Oldham	46	13	7	3	43	23	2	9	12	19	31	61
14 Wycombe	46	10	10	3	32	20	4	8	11	19	33	60
15 Preston	46	10	6	7	29	26	5	8	10	27	30	59
16 York	46	9	7	7	26	21	5	10	8	26	37	59
17 Luton	46	7	7	9	35	38	7	8	8	25	26	57
18 Millwall	46	7	8	8	23	23	7	5	11	20	31	55
19 Walsall	46	10	8	5	26	16	4	4	15	17	36	54
20 Burnley	46	10	9	4	34	23	3	4	16	21	42	52
21 Brentford	46	9	7	7	33	29	2	10	11	17	42	50
22 Plymouth	46	10	5	8	36	30	2	8	13	19	40	49
23 Carlisle	46	8	5	10	27	28	4	3	16	30	45	44
24 Southend	46	8	7	8	29	30	3	3	17	18	49	43
	1104	262	162	128	783	554	128	162	262	554	783	1494

* promoted after play-offs

Odds & ends

Double wins: (7) Wigan, Southend, York, Millwall, Oldham, Bristol Rov, Wycombe.
Double losses: (2) Fulham, Gillingham.

Won from behind: (3) York (h), Burnley (h), Oldham (a).
Lost from in front: (1) Northampton (a).

High spots: Eight consecutive League victories.
Brilliant home win over Grimsby.
Colin Cramb's two goals at Wycombe.
Recovering from half-time deficit to beat Oldham at Boundary Park.
Doing the double over Bristol Rovers.
Celebrations following the Walsall game at Ashton Gate.

Low spots: The loss of Taylor and Welch through injury and the transfer of Shaun Goater during the promotion run-in.
Losing at Northampton, despite taking an early lead.
Twice succumbing to Fulham.
Poor display at Preston that lost the Championship.
Inability to beat Bournemouth in four attempts (League, FA Cup and Autowindscreens Shield).
The disgraceful decision by both Bristol City and Bristol Rovers not to contest what would have been the 100th Gloucestershire Senior Cup Final.

Player of the year: Shaun Taylor.
Ever-presents: (0).
Hat-tricks: Shaun Goater (1).
Leading scorer: Shaun Goater (18).

	Appearances						Goals			
	Lge	*Sub*	LC	*Sub*	FAC	*Sub*	Lge	LC	FAC	Tot
Barclay, Dominic		*8*		*1*		*1*				
Bell, Mickey	**44**		4		2		**10**			**10**
Bent, Junior		*2*		*2*				1		**1**
Brennan, Jim	**4**	*2*			1					
Carey, Louis	**37**	*1*	1	*1*	2					
Cramb, Colin	**34**	*6*	2		1		**9**		1	**10**
Doherty, Tom	**22**	*8*	1		1		**2**			**2**
Dyche, Sean	**10**	*1*	1							
Edwards, Rob	**34**	*3*	3		1		**2**			**2**
Goater, Shaun	**28**	*5*	3		2		**17**	1		**18**
Goodridge, Greg	**28**	*3*	1	*1*	2		**6**	1		**7**
Hewlett. Matt	**27**	*7*	3		1		**4**			**4**
Johansen Stig	**2**	*1*								
Langan, Kevin		*3*				*1*				
Locke, Adam	**35**	*2*	3		2		**1**			**1**
McCarthy Shaun	**7**						**1**			**1**
Murray, Scott	**10**	*13*								
Naylor Stuart	**2**									
Owers, Gary	**20**	*2*	4				**1**			**1**
Paterson Scott	**7**	*3*	3							
Plummer, Dwayne		*1*								
Roberts, Jason	**1**	*2*					**1**			**1**
Shail, Mark	**2**									
Taylor, Shaun	**43**		4		2		**2**	2	1	**5**
Tinnion, Brian	**44**		4		1	*1*	**3**			**3**
Tisdale Paul	**2**	*3*	1	*1*	1					
Torpey, Steve	**19**	*10*	2		1		**8**			**8**
Welch, Keith	**44**		4		2					
(own-goals)							**2**			**2**
28 players used	**506**	***86***	**44**	***6***	**22**	***3***	**69**	**5**	**2**	**76**

No	Date		Att	Pos	Pt	F-A	H-T	Scorers, Times, and Referees	1	2	3	4	5	6	7	8	9	10	11	subs used
1	H	OXFORD			D	2-2	2-1	Andersen 26, 44	Welch	Locke	Bell	Hewlett	**Watts**	Dyche*	Goodridge"	**Hutchings**	**Akinbiyi**	**Anders'n S^**	Tinnion	Carey/**Thorpe**/Doherty
	8/8		13,729		1			*Murphy 18, Windass 48*	*Whitehead*	*Robinson*	*Marsh*	*Gray*	*Davis**	*Gilchrist*	*Banger"*	*Windass*	*Thomson^*	*Murphy*	*Beauchamp*	*Powell/Weatherstone/Smith*
								Ref: R Furnandiz	City's attack looks proficient enough, but against more skilful opponents their defence gives cause for concern as Murphy is unmarked when he turns in Banger's cross. In the wilting heat Hewlett and Hutchings strike the woodwork either side of Andersen's tapped-in early equaliser.											
2	A	QP RANGERS			D	1-1	1-0	Hewlett 28	Welch	Locke	Bell	Hewlett	Watts	Carey	Goodridge^	Doherty	Akinbiyi	Andersen S*	Tinnion	Thorpe/Dyche
	15/8		*13,337*		2			*Ready 90*	*Harper*	*Heinola*	*Baraclough*	*Yates**	*Ready*	*Maddix*	*Murray*	*Peacock*	*Sheron*	*Gallen^*	*Scully*	*Slade/Rowland*
								Ref: A Wiley	Despite Akinbiyi being given offside when he puts the ball in the net, City look set for their first win of the season by virtue of Hewlett's strike when he is played in by Andersen. Unfortunately, the defence falters in final seconds as the unmarked Karl Ready fires into the bottom corner.											
3	H	WATFORD		17	L	1-4	0-1	Andersen 59	Welch	Locke	Bell	Hewlett*	Watts^	Carey	Goodridge	Hutchings	Akinbiyi	Andersen S	Tinnion	Thorpe/Dyche
	22/8		13,063	*3*	2			*Johnson 8, 61, Yates 58, Hazan 79*	*Chamberlain*	*Bazeley*	*Kennedy*	*Palmer*	*Millen**	*Yates*	*Smart"*	*Hyde*	*Ngonge^*	*Johnson*	*Robinson*	*Hazan/Noel-Williams/Daley*
								Ref: B Knight	Watford demonstrate the art of finishing as they expose City's poor defending. Shortly after Andersen's powerful shot hauls City back into the game, Richard Johnson adds to his 30-yard opener with another screamer, but this time from only 25 yards. City are well beaten by the end.											
4	A	TRANMERE		16	D	1-1	1-1	Akinbiyi 32	Welch	Locke	Bell	Hewlett	Watts	Carey	Edwards R	Hutchings	Akinbiyi	Andersen S*	Tinnion	Goodridge
	29/8		*5,960*	*22*	3			*Parkinson 7*	*Coyne*	*Morgan^*	*Thompson*	*Allen*	*Hill*	*Irons*	*Morrissey**	*O'Brien*	*Jones G*	*Parkinson*	*Jones L"*	*Koumas/Mellon/Russell*
								Ref: W Burns	In a contest that fades badly after an action-packed opening, Akinbiyi shows just why City paid a record £1.2 million for him. After Andy Parkinson drives in from John Morrissey's corner, Akinbiyi finishes off Tinnion's inviting free-kick with an unstoppable headed equaliser.											
5	H	HUDDERSFIELD		19	L	1-2	1-0	Goodridge 12	Welch	Locke	Bell	Hewlett	Watts	Carey	Goodridge	Edwards R^	Akinbiyi	Andersen S*	Tinnion	Thorpe/Doherty
	31/8		11,801	*9*	3			*Horne 48, Stewart 52*	*Vaesen*	*Jenkins*	*Edwards*	*Johnson*	*Morrison*	*Collins*	*Browning**	*Horne*	*Stewart*	*Allison*	*Thornley*	*Richardson*
								Ref: A Butler	Marcus Stewart nips in between Bell and Welch to fire home Town's winner as City pay yet again for their defensive shortcomings. Goodridge fires in from 15 yards for the opener, but City's failure to close down opponents allows Barry Horne to net with a screamer just after the break.											
6	A	SWINDON		21	L	2-3	0-3	Akinbiyi 65, Bell 79p	Welch	Locke	Bell	Doherty	Watts	Dyche	Murray	Edwards R*	Akinbiyi	Thorpe^	Tinnion	Hewlett/Cramb
	5/9		*8,537*	*18*	3			*Walters 2p, Ndah 5, Onuora 9*	*Talia*	*Kerslake*	*Hall*	*Leitch^*	*Reeves*	*Borrows**	*Walters*	*Ndah*	*Onuora*	*Bullock*	*Gooden*	*Davis !/Hulbert !*
								Ref: P Rejer	City are lifted by their magnificent fans and nearly complete a stirring comeback. Shortly after Sol Davis is sent off for bringing down Murray to concede City's penalty, Akinbiyi almost breaks the bar with a close-range shot. Hulbert walks at the death for his second bookable offence.											
7	A	SUNDERLAND		20	D	1-1	0-1	Andersen 88	Welch	Locke	Bell	Doherty	Watts*	Dyche	Murray	Hewlett	Akinbiyi	Carey	Tinnion^	Andersen S/Goodidge
	8/9		***32,745***	*2*	4			*Phillips 13*	*Sorensen*	*Williams*	*Gray M*	*Ball*	*Melville*	*Butler P*	*Summerbee*	*Mullin*	*Dichio*	*Phillips*	*Johnson*	
								Ref: D Pugh	A fortuitous point at the Stadium of Light, thanks to Andersen's magnificent shot on the turn. Welch, who saves a 24th-minute penalty from Kevin Phillips, is in great form between the sticks. In front of the Sky TV audience he saves City's over-run side from complete humiliation.											
8	H	WEST BROM		22	L	1-3	0-2	Watts 69	Welch	Locke	Bell	Doherty	Carey	Dyche^	Murray"	Hewlett*	Akinbiyi	Andersen S	Tinnion	Goodridge/Watts/Cramb
	13/9		13,761	*6*	4			*Hughes 11, 33, Quinn 52*	*Miller*	*McDermott*	*Van Blerk*	*Flynn*	*Raven*	*Carbon*	*Quinn*	*De Frietas**	*Hughes^*	*Kilbane*	*Sneekes*	*Bortolazzi/Mardon*
								Ref: S Baines	A 22-hour postponement of this game, due to yesterday's return of The Matthew to home waters, fails to save City from a rout. Watts heads in to give City hope after being caught square time and time again by the pace of Albion's strikers following Lee Hughes' tapped-in opener.											
9	A	IPSWICH		23	L	1-3	0-2	Akinbiyi 88	Welch	Locke^	Bell	**Zwijnenb'rg**	Watts	Carey	Brennan*	Hutchings"	Akinbiyi	Andersen S	Tinnion	Edwards R/Cramb/Murray
	19/9		*13,657*	*10*	4			*Johnson 13, 90, Scowcroft 33*	*Wright*	*Stockwell*	*Taricco*	*Clapham*	*Thetis^*	*Tanner*	*Dyer*	*Holland*	*Johnson*	*Scowcroft*	*Petta**	*Sonner/Holster*
								Ref: P Danson	Welch saves City from an even heavier defeat as they run out of ideas. Starting with a 5-3-2 formation, they progress through a conventional 4-4-2 to finish in 4-3-3 mode, but all to no avail. David Johnson lobs Welch in injury-time to extinguish hopes raised by Akinbiyi's header.											
10	H	CREWE		22	W	**5-2**	3-0	Doherty 13, Goodridge 29, Murray 37,	Welch	Murray	Bell	Doherty	Watts	Carey	Goodridge	Edwards R^	Akinbiyi	Cramb*	Tinnion	Andersen S/Hutchings
	26/9		**9,810**	*20*	7			*Anthrobus 72, 85* [Akin' 78, Hut' 89]	*Kearton*	*Bignot*	*Smith S*	*Unsworth*	*Walton*	*Charnock**	*Wright*	*Johnson^*	*Jack*	*Anthrobus*	*Rivers*	*Little/Lunt*
								Ref: R Styles	The message on Akinbiyi's and Goodridge's tee-shirts demonstrate City's great team spirit as they romp to their first League win of the season. The goal highlights are a spectacular volley from the edge of the box by Steve Anthrobus for his first, and Goodridge's thunderous 25-yarder.											
11	H	BARNSLEY		22	D	1-1	0-0	Bell 69	Welch	Murray	Bell	Doherty	Watts	Carey	Goodridge*	Hutchings	Akinbiyi	Cramb^	Tinnion	Zwijnenberg/Andersen S
	29/9		12,005	*14*	8			*Sheridan 74*	*Leese*	*Eaden*	*De Zeeuw*	*Richardson**	*Morgan*	*Appleby^*	*Hendrie"*	*McClare*	*Ward*	*Bullock M*	*Barnard*	*Sheridan/Liddell/Fjortoft*
								Ref: A Leake	Bell's unstoppable free-kick from just outside the box gives City a surprise lead against a Barnsley side who control the play for long periods. Darren Sheridan brings Barnsley a deserved equaliser with a left-foot volley bent beyond Welch's dive into the top corner from fully 25 yards.											

No		Date	Opponent	Att	Pos	Res	F-A	H-T	Scorers, Times, and Referees												subs used
12	A		BURY		19	W	1-0	0-0	Bell 67p	Welch	Murray	Bell	Doherty	Watts	Carey	Goodridge*	Hutchings	Akinbiyi	Cramb	Tinnion	Edwards R
		3/10		4,794	12	11				Kiely	Woodward	Barrick	Daws	Lucketti	Redmond	Swailes C*	Matthews^	Billy	Patterson	Preece	Baldry"/Avdiu/Jemson
									Ref: A Wiley	City's leaky defence somehow survives a battering at Gigg Lane, and it takes a conga on the terraces by their travelling fans to inspire some attacking ideas. Akinbiyi is brought down outside the area, but the referee's award of a penalty condemns Bury to their first home defeat.											
13	H		PORTSMOUTH		18	D	2-2	1-1	Murray 11, Andersen 85	Welch	Murray	Bell	Doherty^	Watts	Carey	Goodridge	Hutchings	Akinbiyi	Cramb*	Tinnion	Andersen S/Edwards R
		10/10		13,056	15	12			Igoe 18, Claridge 70	Flahavan	Thogersen	Simpson F	Hillier	Whitbread	Awford	Perrett	Peron	Aloisi*	Claridge	Igoe	Durnin
									Ref: A D'Urso	Andersen rescues a point from this noon encounter against a skilful Pompey side prompted by the inspirational Sammy Igoe. He shoots past the advancing keeper to equalise Steve Claridge's header, after Murray's thunderous opener had been countered by Igoe's rounding of Welch.											
14	A		PORT VALE		20	L	2-3	0-1	Murray 55, Akinbiyi 59	Welch	Murray	Bell	Doherty	Watts	Carey	Goodridge*	Edwards R	Akinbiyi	Andersen S	Tinnion^	Hutchings/Cramb
		17/10		6,691	15	12			Beesley 1, Ainsworth 47, 86	Musselwhite	Carragher	Tankard	Bogie	Barnett	Beesley	Ainsworth	Barker	Beadle	Foyle*	McGlinchey	Snijders
									Ref: K Leach	City's spirited fight-back is of no avail as Tinnion's hapless defensive header sets up the Vale winner, with Ainsworth weaving past three men before firing in. After conceding the day's earliest goal, and another straight after the break, Murray's wickedly-deflected shot sparks City.											
15	A		GRIMSBY		22	L	1-2	1-0	Andersen 33	Welch	Murray	Bell	Docherty^	Watts	Carey	Goodridge*	Edwards R	Akinbiyi	Andersen S	Brennan	Thorpe/Hutchings
		20/10		5,082	5	12			Groves 50, 60p	Davison	McDermott	Gallimore	Smith R	Lever	Widdrington	Donovan^	Smith D*	Nogan	Black	Groves	Lester/Livingstone
									Ref: C Foy	City's defence is all of a dither as their old inability to deal with corners allows Paul Groves to net with a stooping header, and then Kevin Donovan wins a penalty without falling down. Andersen punishes the Mariners' lax defending as he is free in the box to head in City's opener.											
16	H		BOLTON		18	W	2-1	2-1	Akinbiyi 28, Bell 45p	Welch	Murray	Bell	Hutchings	Watts	Carey	Goodridge	Edwards R	Akinbiyi^	Andersen S*	Tinnion	Thorpe/Zwijnenberg
		23/10		12,026	7	15			Gunnlaugsson 5	Branagan	Cox	Whitlow	Jensen	Todd	Fish	Johansen	Frandsen^	Blake	Gardner*	Gunnl'gsson	Holdsworth/Taylor
									Ref: M Halsey	Rip-roaring tussle in front of the Sky cameras after a 30-second silence for war victims. City refuse to be dismayed following Bolton's brilliant early strike. After Akinbiyi's poorly-hit shot finds the net with the aid of a deflection, Andersen is flattened for City's match-winning penalty.											
17	A		BRADFORD C		21	L	0-5	0-2	[Beagrie 58, Blake 90]	Welch	Murray*	Bell	Hutchings	Watts	Carey	Goodridge	Edwards R	Akinbiyi	Andersen S	Tinnion	Shail
		31/10		14,468	8	15			Mills 8, Carey 15 (og), Rankin 51,	Walsh	Todd	Jacobs	McCall"	Moore	Dreyer	Rankin	Blake	Mills^	Whalley	Beagrie*	Lawrence/Watson/O'Brien
									Ref: A Bates	A cruel introduction to English football for new boss Benny Lennartsson as City are ripped to shreds at Valley Parade. In contrast to last week's heroics, a gutless performance as defensive frailties resurface. Mills starts the rot by firing in after receiving Moore's 50-yard pass.											
18	H		WOLVES		21	L	**1-6**	1-2	Hutchings 12 [Robinson 80]	Welch	Murray	Bell^	Hutchings	Shail	Carey	Goodridge	Thorpe*	Akinbiyi	Andersen S"	Tinnion	Cramb/**Hill**/Torpey
		7/11		15,432	8	15			Whittingham 19, Connolly 21, 57, 67, 77,	Stowell	Muscat*	Naylor	Emblen	Sedgley	Curle	Corica	Fernando^	Connolly"	Whittingham	Osborn	Robinson/Ferguson/Jones
									Ref: P Taylor	Wolves inflict on an inept and passionless City side their worst home League loss for almost 50 years. Connolly thrives on the amount of space behind Bell to notch a deserved hat-trick. The sponsors show a fine appreciation of irony in their choice of Tinnion as City Man of the Match.											
19	A		CRYS PALACE		23	L	1-2	1-1	Andersen 35	Welch	Murray	Bell	Hutchings	Shail	Carey	Edwards R	Thorpe	Akinbiyi	Andersen S	Brennan	
		14/11		17,821	11	15			Bradbury 5, Jansen 88	Digby	Austin*	Jihal	Petric	Burton	Foster	Lombardo	Rizzo^	Bradbury"	Jansen	Mullins	Tuttle/ Curcic/Morrison
									Ref: R Furnandiz	City battle back well after conceding an early goal. Carey's failure to cut out a through-ball allows Bradbury to curl in a shot past Welch, but Andersen levels with a delightful chip. Unfortunately, straight after Akinbiyi hits the post, Jansen finds himself free to head powerfully home.											
20	H		STOCKPORT		23	D	1-1	1-0	Thorpe 43	Welch	Murray	Bell	Hutchings	Shail	Carey	Edwards R	Thorpe*	Akinbiyi	Andersen S	Brennan^	Goodridge/Tinnion
		21/11		11,032	17	16			Angell 53	Nash	Connelly	Woodthorpe	Cook"	Flynn	McIntosh	Gannon*	Matthews^	Angell	McInnes	Branch	Cooper/Wilbraham/Dinning
									Ref: P Rejer	Akinbiyi's failure to score, perhaps put off by the innovation of a yellow ball, when clean through early in the second half, costs City the points in a game where all the good football is played by Stockport. For the second successive home match Bell fails to make a worthwhile tackle.											
21	A		BIRMINGHAM		23	L	2-4	2-3	Thorpe 4, Andersen 45	Welch	Murray	Bell	Hutchings	Shail	Carey	Edwards R	Thorpe	Akinbiyi	Andersen S*	Brennan^	Goodridge/Tinnion
		28/11		17,577	4	16			Johnson M 5, Ndlovu 14, Forster 42, 72	Poole	Rowett	Charlton*	Purse	Grainger	Johnson M	McCarthy	Holland	Forster^	Robinson	Ndlovu	Hughes/Johnson A
									Ref: B Coddington	For once it is City who take an early lead as Thorpe's half-volley finds the net, but straight away Michael Johnson's header loses them the advantage. Nicky Forster punishes dominant City for spurning many chances after the break by heading in following Akinbiyi's bad miss.											
22	H		SHEFFIELD UTD		23	W	2-0	1-0	Bell 33p, Akinbiyi 65	**Phillips**	Brennan	Bell	Hutchings	Shail	Carey	Edwards R*	Thorpe	Akinbiyi	Andersen S^	Tinnion	Murray/Doherty
		5/12		11,134	9	19				Tracey	O'Connor	Quinn	Henry	Derry	Sandford	Ford	Hamilton	Marcelo	Devlin*	Woodhouse	Twiss
									Ref: A Hall	United, weakened by the loss of eight regulars, have Henry sent off in the 85th minute for his blatant late challenge on Phillips. The crowd are mystified by City's penalty award as Hamilton is adjudged to have pulled Thorpe's shirt. Akinbiyi clinches the points with a powerful header.											
23	H		CRYS PALACE		23	D	1-1	1-1	Akinbiyi 25	Phillips	Brennan	Bell	Murray	Shail	Carey	Edwards R	Thorpe	Akinbiyi*	Andersen S	**Brown**^	Goodridge/Doherty
		12/12		13,014	14	20			Bell 23 (og)	Miller	Amsalem	Crowe	Petric*	Burton	Foster	Rodger	Mullins	Svensson^	Jansen	Tuttle	Bradbury/Thomson
									Ref: E Wolstenholme	A case of two points lost against a Crystal Palace team who run out of steam after the half-time break. Bell supplies the cross for Akinbiyi's headed equaliser within a couple of minutes of conceding an own-goal in his attempts to clear Craig Foster's toe-poke over the diving Phillips.											

No	Date		Att	Pos	Pt	F-A	H-T	Scorers, Times, and Referees	1	2	3	4	5	6	7	8	9	10	11	subs used
24	A	NORWICH		23	L	1-2	1-2	Akinbiyi 20	Phillips	Brennan	Bell	Hutchings	Shail	Carey	Edwards R*	Thorpe	Akinbiyi	Murray	Goodridge^	Andersen S/Torpey
	19/12		17,022	5	20			Roberts 18, 36	Watt	Kenton	Mackay	Grant	Wilson	Jackson	Adams*	Eadie	Roberts	Russell^	Llewellyn	Sutch/Marshall
								Ref: J Brandwood	Akinbiyi is the early hero when latching onto Edwards' through-pass to slide the ball under Michael Watt, but turns villain at the death. He misses two relatively simple chances to equalise, after Iwan Roberts deflects in Matt Jackson's goalward header, to add to his headed opener.											
25	A	WATFORD		23	L	0-1	0-0		Phillips	Brennan	Bell	Hutchings"	Shail	Edwards C	Murray*	Tistimet'u^	Akinbiyi	Torpey	Andersen S	Thorpe/Doherty/Goodridge
	26/12		15,081	3	20			Smart 57	Chamberlain	Bazeley	Kennedy	Page	Palmer	Iroha	Smart	Hyde	N'l-Williams	Johnson	Gudmundss'n	
								Ref: R Styles	City have the better of the early play as Ben Iroha almost heads Bell's centre into his own net. Hutchings has his header cleared off the line, and Andersen's 25-yard drive hits the bar. Watford resort to time-wasting tactics at the end as they hang on to Allan Smart's 15-yard winner.											
26	H	SWINDON		23	W	3-1	1-0	Torpey 8, 51, Akinbiyi 75	Phillips	Brennan*	Bell	Doherty	Shail	Edwards C	Murray	Tistimetanu	Akinbiyi	Torpey	Andersen S	Hutchings
	28/12		16,257	15	23			Ndah 46	Talia	Robinson"	Hall	Hulbert	Taylor	Ndah	Walters	Hay^	Onuora*	Bullock	Davis	Watson/Cowe/Reeves
								Ref: M Pierce	Torpey is City's hero with a bizarre opening goal as his swinging left foot connects 30 yards out to send the ball looping over the advancing Frank Talia to bounce high into the net. George Ndah expertly beats Phillips, but Torpey's header and Akinbiyi's drive tie up City's win.											
27	A	OXFORD		23	D	0-0	0-0		Phillips	Brennan	Bell	Murray	Shail	Edwards C	Hewlett*	Tistimetanu	Akinbiyi	Torpey	Andersen S	Locke
	9/1		9,434	21	24				Gerrard	Robinson	Powell	Warren	Watson	Gilchrist	Remy	Murphy	Banger	Windass	Beauchamp	
								Ref: A Leake	City show few attacking ideas as they end a poor away run. Phillips is in top form to deny Oxford, making a point-blank stop as early as the second minute, while Bell and Murray both effect clearances off the goal-line. Paul Gerrard's finger-tip save denies Torpey a headed goal.											
28	H	TRANMERE		21	D	1-1	1-1	Locke 25	Phillips	Brennan	Bell	Locke^	Shail	Carey	Murray	Tistimetanu	Thorpe	Torpey	Andersen S*	Tinnion/Hutchings
	16/1		13,217	16	25			Mahon 8	Coyne	Allen	Thompson !	McGreal	Challinor	Irons	Mahon	O'Brien^	Parkinson*	Hill	Taylor	Jones L/Jones G
								Ref: M Warren/S Castle	Challinor's missile-like throws cause City problems, but Locke equalises Mahon's early shot, by driving in a loose ball. Steve Castle (a 48th-minute replacement for the injured Mark Warren) harshly sends off Andy Thompson for his second bookable offence near the call of time.											
29	A	HUDDERSFIELD		22	D	2-2	1-1	Akinbiyi 16, Locke 62	Phillips	Brennan	Bell	Locke	Shail	Carey	Edwards R	Tistimetanu*	Akinbiyi^	Torpey	Tinnion	Murray/Andersen S
	30/1		14,034	10	26			Phillips 3, Johnson 60	Vaesen	Jenkins	Edwards	Johnson^	Collins	Gray*	Beech	Phillips	Stewart	Allison	Thornley	Hessey/Beresford
								Ref: G Frankland	The strength, courage and determination of Akinbiyi allows City to recover from the early shock of David Phillips' breathtaking 30-yard strike. He powerfully heads an equaliser, and then, shortly after Grant Johnson had fired Town back in front, flicks on a cross for Locke to stab in.											
30	H	QP RANGERS		22	D	0-0	0-0		Phillips	Brennan	Bell	Locke	Shail	Carey	Murray*	Tistimetanu	Akinbiyi	Torpey	Tinnion	Goodridge
	5/2		13,841	17	27				Miklosko	Heinola*	Baraclough	Morrow	Ready	Maddix	Plummer	Peacock	Dowie	Gallen	Kiwomya^	Murray/Scully
								Ref: J Kirkby	Creativity is at a minimum as these struggling sides fail to serve up a Friday night treat for the live Sky TV audience. City have the best of the chances, Brennan's 20-yarder skimming the bar in the 62nd minute, but the killer touch is lacking as the fear of defeat dominates the action.											
31	H	SUNDERLAND		23	L	0-1	0-0		Phillips	Brennan	Bell*	Locke	Shail	Carey	Murray	Tistimetanu	Akinbiyi	Torpey^	Tinnion	Sebok/Andersen S
	13/2		15,736	1	27			Phillips 89p	Sorensen	Makin	Gray M	Ball	Melville	Butler	Summerbee	Clark	Quinn*	Phillips	Johnston	Dichio
								Ref: K Styles	The dark blue of Sunderland's shirts forces the officials to turn out in green shirts, whilst the keepers perform in yellow jerseys. City are denied a deserved share of the spoils as a reckless challenge by keeper Phillips on his namesake Kevin gifts Sunderland their match-winning penalty.											
32	A	WEST BROM		23	D	2-2	0-1	Akinbiyi 60, 85	Phillips	Brennan	Bell*	Locke	Shail	Carey	Brown	Tistimetanu^	Akinbiyi	Torpey	Tinnion	Sebok/Andersen S
	20/2		16,343	9	28			Hughes 32, 90	Whitehead	Holmes	Van Blerk	Bortolazzi^	Murphy	Raven	Quinn	Sneekes	De Freitas*	Hughes	Kilbane	Flynn/Angel
								Ref: P Walton	In the seventh minute of injury-time, City's sloppy defending allows Lee Hughes to shoot in the Baggies' equaliser. Torpey hits the woodwork before Hughes heads Albion's opener, but Akinbiyi makes amends for early misses by firing in, either side of Brown being denied by a post.											
33	H	IPSWICH		23	L	0-1	0-0		Phillips	Brennan	Sebok	Locke	Shail	Carey	Brown	Edwards R*	Akinbiyi	Torpey	Andersen S	Hill
	27/2		14,065	3	28			Naylor 56	Wright	Wilnis*	Thetis	Clapham	Mowbray	Venus	Dyer	Holland	Naylor	Harewood^	Magilton	Stockwell/Petta
								Ref: B Knight	City's poor finishing, allied to the excellent form of keeper Richard Wright, allows Ipswich to keep their 19th clean sheet of the campaign with this smash and grab win. After Akinbiyi puts his header wide from just six yards, Richard Naylor has time and space to shoot in Dyer's pass.											
34	H	BURY		23	D	1-1	0-1	Andersen 80	Phillips	Brennan	Langan^	Locke	Shail"	Carey	Brown*	Edwards R	Akinbiyi	Torpey	Doherty	Andersen S/ Murray/Hill
	9/3		11,606	22	29			D'Jaffo 17	Kiely	West	Serrant	Daws	Lucketti	Redmond	Swailes C	Hall	D'Jaffo*	Billy	Littlejohn^	Jemson/Preece
								Ref: A D'Urso	A lacklustre display by shapeless City in this aerial encounter. Laurent D'Jaffo's seventh-minute strike is ruled out for handball, but no escape for City shortly after, when his low swerving drive gives Bury a deserved lead. Substitute Andersen rescues a point with his six-yard header.											

No	Date	Opponent	Att	Pos	Pts	F-A	H-T	Scorers, Times, and Referees	1	2	3	4	5	6	7	8	9	10	11	subs used
35	A	WOLVES		23	L	0-3	0-1		Phillips	Brennan	Murray	Locke*	Sebok	Carey	Andersen S	Edwards R	Akinbiyi	Torpey	Tinnion^	Doherty/**Heaney**
	13/3		25,237	6	29			Flo 14, 84, Sebok 53 (og)	Stowell	Atkins	Gilkes	Sedgley	Richards	Curle	Simpson"	Emblen*	Flo	Keane	Osborn^	Robinson/Corica/Connolly
								Ref: D Crick	City's improved display is thwarted by Phillips as he misses his kick in attempting to deal with Sebok's simple back-pass. A long crossfield ball allows Haavard Flo to slide home Wolves' opener, and he adds his second with a clinical volley for a somewhat flattering victory margin.											
36	H	BRADFORD C		24	L	2-3	0-2	Akinbiyi 51, Andersen 81	Phillips	Brennan	Sebok	Doherty	Shail	Carey	Heaney^	Edwards R*	Akinbiyi	Andersen S	Tinnion	Locke/Murray
	20/3		10,870	3	29			Mills 30, Jacobs 40, Whalley 83	Walsh	Todd	Jacobs	McCall	Moore	Dreyer	Lawrence	Windass*	Mills	Whalley	Beagrie	Rankin
								Ref: W Jordan	City's early ineptitude brings down the fans wrath on Benny Lennartsson, but a second-half recovery almost saves the game. Unfortunately, after superb headed goals from Akinbiyi and Andersen, the defence dithers and allows Gareth Whalley the time to drill in Bradford's winner.											
37	A	BARNSLEY		24	L	0-2	0-1		**Andersen B**	Murray	Brennan	Locke	Shail	Carey	Heaney*	Brown^	Akinbiyi	Andersen	Tinnion	Goodridge/Hewlett
	23/3		14,741	15	29			Dyer 32, Hignett 89	Bullock T	Eaden	De Zeeuw	Richardson	Moses	Appleby	Van der L'n*	Hignett	Sheron	Dyer^	Jones	Blackmore/Hristov
								Ref: G Laws	With both sides seeking their first League win in three months, it is City who find themselves in their all-familiar role as the fall guys. After Bruce Dyer shoots in Barnsley's opener, Craig Hignett kills off City by steering the ball in from Mike Sheron's cross to round off a fine move.											
38	H	PORT VALE		24	W	2-0	2-0	Akinbiyi 31, Howells 36	Andersen B	Brennan	Sebok	Locke	Taylor	Carey	**Howells***	Brown	Akinbiyi	Torpey	Tinnion	Goodridge
	3/4		11,039	22	32				Musselwhite	Aspin	Tankard	Brammer	Barnett	Butler"	Talbot	Griffiths^	Bent	Foyle	Widdrington*	Smith/Lee/Beesley
								Ref: S Bennett	Shaun Taylor's return inspires City to their first win of the year, but Vale are far from being outplayed. Brennan has to clear off the line, while both Stewart Taylor and Alan Lee are denied by the woodwork. Akinbiyi's header and a brilliant half-volley by Howells clinch the spoils.											
39	A	PORTSMOUTH		24	W	1-0	0-0	Locke 87	Andersen B	Brennan	Sebok	Locke	Taylor	Carey	Howells	Brown	Akinbiyi	Torpey*	Tinnion	Andersen S
	5/4		13,026	18	35				Knight	Robinson	Simpson	McLoughlin	Whitbread	Awford	Nightingale*	Peron	Viachos	Claridge	Igoe^	Durnin/Phillips
								Ref: F Stretton	City fans are in dreamland as Locke clinches victory at Fratton Park, when he is unmarked at the far post to head in Tinnion's corner. City ride their luck in injury-time as Matthew Robinson's header hits the bar, but straight away Akinbiyi races clear at the other end only to shoot wide.											
40	H	GRIMSBY		23	W	4-1	2-1	Torpey 21, Akinbiyi 43, 62, Tinnion 55	Andersen B	Brennan	Sebok	Locke	Taylor"	Carey	Howells*	Brown	Akinbiyi	Torpey^	Tinnion	Goodridge/Andersen S/Shail
	10/4		11,616	13	38			Ashcroft 13	Love	McDermott*	Gallimore	Livingstone	Lever	Burnett"	Caldicott	Black	Ashcroft	Lester^	Groves	Butterfield/Nogan/Clare
								Ref: S Mathieson	Refusing to be put out of their stride by Lee Ashcroft's stunning 25-yard strike, City hit back as Torpey shoots in at the near post. Grimsby have no answer to City's onslaught as a header and a shot by Akinbiyi, as well as Tinnion's great strike, raise hopes of escape from relegation.											
41	A	BOLTON		23	L	0-1	0-1		Andersen B	Brennan	Sebok	Locke	Taylor	Murray	Howells	Brown^	Akinbiyi*	Torpey	Tinnion	Andersen S/Goodridge
	13/4		14,459	5	38			Gudjohnsen 7	Banks	Cox	Phillips	Frandsen	Todd	Fish	Johnansen	Jensen	Gudjohnsen	Taylor	Gardner	
								Ref: A Hall	At the Reebok Stadium City are caught cold early on as Eidur Gudjohnsen blasts home from close in. Bolton are rampant in the first half, but after the break City make a more even game of it against opponents with only one win in ten games. Locke nets on 51 minutes, but is offside.											
42	A	STOCKPORT		23	D	2-2	0-0	Brennan 58, Tinnion 77	Andersen B	Brennan	Sebok	Locke	Taylor	Carey	Howells	Brown*	Andersen S^	Torpey	Tinnion	Godridge/Cramb
	17/4		7,602	14	39			Ellis 56, 69	Nash	Gannon	Dinning	Smith	Flynn	McIntosh	Cooper	Matthews*	Angell	Ellis	Woodthorpe	Moore
								Ref: B Coddington	Brennan's shot into the far corner and Tinnion's scorching drive enable City to retain an unbeaten record at Edgeley Park that goes back 86 years. Torpey performs wonders to divert Mike Flynn's header for a corner midway through the first half as County threaten to tear City apart.											
43	H	BIRMINGHAM		24	L	1-2	0-0	Akinbiyi 46	Andersen B	Brennan	Sebok	Locke	Taylor	Carey"	Howells	Brown^	Akinbiyi	Torpey	Doherty*	Goodridge/Cramb/Shail
	24/4		15,845	4	39			Grainger 48p, Ndlovu 70	Poole	Rowett	Grainger	Hyde	Holdsworth	Johnson	Bass	Robinson*	Bradbury^	Hughes	Ndlovu	McCarthy/Furlong
								Ref: M Dean	The referee reaches the height of notoriety, giving a pen as Ndlovu is challenged outside the box, after previously disallowing Akinbiyi's 26th-min tap-in and Lee Bradbury's 41st-min header, as well as ignoring Jonathan Bass's handball. Howells' weak back-pass gives away the points.											
44	A	CREWE		24	L	0-1	0-1		Andersen B	Murray	Shail	Locke*	Taylor	Carey	Howells^	Brown"	Akinbiyi	Torpey	Tinnion	Doherty/Edwards R/Cramb
	27/4		5,579	19	39			Johnson 23	Kearton	Wright D	Smith S	Macauley	Walton	Charnock	Wright J	Johnson	Jack*	Murphy	Rivers	Street
								Ref: C Foy	City control most of this game against fellow strugglers, but their inability to get behind Crewe's rearguard all but makes relegation a certainty. Lennartsson bemoans the loss of Brennan and Sebok on international duty as Rodney Jack's cross sets up Seth Johnson to ram the ball home.											
45	A	SHEFFIELD UTD		24	L	1-3	0-1	Akinbiyi 61	Andersen B	Brennan	Shail*	Locke	Taylor"	Carey	Howells^	Brown	Akinbiyi	Torpey	Tinnion	Goodridge/ Doherty !/Cramb
	[illegible]/5		17,316	8	39			Marcelo 44, Morris 55, 64	Kelly	Derry	Kozluk	Dellas	Sandford*	Tebily	Donis	Hunt^	Marcelo"	Devlin	Morris	Jacobsen/Quinn/Katchouro
								Ref: D Pugh	At the last chance saloon Marcelo shoots the Blades ahead as five defenders back off, while City's only reply to two strikes by Morris is Akinbiyi's header. After Doherty's 88th-min sending off for handling Tebily's goal-bound shot, Morris has his penalty saved by Bo Andersen.											
46	H	NORWICH		24	W	1-0	1-0	Pinamonte 40	Andersen B	Brennan	Sebok	Doherty	**Jordan**	Carey	Goodridge^	Brown	Akinbiyi	**Pinamonte**	Bell*	Andersen S/**Meechan**
	3/5		10,856	9	42				Marshall A	Kenton	Fugelstad	Marshall L	Jackson	Mackay	Arselin*	Bellamy	Roberts	Mulryne	Llewellyn	Carey
		Home	Away					Ref: M Halsay	A typical end-of-season non-event enlivened by City's amazing fans who form congas in the stands. Reserve top scorer Lorenzo Pinamonte shows a true striker's instincts, sticking out a foot to divert Akinbiyi's header into the net for a close-range debut goal on his 21st birthday.											
Average		12,818	13,502																	

Worthington Cup						F-A	H-T	Scorers, Times, and Referees	1	2	3	4	5	6	7	8	9	10	11	subs used
1:1	H	SHREWSBURY			W	4-0	3-0	Hutchings 13, Akinbiyi 14, 54, [Andersen 21]	Welch	Locke	Bell	Hewlett	Watts^	Carey	Goodridge"	Hutchings	Akinbiyi	Andersen S*	Tinnion	Thorpe/Dyche/Murray
11/8			3,585						*Edwards*	*Seabury*	*Hanmer*	*Jobling*	*Wilding*	*Gayle*	*Craven*	*Kerrigan^*	*Steele**	*Evans*	*Preece"*	*Jagielka/White/Williams*
								Ref: P Taylor	City put on a classy show on a night where nearly everything goes right. Hutchings opens the scoring with a perfectly-timed run and jump to meet Tinnion's free-kick and angle a header into the bottom corner, and then supplies the pass for Akinbiyi to fire in from the edge of the area.											
1:2	A	SHREWSBURY			L	3-4	2-2	Thorpe 4, Akinbiyi 30, 54, Hewlett 88	Welch	Locke	Brennan	Hewlett	Dyche	Carey !	Murray*	Doherty	Akinbiyi"	Thorpe^	Tinnion	Watts/Edwards R/Cramb
18/8			*1,011*					*Evans 39p, 43, 47p, Jobling 69*	*Edwards*	*Seabury*	*Hanmer*	*Herbert*	*Wilding*	*Gayle*	*Craven*	*Jagieka*	*White*	*Evans*	*Jobling*	
								Ref: M Dean (City won 7-4 on aggregate)	After Thorpe's tap-in and Akinbiyi's conversion of Murray's low centre for a 6-0 aggregate lead, City lose their way. Handball by Akinbiyi and Dyche concede pens, whilst Paul Evans nets in Beckham-like style after the sending off of Carey for his professional foul on Jagielka.											
2:1	H	CREWE		22	D	1-1	1-1	Akinbiyi 15	Welch	Locke	Bell	Hutchings	Watts	Carey*	Goodridge^	Brennan	Akinbiyi	Andersen S	Tinnion	Edwards R/Murray
16/9			3,082	*18*				*Rivers 21*	*Kearton*	*Bignot**	*Smith S*	*Wicks*	*Charnock"*	*Unsworth*	*Rivers*	*Street*	*Little^*	*Wright J*	*Smith P*	*Wright D/Foster/Lunt*
								Ref: M Fletcher	A bore for the fans as boss Ward makes no apology for sacrificing entertainment to halt City's poor run. Akinbiyi has the easiest of tap-ins to put the Robins ahead, but poor defending allows Mark Rivers to collect Colin Little's through-pass and lift the ball over the stranded Welch.											
2:2	A	CREWE		23	L	0-2	0-0		Welch	Murray	Bell	Doherty*	Zwijnenberg	Watts	Goodridge	Edwards R	Akinbiyi	Cramb^	Tinnion	Hutchings/Andersen S
22/9			*3,089*	*11*				*Rivers 62, 64*	*Kearton*	*Bignot*	*Smith S*	*Unsworth*	*Walton*	*Charnock*	*Wright J*	*Johnson*	*Little**	*Anthrobus*	*Rivers*	*Street*
								Ref: R Pearson (City lost 1-3 on aggregate)	In a tight first half City, looking solid at the back, have the better chances, but after the interval Mark Rivers, who switches flanks to escape Murray, turns the game. Watts is deceived by his shot on the turn and a few minutes later he taps the ball over the goal-line after Welch saves.											

FA Cup																				
3	H	EVERTON		23	L	0-2	0-0		Phillips	Locke*	Bell	Murray	Shail	Carey	Hewlett^	Tistimetanu	Akinbiyi	Torpey	Andersen S	Goodridge/Hutchings
2/1			19,608	*P:14*				*Bakayoko 86, 88*	*Myhre*	*Dunne*	*Ball*	*Bilic*	*Watson*	*Unsworth*	*Cadamarei"*	*Barmby^*	*Bakayoko*	*Dacourt**	*Hutchison*	*Grant/Oster/Branch*
								Ref: J Winter	Hewlett hits the post as City dominate this game in front of the Match of the Day cameras, but Everton snatch a late win, much as they did four years previously. Unlucky when ref fails to consult linesman flagging for a penalty, City's hearts are broken by Ibrahim Bakayoko's free-kick.											

		Home						Away					
		P	W	D	L	F	A	W	D	L	F	A	Pts
1	Sunderland	46	19	3	1	50	10	12	9	2	41	18	105
2	Bradford City	46	15	4	4	48	20	11	5	7	34	27	87
3	Ipswich	46	16	1	6	37	15	10	7	6	32	17	86
4	Birmingham	46	12	7	4	32	15	11	5	7	34	22	81
5	Watford *	46	12	8	3	30	19	9	6	8	35	37	77
6	Bolton	46	13	6	4	44	25	7	10	6	34	34	76
7	Wolves	46	11	10	2	37	19	8	6	9	27	24	73
8	Sheffield Utd	46	12	6	5	42	29	6	7	10	29	37	67
9	Norwich	46	7	12	4	34	28	8	5	10	28	33	62
10	Huddersfield	46	11	9	3	38	23	4	7	12	24	48	61
11	Grimsby	46	11	6	6	25	18	6	4	13	15	34	61
12	West Brom	46	12	4	7	43	33	4	7	12	26	43	59
13	Barnsley	46	7	9	7	35	30	7	8	8	24	26	59
14	Crys Palace	46	11	10	2	43	26	3	6	14	15	45	58
15	Tranmere	46	8	7	8	37	30	4	13	6	26	31	56
16	Stockport	46	7	9	7	24	21	5	8	10	25	39	53
17	Swindon	46	7	8	8	40	44	6	3	14	19	37	50
18	Crewe	46	7	6	10	27	35	5	6	12	27	43	48
19	Portsmouth	46	10	5	8	34	26	1	9	13	23	47	47
20	QP Rangers	46	9	7	7	34	22	3	4	16	18	39	47
21	Port Vale	46	10	3	10	22	28	3	5	15	23	47	47
22	Bury	46	9	7	7	24	27	1	10	12	11	33	47
23	Oxford	46	7	8	8	31	30	3	6	14	17	41	44
24	BRISTOL CITY	46	7	8	8	35	36	2	7	14	22	44	42
		1104	250	163	139	846	609	139	163	250	609	846	1493

* promoted after play-offs

Odds & ends

Double wins: (0).
Double loses: (5) Watford, Ipswich, Bradford City, Wolves, Birmingham.

Won from behind: (2) Bolton (h), Grimsby (h).
Lost from in front: (5) Huddersfield (h), Grimsby (a), Wolves (h), Birmingham (a), Birmingham (h).

High spots: Keith Welch's brilliant goalkeeping display and Soren Andersen's great strike at Sunderland.
Beating Bolton 2-1 at Ashton Gate.
Adam Locke's late winner at Portsmouth.
Ade Akinbiyi's enthusiastic play.
The tremendous support given by City fans in a difficult season.
The half-time punch-up between the mascots (Wolfie, Cat and the sponsors' three little pigs) at the Wolves game on 7 November.

Low spots: Being savaged by the Wolves at Ashton Gate.
Dispirited performance in 0-5 defeat at Bradford City.
Inability to get behind Crewe's defence at Gresty Road.
The departure of John Ward.
The failure of Benny Lennartsson to improve results or produce a side playing other than route-one football.

Player of the Year: Ade Akinbiyi.
Ever-presents: (0).
Hat-tricks: (0).
Leading scorer: Ade Akinbiyi (23).

	Appearances						Goals			
	Lge	*Sub*	LC	*Sub*	FAC	*Sub*	Lge	LC	FAC	Tot
Akinbiyi, Ade	**44**		4		1		**19**	4		**23**
Andersen, Bo	**10**									
Andersen, Soren	**26**	*13*	2	*1*	1		**10**	1		**11**
Bell, Mickey	**33**		3		1		**5**			**5**
Brennan, Jim	**29**		2				**1**			**1**
Brown, Aaron	**14**									
Carey, Louis	**40**	*1*	3		1					
Cramb, Colin	**4**	*9*	1	*1*						
Doherty, Tom	**15**	*8*	2				**1**			**1**
Dyche, Sean	**4**	*2*	1	*1*						
Edwards, Christian	**3**									
Edwards, Rob	**19**	*4*	1	*2*						
Goodridge, Greg	**15**	*15*	3			*1*	**2**			**2**
Heaney, Neil	**2**	*1*								
Hewlett, Matt	**8**	*2*	2		1		**1**	1		**2**
Hill, Matt		*3*								
Howells, David	**8**						**1**			**1**
Hutchings, Carl	**16**	*5*	2	*1*		*1*	**2**	1		**3**
Jordan, Andrew	**1**									
Langan, Kevin	**1**									
Locke, Adam	**26**	*2*	3		1		**3**			**3**
Meechan, Alex		*1*								
Murray, Scott	**27**	*5*	2	*2*	1		**3**			**3**
Phillips, Steve	**15**				1					
Pinamonte, Lorenzo	**1**						**1**			**1**
Sebok, Vilmos	**10**	*2*								
Shail, Mark	**21**	*3*			1					
Taylor, Shaun	**8**									
Thorpe , Tony	**9**	*7*	1	*1*			**2**	1		**3**
Tinnion, Brian	**32**	*3*	4				**2**			**2**
Tistimetanu, Ivan	**8**				1					
Torpey, Steve	**19**	*2*			1		**3**			**3**
Watts, Julian	**16**	*1*	3	*1*			**1**			**1**
Welch, Keith	**21**		4							
Zwijnenberg, Clem'	**1**	*2*	1							
35 players used	**506**	***91***	**44**	***10***	**11**	***2***	**57**	**8**		**65**

No	Date		Att	Pos	Pt	F-A	H-T	Scorers, Times, and Referees	SQUAD	NUMBERS	IN	USE								subs used
1	A	READING			L	1-2	0-1	Tinnion 78	Phillips	**Lavin !**	Brennan	**Mortimer**	Taylor	Carey	Goodridge^	Hutchings"	Akinbiyi	Brown A*	Tinnion	Shail/Pinamonte/Murray
	7/8		***13,348***		0			*Brebner 15, Crawford 85*	*Howie*	*Gurney*	*Gray*	*Caskey*	*Hunter*	*Polston*	*McLaren*	*Brebner*	*Scott**	*Williams*	*Hodges^*	*McIntyre/Crawford*
								Ref: G Cain	For both Davidson and Pulis it proves to be a case of engaging the tongue before the brain. They are forced to backtrack from their immediate post-match comments that Lavin would not play for the Club again after his 28th-minute dismissal for kicking the ball into the home crowd.											
2	H	BOURNEMOUTH			W	3-1	2-0	Akinbiyi 24, 44, Brennan 47	Phillips	Carey	Brennan	Sebok	Taylor	Mortimer	Goodridge^	Hutchings	Akinbiyi	Torpey*	Tinnion	Pinamonte/Murray
	14/8		11,315		3			*O'Neill 77*	*Ovendale*	*Young*	*Warren*	*Cox*	*Howe*	*Mean^*	*Hayter"*	*Rawlinson**	*Fletcher*	*Stein*	*Jorgensen*	*Hughes/Huck/O'Neill*
								Ref: S Mathieson	After missing early chances, Akinbiyi fires in Tinnion's cross for the opener, before Mortimer's 40-yard pass sets him free to coolly slide in his second. Brennan's angled drive just after the break allows City to turn on the style, but John O'Neill runs through for the visitors' consolation.											
3	A	WIGAN		14	L	1-2	0-1	Thorpe 72p	Phillips	Carey	Brennan	Sebok	Taylor	Murray	Goodridge	Hutchings	Akinbiyi	Torpey*	Tinnion	Thorpe
	21/8		*7,103*	*2*	3			*Barlow 8, Haworth 90*	*Carroll*	*Green*	*Bowen*	*Kilford**	*McGibbon*	*Balmer*	*O'Neill^*	*Sheridan*	*Haworth*	*Liddell*	*Barlow*	*Porter/Lee*
								Ref: B Burns	At Wigan's new home, the magnificent JJB Stadium, City should have been two up before Stuart Barlow struck with a curled shot. Thorpe levels from the spot after being felled by Roy Carroll, but in injury-time Simon Haworth drills in a rebound off the bar from Barlow's drive.											
4	H	BURY		15	D	1-1	0-0	Taylor 90	Phillips	Brennan	Bell	Sebok	Taylor	Murray"	Goodridge	Hutchings*	Thorpe^	Torpey	Tinnion	Doherty/Meechan/P'monte
	28/8		9,537	*13*	4			*Littlejohn 67*	*Kenny*	*Billy*	*Williams*	*Collins*	*Swailes C*	*Daws*	*Richardson**	*Reid*	*Littlejohn^*	*Lawson*	*James*	*Bullock/Preece*
								Ref: A Butler	Despite Taylor's late-headed leveller for his 50th League goal, both sides squander further chances during four minutes of injury-time. A poor game, in which the ball is often in the air, looked as though it was settled when the lively Adrian Littlejohn brushed past Brennan and shot in.											
5	H	BLACKPOOL		12	W	5-2	0-1	Bell 48, Thorpe 70, 79, Hutchings 83,	Phillips	Lavin	Bell^	Mortimer"	Taylor	Carey	Goodridge	Hutchings	Thorpe	Torpey*	Tinnion	Pinamonte/Brennan/Murray
	4/9		8,439	*20*	7			*Ormerod 15, Murphy 85* [Brennan 89]	*Caig*	*Bryan*	*Hills*	*Clarkson*	*Carlisle*	*Hughes**	*Bent^*	*Couzens*	*Murphy*	*Ormerod*	*Forsyth*	*Robinson !/Nowland*
								Ref: W Jordan	The 48th-min dismissal of Phil Robinson for hauling back Thorpe, and Bell's registering from the resulting free-kick changes the course of this game. Brennan adds to his goal for Canada in midweek by netting a real screamer from a narrow angle after his great dash down the left flank.											
6	H	MILLWALL		14	D	0-0	0-0		Phillips	Lavin^	Brennan	Mortimer	Taylor	Carey*	Goodridge	Murray	Thorpe"	Torpey	Tinnion	Sebok/Bell/**Jones**
	11/9		9,893	*22*	8				*Warner*	*Neill*	*Stuart*	*Cahill*	*Fitzgerald*	*Nethercott*	*Reid**	*Bircham*	*Sadlier*	*Moody^*	*Gilkes"*	*Livermore/Harris/Ryan*
								Ref: A Bates	Head injuries to Carey and Lavin in separate incidents early in the second half help to produce 13 minutes of injury-time in this exciting game. Millwall keeper Tony Warner turns in a Kevin Keelan type performance to deny City, who make 19 goal attempts and twice hit the woodwork.											
7	A	SCUNTHORPE		11	W	2-1	0-0	Jones 79, Taylor 84	Phillips	Brennan	Lavin	Sebok	Taylor	Mortimer !	Goodridge^	Murray	Jones	Torpey*	Tinnion	Bell/Thorpe
	18/9		*4,542*	*20*	11			*Guinan 56*	*Evans*	*Harsley*	*Hope*	*Wilcox*	*Dawson*	*Hodges**	*Guinan*	*Sparrow*	*Stanton*	*Cal'o-Garcia*	*Ipoua*	*Gayle*
								Ref: P Rejer	Perhaps Glanfield Park is more to City's liking than the Old Show Ground. Despite Mortimer's 44th-min red card for a high kick, City notch up their first ever away win over Scunthorpe. Jones' angled shot and Taylor's header tie up the points after Steve Guinan blasted Iron in front.											
8	H	BURNLEY		13	D	0-0	0-0		Philips	Lavin	Brennan	Sebok	Taylor	Mortimer	Goodridge	**Holland***	Jones	Pinamonte^	Tinnion	Hutchings/Thorpe
	25/9		11,510	*2*	12				*Crichton*	*Davis*	*West*	*Armstrong*	*Thomas*	*Cook"*	*Little**	*Mellon*	*Branch^*	*Payton*	*Smith*	*Mullin/Johnrose/Jepson*
								Ref: M Jones	A dire travesty of a match, the only entertainment being a display by the youngsters of King Edmund Gymnastic Club at half-time. Apart from a Taylor header that rebounds off the base of the post, the keepers are rarely troubled, though Paul Crichton does well to save from Goodridge.											
9	A	OXFORD		14	L	0-3	0-2		Phillips	Lavin	Brennan	Sebok	Taylor	Hutchings*	Goodridge"	Thorpe	Jones	Tinnion	Bell^	Tistimetanu/Torpey/Murray
	2/10		*6,638*	*15*	12			*Beauchamp 7, 43, Lilley 66*	*Lundin*	*Folland*	*Powell*	*Robinson*	*Watson*	*Murphy*	*Lambert**	*Lilley^*	*Anthrobus*	*Fear*	*Beauchamp*	*Cook/Abbey*
								Ref: P Richards	City are made to pay for squandering a hatful of chances as they commit suicide at the back. How they miss the departed Welch's assurance on the ball as Phillips is dispossessed in his attempt to dribble round Derek Lilley, who squares the ball for Joey Beauchamp to tap in the opener.											
10	A	PRESTON		15	L	0-1	0-1		Phillips	Lavin	Bell	Carey^	Taylor	Mortimer	Goodridge*	Hutchings"	Jones	Pinamonte	Tinnion	Murray/Sebok/Meechan
	9/10		*10,042*	*7*	12			*Mathie 37*	*Moilanen*	*Alexander*	*Edwards*	*Jackson*	*Kidd*	*Rankine*	*Cartwright*	*Gregan*	*Mathie^*	*Macken*	*McKenna**	*Eyres/Nogan*
								Ref: J Kirby	City's failure to score for the fourth successive game rekindles fears of another relegation fight. Despite City's hard work, the inability of their front players to hold the ball up makes it easy for Preston, who should have registered more than Alex Mathie's shot on the turn from the left.											
11	H	BRISTOL ROV		15	D	0-0	0-0		Phillips	Lavin	Brennan	Carey"	Taylor	Mortimer	Goodridge^	Hutchings	Jones	Thorpe*	Tinnion	**Brown M**/Murray/Sebok
	17/10		**16,011**	*1*	13				*Taylor*	*Pethick*	*Challis"*	*Thomson*	*Tillson*	*Foster*	*Hillier*	*Mauge*	*Cureton^*	*Roberts*	*Pritchard**	*Bryant/Ellington/Leoni*
								Ref: T Heilbron	A much smaller crowd than expected see City dominate this Sky TV game without being able to end their goal drought. Too much air-ball in the first half, in which Jones heads against the crossbar. Then, after the break Goodridge's header suffers the same fate as City turn on the style.											

No	Date	Venue	Opponent	Att	Pos	Res	Pts	F-A	H-T	Scorers, Times, and Referees	1	2	3	4	5	6	7	8	9	10	11	Subs used
12	19/10	H	COLCHESTER	***7,777***	15 / *23*	D	14	1-1	1-0	Tinnion 34 *Duguid 58* Ref: M Warren	Phillips *Brown*	Lavin *Farley*	Brennan *Keith*	Sebok^ *Greene*	Taylor *Skelton^*	Mortimer *Arnott**	Goodridge* *Wilkins*	Hutchings *Gregory*	Jones *Duguid*	**Beadle"** *Dozzell*	Tinnion *Lua Lua*	Thorpe/Murray/Brown M *McGavin/Moralee*
											Tinnion ends City's 490-minute barren spell by driving in a simple chance at the Wedlock Stand end after David Greene got in a tangle. Karl Duguid steers in a well-earned leveller for enterprising Colchester as City's truly appalling performance brought them the jeers they deserved.											
13	23/10	A	BURNLEY	*10,175*	16 / *5*	L	14	0-2	0-1	*Cook 6, Cooke 61* Ref: K Leach	Phillips *Crichton*	Lavin *West*	Brennan *Smith*	Sebok* *Davis*	Taylor *Thomas*	Mortimer *Cook"*	Murray *Little*	Hutchings *Mullin^*	Jones" *Cooke**	Beadle^ *Payton*	Tinnion *Johnrose*	Goodridge/Thorpe/Torpey *Branch/Mellon/Jepson*
											City more than match high-riding Burnley, except in the art of goalscoring. After Paul Cook's 30-yard opener, both Mortimer and Jones miss easy chances before Beadle (£200k ex-Notts) heads against the post just prior to the interval. Andy Cooke's curler ties up the Clarets' victory.											
14	2/11	A	GILLINGHAM	*6,892*	17 / *8*	L	14	0-3	0-0	*Taylor 60, 63, 89* Ref: G Laws	**Mercer** *Bartram*	Lavin *Southall*	Bell *Edge*	Hutchings *Pennock*	Taylor *Ashby*	Mortimer *Butters*	Murray *Saunders^*	Holland *Hessenth'ler*	Jones *Omoyimni**	Meechan* *Thomson"*	Tinnion *Smith*	Thorpe *Taylor/Hodge/Lewis*
											Pulis' return to his old club ends in disappointment after City dominate the first half. Robert Taylor comes off the bench to destroy City after the break. New keeper Mercer, a £275,000 signing from Chesterfield, has no chance as Taylor notches his hat-trick with three fine shots.											
15	6/11	H	CAMBRIDGE	8,646	17 / *22*	D	15	1-1	1-1	Jones 35 *Butler 2* Ref: T Parkes	Mercer *Marshall*	Lavin* *Ashbee*	Bell *Wilson*	Hutchings *McNeil*	Taylor *Joseph*	Mortimer *Mustoe*	Murray *MacKenzie*	Holland *Wanless*	Jones *Butler*	Beadle *Benjamin**	Tinnion^ *Kyd*	Goodridge"/Meechan/**Burns** *Taylor*
											Against the run of play Jones levels Martin Butler's spectacular 20-yard opener, with a first-time shot from eight yards. Unlucky with Jones' header cleared off the line and a Mortimer shot kept out by a post, City fully deserve the boos at the finish for what in truth was a dire display.											
16	14/11	A	STOKE	*10,775*	17 / *7*	D	16	1-1	0-0	Tinnion 85 *Mohan 65* Ref: R Beeby	Mercer *Ward*	Murray* *Short^*	Bell *Clarke*	Hutchings *Mohan*	**Millen** *Dryden*	Holland *Kavanaugh*	Tistimetanu *Keen"*	Beadle *O'Connor*	Jones *Lightbourne*	Mortimer *Thorne*	Tinnion *Bullock**	Goodridge *Jacobson/Robinson/Oldfield*
											Stoke boss Gary Megson in his last game following an Icelandic takeover is cheered by Nicky Mohan's bullet header that gives his side the lead. City save a point with Tinnion's superlative 35-yard lob, but they should have won as Goodridge puts a last min point blank header wide.											
17	23/11	H	OLDHAM	8,214	19 / *15*	D	17	1-1	1-0	Beadle 39 *Allott 84* Ref: G Barber	Mercer *Kelly*	Murray *Rickers*	Bell *Holt*	Millen *McNiven*	Taylor *Garnett*	Holland *Hotte*	Tistim'tanu" *Duxbury*	Beadle *Whitehall**	Jones^ *Allott*	Mortimer* *Sheridan*	Tinnion *Innes^*	Lavin/Torpey/Goodridge *Tipton/Walsh*
											City are booed off after being outplayed by the Latics, but it should have been different after Beadle bundled in his first goal for the Club. Oldham, unbeaten away since losing to the Rovers in September, fully deserved to extend their run, courtesy of Mark Allott's towering header.											
18	27/11	A	NOTTS CO	*5,374*	19 / *6*	D	18	4-4	1-2	Bell 20, 76, Tistimetanu 60, Beadle 64 *Holland 30 (og), Stallard 31, Dyer 72,* Ref: P Walton *[Warren 87]*	Mercer *Ward*	Lavin^ *Holmes"*	Bell *Pearce*	Millen *Warren*	Taylor *Fenton^*	Holland *Redmile*	Tistimetanu *Hughes*	Beadle *Darby**	Jones* *Allsopp*	Mortimer *Owers*	Tinnion *Ramage*	Torpey/Murray *Stallard/Dyer/Tierney*
											City's early dominance is sabotaged by the 27th-minute introduction of substitute Mark Stallard, but after the half-time interval they regain control. Bell's 25-yard screamer should have been a worthy winner, but they fail to close down Mark Warren, who fires in a 30-yard leveller.											
19	4/12	H	READING	8,936	14 / *21*	W	21	3-1	1-0	Torpey 45, Taylor 50, Beadle 76 *Caskey 56* Ref: P Dowd	Mercer *Howie*	Lavin *Gurney*	Bell *Potter*	Millen *Primus*	Taylor *Polston*	Tistim'tanu" *Caskey*	Goodridge^ *Grant^*	Beadle *McIntyre*	Torpey *Williams*	Mortimer* *Bernal*	Tinnion *Evers**	Holland/Murray/Hutchings *Smith/Lisbie*
											Moments after Taylor gets away with his handball to keep out Jimmy McIntyre's shot, Torpey's 18-yarder sets City up for their first League win in twelve attempts. Darren Caskey's free-kick has City rocking until Beadle races through. Mercer saves Caskey's harsh last-min penalty.											
20	7/12	A	CHESTERFIELD	***2,254***	14 / *24*	W	24	2-0	1-0	Galloway 45 (og), Tistimetanu 61 Ref: E Wolstenholme	Mercer *Gayle*	Lavin *Williams D*	Bell *Williams R*	Hutchings *Pearce**	Taylor *Payne*	Millen *Blatherwick*	Tistimetanu *Galloway^*	Beadle *Reeves*	Torpey *Howard*	Holland *D'Auria*	Tinnion *Beaumont*	*Hewitt/Breckin*
											Moldovan international Tistimetanu's 25-yard wonder volley lights up a dismal game. City have the better of the first half, but are fortunate to take the lead when Mick Galloway deflects Lavin's cross into his own net. The post aids City on 72 mins by keeping out Jon Howard's header.											
21	17/12	H	WYCOMBE	8,195	13 / *12*	D	25	0-0	0-0	Ref: A Wiley	Mercer *Taylor*	Lavin *Lawrence*	Bell *Ablett*	Hutchings* *Simpson*	Taylor *Cousins*	Millen *Bates*	**Black^** *Carroll**	Beadle *Baird !*	Torpey *Devine^*	Tistimetanu *Ryan*	Tinnion *Brown*	Holland/Jones *Bulman/Senda*
											Hutchings on 31 mins and loan signing Black (Arsenal) early in the second, are both denied by an upright in an absorbing contest in which the visitors are always a threat. Andrew Baird sent off on 72 mins after a tangle with Man of the Match Black brought forth a second yellow card.											
22	26/12	A	BRENTFORD	*6,942*	14 / *9*	L	25	1-2	0-0	Beadle 90 *Owusa 46, Rowlands 50* Ref: S Bennett	Mercer *Woodman*	Lavin *Quinn*	Bell *Ingimarsson*	Hutchings *Mahon*	Taylor* *Marshall*	Millen *Clement*	Holland *Evans*	Black *Theobald*	Beadle *Partridge^*	Tistim'anu^ *Rowlands*	Tinnion" *Owusa**	Goodridge/Torpey/Mortimer *Agyemang/Charles*
											At Griffin Park keeper Mercer is the fall-guy in a slapstick comedy of errors as woeful City lose their seven-match unbeaten League run. He spills a long shot into the path of Lloyd Owusa, and shortly after is beaten by Martin Rowlands' great angled drive from the edge of the area.											
23	28/12	H	LUTON	11,832	14 / *12*	D	26	0-0	0-0	Ref: M Ryan	Mercer *Abbey*	Lavin* *Taylor*	Bell *Boyce*	Millen *Johnson*	Taylor *Watts*	Mortimer *Doherty*	Black *Spring*	Hutchings^ *White*	Beadle *Gray*	Torpey" *Douglas**	Tinnion *Locke*	Murray/Tistimetanu/Thorpe *Fotiadis*
											Pulis hardly encourages the fans to return with his after-the-match comment that his side are playing good football. Most would disagree after witnessing yet another poor game. Luton have their chances, though City are unlucky with Beadle's first-half effort which cannons off the bar.											

No	Date		Att	Pos	Pt	F-A	H-T	Scorers, Times, and Referees	SQUAD NUMBERS IN USE											subs used
24	A	WREXHAM		14	W	1-0	0-0	Taylor 71	Mercer	Carey	Bell	Millen	Taylor	Mortimer^	Murray	Holland"	Torpey	Black*	Tinnion	Meec'n/Tist'tanu/Hutchings
	3/1		*4,021*	*19*	29				*Dearden*	*McGregor*	*Hardy"*	*Ridler*	*Carey*	*Ferguson*	*Russell^*	*Williams**	*Roberts*	*Stevens*	*Connolly*	*Owen/Chalk/Falconbridge*
								Ref: T Jones	After Mercer's sterling work in almost single-handedly keeping Wrexham at bay, Taylor's ten-yard blaster brings City their first ever success at the Racecourse. A good start to the New Year for City, but Wrexham, without a win in 16 League games, continue their headlong descent.											
25	H	CARDIFF		15	D	0-0	0-0		Mercer	Carey	Bell*	Millen	Taylor	Mortimer^	Murray	Tistimetanu	Torpey	Meechan"	Tinnion !	Holland/Goodridge/Beadle
	9/1		10,568	*17*	30				*Hallworth*	*Low*	*Legg*	*Eckhardt*	*Middleton**	*Perrett*	*Fowler*	*Carpenter*	*Nugent*	*Bowen*	*Hill^*	*Roberts/Bonner*
								Ref: M Dean	After first giving Tistimetanu's 44th-min close-range shot, the referee incurs City's wrath by disallowing same after consulting his insistent linesman and then sending off Tinnion for his remarks to the flag wielding official. Cardiff are unlucky with a long-range shot that hit the bar.											
26	A	BOURNEMOUTH		14	W	3-2	1-0	Millen 32, Thorpe 60, 65p	Mercer	Murray	**Hill**	Millen	Holland	Mortimer	**Burnell**	Thorpe^	Torpey	Tist'tanu*	Tinnion	Hutchings/**Wright**
	15/1		*5,425*	*11*	33			*Robinson 47, O'Neill 86*	*Stewart*	*Warren*	*Mean*	*Broadhurst*	*Cox*	*Elliott**	*O'Neill*	*Robinson*	*Day^*	*Stein*	*Hayter*	*Jorgenson/Fletcher C*
								Ref: A Hall	City respond to the shock departure of Pulis with a style of play more in keeping with the Club's traditions. Millen's six-yard lob sets City on the path to a deserved victory at Dean Court, made sure by Thorpe's neat 20-yarder, that followed his penalty after being pushed to the ground.											
27	H	WIGAN		13	D	0-0	0-0		Mercer	Burnell	Bell	Millen	Hill	Mortimer*	Murray^	Thorpe	Torpey	Burns"	Tinnion	Holland/Goodridge/Tist'tanu
	22/1		10,758	*1*	34				*Carroll*	*McGibbon*	*Green*	*Balmer*	*Sharp*	*McLoughlin*	*O'Neill*	*Barlow**	*Haworth*	*Griffiths*	*Liddell*	*Peron*
								Ref: M Fletcher	The 'feelgood' factor returns to Ashton Gate as City respond to the enthusiastic reception the caretaker management trio of Fawthrop, Rosenior and Burnside received at the start. Unfortunately despite the improved style of football it is still the same old story as the goals just don't come.											
28	A	BURY		14	D	0-0	0-0		Mercer	Burnell	Bell	Millen	Hill*	Mortimer^	Murray	Thorpe"	Torpey	Holland	Hewlett	Carey/**Clist**/Beadle
	29/1		*3,435*	*16*	35				*Kenny*	*Williams*	*Barnes*	*Daws*	*Bullock*	*Reid*	*Avdiu*	*Redmond*	*Barrass*	*Swailes*	*Lawson**	*Preece*
								Ref: P Danson	In the pouring rain City do much better after the break when playing into the gale-force wind. Up front though they offer little, other than Clist's effort which is cleared off the line, whilst Paul Barnes, Ian Lawson, Paul Reid and Andy Preece fail to tuck away easy chances for Bury.											
29	H	CHESTERFIELD		13	W	3-0	2-0	Thorpe 44, Murray 45, Beadle 75	Mercer	Bell*	Burnell	Holland	Millen	Carey	Murray	Thorpe^	Beadle"	Clist	Tinnion	Hill/**Spencer**/**Odejayi**
	5/2		8,837	*23*	38				*Gayle*	*Hewitt*	*Pearce*	*Pointon**	*Blatherwick*	*Williams*	*Galloway*	*Reeves*	*Wilkinson*	*Beaumont*	*Perkins*	*Woods*
								Ref: L Cable	The goals eventually come as City give a solid, but unspectacular display. Thorpe's unerring strike low into the left-hand corner of the Atyeo Stand net raises the fans' spirits, and a minute later they are in dreamland. Murray rides the breaks to surge past three defenders and fire home.											
30	A	BLACKPOOL		11	W	2-1	1-1	Murray 21, Millen 48	Mercer	Burnell	Bell	Carey	Millen	Holland	Murray	Thorpe	Beadle	Clist*	Tinnion	Hewlett
	12/2		*5,066*	*22*	41			*Murphy 41*	*Caig*	*Hills*	*Clarkson*	*Bardsley*	*Carlisle*	*Lumsdon**	*Newell*	*Jaszczun*	*Richardson*	*Murphy*	*Ablett*	*Bent*
								Ref: J Winter	City keep hopes of a play-off place alive with this slick performance at windy Bloomfield Road. Murray's low drive produced early reward for their attack-minded approach, but it takes Millen's looping header to secure the points after John Murphy headed in Pool's simple leveller.											
31	H	NOTTS CO		11	D	2-2	2-0	Holmes 37 (og), Thorpe 42	Mercer	Burnell^	Bell	Hill	Millen	Burns*	Murray	Clist"	Beadle	Thorpe	Tinnion	Goodridge/Carey/Brown A
	19/2		10,029	*7*	42			*Liburd 60, Hughes 77p*	*Ward*	*Holmes**	*Richardson*	*Pearce*	*Warren*	*Hughes*	*Liburd*	*Rapley*	*Dyer"*	*Owers*	*Tierney^*	*Redmile/Ramage/Darby !*
								Ref: P Richards	City struggle against lively opponents and are relieved to hang onto a point after Bell is unfairly adjudged to have tripped Richard Liburd for County's penalty. Richard Holmes heads powerfully into his own net for City's opener, then Thorpe clinically finishes off a through-ball.											
32	A	CARDIFF		10	D	0-0	0-0		Mercer	Burnell	Bell	Carey	Millen	Tist'tanu^	Murray	Clist*	Beadle	Thorpe	Tinnion	Brown A/Burns
	22/2		*6,586*	*21*	43				*Hallworth*	*Legg*	*Ford*	*Young*	*Perrett*	*Bonner*	*Bowen*	*Nugent*	*Carpenter*	*Brazier*	*Fowler**	*Earnshaw*
								Ref: K Lynch	Whilst City stretch their unbeaten run to ten games, spurned chances mean two points lost. Tinnion's immaculate passing with his trusty left foot, makes him the star man, but despite becoming a difficult side to beat, City still have to convince their fans that they have a killer instinct.											
33	H	SCUNTHORPE		10	W	2-1	2-1	Thorpe 18, Murray 40	Mercer	Burnell	Bell	Carey	Millen	Hewlett	Murray	Brown A	Beadle	Thorpe	Tinnion	
	26/2		9,897	*19*	46			*Quailey 43*	*Evans*	*Fickling**	*Hope*	*Logan*	*Housham^*	*Harsley*	*Stanton*	*Ipoua*	*Quailey*	*Hodges*	*Dawson*	*Walker/Sheldon*
								Ref: K Hill	Brian Quailey brings the Iron back into the contest with a vicious 25-yard volley that dips under the bar. Thorpe squanders two open-goal chances after notching City's opener with a quality 12-yard shot, but Murray runs through from the halfway line to double City's advantage.											
34	A	MILLWALL		10	L	**1-4**	1-3	Meechan 45	Mercer	Burnell^	Bell	Carey	Millen	Hewlett	Murray	Brown A*	Beadle	Meechan"	Tinnion	Holland/Hill/Wright
	4/3		*10,141*	*3*	46			*Cahill 8, 34, Ifill 30, Sadlier 57*	*Warner*	*Neill*	*Ryan*	*Tuttle*	*Nethercott*	*Livermore*	*Ifill**	*Cahill*	*Shaw*	*Sadlier^*	*Gilkes*	*Reid/Moody*
								Ref: R Furnadiz	A sorry City display as their 15-match unbeaten run comes to an end. Woeful defending leaves Tim Cahill acres of space to steer in Paul Ifill's cut-back, then Bell's inability to deal with a bouncing ball allows Ifill to net with a fierce shot. Meechan coolly tucks away City's sole reply.											

35	A	CAMBRIDGE		10	L	0-3	1-0		Mercer	Carey	Bell	Hill	Millen	Hewlett	Murray	Holland^	Beadle	Thorpe	Tinnon*	Brown A/Burns
7/3			3,505	20	46			*Youngs 5, 76, Benjamin 87*	*Marshall*	*Chenery*	*Joseph*	*McNeil*	*Eustace*	*Ashbee*	*Mustoe**	*Wanless*	*Taylor^*	*Benjamin*	*Youngs*	*MacKenzie/Preece*
								Ref: S Baines	City's play-off hopes are in tatters as they fail to cope with the more direct style of their opponents. Caught napping when Tom Youngs reacts the quickest to prod in United's opener, City offer little except for a Thorpe effort that is well saved, and Beadle blasting over an open goal.											
36	H	GILLINGHAM		10	L	0-1	0-0		Phillips	Burnell*	Hill	Carey	Millen	Burns	Murray	Tistimetanu	Spencer	Thorpe	Clist	Meechan
11/3			9,332	6	46			*Hessenthaler 78*	*Bartram*	*Southall*	*Pennock*	*Nosworthy*	*Saunders*	*Smith*	*Butters*	*Hesenthaler*	*Asaba^*	*Onuora**	*Lewis*	*Rowe/Butler*
								Ref: A D'Urso	With Mercer injured in the pre-match warm-up, and Phillips not listed on the team sheet, it needs the special permission of the referee for him to play. Even though City are denied a penalty in each half, and Spencer has his 73rd-min header disallowed, the Gills deserve their success.											
37	A	OLDHAM		11	D	1-1	0-0	Brown 77	Phillips	Carey	Hill*	Hewlett^	Jordan	Clist	Murray	Brown A	Beadle	Thorpe	Tinnion	Burnell/**Amankwaah**
18/3			4,808	15	47			*Whitehall 46*	*Kelly*	*Garnett*	*Hotte*	*Duxbury*	*Jones*	*Sheridan*	*McNiven*	*Holt*	*Whitehall*	*Dudley**	*Rickers*	*Allott*
								Ref: P Dowd	Neither keeper is scarcely troubled in the first half, but after the break Thorpe squanders many chances for City. Lee Duxbury's shot is going well wide before Steve Whitehall sticks out his boot to deflect the ball in. Brown levels with a neat shot after outstripping Oldham's defence.											
38	H	BRENTFORD		10	W	1-0	0-0	Murray 77	Phillips	Awankwaah	Bell	Burnell	Jordan	Clist	Murray	Thorpe	Spencer	Holland	Brown A	
25/3			8,804	12	50				*Pearcey*	*Hutchings*	*Anderson*	*Quinn*	*Powell*	*Graham*	*Rowlands*	*Partridge"*	*Owusa*	*Scott*	*Mahon**	*Ing'son^/Kennedy/Pinamonte*
								Ref: G Frankland	At long last City manage to defeat a side higher-placed than themselves at the start of play. Murray's unerring shot into the far corner of the Atyeo Stand net settles this dull game, but ex-City player Scott Partridge has good cause to rue the referee's decision to rule out his header.											
39	H	STOKE		9	D	2-2	1-2	Thorpe 10, 78	Phillips	Amankwaah	Bell	Burnell	Taylor*	Clist^	Murray	Thorpe	Spencer	Holland	Brown A	Hill/Tinnion
28/3			8,103	7	51			*Lightbourne 26, Kavanagh 40*	*Ward*	*Hansson*	*Clake*	*Mohan*	*Dryden**	*Kavanagh*	*Gudjonsson*	*Gunnarsson*	*Thorne*	*Lightbourne*	*O'Connor*	*Gunnlaugsson*
								Ref: B Knight	City look bright early on when Thorpe heads in, but Stoke come back strongly and deservedly lead at the break. Tinnion's entry into the fray sparks City's revival and Thorpe tucks away the equaliser straight after a handball decision had robbed Arnar Gunnlaugsson of a great goal.											
40	A	WYCOMBE		9	W	2-1	1-0	Thorpe 18, Spencer 66	Phillips	Amankwaah	Bell	Millen	Jordan	Tinnion	Murray	Thorpe	Spencer^	Holland	Brown A*	Hewlett/Beadle
1/4			4,754	14	54			*Devine 63*	*Taylor*	*Vinnicombe"*	*Brown^*	*Rogers*	*McCarthy*	*Simpson*	*Carroll*	*Ryan**	*Baird*	*Devine*	*Bulman*	*McSporran/Harkin/Bates*
								Ref: R Styles	Thorpe's shot from the edge of the area is deflected past keeper Martin Taylor as City dominate against poor opposition. After being caught napping by Sean Devine, City's blushes are saved when Spencer (the only player without a name on his back) fires in the deserved winner.											
41	H	WREXHAM		9	W	**4-0**	0-0	Thorpe 53, 83, Beadle 62, Meechan 90	Mercer	Carey	Bell	Millen	Jordan	Burns	Murray	Beadle*	Thorpe^	Holland	Tinnion	Spencer/Meechan
8/4			8,639	18	57				*Dearden*	*McGregor*	*Chalk*	*Hardy*	*Owen**	*Roberts*	*Russell*	*Gibson^*	*Ferguson*	*Ridler*	*Williams"*	*Morrell/Lowe/Thomas*
								Ref: D Crick	City make up for squandering easy chances in the first half with four quality strikes after the break. Referee's assistant Wendy Toms' 29th-min departure with a shoulder injury amuses the crowd, who are captivated by Thorpe's 40-yard lobbed in opener, and Beadle's great 30-yarder.											
42	A	LUTON		9	W	2-1	1-0	Murray 28, Bell 77	Mercer	Carey	Bell	Millen	Jordan	Holland	Murray^	Spencer*	Thorpe"	Beadle	Tinnion	Hill/Burnell/Burns
15/4			4,771	10	60			*Doherty 78*	*Roberts*	*Boyce"*	*White*	*George*	*Watts*	*Spring*	*McLaren**	*Johnson*	*Doherty*	*Taylor*	*Gray^*	*Locke/Douglas/McGowan*
								Ref: T Leake	City put their Auto-Windscreens final loss behind them as Murray takes a long ball in his stride and cuts inside to clip a beauty over the keeper. Bell's strike should have had City coasting, but straight from the re-start Mercer fumbled Gary Doherty's shot to set up a nail-biting finale.											
43	A	BRISTOL ROV		9	L	0-2	0-0		Mercer	Carey	Bell	Jordan	Millen	Tinnion	Murray	Holland	Thorpe^	Beadle*	Brown A	Spencer/Hill
22/4			10,805	3	60			*Roberts 53, Walters 69*	*Jones*	*Andreasson*	*Foster*	*Thomson*	*Tillson*	*Hillier*	*Pethick*	*Cureton*	*Roberts*	*Ellington*	*Walters*	
								Ref: R Baxter	Fortunate to survive a torrid first half, City find there is no escape after the break. Jason Roberts registers with a power shot, and, shortly after Beadle wastes City's only real chance by heading wide, Mark Walters' deflected shot ensures that Rovers end their six-match winless run.											
44	H	OXFORD		9	D	2-2	2-1	Meechan 22, Brown 39	Phillips	Burnell	Bell	Burns^	Millen	Hill"	Murray	Thorpe	Spencer*	Brown A	Tinnion	Meechan/**Hulbert/Coles**
24/4			9,046	20	61			*Powell 10, Davis 68*	*Knight*	*Robinson"*	*Davis*	*Watson*	*Powell*	*Murphy*	*Newton**	*Anthrobus*	*McGowan^*	*Lilley*	*Tait*	*Weatherstone/Folland/Cook*
								Ref: M Fletcher	City are a shambles at the back, but their vibrant attack, especially in the first half, should have secured victory. After Paul Powell slammed the visitors in front when Phillips failed to deal with a deep cross, Meechan did well to deflect in Tinnion's under-hit weak shot for the equaliser.											
45	A	COLCHESTER		9	W	4-3	1-2	Mur' 39, Meech' 63, Ferg' 71(og), Bell 84	Phillips	Burnell	Bell	Millen	Jordan	Holland	Murray	Hulbert*	Brown A^	Meechan	Tinnion	Odejayi/Burns
29/4			4,013	18	64			*Lua Lua 12, Skelton 29p, Duguid 46*	*Brown*	*Dunne*	*Keith^*	*Ferguson*	*Johnson G*	*Skelton*	*Gregory*	*Dozzell*	*McGavin*	*Duguid**	*Lua Lua"*	*Lock/Johnson R/Keeble*
								Ref: C Foy	Bell's direct free-kick from the edge of the area produces an unlikely win after City had twice found themselves two goals behind. Murray's narrow-angled strike hauls City back into the game, after looking all at sea following Jordan's handball, which gave Aaron Skelton his penalty.											
46	H	PRESTON		9	L	0-2	0-1		Phillips	Burnell"	Bell	Millen*	Jordan	Burns	Am'kwaah^	Meechan	Thorpe	Holland	Tinnion	Hill/Odejayi/Tistimetanu
6/5			11,160	1	64			*Angell 14, Appleton 53*	*Moilanen*	*Alexander"*	*Edwards*	*Murdock*	*Jackson*	*McKenna*	*Appleton*	*Rankine*	*Angell**	*Eyres^*	*Macken*	*Basham/Murphy/Parkinson*
		Home	Away					Ref: R Oliver	Despite the hot weather Phillips still plays in his trademark track-suit bottoms as City's bright start comes to nought after Brett Angell's bullet-like header puts Preston in front. Thereafter the Champions dominated and Mike Appleton's sweet strike seals the visitors' impressive display.											
Average		9,803	6,583																	

Worthington Cup			F-A	H-T	Scorers, Times, and Referees	SQUAD	NUMBERS	IN	USE								subs used
1:1 A CAMBRIDGE		D	2-2	0-0	Hutchings 51, Mortimer 90	Phillips	Carey	Brennan	Sebok	Taylor	Mortimer	Murray"	Hutchings^	Akinbiyi	Torpey*	Tinnion	P'monte/Doherty/Goodridge
10/8	*2,813*				*Butler 50, 86*	*Van Hu'sden*	*Chenery*	*Wilson*	*Duncan*	*Eustace*	*Russell*	*Mustoe^*	*Ashbee*	*Benjamin*	*Butler*	*Kyd**	*Taylor/Graham*
					Ref: P Taylor	Mortimer's late header leaves all to play for in the 2nd leg, but in truth City squandered numerous chances. In the first half Murray hits a post and Martin Butler is unfortunate with his shot that hits the crossbar, but makes amends by bundling in the opener and heading the U's in front.											
1:2 H CAMBRIDGE	14	W	2-1	2-0	Torpey 18, Thorpe 36	Phillips	Carey	Brennan	Sebok	Taylor	Murray	Goodridge	Hutchings	Thorpe	Torpey*	Tinnion	Pinamonte
24/8	5,352 *17*				*Butler 87*	*Van Hu'sden*	*Chenery*	*Wilson*	*Eustace*	*Duncan*	*Ashbee*	*Wanless"*	*Mustoe**	*Butler*	*Benjamin*	*Kyd^*	*Taylor/Youngs/Cassidy*
					Ref: C Wilkes (City won 4-3 on aggregate)	With Akinbiyi away on international duty, Thorpe has the chance to show his paces. Only the goalkeeping of Arjan Van Huesden, fortunate when an early shot cannons off his crossbar, thwarts City, but he can do nothing when Torpey and Thorpe are presented with easy tap-ins.											
2:1 A NOTTM FOREST	14	L	1-2	1-1	Jordan 13	Phillips	Sebok	Brennan	Jordan	Taylor	Mortimer^	Murray	Meechan*	Jones	Tinnion	Bell	Brown M/ Brown A
15/9	*5,015 1:9*				*Harewood 12, Rogers 56*	*Crossley*	*Louis-Jean*	*Chettle*	*Scimeca^*	*Hjelde*	*Burns*	*Petrachi**	*Freedman"*	*Harewood*	*Quashie*	*Rogers*	*Allou/Bonalair/Merino*
					Ref: M Messias	Marvin Brown's appearance as a 73rd-min sub makes him City's youngest ever player at 16 years 71 days. Forest's poor finishing keeps City in with a chance after sharp-eyed officials ruled Jordan's header over the line just after Marlon Harewood's low driven opener from 15 yards.											
2:2 H NOTTM FOREST	11	D	0-0	0-0		Phillips	Lavin	Brennan	Sebok	Taylor	Mortimer	Goodridge*	Murray^	Jones	Pinamonte"	Tinnion	Brown A/Thorpe/Torpey
22/9	8,259 *1:11*					*Crossley**	*Louis-Jean*	*Doig*	*Bonalair*	*Hjelde*	*Prutton*	*Allou^*	*Freedman*	*Harewood*	*Quashie*	*Rogers*	*Beasant/Gray*
					Ref: P Durkin (City lost 1-2 on aggregate)	Despite Forest's much superior skill, City with 14 shots on goal (five on target), have the chances to win this exciting game. Dave Beasant took over between the sticks for Forest when Mark Crossley lands awkwardly after tipping over Goodridge's 35-yard dipper in the 16th minute.											

FA Cup (Sponsored by AXA)			F-A	H-T	Scorers, Times, and Referees												subs used
1 H MANSFIELD	16	W	3-2	1-1	Tinnion 44, 50, Murray 65	Phillips	Lavin	Bell	Hutchings	Taylor !	Mortimer"	Murray	Beadle^	Jones*	Holland	Tinnion	M'chan/Goodridge/Tist'tanu
30/10	5,411 *3:18*				*Lormor 10p, Blake 89*	*Bowling*	*Hassell**	*Porter*	*Richardson*	*Linighan*	*Clarke*	*Williams^*	*Disley"*	*Lormor*	*Blake*	*Roscoe*	*Asher/Boulding/Bacon*
					Ref: R Oliver	One short and trailing to Lormor's pen, following Taylor's dismissal for keeping the ball out with his hand, Meechan's 25th-min entry as sub for the injured Jones transforms home fortunes. Tinnion's rarely used right-foot fires in the equaliser, then his left-foot chip puts City ahead.											
2 A BOURNEMOUTH	17	W	2-0	1-0	Murray 22, 53	Mercer	Murray	Bell	Millen	Taylor	Holland	Tist'tanu*	Beadle	Jones	Mortimer	Tinnion	Hutchings
20/11	*5,223 13*					*Ovendale*	*Young*	*Warren**	*Broadhurst*	*Cox*	*Day*	*Jorgensen*	*Robinson*	*Stein*	*Fletcher S*	*Fletcher C !*	*Watson*
					Ref: W Jordan	Third time lucky for City, as they avenge recent FA Cup defeats by the Cherries. Carl Fletcher is dismissed on 72 minutes for his second bookable offence, but by then Murray's cross-shots from the left had clinched victory - his second a scorching 16-yarder into the top corner.											
3 A SHEFFIELD WED	14	L	0-1	0-1		Mercer	Lavin^	Bell	Millen	Taylor	Hutchings	Tist'tanu*	Beadle	Torpey	Holland	Tinnion	Murray/Jones
11/12	*11,644 P:20*				*Booth 25*	*Srnicek*	*Nolan*	*Atherton*	*Thome*	*Walker*	*Hinchcliffe**	*Alexand'son*	*De Bilde"*	*Booth*	*Jonk^*	*Sonner*	*McKeever/Sibon/Quinn !*
					Ref: M Reed	Against opponents lacking in confidence, City's failure to get behind Wednesday's defence often enough proves costly as they fall to Andy Booth's header. The Owls' 88th-minute sub, Alan Quinn, is red carded almost immediately when, with a raised arm, he clatters into Taylor.											

		Home					Away					
	P	W	D	L	F	A	W	D	L	F	A	Pts
1 Preston	46	15	4	4	37	23	13	7	3	37	14	95
2 Burnley	46	16	3	4	42	23	9	10	4	27	24	88
3 Gillingham *	46	16	3	4	46	21	9	7	7	33	27	85
4 Wigan	46	15	3	5	37	14	7	14	2	35	24	83
5 Millwall	46	14	7	2	41	18	9	6	8	35	32	82
6 Stoke	46	13	7	3	37	18	10	6	7	31	24	82
7 Bristol Rov	46	13	7	3	34	19	10	4	9	35	26	80
8 Notts Co	46	9	6	8	32	27	9	5	9	29	28	65
9 BRISTOL CITY	46	7	14	2	31	18	8	5	10	28	39	64
10 Reading	46	10	9	4	28	18	6	5	12	29	45	62
11 Wrexham	46	9	6	8	23	24	8	5	10	29	37	62
12 Wycombe	46	11	4	8	32	24	5	9	9	24	29	61
13 Luton Town	46	10	7	6	41	35	7	3	13	20	30	61
14 Oldham	46	8	5	10	27	28	8	7	8	23	27	60
15 Bury	46	8	10	5	38	33	5	8	10	23	31	57
16 Bournemouth	46	11	6	6	37	19	5	3	15	22	43	57
17 Brentford	46	8	6	9	27	31	5	7	11	20	30	52
18 Colchester	46	9	4	10	36	40	5	6	12	23	42	52
19 Cambridge	46	8	6	9	38	33	4	6	13	26	32	48
20 Oxford	46	6	5	12	24	38	6	4	13	19	35	45
21 Cardiff	46	5	10	8	23	34	4	7	12	22	33	44
22 Blackpool	46	4	10	9	26	37	4	7	12	23	40	41
23 Scunthorpe	46	4	6	13	16	34	5	6	12	24	40	39
24 Chesterfield	46	5	7	11	17	25	2	8	13	17	38	36
	1104	234	155	163	770	634	163	155	234	634	770	1502

* promoted
after play-offs

Odds & ends

Double wins: (5) AFC Bournemouth, Blackpool, Scunthorpe United, Chesterfield, Wrexham.
Double losses: (2) Preston North End, Gillingham.

Won from behind: (3) Blackpool (h), Scunthorpe (a), Colchester Utd (a).
Lost from in front: (0).

High spots: The win at Bournemouth on 15 January.
Winning at Blackpool on 12 February.
The thrilling success at Colchester United on 29 April.
Reaching Wembley in the Freight Rover Trophy.
The departure of manager Tony Pulis and his alien style of football.

Low spots: The first half of the season.
Losing at Cambridge United on 7 March.
The away defeat at Bristol Rovers on 22 April.
Louis Carey's loss of concentration at Wembley that sent City to defeat in the final of the Fright Rover Trophy.

AGM (Sports Hall, St George Community College, 2 November 2000).
Loss: £175,647. Season Ticket Sales (No): 6,000.

Player of the year: Billy Mercer.
Ever-presents: (0).
Hat-tricks: (0).
Leading-scorer: Overall: Tony Thorpe (14). League: (13) Tony Thorpe.

	Appearances						Goals			
	Lge	*Sub*	LC	*Sub*	FAC	*Sub*	Lge	LC	FAC	Tot
Akinbiyi, Ade	3		1				2			2
Amankwaah, Kevin	4	*1*								
Beadle, Peter	22	*3*			3		6			6
Bell, Mickey	34	*2*	1		3		5			5
Black, Tommy	4									
Brennan, Jim	11	*1*	4				2			2
Brown, Aaron	10	*3*		*2*			2			2
Brown, Marvin		*2*		*1*						
Burnell, Joe	15	*2*								
Burns, John	6	*5*								
Carey, Louis	20	*2*	2							
Clist, Simon	8	*1*								
Coles, Danny		*1*								
Doherty, Tommy		*1*		*1*						
Goodridge, Greg	13	*8*	2	*1*		*1*				
Hewlett, Matt	5	*2*								
Hill, Matt	8	*6*								
Holland, Paul	22	*5*			3					
Hulbert, Robin	1	*1*								
Hutchings, Carl	17	*4*	2		2	*1*	1	1		2
Jones, Steve	12	*2*	2		2	*1*	2			2
Jordan, Andrew	8		1					1		1
Lavin, Gerard	18	*1*	1		2					
Meechan, Alex	5	*7*	1			*1*	4			4
Mercer, Billy	25				2					
Millen, Keith	28				2		2			2
Mortimer, Paul	22	*1*	3		2			1		1
Murray, Scott	31	*10*	4		2	*1*	6		3	9
Odejayi, Kayode		*3*								
Phillips, Steve	21		4		1					
Pinamonte, Lorenzo	2	*4*	1	*2*						
Sebok, Vilmos	8	*3*	4							
Shail, Mark		*1*								
Spencer, Damien	6	*3*					1			1
Taylor, Shaun	25		4		3		4			4
Thorpe, Tony	24	*7*	1	*1*			13	1		14
Tinnion, Brian	42	*1*	4		3		3		2	5
Tistimetanu, Ivan	11	*5*			2	*1*	2			2
Torpey, Steve	15	*5*	2	*1*	1		1	1		2
Wright, Ben		*2*								
(own-goals)							3			3
40 players used	**506**	***105***	**44**	***9***	**33**	***6***	**59**	**5**	**5**	**69**

No	Date		Att	Pos	Pt	F-A	H-T	Scorers, Times, and Referees	SQUAD	NUMBERS	IN	USE								subs used
1	A	WREXHAM			W	2-0	1-0	Thorpe 8, Holland 62	Miller	Tistimetanu	Bell	Carey	Lever	Holland	Murray^	Dunning	Peacock	Thorpe*	Tinnion	Goodridge/Spencer
	12/8		5,852		3				Rogers	McGregor	Faulconb'ge	Roberts	Owen	Carey	Ferguson	Gibson	Roche	Blackwood	Sam	
								Ref: A Leake	A backs to the wall performance by City at the Racecourse, where they ride their luck before claiming their first winning start to a season for ten years. After Hector Sam's early strike was surprisingly disallowed, Thorpe seized on Tinnion's through ball to poke home City's opener.											
2	H	STOKE			L	1-2	0-0	Thomas 65 (og)	Miller	Tistimetanu	Bell	Carey	Lever	Holland*	Murray	Dunning	Peacock	Thorpe	Tinnion	Spencer
	19/8		12,590		3			Gudjonsson 75, O'Connor 87	Muggleton	Mohan	Dorigo	Gunnarsson	Gudjonsson	Lightbo'rne*	Risom	O'Connor	Petty	Thordarsson	Thomas^	Connor/Fenton
								Ref: W Jordan	With Wedlock's name now disgracefully omitted from the newly named Dry Blackthorn Stand, City are stunned by Stoke's late double. Bjarni Gudjonsson ghosted in behind City's sleeping defenders to steer in Graham Fenton's cross, then James O'Connor slammed home the winner.											
3	A	CAMBRIDGE		14	L	0-1	0-0		Miller	Lavin	Bell	Carey	Jordan	Hulbert*	Murray	Dunning	Spencer^	Thorpe	Tinnion	Tistimetanu/Brown A
	26/8		3,716	11	3			Wanless 57p	Perez	McAnespie	Ashbee	Mustoe	Duncan	Dreyer	Ussell	Wanless	Youngs	Abbey	Slade*	Axeidal
								Ref: M Halsey	Lacklustre City reaped what they deserved at the Abbey Stadium, where their woeful performance made nonsense of declared promotion aims. United, who hit the bar and had a goal disallowed for offside, deserved to win by more than Paul Wanless' penalty following Bell's handball.											
4	H	ROTHERHAM		20	L	0-1	0-0		Miller	Lavin	Bell	Carey	Millen	Holland	Murray*	Dunning	Peacock	Thorpe^	Tinnion	Goodridge/Odejayi
	28/8		8,280	10	3			Fortune-West 64	Gray	Bryan	Branston	Beach	Wilsterman	Talbot*	Garner	Robins	Fort'e-West	Warne	Watson	Hurst
								Ref: P Dowd	City's dire first-half display is only partially redeemed by Goodridge's appearance after the break. Bell is caught napping by Marvin Bryan's quickly taken free-kick, and Leo Fortune-West steams in at the far post at the Blackthorn end to bring the visitors their first win of the season.											
5	H	SWINDON		22	L	0-1	0-0		Phillips"	Lavin*	Bell	Carey	Millen	Holland	Murray	Dunning	Beadle^	Thorpe	Tinnion	Tistim'anu/Odejayi/Malessa
	9/9		10,110	21	3			Reeves 81	Griemink	Robinson	Davis	Reeves	Willis	Hewlett	O'Halloran	Duke	Williams	Invincible*	Howe	Grazioli
								Ref: C Foy	A moderate Swindon side pile on the problems for City boss Danny Wilson. City waste their chances, including a first-half Murray header that hits a post, and pay the price when Alan Reeves capitalises on some kamikaze defending to head in the decider from a Sol Davis free-kick.											
6	A	OLDHAM		22	D	0-0	0-0		Phillips	Tistimetanu	Bell	Carey	Millen	Holland*	Murray	Dunning	Beadle^	Thorpe	Tinnion	Jordan/Goodridge
	16/9		4,095	21	4				Kelly	Adams	McNiven	Innes	Lightfoot*	Duxbury	Jones	Boshell	Corazzin	Allott^	Rickers"	Hotte/Tipton/Prenderville
								Ref: D Laws	The finishing ability of watching ex-City favourite Shaun Goater is what this game is crying out for. Phillips turns in his best display to date as both keepers are kept busy, but the goals don't come. Beadle's header and Murray's 20-yarder are repelled by the woodwork in the first half.											
7	H	COLCHESTER		23	D	1-1	1-1	Thorpe 21	Phillips	Amankwaah	Bell	Carey	Millen	Tinnion	Murray	Dunning	Beadle^	Thorpe	Goodridge*	Tistimetanu/Brown M
	23/9		7,411	12	5			Lock 2	Brown	Dunne	Johnson	White^	Clark	Skelton	Stockwell	Dozzell	McGavin"	Lock	Gregory*	Keeble/Keith/Opara
								Ref: M Warren	A lamentable performance by sorry City, their worst for many years is the verdict of many, means they still seek their first home win. Ex-City player Lock headed the U's in front, but Thorpe seized on a mistake by Aaron Skelton to skip past a defender and slot home the leveller.											
8	A	OXFORD		18	W	1-0	1-0	Murray 9	Phillips	Amankwaah	Carey	Clist^	Millen	Tinnion	Murray	Dunning	Beadle*	Thorpe"	Bell	Peacock/Tistimetanu/Hill
	30/9		5,308	24	8				Knight	Robertson	Jarman	Ford	Richardson	Tait^	Omoyimni*	Whitehead	Lilley	Mike	Beauchamp	Cook/Fear
								Ref: M Jones	In a match that City had to win the points are theirs' thanks to Murray's tight-angled prod over the advancing keeper early in the first half. With the slope in their favour after the interval, rampant Oxford are let down by a combination of poor finishing and City's good defending.											
9	H	BOURNEMOUTH		18	D	3-3	3-2	Thorpe 24, 30, 38	Phillips	Amankwaah	Carey	Clist	Millen	Tinnion	Murray	Dunning	Beadle^	Thorpe*	Bell	Rodrigues/Peacock
	6/10		8,936	19	9			Fletcher C 32, Jorgensen 45, [O'Connor 89]	Stewart	Purches	Tindall*	Woozley	Smith"	Fletcher C	Jorgensen	Day^	Hayter	Fletcher S	Grant	Broadhurst/Ford/O'Connor
								Ref: M Cowburn	Gareth O'Connor's hopeful shot robs City of a deserved victory in this brilliant advertisement for Second Division soccer. Thorpe fired City in front when Murray's shot hit a post, and he went on to claim a hat-trick with an easy tap-in followed by a bullet-like header to Beadle's cross.											
10	A	WALSALL		20	D	0-0	0-0		Phillips	Amankwaah	Carey	Clist	Millen	Tinnion	Murray	Hulbert*	Peacock	Rodrigues	Bell	Brown A
	14/10		6,576	1	10				Walker	Brightwell	Aranalde	Barras	Tillson	Bukran	Hall*	Bennett	Angell^	Leitao	Mathias	Wrack/Byfield
								Ref: E Wolstenholme	City shut out the Second Division's most potent strike force (24 League goals this season) thanks to inside information from Portuguese Dani Rodrigues. His fellow compatriot, Jorge Leitao, who has found the net on eight occasions this season, is hardly allowed a kick by Carey.											
11	A	MILLWALL		20	D	1-1	0-1	Murray 90	Phillips	Am'kwaah*	Carey	Clist	Millen	Tinnion	Murray	Hulbert^	Peacock"	Rodrigues	Bell	Burnell/Brown A/Beadle
	17/10		9,694	3	11			Parkin 3	Warner	Lawrence	Bull"	Nethercott	Dyche	Cahill	Gilkes*	Livermore	Parkin^	Harris	Neill	Ifill/Sadlier/Stuart
								Ref: R Pearson	Never-say-die City snatch a plucky point at the New Den. Their tenacious late fightback is rewarded when Murray skipped around the back and somehow slotted the ball past Tony Warner for their point saver after Sam Parkin had earlier risen unchallenged to head Millwall in front.											

No	Venue / Date	Opponent / Att	Pos	Res / Pts	F-A	H-T	Scorers, Times, Referees	1	2	3	4	5	6	7	8	9	10	11	Subs used
12	H	READING	17	W	4-0	3-0	Peacock 9, 60, Murray 18, Bell 30	Phillips	Burnell	Carey	Clist	Millen	Tinnion	Murray	Hulbert"	Peacock^	Rodrigues*	Bell	Thorpe/Beadle/Brown A
	21/10	11,134	2	14				*Whitehead*	*Murty"*	*Robinson*	*Viveash*	*Williams**	*Jones*	*Caskey*	*Newman*	*McIntyre^*	*Butler*	*Hodges*	*Gurney/Cureton/Igoe*
							Ref: P Danson	Nice to see that Wedlock's name has now been restored to the old Covered End – the Dry Blackthorn Wedlock Stand. City are well in charge against the high flying Royals, but this exhilarating game is marred by the horrific broken ankle sustained by Rodrigues just prior to half-time.											
13	H	PETERBOROUGH	16	W	2-1	0-1	Peacock 62, Thorpe 86	Phillips	Burnell	Carey	Clist	Millen	Tinnion	Murray	Hulbert*	Peacock^	Thorpe	Bell	Beadle/Brown A
	24/10	9,219	13	17			*Farrell 23*	*Tyler*	*Hooper^*	*Drury*	*Edwards*	*Rae*	*Oldfield*	*Forsyth*	*Shields"*	*Farrell*	*Clarke*	*Green**	*Lee/Gill/Danieisson*
							Ref: M North	After Bell had his fourth-minute shot disallowed for offside, David Farrell's sweet angled drive into the top corner of the Atyeo Stand net gives Posh the lead against the run of play. Peacock levels with a stunning 25-yard half-volley, then Thorpe's low right-footed drive secures victory.											
14	A	WYCOMBE	15	W	2-1	1-1	Thorpe 2p, 70	Phillips	Burnell	Carey	Clist^	Hill	Tinnion	Murray	Hulbert	Peacock*	Thorpe	Bell	Beadle/Brown A
	28/10	*6,051*	*6*	20			*Rammell 45*	*Taylor*	*Cousins*	*McCarthy*	*Simpson*	*Bates*	*Lee*	*Senda*	*Ryan**	*Rammell*	*McSporran*	*Vinnicombe*	*Castledine*
							Ref: A Hall	City have to battle against the wind and driving rain as well as the slope in the first half. Bell (captain for the first time against his old club) is upended by Jamie Bates for the early spot-kick. Thorpe's low diving header secures victory after Andy Rammell had headed Wycombe level.											
15	A	SWANSEA	10	D	2-2	1-1	Carey 35, Smith 74 (og)	Phillips	Burnell	Carey	Clist	Hill*	Tinnion	Murray	Hulbert^	Peacock	Thorpe	Bell	Millen/Brown A
	31/10	*5,286*	*19*	21			*Savarese 9, 65*	*Freestone*	*Howard*	*Smith*	*Romo*	*Bound*	*Roberts*	*Price*	*Jenkins*	*Savarese*	*Watkin*	*Cusack*	
							Ref: G Cain	City do well to weather the storm at the Vetch Field, where poor defending gifts Giovanni Savarese both of his strikes. Carey heads in his first ever goal and then, after Clist's shot from Murray's pull-back is disallowed, Jason Smith diverts in Hill's low cross for a hard-earned point.											
16	H	NOTTS CO	9	W	4-0	2-0	Clist 33, Murray 36, Thorpe 61, [Peacock 88]	Phillips	Carey	Hill	Clist	Millen	Tinnion	Murray^	Thorpe*	Peacock	Brown A	Bell	Beadle/Goodridge
	4/11	10,250	*16*	24				*Gibson*	*McDermott*	*Richardson*	*Owers*	*Jacobsen*	*Ramage*	*Fenton*	*Pearce*	*Farrell*	*Joseph**	*Hamilton*	*Murray*
							Ref: J Brandwood	After Millen's early header is cleared off the line it takes time for City to break down County's hard-tackling display. Clist's first ever goal – reminiscent of Jimmy Greaves – opens the floodgates. Murray has City cruising by punishing Paul Gibson for spilling Thorpe's half-hit effort.											
17	A	LUTON	8	W	3-0	0-0	Murray 55, Peacock 63, Bell 67	Phillips	Carey	Hill	Clist	Millen	Tinnion"	Murray	Thorpe^	Peacock	Brown A*	Bell	Burnell/Beadle/Tistimetanu
	11/11	*6,595*	*23*	27				*Abbey*	*Karisen*	*George*	*McLaren*	*Boyce*	*Spring*	*Helin*	*Taylor*	*Stein^*	*Douglas**	*McGowan*	*Fotiades/Baptiste*
							Ref: M Cooper	Memorable first-half saves by Phillips give City the platform for their swashbuckling display after the break. Murray picks his spot from ten yards to beat a defender on the line for the opener, then his ball into the box allows Peacock to execute a deft finish for his first City away goal.											
18	H	WIGAN	8	D	1-1	1-1	Peacock 7	Phillips	Carey	Hill	Clist	Millen	Tinnion	Murray	Thorpe*	Peacock	Brown A	Bell	Beadle
	25/11	12,708	*3*	28			*Carey 3 (og)*	*Stillie*	*McGibbon*	*De Zeeuw*	*Bidstrup*	*Griffiths*	*Martinez*	*Green*	*Liddell*	*Roberts*	*Kilford*	*Sharp*	
							Ref: R Oliver	City show the leaders too much respect in this absorbing clash. Carey puts into his own net in his attempt to deal with Andy Liddell's cross, but Peacock – who had put an unchallenged header too close to keeper Derek Stillie after just 65 secs – made amends by sliding in Bell's cross.											
19	H	BURY	6	W	4-1	1-0	Carey 45, Thorpe 52, Clist 73, [Murray 90]	Phillips	Carey	Hill	Clist	Millen	Tinnion*	Murray	Thorpe	Peacock	Brown A	Bell	Goodridge
	2/12	9,416	*14*	31			*Reid 50*	*Kenny*	*Swailes C*	*Barrick*	*Swailes D*	*Redmond*	*Daws*	*Billy*	*Bullock**	*Smith^*	*Preece"*	*Reid*	*Littlejohn/James/Barnes*
							Ref: F Stretton	City are dominant, but it is not until first-half injury-time that Carey's header makes the breakthrough. Despite Paul Reid sweeping in Bury's leveller, City are not to be denied. Murray's intersection and run half the length of the field before firing home sets the seal on a great win.											
20	H	BRENTFORD	6	L	1-2	1-1	Peacock 32	Phillips	Carey	Hill	Clist*	Millen	Tinnion	Murray	Thorpe	Peacock	Brown A	Bell	Beadle
	12/12	8,096	*12*	31			*Mahon 41, Partridge 86*	*Gotts'ksson*	*Ingimarsson*	*Marshall*	*Rowlands*	*Mahon*	*Quinn*	*Lovett*	*Partridge*	*Scott*	*Evans*	*Dobson**	*Owusa*
							Ref: A Kaye	Poetic justice perhaps as City undeservedly lose this rearranged game, as many thought they had used the excuse of the 'fuel crisis' to postpone for their injury-hit side in September. Murray's disallowed power-drive summed up City's night, made worse by Scott Partridge's late tap-in.											
21	A	PORT VALE	6	W	2-1	1-0	Peacock 19, 88p	Phillips	Carey	Hill	Clist*	Millen	Tinnion	Murray"	Thorpe^	Peacock	Brown A	Bell	Burnell/Beadle/Goodridge
	13/12	*4,113*	*21*	34			*Bridge-Wilkinson 59*	*Goodlad*	*Walsh*	*Tankard*	*Widdrington*	*Carragher*	*Brammer*	*Cummins*	*B'dge-W'son*	*Naylor**	*Minton*	*Smith*	*Burton*
							Ref: J Robinson	A quick change of fortune for City who survive a real battering. Marc Bridge-Wilkinson's volleyed leveller to Clist's headed opener has City hanging on, with Vale hitting the bar and creating numerous chances before Jeff Minton brought Burnell down in the box for the pen winner.											
22	H	BRISTOL ROV	5	W	3-2	0-1	Millen 49, Beadle 55, Thorpe 74	Phillips	Carey	Hill	Clist	Millen	Tinnion	Murray	Thorpe	Peacock*	Brown A	Bell	Beadle
	23/12	**16,696**	*18*	37			*Bignot 1, Cameron 78*	*Culkin*	*Thomson*	*Jones*	*Hogg*	*Foster*	*Bryant*	*Pethick"*	*Evans^*	*Ellington**	*Cameron*	*Bignot*	*Astafjevs/Meaker/Mauge*
							Ref: C Wilkes	The Sky TV audience witness one of the quickest derby goals as Marcus Bignot bursts through into the box to shoot into the City net after just 27 seconds. Beadle changes the course of the game. Involved in the build-up to Millen's leveller, he puts City ahead with a powerful header.											
23	A	NORTHAMPTON	6	L	0-2	0-2		Phillips	Carey	Hill	Tisti'tanu*	Millen	Thorpe	Amankwaah	Murray	Beadle	Brown A	Bell	Clist
	26/12	*6,064*	*8*	37			*Savage 29, Forrester 30*	*Welch*	*Chivers*	*Spedding*	*Sampson*	*Green*	*Crooks*	*Savage**	*Hunt*	*Forrester*	*Howard*	*Hargreaves*	*Hughes*
							Ref: C Webster	Without the injured Peacock and Tinnion, and with Murray and Beadle playing up front City are made to pay for early missed chances. Hill's miskicked clearance lets in Dave Savage to fire the homesters in front, then within a minute Phillips is beaten by Jamie Forrester's header.											

NATIONWIDE LEAGUE DIVISION 2

Manager: Danny Wilson

SEASON 2000-01

No	Date		Att	Pos	Pt	F-A	H-T	Scorers, Times, and Referees	SQUAD	NUMBERS	IN	USE								subs used
24	A	STOKE		7	L	0-1	0-0		Phillips	Carey	Hill	Clist^	Millen	Tinnion	Murray	Thorpe	Spencer*	Brown A	Bell	Odejayi/Tistimetanu
	30/12		*14,629*	*5*	37			*Gudjonsson 82*	*Kristinsson*	*Mohan*	*Thomas*	*O'Connor*	*Gunnarsson*	*Gudjonsson*	*Hansson"*	*Thorne*	*Cooke^*	*Kavanagh*	*Dorigo**	*Clarke/Dadasun/Rosom*
								Ref: P Richards	City put on an inept display for their travelling fans at the Britannia Stadium, where they hardly manage a worthwhile attack. Resolute defending looked like gaining City an unlikely point, but a moment's slackness cost them when a floated left-wing cross bounced into the net.											
25	H	CAMBRIDGE		7	W	**6-2**	1-1	Murray 31, 48, Thorpe 60p, 78, 81,	Phillips	Carey	Hill	Clist	Millen	Tinnion	Murray	Thorpe	Beadle	Brown A	Bell*	Tistimetanu
	1/1		10,637	*18*	40			*Wanless 32, Connor 59* [Tinnion 83]	*Perez !*	*Duncan*	*Cowan*	*Wanless*	*Joseph*	*Dreyer*	*Wilson**	*Connor"*	*Taylor*	*Ashbee*	*Hansen^*	*Oakes/Traore/Marshall*
								Ref: S Mathieson	Tinnion scores the goal of the game with a fine volley. Beadle sets the ball up for him from the free-kick resulting from Perez's unfortunate sending-off for catching the ball outside of the area. A deceptive scoreline for a game in which the visitors had posed City many problems.											
26	A	ROTHERHAM		7	D	1-1	0-1	Beadle 88	Phillips	Carey	Hill	Clist*	Millen	Tinnion	Murray	Beadle	Peacock	Brown A	Bell	Brown M
	13/1		*5,654*	*4*	41			*Robins 35*	*Gray*	*Artell*	*Scott*	*Hurst*	*Branston*	*Watson*	*Talbot*	*Lee**	*Warne*	*Robins^*	*Garner*	*Sedgwick/Barker*
								Ref: A Leake	The man responsible for City's infamous *Donkey of the Week* award pops up with a dramatic late header to give his team some reward for all their second-half pressure. Surprise side Rotherham, were in control before the break, especially after Mark Robins had headed them in front.											
27	H	NORTHAMPTON		7	W	2-0	0-0	Clist 54, Bell 73	Phillips	Carey	Hill	Clist	Millen	Tinnion	Murray	Beadle*	Peacock	Brown A	Bell	Thorpe
	20/1		11,630	*8*	44				*Welch*	*Chivers*	*Sampson*	*Hunt*	*Spedding*	*Savage*	*Green*	*Crooks**	*Forrester*	*Howard^*	*Hargreaves*	*Hodge/Gabbiadini*
								Ref: L Cable	On the face of it, with two efforts disallowed and thrice being thwarted by the woodwork, it appears that City had an easy victory. This wasn't the case however as the Cobblers played their part in a thrilling contest. Bell made sure of the points with an exquisite shot at the Park end.											
28	H	SWANSEA		7	W	3-1	1-1	Bell 18, Beadle 89, Thorpe 90	Phillips	Carey	Hill*	Clist^	Millen	Tinnion	Murray	Thorpe	Peacock"	Brown A	Bell	Am'kwaah/Brown M/Beadle
	3/2		10,379	*22*	47			*Roberts 11*	*Freestone*	*Smith*	*Howard !*	*Lacey*	*O'Leary*	*Jenkins*	*Price*	*Savarese**	*Roberts*	*Romo*	*Keegan^*	*Watkin/Cusack*
								Ref: M Halsey	City leave it late to dispose of opponents down to ten men from the 17th-min when Michael Howard had tugged back Murray. Indeed Swansea gave City a lot of trouble and it was some relief when sub Beadle headed City in front at the Atyeo Stand end. Thorpe then tapped in another.											
29	A	SWINDON		7	D	1-1	1-1	Beadle 45	Phillips	Carey	Hill	Clist	Millen	Tinnion	Murray	Thorpe	Beadle*	Brown A	Bell^	Peacock/Burnell
	10/2		*10,031*	*19*	48			*Reddy 33*	*Mildenhall*	*Willis*	*Hall**	*Williams*	*Heywood*	*O'Halloran*	*Cowe^*	*Reddy*	*Van Linden*	*Duke*	*Davis*	*Grazioli/Hewlett*
								Ref: D Gallagher	Another late goal for City, but at least this time it is at the end of the first half when flu bug victim Beadle met Brown's perfect cross to steer the ball in at the back post. In the second half City controlled the game, but apart from Peacock's headed opportunity few chances are created.											
30	H	WREXHAM		6	W	2-1	0-0	Peacock 57, Millen 66	Phillips	Carey	Hill	Clist	Millen	Tinnion	Murray	Thorpe	Beadle*	Burnell^	Brown A	Peacock/Amankwaah
	13/2		9,500	*15*	51			*Russell 61*	*Dearden*	*Roche*	*McGregor*	*Ridler*	*Carey*	*Phillips**	*Ferguson*	*Russell*	*F'bridge^*	*Owen"*	*Edwards*	*Barrett/Morrell/Gibson*
								Ref: P Armstrong	City struggled throughout a dire first half, but the arrival of Peacock after the break restored some movement to the side. Brown's magic on the left and his great ground level cross set-up skipper Millen to slam in the winner after Kevin Russell's fierce drive had levelled for the visitors.											
31	A	BRENTFORD		7	L	1-2	1-1	Thorpe 36	Phillips	Carey	Hill	Clist	Millen	Tinnion	Murray	Thorpe*	Peacock	Brown A	Bell	Beadle
	20/2		*4,823*	*10*	51			*O'Connor 3, Partridge 68*	*Gotts'ksson*	*Mahon*	*Marshall*	*Evans*	*Powell*	*O'Connor^*	*Dobson*	*Owusa**	*Partridge*	*Ingimarsson*	*Gibbs*	*McCammon/Lovett*
								Ref: M Warren	Following Kevin O'Connor's early 20-yarder, City offer little, apart from Millen's disallowed eighth-min header, until Thorpe headed in Bell's cross at the far post. Brentford remained in the ascendancy after the break and ex-City player Scott Partridge side-footed in a deserved winner.											
32	A	COLCHESTER		7	L	**0-4**	0-2	*[Conlon 69]*	Phillips	Carey	Am'kwaah*	Clist^	Millen	Tinnion	Murray	Beadle	Peacock	Brown A	**Woodman**	Hill/Thorpe
	24/2		***3,430***	*17*	51			*Gregory 7, Keith 42, Stockwell 57,*	*Woodman*	*Johnson R*	*Fitzgerald*	*Gregory**	*Clark*	*Stockwell^*	*Dunne*	*Duguid"*	*Conlon*	*Skelton*	*Keith*	*J'son G/McGavin/McGleish*
								Ref: T Parkes	It might have been different if Peacock hadn't hit the bar on 23 minutes, but City lacked pace and desire in this sorry display. Murray's failure to track back allowed Joe Keith to put Utd firmly in charge with a stooping header, after an unmarked David Gregory had slotted in the opener.											
33	H	OXFORD		7	D	0-0	0-0		Phillips	Am'kwaah"	Hill	Hulbert	Carey	Tinnion*	Murray	Thorpe	Peacock	Burnell^	Brown A	Beadle/Woodman/Coles
	3/3		9,681	*24*	52				*Knight*	*Robertson*	*Hatswell*	*Richardson*	*Patterson*	*Murphy*	*Scott*	*Tait*	*Gray*	*Whitehead*	*Powell**	*Beauchamp*
								Ref: R Beeby	Tinnion's exit with a strained hamstring midway through the second period is a serious blow for City as they fail to perform against rock bottom Oxford. The desire to win is missing until the final ten minutes. Thorpe has his injury-time penalty saved at the Atyeo Stand End.											
34	H	WALSALL		8	L	1-3	1-2	Thorpe 32	Phillips	Carey	Hill	Clist	Millen	Hulbert*	Murray	Thorpe	Beadle	Burnell	Brown A	Brown M
	6/3		9,263	*3*	52			*Leitao 14, Simpson 16, Carey 74 (og)*	*Walker*	*Roper*	*Barras*	*Simpson*	*Tillson*	*Bennett*	*Brightwell**	*Leitao*	*Byfield*	*Keates*	*Aranalde*	*Marsh*
								Ref: P Prosser	A nightmare night for Carey as his failure to clear gifts Walsall their opener, then after the break he slides in an own-goal at the East End. After Beadle's fierce free-kick that the keeper did well to save, City fought-back with Thorpe's glanced in header and looked likely to level matters.											

No	Date	Opponent	Att	Pos	Res/Pts	F-A	H-T	Scorers, Times, and Referees	1	2	3	4	5	6	7	8	9	10	11	Subs used
35	A	**BOURNEMOUTH**		9	L	**0-4**	0-3	*[Fletcher C 39]*	Phillips	Carey	Hill	Clist	**Coles***	Burnell	Murray	Thorpe	Beadle	Hulbert	Brown A	Amankwaah
	10/3		*4,028*	*11*	52			*Elliott 12, 55, Hughes 17,*	*Menetrier*	*Hayter**	*Howe*	*Jorgensen*	*Tindall*	*Fletcher C*	*Broadhurst*	*Defoe*	*Fletcher S*	*Hughes*	*Elliott^*	*O'Connor/Purchase*
								Ref: A Hall	Another inept passionless display made worse on the day by the fact of a fully committed Wycombe doing what City failed to do at Leicester to progress through to the FA Cup semi-final. Phillips gets the boos of the travelling fans as his mistake gifts Bournemouth their last goal.											
36	H	**MILLWALL**		7	W	2-1	1-0	Carey 4, Matthews 89p	Phillips	Carey	Hill	Clist"	Burnell	**Maddison**	Murray	Thorpe !	Peacock*	Brown A	Bell^	Beadle!/**Matthews**/Hulbert
	16/3		10,395	*1*	55			*Harris 60p*	*Gueret*	*Lawrence*	*Ryan^*	*Cahill*	*Nethercott*	*Dyche*	*Neill*	*Moody !*	*Harris !*	*Livermore*	*Kinet**	*Ifill/Reid*
								Ref: M Jones	Thorpe's 61st-minute red card was deserved for his sly kick on Sean Dyche. Shortly before City's controversial injury-time winner, Beadle and Paul Moody received the same punishment for hitting each other, whilst after there is still time for Neil Harris to go for laying out Murray.											
37	A	**READING**		7	W	3-1	1-1	Thorpe 44, Peacock 53, Matthews 75	Phillips	Carey	Hill	Clist"	Burnell	Maddison	Murray	Thorpe*	Peacock	Brown A^	Bell	Matthews/Tinnion/Hulbert
	23/3		***15,716***	*3*	58			*Murty 8*	*Whitehead*	*Robinson*	*Newman*	*Hunter^*	*Whitbread*	*Parkinson"*	*McIntyre*	*Butler*	*Rougier**	*Harper*	*Murty*	*Cureton/Igoe/Caskey*
								Ref: P Durkin	The Royals dominated much of the first half after Graeme Murty's 25-yard opener. Peacock's good work on the left set up Thorpe's close-in leveller, then he headed City in front shortly after the post had denied Martin Butler. Matthews' angled drive made sure of the points for City.											
38	H	**OLDHAM**		7	D	2-2	1-1	Maddison 1, Peacock 88	Phillips	Carey	Hill	Clist^	Burnell	Maddison*	Murray	Thorpe	Peacock	Tinnion	Bell	Hulbert/Beadle
	27/3		9,568	*13*	59			*Carss 14, Sheridan 69p*	*Kelly*	*Hotte*	*Garnett*	*Sheridan*	*McNiven*	*Carss*	*Eyres*	*Allott**	*Corazzin*	*Innes*	*Rickers*	*Parkin*
								Ref: P Taylor	Despite Maddison's sweetly struck 20-yard half-volley at the start, City are lucky to escape with a point against more determined opponents. Tony Carss rises unchallenged to head in John Sheridan's corner, then Carey grabs Carlo Corazzin to concede Sheridan's cutely taken penalty.											
39	H	**PORT VALE**		7	D	1-1	0-1	Murray 78	Phillips	Carey	Hill	Clist	Burnell	Maddison^	Murray	Matthews"	Peacock	Brown A*	Bell	Tinnion/Hulbert/Brown M
	31/3		11,782	*17*	60			*Brooker 28*	*Delaney*	*Carragher*	*Burton*	*Brammer*	*Walsh*	*Smith*	*Cummins*	*Naylor**	*Twiss*	*Brooker*	*Brisco*	*Widdrington*
								Ref: P Joslin	Murray's classic diving header salvages a point on a frustrating afternoon at Ashton Gate. Against in-form opponents – no goals conceded in six games and thirteen unbeaten – City rarely threatened, although a post denied Matthews shortly after Steve Brooker had fired Vale in front.											
40	A	**BRISTOL ROV**		7	D	1-1	0-0	Peacock 78p	Phillips	Carey	Hill	Clist	Burnell	Tinnion	Murray	Matthews	Peacock	Hulbert	Bell	
	3/4		*9,361*	*21*	61			*Lee 52*	*Culkin*	*Thomson*	*Jones*	*Plummer*	*Foster*	*Mauge*	*Wilson*	*Ellington*	*Lee*	*Hogg**	*Challis*	*Gall*
								Ref: A Wiley	In monsoon-like conditions this game only livens up after the interval. Phillips makes amends for being stranded by Christian Lee's looping header, as after Hill's handball at the death he saves Scott Jones' penalty. No such problem for Peacock who registers for City from the spot.											
41	A	**BURY**		7	W	1-0	0-0	Da Silva 52	Phillips	Carey	Hill	Clist	Burnell	Tinnion	Murray	Matthews	Peacock*	Hulbert	Bell	**Da Silva**
	7/4		*3,729*	*12*	64				*Kenny*	*Daws*	*Reid*	*Swailes C*	*Swailes D**	*Armstrong*	*Hill*	*Preece*	*Cramb*	*Billy*	*Jarrett*	*Jones*
								Ref: M Riley	Portuguese trialist Da Silva is City's hero with the game's only goal. Coming on following Peacock's 20th-min hamstring injury, he nets from a tight angle when Paddy Kenny spilled Tinnion's long-range shot. For Bury, Jason Jarrett was unlucky to be denied by the bar in the first half.											
42	A	**PETERBOROUGH**		7	L	1-2	1-1	Matthews 23	Phillips	Carey	Hill	Clist"	Burnell	Tinnion	Murray	Matthews^	Beadle	Hulbert*	Bell	Brown A/Thorpe/Am'kwaah
	14/4		*6,560*	*11*	64			*McKenzie 29p, Green 64*	*Tyler*	*Hooper*	*Scott*	*Morrow*	*Edwards*	*Shields*	*Hanlon*	*McKenzie**	*Lee^*	*Oldfield*	*Farrell*	*Green /Clarke !*
								Ref: M Cooper	Matthews' tap-in is City's sole reward for their first-half domination. Hill's wayward arms gift McKenzie his pen leveller, then Posh's double substitution on 63 mins sees Green belting in the winner with his first touch. Clarke's second bookable offence on 82 mins brings the red card.											
43	H	**WYCOMBE**		7	L	1-2	0-0	Murray 48	Phillips	Carey	Hill	Clist*	Burnell	Tinnion^	Murray	Thorpe	Beadle	Brown A"	Bell	Hulbert/Maddison/Am'kwah
	16/4		11,643	*18*	64			*Senda 63, Whittingham 90*	*Taylor*	*Marsh*	*Vinnicombe*	*Cousins*	*McCarthy*	*Brown"*	*Carroll^*	*Bulman*	*Rammell**	*Simpson*	*Senda*	*Whitt'gham/Casteldine/Lee*
								Ref: W Burns	Despite the alert Murray prodding in the opener, after Beadle's header hit the post, City lack the desire to press for a play-off place. Danny Senda's great shot brings the visitors level, then Burnell gets caught and Guy Whittingham is set free to stroke in Wycombe's late winner.											
44	A	**NOTTS CO**		8	L	1-2	1-0	Clist 33	Phillips	Carey	Hill	Clist^	Burnell	Tinnion	Murray	Beadle*	Peacock	Brown A	Bell	Da Silva/Thorpe
	21/4		*5,369*	*9*	64			*Nicholson 67, Allsopp 77*	*Ward*	*Pearce*	*Jacobsen*	*Fenton*	*Ireland*	*Owers*	*Newton^*	*Stallard*	*Allsopp*	*Thomas**	*Nicholson*	*Brough/Joseph*
								Ref: C Foy	For the third match running City press the self-destruct button after taking the lead. After Clist fired in for a deserved opener, City's inability to finish off Notts in this game proves costly. Kevin Nicholson's shot and Danny Allsopp's looping header brings to an end City's play-off hopes.											
45	H	**LUTON**		8	W	3-1	1-0	Brown 33, 65, Thorpe 78	Phillips	Carey	Hill	Clist"	Burnell*	Tinnion	Murray	Da Silva^	Peacock	Brown A	Bell	Am'kwah/Thorpe/Maddison
	28/4		9,161	*22*	67			*George 59*	*Ovendale*	*Shepherd*	*Johnson*	*Dryden*	*Boyce*	*Spring*	*Helin"*	*George**	*Howard^*	*McLaren*	*Taylor*	*Stein/Douglas/Locke*
								Ref: P Walton	City owed their win in this poor end of season game to already relegated Luton's poor finishing. The Hatters, who twice in the first half had shots cleared off the line, spurned some easy chances, whilst their sloppy defending gave Brown both his opening volley and his later header.											
46	A	**WIGAN**		9	D	0-0	0-0		Phillips	Carey	Hill	Hulbert*	Burnell	Tinnion^	Murray	Beadle	Peacock	Brown A	Bell	Clist/Maddison
	5/5		*10,048*	*6*	68				*Carroll*	*Bradshaw**	*Sharp*	*McGibbon*	*De Zeeuw*	*Martinez*	*Green*	*Nicholls*	*McCulloch*	*Liddell^*	*Beagrie*	*Haworth/Ashcroft*
Average	Home 10,369		Away 6,814					Ref: M Messias	A nervy game for the homesters, seeking a win to be sure of a place in the play-offs. Wigan dominate the contest, but Phillips frustrates them with his inspired form. In the event Bournemouth's failure to win at Reading, after being 3-1 ahead, means this result is good enough for them.											

Worthington Cup					F-A	H-T	Scorers, Times, and Referees	SQUAD	NUMBERS	IN	USE								subs used
1:1	H	BRENTFORD	8	D	2-2	2-1	Thorpe 29p, Peacock 45p	Malessa	Lavin	Bell	Carey	Lever^	Holland*	Murray	Tistimetanu	Peacock	Thorpe"	Tinnion	Hulbert/Jordan/Spencer
22/8		3,471	*16*				*Rowlands 33, McCammon 90*	*Gottsk'Isson*	*Quinn*	*Ingimarsson*	*Javary*	*Marshall*	*Mahon*	*Gibbs^*	*Evans*	*McCammon*	*Owusa**	*Scott*	*Rowlands/Partridge*
							Ref: P Alcock	City are made to pay for defensive lapses in a game that has 21 mins stoppage time added to the first half. Lloyd Owusa's injury, for which he needed a neck-brace, brought a long delay, but both Holland and Paul Gibbs also received injuries, which necessitated departure on stretchers.											
1:2	A	BRENTFORD	21	L	1-2	1-0	Holland 27	Phillips	Lavin	Hill	Carey	Millen	Bell	Murray	Goodridge*	Beadle	Holland	Tinnion	Hulbert
5/9		*2,310*	*13*				*Scott 79, 90*	*Gottsk'Isson*	*Quinn*	*Marsh*	*Marshall*	*Ingimarsson*	*Mahon*	*Rowlands*	*Scott*	*McCammon*	*Evans*	*Javary**	*Folan*
							Ref: P Rejer (City lost 3-4 on aggregate)	In the fifth min of injury-time Andy Scott's header breaks City's hearts and brings the Bees their first home win in thirteen months. Holland's opening blockbuster had City in control, but Scott's stooped header, after Phillips had misjudged a corner, changed the course of the contest.											

FA Cup (Sponsored by AXA)																			
1	A	CHESTERFIELD	8	W	1-0	0-0	Thorpe 55	Phillips	Carey	Hill	Clist*	Millen	Tinnion	Murray	Thorpe^	Peacock	Brown A	Bell	Burnell/Beadle
18/11		*5,210*	*3:1*					*Pollitt*	*Tutill*	*Breckin*	*Edwards*	*Blatherwick*	*Ebdon*	*Williams*	*Willis^*	*Beckett*	*Parrish*	*Simpkins**	*D'Auria/Jones*
							Ref: P Robinson	Thorpe brings City a hard-earned success against the Third Division leaders, who had lost but once before this season. He ghosts in at the far post to head in Murray's superb cross at Saltergate to end Chesterfield's 13-match unbeaten run and avenge City's cup defeat here in 1996-97.											
2	H	KETTERING	6	W	3-1	0-1	Peacock 55, Clist 65, Thorpe 83	Phillips	Carey	Hill	Clist	Millen	Tinnion	Murray	Thorpe	Peacock^	Brown A*	Bell	Burnell/Beadle
9/12		7,641	*C:22*				*Collins 29*	*Bowling*	*Codner*	*Perkins*	*Fisher^*	*McNamara*	*Brown*	*Vowden*	*Norman*	*Inman"*	*Collins*	*Simba**	*Watkins/Diuk/Shutt*
							Ref: A Bates	Complacent City are suitably punished when Phillips, perhaps feeling the effects of a car crash on the way to the ground, gifts bottom of the Conference visitors their goal with a poor clearance. Peacock, though, is not to be denied after the break when his persistence levels matters.											
3	A	HUDDERSFIELD	7	W	2-0	0-0	Clist 55, Beadle 82	Phillips	Carey	Hill	Clist	Millen	Tinnion	Murray	Thorpe	Beadle	Brown A	Bell*	Burnell
6/1		*9,192*	*1:19*					*Vaesen*	*Heary^*	*Vincent*	*Dyson*	*Gray*	*Armstrong**	*Baldry*	*Facey*	*Gallen*	*Holland*	*Thornley*	*Sellars/Gorre*
							Ref: W Burns	City gain revenge for their semi-final defeat at the hands of the Terriers 80 years ago. Following Clist's left-footed flick that had put them in front, City were fortunate with two Huddersfield efforts that hit the post. Beadle clinched victory with a shot into the far corner of the net.											
4	H	KINGSTONIAN	7	D	1-1	0-0	Thorpe 90	Phillips	Carey"	Hill	Clist^	Millen	Tinnion	Murray	Beadle*	Peacock	Brown A	Bell	Thorpe/Brown M/Am'kwah
27/1		14,787	*C:21*				*Wingfield 57*	*Kelly*	*Allen*	*Harris*	*Pitcher*	*Saunders*	*Patterson*	*Beard*	*Akuamoah*	*Duerden^*	*Wingfield**	*Luckett*	*Bass/Winston*
							Ref: G Poll	Thorpe saves City with his last-kick equaliser after almost four mins of injury-time, not long after Bell had been unfortunate to have his volley disallowed for Tinnion's alleged handball. Carey's mis-hit back-pass set up Phil Wingfield for his well-taken strike into the roof of City's net.											
R	A	KINGSTONIAN	7	W	1-0	0-0	Murray 87	Phillips	Carey	Hill	Clist	Millen	Tinnion	Murray	Thorpe	Beadle	Brown A	Bell	
7/2		*3,341*	*C:21*					*Kelly*	*Allen*	*Harris*	*Pitcher*	*Saunders*	*Patterson*	*Beard*	*Akuamoah*	*Duerden*	*Boyce**	*Luckett*	*Winston*
							Ref: B Knight	Murray's soft daisy-cutter from the edge of the box into the far corner of the net, shortly after Thorpe's strike had been wrongly disallowed for offside, saved City's blushes in front of the Sky TV cameras. City, for all their domination, had rarely looked like breaching the home defence.											
5	A	LEICESTER	7	L	0-3	0-2		Phillips	Carey	Hill	Clist	Millen	Tinnion	Murray	Thorpe	Peacock	Brown A	Bell	
17/2		*20,905*	*P:8*				*Sturridge 10, Hill 15 (og), Izzet 83p*	*Royce*	*Rowett*	*Davidson*	*Jones*	*Elliott**	*Savage*	*Sinclair*	*Sturridge^*	*Akinbiyi"*	*Izzet*	*Guppy*	*Oakes/G'laugsson/Benjamin*
							Ref: P Durkin	Hill's headed deflection of Izzet's cross into his own net following on from Sturridge's simple header has City facing a mountain to climb with the sides barely warmed up. Tinnion early on and Bell after the break are both denied by the woodwork before Hill handles to concede the pen.											

		Home					Away					
	P	W	D	L	F	A	W	D	L	F	A	Pts
1 Millwall	46	17	2	4	49	11	11	7	5	40	27	93
2 Rotherham	46	16	4	3	50	26	11	6	6	29	29	91
3 Reading	46	15	5	3	58	26	10	6	7	28	26	86
4 Walsall*	46	15	5	3	51	23	8	7	8	28	27	81
5 Stoke	46	12	6	5	39	21	9	8	6	35	28	77
6 Wigan	46	12	9	2	29	18	7	9	7	24	24	75
7 Bournemouth	46	11	6	6	37	23	9	7	7	42	32	73
8 Notts Co	46	10	6	7	37	33	9	6	8	25	33	69
9 BRISTOL CITY	46	11	6	6	47	29	7	8	8	23	27	68
10 Wrexham	46	10	6	7	33	28	7	6	10	32	43	63
11 Port Vale	46	9	8	6	35	22	7	6	10	20	27	62
12 Peterborough	46	12	6	5	38	27	3	8	12	23	39	59
13 Wycombe	46	8	7	8	24	23	7	7	9	22	30	59
14 Brentford	46	9	10	4	34	30	5	7	11	22	40	59
15 Oldham	46	11	5	7	35	26	4	8	11	18	39	58
16 Bury	46	10	6	7	25	22	6	4	13	20	37	58
17 Colchester	46	10	5	8	32	23	5	7	11	23	36	57
18 Northampton	46	9	6	8	26	28	6	6	11	20	31	57
19 Cambridge	46	8	6	9	32	31	6	5	12	29	46	53
20 Swindon	46	6	8	9	30	35	7	5	11	17	30	52
21 Bristol Rov	46	6	10	7	28	26	6	5	12	25	31	51
22 Luton	46	5	6	12	24	35	4	7	12	28	45	40
23 Swansea	46	5	9	9	26	24	3	4	16	21	49	37
24 Oxford	46	5	4	14	23	34	2	2	19	30	66	27
	1104	242	151	159	842	624	159	151	242	624	842	1505

* promoted after play-offs

Odds & ends

Double wins: (4) Wrexham, Reading, Luton Town, Bury.
Double losses: (2) Stoke City, Brentford.

Won from behind: (4) Peterborough United (h), Bristol Rovers (h), Swansea City (h), Reading (a).
Lost from in front: (5) Stoke City (h), Brentford (h), Peterborough United (a), Wycombe Wanderers (h), Notts County (a).

High spots: The vibrant 3-3 draw with AFC Bournemouth on 6 October.
Beating Bury 4-1 on 2 December.
Coming back from a goal down to beat the Rovers on 23 December.
Winning at Huddersfield in the FA Cup.

Low spots: The poor form that, despite a winning start to the season for the first time in ten years, left City just one off the bottom of the table on 23 September.
The horrific broken ankle Dani Rodrigues sustained against Reading on 21 October.
The sorry displays in 0-4 hammerings at Colchester and Bournemouth.

Players in the PFA XI: Brian Tinnion (voted best player in the Second Division), Mickey Bell & Scott Murray

AGM (Sports Hall, St George Community College, 29 November 2001).
Loss: £2,684,254. Season Ticket Sales (No): 7,096.

Player of the year: Brian Tinnion.
Ever-presents: (2) Louis Carey and Scott Murray.
Hat-tricks: (2) Tony Thorpe.
Leading scorer: Overall: Tony Thorpe (23). League: Tony Thorpe (19).

	Appearances						Goals			
	Lge	*Sub*	LC	*Sub*	FAC	*Sub*	Lge	LC	FAC	Tot
Amankwaah, Kevin	**8**	*6*				*1*				
Beadle, Peter	**18**	*15*	1		3	*2*	**4**		1	**5**
Bell, Mickey	**41**		2		6		**4**			**4**
Brown, Aaron	**27**	*8*			6		**2**			**2**
Brown, Marvin		*5*				*1*				
Burnell, Joe	**19**	*4*				*3*				
Carey, Louis	**46**		2		6		**3**			**3**
Clist, Simon	**36**	*2*			6		**4**		2	**6**
Coles, Danny	**1**	*1*								
Da Silva, Lourenco	**1**	*2*					**1**			**1**
Dunning, Darren	**9**									
Goodridge, Greg	**1**	*6*	1							
Hill, Matt	**32**	*2*	1		6					
Holland, Paul	**5**		2				**1**	1		**2**
Hulbert, Robin	**14**	*5*		*2*						
Jordan, Andrew	**1**	*1*		*1*						
Lavin, Gerard	**3**		2							
Lever, Mark	**2**		1							
Maddison, Neil	**4**	*3*					**1**			**1**
Malessa, Antony		*1*	1							
Matthews, Lee	**4**	*2*					**3**			**3**
Millen, Keith	**28**	*1*	1		6		**2**			**2**
Miller, Alan	**4**									
Murray, Scott	**46**		2		6		**10**		1	**11**
Odejai, Kayode		*3*								
Peacock, Lee	**31**	*4*	1		4		**13**	1	1	**15**
Phillips, Steve	**42**		1		6					
Rodrigues, Dani	**3**	*1*								
Spencer, Damien	**2**	*2*		*1*						
Thorpe, Tony	**33**	*6*	1		5	*1*	**19**	1	3	**23**
Tinnion, Brian	**40**	*2*	2		6		**1**			**1**
Tistimetanu, Ivan	**4**	*7*	1							
Woodman, Craig	**1**	*1*								
(own-goals)							**2**			**2**
33 players used	**506**	***90***	**22**	***4***	**66**	***8***	**70**	**3**	**8**	**81**

No	Date		Att	Pos	Pt	F-A	H-T	Scorers, Times, and Referees	SQUAD	NUMBERS	IN	USE								subs used
1	A	NORTHAMPTON			W	**3-0**	3-0	Thorpe 6, 22p, 28	**Stowell**	Carey	Hill	Doherty*	Lever	Tinnion	Am'kwaah^	Thorpe	Jones	Brown A	Bell	Clist/Murray
	11/8		*5,528*		3				*Welch*	*Lavin*	*Burgess*	*Spedding**	*Frain*	*Hunt !*	*Hope*	*Forrester*	*Gabbiadini*	*Parkin^*	*Hargreaves*	*Evatt/Asamoah*
								Ref: P Alcock	James Hunt's 34th-min dismissal for a late tackle on Carey has no bearing on the result as by then Thorpe had registered a hat-trick. He opened with a stooped header, which was followed by a cheeky shimmy from the spot after being upended by Richard Hope, and then an easy tap-in.											
2	H	SWINDON			W	3-1	1-0	Tinnion 34, Matthews 61, Jones 74	Stowell	Carey	Hill	Doherty	Lever	Tinnion	Am'kwaah"	Thorpe*	Jones	Brown A^	Bell	Matthews/Clist/Murray
	18/8		13,818		6			*O'Halloran 79p*	*Griemink*	*Gurney*	*Grazioli^*	*Sabin*	*O'Halloran*	*Invincible**	*Hewlett*	*Robinson"*	*Reeves !*	*Heywood*	*Duke*	*Davis/Howe/Brayley*
								Ref: P Dowd	City should have done better following Swindon's skipper Alan Reeves' 58th-min dismissal for his second bookable offence. After Tinnion's steered in right-footed effort, City can only register twice more. Matthews headed in Brown's cross, then Jones masterly slotted the ball home.											
3	A	WIGAN		1	W	2-1	0-0	Murray 47, Thorpe 52	Stowell	Carey	Hill	Doherty*	Lever	Tinnion	Murray^	Thorpe	Jones	Brown A	Bell	Clist/Amankwaah
	25/8		*6,231*	*18*	9			*Ashcroft 73*	*Kerr*	*Adamczuk**	*Sharp*	*Dalglish*	*De Zeeuw*	*McGibbon*	*Mitchell*	*Ashcroft*	*Haworth*	*Kennedy*	*Brannan*	*Roberts*
								Ref: S Baines	Lee Ashcroft gave Wigan a lifeline when he flicked in Neil Roberts' nod down. City weather an anxious finale to escape with the points secured by Murray's shot into an empty net and Thorpe's effort that bounced into the goal after cannoning into the air off of Stewart Kerr.											
4	A	QP RANGERS		2	D	0-0	0-0		Stowell	Carey	Hill	Clist*	Lever	Tinnion	Murray	Thorpe	Jones	Brown A	Bell	Matthews
	30/8		*11,655*	*6*	10				*Day*	*Perry*	*Connolly"*	*Bruce*	*Palmer*	*Forbes*	*Bignot*	*Taylor**	*Askar !*	*Doudou*	*Thomson^*	*Griffiths/McEwan/Bonnot*
								Ref: L Cable	Despite dominating play in front of the Ondigital cameras, and only facing ten men from the 47th min when Aziz Ben Askar was sent off for his second bookable offence, City fail to breach the Rangers defence. Thorpe comes nearest with a header that hits the bar just after the break.											
5	H	PORT VALE		5	D	1-1	0-1	Thorpe 49	Stowell	Carey	Hill	Clist*	Lever	Tinnion	Murray	Thorpe	Jones	Brown A	Bell	Amankwaah
	8/9		12,560	*15*	11			*O'Callaghan 10*	*Goodlad*	*Cummins*	*Carragher*	*Hardy*	*Burns*	*Brisco*	*Ingram*	*McPhee*	*Brooker*	*O'Callaghan*	*Osborn*	
								Ref: A Hall	Vale spoil the carnival atmosphere of City's League Centenary party by easily blunting the home attack. O'Callaghan swept in Brooker's cross for the Valiants early lead and, despite five minutes added time at the end of each half, Thorpe's drilled in leveller is City's only response.											
6	H	COLCHESTER		2	W	3-1	1-1	Murray 14, Jones 47, Clist 88	Stowell	Carey	Hill	Doherty*	Lever	Tinnion	Murray	Thorpe^	Jones	Brown A	Bell	Clist/Matthews
	15/9		9,992	*5*	14			*Rapley 45*	*Woodman*	*Gregory^*	*Clark**	*Pinault*	*Fitzgerald*	*Stockwell*	*Duguid*	*McGleish"*	*Rapley*	*Johnson*	*Keith*	*White/Izzet/Morgan*
								Ref: R Oliver	Intent to prove that their boss, Steve Wignall, should have received the manager of the month award instead of Danny Wilson, the U's provide a stern test after a min's silence for the victims of the hi-jack horror. Clist's low-drive at the end of a 60-yard run makes City's victory certain.											
7	A	BRENTFORD		3	D	2-2	1-2	Tinnion 17, Bell 76p	Stowell	Amankwaah	Hill	Doherty*	Lever	Tinnion	Murray	Thorpe^	Jones	Brown A	Bell	Clist/Goodridge
	18/9		*6,342*	*4*	15			*Burgess 24, Powell 28*	*Gotts'lkssonLovett"*		*Ingimarsson*	*Evans*	*Gibbs*	*Mahon*	*Powell*	*Owusa**	*Burgess*	*Price*	*Caceras^*	*O'Connor/Rowl'ds/Williams*
								Ref: J Brandwood	A cracking contest at Griffin Park where Bell's pen, following a handball, meant that both sides maintained their unbeaten records. A Tinnion special gave City the lead, but Ben Burgess finished a mazy run by curling in a leveller, before Darren Powell headed the Bees in front.											
8	A	PETERBOROUGH		7	L	1-4	0-3	Murray 61	Stowell	Burnell	Hill	Doherty^	Lever	Tinnion	Am'kwaah*	Thorpe	Jones"	Brown A	Bell	Murray/Clist/Matthews
	22/9		*5,550*	*9*	15			*Clarke 14, 42, Joseph 39, Bullard 75*	*Tyler*	*Joseph*	*Williams*	*Edwards*	*Rea*	*Bullard*	*Danielsson*	*Fenn*	*Clarke**	*Forsyth^*	*Farrell*	*Green/Shields*
								Ref: M Clattenburg	Substitute Murray was physically sick at half-time, but City fans were feeling distinctly queasy long before the break at London Road. Barry Fry declared his team's display the best during his time at the club. Free headers for Andy Clarke and Marc Joseph had Peterborough cruising.											
9	H	TRANMERE		3	W	2-0	2-0	Jones 21, Thorpe 45	Stowell	Amankwaah	Hill	Clist	Lever	Tinnion	Murray	Thorpe	Jones	Brown A	Bell*	Doherty
	25/9		9,634	*15*	18				*Murphy*	*Yates*	*Sharps*	*Flynn*	*Allen*	*Henry**	*Roberts*	*N'Diaye"*	*Barlow*	*Parkinson^*	*Koumas*	*Mellon/Allison/Hulme*
								Ref: P Armstrong	Tranmere were played off the park by City's high-quality first-half attacking display. Jones drilled in the opener, then Murray set up Thorpe to blaze in City's second. It wasn't so gripping after the break, though in injury-time Stuart Barlow blasted a penalty high into the Atyeo Stand.											
10	A	HUDDERSFIELD		6	L	0-1	0-0		Stowell*	Amankwaah	Hill	Clist^	Lever	Tinnion	Murray	Thorpe	Jones	Brown A	Bell	Phillips/Matthews
	29/9		*10,652*	*3*	18			*Thorrington 71*	*Margetson*	*Jenkins*	*Evans*	*Clarke*	*Gray*	*Irons*	*Thorrington*	*Schofield*	*Booth*	*Mattis*	*Holland*	
								Ref: F Stretton	Stowell's bizarre early groin injury when he effected a clearance set the scene for Phillips to come on and make a string of spectacular saves to keep City in the contest. Even he, however, was powerless to stop Town's winner when John Thorrington fired in from Chris Holland's cross.											
11	H	CHESTERFIELD		4	W	**3-0**	2-0	Thorpe 31, Jones 38, 49	Phillips	Amankwaah	Hill	**Summ'bell**	Lever	Tinnion"	Murray	Thorpe	Jones^	Brown A*	Bell	Clist/Matthews/Doherty
	5/10		10,718	*17*	21				*Abbey*	*Booty*	*Payne*	*Richardson*	*Breckin*	*Ingledow*	*Williams*	*Willis*	*Beckett*	*Reeves**	*Edwards*	*Jones*
								Ref: S Tomlin	City turned the tables on the sturdy Spireites in this game, switched to a Friday night because of England's vital World Cup Qualifying match against Greece tomorrow. Thorpe's volleyed in opener came out of nothing, then Jones twice fired home to bring City a hard-earned victory.											

No	Date	Venue	Opponent	Att	Pos	Pt	Res	F-A	H-T	Scorers, Times, and Referees	1	2	3	4	5	6	7	8	9	10	11	subs used
12	9/10	H	CARDIFF	13,804	3 / *17*	22	D	1-1	0-1	Bell 56	Phillips	Amankwaah	Hill	Sum'erbell^	Lever	Tinnion	Murray	Thorpe	Jones"	Brown A*	Bell	Clist/Doherty/Matthews
										Earnshaw 45p	*Alexander*	*Weston^*	*Gabbidon*	*Bowen**	*Prior*	*Kavanagh*	*Simpkins*	*Thorne*	*Earnshaw*	*Boland*	*Brayson*	*Bonner/Hamilton*
										Ref: R Harris	The Somerset Cricketers, who show off the Cup won with their recent Lord's success, are unable to inspire City. Decidedly second-best to an impressive Cardiff side, it takes Bell's great 25-yard drive at the Wedlock Stand end to level Cardiff's rather fortunately awarded spot-kick.											
13	13/10	A	OLDHAM	*6,565*	2 / *4*	25	W	1-0	1-0	Murray 39	Phillips	Am'kwaah*	Hill	Summerbell	Lever	Tinnion	Murray	Thorpe	Jones	Clist	Bell	Burnell
											Kelly	*Dudley*	*Balmer*	*Duxbury*	*Holden*	*Gill"*	*Prenderville*	*Corazzin*	*Eyre**	*Rickers^*	*Eyres*	*Richards/Innes/Boshell*
										Ref: P Joslin	Murray darts clear of the Oldham defence and finishes with a left-foot shot to knock the Latics off top spot. A hard-won victory, which took bags of endeavour, commitment and downright stubbornness by a Robins side who exhibited little of their normal slick attacking style.											
14	20/10	H	WYCOMBE	11,452	3 / *6*	25	L	0-1	0-0		Phillips	Burnell	Hill^	Sum'erbell"	Lever	Tinnion	Murray	Thorpe	Jones	Clist*	Bell	Peacock/Coles/Doherty
										McSporran 53	*Taylor*	*Senda*	*Vinnicombe*	*McCarthy*	*Rogers*	*Bulman*	*Currie**	*Simpson*	*Rammell^*	*Brown"*	*McSporran*	*Carroll/Walker/Ryan*
										Ref: G Cain	A siege on the M4 results in this game kicking off 33 minutes late as Wycombe only arrive five minutes before the scheduled 3 o'clock start time. City failed to learn from several narrow escapes before Jermaine McSporran raced away to finish with a crisp low shot past Phillips.											
15	23/10	H	BOURNEMOUTH	9,972	3 / *17*	28	W	1-0	1-0	Tinnion 38	Phillips	Burnell	Hill	Summerbell	Lever	Tinnion	Murray	Thorpe	Peacock*	Doherty^	Bell	Matthews/Clist
											Stewart	*Purches^*	*Tindall*	*Fletcher*	*Broadhurst*	*Elliott*	*Howe*	*Hayter*	*Holmes*	*Stock**	*Narada"*	*Kandol/O'Connor/Eribenne*
										Ref: D Crick	After Tinnion had stolen in behind the Cherries' defence to tuck the ball away with a clinical finish, it needs two quite outstanding second-half saves by Phillips to hold onto the points. A rather fortunate win for an anxious City side who are often outplayed by the impressive visitors.											
16	27/10	A	STOKE	***16,828***	4 / *3*	28	L	0-1	0-0		Stowell	Burnell	Hill	Carey*	Lever	Tinnion	Murray !	Thorpe	Jones^	Brown A	Bell	Doherty/Peacock
										Gunnarsson 87	*Cutler*	*Thomas**	*Clarke^*	*Handyside*	*Shtaniuk*	*Gunnarsson*	*Gudjonsson*	*Iwelumo"*	*Hoekstra*	*O'Connor*	*Vandeurzen*	*Henry/Neal/Cooke*
										Ref: H Webb	Celebrations before kick-off at the Britannia Stadium where Kevin Keegan unveils a statue in honour of Stanley Matthews. Thereafter it's poor fare for the City fans, who see their side out of luck at the death, when instead of being awarded a spot-kick, Murray is sent off for diving.											
17	3/11	H	BRIGHTON	13,955	4 / *2*	28	L	0-1	0-1		Stowell	Carey^	Hill	Doherty	Lever	Tinnion !	Murray	Thorpe	Jones*	Brown A"	Bell	Peacock/Am'kwaah/Coles
										Zamora 38	*Kulpers*	*Watson*	*Mayo*	*Cullip*	*Morgan*	*Carpenter*	*Hart*	*Steele*	*Zamora**	*Oatway*	*Jones*	*Pethick*
										Ref: D Elleray	City's hopes went with Jones' fifth-min hamstring injury. Lacking movement and invention they are easy pickings for the impressive visitors. Hill fails to deal with a high ball and Bobby Zamora coolly side-foots the only goal. Tinnion's second booking brings his 88th-min departure.											
18	10/11	A	READING	*14,060*	7 / *4*	28	L	2-3	1-2	Shorey 34 (og), Thorpe 60	Stowell	Carey	Hill	Doherty	Lever*	Tinnion"	Amankw'h^	Thorpe	Peacock	Brown A	Bell	Coles/Goodridge/Matthews
										Mackie 12, Lever 44 (og), Salako 50	*Whitehead*	*Murty*	*Shorey*	*Viveash*	*Mackie*	*Watson*	*Hughes**	*Cureton^*	*Forster"*	*Smith*	*Salako*	*Igoe/Henderson/Jones*
										Ref: D Gallagher	Thorpe, who squandered a succession of chances before heading in shortly after the break, inspired a City fightback after Lever's spectacular own-goal had left them a mountain to climb. It took a great point-blank save by Phil Whitebread to keep out a late effort from sub Matthews.											
19	20/11	A	BURY	***2,608***	7 / *21*	29	D	2-2	1-1	Peacock 20, 89p	Stowell	Carey	Hill	Doherty	Coles	Clist*	Murray	Thorpe^	Peacock	Brown A	Bell	Burnell/Brown M
										Newby 42p, Singh 49	*Kenny*	*Unsworth*	*Nelson*	*Singh*	*Swailes*	*Borley**	*Redmond*	*Newby*	*Seddon*	*Jarrett*	*Forrest*	*Reid*
										Ref: M Dean	City rode their luck early on, but shortly after Gareth Seddon had his header ruled out for offside, they took the lead when Peacock stabbed the ball past Paddy Kenny. Despite Thorpe having his 22nd-min pen saved, Peacock made no mistake with his effort from the spot to earn a point.											
20	24/11	H	BLACKPOOL	9,876	5 / *14*	32	W	2-1	1-0	Thorpe 45, Murray 90	Stowell	Carey	Hill	Doherty	Coles	Clist*	Murray	Thorpe	Peacock	Brown A	Bell	Matthews
										Simpson 84p	*Barnes*	*O'Kane*	*Coid*	*Marshall*	*Jaszczun*	*Reid**	*Bullock*	*Ormerod*	*Murphy*	*Wellens*	*Simpson^*	*Hughes/Hills*
										Ref: K Hill	Despite an impaired left arm, the ref gets no sympathy following his abject performance in this game. A controversial penalty, when a fierce drive hit Hill on the arm, is the final straw for City fans, but all was well at the finish with Murray's great last-minute strike at the Atyeo end.											
21	1/12	H	NOTTS CO	9,411	5 / *21*	35	W	3-2	1-0	Ireland 11 (og), Peacock 67p, 75	Stowell	Carey	Hill	Doherty	Coles	Clist*	Murray	Thorpe	Peacock	Brown A	Woodman^	Hulbert/Burnell
										Quinn 65, Chivers 74	*Mildenhall*	*Richardson*	*Baraclough*	*Chivers**	*Ireland*	*Owers^*	*Quinn*	*Hackworth*	*Allsopp*	*Caskey*	*Cas*	*Stone/Hefferman*
										Ref: M Fletcher	A stirring game right from Craig Ireland's spectacular headed own-goal opener into the Atyeo end net. City displayed an attacking zeal seldom witnessed this season and deserved to have won by a greater margin than Peacock's ferocious drive after Craig Chivers had shot County level.											
22	8/12	A	WREXHAM	*3,091*	4 / *22*	38	W	2-0	0-0	Roberts 55 (og), Thorpe 62	Stowell	Carey	Hill	Doherty	Coles	Burnell	Murray	Thorpe*	Peacock	Brown A	Woodman	Brown M
											Walsh	*Whitley*	*Holmes**	*Roberts*	*Hill*	*Thomas*	*Chalk^*	*Morrell"*	*Trundle*	*Ferguson*	*Sharp*	*Sam/Blackwood/Gibson*
										Ref: C Webster	There was no way back for Wrexham after Thorpe galloped away to round keeper David Walsh to net at the second attempt. This dull and lifeless spectacle of a game was only slightly enlivened when Steve Roberts, under pressure from Coles, bundled the ball into his own goal.											
23	15/12	A	CAMBRIDGE	*3,516*	4 / *24*	41	W	**3-0**	2-0	Peacock 12, 43, Duncan 88 (og)	Stowell	Carey	Hill	Doherty*	Coles	Burnell	Murray	Thorpe^	Peacock	Brown A	Woodman"	Hulbert/Brown M/Fortune
											Marshall	*Ashbee*	*Murray*	*Duncan*	*Tann*	*Tudor*	*Guttridge^*	*One*	*Kitson**	*Scully*	*Wanless*	*Revell/Taylor*
										Ref: P Rejer	Peacock swivelled on Woodman's miscued drive to fire City into an early lead then headed in a second before the break. Andy Duncan, in only being able to help the want-away Thorpe's shot over his own line, put the seal on a rare, but much deserved, City win at the Abbey Stadium.											

No	Date			Att	Pos	Pt	F-A	H-T	Scorers, Times, and Referees	SQUAD	NUMBERS	IN	USE								subs used
24		H	WREXHAM		3	W	1-0	0-0	Carey 80 (og)	Stowell	Carey	Hill	Doherty	Coles	Burnell	Am'kwaah*	Thorpe	Peacock	Brown A"	Woodman^	Tinnion/Bell/Brown M
	22/12			12,137	22	44				Rogers	Whitley	Sharp	Carey	Roberts	Thomas	Phillips	Sam	Trundle	Morrell^	Chalk*	Blackwood/Gibson
									Ref: W Jordan	City profit from a fourth own-goal in successive games to clinch the points in this poor pre-Christmas entertainment. Wrexham's veteran Brian Carey diverted his namesake's whipped in low-cross into the Atyeo Stand goal, not long after Peacock had hit the bar with an audacious lob.											
25		A	PORT VALE		4	L	0-1	0-0		Stowell	Carey	Hill	Burnell^	Coles	Doherty*	Murray	Thorpe	Peacock	Brown A	Bell	Tinnion/Brown M
	26/12			5,682	17	44			McPhee 63	Goodlad	Walsh	Burton	Durnin	Carragher	Cummins	McClare	Brooker	McPhee	Armstrong*	Rowland	Brisco
									Ref: R Pearson	It's cold comfort for City at Vale Park, where they never got going on an icy pitch. Michael Walsh's long throw in set up Stephen McPhee to swivel and fire in the goal that prevented City from improving on their poor Boxing Day record of only three wins in 28 attempts on the road.											
26		A	CARDIFF		1	W	3-1	0-0	Murray 55, 57, Matthews 60	Stowell	Carey	Hill	Burnell	Coles	Tinnion*	Murray	Thorpe	Matthews^	Brown A	Bell	Lever/Amankwaah
	29/12			16,149	10	47			Kavanagh 47	Alexander	Gabbidon	Gordon	Young	Prior	Kavanagh	Boland	Earnshaw	Gordon^	Bonner*	Bowen"	Fortune-West/Legg/Brayson
									Ref: P Durkin	Few thought City could win this game when Graham Kavanagh headed Cardiff in front just after half-time. Up to this time they had been outplayed, but the complexion of the match changed when Murray jinked through to fire in a leveller. Matthews volleyed in City's third.											
27		H	WIGAN		3	D	2-2	2-0	Peacock 14, 23	Stowell	Am'kwaah*	Hill	Burnell	Coles	Doherty	Murray	Thorpe	Peacock^	Brown A"	Bell	Tinnion/M'thews/Rodriques
	5/1			9,991	13	48			McCulloch 59, De Vos 77	Filan	Greene*	McMillan	Jackson	De Zeeuw	Brannan	Teale"	Liddell	McCulloch^	Dinning	Kennedy	De Vos/Haworth/Dalglish
									Ref: R Beeby	City were fortunate to draw this game shown live on ITV Digital, which kicked-off at midday. Despite Peacock's tap-in and his terrific curling 20-yarder, thrice the woodwork came to their aid. Jason De Vos headed in Wigan's leveller after Lee McCulloch had bundled in their first.											
28		A	SWINDON		2	W	2-1	1-0	Hill 20, Peacock 53	Phillips	Amankwaah	Hill	Burnell	Coles	Tinnon^	Murray	Thorpe*	Peacock	Brown A"	Bell	Rodrigues/Hulbert/Lever
	13/1			7,273	18	51			Foley 58	Griemink	Duke	Reeves !	Davis	Heywood	Invincible	Willis	Foley	Sabin*	Robinson	McAr'vey^	Young/Williams
									Ref: U Rennie	Hill celebrated the birth of his son with his first senior goal. In this game, shown live on HTV, he heads in City's opener, then Peacock doubles their advantage from a free-kick shortly after Reeves had been sent off. City struggled to hold on following Foley's brilliant lob over Phillips.											
29		H	NORTHAMPTON		2	L	1-3	0-2	Thorpe 62	Phillips	Am'kwaah*	Hill	Burnell	Coles	Tinnion^	Murray	Thorpe	Peacock	Brown A	Bell	Carey/Brown M
	19/1			11,733	24	51			Forrester 36p, 37, Hunt 68	Sollitt	Hunter	Carruthers	Burgess	Sampson	Hunt	McGregor	Gabbiadini	Forrester	Parkin	Hargreaves	
									Ref: L Cable	City are not helped by the linesman, who signalled for Northampton's penalty when their player fell over the ball, or Phillips, who needlessly spoons out the ball to present the visitors with their second goal. City failed to show the desire or commitment necessary to win this game.											
30		H	HUDDERSFIELD		4	D	1-1	0-0	Peacock 68	Phillips	Carey	Hill	Burnell	Coles	Tinnion*	Murray	Thorpe	Peacock	Brown A	Bell	Lever
	2/2			10,643	7	52			Knight 89	Margetson	Heary	Evans	Clarke	Moses	Irons	Armstrong	Hay*	Knight	Schofield	Booth	Wijnhard
									Ref: A Leake	City pressed the self-destruct button during two minutes of injury-time. After Peacock rammed them in front at the Atyeo Stand end, they paid the cost of failing to attack the ball from Town's corner on the left. Leon Knight's acute angled shot crashed in off the bar to rob City of a win.											
31		H	QP RANGERS		3	W	2-0	2-0	Murray 8, Thorpe 45	Phillips	Amankwaah	Hill	Doherty*	Carey	Tinnion	Murray	Thorpe	Peacock^	Burnell	Bell	Hulbert/Jones S
	5/2			11,654	8	55				Digby	Forbes	Murphy*	Shittu	Palmer	Rose	Doudou"	Pacquette^	Gallen	Langley	Griffiths	Warren/Thomson/Connolly
									Ref: T Parkes	Slick City turn on the style after Murray rifled home a magnificent early opener into the Wedlock Stand net. They spurned many chances however and were fortunate when, in first-half injury-time, an offside looking Thorpe steered in a ball that broke his way from Peacock's shot.											
32		A	WYCOMBE		4	L	1-2	0-0	Peacock 63	Phillips	Carey	Hill	Burnell	Coles	Tinnion	Murray	Brown M*	Peacock	Brown A^	Bell	Jones S/Clist
	9/2			7,972	11	55			Devine 70, Rogers 73	Taylor	Senda	Vinnicombe	Rogers	Johnson	Currie"	Simpson	Roberts	Devine	Bulman^	McSporran*	Baird/Brown/Ryan
									Ref: P Walton	The travelling fans say that the referee cost City this game, but the truth is that despite dominating most of the proceedings they fail to put away their chances. In torrential conditions after the break, a twice taken free-kick allowed Sean Devine to crash in Wycombe's leveller.											
33		H	OLDHAM		3	W	**3-0**	0-0	Peacock 47, Thorpe 69p, Lever 72	Philips	Carey	Bell	Lever	Coles	Burnell^	Murray*	Thorpe	Peacock	Brown A"	Tinnion	Brown M/Hulbert/Woodman
	16/2			10,849	7	58				Rachubka	McNiven	Armstrong	Beharall	Baudet !	Appleby	Duxbury*	Reeves	Corazzin^	Murray	Eyres"	Holden/Smart/Colusso
									Ref: M Cooper	Oldham got physical when City turned on the style after a dull opening. Five bookings, as well as a sending-off when Aaron Brown was brought down for the pen. The loss of Murray with a fractured cheekbone early on could well prove a fatal blow to City's promotion hopes.											
34		A	COLCHESTER		4	D	0-0	0-0		Phillips	Carey	Hill	Hulbert	Lever	Tinnion	Amankwaah	Thorpe	Peacock	Brown A	Bell	
	23/2			3,558	14	59				Brown	Duguid	White	Stockwell*	Fitzgerald	Pinault	Barrett	Rapley^	McGleish	Izzet	Keith	Bowrey/Coote
									Ref: A Butler	City fail to bounce back from a shock LDV Vans Trophy defeat as they produce another lacklustre performance at Layer Road. As so often happens, the commitment that the supporters expect is lacking. Once again City talk a good game but when it comes to produce they fail badly.											

No	Venue	Opponent	Att	Pos	Res	F-A	H-T	Scorers, Times, and Referees	1	2	3	4	5	6	7	8	9	10	11	subs used
35	H	PETERBOROUGH		3	W	1-0	1-0	Thorpe 15	Phillips	Carey	Hill	Hulbert	Lever	Tinnion	Amankwaah	Peacock	Thorpe^	Brown A*	Bell	Clist/Jones S
26/2			**8,299**	18	62				*Tyler*	*Gill*	*Williams*	*Edwards*	*Joseph*	*Green**	*Shields^*	*Fenn"*	*Forinton*	*Bullard*	*Farrell*	*French/Danielsson/Rea*
								Ref: C Penton	Thorpe silenced the critics with a neat header into the Wedlock Stand net that reignited City's promotion challenge. A welcome three points from a tense and edgy game in which success was achieved the hard way as City struggled to get into their stride against impressive opponents.											
36	H	BRENTFORD		5	L	0-2	0-0		Phillips	Carey	Hill	Hulbert	Lever"	Tinnion^	Am'kwaah*	Peacock	Thorpe	Burnell	Bell	Matthews/Doherty/Jones S
2/3			11,421	4	62			*Rowlands 54, Owusa 56*	*Smith*	*Dobson*	*Anderson*	*Powell*	*Ingimarsson*	*Sidwell*	*Rowlands*	*Burgess*	*Owusa*	*Evans*	*Hunt*	
								Ref: D Gallacher	Fuelled by junk food after getting stuck at the Motorway Services, Brentford secured their first away win since October. Despite Peacock heading against a post, City failed to create much and paid the price when Rowlands volleyed in the Bees terrific opener at the Wedlock End.											
37	A	TRANMERE		5	L	0-1	0-1		Phillips	Carey	Hill	Hulbert	Coles	Tinnion	Burnell"	Peacock	Thorpe*	Doherty^	Bell	JonesS/BrownA/Am'kwaah
5/3			*7,735*	*10*	62			*Haworth 14*	*Achterberg*	*Allen*	*Roberts*	*Hill*	*Sharps*	*Thornton*	*Navarro*	*Barlow*	*Haworth*	*Henry*	*Koumas*	
								Ref: M Messias	Danny Wilson is satisfied with his side's application, but that wasn't the feeling of the City fans. Yet another hapless display by the Robins, who are fortunate that wayward defending didn't produce an even heavier defeat. A needless square ball set up the play for the tap-in winner.											
38	H	CAMBRIDGE		5	W	2-0	2-0	Bell 9, 17	Phillips	Carey	Bell	Hill	Coles	Tinnion	Burnell	Peacock	Matthews*	Doherty^	**Singh**	Hulbert/Amankwaah
9/3			9,817	24	65				*Perez*	*Goodhind*	*Murray*	*Duncan*	*Angus*	*Wanless*	*Guttridge*	*One**	*Youngs*	*Revell^*	*Ashbee*	*Jackman/Tudor*
								Ref: A Bates	A 20-yard free-kick and a fantastic 30-yard volley from the left into the far corner of the Wedlock end net, were well worthy of the admission price, but City failed to capitalise further. Their fans, though, were in joyous mood as they watched a Territorial Army display at half-time.											
39	A	NOTTS CO		6	L	0-2	0-1		Phillips	Carey	Bell	Hill	Coles	Tinnion	Burnell	Peacock	Matthews*	Doherty^	Singh"	Jones S/Hulbert/Brown M
16/3			*7,521*	*20*	65			*Cas 17, Heffernan 73*	*Garden*	*Richardson*	*Nicholson*	*Fenton*	*Ireland*	*Caskey*	*Cas*	*Allsopp*	*Heffernan*	*Brough*	*Liburd**	*Hackworth*
								Ref: M Pike	City are condemned yet again by the travelling fans, who feel that only Hill showed real desire. Against an ordinary, though spirited County side, City should have provided them a sterner test. They didn't have the weaponry to hurt and were twice undone by their poor defending.											
40	A	CHESTERFIELD		6	L	1-2	0-1	Matthews 88	Phillips	Carey	Hill	**Robinson"**	Coles	Burnell	Singh*	Jones S^	Matthews	Tinnion !	Bell	Doherty/Thorpe/Rodrigues
19/3			*3,630*	*16*	65			*Allott 21, Hurst 54*	*Abbey*	*Payne*	*O'Hare*	*Breckin*	*Howson*	*Innes**	*Booty*	*Hurst*	*Allott*	*Ebdon^*	*Burt*	*D'Auria/Rowland*
								Ref: M Warren	A header in the second minute of injury-time is all ten-man City can manage, despite a stirring fight-back following Tinnion's sending off for a late tackle shortly after the break. For the opening 54 minutes though City were terrible and they can have no complaints over the final result.											
41	A	BOURNEMOUTH		6	W	3-1	2-0	Bell 34p, Peacock 44, Thorpe 90	Phillips	Carey	Hill*	Robinson	Lever	Doherty	Murray	Peacock	Matthews^	Tinnion	Bell	Burnell/Thorpe
23/3			*7,033*	*22*	68			*McAnespie 90*	*Stewart*	*Purches^*	*McAnespie*	*Tindall*	*Howe*	*Maher*	*Elliott*	*Hayter*	*Feeney*	*Cooke*	*Thomas**	*Stock/Kandol*
								Ref: B Knight	After surviving the early Cherries onslaught, City took a grip on the proceedings late on in the first half and ran out worthy winners by the finish. Murray turned the game round with one of his trademark runs that finished with him being upended by Jason Tindall in the box.											
42	H	READING		7	D	3-3	2-3	Peacock 6, Bell 12p, Robinson 59	Phillips	Carey	Burnell	Doherty	Lever	Tinnion	Murray	Peacock	Matthews*	Robinson^	Bell	Thorpe/Rodrigues
30/3			**15,609**	*1*	69			*Hughes 2, Forster 5p, Watson 14*	*Whitehead*	*Murty*	*Shorey*	*Williams*	*Mackie*	*Watson*	*Hughes**	*Forster*	*Cureton^*	*Parkinson*	*Salako*	*Harper/Branch"/Rougier*
								Ref: A Hall	City's marking was woeful as Andy Hughes, at back post, gave the Royals the early lead with a free header from Nicky Forster's cross. After falling further behind when Burnell brought down Forster on the edge of the box, Peacock's searing angled shot soon revived City's hopes.											
43	A	BRIGHTON		1	L	1-2	0-1	Doherty 52	Stowell	Carey	Burnell	Doherty"	Lever	Tinnion	Murray	Peacock*	**Roberts^**	Robinson	Bell	Matthews/Thorpe/Doherty
1/4			*6,759*	*7*	69			*Lewis 45, Steele 90*	*Kulpers*	*Watson*	*Mayo*	*Cullip*	*Morgan*	*Lewis*	*Hart*	*Brooker**	*Gray^*	*Carpenter*	*Jones*	*Steele/Hadland*
								Ref: M Fletcher	City outplayed Brighton at the Withdean Stadium, but paid the price for spurning their chances. The homesters rode their luck to grab victory with injury-time goals in each half. Wendy Toms kept her flag down as Les Steele headed in the 91st-minute winner from Gary Hart's cross.											
44	H	BURY		7	W	2-0	0-0	Bell 85, Peacock 90	Stowell	Carey	Burnell	Robinson^	Coles	Doherty	Murray	Peacock	Roberts*	Brown A	Bell	Thorpe/Matthews
6/4			9,449	*21*	72				*Kenny*	*Connell**	*Clegg*	*Forrest*	*Unsworth*	*Nelson^*	*Billy*	*Newby*	*Lawson"*	*Clarkson*	*Borley*	*Barrass/Hill/Nugent*
								Ref: G Hegley	City, who again spurned their chances, were thankful for Bell's weaker right foot that sent a sweetly struck drive soaring gloriously into the top corner of the net. Peacock slotted the ball home from 12 yards to double the advantage and keep City in with a chance of the play-offs.											
45	A	BLACKPOOL		7	L	**1-5**	0-4	Thorpe 61 *[Bullock 34, Hills 50]*	Stowell	Carey	Burnell	Robinson*	Coles^	Doherty	Murray	Peacock	Roberts"	Brown A	Bell	Thorpe/Jones/Matthews
13/4			*9,333*	*15*	72			*Walker 8, Murphy 12, 28,*	*Barnes*	*O'Kane*	*Jaszczun"*	*Reid*	*Clarke*	*Dunning*	*Bullock**	*Walker*	*Murphy J*	*Wellens^*	*Hills*	*Taylor/Collins/Coid*
								Ref: C Webster	Considering the importance of this game City produced a disgraceful and totally unacceptable first half at Bloomfield Road. The players let both themselves and the fans down, many of the City's big travelling support leaving at the interval to a chorus of derision from the Pool fans.											
46	H	STOKE		7	D	1-1	0-1	Brown A 68	Phillips	Carey	Woodman	Jones	Lever	Burnell*	Murray	Peacock	Roberts	Doherty	Brown A^	Rosenior/Brown M
20/4			11,277	*5*	73			*Cooke 16*	*Cutler*	*Brightwell"*	*Vandeurzen*	*Shtaniuk*	*Handyside*	*O'Connor*	*Gudjons'on**	*Iwelumo*	*Cooke^*	*Dinning*	*Goodfellow*	*Miles/Burton/Henry*
Average	Home 11,220		Away 7,620					Ref: D Pugh	A typical end of season affair in many ways, but some positives can be taken by the fact that City fought back well after almost being swept away without trace. Andy Cooke prodded in Chris Iwelumo's nod-down, but Aaron Brown's coolly fired low shot earned City their point.											

Worthington Cup

No	Venue	Opponent	Att / Pos	Res	F-A	H-T	Scorers, Times, and Referees	SQUAD	NUMBERS	IN	USE								subs used
1	H	CHELTENHAM		W	2-1	1-0	Amankwaah 2, Jones 78	Stowell	Carey	Hill	Clist^	Lever	Tinnion	Am'kwaah*	Thorpe	Jones"	Brown A	Bell	Murray/Burnell/Matthews
21/8			5,367				*Grayson 66*	*Muggleton*	*Howarth**	*Victory*	*Walker*	*Banks*	*Yates*	*Duff*	*Naylor*	*Grayson^*	*Milton*	*Devaney"*	*Griffin/White/Alsop*
							Ref: P Rejer												

After Amankwaah's glided header got City off to the best possible start, they dominate the opening half-hour without being able to add to their score. Neil Grayson's spectacular looping 35-yarder brought the visitors level, but Jones saved City blushes by nodding in the winner.

No	Venue	Opponent	Att / Pos	Res	F-A	H-T	Scorers, Times, and Referees	SQUAD	NUMBERS	IN	USE								subs used
2	H	WATFORD	5	L	2-3	0-0	Clist 48, Thorpe 55	Stowell	Carey	Hill	Clist*	Lever	Doherty^	Murray	Thorpe	Jones"	Brown A	Bell	Burnell/Amank'h/Matthews
12/9			7,256 *1:9*				*Gayle 73p, Vega 87, Hyde 90*	*Baardsen*	*Cox*	*Robinson*	*Vega*	*Galli*	*Noble"*	*Wooter*	*Fisken**	*Noel-W'ms^*	*Hyde*	*Glass*	*Gayle/Smith/Helguson*
							Ref: P Danson												

Paul Danson unfairly gets the blame for changing the course of this game with the award of a penalty for Hill's challenge on Smith. Clist's header and Thorpe's shot had put City in control, but as they fell back on defence they succumbed to Vega's shot and Hyde's stooping header.

FA Cup (Sponsored by AXA)

No	Venue	Opponent	Att / Pos	Res	F-A	H-T	Scorers, Times, and Referees												subs used
1	H	ORIENT	7	L	0-1	0-1		Stowell	Carey	Hill	Doherty	Lever*	Coles^	Murray"	Thorpe	Peacock	Brown A	Bell	Clist/Brown M/Goodridge
17/11			6,343 *3:14*				*Watts 31*	*Barrett*	*Jones*	*Smith*	*Dorrian*	*Joseph*	*Martin^*	*McGhee*	*Ibrhre**	*Watts"*	*Minton*	*Harris*	*McLean/Herrera/Hatcher*
							Ref: S Tomlin												

No excuses from the home fans in regard to this defeat by lower League opponents courtesy of a lobbed in effort at the Atyeo Stand end. The boos of the City fans ring out at the end in response to their team's spineless and passionless performance which was embarrassing to witness.

		Home					Away					
	P	W	D	L	F	A	W	D	L	F	A	Pts
1 Brighton	46	17	5	1	42	16	8	10	5	24	26	90
2 Reading	46	12	7	4	36	20	11	8	4	34	23	84
3 Brentford	46	17	5	1	48	12	7	6	10	29	31	83
4 Cardiff	46	12	8	3	39	25	11	6	6	36	25	83
5 Stoke *	46	16	4	3	43	12	7	7	9	24	28	80
6 Huddersfield	46	13	7	3	35	19	8	8	7	30	28	78
7 BRISTOL CITY	46	13	6	4	38	21	8	4	11	30	32	73
8 QP Rangers	46	11	10	2	35	18	8	4	11	25	31	71
9 Oldham	46	14	6	3	47	27	4	10	9	30	38	70
10 Wigan	46	9	6	8	36	23	7	10	6	30	28	64
11 Wycombe	46	13	5	5	38	26	4	8	11	20	38	64
12 Tranmere	46	10	9	4	39	19	6	6	11	24	41	63
13 Swindon	46	10	7	6	26	21	5	7	11	20	35	59
14 Port Vale	46	11	6	6	35	24	5	4	14	16	38	58
15 Colchester	46	9	6	8	35	33	6	6	11	30	43	57
16 Blackpool	46	8	9	6	39	31	6	5	12	27	38	56
17 Peterborough	46	11	5	7	46	26	4	5	14	18	33	55
18 Chesterfield	46	9	3	11	35	36	4	10	9	18	29	52
19 Notts Co	46	8	7	8	28	29	5	4	14	31	42	50
20 Northampton	46	9	4	10	30	33	5	3	15	24	46	49
21 Bournemouth	46	9	4	10	36	33	1	10	12	20	38	44
22 Bury	46	6	9	8	26	32	5	2	16	17	43	44
23 Wrexham	46	7	7	9	29	32	4	3	16	27	57	43
24 Cambridge	46	7	7	9	29	34	0	6	17	18	59	34
	1104	261	152	139	870	602	139	152	261	602	870	1504

* promoted after play-offs

Odds & ends

Double wins: (5) Swindon Town, Oldham Athletic, AFC Bournemouth, Wrexham, Cambridge United.
Double losses: (2) Wycombe Wanderers, Brighton & Hove Albion.

Won from behind: (1) Cardiff City (a).
Lost from in front (1): Wycombe Wanderers (a).

High spots: Winning at Northampton in the season's opener.
Rare wins at the Racecourse and Abbey Stadium in successive games shortly before Christmas.
Hammering Bristol Rovers in the LDV Trophy.

Low spots: City's appalling display in the must-win penultimate game that had many supporters departing Bloomfield Road at half-time.
Cambridge United's stirring display at Ashton Gate that cost City a place in the Leyland Daf Vans final.

Players in the PFA XI: Mickey Bell and Scott Murray.

Scottish Trialist: Scott Murray (played at right-back for the Scottish squad in a 2-0 end of season win versus Dundee United at Stirling).

AGM (Exhibition Hall, Dolman Stand, Ashton Gate, 28 November 2002).
Loss: £3,033,721. Season Ticket Sales (No): 7,600.

Player of the year: Matt Hill.
Ever-presents: (0).
Hat-tricks: (1) Tony Thorpe.
Leading scorer: Overall: Tony Thorpe (17). League: Tony Thorpe (16).

	Appearances						Goals			
	Lge	*Sub*	LC	*Sub*	FAC	*Sub*	Lge	LC	FAC	Tot
Amankwaah, Kevin	**18**	*6*	1	*1*				1		**1**
Bell, Mickey	**41**	*1*	2		1		**7**			**7**
Brown, Aaron	**34**	*2*	2		1		**1**			**1**
Brown, Marvin	**1**	*9*				*1*				
Burnell, Joe	**26**	*4*		*2*						
Carey, Louis	**34**	*1*	2		1					
Clist, Simon	**9**	*11*	2			*1*	**1**	1		**2**
Coles, Danny	**20**	*3*			1					
Doherty, Tommy	**27**	*7*	1		1		**1**			**1**
Fortune, Clayton		*1*								
Goodridge, Greg		*2*				*1*				
Hill, Matt	**40**		2		1		**1**			**1**
Hulbert, Robin	**4**	*7*								
Jones, Darren	**1**	*1*								
Jones, Steve	**17**	*6*	2				**5**	1		**6**
Lever, Mark	**26**	*3*	2		1		**1**			**1**
Matthews, Lee	**6**	*16*		*2*			**3**			**3**
Murray, Scott	**34**	*3*	1	*1*	1		**8**			**8**
Peacock, Lee	**28**	*3*			1		**15**			**15**
Phillips, Steve	**21**	*1*								
Roberts, Christian	**4**									
Robinson, Steve	**6**						**1**			**1**
Rodrigues, Dani		*4*								
Rosenior, Liam		*1*								
Singh, Harpal	**3**									
Stowell, Mike	**25**		2		1					
Summerbell, Mark	**5**									
Thorpe, Tony	**36**	*6*	2		1		**16**	1		**17**
Tinnion, Brian	**35**	*3*	1				**3**			**3**
Woodman, Craig	**5**	*1*								
(own-goals)							**5**			**5**
30 players used	**506**	***102***	**22**	***6***	**11**	***3***	**68**	**4**		**72**

No	Date		Att	Pos	Pt	F-A	H-T	Scorers, Times, and Referees	SQUAD NUMBERS IN USE											subs used
1	H	BLACKPOOL			W	2-0	0-0	Peacock 77, Murray 90	Phillips	Burnell	Hill	Coles	Millen	Doherty	Murray	Roberts^	Peacock	Brown A*	Bell	Rosenior/Lita
	10/8		11,891		3				Barnes	Grayson	Hills	Clarke P	Clarke C	Wellens"	Bullock !	Collins !	Walker*	Southern	Taylor^	Dalglish/Jaszczun/Hughes
								Ref: M Fletcher	City withstood Blackpool's calculated strong-arm display, which resulted in the dismissal of two of their players not long after the break. Murray galloped through at the finish to fire a low shot into the empty net after the keeper had gone forward to try and get a late leveller.											
2	A	BRENTFORD			L	0-1	0-0		Phillips	Burnell*	Hill	Coles	Millen	Doherty	Murray	Roberts^	Peacock	Brown A !	Bell	Rosenior/Lita
	13/8		7,130		3			Hunt 76p	Smith	Hutchinson	Roget	Dobson	Sonko	Smith	O'Connor	Vine	McCammon	Hunt	Somner	
								Ref: P Danson	As well as missing a stack of chances and being thrice thwarted by the post, City had Brown dismissed for a foul just before Hunt secured the points for the Bees. He blasted in from the spot after being brought down by Coles, to keep alive Brentford's run of success against the City.											
3	A	WIGAN	18		L	0-2	0-0		Phillips	Burnell	Hill	Coles !	Millen^	Doherty	Murray	Roberts*	Peacock	Brown A"	Bell	Rosenior/Fortune/Lita
	17/8		6,548	1	3			Green 75, McCulloch 89	Filan	Dinning	Jackson	Brannan*	De Vos	Jarrett^	Green	Ellington	Liddell	McCulloch	Kennedy	Breckin/Flynn
								Ref: U Rennie	The new clampdown shows no sign of abating as a reckless two-footed lunge on ex-Rover Nathan Ellington, early in the second half, brought a red card for Coles at the JJB Stadium. Lee McCulloch's daisy-cutter made the game safe for Wigan after Scott Green bundled in the opener.											
4	H	WYCOMBE	11		W	3-0	1-0	Bell 38, Murray 52, Roberts 72	Phillips	Fortune	Hill	Doherty^	Coles	Bell	Murray	Roberts	Peacock"	Brown A*	Woodman	Hulbert/Rosenior/Matthews
	24/8		**9,597**	20	6				Talia	Vinnicombe	Rogers	Ryan	McCarthy	Brown^	Currie	Devine*	Faul'bridge"	Simpson	Senda	Rammell/Roberts/Harris
								Ref: P Walton	It City can keep up the standard they achieved in this game then they will be in the promotion shake up at the season's end. Bell's ferocious 20-yard volley produced the opener, then after the tunraround Murray fired low past Frank Talia before Roberts netted with a simple tap in.											
5	A	PLYMOUTH	15		L	0-2	0-0		Phillips	Fortune	Hill	Doherty*	Coles	Bell	Murray"	Roberts	Peacock	Brown A	Woodman^	Burnell/Matthews/Beadle
	26/8		11,922	3	6			Wotton 65p, Coughlan 81	Larrieu	Bent*	Wotton	Friio"	Coughlan	Hodges	Phillips	Evans	Lowndes^	Adams	Worrell	Sturrock/Beresford/Broad
								Ref: P Prosser	City's lack of experience in defence was ruthlessly exposed at Home Park. Argyle took the lead when Paul Wotton's free-kick was flicked on by Micky Evans towards David Friio. As the Frenchman prepared to shoot, Fortune held him back to give away an inevitable spot-kick.											
6	H	TRANMERE	10		W	2-0	0-0	Tinnion 70p, Murray 74	Phillips	Burnell	Hill	Hulbert"	**Butler**	Tinnion	Murray	Roberts^	Peacock	Bell*	Woodman	Clist/Matthews/Fortune
	31/8		9,849	7	9				Achterberg	Sharps"	Gray	Mellon	Allen	Curtis^	Hines	Haworth	Barlow	Jones	Nicholson*	Price/Parkinson/Hume
								Ref: M Warren	A somewhat fortunate penalty when Murray's cross cannoned off Kevin Gray and hit Graham Allen's hand, but justice perhaps as earlier Roberts had clearly been brought down in the box with nothing given. Murray's blaster made sure of the points against difficult opponents.											
7	H	NORTHAMPTON	3		W	3-0	1-0	Peacock 7, 76, Clist 89	Phillips	Burnell	Hill	Hulbert	Butler	Tinnion"	Murray	Roberts*	Peacock	Doherty^	Woodman	Matthews/Clist/Beadle
	6/9		11,104	16	12				Harper	Gill	Spedding	Sampson	Burgess !	Harsley	Hargreaves	Gabbiadini^	Asamoah*	Carruthers	McGregor	Forrester/Rickers
								Ref: P Rejer	On a rain-soaked pitch City treated the good-sized Friday night crowd to a dazzling display. Their passing was breathtaking at times, especially that which lead up to Peacock's fired-in opener. Burgess was sent off for bringing down Peacock as he galloped through in the 53rd minute.											
8	A	CHELTENHAM	2		W	3-2	2-2	Murray 3, Coles 42, Matthews 53	Phillips	Coles	Fortune	Doherty	Butler	Burnell	Murray	Matthews*	Peacock	Brown A^	Woodman	Tinnion/Roberts
	14/9		5,895	24	15			Alsop 1, 22	Book	Howarth	Victory	Duff	Walker	Yates	McAuley^	Naylor"	Alsop	Finnigan	Milton*	Brayson/Williams/Spencer
								Ref: P Armstrong	City had to dig very deep to secure the points after some weak first-half defending which Julian Alsop exploited with two thumping headers as well as being denied by a post. However a 30-yard wonder strike by Matthews direct from a free-kick was a goal worthy of winning any game.											
9	A	OLDHAM	6		L	0-1	0-0		Phillips	Coles	Fortune	Doherty !	Butler	Burnell"	Murray	Matthews*	Peacock^	Tinnion	Woodman	Roberts/Lita/Brown A
	17/9		5,583	3	15			Wijnhard 79	Pogliacomi	Hall	Beharall	Sheridan	Hill	Appleby	Low*	Wijnhard	Corazzin^	Eyre	Eyres	Duxbury/Andrews
								Ref: C Webster	Another second-half dismissal and another defeat, an emerging pattern in regard to City away days this season. This dreadful game, littered with stoppages and poor distribution, is settled by Clyde Wijnhard. He found himself in acres of space and registered with a measured shot.											
10	H	QP RANGERS	9		L	**1-3**	1-1	Murray 10	Phillips	Coles	Hill	Doherty	Butler	Burnell	Murray	Matthews*	Peacock^	Tinnion	Woodman"	Roberts/Lita/Rosenior
	21/9		12,221	1	15			Connelly 23, 46, Gallen 52	Royce	Shittu	Palmer	Langley*	Carlisle	Forbes	Williams	Rose	Oli	Gallen	Connelly^	Murphy/Thomson
								Ref: M Messias	After Murray gave City the lead with a lob over the keeper from an acute angle, City are on top for much of the first half when Woodman was twice thwarted by the post. Despite the loss of their injured strikers it is defensive failings that cost City the game immediately after the break.											
11	A	PORT VALE	8		W	3-2	2-0	Beadle 18, Murray 40, Lita 90	Phillips	Coles	Hill	Doherty	Butler	Burnell	Murray*	Roberts^	Beadle	Tinnion	Bell	Lita/Hulbert
	28/9		4,286	13	18			Paynter 61, Cummins 89	Goodlad	Rowland	Collins	Brisco*	Carragher	Armstrong	Brightwell	Angell	Paynter	Br-Wilkinson	Cummins	Charnock
								Ref: R Olivier	A typical game of two halves which should have seen City at least 4-0 up at the break. As it was they had to make do with Beadle's headed opener and Murray's measured drive. Vale fought back in the second half with two shots to level matters before Lita fired in City's winner.											

No	H/A	Opponent	Pos	Res	FT	HT	Scorers, Times, and Referees	1	2	3	4	5	6	7	8	9	10	11	subs used
12	H	CHESTERFIELD	6	W	**4-0**	1-0	Roberts 26, Hill 64, Murray 89, 90	Phillips	Coles	Hill	Burnell	Butler	Tinnion^	Murray	Roberts	Beadle	Brown A*	Bell	Hulbert/Woodman
5/10		10,107	*8*	21				*Muggleton*	*Dawson*	*Howson*	*Ebdon*	*Blatherwick*	*Hudson^*	*Davies**	*Reeves*	*Allott*	*Booty*	*Rushbery*	*Edwards/Brandon*
							Ref: R Beeby	Roberts opened the scoring with a close-range shot after a neat one-two with Beadle. He also had two efforts brilliantly saved and laid on the pass for Murray to fire his first goal in off a defender at the near post. It took a long time coming, but Hill's header rewarded City's dominance.											
13	A	BARNSLEY	5	W	4-1	2-0	Butler 19, Roberts 28, 58, 73	Phillips	Coles	Hill	Doherty*	Butler	Burnell	Murray	Roberts	Beadle^	Tinnion	Bell	Brown A/Hulbert
12/10		*10,495*	*17*	24			*Bertos 49*	*Marriott*	*Austin*	*Curle*	*Gorre*	*Morgan*	*Lumsden*	*Betsy*	*Fallon^*	*Dyer"*	*Jones Gry**	*Williams*	*Burtos/Neil/Jones Griff*
							Ref: D Pugh	City boss Danny Wilson made a triumphant first return to Oakwell where he had made his name. Against the financially troubled Tykes, City excelled as they bulldozed their way to a convincing success after Butler stabbed in the opener. Roberts fired in a free-kick for his hat-trick.											
14	H	SWINDON	3	W	2-0	2-0	Murray 12, Tinnion 38	Phillips	Coles	Hill	Doherty^	Butler	Burnell	Murray	Roberts"	Beadle	Tinnion	Bell*	Woodman/Brown A/Lita
19/10		13,205	*22*	27				*Griemink*	*Gurney*	*Duke*	*Reeves*	*Heywood*	*Hewlett*	*Miglioranzi^*	*Davis*	*Sabin*	*Invincible**	*Robinson*	*Young/Jackson*
							Ref: G Cain	Whilst Swindon had most of the possession they could have been even further behind at the break as Murray squandered two excellent chances. Doherty's astute pass set Murray free to fire in an acute-angled opener, then Tinnion got in on the act with a 25-yard scorcher.											
15	A	PETERBOROUGH	3	W	3-1	2-1	Tinnion 3, Brown 17, Murray 90	Phillips	Coles	Hill	Doherty	Butler	Burnell	Murray	Roberts	Brown A*	Tinnion	Bell	Lita
26/10		*5,332*	*22*	30			*Clarke 43*	*Tyler*	*Joseph*	*Gill*	*Edwards*	*Rea*	*Hyde*	*Semple"*	*Allen*	*Clarke*	*Shields**	*Farrell*	*Danielsson/Lee*
							Ref: M Thorpe	Even the absence of a recognised target-man is not a handicap to a City team who appear to be in unstoppable mood. After Tinnion fired City in front with a real pearler, they looked lethal going forward with Brown and Murray tearing holes at the heart of sorry Posh from all angles.											
16	H	HUDDERSFIELD	3	W	1-0	1-0	Hill 38	Phillips	Coles	Hill	Doherty*	Butler	Burnell	Murray	Robets	Brown A"	Tinnion	Bell^	Lita/Woodman/Hulbert
23/10		*11,494*	*17*	33				*Bevan*	*Jenkins^*	*Sharp*	*Brown*	*Moses*	*Holland*	*Th'rrington**	*Schofield*	*Stead*	*Mattis*	*Smith*	*Baldry/Irons*
							Ref: P Durkin	Not so much a night for the soccer purist, more one for those who enjoy a good hard battle. Right at the death Phillips had to bring off a stunning last-ditch save to prevent Danny Schofield's raking drive from sneaking into the net as City held onto Hill's stunning first-half strike.											
17	A	COLCHESTER	4	D	2-2	1-0	Peacock 42, 57	Phillips	Coles	Hill	Doherty	Butler	Burnell	Murray	Roberts*	Peacock	Tinnion^	Bell	Rosenior/A Brown
9/11		***3,338***	*21*	34			*Pinault 54, Bowry 66*	*Brown*	*Stockwell**	*Baldwin*	*White*	*Keith*	*Bowry*	*Stockley*	*Rapley*	*McGleish*	*Pinault*	*Izzet*	*Morgan*
							Ref: J Ross	It is a measure of the progress made by City this season that the players looked crestfallen as they trouped off with a point at the end of this game. Twice Peacock gave City the lead, a deft side-footed effort, followed by a six-yard header, but Bowry stabbed in the U's point saver.											
18	A	MANSFIELD	3	W	5-4	1-1	Mur'39, Rob' 49, 90, Tin' 86p, Lita 89	Phillips	Coles^	Hill	Burnell	Butler	Tinnion	Murray	Roberts	Beadle	A Brown*	Bell	Rosenior/Lita
23/11		*4,801*	*24*	37			*Corden 38, 67, Christie 62, 76*	*Pilkington*	*Lever*	*Moore*	*Disley*	*Gadsby*	*Williamson ! Clark*		*Larkin**	*Christie^*	*Lawrence*	*Corden*	*Jervis/Bacon*
							Ref: E Ilderton	A strike of stunning ferocity clinched City's last-gasp victory in the fifth minute of added time, just 60 seconds after Lita had touched in the leveller from Murray's cross. It took a dubious penalty to get City back into the game, this making up for Mansfield's equally 'iffy' award.											
19	H	CREWE	4	D	2-2	0-2	Murray 47, Peacock 83	Phillips	Coles	Hill	Doherty*	Butler	Burnell	Murray	Roberts	Beadle"	Tinnion	Bell^	Brown A/Peacock/Lita
30/11		12,585	*5*	38			*Ashton 30, Hulse 35*	*Ince*	*Wright*	*Tierney*	*Foster*	*Walton*	*Brammer*	*Jack*	*Ashton**	*Hulse*	*Lunt*	*Vaughan*	*Sorvel*
							Ref: P Crossley	Yet again City showed great character by producing a storming recovery after the break. Falling behind when Steve Foster's header from a corner was deflected in off striker Dean Ashton, City were really up against it when Rob Hulse pounced on a loose ball shortly afterwards.											
20	H	NOTTS CO	3	W	3-2	1-1	Beadle 33, Richardson 57 (og), [Peacock 83]	Phillips	Coles	Hill	Doherty	Butler	Burnell	Murray	Roberts^	Beadle*	Tinnion	Bell	Peacock/Rosenior
3/12		10,690	*21*	41			*Stallard 19, 80*	*Mildenhall*	*Ashton**	*Richardson*	*Ramsden*	*Fenton*	*Whiteley*	*Jupp*	*Stallard*	*Allsopp*	*Baraclough*	*Riley^*	*Caskey/Francis*
							Ref: S Tomlin	City somehow chalked up another win after a night of sweat and toil at the Gate. As though to give Notts the advantage they held when the first meeting was abandoned a month earlier, City were caught cold when Mark Stannard steered in the opener from Ian Richardson's free-kick.											
21	A	CARDIFF	2	W	2-0	0-0	Tinnion 48p, Roberts 75	Phillips	Coles	Hill	Doherty	Butler	Burnell	Murray	Roberts*	Peacock	Tinnion	Bell	Rosenior
14/12		***15,239***	*3*	44				*Alexander*	*Legg*	*Zhiyl*	*Boland*	*Prior*	*Kavanagh*	*Croft*	*Earnshaw*	*Thorne"*	*Hamilton**	*Barker*	*Maxwell^/Bowen/Campbell*
							Ref: A Wiley	A fevered atmosphere at Ninian Park for the Sky television cameras at the 5.35pm kick-off time. After weathering early pressure caused by Spencer Prior's long throws, ex-Cardiff man Roberts clinched City's victory when Neil Alexander failed to clear from the edge of the box.											
22	H	LUTON	3	D	1-1	0-0	Beadle 90	Phillips	Carey	Hill	Doherty	Coles	Burnell*	Murray	Roberts^	Peacock	Tinnion"	Bell	Brown A/Rosenior/Beadle
21/12		14,057	*8*	45			*Howard 53*	*Emberson*	*Boyce*	*Davis !*	*Neilson**	*Coyne*	*Robinson*	*Crowe*	*Howard*	*Thorpe^*	*Hughes*	*Brkovic*	*Hillier/Kimble*
							Ref: M Cooper	A thunderous last-gasp drive in the sixth min of added time took City's unbeaten run to 17 games against opponents who had Sol Davis sent off for hitting Murray shortly before. A deserved point for City after thrice being foiled by the woodwork as well as having a goal disallowed.											
23	H	PLYMOUTH	2	D	0-0	0-0		Phillips	Coles	Bell	Burnell	Butler	Hill	Murray	Roberts*	Peacock	Doherty^	Tinnion	Rosenior/Beadle
26/12		**18,085**	*3*	46				*Larrieu*	*Worrell*	*Hodges*	*Wotton*	*Barrass**	*Coughlan*	*Norris*	*Keith"*	*Evans^*	*Bent*	*Adams*	*McGl'chey/St'bridge/St'rck*
							Ref: A Hall	This was poor fare for the bumper crowd. Apart from Argyle skipper Paul Wotton's thunderous 35-yard free-kick at the start, and Hill's low drive hitting the post right on half-time, there was little of interest, though in the 64th minute the upright also served to thwart Marino Keith.											

No	Date		Opponent	Att	Pos	Pt		F-A	H-T	Scorers, Times, and Referees	SQUAD	NUMBERS	IN	USE								subs used
24	28/12	A	STOCKPORT	5,100	2 / 14	49	W	4-1	3-0	Peacock 19, Coles 40, Rosenior 40, [Beadle 88]	Phillips	Coles	Bell	Burnell*	Butler	Hill	Murray	Rosenior"	Peacock	Doherty	Tinnion^	Brown A/Carey/Beadle
										Beckett 57	*Jones*	*Gibb*	*Tonkin*	*Lambert^*	*Challinor*	*Hardiker*	*Clare*	*Beckett*	*Burgess*	*Fradin*	*Pemberton**	*Goodwin/Daly*
										Ref: P Robinson	How City must like playing at Edgeley Park, where they added to many wins they have obtained here over the years. As Stockport pressed forward, City picked them off on the counter. All City's goals were outstanding, but the build-up to the one shot in by Coles was sheer class.											
25	1/1	A	WYCOMBE	6,785	3 / 13	49	L	1-2	0-0	Tinnion 87p	Phillips	Coles	Bell	Doherty	Butler	Hill	Murray	Rosenior*	Peacock	Brown A^	Tinnion	Roberts"/Beadle/Carey
										Johnson 49, Brown 68p	*Talia*	*Thomson*	*Johnson*	*Bulman*	*Rogers*	*Simpson*	*Senda*	*Dixon*	*F'conbrdge**	*Brown*	*Ryan*	*Harris*
										Ref: G Salisbury	City looked to be suffering a New Year hangover as they stumbled to defeat against poor opposition. They were made to pay for failing to take their chances when a static defence allowed Roger Johnson to head the Choirboys into the lead with an easy header from Keith Ryan's corner.											
26	10/1	H	WIGAN	13,151	4 / 1	49	L	0-1	0-0		Phillips	Coles"	Bell	Burnell	Butler	Hill	Murray	Beadle*	Peacock^	Doherty	Brown A	Rosenior/Tinnion/Carey
										Kennedy 49	*Filan*	*Eadon*	*Kennedy*	*Mitchell*	*Jackson*	*De Vos*	*Teale^*	*Ellington**	*Liddell*	*Dinning*	*McCulloch*	*Roberts/Jarrett*
										Ref: D Pugh	Whilst City gave their all on a bitterly cold night warmed by this TV thriller, they were again found wanting in front of goal. Wigan's competent and clinical display snatched a narrow victory thanks to Peter Kennedy firing the ball in from a free-kick on the edge of the box.											
27	18/1	A	TRANMERE	7,459	5 / 9	50	D	1-1	1-0	Bell 9	Phillips	Coles	Hill	Burnell	Butler	Carey	Murray	**Fagan^**	Peacock*	Tinnion	Bell	Roberts/Fortune
										Haworth 61	*Achterberg*	*Connelly*	*Roberts*	*Jackson*	*Sharps*	*Jones*	*Hume*	*Barlow^*	*Haworth*	*Mellon*	*Hay**	*Nicholson/Price*
										Ref: B Curson	City got their promotion bid back on the rails with a point from this Prenton Park thriller. Bell put them in front with a fine angled left-footer, but Simon Haworth levelled with an unstoppable shot from the edge of the box. Thereafter Phillips performed wonders between the sticks.											
28	25/1	H	STOCKPORT	10,831	5 / 18	51	D	1-1	0-1	Roberts 50	Phillips	Coles"	Fortune*	Carey	Butler	Hill	Murray	Roberts	Fagan	Burnell^	Bell	Tinnion/Clist/Lita
										Beckett 22	*Tidman*	*Lescott !*	*Tonkin*	*Clare*	*Challinor*	*McLachlan*	*Ellison^*	*Daly**	*Beckett*	*Lambert"*	*Gibb*	*G'dwin/Wilb'ham/Pemb'ton*
										Ref: P Armstrong	Stockport should have been out of sight by the break, but fortunately the visitors, down to ten men following Aaron Lescott's two daft cautions, only had Luke Beckett's header to show for their domination. Roberts buried Murray's miscued effort to salvage City a point.											
29	1/2	A	BLACKPOOL	7,290	5 / 9	52	D	0-0	0-0		Phillips	Coles	Fortune	Carey	Butler	Burnell	Murray	Beadle	Roberts*	Tinnion	Bell	Fagan
											Barnes	*Grayson*	*Richardson*	*Hendry*	*Flynn*	*Southern*	*Wellens*	*Murphy*	*Walker^*	*Evans**	*Thornley"*	*Bullock/Taylor/Coid*
										Ref: C Boyeson	After what happened in this fixture last year it was encouraging that City's defending was such that they hardly gave Blackpool a chance. Unfortunately this was at the expense of the free-flowing attack minded play that had characterised their play in the first part of the season.											
30	8/2	H	COLCHESTER	11,107	5 / 20	52	L	1-2	0-1	Fagan 51	Phillips	Carey	Fortune	Burnell	Hill	Tinnion	Murray	Fagan	Beadle*	Doherty^	Bell	Peacock/Roberts
										McGleish 12, Pinault 82	*Brown*	*Stockley*	*Chivers*	*White*	*Fitzgerald*	*Izzet*	*Stockwell**	*McGleish*	*Morgan^*	*Keith*	*Pinault*	*Bowry/Williams*
										Ref: A Hall	City were totally lacking in any degree of heart or urgency as their poor run of form shows no sign of ending. After Scott McGleish's headed opener, an errant back-pass led to Fagan's rammed in equaliser, before Phillips was surprisingly beaten by Thomas Pinault's 25-yard winner.											
31	11/2	H	BRENTFORD	9,084	5 / 13	53	D	0-0	0-0		Phillips	Coles	Bell	Carey	Hill	Doherty	Murray	Fagan*	Beadle	Burnell^	Tinnion	Roberts/Peacock
											Smith	*Dobson*	*Somner*	*Sonko*	*Marshall*	*Fullarton*	*O'Connor*	*Hunt*	*Vine*	*Smith*	*Evans**	*McCammon*
										Ref: S Mathieson	City made a real effort in this game and in contrast to Saturday's boos the team were applauded off the pitch. Early after the break Murray almost registered with an astonishing bicycle kick from the edge of the box. Despite one heck of a grandstand finish, success just wasn't to be.											
32	15/2	A	NOTTS CO	5,754	5 / 15	53	L	0-2	0-0		Phillips	Carey	Bell	Coles	Butler	Burnell"	Murray	Fagan*	Peacock	Doherty	Brown A^	Roberts/Tinnion/Beadle
										Stallard 50p, Heffernan 66	*Mildenhall*	*Fenton*	*Liburd*	*Baraclough*	*Richardson*	*Brough*	*Bolland**	*Ireland*	*Stallard*	*Heffernan*	*Caskey^*	*Ramsden/Francis*
										Ref: G Hegley	City paid the price for failing to translate their first-half possession into goals. A disputed penalty, following Carey's tangle with Mark Stallard, got County off the mark, then the City defence stood around like statues as Paul Heffernan's lunging header doubled the Magpies' advantage.											
33	22/2	A	NORTHAMPTON	4,688	5 / 23	56	W	2-1	2-1	Robins 12, Tinnion 35	Phillips	Carey	Bell	Burnell^	Butler	Hill	Murray	**Robins***	Peacock	Doherty	Tinnion	Roberts/Coles
										McGregor 45	*Abbey*	*Gill*	*Carruthers*	*Johnson^*	*Burgess*	*Reid*	*Trollope**	*Gabbiadini*	*Asamoah*	*Rahim"*	*McGregor*	*Hargreaves/Harsley/Stamp*
										Ref: A Butler	The arrival of Mark Robins on loan from Rotherham galvanised City, who dominated the first-half play. It was cruel luck when straight after Peacock had his shot struck off for offside, that the Cobblers raced up to the other end where Paul McGregor registered with an 18-yard chip.											
34	1/3	H	CHELTENHAM	11,711	5 / 24	59	W	3-1	2-1	Robins 2, Brown 20, Rosenior 90	Phillips	Carey	Bell	Burnell	Butler	Hill	Roberts^	Robins*	Peacock	Doherty	Brown A	Rosenior/Beadle
										McCann 44	*Book*	*Jones*	*Victory*	*Duff M^*	*Duff S*	*Yates*	*Devaney"*	*Spencer**	*Alsop*	*Finnigan*	*McCann*	*Naylor/Brough/Bird*
										Ref: L Cable	It looked easy for City when, following their 66-second opener, Brown doubled the advantage by coolly firing in a deflection off Bell's shot. Unfortunately Grant McCann's free-kick made for an edgy second half which was finally settled by Rosenior's low drive right at the finish.											

35	H	OLDHAM		5	W	2-0	0-0	Murray 54, Roberts 90	Phillips	Carey	Bell	Burnell	Butler	Hill	Murray	Robins*	Peacock	Doherty^	Brown A	Roberts/Tinnion
	4/3		11,194	*6*	62				*Pogliacomi*	*Hall*	*Beharall**	*Carss*	*Haining*	*Baudet"*	*Murray*	*Andrews^*	*Wijnhard*	*Armstrong*	*Eyres*	*Corazzin/Killen/Duxbury*
								Ref: T Parkes	Murray broke the deadlock and deprived Oldham of their unbeaten away record with a run from one penalty box to the other before registering with a curling strike into the bottom corner of the Atyeo Stand net. Carey's intelligent pass set up Roberts to register with an unerring shot.											
36	A	QP RANGERS		5	L	0-1	0-1		Phillips	Carey	Bell	Burnell"	Butler	Hill	Murray	Robins^	Peacock	Doherty	Brown A*	Tinnion/Roberts/Beadle
	8/3		*14,681*	*6*	62			*Gallen 19p*	*Day*	*Forbes*	*Williams*	*Palmer*	*Carlisle*	*Shittu*	*Bircham*	*Furlong*	*Gallen*	*Langley*	*Cook**	*Griffiths*
								Ref: P Rejer	A strange game which could easily have ended in stalemate but for Hill being adjudged to have nudged the ball with his arm. Rangers' 1-0 win was just about right for a contest of few real chances played in a deafening atmosphere that perhaps made the game appear better than it was.											
37	H	PETERBOROUGH		5	W	1-0	1-0	Robins 12	Phillips	Carey	Bell	Burnell	Butler	Hill	Murray	Robins"	Peacock^	Doherty	Brown A*	Tinnion/Beadle/Roberts
	15/3		11,231	*19*	65				*Tyler*	*Arber*	*Jelleyman"*	*Newton*	*Rea*	*Gill*	*Burton*	*Fotiadis**	*Clarke*	*Scott*	*Danielsson^*	*Lee/Strachan/Farrell*
								Ref: R Olivier	Despite the encouragement of an early goal, when Robins scrambled the ball home from Peacock's neat header, the crowd made little noise. They obviously knew what was coming as City produced a strangely cumbersome display with many misplaced passes and off-target efforts.											
38	A	SWINDON		5	D	1-1	0-0	Robins 48	Phillips	Carey	Hill	Coles	Butler	Burnell	Murray	Robins^	Peacock	Doherty	Brown A*	Tinnion/Roberts
	13/3		*8,629*	*13*	66			*Parkin 66*	*Griemink*	*Ifil*	*Heywood*	*Duke*	*Reeves*	*Miglioranzi*	*Gurney*	*Invincible*	*Parkin*	*Robinson*	*Lewis*	
								Ref: C Penton	Few loan players down the years have made the sort of impact that Mark Robins had during his memorable one-month loan. He signed off here with another goal, a superbly executed header, but it wasn't enough for victory as Sam Parkin equalised matters by firing in from close range.											
39	A	HUDDERSFIELD		5	W	2-1	2-1	Hill 17, Peacock 35	Phillips	Carey	Hill	Coles	Butler	Burnell	Murray	Roberts^	Peacock"	Doherty*	Brown A	Tinnion/Rosenior/Lita
	22/3		*9,467*	*24*	69			*Smith 19p*	*Senior*	*Moses*	*Sharp*	*Gavin*	*Brown*	*Holland*	*Schofield**	*Smith*	*Booth*	*Stead*	*Heary*	*Thorrington*
								Ref: J Robinson	Following their second-half introduction, Rosenior and Lita tormented Town's defenders to keep City on track for a vital win at the McAlpine Stadium. Butler's push on Andy Booth allowed Town to level Hill's close-range shot, but Peacock headed in City's winner from Carey's cross.											
40	H	BARNSLEY		4	W	2-0	1-0	Murray 6, Roberts 63	Phillips	Carey	Bell	Coles"	Butler	Burnell	Murray	Roberts^	Peacock	Doherty	Brown A*	Tinnion/Rosenior/Hill
	29/3		10,232	*16*	72				*Taylor*	*Kay*	*Donovan*	*Austin*	*Morgan*	*Betsy*	*Jones*	*Dyer**	*Sheron*	*Ward^*	*Neil*	*Gorre/Mulligan*
								Ref: A Penn	Just as happened against Peterborough the early breakthrough, courtesy of the alert Murray seizing on Neil Austin's weak back-pass, did little to improve the atmosphere or the quality of the game. Fortunately Martin Taylor marred a brilliant display by fumbling a hopeful Roberts shot.											
41	H	MANSFIELD		4	W	5-2	2-1	Peacock 13, Murray 32, 51, 80, *Disley 37, Butler 61 (og)* [Carey 70]	Phillips	Carey	Bell	Coles	Butler	Burnell	Murray	Roberts"	Peacock	Doherty*	Tinnion^	Brown A/Hill/Rosenior
	12/4		12,013	*23*	75				*Pilkington*	*Hassell*	*Eaton**	*Day*	*Curle*	*Williamson*	*MacKenzie"*	*Curtis^*	*Mendes*	*Disley*	*Corden*	*Gadsby/Christie/White*
								Ref: P Taylor	Murray celebrated last week's LDV Vans Trophy final success with his first ever hat-trick to blaze his way to 25 goals so far this campaign. The Stags refused to wilt after Peacock's opening header and always looked a threat with their lively approach play in this entertaining game.											
42	A	CREWE		4	D	1-1	0-1	Roberts 62	Phillips	Carey	Bell*	Coles	Butler	Burnell	Murray	Roberts^	Peacock	Doherty	Tinnion"	Hill/Rosenior/Brown A
	15/4		*7,901*	*2*	76			*Lunt 14p*	*Ince*	*Sodje*	*Foster*	*Walton*	*Walker*	*Brammer*	*Lunt**	*Ashton"*	*Jack*	*Sorvel*	*Vaughan^*	*Hulse/Oakes/Jones*
								Ref: M Ryan	City kept automatic promotion hopes alive with this fighting draw, but they really needed to win to have a realistic chance. After Bell chopped down Rodney Jack to concede the spot-kick, Roberts rescued a point with a scorcher that Clayton Ince could only watch fizz past his left hand.											
43	A	LUTON		5	D	2-2	0-1	Tinnion 66p, Peacock 75	Phillips	Carey	Hill	Coles	Butler	Burnell	Murray	Roberts^	Peacock	Doherty*	Tinnion"	Brown A/Beadle/Lita
	19/4		*6,381*	*9*	77			*Howard 2, 82*	*Beckwith*	*Boyce*	*Davis*	*Wilmot*	*Neilson*	*Nicholls*	*Holmes**	*Griffiths*	*Howard*	*Spring*	*Hughes^*	*Foley/Kimble*
								Ref: G Salisbury	City, who have proved that they can live with the best footballing sides in the Second Division, were subjected to intense physical intimidation at Kenilworth Road where they nearly came out on top. Unfortunately Steve Howard rose above Butler to head in Luton's late equaliser.											
44	H	CARDIFF		3	W	2-0	0-0	Tinnion 55p, Roberts 73	Phillips	Carey	Hill	Coles	Butler	Burnell	Murray	Roberts^	Peacock	Doherty	Tinnion*	Brown A !/Rosenior
	22/4		15,615	*4*	80				*Alexander*	*Weston*	*Barker*	*Gabbidon*	*Prior*	*Boland**	*Ainsworth !*	*Thorne*	*Earnshaw*	*Kavanagh*	*Legg^*	*Whalley/Campbell*
								Ref: R Styles	City took a while to warm up, but when they did there were no doubts of them extending their unbeaten League run against their old rivals to 22 games. After a handball had produced a controversial penalty for City, Roberts tied matters up by firing in Murray's cross from close range.											
45	A	CHESTERFIELD		4	L	0-2	0-0		Phillips	Carey	Hill	Coles	Butler !	Burnell	Murray	Roberts^	Peacock"	Tinnion*	Brown A !	Beadle/Bell/Rosenior
	26/4		*4,770*	*20*	80			*Hurst 86, Hudson 90*	*Muggleton*	*Booty*	*O'Hare*	*Blatherwick*	*Dawson*	*Close**	*Douglas*	*Hurst*	*Allott^*	*Hudson*	*Innes"*	*Ebdon/Reeves/Edwards*
								Ref: I Williamson	The double sending off of Butler, who was only trying to diffuse the situation, and Brown, who tried to kick the ball trapped by a Chesterfield player's body, ended City's faint hopes of automatic promotion. They paid the price of their indiscipline when Glynn Hurst forced the ball in.											
46	H	PORT VALE		3	W	2-0	2-0	Murray 31, Peacock 43	Phillips	Carey	Hill	Coles	Butler	Burnell	Murray^	Roberts*	Peacock"	Tinnion	Bell	Lita/Amankwaah/Beadle
	3/5		12,410	*17*	83				*Goodlad*	*Brightwell"*	*Collins*	*Durnin^*	*Walsh*	*Charnock**	*Carragher*	*McPhee*	*Littlejohn*	*Cummins*	*Armstrong*	*Paynter/Reid/Brown*
		Home	Away					Ref: M Riley	Rookie striker Lita came on to give an effervescent cameo display for City in this comfortable win. Murray took his goal tally to a remarkable 26 by converting Hill's low cross, then Peacock made the points secure by shooting the ball home after the keeper had blocked his first effort.											
Average		11,890	7,368																	

Play-Offs

Play-Offs	F-A	H-T	Scorers, Times, and Referees	SQUAD	NUMBERS	IN	USE								subs used
SF1 A CARDIFF 3 L	0-1	0-0		Phillips	Carey	Hill	Coles	Butler	Burnell	Murray	Roberts*	Peacock	Doherty^	Bell	Rosenior/Tinnion
10/5 *19,146* *6*			*Thorne 74*	*Alexander*	*Weston*	*Barker*	*Gabbidon*	*Prior*	*Kavanagh*	*Boland*	*Thorne*	*Earnshaw^*	*Whalley*	*Legg**	*Bonner/Campbell*
			Ref: H Webb	City boss Danny Wilson assures us that the heat is on Cardiff despite Peter Thorne's firm header giving the Welshmen a slender advantage for the second leg. The feeling persists however that the odds are with Cardiff, with them having ended City's 32-year dominance of this fixture.											
SF2 H CARDIFF 3 D	0-0	0-0		Phillips	Carey	Hill"	Coles	Butler	Burnell^	Murray	Roberts*	Peacock	Doherty	Tinnion	Lita/Amankwaah/Beadle
13/5 16,307 *6*				*Alexander*	*Weston**	*Barker*	*Gabbidon*	*Prior*	*Kavanagh*	*Boland*	*Thorne*	*Earnshaw"*	*Whalley*	*Legg^*	*Croft/Bonner/Campbell*
			Ref: J Winter (City lost 0-1 on aggregate)	City, scorers of more than 100 goals this season, couldn't score when it mattered. Cardiff obtained sweet revenge for the two league defeats at City's hands this season by surviving this tense affair to reach the final (which they win). In truth, City struggled to make any impression.											

Worthington Cup

Worthington Cup	F-A	H-T	Scorers, Times, and Referees												subs used
1 H OXFORD 4 L	0-1	0-1		Phillips	Burnell	Hill	Hulbert*	Butler	Doherty"	Murray	Roberts^	Peacock	Tinnion	Woodman	Clist/Matthews/Beadle
10/9 4,065 *3:15*			*Hunt 17*	*Woodman*	*McNiven*	*Robinson**	*Crosby*	*Viveash*	*Bound*	*Oldfield*	*Scott !*	*Ford*	*Savage*	*Hunt*	*Powell*
			Ref: T Parkes	Yet again City fail against so-called inferior opposition, as they never looked like doing the business. The poor crowd on a lovely fine evening are short-changed as the flat-footed Phillips is beaten at the Atyeo end when James Hunt's drive from the left takes a slight deflection off Hill.											

FA Cup

FA Cup	F-A	H-T	Scorers, Times, and Referees												subs used
1 A HEYBRIDGE SWIFTS 4 W	7-0	4-0	Roberts 15, 41, Tinnion 39p,	Phillips	Coles"	Hill	Doherty	Butler	Burnell	Murray	Roberts^	Peacock*	Tinnion	Bell	Beadle/Lita/Brown A
16/11 *2,046 RL:20*			[Murray 45, 62, Lita 66, 82]	*Banks*	*Blackwell*	*Barber*	*Culverhouse*	*Pollard*	*Baillie*	*Rainford*	*Tomlinson**	*Abrahams*	*Window"*	*Budge^*	*Hunter/Cobb/Payne*
			Ref: B Curson	After surviving an early scare when Phillips touched a 25-yarder by Jamie Window onto a post, it was easy for City at Scraley Road. Roberts fired in City's opener from close range before Peacock was taken off wearing a neck brace after being clattered by home skipper John Pollard.											
2 A HARROGATE RLWY 3 W	3-1	1-0	Walker 20 (og), Murray 53, Roberts 90	Phillips	Coles*	Hill	Doherty	Butler	Burnell	Murray	Roberts	Peacock	Tinnion	Bell	Carey
8/12 *3,200 NC:10*			*Davey 78*	*Neale*	*Watkinson^*	*Ames*	*Wilson*	*Danby*	*Walker*	*McLean*	*Gore*	*Smith*	*Flynn**	*Stansfield"*	*Davey/Constable/Hart*
			Ref: P Danson	Most of the Sky viewers who witnessed this game, which started at 11 o'clock, were hoping for a giant-killing act at Station View. After Steve Davey had lobbed the Railway back into the game, Roberts ended their hopes deep into stoppage time – slotting the ball in from an acute angle.											
3 A LEICESTER 4 L	0-2	0-1		Phillips	Coles	Bell	Doherty	Butler	Hill	Murray	Roberts*	Peacock	Tinnion^	Bell	Rosenior/Beadle
4/1 *25,868* *1:2*			*Elliott 45, Dickov 75*	*Walker*	*Impey*	*Rogers*	*McKinlay*	*Elliott*	*Sinclair*	*Su'merbee"*	*Dickov*	*Dean*	*Lewis^*	*Stewart**	*Benjamin/Jones/Heath*
			Ref: M Messias	City outplayed the Foxes in midfield, but lacked the cutting edge in this strangely low-key Cup clash. On Leicester's new ground, City fell to a sucker punch in first-half added time. From a free-kick Junior Lewis was unmarked to head across goal for Elliott to fire in from close range.											

Abandoned League Fixture

Abandoned League Fixture	F-A	H-T	Scorers, Times, and Referees												subs used
H NOTTS CO 4	0-1	0-1		Phillips	Coles	Bell	Burnell	Butler	Hill	Murray	Roberts	Peacock	Tinnion	Brown A	
2/11 10,700 18 *(Abandoned 49 mins waterlogged pitch)*			*Heffernan 45*	*Garden*	*Stone*	*Nicholson*	*Richardson*	*Fenton*	*Bolland*	*Brough*	*Heffernan*	*Stallard*	*Whitley*	*Cas*	
			Ref: S Tomlin	After being out with hamstring and back problems, Peacock had an ideal workout in the rain-sodden conditions He could have had a hat-trick but for a certain amount of rustiness. Unfortunately for County's Paul Heffernan, his first-half stoppage time strike will now count for nothing.											

		P	W	D	L	F	A	W	D	L	F	A	Pts
			Home					Away					
1	Wigan	46	14	7	2	37	16	15	6	2	31	9	100
2	Crewe	46	11	5	7	29	19	14	6	3	47	21	86
3	BRISTOL CITY	46	15	5	3	43	15	9	6	8	36	33	83
4	QP Rangers	46	14	4	5	38	19	10	7	6	31	26	83
5	Oldham	46	11	6	6	39	18	11	10	2	29	20	82
6	Cardiff *	46	12	6	5	33	20	11	6	6	35	23	81
7	Tranmere	46	14	5	4	38	23	9	6	8	28	34	80
8	Plymouth	46	11	6	6	39	24	6	8	9	24	28	65
9	Luton	46	8	8	7	32	28	9	6	8	35	34	65
10	Swindon	46	10	5	8	34	27	6	7	10	25	36	60
11	Peterborough	46	8	7	8	25	20	6	9	8	26	34	58
12	Colchester	46	8	7	8	24	24	6	9	8	28	32	58
13	Blackpool	46	10	8	5	35	25	5	5	13	21	39	58
14	Stockport	46	8	8	7	39	38	7	2	14	26	32	55
15	Notts Co	46	10	7	6	37	32	3	9	11	25	38	55
16	Brentford	46	8	8	7	28	21	6	4	13	19	35	54
17	Port Vale	46	9	5	9	34	31	5	6	12	20	39	53
18	Wycombe	46	8	7	8	39	38	5	6	12	20	28	52
19	Barnsley	46	7	8	8	27	31	6	5	12	24	33	52
20	Chesterfield	46	11	4	8	29	28	3	4	16	14	45	50
21	Cheltenham	46	6	9	8	26	31	4	9	10	27	37	48
22	Huddersfield	46	7	9	7	27	24	4	3	16	12	37	45
23	Mansfield	46	9	2	12	38	45	3	6	14	28	52	44
24	Northampton	46	7	4	12	23	31	3	5	15	17	48	39
		1104	236	150	166	793	628	166	150	236	628	793	1506

* promoted after play-offs

Odds & ends

Double wins: (8) Northampton Town, Cheltenham Town, Port Vale, Barnsley, Peterborough United, Huddersfield Town, Mansfield, Cardiff.
Double losses: (2) Wigan Athletic, Queens Park Rangers.

Won from behind: (3) Cheltenham (a), Mansfield Town (a), Notts Co (h).
Lost from in front: (1) Queens Park Rangers (h).

High spots: Winning at Cheltenham on 14 September to spark a sequence of four consecutive away victories.
Six successive League wins, starting at Port Vale on 28 September.
The Field Mill thriller on 23 November.
Beating Cardiff at Ninian Park on 14 December.
City's four-goal haul at Edgeley Park on 28 December.

Low spots: Losing out to Cardiff in the Play-Offs.
Failing to turn possession into goals against Leicester in the FA Cup.
The double sending-off at Saltergate on 26 April.
City's poor display, despite the win, on the occasion of their first ever appearance at the Millennium Stadium.

Players in the PFA XI: Mickey Bell and Scott Murray (third and fourth successive years respectively).

AGM (Exhibition Hall, Dolman Stand, Ashton Gate, 27 November 2003).
Loss: £1,918,154. Season Ticket Sales (No): 8,000+

Internationals: Scottish B: Scott Murray (41st-min substitute in a 3-3 draw with Germany at Mainz on 17 December). Northern Ireland B: Tommy Doherty (1-2 defeat by Scotland at Partick Thistle on 20 May).

Player of the year: Scott Murray.
Ever-presents: (1) Steve Phillips.
Hat-tricks: (2) Christian Roberts (1) and Scott Murray (1).
Leading scorer: Overall: Scott Murray (21). League: Scott Murray (18).

	Appearances								Goals				
	Lge	*Sub*	LC	*Sub*	FAC	*Sub*	PO	*Sub*	Lge	LC	FAC	PO	Tot
Amankwaah, Kevin		*1*						*1*					
Beadle, Peter	**11**	*13*		*1*		*2*		*1*	**4**				**4**
Bell, Mickey	**37**	*1*			3		1		**2**				**2**
Brown, Aaron	**21**	*11*				*1*			**2**				**2**
Burnell, Joe	**43**	*1*	1		3		2						
Butler, Tony	**38**		1		3		2		**1**				**1**
Carey, Louis	**21**	*3*				*1*	2		**1**				**1**
Clist, Simon		*3*		*1*					**1**				**1**
Coles, Danny	**38**	*1*			3		2		**2**				**2**
Doherty, Tommy	**38**		1		3		2						
Fagan, Craig	**5**	*1*							**1**				**1**
Fortune, Clayton	**7**	*3*											
Hill, Matt	**39**	*3*	1		3		2		**3**				**3**
Hulbert, Robin	**2**	*5*	1										
Lita, Leroy		*15*				*1*		*1*	**2**		2		**4**
Matthews, Lee	**3**	*4*		*1*					**1**				**1**
Millen, Keith	**3**												
Murray, Scott	**45**		1		3		2		**18**		3		**21**
Peacock, Lee	**33**	*4*	1		3		2		**12**				**12**
Phillips, Steve	**46**		1		3		2						
Robins, Mark	**6**								**4**				**4**
Roberts, Christian	**31**	*13*	1		3		2		**13**		3		**16**
Rosenior, Liam	**2**	*19*				*1*		*1*	**2**				**2**
Tinnion, Brian	**30**	*10*	1		3		1	*1*	**9**		1		**10**
Woodman, Craig	**7**	*3*	1										
(own-goals)									**1**		1		**2**
25 players used	**506**	***114***	**11**	***3***	**33**	***6***	**22**	***5***	**79**		**10**		**89**

No	Date		Att	Pos	Pt	F-A	H-T	Scorers, Times, and Referees	SQUAD	NUMBERS	IN	USE								subs used
1	H	NOTTS CO			W	5-0	2-0	Peacock 12, 37, Miller 49,	Phillips	Carey	Hill	Coles	Butler	Burnell^	**Wilkshire**	**Miller***	Peacock	Doherty"	Bell	Matthews/Roberts/Tinnion
	9/8		12,050		3			[Matthews 71, 88]	*Garden*	*Jenkins*	*Nicholson*	*Barras*	*Fenton*	*Brough*	*Bolland**	*Platt^*	*Stallard"*	*Richardson*	*Baraclough*	*Francis/Hackw'th/H'ffernan*
								Ref: J Ross	In the oppressive heat Peacock got City's season off to a good start against poor opposition. On receiving Bell's pass he jinked past his marker and confidently slotted home the opener at the Wedlock End before having his header from Wilkshire's corner ruled to have crossed the line.											
2	A	CHESTERFIELD			D	1-1	1-1	Coles 10	Phillips	Carey	Hill	Coles	Butler	Burnell	Wilkshire*	Miller"	Peacock	Doherty	Bell^	Roberts/Tinnion/Matthews
	16/8		*4,302*		4			*O'Hare 31*	*Muggleton*	*Uhlenbeek*	*O'Hare*	*Payne*	*Dawson*	*Searle*	*Hudson*	*Brandon**	*Hurst^*	*Evatt*	*Allott*	*Davies/Burt*
								Ref: G Cain	The famous crooked spire has often cast a shadow over City's fortunes at Saltergate so a point was welcome despite failing to build on their confident start. Following a short corner routine Coles opened the scoring from close range, but Alan O'Hare levelled with a low eight-yarder.											
3	H	HARTLEPOOL		11	D	1-1	0-0	Peacock 56	Phillips	Carey	Hill	Coles	Butler	Burnell"	Wilkshire	Miller*	Peacock	Doherty^	Bell	Matthews/Tinnion/Roberts
	23/8		10,730	*12*	5			*Gabbiadini 73*	*Provett*	*Barron*	*Westwood*	*Nelson*	*Jordan*	*Strachan*	*Clarke^*	*Robinson*	*Henderson**	*Tinkler"*	*Humphreys*	*Gabbiadini/Istead/Robson*
								Ref: A Hall	Peacock gave an awesome display in an otherwise forgettable team performance and was the deserved recipient on the man of the match champagne. His breathtaking 30-yard shot put City in front, but Marco Gabbiadini's glancing header brought Hartlepool a deserved point.											
4	A	COLCHESTER		14	L	1-2	0-0	Peacock 66	Phillips	Carey	Hill	Coles	Butler	Burnell	Wilkshire*	Miller^	Peacock	Doherty	Bell"	Roberts/Matthews/Tinnion
	26/8		***3,079***	*19*	5			*McGleish 47, 55*	*Brown*	*Stockley*	*Myers*	*Fitzgerald*	*Baldwin*	*Pinault*	*Duguid*	*McGleish*	*Andrews**	*Izzet*	*Vine*	*Fagan*
								Ref: M Cooper	City's set-piece demons resurfaced as the U's collected their first points of the season. Failure to deal with a cross led to Scott McGleish opening the scoring with an overhead kick, then doubling the advantage by heading in Karl Duguid's free-kick. Peacock headed in for City.											
5	H	GRIMSBY		7	W	1-0	0-0	Roberts 90	Phillips	Carey	Hill*	Coles	Butler	Burnell	Wilkshire"	Roberts	Peacock	Doherty	Bell^	Brown A/Tinnion/Miller
	30/8		10,033	*10*	8				*Davison*	*McDermott**	*Barnard*	*Ford*	*Crane*	*Groves*	*Crowe*	*Rowan*	*Boulding*	*Bolder^*	*Campbell*	*Parker/Heuvel*
								Ref: P Armstrong	If Danny Wilson had some harsh words for his players in the wake of their bank holiday weekend performances, it's a pretty safe bet that a repeat dose was delivered at half-time in this match. It did the trick as City were a different team after the break and deserved their late winner.											
6	A	BOURNEMOUTH		9	D	0-0	0-0		Phillips	Carey	Hill	Coles	Butler	Burnell	Wilkshire	Roberts*	Peacock	Tinnion	Brown A^	Miller/Bell
	6/9		*6,756*	*17*	9				*Moss*	*Young*	*Cummimgs**	*Fletcher C*	*Broadhurst*	*O'Connor*	*Elliott*	*Fletcher S*	*Hayter*	*Browning*	*Purches*	*Thomas*
								Ref: T Parkes	Defiant City boss Danny Wilson backed his misfiring strike force to rediscover their form after this dire affair, which kicked-off at midday. Both sides failed to impress in front of the Sky TV cameras. Wilkshire's weak shot and Peacock's off-target header were City's best efforts.											
7	A	OLDHAM		9	D	1-1	1-0	Butler 35	Phillips	Carey	Hill^	Coles	Butler	Burnell	Wilkshire*	Roberts	Miller"	Tinnion	Brown A	Lita/Bell/Matthews
	13/9		*5,921*	*19*	10			*Zola 54*	*Pogliacomi*	*Hudson*	*Holden*	*Clegg*	*Hall*	*Sheridan^*	*Eyres*	*Zola"*	*Vernon**	*Murray*	*Eyre*	*Curier/Cooksey/O'Halloran*
								Ref: C Webster	City have a deserved reputation as a crisp passing side with a flair for finding the net, but both qualities were missing at Boundary Park. Despite Butler putting City in front with a free six-yard header, the Latics grabbed a deserved point thanks to Calvin Zola's 16-yard shot.											
8	H	TRANMERE		8	W	2-0	1-0	Brown 23, Peacock 76	Phillips	Carey	Hill	Coles !	Butler	Burnell	Roberts^	Miller*	Peacock	Tinnion"	Brown A	Fortune/Matthews/Doherty
	16/9		**9,365**	*18*	13				*Achterberg*	*Connolly*	*Sharps*	*Allen !*	*Roberts*	*Loran*	*Taylor**	*Dagnall*	*Haworth*	*Jones*	*Nicholson^*	*Mellon/Navaro*
								Ref: S Tomlin	With seven bookings and the dismissal of Coles and Allen in the 53rd and 61st mins respectively, the referee had a truly awful game. Brown's angled drive from the left gave City the lead, then looked suspiciously offside when he ran through to set up Peacock to bundle in the second.											
9	H	PORT VALE		12	L	0-1	0-0		Phillips	Carey	Hill	Coles	Butler	Burnell^	Roberts"	Matthews*	Miller	Tinnion	Brown A	Lita/Doherty/Wilkshire
	20/9		11,369	*1*	13			*Paynter 71*	*Delaney*	*Pilkington*	*Cummins*	*Collins*	*Walsh*	*Lipa*	*Boyd*	*McPhee*	*Brooker*	*Paynter*	*Brown*	
								Ref: B Curson	Whilst booing a team off after a rare home defeat achieves absolutely nothing, it was easy to understand the fans' frustration. City, who are missing the pace of the departed Murray, are not firing on all cylinders, and much superior Vale deserved Billy Paynter's rifled in winner.											
10	A	QP RANGERS		11	D	1-1	0-0	Miller 76	Phillips	Woodman	Bell	Butler	Coles	Doherty	Wilkshire	Roberts*	Miller !	Tinnion	Brown A	Lita
	27/9		*14,913*	*4*	14			*Padula 73*	*Day*	*Edghill**	*Padula*	*Forbes*	*Gnohere*	*Bean*	*Rowlands*	*Furlong*	*Gallen*	*Bircham*	*McLeod^*	*Ainsworth/Palmer*
								Ref: P Prosser	After being completely overrun prior to the interval, City were unlucky to have Miller dismissed for his second bookable offence some fourteen mins from the finish. Gino Padula's angled shot tore in for the opener, but Miller's thunderbolt brought City a somewhat lucky point.											
11	A	PLYMOUTH		7	W	1-0	1-0	Peacock 27	Phillips	Woodman	Bell*	Hill	Butler	Burnell	Wilkshire	Miller	Peacock^	Tinnion	Brown A	Fortune/Lita
	30/9		*13,923*	*8*	17				*McCormick*	*Worrell*	*Gilbert"*	*Coughlan*	*Wotton*	*Adams*	*Norris*	*Evans*	*Keith**	*Bent*	*Capaldi^*	*Stonebdge/Sturrock/Hodges*
								Ref: P Armstrong	A real backs to the wall performance by City after Peacock gave them the first-half lead. The home defenders stood and watched as the City striker slid in at the back post to stab Brown's floated cross through Luke McCormick's legs. City had to withstand a late aerial bombardment.											

No	Ven	Opponent	Pos	Res	FT	HT	Scorers, Times, Referees	1	2	3	4	5	6	7	8	9	10	11	Subs used
12	H	SWINDON	6	W	2-1	0-1	Peacock 52, Brown 74	Phillips	Woodman	Bell*	Butler	Coles	Burnell^	Wilkshire	Miller*	Peacock	Tinnion	Brown A	Hill/Roberts/Lita
	4/10	14,294	*7*	20			*Mooney 34*	*Evans*	*Herring*	*Duke*	*Viveash*	*Heywood*	*Miglioranzi**	*Igoe"*	*Mooney*	*Howard*	*Gurney*	*Hewlett*	*Smith^/Reeves/Stevenson*
							Ref: H Webb	The pivotal moment of this closely fought game came on the stroke of half-time when Butler pulled of a brilliant saving challenge on Tommy Mooney, who had fired in the opener. Peacock's glancing header levelled matters before Brown's superb left-footed strike secured the points.											
13	H	PETERBOROUGH	6	D	1-1	1-0	Tinnion 24	Phillips	Woodman	Bell	Butler	Coles	Burnell	Wilkshire*	Miller^	Peacock	Tinnion	Brown A"	Roberts/Lita/Hill
	10/10	11,053	*19*	21			*Logan 90*	*Tyler*	*Burton*	*Arber*	*Legg*	*Rea**	*Gill*	*Newton"*	*McKenzie*	*Clarke^*	*Thomson*	*Jelleyman*	*Logan/Farrell/Kanu*
							Ref: L Cable	In this excellent game, Tinnion's soft strike looked like being enough, after Phillips had saved Mark Arber's third-minute spot-kick, but City were pegged back right at the death. Chris Kanu's low cross from the right was fired emphatically in from close range by Richard Logan.											
14	A	WREXHAM	7	D	0-0	0-0		Phillips	Carey	Bell	Butler	Coles	Doherty	Wilkshire	Miller^	Peacock	Tinnion	Brown A*	Woodman/Roberts
	18/10	*4,405*	*14*	22				*Dibble*	*Roberts*	*Lawrence C*	*Whitley*	*Carey**	*Ferguson*	*Edwards C^*	*Jones L*	*Sam*	*Llewellyn"*	*Edwards P*	*Morgan/Thomas S/Jones M*
							Ref: M Clattenburg	City survived a few first-half scares before they recovered their form and came close to sneaking a win against a strong home side. Their best chances came after the break when Butler headed against the bar and Peacock shot wide. Despite the dearth of goals, this was an open game.											
15	A	WYCOMBE	9	L	**0-3**	0-1		Phillips	Carey	Bell"	Butler	Coles !	Doherty !	Wilkshire	Miller^	Peacock	Tinnion	Brown A*	Burnell/Roberts/Woodman
	21/10	*4,613*	*22*	22			*Holligan 40, 70, McSporran 90*	*Talia*	*Senda*	*Branston*	*Bulman*	*Vinnicombe*	*Simpson*	*Thomson*	*Holligan*	*McSporran*	*Currie*	*Brown**	*Roberts*
							Ref: M Fletcher	City, bereft of ideas in attack and shaky at the back, were really up against it when Doherty was sent off for head-butting Dannie Bulman in the 37th minute. Gavin Holligan bundled a header over the line for the Choirboys opener. Coles got a red card for a rash lunge a minute from time.											
16	H	SHEFFIELD WED	11	D	1-1	0-1	Peacock 69	Phillips	Coles	Hill	Carey*	Butler	Doherty	Wilkshire	Roberts^	Peacock	Tinnion	Woodman	Amankwaah/Lita
	25/10	13,668	*10*	23			*Proudlock 25*	*Lucas*	*Bromby*	*Lee*	*Reddy*	*Smith*	*Mustoe*	*Geary*	*Proudlock*	*Owusa*	*McLaren*	*Wood*	
							Ref: M Warren	Despite having a lot of possession, City struggled to create chances against a strong Wednesday side, for whom Adam Proudlock shot in the opener. Peacock, unlucky to hit the post with a fine 19th-minute volley from outside the box, equalised after the break with a perfect header.											
17	H	LUTON	9	D	1-1	1-1	Burnell 2	Phillips	Am'kwaah*	Hill	Coles	Butler	Burnell	Wilkshire	Roberts	Peacock	Tinnion	Woodman	Lita^/Miller
	1/11	9,735	*14*	24			*McSheffrey 18*	*Beresford*	*Neilson^*	*Davis*	*Coyne*	*Boyce*	*Robinson*	*Mansell*	*Forbes**	*McSheffrey*	*Spring*	*Brkovic*	*Showunmi/Hillier*
							Ref: T Leake	Danny Wilson scrapped his experimental wing-back system when bringing on Lita in the 41st min. The youngster made a lively contribution, but was booked for diving as he sought a 75th-min match-winning penalty. Burnell's low-drive brought City their opener after just 90 seconds.											
18	A	BRIGHTON	9	W	4-1	3-1	Wilkshire 26, Miller 31, Brown 44,	Phillips	Carey	Woodman*	Amankwaah	Coles	Hill	Wilkshire	Roberts	Miller"	Tinnion^	Brown A	Butler/Burnell/Matthews
	15/11	*6,305*	*7*	27			*Knight 45p* [Hill 85]	Roberts	Hinshelw'd	Mayo	Butters	Cullip	Hart^	Carpenter	Knight	McPhee"	Rehman*	Yeates	*Piercy/Pethick/Robinson*
							Ref: I Williamson	Wilkshire got City off the mark at the Withdean Stadium by sprinting through a gaping hole in the Gulls' defence to collect Roberts' pass and coolly slotting the ball into the net. In a game that hardly had a chance in it, City registered with three headers to tie up a welcome success.											
19	H	BARNSLEY	6	W	2-1	1-0	Miller 38, 90	Phillips	Carey	Woodman^	Amankwaah	Coles	Hill	Wilkshire	Roberts*	Miller	Tinnion	Brown A	Peacock/Lita
	22/11	10,031	*3*	30			*Burns 51*	*Ilic*	*Austin*	*Gallimore*	*Hayward*	*O'Callaghan*	*Ireland*	*Betsy*	*Walters^*	*Rankin*	*Burns*	*Gorre**	*Monk/Kay*
							Ref: A Marriner	The clock was showing that 91 minutes had been played when Miller headed in Tinnion's right-wing corner into the Atyeo Stand net for City's last-gasp winner. Barnsley thus paid for shutting up shop following a brilliant long-range drive, from Jacob Burns, that brought their equaliser.											
20	A	BLACKPOOL	9	L	0-1	0-0		Phillips	Carey	Woodman	Am'kwaah*	Coles	Hill	Wilkshire	Roberts	Miller	Tinnion	Brown A^	Peacock/Bell
	29/11	*5,989*	*11*	30			*Taylor 58*	*Jones B*	*Richardson*	*Evans*	*Bullock^*	*Flynn*	*Elliott*	*Wellens**	*Murphy*	*Taylor*	*Southern*	*Coid*	*Grayson/Davis*
							Ref: M Prosser	Despite dominating the first half and twice hitting the woodwork, City went down to defeat at windswept Bloomfield Road. After the break, Blackpool got on top and Taylor secured the points for them when he slotted the ball home from close range when Phillips spilled a free-kick.											
21	A	RUSHDEN	9	D	1-1	0-1	Miller 71	Phillips	Carey	Woodman	Clist*	Coles	Hill	Wilkshire	Miller^	Peacock	Tinnion	Brown A	Roberts/Lita
	13/12	*4,340*	*13*	31			*Talbot 4*	*Ashdown*	*Bignot*	*Underwood*	*Jack*	*Hunter*	*Dempster*	*Mills*	*Benjamin^*	*Lowe*	*Burgess*	*Talbot**	*Bell/Kitson*
							Ref: F Stretton	Miller rifled in a deserved leveller, but lack of ruthlessness is proving costly to a City side whose solitary goal in the past three games hardly does them justice. Daniel Talbot forced in the Diamond's early opener when Onandi Lowe's header hit a post and struck Phillips on his back.											
22	H	STOCKPORT	6	W	1-0	0-0	Peacock 69	Phillips	Carey	Woodman	Wilkshire	Coles	Hill	Roberts	Miller*	Peacock	Tinnion^	Brown A	Lita/Doherty
	20/12	10,478	*21*	34				*Colgan*	*Hardiker*	*Jackman*	*Goodwin^*	*Heath*	*Clare*	*Gibb*	*Lynch**	*Wilbraham"*	*Lambert*	*Welsh*	*Barlow/Lescott/Daly*
							Ref: S Tomlin	Peacock conjured up a moment of inspiration with a great shot on the turn at the Atyeo End to score what could prove one of City's most important goals of the season. Again, though, City made hard work of matters and at times were outpassed by their enterprising opponents.											
23	A	BRENTFORD	5	W	2-1	0-0	Lita 77, 82	Phillips	Carey	Hill	Wilkshire	Coles	Butler	Roberts"	Miller^	Peacock	Tinnion*	Brown A	Doherty/Lita/Woodman
	26/12	*5,912*	*19*	37			*May 62*	*Smith*	*Dobson*	*Somner*	*Roget*	*Kitamirike*	*Sonko*	*O'Connor*	*Wright*	*May**	*Evans*	*Hunt*	*Rhodes*
							Ref: R Oliver	City, playing in their bright yellow strip, were made to pay for not having made use of their first-half chances when Ben May powered in an unstoppable header. Fortunately super-sub Lita came off the bench to head in an equaliser, before taping in City's rare Griffin Park winner.											

NATIONWIDE LEAGUE DIVISION 2

Manager: Danny Wilson

SEASON 2003-04

No	Date		Att	Pos	Pt	F-A	H-T	Scorers, Times, and Referees	SQUAD	NUMBERS	IN	USE								subs used
24	H	BOURNEMOUTH		3	W	2-0	1-0	Peacock 40, Brown 56	Phillips	Carey	Hill	Wilkshire	Coles	Butler	Roberts	Miller*	Peacock	Doherty	Brown A	Lita
	27/12		13,807	14	40				Moss	Maher	Cummings	Broadhurst	Buxton	Elliott*	Purches	Browning	Feeney	Hayter	Fletcher^	Thomas/Connell
								Ref: C Penton	After a few early jitters, City turned in an almost faultless display. Peacock, with his back to goal on the edge of the area at the Wedlock end, gathered in Hill's pass before turning and lifting the ball in for an excellent opener. Brown jinked past his marker to fire in a venomous second.											
25	A	NOTTS CO		3	W	2-1	1-1	Peacock 11, Goodfellow 90	Phillips	Carey	Hill	Butler	Coles*	Tinnion	Brown M^	Miller"	Peacock	Doherty	Brown A	Bell/**Goodfellow**/Lita
	9/1		6,403	23	43			Butler 40 (og)	Mildenhall	Fenton	Nicholson	Richardson	Barras	Riley	Bolland*	Stallard	Hackworth^	Caskey	Brough	Francis/Harrad
								Ref: G Laws	Despite getting off to a perfect start with Peacock's dipping volley, City's defence looked decidedly shaky all afternoon. Fortunately debutant Goodfellow (Stoke) headed in the late winner. Tinnion received a big ovation from City's large following on his 500th appearance for the club.											
26	H	CHESTERFIELD		3	W	4-0	1-0	Doherty 44, Lita 85, Carey 86, [Goodfellow 89]	Phillips	Carey	Hill	Butler"	Coles	Tinnion	Goodfellow	Miller*	Peacock	Doherty	Brown A^	Lita/Bell/Woodman
	15/1		11,807	23	46				Muggleton	Uhlenbeek	O'Hare	Evatt*	Blatherwick	Innes^	Allott	McMaster"	Hurst	Niven	Brandon	Howson/Hudson/Robinson
								Ref: P Crossley	Miller was unfortunate to have a great diving header disallowed for offside, but Doherty made amends with a left-foot strike from outside the box at the Wedlock end. Lita's half-volley, his first Ashton Gate goal, sparked the late goalrush which was rather unfair on the gutsy Spireites.											
27	A	HARTLEPOOL		3	W	2-1	0-0	Peacock 54, Tinnion 76	Phillips	Carey	Woodman	Hill	Coles	Tinnion	Goodfellow	Miller	Peacock	Doherty	Brown A	
	24/1		5,375	9	49			Tinkler 70	Provett	Barron	Robson"	Nelson	Westwood	Tinkler^	Shuker	Porter*	Williams	Strachan	Humphreys	Istead/Clarke/Robinson
								Ref: A Kaye	Tinnion's 25-yard spectacular strike into the roof of the Hartlepool net enabled City to become only the second team to win a League game at Victoria Park in 16 months. Peacock's low shot put City in front, but Mark Tinkler pegged them back by heading in from a right-wing corner.											
28	H	COLCHESTER		3	W	1-0	1-0	Goodfellow 45	Phillips	Carey	Woodman	Hill	Coles	Tinnion	Goodfellow^	Miller*	Peacock	Doherty"	Brown A	Lita/Roberts/Doherty
	27/1		10,733	13	52				McKinney	Stockley	Duguid	Chivers	White	Izzet^	Fagan !	Andrews*	McGleish	Pinault	Keith	Cade/Halford
								Ref: F Stretton	Marc Goodfellow, City's recent £50,000 signing from Stoke, demonstrated he has a deadly touch with both feet. Having earlier missed a much easier chance with his favoured right, he rifled a left-footed drive into the Wedlock end in first-half added time to clinch a seventh straight win.											
29	H	BRENTFORD		3	W	3-1	1-0	Miller 4, Hill 88, Lita 90	Phillips	Carey	Woodman	Hill	Coles	Wilkshire	Goodf'llow*	Miller^	Peacock	Tinnion"	Brown A	Roberts/Lita/Fortune
	7/2		13,029	18	55			Hutchinson 77	Julian	Dobson	Bull	Kitamirike	Sonko	Hutchinson	Rougier	Wright*	O'Connor	Tabb	Hunt	Peters
								Ref: D Pugh	After Miller's early headed opener, City failed to make their first-half dominance pay. Eddie Hutchinson shocked them by nipping in to put away Michael Dobson's free-kick, but brave Hill headed in during a frantic melee at the Atyeo end to bring City a rare double over the Bees.											
30	A	PETERBOROUGH		3	W	1-0	0-0	Doherty 75	Phillips	Carey	Hill	Butler	Coles	Wilkshire^	Goodfellow"	Miller*	Peacock	Tinnion	Brown A	Lita/Doherty/Brown M
	14/2		4,449	21	58				Tyler	Rea	Legg	Thomson	Arber	Farrell	Newton	Clarke^	Platt*	Woodhouse	Jelleyman	Logan/Willcock
								Ref: G Salisbury	The taking down of the Union flag, which has been flying at half-mast at London Road since the September 11 attacks, did little to change the Posh's ill luck. City were almost overrun before the break, but still managed to capture the points thanks to Doherty's second-half header.											
31	A	GRIMSBY		1	W	2-1	1-1	Miller 11, Brown 88	Phillips	Carey	Hill	Butler*	Coles	Doherty	Wilkshire^	Miller"	Peacock	Tinnion	Brown A	Woodman/Goodfellow/Lita
	17/2		5,272	20	61			Anderson 30p	Davison	Crowe	Young	Crane	Ford	Daws	Anderson^	Rankin	Mansaram"	Coldicott*	Campbell	Hamilton/Jevons/Soames
								Ref: M Jones	City, who felt aggrieved over the award of a penalty for Hill's sliding challenge on Isaiah Rankin, deserved their late winner thanks to Brown's hooking the ball in from six yards. Top of the table at last, City had the chances to have added many more following Miller's headed opener.											
32	H	WREXHAM		1	W	1-0	1-0	Wilkshire 3	Phillips	Carey	Hill	Butler	Coles	Doherty"	Wilkshire	Miller*	Peacock	Tinnion^	Brown A	Lita/Goodfellow/Burnell
	21/2		13,871	9	64				Dibble	Roberts	Whitley	Carey	Edwards C	Ferguson	Whitley	Llewellyn	Armstrong	Thomas*	Edwards P^	Sam/Jones
								Ref: P Danson	Twice at the start Brown's pace on the left opened up opponents who have won eight games on their travels this season. The second time Wilkshire met his cross and smashed the ball into the roof of the net from eight yards. City dominated but were unable to add to their tally.											
33	A	SHEFFIELD WED		2	L	0-1	0-0		Phillips	Carey	Hill*	Butler	Coles	Doherty	Wilkshire^	Miller	Peacock	Tinnion	Brown A	Woodman/Roberts
	28/2		**24,154**	12	64			Lee 90	Pressman	Bromby	Murphy	Wood	Smith	Quinn	Shaw	Haslam	Lee	Chambers	N-Nsunga	
								Ref: M Cowburn	City's super winning run had to end some time, but not in this puerile way. Typical of City, in that against much-weakened opponents they failed to take the game by the throat. Unlucky perhaps in having Miller's 67th-min header disallowed, City paid the price right on the whistle.											
34	H	WYCOMBE		2	D	1-1	0-0	Goodfellow 59	Phillips	Carey	Bell	Wilkshire^	Coles	Hill*	Goodfellow	Miller"	Peacock	Doherty	Brown A	Fortune/Tinnion/Lita
	2/3		12,291	24	65			McSporran 72	Williams	Senda	Vinnicombe	Nethercott	Johnson	Bulman	McSporran	Tyson	Currie^	Bloomfield*	Brown S	Simpemba/Philo
								Ref: T Bates	With City's winning run over, the luck which was theirs has now deserted them. Despite dominating this game against the bottom side, City's attack, as so often this season, fails to put away their chances. Goodfellow's deflected shot from the right at the Atyeo End is their sole reward.											

No	Date	Opponent	Att	Pos	Res	F-A	H-T	Scorers, Times, and Referees	1	2	3	4	5	6	7	8	9	10	11	subs used
35	A	STOCKPORT		2	L	0-2	0-1		Phillips	Carey	Bell	Butler	Coles	Doherty	Wilkshire*	Miller^	Peacock	Tinnion	Brown A"	Roberts/Lita/Goodfellow
	6/3		5,050	23	65			Goodwin 11, Williams C 88	Williams A	Clare	Adams	Watson	Griffin	Goodwin	Cartwright	Wilbraham	Barlow*	Lambert	Jackman	Williams C
								Ref: M Halsey	Against a side who had not won in nine games, and on a ground where they have not tasted defeat since 1913, most City fans could see this result coming. If luck had been against City, that would have been understandable, but not an inept and totally gutless performances like this.											
36	H	RUSHDEN		2	W	1-0	1-0	Lita 29	Phillips	Carey	Hill	Butler	Coles	Doherty"	Roberts	Lita^	Peacock	Tinnion	Brown A*	Goodfellow/Miller/Fortune
	12/3		12,559	13	68				Ashdown	Edwards	Roget	Bell	Hunter	Mills^	Bignot	Jack	Kitson"	Gray*	Underwood	Burgess/Hanlon/Duffy
								Ref: P Taylor	Despite many chances, City, as so often this campaign, rarely looked capable of putting the ball in the back of the net. Brown's broken ankle puts him out for the rest of the season, whilst Doherty's injury is worrying as City held on to take the points thanks to Lita's first-half header.											
37	H	OLDHAM		3	L	0-2	0-2		Phillips	Carey	Hill"	Butler	Coles	Burnell	Roberts	Lita	Peacock*	Tinnion	Wilkshire^	Miller/Bell/Goodfellow
	20/3		11,037	16	68			Cooksey 26, Murray 37	Pogliacomi	Clegg	Griffin	Boshell^	Holden	Owen*	Murray	Vernon	Eyre	Sheridan	Cooksey	Haining/Wilkinson
								Ref: T Kettle	This was a disgraceful performance by City, who barely managed a couple of shots throughout the whole game. A gale-force wind made the conditions difficult, but City, without the services of the injured Doherty, plainly lacked confidence. They were caught napping by both goals.											
38	A	TRANMERE		3	L	0-1	0-0		Phillips	Carey	Hill	Butler	Coles	Fortune	Wilkshire	Miller	Roberts	Tinnion	G'dfellow*	Lita
	24/3		6,712	16	68			Dadi 82	Achterberg	Loran	Goodison	Allen	Sharps	Mellon	Hume*	Jones	Dadi	Harrison	Beresford	Hay
								Ref: E Ilderton	City never looked like ending their dismal record of not having won at Prenton Park. Yet another poor display serves to illustrate that this City side hasn't the skill to be worthy of a place in a higher division, but more crucially lacks the desire. Dadi's thumping header wins it for Rovers.											
39	A	PORT VALE		3	L	1-2	0-0	Peacock 90	Phillips	Carey	Hill	Butler	Coles	Doherty	Murray	Rougier*	Peacock	Wilkshire^	Tinnion	Roberts/Woodman
	27/3		6,724	7	68			Brooker 66, Bridge-Wilkinson 77	Brain	Rowland	James	Collins	Pilkington	Cummins	Paynter	Brooker*	McPhee	Brisco	B-Wilkinson	Birchall
								Ref: K Hill	Murray's return failed to inspire a lacklustre City side who suffered another blow in their promotion bid. Peacock's late tap-in, when keeper Jon Brain tipped Hill's header onto a post, wasn't enough as by then slack defending had twice allowed Vale to fire the ball past Phillips.											
40	H	QP RANGERS		3	W	1-0	1-0	Roberts 40	Phillips	Carey	Hill	Butler	Coles	Doherty	Murray	Roberts^	Peacock	Tinnion*	Bell	Wilkshire/Miller
	4/4		19,041	2	71				Camp	Bignot	Rose	Carlisle	Gnohere	Bean*	Rowlands	Gallen	Furlong	Johnson^	McLeod"	Cureton/Palmer/Thorpe
								Ref: A Leake	A change of month brings an upturn in City's fortunes with this deserved success against their main challengers for the runners-up spot. They should have had more to show than their close-range winner. Just before the finish ex-City hot-shot Tony Thorpe was denied by Phillips.											
41	A	SWINDON		3	D	1-1	1-0	Roberts 45	Phillips	Carey	Hill	Butler	Coles	Doherty	Murray	Roberts*	Peacock	Tinnion	Bell	Miller
	10/4		14,540	5	72			Fallon 74	Evans	O'Hanlon	Nicholas*	Heywood	Gurney	Hewlett	Igoe	Parkin	Mooney	Miglioranzi	Duke	Fallon
								Ref: N Barry	How vital will Miller's late miss prove to be? Deep into injury-time the Scot nodded Peacock's headed cross against a post when it looked certain that he would win the game in front of the City fans massed on the Stratton Bank. Rory Fallon's overhead earned Swindon a point.											
42	H	PLYMOUTH		3	W	1-0	0-0	Peacock 85	Phillips	Carey	Hill	Butler	Coles	Doherty	Murray*	Roberts"	Peacock	Wilkshire^	Bell	Rougier/Tinnion/Miller
	13/4		19,045	1	75				McCormick	Connolly	Gilbert	Wotton	Coughlan	Norris	Bent*	Adams"	Evans	Hodges	Capaldi^	Aljofree/Lowndes/Keith
								Ref: R Pearson	With Plymouth needing just three points to clinch promotion, it seemed strange that they paid City too much respect by lining up in a 4-5-1 formation. However it seemed as though the Pilgrims had done enough to secure a point until Peacock swivelled to find the net with a rasper.											
43	A	LUTON		3	L	2-3	0-1	Roberts 59, Coles 88	Phillips	Carey	Hill	Butler	Coles	Doherty	Rougier	Roberts^	Peacock	Wilkshire*	Bell"	Tinnion/Goodfellow/Miller
	17/4		6,944	8	75			Howard 26, Boyce 56, Keane 90	Hyldaard	Keane	Davis	Coyne	Boyce	Robinson	Nicholls	Howard	Forbes*	Brkovic	Foley	Showunmi
								Ref: M Atkinson	Controversy at Kenilworth Road, where Luton's second goal was allowed despite protests that the ball hadn't crossed the line. Coles headed in City's leveller in the first min of injury-time, but just two mins later Keith Keane's shot hit the ground and amazingly bounced in over Phillips.											
44	H	BRIGHTON		3	D	0-0	0-0		Phillips	Carey	Hill	Butler"	Coles	Doherty	Rougier*	Roberts	Peacock	Wilkshire^	Bell	Murray/Tinnion/Goodfellow
	24/4		17,088	6	76				Roberts	Virgo	Harding	Butters	Cullip	Carpenter	Reid	Knight	Iwelumo*	Oatway	Jones^	Hart/Piercy
								Ref: R Beeby	With QPR losing at Plymouth, City had the opportunity to slip into an automatic promotion place. Unfortunately, as so often this season, their inept attack wasn't up to the task as they failed to put away their chances. City dominated the proceedings, but the goals just wouldn't come.											
45	A	BARNSLEY		3	W	1-0	1-0	Rougier 21	Phillips	Carey	Hill	Butler	Coles	Doherty	Rougier	Roberts*	Peacock	Tinnion	Bell	Lita
	2/5		10,865	13	79				Ward	O'Callaghan	Hayward	Ireland	Kay !	Gorre*	Murphy	Shuker^	Birch	Neil	Betsy	Baker/Monk
								Ref: C Boyeson	On the day that their Women's side secured promotion to the top flight, City did what was required to stay in contention with QPR for the runners-up spot. Only Rougier, who fired into the bottom corner of net, was able to take one of City's many chances in a deserved success.											
46	H	BLACKPOOL		3	W	2-1	2-0	Roberts 19, 21	Phillips	Carey	Hill	Butler	Coles	Doherty	Rougier	Roberts^	Peacock	Tinnion	Bell*	Murray/Miller
	8/5		**19,101**	14	82			Southern 78p	Edge	Richardson	Coid*	Elliott	Flynn	Wellens	Bullock	Murphy	Sheron	Southern	Donnelly^	Burns/Mangon
	Home		Away					Ref: J Robinson	Even though Peacock squandered three excellent chances, City did what they had to with some ease. Unfortunately Queens Park Rangers collected the full quota of points at Sheffield Wednesday and consigned City to the lottery of the Play-Offs for the second successive season.											
Average	12,879		7,693																	

Play-Offs

			F-A	H-T	Scorers, Times, and Referees	SQUAD	NUMBERS	IN	USE								subs used
SF A HARTLEPOOL 1 15/5	3 7,211 6	D	1-1	1-0	Rougier 5	Phillips	Carey	Hill	Butler	Coles	Doherty*	Rougier^	Roberts"	Peacock	Tinnion	Woodman	Burnell/Murray/Wilkshire
					Porter 74	*Provett*	*Barron*	*Robertson*	*Nelson"*	*Westwood*	*Sweeney^*	*Williams*	*Boyd*	*Porter**	*Tinkler*	*Humphreys*	*Robinson/Danns/Clarke*

Ref: P Taylor

Despite the early advantage of Rougier's header, City were on the defensive throughout. Phillips, fortunate not to concede a spot-kick soon after the change of ends, and Butler starred for City, though the keeper's mix-up with Carey brought Hartlepool their fully deserved equaliser.

			F-A	H-T	Scorers												subs used
SF H HARTLEPOOL 2 19/5	3 18,434 6	W	2-1	0-0	Goodfellow 88, Roberts 90	Phillips	Carey	Hill	Butler"	Coles	Doherty	Rougier	Roberts	Peacock*	Tinnion	Woodman^	Murray/Goodfellow/Lita
					Sweeney 63	*Provett*	*Barron^*	*Robertson*	*Nelson*	*Westwood**	*Tinkler*	*Williams*	*Boyd*	*Porter"*	*Sweeney*	*Humphreys*	*Danns/Clarke/Robinson*

Ref: G Poll

(City won 3-2 on aggregate)

City didn't impress as likely winners until the last quarter-of-an-hour, which included six minutes stoppage time. The Pool were unlucky with a shot that hit the post in the first half, but took the lead with a stooping header. City's fight-back made up for all their previous inadequacies.

			F-A	H-T	Scorers												subs used
F N BRIGHTON 30/5 (at Millennium Stadium, Cardiff)	3 65,167 4	L	0-1	0-0		Phillips	Carey	Hill	Butler"	Coles	Doherty	Rougier	Roberts	Miller*	Tinnion^	Woodman	Murray/Wilkshire/G'dfellow
					Knight 84p	*Roberts*	*Virgo*	*Harding*	*Cullip*	*Butters*	*Carpenter**	*Hart*	*Iwelumo*	*Knight*	*Oatway*	*Jones^*	*Reid/Piercy*

Ref: R Beeby

Yet again City are made to pay for their failure to take the game to moderate opposition. Rarely can so many people have witnessed so few moments of genuine excitement as in this triumph for battling Brighton over boring opponents. All in all, a day of bitter City disappointment.

Carling Cup

			F-A	H-T	Scorers												subs used
1 H SWANSEA 13/8	5,807	W	4-1 aet	1-1	Peacock 14, 108, Bell 96p, Coles 103	Phillips	Carey	Hill	Coles	Butler	Burnell^	Wilkshire"	Miller*	Peacock	Doherty	Bell	Roberts/Matthews/Tinnion
					Connolly 18	*Murphy*	*Jones*	*Hylton*	*Johnrose*	*O'Leary*	*Maylett !*	*Connolly**	*Britton*	*Trundle*	*Martinez*	*Durkan^*	*Coates/Nugent*

Ref: C Penton

After Peacock had drilled City into an early lead, the impressive Swans should have won following Karl Connolly's headed leveller. Brad Maylett's sending off, deep into stoppage time, was the turning point. The dubious award of a penalty set up City's extra-time goal flurry.

			F-A	H-T	Scorers												subs used
2 H WATFORD 23/9	12 5,213 1:23	W	1-0 aet	0-0	Miller 94	Phillips	Carey*	Bell	Coles	Butler	Doherty"	Wilkshire	Roberts	Miller	Tinnion^	Brown A	Fortune/Matthews/Hulbert
						Chamberlain	*Doyley*	*Robinson*	*Cox*	*Dyche*	*Fisken**	*Devlin*	*Webber*	*Dyer*	*Mahon*	*Young^*	*Hyde"/Cook/Hand*

Ref: P Crossley

A competent rather than an exhilarating display proved good enough for City to progress through to the third round for the first time in 15 years. Miller's extra-time header did the trick against opponents who played good and comfortable football, but lacked the finishing touch.

			F-A	H-T	Scorers												subs used
3 H SOUTHAMPTON 28/10	11 17,408 P:9	L	0-3	0-1		Phillips	Am'kwaah"	Hill	Coles	Butler	Burnell	Wilkshire^	Roberts*	Peacock	Tinnion	Woodman	Lita/Hulbert/Miller
					Beattie 31, Ormerod 67, Le Saux 89	*Niemi**	*Svensson M*	*Le Saux*	*Lundekvan*	*Dodd*	*Delap*	*Fernandes^*	*Beattie*	*Ormerod*	*Svensson A*	*Marsden*	*Jones/McCann*

Ref: P Walton

Whilst City gave their all, the Saints possessed far too much quality in front of goal. Graeme Le Saux's late free-kick deflected through City's defensive wall secured the victory after James Beattie's first-half strike and Brett Ormerod's measured shot midway through the second period.

FA Cup

			F-A	H-T	Scorers												subs used
1 A BRADFORD 9/11	9 1,945 UB:19	W	5-2	2-2	Am' 6, 8, Stan' 55 (og), Wil' 67, Mat' 83	Phillips	Amankwaah	Hill	Coles	Butler	Burnell	Wilkshire^	Roberts*	Peacock	Brown A"	Woodman	Matthews/Lita/Clist
					Hayward 5, Coles 13 (og)	*Boswell*	*Stansfield*	*Crossley*	*Mitchell*	*Wood"*	*Olek'wycz**	*Collins^*	*Maxwell*	*Hayward*	*Benn*	*Serrant*	*Smith/Wright/Walsh*

Ref: M Pike

Despite having most of the play at the Horsfall Stadium, City were given some early shocks on renewing rivalry with ex-Leaguers Bradford Park Avenue. After Andy Hayward's rifled in opener, City were further embarrassed when Coles knocked the ball between his own posts.

			F-A	H-T	Scorers												subs used
2 H BARNSLEY 6/12	9 6,741 4	D	0-0	0-0		Phillips	Carey	Woodman	Clist*	Coles	Hill	Wilkshire	Miller	Peacock^	Tinnion	Brown A	Roberts/Matthews
						Ilic	*Austin*	*Gallimore*	*Ireland*	*Monk*	*Kay**	*Hayward*	*Walters*	*Betsy*	*O'Callaghan*	*Lumsdon*	*Neil*

Ref: B Curson

Wilkshire's luck in front of goal might be out at the moment, but the City career of the £250,000 summer signing from Middlesbrough is threatening to take off in a big way. He had an outstanding game, displaying a range of passing that should have brought his side victory.

			F-A	H-T	Scorers												subs used
R A BARNSLEY 16/12	9 5,434 4	L	1-2	0-2	Roberts 66	Phillips	Carey	Woodman	Clist*	Coles	Hill	Wilkshire	Miller^	Peacock	Tinnion	Brown A"	Roberts/Lita/Bell
					Kay 24, Monk 43	*Ilic*	*O'Callaghan*	*Austin*	*Burns*	*Ireland*	*Monk*	*Hayward*	*Walters**	*Betsy*	*Kay*	*Carson^*	*Neil/Lumsdon*

Ref: B Curson

A battling second-half fightback failed to save City as they crashed out of the FA Cup at Oakwell. The Tykes demonstrated more attacking intent than in the previous two meetings between the sides and Anthony Kay headed them into the lead from Brian O'Callaghan's cross.

	P	W	D	L	F (Home)	A (Home)	W	D	L	F (Away)	A (Away)	Pts
1 Plymouth	46	17	5	1	52	13	9	7	7	33	28	90
2 QP Rangers	46	16	7	0	47	12	6	10	7	33	33	83
3 BRISTOL CITY	46	15	6	2	34	12	8	7	8	24	25	82
4 Brighton *	46	17	4	2	39	11	5	7	11	25	32	77
5 Swindon	46	12	7	4	41	23	8	6	9	35	35	73
6 Hartlepool	46	10	8	5	39	24	10	5	8	37	37	73
7 Port Vale	46	15	6	2	45	28	6	4	13	28	35	73
8 Tranmere	46	13	7	3	36	18	4	9	10	23	38	67
9 Bournemouth	46	11	8	4	35	25	6	7	10	21	26	66
10 Luton	46	14	6	3	44	27	3	9	11	25	39	66
11 Colchester	46	11	8	4	33	23	6	5	12	19	33	64
12 Barnsley	46	7	12	4	25	19	8	5	10	29	39	62
13 Wrexham	46	9	6	8	27	21	8	3	12	23	39	60
14 Blackpool	46	9	5	9	31	28	7	6	10	27	37	59
15 Oldham	46	9	8	6	37	25	3	13	7	29	35	57
16 Sheffield Wed	46	7	9	7	25	26	6	5	12	23	38	53
17 Brentford	46	9	5	9	34	38	5	6	12	18	31	53
18 Peterborough	46	5	8	10	36	33	7	8	8	22	25	52
19 Stockport	46	6	8	9	31	36	5	11	7	31	34	52
20 Chesterfield	46	9	7	7	34	31	3	8	12	15	40	51
21 Grimsby	46	10	5	8	36	26	3	6	14	19	55	50
22 Rushden & Dia	46	9	5	9	37	34	4	4	15	23	40	48
23 Notts Co	46	6	9	8	32	27	4	3	16	18	51	42
24 Wycombe	46	5	7	11	31	39	1	12	10	19	36	37
	1104	251	166	135	861	599	135	166	251	599	861	1490

* promoted after play-offs

Odds & ends

Double wins: (5) Notts Co, Grimsby, Plymouth, Barnsley, Brentford.
Double losses: (1) Port Vale.

Won from behind: (2) Swindon Town (h), Brentford (a).
Lost from in front: (0).

High spots: The run of eleven successive League wins, starting on 20 December, that propelled City to the top of the table.
The exciting conclusion to the semi-final, 2nd leg, game with unlucky Hartlepool that masked yet another poor City performance.

Low spots: The abject performance in the Play-Off final.
The defeat against a below-strength Sheffield Wednesday at Hillsborough that ended City's eleven-match winning run.
City's lack of attacking flair throughout the season and a negative thinking management that brought ultimate failure.

Players in the PFA XI: Louis Carey, Steve Phillips, Brian Tinnion.
Internationals: Full: Tommy Doherty (Northern Ireland). Under-23: Luke Wilkshire (Australia).
AGM (Exhibition Hall, Dolman Stand, Ashton Gate, 2 December 2004).
Loss: £1,166,341. Season Ticket Sales (No): 8,400.

Player of the Year: Tommy Doherty.
Ever -presents: (1) Steve Phillips.
Hat-tricks: (0).
Leading scorer: Overall: Lee Peacock (16). League: Lee Peacock (14).

	Appearances								Goals				
	Lge	*Sub*	LC	*Sub*	FAC	*Sub*	PO	*Sub*	Lge	LC	FAC	PO	Tot
Amankwaah, Kevin	4	1	1		1						2		2
Bell, Mickey	20	7	2			1				1			1
Brown, Aaron	29	1	1		3				5				5
Brown, Marvin	1	1											
Burnell, Joe	14	3	2		1			1	1				1
Butler, Tony	37	1	3		1		3		1				1
Carey, Louis	41		2		2		3		1				1
Clist, Simon	1				2	1							
Coles, Danny	45		3		3		3		1	1			2
Doherty, Tommy	28	5	2				3		2				2
Fortune, Clayton	1	5		1									
Goodfellow, Marc	7	8						2	5			1	6
Hill, Matt	40	2	2		3		3		2				2
Hulbert, Robin				2									
Lita, Leroy	2	23		1		2		1	5				5
Matthews, Lee	1	7		2		2			2		1		3
Miller, Lee	32	10	2	1	2		1		8	1			9
Murray, Scott	4	2						3					
Peacock, Lee	39	2	2		3		2		14	2			16
Phillips, Steve	46		3		3		3						
Roberts, Christian	24	14	2	1	1	2	3		6		1	1	8
Rougier, Tony	5	1					3		1			1	2
Tinnion, Brian	36	9	2	1	2		3		2				2
Wilkshire, Luke	35	2	3		3			2	2		1		3
Woodman, Craig	14	7	1		3		3						
(own-goals)											1		1
25 players used	**506**	***111***	**33**	***9***	**33**	***8***	**33**	***9***	**58**	**5**	**6**	**3**	**72**

No	Date		Att	Pos	Pt	F-A	H-T	Scorers, Times, and Referees	SQUAD	NUMBERS	IN	USE								subs used
1	H	TORQUAY			D	1-1	0-0	Lita 59	Phillips	**Smith**	Woodman	**Orr**	Coles	Hill	Murray	**Heffernan**^	Lita	Fortune*	Tinnion"	Doherty/Anyinsah/Roberts
	7/8		14,275		1			Woods 72p	Bossu	Canoville	McGinchey	Hockley*	Taylor	Woods	Fowler"	Kuffour	Akinfenwa	Russell	Hill^	Phillips/Gritton/Owen
								Ref: A Hall	An appalling referee who wouldn't allow any sort of bodily contact didn't help but in truth a supposedly committed to attack City were as inept in front of goal as last season. Whilst Torquay's penalty was controversial, City were indebted to a Phillips wonder save just after the interval.											
2	A	BARNSLEY			L	1-2	0-0	Lita 88	Phillips	Smith	Woodman	Orr	Coles	Hill	Murray	Heffernan*	Lita	Doherty	Tinnion^	Miller/Anyinsah
	10/8		10,435		1			Shuker 69, 76	Colgan	Hassell	Vaughan	Wroe	Carbon*	Reid	Williams	Conlon	Boulding^	McPhail	Shuker	Austin/Nardiello
								Ref: G Salisbury	City, the promotion favourites, continued their disappointing start to the season at Oakwell, where they gave another punchless display. Lita gave City some late hope by slotting the ball past Nick Colgan after spinning past marker Paul Reid, but it proved a case of too little too late.											
3	A	BOURNEMOUTH		21	D	2-2	0-1	Lita 77, Smith 90	Phillips	Smith	Hill	Orr	Coles	Fortune	Murray"	Heffernan*	Lita	Doherty	Anyinsah^	Miller/**Gillespie**/Goodfellow
	14/8		6,918	20	2			Fletcher 38, Hayter 87	Moss	Young	Cummings	Broadhurst	Howe	Fletcher C	Browning	Holmes*	Hayter	Stock^	Elliott"	Connell/Rowe/Maher
								Ref: P Crossley	City, who had been totally outplayed in the first half, hit a last-gasp leveller three minutes into added time. Smith's mis-hit left-footer curled just inside the post to bring a fortunate point. Miller's flick-on allowed Lita to get City back into the game by firing the ball high into the net.											
4	H	SWINDON		21	L	1-2	1-1	Doherty 45	Phillips	Smith	Woodman^	Orr	Coles	Hill	Roberts"	Miller	Lita	Doherty	Tinnion*	Murray/Bell/Gillespie
	21/8		13,389	12	2			Henderson 23, 60	Evans	Gurney	Duke	Ifil	O'Hanlon	Hewlett	Igoe	Henderson*	Parkin	Miglioranzi^	Howard"	Fallon/Robinson/Nicholas
								Ref: L Cable	City need 'more bottle' according to striker Leroy Lita as their poor form continues. On-loan striker Darius Henderson was the decisive factor in this exciting derby, heading in the opener and then bundling the ball over the line for the winner after Doherty had fired in City's leveller.											
5	A	PORT VALE		21	L	0-3	0-2		Phillips	Smith	Hill	Butler	Fortune	**Harley***	Gillespie^	Miller"	Lita	Orr	Wilkshire	Tinnion/Roberts/Heffernan
	28/8		5,377	4	2			James 37, Brooker 45, Armstrong 66	Goodlad	Rowland	James	Collins	Pilkington	Hulbert"	Cummins	Matthews*	Brooker	Armstrong^	Reid	Paynter/Smith/Lipa
								Ref: P Armstrong	According to the *Western Daily Press*, City dominated possession in this game as they succumbed to a defeat that led to player-boss Tinnion branding members of his side as 'lacking desire'. A superbly executed free-kick, which Craig James fired in from 25 yards, opened the scoring.											
6	H	BRENTFORD		20	W	4-1	1-0	Wilkshire 25, 69, Murray 48, 73	Phillips	Smith	Hill	Butler	Coles	Tinnion	Murray	Roberts	Lita	Doherty*	Wilkshire	Orr
	30/8		10,296	12	5			O'Connor 61	Nelson	Dobson^	Frampton	Fitzgerald	Turner	Hargreaves	O'Connor	Burton	Rankin"	Sodje	Somner*	Salako/Talbot/Rhodes
								Ref: P Joslin	After an uneasy opening, City settled down when Wilkshire rifled in a fine opener. Straight after the interval Murray skipped away to plant a low ball across the keeper into the bottom corner of the net before Kevin O'Connor set City nerves jangling by heading in for the Bees.											
7	A	PETERBOROUGH		18	W	1-0	0-0	Lita 72	Phillips	Smith	Hill	Butler	Coles	Tinnion^	Murray	Roberts*	Lita	Orr	Wilkshire	Miller/Fortune
	4/9		4,227	16	8				Tyler	Plummer	Ireland	Legg	Rea	Woodhouse	Newton	Const'ntine*	Platt"	Kennedy^	Jelleyman	Logan/Farrell/Clarke
								Ref: A Marriner	City's magnificent defensive display set up a win that looked unlikely early on. Phillips was the hero, saving Curtis Woodhouse's spot-kick on half-time when Smith brought down Leon Constantine. A scrappy game that City finally took by the scruff of the neck with their breakaways.											
8	H	STOCKPORT		13	W	**5-0**	3-0	Tinnion 11, Roberts 24, Lita 31, 81, [Heffernan 79]	Phillips	Smith	Hill"	Butler	Coles	Tinnion*	Murray	Roberts^	Lita	Doherty	Wilkshire	Orr/Heffernan/Fortune
	11/9		10,811	23	11				Spencer	Geary	Adams	Hardiker	Williams	Goodwin	Cartwright	Feeney	Beckett	Lambert	Jackman	
								Ref: A Penn	Leading 3-0, City ran riot in the period up to the break, but were unable to add to the score until Heffernan raced on to Lita's flick to shoot past James Spencer. Lita fired in City's fifth and last with a glorious 30-yard strike but a 10-2 score would have more accurately represented events.											
9	A	BRADFORD C		15	L	1-4	0-2	Murray 88 [Wetherall 61, Adebola 80]	Phillips	Smith	Hill	Butler	Coles	Tinnion	Murray	Roberts*	Lita	Doherty	Wilkshire^	Heffernan/Orr
	18/9		7,235	12	11			Schumacher 30, Roberts 38,	Henderson	Holloway	Jacobs	Bower	Wetherall	Kearney	Summerbee	Roberts*	Adebola	Schumacher	Muirhead	Symes
								Ref: T Parkes	City were made to rue their missed chances at Valley Parade. Poor defending resulted in an emphatic-looking defeat that did not tell the story of a more even contest than that. Murray, who had a goal disallowed for offside, eventually got City on the scoresheet with a fine solo effort.											
10	H	HUDDERSFIELD		17	D	3-3	1-2	Murray 9, Lita 80p, Mirfin 89 (og)	Phillips	Smith"	Hill	Butler	Coles	Orr*	Murray	Roberts^	Lita	Doherty	Wilkshire	Tinnion/Heffernan/Miller
	25/9		10,783	10	12			Schofield 28, Abbott 35, Brandon 60	Gray	Clarke	Yates	Worthington	Mirfin	Schofield	Holdsworth*	Booth^	Abbott	Brandon	Lloyd	Brown/Sodje A
								Ref: I Williamson	City's first League penalty for 17 months when Lita was checked by an innocuous challenge which most referees would have ignored. Poor defending let City down, but they salvaged a point with Wilkshire's shot that took a wicked deflection to loop into the top corner of the net.											
11	A	CHESTERFIELD		15	D	2-2	0-1	Murray 47, Coles 54	Phillips	Smith !	Hill	Butler*	Coles	Tinnion	Murray	**Brooker**	Lita"	Doherty	Wilkshire^	Fortune/Orr/Bell
	2/10		4,854	6	13			Nicholson 33p, Bailey 88	Muggleton	Bailey	Nicholson	Evatt	Blatherwick	Davies^	Allott	N'Toya*	Stallard	Hudson	C'bell-Ryce	Debolla/Smith
								Ref: K Hill	Trailing to Nicholson's spot-kick after Stallard was floored by Phillips, matters got worse for City with Smith's 41st-minute red-card for a reckless challenge. Murray's cross-drive and a close-in shot by Coles, had brave City looking likely victors until Bailey's fierce 30-yarder.											

No Date	Ven	Opponent Att	Pos	Res Pts	F-A	H-T	Scorers, Times, and Referees												subs used
12	H	HULL	12	W	3-1	1-0	Brooker 38, Wilkshire 58, Butler 85	Phillips	Coles	Bell	Tinnion^	Butler	Hill	Murray"	Brooker	Lita	Orr	Wilkshire*	Fortune/**Brown**/Am'kwaah
16/10		12,011	*4*	16			*Facey 54*	*Myhill*	*Joseph*	*Dawson*	*Lewis*	*Cort*	*Delaney*	*France**	*Elliott*	*Facey*	*Green*	*Keane^*	*Allsopp/Price*
							Ref: R Olivier	Given City's wealth of possession, this was more nerve-racking affair than it should have been. Brooker used his head to good effect, nodding in the opener and setting up Wilkshire to turn and fire in the second. City couldn't relax however until Butler's header somehow found the net.											
13	A	OLDHAM	15	D	0-0	0-0		Phillips	Amankwaah	Hill	Butler	Coles	Wilkshire	Murray	Brooker	Lita*	Orr	Bell	Heffernan
19/10		*5,090*	*20*	17				*Pogliacomi*	*Lomax*	*Holden*	*Haining*	*Hall*	*Lee*	*Betsy*	*Vernon*	*Johnson !*	*Appleby*	*Eyres*	
							Ref: M Warren	City huffed and puffed but lacked penetration as they extended their unbeaten run to five games. Chances went begging after doing well to survive an early onslaught from an Oldham side, for whom Johnson was dismissed in the 78th minute, seeking their first win in six games.											
14	A	WALSALL	10	W	2-1	0-0	Lita 64, 89	Phillips	Coles	Bell	Butler	Hill	Orr*	Murray	Brooker	Lita	Doherty	Wilkshire"	Tinnion^/Brown/Fortune
23/10		*7,105*	*17*	20			*Fryatt 48p*	*Murphy*	*Wright*	*Aranalde*	*Emblen*	*Bennett*	*Osborn*	*Merson*	*Birch*	*Fryatt*	*Standing*	*Wrack*	
							Ref: M Cowburn	City's capture of all three points owes as much to the wet weather as well as Lita's confidence. Frustrated in the first half by having a goal disallowed and a fabulous header kept out by the post, he fired in a long-distance shot that slipped through the keeper's hands for the winner.											
15	H	COLCHESTER	12	D	0-0	0-0		Phillips	Smith	Bell"	**Dinning***	Butler	Hill	Murray^	Brooker	Lita	Orr	Wilkshire	Fortune/Gillespie/Cotterill
30/10		11,678	*13*	21				*Gerken*	*Stockley*	*Chilvers*	*Baldwin*	*Brown*	*Watson*	*Keith*	*Halford*	*Fagan*	*Danns*	*Johnson*	
							Ref: P Walton	Gillespie admitted that the headlines were ready to be written in this poor game as he had been on the field a matter of seconds when the ball fell to him unmarked at the far post with time to line up a 77th-minute winner. Unfortunately both his first shot and the rebound were blocked.											
16	H	MK DONS	10	W	4-1	3-0	Lita 4, 25, Brooker 30, Wilkshire 63	Phillips	Coles	Bell*	Dinning	Butler	Hill	Murray	Brooker	Lita^	Doherty"	Wilkshire	Smith/Gillespie/Orr
6/11		10,717	*23*	24			*Small 52*	*Bevan*	*Edds*	*Lewington*	*Johnson*	*Williams*	*Palmer*	*Kamara*	*Small*	*McLeod*	*Chorley*	*Tapp**	*Makofo*
							Ref: K Friend	Both sides went at it hammer and tongs during the early part of the second half. Murray missed a sitter when clean through and the Dons went straight up the Wedlock end where Wade Small netted with a cool shot. Wilkshire restored City's three-goal advantage with a stunning volley.											
17	H	TRANMERE	7	W	4-0	2-0	Brooker 19, 57, Wilkshire 41, 89p	Phillips	Coles	Bell"	Dinning	Butler	Hill	Murray	Brooker*	Lita	Doherty^	Wilkshire	Gillespie/Orr/Smith
9/11		11,098	*3*	27				*Achterberg*	*Taylor*	*Goodison**	*Sharps*	*Jackson*	*McAteer^*	*Hall*	*Jones*	*Hume"*	*Rankine*	*Roberts*	*Ber'sford/Harrison/Haworth*
							Ref: T Kettle	City were given a hard physical workout by a fully committed Tranmere side. Wilkshire's volley from the edge of the centre-circle was one of the best ever Ashton Gate goals. Gillespie's upending saw victory being tied up by a retaken penalty after Wilkshire had netted his first effort.											
18	A	WREXHAM	6	W	3-1	2-0	Bell 36p, Murray 34, Brooker 52	Phillips	Bell	Hill	Coles	Butler	Dinning	Murray^	Brooker	Lita"	Doherty	Wilkshire*	Orr/Smith/Fortune
20/11		*7,833*	*17*	30			*Armstrong 77*	*Baker*	*Hor*	*Lawrence^*	*Pejic*	*Roberts*	*Jones*	*Spender*	*Armstrong*	*Sam**	*Ferguson*	*Llewellyn*	*Ugarte/Morgan*
							Ref: K Hill	With fans from many clubs among the crowd supporting the financially threatened homesters, City did well to put the emotion of the occasion to one side. After Lita, not for the first time in his fledgling career, made a meal of a challenge, Bell's spot-kick got City off to a flying start.											
19	H	SHEFFIELD WED	6	L	1-4	0-1	Murray 56	Phillips	Smith*	Bell	Dinning"	Coles !	Hill	Murray	Brooker	Lita	Doherty^	Wilkshire	Am'kwaah/Tinnion/Fortune
27/11		**14,852**	*7*	30			*Proudlock 15, 63, Brunt 61, Collins 84*	*Lucas*	*Bullen*	*H'k'gbottom*	*Branston*	*Collins*	*McGovern*	*McMahon**	*MacLean*	*Proudlock^*	*Whelan*	*Brunt*	*Hamshaw/Nsunga*
							Ref: M Fletcher	Despite the dismissal of Coles five minutes after the break for elbowing Paul Heckingbottom, City looked set to snatch an unlikely win when Murray fired in an equaliser. Unfortunately Tinnion's wayward pass set up Wednesday to go on and beat a disjointed and pedestrian City side.											
20	A	DONCASTER	6	D	1-1	1-1	Brooker 45	Phillips	Smith	Bell	Dinning	Butler	Hill	Murray^	Brooker	Lita	Doherty"	Wilkshire*	Amankwaah/Brown/Orr
7/12		*5,608*	*12*	31			*Roberts 34*	*Warrington*	*Price*	*Ryan*	*Morley*	*Fenton*	*Ravenhill**	*Johnson*	*Blundell^*	*Roberts*	*Green*	*McIndoe*	*Doolan/Ipoua*
							Ref: T Parkes	Battling City had to fight all the way against opponents who pressed relentlessy, but they can take a lot of heart from this performance at Bellevue. Trailing to a firm header from Neil Roberts, the Robins hit back when Brooker netted with a powerful drive right on half-time.											
21	A	BLACKPOOL	8	D	1-1	1-1	Wilkshire 21	Phillips	Smith	Bell	Dinning	Butler	Hill^	Murray	Brooker*	Lita	Doherty	Wilkshire	Heffernan/Fortune
11/12		*5,220*	*19*	32			*Taylor 45p*	*Jones*	*Clare*	*Evans*	*Clarke*	*McGregor*	*Grayson**	*Southern*	*Parker*	*Taylor*	*Wellens*	*Burns*	*Coid*
							Ref: C Oliver	It looked like City were going to take the full haul of points as they were awarded a somewhat fortuitous last minute spot-kick when Wilkshire was caught by Danny Coid's boot. Fortunately for the Pool, Bell blasted the ball high over the bar, his first penalty failure in over 20 attempts.											
22	H	LUTON	9	L	1-2	0-1	Lita 66	Phillips	Smith*	Bell	Dinning^	Butler	Hill	Murray	Brooker"	Lita	Doherty	Wilkshire	Coles/Tinnion/Heffernan
18/12		13,414	*1*	32			*Coyne 34, Showunmi 89*	*Beresford*	*Foley*	*Davis*	*Coyne*	*Davies*	*Holmes*	*Brkovic*	*Showunmi*	*Vine*	*Nicholls*	*Underwood*	
							Ref: S Mathieson	Scant consolation, but at least hot-shot Lita is back amongst the goals again for City. His wonder-strike, an overhead kick at the Atyeo end, hauled City level, only for the Reds to be undone right at the death when Enoch Showunmi was able to turn in Paul Underwood's low cross.											
23	A	STOCKPORT	9	W	2-1	1-1	Butler 3, Heffernan 55	Phillips	Smith	Bell	Coles	Butler	Dinning^	Murray*	Heffernan	Lita	Orr	Wilkshire"	Fortune/Tinnion/Am'kwaah
26/12		*5,071*	*24*	35			*Feeney 18*	*Cutler*	*Hardiker*	*Adams*	*Griffin*	*Williams*	*Daly*	*B-Wilkinson**	*Allen*	*Jackman*	*Feeney*	*Lambert*	*Barlow*
							Ref: C Webster	Not the prettiest of games as City struggled to make an impact on one of their lucky grounds. After Butler's deft header put them into an early lead, City were pegged back when Warren Feeney beat Phillips with a thunderous drive. Heffernan tapped in a rebound to secure the points.											

No		Date	Att	Pos	Pt	F-A	H-T	Scorers, Times, and Referees	SQUAD	NUMBERS	IN	USE								subs used
24	H	HARTLEPOOL		9	D	0-0	0-0		Phillips	Smith	Hill	Coles	Butler	Tinnion	Wilkshire*	Heffernan	Lita	Orr	Bell^	Murray/**Cotterill**
		28/12	13,034	*5*	36				*Ko'st'poulos*	*Ross*	*Robertson*	*Westwood*	*Nelson*	*Tinkler*	*Williams*	*Boyd**	*Porter^*	*Sweeney*	*Humphreys*	*Appleby/Istead"/Strachan*
								Ref: R Beeby	Whilst City found much needed defensive solidity after consecutive home defeats, it unfortunately came at the expense of creativity. Faced by central defenders Michael Nelson and Chris Westwood in outstanding form, City failed to trouble the Pool keeper Dimitrios Konstantpoulos.											
25	H	PETERBOROUGH		8	W	2-0	2-0	Brooker 30, Heffernan 34	Phillips	Smith	Bell	Coles	Butler*	Dinning^	Murray	Brooker"	Heffernan	Orr	Wilkshire	Fortune/Doherty/Lita
		1/1	10,873	*22*	39				*Tyler*	*Newton*	*Arber*	*Branston*	*Burton*	*Legg^*	*Farrell*	*Platt**	*Logan"*	*Boucard*	*Sonner*	*Willcock/Clarke/Semple*
								Ref: F Graham	A fracas in the tunnel at the interval between Butler and Posh forward Clive Platt, which left the City man having eight teeth displaced, saw both men replaced. In the strong wind and driving rain, Brooker's firm well-placed header from Wilkshire's cross set City on the victory path.											
26	A	HUDDERSFIELD		8	D	2-2	0-1	Lita 71, Clarke 89 (og)	Phillips	Smith	Bell	Dinning	Coles	Fortune	Murray*	Brooker"	Heffernan	Orr	Wilkshire^	Tinnion/Lita/Goodfellow
		3/1	*11,151*	*13*	40			*Dinning 17 (og), Abbott 57*	*Rachubka*	*Holdsworth*	*Mirfin**	*Carss*	*Sodje*	*Clarke*	*Brandon*	*McAliskey^*	*Abbott*	*Scholfield*	*Worthington*	*Brown/Mendes*
								Ref: J Robinson	City's fighting comeback shouldn't disguise the fact that they were very much second-best. Following their late leveller when Clarke, under pressure from Lita, headed into his own net, City were indebted to Phillips for brilliantly touching Brandon's long-range shot onto a post.											
27	A	TRANMERE		5	W	1-0	1-0	Lita 10	Phillips	Smith	Fortune	Coles	**Ireland**	Tinnion*	Orr	Brooker"	Lita	Wilkshire^	Bell	Dinning/Doherty/Murray
		10/1	*8,183*	*3*	43				*Howarth*	*Taylor*	*Goodison*	*Sharps"*	*Jackson*	*Rankine*	*McAteer*	*Hall^*	*Hume*	*Harrison**	*Roberts*	*Whitmore/Dadi/Jones*
								Ref: R Oliver	At the 14th attempt City break their Prenton Park jinx, thanks to Lita's early goal. In this live game on Sky TV the young striker chested down Wilkshire's lofted ball and nudged it past his marker before firing into the bottom corner of the net. Thereafter City had to weather the storm.											
28	H	BRADFORD C		6	D	0-0	0-0		Phillips	Smith	Fortune	Coles	Ireland	Tinnion*	Orr"	Brooker	Lita	Wilkshire	Bell^	Dinning/Murray/Goodfellow
		15/1	11,605	*9*	44				*Henderson*	*Holloway*	*Emanuel**	*Wetherall*	*Bower*	*Crooks*	*Summerbee*	*Windass*	*Cooke"*	*Schumacher*	*Morrison^*	*Tierney/Muirhead/Forrest*
								Ref: A Woolmer	A frustrating afternoon for City fans as the Reds again demonstrate their inability to break down opponents who put two strong ranks of four behind the ball. Starting with a 3-5-2 formation, City switch to 4-4-2 with the introduction of Goodfellow and Murray early in the second half.											
29	A	HARTLEPOOL		7	L	1-2	1-1	Brooker 26	Phillips	Smith	Fortune	Coles	Butler	Dinning*	Orr	Brooker	Lita	Wilkshire^	Bell"	Doherty/Murray/Heffernan
		22/1	*5,399*	*5*	44			*Boyd 16p, Sweeney 71*	*Ko'st'poulos*	*Ross*	*Robertson*	*Westwood*	*Nelson*	*Sweeney^*	*Clark*	*Porter**	*Boyd*	*Tinkler*	*Humphreys*	*Appleby/Istead*
								Ref: B Curson	City can only hope for the play-offs now as this defeat, their first in seven games, extinguishes all thoughts of automatic promotion. Brooker's unstoppable low drive isn't enough as Anthony Sweeney fired in Adam Boyd's sublime reverse pass to bring the Pool their deserved success.											
30	H	CHESTERFIELD		7	L	2-3	0-2	Brooker 67, Smith 70	Phillips	Smith	Bell	Coles	Butler*	Doherty^	Murray	Brooker	Lita	Tinnion"	Goodfellow	Fortune/Dinning/Wilkshire
		28/1	10,103	*13*	44			*Hudson 1, 88, Allison 14*	*Muggleton*	*Bailey*	*Nicholson*	*Evatt*	*O'Hare*	*Niven*	*Allott*	*Folan^*	*Allison*	*Hudson*	*Innes**	*Fowler/N'Toya*
								Ref: A Wiley	City are embarrassed in this live game on Sky TV as Chesterfield, after over 100 years of trying, deservedly chalked up their first ever away win against either of the Bristol clubs. City's storming second-half fight-back is ruined by inane late substitutions and a goalkeeping error.											
31	A	HULL		7	D	1-1	0-0	Lita 76	Phillips	Smith	Fortune	Carey	Ireland	Tinnion	Murray	Brooker	Lita	Orr	Brown*	Bell
		5/2	*17,637*	*2*	45			*Barmby 59*	*Myhill*	*Stockdale^*	*Edge*	*Cort*	*Delaney*	*Lewis*	*France*	*Barmby**	*Wilbraham"*	*Green*	*Ellison*	*Allsopp/Hessenthaler/Facey*
								Ref: E Evans	The manager's fierce response to last week's debacle at least produced a more committed performance from City in this encounter at Hull's impressive KC Stadium. Falling behind to Nicky Barmby's brilliant volley, Brooker's cross set-up Lita to fire in City's deserved point-saver.											
32	H	WALSALL		7	L	0-1	0-0		Phillips	Smith	Fortune"	Carey	Ireland	Tinnion*	Murray	Brooker	Lita	Orr	Brown^	Dinning/Heffernan/**Bell**
		11/2	10,820	*12*	45			*Surnam 75*	*Murphy*	*Wright*	*Aranalde*	*Emblen*	*Roper*	*Taylor K*	*Wrack*	*Taylor D*	*Leitao**	*Osborn*	*Surnam*	*Fryatt*
								Ref: G Salisbury	City's only consolation was that there were no television cameras present to inflict yet another hapless display on the nation. Bereft of form, scarcely any of their players demonstrated any knowledge of their function. Andrew Surnam's header made sure City got what they deserved.											
33	A	COLCHESTER		9	W	2-0	0-0	Brooker 51, Lita 71	Phillips	Carey	Bell	Coles	Ireland	Doherty	Cotterill^	Brooker	Lita"	Wilkshire*	Brown	**Golb'rne/Skuse**/Anyinsah
		19/2	***3,412***	*16*	48				*Gerken*	*Baldwin*	*Chilvers*	*Brown W*	*Hunt^*	*Watson*	*Keith**	*Halford*	*Fagan*	*Danns*	*Johnson*	*N'Sungu/Williams*
								Ref: P Taylor	After enduring a week of strong criticisms and decimated by suspensions and injuries, City responded in the best possible way at Layer Road. Lita set the seal on their fully deserved success by dashing half the length of the field before drilling the ball inside Dean Gerken's near post.											
34	H	OLDHAM		7	W	5-1	3-0	Lita 3, 23, Wilkshire 45, Brooker 52, [Branston 88 (og)]	Phillips	Smith	Bell	Carey	Coles	Dinning	Cotterill"	Brooker*	Lita	Brown	Wilkshire^	Heffernan/Murray/Orr
		22/2	9,007	*19*	51			*Haining 57*	*Mildenhall*	*Bruce*	*Griffin*	*Haining*	*Branston*	*Hughes*	*Holden*	*Cooper*	*Killen*	*Kilkenny*	*Eyres*	
								Ref: A Penn	The Latics, so shaky at the back and bereft of confidence born of a wretched spell of results, wasted numerous opportunities to have pushed City much closer. Lita pounced to finish inside the near post with the outside of his boot and doubled City's advantage with raking low drive.											

No	H/A Date	Opponent Att	Pos	Res Pts	F-A	H-T	Scorers, Times, and Referees	1	2	3	4	5	6	7	8	9	10	11	Subs used
35	H	BLACKPOOL	8	D	1-1	1-0	Brooker 21	Phillips	Smith	Bell	Carey	Coles	Dinning	Cotterill"	Brooker	Lita*	Brown	Wilkshire^	Heffernan/Murray/Anyinsah
	26/2	10,977	*18*	52			*Wellens 60*	*Jones*	*Coid*	*Evans*	*Clarke*	*Butler*	*Southern*	*Bullock*	*Parker*	*Murphy*	*Wellens*	*Burns*	
							Ref: P Joslin	This performance summed up City's season as they were breathtaking, awful and plain ordinary, all in one fluctuating and open encounter. So slick and sharp to start with, when Brooker gave them the lead with a faint flick of the head, after the break they were completely out of sorts.											
36	A	LUTON	9	L	**0-5**	0-3	*[Holmes 61]*	Phillips	Carey	Bell	Fortune	Coles^	Dinning*	Smith	Brooker	Lita	Brown"	Wilkshire	Orr/Skuse/Goodfellow
	5/3	*8,330*	*1*	52			*Brkovic 10, 79, Nicholls 26p, Davis 45,*	*Beresford*	*Keane*	*Davis**	*Perrett*	*Davies*	*Nicholls*	*Brkovic*	*Howard*	*Vine^*	*Holmes"*	*Underwood*	*Showunmi/Andrew/Leary*
							Ref: P Danson	As well as coming under fire from their fans, the City players were also given a verbal blast on the radio by Chairman Steve Lansdown after this truly shocking display. Rarely can City have been so utterly outplayed and devoid of industry and guile. In truth they were a disgrace.											
37	H	BARNSLEY	8	D	0-0	0-0		Phillips	Smith^	Golbourne	Carey*	Coles	Doherty	Cotterill	Brooker	Lita	Brown"	Wilkshire	Fortune/Murray/Heffernan
	12/3	9,321	*13*	53				*Flinders*	*Tonga*	*Williams*	*Reid*	*Hassell*	*McPhail*	*Shuker*	*Chopra !*	*Johnson**	*Burns*	*Wroe*	*Nardiello*
							Ref: M Fletcher	City were expected to bury the bitter memory of last week's Luton nightmare. Instead, despite being denied by the bar on three occasions, they turned in as limp a display as has been witnessed at the Gate this season. Two bookable offences meant a 59th-min departure for Mike Chopra.											
38	A	TORQUAY	8	W	4-0	3-0	Lita 9, 12, 21, Heffernan 54	Phillips	Smith"	Golbourne	Fortune	Coles	Doherty	Murray	Brooker^	Lita*	Brown	**Keith**	Heffernan/Wilkshire/Orr
	19/3	*4,229*	*21*	56				*Marriott*	*Canoville*	*Hill*	*Woods*	*Taylor*	*Garner*	*Phillips"*	*Const'ntine**	*Akinfenwa*	*Russell*	*Kuffour^*	*Woodman/Bedeau/Abbey*
							Ref: M Warren	Despite the impressive scoreline, City were indebted to their keeper in the fog on the Plainmoor ground. After Lita's brilliant 35-yard volleyed opener it was baffling that Torquay didn't manage to get on the scoresheet. Phillips made many fine saves to deny them time and time again.											
39	H	PORT VALE	8	W	2-0	1-0	Lita 14, Heffernan 67	Phillips	Smith	Bell	Carey	Coles	Doherty	Murray"	Brooker	Lita*	Brown	Keith^	Heffernan/Orr/Cotterill
	2/4	10,284	*18*	59				*Goodlad*	*Rowland*	*James**	*Sonner*	*Pilkington*	*Collins*	*Birchall*	*Paynter*	*Matthews*	*Cummins*	*Reid^*	*Abbey/Innes*
							Ref: R Booth	The fact that the Ashton Gate patrons rose at the end to give City an ovation must have been in relief that play-off aspirations had been kept alive, as this was another dire affair. The only highlight was Lita's goal, fired into the Wedlock Stand net from a narrow angle wide on the left.											
40	H	BOURNEMOUTH	8	L	0-2	0-0		Phillips	Smith	Bell"	Carey	Coles	Doherty	Murray	Brooker^	Lita	Brown	Keith*	Cotterill/Heffernan/Golb'rne
	5/4	12,008	*5*	59			*O'Connor 60, 77p*	*Moss*	*Simek*	*Purches*	*Mills*	*Howe*	*Spicer*	*Elliott**	*Fletcher*	*Hayter*	*Stock*	*O'Connor*	*Browning*
							Ref: M Russell	City find themselves chasing shadows as they are given a football lesson by the fast and skilful visitors, who waltzed in the opener. Whilst City had their chances, the Cherries would have scored even more but for the intervention of a post as well as a particularly fine Phillips save.											
41	A	BRENTFORD	9	L	0-1	0-1		Phillips	Smith	Golbourne	Fortune	Coles	Doherty"	Orr	Brooker	Lita	Brown*	Cotterill^	Murray/Heffernan/Skuse
	9/4	*6,780*	*7*	59			*Sodje 12*	*Nelson*	*O'Connor*	*Frampton*	*Turner*	*Sodje*	*Pratley*	*Tabb*	*Fitzgerald^*	*Burton**	*Talbot*	*Gayle*	*Rankin/Harrold*
							Ref: J Ross	Whilst City pretty much matched Brentford's physical approach, they struggled to find any way that might have brought victory over limited opposition. Sam Sodje's neat volley, with the outside of his boot, always looked like being enough to secure all three points for the Bees.											
42	A	SWINDON	8	D	0-0	0-0		Phillips	Orr	Goldbourne	Carey	Fortune	Doherty	Smith	Brooker"	Lita	Wilkshire*	Cotterill^	Brown/Murray/Heffernan
	13/4	*6,977*	*10*	60				*Evans*	*Heywood*	*Ifil*	*Miglioranzi**	*O'Hanlon*	*Howard*	*Jenkins*	*Parkin*	*Fallon*	*Igoe*	*Smith*	*Duke*
							Ref: T Bates	City were almost washed away in the teeming rain, but they showed plenty of spirit and commitment as they hung on for a point. Town striker Rory Fallon could easily have taken home three match balls, such was the amount of chances he had of grabbing victory for the home side.											
43	H	WREXHAM	8	W	1-0	0-0	Murray 66	Phillips	Carey	Goldbourne	Skuse	Fortune	Doherty*	Orr^	Heffernan	Lita	Wilkshire	Cotterill"	Brown/Murray/Harley
	16/4	**8,267**	*22*	63				*Foster*	*Pejic*	*Lawrence*	*Jones**	*Morgan*	*Ferguson*	*Edwards*	*Holt"*	*Llewellyn*	*Ugarte*	*Crowell^*	*Armstrong/Sam/Smith*
							Ref: P Melin	With old City manager Denis Smith in charge, Wrexham, who are struggling against relegation due to having ten points deducted, rarely gave City the chance to shine in this typically poor end of season affair. Hope for the future though. as Cole Skuse makes an impressive full debut.											
44	A	MK DONS	8	W	2-1	1-1	Lita 45, 70	Phillips	Carey	Golbourne	Fortune	Coles	Wilkshire^	Murray	Brooker"	Lita	Skuse	Cotterill*	Brown/Orr/Smith
	23/4	*5,656*	*21*	66			*McLeod 8*	*Baker*	*McCle'han^*	*Crooks**	*Pen'e-Bilong*	*Chorley*	*Smith*	*Small*	*Platt*	*McLeod*	*Edds"*	*Lewington*	*Kamara/Westcarr/Harding*
							Ref: D Drysdale	A series of topsy-turvy results and this fortuitous win restores play-off hopes, but City must be successful in their last two games and look for other results to go their way. Against old boss Danny Wilson at the National Hockey Stadium, keeper Phillips saved City time and time again.											
45	H	DONCASTER	8	D	2-2	0-1	Brooker 62, 90	Phillips	Carey	Golbourne"	Fortune	Coles	Wilkshire	Murray*	Brooker	Heffernan	Skuse	Brown^	Anyinsah/Gillespie/Bell
	30/4	12,375	*10*	67			*Fortune-West 34, 88*	*Turner*	*Mulligan*	*Ryan*	*Fenton*	*Foster*	*Ravenhill !*	*Coppinger^*	*Guy**	*F'tune-West*	*Green*	*McIndoe*	*Blundell/Doolan*
							Ref: F Graham	Despite further failure in another must-win game, amazingly City still have a slim chance of making the play-offs. They were unfortunate as they played well enough, but the ball often didn't fall kindly for them. Brooker's header at the start of three minutes added time saved a point.											
46	A	SHEFFIELD WED	7	W	3-2	2-0	Brooker 24, 45, Wilkshire 81p	Phillips	Carey	Bell^	Fortune	Coles	Wilkshire	Anyinsah"	Brooker	Heffernan*	Skuse	Brown	Gillespie/Orr/Wring
	7/5	***28,798***	*5*	70			*McGovern 52, Wood 61*	*Gallacher !*	*Bruce*	*H'k'gbottom*	*Wood*	*Bullen*	*Whelan*	*Adams"*	*Quinn**	*Talbot^*	*McGovern*	*Brunt*	*Peacock/Barrett/Collins*
	Home	Away					Ref: G Laws	This rare Hillsborough win counted for little as Brentford's midweek success at Wrexham had put a play-off place beyond City's reach. The sending off of the Wednesday keeper for bringing down Brooker, saw ex-City player Lee Peacock failing to keep out the resultant spot-kick.											
	Average 11,391	7,892																	

Carling Cup

No	Venue	Opponent	Att / Pos	Res	F-A	H-T	Scorers, Times, and Referees	SQUAD	NUMBERS	IN	USE								subs used
1	A	WYCOMBE	21	W	1-0	0-0	Lita 70	Phillips	Smith	Woodman	Fortune	Hill	Orr	Murray*	Miller	Lita	Doherty	Roberts^	Gillespie/Tinnion
24/8			1,778 *2:7*					*Talia*	*Uhlenbeek*	*Silk*	*Johnson*	*Nethercott*	*Burnell*	*Senda*	*Birchall*	*Stonebridge*	*Easton*	*Tyson*	
							Ref: P Danson												
2	H	EVERTON	15	D	2-2	0-2	Stubbs 50 (og), Lita 53	Phillips	Smith"	Hill	Butler	Coles	Orr	Murray	Roberts*	Lita	Doherty	Wilkshire^	Heffernan/Fortune/Miller
22/9			15,264 *P:3*		*aet*		*Ferguson 30p, Chadwick 45*	*Wright*	*Hibbert*	*Naysmith^*	*Yobo*	*Stubbs*	*Cahill*	*Watson*	*McFadden*	*Ferguson"*	*Carsley*	*Osman**	*Chadwick/Pistone/Campbell*
							Ref: P Crossley (City lost on penalties 3-4)												

1: Lita's on target again as nervy City notch their first win of the season, but they barely deserved success from this encounter at the Causeway. Wycombe looked the more accomplished side prior to the interval and it took Lita's match-winning header to quell the lower division hosts.

2: City produced a stirring second-half comeback only to lose out 3-4 in the heartbreaking circumstances of a penalty shoot-out. Lita rifled home City's equaliser at the Atyeo End, after which Phillips' brilliant double save from James McFadden's 85th-min pen took the tie into extra-time.

FA Cup

No	Venue	Opponent	Att / Pos	Res	F-A	H-T	Scorers, Times, and Referees	SQUAD	NUMBERS	IN	USE								subs used
1	H	BRENTFORD	7	D	1-1	0-1	Lita 89	Phillips	Coles	Bell"	Orr^	Butler*	Hill	Murray	Brooker	Lita	Doherty	Wilkshire	Smith/Tinnion/Gillespie
12/11			7,547 *6*				*Salako 7*	*Nelson*	*O'Connor*	*Frampton*	*Sodje*	*Turner*	*Talbot*	*Salako**	*Rankin*	*Burton^*	*Hargreaves*	*Tabb*	*Lawrence/Rhodes*
							Ref: A Hall												
R	A	BRENTFORD	6	A	1-1	0-1	Heffernan 77	Phillips	Smith	Fortune	Doherty^	Butler	Hill"	Murray*	Heffernan	Miller	Tinnion	Orr	Lita/Brown/Coles
25/11			3,706 *8*		*aet*		*Frampton 44*	*Nelson*	*O'Connor*	*Frampton*	*Sodje*	*Turner*	*Talbot*	*Lawrence*	*Harrold**	*Rankin^*	*Hargreaves*	*Salako*	*Tabb/Rhodes*
							Ref: A Hall (City lost on penalties 3-4)												

1: The live Sky TV audience see City gifted an FA Cup lifeline when the Brentford keeper, under pressure from Lita, missed his kick and allowed the striker to sprint through and tap in a late equaliser. John Salako curled in a fine left-footed opener for the highly committed Brentford side

R: Yet again the lottery of the penalty shoot-out ensures City's exit from a cup competition. This time though, their fate was fully deserved as they gave an impoverished display in front of a live Sky TV audience. Heffernan's delighful side-foot turn in of Smith's cross was all they offered.

		Home					Away					
	P	W	D	L	F	A	W	D	L	F	A	Pts
1 Luton	46	17	4	2	46	16	12	7	4	41	32	98
2 Hull	46	16	5	2	42	17	10	3	10	38	36	86
3 Tranmere	46	14	5	4	43	23	8	8	7	30	32	79
4 Brentford	46	15	4	4	34	22	7	5	11	23	38	75
5 Sheffield Wed *	46	10	6	7	34	28	9	9	5	43	31	72
6 Hartlepool	46	15	3	5	51	30	6	5	12	25	36	71
7 BRISTOL CITY	46	9	8	6	42	25	9	8	6	32	32	70
8 Bournemouth	46	9	7	7	40	30	11	3	9	37	34	70
9 Huddersfield	46	12	6	5	42	28	8	4	11	32	37	70
10 Doncaster	46	10	11	2	35	20	6	7	10	30	40	66
11 Bradford C	46	9	6	8	40	35	8	8	7	24	27	65
12 Swindon	46	12	5	6	40	30	5	7	11	26	38	63
13 Barnsley	46	7	11	5	38	31	7	8	8	31	33	61
14 Walsall	46	11	7	5	40	28	5	5	13	25	41	60
15 Colchester	46	8	6	9	27	23	6	11	6	33	27	59
16 Blackpool	46	8	7	8	28	30	7	5	11	26	29	57
17 Chesterfield	46	9	8	6	32	28	5	7	11	23	34	57
18 Port Vale	46	13	2	8	33	23	4	3	16	16	36	56
19 Oldham	46	10	5	8	42	34	4	5	14	18	39	52
20 MK Dons	46	8	10	5	33	28	4	5	14	21	40	51
21 Torquay	46	8	5	10	27	36	4	10	9	28	43	51
22 Wrexham**	46	6	8	9	26	37	7	6	10	36	43	43
23 Peterborough	46	5	6	12	27	35	4	6	13	22	38	39
24 Stockport	46	3	4	16	26	46	3	4	16	23	52	26
	1104	244	149	159	868	683	159	149	244	683	868	1497

* promoted after play-offs

** deducted 10 points for entering administration

Odds & ends

Double wins: (5) Stockport County, Milton Keynes Dons, Tranmere Rovers, Peterborough United, Wrexham.
Double losses: (1) Luton Town.

Won from behind: (2) Walsall (a), Milton Keynes Dons (a).
Lost from in front: (0).

High Spots: A thrilling 2-2 draw with Premiership Everton in the League Cup, which culminated in a penalty shoot-out defeat.
Bournemouth's brilliant play at Ashton Gate on 5 April.
The many superb displays between the sticks by Steve Phillips.
Replacing the City Cat matchday mascot with a Robin, although the choice of the name 'Scrumpy', selected when the bird appeared for the first time on 30 April, is somewhat poor.

Low spots: Losing to Sheffield Wed at the Gate on 27 November.
The abysmal FA Cup display at Griffin Park in front of Sky TV cameras.
The abject performance in losing at Luton on 5 March.
City's League defeat at Griffin Park on 9 April.
Failure to reach the play-offs.

Player in the PFA XI: Leroy Lita.
Internationals: Full: Tommy Doherty (Northern Ireland), Luke Wilkshire (Australia). Under-23: Leroy Lita (England), Dave Cotterill (Wales). Under-19: Scott Golbourne (England).

AGM (Exhibition Hall, Dolman Stand, 24 November 2005).
Loss: £1,968,195. Season Ticket Sales (No): 9,000.

Player of the Year: Leroy Lita.
Ever-presents: (1) Steve Phillips.
Hat-tricks: (2) Leroy Lita.
Leading scorer: Overall: Leroy Lita (27). League: Leroy Lita (24).

	Appearances						Goals			
	Lge	*Sub*	LC	*Sub*	FAC	*Sub*	Lge	LC	FAC	Tot
Amankwaah, Kevin	1	*4*								
Anyinsah, Joe	2	*5*								
Bell, Mickey	26	*5*			1		1			1
Brooker, Steve	33				1		16			16
Brown, Scott	13	*6*				*1*				
Butler, Tony	22		1		2		2			2
Carey, Louis	14									
Coles, Danny	37	*1*	1		1	*1*	1			1
Cotterill, Dave	8	*4*								
Dinning, Tony	15	*4*								
Doherty, Tommy	25	*4*	2		2		1			1
Fortune, Clayton	17	*13*	1	*1*	1					
Gillespie, Steve	1	*7*		*1*		*1*				
Goodfellow, Marc	1	*4*								
Golbourne, Scott	7	*2*								
Harley, Ryan	1	*1*								
Heffernan, Paul	10	*17*		*1*	1		5		1	6
Hill, Matt	23		2		2					
Ireland, Craig (loan)	5									
Keith, Joe (loan)	3									
Lita, Leroy	42	*2*	2		1	*1*	24	2	1	27
Miller, Lee	2	*5*	1	*1*	1					
Murray, Scott	31	*11*	2		2		8			8
Orr, Bradley	23	*14*	2		2					
Phillips, Steve	46		2		2					
Roberts, Christian	6	*2*	2				1			1
Skuse, Cole	4	*3*								
Smith, Jamie	35	*4*	2		1	*1*	2			2
Tinnion, Brian	15	*7*		*1*	1	*1*	1			1
Wilkshire, Luke	35	*2*	1		1		9			9
Woodman, Craig	3		1							
Wring, Danny		*1*								
(own-goals)							3	1		4
32 players used	**506**	***131***	**22**	***5***	**22**	***6***	**74**	**3**	**2**	**79**

No	Date		Att	Pos	Pt	F-A	H-T	Scorers, Times, and Referees	SQUAD	NUMBERS	IN	USE								subs used
1	H	DONCASTER			D	0-0	0-0		Phillips	Carey	Woodman	Fortune	**Heywood**	Skuse	Cotterill^	**Stewart**	**Bridges***	Wilkshire	Smith G	Brooker/Murray
	6/8		15,481		1				*Warrington*	*McGuire*	*Ryan*	*Foster*	*Fenton*	*Green*	*Mulligan*	*Roberts N^*	*Heffernan"*	*Thornton**	*McIndoe*	*Roberts S/F-West/Guy*
								Ref: C Penton	Despite being assured that City were focused on winning the League the home fans suffered what is becoming all-too-habitual bad early season form. Against a Donnie side who had a first-half shot cleared off the line and were denied by the crossbar after the break, the Reds were inept.											
2	A	HUDDERSFIELD			L	0-1	0-0		Phillips	Carey	Woodman	Fortune	Heywood	Skuse	Cotterill^	Stewart	Brooker"	Wilkshire !	Smith G*	Brown/Smith J/Bridges
	9/8		*11,138*		1			*Abbott 89*	*Rachubka*	*Mirfin**	*Adams*	*McIntosh*	*Clarke*	*Worthington*	*Brandon*	*Booth*	*Abbott*	*Hudson"*	*Schofield^*	*Holdsworth/Fletcher/Carss*
								Ref: A Hall	City thought themselves unlucky to lose this game right at the finish. In truth City performed better following Wilkshire's 50th-min dismissal for a second bookable offence and it was only the fact of Pawel Abbott failing to put away six relatively easy chances that kept the score down.											
3	A	BOURNEMOUTH		24	L	0-2	0-1		Phillips	Carey	Woodman^	**Partridge**	Heywood	Skuse	Cotterill	Bridges	Brooker	Brown	Stewart*	Murray/Golbourne
	13/8		*6,544*	*7*	1			*Stock 19, Hayter 48p*	*Moss*	*Young*	*O'Connor*	*Howe*	*Maher*	*Browning*	*Spicer^*	*Hayter"*	*Fletcher*	*Stock*	*Surman**	*Rodrigues/Cooke/Coutts*
								Ref: D Gallagher	City, in their new sandy away kit, are their own worst enemies, gifting Bournemouth two soft goals. Despite being second best all afternoon, it is City's continuing frailties in the face of set-piece routines that are of as much concern as the ongoing failure to find the net at the other end.											
4	H	PORT VALE		17	W	4-2	4-2	Brooker 3, 28, Stewart 6, Murray 13	Phillips	Carey	Golbourne	Partridge	Heywood*	Skuse	Murray"	Stewart	Brooker	Wilkshire	Brown^	Fortune/Smith G/Cotterill
	20/8		11,120	*7*	4			*Lowndes 35, Bell 39*	*Goodland*	*Abbey^*	*Bell*	*Collins*	*Pilkington*	*Dinning*	*Cummins*	*Paynter*	*Lowndes*	*Sonner*	*Innes**	*Smith/Birchall*
								Ref: M Fletcher	Aided and abetted by some slapstick Vale defending, City flattered to deceive with their storming start. They allowed the visitors a way back by choosing to ease off and admire their handiwork. After the break City were lucky not to concede as they rarely got outside their own half.											
5	H	MK DONS		17	D	2-2	0-2	Brooker 53, Heywood 60	Phillips	Smith J	Golbourne	Carey	Heywood	Skuse	Murray	Stewart^	Brooker	Brown	Wilkshire*	Bridges/Cotterill
	27/8		10,011	*21*	5			*Platt 7, 18*	*Baker*	*McClenahan*	*Lewington*	*Crooks*	*Morgan*	*Edds*	*Small*	*Platt*	*Wilbraham**	*Mitchell^*	*McKoy*	*Kamara/Carriho*
								Ref: K Stroud	After the crowd gave a hero's welcome to their ex-manager, Danny Wilson, now in charge of the Dons, a share of the spoils was a fair reward for City's second-half spirit. Errors at the back cost them and successive wins are much needed if their sagging confidence isn't to plummet.											
6	H	COLCHESTER		18	D	0-0	0-0		Phillips	Murray	Golbourne^	Carey	Heywood	**Keogh**	Orr	Bridges	Brooker*	Brown	Skuse	Gillespie/Smith G
	3/9		10,180	*20*	6				*Davison*	*Richards*	*Elokobi*	*Brown*	*Baldwin^*	*Watson*	*Halford*	*Izzet*	*Iwelumo*	*White*	*Yeates**	*Howell/King*
								Ref: R Oliver	Yet another Jekyll and Hyde performance from City, although the second half was more about guts and desperation to score than anything particularly fluent. City's dire first-half display in this midday kick-off game must have had the Sky TV viewers switching off in their droves.											
7	A	SWANSEA		22	L	**1-7**	0-1	Cotterill 81 *[Trundle 58p, 71, Britton 75]*	Phillips	Smith J	Golbourne	Carey*	Keogh	Fortune	Orr"	Bridges	Gillespie^	Brown	Cotterill	Murray/Stewart/Wilkshire
	10/9		*13,662*	*4*	6			*McLeod 44, 69, 87, Akinfenwa 51,*	*Gueret*	*Tate*	*Ricketts**	*Austin !*	*Iriekpen*	*Bean*	*Britton"*	*Trundle*	*Akinfenwa^*	*Martinez*	*McLeod*	*Anderson/Connor/Robinson*
								Ref: A Bates	Shambolic City are cut to ribbons at Swansea's impressive new home. Whilst this woeful display wasn't entirely unexpected after what has gone before this season, there can be no excuse for a gutless and leaderless performance which saw the Swans have an eighth goal disallowed.											
8	H	BLACKPOOL		23	D	1-1	0-0	Cotterill 85	Phillips	Carey	Woodman	Partridge	Heywood*	Skuse	Murray^	Stewart	Gillespie"	Brown	Smith G	Orr/Cotterill/Wilkshire
	17/9		9,576	*17*	7			*Blinkhorn 90*	*Pogliacomi*	*McGregor*	*Edwards*	*Clarke*	*Butler*	*Grayson*	*Wiles^*	*Parker**	*Wright*	*Southern*	*Donnelly*	*Blinkhorn/Prendergast*
								Ref: P Melin	Under the control of caretaker boss Keith Millen, following Tinnion's departure, City's long-standing frailty at defending set-pieces cost them after Cotterill had tapped them in front. From a corner, at the start of four minutes stoppage time, the unmarked Matthew Blinkthorn headed in.											
9	A	NOTT'M FOREST		23	L	1-3	1-2	Gillespie 15	Phillips	Smith J	Woodman	Keogh	Partridge	Skuse	Murray"	Stewart	Gillespie^	Brown	Smith G*	Wilkshire/Bridges/Cotterill
	20/9		***16,666***	*13*	7			*Lester 25p, Perch 27, Commons 56*	*Hoult*	*Eaden*	*Thompson**	*Breckin*	*Morgan*	*Frilo*	*Southall*	*Johnson*	*Lester"*	*Perch*	*Commons^*	*Gardner/Bopp/Dadi*
								Ref: S Mathieson	Despite taking the lead when Gillespie thumped the ball home on the run, yet again City struggled to show any fluency. Forest levelled from the spot when Kris Commons was upended. Following the interval Phillips, who became a father earlier in the day, was beaten by a 25-yarder.											
10	A	BRENTFORD		22	W	3-2	2-0	Stewart 12, Wilkshire 40, Brooker 74	Phillips	Orr	Woodman	Partridge	Heywood	Wilkshire	Cotterill"	Stewart*	**Madjo^**	Skuse	Brown	Brooker/Keogh/Murray
	24/9		*6,413*	*4*	10			*Brooker 67, Sodje 80*	*Nelson*	*Osborne*	*Tillen*	*Turner*	*Sodje*	*Lewis*	*Rankin**	*Owusu^*	*Gayle*	*Pratley"*	*Tabb*	*Campbell/Brooker/Rhodes*
								Ref: K Wright	Under new boss Gary Johnson (Yeovil), City's luck changed with this well-deserved success on their bogey ground at Griffin Park. They failed to convert their chances in the early stages of the second half when Stewart had a goal ruled out. Wilkshire later had a 76th-min penalty saved.											
11	H	BARNSLEY		19	W	3-0	3-0	Brooker 24, Stewart 38p, 45	Phillips	Orr	Woodman	**Sankofa**	Partridge	Wilkshire	Cotterill^	Stewart*	Brooker"	Skuse	Brown	Madjo/Murray/Bridges
	27/9		10,771	*14*	13				*Colgan*	*Tonge*	*Williams*	*Hassell*	*Reid*	*Wroe*	*Shuker*	*Conlon"*	*Hayes^*	*Burns*	*Devaney**	*Howard/Nardiello/Richards*
								Ref: M Clattenburg	Against lacklustre opposition, City gave a solid and enterprising display in notching up only their second home win of the season. Young Osei Sankofa, on loan from Charlton Athletic, impressed on his debut. Stewart tucked away the spot-kick after being scythed down by Dale Tonge.											

No	Venue	Opponent	Att	Pos	Res/Pts	F-A	H-T	Scorers, Times, and Referees	1	2	3	4	5	6	7	8	9	10	11	Subs used
12	H	HARTLEPOOL		21	L	0-1	0-0		Phillips	Orr	Woodman"	Sankofa	Partridge	Wilkshire	Cotterill*	Stewart^	Brooker	Skuse	Brown	Murray/Madjo/Bridges
1/10			11,365	*18*	13			*Proctor 54*	*Ko'st'poulos*	*Williams D*	*Humphreys*	*Collins*	*Nelson*	*Turnbull*	*Proctor^*	*Bullock*	*Daly"*	*Sweeney**	*Llewellyn*	*Tinkler/Williams E/Maidens*
								Ref: I Williamson	A smash and grab success for Hartlepool as City exhibited familiar failings against defensive opponents. The Reds were unlucky to be beaten by Mike Proctor's angled strike at the Wedlock End as they produced some slick passing routines in their disciplined and hard-working show.											
13	H	TRANMERE		18	W	1-0	0-0	Wilkshire 65	Phillips	Carey	Woodman	Youga*	Sankofa	Wilkshire	Murray	Stewart^	Brooker	Skuse	Cotterill"	Fortune/Bridges/Smith G
15/10			10,495	*23*	16				*Achterberg*	*Sharps*	*Goodison^*	*Rankine"*	*Jackson*	*Jennings*	*Bruce*	*Zola**	*Facey*	*Greenacre*	*Roberts*	*Theodore/Sumr'bee/Aiston*
								Ref: G Lewis	City, who gave but a reasonable performance, have cause to be thankful to the alert Luke Wilkshire. When his rasping effort ricocheted off the base of a post, the Aussie International kept his cool to get onto the rebound and strike the leather low and true into the net at the Atyeo end.											
14	A	OLDHAM		19	L	3-4	0-2	Brown 49, Quinn 78, Murray 90	Phillips	Carey^	Woodman"	Sankofa	Partridge	Wilkshire	Murray	Stewart*	Cotterill	Skuse	Brown	Quinn/Orr/Bridges
22/10			*5,456*	*10*	16			*Hughes 4, Wel' 25, Porter 56, Liddell 87*	*Day*	*Scott*	*Tierney*	*Branston*	*Hall*	*Wellens^*	*Warne*	*Porter*	*Liddell*	*Hughes*	*Eyres**	*Edwards/Forbes*
								Ref: P Robinson	For all City's promising approach play, they are yet again let down by defensive deficiencies that need serious shoring-up. For example, Chris Porter was left unmarked to guide his header past Phillips when David Eyres slung in a free-kick. Brown's first senior goal was a real scorcher.											
15	A	CHESTERFIELD		20	L	0-3	0-0		Phillips	Orr"	Fortune	Sankofa	Partridge	Skuse	Murray	Cotterill	**Quinn**	Wilkshire^	Brown*	Madjo/Smith G/Keogh
26/10			*5,027*	*5*	16			*Allison 57, Nicholson 66, 87p*	*Roche*	*Bailey*	*Nicholson*	*Hazell*	*Blatherwick*	*Allott*	*Hall**	*Larkin*	*Allison*	*Niven*	*Hurst*	*Clingan*
								Ref: C Oliver	City, who huffed and puffed to hold their own in a dour first half, once again fell apart alarmingly from the moment Wayne Allison headed the Spireites in front. Indeed, so poor was their display that boss Johnson apologised to the travelling fans who had angrily protested at the finish.											
16	H	SOUTHEND		22	L	0-3	0-1		Phillips	Orr*	Carey	Sankofa	Partridge	Skuse	Murray	Cotterill	Quinn"	Wilkshire	Brown^	Woodman/Stewart/Madjo
29/10			10,625	*1*	16			*Eastwood 25, 47, 76*	*Griemink*	*Hunt*	*Wilson*	*Barrett*	*Edwards*	*Maher*	*C'bell-Ryce"*	*Goater**	*Eastwood*	*Guttridge*	*Cole^*	*Gray/Lawson/Gower*
								Ref: B Curson	At the interval City are only trailing to Freddy Eastwood's rifled in left-footer when Phillips fumbled Luke Gutteridge's drive into his path, but it should have been worse. Following the change of ends, birthday boy Eastwood forced the ball in from close range before adding a 30-yarder.											
17	A	SWINDON		22	L	1-2	1-2	Murray 4p	**Basso**	Sankofa !	**Youga**	**Joseph**	Partridge^	Orr"	Cotterill	Murray*	Brooker	Brown	**Russell**	Smith G/Heywood/Stewart
11/11			*7,572*	*24*	16			*McDermott 12, Fallon 31*	*Heaton*	*Smith^*	*Gurney*	*Ifil*	*O'Hanlon*	*Miglioranzi*	*McDermott"*	*Pook**	*Fallon*	*Nicholas*	*Bouazza*	*Roberts/Jenkins/Platt*
								Ref: A Hall	The City boss moans about the officials in a forlorn attempt to excuse a sixth successive defeat, but completely failed to acknowledge his side's good fortune when Murray's saved spot-kick was ordered to be retaken. In truth it was slack defending and inability to create that cost City.											
18	H	CHESTERFIELD		23	L	2-4	1-3	Wilkshire 6, Cotterill 85	Basso	Orr	Youga^	Joseph	Heywood	Skuse	Murray"	Stewart	Brooker*	Brown	Wilkshire	Cotterill/Smith G/Russell
19/11			9,752	*4*	16			*Hall 18, 29p, 60, Hurst 25*	*Roche*	*Bailey*	*Picken*	*Blatherwick*	*Hazell*	*Clingan*	*Allott*	*Hall*	*Larkin*	*Niven*	*Hurst**	*Davies*
								Ref: A Penn	City played some crisp and exciting soccer at the start and deservedly went in front when Wilkshire found the back of the Wedlock Stand net with a curling free-kick. Unfortunately after an unlucky deflection set up Hall to fire in an equaliser, City just crumbled and showed little fight.											
19	A	DONCASTER		24	L	0-2	0-1		Basso	Carey	Youga"	Joseph^	Sankofa	**Noble**	Murray	Cotterill*	Brooker	Skuse	Wilkshire	**Savage**/Heywood/Orr
26/11			*7,876*	*9*	16			*Heffernan 4, Coppinger 67*	*Seremet*	*Fenton*	*McDaid**	*Foster*	*Roberts S*	*Thornton*	*Coppinger*	*Heffernan*	*Guy^*	*Ravenhill*	*McIndoe*	*Green/Roberts N*
								Ref: S Mathieson	Doncaster's debutant goalkeeper looked shaky throughout, but City failed to take advantage. Spurning their chances, City succumbed to their eighth successive defeat. Paul Heffernan shot in Doncaster's opener via Sankofa's deflection and James Coppinger headed in their second.											
20	H	BRADFORD C		24	L	0-1	0-0		Basso	Orr	Woodman	Noble	Heywood	Carey	Cotterill	Stewart*	Brooker	Russell^	Wilkshire"	Savage/Smith G/Smith J
6/12			**9,103**	*10*	16			*Carey 79 (og)*	*Ricketts*	*Edghill*	*Taylor*	*Bower*	*Wetherall*	*Bdge-Wknsn*	*Morrison**	*Cadamarteri*	*Windass*	*Schumacher*	*Muirhead^*	*Cooke/Kearney*
								Ref: P Melin	Seeking to end their club record run of defeats, City were cruelly robbed in this game, which started some 20 mins late as Bradford were held up on the motorway. City, who totally dominated the play, are made to pay for their lack of punch when Carey sliced the ball into his own net.											
21	H	HUDDERSFIELD		23	W	2-0	1-0	Murray 5, Cotterill 80	Basso	Orr	Woodman	Noble	Heywood	Carey	Cotterill	Stewart	Brooker	Russell	Murray	
10/12			9,949	*2*	19				*Rachubka*	*Holdsworth*	*Adams^*	*Clarke T*	*Clarke N*	*Hudson*	*Fletcher**	*Abbott"*	*Booth*	*Worthington*	*Schofield*	*Carss/Ahmed/McAliskey*
								Ref: M Russell	Cotterill's one moment of quality sealed this win. Securing the ball on the edge of the centre-circle, he set off on a mazy run and burst into the box to fire an exquisite low shot into the far bottom corner of the Atyeo Stand net. A deserved victory for City, for whom keeper Basso starred.											
22	A	PORT VALE		23	W	1-0	1-0	Brooker 44	Basso	Orr	Woodman	Noble	Heywood	Carey	Cotterill	Savage*	Brooker	Russell	Murray	Keogh
17/12			*4,214*	*16*	22				*Goodland*	*Rowland*	*Bell**	*Pilkington*	*James*	*Porter^*	*Togwell*	*Const'ntine"*	*Lowndes*	*Sonner*	*Birchall*	*Husbands/Cardle/Briscoe*
								Ref: D Deadman	The Reds made hard work of beating a Vale side much weakened by injuries and suspensions. After surviving an anxious opening, City took control of the game only to be let down by poor finishing. Fortunately Brooker was able to turn on a ball in the box and fire it into the net.											
23	A	GILLINGHAM		23	D	1-1	1-0	Murray 10	Basso*	Orr	Woodman	Noble^	Heywood	Carey	Cotterill	Savage	Brooker	Russell"	Murray	Phillips/Skuse/Wilkshire
26/12			*7,786*	*18*	23			*Flynn 69*	*Brown*	*Wallis**	*Johnson*	*Cox"*	*Jackman*	*Flynn*	*Jarvis*	*Shields^*	*Harris*	*Crofts*	*Spiller*	*Clohessy/Edusei/Sancho*
								Ref: A D'Urso	It was a pity that City were unable to hang onto Murray's fired-in goal, as they looked staunch and disciplined at the back. The Gills started the brighter and Danny Spiller had a fifth-minute goal ruled out. Losing Basso with a dislocated finger was a blow as Phillips let in a soft leveller.											

No	Date		Att	Pos	Pt	F-A	H-T	Scorers, Times, and Referees	SQUAD	NUMBERS	IN	USE								subs used
24	H	ROTHERHAM		20	W	3-1	1-1	Brooker 11, 77, Murray 48	Basso	Orr	Woodman	Noble	Heywood	Carey	Cotterill"	Savage*	Brooker	Russell	Murray^	Stewart/Wilkshire/Skuse
	28/12		12,510	*22*	26			*Murdock 26*	*Montgom'ry*	*Worrell*	*Robertson"*	*Gilchrist^*	*Murdock*	*Williamson*	*Mullin*	*Burton*	*Butler*	*McLaren*	*Keane**	*Hurst/Barker/Hoskins*
								Ref: G Sutton	Individual excellence, including much excellent headwork by the ungainly Savage, was the key to this victory, which kept up City's 100 per cent *Red 'N' White* nights record. The Millers more than played their part as City had to fight every inch of the way to achieve this success.											
25	A	YEOVIL		20	D	1-1	0-1	Heywood 51	Basso*	Orr	Woodman	Noble"	Heywood	Carey	Cotterill	Savage^	Brooker	Russell	Murray	Phillips/Stewart/Skuse
	31/12		*9,178*	*18*	27			*Poole 2*	*Collis*	*Amankwaah*	*Jones*	*Skiverton*	*Miles**	*Cohen*	*Terry*	*Jevons"*	*Harrold*	*Johnson*	*Poole^*	*Guyett/Gall/Bastianni*
								Ref: K Stroud	As in the previous away game, Basso, who pulled off some excellent saves, was in the wars again, this time being forced off after being briefly knocked out. Against a lively Yeovil side this was a rather lucky point for City, thanks to Heywood's glancing header from Russell's corner.											
26	H	WALSALL		20	W	3-0	2-0	Murray 10, 30, Wilkshire 88	Basso	Orr	Woodman	Noble	Heywood	Carey	Cotterill*	Savage	Brooker	Russell^	Murray	Wilkshire/Skuse
	2/1		12,652	*12*	30				*Murphy*	*Pead*	*Bennett*	*Gerrard*	*Westwood*	*Kinsella^*	*Leitao**	*Constable*	*Nicholls*	*Taylor K"*	*Harkness*	*Taylor D/Osborn/Standing*
								Ref: P Dowd	Murray, who has looked a new man since switching from the right flank, opened the scoring when he latched onto Russell's threaded pass and swept the ball over the advancing Joe Murphy into the Wedlock Stand net. He lashed in a magnificent second from Cotterill's hanging centre.											
27	H	SCUNTHORPE		20	D	1-1	0-1	Savage 62	Basso	Orr	Woodman	Noble	Heywood	Carey	Cotterill^	Savage"	Brooker	Russell*	Murray	Skuse/Wilkshire/Stewart
	14/1		11,692	*18*	31			*Keogh 5*	*Evans*	*Hinds*	*Rose*	*Crosby*	*Butler**	*Goodwin^*	*Taylor*	*Sharp*	*Keogh*	*MacKenzie*	*Beagrie"*	*Byrne/Sparrow/Torpey*
								Ref: P Miller	Despite a four-day break on the Algarve, City were unable to rouse themselves in this scrappy affair. Basso's misplaced clearance gifted the Iron the early lead, but the towering Savage was able to save City's blushes by heading in from Noble's free-kick for his first-ever senior goal.											
28	A	COLCHESTER		20	L	2-3	1-2	Murray 2, Stewart 90	Basso	Orr	Woodman	Noble	Heywood	Carey	Cotterill*	Savage^	Brooker	Skuse"	Murray	Brown/Stewart/Russell
	17/1		*4,022*	*2*	31			*Williams 27, Danns 45, 61*	*Davison*	*Duguid*	*White*	*Baldwin*	*Brown*	*Watson*	*Halwood"*	*Iwelumo*	*Williams**	*Danns^*	*Yeates*	*Garcia/Izzet/Thorpe*
								Ref: P Armstrong	Another poor display suggests that City are on the slide again. Despite Murray's deflected early opener, the Reds, against opponents who looked unworthy of their lofty position, were but a pale shadow of the side that swept opponents aside during their seven-match unbeaten run.											
29	A	BLACKPOOL		20	D	1-1	1-1	Brooker 26	Basso	Orr	Woodman	Noble	Heywood	Carey	Cotterill^	Savage*	Brooker	Russell"	Murray	Stewart/Skuse/Wilkshire
	21/1		*4,842*	*21*	32			*Murphy 5*	*Jones*	*Joseph*	*Wilcox*	*Clarke*	*Butler*	*Wood^*	*Donnelly**	*Parker"*	*Murphy*	*Southern*	*Morris*	*Wiles/Fox/Vernon*
								Ref: M Jones	Despite a powered equaliser from City's clever free-kick routine, Brooker again demonstrated need for a consistent goalscorer with a series of missed opportunities. After Basso's slip – on what must be one of the worst pitches in the league – gifted the opener, City were well in control.											
30	H	SWANSEA		19	W	1-0	1-0	Carey 45	Basso	Orr	Woodman	Noble*	Heywood	Carey	Cotterill	Savage^	Brooker	Russell	Murray	Skuse/**Fontaine**
	28/1		12,859	*4*	35				*Gueret*	*Iriekpen*	*Austin*	*Monk*	*Watt**	*Robinson*	*Forbes"*	*Fallon*	*Trundle*	*Martinez^*	*Williams !*	*Britton/Way/Knight*
								Ref: C Penton	City proved that they had the will to win as they battled to victory in this torrid affair, which brought the Swans seven bookings. Early on, Cotterill had his weak shot kicked off the line by Kevin Austin, but on the stroke of half-time Carey was able to prod in the close-range winner.											
31	A	BARNSLEY		20	L	0-2	0-1		Phillips	Smith J^	Woodman	Skuse	Heywood	Carey !	Cotterill*	Savage	**Andrew**	Russell	Murray	Stewart/Brown
	4/2		*8,092*	*4*	35			*Richards 27, 81p*	*Colgan*	*Hassell*	*H'kingb'tom*	*Kay*	*Reid^*	*Burns*	*Shuker**	*Hayes*	*Richards*	*Howard*	*Williams*	*Wright/Laight*
								Ref: N Miller	The fates conspire to make City quickly pay for their failure to secure a quality striker during the transfer window. They dominated this game, but Brooker's absence due to injury fully exposed their lack of punch. An unlucky day with goalkeeper Basso being injured in the warm-up.											
32	H	BRENTFORD		22	L	0-1	0-0		Basso	Orr	**Green**	Fontaine	Heywood	Noble	Murray*	Savage^	Brooker	Russell	Wilkshire"	Andrew/Stewart/Cotterill
	11/2		10,854	*4*	35			*Owusu 78*	*Nelson*	*O'Connor*	*Tillen*	*Sodje*	*Turner*	*Pratley*	*Mousinho^*	*Willock**	*Newman*	*Owusu*	*Tabb*	*Peters/Gayle*
								Ref: P Joslin	There is no rest for woeful City after this display as the squad are called in for Sunday training at the club's Abbots Leigh training ground. The Robins lacked invention and creativity in this surprisingly passionless affair, which Lloyd Owusu settled by hooking the ball in from a corner.											
33	A	SCUNTHORPE		18	W	2-0	1-0	Cotterill 32, Murray 79	Basso	Orr	Woodman	Noble	Fontaine	Carey	Brown^	Stewart*	Brooker"	Skuse	Murray	Cotterill/Wilkshire/Green
	14/2		***3,786***	*20*	38				*Evans*	*Byrne**	*Rose^*	*Foster*	*Hinds*	*MacKenzie*	*Taylor*	*Johnson*	*Sharp*	*Goodwin**	*Sparrow*	*Stanton/Williams/Torpey*
								Ref: K Hill	Stewart's limping out of the action after just 22 minutes set up City's vital win. His replacement profited from a comedy of errors in the Iron's area to sweep the ball in from close range. Murray left a forest of claret and blue shirts standing as he raced through to steer in City's second.											
34	A	BRADFORD C		16	D	1-1	1-0	Brooker 16	Basso	Orr	Woodman	Noble	Fontaine	Carey	Brown^	Cotterill	Brooker	Skuse*	Murray"	Russell/W'ksh/**McCammon**
	18/2		*7,917*	*12*	39			*Wetherall 52*	*Ricketts*	*Holloway*	*Bower*	*Stewart*	*Wetherall*	*Penford*	*Petta**	*Cadamarteri*	*Windass*	*B-Wilkinson*	*Emanuel*	*Colbeck*
								Ref: M Jones	City had the better of the game but, apart from Brooker's right-footed 20-yarder, failed to turn their possession into goals. Indeed, after David Wetherall had headed the Bantams' leveller, they had to be thankful for Basso's wonder save for getting away from Valley Parade with a point.											

No	Venue	Opponent	Pos	Res	F-A	H-T	Scorers, Times, Referee	1	2	3	4	5	6	7	8	9	10	11	Subs used
35	H	BOURNEMOUTH	13	W	3-1	1-1	McCammon 7, Brooker 56, 64	Basso	Orr	Woodman	Noble"	Fontaine	Carey	Cotterill	McCam'on^	Brooker	Skuse*	Murray	Russell/Savage/Brown
26/2		11,058	*15*	42			*Hayter 45*	*Stewart*	*Purches*	*Hart*	*Brown*	*Young*	*Browning*	*Cooke*	*Fletcher*	*Hayter*	*Rix**	*Foley*	*Griffiths*
							Ref: M Fletcher	City who had squandered five good chances looked to have paid the price when James Hayter's levelled for the visitors with a magnificent 35-yarder into the Wedlock net right on the interval. Fortunately Brooker's shot took a huge deflection off Neil Young to put City back in charge.											
36	H	NOTT'M FOREST	13	D	1-1	0-0	Russell 78	Basso	Orr^	Woodman	Russell	Fontaine	Carey	Cotterill	Savage*	Brooker	Skuse	Murray	Stewart/Wilkshire
4/3		14,397	*10*	43			*Perch 66*	*Pederson*	*Curtis*	*Bennett*	*Breckin*	*Morgan*	*Perch*	*Southall**	*Tyson*	*Holt, Grant*	*Holt, Gary*	*Commons^*	*Clingan/Bastians"/Thompson*
							Ref: A Penn	With the new ruling, many goals have been allowed this season when others rather than the scorer have been offside, but not in this game when Brooker timed his run perfectly to powerful head in Orr's 25th-minute cross. Russell's 25-yarder saved City a point in this high-tempo affair.											
37	A	MK DONS	12	W	1-0	1-0	Brooker 4	Basso	Orr	Woodman	Russell	Fontaine	Carey	Cotterill*	Savage"	Brooker	Skuse	Murray^	Wilkshire/Keogh/Noble
10/3		*6,855*	*24*	46				*Batista*	*McClenahan*	*Lewington*	*Morgan*	*Chorley*	*Harding"*	*Small^*	*McLeod*	*Taylor**	*Edds*	*Morais*	*Platt/Rizzo/Kamara*
							Ref: M Thorpe	With the Dons due to move into their new home next season, City made sure that their final visit to the National Hockey Stadium was marked with a win. While indebted to Basso's display after the break, in the first half they should have scored more than Brooker's left-footed effort.											
38	H	GILLINGHAM	12	W	**6-0**	3-0	Brooker 11, Carey 18, 50, Skuse 45p, [Wilkshire 67, McCammon 87]	Basso	Orr	Woodman	Russell	Fontaine	Carey	Cotterill^	Savage"	Brooker	Skuse	Murray*	Wilk're/Andrew/McCammon
18/3		10,932	*21*	49				*Brown*	*Clohessy*	*Johnson !*	*Cox*	*Hope"*	*Crofts*	*Spiller*	*Harris**	*Mulligan*	*Poulton*	*Black^*	*Jackman/Jarvis/B-Sancho*
							Ref: C Penton	Relegation-threatened Gillingham looked a poor side, but they were not helped by a rather harsh sending-off. The lacklustre Cotterill, who managed to put in an inept shot as he was tackled by Leon Johnson, was reprieved by the referee's spot-kick award and the defender's red card.											
39	A	ROTHERHAM	13	L	1-3	0-2	Skuse 80	Basso	Orr	Woodman	Russell	Fontaine	Carey	Cotterill"	Savage^	Brooker	Skuse	Murray*	Wilk're/McCammon/Brown
25/3		*6,682*	*20*	49			*Forte 27, 47, Shaw 39*	*Montg'mery*	*Hurst*	*Robertson*	*Murdock*	*Barker*	*Quinn*	*Mullin*	*Williamson*	*Forte*	*McLaren**	*Keane*	*Shaw*
							Ref: P Miller	In being set a target to win their final eight games, it was typical of City to fall at the first hurdle. Against opponents given a stay of execution from their financial problems a few days ago, City were not at the races. McCammon's knockdown allowed Skuse to net City's consolation.											
40	H	YEOVIL	11	W	2-1	2-0	Orr 12, McCammon 21	Basso	Orr	Woodman	Noble^	Fontaine	Carey	Brown"	McCammon	Brooker*	Skuse	Wilkshire	Cotterill/Russell/Savage
1/4		**15,889**	*19*	52			*Davies 64*	*Collis*	*Am'kwaah"*	*Miles**	*Lockwood*	*Guyett*	*Rocastle*	*Jones*	*Harrold^*	*Davies*	*Cohen*	*Terry*	*Poole/Jevons/Lindegaard*
							Ref: G Salisbury	Orr's cross-cum-shot from wide out right looped high over the keeper into the Atyeo Stand net to get City off to a flier in this West Country derby. It looked all too easy when McCammon headed in the second, but Yeovil made City sweat with their determined second-half display.											
41	A	WALSALL	10	W	3-0	1-0	Cotterill 44, Russell 51p, Keogh 90	Basso	Orr	Woodman	Noble	Fontaine^	Carey	Brown"	McCammon	Cotterill	Skuse*	Wilkshire	Russell/Keogh/Savage
8/4		*5,402*	*23*	55				*Oakes*	*Wright*	*Fox*	*Leary*	*Roper*	*Gerrard*	*Devlin*	*Claridge*	*Constable^*	*Mills**	*Keates*	*Demontagnac/Osborn*
							Ref: C Webster	City were always in charge of this one-way contest against opponents who look destined for relegation. Welsh international Cotterill, playing in place of the injured Brooker, always had far too much pace for the Walsall rearguard and he opened the scoring by guiding in a fine shot.											
42	A	HARTLEPOOL	9	W	2-1	2-0	Noble 13, Russell 38	Basso	Orr	Woodman	Noble	Fontaine	Carey	Brown*	McCam'on^	Cotterill	Russell	Wilkshire	Keogh/Savage
15/4		*5,039*	*21*	58			*Williams 84*	*Ko'st'poulos*	*Barron*	*Robertson"*	*Turnbull*	*Nelson*	*Clark*	*Butler*	*Boyd^*	*Williams*	*Bullock**	*Humphreys*	*Robson/Brown/Proctor*
							Ref: N Swarbrick	After Noble had got City off to a good start with a left-footed shot that went in off the far post, chances were spurned until Russell was able to pick his spot from McCammon's low cross. Eifion Williams bundled the ball in for Hartlepool to make things hot for City in the closing stages.											
43	H	OLDHAM	9	W	2-1	0-1	Russell 57p, Brooker 76	Basso	Orr	Woodman	Noble	Fontaine	Carey	Brown	M'Cam'on^	Cotterill	Russell	Wilkshire*	Brooker/Savage
17/4		12,779	*8*	61			*Beckett 45*	*Grant*	*Forbes*	*Edwards*	*Haining*	*Branston*	*Wellens*	*Warne**	*Porter*	*Beckett*	*Hughes*	*Eyres^*	*Taylor/Butcher*
							Ref: P Crossley	City paid the price for their poor first-half display when, in added time, Luke Beckett headed the visitors in front from a David Eyres corner. Following the interval Guy Branston's handling offence brought City their spot-kick leveller, despite Grant saving Russell's initial attempt.											
44	A	TRANMERE	8	W	3-0	2-0	Brooker 17, McCammon 34, [Woodman 88p]	Basso	Orr	Woodman	Noble	Fontaine	Carey	Cotterill	McCammon	Brooker^	Russell	Brown*	Wilkshire/Skuse
22/4		*6,288*	*19*	64				*Murray*	*Raven*	*Roberts*	*Sharps*	*Goodison*	*McAteer !*	*Jennings*	*Greenacre*	*Davies**	*Facey*	*Harrison*	*Tremarco*
							Ref: P Melin	Amazingly, with other results going their way, City find themselves in with a chance of making the play-offs after this well-deserved success. Headers by Brooker and McCammon have City cruising before Jason McAteer's 36th-minute sending-off for use of an elbow on McCammon.											
45	H	SWINDON	9	D	1-1	0-0	Cotterill 68	Basso	Orr^	Woodman	Noble	Fontaine	Carey	Cotterill	M'Cammon"	Brooker	Russell	Brown*	Wilkshire/Skuse/Savage
29/4		15,632	*23*	65			*Brown 49*	*Evans*	*Ifil*	*O'Hanlon*	*Diagouraga^*	*Jenkins**	*Comyn-Platt*	*Smith*	*McPhee*	*Jutkiewicz*	*Whalley"*	*Brown*	*Gurney/Pook/Cureton*
							Ref: K Hill	The usual City scenario as they disappoint a large crowd with a poor display to drop out of play-off contention. Their hopes are not helped, a few minutes before the close, by Cotterill's crass dive in the penalty area at the Atyeo End when it would have been far easier to have scored.											
46	A	SOUTHEND	9	L	0-1	0-0		Basso^	Orr	Woodman	Noble	Keogh	Carey	Cotterill	M'Cammon*	Brooker	Skuse	Wilkshire"	M-Williams/**Abbey**/Brown
6/5		*11,387*	*1*	65			*Gray 87*	*Flahaven*	*Jupp*	*Wilson*	*Guttridge^*	*Hunt*	*Barrett*	*Bradbury*	*Goater"*	*Eastwood*	*Maher*	*Gower**	*Cole/Bentley/Gray*
	Home	Away					Ref: K Stroud	Having dominated the proceedings, the blow of losing to a late deflected goal was bad enough for the City players, but being made to witness Southend's Championship celebrations was doubly painful. Nevertheless, a fine ending to the career of former City favourite Shaun Goater.											
Average	11,725	7,471																	

Carling Cup			F-A	H-T	Scorers, Times, and Referees	SQUAD	NUMBERS	IN	USE								subs used
1 H BARNET	17	L	2-4	1-1	Golbourne 14, Bridges 64	Phillips	Carey	Golbourne	Fortune	Partridge*	Skuse	Murray	Stewart	Brooker	**Grant**	Smith G	Bridges
23/8	3,383 *2:1*				*Lee 16, 53, Bailey 58, Roache 82*	*Flitney*	*Hendon*	*Gross*	*King*	*Charles*	*Lee*	*Strevens*	*Bowditch^*	*Grazioli**	*Bailey*	*Graham*	*Roache/Norville*
					Ref: P Armstrong	There have been some woeful nights at the Gate down the years, but this display, against last season's Conference winners, took the biscuit as far as City fans are concerned. Defensively City were all over the place with Nicky Bailey running them ragged and scoring a really fine goal.											

FA Cup																	
1 H NOTTS CO	22	L	0-2	0-1		Phillips	Orr	Carey^	Youga	Partridge"	Skuse !	Murray	Quinn	Brooker	Wilkshire	Cotterill*	Gillespie/Heywood/Russell
5/11	4,221 *2:12*				*Tann 45, Baudet 68*	*Pilkington*	*Tann*	*Pipe*	*Edwards*	*Baudet*	*Long*	*McMahon^*	*Hurst*	*Scoffham**	*Gill*	*Ullathorne*	*White/O'Callaghan*
					Ref: A Woolmer	Exactly 45 years on from depositing eleven goals in Chichester's net, City rarely looked like scoring in this Guy Fawkes Day clash. Again they let down their fans with a sorry display. Against so-called inferior opposition, they lacked both the skill as well as the necessary commitment.											

	P	W	D	L	F	A	W	D	L	F	A	Pts
		Home					Away					
1 Southend	46	13	6	4	37	16	10	7	6	35	27	82
2 Colchester	46	15	4	4	39	21	7	9	7	19	19	79
3 Brentford	46	10	8	5	35	23	10	8	5	37	29	76
4 Huddersfield	46	13	6	4	40	25	6	10	7	32	34	73
5 Barnsley *	46	11	11	1	37	19	7	7	9	25	25	72
6 Swansea	46	11	9	3	42	23	7	8	8	36	32	71
7 Nott'm Forest	46	14	5	4	40	15	5	7	11	27	37	69
8 Doncaster	46	11	6	6	30	19	9	3	11	25	32	69
9 BRISTOL CITY	46	11	7	5	38	22	7	4	12	28	40	65
10 Oldham	46	12	4	7	32	24	6	7	10	26	36	65
11 Bradford C	46	8	9	6	28	25	6	10	7	23	24	61
12 Scunthorpe	46	8	8	7	36	33	7	7	9	32	40	60
13 Port Vale	46	10	5	8	30	26	6	7	10	19	28	60
14 Gillingham	46	13	4	6	31	21	3	8	12	19	43	60
15 Yeovil	46	8	8	7	27	24	7	3	13	27	38	56
16 Chesterfield	46	6	7	10	31	37	8	7	8	32	36	56
17 Bournemouth	46	7	11	5	25	20	5	8	10	24	33	55
18 Tranmere	46	7	8	8	32	30	6	7	10	18	22	54
19 Blackpool	46	9	8	6	33	27	3	9	11	23	37	53
20 Rotherham	46	7	9	7	31	26	5	7	11	21	36	52
21 Hartlepool	46	6	10	7	28	30	5	7	11	16	29	50
22 MK Dons	46	8	8	7	28	25	4	6	13	17	41	50
23 Swindon	46	9	5	9	31	31	2	10	11	15	34	48
24 Walsall	46	7	7	9	27	34	4	7	12	20	36	47
	1104	234	173	145	788	596	145	173	234	596	788	1483

* promoted after play-offs

Odds & ends

Double wins: (3) Port Vale, Tranmere Rovers, Walsall.
Double losses: (2) Chesterfield, Southend United.

Won from behind: (1) Oldham Athletic (h).
Lost from in front: (4) Nottingham Forest (a), Swindon Town (a), Chesterfield (h), Colchester United (a).

High spots: Celebrating Gary Johnson's appointment as manager by winning 3-2 at Griffin Park on 24 September.
Dave Cotterill's brilliant home goal against Huddersfield, stopping City's club record run of successive defeats reaching double figures.
Beating Gillingham 6-0 at Ashton Gate on 18 March.
The pleasure, despite the defeat, of being part of Southend's promotion celebration at Roots Hall on 6 May which coincided with the retirement of the popular ex-City striker Shaun Goater.
The recovery from looking like relegation certainties shortly before Christmas to almost qualifying for the play-offs.
Adriano Basso's displays between the sticks.
The Ashton Gate pitch being voted the best in League One.

Low spots: The defensive shambles at Swansea on 10 September.
Louis Carey's unfortunate own-goal against Bradford City that brought an undeserved defeat on 6 December.
Succumbing to Barnet in both the Coca-Cola Cup and the LDV Trophy.
Losing to Notts County in the FA Cup to complete City's tale of woe against lower League opposition in all the knockout competitions.
Losing at home to Brentford on 11 February.
The decision to put the East Stand project on hold, choosing to revamp the Williams Stand instead.

AGM (Exhibition Hall, Dolman Stand, Ashton Gate, 30 November 2006).
Loss: £1,176,139. Season Ticket Sales (No): 7,700.

Player of the Year: Steve Booker.
Ever-presents: (0).
Hat-tricks: (0).
Leading-scorer: Overall: Steve Booker (16). League: Steve Booker (16).

	Appearances Lge	*Sub*	LC	*Sub*	FAC	*Sub*	Goals Lge	LC	FAC	Tot
Abbey, Nathan		*1*								
Andrew, Calvin (loan)	1	*2*								
Basso, Adriano	29									
Bridges, Michael	4	*7*		*1*				1		1
Brooker, Steve	34	*1*	1		1		16			16
Brown, Scott	23	*6*					1			1
Carey, Louis	38		1		1		3			3
Cotterill, Dave	37	*8*			1		7			7
Fortune, Clayton	4	*2*	1							
Fontaine, Liam (loan)	14	*1*								
Gillespie, Steven	3	*1*				*1*	1			1
Golbourne, Scott	4	*1*	1					1		1
Grant, Tony			1							
Green, Adam (loan)	1	*1*								
Heywood, Matt	22	*2*				*1*	2			2
Joseph, Marc (loan)	3									
Keogh, Richard	4	*6*					1			1
McCammon, Mark(ln)	8	*3*					4			4
Madjo, Guy	1	*4*						1		1
Murray, Scott	31	*6*	1		1		10	1		11
M-Williams, Jennison		*1*								
Noble, Dave	23	*1*					1			1
Orr, Bradley	35	*3*			1		1			1
Partridge, Dave	11		1		1					
Phillips, Steve	17	*2*	1		1					
Quinn, James (loan)	2	*1*			1		1			1
Russell, Alex	21	*6*				*1*	4			4
Sankofa, Osei (loan)	8									
Savage, Bas	15	*8*					1			1
Skuse, Cole	29	*9*	1		1		2			2
Smith, Grant	4	*7*	1							
Smith, Jamie	4	*2*								
Stewart, Marcus	16	*11*	1				5			5
Wiltshire, Luke	20	*16*			1		5			5
Woodman, Craig	36	*1*					1			1
Youga, Kelly (loan)	4				1					
36 players used	**506**	***120***	**11**	***1***	**11**	***3***	**66**	**4**		**70**

No	Date		Att	Pos	Pt	F-A	H-T	Scorers, Times, and Referees	1	2	3	4	5	6	7	8	9	10	11	subs used
1	H	SCUNTHORPE			W	1-0	0-0	Showunmi 69	Basso	Orr	Woodman	Carey	Fountaine	Skuse	Cotterill"	**Jevons^**	Brooker	Noble	Murray*	**Sh'nmi/McCombe**/Brown
	5/8		13,268		3				*Murphy*	*Hinds*	*Ridley*	*Crosby*	*Foster*	*Baraclough"*	*Mulligan^*	*Keogh*	*Sharp*	*Goodwin**	*Sparrow*	*Taylor/Torpey !/MacKenzie*
								Ref: R Lewis	Whilst this hard-earned win was welcome for a City side playing in red and white again after five years of all red, it is hard to see where the goals are going to come from this season. As it was, Showunmi looked offside when he ran through to round the keeper and tuck the ball away.											
2	A	BRADFORD C			L	1-2	1-2	Murray 2	Basso	Orr	Woodman	Carey	Fontaine	Skuse"	Cotterill*	Showunmi	Brooker	Noble	Murray^	Jevons/McCombe/Russell
	8/8		*7,356*		3			*Windass 41, Graham 42*	*Ricketts*	*Edghill*	*Parker*	*Wetherall**	*Bower*	*Schumacher*	*Johnson*	*Graham*	*Windass*	*B-Wilkinson*	*Holmes*	*Doyle*
								Ref: E Ilderton	Following Murray's headed opener, City's lightweight attack fail to add to their score, despite a host of chances. A minute's madness turns this game on its head. After Dean Windass levelled from a quickly taken free-kick, Cotterill carelessly lost possession of the ball from the re-start.											
3	A	HUDDERSFIELD		14	L	1-2	0-0	Jevons 48	Basso	Orr	Woodman	Carey	Fontaine	Skuse	Murray"	Jevons*	Brooker	Noble	**McAl'ster^**	Johnson/Sh'wunmi/Cotterill
	12/8		*10,492*	*6*	3			*Beckett 63, Abbott 90*	*Glennon*	*Holdsworth*	*Adams*	*Clarke*	*Mirfin*	*Hudson*	*T-Fletcher^*	*Abbott*	*Beckett"*	*Worthington*	*Brandon**	*Schofield/Collins/McAliskey*
								Ref: P Taylor	Yet again the City are off the pace as they fail to capitalise on an excellent strike by the grounded Jevons. Their season is already showing signs of disintegration as they slump from promotion favourites to chumps. Sleepy Woodman took too long to clear Abbot's shot at the death.											
4	H	BLACKPOOL		20	L	2-4	1-1	Showunmi 43, 64p *[Graham 89]*	Basso	Orr"	Woodman	Carey	Fontaine	Noble	Skuse*	Jevons^	Brooker	Johnson	Showunmi	Cotterill/M-Williams/Keogh
	19/8		10,630	*18*	3			*Vernon 27, Jackson 50, Parker 78,*	*Evans*	*Barker*	*Tierney^*	*Jackson*	*Evatt*	*Fox*	*Gillett*	*Morrell"*	*Vernon*	*Southern*	*Forbes**	*Parker/Joseph/Graham*
								Ref: M Russell	After this match the City boss took the stinging criticism from the fans on the chin and admitted it was fully deserved. It was embarrassing, as City's team of fancied promotion chasers was ripped apart by opponents who arrived without a point or a goal from their three previous games.											
5	A	NORTHAMPTON		13	W	3-1	1-1	Jevons 32p, Brooker 71, Cotterill 90p	Basso	Orr	McAllister	Carey	Fontaine	Noble	Cotterill	Jevons^	Brooker"	Johnson	Showunmi*	Keogh/M-Wiiliams/Brown
	29/8		*4,919*	*21*	6			*Kirk 18*	*Bunn*	*Chambers**	*Doig*	*Crowe*	*Dyche*	*Burnell*	*Taylor"*	*Quinn^*	*Kirk*	*Aiston*	*Holt*	*Jess/Gilligan/Bojic*
								Ref: M Jones	Despite Orr's sending off for head-butting teammate Carey almost on half-time, ten-man City clinched a well-merited victory in front of the Sky TV cameras. Welsh international Cotterill set up City's penalty equaliser, being brought down after weaving his way past three defenders.											
6	H	BRIGHTON		8	W	1-0	1-0	Brown 21	Basso	Keogh	McAllister	Carey	Fontaine	Noble"	Murray	Jevons*	M-Williams	Johnson^	Brown	Skuse/Russell/Woodman
	4/9		10,552	*16*	9				*Kulpers*	*Reid*	*El-Abd*	*Santos*	*Lynch**	*Hammond*	*Frutos^*	*Loft"*	*Revell*	*Carpenter*	*Cox*	*Rents/Robinson/Stokes*
								Ref: C Foy	With Friday's shock jailing of Brooker, Orr and Partridge following last October's pub brawl and the £2 million transfer of Cotterill to Wigan Athletic, a depleted City side did well to win this fixture. A Jevons shot was brilliantly parried, but Brown pounced to sweep the ball home.											
7	A	TRANMERE		8	L	0-1	0-0		Basso	Keogh"	McAllister*	Carey	Fontaine	Noble	Murray^	Jevons	M-Williams	Johnson	Brown	McCombe/Skuse/Woodman
	8/9		*8,111*	*2*	9			*Mullin 84*	*Ward*	*Stockdale*	*Sherriff*	*Goodison*	*McCready*	*Mullin*	*Shuker*	*Greenacre*	*Taylor*	*McLaren*	*Ellison*	
								Ref: P Robinson	Friday night football again on the Wirral made it like old times at Prenton Park, where City are denied by midfielder John Mullin's superb late volley. A fine defensive performance by the visitors, but they could have few complaints however as their attack rarely looked likely to score.											
8	H	ORIENT		7	W	2-1	2-0	Jevons 19, Showunmi 44	Basso	Keogh	McAllister	Carey	McCombe	Noble*	Brown	Jevons"	Showunmi^	Johnson	M-Williams	Russell/Skuse/Fontaine
	12/9		9,726	*21*	12			*Lockwood 65p*	*Garner*	*Miller*	*Lockwood*	*Mackie"*	*Tann*	*Chambers*	*Corden**	*Connor^*	*Alexander*	*Simpson*	*Keith*	*Tudor/Ibehre/Saah*
								Ref: R Beeby	City just about deserved to win this high-tempo game, which was well refereed by Richard Beeby of Northamptonshire. A spectacular diving header got City off to a good start, but it needed a couple of great second-half saves from Basso to make sure that the game didn't slip away.											
9	H	CHESTERFIELD		3	W	3-1	2-1	Carey 4, Brown 40, Myrie-Williams 51	Basso	Keogh	McAllister	Carey	McCombe	Russell	Brown*	Jevons	Brooker^	Johnson	M-Williams	Murray/Woodman
	16/9		10,398	*17*	15			*Larkin 21*	*Roche*	*Bailey*	*Picken*	*Downes*	*Hazell*	*Niven*	*Hall*	*Larkin^*	*Allison**	*Allott*	*Hurst*	*Folan/Smith*
								Ref: K Stroud	Twice in each half the woodwork came to Chesterfield's rescue, but despite Colin Larkin's tapped in leveller there was no way that the visitors could resist City's cultured display. Carey headed in the opener and Myrie-Williams tied up City's success with the coolest of lobs over Roche.											
10	A	PORT VALE		3	W	2-0	1-0	Brown 45, Jevons 76	Basso	Keogh	McAllister	Carey	McCombe	Russell	Brown^	Jevons"	Brooker*	Johnson	M-Williams	Murray/Skuse/Fontaine
	23/9		*5,295*	*7*	18				*Goodlad*	*Talbot*	*McGregor*	*Pilkington*	*Walker*	*Harsley^*	*Whitaker*	*Sodje**	*Constantine*	*Sonner"*	*Smith*	*Moore/Husb'nds/Humphr'ys*
								Ref: E Ilderton	Brown's venomous 25-yard curler into the top right-hand corner of Mark Goodlad's goal in first-half injury-time set up this well-deserved win at Vale Park. Jevons, though, was fortunate with his strike, as he knew little about George Pilkington's clearance that ricocheted off of his boot.											
11	A	BOURNEMOUTH		3	W	1-0	0-0	Jevons 70	Basso	Keogh	McAllister	Carey	McCombe	Russell	Murray	Jevons	M-Williams*	Johnson	Brown"	Skuse^/Noble/Orr
	26/9		*6,484*	*14*	21				*Stewart*	*Broadhurst*	*Cummings*	*Young*	*Gowling*	*Anderton^*	*Purches*	*Fletcher**	*Hayter*	*Cooper*	*Foley"*	*Best/Hollands/Ainsworth*
								Ref: G Hegley	With City denied a spot-kick soon after the break when Murray's cross was handled by Stephen Purches, and Brown hitting the woodwork a minute later, the travelling fans feared the worst. Fortunately, Jevons got on the end of Johnson's cross to grab the points with a diving header.											

No	Venue	Date	Opponent	Att	Pos	Res	F-A	H-T	Scorers, Times, Referees	1	2	3	4	5	6	7	8	9	10	11	Subs used
12	H		OLDHAM		3	D	0-0	0-0		Basso	Keogh	McAllister	Carey	McCombe	Russell*	Brown	Jevons	Showunmi^	Johnson	Murray	Skuse/M-Williams
		30/9		11,656	*9*	22				*Poglicami*	*Eardley*	*Charlton*	*Haning*	*Stam*	*McDonald*	*Liddell*	*Warne**	*Porter*	*Wellens*	*Taylor*	*Grabban*
									Ref: J Singh	The whistle-happy referee compounded his poor performance by waiting until the interval to change his black kit which clashed with Oldham's dark blue. A draw was a fair result, but it took Basso's late wonder save at the Wedlock end to ensure that City held on to a share of the spoils.											
13	A		BRENTFORD		2	D	1-1	1-0	McCombe 41	Basso	Orr	McAllister	Keogh	McCombe	Russell*	Brown	Jevons	Showunmi	Johnson"	M-Williams^	Skuse/Noble/Murray
		7/10		*6,740*	*16*	23			*O'Connor 68p*	*Nelson*	*O'Connor*	*Frampton*	*Griffiths*	*Heywood*	*Pinault*	*Brooker^*	*Kuffour*	*Wijnhard"*	*Skulason*	*Rhodes**	*Tillen/Peters/Moore*
									Ref: D Whitestone	Against opponents wrecked by injuries, a succession of misplaced passes produced an impoverished City display. Amazingly they were a goal to the good at the break and on top the league, but they were fortunate right at the finish when Jo Kuffour's free header skimmed by the post.											
14	H		CREWE		2	W	2-1	2-0	Murray 26, Brown 32	Basso	Orr	McAllister	Carey	McCombe	Johnson	Murray^	Jevons	M-Williams	Skuse	Brown*	**Wright**/Fontaine
		14/10		11,899	*10*	26			*Varney 59*	*Williams*	*Baudet*	*Ostemobor*	*O'Donnell**	*Cox*	*Roberts !*	*O'Connor^*	*Varney*	*Lowe*	*Vaughan*	*Maynard*	*Jack/Rix*
									Ref: P Crossley	Despite falling behind to Murray's header and Brown's close in side-footer, after Myrie-Williams produced an electrifying turn of pace down the left, the skilful Crewe side gave City a real test. Unlucky to have Gary Roberts sent off on 69 minutes, Crewe often had City on the run.											
15	A		NOTT'M FOREST		3	L	0-1	0-1		Basso	Orr*	Woodman	Carey	McCombe	Johnson	Murray	Jevons"	M-Williams	Skuse	Brown^	Keogh/Wright/Fontaine
		21/10		*23,466*	*1*	26			*Southall 9*	*Smith*	*Morgan*	*Cullip*	*Perch*	*Breckin*	*Clingan*	*Southall*	*Commons^*	*Agogo**	*Harris"*	*Curtis*	*Holt/Bennett/Thompson*
									Ref: M Halsey	City's attack is found wanting in this vital top-of-the-table clash. Falling behind to Nicky's Southall's free-kick, it wasn't until the second half that they woke up. Towards the finish it was like the siege of the Alamo as Forest were pressed back, but City were unable to break through.											
16	H		DONCASTER		2	W	1-0	1-0	Carey 37	Basso	Keogh	McAllister	Carey	McCombe	Johnson	Murray	Jevons"	M-Williams	Skuse^	Brown*	Wright/Russell/**Corr**
		23/10		11,909	*18*	29				*Smith*	*Roberts S*	*Lee"*	*Green*	*Lockwood*	*McDaid**	*O'Connor*	*Forte*	*Guy^*	*Stock*	*Roberts G*	*Price/Coppinger/Heffernan*
									Ref: P Walton	Despite Carey's fierce shot at the Wedlock end, that found the net off the underside of the bar, City should have been made to pay for failing to inject any tempo into their play. As it was, Basso turned in a great display to keep out the vibrant visitors who overran them after the interval.											
17	A		YEOVIL		4	L	1-2	0-0	Jevons 90p	Basso	Keogh	McAllister	Carey !	McCombe	Johnson	Wright*	Jevons	Corr	Skuse	M-Williams	Noble
		4/11		*9,009*	*2*	29			*Davies 73, Gray 88*	*Mildenhall*	*Lynch*	*Jones"*	*Forbes*	*Skiverton**	*Barry*	*Brittain*	*Morris^*	*Gray*	*Terry*	*Cohen*	*Guyett !/Tonkin/Davies*
									Ref: A Marriner/S Tomlinson	City fail to profit by their refusal for Yeovil to play on-loan Marcus Stewart. Despite a double sending-off just before the break, it wasn't until the change of referee - the official pulling a muscle on 59 minutes - that matters livened up. Two goals come in the four minutes of added time.											
18	H		GILLINGHAM		3	W	3-1	1-1	Keogh 28, Showunmi 76, Murray 89	Basso	Keogh	McAllister	Fontaine	McCombe	Russell	Skuse	Showunmi^	M-Williams*	Johnson	Jevons"	Murray/Corr/Orr
		18/11		11,823	*13*	32			*Flynn 15*	*Jack*	*Chorley*	*Cox*	*Crofts*	*Sancho**	*Flynn*	*Jupp*	*Jarvis*	*Mulligan*	*Bentley*	*Easton^*	*Ndumbu-Nsungu/Savage*
									Ref: D Gallagher	Despite Showunmi's return, City's attack still lacks physical presence in the box. It took Keogh's stunning volley from the edge of the area to wake up a City side who were trailing to Michael Flynn's powerful 20-yarder. Showunmi's angled drive and Murray's tap-in tied up the points.											
19	A		SWANSEA		4	D	0-0	0-0		Basso	Keogh	McAllister	Fontaine	McCombe	Russell^	Skuse	Jevons*	Brooker"	Johnson	Showunmi	M-Wil'ms/Murray/Woodman
		26/11		*15,531*	*6*	33				*Gueret*	*Amankw'h^*	*Painter*	*Austin*	*Lawrence**	*Tate*	*Britton*	*Trundle*	*Fallon"*	*Praley*	*Robinson*	*Iriekpen/Craney/Akinfenwa*
									Ref: P Taylor	City fail to gain revenge for last season's mauling at the Liberty Stadium, but at least they come away with a point. City should have been two up at the break, but in the second half they were indebted to McCombe's rock-solid display and Basso's great save from Trundle at the death.											
20	H		CARLISLE		3	W	1-0	0-0	Showunmi 85	Basso	Keogh"	Fontaine	Carey	McCombe	Russell	Skuse	Jevons	Showunmi	Johnson^	M-Williams*	Brooker/Murray/Orr
		5/12		10,792	*8*	36				*Westwood*	*Murphy*	*Aranalde*	*Gray"*	*Livesey*	*Lumsdon^*	*Gall*	*Billy*	*Hawley*	*Thirlwell*	*Harper**	*Hackney/Holmes/Grand*
									Ref: D McDermid	Whilst City improved on a dire first-half display, Showunmi's diving-header scarcely deserved to win them this encounter. The Cumbrians were much the brighter team and Kevin Harper was a real thorn in City's side until being rather inexplicably substituted in the 74th minute.											
21	A		ROTHERHAM		3	D	1-1	0-0	Murray 72	Basso	Keogh	McAllister	Fontaine	McCombe	Russell	Murray	Jevons	Showunmi	Skuse	Brown*	Brooker
		9/12		*4,862*	*19*	37			*Facey 53*	*Cutler*	*Worrell*	*Robertson*	*Sharps*	*Mills*	*Cochrane*	*Partridge*	*Hoskins*	*Facey*	*Bopp*	*Woods*	
									Ref: P Walton	Murray's cracker earns a point at Millmoor, against opponents who would be in seventh place but for having ten points deducted for entering administration. Unfortunately it is not enough as both Nott'm Forest and Scunthorpe win away to leave City trailing even further in their wake.											
22	H		MILLWALL		2	W	1-0	1-0	Murray 1	Basso	Keogh	McAllister	Fontaine	McCombe	Russell	Murray^	Jevons*	Showunmi	Johnson	Skuse	Orr/Brooker
		16/12		12,067	*23*	40				*Pidgeley*	*Senda*	*Phillips*	*Lee"*	*Robinson*	*Dunne*	*Hackett*	*May^*	*Byfield*	*Elliott*	*Morais**	*Zebroski/Hubertz/Grant*
									Ref: R Shoebridge	With second place up for grabs, following Scunthorpe's defeat last night, Murray's angled-shot into the Wedlock end net after just 15 seconds got City off to a great start. Unfortunately they rarely looked like adding to the score, a situation which negative substitutions didn't improve.											
23	A		CHELTENHAM		3	D	2-2	0-2	Orr 53, McCombe 90	Basso	Orr	McAllister^	Fontaine*	McCombe	Russell	Murray	Jevons	Showunmi	Johnson	Skuse"	Carey/M-Williams/Brooker
		23/12		*5,863*	*21*	41			*O'Leary 36, Bird 38*	*Higgs*	*Wilson"*	*Armstrong**	*Townsend*	*Duff*	*O'Leary*	*Bird*	*Finnigan*	*Odejayi*	*Guinan^*	*Spencer*	*Gill/Gillespie/Caines*
									Ref: M Russell	City's dire first-half performance is redeemed by their determined display after the break. McCombe's fired in leveller in the second minute of added time salvages a point, but it is now six away League games without a win – a worrying statistic for a side with promotion aspirations.											

No	Date		Att	Pos	Pt	F-A	H-T	Scorers, Times, and Referees	1	2	3	4	5	6	7	8	9	10	11	subs used
24	H	BOURNEMOUTH		4	D	2-2	0-1	Murray 74, Johnson 79	Basso	Orr	McAllister	Carey	McCombe	Russell	Murray	Jevons	Brooker	Johnson	Skuse*	M-Williams
	26/12		13,848	*23*	42			*Pitman 16, Browning 48*	*Moss*	*Purches*	*Hart*	*Broadhurst**	*Young*	*Browning*	*Hollands*	*Hayter*	*Pitman^*	*Cooper*	*Gillett"*	*Gowling/Vokes/Connolly*
								Ref: J Singh	Against opponents seeking their first away win of the season, City almost meet their Waterloo. The shambolic homesters are given hope by Murray's angled shot into the Wedlock Stand net and Johnson's 20-yard straight drive through a crowded box salvages an unlikely point.											
25	H	PORT VALE		4	W	2-1	0-0	Brooker 69, Murray 76	Basso	Orr*	McAllister	Carey	McCombe	Russell^	Murray	Showunmi	Brooker"	Johnson	M-Williams	Jevons/Skuse/Keogh
	30/12		12,776	*11*	45			*Smith 68*	*Goodlad**	*Abbey*	*Miles A^*	*Fortune*	*Pilkington*	*Hulbert*	*Gardner*	*Sodje*	*Whitaker*	*Harsley*	*Smith*	*Anyon/McGregor"/Walker*
								Ref: R Lee	The monsoon conditions took their toll as early as the third minute when Vale keeper Mark Goodlad ruptured his Achilles tendon. His deputy Joe Anyon impressed on his League debut, but City spoilt his day by recovering well after falling behind to Jeff Smith's stunning free-kick.											
26	A	ORIENT		4	D	1-1	0-0	Johnson 68	Basso	Orr	McAllister	Carey*	McCombe	Skuse	Murray	Jevons	Showunmi	Johnson"	M-Williams^	Keogh/Brown/Noble
	1/1		*4,814*	*20*	46			*Lockwood 61p*	*Garner*	*Miller*	*Lockwood*	*Saah*	*Mackie*	*Corden"*	*Chambers*	*Walker**	*Alexander^*	*Easton*	*Guttridge*	*Ibhehre/Connor/Duncan*
								Ref: D Drysdale	Gary Johnson bemoans City's lack of consistency in this patchy display as yet again they fail to beat a club near the bottom of the table. It is to be hoped that the manager will address the club's consistent failure in the scoring stakes, which threatens to scupper their promotion hopes.											
27	H	TRANMERE		4	W	3-2	0-2	Show' 49, Jevons 58, M-Williams 68	Basso	Orr*	McAllister	Carey	McCombe	Skuse	Murray	Jevons^	Brooker	Johnson"	Showunmi	**Wilson**/M-Williams/Keogh
	13/1		10,822	*9*	49			Carey 25 (og), McLaren 44	*Hart*	*Sherriff*	*Tremarco*	*McCready*	*Goodison*	*Harrison*	*Shuker**	*Zola*	*Taylor*	*McLaren*	*Davies^*	*Ellison/Curran*
								Ref: P Melin	After Showunmi's header from almost on the goal-line got City up and running, an angled drive soon equalised matters. Sub Myrie-Williams completed the amazing fight-back by stroking in the winner with his first touch of the game when Brooker's shot rebounded off the woodwork.											
28	A	OLDHAM		2	W	3-0	2-0	Showunmi 9, McAllister 37, [Andrews 65]	Basso	Orr	McAllister	Carey	McCombe	Skuse"	Murray	Showunmi	Brooker*	Johnson^	Wilson	**Andrews**/Keogh/Noble
	20/1		*6,924*	*4*	52				*Pogliacomi*	*Eardley*	*Charlton*	*Gregan*	*Haining**	*Wellens*	*Liddell^*	*Warne*	*Porter*	*McDonald"*	*Taylor*	*Stam/Hall/Edwards*
								Ref: M Thorpe	This win against in-form Oldham, might well prove to be City's most important of the season. Keeper Les Pogliacomi was badly caught out by the 25-yard opener, but, following Simon Charlton's foul on Murray, he made amends by brilliantly saving Showunmi's 16th-minute penalty.											
29	H	CHELTENHAM		3	L	0-1	0-1		Basso	Orr	McAllister^	Carey	McCombe	Skuse	Murray	Andrews*	Showunmi	Johnson"	Wilson	**Betsy**/Noble/Russell
	31/1		12,227	*21*	52			*Spencer 44*	*Higgs*	*Gill*	*Armstrong*	*Duff*	*Townsend*	*Bird*	*Melligan^*	*Spencer"*	*Connor*	*Finnigan*	*Brown**	*Yao/Odejayi/Caines*
								Ref: R Styles	Against opponents seeking their first away win, it just had to happen as City's unbeaten run comes to grief just one short of equalling their 19-game post-war best. Cheltenham did well to overcome the early loss of Scott Brown with a broken leg, but in truth City were absolutely dire.											
30	A	SCUNTHORPE		4	L	0-1	0-1		Basso	Orr*	McAllister	Carey	McCombe	Skuse^	Murray	Betsy	Showunmi	Johnson	Wilson"	Andrews/Noble/Keogh
	5/2		*5,108*	*1*	52			*Sharp 41*	*Murphy*	*Byrne*	*Ridley*	*Foster*	*Crosby*	*Hinds*	*Taylor*	*Beckford*	*Sharp^*	*Goodwin*	*Hurst**	*Morris/Butler*
								Ref: R Booth	It was embarrassing that this game was shown live on Sky television as City failed to trouble the Scunthorpe keeper. Whist the rutted pitch was hardly conducive to good football, City's failure to take advantage of opponents decimated by injury and discipline problems was inexcusable.											
31	H	HUDDERSFIELD		5	D	1-1	0-0	Johnson 88	Basso !	Orr	McAllister^	Carey	McCombe	Skuse	Murray	Jevons"	Showunmi*	Johnson	Betsy	Andrews/**Weale**/Wilson
	10/2		11,636	*11*	53			*Taylor-Fletcher 51*	*Glennon*	*Holdsworth*	*Taylor*	*Sinclar*	*Mirfin*	*Collins*	*Young**	*Beckett*	*Booth*	*T-Fletcher*	*Schofield*	*Ahmed*
								Ref: P Armstrong	Johnson's fit of pique in failing to celebrate his 25-yard strike that salvaged an undeserved point is hardly likely to get the boo boys off his back. City's inept display so incensed one fan that he got near enough to Orr, one few players who didn't let his side down, to throw a punch.											
32	A	BLACKPOOL		3	W	1-0	0-0	Andrews 54	Basso	Keogh	Wilson	Fontaine	McCombe"	Johnson^	Russell*	Andrews	Brooker	Noble	Betsy	Murray/Orr/Woodman
	17/2		*6,696*	*8*	56				*Evans*	*Barker*	*Tierney"*	*Evatt*	*Jackson*	*Southern*	*Forbes^*	*Parker*	*Vernon*	*Fox**	*Hoolahan*	*Gillett/Burgess/Jorgensen*
								Ref: C Oliver	With three of their promotion rivals losing, this was a vital win for City at Bloomfield Road where they rode their luck at times. Andrews settled this incident-packed affair when he outpaced his man and swerved past the onrushing keeper before passing the ball into an empty net.											
33	A	BRIGHTON		4	W	2-0	1-0	Jevons 43, 84p	Basso	Orr	Fontaine	Carey	Keogh	Skuse	Wilson	Andrews*	Brooker^	Noble"	Betsy	Jevons/**Smith**/Woodman
	24/2		*6,280*	*12*	59				*Flinders*	*El-Abd*	*Mayo*	*O'Cearuill*	*Butters"*	*Bertin*	*Ward^*	*Gatting**	*Savage*	*Hammond*	*Cox*	*Revell/Fraser !/Elder*
								Ref: M Riley	Following their dire derby performance in the Johnson's Paint Trophy, City responded in the best possible fashion with this deserved success at the Withdean Stadium. An unstoppable volley opened City's account; this being doubled by a cheeky penalty when Wilson was scythed down.											
34	H	NORTHAMPTON		3	W	1-0	1-0	Betsy 19	Basso	Keogh	Wilson	Carey	McCombe	Johnson^	Betsy	Smith*	Brooker"	Noble	Skuse	Jevons/Fontaine/Andrews
	3/3		11,965	*17*	62				*Bunn*	*Crowe*	*Holt*	*Pearce*	*Hughes*	*Doig*	*Taylor^*	*Robertson**	*Deuchar*	*Aiston*	*Johnson*	*Kirk/Hunt*
								Ref: G Hegley	Incompetence ruled throughout the first half, with the City keeper clad all in an all-black kit almost identical to that worn by the visitors. A high-tempo performance deservedly brought the points, even though Wilson was unfortunate to have a 46th-minute strike ruled out for offside.											

35	A	CHESTERFIELD		2	W	3-1	3-0	Keogh 8, Johnson 36, Noble 45	Basso	Keogh	Wilson	Carey	McCombe	Johnson	Betsy	Smith"	Brooker*	Noble^	Skuse	Jevons/Orr/Showunmi
	7/3		*3,471*	*20*	65			*Allison 59*	*Roche*	*Critchell*	*Picken"*	*Grimaldi*	*Downes*	*Niven*	*Hall*	*Larkin**	*Allison*	*Allott*	*Holmes^*	*Jackson/Davies/Bailey*
								Ref: D Deadman	Fielding an unchanged side for the first time in five months and keeping the 3-5-2 formation that has served them so well of late, City turned in a super first-half show. After the break though ex-City man Wayne Allison, playing his 739th League game, pulled one back for the Spireites.											
36	H	BRENTFORD		2	W	1-0	1-0	Jevons 5p	Basso	Orr	Wilson	Fontaine	McCombe	Johnson	Betsy	Jevons"	Showunmi	Noble*	Skuse^	Russell/McAllister/Smith
	10/3		11,826	*23*	68				*Abbey*	*O'Connor*	*Tillen*	*Griffiths**	*Richards*	*Frampton*	*Ide*	*Shipperley*	*Taylor*	*Mousinho*	*Leary^*	*Keith/Heywood*
								Ref: P Taylor	This week it is only the City keeper's shorts that clash with the visitors' all-black kit. Strangely the referee doesn't enforce a half-time change, but he had probably gone to sleep as City serve up yet more poor home fare. They started well enough, but faded after their early spot-kick.											
37	H	BRADFORD C		2	L	2-3	1-1	Jevons 13, Russell 90	Basso	Orr	Wilson	Fontaine^	McCombe	Johnson"	Betsy	Jevons	Showunmi	Noble*	Skuse	Smith/Carey/Russell
	13/3		13,201	*19*	68			*Paynter 44, Ashikodi 49, Schumac' 55*	*Ricketts*	*Youga*	*Parker*	*Bower*	*Wetherall*	*B-Wilkinson*	*Colbeck*	*Paynter^*	*Ashikodi**	*Schumacher*	*Bentham*	*Johnson/Ainge*
								Ref: N Swarbrick	On-loan Billy Paynter's stunning 30-yard leveller turned this game on its head. City should have been well in front by the interval but for their strikers, who again offered little. Basso fumbled Steve Schumacher's 25-yarder over the line, but the Bradford man was allowed acres of space.											
38	A	CREWE		2	W	1-0	0-0	Showunmi 85	Basso	Orr	McAllister	Carey	McCombe	Johnson	Russell*	Showunmi"	Smith^	Skuse	Wilson	M-Williams/Fontaine/Jevons
	17/3		*5,731*	*13*	71				*Williams*	*Woodwards*	*Bignot*	*Baudet**	*O'Donnell*	*Jones*	*Lowe*	*Jack^*	*Higdon"*	*Cox*	*Roberts*	*Rix/Miller/Pope*
								Ref: R Beeby	Missing many key players due to injury, sickness and even childbirth, City are relieved that Crewe are without their two top strikers. Certainly strikers are what this mundane game lacked, but thankfully Showunmi is in the right place to chest the ball in and bring City three vital points.											
39	A	DONCASTER		2	W	1-0	0-0	McCombe 87	Basso	Orr	Fontaine	Carey	McCombe	Johnson	Betsy	Showunmi"	Brooker*	Russell^	Skuse	Smith/Noble/Jevons
	24/3		*7,945*	*10*	74				*Sullivan*	*O'Connor*	*McDaid*	*Lee*	*Lockwood*	*Stock*	*Green**	*Thornton*	*Cadamarteri*	*Dyer*	*Forte^*	*Wilson/Nelthorpe*
								Ref: G Salisbury	City's display on their first visit to the Keepmoat Stadium is almost as leaden as the sky. Persisting in the 3-5-2 mode that has secured them so many points recently, a header settles this affair. A satisfactory outcome for the many travelling fans, but do the ends really justify the means?											
40	H	NOTT'M FOREST		2	D	1-1	1-1	Orr 37	Basso	Orr	Fontaine	Carey	McCombe	Johnson	Betsy	Jevons	Brooker*	Skuse	Wilson	Showunmi
	31/3		19,249	*3*	75			*Holt 4*	*Smith*	*Curtis"*	*Wright*	*Chambers*	*Breckin*	*Holt Gary*	*Perch*	*Lester**	*Holt Grant*	*McGugan^*	*Commons*	*Prutton/Tyson/Morgan*
								Ref: A Bates	Whilst a draw is a more satisfactory outcome for City than Forest, this result has the potential to scupper either of their promotion hopes. In this all-action affair, City were stunned early on by Grant Holt's stooping header. Fortunately, Orr had his shooting boots on to grab the leveller.											
41	H	SWANSEA		2	D	0-0	0-0		Basso	Orr	Fontaine^	Carey	McCombe	Johnson	Betsy	Jevons"	Brooker*	Skuse	Wilson	Showunmi/Keogh/Smith
	7/4		14,025	*7*	76				*Gueret*	*Am'kwaah"*	*Painter*	*O'Leary*	*Iriekpen*	*Lawrence*	*Britton*	*Trundle*	*Abbett**	*Craney*	*Butler^*	*Duffy D/Robinson/Duffy R*
								Ref: M Jones	Notwithstanding that for the fifth home game running the opposition turn out in an all-black kit, the City goalkeeper persists in wearing shorts which clash. After last week's stirring display, the Ashton Gate faithful are disappointed by City's impoverished and punchless performance.											
42	A	GILLINGHAM		2	L	0-1	0-0		Basso	Orr	Keogh	Carey	McCombe	Johnson	Betsy	Jevons*	Showunmi^	Skuse"	Wilson	Smith/M-Williams/Russell
	9/4		*6,292*	*17*	76			*McDonald 55*	*Larrieu*	*Southall*	*Jackman*	*Cox*	*Chorley*	*Crofts*	*Bentley*	*Spiller*	*N-Nzunga**	*Flynn*	*Bastians^*	*McDonald"/Easton/Collin*
								Ref: J Singh	It's a bit late now as City boss Johnson at last expresses concerns in regard to his goal-shy team. 'Sometimes you can unlucky but today I don't feel we did enough early on'. Dean McDonald heads in the Gills' winner and it is now 20 years since City last won at the Priestfield Stadium.											
43	H	YEOVIL		2	W	2-0	1-0	Johnson 43, Orr 71p	Basso	Orr	Fontaine	Carey	McCombe	Johnson	Betsy	Russell	Showunmi"	Noble*	Wilson^	Keogh/M-Williams/Jevons
	14/4		19,002	*5*	79				*Mildenhall*	*Rose*	*Jones*	*Skiverton**	*Forbes*	*Barry*	*Davies*	*Stewart*	*Gray"*	*Kalala^*	*Cohen*	*Guyett !/Lindegaard/Morris*
								Ref: M Dean	An excellent referee, though many home fans thought him at fault for disallowing Carey's 65th-minute header. No complaints, though, for him striking off McCombe's tap-in right on the interval. City captain Carey was outstanding, but it was Orr who was named as man of the match.											
44	A	CARLISLE		2	W	3-1	1-1	McCombe 45, Showunmi 65, Orr 84	**Ruddy**	Orr	Fontaine	Carey	McCombe	Johnson	Wilson^	Russell"	Showunmi	Noble*	Betsy	Skuse/McAllister/Keogh
	21/4		*10,232*	*8*	82			*Graham 5*	*Westwood*	*Raven"*	*Aranalde*	*Murphy*	*Livesey*	*Lumsdon*	*Gall**	*Garner*	*Graham^*	*Thirwell*	*Smith, Jeff*	*Smith, J'n/Hawley/Holmes*
								Ref: S Mathieson	McCombe's header, late in first-half added time, turned this game on its head. With Ruddy on loan from Everton, City were out of sorts before the break, but thereafter Showunmi's angled drive between the keeper's legs and Orr's fine left-footer ended Carlisle's five-match winning run.											
45	A	MILLWALL		2	L	0-1	0-0		Basso	Orr	McAllister	Fontaine	McCombe	Johnson	Wilson^	Russell*	Showunmi	Noble	Betsy"	Skuse/Jevons/Smith
	28/4		*12,547*	*9*	82			*Robinson 78*	*Pidgeley*	*Senda*	*Craig*	*Shaw*	*Robinson*	*Brammer*	*Elliott**	*Harris*	*Byfield"*	*Dunne*	*Smith^*	*Hubertz/Hackett/Williams*
								Ref: R Shoebridge	Looking for the win to clinch promotion, the many late-arriving fans caught up in the traffic chaos probably knew it wouldn't be City's day. Not for the first time this season, City suffer for the lack of a quality striker. With Forest and Blackpool on top form, it's win or bust next week.											
46	H	ROTHERHAM		2	W	3-1	2-0	Noble 8, 44, Russell 55	Basso	Orr	McAllister"	Carey	McCombe	Johnson*	Betsy	Russell	Showunmi	Noble^	Wilson	Skuse/Jevons/Fontaine
	5/5		**19,517**	*23*	85			*Newsham 58*	*Cutler*	*Wilson*	*Brogan*	*Sharps*	*Fleming**	*Cochrane*	*Henderson"*	*Jarvis*	*Newsham^*	*Facey*	*Woods*	*Kerr/Taylor/Yates*
		Home	Away					Ref: M Russell	Not quite a stroll in the sunshine but City get the victory to clinch promotion. Noble's angled volley settles the nerves, and all is well with the world when he runs through to slide in another just before the break. At the finish the players are submerged by an ecstatic flood of humanity.											
Average		12,818	8,007																	

Carling Cup					F-A	H-T	Scorers, Times, and Referees	1	2	3	4	5	6	7	8	9	10	11	subs used
1	A	CHELTENHAM	10	L	1-2	1-2	Cotterill 39	Basso	Keogh"	McAllister	Carey	Fontaine	Noble^	Cotterill	Jevons	Showunmi	Johnson	Murray*	M-Williams/Skuse/Brown
	22/8		*3,713 20*				*Guinan 24, Wilson 33*	*Higgs*	*Gill*	*Armstrong*	*Victory*	*Caines*	*Finnigan*	*Melligan**	*Guinan^*	*Odejayi*	*McCann*	*Wilson*	*Vincent/Gillespie*
							Ref: A Woolmer	Quite how this game only produced three goals will remain a mystery. City should have had three or four, given their number of chances, but more worrying is the fact that the hosts could have had even more. Brian Wilson volleyed in Cheltenham's second from Basso's poor palm out.											

FA Cup (Sponsored by E-on)					F-A	H-T	Scorers, Times, and Referees	1	2	3	4	5	6	7	8	9	10	11	subs used
1	A	YORK	4	W	1-0	0-0	McCombe 53	Basso	Keogh	McAllister*	Fontaine	McCombe	Johnson	Skuse	Jevons^	Showunmi	Russell	Woodman	Brown/M-Williams
	11/11		*3,525 NC:5*					*Evans*	*Craddock*	*Lloyd*	*Goodliffe*	*Foster*	*Bowey*	*Bishop*	*Donaldson*	*Farrell**	*Panther*	*Woolford*	*Stamp*
							Ref: M Oliver	On a cold and windy Remembrance Day, the boggy pitch made things difficult for City against Conference side York. Despite Showunmi's return from injury, the attack was still lacking and it took defender McCombe, who was captain for the day, to head City into the next round.											
2	H	GILLINGHAM	4	W	4-3	3-0	Jevons 21, 44, 45, Showunmi 64	Basso	Keogh	McAllister^	Carey	McCombe	Johnson	Skuse*	Jevons"	Showunmi	Russell	M-Williams	Murray/Fontaine/Brown
	3/12		5,663 *10*				*Mulligan 49, Flynn 66, 90p*	*Jack*	*Jupp*	*Easton*	*Sancho*	*Johnson*	*Flynn*	*Bentley*	*McDonald**	*Mulligan*	*Crofts*	*Jarvis*	*N-Nsungu*
							Ref: S Mathieson	It's been a long time coming, some 60 years in fact, for City to avenge their last-ever defeat by a non-League club. This time the sides meet on equal terms, but City almost threw it away in the second half against opponents whose keeper was suffering from the effects of concussion.											
3	H	COVENTRY	4	D	3-3	3-2	Brooker 14, Showunmi 18, Jevons 21	Basso	Orr	McAllister	Keogh	McCombe	Russell	Murray	Jevons*	Brooker	Johnson	Showunmi	Skuse
	6/1		13,336 *CC:16*				*Cameron 13, McKenzie 33, John 81*	*Steele*	*Virgo*	*Whing*	*Turner*	*Page*	*Doyle*	*Cameron*	*Kyle^*	*Adebola**	*Osbourne*	*McKenzie*	*John/Andrews*
							Ref: P Joslin	Against the struggling Championship visitors, City rediscover their shooting boots, but are let down by their defence. Not for the first time this season, negative substitutions invite the pressure on themselves and they pay the price with Stern John knocking in Coventry's equaliser.											
3R	A	COVENTRY	4	W	2-0	1-0	Murray 39, Showunmi 54	Basso	Orr	McAllister	Carey	McCombe	Skuse^	Murray	Jevons*	Brooker"	Johnson	Showunmi	M-Williams/Russell/Keogh
	16/1		*13,055 CC:16*					*Steele*	*Whing*	*Hall*	*Turner*	*Page*	*Doyle**	*Tabb^*	*Kyle"*	*John*	*Osbourne*	*McKenzie*	*Thornton/Birchall/Adebola*
							Ref: N Miller	At the impressive Ricoh Arena, Murray's 20-yarder and Showunmi's header bring City a deserved success as they extend their unbeaten run to 15 games. Strong in defence the impressive Basso pulled off fine saves on the few occasions the Bantams were able to breach City's rearguard.											
4	H	MIDDLESBROUGH	2	D	2-2	0-2	Keogh 53, Murray 59	Basso	Orr	Fontaine"	Carey	Keogh	Skuse^	Murray	Noble	Showunmi	Johnson	McAllister	M-Williams/Russell/W'dman
	27/1		19,008 *P:11*				*Yakubu 4, Christie 23*	*Schwarzer*	*Xavier*	*Taylor*	*Pogatetz*	*Woodgate*	*Arca*	*Morrison^*	*Yakubu*	*Christie**	*Cattermole*	*Downing*	*Euell/Johnson*
							Ref: G Poll	The comeback kings are at it again, this time against Premiership opposition. After paying the penalty for their habit of playing square balls across the back, City came out all guns blazing in the second half. Keogh's back-header and Murray's wonder half-volley leaves all to play for.											
4R	A	MIDDLESBROUGH	5	D	2-2	1-0	Noble 23, McCombe 117	Weale	Orr	Fontaine"	Keogh	McCombe	Russell	Murray	Noble^	Jevons	Johnson	McAllister*	W'dman/M-W'lms/Partridge
	13/2		*26,328 P:12*		*aet*		*Viduka 69, Yakubu 102*	*Schwarzer*	*Hines**	*Taylor*	*Pogatetz*	*Xavier*	*Rochemback*	*Cattermole"*	*Yakubu*	*Christie^*	*Boateng*	*Downing*	*Davies/Viduka/Johnson*
							Ref: P Dowd (City lost 4-5 on penalties)	City's great fighting spirit almost pulled off a Cup shock but, despite scoring twice and having good midfield possession, they offered little at the sharp end. Yakubu had his 94th-minute penalty saved by the City keeper, whilst in the shoot-out he put his side's fifth effort against a post.											

	P	W	D	L	F	A	W	D	L	F	A	Pts
				Home					Away			
1 Scunthorpe	46	15	6	2	40	17	11	7	5	33	18	91
2 BRISTOL C	46	15	5	3	35	20	10	5	8	28	19	85
3 Blackpool*	46	12	6	5	40	25	12	5	6	36	24	83
4 Nott'm Forest	46	14	5	4	37	17	9	8	6	28	24	82
5 Yeovil	46	14	3	6	22	12	9	7	7	33	27	79
6 Oldham	46	13	4	6	36	18	8	8	7	33	29	75
7 Swansea	46	12	6	5	36	20	8	6	9	33	33	72
8 Carlisle	46	12	5	6	35	24	7	6	10	19	31	68
9 Tranmere	46	13	5	5	33	22	5	8	10	25	31	67
10 Millwall	46	11	8	4	33	19	8	1	14	26	43	66
11 Doncaster	46	8	10	5	30	23	8	5	10	22	24	63
12 Port Vale	46	12	3	8	35	26	6	3	14	29	39	60
13 Crewe	46	11	4	8	39	38	6	5	12	27	34	60
14 Northampton	46	8	5	10	27	28	7	9	7	21	23	59
15 Huddersfield	46	9	8	6	37	33	5	9	9	23	36	59
16 Gillingham	46	14	2	7	29	24	3	6	14	27	53	59
17 Cheltenham	46	8	6	9	25	27	7	3	13	24	34	54
18 Brighton	46	5	7	11	23	34	9	4	10	26	24	53
19 Bournemouth	46	10	5	8	28	27	3	8	12	22	37	52
20 Leyton Orient	46	6	10	7	30	32	6	5	12	31	45	51
21 Chesterfield	46	9	5	9	29	22	3	6	14	16	31	47
22 Bradford C	46	5	9	9	27	31	6	5	12	20	34	47
23 Rotherham^	46	8	4	11	37	39	5	5	13	21	36	38
24 Brentford	46	5	8	10	24	41	3	5	15	16	38	37
	1104	249	139	164	767	619	164	139	249	619	767	1507

* promoted after play-offs
^ 10 points off: Administration

Odds & ends

Double wins: (7) Northampton Town, Brighton & HA, Chesterfield, Port Vale, Crewe Alexandra, Doncaster Rovers, Carlisle United.
Double losses: (1) Bradford C.

Won from behind: (5) Northampton T (a), Gillingham (h), Port Vale (h), Tranmere Rovers (h), Carlisle United (a).
Lost from in front: (3) Bradford C (a), Huddersfield (a), Bradford C (h).

High spots: City's 10-man win at Northampton on 29 August.
The post-Christmas improved away form that produced vital wins at Oldham, Blackpool, Brighton, Chesterfield, Crewe and Doncaster.
City's fight-back to win 3-1 at in-form Carlisle on 21 April.
A great goal, pity it was Billy Paynter's for Bradford City which sparked their winning fight-back at Ashton Gate on 13 March.
The great scenes at Ashton Gate on the clinching of promotion.
An FA Cup campaign that brought a superb win at Coventry and a fine display at Premiership Middlesbrough.

Low spots: The sloppy display at home to Blackpool on 19 August.
The bust-up between Carey and Orr at Northampton
City's inept displays at Yeovil, Cheltenham and Scunthorpe.
The loss at Millwall that delayed the promotion celebrations.
City's failure to mount a realistic challenge for the title.
Twice failing against Bristol Rovers in the Johnston's Paint Trophy.

Player of the year: Jamie McCombe.
Ever presents: (0).
Hat-tricks: (1) Phil Jevons.
Leading scorer: Phil Jevons (15).

	Appearances						Goals			
	Lge	*Sub*	LC	*Sub*	FAC	*Sub*	**Lge**	LC	FAC	**Tot**
Andrews, Wayne	**3**	*4*					**2**		1	**3**
Basso, Adriano	**45**		1		5					
Betsy, Kevin	**16**	*1*					**1**			**1**
Brooker, Steve	**19**	*4*			2		**2**		1	**3**
Brown, Scott	**12**	*3*		*1*		*2*	**4**			**4**
Carey, Louis	**36**	*2*	1		3		**2**			**2**
Corr, Barry	**1**	*2*								
Cotterill, Dave	**3**	*2*	1				**1**	1		**2**
Fontaine, Liam	**23**	*7*	1		3	*1*				
Jevons, Phil	**31**	*10*	1		5		**11**		4	**15**
Johnson, Lee	**41**	*1*	1		6		**5**			**5**
Keogh, Richard	**20**	*11*	1		5	*1*	**2**		1	**3**
McAllister, James	**29**	*2*	1		6		**1**			**1**
McCombe, Jamie	**38**	*3*			5		**4**		2	**6**
Murray, Scott	**21**	*7*	1		4	*1*	**7**		2	**9**
M-Williams, Jennison	**15**	*10*		*1*	1	*4*	**2**			**2**
Noble, David	**18**	*8*	1		2		**3**			**3**
Orr, Bradley	**29**	*6*			4		**4**			**4**
Partridge, Dave						*1*				
Ruddy, John	**1**									
Russell, Alex	**20**	*8*			4	*2*	**2**			**2**
Showunmi, Enoch	**28**	*5*	1		5		**10**		3	**13**
Skuse, Cole	**31**	*11*		*1*	4	*1*				
Smith, Andy	**3**	*7*								
Weale, Chris		*1*			1					
Wilson, Brian	**17**	*2*								
Woodman, Craig	**5**	*6*			1	*2*				
Wright, Nick	**1**	*3*								
28 players used	**506**	***126***	**11**	***3***	**66**	***15***	**63**	**1**	**14**	**78**

Action shots from two matches against Bristol Rovers.
Top: City lose 2-4 at home in the League Cup (October 1991);
Bottom: City lose 2-3 at Twerton Park in the League (December 1991)